Red Book®:

2006 REPORT OF THE COMMITTEE ON INFECTIOUS DISEASES
TWENTY-SEVENTH EDITION

Author: Committee on Infectious Diseases
American Academy of Pediatrics

Larry K. Pickering, MD, FAAP, Editor

Carol J. Baker, MD, FAAP, Associate Editor
Sarah S. Long, MD, FAAP, Associate Editor
Julia A. McMillan, MD, FAAP, Associate Editor

American Academy of Pediatrics
141 Northwest Point Blvd
Elk Grove Village, IL 60007-1098

Suggested Citation: American Academy of Pediatrics. [Chapter title]. In: Pickering LK, Baker CJ, Long SS, McMillan JA, eds. *Red Book: 2006 Report of the Committee on Infectious Diseases*. 27th ed. Elk Grove Village, IL: American Academy of Pediatrics; 2006:[page numbers]

27th Edition
1st Edition – 1938
2nd Edition – 1939
3rd Edition – 1940
4th Edition – 1942
5th Edition – 1943
6th Edition – 1944
7th Edition – 1945
8th Edition – 1947
9th Edition – 1951
10th Edition – 1952
11th Edition – 1955
12th Edition – 1957
13th Edition – 1961
14th Edition – 1964
15th Edition – 1966
16th Edition – 1970
16th Edition Revised – 1971
17th Edition – 1974
18th Edition – 1977
19th Edition – 1982
20th Edition – 1986
21st Edition – 1988
22nd Edition – 1991
23rd Edition – 1994
24th Edition – 1997
25th Edition – 2000
26th Edition – 2003

ISSN No. 1080-0131
ISBN-10 No. 1-58110-207-0 hardcover
ISBN-13 No. 978-1-58110-207-9 hardcover
ISBN-10 No. 1-58110-194-5 softcover
ISBN-13 No. 978-1-58110-194-2 softcover
MA0340 hardcover
MA0332 softcover

Quantity prices on request. Address all inquiries to:
American Academy of Pediatrics
PO Box 927, 141 Northwest Point Blvd
Elk Grove Village, IL 60007-1098

or Phone:
1-888-227-1770 Publications

Committee on Infectious Diseases
2004–2006

Collaborators

M. Abdy, DVM, PhD, Food and Drug Administration, Rockville, MD
Mark Abramowicz, MD, The Medical Letter Inc, New Rochelle, NY
Jon Abramson, MD, Wake Forest University School of Medicine, Winston-Salem, NC
Alice D. Ackerman, MD, University of Maryland School of Medicine, Baltimore, MD
David Adamkin, MD, University of Louisville, Louisville, KY
David G. Addiss, MD, MPH, Centers for Disease Control and Prevention, Atlanta, GA
Lisa M. Hoeft Albers, MD, Harvard Medical School, Children's Hospital, Boston, MA
James P. Alexander, MD, Center for Disease Control and Prevention, Atlanta, GA
John J. Alexander, MD, MPH, Food and Drug Administration, Rockville, MD
Donna Ambrosino, MD, University of Massachusetts Medical School, Jamaica Plain, MA
Nilesh H. Amin, PharmD, Department of Pharmacy Services, Yale-New Haven Hospital, New Haven, CT
Larry J. Anderson, MD, Centers for Disease Control and Prevention, Atlanta, GA
Warren A. Andiman, MD, Yale School of Medicine, New Haven, CT
Paul Arguin, MD, Centers for Disease Control and Prevention, Atlanta, GA
Gregory L. Armstrong, MD, Centers for Disease Control and Prevention, Atlanta, GA
Jane Aronson, DO, Cornell Weill Medical College, New York, NY
Susan S. Aronson, MD, University of Pennsylvania, The Children's Hospital of Philadelphia, Narbeth, PA
David M. Asher, MD, Food and Drug Administration, Rockville, MD
William L. Atkinson, MD, MPH, Centers for Disease Control and Prevention, Atlanta, GA
Chintamani D. Atreya, PhD, Food and Drug Administration, Bethesda, MD
Francisco Averhoff, MD, MPH, Center for Disease Control and Prevention, Atlanta, GA
Kassa Ayalew, MD, Food and Drug Administration, Rockville, MD
Robert Ball, MD, MPH, ScM, Food and Drug Administration, Rockville, MD
Ezra J. Barzilay, MD, Center for Disease Control and Prevention, Atlanta, GA
Margaret C. Bash, MD, MPH, Food and Drug Administration, Rockville, MD
Daniel G. Batton, MD, William Beaumont Hospital, Royal Oak, MI
Melisse S. Baylor, MD, Food and Drug Administration, Rockville, MD
Michael J. Beach, PhD, Centers for Disease Control and Prevention, Atlanta, GA
Charles Beard, BS, MS, PhD, Centers for Disease Control and Prevention, Fort Collins, CO
Judy Beeler, MD, Food and Drug Administration, Rockville, MD

Ermias D. Belay, MD, Centers for Disease Control and Prevention, Atlanta, GA

Beth P. Bell, MD, MPH, Centers for Disease Control and Prevention, Atlanta, GA

Edward Bell, MD, University of Iowa, Iowa City, IA

Catherine M. Bendel, MD, University of Minnesota Medical School, Minneapolis, MN

Stuart M. Berman, MD, ScM, Centers for Disease Control and Prevention, Atlanta, GA

Caryn Bern, MD, MPH, Centers for Disease Control and Prevention, Atlanta, GA

Richard E. Besser, MD, Centers for Disease Control and Prevention, Atlanta, GA

Achal Bhatt, PhD, Center for Disease Control and Prevention, Atlanta, GA

Oleg Bilukha, MD, PhD, Centers for Disease Control and Prevention, Atlanta, GA

Robin M. Biswas, MD, Food and Drug Administration, Rockville, MD

Brian Blackburn, MD, Centers for Disease Control and Prevention, Atlanta, GA

Lillian R. Blackmon, MD, University of Maryland School of Medicine, Baltimore, MD

David Blair, PhD, Cook University, Townsville School of Tropical Biology, James Cook University, Townsville, Australia

Martin J. Blaser, MD, New York University Medical Center, New York, NY

Margaret Blythe, MD, Indiana University Medical Center, Indianapolis, IN

Elizabeth A. Bolyard, RN, MPH, Centers for Disease Control and Prevention, Atlanta, GA

Robert Bortolussi, MD, Dalhousie University, Halifax, Canada

Anna B. Bowen, MD, MPH, Centers for Disease Control and Prevention, Atlanta, GA

Christopher Braden, MD, Centers for Disease Control and Prevention, Atlanta, GA

Paul Jeffrey Brady, MD, MPH, Food and Drug Administration, Rockville, MD

M. Miles Braun, MD, MPH, Food and Drug Administration, Rockville, MD

George R. Brenneman, MD, Indian Health Service, Elkridge, MD

Joseph S. Bresee, MD, Centers for Disease Control and Prevention, Atlanta, GA

Carolyn Bridges, MD, Centers for Disease Control and Prevention, Atlanta, GA

Karen R. Broder, MD, Centers for Disease Control and Prevention, Atlanta, GA

June M. Brown, BS, Centers for Disease Control and Prevention, Atlanta, GA

Marc Bulterys, MD, PhD, Centers for Disease Control and Prevention, Atlanta, GA

Jane L. Burns, MD, University of Washington, Seattle, WA

Deron C. Burton, MD, JD, MPH, Centers for Disease Control and Prevention, Atlanta, GA

Lauren Anne Burwell, MD, Centers for Disease Control and Prevention, Atlanta, GA

Jay C. Butler, MD, Centers for Disease Control and Prevention, Anchorage, AK

Angela Calugar, MD, Centers for Disease Control and Prevention, Atlanta, GA

William Cameron, MD, The Ottawa Hospital, Ottawa, Canada

Grant Campbell, MD, Centers for Disease Control and Prevention, Fort Collins, CO

Christine G. Casey, MD, FAAP, ACP, Centers for Disease Control and Prevention, Atlanta, GA

Donna Chandler, PhD, Food and Drug Administration, Rockville, MD

Michelle A. Chang, MD, Centers for Disease Control and Prevention, Atlanta, GA

Alice S. Chapman, DVM, MPH, Centers for Disease Control and Prevention, Atlanta, GA

Robert T. Chen, MD, MA, Centers for Disease Control and Prevention, Atlanta, GA

Tom M. Chiller, MD, MPHTM, Centers for Disease Control and Prevention, Atlanta, GA

Lance Chilton, MD, University of New Mexico School of Medicine, Lovelace Medical Center, Albuquerque, NM

Thomas A. Clark, MD, Centers for Disease Control and Prevention, Atlanta, GA

William L. Clarke, MD, University of Virginia, Charlottesville, VA

Thomas G. Cleary, MD, University of Texas Medical School, Houston, TX

Susan E. Coffin, MD, MPH, Children's Hospital of Philadelphia, University of Pennsylvania School of Medicine, Philadelphia, PA

Joanne Cono, MD, ScM, Centers for Disease Control and Prevention, Atlanta, GA

Armando Correa, MD, Mayo Eugenio Litta Children's Hospital, Rochester, MN

Margaret Mary Cortese, MD, Centers for Disease Control and Prevention, Atlanta, GA

Elliot P. Cowan, PhD, Food and Drug Administration, Rockville, MD

James E. Crowe, Jr, MD, Vanderbilt University School of Medicine, Vanderbilt University Medical Center, Nashville, TN

Coleen K. Cunningham, MD, Duke University Medical Center, Durham, NC

Inger Damon, MD, PhD, Centers for Disease Control and Prevention, Atlanta, GA

Gregory A. Dasch, PhD, Centers for Disease Control and Prevention, Atlanta, GA

Jon R. Daugherty, PhD, Food and Drug Administration, Rockville, MD

Alma C. Davidson, MD, Food and Drug Administration, Rockville, MD

Lora Baker Davis, DVM, MPH, Centers for Disease Control and Prevention, Fort Collins, CO

Amy M. Dechet, MD, Centers for Disease Control and Prevention, Atlanta, GA

Linda J. Demma, PhD, Centers for Disease Control and Prevention, Atlanta, GA

Anita Denson, MD, Food and Drug Administration, Rockville, MD

Susan E. Denson, MD, University of Texas Medical School, Houston, TX

Dickson Despommier, BS, MS, PhD, Columbia University, Department of Environmental Health Services, New York City, NY

Frank DeStefano, MD, Centers for Disease Control and Prevention, Atlanta, GA

Douglas S. Diekema, MD, MPH, University of Washington, Kenmore, WA

Joseph Domachowske, MD, SUNY Upstate Medical University Syracuse, NY

Kenneth L. Dominguez, MD, MPH, Centers for Disease Control and Prevention, Atlanta, GA

Amy Dubois, MD, MPH, Centers for Disease Control and Prevention, Atlanta, GA

John R. Dunn, DVM, PhD, Centers for Disease Control and Prevention, Atlanta, GA

Eileen F. Dunne, MD, MPH, Centers for Disease Control and Prevention, Atlanta, GA

Anna Durbin, MD, Johns Hopkins University, Baltimore, MD

Clare A. Dykewicz, MD, MPH, Centers for Disease Control and Prevention, Atlanta, GA

Morven S. Edwards, MD, Baylor College of Medicine, Houston, TX

Lawrence F. Eichenfield, MD, University of California, San Diego School of Medicine, San Diego, CA

William Engle, MD, Indiana University School of Medicine, Indianapolis, IN

Marina E. Eremeeva, MD, PhD, Centers for Disease Control and Prevention, Atlanta, GA

Geoffrey Evans, MD, Vaccine Injury Compensation Program, Health Resources and Services Administration, Rockville, MD

Karen M. Farizo, MD, Food and Drug Administration, Rockville, MD

Mahmood Farshid, PhD, Food and Drug Administration, Rockville, MD

Stephen A. Feig, MD, David Geffen School of Medicine at UCLA, Los Angeles, CA

Stephen M. Feinstone, MD, Food and Drug Administration, Bethesda, MD

Jane D. Filie, MD, Food and Drug Administration, Rockville, MD

Theresa M. Finn, PhD, Food and Drug Administration, Rockville, MD

Anthony E. Fiore, MD, MPH, Centers for Disease Control and Prevention, Atlanta, GA

Brendan L. Flannery, PhD, Centers for Disease Control and Prevention, Atlanta, GA

Patricia M. Flynn, MD, St. Jude's Children's Research Hospital, Memphis, TN

Barbara Frankowski, MD, University Pediatrics, Vermont Children's Hospital, Burlington, VT

Scott K. Fridkin, MD, Centers for Disease Control and Prevention, Atlanta, GA

Alicia M. Fry, MD, MPH, Centers for Disease Control and Prevention, Atlanta, GA

Vincent A. Fulginiti, MD, MS, University of Arizona Health Sciences Center, Tucson, AZ

Francis Gigliotti, MD, University of Rochester Medical Center, School of Medicine, Rochester, NY

Laurence B. Givner, MD, Wake Forest University School of Medicine, Winston-Salem, NC

Danette Glassy, MD, University of Washington, Mercer Island, WA

Basil Golding, MD, Food and Drug Administration, Rockville, MD

Rachel J. Gorwitz, MD, MPH , Centers for Disease Control and Prevention, Atlanta, GA

David P. Greenberg, MD, Children's Hospital of Pittsburgh, Pittsburgh, PA

Michael Greenberg, MD, MPH, Centers for Disease Control and Prevention, Atlanta, GA

Carolyn M. Greene, MD, Centers for Disease Control and Prevention, Atlanta, GA

Patricia M. Griffin, MD, Centers for Disease Control and Prevention, Atlanta, GA

Kevin S. Griffith, MD, MPH, Centers for Disease Control and Prevention, Fort Collins, CO

Diane K. Gross, DVM, PhD, Centers for Disease Control and Prevention, Atlanta, GA

Marion F. Gruber, PhD, Food and Drug Administration, Rockville, MD

Sundeep K. Gupta, MD, MPH, Centers for Disease Control and Prevention, Atlanta, GA

Dalya Guris, MD, MPH, Centers for Disease Control and Prevention, Atlanta, GA

Deborah Gust, MD, Centers for Disease Control and Prevention, Atlanta, GA

Jeffrey C. Hageman, MHS, Centers for Disease Control and Prevention, Atlanta, GA

Neal Halsey, MD, Johns Hopkins University, Baltimore, MD

Peter L. Havens, MD, Medical College of Wisconsin, Milwaukee, WI

Edward B. Hayes, MD, Centers for Disease Control and Prevention, Fort Collins, CO

Rita F. Helfand, MD, Centers for Disease Control and Prevention, Atlanta, GA

Barbara L. Herwaldt, MD, MPH, Centers for Disease Control and Prevention, Atlanta, GA

Lauri A. Hicks, DO, Centers for Disease Control and Prevention, Atlanta, GA

Steve Holve, MD, Tuba City Regional Healthcare Corporation, Tuba City, AZ

Peter J. Hotez, MD, PhD, George Washington University, Medical Center, Washington, DC

John J. Hutter, MD, University of Arizona, Tucson, AZ

Ekopimo O. Ibia, MD, MPH, Food and Drug Administration, Rockville, MD

Menfo A. Imoisili, MD, MPH, Food and Drug Administration, Silver Spring, MD

John K. Iskander, MD, MPH, Centers for Disease Control and Prevention, Atlanta, GA

Martha Iwamoto, MD, MPH, Centers for Disease Control and Prevention, Atlanta, GA

Mary Anne Jackson, MD, Children's Mercy Hospitals and Clinics, University of Missouri-Kansas City School of Medicine, Kansas City, MO

Richard F. Jacobs, MD, Arkansas Children's Hospital, Little Rock, AR

Hamid S. Jafari, MBBS, Centers for Disease Control and Prevention, Atlanta, GA

Jerri Ann Jenista, MD, St Joseph Mercy Hospital, Ann Arbor, MI

Daniel B. Jernigan, MD, MPH, Centers for Disease Control and Prevention, Atlanta, GA

Robert Jerris, PhD, Emory University School of Medicine, Atlanta, GA

Rosemary Johann-Liang, MD, Food and Drug Administration, Rockville, MD

Robert E. Johnson, MD, MPH, Centers for Disease Control and Prevention, Atlanta, GA

James Jones, MD, Centers for Disease Control and Prevention, Atlanta, GA

Jeffrey L. Jones, MD, MPH, Centers for Disease Control and Prevention, Atlanta, GA

M. Patricia Joyce, MD, Centers for Disease Control and Prevention, Atlanta, GA

Dennis D. Juranek, DVM, MSc, Centers for Disease Control and Prevention, Atlanta, GA

Pavani Kalluri, MD, Centers for Disease Control and Prevention, Atlanta, GA

Sheldon L. Kaplan, MD, Baylor College of Medicine, Texas Children's Hospital, Houston, TX

Ruth Karron, MD, Center for Immunization Research, Baltimore, MD

Julie Katkin, MD, Clinical Care Center, Texas Children's Hospital, Houston, TX

Nino Khetsuriani, MD, PhD, Centers for Disease Control and Prevention, Atlanta, GA

Peter W. Kim, MD, MS, Food and Drug Administration, Rockville, MD

Martin B. Kleiman, MD, Indiana University, Riley Hospital for Children, Indianapolis, IN

Karl C. Klontz, MD, MPH, Food and Drug Administration, College Park, MD

Katrin Kohl, MD, MPH, DTM, Centers for Disease Control and Prevention, Atlanta, GA

Emilia H. Koumans, MD, MPH, Centers for Disease Control and Prevention, Atlanta, GA

Carl Kraus, MD, Food and Drug Administration, Rockville, MD

Philip R. Krause, MD, Food and Drug Administration, Bethesda, MD

John W. Krebs, MS, Centers for Disease Control and Prevention, Atlanta, GA

Katrina Kretsinger, MD, MA, Centers for Disease Control and Prevention, Atlanta, GA

Thomas G. Ksiazek, DVM, PhD, Centers for Disease Control and Prevention, Atlanta, GA

Matthew J. Kuehnert, MD, Centers for Disease Control and Prevention, Atlanta, GA

Nicole M.A. Le Saux, MD, Children's Hospital of Eastern Ontario, Ottawa, Ontario, Canada

Ellen Hyun-Ju Lee, MD, Centers for Disease Control and Prevention, Atlanta, GA

Lucia Lee, MD, Food and Drug Administration, Rockville, MD

Roland A. Levandowski, MD, Food and Drug Administration, Bethesda, MD

Linda L. Lewis, MD, Food and Drug Administration, Bethesda, MD

Jay M. Lieberman, MD, Miller Children's Hospital, University of California Irvine, Long Beach, CA

Michael Light, MD, University of Miami, Sunny Isles, FL

Mark N. Lobato, MD, Centers for Disease Control and Prevention, Atlanta, GA

Ann M. Loeffler, MD, Legacy Emanuel Children's Hospital, Portland, OR

Michael Lynch, MD, Centers for Disease Control and Prevention, Atlanta, GA

Gavin MacGregor-Skinner, BVSc, MSc, MPH, MRCVS, Centers for Disease Control and Prevention, Atlanta, GA

James H. Maguire, MD, MPH, Centers for Disease Control and Prevention, Atlanta, GA

Susan A. Maloney, MD, MHSc, Centers for Disease Control and Prevention, Atlanta, GA

Thomas T. Mancuso, MD, Children's Hospital of Boston, Boston, MA

Anna M. Mankalakas, MD, MS, Case Western Reserve University, Kirtland, OH

Susan E. Manning, MD, MPH, Centers for Disease Control and Prevention, Atlanta, GA

Charles Maplethorpe, MD, Food and Drug Administration, Rockville, MD

Lewis J. Markoff, MD, Food and Drug Administration, Bethesda, MD

Gilbert Martin, MD, Citrus Valley Medical Center, West Covina, CA

Els Mathieu, MD, MPH, Centers for Disease Control and Prevention, Atlanta, GA

Lisa L. Mathis, MD, Food and Drug Administration, Rockville, MD

Leonard W. Mayer, PhD, Centers for Disease Control and Prevention, Atlanta, GA

Anne E. McCarthy, MD, FRCPC, DTM&H, Ottawa Hospital, Ottawa, Ontario, Canada

George H. McCracken, Jr, MD, University of Texas Southwestern Medical Center at Dallas, Dallas, TX

L. Clifford McDonald, MD, Centers for Disease Control and Prevention, Atlanta, GA

Jennifer H. McQuiston, DVM, MS, Centers for Disease Control and Prevention, Atlanta, GA

Paul Mead, MD, MPH, Centers for Disease Control and Prevention, Fort Collins, CO

Joette M. Meyer, PharmD, Food and Drug Administration, Rockville, MD

Nancy Miller, MD, Food and Drug Administration, Rockville, MD

ChrisAnna Marie Mink, MD, Food and Drug Administration, Rockville, MD

Eric D. Mintz, MD, MPH, Centers for Disease Control and Prevention, Atlanta, GA

John F. Modlin, MD, Dartmouth Hitchcock Medical Center, Lebanon, NH

Nasim Moledina, MD, Food and Drug Administration, Silver Spring, MD

Susan P. Montgomery, DVM, MPH, Centers for Disease Control and Prevention, Atlanta, GA

Anne C. Moore, MD, PhD, Centers for Disease Control and Prevention, Atlanta, GA

Gina T. Mootrey, DO, MPH, Centers for Disease Control and Prevention, Atlanta, GA

John S. Moran, MD, MPH, Centers for Disease Control and Prevention, Atlanta, GA

Juliette Morgan, MD, Centers for Disease Control and Prevention, Atlanta, GA

Ardythe L. Morrow, PhD, MSc, Children's Hospital Medical Center, Center for Epidemiology and Biostatistics, Cincinnati, OH

Mary Mulholland, MA, Centers for Disease Control and Prevention, Atlanta, GA

Trudy V. Murphy, MD, Centers for Disease Control and Prevention, Atlanta, GA

Dennis Murray, MD, Medical College of Georgia, Children's Medical Center, Augusta, GA

Sumathi Nambiar, MD, MPH, Food and Drug Administration, Silver Spring, MD

Michael R. Narkewicz, MD, The Pediatric Liver Center, Children's Hospital, Denver, CO

James P. Nataro, MD, PhD, University of Maryland School of Medicine, Baltimore, MD

Eileen E. Navarro, MD, Food and Drug Administration, Rockville, MD

William Nicholson, BSc, MSc, PhD, Centers for Disease Control and Prevention, Atlanta, GA

Glen J. Nowak PhD, Centers for Disease Control and Prevention, Atlanta, GA

Pekka Nuorti, MD, DSc, Centers for Disease Control and Prevention, Atlanta, GA

Thomas B. Nutman, MD, National Institutes of Health, Bethesda, MD

Rosalyn E. O'Loughlin, PhD, Centers for Disease Control and Prevention, Atlanta, GA

Ciara O'Reilly, BSc, PhD, Centers for Disease Control and Prevention, Atlanta, GA

Elizabeth O'Shaughnessy, MD, Food and Drug Administration, Rockville, MD

Walter A. Orenstein, MD, Emory Vaccine Center, Atlanta, GA

Michael Osterholm, MD, PhD, University of Minnesota, Minneapolis, MN

Gary Overturf, MD, University of New Mexico—HSC, Department of Pediatrics, Albuquerque, NM

John A. Painter, DVM, MS, Centers for Disease Control and Prevention, Atlanta, GA

Adelisa L. Panlilio, MD, MPH, Centers for Disease Control and Prevention, Atlanta, GA

Mark Papania, MD, MPH, Centers for Disease Control and Prevention, Atlanta, GA

Monica E. Parise, MD, Centers for Disease Control and Prevention, Atlanta, GA

Benjamin J. Park, MD, Centers for Disease Control and Prevention, Atlanta, GA

Andrew T. Pavia, MD, University of Utah, Salt Lake City, UT

Teresa Peret, PhD, Centers for Disease Control and Prevention, Atlanta, GA

Christina R. Phares, PhD, Centers for Disease Control and Prevention, Atlanta, GA

Joseph Piesman, DSc, Centers for Disease Control and Prevention, Fort Collins, CO

Andreas Pikis, MD, Food and Drug Administration, Rockville, MD

Fernando Polack, MD, John Hopkins University, Baltimore, MD

Nancy Powers, MD, Neonatology-Wesley Medical Center, Wichita, KS

Charles Prober, MD, Stanford University, Stanford, CA

Robert E. Quick, MD, MPH, Centers for Disease Control and Prevention, Atlanta, GA

Tonse N.K. Raju, MD, National Institute of Child Health and Human Development/National Institutes of Health, Bethesda, MD

Gopa Raychaudhuri, PhD, Food and Drug Administration, Rockville, MD

Sarah Reagan, MPH, Centers for Disease Control and Prevention, Atlanta, GA

Susan Reef, MD, Centers for Disease Control and Prevention, Atlanta, GA

Frank O. Richards, Jr, MD, Centers for Disease Control and Prevention, Atlanta, GA

Laura E. Riley, MD, Massachusetts General Hospital, Boston, MA

Lance Rodewald, MD, Centers for Disease Control and Prevention, Atlanta, GA

Patricia J. Rohan, MD, Food and Drug Administration, Rockville, MD

Pierre Rollin, MD, Centers for Disease Control and Prevention, Atlanta, GA

Martha Roper, MD, MPH, Centers for Disease Control and Prevention, Atlanta, GA

Nancy E. Rosenstein, MD, Centers for Disease Control and Prevention, Atlanta, GA

Steven R. Rosenthal, MD, MPH, Food and Drug Administration, Rockville, MD

Jennifer J. Ross, PhD, Food and Drug Administration, Rockville, MD

Larry A. Ross, MD, Childrens Hospital Los Angeles, Los Angeles, CA

Sharon L. Roy, MD, MPH, Centers for Disease Control and Prevention, Atlanta, GA

Charles E. Rupprecht, VMD, MS, PhD, Centers for Disease Control and Prevention, Atlanta, GA

Hari C. Sachs, MD, Food and Drug Administration, Rockville, MD

Leonard V. Sacks, MBBCh, Food and Drug Administration, Rockville, MD

Erika Samoff, Centers for Disease Control and Prevention, Atlanta, GA

Gary Sanden, MS, PhD, Centers for Disease Control and Prevention, Atlanta, GA

Jeanne M. Santoli, MD, MPH , Centers for Disease Control and Prevention, Atlanta, GA

Lawrence A. Schachner, MD, University of Miami School of Medicine, Miami, FL

Peter M. Schantz, VMD, PhD , Centers for Disease Control and Prevention, Atlanta, GA

Lawrence B. Schonberger, MD, MPH, Centers for Disease Control and Prevention, Atlanta, GA

Stephanie J. Schrag, DPhil, Centers for Disease Control and Prevention, Atlanta, GA

Anne Schuchat, MD, Centers for Disease Control and Prevention, Atlanta, GA

Seth Schulman, MD, University of Pennsylvania School of Medicine, Philadelphia, PA

Gordon G. Schutze, MD, Arkansas Children's Hospital, Little Rock, AR

Ann Schwartz, MD, Food and Drug Administration, Rockville, MD

Jane E. Seward, MBBS, MPH, Centers for Disease Control and Prevention, Atlanta, GA

Michael Shannon, MD, MPH, Children's Hospital of Boston, Boston, MA

Eugene D. Shapiro, MD, Yale Department of Pediatrics, New Haven, CT

Abigail Shefer, MD, Centers for Disease Control and Prevention, Atlanta, GA

Donald Shifrin, MD, University of Washington School of Medicine, Bellevue, WA

George Siberry, MD, MPH, Johns Hopkins Medical Institutions, Baltimore, MD

Toby A. Silverman, MD, Food and Drug Administration, Rockville, MD

Mary E. Singer, MD, PhD, Food and Drug Administration, Rockville, MD

Rosalyn Singleton, MD, MPH, Centers for Disease Control and Prevention, Anchorage, AK

Barbara A. Slade, MD, MS, Centers for Disease Control and Prevention, Atlanta, GA

Thomas D. Smith, MD, Food and Drug Administration, Rockville, MD

Jeremy Sobel, MD, MPH, Centers for Disease Control and Prevention, Atlanta, GA

Sunil K. Sood, MD, Albert Einstein College of Medicine, North Shore University Hospital, Manhasset, NY

Alfred F. Sorbello, DO, Food and Drug Administration, Rockville, MD

Montse Soriano-Gabarró, MD, MSc, Centers for Disease Control and Prevention, Atlanta, GA

Sarah Springer, MD, International Adoption Health Services of Western Pennsylvania, Pittsburgh, PA

Arjun Srinivasan, MD, Centers for Disease Control and Prevention, Atlanta, GA

Joseph W. St. Geme, MD, Washington University School of Medicine, St. Louis, MO

Mary Allen Staat, MD, MPH, Children's Hospital Medical Center, Cincinnati, OH

J. Erin Staples, MD, PhD, Centers for Disease Control and Prevention, Fort Collins, CO

Ann Stark, MD, Baylor College of Medicine Houston, TX

William J. Steinbach, MD, Duke University Medical Center, Durham, NC

David S. Stephens, MD, Centers for Disease Control and Prevention, Atlanta, GA

E. Richard Stiehm, MD, Mattel Children's Hospital at UCLA, Los Angeles, CA

Peter M. Strebel, MBChB, MPH, Centers for Disease Control and Prevention, Atlanta, GA

Raymond Strikas, MD, Centers for Disease Control and Prevention, Atlanta, GA

Madeline Y. Sutton, MD, MPH, Centers for Disease Control and Prevention, Atlanta, GA

David L. Swerdlow, MD, Centers for Disease Control and Prevention, Atlanta, GA

Rolf E. Taffs, BS, MS, PhD, Food and Drug Administration, Rockville, MD

Robert V. Tauxe, MD, MPH, Centers for Disease Control and Prevention, Atlanta, GA

Joseph John Temenak, PhD, Food and Drug Administration, Rockville, MD

Michael Craig Thigpen, MD, Centers for Disease Control and Prevention, Atlanta, GA

Charlis Thompson, MEd, Centers for Disease Control and Prevention, Atlanta, GA

Herbert A. Thompson, BA, MA, PhD, Centers for Disease Control and Prevention, Atlanta, GA

Susan D. Thompson, MD, Food and Drug Administration, Rockville, MD

Rosemary Tiernan, MD, MPH, Food and Drug Administration, Rockville, MD

Maureen R. Tierney, MD, MSc, Food and Drug Administration, Rockville, MD

Tejpratap S.P. Tiwari, MD, Centers for Disease Control and Prevention, Atlanta, GA

James Todd, MD, The Children's Hospital, Denver, CO

Joseph G. Toerner, MD, MPH, Food and Drug Administration, Rockville, MD

Kay M. Tomashek, MD, MPH, Centers for Disease Control and Prevention, Atlanta, GA

Kristin B. Uhde, PhD, MPH, Centers for Disease Control and Prevention, Atlanta, GA

Elizabeth R. Unger, PhD, MD, Centers for Disease Control and Prevention, Atlanta, GA

Gary A. Urquhart, MPH, Centers for Disease Control and Prevention, Atlanta, GA

Timothy M. Uyeki, MD, MPH, Centers for Disease Control and Prevention, Atlanta, GA

Chris A. Van Beneden, MD, MPH, Centers for Disease Control and Prevention, Atlanta, GA

Govinda S. Visvesvara, PhD, Centers for Disease Control and Prevention, Atlanta, GA

Robert G. Voigt, MD, Division of Developmental and Behavioral Pediatrics, Mayo Clinic, Rochester, MN

Gregory Wallace, MD, MPH, MS, Centers for Disease Control and Prevention, Atlanta, GA

Richard J. Wallace, MD, University of Texas Health Center, Microbiology, Tyler, TX

Carol M. Wallman, MS, RNC, NNP, The Children's Hospital, Denver, CO

David W. Warnock, PhD, Centers for Disease Control and Prevention, Atlanta, GA

Steven Wassner, MD, Penn State Children's Hospital, Hershey, PA

Cindy M. Weinbaum, MD, MPH, Centers for Disease Control and Prevention, Atlanta, GA

Jerry P. Weir, PhD, Food and Drug Administration, Rockville, MD

Bruce G. Weniger, MD, Centers for Disease Control and Prevention/World Health Organization, Atlanta, GA

Richard Wenzel, MD, Virginia Commonwealth University, Richmond, VA

A. Clinton White, Jr, MD, Baylor College of Medicine, Houston, TX

Richard Whitley, MD, The University of Alabama at Birmingham, Birmingham, AL

Cynthia G. Whitney, MD, MPH, Centers for Disease Control and Prevention, Atlanta, GA

Ian Williams, PhD, MS, Centers for Disease Control and Prevention, Atlanta, GA

Kirk P. Winger, DVM, MPH, Centers for Disease Control and Prevention, Atlanta, GA

Robert A. Wood, MD, Johns Hopkins University School of Medicine, Baltimore, MD

Kimberly A. Workowski, MD, Centers for Disease Control and Prevention, Atlanta, GA

Fujie Xu, MD, PhD, Centers for Disease Control and Prevention, Atlanta, GA

Edward J. Young, MD, VA Medical Center, Houston, TX

Committee on Infectious Diseases, 2004-2006

SEATED, LEFT TO RIGHT: Caroline B. Hall, Trudy V. Murphy, Mamodikoe Makhene, Julia A. McMillan, Carol J. Baker, Larry K. Pickering, Margaret B. Rennels, Sarah S. Long, H. Cody Meissner, Joanne Embree, Penelope H. Dennehy, Edgar O. Ledbetter

STANDING, LEFT TO RIGHT: Benjamin Schwartz, Marc A. Fischer, Jack Swanson, Jeffrey R. Starke, Joseph A. Bocchini, Keith R. Powell, Lorry G. Rubin, Robert S. Baltimore, John S. Bradley, Robert W. Frenck, Jr, Douglas R. Pratt

NOT PICTURED: Richard D. Clover, Steven Cochi

Dedication

This edition of the *Red Book* is dedicated to Caroline Breese Hall, MD, FAAP, who served the Committee on Infectious Diseases (COID) as member and chairman (her preferred term) from 1984–1995 and was associate editor of the *Red Book* for the 1986, 1988, and 1997 editions. Caren also was the principal, or a contributing author, on more than 50 COID statements and guidelines. Although impressive, numbers cannot capture Caren's passion for the work of the COID, her love for her work, and her sincerity and kindness toward the people with whom she works. Knowing the time and energy that Caren dedicated to the COID, some will find it difficult to believe that the work of the committee always was superseded by family and primary responsibilities as a full-time tenured faculty member at the University of Rochester School of Medicine.

Some experts say that being an academic "triple threat"—clinician, teacher, and investigator—no longer is possible. Caren has been listed in each edition of "The Best Doctors in America" since 1993, has received the annual teaching award from the pediatric house staff 9 times, and has published more than 500 scholarly works (not including her published poetry). Caren helped found the Pediatric Infectious Diseases Society, was the first secretary-treasurer and then was president, established the Breese Award, and has been on the council continuously since the Society began in 1983. Caren has served on the American Board of Pediatrics, the Board of Scientific Counselors of the National Center for Infectious Diseases of the Centers for Disease Control and Prevention (CDC), the Vaccines and Related Biological Products Advisory Committee of the US Food and Drug Administration, and the Advisory Committee on Immunization Practices of the CDC and was elected to the Institute of Medicine. Caren also is the recipient of many other national and international awards and honors.

So much for the demise of the triple threat. But is triple the correct designation for Caren? With her husband Bill, Caren raised 3 wonderful children who have grown into an attorney, a physician, and a world-class tri-athlete. Caren has been and is a friend, a mentor, and a confidant to residents, fellows, and colleagues. Caren gives time, energy, love, and passion to her family; patient care; teaching; research; and service in local, national, and international venues. This edition of the *Red Book* is dedicated to Caren to recognize and thank her for the time, energy, powerful intellect, passion, and love that she has given so freely to the COID, the *Red Book*, the American Academy of Pediatrics, and children worldwide over the past 23 years.

Preface

The Committee on Infectious Diseases of the American Academy of Pediatrics (AAP) is dedicated to providing practitioners with the most current and accurate information available. Because the practice of pediatric infectious diseases is changing rapidly and because of the emergence of new infectious diseases and immunizations, the ability to obtain information quickly is paramount. Although the *Red Book* is updated every 3 years, practitioners who care for children should visit periodically the AAP Web site (www.aap.org) and the Red Book Online Web site (www.aapredbook.org), where interim updates will be provided.

The Committee on Infectious Diseases relies on information and advice from many experts as evidenced by the lengthy list of contributors. We especially are indebted to the many contributors from other AAP committees, the Centers for Disease Control and Prevention, the Food and Drug Administration, the National Institutes of Health, the Canadian Paediatric Society, the World Health Organization, and many other organizations that have made this edition possible. In addition, many suggestions made by individual AAP members to improve the presentation of information on specific issues have been taken into account under the able leadership of Larry K. Pickering, MD, editor, and associate editors Carol J. Baker, MD, Sarah S. Long, MD, and Julia A. McMillan, MD. We also are indebted to Edgar O. Ledbetter, MD, who spent many hours gathering the slide materials that are part of the electronic versions of the *Red Book* and provided other invaluable assistance with this edition.

As noted in previous editions of the *Red Book*, some omissions and errors are inevitable in a book of this type. We hope that AAP members will continue to assist the committee actively by suggesting specific ways to improve the quality of future editions.

Keith R. Powell, MD, FAAP
Chairperson, Committee on Infectious Diseases

Introduction

The Committee on Infectious Diseases (COID) of the American Academy of Pediatrics (AAP) is responsible for developing and revising guidelines of the AAP for control of infectious diseases in children. At intervals of approximately 3 years, the committee issues the *Red Book: Report of the Committee on Infectious Diseases,* which contains a composite summary of current AAP recommendations concerning infectious diseases in and immunizations for infants, children, and adolescents. These recommendations represent a consensus of opinions developed by members of the committee in conjunction with liaison representatives from the Centers for Disease Control and Prevention (CDC), the Food and Drug Administration (FDA), the National Institutes of Health, the National Vaccine Program Office, the Canadian Paediatric Society, *Red Book* consultants, and numerous collaborators. This edition is based on information available as of January 2006.

Unanswered scientific questions, the complexity of medical practice, the explosion of new information, and inevitable differences of opinion among experts result in inherent limitations of the *Red Book*. In the context of these limitations, the committee endeavors to provide current, relevant, and defensible recommendations for prevention and management of infectious diseases in infants, children, and adolescents. In some cases, other committees and experts may differ in their interpretation of data and resulting recommendations. In some instances, no single recommendation can be made because several options for management are equally acceptable.

In making recommendations in the *Red Book*, the committee acknowledges these differences in viewpoints by use of the phrases "most experts recommend..." and "some experts recommend..." Both phrases indicate valid recommendations, but the first signifies more support among experts, and the second, less support. Hence "some experts recommend..." indicates a minority view that is based on data and/or experience and is sufficiently valid to warrant consideration.

Inevitably in clinical practice, questions arise that cannot be answered on the basis of currently available data. In such cases, the committee attempts to provide guidelines and information that, in conjunction with clinical judgment, will facilitate well-reasoned decisions. We appreciate the questions, different perspectives, and alternative recommendations that we have received, and encourage any suggestions or correspondence that will improve future editions of the *Red Book*. Through this process, the committee seeks to provide a practical and authoritative guide for physicians and other health care professionals in their care of infants, children, and adolescents.

To aid physicians and other health care professionals in assimilating current changes in the recommendations in the *Red Book*, a list of major changes has been compiled (see Summary of Major Changes, p xxix). However, this listing does not include many changes of lesser importance, and health care professionals should consult individual chapters and sections of the book for current guidelines. In addition, new information inevitably begins to outdate some recommendations in the *Red Book*, and necessitates that health care professionals remain informed of new developments and resulting changes in recommendations. Between editions, the AAP publishes new recommendations from the committee in *Pediatrics*, in *AAP News*, and on the *Red Book* Online Web site (www.aapredbook.org). In this edition, we have provided Web site addresses throughout the text to enable early access to new information. For the most up-to-date list of important *Red Book* errata, please visit the *Red Book* Online Web site at www.aapredbook.org. The list of errata is available in standard HTML format and as an easy-to-navigate and easy-to-print PDF file and is freely accessible to all visitors to the site. On *Red Book* Online, you can sign up for e-mail alerts to be notified automatically when new errata have been announced.

When using antimicrobial agents, physicians should review the package inserts (product labels) prepared by manufacturers, particularly for information concerning contraindications and adverse reactions. No attempt has been made in the *Red Book* to provide this information, because it is readily available in the *Physicians' Desk Reference*, online (www.pdr.net), and in package inserts (product labels). As in previous editions, recommended dosage schedules for antimicrobial agents are given (see Section 4, Antimicrobial Agents and Related Therapy). Recommendations in the *Red Book* for drug dosages may differ from those of the manufacturer in the package insert. Physicians also should be familiar with information in the package insert for vaccines and immune globulins as well as recommendations of other committees (see Sources of Vaccine Information, p 2).

This book could not have been prepared without the dedicated professional competence of Edgar O. Ledbetter, MD, who served as the *Red Book* reviewer appointed by the AAP Board of Directors, who led the charge in gathering and organizing the new slide materials for the electronic part of the *Red Book*, and who provided valuable suggestions and support. The AAP staff has been outstanding in its committed work and contributions, particularly Martha Cook and Alison Siwek, managers, who served as the administrative directors for the committee and coordinated the preparation of the *Red Book*; Jennifer Pane, senior medical copy editor; Darlene Mattefs, department assistant; Barbara Drelicharz, division assistant; and Mark Ruthman and Mark Grimes, Department of Marketing, who make the *Red Book* Online and other *Red Book* products possible. Special thanks are given to Stephanie Renna, assistant to the editor, for her work, patience, and support. Marc Fischer, MD, and Douglas Pratt, MD, of the CDC and FDA, respectively, devoted a great deal of time and effort in providing input from their organizations. I am especially indebted to the associate editors Carol J. Baker, MD, Sarah S. Long, MD, and Julia A. McMillan, MD, for their expertise, tireless work, good humor, and immense contributions in their editorial and committee work. Georges Peter, MD, and Margaret Rennels, MD, continue to provide constant support and advice. Members of the committee contributed countless hours and deserve appropriate recognition for their patience, dedication, revisions, and reviews. As a committee, we particularly appreciate the guidance and dedication of the current committee chairperson, Keith R. Powell, MD, whose knowledge, dedication, insight, and leadership are reflected in the quality and productivity of the committee's work. The patience, tolerance, and support of Mimi are beyond words.

These individuals are only a few of the many contributors whose professional work and commitment have been essential in the committee's preparation of the *Red Book*.

Larry K. Pickering, MD, FAAP
Editor

Table of Contents

SECTION 2
RECOMMENDATIONS FOR CARE OF CHILDREN
IN SPECIAL CIRCUMSTANCES

SECTION 3
SUMMARIES OF INFECTIOUS DISEASES

SECTION 4
ANTIMICROBIAL AGENTS AND RELATED THERAPY

SECTION 5
ANTIMICROBIAL PROPHYLAXIS

APPENDICES

Summary of Major Changes in the 2006 *Red Book*

MAJOR CHANGES: GENERAL

1. All chapters and sections are updated.
2. Many new Web sites are added and are placed in bold throughout the text for ease of access.
3. The electronic image library, available through *Red Book* Online (**www.aapredbook.org**) and *Red Book Plus*, has been expanded with over 1800 slides, including more than 500 new slides, and reorganized to better complement the text subsections of chapters in Section 3.

SECTION 1. ACTIVE AND PASSIVE IMMUNIZATION

1. **Prologue.** Table 1.1 is updated to include the baseline 20th century annual morbidity and 2004 morbidity from 10 diseases with vaccines recommended before 1990 for universal use in children in the United States.
2. **Sources of Vaccine Information.** A Web site is added that provides the CDC and private sector costs of pediatric and adolescent vaccines.
3. **Informing Patients and Parents.** A Web site is added to Table 1.2 that provides the status of vaccine information sheets.
4. **Parental Concerns About Immunization** and **Parental Refusal of Immunization.** Previously titled Risk Communication, these portions describe factors that contribute to concerns parents have about immunization.
5. **Vaccines Licensed and Distributed in the United States.** Table 1.3 (p 10) lists vaccines produced and/or licensed in the United States. Additions since 2003 include tetanus and diphtheria toxoids and acellular pertussis (Tdap) vaccines for adolescents and adults, meningococcal conjugate vaccine, measles-mumps-rubella-varicella (MMRV) vaccine, and rotavirus vaccine.
6. **Vaccine Handling and Storage.** Information is updated to clarify appropriate equipment for storing vaccines, describe the role of personnel who handle vaccines, and update procedures that should be used to store vaccines. Table 1.4 (p 13) is updated and simplified.
7. **Site and Route of Immunization.** An intranasal vaccine section is added for live-attenuated influenza vaccine. Table 1.5 (p 21) is added showing site and needle length by age for administering vaccines.
8. **Scheduling Immunizations.** The 2006 Recommended Childhood and Adolescent Immunization Schedule (Fig 1.1) is given. Table 1.7 (p 28), Catch-up Immunization Schedules for Children and Adolescents Who Start Late or Who

Are >1 Month Behind, is updated. Table 1.8 (p 31), Recommended and Minimum Ages and Intervals Between Vaccine Doses, is updated.

9. The portion describing the **Institute of Medicine Immunization Safety Review Committee** (p 40) is updated and a link is provided to access the executive summary of each report from the Institute of Medicine.

10. **Reporting of Adverse Events.** The list of vaccines that are covered under the National Vaccine Injury Compensation Program is updated and Web sites to access information are added.

11. **Vaccine Adverse Event Reporting System (VAERS).** This portion is updated and reporting mechanisms are clarified.

12. **Hypersensitivity Reactions to Vaccine Constituents.** The portion on thimerosal content of biologicals is updated to clarify that all vaccines, except for some influenza preparations, routinely recommended for infants and children as well as Immune Globulin preparations are available only as thimerosal-free formulations or contain only trace amounts of thimerosal.

13. **Pregnancy.** Recommendations for use of Tdap in pregnant women are added (p 69).

14. **Immunocompromised Children.** This section is updated and Table 1.14 (p 73) showing immunization of children and adolescents with primary and secondary immune deficiences is expanded.

15. **American Indian/Alaska Native Children.** This section is updated to describe the effectiveness of immunization programs in American Indian/Alaska Native children and to include current vaccine recommendations for hepatitis A and hepatitis B.

16. **Children Living Outside the United States.** This new chapter replaces and expands Children in Military Populations.

17. **International Travel.** This portion is updated to include new travel regulations and immunization recommendations. Web sites are added where additional data can be obtained.

18. **New Chapters and Tables**
    - Table 1.5 (p 21) shows recommended site of administration and needle length by age for intramuscular injections.
    - **Parental Refusal of Immunization** (p 7) outlines responses to parenteral refusals of immunization of their children.

SECTION 2. RECOMMENDATIONS FOR CARE OF CHILDREN IN SPECIAL CLINICAL CIRCUMSTANCES

1. **Biological Terrorism.** The tables showing clinical manifestations, diagnostic procedures, isolation precautions, and treatment and prophylaxis of children are consolidated, condensed, and updated.

2. **Blood Safety.** This chapter is updated to include use of diagnostic assays that permit more rapid detection of human immunodeficiency virus and hepatitis C virus, information about screening blood for West Nile virus, new standards to detect and limit bacterial contamination of platelet components, current information about sporadic and variant Creutzfeldt-Jakob disease, current good tissue

practice for safety of transplantation of human cells, tissue, and cellular and tissue-based products.

3. **Children in Out-of-Home Child Care.** Recommendations are added for use of varicella vaccine during a varicella outbreak and Tdap vaccine use in child care providers. Guidance is provided on the approach to a situation in which an infant inadvertently is fed human milk from another mother.

4. **Infection Control for Hospitalized Children.** This chapter is updated in accordance with new guidelines from the Healthcare Infection Control Practices Advisory Committee (HICPAC). Table 2.7 (p 155) shows recommendations for application of standard precautions for care of patients in all health care settings.

5. **Infection Control and Prevention in Ambulatory Settings** (previously Infection Control in Physicians' Offices). This chapter is updated to reflect the 2006 AAP guidelines for children in ambulatory settings.

6. **Sexually Transmitted Infections in Adolescents and Children.** This chapter replaces Sexually Transmitted Diseases and is updated to reflect the 2006 Sexually Transmitted Infections Guidelines from the CDC.

7. **Hepatitis and Youth in Corrections Settings.** The hepatitis portions of this chapter are updated in accordance with the new CDC guidelines on hepatitis A and B.

8. **New Chapters**
   • **Prevention of Mosquitoborne Infections** (p 197)
   • **Prevention of Illnesses Associated With Recreational Water Use** (p 199)

SECTION 3. SUMMARIES OF INFECTIOUS DISEASES

1. **Amebiasis**. Tinidazole is added as a therapeutic option for patients with mild or moderate intestinal symptoms or extraintestinal tract disease attributable to *Entamoeba histolytica*.

2. **Arboviruses.** This chapter is updated, and West Nile virus information has been placed in a separate chapter.

3. **Aspergillosis.** Treatment of children and adolescents with various clinical manifestations of aspergillosis is updated.

4. **Candidiasis.** Treatment of children and adolescents with various clinical manifestations of infections with *Candida* species is updated.

5. **Coronaviruses.** This chapter is expanded to include severe acute respiratory syndrome (SARS) coronaviruses.

6. **Cryptosporidiosis.** Therapy with nitazoxanide and methods of water purification are added.

7. **Cytomegalovirus Infection.** Antiviral therapy for cytomegalovirus infections is updated.

8. **Diphtheria.** Recommendations for use of Tdap vaccine in adolescents and adults are added.

9. ***Ehrlichia* and *Anaplasma* Infections (Human Ehrlichioses).** The nomenclature of the 3 causes of human ehrlichiosis is clarified and the chapter is updated.

10. **Enterovirus (Nonpoliovirus) Infections.** The diagnosis section of this chapter is updated.

11. ***Escherichia coli* and Other Gram-Negative Bacilli.** This chapter is expanded to include information about extended-spectrum beta-lactamases.

12. ***Giardia intestinalis* Infections.** The chapter includes drugs (tinidazole, albendazole, and nitazoxanide) approved for treatment since the last edition and control measures for water treatment when camping to prevent *Giardia* infections.

13. ***Haemophilus influenzae* Infections.** The vaccines available to prevent infections with *Haemophilus influenzae* type b are updated, and Tables 3.11 (p 315) and 3.12 (p 316) are simplified.

14. **Hepatitis A.** The licensure of hepatitis A virus vaccine for children beginning at 1 year (12–23 months of age) and recommendations for use are included.

15. **Hepatitis B.** This chapter is updated in accordance with the revised CDC hepatitis B recommendations, including addition of Table 3.19 (p 348), showing hepatitis B vaccine schedule for infants by maternal hepatitis B surface antigen status, and recommendations for use of all hepatitis B-containing vaccines in all ages.

16. **Hepatitis G.** This chapter is deleted.

17. **Herpes Simplex.** Table 3.22 (p 365), showing types of infection and recommended antiviral therapy, is added.

18. **Human Immunodeficiency Virus Infection.** This chapter is extensively updated to provide current epidemiology, diagnosis, treatment, and prevention of human immunodeficiency virus (HIV) infection. The tables of antiretroviral drugs have been deleted, and a Web site that permits access to current drug therapy is added.

19. **Influenza.** Updates are provided on the epidemiology of disease in children, chemoprophylaxis, vaccines, and pandemic influenza. Influenza vaccine recommendations are expanded to include 24 to 59 months of age.

20. **Kawasaki Disease** (Kawasaki syndrome). Information about incomplete Kawasaki disease is added.

21. ***Legionella pneumophila* Infections.** Updates include current recommendations for control measures to prevent transmission through municipal and potable water supplies.

22. **Leishmaniasis.** The epidemiology and control measures portions are updated.

23. **Leprosy.** This chapter highlights changes in diagnosis and therapy. The classification and epidemiology portions contain updated information.

24. **Lyme Disease.** Methods of diagnosis are refined and clarified.

25. **Malaria.** Updates to treatment and prevention are added.

26. **Measles.** This chapter is updated to include recommendations for use of measles-mumps-rubella-varicella (MMRV) vaccine.

27. **Meningococcal Infections.** Recommendations for use of meningococcal vaccines, including meningococcal conjugate vaccine, are included in the text and in the new Table 3.37 (p 458).

28. **Pediculosis Capitis.** The portion of this chapter on treatment is updated.

29. **Pertussis.** This chapter includes new information on the epidemiology, diagnosis, and treatment. Recommendations for use of Tdap vaccine in adolescents and adults are provided, including contraindications and precautions to immunization. Table 3.42 (p 501) is added to show recommended antimicrobial therapy and postexposure prophylaxis for pertussis.

30. **Pneumococcal Infections.** This chapter is updated to include current epidemiology and expansion of vaccine recommendations to include children with cochlear implants. Table 3.48 (p 533) is expanded to include additions and catch-up immunizations scenarios.

31. **Rabies.** Update is included on available rabies vaccines.

32. **Respiratory Syncytial Virus.** Guidelines from the American Academy of Pediatrics are updated for appropriate use of palivizumab.

33. **Rickettisial Diseases.** This chapter is reorganized and expanded to follow the format used for chapters in section 3.

34. **Rotavirus.** This chapter is updated to include the AAP and CDC recommendations for use of rotavirus vaccine.

35. **Staphylococcal Infections**. This chapter is updated to include an approach for diagnosis and treatment of children and adolescents infected with methicillin-resistant *Staphylococcus aureus*.

36. **Non-Group A or B Streptococcal and Enterococcal Infections.** This chapter includes information about the association between *Streptococcus mutans* and dental caries.

37. **Pityriasis Versicolor** is the new name for Tinea versicolor.

38. **Syphilis.** Treatment guidelines reflect the 2006 Sexually Transmitted Infections Guidelines from the CDC. Tables 3.61 (p 638) and 3.62 (p 640) are updated.

39. **Tetanus**. Use of Tdap vaccine in prevention and control of tetanus is added in the text and in Table 3.63 (p 650).

40. **Tinea Capitis**. The treatment section is updated.

41. ***Toxoplasma gondii* Infections.** Table 3.68 (p 670) is added to show drugs recommended to prevent first and recurrent episodes of toxoplasmosis in children.

42. **Tuberculosis**. Advances in diagnosis of tuberculosis include use of an enzyme immunoassay test that detects release of interferon-gamma from white blood cells in response to *Mycobacterium tuberculosis* antigens. Information about infection attributable to *Mycobacterium bovis* is added. Table 3.71 (p 684) shows validated questions for determining risks of latent tuberculosis infection in chidren.

43. **Diseases Caused by Nontuberculous Mycobacteria**. The table updates treatment of nontuberculous mycobacteria infection in children.

44. **Varicella**. The epidemiology, diagnosis, and prevention portions are updated. The table shows expanded diagnostic tests for varicella-zoster infections. Recommendations for expanded use of varicella-zoster vaccine, recommendations for use of measles-mumps-rubella-varicella (MMRV) vaccine, guidance for management of susceptible people exposed to varicella, and a revised definition for evidence of immunity to varicella are added.

45. **New Chapters**
    - *Baylisascaris* **Infections**
    - **Metapneumovirus, Human**
    - **West Nile Virus**

SECTION 4. ANTIMICROBIAL AGENTS AND RELATED THERAPY

1. **Fluoroquinolones.** This section is updated to include indications approved by the Food and Drug Administration for use of fluoroquinolones in children and recommendations in the AAP statement on fluoroquinolone use in children.

2. **Appropriate Use of Antimicrobial Agents.** Guidelines from the American Academy of Pediatrics for treatment of children with otitis media are incorporated.

3. **The following have been updated:**
   - Tables of Antibacterial Drug Dosages (Tables 4.2, p 751, and 4.3, p 753)
   - Sexually Transmitted Infections (Table 4.4, p 766). This table includes the 2006 CDC treatment guidelines for sexually transmitted infections.
   - Antifungal Drugs for Systemic Fungal Infections. Caspofungin, voriconazole, micafungin, and anidulafungin are added and therapy for specific fungal infections is updated.
   - Antiviral Drugs (Table 4.9, p 785). Doses and specific therapeutic options are updated.
   - Tables 4.10 (p 791) and 4.11 (p 818), Drugs for Parasitic Infections include recommendations from the 2004 *Medical Letter on Drugs and Therapeutics*.

4. **Antiretroviral Therapy.** These tables are eliminated and replaced with a Web site that provides current information.

5. **New Chapter and Table**
   - Drug Interactions (p 742) and Table 4.1 (p 743) are added and include information about inhibition or induction of cytochrome P450 enzymes.

SECTION 5. ANTIMICROBIAL PROPHYLAXIS

1. **Antimicrobial Prophylaxis in Pediatric Surgical Patients.** Table 5.1, Recommendations for Preoperative Antimicrobial Prophylaxis, are updated as provided in the 2004 *Medical Letter on Drugs and Therapeutics* recommendations.

APPENDICES

1. **Appendix I. Directory of Services** is updated to include current contact information.

2. **Appendix III. Guide to Contraindications and Precautions to Immunizations** is updated to include Tdap, MCV4, PCV7, MMRV, and rotavirus vaccines.

3. **Appendix IV. National Vaccine Injury Act Reporting and Compensation Table** now includes inactivated and attenuated influenza vaccine and hepatitis A vaccine.

4. **Appendix IX. Nationally Notifiable Infectious Diseases in the United States** now includes Shiga toxin-positive, nonserogrouped enterohemorrhagic *Escherichia coli*; SARS-associated coronavirus disease; *Staphylococcus aureus* (both vancomycin-intermediately susceptible *S aureus* and vancomycin-resistant *S aureus*); and pediatric deaths attributable to influenza. A Web site is provided to access notifiable infectious diseases listed by year.

OTHER

The Committee on Infectious Diseases expects that other vaccines will be licensed by the Food and Drug Administration before the next edition of the *Red Book* is published. Current status of licensure and approval of new vaccines can be found at **www.aapredbook.org/news/vaccstatus.pdf** and recommendations for use of these vaccines can be found on the AAP Web site (**www.aap.org**).

Active and Passive Immunization

‥‥‥‥‥‥‥‥
PROLOGUE

The ultimate goal of immunization is eradication of disease; the immediate goal is prevention of disease in individuals or groups. To accomplish these goals, physicians must make timely immunization, including active and passive immunoprophylaxis, a high priority in the care of infants, children, adolescents, and adults. The global eradication of smallpox in 1977 and elimination of poliomyelitis disease from the Americas in 1991 serve as models for fulfilling the promise of disease control through immunization. Both of these accomplishments were achieved by combining a comprehensive immunization program providing consistent, high levels of vaccine coverage with intensive surveillance and effective public health disease control measures. Future success in the worldwide elimination of measles, rubella, and hepatitis B is possible through implementation of similar prevention strategies.

High immunization rates have reduced dramatically the incidence of diphtheria, measles, mumps, polio, rubella (congenital and acquired), tetanus, and *Haemophilus influenzae* type b disease (see Table 1.1, p 2) in the United States. Declines in the incidence of varicella, invasive pneumococcal disease, and hepatitis A also have occurred. Yet, because organisms that cause these diseases persist in the United States and elsewhere around the world, continued immunization efforts must be maintained and strengthened. Discoveries in immunology, molecular biology, and medical genetics have resulted in burgeoning vaccine research. Licensing of new, improved, and safer vaccines; anticipated arrival of additional combination vaccines; and application of novel vaccine delivery systems promise a new era of preventive medicine. The advent of population-based postlicensure studies of new vaccines facilitates detection of rare adverse events temporally associated with immunization that were undetected during prelicensure clinical trials. Studies of the rare occurrence of intussusception after administration of the oral rhesus rotavirus vaccine confirmed the value of such surveillance systems. Physicians must regularly update their knowledge about specific vaccines, including information about their recommended use, safety, and effectiveness.

Each edition of the *Red Book* provides recommendations for immunization of infants, children, and adolescents. These recommendations, which are harmonized among the Advisory Committee on Immunization Practices of the Centers for Disease Control and Prevention, the American Academy of Family Physicians, and the American Academy of Pediatrics (AAP), are based on careful analysis of disease epidemiology, the benefits and risks of immunization, and the feasibility of implementation. Whereas immunization recommendations represent the best approach to disease prevention on a population basis, in rare circumstances, individual considerations may warrant a different approach.

Use of trade names and commercial sources in the *Red Book* is for identification purposes only and does not imply endorsement by the AAP. References to Internet

Table 1.1. Baseline 20th Century Annual Morbidity and 2004 Morbidity From 10 Diseases With Vaccines Recommended Before 1990 for Universal Use in Children: United States[1]

Disease	Baseline 20th Century Annual Morbidity	2004 Morbidity	% Decrease
Smallpox	48 164[2]	0	100
Diphtheria	175 885[3]	0	100
Pertussis	147 271[4]	25 827	82
Tetanus	1314[5]	34	97
Poliomyelitis (paralytic)	16 316[6]	0	100
Measles	503 282[7]	37	>99
Mumps	152 209[8]	258	>99
Rubella	47 745[9]	10	>99
Congenital rubella syndrome	823[10]	0	100
Haemophilus influenzae type b	20 000[11]	196[12]	>99

[1] Adapted from Centers for Disease Control and Prevention. Impact of vaccines universally recommended for children— United States, 1990–1998. *MMWR Morb Mortal Wkly Rep.* 1999;48:243–248; and Centers for Disease Control and Prevention. Notice to readers: final 2004 reports of notifiable diseases. *MMWR Morb Mortal Wkly Rep.* 2005;54:770–780.
[2] Average annual number of cases during 1900–1904.
[3] Average annual number of reported cases during 1920–1922, 3 years before vaccine development.
[4] Average annual number of reported cases during 1922–1925, 4 years before vaccine development.
[5] Estimated number of cases based on reported number of deaths during 1922–1926, assuming a case-fatality rate of 90%
[6] Average annual number of reported cases during 1951–1954, 4 years before vaccine licensure.
[7] Average annual number of reported cases during 1958–1962, 5 years before vaccine licensure.
[8] Number of reported cases in 1968, the first year reporting began and the first year after vaccine licensure.
[9] Average annual number of reported cases during 1966–1968, 3 years before vaccine licensure.
[10] Estimated number of cases based on seroprevalence data in the population and on the risk that women infected during a childbearing year would have a fetus with congenital rubella syndrome.
[11] Estimated number of cases from population-based surveillance studies before vaccine licensure in 1985.
[12] Represents invasive disease in children younger than 5 years of age and includes *H influenzae* strains that were not serotyped.

sites in the *Red Book* are provided as a service to readers and do not constitute AAP endorsement of these sites.

SOURCES OF VACCINE INFORMATION

In addition to the *Red Book*, which is published at intervals of approximately 3 years, physicians should use evidence-based literature and other sources for data to answer specific vaccine questions encountered in practice. Such sources include the following:
• ***Pediatrics.*** Policy statements developed by the Committee on Infectious Diseases (COID) providing updated recommendations are published in *Pediatrics* between editions of the *Red Book*. Policy statements also may be accessed via the American Academy of Pediatrics (AAP) Web site (**www.aap.org**).

The updated recommended childhood and adolescent immunization schedule for the United States is published annually in the January issue of *Pediatrics* and elsewhere (see Scheduling Immunizations, p 23).

- *AAP News.* Policy statements (or statement summaries) from the COID often are published initially in *AAP News*, the Academy's monthly newsmagazine (**www.aapnews.org**), to inform the AAP membership promptly of new recommendations.

- *Morbidity and Mortality Weekly Report (MMWR).* Published weekly by the Centers for Disease Control and Prevention (CDC), *MMWR* contains current vaccine recommendations; reports of specific disease activity; alerts concerning vaccine availability; changes in vaccine formulations, vaccine safety issues, and policy statements; and other infectious disease and vaccine information. Recommendations of the Advisory Committee on Immunization Practices (ACIP) of the CDC are published periodically, often as supplements to the *MMWR*, and are posted on the CDC Web site (**www.cdc.gov/mmwr**). Recommendations of the ACIP are not official until approved by the CDC director and the Department of Health and Human Services and published in the *MMWR*.

- **Manufacturers' package inserts (product labels).** Manufacturers provide product-specific information with each vaccine product. This information also is published in the *Physicians' Desk Reference*, which is published annually. The product label must be in full compliance with US Food and Drug Administration (FDA) regulations pertaining to labeling for prescription drugs, including indications and usage, dosages, routes of administration, clinical pharmacology, contraindications, and adverse events. Each package insert lists contents of the vaccine, including preservatives, stabilizers, antimicrobial agents, adjuvants, and suspending fluids. Health care professionals should be familiar with the label for each product they administer. Most manufacturers maintain Web sites with current information concerning new vaccine releases and changes in labeling. Additionally, 24-hour contact telephone numbers for medical questions are available in the *Physicians' Desk Reference* (**www.pdr.net**).

- *Health Information for International Travel.* This useful monograph is published approximately every 2 years by the CDC as a guide to requirements of various countries for specific immunizations. The monograph also provides information about other vaccines recommended for travel in specific areas and other information for travelers. This document can be purchased from the Superintendent of Documents, US Government Printing Office, Washington, DC 20402–9235. This information also is available on the CDC Web site (**www.cdc.gov/travel**). For further sources of information on international travel, see International Travel (p 98).

- **CDC materials.** A CDC textbook, *Epidemiology and Prevention of Vaccine-Preventable Diseases*, also referred to as the Pink Book, provides detailed information on the use and administration of childhood vaccines as well as selected ACIP statements and other vaccine-related information (for copies of the Pink Book, contact the Public Health Foundation at 877-252-1200 or access **www.cdc.gov/nip/publications/pink**). A CDC publication titled *Manual for Surveillance of Vaccine-Preventable Diseases* provides insight into principles used to investigate and control outbreaks of disease when immunization levels decrease. The CDC's National Immunization Program (NIP) publishes a series of brochures on immunization topics and produces a CD-ROM that contains a wide range of resources, including vaccine information statements (VISs) and the complete text of the Pink Book. To obtain CDC materials, contact the CDC information center at 1-800-CDC-INFO (1-800-232-4636), or access the NIP Web site (**www.cdc.gov/nip**).

- **Satellite broadcasts and Web-based training courses.** The NIP, in conjunction with the Public Health Training Network, conducts several immunization-related "train the trainer" courses live via satellite and over the Internet each year. Annual course offerings include the Immunization Update, Vaccines for International Travel, Influenza, and a 4-part introductory course on the Epidemiology and Prevention of Vaccine-Preventable Diseases. The course schedule, slide sets, and written materials can be accessed on the Internet (**www.cdc.gov/nip/ed/_satellite_broadcasts.htm**).
- **Immunization information e-mail–based inquiry system.** The NIP is available to respond to immunization-related questions submitted from health care professionals and members of the public. Individualized responses to inquiries typically are sent within 24 hours. Inquiries should be sent via e-mail (**NIPINFO@cdc.gov**).
- **CDC Telephone Hotline.** The hotline is a telephone-based resource available to answer immunization-related questions from health care professionals and members of the public. The hotline may be reached at 1-800-CDC-INFO (1-800-232-4636) and is available in English and Spanish.

  Printed information on immunizations also can be obtained from the NIP through the Web site (**www.cdc.gov/nip**) or by fax at 1-888-CDC-FAXX (1-888-232-3299).
- **Independent sources of reliable immunization information.** Appendix I (p 839) provides a list of reliable immunization information resources including facts concerning vaccine efficacy, clinical applications, schedules, and unbiased information about safety. Two organizations particularly are comprehensive in addressing concerns of practicing physicians: the National Network for Immunization Information (**www.immunizationinfo.org**) and the Immunization Action Coalition (**www.immunize.org**).
- **Vaccine price list.** Information about pediatric and adolescent vaccines, types of packaging, CDC costs, and private sector costs is available at **www.cdc.gov/nip/vfc/cdc_vac_price_list.htm**.

Other resources* include the FDA and Institute of Medicine; infectious disease experts at university-affiliated hospitals, at medical schools, and in private practice; and state immunization programs and local public health departments. Information can be obtained from state and local health departments about current epidemiology of diseases, immunization recommendations, legal requirements, public health policies, and nursery school, child care, and school health concerns or requirements.

---

* Appendix I, Directory of Resources, p 839.

INFORMING PATIENTS AND PARENTS

Parents and patients should be informed about the benefits and risks of disease preventive and therapeutic procedures, including immunization. The patient, parents, and/or legal guardian should be informed about benefits to be derived from vaccines in preventing diseases in immunized people and in the community where they live and about the risks of those vaccines. Questions should be encouraged and adequate time should be allowed so that information is understood.

The National Childhood Vaccine Injury Act (NCVIA) of 1986 included requirements for notifying *all* patients and parents about vaccine benefits and risks. Whether vaccines are purchased with private or public funds, this legislation mandates that a vaccine information statement (VIS) be provided each time a vaccine covered under the National Vaccine Injury Compensation Program (VICP) is administered (see Table 1.2). This applies in all settings, such as clinics, offices, and hospitals (eg, for the birth dose of hepatitis B vaccine). Providing this information before the day of immunization is desirable. For vaccines not yet included in the VICP, VISs are available but are not mandated unless the vaccine is purchased through a contract with the Centers for Disease Control and Prevention (CDC [ie, the Vaccines for Children Program, state immunization grants, or state purchases through the CDC]). Copies of current VISs are available on the NIP Web site (**www.cdc.gov/nip/publications/ VIS/default.htm**) and the Immunization Action Coalition Web site (**www.immunize.org**) in English and many other languages. Copies also can be obtained from the American Academy of Pediatrics (AAP), state and local health departments, and vaccine manufacturers or by calling the CDC telephone hotline (1-800-232-4636). Information is available in English and in Spanish. Physicians need to ensure that the VIS provided is the current version by noting the date of publication. The latest version can be determined by accessing the NIP Web site (**www.cdc.gov/ nip/publications/VIS/default.htm**) or by calling the CDC telephone hotline.

The NCVIA requires physicians administering vaccines covered by the VICP, whether purchased with private or public funds, to record in the patient's medical record information shown in Table 1.2 as well as confirmation that the relevant VIS was provided at the time of immunization. For vaccines purchased through CDC contract, physicians are required to record the VIS date of publication as well as the date on which the VIS was provided to the patient, parent, and/or legal guardian. Although VIS distribution and vaccine record-keeping requirements do not apply to privately purchased vaccines not covered by the VICP, the American Academy of Pediatrics (AAP) recommends following the same record-keeping practices for all vaccines. The AAP also recommends recording the site and route of administration and vaccine expiration date when administering any vaccine.

New VISs do not require parents' or patients' signatures to indicate that they have read and understood the material. However, the health care professional has the option to obtain a signature. Providers should be familiar with requirements of the state in which they practice. Whether or not a signature is obtained, health care professionals should document in the chart that the VIS has been provided and discussed with the patient, parent, and/or legal guardian.

Table 1.2. Guidance in Using Vaccine Information Statements (VISs)[1]

Distribution	Documentation in the Patient's Medical Record
Must be provided each time a VICP-covered vaccine is administered[2]	Vaccine manufacturer, lot number, and date of administration[2]
Given to patient (nonminor), parent, and/or legal guardian[2]	Name and business address of the health care professional administering the vaccine[2]
Must be the current version[3]	Date that VIS is provided (and VIS publication date[3])
Can provide (not substitute) other written materials or audiovisual aids in addition to VISs	Site (eg, deltoid area) and route (eg, intramuscular) of administration and expiration date of the vaccine[4]

VICP indicates Vaccine Injury Compensation Program.

[1] VISs are available at **www.cdc.gov/nip/publications/vis/default.htm**.

[2] Required under the National Childhood Vaccine Injury Act.

[3] Required by Centers for Disease Control and Prevention (CDC) regulations for vaccines purchased through CDC contract.

[4] Recommended by the American Academy of Pediatrics.

Parental Concerns About Immunization

Health care professionals should anticipate that some parents will question the need for or the safety of immunizations, refuse certain vaccines, or even decide to reject all immunizations for their child. Some parents may have religious or philosophic objections to immunization, which are permitted by some states. Other parents want only to enter into a dialogue with their child's physician about the risks and benefits of one or more of the vaccines. Several factors contribute to parental vaccine concerns, including: (1) lack of information about the vaccine being given and about immunizations in general; (2) opposing information from other sources (eg, alternative medicine providers, antivaccination organizations, and some religious groups); (3) mistrust of the source of information (eg, child's health care professional); (4) perceived risk of serious vaccine adverse events; (5) concern regarding number of injections; (6) information being delivered in a way not tailored to individual concern; (7) information being delivered at an inconvenient time (eg, the day of the immunization); (8) not perceiving risk of vaccines accurately; and (9) lack of appreciation of the severity of vaccine-preventable diseases. One important aspect physicians can control is their relationship with their patients and parents. Physicians are the most trusted source of health information for parents. If parents trust their child's physician, information presented to them by the physician in support of vaccines is accepted more readily. A nonjudgmental approach is best for parents who question the need for immunizations. Ideally, health care professionals should determine in general terms what parents understand about vaccines their children will be receiving, the nature of their concerns, their health beliefs, and what information they find credible.

People understand and react to vaccine information on the basis of a variety of factors, including previous experiences, attitudes, health beliefs, personal values, and education. The method in which data are presented about immunizations as well as a person's perceptions of the risks of disease, perceived ability to control those risks, and risk preference also contribute to understanding of immunizations. For some people, the risk of immunization can be viewed as disproportionately greater so that immunization is not perceived as beneficial, in part because of the relative infrequency of vaccine-preventable diseases in the United States. Others can dwell on sociopolitical issues, such as mandatory immunization, informed consent, and the primacy of individual rights over that of societal benefit.

Parents may be aware through the media or information from nonauthoritative Web sites of controversial issues about vaccines their child is scheduled to receive. Many issues about childhood vaccines communicated by these means are presented incompletely or inaccurately. When a parent initiates discussion about a vaccine controversy, the health care professional should discuss specific concerns and provide factual information, using language appropriate for parents. Through direct dialogue with parents and the use of available resources, health care professionals can help reduce and possibly prevent acceptance of inaccurate media reports and information from nonauthoritative sources.

Helpful information sources that can be provided to parents or to which parents can be directed are the National Immunization Program's "Parent's Guide to Childhood Immunization" (**www.cdc.gov/nip** or contact the CDC telephone hotline at 1-800-232-4636), the National Partnership for Immunizations' "Reference Guide . . . to Vaccines and Vaccine Safety" (**www.partnersforimmunization.org** or telephone 301-656-0003), and the AAP Immunization Initiatives Web site (**www. cispimmunize.org/fam/fam_main.html**). Parents should be advised of state laws pertaining to school or child care entry, which can require that unimmunized children stay home from school during disease outbreaks. Documentation of such discussions in the patient's record may help to decrease any potential liability should a vaccine-preventable disease occur in an unimmunized patient. This *informed refusal* documentation should note that the parent was informed why the immunization was recommended, the risk and benefits of immunization, and the possible consequences of not allowing the vaccine to be administered. A sample Refusal to Vaccinate form can be found on the AAP Web site at **www.cispimmunize.org/pro/pdf/ RefusaltoVaccinate_2pageform.pdf**.

PARENTAL REFUSAL OF IMMUNIZATION

The approach of a health care professional to a parent who refuses immunization of his or her child is complex and should be based on the reason for the refusal and the knowledge of the parent. Suggested responses to parental refusals of immunization of children are outlined as follows*:

---

* Diekema DS, American Academy of Pediatrics Committee on Bioethics. Responding to parental refusals of immunization of children. *Pediatrics*. 2005;115:1428–1431

- The pediatrician should listen carefully and respectfully to the parent's concerns, recognizing that some parents may not use the same decision criteria as the physician and may weigh evidence differently than does the physician.
- The pediatrician should share honestly what is and is not known about the risks and benefits of the vaccine in question and attempt to correct any misperceptions and misinformation.
- The pediatrician should assist parents in understanding that the risks of any vaccine should not be considered in isolation but in comparison with the risks to the child and community should the child remain unimmunized.
- Parents can be referred to one of several reputable and data-based Web sites for additional information on specific immunizations and the diseases they prevent (see Internet Resources for Immunization Information, p 53).
- Many parents have concerns related to 1 or 2 specific vaccines. The pediatrician should discuss the benefits and risks of each vaccine, because a parent who is reluctant to accept the administration of 1 vaccine may be willing to allow others.
- Parents who have concerns about administering multiple vaccines to a child in a single visit may have their concerns addressed by using methods to reduce the pain of injection (see Managing Injection Pain, p 22) or by developing a schedule of immunizations that does not require multiple injections at a single visit.
- Physicians also should explore the possibility that cost is a reason for refusing immunization and assist the parents to by helping them obtain recommended immunizations for their children.
- For all cases in which parents refuse vaccine administration, pediatricians should take advantage of their ongoing relationship with the family and revisit the immunization discussion on subsequent visits.
- Continued refusal after adequate discussion should be respected unless the child is put at significant risk of serious harm (eg, during an epidemic). Only then should state agencies be involved to override parental discretion on the basis of medical neglect.
- Physician concerns about liability should be addressed by appropriate documentation of the discussion of benefits of immunization and risks associated with remaining unimmunized.
- Physicians also may wish to consider having the parents sign a refusal waiver (a sample refusal-to-vaccinate waiver can be found at **www.cispimmunize.org/pro/ pdf/RefusaltoVaccinate_2pageform.pdf**).
- In general, pediatricians should avoid discharging a patient from their practice solely because a parent refuses immunizations for the child. However, when a substantial level of distrust develops, significant differences in the philosophy of care emerge, or poor quality of communication persists, the pediatrician can encourage the family to find another physician or practice after providing sufficient advance notice in writing to the patient or custodial parent or legal guardian to permit another health care professional to be secured.

ACTIVE IMMUNIZATION

Active immunization involves administration of all or part of a microorganism or a modified product of that microorganism (eg, a toxoid, a purified antigen, or an antigen produced by genetic engineering) to evoke an immunologic response that mimics that of natural infection but that usually presents little or no risk to the recipient. Immunization can result in antitoxin, antiadherence, anti-invasive, or neutralizing activity or other types of protective humoral or cellular responses in the recipient. Some immunizing agents provide nearly complete lifelong protection against disease, some provide partial protection, and some must be readministered at regular intervals to maintain protection. The effectiveness of a vaccine is assessed by evidence of protection against the natural disease. Induction of antibodies commonly is an indirect measure of protection (eg, antitoxin against *Clostridium tetani* or neutralizing antibody against measles virus), but for some conditions (eg, pertussis), the immunologic response that correlates with protection is poorly understood, and serum antibody concentration does not always predict protection.

Vaccines incorporating an intact infectious agent may be live-attenuated (weakened) or killed (inactivated). Vaccines licensed for immunization in the United States are listed in Table 1.3 (p 10). The US Food and Drug Administration (FDA) maintains and updates a Web site listing vaccines licensed for immunization in the United States (**www.fda.gov/cber/vaccine/licvacc.htm**). Many viral vaccines contain live-attenuated virus. Although active infection (with viral replication) ensues after administration of these vaccines, usually little or no adverse host reaction occurs. The vaccines for some viruses and most bacteria are inactivated (killed) components, subunit (purified components) preparations, or inactivated toxins or are conjugated chemically to immunobiologically active proteins (eg, tetanus toxoid, nontoxic variant of mutant diphtheria toxin, or meningococcal outer membrane protein complex). Viruses and bacteria in inactivated, subunit, and conjugate vaccine preparations are not capable of replicating in the host; therefore, these vaccines must contain a sufficient antigenic mass to stimulate a desired response. Maintenance of long-lasting immunity with inactivated viral or bacterial vaccines may require periodic administration of booster doses. Inactivated vaccines may not elicit the range of immunologic response provided by live-attenuated agents. For example, an injected inactivated viral vaccine may evoke sufficient serum antibody or cell-mediated immunity but evoke only minimal local antibody in the form of secretory immunoglobulin (Ig) A. Thus, mucosal protection after administration of inactivated vaccines generally is inferior to mucosal immunity induced by live vaccines. Although systemic infection is prevented or ameliorated by the presence of serum and cellular factors, local infection or colonization with the agent can occur. However, viruses and bacteria in inactivated vaccines cannot replicate in or be excreted by the vaccine recipient as infectious agents and, thereby, cannot adversely affect immunosuppressed vaccinees or contacts of vaccinees.

Recommendations for dose, vaccine storage and handling, route and technique of administration, and immunization schedules should be followed for predictable, effective immunization (see disease-specific chapters in Section 3). Adherence to recommended guidelines is critical to the success of immunization practices.

Table 1.3. Vaccines Licensed for Immunization and Distributed in the United States and Their Routes of Administration[1]

Vaccine	Type	Route
BCG	Live bacteria	ID (preferred) or SC
Diphtheria-tetanus (DT, Td)	Toxoids	IM
DTaP	Toxoids and inactivated bacterial components	IM
DTaP, hepatitis B, and IPV	Toxoids and inactivated bacterial components, recombinant viral antigen, inactivated virus	IM
Hepatitis A	Inactivated viral antigen	IM
Hepatitis B	Recombinant viral antigen	IM
Hepatitis A-hepatitis B	Inactivated and recombinant viral antigens	IM
Hib conjugates[2]	Polysaccharide-protein conjugate	IM
Hib conjugate-DTaP (PRP-T[2] reconstituted with DTaP)	Polysaccharide-protein conjugate with toxoids and inactivated bacterial components	IM
Hib conjugate (PRP-OMP[2]) -hepatitis B	Polysaccharide-protein conjugate with recombinant viral antigen	IM
Influenza	Inactivated viral components	IM
Influenza	Live-attenuated virus	Intranasal
Japanese encephalitis	Inactivated virus	SC
Measles	Live-attenuated virus	SC
Meningococcal	Polysaccharide	SC
Meningococcal	Polysaccharide-protein conjugate	IM
MMR	Live-attenuated viruses	SC
MMRV	Live-attenuated viruses	SC
Mumps	Live-attenuated virus	SC
Pneumococcal	Polysaccharide	IM or SC
Pneumococcal	Polysaccharide-protein conjugate	IM
Poliovirus (IPV)	Inactivated virus	SC or IM
Rabies	Inactivated virus	IM
Rotavirus	Live-attenuated virus	Oral
Rubella	Live-attenuated virus	SC
Tdap	Toxoids and inactivated bacterial component	IM
Tetanus	Toxoid	IM
Typhoid Parenteral	Capsular polysaccharide	IM
Oral	Live-attenuated bacteria	Oral
Varicella	Live-attenuated virus	SC
Yellow fever	Live-attenuated virus	SC

BCG indicates bacille Calmette-Guérin; ID, intradermal; SC, subcutaneous; DT, diphtheria and tetanus toxoids (for children younger than 7 years of age); Td, diphtheria and tetanus toxoids (for children 7 years of age or older and adults); IM, intramuscular; DTaP, diphtheria and tetanus toxoids and acellular pertussis, adsorbed; Hib, *Haemophilus influenzae* type b; PRP-T, polyribosylribitol phosphate-tetanus toxoid; PRP-OMP, polyribosylribitol phosphate-meningococcal outer membrane protein; MMR, live measles-mumps-rubella; MMRV, live measles-mumps-rubella-varicella; IPV, inactivated poliovirus; Tdap, tetanus toxoid, reduced diphtheria toxoid, and acellular pertussis.

[1] Other vaccines licensed in the United States but not distributed include anthrax, smallpox, rhesus tetravalent rotavirus, and oral poliovirus (OPV) vaccines. The FDA maintains a Web site listing currently licensed vaccines in the United States (**www.fda.gov/cber/vaccine/licvacc.htm**). The AAP maintains a Web site (**www.aapredbook.org/news/vaccstatus.shtml**) showing status of licensure and recommendations for new vaccines.

[2] See Table 3.11, p 315.

Immunizing Antigens

Physicians should be familiar with the major constituents of the products they use. The major constituents, including cell line derivation or animal derivatives as relevant, are listed in the package inserts. If a vaccine is produced by different manufacturers, differences may exist in the active and/or inert ingredients and the relative amounts contained in the various products. The major constituents of vaccines include the following:

- **Active immunizing antigens.** Some vaccines consist of a single antigen that is a highly defined constituent (eg, tetanus or diphtheria toxoid). In other vaccines, antigens that provoke protective immune responses vary substantially in chemical composition and number (eg, acellular pertussis components, *Haemophilus influenzae* type b, and pneumococcal and meningococcal products). Vaccines containing live-attenuated viruses (measles-mumps-rubella [MMR], measles-mumps-rubella-varicella [MMRV], varicella, oral poliovirus [OPV], live-attenuated influenza vaccine, oral rotavirus vaccine), killed viruses or portions of virus (eg, enhanced inactivated poliovirus [IPV], hepatitis A, and inactivated influenza vaccines), and viral proteins incorporated into a vaccine through recombinant technology (eg, hepatitis B vaccine) produce both humoral and cellular-mediated responses to ensure long-term protection.

- **Conjugating agents.** Carrier proteins of proven immunologic potential (eg, tetanus toxoid, nontoxic variant of diphtheria toxin, meningococcal outer membrane protein complex), when chemically combined to less immunogenic polysaccharide antigens (eg, *H influenzae* type b, meningococcal and pneumococcal polysaccharides), enhance the type and magnitude of immune responses in people with immature immune systems, particularly children younger than 2 years of age.

- **Suspending fluid.** The suspending fluid commonly is as simple as sterile water for injection or saline solution, but it may be a complex tissue-culture fluid. This fluid may contain proteins or other constituents derived from the medium and biological system in which the vaccine is produced (eg, egg antigens, gelatin, or cell culture-derived antigens).

- **Preservatives, stabilizers, and antimicrobial agents.** Trace amounts of thimerosal (less than 0.5 µg/0.25 mL of vaccine), other chemicals, and certain antimicrobial agents (such as neomycin or streptomycin sulfate) may be included in some vaccines and immune globulin preparations to prevent bacterial growth or to stabilize an antigen. Allergic reactions may occur if the recipient is sensitive to one or more of these additives. Whenever feasible, these reactions should be anticipated by screening the potential vaccinee for known severe allergy to specific vaccine components. Standardized forms are available to assist clinicians in screening for allergies and other potential contraindications to immunization (**www.immunize.org/catg.d/p4060scr.pdf**).

- **Adjuvants.** An aluminum salt commonly is used in varying amounts to increase immunogenicity and to prolong the stimulatory effect, particularly for vaccines containing inactivated microorganisms or their products (eg, hepatitis B and diphtheria and tetanus toxoids).

Vaccine Handling and Storage

Vaccines should be stored at recommended temperatures. Inattention to vaccine storage conditions can contribute to vaccine failure. Exposure of inactivated vaccines to freezing temperature (0.0°C [32.0°F] or colder) is the most common storage error. Live-virus vaccines, including MMR, MMRV, varicella, yellow fever, live-attenuated influenza, and OPV vaccines, are sensitive to increased temperature (heat sensitive). Inactivated vaccines may tolerate limited exposure to elevated temperatures but are damaged rapidly by freezing (cold sensitive). Examples of cold-sensitive vaccines include diphtheria and tetanus toxoids and acellular pertussis (DTaP and tetanus toxoid, reduced diphtheria toxoid, and acellular pertussis [Tdap]) vaccines, IPV vaccine, *H influenzae* type b (Hib) vaccine, pneumococcal polysaccharide and conjugate vaccines, hepatitis A and hepatitis B vaccines, inactivated influenza vaccine, and meningococcal polysaccharide and conjugate vaccines. Some products may show physical evidence of altered integrity, and others may retain their normal appearance despite a loss of potency. Physical appearance is not an appropriate basis for determining vaccine acceptability. Therefore, all personnel responsible for handling vaccines in an office or clinic setting should be familiar with standard procedures designed to minimize risk of vaccine failure. Recommended storage conditions for commonly used vaccines are listed in Table 1.4 (p 13); new vaccines and new formulations of currently available products may have storage requirements different from those listed. In addition, storage recommendations may be revised by the manufacturer. Revisions require approval by the FDA.

Recommendations for handling and storage of selected biologicals are summarized in several areas, including the package insert for each product; in a publication titled *Vaccine Management*, available from the Centers for Disease Control and Prevention (CDC)*; and in a Web-based toolkit available at **www2a.cdc.gov/nip/isd/ shtoolkit/splash.html**. The most current information about recommended vaccine storage conditions and handling instructions can be obtained directly from manufacturers; their telephone numbers are listed in product labels (package inserts) and in the *Physicians' Desk Reference*, which is published yearly. The following guidelines are suggested as part of a quality control system for safe handling and storage of vaccines in an office or clinic setting.

PERSONNEL

- Designate one person as the vaccine coordinator, and assign responsibility for ensuring that vaccines and other biological agents and products are handled and stored in a careful, safe, recommended, and documentable manner. Assign a backup person to assume these responsibilities during times of illness or vacation.
- Inform all people who will be handling vaccines about specific storage requirements and stability limitations of the products they will encounter (see Table 1.4, p 13). The details of proper storage conditions should be posted on or near each refrigerator or freezer used for vaccine storage or should be readily available to staff.

---

* Centers for Disease Control and Prevention. *Vaccine Management: Recommendations for Handling and Storage of Selected Biologicals.* Atlanta, GA: US Department of Health and Human Services, Public Health Service; 2005

Table 1.4. Recommended Storage of Commonly Used Vaccines[1]

Vaccine	Storage	Normal Appearance
Diphtheria and tetanus toxoids and acellular pertussis (DTaP and Tdap) vaccines, adsorbed	2°C–8°C (35°F–46°F). Do not freeze. As little as 24 h at <2°C (<35°F) or >25°C (>77°F) may cause antigens to fall from suspension and be difficult to resuspend.	Markedly turbid and whitish suspension. If product contains clumps of material that cannot be resuspended with vigorous shaking, it should NOT be used.
Diphtheria toxoid, adsorbed	2°C–8°C. Do not freeze.	Turbid and white, slightly gray, or slightly pink suspension.
DTaP, hepatitis B virus vaccine inactivated (recombinant), and inactivated poliovirus vaccine	2°C–8°C. Do not freeze	Turbid, white suspension.
DTaP and Hib conjugate vaccine	Do not freeze. Reconstituted product must be used within 30 min.	After reconstitution and agitation, the vaccine will appear whitish in color.
Hepatitis A virus vaccine, inactivated	2°C–8°C. Do not freeze.	Opaque, white suspension.
Hepatitis A-hepatitis B combination vaccine	2°C–8°C. Do not freeze.	Homogeneous white turbid suspension.
Hepatitis B virus vaccine inactivated (recombinant)	2°C–8°C. Do not freeze.	After thorough agitation, a slightly opaque, white suspension.
Hib conjugate vaccine: HbOC (diphtheria CRM197 protein conjugate)	2°C–8°C. Do not freeze.	Clear, colorless liquid.
Hib conjugate vaccine (meningococcal protein conjugate) and hepatitis B (recombinant) vaccine	2°C–8°C. Do not freeze.	Slightly opaque, white suspension.
Hib conjugate vaccine: PRP-OMP (meningococcal protein conjugate)	2°C–8°C. Do not freeze.	Clear, colorless liquid.

Table 1.4. Recommended Storage of Commonly Used Vaccines, continued

Vaccine	Storage	Normal Appearance
Hib conjugate vaccine: PRP-T (tetanus toxoid conjugate)	Lyophilized formulation: 2°C–8°C. Do not freeze. Reconstituted formulation: 2°C–8°C. Do not freeze. Store diluent with product. Vaccine should be used within 24 h when reconstituted.	Lyophilized: white, lyophilized cake. Reconstituted: clear and colorless.
Influenza virus vaccine (subvirion)	2°C–8°C. Do not freeze.	Clear, colorless liquid.
Influenza virus vaccine (live-attenuated)	Keep frozen at −15°C (5°F) or colder. Storage in a frost-free freezer with a separate exterior door. May be stored in a frost-free freezer; the manufacturer-supplied freezer box no longer is required. Use of vaccine is recommended only during the influenza season for which it is manufactured. May be thawed in a refrigerator and stored at 2°C–8°F (36°–46°F) for no more than 60 h before use. Do not refreeze.	When thawed for administration, this product is a colorless to pale yellow liquid and is clear to slightly cloudy; some white proteinaceous particles may be present but do not affect use of the product.
Measles-mumps-rubella virus (MMR) vaccine, live	Lyophilized formulation: 2°C–8°C, but may be frozen. Protect from light, which may inactivate virus. Diluent: store at room temperature or refrigerate. Reconstituted formulation: 2°C–8°C. Discard reconstituted vial if not used within 8 h (keep refrigerated and protect from light).	Lyophilized: light yellow compact crystalline plug. Diluent: clear, colorless liquid. Reconstituted: clear, yellow solution.
Measles-mumps-rubella-varicella (MMRV) vaccine	See Varicella virus vaccine.	See Varicella virus vaccine.
Measles virus vaccine, live	See MMR.	See MMR.
Meningococcal conjugate vaccine	2°C–8°C. Do not freeze. Protect from light.	Homogeneous white suspension after vigorous shaking.
Meningococcal polysaccharide vaccine	Lyophilized or reconstituted formulation: 2°C–8°C. Do not freeze. Discard reconstituted multidose vials after 35 days; use single-dose vial within 30 min.	Lyophilized: white pellet. Reconstituted: clear, colorless.
Mumps virus vaccine, live	See MMR.	See MMR.
Rubella virus vaccine, live	See MMR.	See MMR.

Table 1.4. Recommended Storage of Commonly Used Vaccines, continued

Vaccine	Storage	Normal Appearance
Pneumococcal polysaccharide vaccine	2°C–8°C. Do not freeze.	Clear, colorless, or slightly opalescent liquid.
Pneumococcal conjugate vaccine	2°C–8°C. Do not freeze.	Homogeneous white suspension after vigorous shaking.
Poliovirus vaccine, inactivated (IPV)	2°C–8°C. Do not freeze.	Clear, colorless suspension. If product contains particulate matter, develops turbidity, or changes color it should NOT be used.
Rotavirus vaccine, live	Store and transport at 2°C–8°C (36°F–46°F). Administer as soon as possible after removal from refrigeration. Protect from light.	Pale yellow clear liquid that may have a pink tint.
Tetanus and diphtheria toxoids, adsorbed (Td)	2°C–8°C. Do not freeze.	Markedly turbid and white suspension. If product contains clumps of material that cannot be resuspended with vigorous shaking, it should NOT be used.
Varicella virus vaccine[2]	Lyophilized formulation: keep frozen at −15°C (5°F) or colder. Protect from light. Store only in freezer with a separate exterior door. Diluent: store at room temperature or refrigerate. For temporary storage, unreconstituted vaccine may be stored at 2°C–8°C for a maximum of 72 h. Discard unreconstituted vaccine if not used within 72 h (do not refreeze). Reconstituted formulation: use immediately; do not store. Discard reconstituted vials if not used within 30 min.	Lyophilized formulation: whitish powder. Clear, colorless liquid. Reconstituted formulation: clear, colorless to pale yellow liquid.

Hib indicates *Haemophilus influenzae* type b.

[1] See expiration date on vial for duration of stability. For recently licensed vaccines, see package inserts; instructions may be different from those for products listed in the table. Also, any changes in the formulation of available immunizing agents may alter their appearance, stability, and storage requirements. Questions about the stability of biological agents subjected to potentially harmful environmental conditions should be addressed to the manufacturer of the product in question. Parenteral drug products should be inspected visually for extraneous particulate matter and/or discoloration before administration. If these conditions exist, the product should not be administered.

[2] For questions about stability, contact the manufacturer by calling 1-800-9-VARIVAX or visit **www.varivax.com**.

Receptionists, mail clerks, and other staff members who may receive shipments also should be educated.

EQUIPMENT

- Ensure that refrigerators and freezers in which vaccines are to be stored are working properly and are capable of meeting storage requirements.
- Do not connect refrigerators or freezers to an outlet with a ground-flow circuit interrupter or one activated by a wall switch. Use plug guards and warning signs to prevent accidental dislodging of the wall plug. Post "Do not unplug" warning signs on circuit breakers.
- Equip each refrigerator and freezer compartment with a certified thermometer located at the center of the storage compartment. A certified thermometer has been individually tested against a reference standard, such as the National Institute of Standards and Technology or ASTM International. These thermometers are sold with an individually numbered certificate documenting this testing. A calibrated, constant-recording thermometer with graphical readings or a thermometer that indicates upper and lower extremes of temperature during an observation period ("minimum-maximum" thermometer) will provide more information as to whether vaccines have been exposed to potentially harmful temperatures than single-reading thermometers. Placement of vaccine cold-chain monitor cards* in refrigerators and freezers can serve to detect potentially harmful increases in temperature but should not be a substitute for use of certified thermometers.
- Maintain a logbook in which temperature readings are recorded at the beginning and end of the clinic day and in which the date, time, and duration of any mechanical malfunctions or power outages are noted. The current temperature log should be posted on the door to remind staff to monitor and record temperatures. Previous logs should be stored for a minimum of 3 years.
- Place all opened vials of vaccine in a refrigerator tray. To avoid mishaps, do not store other pharmaceutical products in the same tray. Store unopened vials in the original packaging. This facilitates inventory management and rotation of vaccine by expiration date and also protects MMR and MMRV vaccines from light.
- Equip refrigerators with several bottles of chilled water and freezers with several ice trays or ice packs to fill empty space, which will help to minimize temperature fluctuations during brief electrical or mechanical failures.

PROCEDURES

- Acceptance of vaccine on receipt of shipment:
  - Ensure that the expiration date of the delivered product has not passed.
  - Examine the merchandise and its shipping container for any evidence of damage during transport.
  - Consider whether the interval between shipment from the supplier and arrival of the product at its destination is excessive (more than 48 hours) and whether the product has been exposed to excessive heat or cold that might alter its integrity.

---

* Available from 3M Pharmaceuticals.

Review vaccine time and temperature indicators, both chemical and electronic, if included in the vaccine shipment.

- Do not accept the shipment if reasonable suspicion exists that the delivered product may have been damaged by environmental insult or improper handling during transport.
- Contact the vaccine supplier or manufacturer when unusual circumstances raise questions about the stability of a delivered vaccine. Store suspect vaccine under proper conditions and label it "Do not use" until the viability has been determined.
- Refrigerator and freezer inspection:
  - Measure the temperature of the central part of the storage compartment twice a day, and record this temperature on a temperature log. If a minimum-maximum thermometer is available, record extremes in temperature fluctuation and reset to baseline. The refrigerator temperature should be maintained between 2°C and 8°C (35°F and 46°F) with a target temperature of 40°F, and the freezer temperature should be −15°C (5°F) or colder.
  - Train staff to respond immediately to temperature recordings outside the recommended range and to document response and outcome.
  - Inspect the unit weekly for outdated vaccine and either dispose of or return expired products appropriately.
- Routine procedures:
  - Store vaccines according to temperatures recommended in the package insert.
  - Rotate vaccine supplies so that the shortest-dated vaccines are in front to reduce wastage because of expiration.
  - Promptly remove expired (outdated) vaccines from the refrigerator or freezer and dispose of them appropriately or return to manufacturer to avoid accidental use.
  - Keep opened vials of vaccine in a tray so that they are readily identifiable.
  - Store unopened vials in the original packaging.
  - Indicate on the label of each vaccine vial the date and time the vaccine was reconstituted or first opened.
  - Avoid reconstituting multiple doses of vaccine or drawing up multiple doses of vaccine in multiple syringes before immediate use. Predrawing vaccine increases the possibility of medication errors and causes uncertainty of vaccine stability.
  - When feasible, use prefilled unit-dose syringes to prevent contamination of multidose vials and errors in labeling syringes.
  - Discard reconstituted live-virus and other vaccines if not used within the interval specified in the package insert. Examples of discard times include varicella vaccine after 30 minutes and MMR vaccine after 8 hours. All reconstituted vaccines should be refrigerated during the interval in which they may be used.
  - Always store vaccines in the refrigerator or freezer as indicated, including throughout the office day.
  - Do not open more than 1 vial of a specific vaccine at a time.
  - Store vaccine only in the central storage area of the refrigerator, not on the door shelf or in peripheral areas, where temperature fluctuations are greater.
  - Do not keep food or drink in refrigerators in which vaccine is stored; this will limit frequent opening of the unit that leads to thermal instability.

- Do not store radioactive materials in the same refrigerator in which vaccines are stored.
- Discuss with all clinic or office personnel any violation of protocol for handling vaccines or any accidental storage problem (eg, electrical failure), and contact vaccine suppliers for information about disposition of the affected vaccine.
- Develop a written plan for emergency storage of vaccine in the event of a catastrophic occurrence. Office personnel should have a written and easily accessible procedure that outlines vaccine packing and transport. Vaccines that have been exposed to temperatures outside the recommended storage range may be ineffective. Vaccines should be packed in an appropriate insulated storage box and moved to a location where the appropriate storage temperatures can be maintained. Office personnel need to be aware of alternate storage sites and trained in the correct techniques to store and transport vaccines to avoid warming vaccines that need to be refrigerated or frozen and to avoid freezing vaccines that should be refrigerated (see Table 1.4, p 13). After a power outage or mechanical failure, do not assume that vaccine exposed to temperature outside the recommended range is unusable. Contact the vaccine manufacturer for guidance before discarding vaccine.

Other resources on vaccine storage and handling are available, including a video from the CDC National Immunization Program, "How to Protect Your Vaccine Supply," (available at **http://video.cdc.gov/asxgen/nip/isdvacstorage/VacStorage. wmv**). Additional materials are available at **www.cdc.gov/nip/menus/vaccines. htm#Storage**.

Vaccine Administration

GENERAL INSTRUCTIONS FOR VACCINE ADMINISTRATION

Personnel administering vaccines should take appropriate precautions to minimize risk of spread of disease to or from patients. Hand hygiene should be used before and after each new patient contact. Gloves are not required when administering vaccines unless the health care professional has open hand lesions or will come into contact with potentially infectious body fluids. Syringes and needles must be sterile and preferably disposable. To prevent inadvertent needlesticks or reuse, a needle should **not** be recapped after use, and disposable needles and syringes should be discarded promptly in puncture-proof, labeled containers. Changing needles between drawing a vaccine into a syringe and injecting it into the child is not necessary. Different vaccines should not be mixed in the same syringe unless specifically licensed and labeled for such use. Occupational Safety and Health Administration recommendations for use of gloves and needle devices are available, which are aimed at decreasing transmission of infectious agents by exposure to body fluids (**www.osha.gov/ pls/oshaweb**).

Because of the rare possibility of a severe allergic reaction to a vaccine component, people administering vaccines or other biological products should be prepared to recognize and treat allergic reactions, including anaphylaxis (see Hypersensitivity Reactions to Vaccine Constituents, p 46). Facilities and personnel should be available for treating immediate allergic reactions. This recommendation does not preclude administration of vaccines in school-based or other nonclinic settings. When possible, patients should be observed for an allergic reaction and syncope for 15 to 20 minutes after receiving immunization(s).

Syncope may occur after immunization, particularly in adolescents and young adults. Personnel should be aware of presyncopal manifestations and take appropriate measures to prevent injuries if weakness, dizziness, or loss of consciousness occurs. The relatively rapid onset of syncope in most cases suggests that having vaccine recipients *sit or lie down for 15 minutes* after immunization could avert many syncopal episodes and secondary injuries. If syncope develops, patients should be observed until they are asymptomatic.

SITE AND ROUTE OF IMMUNIZATION (ACTIVE AND PASSIVE)

ORAL VACCINES. Breastfeeding does not interfere with successful immunization with OPV or rotavirus vaccine. Vomiting within 10 minutes of receiving an oral dose is an indication for repeating the dose of OPV but not rotavirus vaccine. If the second dose of OPV vaccine is not retained, neither dose should be counted, and the vaccine should be readministered.

INTRANASAL VACCINE. Live-attenuated influenza vaccine is the only vaccine licensed for intranasal administration. This vaccine is licensed for healthy people 5 through 49 years of age. With the recipient in the upright position, approximately 0.25 mL (ie, half of the total sprayer contents) is sprayed into one nostril. An attached dose-divider clip is removed from the sprayer to administer the second half of the dose into the other nostril. If the recipient sneezes after administration, the dose should not be repeated. The vaccine can be administered during minor illnesses. However, if clinical judgment indicates that nasal congestion might impede delivery of the vaccine to the nasopharyngeal mucosa, deferral should be considered until resolution of the illness.

PARENTERAL VACCINES.* Injectable vaccines should be administered using aseptic technique in a site as free as possible from risk of local neural, vascular, or tissue injury. Data do not warrant recommendation of a single preferred site for all injections, and product recommendations of many manufacturers allow flexibility in the site of injection. Preferred sites for vaccines administered subcutaneously or intramuscularly include the anterolateral aspect of the upper thigh and the deltoid area of the upper arm.

Recommended routes of administration are included in package inserts of vaccines and are listed in Table 1.3 (p 10). The recommended route is based on studies designed to demonstrate maximum safety and efficacy. To minimize untoward local or systemic effects and ensure optimal efficacy of the immunizing procedure, vaccines should be given by the recommended route.

For intramuscular (IM) injections, the choice of site is based on the volume of the injected material and the size of the muscle. In children younger than 1 year of age

---

* For a review on intramuscular injections, see Centers for Disease Control and Prevention. *Epidemiology and Prevention of Vaccine-Preventable Diseases (Pink Book)*. Atlanta, GA: Centers for Disease Control and Prevention. For copies, contact the Public Health Foundation at 877-252-1200 or visit **www.cdc.gov/nip/ publications/pink/**.

(ie, infants), the anterolateral aspect of the thigh provides the largest muscle and is the preferred site. In older children, the deltoid muscle is usually large enough for IM injection. Some health care professionals prefer to use the anterolateral thigh muscles for toddlers. Parents and children, however, often prefer use of the deltoid muscle for immunization at 18 months of age and older, because it is associated with less pain in the affected extremity when ambulating.

Ordinarily, the upper, outer aspect of the buttocks should not be used for active immunization, because the gluteal region is covered by a significant layer of subcutaneous fat and because of the possibility of damaging the sciatic nerve. However, clinical information on the use of this area is limited. Because of diminished immunogenicity, hepatitis B and rabies vaccines should not be given in the buttocks at any age. People, especially adults, who were given hepatitis B vaccine in the buttocks should be tested for immunity and reimmunized if antibody concentrations are inadequate (see Hepatitis B, p 335).

When the upper, outer quadrant of the buttocks is used for large-volume passive immunization, such as IM administration of large volumes of Immune Globulin (IG), care must be taken to avoid injury to the sciatic nerve. The site selected should be well into the upper, outer mass of the gluteus maximus, away from the central region of the buttocks, and the needle should be directed anteriorly, that is, if the patient is lying prone, the needle is directed perpendicular to the table's surface, not perpendicular to the skin plane. The ventrogluteal site may be less hazardous for IM injection, because it is free of major nerves and vessels. This site is the center of a triangle for which the boundaries are the anterior superior iliac spine, the tubercle of the iliac crest, and the upper border of the greater trochanter.

Vaccines containing adjuvants (eg, aluminum, which most vaccines recommended for IM injection include) must be injected deep into the muscle mass. These vaccines should not be administered subcutaneously or intracutaneously, because they can cause local irritation, inflammation, granuloma formation, and tissue necrosis. Immune Globulin, Rabies Immune Globulin (RIG), Hepatitis B Immune Globulin, palivizumab, and other similar products for passive immunoprophylaxis also are injected intramuscularly, except when RIG is infiltrated around the site of a bite wound.

The needles used for IM injections should be long enough to reach the muscle mass to prevent vaccine from seeping into subcutaneous tissue and, therefore, minimize local reactions and not so long as to involve underlying nerves, blood vessels, or bone. Suggested needle lengths are shown in Table 1.5 (p 21).

Serious complications resulting from IM injections are rare. Reported adverse events include broken needles, muscle contracture, nerve injury, bacterial (staphylococcal, streptococcal, and clostridial) abscesses, sterile abscesses, skin pigmentation, hemorrhage, cellulitis, tissue necrosis, gangrene, local atrophy, periostitis, cyst or scar formation, and inadvertent injection into a joint space.

Subcutaneous (SC) injections can be administered at a 45° angle into the anterolateral aspect of the thigh or the upper outer triceps area by inserting the needle in a pinched-up fold of skin and SC tissue. A 23- or 25-gauge needle, 5/8 to 3/4 inch long, is recommended. Immune responses after SC administration of hepatitis B or recombinant rabies vaccine are decreased compared with those after IM administration of either of these vaccines; therefore, these vaccines should not be given subcutaneously. In patients with a bleeding diathesis, the risk of bleeding after IM injection

Table 1.5. Site and Needle Length by Age for Intramuscular Immunization

Age Group	Needle Length, inches (mm)	Suggested Injection Site
Preterm newborn[1]	5/8 (16)	Anterolateral thigh muscle
Term newborn[1]	5/8 (16)	Anterolateral thigh muscle
Term, age 2–12 mo	1 (25)	Anterolateral thigh muscle
Toddlers and children	5/8–1 (16–25)	Deltoid muscle of the arm
	1–1¼ (25–32)	Anterolateral thigh muscle
Adolescents and young adults		
Female and male, weight <60 kg	5/8–1 (16–25)	Deltoid muscle of the arm
Female, weight 60–90 kg	1 (25)	Deltoid muscle of the arm
Female, weight >90 kg	1½ (38)	Deltoid muscle of the arm
Male, weight 60–118 kg	1 (25)	Deltoid muscle of the arm
Male, weight >118 kg	1½ (38)	Deltoid muscle of the arm

[1] Newborn is first 28 days of life.

can be minimized by vaccine administration immediately after the patient's receipt of replacement factor, use of a 23-gauge (or smaller) needle, and immediate application of direct pressure to the immunization site for at least 2 minutes. Certain vaccines (eg, Hib vaccines except PRP-OMP [PedvaxHIB]) recommended for IM injection may be given subcutaneously to people at risk of hemorrhage after IM injection, such as people with hemophilia. For these vaccines, immune responses and clinical reactions after IM or SC injection generally have been reported to be similar.

Intradermal (ID) injections usually are given on the volar surface of the forearm. Because of the decreased antigenic mass administered with ID injections, attention to technique is essential to ensure that material is not injected subcutaneously. A 25- or 27-gauge needle is recommended. No vaccine licensed in the United States is approved for intradermal administration, and deviation from the FDA-approved route of administration is not recommended routinely.

A patient should be restrained adequately if indicated before any injection.

When multiple vaccines are administered, separate sites ordinarily should be used if possible, especially if one of the vaccines contains DTaP. When necessary, 2 or more vaccines can be given in the same limb at a single visit. The anterolateral aspect of the thigh is the preferred site for multiple simultaneous IM injections because of its greater muscle mass. The distance separating the injections is arbitrary but should be at least 1 inch if possible so that local reactions are unlikely to overlap. Multiple vaccines should not be mixed in a single syringe unless specifically licensed and labeled for administration in 1 syringe. A different needle and syringe should be used for each injection.

Aspiration before injection of vaccines or toxoids (ie, pulling back on the syringe plunger after needle insertion, before injection) is not required because there are no large blood vessels at the preferred injection sites.

A brief period of bleeding at the injection site is common and usually can be controlled by applying gentle pressure.

Managing Injection Pain

Concerns and resulting anxiety about injections are common at any age. Current immunization schedules sometimes require children to receive 4 or more injections during a single visit. Although most children older than 5 years of age usually accept immunization with minimal opposition, some children react vigorously or refuse to receive injections. Effective practical techniques can be used to ameliorate some discomfort of injections.

A planned approach to managing the child before, during, and after immunization is helpful for children of any age. Truthful and empathetic preparation for injections is beneficial. Parents should be advised not to threaten children with injections or use them as a punishment for inappropriate behavior. If possible, parents should have a role in comforting rather than restraining their child. For younger children, parents may soothe, stroke, and calm the child. For older children, parents should be coached to distract the child (see Nonpharmacologic Techniques, p 23).

INJECTION TECHNIQUE AND POSITION

A rapid plunge of the needle through the skin may decrease discomfort associated with skin penetration. The Z-track method of injection also is reported to decrease associated pain; traction is applied to the skin and subcutaneous tissues before insertion of the needle and released after the needle is withdrawn so that the injection track superficial to the muscle is displaced from the track within the muscle to seal vaccine into the muscle. The limb should be positioned to allow relaxation of the muscle to be injected. For the deltoid, some flexion of the arm may be required. For the anterolateral thigh, some degree of internal rotation may be helpful. Infants may exhibit less pain behavior when held on the lap of a parent or other caregiver. Older children may be more comfortable sitting on a parent's lap or examination table edge, hugging their parent chest to chest while an immunization is administered.

If multiple injections are to be given, having different health care professionals administer them simultaneously at multiple sites (eg, right and left anterolateral thighs) may lessen anticipation of the next injection. Allowing older children some choice in selecting the injection site may be helpful by allowing a degree of control.

TOPICAL ANESTHETIC TECHNIQUES

Some physical techniques and topically applied agents reduce the pain of injection. Applying pressure at the site for 10 seconds before injection reduces the pain of injection. Ice or vapocoolant provide only brief analgesia at the injection site and, therefore, are not recommended. Local anesthetic agents may be administered by several routes. Topical anesthetics have been evaluated in placebo-controlled, randomized clinical trials and have been demonstrated to provide pain relief. Because topical anesthetics require 30 to 60 minutes to provide adequate anesthesia, planning is necessary, such as applying the cream before an office visit or immediately on arrival.

Additional studies need to be performed on the use of local anesthetic agents to better establish their safety and effectiveness when used to manage injection pain and to ensure that their use does not interfere with the immune response, particularly to SC injections.

NONPHARMACOLOGIC TECHNIQUES

Sucrose placed on the tongue or on a pacifier ameliorates discomfort in newborn infants but has little effect beyond the immediate postnatal period. Skin-to-skin contact between mothers and their infants significantly reduces crying and lowers heart rate during heel strike. In addition, breastfeeding is a potent analgesic intervention in newborn infants during blood collection. Stroking or rocking a child after an injection decreases crying and other pain behaviors. For older children, breathing and distraction techniques, such as "blowing the pain away"; use of pinwheels or soap bubbles; telling children stories; reading books; or use of music, are all effective. Techniques that involve the child in a fantasy or reframe the experience with the use of suggestion ("magic love" or "pain switch") also are effective but may require training.

The younger the child, the greater the reliance on injection techniques and pharmacologic approaches. As the child becomes older, distraction and other psychologic approaches, in addition to pharmacologic and technical approaches to pain reduction, are increasingly effective.

Scheduling Immunizations

A vaccine is intended to be administered to a person who is capable of an appropriate immunologic response and who likely will benefit from the protection given. However, optimal immunologic response for the person must be balanced against the need to achieve effective protection against disease. For example, pertussis-containing vaccines may be less immunogenic in early infancy than in later infancy, but the benefit of conferring protection in young infants mandates that immunization should be given early despite a lessened serum antibody response. For this reason, in some developing countries, OPV vaccine is given at birth, in accordance with recommendations of the World Health Organization.

With parenterally administered live-virus vaccines, the inhibitory effect of residual specific maternal antibody determines the optimal age of administration. For example, live-virus measles-containing vaccine in use in the United States provides suboptimal rates of seroconversion during the first year of life mainly because of interference by transplacentally acquired maternal antibody. If a measles-containing vaccine is administered before 12 months of age, the child should be reimmunized at 12 to 15 months of age with MMR or MMRV; a third dose of MMR is indicated at 4 to 6 years of age but may be administered as early as 4 weeks after the second dose.

An additional factor in selecting an immunization schedule is the need to achieve a uniform and regular response. With some products, a response is achieved after 1 dose. For example, live-virus rubella vaccine evokes a predictable response at high rates after a single dose. A single dose of some vaccines confers less-than-optimal response in the recipient. As a result, several doses are needed to complete primary immunization. For example, some people respond only to 1 or 2 types of poliovirus after a single dose of poliovirus vaccine, so multiple doses are given to produce antibody against all 3 types, thereby ensuring complete protection for the person and maximum response rates for the population. For some vaccines, periodic booster doses (eg, with tetanus and diphtheria toxoids) are administered to maintain immunologic protection.

Most vaccines are safe and effective when administered simultaneously, although limited data are available for some products. This information is particularly important for scheduling immunizations for children with lapsed or missed immunizations and for people preparing for international travel (see Simultaneous Administration of Multiple Vaccines, p 34). Data indicate possible impaired immune responses when 2 or more live-virus vaccines are given nonsimultaneously but within 28 days of each other; therefore, live-virus vaccines not administered on the same day should be given at least 28 days (4 weeks) apart whenever possible (Table 1.6).

The recommended childhood and adolescent immunization schedule in Fig 1.1 (p 26) represents a consensus of the American Academy of Pediatrics (AAP), the Advisory Committee on Immunization Practices (ACIP) of the CDC, and the American Academy of Family Physicians (AAFP) for routine childhood immunizations in the year 2006. This schedule is reviewed regularly, and an updated national schedule is issued annually in January (and occasionally is updated again within the year) to incorporate new vaccines and revised recommendations. Special attention should be given to footnotes on the schedule, because they summarize major recommendations for routine childhood immunizations. Combination vaccine products may be given whenever any component of the combination is indicated and its other components are not contraindicated, provided they are licensed by the FDA for that dose in the schedule for each component vaccine* and for the child's age.[†] A Web-based childhood immunization scheduler using the current vaccine recommendations is available for parents, caregivers, and health care professionals to make instant immunization schedules for any child 5 years of age or younger (**www.cdc.gov/nip/kidstuff/**

Table 1.6. Guidelines for Spacing of Live and Inactivated Antigens

Antigen Combination	Recommended Minimum Interval Between Doses
≥2 inactivated[1]	None; can be administered simultaneously or at any interval between doses
Inactivated and live	None; can be administered simultaneously or at any interval between doses
≥2 live[2]	28-day minimum interval if not administered at the same visit

[1] If simultaneous administration of Tdap and MCV4 is not feasible (a vaccine is not available), the American Academy of Pediatrics recommends administration be separated by at least 28 days.
[2] Some live oral vaccines (eg, Ty21a typhoid vaccine, oral poliovirus vaccine, rotavirus vaccine) can be administered simultaneously or at any interval before or after inactivated or live parenteral vaccines.

---

* American Academy of Pediatrics, Committee on Infectious Diseases. Combination vaccines for childhood immunization: recommendations of the Advisory Committee on Immunization Practices (ACIP), the American Academy of Pediatrics (AAP), and the American Academy of Family Physicians (AAFP). *Pediatrics.* 1999;103:1064–1077 (Reaffirmed 2002)
† For example, Pediarix (DTaP-IVP-hepatitis B) is licensed for the first 3 doses of the DTaP and IVP series. It should not be used for the fourth or fifth doses of the DTaP series or for the fourth IPV dose.

scheduler.html). An adult immunization schedule, which is updated yearly, also is available (**www.cdc.gov/nip**).

Table 1.7 (p 28) gives the recommended schedule for children who were not immunized appropriately during the first year of life.

For children in whom early or rapid immunization is urgent or for children not immunized on schedule, simultaneous immunization with multiple products allows for more rapid protection. In addition, in some circumstances, immunization can be initiated earlier than at the usually recommended time or schedule and doses can be given at shorter intervals than are recommended routinely (for guidelines, see Table 1.8, p 31, and the immunization recommendations in the disease-specific chapters in Section 3).

Influenza vaccine should be administered before the start of the influenza season but also provides benefit if administered any time before the occurrence of peak disease in a local area (see Influenza, Vaccine Administration, p 409).

The immunization schedule issued by the AAP, ACIP, and AAFP primarily is intended for children in the United States. In many instances, the guidelines will be applicable to children in other countries, but individual pediatricians and recommending bodies in each country are responsible for determining the appropriateness of the recommendations for their setting. The schedule recommended by the Expanded Programme on Immunization of the World Health Organization should be consulted (**www.who.org**). Modifications may be made by the ministries of health in individual countries on the basis of local considerations.

Minimum Ages and Minimum Intervals Between Vaccine Doses

Immunizations are recommended for members of the youngest age group at risk of experiencing the disease for whom efficacy, immunogenicity, and safety have been demonstrated. Most vaccines in the childhood and adolescent immunization schedule require 2 or more doses for stimulation of an adequate and persisting antibody response. Studies have demonstrated that the recommended age and interval between doses of the same antigen(s) provide optimal protection and efficacy. Table 1.8 lists the recommended minimum ages and intervals between immunizations for vaccines in the recommended childhood immunization schedule. Administering doses of a multidose vaccine at intervals shorter than those in the recommended childhood and adolescent immunization schedule might be necessary in circumstances in which an infant or child is behind schedule and needs to be brought up to date quickly or when international travel is pending. In these cases, an accelerated schedule using minimum age or interval criteria can be used. These accelerated schedules should not be used routinely.

Vaccines should not be administered at intervals less than the recommended minimum or at an earlier age than the recommended minimum (eg, accelerated schedules). Two exceptions to this may occur. The first is for measles vaccine during a measles outbreak, in which case the vaccine may be administered before 12 months of age. However, if a measles-containing vaccine is administered before 12 months of age, the dose is not counted and the child should be reimmunized at 12 to 15 months of age with MMR or MMRV vaccine (see Measles, p 441). The second consideration involves administering a dose a few days earlier than the minimum interval or age, which is unlikely to have a substantially negative effect on the immune response to

FIGURE 1.1. CHILDHOOD AND ADOLESCENT IMMUNIZATION SCHEDULE

Recommended Childhood and Adolescent Immunization Schedule   UNITED STATES • 2006

Vaccine ▼ Age ▶	Birth	1 month	2 months	4 months	6 months	12 months	15 months	18 months	24 months	4–6 years	11–12 years	13–14 years	15 years	16–18 years
Hepatitis B[1]	HepB	HepB		HepB[1]		HepB					HepB Series	HepB Series		HepB Series
Diphtheria, Tetanus, Pertussis[2]			DTaP	DTaP	DTaP		DTaP	DTaP		DTaP	Tdap	Tdap	Tdap	Tdap
Haemophilus influenzae type b[3]			Hib	Hib	Hib[3]		Hib							
Inactivated Poliovirus[4]			IPV	IPV	IPV		IPV			IPV				
Measles, Mumps, Rubella[4]						MMR				MMR		MMR		
Varicella[5]						Varicella					Varicella	Varicella		
Meningococcal[6]										MPSV4	MCV4	MCV4	MCV4	MCV4
Pneumococcal[7]			PCV	PCV	PCV	PCV	PCV		PCV	PCV	PPV			
Influenza[8]					Influenza (Yearly)	Influenza (Yearly)					Influenza (Yearly)			
Hepatitis A[9]									HepA Series	HepA Series				

Vaccines within broken line are for selected populations

Range of recommended ages   **Catch-up immunization**   **11–12 year old assessment**

This schedule indicates the recommended ages for routine administration of currently licensed childhood vaccines, as of December 1, 2005, for children through age 18 years. Any dose not administered at the recommended age should be administered at any subsequent visit when indicated and feasible. ▒ Indicates age groups that warrant special effort to administer those vaccines not previously administered. Additional vaccines may be licensed and recommended during the year. Licensed combination vaccines may be used whenever any components of the combination are

indicated and other components of the vaccine are not contraindicated and if approved by the Food and Drug Administration for that dose of the series. Providers should consult the respective ACIP statement for detailed recommendations. Clinically significant adverse events that follow immunization should be reported to the Vaccine Adverse Event Reporting System (VAERS). Guidance about how to obtain and complete a VAERS form is available at www.vaers.hhs.gov or by telephone, 800-822-7967.

FIG 1.1. CHILDHOOD AND ADOLESCENT IMMUNIZATION SCHEDULE, CONTINUED

1. **Hepatitis B vaccine (HepB).** *AT BIRTH:* **All newborns** should receive monovalent HepB soon after birth and before hospital discharge. **Infants born to mothers who are HBsAg-positive** should receive HepB and 0.5 mL of hepatitis B immune globulin (HBIG) within 12 hours of birth. **Infants born to mothers whose HBsAg status is unknown** should receive HepB within 12 hours of birth. The mother should have blood drawn as soon as possible to determine her HBsAg status; if HBsAg-positive, the infant should receive HBIG as soon as possible (no later than age 1 week). **For infants born to HBsAg-negative mothers,** the birth dose can be delayed in rare circumstances but only if a physician's order to withhold the vaccine and a copy of the mother's original HBsAg-negative laboratory report are documented in the infant's medical record. *FOLLOWING THE BIRTHDOSE:* The HepB series should be completed with either monovalent HepB or a combination vaccine containing HepB. The second dose should be administered at age 1–2 months. The final dose in the series should be given at age ≥24 weeks. It is permissible to administer 4 doses of HepB (e.g., when combination vaccines are given after the birth dose); however, if monovalent HepB is used, a dose at age 4 months is not needed. **Infants born to HBsAg-positive mothers** should be tested for HBsAg and antibody to HBsAg after completion of the HepB series, at age 9–18 months (generally, at the next well-child visit after completion of the vaccine series).

2. **Diphtheria and tetanus toxoids and acellular pertussis vaccine (DTaP).** The fourth dose of DTaP may be administered as early as age 12 months, provided 6 months have elapsed since the third dose and the child is unlikely to return at age 15–18 months. The final dose in the series should be given at age ≥4 years. **Tetanus and diphtheria toxoids and acellular pertussis vaccine (Tdap – adolescent preparation)** is recommended at age 11–12 years for those who have completed the recommended childhood DTP/DTaP vaccination series and have not received a Td booster dose. Adolescents 13–18 years who missed the 11–12-year Td/Tdap booster dose should also receive a single dose of Tdap if they have completed the recommended childhood DTP/DTaP vaccination series. Subsequent **tetanus and diphtheria toxoids (Td)** are recommended every 10 years.

3. **Haemophilus influenzae type b conjugate vaccine (Hib).** Three Hib conjugate vaccines are licensed for infant use. If PRP-OMP (PedvaxHIB® or ComVax® [Merck]) is administered at ages 2 and 4 months, a dose at age 6 months is not required. DTaP/Hib combination products should not be used for primary immunization in infants at ages 2, 4, or 6 months but can be used as boosters after any Hib vaccine. The final dose in the series should be administered at age ≥12 months.

4. **Measles, mumps, and rubella vaccine (MMR).** The second dose of MMR is recommended routinely at age 4–6 years but may be administered during any visit, provided at least 4 weeks have elapsed since the first dose and both doses are administered beginning at or after age 12 months. Those who have not previously received the second dose should complete the schedule by age 11–12 years.

5. **Varicella vaccine.** Varicella vaccine is recommended at any visit at or after age 12 months for susceptible children (i.e., those who lack a reliable history of chickenpox). Susceptible persons aged ≥13 years should receive 2 doses administered at least 4 weeks apart.

6. **Meningococcal vaccine (MCV4).** Meningococcal conjugate vaccine (MCV4) should be given to all children at the 11–12 year old visit as well as to unvaccinated adolescents at high school entry (15 years of age). Other adolescents who wish to decrease their risk for meningococcal disease may also be vaccinated. All college freshmen living in dormitories should also be vaccinated, preferably with MCV4, although **meningococcal polysaccharide vaccine (MPSV4)** is an acceptable alternative. Vaccination against invasive meningococcal disease is recommended for children and adolescents aged ≥2 years with terminal complement deficiencies or anatomic or functional asplenia and certain other high risk groups (see *MMWR* 2005;54 [RR-7]:1-21); use MPSV4 for children aged 2–10 years and MCV4 for older children, although MPSV4 is an acceptable alternative.

7. **Pneumococcal vaccine.** The heptavalent **pneumococcal conjugate vaccine (PCV)** is recommended for all children aged 2–23 months and for certain children aged 24–59 months. The final dose in the series should be given at age ≥12 months. **Pneumococcal polysaccharide vaccine (PPV)** is recommended in addition to PCV for certain high-risk groups. See *MMWR* 2000;49(RR-9):1-35.

8. **Influenza vaccine.** Influenza vaccine is recommended annually for children aged ≥6 months with certain risk factors (including, but not limited to, asthma, cardiac disease, sickle cell disease, human immunodeficiency virus [HIV], diabetes, and conditions that can compromise respiratory function or handling of respiratory secretions or that can increase the risk for aspiration), healthcare workers, and other persons (including household members) in close contact with persons in groups at high risk (see *MMWR* 2005;54[RR-8]:1-55). In addition, healthy children aged 6–23 months and close contacts of healthy children aged 0–5 months are recommended to receive influenza vaccine because children in this age group are at substantially increased risk for influenza-related hospitalizations. For healthy persons aged 5–49 years, the intranasally administered, live, attenuated influenza vaccine (LAIV) is an acceptable alternative to the intramuscular trivalent inactivated influenza vaccine (TIV). See *MMWR* 2005;54(RR-8):1-55. Children receiving TIV should be administered a dosage appropriate for their age (0.25 mL if aged 6–35 months or 0.5 mL if aged ≥3 years). Children aged ≤8 years who are receiving influenza vaccine for the first time should receive 2 doses (separated by at least 4 weeks for TIV and at least 6 weeks for LAIV).

9. **Hepatitis A vaccine (HepA).** HepA is recommended for all children at 1 year of age (i.e., 12–23 months). The 2 doses in the series should be administered at least 6 months apart. States, counties, and communities with existing HepA vaccination programs for children 2–18 years of age are encouraged to maintain these programs. In these areas, new efforts focused on routine vaccination of 1-year-old children should enhance, not replace, ongoing programs directed at a broader population of children. HepA is also recommended for certain high risk groups (see *MMWR* 1999;48[RR-12]:1-37).

Additional information about vaccines, including precautions and contraindications for vaccination and vaccine shortages, is available at http://www.cdc.gov/nip or from the National Immunization Information Hotline, 800-232-2522 (English) or 800-232-0233 (Spanish). Approved by the **Advisory Committee on Immunization Practices** (http://www.cdc.gov/nip/acip), the **American Academy of Pediatrics** (http://www.aap.org), and the **American Academy of Family Physicians** (http://www.aafp.org).

Table 1.7. Catch-up Immunization Schedules for Children and Adolescents Who Start Late or Who Are >1 Month Behind*

Dose 1	Children 4 Months Through 6 Years of Age				
	Minimum Interval Between Doses				
(Minimum Age)	Dose 1 to Dose 2	Dose 2 to Dose 3	Dose 3 to Dose 4	Dose 4 to Dose 5	
DTaP (6 wk)	4 wk	4 wk	6 mo	6 mo[1]	
IPV (6 wk)	4 wk	4 wk	4 wk[2]		
HepB[3] (birth)	4 wk	8 wk (and 16 wk after first dose)			
MMR (12 mo)	4 wk[4]				
Varicella (12 mo)					
Hib[5] (6 wk)	4 wk: if first dose given at younger than 12 mo of age	4 wk[6]: if current age younger than 12 mo	8 wk (as final dose): this dose only necessary for children 12 mo to 5 y of age who received 3 doses before 12 mo of age		
	8 wk (as final dose): if first dose given at 12 to 14 mo of age	8 wk (as final dose)[6]: if current age 12 mo or older and second dose given at younger than 15 mo of age			
	No further doses needed: if first dose given at 15 mo of age or older	No further doses needed: if previous dose given at 15 mo of age or older			
PCV[7]: (6 wk)	4 wk: if first dose given at younger than 12 mo of age and current age younger than 24 mo	4 wk: if current age younger than 12 mo	8 wk (as final dose): this dose only necessary for children 12 mo to 5 y of age who received 3 doses before 12 mo of age		

Table 1.7. Catch-up Immunization Schedules for Children and Adolescents Who Start Late or Who Are >1 Month Behind,* continued

Children 4 Months Through 6 Years of Age

Dose 1 (Minimum Age)	Minimum Interval Between Doses			
	Dose 1 to Dose 2	Dose 2 to Dose 3	Dose 3 to Dose 4	Dose 4 to Dose 5
	8 wk (as final dose): if first dose given at 12 mo of age or older or current age 24 to 59 mo **No further doses needed:** for healthy children if first dose given at 24 mo of age or older	**8 wk (as final dose):** if current age 12 mo or older **No further doses needed:** for healthy children if previous dose given at 24 mo of age or older		

Children 7 Through 18 Years of Age

Dose 1 to Dose 2	Dose 2 to Dose 3	Dose 3 to Booster Dose
Minimum Interval Between Doses		
Td: **4 wk**	Td: **6 mo**	Td[8]: **6 mo:** if first dose given at younger than 12 mo of age and current age younger than 11 y **Otherwise: 5 y** IPV[7,9]
IPV[9]: **4 wk** HepB: **4 wk** MMR: **4 wk** Varicella[10]: **4 wk**	IPV[9]: **4 wk** HepB: **8 wk** (and 16 wk after first dose)	

Table 1.7. Catch-up Immunization Schedules for Children and Adolescents Who Start Late or Who Are >1 Month Behind,* continued

* Catch-up schedules and minimum intervals between doses for children who have delayed immunizations. There is no need to restart a vaccine series regardless of the time that has elapsed between doses. Use the chart appropriate for the child's age. For additional information about vaccines, including precautions and contraindications for immunization and vaccine shortages, please visit the National Immunization Program Web site at www.cdc.gov/nip or call the CDC telephone hotline (1-800-232-4636). Report adverse reactions to vaccines through the federal Vaccine Adverse Event Reporting System. For information on reporting reactions following vaccines, please visit http://vaers.hhs.gov or call the 24-hour national toll-free information line at 800-822-7967. Report suspected cases of vaccine-preventable diseases to your state or the local health department.

[1] **Diphtheria and tetanus toxoids and acellular pertussis (DTaP) vaccine:** The fifth dose is not necessary if the fourth dose was given after the fourth birthday.

[2] **Inactivated poliovirus (IPV) vaccine:** For children who received an all-IPV or all-oral poliovirus (OPV) series, a fourth dose is not necessary if third dose was given at 4 years of age or older. If both OPV and IPV were given as part of a series, a total of 4 doses should be given, regardless of the child's current age.

[3] **Hepatitis B (HepB) vaccine:** Administer the 3-dose series to all children and adolescents younger than 19 years of age if they were not immunized previously.

[4] **Measles-mumps-rubella (MMR) vaccine:** The second dose of MMR is recommended routinely at 4 to 6 years of age but may be given earlier if desired.

[5] *Haemophilus influenzae* type b **(Hib) vaccine:** Vaccine generally is not recommended for children 5 years of age or older.

[6] **Hib:** If current age younger than 12 months and the first 2 doses were PRP-OMP (PedvaxHIB or ComVax), the third (and final) dose should be given at 12 to 15 months of age and at least 8 weeks after the second dose.

[7] **Pneumococcal conjugate vaccine (PCV):** Vaccine generally is not recommended for children 5 years of age or older.

[8] **Tetanus and diphtheria toxoids (Td) vaccine:** Adolescent tetanus, diphtheria, and pertussis (Tdap) vaccine may be substituted for any dose in a primary catch-up series or as a booster if age appropriate for Tdap. A 5-year interval from the last Td dose is encouraged when Tdap is used as a booster dose.

[9] **IPV:** Vaccine generally is not recommended for people 18 years of age or older.

[10] **Varicella:** Give 2-dose series to all susceptible adolescents 13 years of age or older.

Table 1.8. Recommended and Minimum Ages and Intervals Between Vaccine Doses[1]

Vaccine and Dose Number	Recommended Age for This Dose	Minimum Age for This Dose	Recommended Interval to Next Dose	Minimum Interval to Next Dose
Hepatitis B1[2]	Birth	Birth	1–4 mo	4 wk
Hepatitis B2	1–4 mo	4 wk	2–17 mo	8 wk (and 16 wk after the first dose)
Hepatitis B3[3]	6–18 mo	24 wk	—	—
Diphtheria and tetanus toxoids and acellular pertussis (DTaP)[1,2]	2 mo	6 wk	2 mo	4 wk
DTaP2	4 mo	10 wk	2 mo	4 wk
DTaP3	6 mo	14 wk	6–12 mo	6 mo[4]
DTaP4	15–18 mo	12 mo	3 y	6 mo
DTaP5	4–6 y	4 y	—	—
Haemophilus influenzae type b (Hib)[1,2,5]	2 mo	6 wk	2 mo	4 wk
Hib2	4 mo	10 wk	2 mo	4 wk
Hib3[6]	6 mo	14 wk	6–9 mo	8 wk
Hib4	12–15 mo	12 mo	—	—
Inactivated poliovirus (IPV)[1,2]	2 mo	6 wk	2 mo	4 wk
IPV2	4 mo	10 wk	2–14 mo	4 wk
IPV3	6–18 mo	14 wk	3–5 y	4 wk
IPV4	4–6 y	18 wk	—	—
Pneumococcal conjugate vaccine (PCV)[1,5]	2 mo	6 wk	2 mo	4 wk
PCV2	4 mo	10 wk	2 mo	4 wk
PCV3	6 mo	14 wk	6 mo	8 wk
PCV4	12–15 mo	12 mo	—	—
Measles-mumps-rubella (MMR)1	12–15 mo[7]	12 mo	3–5 y	4 wk
MMR2	4–6 y	13 mo	—	—
Varicella[8]	12–18 mo	12 mo	4 wk[8]	4 wk[8]
Hepatitis A1	12–23 mo	12 mo	6–18 mo	6 mo
Hepatitis A2	18–41 mo	18 mo	—	—
Influenza, trivalent inactivated[9]	6–23 mo (annually)	6 mo[4]	4 wk	4 wk

Table 1.8. Recommended and Minimum Ages and Intervals Between Vaccine Doses,[1] continued

Vaccine and Dose Number	Recommended Age for This Dose	Minimum Age for This Dose	Recommended Interval to Next Dose	Minimum Interval to Next Dose
Influenza, trivalent live-attenuated[9]	—	5 y	6–10 wk	6 wk
Meningococcal conjugate vaccine (MCV4)	11–12 y	11 y	—	—
Meningococcal polysaccharide vaccine (MPSV4)-1	—	2 y	5 y	5 y
MPSV4-2	—	7 y[10]	—	—
Tetanus toxoid, reduced diptheria toxoid, and reduced acellular pertussis (Tdap)	≥11 y	11 y	10 y[11]	—
Pneumococcal polysaccharide vaccine (PPV)[1]	—	2 y	5 y[12]	5 y
PPV2	—	7 y[12]	—	—

1 Combination vaccines are available. Use of licensed combination vaccines is preferred over separate injections of their equivalent component vaccines (Source: Centers for Disease Control and Prevention. Combination vaccines for childhood immunization: recommendations of the Advisory Committee on Immunization Practices (ACIP), the American Academy of Pediatrics (AAP), and the American Academy of Family Physicians (AAFP). *MMWR Recomm Rep.* 1999;48(RR-5):1–15). When administering combination vaccines, the minimum age for administration is the oldest age for any of the individual components; the minimum interval between doses is equal to the greatest interval of any of the individual antigens.

2 A combination hepatitis B-Hib vaccine is available (Comvax) and a combination DTaP/hepatitis B/IPV vaccine is available (Pediarix). These vaccines should not be administered to infants younger than 6 weeks of age.

3 Hepatitis B3 should be administered ≥8 weeks after hepatitis B2 and 16 weeks after hepatitis B1, and it should not be administered before 24 weeks of age.

4 The minimum interval between DTaP3 and DTaP4 is recommended to be ≥6 months. However, DTaP4 does not need to be repeated if administered ≥4 months after DTaP3.

5 For Hib and PCV, children receiving the first dose of vaccine at 7 months of age or older require fewer doses and different minimum intervals to complete the series (see Centers for Disease Control and Prevention. *Haemophilus influenzae*, type b disease among infants and children two months of age and older: recommendations of the ACIP. *MMWR Recomm Rep.* 1991;40(RR-1):1–7; and Centers for Disease Control and Prevention. Preventing pneumococcal disease among infants and young children: recommendations of the Advisory Committee on Immunization Practices [ACIP]. *MMWR Recomm Rep.* 2000;49(RR-9):1–38).

6 For a regimen of only polyribosylribitol phosphate-meningococcal outer membrane protein (PRP-OMP [PedvaxHIB]), a dose administered at 6 months of age is not required.

7 During a measles outbreak, if cases are occurring among infants younger than 12 months of age, measles immunization of infants 6 months of age and older can be undertaken as an outbreak control measure. However, doses administered at younger than 12 months of age should not be counted as part of the series (Source: Centers for Disease Control and Prevention. Measles, mumps, and rubella—vaccine use and strategies for elimination of measles, rubella, and congenital rubella syndrome and control of mumps: recommendations of the Advisory Committee on Immunization Practices [ACIP]. *MMWR Recomm Rep.* 1998;47(RR-8):1–57). A combination measles-mumps-rubella-varicella (MMRV) vaccine is available and can be used when MMR and varicella vaccines are indicated.

8 Children 12 months to 12 years of age require only 1 dose of varicella vaccine. People 13 years of age and older should receive 2 doses separated by ≥4 weeks. A combination MMRV vaccine is available and can be used when MMR and varicella vaccines are indicated.

9 Two doses of inactivated influenza vaccine, separated by 4 weeks, are recommended for children 6 months to 9 years of age who are receiving the vaccine for the first time. Children 6 months to 9 years of age who previously have received influenza vaccine and people 9 years of age and older require only 1 dose per influenza season.

10 Second dose of MPSV4 is recommended for people at high risk of meningococcal disease (Centers for Disease Control and Prevention. Prevention and control of meningococcal disease: recommendations of the Advisory Committee on Immunization Practices [ACIP]. *MMWR Recomm Rep.* 2005;54[RR-7]:1–14).

11 Only one dose of Tdap vaccine is recommended. Subsequent doses should be given as Td vaccine. If immunization to prevent tetanus and/or diphtheria disease is required during the ages 7–10 years, Td vaccine should be given. The preferred interval between Tdap vaccine and a previous dose of Td vaccine is 5 years.

12 Second doses of PPV are recommended for people at highest risk of serious pneumococcal infection and people who are likely to have a rapid decrease in pneumococcal antibody concentration. Reimmunization 3 years after the previous dose can be considered for children at highest risk of severe pneumococcal infection who would be younger than 10 years of age at the time of reimmunization (see Centers for Disease Control and Prevention. Prevention of pneumococcal disease: recommendations of the Advisory Committee on Immunization Practices [ACIP].

that dose. Although immunizations should not be scheduled at an interval or age less than the minimums listed in Table 1.8 (p 31), a child may be in the office early or for an appointment not specifically for immunization (eg, recheck of otitis media). In this situation, the clinician can consider administering the vaccine before the minimum interval or age. If the child is known to the clinician, rescheduling the child for immunization closer to the recommended interval is preferred. If the parent or child is not known to the clinician or follow-up cannot be ensured (eg, habitually misses appointments), administration of the vaccine at that visit rather than rescheduling the child for a later visit is preferable. Vaccine doses administered 4 days or fewer before the minimum interval or age can be counted as valid. This 4-day recommendation does not apply to rabies vaccine because of the unique schedule for this vaccine. Doses administered 5 days or more before the minimum interval or age should not be counted as valid doses and should be repeated as age appropriate. The repeat dose should be spaced after the invalid dose by at least 4 weeks (Table 1.8, p 31). In certain situations, local or state requirements might mandate that doses of selected vaccines (in particular, MMR) be administered on or after specific ages, precluding these 4-day recommendations.

Interchangeability of Vaccine Products

Similar vaccines made by different manufacturers may differ in the number and amount of their specific antigenic components and formulation of adjuvants and conjugating agents, thereby eliciting different degrees of immune response. However, such vaccines have been considered interchangeable by most experts when administered according to their licensed indications, although data documenting the effects of interchangeability are limited. Licensed vaccines that may be used interchangeably during a vaccine series from different manufacturers, according to recommendations from the ACIP or AAP, include diphtheria and tetanus toxoids vaccines, hepatitis A vaccines, hepatitis B vaccines for infants, and rabies vaccines (see Rabies, p 552). An example of similar vaccines used in different schedules that are not recommended as interchangeable is the 2 hepatitis B vaccine option currently available for adolescents 11 through 15 years of age. Adolescent patients begun on a 3-dose hepatitis B regimen are not candidates to complete their series with hepatitis B vaccine used in the 2-dose protocol, and vice versa, and the 2-dose schedule is applicable only to Recombivax HB (see Hepatitis B, p 335).

Licensed Hib conjugate vaccines are considered interchangeable for primary as well as for booster immunization as long as recommendations concerning conversion from a 3-dose regimen (PRP-OMP) to a 4-dose regimen (all other conjugated polyribosylribitol [PRP] preparations) are followed (see *Haemophilus influenzae* Infections, p 310).

Minimal data on safety and immunogenicity and no data on efficacy are available for different DTaP vaccines when administered interchangeably (see Pertussis, p 498). However, in circumstances in which the type of DTaP product(s) received previously is not known or the previously administered product(s) is not readily available, any of the DTaP vaccines may be used. For interchangeability of the DTaP, hepatitis B, and IPV combination vaccine, see Pertussis (p 498). These recommendations may change as additional data become available.

Simultaneous Administration of Multiple Vaccines

Most vaccines safely and effectively can be administered simultaneously. Infants and children have sufficient immunologic capacity to respond to multiple vaccines. No contraindications to the simultaneous administration of multiple vaccines routinely recommended for infants and children are known. Immune responses to one vaccine generally do not interfere with responses to other vaccines. Simultaneous administration of IPV, MMR, varicella, or DTaP vaccines results in rates of seroconversion and of adverse effects similar to those observed when the vaccines are administered at separate visits. For some other routinely administered vaccines, data on simultaneous administration are limited or not available. Because simultaneous administration of common vaccines is not known to affect the efficacy or safety of any of the recommended childhood vaccines, simultaneous administration of all vaccines, including DTaP, Tdap, IPV, MMR, MMRV, varicella, hepatitis A, hepatitis B, Hib, oral rotavirus, influenza, and pneumococcal and meningococcal conjugate and polysaccharide vaccines that are appropriate for the age and immunization status of the recipient, is recommended. When vaccines are administered simultaneously, separate syringes and separate sites should be used, and injections into the same extremity should be separated by at least 1 inch so that any local reactions can be differentiated. Simultaneous administration of multiple vaccines can increase immunization rates significantly. Individual vaccines should never be mixed in the same syringe unless they are specifically licensed and labeled for administration in one syringe. For people preparing for international travel, multiple vaccines can be given concurrently. If live-virus vaccines are not administered concurrently, 4 weeks should be allowed to elapse between sequential immunizations.

Combination Vaccines*

An increasing number of new vaccines to prevent childhood diseases have been or will be licensed and recommended for use. Combination vaccines represent one solution to the issue of increased numbers of injections during single clinic visits.[†] To minimize the number of injections children receive, parenteral combination vaccines should be used, if licensed and indicated for the patient's age, instead of their equivalent component vaccines. Table 1.3 (p 10) lists combination vaccines licensed in the United States. Immunization providers should stock sufficient types of combination and monovalent vaccines needed to immunize children against all diseases for which vaccines are recommended, but they need not stock all available types or brand-name products. When patients already have received the recommended immunizations for some of the components in a combination vaccine, administering the extra antigen(s) in the combination vaccine is permissible if doing so will reduce the number of injections required. Excessive doses of toxoid vaccines (diphtheria and tetanus) may result in extensive local reactions. To overcome recording errors and ambiguities in the

---

* American Academy of Pediatrics, Committee on Infectious Diseases. Combination vaccines for childhood immunization: recommendations of the Advisory Committee on Immunization Practices (ACIP), the American Academy of Pediatrics (AAP), and the American Academy of Family Physicians (AAFP). *Pediatrics.* 1999;103:1064–1077 (Reaffirmed 2002)

† Santoli JM, Peter G, Arvin AM, et al. Strengthening the supply of routinely recommended vaccines in the United States: recommendations from the National Vaccine Advisory Committee. *JAMA.* 2003;290:3122–3128

names of vaccine combinations, improved systems are needed to enhance the convenience and accuracy of transferring vaccine-identifying information into medical records and immunization information systems.

Lapsed Immunizations

A lapse in the immunization schedule does not require reinstitution of the entire series or addition of doses to the series. If a dose of DTaP, IPV, Hib, pneumococcal conjugate, hepatitis A, or hepatitis B vaccine is missed, subsequent immunizations should be given at the next visit as if the usual interval had elapsed. The medical charts of children in whom immunizations have been missed or postponed should be flagged to remind health care professionals to resume the child's immunization regimen at the next available opportunity. Minimum age and interval criteria should be adhered to for administration of all doses (see Table 1.8, p 31).

Unknown or Uncertain Immunization Status

A physician may encounter children with an uncertain immunization status. Many children, adolescents, and young adults do not have adequate documentation of their immunizations. Parent or guardian recollection of a child's immunization history and the specific vaccines used may not be accurate. Only written, dated records should be accepted as evidence of immunization. In general, when in doubt, a person with unknown or uncertain immunization status should be considered disease susceptible, and recommended immunizations should be initiated without delay on a schedule commensurate with the person's current age. There is no evidence that administration of most vaccines to already immune recipients is harmful; adult-type tetanus and diphtheria toxoids (Td), rather than DTaP, should be given to people 7 years of age or older, and Tdap is available for people 10 years of age and older (see Pertussis, p 498). Reimmunization with multiple doses of DTaP or Td may result in increased incidence and severity of local reactions, including swollen limb reactions; serologic testing for specific antibody to tetanus and diphtheria toxins may be considered before administering additional doses (see Medical Evaluation of Internationally Adopted Children, p 182).

Immunizations Received Outside the United States

People immunized in other countries, including internationally adopted children, refugees, and exchange students, should be immunized according to recommended schedules in the United States for healthy infants, children, and adolescents (see Fig 1.1, p 26, and Table 1.7, p 28). In general, only written documentation should be accepted as evidence of previous immunization. Written records may be considered valid if the vaccines, dates of administration, numbers of doses, intervals between doses, and age of the patient at the time of immunization are comparable with those of the current US schedule. Although some vaccines with inadequate potency have been produced in other countries, most vaccines used worldwide are produced with adequate quality-control standards and are reliable. However, immunization records for certain children, especially for children from orphanages, may not accurately reflect protection because of inaccuracies, lack of vaccine potency, or other problems, such as recording MMR but giving a product that did not contain one of the components (eg, rubella). Therefore, reimmunization or serologic testing may be reasonable for these children (see Unknown or Uncertain Immunization Status, p 35). For any child who has received immunizations outside the United States, if any question exists about whether immunizations were administered or were immunogenic, the best course for most vaccines is to repeat administration of the immunizations in question (see Medical Evaluation of Internationally Adopted Children, p 182).

Vaccine Dose

Reduced or divided doses of DTaP or any other vaccine, including those given to preterm or low birth weight infants, should not be administered. The efficacy of this practice in decreasing the frequency of adverse events has not been demonstrated. Also, such a practice may confer less protection against disease than that achieved with recommended doses. A diminished antibody response in both term and preterm infants to reduced doses of diphtheria and tetanus and whole-cell pertussis (DTP) vaccine has been reported. A previous immunization with a dose that was less than the standard dose or one administered by a nonstandard route should not be counted, and the person should be reimmunized as recommended for age; a general exception is that repeating doses of vaccine administered by the intramuscular route rather than by the subcutaneous route is unnecessary. Exceeding a recommended dose volume also may be hazardous. Excessive local concentrations of injectable inactivated vaccines might result in enhanced tissue or systemic reactions, whereas administering an increased dose of a live vaccine constitutes a theoretic but unproven risk.

Active Immunization of People Who Recently Received Immune Globulin

Live-virus vaccines may have diminished immunogenicity when given shortly before or during the several months after receipt of IG (both intramuscular and intravenous preparations). In particular, IG administration has been demonstrated to inhibit the response to measles vaccine for a prolonged period. Inhibition of immune response to rubella vaccine also has been demonstrated. The appropriate suggested interval between IG administration and measles immunization will vary with the indication for, and dose of, IG and the specific product; suggested intervals are given in Table 3.32 (p 445). If IG must be given within 14 days after administration of measles or measles-containing vaccines, these live-virus vaccines should be administered again after the period specified in Table 3.32 (p 445) unless serologic testing at an appropriate interval after IG administration indicates that adequate serum antibodies were produced.

The effect of administration of IG on antibody response to varicella vaccine is not known. Because of potential inhibition, varicella vaccine administration should be delayed after receipt of an IG preparation or a blood product (except washed Red Blood Cells), as recommended for measles vaccine (see Table 3.32, p 445). In addition, IG preparations ideally should not be administered for 14 days after varicella immunization. If an IG preparation is given in this interval, the vaccine recipient should be reimmunized after the period specified in Table 3.32 (p 445) or tested for varicella immunity at that time and reimmunized if seronegative.

Administration of IG preparations does not interfere with antibody responses to yellow fever, OPV, or oral rotavirus vaccines. Hence, these vaccines can be administered simultaneously with or at any time before or after IG.

In contrast with live-virus vaccines, administration of IG preparations has not been demonstrated to cause significant inhibition of the immune responses to inactivated vaccines and toxoids. Concurrent administration of recommended doses of Hepatitis B Immune Globulin, Tetanus Immune Globulin, or Rabies Immune Globulin and the corresponding inactivated vaccine or toxoid for postexposure prophylaxis does not impair the efficacy of vaccine and provides immediate and long-term immunity. Standard doses of the corresponding vaccines are recommended. Increases in vaccine dose volume or number of immunizations are not indicated. Vaccines should be administered at sites different from those of intramuscularly administered IG. For further information, see chapters on specific diseases in Section 3.

Administration of hepatitis A vaccine together with IG has been recommended for situations in which immediate *and* prolonged protection against hepatitis A virus infection is desired. Although this combined active-passive immunization has been demonstrated to result in lower serum antibody concentrations than those induced by vaccine administration alone, antibody concentrations still are high enough to be considered protective, and seroconversion rates are not affected.

The respiratory syncytial virus monoclonal antibody (palivizumab) does not interfere with response to inactivated or live vaccines.

Tuberculin Testing

Recommendations for use of the tuberculin skin test (see Tuberculosis, p 678) are independent of those for immunization. Tuberculin testing at any age is not required before administration of live-virus vaccines. A tuberculin skin test (TST) can be applied at the same visit during which these vaccines are administered. Measles vaccine temporarily can suppress tuberculin reactivity for at least 4 to 6 weeks. The effect of live-virus varicella, yellow fever, and live-attenuated influenza vaccines on tuberculin skin test reactivity is not known. In the absence of data, the same TST spacing recommendation should be applied to these vaccines as described for MMR. There is no evidence that inactivated vaccines, polysaccharide vaccines, or recombinant or subunit vaccines or toxoids interfere with immune response to TST.

Record Keeping and Immunization Information Systems

The National Vaccine Advisory Committee (NVAC) in 1993 recommended a set of standards to improve immunization practices for health care professionals serving children and revised the standards in 2002 (see p 844). The standards include the recommendation that immunizations of patients be documented through use of immunization records that are accurate, complete, and easily accessible. In addition, the standards also recommend use of tracking systems to provide reminder/recall notices to parents/guardians and physicians when immunizations are due or overdue. Immunization information systems address record-keeping needs and tracking functions and have additional capacities such as adverse event reporting, interoperability with electronic medical records, emergency preparedness functions, and linkage with other public health programs.

PERSONAL IMMUNIZATION RECORDS OF PATIENTS

The AAP and state health departments have developed an official immunization record. This record should be given to parents of every newborn infant and should be accorded the status of a birth certificate or passport and retained with vital documents for subsequent referral. Physicians should cooperate with this endeavor by recording immunization data in this record and by encouraging patients not only to preserve the record but also to present it at each visit to a health care professional.

The immunization record especially is important for people who frequently move or change health care professionals. The record facilitates maintaining an accurate patient medical history, enables the physician to evaluate a child's immunization status, and fulfills the need for documentation of immunizations for child care and school attendance and for admission to other institutions and organizations.

Although still necessary, paper-based immunization records are not always kept up-to-date and may be misplaced, and the absence of an immunization card may result in missed opportunities or extraimmunization.

All states and many large metropolitan areas are developing population-based computerized immunization information systems to record and track immunizations regardless of where in the state or metropolitan area the immunization services are provided. Most immunization information systems can consolidate records from physician offices, help remind parents and health care professionals when immunizations are due or overdue, help health care professionals determine the immunization needs of their patients at each visit, and generate official immunization records to meet child care or school requirements. Immunization information systems also can provide measurements of immunization coverage and rates by age, immunization series, and physician or clinic practice. The AAP urges physicians to cooperate with state and local health officials in providing immunization data for state or local immunization information systems.

IMMUNIZATION RECORDS OF PHYSICIANS

Every physician should ensure that the immunization history of each patient is maintained in a permanent, confidential record that can be reviewed easily and updated when subsequent immunizations are administered. The medical record maintained by the primary health care professional should document all vaccines received, including vaccines received in another health care setting. The format of the record should facilitate identification and recall of patients in need of immunization.

Records of children whose immunizations have been delayed or missed should be flagged to indicate the need to complete immunizations. For data that are required by the National Childhood Vaccine Injury Act of 1986, as well as data recommended by the AAP to be recorded in each patient's medical record for each immunization, see Informing Patients and Parents (p 5).

Interest in the use of electronic medical record (EMR) systems prompted the AAP Task Force on Medical Informatics to issue a statement in 2001 outlining functions that would need to be performed in a pediatric practice for EMR systems to be useful. More recently, the president issued an executive federal order calling for the widespread adoption of interoperable electronic health records (EHRs) within the next 10 years. Electronic medical record systems that can send and receive data from population-based immunization information systems will further enhance complete immunization record keeping and facilitate reminder/recall functions to ensure complete immunization coverage and prevent administration of excessive doses.

Vaccine Shortages

Unprecedented and unanticipated shortages of vaccines in the recommended childhood and adolescent immunization schedule have occurred. When shortages occur, temporary changes in childhood immunization recommendations by the AAP, ACIP, and National Immunization Program at the CDC may be necessary, including deferral of certain immunizations in some children, establishment of vaccine priorities for high-risk children, and suspension in some states of school and child care entry immunization requirements. Several national committees and organizations, including the National Vaccine Advisory Committee and the US General Accounting Office, have proposed comprehensive strategies to prevent future shortages and encourage key stakeholders to work together to develop corrective action.

When vaccines are in short supply, physicians and other health care professionals should maintain lists of children and adolescents who do not receive vaccines at the recommended time or age so they can be recalled when the vaccine supply becomes adequate. For current information about vaccine shortages and resulting recommendations, see the Web sites of the National Immunization Program (**www.cdc.gov/nip**) or FDA (**www.fda.gov/cber/vaccines.htm**). For analyses of vaccine shortages and recommended solutions, see the Web site of the National Vaccine Program Office (**www.hhs.gov/nvpo**) or published recommendations from the National Vaccine Advisory Committee.*

Vaccine Safety and Contraindications

RISKS AND ADVERSE EVENTS

All licensed vaccines in the United States are safe and effective, but no vaccine is completely safe and effective in every person. Some vaccine recipients will have an adverse reaction, and some will not always be protected fully. The goal of vaccine development is to achieve the highest degree of protection with the lowest rate of adverse events. Adverse events after immunization include both true vaccine reactions and coincidental events blamed on the vaccine. As immunizations successfully eliminate their target vaccine-preventable diseases, vaccine safety issues have increased in relative prominence, increasing the need for immunization providers to communicate the risks and benefits of immunizations to a population whose first-hand experience with vaccine-preventable diseases is increasingly rare.

Risks of immunization may vary from trivial and inconvenient to severe and life threatening. When developing immunization recommendations, vaccine benefits and risks are weighed against the risks of natural disease to the person and the community. Many families lack awareness of the continued threat of certain vaccine-preventable diseases (eg, pertussis and measles) in their community and the risk of tetanus among unimmunized people. Recommendations are made to maximize pro-

---

* Santoli JM, Peter G, Arvin AM, et al. Strengthening the supply of routinely recommended vaccines in the United States: recommendations from the National Vaccine Advisory Committee. *JAMA*. 2003;290:3122–3128

tection and minimize risk by providing specific advice on dose, route, and timing of the vaccine and by delineating people who should be immunized and circumstances that warrant precaution or contraindication to immunization.

Common vaccine adverse reactions usually are mild to moderate in severity (eg, fever or local swelling, redness, and pain at the injection site) and have no permanent sequelae. Because such reactions reflect the body's immune system in maintaining the desired response to the immunizing agent or some other component of the vaccine, reactions occur frequently and are unavoidable. Examples include local inflammation after administration of DTaP, Td, or Tdap vaccines and fever and rash 1 to 2 weeks after administration of MMR or MMRV vaccines.

Sterile abscesses have occurred at the site of injection of certain inactivated vaccines. These abscesses presumably result from an inflammatory response to the vaccine or its adjuvant; in some instances, these reactions may be caused by inadvertent subcutaneous inoculation of a vaccine intended for intramuscular use. Administration of bacille Calmette-Guérin (BCG) vaccine often is followed by occurrence of local cysts, abscesses, and/or regional lymphadenopathy that will resolve spontaneously (see Tuberculosis, p 678).

Rarely, serious adverse effects of immunization occur, resulting in permanent sequelae or life-threatening illness. The occurrence of an adverse event after immunization does not prove that the vaccine caused the symptoms or signs. Vaccines are administered to infants and children during a period in their lives when certain conditions most commonly become clinically apparent (eg, seizure disorders). Because chance association of an adverse event to the timing of administration of a specific vaccine commonly occurs, a true causal association usually requires that the event occur at a significantly higher rate in vaccine recipients than in unimmunized groups of similar age and residence. This excess risk can be demonstrated in clinical trials or in postmarketing epidemiologic studies. More rarely, recovery of a vaccine virus from the ill child with compatible symptoms also may provide support for a causal link with a live-virus vaccine (eg, vaccine-associated polio with OPV). Clustering in time of unusual adverse events after immunizations or repeat of the adverse event with another dose of the same vaccine (eg, alopecia after hepatitis B vaccine) also are suggestive of causal relationships.

Reporting of any clinically significant adverse event after immunization to the Vaccine Adverse Event Reporting System (VAERS, see p 42) is important, because in conjunction with other reports, reporting may provide clues to an unanticipated adverse reaction. A reportable vaccine-preventable disease that occurs in a child or adolescent anytime, including after immunization (vaccine failure), should be reported to the local or state health department and may be reported to the VAERS (see Appendix IX, p 870).

INSTITUTE OF MEDICINE IMMUNIZATION SAFETY REVIEW COMMITTEE

The CDC and the National Institutes of Health commissioned the National Academy of Sciences' Institute of Medicine (IOM) to convene an Immunization Safety Review Committee in 2000. This committee was charged with providing independent advice to vaccine policy makers as well as health care professionals, the public, and the

media. The committee reviewed the following 8 specific topics about existing and emerging vaccine safety concerns.
• Measles-Mumps-Rubella Vaccine and Autism
• Thimerosal-Containing Vaccines and Neurodevelopmental Disorders
• Multiple Immunizations and Immune Dysfunction
• Hepatitis B Vaccine and Demyelinating Neurological Disorders
• SV40 Contamination of Polio Vaccine and Cancer
• Vaccinations and Sudden Unexpected Death in Infancy
• Influenza Vaccines and Neurological Complications
• Vaccines and Autism

On the basis of their conclusions, the committee made recommendations for future activities, including surveillance, research, and communication regarding safety concerns. The committee did not recommend a policy review of the childhood and adolescent immunization schedule or of recommendations for administration of routine childhood vaccines. Executive summaries of each of the committee's 8 reports are available online (**www.iom.edu/imsafety**).

THE BRIGHTON COLLABORATION

The Brighton Collaboration is an international voluntary collaboration formed to develop globally accepted and standardized case definitions for adverse events after immunization, known as the Brighton Standardized Case Definitions. The project began in 2000 with formation of a steering committee and creation of working groups, composed of international volunteers with expertise in vaccine safety, patient care, pharmaceuticals, regulatory affairs, public health, and vaccine delivery. The guidelines for collecting, analyzing, and presenting safety data developed by the collaboration will facilitate sharing and comparison of vaccine data among vaccine safety professionals worldwide. Additional information, including current definitions and updates of progress, can be found online (**www.brightoncollaboration.org**).

Reporting of Adverse Events

Before administering a dose of any vaccine, parents and patients should be questioned about adverse events and possible reactions after previous doses. No recommendations can anticipate all possible adverse events, particularly with newly licensed vaccines or a dose being administered as the first in a series. Unexpected events after administration of any vaccine, particularly events judged to be clinically significant, should be described in detail in the patient's medical record, and a VAERS report should be made. There is no time limit for reporting an adverse event. A possible reaction should be reported when the reaction is recognized.

The National Childhood Vaccine Injury Act of 1986 requires physicians and other health care professionals who administer vaccines covered under the National Vaccine Injury Compensation Program to maintain permanent immunization records and to report to the VAERS any condition listed on the reportable events table (see Appendix IV, p 852) or listed as a contraindication to additional doses of vaccine in the manufacturers package insert. The vaccines to which these requirements apply, as of January 2006, are measles, mumps, rubella, varicella, poliovirus, hepatitis A, hepatitis B, pertussis, diphtheria, tetanus, rotavirus, Hib, pneumococcal conjugate, meningococcal conjugate, and influenza vaccines (see Record Keeping and Immunization Information Systems, p 37).

VACCINE ADVERSE EVENT REPORTING SYSTEM (VAERS)

Clinically significant adverse events other than those listed in Appendix IV (p 852), as well as those occurring after administration of other vaccines not listed in Appendix IV, also should be reported to the VAERS. Vaccine failures (disease in an immunized person who received 1 dose or more of vaccine) and vaccine administration errors also may be reported. Forms (see Fig 1.2, p 43) can be obtained from the VAERS at 1-800-822-7967 and can be mailed or faxed. Reports also can be obtained and submitted electronically through a secure Web site (**http://vaers.hhs.gov**). The VAERS data, stripped of personal identifiers, also can be reviewed by the public by accessing the same Web site.

The VAERS, under the joint administration of the CDC and FDA, accepts reports of suspected adverse events after administration of any vaccine. Reports may be submitted by anyone suspecting that an adverse event might have been caused by immunization, including physicians, patients, parents, caregivers, and others.

All reports of possible adverse events after administration of any vaccine, regardless of the age of the recipient, are accepted. Submission of a report does not necessarily indicate that the vaccine caused the adverse event. All patient-identifying information is kept confidential. Written notification that the report has been received is provided to the person submitting the form. Staff from VAERS will contact the reporter by letter for follow-up of the patient's condition at 60 days and at 1 year after serious adverse events occur. Reports of serious adverse events and death reports also may be followed up by VAERS staff to obtain additional information about the event.

Important uses of VAERS data include detecting previously unrecognized adverse events, monitoring known reactions, identifying possible risk factors, and performing vaccine lot surveillance. Like all passive surveillance systems, VAERS is subject to limitations, including underreporting, reporting of temporal associations or unconfirmed diagnoses, lack of denominator data, and absence of an unimmunized control group. Because of these limitations, determining causal associations between vaccines and adverse events from VAERS reports usually is not possible, except for conditions such as injection site reactions, immediate hypersensitivity, and illnesses consistent with the naturally occurring disease and for which vaccine components can be recovered from tissue specimens (eg, measles vaccine-associated disease in an immunodeficient individual).

All reports of serious adverse events and death after immunization are reviewed by the FDA as received and are evaluated to detect adverse event reporting by vaccine lot. The FDA and CDC periodically prepare vaccine and adverse event specific surveillance summaries, which describe reported adverse events and look for unexpected patterns ("signals") that might suggest a possible causal link between the vaccine and an adverse event. Vaccine safety concerns identified through adverse event monitoring nearly always require confirmation using an epidemiologic or other (eg, laboratory) study by the Vaccine Safety Datalink, by the Clinical Immunization Safety Assessment (CISA) Network, or by other means.

FIGURE 1.2 VAERS FORM

FOR DIRECTIONS FOR COMPLETING FORM AND FOR A NEW ELEC-
TRONIC REPORTING FORM, SEE HTTP://VAERS.HHS.GOV.

WEBSITE: www.vaers.org   E-MAIL: info@vaers.org   FAX: 1-877-721-0366

VACCINE ADVERSE EVENT REPORTING SYSTEM
24 Hour Toll-Free Information 1-800-822-7967
P.O. Box 1100, Rockville, MD 20849-1100
VAERS
PATIENT IDENTITY KEPT CONFIDENTIAL

For CDC/FDA Use Only
VAERS Number _____
Date Received _____

Patient Name:

Last   First   M.I.

Address

City   State   Zip

Telephone no. (___) _____

Vaccine administered by (Name):

Responsible
Physician _____
Facility Name/Address

City   State   Zip

Telephone no. (___) _____

Form completed by (Name):

Relation   ☐ Vaccine Provider   ☐ Patient/Parent
to Patient   ☐ Manufacturer   ☐ Other
Address *(if different from patient or provider)*

City   State   Zip

Telephone no. (___) _____

1. State
2. County where administered
3. Date of birth ___/___/___ mm dd yy
4. Patient age
5. Sex ☐ M ☐ F
6. Date form completed ___/___/___ mm dd yy

7. Describe adverse events(s) (symptoms, signs, time course) and treatment, if any

8. Check all appropriate:
☐ Patient died (date ___/___/___ mm dd yy)
☐ Life threatening illness
☐ Required emergency room/doctor visit
☐ Required hospitalization (_____days)
☐ Resulted in prolongation of hospitalization
☐ Resulted in permanent disability
☐ None of the above

9. Patient recovered   ☐ YES ☐ NO ☐ UNKNOWN

10. Date of vaccination ___/___/___ mm dd yy   Time ___ AM PM
11. Adverse event onset ___/___/___ mm dd yy   Time ___ AM PM

12. Relevant diagnostic tests/laboratory data

13. Enter all vaccines given on date listed in no. 10

	Vaccine (type)	Manufacturer	Lot number	Route/Site	No. Previous Doses
a.					
b.					
c.					
d.					

14. Any other vaccinations within 4 weeks prior to the date listed in no. 10

	Vaccine (type)	Manufacturer	Lot number	Route/Site	No. Previous doses	Date given
a.						
b.						

15. Vaccinated at:
☐ Private doctor's office/hospital   ☐ Military clinic/hospital
☐ Public health clinic/hospital   ☐ Other/unknown

16. Vaccine purchased with:
☐ Private funds   ☐ Military funds
☐ Public funds   ☐ Other/unknown

17. Other medications

18. Illness at time of vaccination (specify)

19. Pre-existing physician-diagnosed allergies, birth defects, medical conditions (specify)

20. Have you reported this adverse event previously?
☐ No   ☐ To health department
☐ To doctor   ☐ To manufacturer

Only for children 5 and under

22. Birth weight _____ lb. _____ oz.
23. No. of brothers and sisters

21. Adverse event following prior vaccination (check all applicable, specify)

Only for reports submitted by manufacturer/immunization project

	Adverse Event	Onset Age	Type Vaccine	Dose no. in series
☐ In patient				
☐ In brother or sister				

24. Mfr./imm. proj. report no.
25. Date received by mfr./imm.proj.

26. 15 day report?   ☐ Yes ☐ No
27. Report type   ☐ Initial ☐ Follow-Up

Health care providers and manufacturers are required by law (42 USC 300aa-25) to report reactions to vaccines listed in the Table of Reportable Events Following Immunization. Reports for reactions to other vaccines are voluntary except when required as a condition of immunization grant awards.

Form VAERS-1(FDA)

VACCINE SAFETY DATALINK PROJECT

To supplement the VAERS program, which is a passive surveillance system, the CDC in 1990 formed partnerships with several large health maintenance organizations to establish the Vaccine Safety Datalink (VSD) project, an active surveillance system designed to evaluate vaccine safety continually. The VSD project includes data on more than 10 million people. Claims data of the study population can be monitored for potential adverse events resulting from immunization. The VSD project allows for both retrospective and prospective observational vaccine safety studies as well as for timely investigations of emerging vaccine safety concerns. The VSD concept to evaluate vaccine safety has been proven to be valuable for many vaccines. Information about the VSD can be found at **www.cdc.gov/nip/vacsafe/#VSD**.

CLINICAL IMMUNIZATION SAFETY ASSESSMENT (CISA) NETWORK

Clinically significant adverse events after immunization rarely occur in prelicensure clinical trials, and health care professionals see them too infrequently to be able to provide standardized evaluation, diagnosis, and management. The CISA Network was established by the CDC in 2001 with primary goals including: (1) developing research protocols for clinical evaluation, diagnosis, and management of vaccine adverse events; (2) improving the understanding of vaccine adverse events at the individual level, including determining possible genetic and other risk factors for predisposed individuals and high-risk subpopulations; and (3) serving as public health regional referral centers for clinical vaccine safety inquiries.

The CISA Network will advise clinicians on the evaluation, diagnosis, and management of adverse events after immunization. The network will conduct research through establishment of a registry for clinical consultations, creation of standardized protocols for evaluation of specific events, and direct patient evaluation to generate increased case series of clinically significant adverse events after immunization. These data will be used to improve the scientific understanding of these events and to develop protocols or guidelines for health care professionals that will assist in evaluation, diagnosis, and management of similarly affected people. In addition, the CISA Network will serve as regional clinical vaccine safety resources for clinicians. Current information about the CISA Network can be found online (**www.vaccinesafety.org**).

VACCINE INJURY COMPENSATION

The National Vaccine Injury Compensation Program is a no-fault system in which people may seek compensation if they are thought to have suffered an injury, or a recipient is thought to have died, as a result of administration of a covered vaccine. Claims must be filed within 36 months after the first symptom appeared after immunization, and death claims must be filed within 24 months of the death and within 48 months after the onset of the vaccine-related injury from which death occurred. Claims arising from covered vaccines must be adjudicated through the program before civil litigation can be pursued. Developed as an alternative to civil litigation and operational since 1988, the program has decreased the number of lawsuits against health care professionals and vaccine manufacturers and has assisted establishment of a stable vaccine supply and marketplace while ensuring access to compensation for vaccine-associated injury and death.

The program is based on a Vaccine Injury Table (VIT [see Appendix IV, p 852]) listing the vaccines covered by the program as well as injuries, disabilities, illnesses, and conditions (including death) for which compensation may be awarded. The VIT defines the time during which the first symptoms or significant aggravation of an injury must appear after immunization. If an injury listed in the VIT is proven, claimants receive a "legal presumption of causation," thus avoiding the need to prove causation in an individual case. If the claim pertains to conditions not listed in the VIT, claimants may prevail if they prove causation. Any vaccine that is recommended by the CDC for routine use in children and has an excise tax placed on it by Congress is eligible for coverage by the program.

Program and contact information about the National Vaccine Injury Compensation Program and the VIT are in Appendix I:

Parklawn Building
5600 Fishers Lane
Room 11C-26
Rockville, MD 20857
Telephone: 800-338-2382
Web site: **www.hrsa.gov/osp/vicp**

People wishing to file a claim for a vaccine injury should telephone or write to the following:

United States Court of Federal Claims
717 Madison Place, NW
Washington, DC 20005-1011
Telephone: 202-219-9657

PRECAUTIONS AND CONTRAINDICATIONS

Precautions and contraindications to immunization are described in specific chapters on vaccine-preventable diseases. A contraindication indicates that a vaccine should not be administered. In contrast, a precaution specifies a situation in which a vaccine may be indicated if, after careful assessment, the benefit of immunization to the individual is judged to outweigh the risk of complications. Some contraindications and many precautions are temporary. Contraindications and precautions may be generic, applying to all vaccines, or may be specific to one or more vaccines.

MINOR ILLNESS WITH OR WITHOUT FEVER DOES NOT CONTRAINDICATE IMMUNIZATION. Most vaccines are intended for use in healthy people or in people whose diseases or conditions are not affected by immunization. For optimal safety, vaccines should not be used if an adverse reaction to the vaccine may seriously affect or be confused with an underlying illness. Most evidence does not indicate an increased risk of adverse events or a decrease in effectiveness associated with immunization administered during a minor illness with or without fever (body temperature $\geq38°C$ [$\geq100.4°F$]). Deferring immunization in such situations contributes to missed opportunities and frequently results in unimmunized or inadequately immunized children who may develop or transmit vaccine-preventable disease.

FEVER, PER SE, IS NOT A CONTRAINDICATION TO IMMUNIZATION. For a child with an acute febrile illness (body temperature ≥38°C [≥100.4°F]), guidelines for immunization are based on the physician's assessment of the child's illness and the specific vaccines the child is scheduled to receive. However, if fever or other manifestations suggest a moderate or serious illness, the child should not be immunized until recovered. Specific recommendations are as follows:

- *Live-virus vaccines.* Minor respiratory, gastrointestinal, or other illnesses with or without fever do not contraindicate use of live-virus vaccines, such as MMR, MMRV, varicella, or rotavirus. Children with febrile upper respiratory tract infections have serologic responses similar to responses of well children after immunization. The potential benefit of immunization at the recommended age, regardless of the presence of a minor illness, outweighs the possible increased risk of vaccine failure.

- *DTaP vaccine.* Mild illnesses (eg, upper respiratory tract illnesses) do not contraindicate administration of DTaP or Tdap. However, a moderate or severe illness with or without fever is a reason to delay immunization, in part because evolving signs and symptoms associated with the illness may be difficult to distinguish from a vaccine adverse event. Currently available DTaP vaccines have rates of adverse events that are much less than previously licensed DTP vaccines.

- *Child with frequent febrile illnesses.* A child who has moderate or severe febrile illness at the time of scheduled immunizations should be asked to return as soon as the acute phase of the illness resolves so that immunization can be completed.

- *Immunocompromised children.* Special consideration needs to be given to immunocompromised children, including children with congenital immunodeficiencies, human immunodeficiency virus (HIV) infection, or malignant neoplasm or who are recipients of immunosuppressive therapy (see Immunocompromised Children, p 71).

A concise summary of contraindications to and precautions for immunizations is given in Appendix III (p 847).

HYPERSENSITIVITY REACTIONS TO VACCINE CONSTITUENTS

Hypersensitivity reactions to constituents of vaccines are rare. Facilities and health care professionals should be available for treating immediate hypersensitivity reactions in all settings in which vaccines are administered. This recommendation does not preclude administration of vaccines in school-based or other nonclinic settings.

The 4 types of hypersensitivity reactions considered related to vaccine constituents are (1) allergic reactions to egg-related antigens; (2) mercury sensitivity in some recipients of mercury-containing IG and vaccines (see Thimerosal Content of Some Vaccines and Immune Globulin Preparations, p 48); (3) antimicrobial-induced allergic reactions; and (4) hypersensitivity to other vaccine components, including gelatin, yeast protein, and the infectious agent itself.

ALLERGIC REACTIONS TO EGG-RELATED ANTIGENS. Current measles and mumps vaccines are derived from chicken embryo fibroblast tissue cultures but do not contain significant amounts of egg cross-reacting proteins. Studies indicate that children with egg allergy, even children with severe hypersensitivity, are at low risk of anaphylactic reactions to these vaccines, singly or in combination (eg, MMR) and that skin testing with dilute vaccine is not predictive of an allergic reaction to immunization. Most immediate hypersensitivity reactions after MMR immunization appear to be reactions to other vaccine components, such as gelatin or neomycin. Therefore, children with egg allergy routinely may be given MMR, MMRV, measles, or mumps vaccines without previous skin testing.

Yellow fever and inactivated and live-attenuated influenza vaccines prepared in eggs contain egg proteins and, on rare occasions, may induce immediate allergic reactions, including anaphylaxis. Skin testing with yellow fever vaccines is recommended before administration to people with a history of systemic anaphylactic symptoms (generalized urticaria, hypotension, or manifestations of upper or lower airway obstruction) after egg ingestion. Skin testing also has been used for children with severe anaphylactic reactions to eggs who are to receive inactivated influenza vaccine. However, these children generally should not receive inactivated or live-attenuated influenza vaccines because of a risk of adverse reaction, the likely need for yearly immunization, and availability of chemoprophylaxis against influenza infection (see Influenza, p 401). History of severe egg allergy in a family member is not a contraindication to influenza vaccines. Less severe or local manifestations of allergy to egg or feathers are not contraindications to administration of yellow fever or influenza vaccines and do not warrant vaccine skin testing.

An egg-sensitive person can be tested with vaccine (eg, yellow fever vaccine) before its use as follows.

- **Scratch, prick, or puncture test.** A drop of a 1:10 dilution of vaccine in physiologic saline solution is applied at the site of a superficial scratch, prick, or puncture on the volar surface of the forearm. Positive (histamine) and negative (physiologic saline solution) control tests also should be used. The test is read after 15 to 20 minutes. A positive test result is a wheal 3 mm larger than that of the saline control area, usually with surrounding erythema. The histamine control test result must be positive for valid interpretation. If the result of this test is negative, an ID test is performed.

- **Intradermal test.** A dose of 0.02 mL of a 1:100 dilution of the vaccine in physiologic saline solution is injected intradermally on the volar surface of the forearm; positive- and negative-control skin tests are performed concurrently as described previously. A wheal 5 mm or larger than the negative control area with surrounding erythema is considered a positive reaction.

If these test results are negative, the vaccine may be given. If the child's test result is positive, the vaccine still may be given using a desensitization procedure if immunization is considered warranted because of a person's risk of complications resulting from the disease. A suggested protocol is SC administration of the following successive doses of vaccine at 15- to 20-minute intervals:

1. 0.05 mL of a 1:10 dilution
2. 0.05 mL of full-strength vaccine
3. 0.10 mL of full-strength vaccine
4. 0.15 mL of full-strength vaccine
5. 0.20 mL of full-strength vaccine

Scratch, prick, or puncture tests with other allergens have resulted in fatalities in highly allergic people. Although such untoward effects have not been reported for vaccine testing, all skin tests and desensitization procedures should be performed by trained personnel experienced in management of anaphylaxis. Necessary medications and equipment for treatment of anaphylaxis should be readily available (see Treatment of Anaphylactic Reactions, p 64).

THIMEROSAL CONTENT OF SOME VACCINES AND IG PREPARATIONS. Thimerosal is a mercury-containing preservative that has been used as an additive to biological agents and vaccines since the 1930s because of its effectiveness in preventing bacterial and fungal contamination, particularly in open multidose containers. All routinely recommended vaccines for US infants and children are available only as thimerosal-free formulations or contain only trace amounts of thimerosal, with the exception of some inactivated influenza vaccines. Inactivated influenza vaccine for pediatric use is available as a thimerosal-preservative containing formulation and a trace thimerosal-containing formulation, but the latter is in more limited supply.

The only nonvaccine biological agents presently distributed in the United States that contain thimerosal in active production and US distribution are certain antivenins. Immune Globulin Intravenous does not contain thimerosal or other preservatives, and none of the Rh_o (D) Immune Globulin (Human) products contain thimerosal (**www.fda.gov/cber/blood/mercplasma.htm**).

ANTIMICROBIAL-INDUCED ALLERGIC REACTIONS. Antimicrobial-induced reactions have been suspected in people with known allergies who received vaccines containing trace amounts of antimicrobial agents (see package insert for each product for specific listing). Proof of a causal relationship is difficult and often impossible to confirm.

The IPV vaccine contains trace amounts of streptomycin, neomycin, and polymyxin B. Live-attenuated measles, mumps, and rubella (singly or in combination as MMR) and varicella vaccines contain a trace quantity of neomycin. Some people who are allergic to neomycin may experience a delayed-type local reaction 48 to 96 hours after administration of IPV, MMR, MMRV, or varicella vaccines. The reaction consists of an erythematous, pruritic papule. This minor reaction is of little importance compared with the benefit of immunization and should not be considered a contraindication. However, if a person has a history of anaphylactic reaction to neomycin, neomycin-containing vaccines should not be used. No currently recommended vaccine contains penicillin or its derivatives.

HYPERSENSITIVITY TO OTHER VACCINE COMPONENTS, INCLUDING THE INFECTIOUS AGENT. Some live-virus vaccines, such as MMR, MMRV, varicella, and yellow fever vaccines, contain gelatin as a stabilizer. People with a history of food allergy to gelatin rarely develop anaphylaxis after receipt of gelatin-containing vaccines. Skin testing is a consideration for these people before administration of a gelatin-containing vaccine, but no protocol or reported experience is available. Because gelatin used in the United States as a vaccine stabilizer usually is porcine and food gelatins may be derived solely from bovine sources, a negative food history does not exclude the possibility of an immunization reaction.

Hepatitis B vaccines are manufactured using recombinant technology by harvesting purified hepatitis B surface antigen from genetically engineered yeast cells containing the hepatitis B surface antigen gene. Purification results in a substantial reduction of yeast protein contained in the vaccine, but in rare instances, vaccine recipients with a significant hypersensitivity to yeast products may experience an allergic reaction to hepatitis B vaccine that would contraindicate receiving additional doses.

Reactions occur with DTaP vaccines but are much less common than with DTP vaccines. On occasion, urticarial or anaphylactic reactions have occurred in recipients of DTP, DTaP, DT, Td, or tetanus toxoid vaccine. Tetanus and diphtheria antigen-specific antibodies of the IgE type have been identified in some of these patients. Although attributing a specific sensitivity to vaccine components is difficult, an immediate, severe, or anaphylactic allergic reaction to any vaccine or vaccine component is a contraindication to subsequent immunization of the patient with the specific product. A transient urticarial rash, however, is not a contraindication to further doses (see Appendix III, p 847).

People who have high serum concentrations of tetanus IgG antibody, usually as the result of frequent booster immunizations, have an increased incidence and severity of adverse reactions to subsequent vaccine administration (see Tetanus, p 648). These Arthus-like reactions present as extensive painful swelling, often from shoulder to elbow.

Reactions resembling serum sickness have been reported in approximately 6% of patients after a booster dose of human diploid rabies vaccine, probably resulting from sensitization to human albumin that had been altered chemically by the virus-inactivating agent.

Measles vaccines, including MMR and MMRV, and rabies vaccines contain Albumin, a derivative of human blood. Because of effective donor screening and product manufacturing processes, the FDA believes the risk of transmission of any viral disease from Albumin in these vaccines is remote.

Japanese encephalitis virus vaccine has been associated with generalized urticaria and angioedema, sometimes with respiratory distress and hypotension, occurring within minutes of immunization to as long as 2 weeks after immunization. The pathogenesis of such reactions is not understood. People with a history of urticaria are at increased risk of this adverse reaction, so vaccine recipients with this history should be observed for 30 minutes after immunization and warned about the possibility of delayed urticaria and potentially life-threatening angioedema.

MISCONCEPTIONS ABOUT VACCINE CONTRAINDICATIONS

Contraindications to immunization often are misunderstood by health care professionals and parents. Common conditions or circumstances that are **not** contraindications include:

- Mild acute illness with low-grade fever or mild diarrheal illness in an otherwise well child.
- The convalescent phase of illness.
- Currently receiving antimicrobial therapy.
- Reaction to a previous vaccine dose that involved only soreness, redness, or swelling in the immediate vicinity of the immunization site or temperature of less than 40.5°C (105°F).

- Preterm birth—the appropriate age for initiating most immunizations in the preterm infant usually is the recommended chronologic age; vaccine doses should not be reduced for preterm infants (see Preterm Infants, p 67, and Hepatitis B, p 335).
- Pregnancy in a household contact is not a contraindication to administration of any routinely recommended live-virus vaccine, including MMR, MMRV, varicella, rotavirus, or live-attenuated influenza vaccine, to a child or other nonpregnant household contact as recommended. Vaccine viruses in MMR vaccine are not transmitted by vaccine recipients, and although varicella vaccine virus and influenza vaccine virus can be transmitted by healthy vaccine recipients to contacts, the frequency is rare and only mild or asymptomatic infection has been reported (see Varicella-Zoster Infections, p 711).
- Immunosuppression of a household contact is not a contraindication to administration of any routinely recommended live-virus vaccines, including MMR, MMRV, varicella, and rotavirus; inactivated influenza vaccines, when available, are preferred to live-attenuated influenza vaccine.
- Recent exposure to an infectious disease.
- Breastfeeding—the only vaccine virus that has been isolated from human milk is rubella; no evidence indicates that human milk from women immunized against rubella is harmful to infants. If rubella infection does occur in an infant as a result of exposure to the vaccine virus in human milk, infection likely would be well tolerated, because the vaccine virus is attenuated.
- History of nonspecific allergies or relatives with allergies.
- History of allergies to penicillin or any other antimicrobial agent, except anaphylactic reactions to neomycin or streptomycin (see Hypersensitivity Reactions to Vaccine Constituents, p 46)—these reactions occur rarely, if ever; none of the vaccines licensed in the United States contain penicillin.
- Allergies to duck meat or duck feathers—no vaccine available in the United States is produced in substrates containing duck antigens.
- Family history of seizures in a person considered for pertussis or measles immunization (see Children With a Personal or Family History of Seizures, p 85).
- Family history of sudden infant death syndrome in children considered for DTaP immunization.
- Family history of an adverse event after immunization.
- Malnutrition.

Reporting of Vaccine-Preventable Diseases

Most vaccine-preventable diseases are reportable throughout the United States (see Appendix IX, p 870). Public health officials depend on health care professionals to report promptly to state or local health departments suspected cases of vaccine-preventable disease. These reports are transmitted weekly to the CDC and are used to detect outbreaks, monitor disease-control strategies, and evaluate national immunization practices and policies. Reports provide useful information about vaccine efficacy, changing or current epidemiology of vaccine-preventable diseases, and possible epidemics that could threaten public health. Reporting confirmed and suspected vaccine-preventable diseases is a legal obligation of the physician.

Standards for Child and Adolescent Immunization Practices (see Appendix II, p 844)

The national *Standards for Pediatric Immunization Practices* were revised by the National Vaccine Advisory Committee, endorsed by the AAP and numerous other medical and public health organizations, and published in *Pediatrics.** As part of this revision, the standards were renamed *Standards for Child and Adolescent Immunization Practices.* These standards include the most essential and desirable immunization practices and are recommended for use by all health care professionals providing care in public or private health care settings who are involved in administration of vaccines or management of immunization services for children. Their use is intended to help identify needed changes in office practices, to improve preschool immunization rates, to prevent vaccine-preventable disease outbreaks, and to achieve national objectives for immunization. The revised standards reflect the increasing role of private practitioners, the importance of adolescent immunization, and recent increases in vaccine safety concerns among the general public.

Parental Misconceptions About Immunizations

Misconceptions about the need for and safety of recommended childhood and adolescent immunizations are potential causes of delayed immunization, underimmunization, or both. Several common misconceptions of parents have been addressed by the CDC.[†] To inform parents further, the AAP has published a brochure titled *Immunizations: What You Need to Know,*[‡] which addresses common questions about recommended childhood and adolescent immunizations, including the following.

- **"Why should children be immunized when most vaccine-preventable diseases have been eliminated in the United States?"** Although immunizations dramatically have decreased the incidence of a number of childhood diseases in the United States, many of these diseases remain prevalent in other areas of the world and could be reintroduced easily into the United States and, without immunization, could spread quickly. Unimmunized children also will be at risk throughout their lives, including when they travel to countries where vaccine-preventable diseases are endemic.

- **"Do immunizations work? Haven't most people who get a vaccine-preventable disease been immunized?"** A few people do not respond immunologically to vaccines, but most childhood vaccines are more than 90% effective. An unimmunized child has a greater risk of contracting a vaccine-preventable disease if exposed. Most people who get a vaccine-preventable disease have not been fully immunized. Failure to immunize a child leaves them with no protection against being affected with one or more of these diseases.

---

* The National Vaccine Advisory Committee. Standards for child and adolescent immunization practices. *Pediatrics.* 2003;112:958–963

[†] National Immunization Program. *Six Common Misconceptions About Vaccination and How to Respond to Them.* Atlanta, GA: Centers for Disease Control and Prevention; 1996. Available at: **www.cdc.gov/nip/publications/6mishome.htm**

[‡] For copies, contact the AAP at 866-843-2271.

- **"Aren't some vaccine lots more dangerous than others?"** All vaccines are reviewed extensively for safety and efficacy before being licensed by the FDA and recommended for use. There is no evidence to support the theory that individual lots of commonly used vaccines differ in safety. The FDA and CDC conduct programs to continue surveillance after licensure for safety and efficacy of all recommended vaccines. Active surveillance for vaccine-associated adverse events after licensure involves numbers of subjects far greater than for many other types of therapeutic agents, reflecting the high standard to which vaccines are held.
- **"Isn't giving children more than one immunization at a time dangerous?"** Numerous studies have shown that multiple recommended childhood and adolescent immunizations can be given safely at the same time. Scientists estimate that the immune system can recognize and respond to hundreds of thousands, if not millions, of antigens. Recommended vaccines use only a small portion of the "memory" of the immune system. The Safety Review Committee of the Institute of Medicine (IOM) found no evidence to support the theory that multiple immunizations increase the risk of immune dysfunction (see p 40).
- **"Do vaccines cause autism?"** The concerns about potential associations of MMR vaccine and autism as well as thimerosal-containing vaccines and autism have been evaluated in many studies. In addition, the Vaccine Safety Committee of the IOM examined the hypothesis that MMR vaccine and thimerosal-containing vaccines are associated with autism. The IOM Vaccine Safety Committee developed and published several conclusions and recommendations, including the following:
  - Scientific evidence favors rejection of a causal relationship between thimerosal-containing vaccines and autism.
  - Scientific evidence favors rejection of a causal relationship between MMR vaccine and autism.
  - Available funding for autism research should be channeled to more promising areas of inquiry.
  - Risk-benefit communication requires attention to the needs of both the scientific community and public communities.
  - Chelation therapy has potentially serious adverse effects and, therefore, should be used in children with autism only in carefully controlled research settings with appropriate oversight by institutional review boards to protect the interests of the children who participate.

Although parents receive information from multiple sources, they consider health care professionals their most trusted source of health information. Health care professionals should obtain and distribute copies of available AAP and CDC immunization documents as well as the required vaccine information statements (VISs) to parents to address their questions and concerns. These resource materials can help parents make informed decisions about immunizing their children. Other sources of objective vaccine information are available (see the list of selected authoritative Web sites, p 53) that can help health care professionals respond to questions and misconceptions about immunizations and vaccine-preventable diseases. Approaches to informing patients and parents about the benefits and risks of disease prevention, including immunizations (see Informing Patients and Parents, p 5), and approaches to parents who refuse immunizations for their child (see Parental Refusal of Immunization, p 7) are available.

The **National Network for Immunization Information** (NNii) provides up-to-date, science-based information to health care professionals, the media, policy makers, and the public. The NNii also provides additional reliable resources for current immunization information and has published a resource kit, "Communicating With Patients About Immunization." Immunization information can be found on the NNii Web site (**www.immunizationinfo.org**).

INTERNET RESOURCES FOR IMMUNIZATION INFORMATION

Several health professional associations, nonprofit groups, universities, and government organizations provide Internet resources containing immunization information.

HEALTH PROFESSIONAL ASSOCIATIONS

American Academy of Family Physicians (AAFP)
www.familydoctor.org
American Academy of Pediatrics (AAP)
www.aap.org
www.cispimmunize.org (AAP Childhood Immunization Support Program)
American Medical Association (AMA)
www.ama-assn.org
American Nurses Association (ANA)
www.nursingworld.org
Association of State and Territorial Health Officials (ASTHO)
www.astho.org
Association of Teachers of Preventive Medicine (ATPM)
www.atpm.org/education/education.htm
National Medical Association (NMA)
www.nmanet.org

NONPROFIT GROUPS AND UNIVERSITIES

Albert B. Sabin Vaccine Institute
www.sabin.org
Allied Vaccine Group (AVG)
www.vaccine.org
Children's Vaccine Program
www.childrensvaccine.org
Every Child By Two (ECBT)
www.ecbt.org
Global Alliance for Vaccines and Immunization (GAVI)
www.vaccinealliance.org
Health on the Net Foundation (HON)
www.hon.ch
National Healthy Mothers, Healthy Babies Coalition (HMHB)
www.hmhb.org
Immunization Action Coalition (IAC)
www.immunize.org

Institute for Vaccine Safety (IVS), Johns Hopkins University
www.vaccinesafety.edu
Institute of Medicine
**www.iom.edu/IOM/IOMHome.nsf/Pages/immunization +
safety + review**
National Alliance for Hispanic Health
www.hispanichealth.org
National Network for Immunization Information (NNii)
www.immunizationinfo.org
Parents of Kids with Infectious Diseases (PKIDS)
www.pkids.org
The Vaccine Education Center at the Children's Hospital of Philadelphia
www.vaccine.chop.edu
The Vaccine Page
www.vaccines.com
World Health Organization
www.who.int/mediacentre/news/notes/2005/np09/en

GOVERNMENT ORGANIZATIONS

Centers for Disease Control and Prevention (CDC)
http://phil.cdc.gov/phil (Image Library)
www.cdc.gov/travel/vaccinat.htm
National Center for Infectious Diseases (NCID)
www.cdc.gov/ncidod
National Immunization Program (NIP)
www.cdc.gov/nip
www.cdc.gov/nip/publications
National Vaccine Program Office (NVPO)
www.hhs.gov/nvpo/
National Institute of Allergy and Infectious Diseases (NIAID)
www.niaid.nih.gov/dmid/vaccines
World Health Organization
www.who.int/vaccines

PASSIVE IMMUNIZATION

Passive immunization entails administration of preformed antibody to a recipient. Passive immunization is indicated in the following general circumstances for prevention or amelioration of infectious diseases:

• When people are deficient in synthesis of antibody as a result of congenital or acquired B-lymphocyte defects, alone or in combination with other immunodeficiencies.
• Prophylactically, when a person susceptible to a disease is exposed to or has a high likelihood of exposure to that infection, especially when that person has a high risk of complications from the disease or when time does not permit adequate protection by active immunization alone.

• Therapeutically, when a disease is already present, antibody may ameliorate or aid in suppressing the effects of a toxin (eg, foodborne or wound botulism, diphtheria, or tetanus) or suppress the inflammatory response (eg, Kawasaki disease).

Passive immunization has been accomplished with several types of products. The choice is dictated by the types of products available, the type of antibody desired, the route of administration, timing, and other considerations. These products include Immune Globulin (IG) and specific ("hyperimmune") IG preparations given intramuscularly, Immune Globulin Intravenous (IGIV), specific (hyperimmune) IG given by the intravenous (IV) route, and antibodies of animal origin and monoclonal antibodies.

Indications for administration of IG preparations other than those relevant to infectious diseases are not reviewed in the *Red Book*.

Whole blood and blood components for transfusion (including plasma) from US registered blood banks are tested for the presence of bloodborne pathogens, including syphilis, hepatitis B virus, hepatitis C virus (HCV), human immunodeficiency virus (HIV)-1, HIV-2, and human T-lymphotropic viruses (HTLV)-1 and HTLV-2. Whole blood and blood components also are batch tested for West Nile virus; during an outbreak in a particular geographic area, units may be tested by individual unit nucleic acid amplification (NAA) testing (see Blood Safety, p 106; and West Nile Virus, p 729). A similar array of tests is performed by US-licensed establishments that collect plasma used only to manufacture plasma derivatives, such as IGIV, IG, and specific immune globulins. United States-licensed IG and specific immune globulin preparations have not been associated with transmission of any of these diseases. Hepatitis C virus transmission in 1994 was associated with administration of IGIV produced by a single manufacturer. The US Food and Drug Administration (FDA) now requires that IGIV and other immune globulin preparations for IV or intramuscular (IM) administration undergo additional manufacturing procedures that inactivate or remove viruses.

Immune Globulin (Intramuscular)

Immune Globulin (intramuscular) is derived from the pooled plasma of adults by an alcohol-fractionation procedure. Immune Globulin consists primarily of the immunoglobulin (Ig) fraction (at least 96% IgG and trace amounts of IgA and IgM), is sterile, and is not known to transmit hepatotropic viruses, HIV, or any other infectious disease agents. Immune Globulin is a concentrated protein solution (approximately 16.5% or 165 mg/mL) containing specific antibodies that reflect the infectious and immunization experience of the population from whose plasma the IG was prepared. Many donors (at least 1000 donors per lot of final product) are used to include a broad spectrum of antibodies.

Immune Globulin is licensed and recommended for IM administration. Therefore, IG should be administered deep into a large muscle mass, usually in the gluteal region or anterior thigh of a child (see Site and Route of Immunization, p 19). Ordinarily, no more than 5 mL should be administered at one site in an adult, adolescent, or large child; a lesser volume per site (1–3 mL) should be given to small children and infants. Administration of more than 15 mL at any one time is seldom, if ever, warranted. Peak serum concentrations of antibodies usually are achieved 3 to 5 days after IM administration.

Intravenous use of human IG is contraindicated. Intradermal use of IG is not recommended.

INDICATIONS FOR THE USE OF IG

REPLACEMENT THERAPY IN ANTIBODY DEFICIENCY DISORDERS. The usual dose (limited by muscle mass and the volume that should be administered) is 100 mg/kg (equivalent to 0.66 mL/kg) per month intramuscularly. Customary practice is to administer twice this dose initially and to adjust the interval between administration of the doses (2–4 weeks) on the basis of trough IgG concentrations and clinical response (absence of or decrease in infections). For most cases, IG has been replaced by IGIV, because higher plasma Ig concentrations and greater efficacy can be achieved by the administration of IGIV.

HEPATITIS A PROPHYLAXIS. Hepatitis A immunization is the preferred method of prophylaxis against hepatitis A infection. However, when given within 2 weeks of exposure, IG can prevent hepatitis A in susceptible people for whom immunization is contraindicated. Indications include international travel by children younger than 1 year of age and postexposure prophylaxis (see Hepatitis A, p 326).

MEASLES PROPHYLAXIS. Immune Globulin administered to exposed, measles-susceptible people will prevent or attenuate infection if given within 6 days of exposure (see Measles, p 441).

RUBELLA PROPHYLAXIS. Immune Globulin administered to rubella-susceptible pregnant women after rubella exposure may decrease the risk of fetal infection (see Rubella, p 574).

ADVERSE REACTIONS TO IG

- Most recipients experience local discomfort, and some experience pain at the site of administration (which are lessened if the preparation is at room temperature at the time of injection). Less common reactions include flushing, headache, chills, and nausea.
- Serious reactions are uncommon; these reactions may involve chest pain or constriction, dyspnea, anaphylaxis, or hypotension and shock. An increased risk of systemic reaction results from inadvertent IV administration. People requiring repeated doses of IG have been reported to experience systemic reactions, such as fever, chills, sweating, and shock.
- Because IG contains trace amounts of IgA, people who have selective deficiency of serum IgA can develop anti-IgA antibodies on rare occasions and react to a subsequent dose of IG, whole-blood transfusion, or plasma infusion. These reactions include systemic symptoms such as chills, fever, and shock-like symptoms. In rare cases in which reactions related to anti-IgA antibodies have occurred, use of IgA-depleted IGIV preparations may decrease the likelihood of further reactions. Because these reactions are rare, routine screening for IgA deficiency is not recommended.

PRECAUTIONS FOR THE USE OF IG

- Caution should be used when giving IG to a patient with a history of adverse reactions to IG.
- Although systemic reactions to IG are rare (see Adverse Reactions to IG, p 56), epinephrine and other means of treating serious acute reactions should be available immediately. Health care professionals administering IG should have training to manage emergencies appropriately.
- Immune Globulin should not be used in patients with severe thrombocytopenia or any coagulation disorder that would preclude IM injection. In such cases, use of IGIV is recommended.
- Screening of potential recipients of IG for IgA deficiency is not recommended routinely (see Adverse Reactions to IG, p 56).

Specific Immune Globulins

Specific immune globulins, termed "hyperimmune globulins," differ from other preparations in the selection of donors and may differ in the number of donors whose plasma is included in the pool from which the product is prepared. Donors known to have high titers of the desired antibody, naturally acquired or stimulated by immunization, are selected. Specific immune globulins are prepared by the same procedure as other immune globulin preparations. Specific immune globulin preparations for use in infectious diseases include Hepatitis B Immune Globulin, Rabies Immune Globulin, Tetanus Immune Globulin, Varicella-Zoster Immune Globulin (if available), Cytomegalovirus Immune Globulin Intravenous, and Botulism Immune Globulin Intravenous (for infant botulism). An intramuscularly administered monoclonal antibody preparation for prevention of respiratory syncytial virus is available. Recommendations for use of these immune globulins are given in the discussions of specific diseases in Section 3. The precautions and adverse reactions for IG and IGIV are applicable to specific immune globulins.

Immune Globulin Intravenous

Immune Globulin Intravenous is made by individual manufacturers from pooled plasma of adults using methods designed to prepare a product suitable for IV use. The donor pool is similar to that of IG. Immune Globulin Intravenous consists primarily of the immunoglobulin fraction (more than 95% IgG and trace amounts of IgA and IgM). Protein content varies between 3% and 12%, depending on the product; liquid and dried products are available. Immune Globulin Intravenous does not contain thimerosal. The FDA specifies that all IGIV preparations must have a minimum concentration of antibodies to measles virus, *Corynebacterium diphtheriae*, poliovirus, and hepatitis B virus. Antibody concentrations against common pathogens such as *Streptococcus pneumoniae* vary widely among products and even among lots of the same product.

INDICATIONS FOR THE USE OF IGIV

Initially, IGIV was developed as an infusion product that allowed patients with primary immunodeficiencies to receive enough IG at monthly intervals to protect them from infection until their next infusion. Subsequently, the FDA and the National Institutes of Health convened a consensus development conference; panel members concluded that there were data to support some of the uses for IGIV listed in Table 1.9. Immune Globulin Intravenous products also may be useful for other conditions, although demonstrated efficacy from controlled trials is not available in all cases.

Licensure by the FDA of specific indications for a manufacturer's IGIV product is based on availability of data from one or more clinical trials that demonstrate that the product has the effect it is represented to have under the conditions of use specified in the labeling. All IGIV products are licensed for primary immunodeficiencies and most are licensed for immune-mediated thrombocytopenia, but not all licensed products are approved for the other indications listed in Table 1.9 (see previous paragraph). In some cases, only a single product has the indication in its product label. Therapeutic differences among IGIV products from different manufacturers are likely to exist but may not have been demonstrated in any clinical trials designed to determine if such differences exist. Among the licensed IGIV products, but not necessarily for each product individually, indications for prevention or treatment of infectious diseases in children and adolescents include the following:

- **Replacement therapy in antibody deficiency disorders**. The usual dosage of IGIV in immunodeficiency syndromes is 400 to 600 mg/kg administered approximately once a month by infusion. Effective dosages have ranged from 200 to 800 mg/kg monthly. Maintenance of a trough IgG concentration of at least 500 mg/dL (5 g/L) has been demonstrated to correlate with clinical response. Dosage and frequency of infusions should be based on clinical effectiveness in the individual patient.
- **Kawasaki disease**. Administration of IGIV and aspirin within the first 10 days of onset of fever decreases the frequency of coronary artery abnormalities and shortens the duration of symptoms (see Kawasaki Disease, p 412).
- **Pediatric HIV infection**. In children with HIV infection and hypogammaglobulinemia, IGIV may be used to prevent serious bacterial infection. Immune Globulin

Table 1.9. Uses of Immune Globulin Intravenous (IGIV) for Which There Are Data to Suggest Efficacy (NIH Consensus Conference)[1]

Primary immunodeficiencies

Kawasaki disease

Pediatric human immunodeficiency virus infection

Chronic B-cell lymphocytic leukemia

Recent stem cell transplantation in adults

Immune-mediated thrombocytopenia

Chronic inflammatory demyelinating polyneuropathy[2]

[1] From Centers for Disease Control and Prevention. Availability of immune globulin intravenous for treatment of immune deficient patients: United States, 1997–1998. *MMWR Morb Mortal Wkly Rep*. 1999;48:159–162

[2] Recommended only by NIH Consensus Development Conference. Intravenous immunoglobulin. Prevention and treatment of disease. *JAMA*. 1990;264:3189-3193

Intravenous also might be considered for HIV-infected children who have recurrent serious bacterial infection* (see Human Immunodeficiency Virus Infection, p 378).

• **Hypogammaglobulinemia in chronic B-cell lymphocytic leukemia**. Administration of IGIV to adults with this disease has been demonstrated to decrease the incidence of serious bacterial infections, although its cost-effectiveness has been questioned.

• **Stem cell transplantation**. Immune Globulin Intravenous may decrease the incidence of infection and death but does not decrease the incidence of acute graft-versus-host disease (GVHD) in pediatric stem cell transplant recipients. In adult transplant recipients, IGIV decreases the incidence of interstitial pneumonia (presumably caused by cytomegalovirus [CMV]), decreases the risk of sepsis and other bacterial infections, decreases the incidence of acute GVHD (but not overall mortality), and in conjunction with ganciclovir, is effective in treatment of some patients with CMV pneumonia.

If VariZIG is not available, IGIV is approved by the Advisory Committee on Immunization Practices of the Centers for Disease Control and Prevention (CDC) for certain people up to 96 hours after exposure to varicella (see Varicella-Zoster Infections, p 711).

Immune Globulin Intravenous also has been used for many other conditions, some of which are listed below.

• **Low birth weight infants**. Results of most clinical trials have indicated that IGIV does not decrease the incidence or mortality rate of late-onset infections in infants who weigh less than 1500 g at birth. Trials have varied in IGIV dosage, time of administration, and other aspects of study design. Immune Globulin Intravenous is not recommended for routine use in preterm infants to prevent late-onset infection.

• **Guillain-Barré syndrome**. In Guillain-Barré syndrome and chronic inflammatory demyelinating polyneuropathy, IGIV treatment has been demonstrated to have efficacy equivalent to that of plasmapheresis.

• **Toxic shock syndrome**. Immune Globulin Intravenous has been administered to patients with severe staphylococcal or streptococcal toxic shock syndrome. Therapy appears most likely to be beneficial when used early in the course of illness.

• **Other potential uses**. Immune Globulin Intravenous may be useful for severe anemia caused by parvovirus B19 infection and for neonatal alloimmune thrombocytopenia that is unresponsive to other treatments, immune-mediated neutropenia, decompensation in myasthenia gravis, dermatomyositis, polymyositis, and severe thrombocytopenia that is unresponsive to other treatments.

For several years after November 1997, periodic shortages of IGIV existed in the United States because of production impediments related to compliance and product recall based on the theoretic risk of contamination with the Creutzfeldt-Jakob disease (CJD) agent. In August 1998, the US Surgeon General recommended that plasma derivatives including IGIV be withdrawn only if the blood donor developed variant CJD (see Blood Safety, p 106). Other problems that may cause short supply of IGIV include increased administration for approved and unapproved uses, wastage, and

---

* US Public Health Service and Infectious Diseases Society of America. Guidelines for preventing opportunistic infections among HIV-infected persons—2002. *MMWR Recomm Rep.* 2002;51(RR-8):1–46

export of IGIV. The FDA is using several methods to improve IGIV distribution to patients. Clinicians should review their IGIV use to ensure consistency with current recommendations. Off-label use of IGIV should be limited until there is adequate scientific evidence of effectiveness.

An outbreak of HCV infection occurred in the United States in 1994 among recipients of IGIV lots from a single domestic manufacturer. Changes in the preparation of IGIV subsequent to this episode have been instituted to prevent transmission of HCV by IGIV infusion.

ADVERSE REACTIONS TO IGIV

The reported incidence of adverse events associated with administration of IGIV ranges from 1% to 15%. Reactions such as fever, headache, myalgia, chills, nausea, and vomiting often are related to the rate of IGIV infusion and usually are mild to moderate and self-limited. These reactions may result from formation of IgG aggregates during manufacture or storage. Less common and more severe reactions include hypersensitivity and anaphylactoid reactions marked by flushing, changes in blood pressure, and tachycardia; thromboembolic events; aseptic meningitis; and renal insufficiency and failure. The causes of these reactions are unknown. Adverse events often can be decreased by following the package insert for the individual product carefully with regard to rate of administration.

Anaphylactic reactions induced by anti-IgA can occur in patients with primary antibody deficiency who have a total absence of circulating IgA and develop IgG antibodies to IgA. These reactions are rare in patients with panhypogammaglobulinemia and potentially are more common in patients with selective IgA deficiency and subclass IgG deficiencies. In rare instances in which reactions related to anti-IgA antibodies have occurred, use of IgA-depleted IGIV preparations may decrease the likelihood of further reactions. Because of the extreme rarity of these reactions, however, screening for IgA deficiency is not recommended routinely.

PRECAUTIONS FOR THE USE OF IGIV

- Caution should be used when giving IGIV to a patient with a history of adverse reactions to immune globulin.
- Because systemic reactions to IGIV may occur (see Adverse Reactions to IGIV), epinephrine and other means of treating acute reactions should be available immediately.
- Adverse reactions often can be alleviated by reducing either the rate or the volume of infusion. For patients with repeated severe reactions unresponsive to these measures, hydrocortisone at a dosage of 1 to 2 mg/kg can be given intravenously 30 minutes before infusion. Using a different IGIV preparation or pretreatment with diphenhydramine, acetaminophen, or aspirin also may be helpful.
- Seriously ill patients with compromised cardiac function who are receiving large volumes of IGIV may be at increased risk of vasomotor or cardiac complications manifested by elevated blood pressure, cardiac failure, or both.
- Screening for IgA deficiency is not recommended routinely for potential recipients of IGIV (see Adverse Reactions to IGIV).

Antibodies of Animal Origin (Animal Antisera)

Products of animal origin used for neutralization of toxins or prophylaxis of diseases are derived from serum of horses immunized with the agent/toxoid of interest. Experimental products prepared in other species also may be available. These products are derived by concentrating the serum globulin fraction with ammonium sulfate. Some, but not all, products are subjected to an enzyme digestion process to decrease clinical reactions to administered foreign proteins. These animal-derived immunoglobulin products are referred to here as serum, for convenience.

Use of the following products is discussed in the disease-specific chapters in Section 3:

- Botulism Antitoxin (Equine), available from the CDC.
- Diphtheria Antitoxin (Equine), available from the CDC. The currently available product is manufactured in Brazil and is available only under an investigational new drug protocol.

INDICATIONS FOR USE OF ANIMAL ANTISERA

Antibody-containing products prepared from animal sera pose a special risk to the recipient, and the use of such products should be limited strictly to certain indications for which specific IG preparations of human origin are not available (eg, diphtheria and botulism other than infant botulism).

REACTIONS TO ANIMAL SERA

Before any animal serum is injected, the patient must be questioned about his or her history of asthma, allergic rhinitis, and urticaria after previous exposure to animals or injections of animal sera. Patients with a history of asthma or allergic symptoms, especially from exposure to horses, can be dangerously sensitive to equine sera and should be given these products with the utmost caution. People who previously have received animal sera are at increased risk of developing allergic reactions and serum sickness after administration of sera from the same animal species.

SENSITIVITY TESTS FOR REACTIONS TO ANIMAL SERA

Each patient who is to be given animal serum should be skin tested before administration of that animal serum. Intradermal (ID) skin tests have resulted in fatalities, but the scratch test usually is safe. Therefore, scratch tests always should precede ID tests. Nevertheless, any sensitivity test always should be performed by trained personnel familiar with treatment of acute anaphylaxis; necessary medications and equipment should be readily available (see Treatment of Anaphylactic Reactions, p 64).

SCRATCH, PRICK, OR PUNCTURE TEST.* Apply 1 drop of a 1:100 dilution of serum in preservative-free isotonic sodium chloride solution to the site of a superficial scratch, prick, or puncture on the volar aspect of the forearm. Positive (histamine) and negative (physiologic saline solution) control tests for the scratch test also should be applied. A positive test result is a wheal with surrounding erythema at least 3 mm

---

* Antihistamines may inhibit reactions in the scratch, prick, or puncture test and in the ID test; hence, testing should not be performed for at least 24 hours or, preferably, 48 hours after receipt of these drugs.

larger than the negative control test area, read at 15 to 20 minutes. The histamine control must be positive for valid interpretation. If the scratch test result is negative, an ID test is performed.

INTRADERMAL TEST.* A dose of 0.02 mL of a 1:1000 dilution of serum in preservative-free isotonic saline-diluted serum (enough to raise a small wheal) is administered. Positive and negative control tests as described for the scratch test also should be applied. If the test result is negative, it should be repeated using a 1:100 dilution. For people with negative history for both animal allergy and previous exposure to animal serum, the 1:100 dilution may be used initially if a scratch, prick, or puncture test result with the serum is negative. Interpretation is the same as for the scratch test.

Positive test results not attributable to an irritant reaction indicate sensitivity, but a negative skin test result is not an absolute guarantee of lack of sensitivity. Therefore, animal sera should be administered with caution even to people whose test results are negative. Immediate hypersensitivity testing is performed to identify IgE-mediated disease and does not predict other immune reactions, such as serum sickness.

If the ID test result is positive or if the history of systemic anaphylaxis after previous administration of serum is highly suggestive in a person for whom the need for serum is unquestioned, desensitization can be undertaken (see Desensitization to Animal Sera).

If history and sensitivity test results are negative, the indicated dose of serum can be given intramuscularly. The patient should be observed afterward for at least 30 minutes. Intravenous administration may be indicated if a high concentration of serum antibody is imperative, such as for treatment of diphtheria or botulism. In these instances, serum should be diluted and slowly administered intravenously according to the manufacturer's instructions. The patient should be monitored carefully for signs or symptoms of anaphylaxis.

DESENSITIZATION TO ANIMAL SERA

Tables 1.10 (p 63) and 1.11 (p 64) serve as guides for desensitization procedures for administration of animal sera. Intravenous (Table 1.10) or ID, subcutaneous, or IM (Table 1.11) regimens may be chosen. The IV route is considered safest, because it offers better control. The desensitization procedure should be performed by trained personnel familiar with treatment of anaphylaxis and with appropriate drugs and available equipment (see Treatment of Anaphylactic Reactions, p 64). Some physicians advocate concurrent use of an oral or parenteral antihistamine (such as diphenhydramine) during the procedure, with or without IV hydrocortisone or methylprednisolone. If signs of anaphylaxis occur, aqueous epinephrine should be administered immediately (see Treatment of Anaphylactic Reactions, p 64). Administration of sera during a desensitization procedure must be continuous, because if administration is interrupted, protection achieved by desensitization will be lost.

TYPES OF REACTIONS TO ANIMAL SERA

The following reactions can occur as the result of administration of animal sera. Of these, only anaphylaxis is mediated by IgE antibodies, and thus, occurrence can be predicted by previous skin testing results.

---

* Antihistamines may inhibit reactions in the scratch, prick, or puncture test and in the ID test; hence, testing should not be performed for at least 24 hours or, preferably, 48 hours after receipt of these drugs.

ACUTE FEBRILE REACTIONS. These reactions usually are mild and can be treated with antipyretic agents. Severe febrile reactions should be treated with antipyretic agents or other safe available methods to decrease temperature physically.

SERUM SICKNESS. Manifestations, which usually begin 7 to 10 days (occasionally as late as 3 weeks) after primary exposure to the foreign protein, consist of fever, urticaria, or a maculopapular rash (90% of cases); arthritis or arthralgia; and lymphadenopathy. Local edema can occur at the serum injection site a few days before systemic signs and symptoms appear. Angioedema, glomerulonephritis, Guillain-Barré syndrome, peripheral neuritis, and myocarditis also can occur. However, serum sickness may be mild and resolve spontaneously within a few days to 2 weeks. People who previously have received serum injections are at increased risk after readministration; manifestations in these patients usually occur shortly (from hours to 3 days) after administration of serum. Antihistamines can be helpful for management of serum sickness for alleviation of pruritus, edema, and urticaria. Fever, malaise, arthralgia, and arthritis can be controlled in most patients by administration of aspirin or other nonsteroidal anti-inflammatory agents. Corticosteroids may be helpful for controlling serious manifestations that are controlled poorly by other agents; prednisone or prednisolone in therapeutic dosages (1.5–2 mg/kg per day; maximum 60 mg/day) for 5 to 7 days is an appropriate regimen.

ANAPHYLAXIS. The rapidity of onset and overall severity of anaphylaxis may vary considerably. Anaphylaxis usually begins within minutes of exposure to the causative agent, and in general, the more rapid the onset, the more severe the overall course.

Table 1.10. Desensitization to Serum— Intravenous (IV) Route

Dose Number[1]	Dilution of Serum in Isotonic Sodium Chloride	Amount of IV Injection, mL
1	1:1000	0.1
2	1:1000	0.3
3	1:1000	0.6
4	1:100	0.1
5	1:100	0.3
6	1:100	0.6
7	1:10	0.1
8	1:10	0.3
9	1:10	0.6
10	Undiluted	0.1
11	Undiluted	0.3
12	Undiluted	0.6
13	Undiluted	1.0

[1]Administer consistently at 15-minute intervals.

Table 1.11. Desensitization to Serum—Intradermal (ID), Subcutaneous (SC), and Intramuscular (IM) Routes

Dose Number[1]	Route of Administration	Dilution of Serum in Isotonic Sodium Chloride	Amount of ID, SC, or IM Injection, mL
1	ID	1:1000	0.1
2	ID	1:1000	0.3
3	SC	1:1000	0.6
4	SC	1:100	0.1
5	SC	1:100	0.3
6	SC	1:100	0.6
7	SC	1:10	0.1
8	SC	1:10	0.3
9	SC	1:10	0.6
10	SC	Undiluted	0.1
11	SC	Undiluted	0.3
12	IM	Undiluted	0.6
13	IM	Undiluted	1.0

[1]Administer consistently at 15-minute intervals.

Major symptomatic manifestations include (1) cutaneous: pruritus, flushing, urticaria, and angioedema; (2) respiratory: hoarse voice and stridor, cough, wheeze, dyspnea, and cyanosis; (3) cardiovascular: rapid weak pulse, hypotension, and arrhythmias; and (4) gastrointestinal: cramps, vomiting, diarrhea, and dry mouth. Anaphylaxis is a medical emergency.

Treatment of Anaphylactic Reactions

Personnel administering biological products or serum should be able to recognize and be prepared to treat systemic anaphylaxis. Medications, equipment, and competent staff necessary to maintain the patency of the airway and to manage cardiovascular collapse must be available.

The emergency treatment of systemic anaphylactic reactions is based on the type of reaction. In all instances, epinephrine is the primary drug. Mild symptoms of pruritus, erythema, urticaria, and angioedema should be treated with epinephrine injected intramuscularly, followed by diphenhydramine, hydroxyzine, or other antihistamine given orally or parenterally (see Tables 1.12, p 65, and 1.13, p 66). Because concentrations of epinephrine are higher and achieved more rapidly after IM administration, subcutaneous administration no longer is recommended. If symptoms persist or recur, epinephrine administration may be repeated every 10 to 20 minutes for up to 3 doses. If the patient's condition improves and remains stable, oral antihistamines and possibly oral corticosteroids (1.5–2.0 mg/kg per day of prednisone; maximum 60 mg/day) can be given for an additional 24 to 48 hours.

Table 1.12. Epinephrine in the Treatment of Anaphylaxis[1]

Intramuscular (IM) administration
Epinephrine 1:1000 (aqueous): 0.01 mL/kg per dose, up to 0.5 mL, repeated every 10–20 min up to 3 doses.[2]

Intravenous (IV) administration
An initial bolus of IV epinephrine is given to patients not responding to IM epinephrine using a dilution of 1:10 000 rather than a dilution of 1:1000. This dilution can be made using 1 mL of the 1:1000 dilution in 9 mL of physiologic saline solution. The dose is 0.01 mg/kg or 0.1 mL/kg of the 1:10 000 dilution. A continuous infusion should be started if repeated doses are required. One milligram (1 mL) of 1:1000 dilution of epinephrine added to 250 mL of 5% dextrose in water, resulting in a concentration of 4 μg/mL, is infused initially at a rate of 0.1 μg/kg per minute and increased gradually to 1.5 μg/kg per minute to maintain blood pressure.

---

[1] In addition to epinephrine, maintenance of the airway and administration of oxygen are critical.
[2] If agent causing anaphylactic reaction was given by injection, epinephrine can be injected into the same site to slow absorption.

More severe or potentially life-threatening systemic anaphylaxis involving severe bronchospasm, laryngeal edema, other airway compromise, shock, and cardiovascular collapse necessitates additional therapy. Maintenance of the airway and administration of oxygen should be instituted promptly. Intravenous epinephrine may be indicated; for this use, the epinephrine must be diluted from 1:1000 aqueous base to a dilution of 1:10 000 using physiologic saline solution (see Table 1.12). A slow, continuous infusion is preferable to repeated bolus administration. Nebulized albuterol is indicated for bronchospasm (see Table 1.13, p 66). Rapid IV infusion of physiologic saline solution, lactated Ringer solution, or other isotonic solution adequate to maintain blood pressure must be instituted to compensate for the loss of circulating intravascular volume.

In some cases, the use of inotropic agents, such as dopamine (see Table 1.13, p 66), may be necessary for blood pressure support. The combination of histamine H_1 and H_2 receptor-blocking agents (see Table 1.13, p 66) can be synergistic in effect and should be used. Corticosteroids should be used in all cases of anaphylaxis except cases that are mild and have responded promptly to initial therapy (see Table 1.13, p 66). However, no data support the usefulness of corticosteroids in treating anaphylaxis, and therefore, they should not be considered primary drugs.

All patients showing signs and symptoms of systemic anaphylaxis, regardless of severity, should be observed for several hours in an appropriate facility. Biphasic and protracted anaphylaxis may be mitigated with early administration of oral corticosteroids; however, usefulness of corticosteroids for these 2 conditions has not been established fully. Therefore, patients should be observed even after remission of immediate symptoms. Although a specific period of observation has not been established, a period of observation of 4 hours would be reasonable for mild episodes and as long as 24 hours would be reasonable for severe episodes.

Table 1.13. Dosages of Commonly Used Secondary Drugs in the Treatment of Anaphylaxis

Drug	Dose
H_1 receptor-blocking agents (antihistamines)	
Diphenhydramine	Oral, IM, IV: 1–2 mg/kg, every 4–6 h (100 mg, maximum single dose)
Hydroxyzine	Oral, IM: 0.5–1 mg/kg, every 4–6 h (100 mg, maximum single dose)
H_2 receptor-blocking agents (also antihistamines)	
Cimetidine	IV: 5 mg/kg, slowly over a 15-min period, every 6–8 h (300 mg, maximum single dose)
Ranitidine	IV: 1 mg/kg, slowly over a 15-min period, every 6–8 h (50 mg, maximum single dose)
Corticosteroids	
Hydrocortisone	IV: 100–200 mg, every 4–6 h
Methylprednisolone	IV: 1.5–2 mg/kg, every 4–6 h (60 mg, maximum single dose)
Prednisone	Oral: 1.5–2 mg/kg, single morning dose (60 mg, maximum single dose); use corticosteroids as long as needed
B_2-agonist	
Albuterol	Nebulizer solution: 0.5% (5 mg/mL), 0.05–0.15 mg/kg per dose in 2–3 mL isotonic sodium chloride solution, maximum 5 mg/dose every 20 min over a 1-h to 2-h period or 0.5 mg/kg per hour by continuous nebulization (15 mg/h, maximum dose)
Other	
Dopamine	IV: 5–20 μg/kg per minute. Mixing 150 mg of dopamine with 250 mL of saline solution or 5% dextrose in water will produce a solution that, if infused at the rate of 1 mL/kg per hour, will deliver 10 μg/kg per min. The solution must be free of bicarbonate, which may inactivate dopamine.

IM indicates intramuscular; IV, intravenous.

Anaphylaxis occurring in people who are already taking beta-adrenergic–blocking agents presents a unique situation. In such people, the manifestations are likely to be more profound and significantly less responsive to epinephrine and other beta-adrenergic agonist drugs. More aggressive therapy with epinephrine may override receptor blockade in some patients. Some experts recommend use of IV glucagon for cardiovascular manifestations and inhaled atropine for management of brady-cardia or bronchospasm.

IMMUNIZATION IN SPECIAL CLINICAL CIRCUMSTANCES

Preterm and Low Birth Weight Infants*

Preterm infants less than 37 weeks' gestation and infants of low birth weight (<2500 g) should, with few exceptions, receive all routinely recommended childhood vaccines at the same chronologic age as full-term infants. Gestational age and birth weight are not limiting factors when deciding whether a clinically stable preterm infant is to be immunized on schedule. Although studies have shown decreased immune responses to some vaccines given to very low birth weight (<1500 g) and very early gestational age (<29 weeks) neonates, most preterm infants, including infants who receive dexamethasone for chronic lung disease, produce sufficient vaccine-induced immunity to prevent disease. Vaccine dosages given to full-term infants should not be reduced or divided when given to preterm and low birth weight infants.

Preterm and low birth weight infants tolerate most childhood vaccines as well as full-term infants. Apnea, reported to have occurred in some extremely low birth weight (<1000 g) infants of fewer than 31 weeks' gestation after use of diphtheria and tetanus toxoids and whole-cell pertussis (DTP) vaccine, has not been reported after use of acellular pertussis-containing vaccines in small numbers of extremely low birth weight infants. However, preterm infants given heptavalent pneumococcal conjugate vaccine (PCV7) concomitantly with DTP and *Haemophilus influenzae* type b (Hib) vaccine also were reported to experience benign febrile seizures more frequently than were full-term infants given the same vaccines. Cardiorespiratory events, including apnea and bradycardia with oxygen desaturation, frequently increase in very low birth weight infants given combination diphtheria and tetanus toxoids and acellular pertussis (DTaP), inactivated poliovirus, hepatitis B, and Hib conjugate vaccine. However, these episodes do not have a detrimental effect on the clinical course of immunized infants.

Medically stable preterm infants who remain in the hospital at 2 months of chronologic age should be given all vaccines recommended at that age (see Recommended Childhood and Adolescent Immunization Schedule, Fig 1.1, p 26). A medically stable infant is defined as one who does not require ongoing management for serious infection; metabolic disease; or acute renal, cardiovascular, or respiratory tract illness and who demonstrates a clinical course of sustained recovery and pattern of steady growth. All immunizations required at 2 months of age may be administered simultaneously to preterm and low birth weight infants. The number of injections at the 2-month visit can be minimized by using combination vaccines. When it is difficult to administer 3 to 4 injections simultaneously to hospitalized preterm infants because of limited injection sites, the vaccines recommended at 2 months of age can be separated. Because all the vaccines are inactivated, any interval between doses is acceptable. However, to avoid superimposing local reactions, 2-week intervals may be reasonable. The choice of needle lengths used for intramuscular (IM) vaccine

---

* Saari TN, American Academy of Pediatrics, Committee on Infectious Diseases. Immunization of preterm and low birth weight infants. *Pediatrics*. 2003;112:193–198

administration is determined by available muscle mass of the preterm infant (see Table 1.5, p 21).

All preterm and low birth weight infants are considered at increased risk of invasive pneumococcal disease, and if medically stable at 2 months of chronologic age, these infants should receive full doses of PCV7. Increasing numbers of infants younger than 6 months of age with fatal pertussis have been reported; all preterm and low birth weight infants should receive DTaP at 2 months of chronologic age.

Hepatitis B vaccine given to preterm and low birth weight infants weighing more than 2000 g at birth produces an immune response comparable to that in full-term infants. Therefore, medically stable preterm infants weighing more than 2000 g born to hepatitis B surface antigen (HBsAg)-negative mothers may receive the first dose of hepatitis B vaccine at birth or shortly thereafter. For medically unstable preterm infants weighing more than 2000 g born to HBsAg-negative mothers, hepatitis B immunization may be deferred until their clinical condition has stabilized. Seroconversion rates and antibody concentrations in infants weighing 2000 g or less at birth immunized with hepatitis B vaccine shortly after birth often are lower than those seen in full-term infants immunized at birth and in preterm infants immunized at a later age. Nonetheless, hepatitis B vaccine appears to protect preterm infants born to HBsAg-positive mothers from complications related to perinatal exposure to hepatitis B infection, regardless of birth weight. Several studies confirm that the chronologic age of the medically stable preterm infant at the time of the first dose of hepatitis B vaccine is the best predictor of successful seroconversion regardless of birth weight or gestational age at birth. Consistent weight gain by preterm infants before receipt of the first dose of hepatitis B vaccine also is predictive of immune responsiveness.

Medically stable, thriving infants weighing less than 2000 g demonstrate predictable, consistent, and sufficient hepatitis B antibody responses and should receive the first dose of hepatitis B vaccine as early as 30 days of chronologic age regardless of gestational age or birth weight. Preterm infants weighing less than 2000 g who are healthy enough to be released from the hospital before a chronologic age of 30 days may receive hepatitis B vaccine at discharge (see Hepatitis B, p 335). Starting the hepatitis B series at 1 month of age, regardless of the weight of the preterm infant, offers more options for implementing the immunization schedule in the special care nursery setting, lessens the number of simultaneous injections at 2 months of age (when other recommended childhood immunizations are due), provides earlier protection to vulnerable preterm infants more likely to receive multiple blood products and undergo surgical interventions, and decreases the risk of horizontal transmission from occult hepatitis B chronic carriers among family members, hospital visitors, and other caregivers. Studies also have shown that the closer hepatitis B vaccine is given to the infant's birth, the greater the likelihood the complement of childhood vaccines will be completed on time.

All preterm and low birth weight infants born to HBsAg-positive mothers should receive Hepatitis B Immune Globulin (HBIG) within 12 hours of birth and hepatitis B vaccine (see Hepatitis B, p 335). If maternal HBsAg status is unknown at birth, preterm or low birth weight infants should receive hepatitis B vaccine in accordance with recommendations for infants born to HBsAg-positive mothers. Preterm and low birth weight infants given a birth dose of hepatitis B vaccine should receive 3 additional doses. For hepatitis B immunoprophylaxis schemes for preterm and low birth weight infants born to mothers who are HBsAg negative, HBsAg positive, and HBsAg unknown, see Table 3.18 (p 347) and Hepatitis B, Special Considerations (p 345).

Only monovalent hepatitis B vaccine should be used for infants from birth to 6 weeks of age. Giving a birth dose of monovalent hepatitis B vaccine when a combination vaccine containing hepatitis B vaccine subsequently is used means that 4 total doses will be administered. Combination vaccines containing a hepatitis B component have not been assessed for efficacy when given to infants born to HBsAg-positive mothers.

Because all preterm infants are considered at increased risk of complications of influenza, 2 doses of inactivated influenza vaccine given 1 month apart should be offered for these infants beginning at 6 months of chronologic age, before the onset of the influenza season (see Influenza, p 401). Because preterm infants younger than 6 months of age and infants of any age with chronic complications of preterm birth are extremely vulnerable when exposed to influenza virus, household contacts, child care providers, and hospital nursery personnel caring for preterm infants should receive inactivated influenza vaccine (see Influenza, p 401). Preterm infants younger than 32 weeks of gestational age and infants with chronic lung disease and specified cardiovascular conditions up to 2 years of age may benefit from monthly immunoprophylaxis with palivizumab (respiratory syncytial virus monoclonal antibody) during respiratory syncytial virus season (see Respiratory Syncytial Virus, p 560). Palivizumab use does not interfere with the provision of routine childhood immunizations to preterm or low birth weight infants.

Pregnancy*

Immunization during pregnancy poses theoretic risks to the developing fetus. Although no evidence indicates that vaccines in use today have detrimental effects on the fetus, pregnant women should receive a vaccine only when the vaccine is unlikely to cause harm, the risk for disease exposure is high, and the infection would pose a significant risk to the mother or fetus. When a vaccine is to be given during pregnancy, delaying administration until the second or third trimester, when possible, is a reasonable precaution to minimize concern about possible teratogenicity.

The only vaccines recommended for routine administration during pregnancy in the United States, provided they are indicated (either for primary or booster immunization), are adult-type tetanus and diphtheria toxoids (Td); tetanus toxoid, reduced diphtheria toxoid, and acellular pertussis (Tdap); and inactivated influenza vaccines. Pregnant women who have not received a Td-containing booster during the previous 10 years should be given Tdap, and women who are unimmunized or only partially immunized should complete the primary series. For complete recommendations regarding Td and Tdap use in pregnancy, see Pertussis, p 498. In developing countries with a high incidence of neonatal tetanus, Td routinely is administered during pregnancy without evidence of adverse effects and with striking decreases in the occurrence of neonatal tetanus.

---

* See adult immunization schedule available at **www.cdc.gov/nip**.

Studies indicate that women who are pregnant or who are in early puerperium with absence of other underlying risk factors are at increased risk of complications and hospitalization from influenza. Therefore, the Advisory Committee on Immunization Practices (ACIP) of the Centers for Disease Control and Prevention (CDC) recommends that inactivated influenza vaccine be administered to all women who will be pregnant during the influenza season (see Influenza, p 401). Influenza immunization of pregnant women also protects infants younger than 6 months of age who cannot be actively immunized or receive antiviral prophylaxis. Live-attenuated influenza vaccine should not be given to pregnant women.

Pneumococcal and meningococcal vaccines can be given to a pregnant woman at high risk of serious or complicated illness from infection with *Streptococcus pneumoniae* or *Neisseria meningitidis*. Meningococcal polysaccharide or meningococcal conjugate vaccines can be given to a pregnant woman when there is substantial risk of disease, such as during epidemics or travel to an area with endemic infection. Hepatitis A or hepatitis B immunizations, if indicated, can be given to pregnant women. Although data on safety of these vaccines for the developing fetus are not available, no risk would be expected, because the vaccines contain polysaccharide antigens (pneumococcal and meningococcal), a toxoid (meningococcal conjugate), formalin-inactivated virus (hepatitis A), or noninfectious surface antigen (hepatitis B). In contrast, infection with hepatitis A or hepatitis B in a pregnant woman can result in severe disease in the mother and, in the case of hepatitis B, chronic infection in the newborn infant.

Pregnancy is a contraindication to administration of all live-virus vaccines, except when susceptibility and exposure are highly probable and the disease to be prevented poses a greater threat to the woman or fetus than does the vaccine. Although only a theoretic risk to the fetus exists with a live-virus vaccine, the background rate of anomalies in uncomplicated pregnancies may result in a defect that could be attributed inappropriately to a vaccine. Therefore, live-virus vaccines should be avoided during pregnancy. Inactivated poliovirus (IPV) vaccine can be given to pregnant women who never have received poliovirus vaccine who are partially immunized or completely immunized but require an additional dose (see Poliovirus Infections, p 542).

Because measles, mumps, rubella, and varicella vaccines are contraindicated for pregnant women, efforts should be made to immunize susceptible women against these illnesses before they become pregnant or after pregnancy. Although of theoretic concern, no case of embryopathy caused by rubella vaccine has been reported. Although no infants have been reported with congenital defects attributable to inadvertent administration of rubella vaccine to pregnant women, a rare theoretic risk of embryopathy cannot be excluded. The effect of varicella vaccine on the fetus, if any, is unknown. The manufacturer, in collaboration with the CDC, has established the VARIVAX Pregnancy Registry to monitor the maternal and fetal outcomes of women who inadvertently are given varicella vaccine from 3 months before or at any time during pregnancy. From March 1995 to March 2005, 587 women (137 of whom were seronegative) who inadvertently received varicella vaccine before or during pregnancy and whose pregnancy outcomes are known were reported to this registry. No offspring had clinical features of congenital varicella, although 11 had congenital malformations, which is the rate of congenital anomalies in the general population.

Reporting of cases by telephone is encouraged (1-800-986-8999). A pregnant mother or other household member is not a contraindication for varicella immunization of a child in that household. Transmission of vaccine virus from an immunocompetent vaccine recipient to a susceptible person has been reported only rarely and only in the presence of a vaccine-associated rash (see Varicella-Zoster Infections, p 711). Breastfeeding is not a contraindication for immunization of varicella-susceptible women after pregnancy. Varicella has not been detected by polymerase chain reaction assay in human milk specimens after immunization, and infants breastfed by mothers immunized with varicella do not seroconvert to varicella.

Pregnant women at risk of exposure to unusual pathogens may need to be considered for immunization when the potential benefits outweigh the potential risks to the mother and fetus.

- Vaccinia virus should be given only when there is a definite and significant exposure to smallpox. Because smallpox causes more severe disease in pregnant than nonpregnant women, the potential risks of immunization may be outweighed by the risk of disease.
- Rabies vaccine should be given to pregnant women after exposure to rabies under the same circumstances as nonpregnant women. There has been no reported association between rabies immunization and adverse fetal outcomes.
- Yellow fever vaccine is a live-attenuated virus vaccine, but if travel of a pregnant woman cannot be postponed and mosquito exposure cannot be avoided, immunization should be considered.
- Japanese encephalitis virus vaccine contains inactivated virus, but there are no safety data for pregnant women. Women should be immunized before conception, if possible, but Japanese encephalitis virus vaccine may be considered if travel to regions with endemic infection and mosquito exposure are unavoidable.
- The parenteral typhoid vaccine should be considered on a case-by-case basis; oral typhoid vaccine is contraindicated in pregnant women.
- Anthrax vaccine contains no live bacteria and no theoretic risk to the fetus, but this vaccine has not been evaluated for safety in pregnant women.

Immunocompromised Children

PRIMARY AND SECONDARY IMMUNE DEFICIENCIES

The safety and effectiveness of vaccines in people with immune deficiency are determined by the nature and degree of immunosuppression. Immunocompromised people vary in their degree of immunosuppression and susceptibility to infection. Immunocompromised children represent a heterogeneous population with regard to immunization. Immunodeficiency conditions can be grouped into primary and secondary (acquired) disorders. Primary disorders of the immune system generally are inherited, usually as single-gene disorders; may involve any part of the immune defenses, including B-lymphocyte (humoral) immunity, T-lymphocyte (cell)-mediated immunity, complement, and phagocytic function as well as other, unique abnormalities of innate immunity; and share the common feature of susceptibility to infection.* Secondary

* Centers for Disease Control and Prevention. Applying public health strategies to primary immunodeficiency diseases: a potential approach to genetic disorders. *MMWR Recomm Rep.* 2004;53(RR-1):1–29

disorders of the immune system are acquired and occur in people with human immu-nodeficiency virus (HIV) infection/acquired immunodeficiency syndrome (AIDS) or malignant neoplasms; people who have undergone transplantation or splenectomy; people receiving immunosuppressive, antimetabolic, or radiation therapy; and people with a variety of other illnesses, such as severe malnutrition, protein loss, and uremia (see Table 1.14, p 73). Published studies of experience with vaccine administration in immunocompromised children are limited. In most situations, theoretic considerations are the primary guide to vaccine administration, because experience with specific vac-cines in people with a specific disorder is lacking. However, considerable experience in HIV-infected children provides reassurance about the low risk of adverse events in these children after immunization.

LIVE VACCINES. In general, people who are severely immunocompromised or in whom immune status is uncertain should not receive live vaccines, either viral or bac-terial, because of the risk of disease caused by the vaccine strains. Although precau-tions, contraindications, and suboptimal efficacy of immunizations in less severely immunocompromised children and adolescents are of concern, benefits may outweigh risks for use of routinely recommended live vaccines.

INACTIVATED VACCINES AND PASSIVE IMMUNIZATION. Inactivated vaccines and Immune Globulin (IG) preparations should be used when appropriate, because the risk of complications from these preparations is not increased in immunocompro-mised people. However, immune responses of immunocompromised children to inac-tivated vaccines (eg, DTaP, Tdap, hepatitis B, hepatitis A, IPV, Hib, pneumococcal, meningococcal, and influenza) may be inadequate. In children with secondary immu-nodeficiency, the ability to develop an adequate immunologic response depends on the presence of immunosuppression during or within 2 weeks of immunization. In children in whom immunosuppressive therapy is discontinued, an adequate response usually occurs between 3 months and 1 year after discontinuation. Inactivated influ-enza vaccine should be given yearly to immunosuppressed children 6 months of age and older before each influenza season. In children with malignant neoplasms, if pos-sible, inactivated influenza immunization should be given no sooner than 3 to 4 weeks after chemotherapy is discontinued and when peripheral granulocyte and lym-phocyte counts greater than 1000 cells/μL (1.0×10^9/L) are achieved.

All children and adolescents with primary and secondary immunodeficiencies should receive an annual age-appropriate influenza vaccine to prevent influenza and secondary bacterial infections associated with influenza disease.

PRIMARY IMMUNODEFICIENCIES. Measles and varicella vaccines should be consid-ered for children with B-lymphocyte disorders. However, optimal antibody response may not occur because of the underlying disease and because the patient may be receiving Immune Globulin Intravenous (IGIV) periodically. Oral poliovirus (OPV) vaccine is contraindicated because it has been associated with an increased incidence of paralytic disease in people with B-lymphocyte or combined immunodeficiency disorders. Other live vaccines also are contraindicated for most patients with B-lymphocyte defects except immunoglobulin (Ig) A deficiency. Live vaccines are con-traindicated for all patients with T-lymphocyte–mediated disorders of immune

Table 1.14. Immunization of Children and Adolescents With Primary and Secondary Immune Deficiencies

Category	Examples of Specific Immunodeficiency	Vaccine Contraindications	Effectiveness and Comments
Primary[1]			
B-lymphocyte (humoral)	Severe antibody deficiencies (eg, X-linked agammaglobulinemia and common variable immunodeficiency)	OPV,[2] smallpox, LAIV, rotavirus, and live-bacteria vaccines[3]; consider measles vaccine; no data for varicella vaccine	Effectiveness of any vaccine dependent only on humoral response is doubtful; IGIV therapy interferes with measles and possibly varicella immune response.
	Less severe antibody deficiencies (eg, selective IgA deficiency and IgG subclass deficiencies)	OPV,[2] other live vaccines[4] seem to be safe, but caution is urged	All vaccines probably effective. Immune response may be attenuated.
T-lymphocyte (cell-mediated and humoral)	Complete defects (eg, severe combined immunodeficiency; complete DiGeorge syndrome)	All live vaccines[3,4]	All vaccines ineffective.
	Partial defects (eg, most patients with DiGeorge syndrome, Wiskott-Aldrich syndrome, ataxia telangiectasia)	All live vaccines[3,4]	Effectiveness of any vaccine depends on degree of immune suppression. Recommend inactivated vaccines.
Complement	Deficiency of early components (C1, C4, C2, C3)	None	All routine vaccines probably effective. Pneumococcal and meningococcal vaccines are recommended.
	Deficiency of late components (C5–C9), properdin, factor B	None	All routine vaccines probably effective. Meningococcal and pneumococcal vaccines are recommended.

Table 1.14. Immunization of Children and Adolescents With Primary and Secondary Immune Deficiencies, continued

Category	Examples of Specific Immunodeficiency	Vaccine Contraindications	Effectiveness and Comments
Phagocytic function	Chronic granulomatous disease Leukocyte adhesion defects Myeloperoxidase deficiency	Live-bacteria vaccines[3]	All inactivated vaccines safe and probably effective. Live viral vaccines probably safe and effective.
Secondary[1]			
	HIV/AIDS	OPV,[2] smallpox, BCG, LAIV[4]; withhold MMR, varicella, and rotavirus in severely immunocompromised children	MMR, varicella, rotavirus, and all inactivated vaccines, including influenza, may be effective.[5]
	Malignant neoplasm, transplantation, autoimmune disease, immuno-suppressive or radiation therapy	Live-virus and -bacteria, depending on immune status[3,4]	Effectiveness of any vaccine depends on degree of immune suppression.

OPV indicates oral poliovirus; LAIV, live-attenuated influenza vaccine; IGIV, Immune Globulin Intravenous; Ig, immunoglobulin; HIV, human immunodeficiency virus; AIDS, acquired immunodeficiency syndrome; BCG, bacille Calmette-Guérin; MMR, measles-mumps-rubella.

[1] All children and adolescents should receive an annual age-appropriate inactivated influenza vaccine. LAIV is indicated only for healthy people 5 to 49 years of age.

[2] OPV vaccine no longer is recommended for routine use in the United States.

[3] Live-bacteria vaccines: BCG and Ty21a *Salmonella typhi* vaccine.

[4] Live-virus vaccines: LAIV, MMR, OPV, varicella, yellow fever, vaccinia (smallpox), and rotavirus.

[5] HIV-infected children should receive Immune Globulin after exposure to measles (see Measles, p 441) and may receive varicella vaccine if CD4+ lymphocyte count ≥15% of expected for age (see Varicella-Zoster Infections, p 711).

function (see Table 1.14, p 73). Fatal or chronic poliomyelitis, measles, and vaccinia after smallpox immunization have occurred in children with disorders of T-lymphocyte function after administration of the respective live-virus vaccines. Oral poliovirus vaccine no longer is recommended for routine use in the United States. Inactivated poliovirus vaccine should be administered. Live-attenuated influenza vaccine (LAIV) should not be given to children with immunodeficiencies. These patients should be given trivalent inactivated influenza vaccine. Children with deficiency in antibody-synthesizing capacity are incapable of developing an antibody response to vaccines and should receive regular doses of IG (usually IGIV) to provide passive protection against many infectious diseases. Specific immune globulins are available for postexposure prophylaxis for some infections (see Specific Immune Globulins, p 57). Children with milder B-lymphocyte and antibody deficiencies have an intermediate degree of vaccine responsiveness and may require monitoring of postimmunization antibody concentrations to confirm vaccine immunogenicity.

Most experts believe that live-virus vaccines are safe to administer to children with complement deficiencies and disorders of phagocyte function. Children with early or late complement deficiencies can receive all immunizations, including live vaccines. Children with phagocytic function disorders, including chronic granulomatous disease and leukocyte adhesion defects, can receive all immunizations except live-bacteria vaccines (bacille Calmette-Guérin [BCG] and Ty21a *Salmonella typhi*).

SECONDARY (ACQUIRED) IMMUNODEFICIENCIES. Several factors should be considered in immunization of children with secondary immunodeficiencies, including the underlying disease, the specific immunosuppressive regimen (dose and schedule), and the infectious disease and immunization history of the person. Live vaccines generally are contraindicated because of an increased risk of serious adverse effects. Exceptions are children with HIV infection who are not severely immunocompromised, in whom measles-mumps-rubella (MMR) vaccine is recommended (see Human Immunodeficiency Virus Infection, p 378) and in whom varicella vaccine should be considered if CD4+ lymphocyte counts are 25% or greater than expected for age (see Varicella-Zoster Infections, p 711). The use of varicella vaccine in children with acute lymphocytic leukemia in remission should be considered, because the risk of natural varicella disease outweighs the risk from the live-attenuated vaccine virus (see Varicella-Zoster Infections, p 711).

Live-virus vaccines usually are withheld for an interval of at least 3 months after immunosuppressive cancer chemotherapy has been discontinued. For corticosteroid therapy (see Corticosteroids, p 76), the interval is based on the assumption that immune response will have been restored in 3 months and that the underlying disease for which immunosuppressive therapy was given is in remission or under control. Immunodeficiency that follows use of recombinant human proteins with anti-inflammatory properties, including tumor necrosis factor alpha antagonists (eg, adalimumab, infliximab, and etanercept) or anti–B-lymphocyte monoclonal antibodies (eg, rituximab), appears to be prolonged. The interval until immune reconstitution varies with the intensity and type of immunosuppressive therapy, radiation therapy, underlying disease, and other factors. Therefore, it often is not possible to make a definitive recommendation for an interval after cessation of immunosuppressive therapy when live-virus vaccines can be administered safely and effectively. In vitro testing of immune function may provide guidelines for optimal timing of immunizations in individual patients.

OTHER CONSIDERATIONS. Because patients with congenital or acquired immuno-deficiencies may not have an adequate response to an immunizing agent, they may remain susceptible despite having received an appropriate vaccine. If there is a known antibody correlate of protection, specific serum antibody titers should be determined 4 to 6 weeks after immunization to assess immune response and guide further immunization and management of future exposures.

People with certain immune deficiencies may benefit from specific immunizations directed at preventing infections by organisms to which they are particularly susceptible. Examples include administration of pneumococcal and meningococcal vaccines to people with splenic dysfunction, asplenia (see Children With Asplenia, p 83), and complement deficiencies, because they are at increased risk of infection with encapsulated bacteria. Also, annual inactivated influenza immunization is indicated for children 6 months of age and older with immune deficiencies, including splenic dysfunction, asplenia, and phagocyte function deficiencies, to prevent influenza and decrease the risk of secondary bacterial infections (see Influenza, p 401).

HOUSEHOLD CONTACTS. Immunocompetent siblings and other household contacts of people with an immunologic deficiency should not receive smallpox vaccine or OPV vaccine, because vaccine virus may be transmitted to immunocompromised people. However, siblings and household contacts should receive MMR, varicella, and rotavirus vaccines if indicated, because transmission of the vaccine viruses rarely occurs. Household contacts 6 months of age and older should receive yearly inactivated influenza vaccine to prevent infection and subsequent transmission to the immunocompromised person. Limited data are available assessing the risk of transmission of LAIV virus from vaccine (FluMist) recipients to immunosuppressed contacts. Inactivated influenza vaccine is recommended for immunizing household members of immunosuppressed people. Varicella vaccine is recommended for susceptible contacts of immunocompromised children, because transmission of varicella vaccine virus from healthy people is rare, and vaccine-associated illness, if it develops, is mild. No precautions need to be taken after immunization unless the vaccine recipient develops a rash, particularly a vesicular rash. In such instances, the vaccine recipient should avoid direct contact with immunocompromised, susceptible hosts for the duration of the rash. If contact inadvertently occurs, administration of VariZIG, if available, or IGIV is not indicated, because risk of transmission is low. Also, when transmission has occurred, the virus has maintained its attenuated characteristics. In most instances, antiviral therapy is not necessary but can be initiated if illness occurs (see Varicella-Zoster Infections, p 711).

CORTICOSTEROIDS

Children who receive systemic corticosteroid therapy can become immunocompromised. The minimal amount of systemic corticosteroids and duration of administration sufficient to cause immunosuppression in an otherwise healthy child are not well defined. The frequency and route of administration of corticosteroids, the underlying disease, and concurrent therapies are additional factors affecting immunosuppression. Despite these uncertainties, sufficient experience exists to recommend empiric guidelines for administration of live-virus vaccines to previously healthy children receiving corticosteroid therapy. A dosage equivalent to ≥2 mg/kg per day of prednisone or equivalent to a total of ≥20 mg/day for children who weigh more than 10 kg, particularly when given for more than 14 days, is considered sufficient to raise concern about the safety of immunization with live-virus vaccines. Accordingly, guidelines for administration of live-virus vaccines to recipients of corticosteroids are as follows:

- **Topical therapy, local injections, or aerosol use of corticosteroids.** Application of low-potency topical corticosteroids to focal areas on the skin; administration by aerosolization in the respiratory tract; application on conjunctiva; or intra-articular, bursal, or tendon injections of corticosteroids usually do not result in immunosuppression that would contraindicate administration of live-virus vaccines. However, live-virus vaccines should not be administered if clinical or laboratory evidence of systemic immunosuppression results from prolonged application until corticosteroid therapy has been discontinued for at least 1 month.
- **Physiologic maintenance doses of corticosteroids.** Children who are receiving only maintenance physiologic doses of corticosteroids can receive live-virus vaccines during corticosteroid treatment.
- **Low or moderate doses of systemic corticosteroids given daily or on alternate days.** Children receiving <2 mg/kg per day of prednisone or its equivalent, or <20 mg/day if they weigh more than 10 kg, can receive live-virus vaccines during corticosteroid treatment.
- **High doses of systemic corticosteroids given daily or on alternate days for fewer than 14 days.** Children receiving ≥2 mg/kg per day of prednisone or its equivalent, or ≥20 mg/day if they weigh more than 10 kg, can receive live-virus vaccines immediately after discontinuation of treatment. Some experts, however, would delay immunization until 2 weeks after corticosteroid therapy has been discontinued, if possible (ie, if the patient's condition allows temporary cessation).
- **High doses of systemic corticosteroids given daily or on alternate days for 14 days or more.** Children receiving ≥2 mg/kg per day of prednisone or its equivalent, or ≥20 mg/day if they weigh more than 10 kg, should not receive live-virus vaccines until corticosteroid therapy has been discontinued for at least 1 month.
- **Children who have a disease that, in itself, is considered to suppress the immune response and who are receiving systemic or locally administered corticosteroids.** These children should not be given live-virus vaccines, except in special circumstances.

These guidelines are based on concerns about vaccine safety in recipients of high doses of corticosteroids. When deciding whether to administer live-virus vaccines, the potential benefits and risks of immunization for an individual patient and the specific circumstances should be considered. For example, some experts recommend immunization of a patient at increased risk of a vaccine-preventable infection (and its complications) if, despite corticosteroid therapy, the patient does not have clinical evidence of immunosuppression.

The guidelines also are based on considerations of safety concerning live-virus vaccines and do not necessarily correlate with those for optimal vaccine immunogenicity. For example, some children receiving moderate doses of prednisone, such as 1.5 mg/kg per day for several weeks or longer, may have a less-than-optimal immune response to some vaccine antigens. In contrast, some children receiving relatively high doses of corticosteroids (eg, 30 mg/day of prednisone) may respond adequately to immunization. Immunization can be deferred temporarily until corticosteroids are discontinued if timely return for immunization is ensured. Otherwise, children should be immunized despite corticosteroid use to enhance the likelihood of protection in the case of exposure to disease.

HODGKIN DISEASE

Patients with Hodgkin disease are at increased risk of invasive pneumococcal infection, and most experts believe they also are at increased risk of invasive Hib infection. Thus, immunization with pneumococcal conjugate and/or polysaccharide vaccine and Hib vaccine according to age-specific guidelines are recommended (see Pneumococcal Infections, p 525, and *Haemophilus influenzae* Infections, p 310) Antibody response is likely to be best when patients are immunized at least 10 to 14 days before initiation of therapy for Hodgkin disease. During active chemotherapy and shortly thereafter, antibody responses to the pneumococcal and Hib vaccines are impaired. However, the ability of these patients to respond improves rapidly, and immunization as early as 3 months after cessation of chemotherapy is reasonable. Patients who received pneumococcal or other polysaccharide vaccines during chemotherapy or radiation therapy should be reimmunized 3 months after discontinuation of the therapy.

HEMATOPOIETIC STEM CELL AND OTHER TRANSPLANT RECIPIENTS

Many factors can affect immunity to vaccine-preventable diseases for a child recovering from successful hematopoietic stem cell transplantation (HSCT), including bone marrow transplantation. These include the donor's immunity, type of transplantation (ie, autologous or allogeneic, blood or hematopoietic stem cell*), interval since the transplantation, receipt of immunosuppressive medications, and presence of graft-versus-host disease (GVHD). Although many children who are transplant recipients acquire the immunity of the donor, some will lose serologic evidence of immunity. Retention of donor immune memory can be facilitated if recalled by antigenic stimulation soon after transplantation. Clinical studies of stem cell transplant recipients indicate that administration of diphtheria and tetanus toxoids to the donor before harvest and immediate administration to the recipient after transplantation can facilitate response to these antigens; serum antibody titers did not increase when immunization of the recipient was delayed until 5 weeks after transplantation. In theory, these results could be expected with other inactivated vaccine antigens, including pertussis, Hib, influenza, hepatitis B, hepatitis A, IPV, and pneumococcal and meningococcal conjugate and polysaccharide vaccines.

---

* Centers for Disease Control and Prevention, Infectious Disease Society of America, and the American Society of Blood and Marrow Transplantation. Guidelines for preventing opportunistic infections among hematopoietic stem cell transplant recipients. *MMWR Recomm Rep.* 2000;49(RR-10):1–125, CE1-CE7

The risk of acquiring diphtheria or tetanus during the year after HSCT is low. Some experts elect to reimmunize all children without serologic evaluation, and others base the decision to reimmunize against diphtheria and tetanus on adequacy of serologic titers obtained 1 year after transplantation. Adequate immune responses can be obtained with 3 doses of Td at 12, 14, and 24 months after transplantation in people 7 years of age or older. In people younger than 7 years of age, DTaP or DT should be used. No data are available on safety and immunogenicity of pertussis immunization for stem cell transplant recipients. People with tetanus-prone wounds sustained during the first year after transplantation should be given Tetanus Immune Globulin, regardless of their tetanus immunization status.

Data on which to base recommendations for reimmunization against Hib or *S pneumoniae* are limited. Doses of Hib conjugate vaccine appear to provide some protection if given at 12, 14, and 24 months after HSCT for recipients of any age. In one study, time after transplantation was the most important factor in determining the immune response to pneumococcal polysaccharide vaccine, with the greatest response observed when the vaccine was administered 2 or more years after transplantation. In another study, Hib conjugate and tetanus toxoid vaccines given 12 and 24 months after HSCT induced adequate immune responses. Some experts recommend a multiple-dose schedule of pneumococcal conjugate and/or polysaccharide vaccine at 12 and 24 months after transplantation, depending on the age of the person (see Pneumococcal Infections, p 525). The second dose of pneumococcal vaccine provides a second opportunity for pneumococcal immunization for people who fail to respond to the first dose. In patients undergoing autologous HSCT, preharvest immunization with Hib conjugate vaccine resulted in higher anti-Hib antibody concentrations for 2 years after transplantation, compared with patients who were not immunized before harvest. Similar benefit in transplant recipients was noted when allogenic stem cell donors were immunized before harvest.

Recovery of immune function after HSCT is variable depending on interaction of several factors. Relying on a generalized schedule for immunization is problematic. Some experts suggest a trial of assessing antibody response to tetanus or diphtheria and tetanus toxoids; a positive result would indicate probable safety of administration of live-virus vaccines. Receipt of IGIV may compromise interpretation of this test. Data indicate that healthy survivors can be immunized with inactivated bacterial and viral vaccines 1 year after HSCT and can receive MMR vaccine 2 years after HSCT. Insufficient data are available for recommendations regarding varicella-zoster virus vaccine. Inactivated influenza vaccine can be given 6 months or longer after HSCT. A second dose of MMR vaccine should be given 1 month (4 weeks) or more after the first dose unless serologic response to measles is demonstrated after the first dose. The benefit of a second dose in this population has not been evaluated. Patients with chronic GVHD should not receive MMR vaccine because of concern about resulting latent virus infection and its sequelae. Susceptible people who are exposed to measles should receive passive immunoprophylaxis (see Measles, p 441). Varicella vaccine is contraindicated for stem cell transplant recipients less than 24 months after transplantation. Use of varicella vaccine for stem cell transplant recipients is restricted to research protocols in which the vaccine may be considered 24 months or more after HSCT for recipients who are presumed immunocompetent. Passive immunization is recommended for susceptible people with known exposure to varicella (see Varicella-Zoster Infections, p 711).

Only IPV vaccine should be given to transplant recipients and their household contacts. Stem cell transplant recipients should be immunized with IPV vaccine at 12, 14, and 24 months after transplantation. The effectiveness of giving additional doses is not known; more data are needed on optimal methods and timing of IPV immunization. Recipients can be tested for type-specific antibodies, but serologic tests for antibody titers against polioviruses are not readily available.

Inactivated influenza vaccine is not effective when given within the initial 6 months after HSCT, but immunization may provide protection when given 1 year after HSCT. Because the risk of disease is substantial, inactivated influenza vaccine should be administered annually during early autumn (see Influenza, p 401) to people who underwent HSCT more than 6 months previously, even if the interval is fewer than 12 months. For children and adolescents fewer than 6 months after HSCT, influenza chemoprophylaxis should be considered (see Influenza, p 401). Live-attenuated influenza vaccine should not be administered to children and adolescents who have undergone HSCT.

The immunogenicity of hepatitis B vaccine in stem cell transplant recipients has not been assessed adequately. On the basis of the response of these patients to other protein antigens, initiation of a 3-dose series at 12, 14, and 24 months after HSCT followed by postimmunization serologic testing for antibody to HBsAg is reasonable. Additional doses (maximum of 3) should be given to vaccine nonresponders. Routine administration of hepatitis A vaccine is not recommended but may be considered 12 months or longer after HSCT for people who have chronic liver disease or chronic GVHD or people from areas with endemic infection or outbreaks of hepatitis A. Hepatitis A immunization requires 2 doses (see Hepatitis A, p 326). Household and health care worker contacts of stem cell and solid organ transplant recipients should have immunity to or be immunized against poliovirus, measles, mumps, rubella, varicella, influenza, and hepatitis A.

SOLID ORGAN TRANSPLANT RECIPIENTS

Children and adolescents being considered for solid organ transplantation should receive immunizations recommended for their age before the transplantation is performed. In general, vaccines will be more immunogenic before transplantation because the medications given after transplantation to prevent and treat organ rejection adversely affect T- and B-lymphocyte numbers and/or function. Live-virus vaccines should be given at least 1 month before transplantation and, in general, should not be given to patients receiving immunosuppressive medications after transplantation. Monovalent measles (or if not available, MMR) vaccine may be given before transplantation to patients as young as 6 months of age if transplantation is anticipated before 12 to 15 months of age. For transplantation candidates who are older than 12 months of age, if previously immunized, serum concentrations of antibody to measles, mumps, rubella, and varicella should be measured. Children who are susceptible should be given the needed vaccines before transplantation.

Information about the use of live-virus vaccines in patients after solid organ transplantation is limited. Some transplant centers have reported administration of live-virus vaccines (eg, MMR and varicella vaccines) in patients who are stable at least 6 months after transplantation, who are receiving minimal immunosuppressive agents, and who have not had recent episodes of organ rejection. No serious adverse reactions have been reported among these children, but too few children have been studied to recommend general use of live-virus vaccines in this population. Measles-mumps-rubella vaccine may be considered for susceptible solid organ transplant recipients in the event of an outbreak of measles, mumps, or rubella in the local community. Serum antibody concentrations for measles, mumps, rubella, and varicella should be measured in all patients 1 year or more after transplantation. Household and close contacts of a solid organ recipient should receive MMR and varicella vaccines, if susceptible, to prevent transmission of wild-type virus to the immunosuppressed child. Oral poliovirus vaccine is contraindicated for transplant recipients and their household contacts. Inactivated poliovirus should be used for protection against poliovirus. Live-bacteria vaccines (eg, BCG and Ty21a *S typhi*) are contraindicated in patients receiving immunosuppressive medications after transplantation.

Killed and subunit vaccines should not pose a risk to solid organ transplant recipients. After transplantation, DTaP, Hib, hepatitis B, hepatitis A, inactivated influenza, and pneumococcal and meningococcal conjugate and polysaccharide vaccines can be administered, if indicated. Safety and immunogenicity data for these vaccines in children after transplantation are limited. Most experts wait at least 6 months after transplantation, when immune suppression is less intense, for resumption of immunization schedules. However, immunization schedules vary in different transplant centers, and immune responses to some inactivated vaccines are diminished compared with healthy controls. Hepatitis A vaccine should be considered for patients undergoing liver transplantation because of an increased mortality rate associated with hepatitis A infection in patients with chronic liver disease. Annual influenza immunization with inactivated vaccine is indicated before and after solid organ transplantation. Live-attenuated influenza vaccine is contraindicated for solid organ transplant recipients. Solid organ transplant recipients at highest risk of infection with *S pneumoniae* appear to be those who have undergone cardiac transplantation or splenectomy. Pneumococcal conjugate or polysaccharide vaccine should be considered in all transplant recipients (see Pneumococcal Infections, p 525).

The decision to use passive immunization with an IG preparation (see Immune Globulin, p 55) should be made on the basis of serologic evidence of susceptibility and exposure to disease. Household and health care worker contacts of stem cell and solid organ transplant recipients should have immunity to or be immunized against poliovirus, measles, mumps, rubella, varicella, influenza, and hepatitis A.

HUMAN IMMUNODEFICIENCY VIRUS INFECTION (SEE ALSO HUMAN IMMUNODEFICIENCY VIRUS INFECTION, P 378)

Data on use of currently available live-virus and live-bacteria vaccines in HIV-infected children are limited, but complications have been reported after BCG and measles immunizations, including vaccine-related measles pneumonitis in a severely immunocompromised child 1 year after measles immunization. Because there have been reports of severe wild-type measles in symptomatic HIV-infected children, with fatalities in as many as 40% of cases, measles immunization (given as MMR vaccine) is recommended for most HIV-infected children, including children who are symptomatic but are not severely immunocompromised and children who are asymptomatic. Measles-mumps-rubella vaccine should be given at 12 months of age to enhance the likelihood of an appropriate immune response. The second dose after the 12-month immunization can be administered as soon as 1 month (28 days) later to induce seroconversion as early as possible. In a measles epidemic, monovalent measles vaccine or MMR, if monovalent vaccine is not available, may be given to infants as young as 6 months of age. Children immunized before their first birthday should be immunized with 2 additional doses of MMR vaccine (see Measles, Immunization During an Outbreak, p 448). Severely immunocompromised patients with HIV infection, as defined by age-specific low CD4 + T-lymphocyte counts or low percentage of total circulating lymphocytes, should not receive measles vaccine (see Human Immunodeficiency Virus Infection, p 378, and Table 3.26, p 386).

After the potential risks and benefits are weighed, varicella vaccine should be considered for asymptomatic or mildly symptomatic HIV-infected children with CD4 + T-lymphocyte percentages of 15% or more expected for age (see Varicella-Zoster Infections, p 711). Children and adolescents with asymptomatic or symptomatic HIV infection also should receive other routinely recommended vaccines, including DTaP, Tdap, IPV, hepatitis B, hepatitis A, Hib, and pneumococcal and meningococcal conjugate and/or polysaccharide vaccines, according to the recommended schedule (see Fig 1.1, p 26). Annual inactivated influenza immunization of HIV-infected children 6 months of age or older and adolescents is recommended; LAIV is contraindicated in this population (see Influenza, p 401). Household contacts of any child infected with HIV should receive inactivated influenza vaccine annually. Immunization with pneumococcal conjugate and/or polysaccharide vaccine is indicated on the basis of age- and vaccine-specific recommendations (see Pneumococcal Infections, p 525). Data are limited on the effect of routine immunizations on HIV RNA viral load in children. Some studies in adults have demonstrated transient increases of HIV RNA concentrations after immunization with influenza or pneumococcal vaccine, but other studies have shown no increase. No evidence indicates that this transient increase enhances progression of disease. Results of increases in HIV RNA concentrations in children after immunization are variable. Additional studies are needed in infants and children who receive recommended immunizations.

In the United States, BCG vaccine is contraindicated for HIV-infected patients. In areas of the world with a high incidence of tuberculosis, the World Health Organization (WHO) recommends giving BCG vaccine to HIV-infected children who are asymptomatic.

Routine or widespread screening to detect HIV infection in asymptomatic children before routine immunizations is not recommended. Children without clinical manifestations of or known risk factors for HIV infection should be immunized in accordance with the recommended childhood and adolescent immunization schedule.

Because the ability of HIV-infected children to respond to vaccine antigens likely is related to the degree of immunosuppression at the time of immunization and may be inadequate, these children should be considered potentially susceptible to vaccine-preventable diseases, even after appropriate immunization, unless a recent serologic test demonstrates adequate antibody concentrations. Hence, passive immunoprophylaxis or chemoprophylaxis after exposure to these diseases should be considered, even if the child previously has received the recommended vaccines. Children with HIV infection given recommended vaccines when they had high HIV RNA concentrations and/or low CD4+ lymphocyte percentages (eg, before the diagnosis of HIV infection was made or before institution of therapy) may benefit from reimmunization after improvement of their immune status (eg, after institution of highly active antiretroviral therapy).

Vaccine-type varicella-zoster virus rarely has been transmitted from healthy people. Therefore, household contacts of HIV-infected people can be immunized with live-virus varicella vaccine (see Varicella-Zoster Infections, p 711). No precautions are needed after immunization of healthy children who do not develop a rash. Vaccine recipients who develop a rash should avoid direct contact with susceptible immunocompromised hosts for the duration of the rash. If the immunocompromised contact develops varicella, disease will be mild, and use of VariZIG, if available, or IGIV to prevent transmission is not indicated.

CHILDREN WITH ASPLENIA

The asplenic state results from the following: (1) surgical removal of the spleen; (2) certain diseases, such as sickle cell disease (functional asplenia); or (3) congenital asplenia. All infants, children, adolescents, and adults with asplenia, regardless of the reason for the asplenic state, have an increased risk of fulminant bacteremia, especially associated with encapsulated bacteria, which is associated with a high mortality rate. Susceptibility to fulminant septicemia is determined largely by the underlying disease. In comparison with immunocompetent children who have not undergone splenectomy, the incidence of and mortality rate from septicemia are increased in children who have had splenectomy after trauma and in children with sickle cell disease by as much as 350-fold, and the rate may be even higher in children who have had splenectomy for thalassemia. The risk of bacteremia is higher in younger children than in older children, and risk may be greater during the years immediately after splenectomy. Fulminant septicemia, however, has been reported in adults as many as 25 years after splenectomy.

Streptococcus pneumoniae is the most common pathogen that causes bacteremia in children with asplenia. Less common causes of bacteremia include Hib, *N meningitidis*, other streptococci, *Escherichia coli*, *Staphylococcus aureus*, and gram-negative bacilli, such as *Salmonella* species, *Klebsiella* species, and *Pseudomonas aeruginosa*. People with functional or anatomic asplenia also are at increased risk of fatal malaria and severe babesiosis.

Pneumococcal conjugate and/or polysaccharide vaccine is indicated for all children with asplenia at the recommended age (see Pneumococcal Infections, p 525). For children with asplenia who received conjugate and/or polysaccharide vaccine before 24 months of age, additional immunization should be considered in reference to age and products received (see Pneumococcal Infections, p 525). Immunization against Hib infections should be initiated at 2 months of age, as recommended for otherwise healthy young children (see Fig 1.1, p 26), and for all previously unimmunized children with asplenia. Tetravalent meningococcal polysaccharide vaccine also should be administered to children with asplenia who are 2 through 10 years of age. Meningococcal conjugate vaccine should be given to adolescents (see Meningococcal Infections, p 452). The efficacy of meningococcal vaccines in children with asplenia has not been established. No known contraindication exists to giving these vaccines at the same time in separate syringes at different sites.

Daily antimicrobial prophylaxis against pneumococcal infections is recommended for many children with asplenia, regardless of immunization status. For infants with sickle cell anemia, oral penicillin prophylaxis against invasive pneumococcal disease should be initiated as soon as the diagnosis is established and preferably by 2 months of age. Although the efficacy of antimicrobial prophylaxis has been proven only in patients with sickle cell anemia, other children with asplenia at particularly high risk, such as children with malignant neoplasms or thalassemia, also should receive daily chemoprophylaxis. Less agreement exists about the need for prophylaxis for children who have had splenectomy after trauma. In general, antimicrobial prophylaxis (in addition to immunization) should be considered for all children with asplenia younger than 5 years of age and for at least 1 year after splenectomy.

The age at which chemoprophylaxis is discontinued often is an empiric decision. On the basis of a multicenter study, prophylactic penicillin can be discontinued at 5 years of age in children with sickle cell anemia who are receiving regular medical attention and who have not had a severe pneumococcal infection or surgical splenectomy. The appropriate duration of prophylaxis for children with asplenia attributable to other causes is unknown. Some experts continue prophylaxis throughout childhood and into adulthood for particularly high-risk patients with asplenia.

For antimicrobial prophylaxis, oral penicillin V (125 mg, twice a day, for children younger than 5 years of age and 250 mg, twice a day, for children 5 years of age and older) is recommended. Some experts recommend amoxicillin (20 mg/kg per day). In recent years, the proportion of pneumococcal isolates that have intermediate or high-level resistance to penicillin has increased in most areas of the United States. Administration of conjugate pneumococcal vaccine reduces carriage of penicillin-nonsusceptible vaccine strains of pneumococci. Ongoing surveillance for resistant pneumococci is needed to determine whether changes to the recommended chemoprophylaxis will be required.

When antimicrobial prophylaxis is used, the limitations must be stressed to parents and patients, who should recognize that some bacteria capable of causing fulminant septicemia are not susceptible to the antimicrobial agents given for prophylaxis. Parents should be aware that all febrile illnesses potentially are serious in children with asplenia and that immediate medical attention should be sought, because the initial signs and symptoms of fulminant septicemia can be subtle. When bacteremia is a possibility, the physician should hospitalize the child, obtain specimens for blood and other cultures as indicated, and immediately begin treatment with an antimicrobial regimen effective against *S pneumoniae*, Hib, and *N meningitidis*. In some clinical situations, other antimicrobial agents, such as aminoglycosides, may be indicated. If a child with asplenia travels to or resides in an area where medical care is not accessible, an appropriate antimicrobial agent should be readily available, and the child's caregiver should be instructed in appropriate use.

Whenever possible, alternatives to splenectomy should be considered. Management options include postponement of splenectomy for as long as possible in congenital hemolytic anemias, preservation of accessory spleens, performance of partial splenectomy for benign tumors of the spleen, conservative (nonoperative) management of splenic trauma, or when feasible, repair rather than removal and, if possible, avoidance of splenectomy when immunodeficiency is present (eg, Wiskott-Aldrich syndrome). When surgical splenectomy, planned or emergent, is imminent, immediate administration of needed vaccines (eg, Hib, pneumococcal, and/or meningococcal) may be recommended.

Children With a Personal or Family History of Seizures

Infants and children with a personal or family history of seizures are at increased risk of having a seizure after receipt of DTP or measles (usually as MMR) vaccines. In most cases, these seizures are brief, self-limited, and generalized and occur in conjunction with fever, indicating that such vaccine-associated seizures usually are febrile seizures. No evidence indicates that these seizures cause permanent brain damage or epilepsy, aggravate neurologic disorders, or affect the prognosis for children with underlying disorders. Universal use of DTaP has reduced greatly the incidence of febrile seizures associated with DTP immunization.

In the case of pertussis immunization during infancy, administration of DTaP could coincide with or hasten the recognition of a disorder associated with seizures, such as infantile spasms or epilepsy, and cause confusion about the role of pertussis immunization. Hence, pertussis immunization in infants with a history of recent seizures should be deferred until a progressive neurologic disorder is excluded or the cause of the earlier seizure has been determined. In contrast, measles immunization is given at an age when the cause and nature of any seizures and related neurologic status are more likely to have been established. This difference provides basis for the recommendation that measles immunization should not be deferred for children with a history of recent seizures.

A family history of a seizure disorder is not a contraindication to pertussis or measles immunization or a reason to defer immunization. Postimmunization seizures in these children usually are febrile in origin, have a benign outcome, and are not likely to be confused with manifestations of a previously unrecognized neurologic disorder. In addition, many children have a family history of seizures and would remain susceptible to pertussis and measles if family history were a contraindication to immunization.

Specific recommendations for pertussis and measles immunization of children with a personal or family history of seizures are given in the respective disease-specific chapters (see Pertussis, p 498, and Measles, p 441); a detailed discussion and recommendations about pertussis immunization of children with neurologic disorders also are given in the chapter on Pertussis (p 498).

Children With Chronic Diseases

Some chronic diseases make children more susceptible to the severe manifestations and complications of common infections. Unless specifically contraindicated, immunizations recommended for healthy children should be given to children with chronic diseases. For children with conditions that may require organ transplantation or immunosuppression, administering recommended immunizations before the start of immunosuppressive therapy is important. However, for children with immunologic disorders, live-virus vaccines usually are contraindicated; the major exceptions are MMR and varicella vaccines for HIV-infected children who are not immunocompromised severely (see Immunocompromised Children, p 71). Children with certain chronic diseases (eg, cardiorespiratory, allergic, hematologic, metabolic, and renal disorders; cystic fibrosis; and diabetes mellitus) are at increased risk of complications of influenza, varicella, and pneumococcal infection and should receive inactivated influenza vaccine and live varicella vaccine and/or pneumococcal conjugate or polysaccharide vaccine as recommended for age and immunization status (see Influenza, p 401, Varicella-Zoster Infections, p 711, and Pneumococcal Infections, p 525). People with chronic liver disease are at risk of severe clinical manifestations of acute infection with hepatitis A virus (HAV). Therefore, children 1 year of age and older should be immunized with HAV vaccine (see Hepatitis A, p 326). Siblings of children with chronic diseases should be immunized as recommended (see Fig 1.1, p 26, and Immunocompromised Children, p 71).

Determining the appropriateness of administering a live-virus vaccine to a specific child with a rare disorder (eg, galactosemia) is problematic, particularly if the disease might impair the immune response to the vaccine. Documented experience with immunization of children with some of these disorders is minimal or nonexistent, and the physician should seek guidance from a specialist before administering the vaccine(s).

Active Immunization After Exposure to Disease

Because not all susceptible people receive vaccines before exposure, active immunization may be considered for a person who has been exposed to a specific disease. The following situations are the most commonly encountered (see the disease-specific chapters in Section 3 for detailed recommendations).

- **Measles**. Live-virus measles vaccine given to susceptible immunocompetent children 1 year of age and older, adolescents, and adults within 72 hours of exposure will provide protection against measles in some cases (see Measles, p 441). Determining the time of exposure may be difficult, because infected people can spread measles virus for 3 to 5 days before the appearance of a rash and for 1 to 2 days before the onset of symptoms.

  Immune Globulin, administered intramuscularly within 6 days of exposure, also can prevent or attenuate measles in an immunocompetent or immunocompromised susceptible person (see Measles, p 441). Because measles morbidity rate is high in children younger than 1 year of age, administration of IG is recommended for infants, immunocompromised people at any age, and pregnant women exposed to measles. Immunocompromised children who receive IGIV regularly are considered to be protected against measles.

- **Varicella**. Susceptible immunocompetent children 12 months of age or older and household contacts exposed to a person with varicella disease should be given varicella vaccine within 72 hours of the appearance of the rash in the index case (see Varicella-Zoster Infections, p 711). If exposure to varicella does not result in infection, immunization should protect against subsequent exposures. Immunization is safe even in the event that the exposure results in clinical varicella disease. Susceptible immunocompromised children should be given passive protection as soon as possible but within 96 hours after contact with an infected person (see Varicella-Zoster Infections, p 711). Immunocompromised children who receive IGIV regularly are considered to be protected against varicella.

- **Hepatitis B.** Postexposure immunization is highly effective if combined with administration of antibody. Administration of HBIG does not inhibit active immunization with HBV vaccine. For postexposure prophylaxis in a newborn infant whose mother is an HBsAg carrier, administration of HBIG and hepatitis B immunization is essential. For percutaneous or mucosal exposure to HBV, combined active and passive immunization is recommended for susceptible people (see Hepatitis B, p 335). People with continuing household or sexual contact with an HBsAg carrier also should be immunized.

- **Hepatitis A.** Available data are insufficient to recommend HAV vaccine alone for postexposure prophylaxis. However, HAV vaccine alone may provide better protection against disease than IG plus immunization, which produces lower antibody titers. Immune Globulin should be administered to household, sexual, and other contacts of HAV-infected people as soon as possible after exposure. If ongoing exposure to HAV is likely, IG and the first dose of HAV vaccine may be administered simultaneously at different sites. Clinical trials are in progress to determine the effectiveness of HAV compared with IG after exposure.

- **Tetanus.** In wound management, cleaning and débriding all dirty wounds as soon as possible is essential. Unimmunized and incompletely immunized people, or people who have not received a booster dose in the past 5 years, should be given a tetanus toxoid-containing vaccine immediately. Some people may require Tetanus Immune Globulin in addition to immunization (see Table 3.63, p 650).

- **Rabies.** Thorough local cleansing and débridement of the wound and postexposure active and passive immunization are essential aspects of immunoprophylaxis for rabies after proven or suspected exposure to rabid animals (see Rabies, p 552).

- **Mumps and Rubella.** Exposed susceptible people are not necessarily protected by postexposure administration of live-virus vaccine. However, a common practice for people exposed to mumps or rubella is to administer vaccine to presumed susceptible people so that permanent immunity will be afforded by immunization if mumps or rubella does not result from the current exposure. Administration of live-virus vaccine is recommended for exposed adults born in the United States in 1957 or after who previously have not had or been immunized against mumps or rubella.

American Indian/Alaska Native Children

Compared with children from other ethnic groups, American Indian/Alaska Native (AI/AN) children historically have been at greater risk of acquiring certain vaccine-preventable diseases, such as hepatitis A and hepatitis B, Hib, and *S pneumoniae* infections, and being hospitalized for respiratory syncytial virus infection and other lower respiratory tract infections (LTRIs). Increased risk of acquiring vaccine-preventable diseases has been demonstrated among AI/AN children who live on reservations or in traditional rural villages. However, high incidences of hepatitis A and hepatitis B infections also have been demonstrated among urban AI/AN children, which may result from frequent visits to extended family members who reside in rural and reservation communities with crowded living conditions and lack of indoor plumbing. In addition, there may be some geographic differences in disease risk.

During the past decade, universal childhood immunization for hepatitis B and targeted immunization for hepatitis A in the United States have eliminated disease disparities for these pathogens in most AI/AN children, and significant decreases in disease have been demonstrated for Hib and *S pneumoniae*. Continued immunization is critical to maintaining this success and eliminating other disparities. Because of the difficulty in ascertaining disease risk as well as the high degree of mobility of the AI/AN population among reservations, rural villages, and urban settings, all physicians caring for AI/AN children should consider the following special immunization recommendations.

HEPATITIS A. Historically, hepatitis A incidence has been substantially higher among AI/AN people than among people from other racial or ethnic groups in the United States. During 1990–1995, reported cases of hepatitis A among AI/AN individuals accounted for 5% to 8% of all cases in the United States, although the AI/AN population constituted less than 1% of the total US population. These high rates largely were the result of periodic community-wide epidemics on reservations and in rural Alaskan communities. Rates among urban AI/AN people were several-fold higher than rates among other people living in the same areas. Hepatitis A vaccine was licensed in 1995 and recommended by the ACIP for routine immunization of children in populations with high rates of hepatitis A infection, including AI/AN children. During 1997–2001, hepatitis A infection rates among AI/AN decreased 20-fold to a level similar to the overall US rate. This represents the largest decrease in the hepatitis A rate that has occurred in children. Sustained routine immunization of all young AI/AN children will be necessary to maintain high levels of population immunity and the low disease rates currently observed in AI/AN communities. In 2005, the ACIP approved addition of hepatitis A vaccine to the recommended childhood and adolescent immunization schedule.

HEPATITIS B. Alaska Native children had a high prevalence of chronic HBV infection before implementation of universal infant HBV immunization. Universal immunization of Alaska Native children starting in 1984 decreased the rate of HBV infection in the Alaska Native population to rates similar to those in the general population (from 200 per 100 000 to <5 per 100 000). Although the rate of chronic HBV infection has decreased in young Alaska Native children, a high incidence of HBV infection has been observed among older American Indian adolescents and young adults, which is associated with high-risk behaviors, such as injection drug use. All AI/AN children should be given the HBV immunization series as infants, preferably starting in the newborn period. In addition, special efforts should be made to ensure catch-up HBV immunization of previously unimmunized adolescents, especially those in correctional settings or treatment programs for substance abuse. In 2005, the ACIP approved the recommendation that unimmunized adults at high risk of hepatitis B infection and all adults seeking protection from hepatitis B should be immunized.

HAEMOPHILUS INFLUENZAE TYPE B. Before availability and public use of conjugated Hib vaccines, the incidence of invasive Hib disease was up to 10 times higher among young AI/AN children compared with the general US population. Because of the high risk of invasive Hib disease within the first 6 months of life in many AI/AN infant populations, the Indian Health Service and the American Academy of Pediatrics (AAP) recommend that the first dose of Hib conjugate vaccine contain polyribosylribitol phosphate-meningococcal outer membrane protein (PRP-OMP) as a single-antigen vaccine or in a combination vaccine with other antigens. The administration of a PRP-OMP–containing vaccine leads to more rapid seroconversion to protective concentrations of antibody within the first 6 months of life, and failure of use has been associated with excess cases of Hib disease in young infants in this population. For subsequent doses, PRP-OMP or any of the other Hib conjugate vaccines can be used with apparently equal efficacy (see *Haemophilus influenzae* Infections, p 310). However, availability of more than one Hib vaccine in a clinic can be confusing, so strict attention must be paid to vaccine type. Sequential immunization with PRP-OMP for the first dose and *Haemophilus influenzae* type b oligosaccharide conjugate (HbOC) for the following doses was performed in Alaska during 1997–1999. During this time, 3 of 6 cases of invasive Hib disease in partially immunized infants occurred in infants who inadvertently were given HbOC for their first dose. Thus, for clinics that serve predominantly AI/AN children, it may be prudent to use only a PRP-OMP Hib vaccine.

STREPTOCOCCUS PNEUMONIAE. The incidence of invasive pneumococcal disease in certain AI/AN children was 5 to 24 times higher than the incidence among other US children before use of the conjugate pneumococcal vaccine. Use of this vaccine in AI/AN infants has resulted in decreased incidence of invasive pneumococcal disease in AI/AN children. However, despite this, AI/AN children continue to have an increased risk of acquiring invasive pneumococcal disease—more than twice the national average. Therefore, Alaska Native children and American Indian children in the southwest should receive the standard 4-dose PCV7 series, even in times of vaccine shortages, as recommended by the ACIP and the AAP.

Because older AI/AN children also are at higher risk of acquiring pneumococcal disease than are other US children, immunization of AI/AN children 2 to 5 years of age with PCV7 or pneumococcal polysaccharide vaccine should be considered.

RESPIRATORY SYNCYTIAL VIRUS AND LOWER RESPIRATORY TRACT
INFECTIONS. The rate of hospitalization for respiratory syncytial virus (RSV) infection is higher for AI/AN children than for other US children. The greatest disparities have been documented among AI/AN infants living in the Alaska and southwest Indian Health Service regions (71 and 48 RSV hospitalizations per 1000 births, respectively, compared with 27 per 1000 births for the general US population). The higher rates underscore the importance of maximizing AAP-recommended use of RSV-specific monoclonal antibody prophylaxis among high-risk AI/AN infants, including preterm infants, in these regions.

American Indian/Alaska Native infants born at 32 and 35 weeks' gestation often have at least 2 risk factors, such as school-aged siblings and exposure to environmental air pollution. American Indian/Alaska Native infants are at higher risk of being hospitalized because of RSV and LRTIs. Respiratory syncytial virus prophylaxis should be considered for AI/AN infants born at 32 to 35 weeks' gestation who will be younger than 6 months of age at the start of the RSV season (if 2 or more risk factors are present [see Respiratory Syncytial Virus, p 560]).

INFLUENZA. Hospitalization rates for all LRTIs are higher in AI/AN children. Like other US children, AI/AN children between 6 and 23 months of age should receive annual influenza vaccine, and household contacts of infants 0 to 23 months of age should receive annual influenza vaccine.

Children in Residential Institutions

Children housed in institutions pose special problems for control of certain infectious diseases. Ensuring appropriate immunization is important because of the risk of transmission within the facility and because conditions that led to institutionalization may increase the risk of complications from the disease. All children entering a residential institution should have received recommended immunizations for their age (see Fig 1.1, p 26, and Table 1.7, p 28). If they have not been immunized appropriately, arrangements should be made to administer these immunizations as soon as possible. Staff members should be familiar with standard precautions and procedures for handling contaminated blood and body fluids as well as trauma with bleeding. For residents who acquire potentially transmissible infectious agents while living in an institution, isolation precautions similar to those recommended for hospitalized patients should be followed (see Infection Control for Hospitalized Children, p 153). Specific diseases of concern include the following (see the disease-specific chapters in Section 3 for detailed recommendations).

- **Measles**. Epidemics can occur among susceptible children in institutional settings. Recommendations for managing children in an institutional setting when a case of measles is recognized are as follows: (1) within 72 hours of exposure, administer live measles virus vaccine (as MMR) to all susceptible children 1 year of age or older for whom immunization is not contraindicated; and (2) administer IG to immunocompromised children (see Measles, p 441) as soon as possible and within 6 days of exposure to all exposed susceptible children younger than 1 year of age. These IG recipients also will require live-virus vaccine (as MMR vaccine) at 12 months of age or thereafter, depending on the age and dose of IG administration (see Table 3.32, p 445, for the appropriate interval between IG administration and MMR immunization).
- **Mumps**. Epidemics can occur among susceptible unimmunized children in institutions. Major hazards are disruption of activities, the need for acute nursing care in difficult settings, and occasional serious complications (eg, in susceptible adult staff).

  If mumps is introduced, prophylaxis is not available to limit the spread or to attenuate the disease in a susceptible person. Immune Globulin is not effective, and Mumps Immune Globulin is not available. Although mumps virus vaccine may not be effective after exposure, the vaccine should be administered to susceptible people to protect against infection from future exposures.
- **Influenza**. Influenza can be unusually severe in a residential or custodial institutional setting. Rapid spread, intensive exposure, and underlying disease can result

in a high risk of severe illness that may affect many residents simultaneously or in close sequence. Current measures for control of influenza in institutions include: (1) a program of annual influenza immunization of residents and staff; and (2) appropriate use of chemoprophylaxis during influenza epidemics (see Influenza, p 401).

- **Pertussis**. Because progressive developmental delay may have resulted in a deferral of pertussis immunization, many children in an institutional setting may not be appropriately immunized against pertussis. Because pertussis vaccine does not cause progressive neurologic disease and because pertussis disease poses a greater risk than does pertussis immunization, children who are not immunized fully and who are younger than 7 years of age or 11 years of age and older should be immunized against pertussis. If pertussis is recognized, infected people and their close contacts should receive chemoprophylaxis (see Pertussis, p 498).

- **Hepatitis A**. Outbreaks of hepatitis A affecting residents and staff can occur in institutions for custodial care by fecal-oral transmission. Infection usually is mild or asymptomatic in young children but can be severe in adults. Hepatitis A vaccine, in addition to IG, may be indicated for postexposure prophylaxis for staff and children 1 year of age or older in institutions in which a hepatitis A outbreak is occurring. If an outbreak occurs, susceptible residents and staff members in close personal contact with patients should receive IG (see Hepatitis A, p 326).

- **Hepatitis B**. Children living in residential institutions for children with developmental disabilities and their caregivers are assumed to be at increased risk of acquiring HBV infection. The high prevalence of markers of HBV infection among children living in these facilities indicates that HBV infections have the propensity for spread in an institutional setting, presumably by exposure to blood and body fluids containing HBV. Factors associated with high prevalence of HBV markers include crowding, high resident-to-staff ratios, and lack of in-service educational programs for staff. In the presence of such factors, the prevalence of HBV increases with the duration of time spent at the institution. Thus, susceptible residents entering or already residing and staff in institutions for children with developmental disabilities should be immunized against HBV; preimmunization serologic screening for HBV markers probably is not cost-effective.

  After parenteral or sexual exposure to an institutionalized patient recognized to be an HBsAg carrier, patients or staff members who are unimmunized and susceptible should receive active and passive immunoprophylaxis (see Hepatitis B, p 335, for recommendations for previously immunized individuals).

- **Pneumococcal Infections**. Children with severe physical or mental disabilities, particularly children who are bedridden, who suffer from a compromised respiratory status, or who are capable of only limited physical activity, may benefit from influenza vaccine and pneumococcal conjugate or polysaccharide vaccine (see Pneumococcal Infections, p 525).

- **Varicella**. Because varicella is highly contagious, disease can occur in a large proportion of susceptible people in an institutional setting. All healthy individuals 1 year of age or older who lack a reliable history of varicella disease or immunization should be immunized. In addition, during a varicella outbreak, a second dose of varicella vaccine is recommended for people who have received 1 dose of varicella vaccine, resources permitting, provided the appropriate interval has elapsed since the first dose (3 months for people 12 months through 12 years of age and at least 4 weeks for people 13 years of age and older). Passive immunization during outbreaks currently is recommended only for immunocompromised, susceptible children at risk of serious complications or death from varicella (see Varicella-Zoster Infections, p 711).

- **Other Infections.** Other organisms causing diseases that spread in institutions and for which no immunizations are available include *Shigella* species, *E coli* O157:H7, other enteric pathogens, *Streptococcus pyogenes*, *S aureus*, respiratory tract viruses, cytomegalovirus, scabies, and lice.

Children Living Outside the United States

In general, children of active-duty military personnel require the same immunizations as their civilian counterparts. If delay in pertussis immunization is recommended for any reason, parents should be warned that the risk of contracting the disease in countries where pertussis immunization is not administered routinely is significantly higher than that in countries where effective vaccine is used. For military dependents traveling internationally, the risk of exposure to HAV, HBV, measles, pertussis, diphtheria, poliovirus, yellow fever, Japanese encephalitis, and other infections may be increased and may necessitate additional immunizations (see International Travel, p 98). In these instances, the choice of immunizations will be dictated by the country of proposed residence, expected travel, and the age and health of the child. For information on the risk of specific diseases in different countries and preventive measures, see International Travel (p 98) or consult the CDC Web site (**www.cdc.gov/travel**) or the WHO Web site (**www.WHO.int/ith**).

Adolescent* and College Populations

Adolescents and young adults may not be protected against all vaccine-preventable diseases. This age group may include people who escaped natural infection and who (1) were not immunized with all recommended vaccines; (2) received appropriate vaccines but at too young an age (eg, measles vaccine before 12 months of age); (3) received incomplete immunization regimens (eg, only 1 or 2 doses of HBV vaccine); (4) failed to respond to vaccines administered at appropriate ages; or (5) have waned immunity despite appropriate immunization.

To ensure age-appropriate immunization, all children should have a routine appointment at 11 to 12 years of age for the following purposes: (1) to immunize people who previously have not received 2 doses of MMR vaccine; (2) to give varicella and/or hepatitis B vaccine and meningococcal conjugate vaccine as indicated; (3) to provide a dose of Tdap vaccine; and (4) to provide other immunizations and preventive services that are indicated. Additional vaccines that may be indicated at this preadolescent visit include influenza, pneumococcal, and hepatitis A vaccines. Specific indications for each of these vaccines are given in the respective disease-specific chapters in Section 3.

---

* Centers for Disease Control and Prevention. Vaccine-preventable diseases: improving vaccination coverage in children, adolescents, and adults. A report on recommendations from the Task Force on Community Preventive Services. *MMWR Recomm Rep*. 1999;48(RR-8):1–15

Appointments for needed doses of vaccines that are not administered during the aforementioned visit should be scheduled. During all subsequent adolescent visits, immunization status should be reviewed and deficiencies should be corrected, including completion of the 3-dose HBV vaccine series and administration of meningococcal conjugate vaccine and Tdap vaccine as recommended.

School immunization laws encourage "catch-up" programs for older adolescents. Accordingly, school and college health services should establish a system to ensure that all students are protected against vaccine-preventable diseases. Many colleges are implementing the American College Health Association (ACHA) recommendations for prematriculation immunization requirements, mandating protection against measles, mumps, rubella, tetanus, diphtheria, polio, varicella, and HBV (**www.acha.org**). In addition, *N meningitidis* vaccine is required by some colleges and universities; many states have laws requiring prematriculation immunization (**www.immunize.org/ laws**). Meningococcal conjugate vaccine is preferred, but meningococcal polysaccharide vaccine also is acceptable.

- *Measles*. In the 1990s, many colleges and universities experienced measles outbreaks; such outbreaks could recur if the proportion of susceptible people increases. Additionally, students traveling internationally have been victims of measles and sources of importation into the United States. To prevent measles outbreaks and ensure high levels of immunity among young adults on college and university campuses, the ACHA has recommended that colleges and universities require 2 doses of measles vaccine as a condition for matriculation. The first dose must have been given on or after the first birthday; the interval between the first and second dose must have been at least 1 month. Similarly, in postsecondary school educational settings, the AAP recommends a 2-dose measles immunization schedule, given as MMR vaccine, for people born in 1957 or after.
- *Rubella*. Adolescents and adults should be considered susceptible to rubella if documentation of receipt of one dose of vaccine or serologic evidence of antibody is lacking. Immunizing susceptible adolescents and adults in college decreases the chance of outbreaks and helps to prevent congenital rubella syndrome.
- *Varicella*. Varicella immunity is desirable in adolescents and adults, especially adults in colleges and universities and women of childbearing age. Adults, adolescents, and children with a reliable history of varicella disease can be assumed to be immune, and immunization is not necessary. Because approximately 70% to 90% of people 18 years of age or older without a reliable history of varicella disease also will be immune and because 2 doses of vaccine are needed for people 13 years of age and older, serologic testing of people 13 years of age or older and immunization of people who are seronegative may be cost-effective. If serologic testing is performed, a tracking system to access seronegative people should be in place to ensure that susceptible people are immunized. However, serologic testing is not required, because varicella vaccine is well tolerated in people who are immune from immunization or previous disease. In many situations, especially for young adolescents, universal immunization rather than serologic testing and tracking may be easier to implement. People older than 12 years of age will require 2 doses of vaccine separated by 4 to 8 weeks.

- *Hepatitis B*. Hepatitis B virus vaccine is recommended for administration to all susceptible adolescents, especially adolescents who have one or more risk factors for HBV infection. Risk factors include multiple sexual partners (defined as more than 1 partner within the previous 6 months), a sexually transmitted disease, sexually active homosexual or bisexual behavior, injection drug use, institutionalization or incarceration, and occupation or training involving contact with blood or body fluids. In 2005, the ACIP recommended that unimmunized adults at high risk and all adults seeking protection from hepatitis B should be immunized.
- *Diphtheria, Tetanus, and Pertussis*. Adolescents 11 to 18 years of age should receive a single dose of Tdap instead of Td vaccine for booster immunization. For complete recommendations, see Pertussis, p 498.
- *Influenza*. Epidemic influenza can affect any closed population. Physicians responsible for health care in schools and colleges should consider annual influenza immunization of students, particularly students residing in dormitories or students who are members of athletic teams, to decrease morbidity and to minimize disruption of routine activities during epidemics. Students with chronic medical conditions should be immunized annually (see Influenza, p 401).
- **Neisseria meningitidis**. Immunization of college freshmen living in dormitories is recommended by the AAP and the ACIP. Because of the feasibility constraints of targeting freshmen in dormitories, colleges may elect to target all matriculating freshmen. Use of meningococcal conjugate vaccine (MCV4) is preferred; but if MCV4 is unavailable, meningococcal polysaccharide vaccine is an acceptable alternative (see Meningococcal Infections, p 452).
- *Other recommendations*. Because adolescents and young adults commonly travel internationally, their immunization status and travel plans should be reviewed 2 or more months before departure to allow time to administer any needed vaccines (see International Travel, p 98).

Some physicians are unaware that adolescents and young adults have risks of vaccine-preventable diseases and do not give priority to immunization. Pediatricians should assist in providing information on benefits and risks of immunization. People with religious or philosophic exemptions have been victims and sources of vaccine-preventable diseases. Therefore, reasons for and risks of administering recommended vaccines should be reviewed, refusal should be documented, and the importance of immunization should be emphasized.

The possible occurrence of diseases such as measles, mumps, rubella, hepatitis A, hepatitis B, pertussis, influenza, and *N meningitidis* infections in a school or college should be reported promptly to local health officials according to individual state guidelines.

Health Care Personnel*

Adults whose occupations place them in contact with patients with contagious diseases are at increased risk of contracting vaccine-preventable diseases and, if infected, transmitting them to their patients. All health care personnel should protect them-

---

* Centers for Disease Control and Prevention. Immunization of health-care workers: recommendations of the Advisory Committee on Immunization Practices (ACIP) and the Hospital Infection Control Practices Advisory Committee (HICPAC). *MMWR*. 1997;46(RR-18):1–42

selves and susceptible patients by receiving appropriate immunizations. Physicians, health care facilities, and schools for health care professionals should play an active role in implementing these policies. Vaccine-preventable infections of special concern to people involved in the health care of children are as follows (see the disease-specific chapters in Section 3 for further recommendations).

- **Rubella**. Outbreaks of rubella among health care personnel have been reported. Although the disease is mild in adults, the risk to a fetus necessitates documentation of rubella immunity in health care personnel of both sexes. People should be considered immune on the basis of serologic tests or documented proof of rubella immunization on or after the first birthday. A history of rubella disease is unreliable and should not be used in determining immune status. All susceptible people should be immunized with MMR vaccine (or monocomponent rubella vaccine if immunity to measles and mumps has been documented) before initial or continuing contact with pregnant patients.

- **Measles**. Because measles in health care personnel has contributed to spread of this disease during outbreaks, evidence of immunity to measles should be required for health care personnel born after 1957. Proof of immunity is established by physician-documented measles, a positive serologic test for measles antibody, or documented receipt of 2 doses of live-virus measles vaccine, the first of which is given on or after the first birthday. Health care personnel born before 1957 generally have been considered immune to measles. However, because measles cases have occurred in health care personnel in this age group, health care facilities should consider offering at least 1 dose of measles-containing vaccine to workers who lack proof of immunity to measles, particularly in communities with documented measles outbreaks.

- **Mumps**. Transmission of mumps in health care facilities can be disruptive and costly. Adults born before 1957 generally have been considered immune to mumps; adults born in 1957 or after are considered immune if they have documentation of a single dose of mumps vaccine received on or after their first birthday or laboratory evidence of immunity.

- **Hepatitis B**. Vaccine is recommended for all health care personnel who are likely to be exposed to blood or blood-containing body fluids. The Occupational Safety and Health Administration of the US Department of Labor has issued a regulation requiring employers of workers at risk of occupational exposure to HBV to offer HBV immunization to employees at the employer's expense. Employees who refuse recommended immunizations should sign a refusal document.

  In some cases, susceptible health care personnel immunized appropriately with HBV vaccines fail to develop serologic evidence of immunity against HBsAg (anti-HBs). Serologic evidence of immunity is defined as serum anti-HBs concentration ≥ 10 mIU/mL. People who do not respond to the primary immunization series should complete a second 3-dose vaccine series with reevaluation of anti-HBs titers 1 to 2 months after the series is completed. People who do not respond to the second series and are HBsAg negative should be considered susceptible to HBV infection and need to receive HBIG prophylaxis for any known or probable exposure to blood or body fluids infected with HBV.*

---

* Hepatitis B virus infection: a comprehensive immunization strategy to eliminate transmission in the US. Part II: immunization of adults. *MMWR*. 2006; in press (see **www.cdc.gov/mmwr**)

- *Influenza*. Certain groups of patients, such as people with chronic cardiovascular or pulmonary disease, are at increased risk of serious or complicated influenza infection. Because health care personnel can transmit influenza to their patients and nosocomial outbreaks can occur, influenza immunization should be recommended and encouraged for all hospital personnel and other health care professionals with direct patient contact each autumn. Influenza vaccine should be available to personnel on all shifts in a convenient manner and location, such as through use of mobile immunization carts.
- *Varicella*. Proof of varicella immunity is recommended for all health care personnel. In health care institutions, serologic screening of personnel who have an uncorroborated negative or uncertain history of varicella before immunization is likely to be cost-effective but need not be done. Varicella immunization is recommended for all immunocompetent people.
- *Tuberculosis*.* Early detection and treatment of patients (or visitors) with communicable tuberculosis is recommended to prevent tuberculosis infection in health care personnel. The risk of transmission of tuberculosis in hospitals varies greatly and is determined by local epidemiologic data. Policies for tuberculin skin testing for health care personnel should conform to CDC guidelines. According to current CDC recommendations, BCG immunization should be considered on an individual basis in settings with a high prevalence of multidrug-resistant *Mycobacterium tuberculosis* infection, in situations in which transmission of resistant organisms is likely, and in facilities where comprehensive infection-control precautions against *M tuberculosis* transmission have been implemented and have failed.†

Refugees and Immigrants

Prevention of infectious diseases in refugee and immigrant children presents special challenges because of the diseases to which these children may have been exposed and the different immunization practices in their native countries. In addition, other aspects of providing care to immigrant, refugee, homeless, and immigrant children should be considered.‡ Since 1996, people seeking an immigrant visa for permanent residency must show proof of receipt of at least the first dose of all vaccines in the recommended immunization series. Although these regulations apply to most immigrant children entering the United States, internationally adopted children who are younger than 10 years of age are exempt from these requirements. Adoptive parents are required to sign a waiver indicating their intention to comply with the ACIP immunization requirements after the child's arrival in the United States. Refugees are not required to meet immunization requirements of the Immigration and Nationality

---

* Centers for Disease Control and Prevention. Controlling tuberculosis in the United States: recommendations from the American Thoracic Society, CDC, and the Infectious Diseases Society of America. *MMWR Recomm Rep*. 2005;54(RR-12):1–81

† Centers for Disease Control and Prevention. The role of BCG vaccine in the prevention and control of tuberculosis in the United States: a joint statement by the Advisory Council for the Elimination of Tuberculosis and the Advisory Committee on Immunization Practices. *MMWR Recomm Rep*. 1996;45(RR-4):1–18

‡ American Academy of Pediatrics, Committee on Community Health Services. Providing care for immigrant, homeless, and migrant children. *Pediatrics*. 2005;115:1095–1100

Act at the time of initial entry into the United States but must show proof of immunization when they apply for permanent residency, typically within 3 years of arrival.

Children who have resided in refugee processing camps for a few months often have had access to medical and treatment services, which may have included some immunizations. However, these children almost universally are incompletely immunized and often have no immunization records. For refugee children whose immunizations are not up-to-date, as documented by a written immunization record (see Immunizations Received Outside the United States, p 35), vaccines as recommended for their age should be administered (see Fig 1.1, p 26, and Table 1.7, p 28). For children without documentation of immunizations, a new vaccine schedule may be initiated. Alternatively, measurement of antibody concentrations to diphtheria, tetanus, measles, mumps, rubella, varicella, and poliovirus (each serotype) and anti-HBs as well as HBsAg and anti-HBc, if from an area with endemic hepatitis B infection, may be considered to determine whether the child needs additional immunizations or initiation of the immunization schedule appropriate for that child's age (see Table 2.18, Approaches to the Evaluation and Immunization of Internationally Adopted Children, p 189). Although many children will have received DTP, poliovirus, measles, and hepatitis B vaccines, most will not have received Hib, pneumococcal, hepatitis A, rubella, mumps, and varicella vaccines. Measles antibody may be measured to determine whether the child is immune; however, many children may need a dose of mumps and rubella vaccines, because these vaccines are not given routinely in developing countries. A clinical diagnosis of rubella without serologic testing should not be accepted as evidence of rubella immunity. Varicella vaccine is not administered in most countries, and history of varicella infection may be unavailable or unreliable in these populations; therefore, children should be immunized for varicella or have antibody testing performed.

All refugees and immigrants from areas with endemic hepatitis B infection, particularly Asia and Africa, should be screened for hepatitis B with serologic tests for HBsAg, anti-HBs, and antibody to hepatitis B core antigen (anti-HBc). A child who tests positively for HBsAg has active infection and may be defined as a chronic carrier if the HBsAg persists for longer than 6 months. Most children who are HBsAg carriers are asymptomatic. Therefore, screening is important to identify children who need follow-up and management and to limit transmission of disease. Transmission risks should be minimal among children in the United States because of universal infant HBV immunization programs. However, adult caregivers may be unimmunized and should be given hepatitis B vaccine if they are susceptible and HBIG if they have had a significant exposure to blood of a carrier (see Hepatitis B, p 335). Serologic screening of all pregnant refugees and immigrants for HBsAg is imperative to identify women whose infants need passive as well as active immunoprophylaxis.

Tuberculosis and HIV infection also are important public health concerns, because many refugees and immigrants come from countries with high prevalences of tuberculosis and HIV infection. Tuberculosis cases in foreign-born people now account for more than 50% of all tuberculosis cases in the United States. Although tuberculosis rates have decreased among children born in the United States in the last decade, rates remain high among children from developing countries. The risk of

HIV infection among refugees and immigrants depends on the country of origin and on individual risk factors, especially among vulnerable refugee populations. The decision to screen children for HIV should depend on history and risk factors (eg, receipt of blood products, maternal drug use), physical examination findings, and prevalence of HIV infection in the child's country of origin. If there is a suspicion of HIV infection, testing should be performed before administration of live vaccines.

International Travel

Children and adolescents should be up-to-date on routinely recommended immunizations before international travel. In addition, travel requires consideration of additional vaccines to prevent hepatitis A, yellow fever, meningococcal disease, typhoid fever, cholera, rabies, and Japanese encephalitis. Vaccines may be required or recommended depending on the destination and type of international travel (see Table 1.15, p 21). Travelers to tropical and subtropical areas often risk exposure to malaria, dengue fever, other vectorborne pathogens, leptospirosis, diarrhea, and other diseases for which vaccines are not available. For travelers to areas with endemic malaria, antimalarial chemoprophylaxis and insect precautions are vitally important (see Malaria, p 435). Attention to hand hygiene and choosing safer foods and beverages for consumption also can reduce travelers' risk of acquiring other communicable diseases.

Up-to-date information, including alerts about current disease outbreaks that may affect international travelers, is available on the CDC Travelers' Health Web site at **www.cdc.gov/travel** or the WHO Web site at **www.who.intl/ith/**. *Health Information for International Travel* (the "Yellow Book") is published every 2 years by the CDC and is an excellent reference for travelers and for practitioners who advise international travelers of health risks. To enhance the usefulness of travel notices, the CDC Travelers' Health Web site issues and removes travel notices under 1 of 4 levels: in the news, outbreak notice, travel health precaution, and travel health warning. Travel information and recommendations can be obtained from the CDC by fax (888-232-3299) or telephone recording (877-394-8747, or 877-FYI-TRIP). Local and state health departments and travel clinics also can provide updated information. Information about cruise ship sanitation inspection scores and reports can be found at **www2.cdc.gov/nceh/vsp/vspmain.asp/**.

RECOMMENDED IMMUNIZATIONS

Infants and children embarking on international travel should be up-to-date on receipt of immunizations recommended for their age. For travel to many countries with highly endemic rates of hepatitis A infection, HAV immunization also may be recommended (see Hepatitis A, p 326). Duration of travel is only one indicator of risk of acquiring infections. Depending on the situation, people can be at high risk even if their stay in the area with endemic infection is brief. Destination, activities, and exposures, as well as host factors, are important in deciding whether to immunize against certain diseases. To optimize immunity before departure, vaccines may need to be given on an accelerated schedule (see Table 1.15, p 99).

Worldwide poliovirus eradication efforts have decreased the number of countries where travelers are at risk of poliovirus infection. Most wild-type poliovirus is found in 6 countries: Afghanistan, India, Pakistan, Nigeria, Niger, and Egypt. The Western

Table 1.15. Recommended Immunizations for Travelers to Developing Countries[1]

Immunizations	Brief, <2 wk	Intermediate, 2 wk to 3 mo	Long-term Residential, >3 mo
Review and complete age-appropriate childhood schedule (see text for details)	+	+	+
• DTaP, poliovirus, pneumococcal, and *Haemophilus influenzae* type b vaccines may be given at 4-wk intervals if necessary to complete the recommended schedule before departure			
• Measles: 2 additional doses given if younger than 12 mo of age at first dose			
• Varicella			
• Hepatitis B[2]			
Yellow fever[3]	+	+	+
Hepatitis A[4]	+	+	+
Typhoid fever[5]	±	+	+
Meningococcal disease[6]	±	±	±
Rabies[7]	±	+	+
Japanese encephalitis[8]	±	±	+

DTaP indicates diphtheria and tetanus toxoids and acellular pertussis; +, recommended; ±, consider.

[1] See disease-specific chapters in Section 3 for details. For further sources of information, see text.

[2] If insufficient time to complete 6-month primary series, accelerated series can be given (see text for details).

[3] For regions with endemic infection (see Health Information for International Travel, p 3).

[4] Indicated for travelers to areas with intermediate or high endemic rates of HAV infection.

[5] Indicated for travelers who will consume food and liquids in areas of poor sanitation.

[6] Recommended for regions of Africa with endemic infection and during local epidemics, and required for travel to Saudi Arabia for the Hajj.

[7] Indicated for people with high risk of animal exposure (especially to dogs) and for travelers to countries with endemic infection.

[8] For regions with endemic infection (see Health Information for International Travel, p 3). For high-risk activities in areas experiencing outbreaks, vaccine is recommended, even for brief travel.

Hemisphere was declared free of wild-type poliovirus in 1994, and the Western Pacific Region was declared free in 2000. The finding of vaccine-derived poliovirus (VDPV) in stool samples from several asymptomatic unimmunized people in a community is the first occurrence of VDPV transmission in a community in the United States since OPV immunizations were discontinued in 2000.* This finding raises

* Centers for Disease Control and Prevention. Poliovirus infections in four unvaccinated children-Minnesota, August–October 2005. *MMWR Morb Mortal Wkly Rep.* 2005;54:1053–1055

concerns about the risk of transmission to other communities with a low level of transmission and the risk of a polio outbreak occurring in the United States. To ensure protection, all children, including pediatric travelers, should be fully immunized against poliovirus. Three doses of IPV vaccine should be administered before departure as shown in the Recommended Childhood and Adolescent Immunization Schedule (Fig 1.1, p 26). If necessary, the doses may be given at 4-week intervals, although 6- to 8-week intervals are preferred. Children should receive a supplemental fourth dose at 4 to 6 years of age (see Poliovirus Infections, p 542).

Importation of measles remains an important source for measles cases in the United States. Therefore, people traveling abroad should be immune to measles to provide personal protection and minimize importation of measles. People should be considered susceptible to measles unless they have documentation of appropriate immunization, physician-diagnosed measles, or laboratory evidence of immunity to measles or were born in the United States before 1957. For people born in the United States in 1957 or after, 2 doses of measles vaccine, the first administered at or after 12 months of age, are required to ensure immunity (see Measles, p 441). The age of initiation of measles immunization can be lowered for children traveling to areas with a high rate of measles transmission. Infants 6 to 11 months of age should receive 1 dose of a measles-containing vaccine, preferably monovalent if available. Children receiving measles vaccine before 12 months of age require 2 additional doses of a measles-containing vaccine separated by at least 1 month starting at 12 to 15 months of age.

Hepatitis B vaccine is recommended routinely for all children in the United States but should be considered for susceptible travelers of all ages visiting areas where hepatitis B infection is highly endemic, such as countries in Asia, Africa, and some parts of South America (see Hepatitis B, p 335). Risk factors for hepatitis B infection include close contact with the local population for a prolonged period (>6 months), contact with blood or blood-containing body fluids, or sexual contact with residents of these areas. An accelerated dosing schedule is licensed for one hepatitis B vaccine (Engerix-B), during which the first 3 doses are given at 0, 1, and 2 months. This schedule may benefit travelers who have insufficient time (ie, <6 months) to complete a standard 3-dose schedule before departure. If the accelerated schedule is used, a fourth dose should be given 12 months after the third dose (see Hepatitis B, p 335).

REQUIRED OR RECOMMENDED TRAVEL-RELATED IMMUNIZATIONS

Depending on the destination, planned activity, and length of stay, other immunizations may be required or recommended (see Table 1.15, p 99, and disease-specific chapters in Section 3).

Immunoprophylaxis against HAV infection is indicated for susceptible people traveling internationally to areas with intermediate or high rates of HAV infection. These include all areas of the world except Australia, Canada, Japan, New Zealand, and Western Europe. Inactivated vaccines and intramuscular IG are effective for immunoprophylaxis; however, only inactivated vaccines will provide long-term protection. For people 1 year of age and older, vaccine is preferred. To ensure immediate protection for people whose departure is imminent, IG and vaccine may be given concurrently at different sites (see Hepatitis A, p 326). For children younger than 1 year of age, IG is indicated, because HAV vaccine is not licensed in the United States for use in this age group. Simultaneous administration of IG may interfere with the immune response to varicella and MMR vaccines.

Yellow fever vaccine, a live-attenuated virus vaccine, is required by some countries as a condition of entry, including travelers arriving from regions with endemic infection.* The vaccine is available in the United States only in centers designated by state health departments. Current requirements and recommendations for yellow fever immunization based on travel destination can be obtained from the CDC Travelers' Health Web site (**www.cdc.gov/travel**) or from the CDC Yellow Book, *Health Information for International Travel*. Yellow fever occurs year-round in predominantly rural areas of sub-Saharan Africa and South America; in recent years, outbreaks have been increasing, including in some urban areas. Although rare, yellow fever continues to be reported among travelers, particularly unimmunized travelers, and may be fatal. Prevention measures against yellow fever should include immunization and protection against mosquitoes (see Prevention of Mosquitoborne Infections, p 197). Yellow fever vaccine generally is considered to be a safe and effective vaccine. However, the vaccine rarely has been found to be associated with a risk of viscerotropic disease (multiple organ system failure) and neurotropic disease (postvaccinal encephalitis). There is increased risk of adverse events in individuals of any age with thymic dysfunction and people older than 60 years of age. The vaccine should not be used in children younger than 6 months of age and should be used with caution in children younger than 9 months of age and only after consultation with a travel medicine expert and/ or the CDC Vector-Borne Diseases Branch (970-221-6400) to weigh risks and benefits (ie, consider immunization if travel to an area of ongoing yellow fever transmission cannot be avoided and a high level of protection against mosquito bites is not possible). Whenever possible, immunization should be delayed until 9 months of age to minimize the risk of vaccine-associated encephalitis. Medical waivers can be given to children who are too young for immunization and to people who have other contraindications to immunization, such as immunodeficiency. The CDC has stated that, given the risk of serious illness and death attributable to yellow fever, evidence of increasing transmission of the disease, and the known effectiveness of the vaccine, clinicians should continue to use yellow fever vaccine to protect travelers. However, the CDC recommends that health care professionals carefully review travel itineraries so that only people traveling to areas with endemic yellow fever infection or areas where there is reported yellow fever activity receive yellow fever vaccine.

The whole-cell inactivated cholera vaccine no longer is produced in the United States. According to WHO regulations, no country may require cholera immunization as a condition for entry. However, despite WHO recommendations, some local authorities may require documentation of immunization. In such cases, a notation of vaccine contraindication should be sufficient to satisfy local requirements.

Typhoid vaccine is recommended for travelers who may be exposed to contaminated food or water. In particular, people with anticipated long-term travel or resi-

---

* Centers for Disease Control and Prevention. Yellow fever vaccine. Recommendations of the Advisory Committee on Immunization Practices, 2002. *MMWR Recomm Rep.* 2002;51(RR-17):1–10

dence in areas with poor sanitation and people who visit remote areas are at greatest risk. Two typhoid vaccines are available for civilian use in the United States: an oral vaccine containing live-attenuated *S typhi* (Ty21a strain) and a parenteral Vi capsular polysaccharide (ViCPS) vaccine. For specific recommendations, see *Salmonella* Infections (p 579). Because antimicrobial agents and the antimalarial drug mefloquine (but not chloroquine) can inhibit the growth of the vaccine strain of *S typhi*, the orally administered vaccine should be given at least 24 hours before or after administration of any of these agents. The oral vaccine capsules need to be refrigerated. Because the vaccine is not completely efficacious, typhoid immunization is not a substitute for careful selection of food and drink.

Meningococcal tetravalent (groups A, C, Y, and W-135) vaccine (polysaccharide or conjugate) should be offered for travelers to areas where epidemics of meningococcal infection occur frequently, such as sub-Saharan Africa, and countries with current meningococcal epidemics. Saudi Arabia requires a certificate of immunization for pilgrims to Mecca or Medina, where outbreaks with serogroups A and W-135 have been reported in travelers participating in the Hajj.

Rabies immunization should be considered for children who will be traveling to areas where they may encounter wild or domestic animals (particularly dogs in developing countries) or where they may engage in activities involving increased risk of rabies transmission (eg, spelunking and camping). The 3-dose preexposure series is given by IM injection (see Rabies, p 552). In the event of a bite by a potentially rabid animal, all travelers (whether they have received preexposure rabies vaccine or not) should be counseled to clean the wound thoroughly with soap and water and then promptly receive postexposure treatment, including booster doses of rabies vaccine.

Japanese encephalitis virus, which is spread primarily by dusk-to-dawn-biting *Culex* species mosquitoes, is a potential risk in Southeast Asia, China, eastern Russia, and the Indian subcontinent. Vaccine should be offered to travelers with prolonged residence ($\geq$4 weeks) in areas where Japanese encephalitis is endemic or epidemic (particularly rural farming areas) during transmission season and to travelers who will engage in high-risk activities with extensive outdoor exposure, such as camping, bicycling, and field work, regardless of the duration of travel. Geographic and seasonal risks are discussed on the CDC Travelers' Health Web site. Because potentially severe immediate and delayed allergic reactions to Japanese encephalitis vaccine occur in approximately 0.5% of vaccine recipients, potential benefits and risks of vaccine use should be considered. Data are not available on vaccine safety and efficacy in infants younger than 1 year of age. Immunization requires 3 doses administered subcutaneously on days 0, 7, and 30 and should be completed at least 10 days before travel to an area with endemic infection so the patient may be observed for potential delayed allergic reactions. If time constraints necessitate an abbreviated schedule, vaccine can be given at 0, 7, and 14 days (see Arboviruses, p 211).

In addition to routine annual influenza immunization, vaccine may be warranted for international travelers, depending on the destination, duration of travel, risk of acquisition of disease (in part on the basis of the season of the year), and the traveler's underlying health status. Because the influenza season is different in the northern and southern hemispheres and epidemic strains may differ, the antigenic composition of influenza vaccines used in North America may be different from those used in the southern hemisphere, and timing of administration may vary (see Influenza, p 401).

The risk of acquiring latent tuberculosis infection (LTBI) during international travel depends on the activities of the traveler and the epidemiology of tuberculosis in the areas in which travel occurs. In general, the risk of acquiring LTBI during usual tourism activities appears to be low, and no pre- or post-travel testing is recommended routinely. When travelers live or work among the general population of a high-prevalence country, the risk may be appreciably higher. In most high-prevalence countries, contact investigation of tuberculosis cases is not performed, and treatment of LTBI is not available. Children returning to the United States who have signs or symptoms compatible with tuberculosis should be evaluated appropriately for tuberculosis disease. It may be prudent to perform a tuberculin skin test 8 to 12 weeks after return for children who spent ≥6 months in a high-prevalence country. Pre-travel administration of BCG vaccine generally is not recommended. However, some countries may require BCG vaccine for issuance of work and residency permits for expatriate workers and their families.

OTHER CONSIDERATIONS. In addition to vaccine-preventable diseases, travelers to the tropics will be exposed to other diseases, such as malaria, which can be life threatening. Prevention strategies for malaria are twofold: prevention of mosquito bites and use of antimalarial chemoprophylaxis. For recommendations on appropriate use of chemoprophylaxis, including recommendations for pregnant women, infants, and breastfeeding mothers, see Malaria (p 435). Prevention of mosquito bites will decrease the risk of malaria, dengue fever, and other mosquito-transmitted diseases (see Prevention of Mosquitoborne Infections, p 197). Appropriate personal protective measures, particularly during the malaria mosquito-biting period from dusk to dawn, can be highly effective. These preventive measures include wearing long-sleeved shirts and long trousers; application of insect repellent, such as diethyltoluamide (DEET), to exposed skin; and use of window screens and bed nets. Insect sprays and soaks containing the residual insecticide permethrin may be applied to clothing and bed nets.

Traveler's diarrhea is a significant problem that may be mitigated by attention to foods and beverages ingested and appropriately treating suspected water sources. Chemoprophylaxis generally is not recommended. Educating families about self-treatment, particularly oral rehydration, is critical. Packets of oral rehydration salts can be obtained before travel or are readily available in most pharmacies throughout the world, especially developing countries where diarrheal diseases are most common. During international travel, families may want to carry an antimicrobial agent (eg, fluoroquinolone for those 16 years of age and older and azithromycin for younger children) for treatment of significant diarrheal symptoms. Antimotility agents may be considered for older children and adolescents (see *Escherichia coli* Diarrhea, p 291) but should not be used if diarrhea is bloody.

Travelers should be aware of potential acquisition of respiratory tract viruses, such as severe acute respiratory syndrome (SARS) and avian influenza. They should be counseled on hand hygiene and avoidance of close contact with animals (dead or live). Swimming, other recreational water sports, and ecotourism carry risks of acquisition of infections from environmental contamination.

Recommendations for Care of Children in Special Circumstances

••
BIOLOGICAL TERRORISM

Some infectious agents have the potential to be used in acts of bioterrorism. The Centers for Disease Control and Prevention (CDC) has designated 3 categories of biological agents according to their potential as weapons of terrorism* and has described the relationships between the CDC, medical examiners and coroners, public health departments, emergency management agencies, emergency operations centers, and the Incident Command System.† The highest-priority agents are designated category A, because they can be disseminated or transmitted person-to-person easily, cause high rates of mortality with potential for major public health effects, could cause public panic and social disruption, and require special action for public health preparedness. Category A agents include organisms that cause anthrax, smallpox, plague, tularemia, botulism, and viral hemorrhagic fevers, including Ebola, Marburg, Lassa, Junin, and other related viruses. Category B agents are moderately easy to disseminate, cause moderate morbidity and low mortality rates, and require enhanced diagnostic capacity and disease surveillance. These agents include *Coxiella burnetti* (Q fever), *Brucella* species (brucellosis), *Burkholderia mallei* (glanders), alphaviruses (Venezuelan equine, eastern equine, and western equine encephalomyelitis occur in the United States), *Rickettsia prowazekii* (typhus), *Chlamydophila psittaci* (psittacosis), ricin toxin from *Ricinus communis* (castor beans), epsilon toxin of *Clostridium perfringens*, and *Staphylococcus* enterotoxin B. Additional category B agents that are foodborne or waterborne include, but are not limited to, *Salmonella* species, *Shigella dysenteriae*, *Escherichia coli* O157:H7, *Vibrio cholerae*, and *Cryptosporidium parvum*. Category C agents include emerging pathogens that could be engineered for mass dissemination in the future because of availability, ease of production and dissemination, and potential for high morbidity and mortality rates and major health effects. These include Nipah virus, hantavirus, tickborne hemorrhagic fever viruses, tickborne encephalitis viruses, yellow fever virus, and multidrug-resistant *Mycobacterium tuberculosis*.

Children may be particularly vulnerable to a bioterrorist attack, because children have a more rapid respiratory rate, increased skin permeability, higher ratio of skin surface area to mass, and less fluid reserve compared with adults. Accurate and rapid diagnosis may be more difficult in children because of their inability to describe symptoms. In addition, the adults on whom children depend for their health and safety may become ill or require quarantine during a bioterrorist event. Many preventive and therapeutic agents recommended for adults exposed or potentially

---

* Centers for Disease Control and Prevention. Biological and chemical terrorism: strategic plan for preparedness and response. Recommendations of the CDC Strategic Planning Workgroup. *MMWR Recomm Rep.* 2000;49(RR-4):1–14
† Nolte KB, Hanzlick RL, Payne DC, et al. Medical examiners, coroners, and biologic terrorism. *MMWR Recomm Rep.* 2004;53(RR-8):1–27

exposed to agents of bioterrorism have not been studied in infants and children, and pediatric doses have not been established.* In addition, parents, pediatricians, and other adults should be cognizant of the psychological responses of children to a disaster or terrorist incident to reduce the possibility of long-term psychological morbidity.†

Fever, malaise, headache, vomiting, and diarrhea are common early manifestations of many infectious diseases. Table 2.1 (p 107) describes typical distinctive signs and symptoms, incubation periods, diagnostic tests, isolation, and recommended treatment and prophylaxis for biological agents included in the CDC's category A and category B lists. More extensive discussion of the clinical illnesses associated with these agents can be found in the disease-specific chapters in Section 3. Table 2.2 (p 112) lists resources, including telephone numbers and Internet sites, that provide updated information concerning clinical recognition, prevention, diagnosis, and treatment of illness caused by potential agents of bioterrorism.

When clinicians suspect that illness is caused by an act of biological terrorism, they should contact their local and state public health authorities immediately so that appropriate infection control measures and outbreak investigations can begin. In the event of a biological terrorist attack, clinicians should check the CDC Emergency Preparedness and Response Web site (**www.bt.cdc.gov**) for current information and specific prophylaxis and treatment guidelines. Public health authorities should be contacted before obtaining and submitting patient specimens for identification of suspected agents of bioterrorism.

The AAP has prepared a policy statement outlining recommendations to pediatricians and the government to ensure that the needs of children and families are met in the event of chemical or biological terrorism.[3]

BLOOD SAFETY: REDUCING THE RISK OF TRANSFUSION-TRANSMITTED INFECTIONS

In the United States, the risk of transmission of infectious agents through transfusion of blood components (Red Blood Cells, Platelets, and Plasma) and plasma derivatives (clotting factor concentrates, immune globulins, and protein-containing plasma volume expanders) is extremely low. Nevertheless, continued vigilance, including improved surveillance and reporting, is crucial because there is no uniform system for transfusion reaction surveillance in the United States, and the blood supply remains vulnerable to organisms associated with newly identified or emerging infections. This chapter will review blood and plasma collection procedures in the United States, factors that have contributed to enhancing the safety of the blood supply, some of the known and emerging infectious agents and related blood safety concerns, and approaches to decreasing the risk of transfusion-transmitted infections.

---

* American Academy of Pediatrics, Committee on Environmental Health and Committee on Infectious Diseases. Chemical-biological terrorism and its impact on children. *Pediatrics*. 2006; in press

† Hagan JF Jr, and American Academy of Pediatrics, Committee on Psychosocial Aspects of Child and Family Health. Psychosocial implications of disaster or terrorism on children: a guide for the pediatrician. *Pediatrics*. 2005;116:787–795

Table 2.1. Biological Weapons: Recommended Diagnostic Procedures, Isolation Precautions, and Treatment and Prophylaxis of Children

Agent	Incubation Period	Diagnostic Specimen(s)[1]	Isolation Precautions	Treatment Options	Postexposure Prophylaxis[2]	Distinctive Findings	Comments
Alpha-viruses (see Table 3.3, p 214)	2–10 days	CSF for viral isolation, anti-body detection in CSF and acute and convalescent serum	Standard; respiratory precautions for western equine encephalitis virus	Supportive		Acute febrile illness with headache, vomiting, encephalopathy	
Anthrax	1–60 days	Gram stain of buffy coat, CSF, pleural fluid, swab of skin lesion; culture of blood, CSF, pleural fluid, skin biopsy	Standard; contact for skin lesions	Ciprofloxacin[3] or doxycycline[4]; combine with 1 or 2 additional antimicrobial agents for inhalational, gastrointestinal, or oropharyngeal disease[5]	Ciprofloxacin[3] or doxycycline[4] or amoxicillin[6]; anthrax vaccine	*Inhalational:* Fever, chest pain, dyspnea, hypoxia ± hemoptysis, with chest radiograph demonstrating widened mediastinum. *Cutaneous:* Vesicular lesion, which develops into necrotic ulceration with black eschar	Additional antimicrobial agents to be used for inhalational, gastrointestinal, or oropharyngeal disease include rifampin, vancomycin, penicillin, ampicillin, chloramphenicol, imipenem, clindamycin, and clarithromycin
Botulism	Foodborne: 2 h–8 days; inhalational: 24–72 h	Toxin detection from serum, stool, enema fluid, gastric fluid, vomitus, or suspected food samples; culture of stool or gastric secretions; nerve conduction testing	Standard	Supportive care; mechanical ventilation and parenteral nutrition may be required. Equine botulism antitoxin given as soon as possible (CDC)[7]	Type-specific antitoxin should be administered if available; antitoxin prevents additional nerve damage but does not reverse existing paralysis	Descending flaccid paralysis, which begins with dysphagia, dysarthria, diplopia, dysphonia, and ptosis	

Table 2.1. Biological Weapons: Recommended Diagnostic Procedures, Isolation Precautions, and Treatment and Prophylaxis of Children, continued

Agent	Incubation Period	Diagnostic Specimen(s)[1]	Isolation Precautions	Treatment Options	Postexposure Prophylaxis	Distinctive Findings	Comments
Brucellosis	5–60 days	Culture of blood or bone marrow; acute and convalescent serum for antibody testing	Standard; contact for draining skin lesions	Doxycycline[4] and rifampin; if younger than 8 years of age, use trimethoprim-sulfamethoxazole (TMP-SMX)	Doxycycline[4] and rifampin	Fever, sweats, malaise, headache, myalgia, which may be accompanied by focal involvement of meninges, heart, and/or bone	TMP-SMX may substitute for rifampin with doxycycline
Plague	1–6 days (pneumonic); 2–8 days (bubonic)	Culture or fluorescent antibody staining of blood, sputum, lymph node aspirate[8]	Droplet	Streptomycin or gentamicin; doxycycline[4] or tetracycline[4]	Doxycycline[2]; tetracycline[4]	*Inhalational exposure:* Fever, cough, hemoptysis, chest pain, with chest radiograph showing bronchopneumonia *Cutaneous exposure:* Swollen regional lymph nodes *Septicemic (following inhalational or cutaneous exposure):* Hypotension, acute respiratory distress, intravascular coagulopathy	TMP-SMX is an alternative; chloramphenicol for meningitis
Q fever	10–40 days	Acute and convalescent serum samples	Standard	Doxycycline[4] or tetracycline[4]	Doxycycline[4] or tetracycline[3]	Fever, chills, headache, weakness, and sweating with elevated hepatic enzymes	Chloramphenicol is an alternative for treatment or prophylaxis

Table 2.1. Biological Weapons: Recommended Diagnostic Procedures, Isolation Precautions, and Treatment and Prophylaxis of Children, continued

Agent	Incubation Period	Diagnostic Specimen(s)[1]	Isolation Precautions	Treatment Options	Postexposure Prophylaxis	Distinctive Findings	Comments
Smallpox	7–17 days	PCR and culture of pharyngeal swab or skin lesions[8]	Airborne, contact	Supportive care	Vaccine if administered within 4 days	Fever, headache, backache, abdominal pain, malaise, followed by a rash that begins on the face and progresses in a centrifugal fashion to involve extremities and then trunk. The lesions evolve from papules to firm vesicles, and then deep-seated, hard pustules	
Staphylo-coccal entero-toxin B	3–12 h	Serum, urine, and respiratory secretions for toxin; acute and convalescent serum for antibodies	Standard	Supportive care	None available	*Ingestion:* Abrupt onset of nausea, abdominal cramps, vomiting, and prostration, often accompanied by diarrhea *Inhalational:* nonproductive cough, retrosternal chest pain, dyspnea, and fever, usually without evidence of pulmonary involvement on chest radiograph	

Table 2.1. Biological Weapons: Recommended Diagnostic Procedures, Isolation Precautions, and Treatment and Prophylaxis of Children, continued

Agent	Incubation Period	Diagnostic Specimen(s)[1]	Isolation Precautions	Treatment Options	Postexposure Prophylaxis	Distinctive Findings	Comments
Ricin	4–8 h	Serum and/or respiratory secretions for EIA	Standard	Supportive care; gastric lavage and cathartics if toxin is ingested	Protective mask	*Ingestion:* Vomiting, hemorrhagic gastroenteritis, shock, and cardiovascular collapse *Inhalational:* Respiratory distress with necrotizing pneumonitis *Injection:* Rapid onset of shock and cardiovascular collapse	
Tularemia	3–5 days (may be as long as 21 days)	Gastric aspirate, sputum, pharyngeal exudates, conjunctival exudates, lymph node aspirate, swab from ulcer and blood for culture,[9] direct fluorescent antibody staining, PCR; blood for antibody testing	Standard precautions	Gentamicin	Doxycycline[4]	*Inhalational exposure:* Atypical pneumonia with hilar adenopathy and pleuritis *Cutaneous exposure:* Systemic illness with painful regional lymphadenopathy with or without cutaneous ulcers. *Ocular exposure:* Purulent conjunctivitis with chemosis, periorbital edema, and conjunctival nodules or ulceration and accompanying preauricular or cervical	Doxycycline, ciprofloxacin,[10] and chloramphenicol are alternatives for treatment

Table 2.1. Biological Weapons: Recommended Diagnostic Procedures, Isolation Precautions, and Treatment and Prophylaxis of Children, continued

Agent	Incubation Period	Diagnostic Specimen(s)[1]	Isolation Precautions	Treatment Options	Postexposure Prophylaxis	Distinctive Findings	Comments
						Oropharyngeal exposure: Acute exudative or membranous tonsillitis with cervical lymphadenopathy. *Typhoidal (as complication of any type of exposure:* Headache, chills, rigors, myalgia, arthralgia.	
Viral hemorrhagic fevers	6–17 days	Culture and/or antigen detection of blood and other body tissues[11]; serum[11] for acute and convalescent antibody detection	Standard, droplet, and contact precautions[12]	IV ribavirin for Lassa fever; plasma from convalescent patients for Argentine hemorrhagic fever; supportive care		Fever, myalgia, prostration, petechiae progressing to shock, mucous membrane hemorrhage, with or without renal involvement.	

CSF indicates cerebrospinal fluid; CDC, Centers for Disease Control and Prevention; EIA, enzyme immunoassay; IV, intravenous.

[1] CDC Web site (**www.bt.cdc.gov**) should be consulted to determine routing of specimens, handling instructions, and when isolation at local hospitals should not be attempted.

[2] Prophylaxis should be administered only after consultation with public health officials and only in situations in which exposure is highly likely. The duration of prophylaxis has not been determined for most agents.

[3] If susceptibility is unknown or indicates resistance to other agents. Ciprofloxacin is approved for use in children as prophylaxis against inhalational anthrax.

[4] Tetracyclines, including doxycycline, carry the risk of tooth discoloration in young children but are approved for treatment and postexposure prophylaxis of anthrax. Dosage for children ≥100 lb is as for an adult. For children <100 lb, dosage is 1 mg/lb (2.2 mg/kg), twice daily, for 60 days.

[5] Treatment should be administered parenterally initially but may be changed to oral therapy for cutaneous infection without dissemination.

[6] Amoxicillin may be used as prophylaxis if the organism is known to be susceptible.

[7] Botulism antitoxin must be obtained from the CDC Drug Service, 404-639-3670 (weekdays, 8:00 AM–4:30 PM) or 404-639-2888 (weekends, nights, and holidays).

[8] Notify the laboratory of suspected etiologic agent so that appropriate safety precautions may be implemented.

[9] Isolation should be attempted only under biosafety level-3 conditions.

[10] Ciprofloxacin is approved only for specific indications in patients younger than 18 years of age.

[11] Isolation should be attempted only under biosafety level-4 conditions.

[12] Because of the risk of nosocomial transmission, the state health department and the CDC should be contacted for specific advice about management and diagnosis of suspected cases.

Table 2.2. Emergency Contacts and Educational Resources

Health Department Information
• State Health Department Web sites, **www.cdc.gov/other.htm#states**

Emergency Contacts
• CDC 24-Hour Emergency Operations Center, **770-488-7100**
• USAMRIID Emergency Response Line, **888-872-7443**
• National Response Center, **800-424-8802** or **202-267-2675**
• National Disaster Medical System, **800-USA-NDMS** or **www.ndms.dhhs.gov**

Selected Web Information Resources
• American Academy of Pediatrics bioterrorism information, **www.aap.org/terrorism**
• CDC Emergency Preparedness and Response, **www.bt.cdc.gov/**
• Infectious Diseases Society of America Web site, **www.idsociety.org/BT/ToC.htm**
• American Society for Microbiology Web site, **www.asm.org/Policy/index.asp?bid 20**
• University of Pittsburgh Medical Center, Center for Biosecurity, **www.upmc-biosecurity. org**
• US Army Medical Research Institute of Infectious Disease (USAMRIID), **www.usamriid. army.mil/**

Blood Components and Plasma Derivatives

Blood collection, preparation, and testing are regulated by the US Food and Drug Administration (FDA). In the United States, whole blood is collected from volunteer donors and separated into **components**, including Red Blood Cells, Platelets, Plasma, and White Blood Cells. Platelets, and less commonly, Red Blood Cells and Plasma, also can be collected through apheresis, in which blood passes through a machine that separates blood components and returns uncollected components to the donor. Plasma for transfusion or further manufacturing into plasma derivatives can be prepared from Whole Blood or collected by apheresis. Most Plasma in the United States is obtained from paid donors at specialized collection centers. **Plasma derivatives** are prepared by pooling plasma from many donors and subjecting the plasma to a fractionation process that separates the desired proteins, including Gamma Globulin.

From an infection standpoint, plasma derivatives differ from blood components in several ways. For economic and therapeutic reasons, plasma from thousands of donors is pooled, and therefore, recipients of plasma derivatives have vastly greater donor exposure than do blood component recipients. However, plasma derivatives are able to withstand vigorous viral inactivation processes that would destroy Red Blood Cells and Platelets. Development and evaluation of various strategies for inactivation of infectious agents are ongoing.

Current Blood Safety Measures

The safety of the blood supply relies on multiple steps, including donor interview and selection, donor screening by serologic tests, screening of collected blood components for markers of infection, inactivation procedures for plasma-derived products, and leukodepletion of certain blood components (see Table 2.3, p 114). Blood donors are interviewed in an attempt to exclude people with a history of exposures or behaviors that increase the risk that their blood will contain an infectious agent. All blood donations are tested routinely for syphilis, hepatitis B virus (HBV), hepatitis C virus (HCV), human T-lymphotropic virus (HTLV) types 1 and 2, and human immunodeficiency virus (HIV) types 1 and 2; selected donations are tested for cytomegalovirus (CMV). Since July 2003, most donations are tested for West Nile virus.

Transfusion-Transmitted Agents: Known Threats and Potential Pathogens

Any infectious agent that has a blood phase potentially can be transmitted by blood transfusion. Factors that influence the risk of transmission by transfusion of an infectious agent and development of clinical disease in the recipient include prevalence and incidence of the agent in donors, duration of hematogenous phase, tolerance of the agent to processing and storage, infectivity and pathogenicity of the agent, and recipient's health status. Table 2.4 (p 115) lists major known transfusion-transmitted infections and some of the emerging agents under investigation.

VIRUSES

HUMAN IMMUNODEFICIENCY VIRUS (P 378), HCV (P 355), HBV (P 335). The probability of infection in recipients who are exposed to these viruses in transfused blood products is approximately 90%. Although blood donations are screened for these viruses, there is a small residual risk of infection resulting almost exclusively from donations collected during the "window period" of infection, the period soon after infection during which a blood donor is infectious but screening results are negative.

To decrease the time period when donor HIV and HCV infection can go undetected, nucleic acid amplification (NAA) testing of blood and plasma donations was implemented beginning in 1999 in the United States and is performed on blood and plasma donations. In addition, NAA testing for HBV is being performed in selected centers under an investigational protocol, although cost-effectiveness of universal NAA testing for HBV is controversial. Various estimates suggest that NAA testing on pooled units can decrease the preantibody seroconversion "window period" from 22 days to 13 to 15 days for HIV and from 70 days to 10 to 29 days for HCV. Mathematic models have been developed to estimate the current very low risks of transfusion transmission of HIV, HCV, and HBV using currently accepted screening policies (Table 2.4).

HUMAN T-LYMPHOTROPIC VIRUS TYPES 1 AND 2. Infections with HTLV are relatively common in certain geographic areas of the world and in specific populations. For example, HTLV-1 is more common in Japan, the Caribbean, and the

Table 2.3. Blood Donor Screening Measures[1]

Measure	Targeted Infectious Agents
General interview and screening • Previous donor history (ie, no deferral in effect) • General health, current illness, temperature at time of donation • Donor confidential unit exclusion option[2] • Reminder to notify blood collector of illness (eg, fever, diarrhea) after donation or of any other pertinent information recalled	Bloodborne phase of multiple agents
Specific risk factor history	
• High-risk sexual behaviors or injection drug use in donor or donor's partner(s)	HIV, HCV, HBV, HTLV
• Geographic risks (travel and residence)	Malaria, vCJD, leishmaniasis
• History of specific infections	HIV, HBV, HCV, other hepatitis agents, parasites (those causing malaria, Chagas disease, babesiosis, and leishmaniasis)
• Previous parenteral exposure to blood via transfusion or occupational exposure; not lifetime deferral	HIV, HCV, HBV
Laboratory screening	HIV-1 and HIV-2 (HIV antibody and HIV-1 NAA testing), HCV (antibody), HIV and HCV NAA testing; HBV (HBsAg and anti-HBc) (ALT generally is performed but not recommended by the FDA), HTLV-1 and HTLV-2 (antibodies), syphilis (antibodies), WNV (NAA testing), screens for bacteria

HIV indicates human immunodeficiency virus; HCV, hepatitis C virus; HBV, hepatitis B virus; HTLV, human T-lymphotropic virus; vCJD, variant Creutzfeldt-Jakob disease; NAA, nucleic acid amplification; HBsAg, hepatitis B surface antigen; anti-HBc, antibody to hepatitis B core antigen; ALT, alanine transaminase; FDA, US Food and Drug Administration; WNV, West Nile Virus.

[1] Screening of Plasma (paid) donors is similar but not identical. For example, because HTLV-1 and HTLV-2 are cellborne agents, Plasma donations are not tested for anti-HTLV-1 and HTLV-2. Donors are tested for syphilis at least every 4 months.

[2] Donor is given the opportunity during the screening process to exclude himself or herself without disclosing the reason.

southern United States, and HTLV- 2 is more common in indigenous people of North America, Central America, and South America and among injection drug users in the United States and Europe. Human T-lymphotropic virus types 1 and 2 are transmitted by transfusion of cellular components of blood but not by plasma or plasma derivatives. The risk of HTLV transmission from screened blood donated during the "window period" has been estimated at 1 per 641 000 units screened. However, transmission of HTLV is less likely to lead to infection than is transmission of

Table 2.4. Selected Known and Potential Transfusion-Transmitted Agents[1]

Agents and Products	Transfusion-Transmitted	Pathogenic	Estimated per-Unit Risk of Contamination (US Studies, Except as Noted)
Viruses for which all blood donors tested			
HIV	Yes	Yes	1 in 2 million
HCV	Yes	Yes	1 in 2 million
HBV	Yes	Yes	1 in 63 000–500 000
HTLV-1 and HTLV-2	Yes	Yes	1 in 641 000
Other viruses			
CMV	Yes	Yes	Most donors harbor virus
Parvovirus B19	Yes	Yes	1 in 10 000
HAV	Yes	Yes	<1 in 1 million contaminated per unit transfused
TT virus	Yes	Unknown	1 in 10 (Japan), 1 in 50 (Scotland)
SEN virus	Yes	Unknown	Unknown
HHV-8	Probable	Yes	Unknown
Bacteria			
Red Blood Cells	Yes	Yes	>1 in 1 million contaminated per unit transfused
Platelets	Yes	Yes	>1 in 1 million contaminated per unit transfused
Parasites[2]			
Malaria (*Plasmodium falciparum*)	Yes	Yes	Varies widely depending on location
Chagas disease (*Trypanosoma cruzi*)	Yes	Yes	Unknown
Prion diseases			
CJD/vCJD	Yes	Yes	Unknown
Tickborne (in nature)			
Babesia species	Yes	Yes	Unknown
Rickettsia rickettsii	Yes	Yes	Unknown
Colorado tick fever virus	Yes	Yes	Unknown
Borrelia burgdorferi	Unknown	Yes	Unknown
Ehrlichia species	Unknown	Yes	Unknown
Mosquitoborne			
West Nile virus	Yes	Yes	Variable (depends on epidemic year)

HIV indicates human immunodeficiency virus; HCV, hepatitis C virus; HBV, hepatitis B virus; HTLV, human T-lymphotropic virus; CMV, cytomegalovirus; HAV, hepatitis A virus; HGV, hepatitis G virus; HHV, human herpesvirus; CJD, Creutzfeldt-Jakob disease; and vCJD, variant CJD. (TT and SEN viruses were named for the initials of patients from whom the viruses first were isolated.)

[1] For additional information, see Goodnough LT, Brecher ME, Kanter MH, AuBuchon JP. Transfusion medicine: first of two parts: blood transfusion. *N Engl J Med.* 1999;340:438-447; and Goodnough LT, Brecher ME, Kanter MH, AuBuchon JP. Transfusion medicine: second of two parts: blood conservation. *N Engl J Med.* 1999;340:525–533.

[2] Other transfusion-transmitted agents include *Toxoplasma gondii* and leishmanial species.

HIV, HBV, or HCV, with an approximate 27% seroconversion rate in people in the United States who receive nonleukocyte reduced cellular blood components from infected donors.

CYTOMEGALOVIRUS (P 273). Immunocompromised people, including preterm infants, stem cell and solid organ transplant recipients, and others, are at risk of severe, life-threatening illness from transfusion-transmitted CMV. Consequently, in many centers, only blood from donors who lack CMV antibodies is given to these people. Leukoreduction decreases the risk of CMV transmission, because CMV resides in a latent phase within white blood cells.

PARVOVIRUS B19 (P 484). Blood donations are not screened for parvovirus B19, because infection with this virus is common in humans. Seroprevalence rates in adult blood donors range from 29% to 79%. Estimates of parvovirus B19 viremia in blood donors have ranged from 0 to 2.6 per 10 000. Parvovirus, like CMV, usually does not cause severe disease in immunocompetent hosts but may be a threat to certain people (eg, fetuses of nonimmune pregnant women; people with hemoglobinopathies, such as sickle cell disease and thalassemia; and immunocompromised patients). Transmission of parvovirus B19 from single-donor specimens is thought to occur rarely. However, pooled plasma derivatives commonly are positive for parvovirus B19 DNA, because parvovirus B19 lacks a lipid envelope, making it resistant to solvent/detergent treatment. To increase safety, manufacturers of plasma derivatives test plasma minipools for parvovirus DNA and exclude those containing parvovirus above a threshold concentration.

HEPATITIS A VIRUS (P 326). Infection with hepatitis A virus (HAV) leads to a relatively short period of viremia, and a chronic carrier state does not occur. Cases of post-transfusion HAV infection have been reported but are rare. Clusters of HAV infections transmitted from clotting factor concentrates occurred among people with hemophilia in Europe during the early 1990s, in South Africa, and more recently, in the United States. Like parvovirus, HAV lacks a lipid envelope and may survive solvent/detergent treatment.

NON-A THROUGH -E HEPATITIS VIRUSES. A small proportion of people with post-transfusion hepatitis as well as community-acquired hepatitis test negative for all known hepatitis agents. In recent years, several newly discovered viruses have been evaluated as possible etiologic agents. Although 3 of these viruses, hepatitis G virus/ GB virus type C (strain variants of a member of the *Flaviviridae* family), TT virus (TTV) (named for the patient from whom the virus was first isolated in Japan), and SEN virus can be found in blood donors and can be transmitted by transfusion, none of these viruses has been found to be associated with development of post-transfusion hepatitis and, hence, are not "hepatitis" viruses. There are no approved tests for screening donors for any of these viruses, and there are no data to suggest that such tests would be beneficial.

HUMAN HERPESVIRUS 8. Human herpesvirus 8 (HHV-8) is associated with Kaposi sarcoma in people with HIV infection, non-HIV Kaposi sarcoma, and certain rare malignant neoplasms. The predominant modes of transmission are male-to-male sexual contact in the United States and close, nonsexual contact in Africa. Because HHV-8 DNA has been detected in peripheral blood mononuclear cells and serum specimens, there is concern that HHV-8 could be transmitted through blood and blood products. Serologic evidence of HHV-8 infection has been associated with receipt of transfused and nonleukocyte-reduced blood components as well as with injection drug use. However, HHV-8 transmission has not been detected in studies of small numbers of recipients of blood from known HHV-8–seropositive donors. Among people with exposure to blood and blood products (eg, people with hemophilia), HHV-8 seroprevalence generally is comparable to that among healthy, HIV-seronegative people. Study of larger populations of recipients of blood or blood products from HHV-8–positive people will be needed to more completely evaluate this risk.

WEST NILE VIRUS. West Nile virus (WNV) has been shown to be transmitted through blood transfusions. To reduce transfusion-associated transmission, blood collection agencies (BCAs) have implemented NAA testing for WNV. Blood collection agencies primarily use an algorithm starting with minipools of donation samples. Donations making up a reactive minipool are retested individually and removed from the blood supply if still positive. If there is evidence of local epidemic WNV transmission, local BCAs switch to individual donation testing to improve the sensitivity of finding blood donations containing WNV. These steps have reduced but not eliminated the risk of WNV transmission via blood products. Cases of WNV disease in patients who have received blood transfusions within 28 days before illness onset should be promptly reported to the Centers for Disease Control and Prevention (CDC) through state and local public health authorities. Serum and tissue samples should be retained for later studies. Also, cases of WNV disease diagnosed in people who have donated blood within 2 weeks before the onset of illness should be reported promptly.

BACTERIA

Although major advances in blood safety have been made, bacterial contamination of blood products remains an important cause of transfusion reaction. Bacterial contamination can occur during collection, processing, and transfusion of blood components.

Platelets are stored at room temperature, which can facilitate growth of contaminating bacteria. Bacterial contamination of blood products previously was underestimated. The predominant bacterium that contaminates Platelets is *Staphylococcus epidermidis*. *Bacillus* species; more virulent organisms, such as *Staphylococcus aureus;* and various gram-negative bacteria, including *Salmonella* and *Serratia* species, also have been reported. Transfusion reactions attributable to contaminated Platelets potentially are underrecognized, because episodes of bacteremia with skin organisms are common in patients requiring platelets, and the link to the transfusion may not be suspected.

Red Blood Cell units are much less likely than are Platelets to contain bacteria at the time of transfusion, because refrigeration kills or inhibits growth of many bacteria. However, certain bacteria, most notably gram-negative organisms, such as *Yersinia enterocolitica*, may contaminate Red Blood Cells, because they survive cold storage.

Cases of septic shock and death attributable to transfusion-transmitted *Y enterocolitica* and other gram-negative organisms have been documented.

Reported rates of transfusion-associated bacterial sepsis have varied widely depending on study methodology and microbial detection methods used. A prospective, multisite study (the Assessment of the Frequency of Blood Component Bacterial Contamination Associated with Transfusion Reaction [BaCon] Study) estimated the rate of transfusion-transmitted bacteremia to be 1 in 100 000 units for single-donor and pooled Platelets and 1 in 5 million units for Red Blood Cells. Other studies that did not require matching bacterial cultures and/or molecular typing of both the component and the recipient's blood as in the BaCon Study have found higher rates of infection.

On March 1, 2004, the American Association of Blood Banks (AABB) adopted a new standard that requires member blood banks and transfusion services to implement measures to detect and limit bacterial contamination of all Platelet components. As blood banks and transfusion services work to implement the new AABB standard, hospitals should ensure that protocols are in place to communicate results of bacterial contamination, both for quarantine of components from that donor and prompt treatment of any transfused recipients. Post-transfusion notification of appropriate personnel is required if cultures identify slow-growing bacteria after product release or transfusion. If bacterial contamination of a component is suspected, the transfusion should be stopped immediately, the unit should be saved for further testing, and blood cultures should be obtained from the recipient. Bacterial isolates from cultures of the recipient and unit should be saved for further investigation.

To improve bacterial screening and reporting, the AABB has provided additional guidance on standardized definitions for test results, investigation and management of implicated units and associated components, and laboratory testing of detected organisms. Current recommendations for clinicians address situations in which (1) a positive test result is encountered only after transfusion of the unit; or (2) a recipient develops post-transfusion bacteremia after receiving Platelets that tested negative (**www.aabb.org/**). Additional guidance includes management of potentially infected donors and algorithms to be followed when organisms found on donor screening are of clinical concern or public health importance (eg, organisms that are notifiable nationally to state and local health departments).

PARASITES

Several parasitic agents have been reported to cause transfusion-transmitted infections, including malaria, Chagas disease, babesiosis, toxoplasmosis, and leishmaniasis. Increasing travel to and immigration from areas with endemic infection has led to a need for increased vigilance in the United States.

MALARIA (SEE P 435). The incidence of transfusion-associated malaria has decreased over the last 30 years in the United States. During the last decade, the rate has ranged from 0 to 0.18 cases per million units transfused, that is, no more than 1 to 2 cases per year. Most cases are attributed to infectious donors who have immigrated to the United States rather than people born in the United States who traveled to areas with endemic infection. *Plasmodium falciparum* is the species most commonly transmitted. Prevention of transfusion-transmitted malaria relies on interviewing donors for risk factors related to residence in or travel to areas with endemic infection or previous treatment for malaria. There is no approved laboratory test to screen donated blood for malaria.

CHAGAS DISEASE (SEE AMERICAN TRYPANOSOMIASIS, P 676). The immigration of millions of people from areas with endemic *Trypanosoma cruzi* infection (parts of Central America, South America, and Mexico) and increased international travel have raised concern about the potential for transfusion-transmitted Chagas disease. To date, fewer than 10 cases of transfusion-transmitted Chagas disease have been reported in North America. Studies of blood donors likely to have been born in or to have traveled to areas with endemic infection have found antibodies to *T cruzi* in as many as 0.5% of people tested. Although transfusion transmission of *T cruzi* in the United States appears to be rare, the lack of adequately sensitive and specific donor history questions and/or licensed tests has limited efforts to identify donors who may be at increased risk of infection.

BABESIOSIS (SEE P 223). The most commonly reported transfusion-associated tick-borne infection in the United States is babesiosis. More than 30 cases of transfusion-induced babesiosis have been documented; most were attributed to *Babesia microti*, but the WA1-type *Babesia* parasite also has been implicated. *Babesia* organisms are intracellular parasites that infect Red Blood Cells. However, at least 4 cases have been associated with receipt of Platelets, which often contain a small number of Red Blood Cells. Although most infections are asymptomatic, *Babesia* infection can cause severe, life-threatening disease, particularly in elderly or splenectomized patients. Severe infection can result in hemolytic anemia, thrombocytopenia, and renal failure. Surveys using indirect immunofluorescent antibody (IFA) assays in areas of Connecticut and New York with highly endemic infection have revealed seropositivity rates for *B microti* in approximately 1% and 4%, respectively. In a study of blood donors in Connecticut, 19 (56%) of 34 seropositive donors had positive results for nucleic acid, as determined by polymerase chain reaction (PCR) assay. Blood from 3 (20%) of 15 donors with positive PCR assay results was infectious when inoculated into hamsters, and infection was transmitted to recipients of blood from approximately 1 in 4 donors with positive PCR assay results.

No licensed test is available to screen donors for *Babesia* organisms. Donors with a history of babesiosis are deferred indefinitely from future donation. Although people with acute illness or fever are not eligible to donate, infected individuals commonly are asymptomatic or experience only mild and nonspecific clinical symptoms. In addition, *Babesia* species can cause chronic, asymptomatic infection for years in otherwise healthy people. Questioning donors about recent tick bites has been shown to be ineffective, because donors who are seropositive for antibody to tickborne agents are no more likely than seronegative donors to recall tick bites.

TRANSMISSIBLE SPONGIFORM ENCEPHALOPATHIES: PRION DISEASE

CREUTZFELDT-JAKOB DISEASE AND VARIANT CREUTZFELDT-JAKOB DISEASE (P 547). Creutzfeldt-Jakob disease (CJD) and variant CJD (vCJD) are fatal neurologic illnesses believed to be caused by unique agents known as prions (see Transmissible Spongiform Encephalopathies, p 547).

SPORADIC CJD. The risk of CJD transmission through blood is considered theoretic. No cases of CJD resulting from receipt of blood transfusion have been documented, and case-control studies have not found an association between receipt of blood and development of CJD.

Nevertheless, because blood of animals with a number of naturally acquired and experimental transmissible spongiform encephalopathies (TSEs) may be infective, concerns remain about the theoretic risk of transmitting CJD by blood transfusion. This concern increased after reports of transfusion-transmitted variant CJD (see next paragraph). For that reason, people with or at increased risk of other forms of CJD (eg, receipt of pituitary-derived growth hormone or dura mater transplant or family history of CJD) are deferred from donation. In addition, if postdonation information reveals that a donor should have been deferred because of increased CJD risk, in-date Whole Blood and components, including unpooled Plasma remaining from previous donations, should be retrieved and discarded; if those units already have been distributed, a biological product deviation report (BPDR) should be submitted to the FDA by the blood establishment. However, withdrawal of plasma derivatives no longer is recommended in that situation, because epidemiologic and laboratory data suggest that most plasma derivatives are less likely to transmit TSE agents than are blood components, because Plasma undergoes extensive processing during fractionation.

VARIANT CJD. In 1996, cases of a new clinically and histopathologically distinct variant form of CJD (vCJD) were first reported in the United Kingdom. The agent causing this new TSE is believed to be the same as that of bovine spongiform encephalopathy (BSE). Bovine spongiform encephalopathy in cattle first was recognized in the United Kingdom in 1986 and later in more than 20 other countries. Four Canadian-born cows, 1 of which was slaughtered in the United States, were found to have BSE. As of December 2005, 185 cases of vCJD have been reported, 158 from the United Kingdom, 15 from France, 3 from Ireland, 2 from the United States, and 1 each from Italy, Japan, the Netherlands, Portugal, Saudi Arabia, Canada, and Spain. The total of 4 patients from Canada, Japan, and the United States and 1 of 3 patients from Ireland likely acquired the disease during their past residence in the United Kingdom. Most patients with vCJD have been younger than 35 years of age, and several were adolescents.

Transmission of vCJD to 2 elderly people in the United Kingdom presumptively has been attributed to transfusions years earlier with nonleukocyte-reduced Red Blood Cells from healthy donors who became ill with vCJD 18 months and 3 years after the donations. Recipients of blood components from other donors later diagnosed with vCJD are under surveillance in the United Kingdom and France. As a precaution, authorities in the United Kingdom have notified recipients of plasma derivatives that they also may be at increased risk of vCJD; the magnitude of that risk is uncertain.

In the United States, the following categories of potential blood and plasma donors are deferred indefinitely: people who received a blood or blood component transfusion in the United Kingdom after January 1, 1980 (when the BSE epidemic is thought to have begun); people who have lived in the United Kingdom for any combined period of 3 months or more from the beginning of 1980 until the end of 1996 (after which rigorous food protection measures were implemented fully throughout the United Kingdom); people who spent a total of 5 years or more in most other European countries (excluding countries of the former Soviet Union) from 1980 to the present; people injected with bovine insulin, unless it is confirmed that the insulin was not manufactured from cattle in the United Kingdom; and military personnel, civilian employees, and dependents who resided or worked on US military bases from 1980 through the end of 1990 in northern Europe or the end of 1996 in southern Europe (as defined by the US Department of Defense). Donors of apheresis plasma (Source Plasma) resident in most European countries are not deferred, but apheresis donors resident in the United Kingdom for 3 months or more in the years noted previously and donors resident in France for 5 years or more after the beginning of 1980 are deferred. Plasma derivatives generally are not withdrawn from the market when postdonation information reveals that a donor should have been deferred. Should postdonation information reveal a diagnosis of vCJD in any donor contributing to a Plasma pool, all in-date Plasma derivatives manufactured from that pool are to be withdrawn from the market; fortunately, that has never been necessary in the United States. Policies regarding CJD donor deferral may change, and blood and Plasma programs are expected to remain informed about such changes, which are announced promptly by trade organizations and the FDA.

Improving Blood Safety

A number of strategies have been proposed or implemented to further decrease the risk of transmission of infectious agents through blood and blood products. Various safety strategies are as follows.

ELIMINATION OF INFECTIOUS AGENTS

AGENT INACTIVATION. Virtually all Plasma derivatives, including Immune Globulin Intravenous (IGIV) and clotting factors, are treated to eliminate infectious agents that may be present despite screening measures. Methods used for this include wet and dry heat and treatment with a solvent/detergent. Solvent/detergent-treated pooled Plasma for transfusion is available in the United States, and methods of treating single-donor Plasma are under study. Solvent/detergent treatment dissolves the lipid envelope of HIV, HBV, and HCV but is not effective against nonlipid-enveloped viruses, such as HAV and parvovirus B19.

Because of their fragility, pathogen inactivation of Red Blood Cells and Platelets is more difficult. However, several methods have been developed, such as addition of psoralens followed by exposure to ultraviolet A, which binds the nucleic acids and blocks replication of bacteria and viruses. Clinical trials of these treated components are underway.

AGENT REMOVAL. Leukoreduction, whereby filters are used to remove donor white blood cells, is increasingly performed in the United States. Benefits of this process include decreasing febrile transfusion reactions related to white blood cells and their products and decreasing the immune modulation associated with transfusion. Leuko-reduction also decreases intracellular or cell-associated agents (eg, viruses such as CMV, Epstein-Barr virus, HHV-8, and HTLV). Several countries have adopted this practice.

DECREASING EXPOSURE TO BLOOD PRODUCTS

ALTERNATIVES TO HUMAN BLOOD PRODUCTS. Many alternatives to human blood products have been developed. Established alternatives include recombinant clotting factors for patients with hemophilia and factors such as erythropoietin used to stimulate red blood cell production. Other agents include Red Blood Cell substitutes in clinical trials, such as human hemoglobin extracted from Red Blood Cells, recombinant human hemoglobin, animal hemoglobin, and various oxygen-carrying chemicals.

AUTOLOGOUS TRANSFUSION. Another means of decreasing recipient exposure is autologous transfusion. Blood may be donated by the patient several weeks before a surgical procedure (preoperative autologous donation) or, alternatively, donated immediately before surgery and replaced with a volume expander (acute normovolemic hemodilution). In either case, the patient's blood can be reinfused if needed. Autologous blood is not completely risk free, because bacterial contamination may occur.

Blood recycling techniques (autotransfusion) also are in this category. During surgery, blood lost by the patient may be collected, processed, and reinfused to the patient.

SURVEILLANCE FOR TRANSFUSION-TRANSMITTED INFECTION

Transfusion-transmitted infection surveillance is crucial and must be coupled with the capacity to rapidly investigate reported cases and to implement measures needed to prevent additional infections. Serious adverse reactions and product problems should be reported to the manufacturer (or, alternatively, to the supplier for transmission to the manufacturer). Health care professionals also may report such information directly to the FDA through MedWatch. This can be done by telephone (1-800-FDA-1088), fax (1-800-FDA-0178), Internet (**www.fda.gov/medwatch/report/ hcp.htm**), or mail (see MedWatch, p 821). This voluntary reporting is considered vital for monitoring product safety.

ORGAN AND TISSUE TRANSPLANTATION

More than 20 000 organ and 1 000 000 tissue transplantations (eg, musculoskeletal allografts, cornea, and skin) and numerous cell therapy infusions (eg, bone marrow and peripheral stem cell transplants) occur each year. Advances in health care technology have led to a proliferation in the use of biological products from human sources. Although these advances in technology have been essential to sustain and improve the quality of human life, the proliferation of these products also has increased the opportunities for transmission of infectious pathogens, including bacteria, viruses, and parasites. Examples of diseases or organisms transmitted through blood, organs, tissues, or cells include rabies virus, lymphocytic choriomeningitis (LCM) virus, WNV, HCV, *Clostridium sordellii*, group A streptococcal infection, malaria, babesiosis, and *T cruzi*, the etiologic agent of Chagas disease. For many tissues, surveillance for recipient infection depends on voluntary reporting by clinicians, and it is likely that many transmission events go undetected. Health care professionals should be aware that a spectrum of infectious pathogens can be transmitted through transplantation of organs, tissues, and cells.

In 2005, the FDA's final rule, Current Good Tissue Practice (CGTP) for Human Cells, Tissues, and Cellular and Tissue-Based Products (HCT/Ps), became effective. The purpose of this rule is to improve the safety of HCT/Ps by preventing introduction, transmission, and spread of communicable disease through transplantation of HCT/Ps.* The Joint Commission on Accreditation of Healthcare Organizations adopted some of these standards, which will apply to accredited organizations that store or use tissue. Along with receiving mandatory reports of adverse events from HCT/P establishments that manufacture tissue, the FDA encourages direct voluntary reporting through its MedWatch program by using MedWatch Form FDA-3500 (available at **www.fda.gov/medwatch**). Additional information about the FDA and HCT/Ps is available at **www.fda.gov/cber/tiss.htm**.

••••••••••••••••••••••••
HUMAN MILK

Breastfeeding provides numerous health benefits to infants, including protection against morbidity and mortality from infectious diseases of bacterial, viral, and parasitic origin. In addition to providing an ideal source of infant nutrition, largely uncontaminated by environmental pathogens, human milk contains protective factors, including cells, specific secretory antibodies, innate factors such as glycoconjugates, and anti-inflammatory components. Breastfed infants have high concentrations of protective bifidobacteria and lactobacillus in their gastrointestinal tracts, which increase resistance to pathogenic organisms. Evidence also indicates that human milk may modulate development of the immune system of infants. Protection by human milk is established most clearly for pathogens causing gastrointestinal tract infection. In addition, human milk seems to provide protection against otitis media, invasive *Haemophilus influenzae* type b infection, respiratory syncytial virus infection, and other causes of upper and lower respiratory tract infections.

The American Academy of Pediatrics (AAP) issues statements and publishes a manual on infant feeding that provides further information about the benefits of

---

* Centers for Disease Control and Prevention. Notice to Readers: FDA Rule for Current Good Tissue Practice for Human Cells, Tissues, and Cellular and Tissue-Based Products. *MMWR Morb Mortal Wkly Rep.* 2005;54:490

breastfeeding and recommended feeding practices.* In the *Pediatric Nutrition Handbook*[†] and in the AAP policy statement on human milk,[‡] issues regarding immunization of lactating mothers and breastfeeding infants, transmission of infectious agents via human milk, and potential effects on breastfed infants of antimicrobial agents administered to lactating mothers also are addressed.

Immunization of Mothers and Infants

EFFECT OF MATERNAL IMMUNIZATION

Women who have not received recommended immunizations before or during pregnancy may be immunized during the postpartum period regardless of lactation status. No evidence exists to validate concern about the potential presence of live viruses from vaccines in maternal milk if the mother is immunized during lactation. Lactating women may be immunized as recommended for adults and adolescents to protect against measles, mumps, rubella, tetanus, diphtheria, pertussis, influenza, *Streptococcus pneumoniae, Neisseria meningitidis*, hepatitis A, hepatitis B, and varicella (**www.cdc.gov/ nip** [see adult immunization schedule]). If previously unimmunized or if traveling to an area with endemic infection, a lactating mother may be given inactivated poliovirus vaccine. Rubella-seronegative mothers who could not be immunized during pregnancy should be immunized during the early postpartum period.

EFFICACY OF IMMUNIZATION IN BREASTFED INFANTS

Infants should be immunized according to the recommended childhood and adolescent immunization schedule regardless of the mode of infant feeding. The immunogenicity of some currently recommended vaccines is enhanced by breastfeeding, but data are lacking as to whether the efficacy of these vaccines is enhanced. Although high concentrations of antipoliovirus antibody in milk of some mothers theoretically could interfere with the immunogenicity of oral poliovirus vaccine, no such association has been demonstrated. This is not a concern with inactivated poliovirus vaccine. Although the immunogenicity of rotavirus immunization of breastfed infants may be affected, the effectiveness of rotavirus vaccine in breastfed infants is not affected.

Transmission of Infectious Agents via Human Milk

BACTERIA

Mastitis and breast abscesses have been associated with the presence of bacterial pathogens in human milk. In general, infectious mastitis resolves with continued lactation during antimicrobial therapy and does not pose a significant risk for the healthy term infant. Breast abscesses occur rarely and have the potential to rupture into the ductal system, releasing large numbers of organisms, such as *Staphylococcus aureus*, into milk.

---

* American Academy of Pediatrics. *Breastfeeding Handbook for Physicians*. Schanler RJ, Gartner LM, Krebs NF, Dooley S, Mass SB, eds. Elk Grove Village, IL: American Academy of Pediatrics; 2005

† American Academy of Pediatrics, Committee on Nutrition. *Pediatric Nutrition Handbook*. 5th ed. Elk Grove Village, IL: American Academy of *Pediatrics*; 2004:55–84

‡ American Academy of Pediatrics, Section on Breastfeeding. Breastfeeding and the use of human milk. *Pediatrics*. 2005;115:496–506

Temporary discontinuation of breastfeeding on the affected breast for 24 to 48 hours after surgical drainage and appropriate antimicrobial therapy may be necessary. Even when breastfeeding is interrupted on the affected breast, breastfeeding may continue on the opposite (unaffected) breast.

Women with tuberculosis who have been treated appropriately for 2 or more weeks and who are not considered contagious may breastfeed. Women with tuberculosis disease suspected of being contagious should refrain from breastfeeding or any other close contact with the infant because of potential transmission through respiratory tract droplets (see Tuberculosis, p 678). *Mycobacterium tuberculosis* rarely causes mastitis or a breast abscess, but if a breast abscess caused by *M tuberculosis* is present, breastfeeding should be discontinued until the mother no longer is contagious.

Expressed human milk can become contaminated with a variety of bacterial pathogens, including *Staphylococcus* species and gram-negative bacilli. Outbreaks of gram-negative bacterial infections in neonatal intensive care units occasionally have been attributed to contaminated human milk specimens that have been collected or stored improperly. Human milk fed to infants from women other than the biologic mother should be treated according to the guidelines of the Human Milk Banking Association of North America. Routine culturing or heat treatment of a mother's milk fed to her infant has not been demonstrated to be necessary or cost-effective (see Human Milk Banks, p 127).

VIRUSES

CYTOMEGALOVIRUS. Cytomegalovirus (CMV) may be shed intermittently in human milk. Although transmission of CMV through human milk has occurred, disease in neonates is uncommon, presumably because of passively transferred maternal antibody. Very low birth weight preterm infants, however, are at greater potential risk of symptomatic disease. Decisions about breastfeeding of preterm infants by mothers known to be CMV seropositive should include consideration of the potential benefits of human milk and the risk of CMV transmission. Holder pasteurization (62.5°C [144.5°F] for 30 minutes) and short-term pasteurization (72°C [161.6°F] for 5 seconds) of milk seems to inactivate CMV; short-term pasteurization may be less harmful to the beneficial constituents of human milk. Freezing milk at −20°C (−4°F) will decrease viral titers but does not reliably eliminate CMV.

HEPATITIS B VIRUS. Hepatitis B surface antigen (HBsAg) has been detected in milk from HBsAg-positive women. However, studies from Taiwan and England have indicated that breastfeeding by HBsAg-positive women does not increase significantly the risk of infection among their infants. In the United States, infants born to known HBsAg-positive women should receive Hepatitis B Immune Globulin (HBIG) and the recommended series of 3 doses of hepatitis B virus vaccine, effectively eliminating any theoretic risk of transmission through breastfeeding. There is no need to delay initiation of breastfeeding until after the infant is immunized. Immunoprophylaxis of infants with hepatitis B virus vaccine alone also provides protection, but optimal therapy of infants born to HBsAg-positive mothers includes HBIG and the 3-dose series of hepatitis B virus vaccine (see Hepatitis B, p 335).

HEPATITIS C VIRUS. Hepatitis C virus (HCV) RNA and antibody to HCV have been detected in milk from mothers infected with HCV. Transmission of HCV via breastfeeding has not been documented in mothers who test positive for anti-HCV but test negative for human immunodeficiency virus (HIV) antibody. Mothers infected with HCV should be counseled that transmission of HCV by breastfeeding theoretically is possible but has not been documented. According to current guidelines of the US Public Health Service, maternal HCV infection is not a contraindication to breastfeeding. The decision to breastfeed should be based on informed discussion between a mother and her health care professional.

HUMAN IMMUNODEFICIENCY VIRUS. Human immunodeficiency virus has been isolated from human milk and can be transmitted through breastfeeding. The risk of transmission is higher for women who acquire HIV infection during lactation (ie, postpartum) than for women with preexisting infection. In populations such as the United States, in which the risk of infant mortality from infectious diseases and malnutrition is low and in which safe and effective alternative sources of feeding are available readily, HIV-infected women should be counseled not to breastfeed their infants or donate milk. All pregnant women in the United States should be counseled and encouraged to be tested for HIV infection. Data are not available about the safety of breastfeeding by mothers on highly active antiretroviral therapy. In areas where infectious diseases and malnutrition are important causes of mortality early in life, the feeding decision may be more complex. Women whose HIV status is unknown are encouraged to continue breastfeeding, because the morbidity associated with artificial feeding is unacceptably high in resource-poor locations. For HIV-infected mothers, one study in Africa found that exclusive breastfeeding for the first 3 to 6 months after birth did not increase the risk of HIV transmission to the infant, whereas infants who received mixed feedings (breastfeeding with other foods or milks) had a higher rate of HIV infection, compared with infants who were exclusively formula fed. The World Health Organization states that if a mother is infected with HIV, replacement of human milk to decrease the risk of HIV transmission may be preferable to breastfeeding provided that the risk associated with replacement feeding is less than the potential risk of HIV transmission. Implementation of this suggestion has many obstacles. The World Health Organization policy stresses the need for continued support for breastfeeding by mothers who are HIV negative or of unknown HIV status, improved access to HIV counseling and testing, and government efforts to ensure uninterrupted access to nutritionally adequate human milk substitutes (see Human Immunodeficiency Virus Infection, p 378).

HUMAN T-LYMPHOTROPIC VIRUS TYPE 1. This retrovirus, which is endemic in Japan, the Caribbean, and parts of South America, is associated with development of malignant neoplasms and neurologic disorders among adults. Epidemiologic and laboratory studies suggest that mother-to-infant transmission of human T-lymphotropic virus (HTLV) type 1 occurs primarily through breastfeeding. Women in the United States who are HTLV-1 seropositive should be advised not to breastfeed.

HUMAN T-LYMPHOTROPIC VIRUS TYPE 2. Human T-lymphotropic virus type 2, also a retrovirus, has been detected among American and European injection drug users and some American Indian/Alaska Native groups. Although apparent maternal-infant transmission has been reported, the rate and timing of transmission have not been established. Until additional data about possible transmission through breast-feeding become available, women in the United States who are seropositive should be advised not to breastfeed.

HERPES SIMPLEX VIRUS TYPE 1. Women with herpetic lesions may transmit her-pes simplex virus (HSV) to their infants by direct contact with the lesions. Whenever a woman has herpes lesions, she must use careful hand hygiene and cover any lesions that might come into contact with the infant. Women with herpetic lesions on a breast or nipple should refrain from breastfeeding an infant until all lesions have resolved.

RUBELLA. Wild and vaccine strains of rubella virus have been isolated from human milk. However, the presence of rubella virus in human milk has not been associated with significant disease in infants, and transmission is more likely to occur via other routes. Women with rubella or women who have just been immunized with live-attenuated rubella virus vaccine need not refrain from breastfeeding.

VARICELLA. Whether varicella vaccine virus is secreted in human milk or whether the virus would infect a breastfeeding infant is unknown. Varicella vaccine may be considered for a susceptible breastfeeding mother if the risk of exposure to natural varicella-zoster virus is high. Recommendations for use of passive immunization and varicella vaccine for breastfeeding mothers who have had contact with people in whom varicella has developed or for contacts of a breastfeeding mother in whom var-icella has developed are available (see Varicella-Zoster Infections, p 711).

WEST NILE VIRUS. West Nile virus RNA has been detected in human milk collected from a woman with disease attributable to West Nile virus; her breastfed infant devel-oped West Nile virus immunoglobulin M antibodies but remained asymptomatic. Ani-mal experiments have shown that West Nile virus can be transmitted in animal milk, and other related flaviviruses can be transmitted to humans via unpasteurized milk from ruminants. The degree to which West Nile virus is transmitted in human milk and the extent to which breastfeeding infants become infected are unknown.

HUMAN MILK BANKS

Some circumstances, such as preterm delivery, may preclude breastfeeding, but infants in these circumstances still may be fed milk collected from their own mothers or from individual donors. The potential for transmission of infectious agents through human milk requires appropriate selection and screening of donors and careful collec-tion, processing, and storage of milk. Currently, US donor milk banks that belong to the Human Milk Banking Association of North America voluntarily follow guidelines drafted in consultation with the US Food and Drug Administration and the Centers for Disease Control and Prevention. These guidelines include screening of all donors for HBsAg and antibodies to HIV-1, HIV-2, HTLV-1, HTLV-2, hepatitis C, and syphilis. Donor milk is dispensed only by prescription after it is heat treated at $\geq 56°C$ ($\geq 133°F$) for 30 minutes and bacterial cultures reveal no growth. Milk from the birth mother of a preterm infant does not require processing if fed to her infant, but proper collection and storage need to be ensured. Some neonatal intensive care units have adopted policies to cover occasions when an infant is wrongly fed another mother's milk. These policies require documentation, counseling, observation of the affected infant for signs of infection, and potential testing of the mothers for HIV infection.

Heat treatment at ≥56°C (≥133°F) for 30 minutes reliably eliminates bacteria, inactivates HIV, and decreases titers of other viruses but in 1 study did not completely eliminate CMV. Holder pasteurization (62.5°C [144.5°F] for 30 minutes) reliably inactivates HIV and CMV and eliminates or significantly decreases titers of most other viruses. Short-term pasteurization (72°C [161.6°F] for 5 seconds) also appears to inactivate CMV.

Freezing at –20°C (–4°F) eliminates HTLV-1 and decreases the concentration of CMV but does not destroy most other viruses or bacteria. Microbiologic quality standards for fresh, unpasteurized, expressed milk are not available. The presence of gram-negative bacteria, *S aureus*, or alpha- or beta-hemolytic streptococci may preclude use of the milk. Routine culture of milk that a birth mother provides to her own infant is not warranted.

Antimicrobial Agents in Human Milk

Antimicrobial agents often are prescribed for lactating women. Although these drugs may appear in milk, the potential risk to an infant must be weighed against the known benefits of continued breastfeeding. As a general guideline, an antimicrobial agent is safe to administer to a lactating woman if it is safe to administer to an infant. The AAP Committee on Drugs has reviewed the risks to infants of specific antimicrobial agents taken by lactating mothers.* Recommendations are included in Table 2.5 (p 129). Although important exceptions exist, only in rare cases will interruption of breastfeeding be necessary because of maternal medications. When treatment with metronidazole is indicated for a lactating mother, the infant's exposure can be minimized by alteration of the dosing schedule and temporary interruption of breastfeeding. For example, for treatment of *Trichomonas vaginalis* infection, a single 2-g dose of metronidazole may be taken by the lactating mother. She then should pump and discard her milk for 12 to 24 hours to allow excretion of the antimicrobial agent and its metabolites and then resume breastfeeding. Women receiving chloramphenicol should not breastfeed because of the theoretic risk of idiosyncratic or dose-related bone marrow suppression in the breastfeeding infant.

The AAP Committee on Drugs considers maternal use of isoniazid to be compatible with breastfeeding. Although potential hepatotoxic effects in breastfeeding infants are a concern, no adverse effects have been documented. Some experts recommend that the infant receive pyridoxine (see Tuberculosis, p 678). The use of ciprofloxacin and ofloxacin by the lactating mother is reported by the Committee on Drugs to be safe for her breastfeeding infant. Data are not available on other fluoroquinolones.

Maternal use of doxycycline or other tetracyclines may be compatible with breastfeeding, because absorption of the drugs by the breastfeeding infant is negligible. Some experts recommend that use of tetracycline or doxycycline by a lactating

---

* American Academy of Pediatrics, Committee on Drugs. The transfer of drugs and other chemicals into human milk. *Pediatrics*. 2001;108:776–789

mother be avoided, if possible, because of the potential for staining of the infant's unerupted teeth.

The amount of drug an infant receives from a lactating mother depends on a number of factors, including maternal dose, frequency and duration of administration, absorption, and distribution characteristics of the drug. When a lactating woman receives appropriate doses of an antimicrobial agent, the concentration of the compound in her milk usually is less than the equivalent of a therapeutic dose for the infant. A breastfed infant who requires antimicrobial therapy should receive the recommended doses, even if the same agent is administered to the mother.

Characteristics of the breastfeeding infant should be considered when assessing the potential effect of specific antimicrobial agents taken by the mother. The infant's gestational age, postpartum age, and clinical status and the pattern of breastfeeding will alter the possible risks to the infant. If an infant has glucose-6-phosphate dehy-

Table 2.5. Antimicrobial Agents Taken by Mothers That May Be Cause for Concern During Breastfeeding

Maternal Antimicrobial Agent	Reported Sign or Symptom in Infant or Possible Cause for Concern	AAP Committee on Drugs Evaluation
Chloramphenicol	Possible idiosyncratic bone marrow suppression	Unknown effect on breastfeeding infant but may be of concern
Metronidazole	In vitro mutagen	Unknown effect on breastfeeding infant but may be of concern; may discontinue breastfeeding for 12–24 h to allow excretion of dose when single-dose therapy is given to mother
Fluoroquinolones	None for ciprofloxacin or ofloxacin	Data not available for other fluoroquinolones
Isoniazid	None; acetyl metabolite secreted, but no hepatotoxicity reported in infants	Usually compatible with breastfeeding; some experts would give infant pyridoxine
Nalidixic acid	Hemolysis in infant with G6PD deficiency	Usually compatible with breastfeeding
Nitrofurantoin	Hemolysis in infant with G6PD deficiency	Usually compatible with breastfeeding
Sulfonamides	Caution in infant with jaundice or G6PD deficiency and in ill, stressed, or premature infant	Usually compatible with breastfeeding
Tinidazole	See metronidazole	

AAP indicates American Academy of Pediatrics; G6PD, glucose-6-phosphate dehydrogenase.

drogenase deficiency, maternal use of nalidixic acid, nitrofurantoin, or sulfonamides should be avoided (see Table 2.5, p 129). With preterm, jaundiced, stressed, or ill infants, maternal use of sulfonamide compounds should be avoided. In addition, pharmacokinetic properties of the antimicrobial agent may be helpful for determining the safety of a new agent for which appearance in milk is unknown. If the drug is not bioavailable orally (ie, it must be given parenterally), it will not be absorbed from milk by the infant.

Another consideration is the potential for interaction between drugs the mother is receiving and drugs her infant is receiving. Hence, physicians caring for infants who are breastfeeding should be aware of the medications the mother is taking and their potential for adverse interaction with drugs being administered to the infant. When making the decision about use of antimicrobial agents for a lactating woman, the physician should weigh benefits of breastfeeding against the potential risk to the breastfeeding infant of exposure to a drug. In most cases, the benefits exceed the risks. The circumstance would be rare in which the only effective medication for treatment of maternal infection would be contraindicated because of risks to the infant.

CHILDREN IN OUT-OF-HOME CHILD CARE*†

Infants and young children who are cared for in group settings have an increased rate of certain infectious diseases and an increased risk of acquiring antimicrobial-resistant organisms. Prevention and control of infection in out-of-home child care settings is influenced by several factors, including the following: (1) caregivers' practice of personal hygiene and immunization status; (2) environmental sanitation; (3) food handling procedures; (4) ages and immunization statuses of children; (5) ratio of children to caregivers; (6) physical space and quality of facilities; and (7) frequency of use of antimicrobial agents in children in child care. Adequately addressing problems of infection control in child care settings requires collaborative efforts of public health officials, licensing agencies, child care providers, physicians, nurses, parents, employers, and other members of the community.

Child care programs should require that all children and staff members receive age-appropriate immunizations and routine health care. In addition, these programs have the opportunity to provide young, inexperienced parents with ongoing instruction in child development, hygiene, appropriate nutrition, and management of minor illnesses. Many early education and child care programs have access to health consultants who can assist with these issues.

---

* For more details see American Academy of Pediatrics, American Public Health Association, and Maternal and Child Health Bureau. *Caring for Our Children. National Health and Safety Performance Standards: Guidelines for Out-of-Home Child Care Programs*. 2nd ed. Elk Grove Village, IL: American Academy of Pediatrics; 2002.

† American Academy of Pediatrics. *Health in Child Care Manual*. Murph JR, ed. Elk Grove Village, IL: American Academy of Pediatrics; 2005

Classification of Care Service

Child care services commonly are classified by the type of setting, number of children in care, and ages and health statuses of the children. **Small family child care homes** provide care and education for up to 6 children at a time, including any preschool children of the care provider, in a residence that usually is the home of the care provider. **Large family child care homes** provide care and education for between 7 and 12 children at a time, including any preschool children of the care provider, in a residence that is usually the home of one of the care providers. A **child care center** is a facility that provides care and education to any number of children in a nonresidential setting, or 13 or more children in any setting if the facility is open on a regular basis. A **facility for ill children** provides care for 1 or more children who temporarily are excluded from their regular child care setting for health reasons. All 50 states license out-of-home child care; however, licensing is directed toward center-based child care; few states or municipalities license small or large family child care homes. A facility for children with special needs provides specialized care and education for 1 child or more who cannot be accommodated in a setting with typically developing children. Licensing requirements for every state can be accessed through the AAP Web site (**www.healthychildcare.org/**).

Grouping of children by age varies, but in child care centers, common groups consist of **infants** (birth–12 months of age), **toddlers** (13–35 months of age), **preschoolers** (36–59 months of age), and **school-aged children** (5–12 years of age).

Infants and toddlers require diapering or assistance in using a toilet, explore the environment with their mouths, have poor control over their secretions and excretions, have immunity to fewer common pathogens, and require hands-on contact with care providers. In addition, toddlers have frequent direct contact with other toddlers. Therefore, child care programs that provide infant and toddler care need to give special attention to infection control measures.

Management and Prevention of Illness

The modes of transmission of bacteria, viruses, parasites, and fungi within child care settings are listed in Table 2.6 (p 132). In most instances, the risk of introducing an infectious agent into a child care group is related directly to prevalence of the agent in the population and to the number of susceptible children in that group. Transmission of an agent within the group depends on the following: (1) characteristics of the organism, such as mode of spread, infective dose, and survival in the environment; (2) frequency of asymptomatic infection or carrier state; and (3) immunity to the respective pathogen. Transmission also can be affected by behaviors of the child care providers, particularly hygienic aspects of child handling; by environmental sanitation practices; and by ages and immunization statuses of children enrolled. Appropriate hand hygiene is the most important factor for decreasing transmission of disease in child care settings. Children infected in a child care group subsequently can transmit organisms not only within the group but also within their households and the community.

Major options for management of ill or infected children in child care and for controlling spread of infection include the following: (1) antimicrobial treatment or

Table 2.6. Modes of Transmission of Organisms in Child Care Settings

Usual Route of Transmission[1]	Bacteria	Viruses	Other[2]
Fecal-oral	Campylobacter organisms, Clostridium difficile, Escherichia coli O157:H7, Salmonella organisms, Shigella organisms	Astrovirus, calicivirus, enteric adenovirus, enteroviruses, hepatitis A virus, rotaviruses	Cryptosporidium parvum, Enterobius vermicularis, Giardia lamblia
Respiratory	Bordetella pertussis, Haemophilus influenzae type b, Mycobacterium tuberculosis, Neisseria meningitidis, Streptococcus pneumoniae, group A streptococcus, Kingella kingae	Adenovirus, influenza virus, human metapneumovirus, measles virus, mumps virus, parainfluenza virus, parvovirus B19, respiratory syncytial virus, rhinovirus, rubella virus, varicella-zoster virus	…
Person-to-person contact	Group A streptococcus, Staphylococcus aureus	Herpes simplex virus, varicella-zoster virus	Agents causing pediculosis, scabies, and ringworm
Contact with blood, urine, and/or saliva	…	Cytomegalovirus, herpes simplex virus	…
Bloodborne	…	Hepatitis B virus	…

[1] The potential for transmission of microorganisms in the child care setting by food and animals also exists (see Appendix VI, Clinical Syndromes Associated With Foodborne Diseases, p 861, and Appendix VIII, Diseases Transmitted by Animals, p 864).

[2] Parasites, fungi, mites, and lice.

prophylaxis; (2) immunization when appropriate; (3) exclusion of ill or infected children from the facility; (4) provision of alternative care at a separate site; (5) cohorting to provide care (eg, segregation of infected children in a group with separate staff and facilities); (6) limiting new admissions; and (7) closing the facility (a rarely exercised option). Recommendations for controlling the spread of specific infectious agents differ according to the epidemiology of the pathogen (see disease-specific chapters in Section 3) and nature of the setting.

Certain general and disease-specific infection control procedures in child care programs decrease acquisition and transmission of communicable diseases; procedures include: (1) periodic review of center-maintained child and employee illness records, including current immunization status; (2) hygienic and sanitary procedures for toilet use and toilet training; (3) review and enforcement of hand-hygiene procedures; (4) environmental sanitation; (5) personal hygiene for children and staff; (6) sanitary preparation and handling of food; (7) communicable disease surveillance and reporting; and (8) management of pets. Specific staff policies that include training procedures for full- and part-time employees and staff illness exclusion policies also aid in control of infectious diseases. Health departments should have plans for responding to reportable and nonreportable communicable diseases in child care programs and should provide training, written information, and technical consultation to child care programs when requested. Evaluation of the health status of each child should be performed by a trained staff member each day as the child enters the site and throughout the day. Parents should be encouraged to share information with child care staff about their child's acute and chronic illnesses and medication use. Parents should be required to report their child's immunization status on an ongoing basis.

Recommendations for Inclusion or Exclusion

Mild illness is common among children. Most children will not need to be excluded from their usual source of care for mild respiratory tract illnesses, because transmission is likely to have occurred before symptoms developed in the child. Disease may occur as a result of contact with children with asymptomatic infection. The risk of illness can be decreased by following common-sense hygienic practices.

Exclusion of sick children and adults from out-of-home child care settings has been recommended when such exclusion could decrease the likelihood of secondary cases. In many situations, the expertise of the program's medical consultant and that of the responsible local and state public health authorities are helpful for determining the benefits and risks of excluding children from their usual care program. Most states have laws about isolation of people with specific communicable diseases. Local or state health departments should be contacted about these laws, and public health authorities in these areas should be notified about cases of reportable communicable diseases and unusual outbreaks of other illnesses involving children or adults in the child care environment (see Appendix IX, Nationally Notifiable Infectious Diseases in the United States, p 870).

Children should be excluded from the child care setting for the following:
- Illness that prevents the child from participating comfortably in program activities.
- Illness that results in a need for care that is greater than the staff can provide without compromising the health and safety of other children.

- Any of the following conditions suggesting possible severe illness: fever accompanied by behavior changes or other signs or symptoms of illness, lethargy, irritability, persistent crying, difficult breathing, or other manifestations of possible severe illness, such as a quickly spreading rash.
- Diarrhea or stools that contain blood or mucus.
- Shiga toxin-producing *Escherichia coli*, including *E coli* O157:H7, or *Shigella* infection, until diarrhea resolves and results of 2 stool cultures are negative for these organisms.
- *Salmonella* infection, until diarrhea resolves and 3 stool cultures test negative for *Salmonella typhi*; other types of *Salmonella* infection do not require negative stool culture results.
- Vomiting 2 or more times during the previous 24 hours, unless the vomiting is determined to be caused by a noncommunicable condition and the child is not in danger of dehydration.
- Mouth sores associated with drooling, unless the child's physician or local health department authority states that the child is noninfectious.
- Rash with fever or behavioral change, until a physician has determined the illness is not a communicable disease.
- Purulent conjunctivitis (defined as pink or red conjunctiva with white or yellow eye discharge, often with matted eyelids after sleep and eye pain or redness of the eyelids or skin surrounding the eye), until examined by a physician and approved for readmission.
- Tuberculosis, until the child's physician or local health department authority states that the child is noninfectious.
- Impetigo, until 24 hours after treatment has been initiated.
- Streptococcal pharyngitis, until 24 hours after treatment has been initiated.
- Head lice (pediculosis), at the end of the program or school day and until after the first treatment.
- Scabies, until after treatment has been given.
- Varicella, until all lesions have dried and crusted (usually 6 days after onset of rash; see Varicella-Zoster Infections, p 711).
- Persistent abdominal pain (continues for ≥2 hours) or intermittent abdominal pain associated with fever, dehydration, or other systemic signs or symptoms.
- Rubella, until 6 days after onset of rash.
- Pertussis, until 5 days of appropriate antimicrobial therapy have been completed (see Pertussis, p 498).
- Mumps, until 9 days after onset of parotid gland swelling.
- Measles, until 4 days after onset of rash.
- Hepatitis A virus (HAV) infection, until 1 week after onset of illness or jaundice (if symptoms are mild).

Most minor illnesses do not constitute a reason for excluding a child from child care. Examples of illnesses and conditions that do not necessitate exclusion include the following:

- Nonpurulent conjunctivitis (defined as pink conjunctiva with a clear, watery eye discharge without fever, eye pain, or eyelid redness).
- Rash without fever and without behavioral change.

- Parvovirus B19 infection in an immunocompetent host.
- Cytomegalovirus (CMV) infection.
- Chronic hepatitis B virus (HBV) infection (see p 139 for possible exceptions).
- Human immunodeficiency virus (HIV) infection (see p 140 for possible exceptions).

Asymptomatic children who excrete an enteropathogen usually do not need to be excluded, except when an infection with Shiga toxin-producing *E coli* or with *Shigella* species has occurred in the child care program. Because these infections are transmitted easily and can be severe, exclusion is warranted until results of 2 stool cultures are negative for the organism (see *Escherichia coli* Diarrhea, p 291, and *Shigella* Infections, p 589). Local health ordinances may be more stringent with respect to number and timing of specimens.

During the course of an identified outbreak of any communicable illness in a child care setting, a child determined to be contributing to transmission of organisms causing the illness at the program may be excluded. The child may be readmitted when the risk of transmission is determined no longer to be present.

Infectious Diseases—Epidemiology and Control*

(See also disease-specific chapters in Section 3.)

ENTERIC DISEASES

The close personal contact and poor hygiene of young children provide ready opportunities for spread of enteric bacteria, viruses, and parasites in child care settings. Enteric pathogens transmitted by the person-to-person route, such as rotaviruses, enteric adenoviruses, astroviruses, noroviruses, *Shigella* species, *E coli* O157:H7, *Giardia lamblia*, *Cryptosporidium parvum*, and HAV have been the principal organisms implicated in outbreaks. *Salmonella* species, *Clostridium difficile*, and *Campylobacter* species infrequently have been associated with outbreaks of disease in children in child care. Most reptiles and rodents carry *Salmonella* organisms, and small reptiles and rodents (eg, hampsters, mice, rats) that could be handled by children can transmit *Salmonella* organisms (or other bacteria) or lymphocytic choriomeningitis (or other viruses) to children.

There is an increased frequency of diarrhea and of HAV infection in young children who are not toilet trained. Fecal contamination of the environment is common in child care programs and is highest in infant and toddler areas. Enteropathogens are spread by the fecal-oral route, either directly by person-to-person transmission or indirectly via fomites, environmental surfaces, and food. The risk of food contamination can be increased when staff members who care for diapered children also prepare or serve food. Several enteric pathogens, including rotaviruses, HAV, *G lamblia* cysts, and *C parvum* oocysts, survive on environmental surfaces for periods ranging from hours to weeks.

Child care programs can be a major source of HAV spread within the community. Hepatitis A virus infection differs from most other diseases in child care centers, because symptomatic illness occurs primarily among adult contacts of infected asymp-

---

* Also see American Academy of Pediatrics. *Managing Infectious Diseases in Child Care and Schools: A Quick Reference Guide.* Aronson SS, Shope TR, eds. Elk Grove Village, IL: American Academy of Pediatrics; 2004

tomatic children. To recognize outbreaks and initiate appropriate control measures, health care professionals and child care providers need to be aware of this epidemiologic characteristic (see Hepatitis A, p 326). Vaccine for HAV should be considered for the staff of child care centers with ongoing or recurrent outbreaks and in communities where cases in a child care center are a major source of HAV infection and routinely for children beginning at 1 to 2 years of age (see Hepatitis A, p 326).

The single most important procedure to minimize fecal-oral transmission is frequent hand hygiene measures combined with staff training and monitoring of staff procedures. A child in whom acute diarrhea or jaundice develops should be moved to a separate area, away from contact with other children, until the child can be removed by a parent or guardian. Exclusion criteria are provided under Recommendations for Inclusion or Exclusion (p 133).

RESPIRATORY TRACT DISEASES

Organisms spread by the respiratory route include those causing acute upper respiratory tract infections or those associated with serious infections, such as infections caused by *Haemophilus influenzae* type b (Hib), *Streptococcus pneumoniae, Neisseria meningitidis, Bordetella pertussis, Mycobacterium tuberculosis,* and *Kingella kingae.* Possible modes of spread of respiratory tract viruses include aerosols, respiratory droplets, and direct hand contact with contaminated secretions and fomites. The viral pathogens responsible for respiratory tract disease in child care settings are those that cause disease in the community, including respiratory syncytial virus, parainfluenza virus, influenza virus, human metapneumovirus, adenovirus, and rhinovirus. The incidence of viral infections of the respiratory tract is increased in child care settings. Hand hygiene measures can decrease the incidence of acute respiratory tract disease among children in child care (see Recommendations for Inclusion and Exclusion, p 133).

Transmission of Hib may occur among unimmunized young children in group child care settings, especially children younger than 24 months of age. Appropriate immunization of children with an Hib conjugate vaccine prevents the occurrence of disease and decreases the rate of carriage, thereby decreasing the risk of transmission to others. In an outbreak of invasive Hib disease in child care, rifampin prophylaxis may be indicated for all nonpregnant contacts (see *Haemophilus influenzae* Infections, p 310), especially when unimmunized or incompletely immunized children attend the child care facility.

Infections caused by *N meningitidis* occur in all age groups. The highest attack rates are in children younger than 1 year of age. Extended close contact between children and staff exposed to an index case of meningococcal disease predisposes to secondary transmission. Because outbreaks may occur in child care settings, chemoprophylaxis is indicated for exposed child care contacts (see Meningococcal Infections, p 452).

The risk of primary invasive disease attributable to *S pneumoniae* among children in child care settings is increased compared with children not in child care settings. Secondary spread of *S pneumoniae* in child care centers has been reported, but the degree of risk of secondary spread in child care facilities is unknown. Prophylaxis for contacts after the occurrence of one or more cases of invasive *S pneumoniae* disease is not recommended. Use of *S pneumoniae* conjugate vaccine has decreased the incidence of invasive disease and decreased carriage of the serotypes of *S pneumoniae* contained in the vaccine.

Group A streptococcal infection among children in child care has been reported. A child with proven group A streptococcal infection should be excluded from classroom contact until 24 hours after initiation of antimicrobial therapy. Although outbreaks of streptococcal pharyngitis in these settings have occurred, the risk of secondary transmission after a single case of mild or even severe invasive group A streptococcal infection remains low. Chemoprophylaxis for contacts after group A streptococcal infection in child care facilities generally is not recommended (see Group A Streptococcal Infections, p 610).

Infants and young children with tuberculosis disease are not as contagious as are adults, because children are less likely to have cavitary pulmonary lesions and are unable to forcefully expel large numbers of organisms into the air. If approved by health officials, children with tuberculosis disease may attend group child care after chemotherapy has begun, ongoing adherence to therapy is documented, clinical symptoms have resolved, and they are considered noninfectious to others. Because an adult with tuberculosis poses a hazard to children in group child care, tuberculin screening with a tuberculin skin test (TST) of all adults who have contact with children in a child care setting is recommended before contact is initiated. However, adults with tuberculosis may not have a reaction to a TST (see Tuberculosis, p 678). The need for periodic subsequent TST of people without clinically important reactions should be determined on the basis of their risk of acquiring a new infection and local or state health department recommendations. Adults with symptoms compatible with tuberculosis should be evaluated for the disease as soon as possible. Child care providers found to have tuberculosis disease should be excluded from the center and should not be allowed to care for children until chemotherapy has rendered them noninfectious (see Tuberculosis, p 678). The need for subsequent periodic TST of adults with an initial negative test result and no clinical symptoms of disease should be determined on the basis of their risk of acquiring a new infection and local or state health department recommendations.

OTHER CONDITIONS

PARVOVIRUS B19. Isolation or exclusion of immunocompetent people with parvovirus B19 infection in child care settings is unwarranted, because little or no virus is present in respiratory tract secretions at the time of occurrence of the rash of erythema infectiosum. In addition, because fewer than 1% of pregnant teachers during erythema infectiosum outbreaks would be expected to experience an adverse fetal outcome, exclusion of pregnant women from employment in child care or teaching is not recommended (see Parvovirus B19, p 484). Also, during outbreaks in the community, there is risk of acquisition of parvovirus B19 outside the child care center.

VARICELLA-ZOSTER VIRUS. Children with varicella who have been excluded from child care may return after all lesions have dried and crusted, which usually occurs on the sixth day after onset of rash. All staff members and parents should be notified when a case of varicella occurs; they should be informed about the greater likelihood of serious infection in susceptible adults and adolescents and in susceptible immunocompromised people in addition to the potential for fetal damage if infection occurs during pregnancy. Approximately 5% to 10% of adults may be susceptible to varicella-zoster virus. Susceptible adults should be offered varicella vaccine unless contraindicated. Susceptible child care staff members who are pregnant and exposed to children with varicella should be referred promptly to a qualified physician or other health care professional for counseling and management. The Centers for Disease Control and Prevention (CDC) and the American Academy of Pediatrics (AAP) recommend the use of varicella vaccine in nonpregnant immunocompetent susceptible people 12 months of age or older within 72 hours after exposure to varicella (see Varicella-Zoster Infections, p 711). During a varicella outbreak, people who have received 1 dose of varicella vaccine should, resources permitting, receive a second dose of vaccine, provided the appropriate interval has elapsed since the first dose (3 months for children 12 months to 12 years of age and at least 4 weeks for people older than 13 years of age).

The decision to exclude staff members or children with herpes zoster infection (shingles) whose lesions cannot be covered should be made on the basis of criteria similar to criteria for varicella. Herpes zoster lesions that can be covered pose little risk to susceptible people, because transmission usually occurs as a result of direct contact with fluid from lesions (see Varicella-Zoster Infections, p 711).

HERPES SIMPLEX VIRUS. Children with herpes simplex virus (HSV) gingivostomatitis who do not have control of oral secretions (drooling) should be excluded from child care when active lesions are present. Although HSV can be transmitted from a mother to her fetus or newborn infant, maternal HSV infections that are a threat to offspring usually are acquired by the infant during birth from genital tract infections of the mother; therefore, exposure of a pregnant woman to HSV in a child care setting carries little risk for her fetus. Child care providers should be educated on the importance of hand hygiene and other measures for limiting transfer of infected material from children with varicella-zoster virus or HSV infection (eg, saliva, tissue fluid, or fluid from a skin lesion).

CYTOMEGALOVIRUS INFECTION. Spread of CMV from asymptomatic infected children in child care to their mothers or to child care providers is the most important consequence of child care-related CMV infection (see Cytomegalovirus Infection, p 273). Children enrolled in child care programs are more likely to acquire CMV than are children primarily cared for at home. The highest rates (eg, 70%) of viral excretion occur in children between 1 and 3 years of age, and excretion commonly continues for years. Studies of CMV seroconversion among child care providers have found annualized seroconversion rates of 8% to 20%. Exposure to CMV with the increased rate of acquisition that occurs in child care staff most likely leads to an increased rate of gestational CMV infection in seronegative female staff members and an increased risk of congenital CMV infection in their offspring.

Cytomegalovirus excretion is so prevalent that attempts at isolation or segregation of children who excrete CMV are impractical and inappropriate. Similarly, testing of children to detect CMV excretion is inappropriate, because excretion often is intermittent and results of testing can be misleading. In view of the risk of CMV infection in child care staff and the potential consequences of gestational CMV infection, child care staff members should be counseled about the risks. This counseling may include testing for serum antibody to CMV to determine the child care provider's protection against primary CMV infection, but routine serologic testing is not recommended.

BLOODBORNE VIRUS INFECTIONS

Hepatitis B virus, HIV, and hepatitis C virus (HCV) are bloodborne pathogens. Although the risk of contact with blood containing one of these viruses is low in the child care setting, appropriate infection control practices will prevent transmission of bloodborne pathogens if exposure occurs. All child care providers should receive regular training on how to prevent transmission of bloodborne diseases.

HEPATITIS B VIRUS. Transmission of HBV in the child care setting has been described but occurs rarely. Because of the low risk of transmission, high immunization rates against HBV in children, and implementation of infection control measures, children known to have chronic HBV infection (hepatitis B surface antigen [HBsAg] positive) may attend child care in most circumstances.

Transmission of HBV in a child care setting is most likely to occur through direct exposure to blood after an injury or from bites or scratches that break the skin and introduce blood or body secretions from an HBV carrier into another person. Indirect transmission through environmental contamination with blood or saliva is possible. This occurrence has not been documented in a child care setting in the United States. Because saliva contains much less virus than does blood, the potential infectivity of saliva is low. Infectivity of saliva has been demonstrated only when inoculated through the skin of gibbons and chimpanzees.

On the basis of limited data, the risk of disease transmission from a child or staff member who has chronic HBV infection but who behaves normally and is without injury, generalized dermatitis, or bleeding problems is minimal. This slight risk usually does not justify exclusion of a child who has chronic HBV infection from child care or the necessity of HBV immunization of the child's contacts at the care program, most of whom already should be protected by previous HBV immunization as part of their routine immunization schedule.

Routine screening of children for HBsAg before admission to child care is not justified. Admission of a child previously identified to have chronic HBV infection with one or more risk factors for transmission of bloodborne pathogens (eg, biting, frequent scratching, generalized dermatitis, or bleeding problems) should be determined by the child's physician, child care provider, or program director. The responsible public health authority or child care health consultant should be consulted when appropriate. Regular assessment of behavioral risk factors and medical conditions of enrolled children with chronic HBV infection is necessary.

Children who bite pose an additional concern. Existing data in humans suggest a small risk of HBV transmission from the bite of a child with chronic HBV infection. For susceptible victims (not fully immunized with HBV vaccine) of bites by children with chronic HBV infection, prophylaxis with Hepatitis B Immune Globulin (HBIG) and hepatitis B immunization is recommended (see Hepatitis B, p 335).

The risk of HBV acquisition when a susceptible child bites a child who has chronic HBV infection is unknown. A theoretic risk exists if HBsAg-positive blood enters the oral cavity of the biter, but transmission by this route has not been reported. Most experts would initiate the hepatitis B vaccine series but not give HBIG to a susceptible biting child who does not have oral mucosal disease when the amount of blood transferred from a child with chronic HBV infection is small.

In the common circumstance in which the HBsAg status of both the biting child and the victim is unknown, the risk of HBV transmission is extremely low because of the expected low seroprevalence of HBsAg in most groups of preschool-aged children, the low efficiency of disease transmission from bites, and routine HBV immunization of preschool children. Serologic testing generally is not warranted for the biting child or the recipient of the bite, but each situation should be evaluated individually.

Efforts to decrease the risk of disease transmission in child care through hygienic and environmental standards generally should focus primarily on precautions for blood exposures and limiting potential saliva contamination of the environment. Toothbrushes should be labeled individually and should not be shared among children. Accidents that lead to bleeding or contamination with blood-containing body fluids by any child should be handled as follows: (1) disposable gloves should be used when cleaning or removing any blood or blood-containing body fluid spills; (2) the area should be disinfected with a freshly prepared solution of a 1:10 dilution of household bleach applied for at least 30 seconds and wiped after the minimum contact time; (3) people involved in cleaning contaminated surfaces should avoid exposure of open skin lesions or mucous membranes to blood or blood-containing body fluids and to wound or tissue exudates; (4) hands should be washed thoroughly after exposure to blood or blood-containing body fluids after gloves are removed and discarded properly; (5) disposable towels or tissues should be used and properly discarded and mops should be rinsed in disinfectant; (6) blood-contaminated paper towels, diapers, gloves, and other materials should be placed in a leak-proof plastic bag with a secure tie for disposal; and (7) staff members should be educated about standard precautions for handling blood or blood-containing material.

HIV INFECTION (SEE ALSO HUMAN IMMUNODEFICIENCY VIRUS INFECTION, P 378). Children who enter child care should not be required to be HIV tested or to disclose their HIV status. There is no need to restrict placement of HIV-infected children without risk factors for transmission of bloodborne pathogens in child care facilities to protect other children or staff members in these settings. Because HIV-infected children whose status is unknown may attend child care, standard precautions should be adopted for handling all spills of blood and blood-containing body fluids and wound exudates of all children, as described in the preceding HBV section.

The decision to admit known HIV-infected children to child care is best made on an individual basis by qualified people, including the child's physician, who are able to evaluate whether the child will receive optimal care in the program and whether an HIV-infected child poses a significant risk to others. Specifically, admission of each HIV-infected child with one or more potential risk factors for transmission of bloodborne pathogens (eg, biting, frequent scratching, generalized dermatitis, or bleeding problems) should be assessed by the child's physician and the program director. A responsible public health authority should be consulted as appropriate. If a bite results in blood exposure to either individual involved, the US Public Health Service recommends postexposure follow-up, including consideration of postexposure prophylaxis (see Human Immunodeficiency Virus Infection, p 378). Information about a child who has immunodeficiency, regardless of cause, should be available to caregivers who need to know how to help protect the child against other infections. For example, immunodeficient children exposed to measles or varicella should receive postexposure immunoprophylaxis immediately (see Measles, p 441, and Varicella-Zoster Infections, p 711).

Available data provide no reason to support the contention that HIV-infected adults will transmit HIV to children during the course of their normal duties. Therefore, HIV-infected adults who do not have open and uncoverable skin lesions, other conditions that would allow contact with their body fluids, or a transmissible infectious disease may care for children in child care programs. However, immunosuppressed adults with HIV infection may be at increased risk of acquiring infectious agents from children and should consult their physician about the safety of continuing to work in child care. All child care providers, especially providers known to be HIV-infected, should be notified immediately if they have been exposed to varicella, parvovirus B19, tuberculosis, diarrheal disease, or measles through children in the facility.

HEPATITIS C VIRUS. Transmission risks of HCV infection in child care settings are unknown. The general risk of HCV infection from percutaneous exposure to infected blood is estimated to be 10 times greater than that of HIV but lower than that of HBV. The risk of transmission of HCV via contamination of mucous membranes or broken skin probably is between the risk of transmission of HIV and the risk of transmission of HBV via contaminated blood. Standard precautions (see Hepatitis C, p 355) should be followed to prevent infection with HCV.

IMMUNIZATIONS

Routine immunization at appropriate ages is important for children in child care, because preschool-aged children can have high age-specific incidence rates of measles, rubella, Hib disease, hepatitis A, invasive *S pneumoniae* disease attributable to serotypes contained in the vaccine, varicella, pertussis, and rotavirus.

Written documentation of immunizations appropriate for age should be provided by parents or guardians of all children enrolling in child care. Unless contraindications exist or children have received medical, religious or philosophic exemptions, immunization records should demonstrate immunizations as shown in the Recommended Childhood and Adolescent Immunization Schedule (see Fig 1.1, p 26). Immunization mandates by state for children in child care can be found online (**www.immunize.org/laws**).

Children who have not received recommended age-appropriate immunizations before enrollment should be immunized as soon as possible, and the series should be completed according to Fig 1.1 (p 26) and Table 1.7 (p 28). In the interim, unimmunized or inadequately immunized children should be allowed to attend child care unless a vaccine-preventable disease to which they may be susceptible occurs in the child care program. In such a situation, all underimmunized children should be excluded for the duration of possible exposure or until they have completed their immunizations.

Child care providers and staff members should have received all immunizations routinely recommended for adults (**www.cdc.gov/nip** [see adult immunization schedule]) according to guidelines for adult immunization of the Advisory Committee on Immunization Practices of the CDC and the American College of Physicians. Child care providers should be immunized against influenza annually. Hepatitis B virus immunization also should be considered, especially for providers who may manage blood spills. All providers should receive written information about hepatitis B disease and its complications as well as means of prevention.

Child care providers should be asked about a history of varicella. Child care providers with a negative or uncertain history of varicella should be immunized or undergo serologic testing for susceptibility; providers who are not immune should be offered varicella vaccine unless it is contraindicated medically. All child care providers should receive written information about varicella, particularly disease manifestations in adults, complications, and means of prevention.

Because HAV can cause symptomatic illness in adult contacts and because child care programs have been a source of infection in the community, HAV vaccine in some circumstances may be justified (see Hepatitis A, p 326). However, because the prevalence of HAV infection does not seem significantly increased in staff members of child care centers in comparison with the prevalence in the general population, routine immunization of staff members is not recommended. During HAV outbreaks, immunization should be considered (see Hepatitis A, p 326).

Adult child care providers who received their last dose of Td 10 years or more earlier should receive a single dose of Tdap to replace a single dose of Td for booster immunization against tetanus, diphtheria, and pertussis. For other recommendations for Tdap use in adults, see Pertussis, p 498.

General Practices

The following practices are recommended to decrease transmission of infectious agents in a child care setting:

- Each child care facility should have **written policies** for managing child and employee illness in child care.
- **Toilet areas and toilet training equipment** should be maintained in sanitary condition.
- **Diaper-changing surfaces** should be nonporous and sanitized between uses. Alternatively, the diaper changing surface should be covered with disposable paper pads, which are discarded after each use. If the surface becomes wet or soiled, it should be cleaned and sanitized.
- **Diaper-changing procedures** should be posted at the changing area. Soiled disposable diapers and soiled disposable wiping cloths should be discarded in a secure, foot-activated, plastic-lined container. Diapers should contain all urine and stool and minimize fecal contamination of children, providers, environmental surfaces, and objects in the child care program. Diapers that should be used are modern disposable paper diapers with absorbent gelling material or carboxymethylcellulose and single-unit reusable systems with an inner cotton lining attached to an outer waterproof covering that are changed as a unit. Clothes should be worn over dia-

pers while the child is in the child care facility. Soiled reusable diapers should be bagged and sent home for laundering. Both the child's and caregiver's hands should be washed after changing a diaper.

• **Diaper-changing areas** never should be located in food preparation areas and never should be used for temporary placement of food, drinks, or eating utensils.

• The use of **child-sized toilets** or access to steps and modified toilet seats that provide for easier maintenance should be encouraged in child care programs. The use of potty chairs should be discouraged, but if used, potty chairs should be emptied into a toilet, cleaned in a utility sink, and disinfected after each use. Staff members should sanitize potty chairs, toilets, and diaper changing areas with a freshly prepared solution of a 1:64 dilution of household bleach (one quarter cup of bleach diluted in 1 gallon of water) applied for 2 minutes, rinsed, and dried.

• **Written procedures for hand hygiene** should be established and enforced.[*] Hand-washing sinks should be adjacent to all diaper-changing and toilet areas. These sinks should be washed and disinfected at least daily and should not be used for food preparation. Food and drinking utensils should not be washed in sinks in diaper-changing areas. These sinks should not be used for rinsing soiled clothing or for cleaning potty chairs. Children should have access to height-appropriate sinks, soap dispensers, and disposable paper towels.

Written **personal hygiene policies** for staff and children are necessary.

Written **environmental sanitation policies and procedures** should include cleaning and disinfecting floors, covering sandboxes, cleaning and sanitizing play tables, and cleaning and disinfecting spills of blood or body fluids and wound or tissue exudates. In general, routine housekeeping procedures using a freshly prepared solution of commercially available cleaner (eg, detergents, disinfectant-detergents, or chemical germicides) compatible with most surfaces are satisfactory for cleaning spills of vomitus, urine, and feces. For spills of blood or blood-containing body fluids and of wound and tissue exudates, the material should be removed using gloves to avoid contamination of hands, and the area then should be disinfected using a freshly prepared solution of a 1:10 dilution of household bleach applied for 30 seconds and wiped with a disposable cloth after the minimum contact time.

Each item of **sleep equipment** should be used only by a single child and should be cleaned and sanitized before being assigned to another child. Crib mattresses should have a nonporous easy-to-wipe surface and should be cleaned and sanitized when soiled or wet. Sleeping mats should be stored so contact with the sleeping surface of another mat does not occur. Bedding (sheets and blankets) should be assigned to each child and cleaned and sanitized when soiled or wet.

Optimally, **toys** that are placed in children's mouths or otherwise contaminated by body secretions should be cleaned with water and detergent, disinfected, rinsed and air-dried before handling by another child. All frequently touched toys in rooms that house infants and toddlers should be cleaned and disinfected daily. Toys

---

* Centers for Disease Control and Prevention. Guideline for hand hygiene in health-care settings. Recommendations of the Healthcare Infection Control Practices Advisory Committee and the HICPAC/SHEA/APIC/IDSA Hand Hygiene Task Force. *MMWR Recomm Rep.* 2002;51(RR-16):1–45

in rooms for older (nondiapered) children should be cleaned at least weekly and when soiled. The use of soft, nonwashable toys in infant and toddler areas of child care programs should be discouraged.

Food should be handled safely and appropriately to prevent growth of bacteria and to prevent contamination by other enteropathogens, insects, or rodents.* Tables and countertops used for food preparation and food service should be cleaned and sanitized between uses, between preparation of raw and cooked food, and before and after eating. No one who has signs or symptoms of illness, including vomiting, diarrhea, or infectious skin lesions that cannot be covered, or who is infected with potential foodborne pathogens should be responsible for food handling. Hands should be washed using soap and water before handling food. Because of their frequent exposure to feces and children with enteric diseases, staff members who work with diapered children should not prepare food for others. Caregivers who prepare food for infants especially should be aware of the importance of careful hand hygiene. No unpasteurized milk, milk products, or juice should be served (see Appendix VII, Potentially Contaminated Food Products, p 861).

- The living quarters of **pets** should be enclosed and kept clean of waste to decrease the risk of human contact with the waste. Hands should be washed after handling all animals or animal wastes. Dogs and cats should be in good health and immunized appropriately for age and should be kept away from child play areas and handled only with staff supervision. Such animals should be given flea, tick, and worm control programs. Reptiles and rodents should not be handled by children.
- Written policies that comply with local and state regulations for filing and regularly updating **immunization records** of each child and child care provider should be maintained.
- Each child care program should use the services of a **health consultant** to assist in development and implementation of written policies for prevention and control of communicable diseases and provision of related health education to children, staff, and parents.
- The child care provider should, when registering each child, **inform parents of the need to share information about illnesses** that could be communicable in the child or in any member of the immediate household to facilitate prompt reporting of disease and institution of any measures necessary to prevent transmission to others. The child care provider or program director, after consulting with the program's health consultant or the responsible public health official, should follow recommendations of the consultant or public health official for **notification of parents** of children who attend the program about exposure of their child to a communicable disease.
- Local and/or state **public health authorities should be notified** about cases of reportable diseases involving children or care providers in the child care setting.
- In settings where human milk is stored and delivered to infants, there should be a written policy and a quality improvement program (as is done routinely for blood products) to minimize administration of human milk to the wrong infant, monitor

---

* Centers for Disease Control and Prevention. Diagnosis and management of foodborne illnesses: a primer for physicians and other health care professionals. *MMWR Recomm Rep.* 2004;53(RR-4):1–33

the program results, and develop protocols to deal with incidents when human milk inadvertently is fed to an infant from the wrong mother. Some neonatal intensive care units have adopted policies to address such occasions. These policies require documentation, counseling, observation of the affected infant for signs of infection, and verification of the donor mother's HIV status.

SCHOOL HEALTH

Although clustering of children together in the school setting provides opportunities for spread of infectious diseases, school attendance is important for children and adolescents, and unnecessary barriers and impediments to attending school should be minimized. Determining the likelihood that infection in one or more children will pose a risk for schoolmates depends on an understanding of several factors, including the following: (1) the mechanism by which the organism causing the infection is spread; (2) the ease with which the organism is spread (contagion); and (3) the likelihood that classmates are immune because of immunization or previous infection. Decisions to intervene to prevent spread of infection within a school should be made through collaboration among school officials, local public health officials, and health care professionals, considering the availability and effectiveness of specific methods of prevention and the risk of serious complications from infection.

Generic methods for control and prevention of spread of infection in the school setting include the following:

- For vaccine-preventable diseases, documentation of the immunization status of enrolled children should be reviewed. Schools have a legal responsibility to ensure that students have been immunized against vaccine-preventable diseases at the time of enrollment, in accordance with state requirements (see Appendix V, State Immunization Requirements for School Attendance, p 856). Although specific laws vary by state, most states require proof of protection against poliomyelitis, tetanus, pertussis, diphtheria, measles, mumps, and rubella. Hepatitis B immunization and immunization against varicella and meningococcal disease are mandatory in many states (**www.immunize.org/laws** or **www.cdc.gov/other.htm#states**). Hepatitis A virus (HAV) immunization is required for school entry in some states. The Centers for Disease Control and Prevention recommends that all states require that children entering elementary school have received varicella vaccine or have other evidence of immunity to varicella. Policies established by a state health department about exclusions of unimmunized children and exemptions for children with certain underlying medical conditions and families with religious or philosophic objection to immunization should be followed.
- Infected children should be excluded from school until they no longer are considered contagious (for recommendations on specific diseases, see relevant disease-specific chapters in Section 3).
- In some instances, administration of appropriate antimicrobial therapy will limit further spread of infection (eg, streptococcal pharyngitis and pertussis).

- Antimicrobial prophylaxis given to close contacts of children with infections caused by specific pathogens may be warranted in some circumstances (eg, meningococcal infection).
- Temporary school closing can be used in limited circumstances: (1) to prevent spread of infection; (2) when an infection is expected to affect a large number of susceptible students and available control measures are considered inadequate (eg, outbreak of influenza); or (3) when an infection is expected to have a high rate of morbidity or mortality.

Physicians involved with school health should be aware of current public health guidelines to prevent and control infectious diseases. In all circumstances requiring intervention to prevent spread of infection within the school setting, the privacy of children who are infected should be protected.

Diseases Preventable by Routine Childhood Immunization

Students who have received 1 dose of varicella vaccine (2 doses for children immunized after their 13th birthday) and 2 doses of measles-mumps-rubella (MMR) vaccine should be considered immune to these diseases. Students with a history of physician-documented infection or serologic evidence of immunity also are considered immune. For the ACIP-approved, revised definitions for evidence of immunity to varicella, see Varicella-Zoster Infections, p 711.

Measles and varicella vaccines have been demonstrated to provide protection in some susceptible people if administered within 72 hours after exposure. Measles or varicella immunization should be recommended immediately for all nonimmune people during a measles or varicella outbreak, respectively, except for people with a contraindication to immunization. Students immunized for measles or varicella for the first time under these circumstances should be allowed to return to school immediately.

Mumps vaccine given after exposure has not been demonstrated to prevent infection among susceptible contacts, but immunization should be administered to unimmunized students to protect them from infection from subsequent exposure.

Although rubella infection usually does not pose a major risk to preadolescent school-aged children, the immunization status of contacts should be reviewed, and documentation of rubella immunization should be required for previously unimmunized students. Pregnant contacts who have serologically confirmed immunity against rubella early in pregnancy can be reassured that they are sufficiently protected. Physician consultation should be recommended for susceptible pregnant women who are exposed to rubella (see Rubella, p 574).

Other Infections Spread by the Respiratory Route

Some pathogens that cause severe lower respiratory tract disease in infants and toddlers, such as respiratory syncytial virus, are of less concern in healthy school-aged children. Respiratory tract viruses, however, are associated with exacerbations of reactive airway disease and an increase in the incidence of otitis media and can cause significant complications for children with chronic respiratory tract disease, such as cystic fibrosis, or for children who are immunocompromised.

Although influenza virus infection is a common cause of febrile respiratory tract disease and school absenteeism, mandatory exclusion of children with suspected influenza infection from school is not warranted. Annual influenza immunization should be given to recommended age groups and to targeted high-risk groups (see Influenza Vaccine, p 405).

Mycoplasma pneumoniae causes upper and lower respiratory tract infection in school-aged children, and outbreaks of *M pneumoniae* infection occur in communities and schools. The nonspecific symptoms and signs of this infection and the lack of a rapid diagnostic test make distinguishing *M pneumoniae* infection from other causes of respiratory tract illness difficult. Antimicrobial therapy does not eradicate the organism or prevent spread necessarily. Thus, intervention to prevent secondary infection in the school setting is difficult. Mass prophylaxis may be considered in certain limited outbreak situations. Mycoplasma outbreaks in schools should be reported to the local health department.

Symptomatic contacts of students with pharyngitis attributable to group A streptococcal infection should be evaluated and treated if streptococcal infection is demonstrated. Infected students may return to school 24 hours after initiation of antimicrobial therapy. Students awaiting results of culture or antigen detection tests who are not receiving antimicrobial therapy may attend school during the culture incubation period unless there is an associated fever or the infection involves a young child with poor hygiene and poor control of secretions. Asymptomatic contacts usually require neither evaluation nor therapy.

Bacterial meningitis in school-aged children often is caused by *Neisseria meningitidis*. Infected people are not considered contagious after 24 hours of appropriate antimicrobial therapy. After discharge from the hospital, they pose no risk to classmates and may return to school. Prophylactic antimicrobial therapy is not recommended for school contacts in most circumstances. Close observation of contacts is recommended, and they should be evaluated promptly if a febrile illness develops. Students who have been exposed to oral secretions of an infected student, such as through kissing or sharing of food and drink, should receive chemoprophylaxis (see Meningococcal Infections, p 452). Immunization of school contacts with meningococcal vaccine, which contains antigens for serogroups A, C, Y, and W-135, should be considered, in consultation with local public health authorities, if evidence suggests an outbreak within a school attributable to one of the meningococcal serogroups contained in the vaccine. Immunization recommendations for use of conjugated meningococcal vaccine beginning at 11 years of age should be followed (see Meningococcal Infections, p 452).

Students and staff members with documented pertussis should be excluded until they have received 5 of the total 14 days of azithromycin, clarithromycin, or erythromycin therapy. In some circumstances, chemoprophylaxis is recommended for their school contacts (see Pertussis, p 498).

Children with tuberculosis generally are not contagious, but students who are in close contact with a child, teacher, or other adult with tuberculosis should be evaluated for infection, including tuberculin skin testing (see Tuberculosis, p 678). An adolescent or adult with tuberculosis almost always is the source of infection for young children. If an adult source outside the school is identified (eg, parent or grandparent of a student), efforts should be made to determine whether other students have been exposed to the same source and whether they warrant evaluation for infection.

Children with erythema infectiosum should be allowed to attend school, because the period of contagion occurs before a rash is evident. Parvovirus B19 infection poses no risk of significant illness for healthy classmates, although aplastic crisis can develop in infected children with sickle cell disease and other hemoglobinopathies. The relatively low risk of fetal damage should be explained to pregnant students and teachers exposed to children in the early stages of parvovirus B19 infection, 5 to 10 days before appearance of the rash. Exposed women should be referred to their physician for counseling and possible serologic testing.

Infections Spread by Direct Contact

Infection and infestation of skin, eyes, and hair can spread through direct contact with the infected area or through contact with contaminated hands or fomites, such as hair brushes, hats, and clothing. *Staphylococcus aureus* and group A streptococcal organisms may colonize the skin or the oropharynx of asymptomatic people. Lesions may develop when these organisms are passed from a person with infected skin to another person. Organisms also can be transmitted to open skin lesions in the same child or to other children. Although most skin infections attributable to *S aureus* and group A streptococcal organisms are minor and require only topical or oral antimicrobial therapy, person-to-person spread should be interrupted by appropriate treatment whenever lesions are recognized. Local and systemic infections associated with methicillin-resistant *S aureus* pose a diagnostic and therapeutic challenge (see Staphylococcal Infections, p 598). Exclusion of any affected children before initiation of therapy is necessary unless the risk of skin contact is low on the basis of location of the lesion and age of the child. Severe and disseminated disease from *S aureus* and group A streptococcus, including toxic shock syndrome and necrotizing fasciitis, occurs rarely.

Herpes simplex virus (HSV) infection of the mouth and skin is common among school-aged children. Infection usually is spread through direct contact with infected lesions. In addition, asymptomatic shedding of virus from oral secretions is common. Infection of the fingers (herpetic whitlow) can occur after direct contact with oral or genital secretions. Cutaneous infection can occur after direct contact with infected lesions or after contact of abraded skin with a contaminated surface, as occurs among wrestlers (herpes gladiatorum) and rugby players (scrum pox). Although asymptomatic shedding of virus from pharyngeal and oral secretions is common, spread of infection requires direct contact with these secretions and, thus, is unlikely to occur during normal school activities. "Cold sore" lesions of herpes labialis identify people with active, and probably recurrent, infection, but no evidence suggests that these students pose any greater risk to their classmates than the unidentified asymptomatic shedders. Herpes simplex virus type 1, the usual cause of oropharyngeal and cutaneous lesions, will infect most people by adulthood. Most of these infections are asymptomatic, and although sometimes painful, even symptomatic infection poses virtually no risk of serious disease to a healthy school-aged child. All children should be advised to avoid direct or indirect (eg, sharing cups and bottles) oral contact with other children and to wash their hands, but excluding symptomatic children with HSV infection from normal school activities is not justified. Exclusion of students with obvious skin or oral lesions from wrestling or rugby and careful cleaning of wrestling mats after use with a freshly prepared solution of a 1:64 dilution of household bleach (one quarter cup of bleach diluted in 1 gallon of water) for a minimum of 30 seconds is reasonable. The bleach solution may be wiped off after the minimum contact time or allowed to air dry.

For immunocompromised children and for children with open skin lesions (eg, severe eczema), HSV infection may pose an increased risk of HSV acquisition and of severe or disseminated infection. Because of the frequency of symptomatic and asymptomatic shedding of HSV among classmates and staff members, careful hygienic practices are the best means of preventing infection.

Infectious conjunctivitis can be caused by bacterial (eg, nontypeable *Haemophilus influenzae* and *Streptococcus pneumoniae*) or viral (eg, adenoviruses, enteroviruses, HSV) pathogens. Bacterial conjunctivitis is less common in children older than 5 years of age. Infection occurs through direct contact or through contamination of hands followed by autoinoculation. Respiratory tract spread from large droplets also may occur. Topical antimicrobial therapy is indicated for bacterial conjunctivitis, which usually is distinguished by a purulent exudate. Herpes simplex virus conjunctivitis usually is unilateral and may be accompanied by vesicles on adjacent skin. Evaluation of HSV conjunctivitis by an ophthalmologist and administration of specific antiviral therapy are indicated. Conjunctivitis attributable to adenoviruses or enteroviruses is self-limited and requires no specific antiviral therapy. Spread of infection is minimized by careful hand hygiene, and infected people should be presumed contagious until symptoms have resolved. Except when viral or bacterial conjunctivitis is accompanied by systemic signs of illness, infected children should be allowed to remain in school once any indicated therapy is implemented, unless their behavior is such that close contact with other students cannot be avoided.

Fungal infections of the skin and hair are spread by direct person-to-person contact and through contact with contaminated surfaces or objects. *Trichophyton tonsurans*, the predominant cause of tinea capitis, remains viable for long periods on combs, hair brushes, furniture, and fabric. The fungi that cause tinea corporis (ringworm) are transmissible by direct contact. Tinea cruris (jock itch) and tinea pedis (athlete's foot) occur in adolescents and young adults. The fungi that cause these infections have a predilection for moist areas and are spread through direct contact and contact with contaminated surfaces. Students with fungal infections of the skin or scalp should be treated for their benefit and to prevent spread of infection. Spread of infection by students with tinea capitis may be decreased by use of selenium sulfide shampoos, but treatment requires systemic antifungal therapy (see Tinea Capitis, p 654). Students with tinea capitis who receive treatment may attend school and participate in their usual activities. Children who fail to obtain treatment do not need to be excluded unless the nature of their contact with other students could potentiate spread. Students with tinea cruris, tinea corporis, or tinea pedis should not be excluded from school even before initiation of therapy. Students with tinea capitis should be instructed not to share combs, hair brushes, hats, or hair ornaments with classmates until they have been treated. Students with tinea pedis should be excluded from swimming pools and from walking barefoot on locker room and shower floors until treatment has been initiated.

Sarcoptes scabiei (scabies) and *Pediculus capitis* (head lice) are transmitted primarily through person-to-person contact. Combs, hair brushes, hats, and hair ornaments can transmit head lice, but away from the scalp, lice do not remain viable. Shampooing with an appropriate pediculocide and manually removing nits by combing usually are effective in eradicating viable lice. Manual removal of nits after treatment with a pediculicide is not necessary to prevent reinfestation (see Pediculosis Capitis, p 488).

Scabies can be transmitted via clothing and bedding to household contacts, but direct skin contact is the predominant means of transmission in the school setting. The parasite survives on clothing for only 3 to 4 days without skin contact. Caregivers who have prolonged skin-to-skin contact with infested students during the school day because of students' physical or mental disabilities may benefit from prophylactic treatment (see Scabies, p 584).

Children identified as having scabies or head lice should be referred for treatment at the end of the school day and subsequently excluded from school only until treatment recommended by the child's health care professional has been started. School contacts generally should not be treated prophylactically.

Infections Spread by the Fecal-Oral Route

For developmentally appropriate school-aged children, pathogens spread via the fecal-oral route constitute a risk only if the infected person fails to maintain good hygiene, including hand hygiene after toilet use, or if contaminated food is shared between or among schoolmates.

Outbreaks attributable to HAV can occur in schools, but these outbreaks usually are associated with community outbreaks. Schoolroom exposure generally does not pose an appreciable risk of infection, and Immune Globulin (IG) administration is not indicated. However, if transmission within a school is documented, IG could be used to limit spread (see Hepatitis A, p 326). Alternatively, HAV vaccine should be considered as a means of prophylaxis and prolonged protection. If an outbreak occurs, consultation with local public health authorities is indicated before initiating interventions.

Enteroviral infections probably are spread via the oral-oral route as well as by the fecal-oral route. The attack rate is so high during summer and fall epidemics that control measures specifically aimed at the school classroom likely would be futile. Person-to-person spread of bacterial, viral, and parasitic enteropathogens within school settings occurs infrequently, but foodborne outbreaks attributable to enteric pathogens can occur. Symptomatic people with gastroenteritis attributable to an enteric pathogen should be excluded until symptoms resolve.

Children in diapers at any age and in any setting constitute a far greater risk for spread of gastrointestinal tract infection attributable to enteric pathogens. Guidelines for control of these infections in child care settings should be applied for developmentally disabled school-aged students in diapers (see Children in Out-of-Home Child Care, p 130).

Infections Spread by Blood and Body Fluids*

Contact with blood and other body fluids of another person requires more intimate exposure than usually occurs in the school setting. The care required for children with developmental disabilities, however, may result in exposure of caregivers to urine, saliva, and in some cases, blood. The application of Standard Precautions for prevention of transmission of bloodborne pathogens, as recommended for children in out-of-home child care, prevents spread of infection from these exposures (see Children in Out-of-Home Child Care, p 130). School staff members who routinely provide acute care for children with epistaxis or bleeding from injury should wear disposable gloves and use appropriate hand hygiene measures immediately after glove removal to protect themselves from bloodborne pathogens. Staff members at the scene of an injury or bleeding incident who do not have access to gloves need to use some type of barrier to avoid exposure to blood or blood-containing materials, use appropriate hand hygiene measures, and adhere to proper protocols for handling contaminated material. Routine use of these precautions helps avoid the necessity of identifying children known to be infected with human immunodeficiency virus (HIV), hepatitis B virus (HBV), or hepatitis C virus (HCV) and acknowledges that unrecognized exposure poses at least as much risk as does exposure from an identified infected child.

During adolescence, the likelihood of infection attributable to HBV, HIV, and other sexually transmitted infections (STIs) increases in proportion to sexual activity. All children should be immunized against HBV before 13 years of age, and adolescents should be instructed in appropriate methods of prevention of STIs.

Students infected with HIV, HBV, or HCV do not need to be identified to school personnel. Because HIV-, HBV-, and HCV-infected children and adolescents will not be identified, policies and procedures to manage all potential exposures to blood or blood-containing materials should be established and implemented. Parents and students should be educated about the types of exposure that present a risk for school contacts. Although a student's right to privacy should be maintained, decisions about activities at school should be made by parents or guardians together with a physician on a case-by-case basis, keeping the health needs of the infected student and the student's classmates in mind.

Prospective studies to aid in determining the risk of transmission of HIV, HBV, or HCV during contact sports among high school students have not been performed, but the available evidence indicates that the risk is low. Guidelines for management of bleeding injuries have been developed for college and professional athletes in recognition of the possibility of unidentified HIV, HBV, or HCV infection in any competitor. Recommendations developed by the American Academy of Pediatrics (AAP) for prevention of transmission of HIV and other bloodborne pathogens in the athletic setting were issued in 1999.[†]

---

* See also American Academy of Pediatrics, Committee on Pediatric AIDS and Committee on Infectious Diseases. Issues related to human immunodeficiency virus transmission in schools, child care, medical settings, the home, and community. *Pediatrics*. 1999;104:318–324 (Reaffirmed 2002)

† American Academy of Pediatrics, Committee on Sports Medicine and Fitness. Human immunodeficiency virus and other blood-borne viral pathogens in the athletic setting. *Pediatrics*. 1999;104:1400–1403 (Reaffirmed 2004)

- Athletes infected with HIV, HBV, or HCV should be allowed to participate in all competitive sports.
- The physician should respect the right of infected athletes to confidentiality. This includes not disclosing the patient's infection status to other participants or the staff of athletic programs.
- Testing for bloodborne pathogens should not be mandatory for athletes or sports participants.
- Pediatricians are encouraged to counsel athletes who are infected with HIV, HBV, or HCV and assure them that they have a low risk of infecting other competitors. Infected athletes can consider choosing a sport in which this risk is relatively low. This may be protective for other participants and for infected athletes themselves, decreasing their possible exposure to bloodborne pathogens other than the one(s) with which they are infected. Wrestling and boxing probably have the greatest potential for contamination of injured skin by blood. The AAP opposes boxing as a sport for youth for other reasons.
- Athletic programs should inform athletes and their parents that the program is operating under the policies of the aforementioned recommendations and that the athletes have a low risk of becoming infected with a bloodborne pathogen.
- Clinicians and staff of athletic programs should promote HBV immunization aggressively among all athletes and among coaches, athletic trainers, equipment handlers, laundry personnel, and any other people at risk of exposure to blood of athletes as an occupational hazard.
- Each coach and athletic trainer must receive training in first aid and emergency care and in prevention of transmission of bloodborne pathogens in the athletic setting. These staff members then can help implement these recommendations.
- Coaches and members of the health care team should educate athletes about precautions described in these recommendations. Such education should include the greater risks of transmission of HIV and other bloodborne pathogens through sexual activity and needle sharing during the use of injection drugs, including anabolic steroids. Athletes should be told not to share personal items, such as razors, toothbrushes, and nail clippers, that might be contaminated with blood.
- Depending on law in some states, schools may need to comply with Occupational Safety and Health Administration (OSHA) regulations* for prevention of bloodborne pathogens. The athletic program must determine what rules apply. Compliance with OSHA regulations is a reasonable and recommended precaution even if this is not required specifically by the state.
- The following precautions should be adopted in sports with direct body contact and other sports in which an athlete's blood or other body fluids visibly tinged with blood may contaminate the skin or mucous membranes of other participants or staff members of the athletic program. Even if these precautions are adopted, the risk that a participant or staff member may become infected with a bloodborne pathogen in the athletic setting will not be eliminated entirely.
  - Athletes must cover existing cuts, abrasions, wounds, or other areas of broken skin with an occlusive dressing before and during participation. Caregivers should

---

* Occupational Safety and Health Administration (**www.osha.gov**)

cover their own damaged skin to prevent transmission of infection to or from an injured athlete.

- Disposable, water-impervious vinyl or latex gloves should be worn to avoid contact with blood or other body fluids visibly tinged with blood and any objects, such as equipment, bandages, or uniforms, contaminated with these fluids. Hands should be cleaned with soap and water or an alcohol-based antiseptic agent as soon as possible after gloves are removed.
- Athletes with active bleeding should be removed from competition as soon as possible and bleeding should be stopped. Wounds should be cleaned with soap and water. Skin antiseptic agents may be used if soap and water are not available. Wounds must be covered with an occlusive dressing that will remain intact and not become soaked through during further play before athletes return to competition.
- Athletes should be advised to report injuries and wounds in a timely fashion before or during competition.
- Minor cuts or abrasions that are not bleeding do not require interruption of play but can be cleaned and covered during scheduled breaks. During these breaks, if an athlete's equipment or uniform fabric is wet with blood, the equipment should be cleaned and disinfected (see next bullet), or the uniform should be replaced.
- Equipment and playing areas contaminated with blood must be cleaned until all visible blood is gone and then disinfected with an appropriate germicide, such as a freshly made bleach solution containing 1 part bleach in 10 parts of water. The decontaminated equipment or area should be in contact with the bleach solution for at least 30 seconds. The area then may be wiped with a disposable cloth after the minimum contact time or allowed to air dry.
- Emergency care must not be delayed because gloves or other protective equipment is not available. If the caregiver does not have appropriate protective equipment, a towel may be used to cover the wound until an off-the-field location is reached where gloves can be used during more definitive treatment.
- Breathing bags (eg, Ambu manual resuscitators and oropharyngeal airways should be available for giving resuscitation. Mouth-to-mouth resuscitation is recommended only if this equipment is not available.
- Equipment handlers, laundry personnel, and janitorial staff must be educated in proper procedures for handling washable or disposable materials contaminated with blood.

INFECTION CONTROL FOR HOSPITALIZED CHILDREN

Health care-associated infections are a major cause of morbidity and mortality in hospitalized children, particularly children in intensive care units. Hand hygiene before and after each patient contact remains the single most important practice in prevention and control of health care-associated infections. A comprehensive set of guidelines for preventing and controlling health care-associated infections, including isolation precautions, personnel health recommendations, and guidelines for prevention of postoperative and device-related infections, can be found on the Centers for Disease Control and Prevention (CDC) Web site (**www.cdc.gov/ncidod/hip/guide/ guide.htm**). Additional guidelines are available from the principal infection control societies in the United States, the Society for Healthcare Epidemiology of America and the Association for Professionals in Infection Control and Epidemiology, as well as specialty societies and regulatory agencies, such as the Occupational Safety and Health Administration (OSHA). The Cystic Fibrosis Foundation publishes an evidence-based guideline for prevention of transmission of infectious agents among cystic fibrosis patients in 2003. The Joint Commission on Accreditation of Healthcare Organizations also has established infection control standards. Physicians and infection control professionals should be familiar with this increasingly complex array of guidelines, regulations, and standards.

Isolation Precautions

The Healthcare Infection Control Practices Advisory Committee (HICPAC) isolation guidelines for preventing transmission of infectious agents in health care settings[*] recommends preventive practices to be implemented according to the strength of evidence available. Adherence to these isolation policies, supplemented by health care facility policies and procedures for other aspects of infection and environmental control and occupational health, should result in reduced transmission and safer patient care. Adaptations must be made according to the conditions and population served by each facility.

Routine and optimal performance of **Standard Precautions** is appropriate for the care of all patients regardless of their diagnosis or suspected or confirmed infection status. Pathogen- and syndrome-based **Transmission-Based Precautions** are used in addition to Standard Precautions when caring for patients who are infected or colonized with pathogens transmitted by the airborne, droplet, or contact routes.

STANDARD PRECAUTIONS

These precautions are used to prevent transmission of all infectious agents through contact with any body fluid except sweat (regardless of whether these fluids contain visible blood), nonintact skin, or mucous membranes. Barrier techniques are recommended to decrease exposure of health care personnel to body fluids. Precautions are used with all patients when exposure to blood and body fluids is anticipated, because medical history and examination cannot reliably identify all patients infected with human immunodeficiency virus or other infectious agents. **Standard Precautions** decrease transmission of microorganisms from patients who are not recognized as harboring potential pathogens, such as antimicrobial-resistant bacteria. See Table 2.7 for new elements added to Standard Precautions (respiratory hygiene/cough etiquette). Standard Precautions include the following practices:

---

[*] Centers for Disease Control and Prevention. Guideline for isolation precautions: preventing transmission of infectious agents in health care settings. Recommendations of the Healthcare Infection Control Practice Advisory Committee. *MMWR.* 2006; in press (see **www.cdc.gov/mmwr**)

Table 2.7. Recommendations for Application of Standard Precautions for Care of All Patients in All Health Care Settings

Component	Recommendations
Hand hygiene	After touching blood, body fluids, secretions, excretions, or contaminated items; immediately after removing gloves; between patient contacts. Alcohol-containing antiseptic hand rubs preferred except when hands visibly are soiled with blood or other proteinaceous materials or if exposure to spores (eg, *Clostridium difficile, Bacillus anthracis*) is likely to have occurred
Personal protective equipment (PPE)	
Gloves	For touching blood, body fluids, secretions, exrections, or contaminated items; for touching mucous membranes and nonintact skin
Gown	During procedures and patient-care activities when contact of clothing/exposed skin with blood/body fluids, secretions, and excretions is anticipated
Mask, eye protection (goggles), face shield	During procedures and patient-care activities likely to generate splashes or sprays of blood, body fluids, or secretions, especially suctioning and endotracheal intubation, to protect health care personnel. For patient protection, use of a mask by the individual inserting an epidural anesthesia needle or performing myelograms when prolonged exposure of the puncture site is likely to occur.
Soiled patient-care equipment	Handle in a manner that prevents transfer of microorganisms to others and to the environment; wear gloves if visibly contaminated; perform hand hygiene
Environmental control	Develop procedures for routine care, cleaning, and disinfection of environmental surfaces, especially frequently touched surfaces in patient care areas
Textiles (linens) and laundry	Handle in a manner that prevents transfer of microorganisms to others and the environment
Injection practices (use of needles and other sharps)	Do not recap, bend, break, or hand manipulate used needles; if recapping is required, use a one-handed scoop technique only; use needle-free safety devices when available; place used sharps in puncture-resistant container. Use a sterile, single-use, disposable needle and syringe for each injection given. Single-dose medication vials are preferred when medications are administered to more than one patient.
Patient resuscitation	Use mouthpiece, resuscitation bag, other ventilation devices to prevent contact with mouth and oral secretions
Patient placement	Prioritize for single-patient room if patient is at increased risk of transmission, is likely to contaminate the environment, does not maintain appropriate hygiene, or is at increased risk of acquiring infection or developing adverse outcome following infection.
Respiratory hygiene/cough etiquette (source containment of infectious respiratory secretions in symptomatic patients) beginning at the initial point of encounter (eg, triage and reception areas in emergency departments and physician offices)	Instruct symptomatic people to cover mouth/nose when sneezing/coughing; use tissues and dispose in no-touch receptacal; observe hand hygiene after soiling of hands with respiratory secretions; wear surgical mask if tolerated or maintain spatial separation (>3 feet if possible).

- **Hand hygiene*** is necessary before and after all patient contacts and after touching blood, body fluids, secretions, excretions, and contaminated items, whether gloves are worn or not. Hand hygiene should be performed either with waterless antiseptic agents or soap and water immediately after removing gloves, between patient contacts, and when otherwise indicated to avoid transfer of microorganisms to other patients and to items in the environment. Hand washing with soap and water is necessary when hands are visibly dirty or contaminated with proteinaceous material such as blood or other body fluids. When exposure to spores (eg, *Clostridium difficile*) is likely, handwashing with soap and water is preferred, because alcohol is not sporicidal and the friction of handwashing is more effective in removing spores.
- **Gloves** (clean, nonsterile) should be worn when touching blood, body fluids, secretions, excretions, and items contaminated with these fluids. Clean gloves should be used before touching mucous membranes and nonintact skin. Gloves should be changed between tasks and procedures on the same patient after contact with material that may contain a high concentration of microorganisms.
- **Masks, eye protection, and face shields** should be worn to protect mucous membranes of the eyes, nose, and mouth during procedures and patient care activities likely to generate splashes or sprays of blood, body fluids, secretions, or excretions.
- **Nonsterile gowns** that are fluid-resistant will protect skin and prevent soiling of clothing during procedures and patient care activities likely to generate splashes or sprays of blood, body fluids, secretions, or excretions. Soiled gowns should be removed promptly.
- **Patient care equipment** that has been used should be handled in a manner that prevents skin or mucous membrane exposures and contamination of clothing.
- **All used textiles (linens)** are considered to be contaminated and should be handled, transported, and processed in a manner that prevents skin and mucous membrane exposure and contamination of clothing.
- **Safe injection practices:** Bloodborne pathogen exposure should be avoided by taking precautions to prevent injuries caused by needles, scalpels, and other sharp instruments or devices during procedures; when cleaning used instruments; during disposal of used needles; and when handling sharp instruments after procedures. Needle-free safety devices are preferred whenever devices with function equivalent to those containing needles are available. To prevent needlestick injuries, needles should not be recapped, purposely bent or broken by hand, removed from disposable syringes, or otherwise manipulated by hand. After they are used, disposable syringes and needles, scalpel blades, and other sharp items should be placed in puncture-resistant containers for disposal; the puncture-resistant containers should be located as close as practical to the use area. Large-bore reusable needles should be placed in a puncture-resistant container located close to the site of use for transport to the reprocessing area. Single-dose vials are preferred when medications are to be given to more than one patient.

---

* Centers for Disease Control and Prevention. Guideline for hand hygiene in health-care settings. Recommendations of the Healthcare Infection Control Practices Advisory Committee and the HICPAC/SHEA/APIC/IDSA Hand Hygiene Task Force. *MMWR Recomm Rep.* 2002;51(RR-16):1–45

- **Mouthpieces, resuscitation bags, and other ventilation devices** should be available in all patient care areas and used instead of mouth-to-mouth resuscitation.

TRANSMISSION-BASED PRECAUTIONS

Transmission-Based Precautions are designed for patients documented or suspected to have colonization or infection with pathogens for which additional precautions beyond **Standard Precautions** are recommended to prevent transmission. The 3 types of transmission routes on which these precautions are based are airborne, droplet, and contact.

- **Airborne transmission** occurs by dissemination of airborne droplet nuclei (small-particle residue [≤5 μm in size] of evaporated droplets containing microorganisms that remain suspended in the air for long periods) or dust particles containing the infectious agent or spores. Microorganisms transmitted by the airborne route can be dispersed widely by air currents and can be inhaled by a susceptible host within the same room or a long distance from the source patient, depending on environmental factors. Special air handling and ventilation are required to prevent airborne transmission. Examples of microorganisms transmitted by airborne droplet nuclei are *Mycobacterium tuberculosis*, rubeola (measles) virus, and varicella-zoster virus. Specific recommendations for **Airborne Precautions** are as follows:
  - Provide infected or colonized patients with a single-patient room (if unavailable, consult with an infection control professional).
  - Use negative air-pressure ventilation (6–12 air changes per hour), with air exhausted directly to the outside or high-efficiency particulate air (HEPA) filtration if air must be recirculated.
  - If infectious pulmonary tuberculosis is suspected or proven, respiratory protective devices (ie, National Institute for Occupational Safety and Health-certified personally "fitted" and "sealing" respirator, such as the N95 or N100 respirators, powered air-purifying respirators) should be worn while inside the patient's room.
  - Susceptible health care personnel should not enter rooms of patients with measles or varicella-zoster virus infections. If susceptible people must enter the room of a patient with measles or varicella infection or an immunocompromised patient with local or disseminated zoster infection, a mask should be worn. People with proven immunity to these viruses need not wear a mask.
- **Droplet transmission** occurs when droplets containing microorganisms generated from an infected person, primarily during coughing, sneezing, or talking and during the performance of certain procedures, such as suctioning and bronchoscopy, are propelled a short distance (≤3 feet) and deposited on the conjunctivae, nasal mucosa, and/or mouth. Because these relatively large droplets do not remain suspended in air, special air handling and ventilation are not required to prevent droplet transmission. Droplet transmission should not be confused with airborne transmission via droplet nuclei, which are much smaller. Specific recommendations for Droplet Precautions are as follows:
  - Provide the patient with a single-patient room. If unavailable, consider cohorting patients infected with the same organism in one room with more than 3 feet between patients and use of precautions between patients.
  - Don a mask or entry into the room or into the cubical space.

If a patient with influenza, severe acute respiratory syndrome (SARS), or viral hemorrhagic fever is to undergo an aerosol-generating procedure (eg, bronchoscopy, intubation, nebulizer treatments), N95 or higher respirators should be used by people in the vicinity of the patient, because small droplet nuclei may be generated by such procedures and could be transmitted to others.

Specific illnesses and infections requiring **Droplet Precautions** include the following:

- Adenovirus
- Diphtheria (pharyngeal)
- *Haemophilus influenzae* type b (invasive)
- Hemorrhagic fever viruses
- Influenza
- Mumps
- *Mycoplasma pneumoniae*
- *Neisseria meningitidis* (invasive)
- Parvovirus B19 during the phase of illness before onset of rash in immunocompetent patients; see Parvovirus B19 (p 484)
- Pertussis
- Plague (pneumonic)
- Rubella
- SARS
- Streptococcal pharyngitis, pneumonia, or scarlet fever

- **Contact Transmission** is the most common route of transmission of health care-associated infections. *Direct-contact* transmission involves a direct body surface-to-body contact and physical transfer of microorganisms between an infected or colonized person and a susceptible host, such as occurs when a health care worker turns a patient, gives a patient a bath, or performs other patient care activities that require direct personal contact. Direct-contact transmission also can occur between 2 patients when one serves as the source of the infectious microorganisms and the other serves as a susceptible host. *Indirect-contact* transmission involves contact of a susceptible host with a contaminated intermediate object, usually inanimate, such as contaminated instruments, needles, dressings, toys, or contaminated hands that are not cleansed or gloves that are not changed between patients. Specific recommendations for **Contact Precautions** are as follows:
  - Provide the patient with a single-patient room (if unavailable, cohorting patients likely to be infected with the same agent and using precautions between contacts with patients is permissible).
  - Gloves (clean, nonsterile) should be used at all times.
  - Hand hygiene should be used after glove removal.
  - Gowns should be used during direct contact with a patient, environmental surfaces, or items in the patient room. Gowns should be donned on entry into the room and should be removed before leaving the patient's room or area.

    Specific illnesses and infections with organisms requiring **Contact Precautions** include the following:
  - Multidrug-resistant bacteria judged by the infection control program on the basis of current state, regional, or national recommendations to be of special clinical and epidemiologic significance (eg, vancomycin-resistant enterococci; methicillin-

resistant *Staphylococcus aureus*; multidrug-resistant, gram-negative bacilli) or other epidemiologically important susceptible bacteria
- *Clostridium difficile*
- Conjunctivitis, viral and hemorrhagic
- Diphtheria (cutaneous)
- Enteroviruses
- *Escherichia coli* O157:H7 and other Shiga toxin-producing *E coli*
- Hepatitis A virus
- Herpes simplex virus (neonatal, mucocutaneous, or cutaneous)
- Herpes zoster (localized with no evidence of dissemination)
- Impetigo
- Major (noncontained) abscess, cellulitis, or decubitus ulcer
- Parainfluenza virus
- Pediculosis (lice)
- Respiratory syncytial virus
- Rotavirus
- Scabies
- *Shigella*
- *Staphylococcus aureus* (cutaneous or draining wounds)
- Viral hemorrhagic fevers (Ebola, Lassa, or Marburg)

Airborne, Droplet, and **Contact Precautions** should be combined for diseases caused by organisms that have multiple routes of transmission. When used alone or in combination, these transmission-based precautions always are to be used in addition to **Standard Precautions**, which are recommended for all patients. The specifications for these categories of isolation precautions are summarized in Table 2.7 (p 155) and Table 2.8 (p 160). Table 2.9 (p 161) lists syndromes and conditions that are suggestive of contagious infection and require empiric isolation precautions pending identification of a specific pathogen. When the specific pathogen is known, isolation recommendations and duration of isolation are given in the pathogen- or disease-specific chapters in Section 3.

PEDIATRIC CONSIDERATIONS

Unique differences in pediatric care necessitate modifications of these guidelines, including the following: (1) diaper changing; (2) use of single-patient room isolation; and (3) use of common areas, such as hospital waiting rooms, play rooms, and schoolrooms.

Because diapering does not soil hands routinely, wearing gloves is not mandatory except when gloves are required as part of transmission-based precautions. However, it may be prudent for individuals who are pregnant or likely to be pregnant to use gloves when changing diapers because of the high prevalence of shedding of cytomegalovirus by healthy infants and toddlers.

Single-patient rooms are recommended for all patients for **Transmission-Based Precautions** (ie, **Airborne, Droplet**, and **Contact**). Patients placed on transmission-based precautions may not leave their rooms to use common areas, such as child life playrooms, schoolrooms, or waiting areas, except under special circumstances as defined by the facility infection control personnel. The guidelines for **Standard Pre-**

Table 2.8. Transmission-Based Precautions for Hospitalized Patients[1]

Category of Precautions	Single-Patient Room	Respiratory Tract/Mucous Membrane Protection	Gowns	Gloves
Airborne	Yes, with negative air-pressure ventilation, 6–12 air exchanges per hour, and HEPA filtration	Respiratiors: N95 or higher level	No[2]	No[2]
Droplet	Yes[3]	Surgical masks[4]	No[2]	No[2]
Contact	Yes[3]	No	Yes	Yes

HEPA indicates high-efficiency particulate air.

[1] These recommendations are in addition to those for **Standard Precautions** for all patients.

[2] Gowns and gloves may be required as a component of **Standard Precautions** (eg, for blood collection or during procedures likely to cause blood splashes or if there are skin lesions containing transmissible infectious agents).

[3] Preferred. Cohorting of children infected with the same pathogen is acceptable if a single-patient room is not available, a distance of >3 feet between patients can be maintained, and precautions are observed between all contacts with different patients in the room.

[4] Masks should be donned on entry into the room.

cautions state that patients who cannot control body excretions should be in single-patient rooms. Because most young children are incontinent, this recommendation does not apply to routine care of uninfected children.

The CDC isolation guidelines were developed for preventing transmission of infection in hospitals and other settings in which health care is delivered. These recommendations do not apply to schools, out-of-home child care centers, and other settings in which healthy children congregate in shared space.

Occupational Health

Standard precautions and transmission-based precautions are designed to prevent transmission of infectious agents in health care settings to limit transmission among patients and health care personnel.

Transmission of infectious agents within health care settings is facilitated by close contact between patients and health care personnel and lack of hygienic practices by infants and young children.

To limit risks of transmission of organisms between children and health care personnel, health care facilities should have established personnel health policies and services. It is important particularly to ensure that personnel are protected against vaccine-preventable diseases by establishing appropriate screening and immunization policies (see adult immunization schedule at **www.cdc.gov/nip** or **www.cdc.gov/mmwr**).

For infections that are not vaccine preventable, personnel should be counseled about exposures and the possible need for leave if they are exposed to, ill with, or a carrier of a specific pathogen, whether the exposure occurs in the home, community, or health care setting.

Table 2.9. Clinical Syndromes or Conditions Warranting Precautions in Addition to *Standard Precautions* to Prevent Transmission of Epidemiologically Important Pathogens Pending Confirmation of Diagnosis[1]

Clinical Syndrome or Condition[2]	Potential Pathogens[3]	Empiric Precautions[4]
Diarrhea		
Acute diarrhea with a likely infectious cause	Enteric pathogens[5]	Contact
Diarrhea in patient with a history of recent antimicrobial use	*Clostridium difficile*	Contact; use soap and water for handwashing
Meningitis	*Neisseria meningitidis*	Droplet
	Enteroviruses	Contact
Rash or exanthems, generalized, cause unknown		
Petechial or ecchymotic with fever	*N meningitidis, Haemophilus influenzae*	Droplet
	Hemorrhagic fever viruses	Add contact plus face/eye protection
Vesicular	Varicella virus	Airborne and contact
Maculopapular with coryza and fever	Measles virus	Airborne
Respiratory tract infections		
Pulmonary cavitary disease	*Mycobacterium tuberculosis*	Airborne
Paroxysmal or severe persistent cough during periods of pertussis activity in the community	*Bordetella pertussis*	Droplet
Viral infections, particularly bronchiolitis and croup, in infants and young children	Respiratory viral pathogens	Contact plus droplet until adenovirus and influenza virus ruled out[6]
Risk of multidrug-resistant microorganisms[7]		
History of infection or colonization with multidrug-resistant organisms	Resistant bacteria	Contact
Skin, wound, or urinary tract infection in a patient with a recent stay in a hospital or chronic care facility	Resistant bacteria	Contact until resistant organism is ruled out by surveillance cultures
Skin or wound infection		
Abscess or draining wound that cannot be covered	*Staphylococcus aureus,* group A streptococcus	Contact Droplet precautions for the first 24 hours of appropriate antimicrobial therapy if invasive group A streptococcal disease is suspected

[1] Infection control professionals are encouraged to modify or adapt this table according to local conditions. To ensure that appropriate empiric precautions are implemented, hospitals must have systems in place to evaluate patients routinely according to these criteria as part of their preadmission and admission care.

[2] Patients with the syndromes or conditions listed may have atypical signs or symptoms (eg, pertussis in neonates, absence of paroxysmal or severe cough in adults). The clinician's index of suspicion should be guided by the prevalence of specific conditions in the community and clinical judgment.

[3] The organisms listed in this column are not intended to represent the complete or even most likely diagnoses but, rather, possible causative agents that require additional precautions beyond **Standard Precautions** until a causative agent can be excluded.

[4] Duration of isolation varies by agent.

[5] These pathogens include Shiga toxin-producing *Escherichia coli* including *E coli* O157:H7, *Shigella* organisms, *Salmonella* organisms, *Campylobacter* organisms, hepatitis A virus, enteric viruses including rotavirus, *Cryptosporidium* organisms, and *Giardia* organisms. Use masks when cleaning up vomitus or stool during norovirus outbreak.

[6] If influenza or adenovirus suspected or proven.

[7] Resistant bacteria judged by the infection control program on the basis of current state, regional, or national recommendations to be of special clinical or epidemiologic significance.

The frequency and need for screening of health care personnel for tuberculosis should be determined by local epidemiologic data as described in the updated CDC guideline for prevention of transmission of tuberculosis in health care settings.* People with frequently occurring infections, such as gastroenteritis, dermatitis, herpes simplex lesions on exposed skin, or upper respiratory tract infections, should be evaluated to determine the resulting risk of transmission to patients or to other health care personnel.

Health care personnel, including pregnant women, should be educated about pathogens for which they are (and are not) at increased risk if they follow Standard Precautions.

Health care personnel education, including understanding of hospital policies, is of paramount importance in infection control. Pediatric health care professionals should be knowledgeable about the modes of transmission of infectious agents, proper hand hygiene techniques, and serious risks to children from certain mild infections in adults. Frequent educational sessions will reinforce safe techniques and the importance of infection control policies. Written policies and procedures relating to needlestick or sharp injuries are mandated by OSHA.† Recommendations for postinjury prophylaxis are available (see Human Immunodeficiency Virus Infection, p 378, and Table 3.27, p 394).‡§

Pregnant health care personnel who follow recommended precautions should not be at increased risk of infections that have possible adverse effects on the fetus (eg, parvovirus B19, cytomegalovirus, rubella, and varicella). Personnel who are immunocompromised and at increased risk of severe infection (eg, *Mycobacterium tuberculosis*, measles virus, herpes simplex virus, and varicella-zoster virus), should seek advice from their health care professional. Special recommendations for infection control for patients/personnel with cystic fibrosis should be consulted.

The consequences to pediatric patients of acquiring infections from adults can be significant. Mild illness in adults, such as viral gastroenteritis, upper respiratory tract viral infection (eg, with respiratory syncytial virus), pertussis, or herpes simplex infection, can cause life-threatening disease in infants and children. People at greatest risk are preterm infants, children who have heart disease or chronic pulmonary disease, and immunocompromised patients.

Sibling Visitation

Sibling visits to birthing centers, postpartum rooms, pediatric wards, and intensive care units are encouraged. Neonatal intensive care, with its increasing sophistication, often results in long hospital stays for the preterm or sick newborn, making family visits important. If guidelines are followed, subsequent infection is not increased in the sick or preterm newborn infant visited by siblings.

---

* Centers for Disease Control and Prevention. Guidelines for preventing the transmission of *Mycobacterium tuberculosis* in health-care settings, 2005. *MMWR Recomm Rep.* 2005;54(RR-17):1–141

† Occupational Safety and Health Administration (**www.osha.gov**)

‡ American Academy of Pediatrics, Committee on Pediatric AIDS. Postexposure prophylaxis in children and adolescents for nonoccupational exposure to human immunodeficiency virus. *Pediatrics.* 2003;111:1475–1489

§ Centers for Disease Control and Prevention. Updated U.S. Public Health Service guidelines for the management of occupational exposures to HIV and recommendations for postexposure prophylaxis. *MMWR Recomm Rep.* 2005;54(RR-9):1–17

Guidelines for sibling visits should be established to maximize opportunities for visiting and to minimize the risks of transmission of pathogens brought into the hospital by young visitors. Guidelines may need to be modified by local nursing, pediatric, obstetric, and infectious diseases staff members to address specific issues in their hospital settings. Basic guidelines for sibling visits to pediatric patients are as follows:

- Sibling visits should be encouraged for all hospitalized infants and children.
- Before the visit, a trained health care professional should interview the parents at a site outside the unit to assess the health of each sibling visitor. These interviews should be documented in the patient's record, and approval for each sibling visit should be noted. No child with fever or symptoms of an acute illness, including upper respiratory tract infection, gastroenteritis, or dermatitis, should be allowed to visit. Siblings who recently have been exposed to a person with a known communicable disease and are susceptible should not be allowed to visit.
- Siblings who are visiting should have received all vaccines recommended for age. During influenza season, it is prudent for siblings who visit to have received influenza vaccine.
- Asymptomatic siblings who recently have been exposed to varicella but have been immunized previously can be assumed to be immune.
- The visiting sibling should visit only his or her sibling and not be allowed in playrooms with groups of patients.
- Children should perform recommended hand hygiene before any patient contact.
- Throughout the visit, sibling activity should be supervised by parents or a responsible adult and limited to the mother's or patient's single-patient room or other designated areas.

Adult Visitation

Guidelines should be established for visits by other relatives and close friends. Anyone with fever or contagious illnesses ideally should not visit. Medical and nursing staff members should be vigilant about potential communicable diseases in parents and other adult visitors (eg, a relative with a cough who may have pertussis or tuberculosis; a parent with a cold visiting a highly immunosuppressed child). During influenza season, it is prudent to encourage all visitors to receive influenza vaccine. Adherence to these guidelines especially is important for oncology and hematopoietic stem cell transplant units.

Pet Visitation

Pet visitation in the health care setting can be separated into 2 categories: visits by a child's personal pet and pet visitation as a part of child life therapeutic programs. Guidelines for pet visitation should be established to minimize risks of transmission of pathogens from pets to humans or injury from animals. The specific health care setting and the level of concern for zoonotic disease will influence establishment of pet visitation policies. The pet visitation policy should be developed in consultation with pediatricians, infection control professionals, nursing staff, the hospital epidemiologist, and veterinarians. Basic principles for pet visitation policies in health care settings are as follows:

- Personal pets other than cats and dogs should be excluded from the hospital. No reptiles (eg, iguanas, turtles, snakes), amphibians, birds, primates, ferrets, or rodents should be allowed to visit. Exceptions may be made for end-of-life patients who are in single-patient rooms.
- Visiting pets should have a certificate of immunization from a licensed veterinarian and verification that the pet is free from contagious diseases.
- The pet should be bathed and groomed for the visit.
- Pet visitation is inappropriate in the intensive care unit.
- The visit of a pet should be approved by appropriate personnel (for example, the director of the child life therapeutic program), who should observe the pet for temperament and general health at the time of visit. The pet should be free of obvious bacterial skin infections, infections caused by superficial dermatophytes, and ecto-parasitic infections (fleas and ticks).
- Pet visitation should be confined to designated areas. Contact should be confined to the petting and holding of animals, as appropriate. All contact should be supervised throughout the visit by appropriate personnel and should be followed by hand hygiene performed by all who had contact with the pet. Supervisors should be familiar with institutional policies for managing animal bites and cleaning pet urine, feces, or vomitus.
- Patients having contact with pets must have approval from a physician or physician representative before animal contact. Documented allergy to dogs or cats should be considered before approving contact. For patients who are immunodeficient or for people receiving immunosuppressive therapy, the risks of exposure to the microflora of pets may outweigh the benefits of contact. Contact of children with pets should be approved on a case-by-case basis.
- Care should be taken to protect indwelling catheter sites (eg, central venous catheters, peritoneal dialysis catheters). These sites should have dressings that provide an effective barrier to pet contact, including licking, and be covered with clothing or gown. Concern for contamination of other body sites should be considered on a case-by-case basis.
- Patients should perform appropriate hand hygiene after contact with pets.
- The pet policy should not apply to professionally trained service animals, such as "seeing eye" dogs. These animals are not pets, and separate policies should govern their uses and presence in the hospital.

INFECTION CONTROL AND PREVENTION IN AMBULATORY SETTINGS

Infection control is an integral part of pediatric practice in ambulatory settings as well as in hospitals. All health care professionals should be aware of the routes of transmission and techniques used to prevent transmission of infectious agents. Written policies and procedures for infection control and prevention should be developed, implemented, and reviewed at least every 2 years. Standard precautions, as outlined for the hospitalized child (see Infection Control for Hospitalized Children, p 153) and by the

Centers for Disease Control and Prevention,* with a modification by the American Academy of Pediatrics exempting the use of gloves for routine diaper changes and wiping a child's nose or tears,† are appropriate for most patient encounters. Key principles of infection control in an outpatient setting are as follows:

- Infection control should begin when the child enters the office or clinic. Standard precautions should be used when caring for all patients.
- Contact between contagious children and uninfected children should be minimized. Policies for children who are suspected of having contagious infections, such as varicella or measles, should be implemented. Immunocompromised children should be kept away from people with potentially contagious infections.
- In waiting rooms of ambulatory facilities, use of some or all components of respiratory hygiene/cough etiquette should be considered for patients and accompanying people with suspected respiratory tract infection when influenza is circulating in the community.‡
- All health care professionals should use hand hygiene before and after patient contact. In health care settings, alcohol-based rub products are preferred for decontaminating hands routinely. Soap and water are preferred when hands are visibly dirty or contaminated with proteinaceous material, such as with blood or other body fluids. Parents and children should be taught the importance of hand hygiene.§
- Staff should receive influenza immunization annually as well as immunizations against other vaccine-preventable infections that can be transmitted in an ambulatory setting.
- Physicians should be familiar with aseptic technique, particularly regarding entry or manipulation of intravascular catheters.
- Alcohol is preferred for skin preparation before immunization or routine venipuncture. Skin preparation for incision, suture, or collection of blood for culture requires 10% povidone-iodine, 70% alcohol, alcohol tinctures of iodine, or 2% chlorhexidine. After application of iodophor skin preparations, the skin should dry for 2 minutes.
- Needles and sharps should be handled with great care. The use of safer medical devices designed to reduce the risk of needlesticks should be evaluated and implemented. Needle disposal containers that are impermeable and puncture proof should be available adjacent to the areas where injections or venipunctures are performed. The containers should not be overfilled and should be kept out of reach of

---

* Centers for Disease Control and Prevention. Guideline for isolation precautions: preventing transmission of infectious agents in healthcare settings. Recommendations of the Healthcare Infection Control Practice Advisory Committee, 2006. *MMWR*. 2006; in press (see **www.cdc.gov/mmwr**)

† American Academy of Pediatrics, Committee on Infectious Diseases and Committee on Practice and Ambulatory Medicine. Infection control and prevention in ambulatory settings. *Pediatrics*. 2006; in press

‡ Centers for Disease Control and Prevention. Respiratory Hygiene/Cough Etiquette in Healthcare Settings. Available at: **www.cdc.gov/flu/professionals/infectioncontrol/resphygiene.htm**

§ Centers for Disease Control and Prevention. Guideline for hand hygiene in health-care settings. Recommendations of the Healthcare Infection Control Practices Advisory Committee and the HICPAC/SHEA/APIC/IDSA Hand Hygiene Task Force. *MMWR Recomm Rep*. 2002;51(RR-16):1–45

young children. Policies should be established for removal and incineration or sterilization of contents.

- A written bloodborne pathogens exposure control plan that includes policies for
management of contaminated sharp object injuries should be developed, readily
available to all staff, and reviewed regularly (see Hepatitis B, p 335; Hepatitis C,
p 355; and Human Immunodeficiency Virus Infection, p 378).
- Standard guidelines for decontamination, disinfection, and sterilization should be
followed.
- Appropriate use of antimicrobial agents is essential to limit the emergence and
spread of drug-resistant bacteria (see Appropriate Use of Antimicrobial Agents,
p 737).
- Policies and procedures should be developed for communication with local and
state health authorities about reportable diseases and suspected outbreaks.
- Ongoing educational programs that encompass appropriate aspects of infection
control should be implemented, reinforced, documented, and evaluated on a regular basis.
- Physicians should be aware of requirements of government agencies, such as the
Occupational Safety and Health Administration (OSHA), as they relate to the
operation of physicians' offices.

SEXUALLY TRANSMITTED INFECTIONS IN ADOLESCENTS AND CHILDREN

Physicians and other health care professionals perform a critical role in preventing
and treating sexually transmitted infections (STIs) in the pediatric population. Sexually transmitted infections are a major problem for adolescents; an estimated 25% of
adolescents will develop an STI before graduating from high school. For infants and
children, detection of an STI is an important warning signal of sexual abuse. Sexual
abuse of children has been endemic for generations, but the prevalence and potentially devastating psychologic effects of sexual abuse have been recognized recently.
Whenever sexual abuse is suspected, appropriate social service and law enforcement
agencies must be involved to ensure the child's protection and to provide appropriate
counseling.

Sexually Transmitted Infections in Adolescents

EPIDEMIOLOGY

Although the incidence of all reported STIs in the United States has decreased during the past decade, adolescents and young adults continue to have higher rates of
STIs than any other age group. Adolescents are at greater risk of STIs, because they
frequently have unprotected intercourse, biologically may be more susceptible to
infection, often are engaged in multiple sequential monogamous partnerships of lim-

ited duration, and face multiple obstacles in accessing confidential health care services. In the United States in 2004, case report rates for gonorrhea were 147 per 100 000 for people between 30 and 34 years of age, 286 per 100 000 for people between 25 and 29 years of age, 498 per 100 000 for people between 20 and 24 years of age, and 427 per 100 000 for people between 15 and 19 years of age. The highest age-specific incidence rate for acquired immunodeficiency syndrome (AIDS) in 2000 was 34 per 100 000, which occurred among young adults 25 to 39 years of age who presumably acquired human immunodeficiency virus (HIV) infection over the previous decade—commonly during adolescence. In 2000, reports based on AIDS surveillance data indicated a substantial decrease in the number of perinatally acquired AIDS cases, reflecting a decreasing rate of perinatal HIV transmission. In the United States in 2004, the rates of chlamydial infection were 1579 per 100 000 for people between 15 and 19 years of age, 1601 per 100 000 for people 20 to 24 years of age, and 715 per 100 000 for people 25 to 29 years of age. Diagnosed infection is higher in women than in men by a factor of 5:1. These data underestimate the incidence of STIs among sexually experienced adolescents, because *all* adolescents, including the one third of US 10th, 11th, and 12th grade students who never have had sexual intercourse, are included in the denominators used to calculate age-specific STI rates and because many cases are not diagnosed or reported.

MANAGEMENT

Pediatricians should screen for risk of STIs by asking all adolescent patients whether they ever have had sexual intercourse or been sexually active. It is important that adolescents recognize that oral and anal intercourse, as well as vaginal intercourse, put them at risk of STIs. Adolescents at increased risk of STIs are listed in Table 2.10, p 168. Physicians can prepare patients for this sensitive question by educating both parents and adolescents about confidentiality. At each annual checkup and at visits for acute illness, a private interview should occur. More detailed recommendations for preventive health care for adolescents are contained in the American Academy of Pediatrics' *Guidelines for Health Supervision III** and the American Medical Association's *Guidelines for Adolescent Preventive Services.*† All 50 states allow minors to give their own consent for confidential STI screening, diagnosis, and treatment. Despite the high prevalence of STIs among adolescents, health care professionals frequently fail to inquire about sexual behavior, assess STI risks, counsel about risk reduction, and screen for STIs.

Within 3 years of initiation of consensual or nonconsensual sexual intercourse, all adolescent females should begin having annual Papanicolaou smears to screen for cervical dysplasia associated with human papillomavirus infection. For adolescent females who are immunosuppressed or immunocompromised, yearly Papanicolaou smears should begin with the initiation of consensual or unconsensual sexual intercourse. All young adult females should begin yearly Papanicolaou smear screening by 21 years of age. Sexually active adolescent females should be screened annually for

---

* American Academy of Pediatrics, Committee on Psychosocial Aspects of Child and Family Health. *Guidelines for Health Supervision III.* Elk Grove Village, IL: American Academy of Pediatrics; 1997 (updated 2002)
† Elster AB, Kuznets NJ, eds. *AMA Guidelines for Adolescent Preventive Services (GAPS) Recommendations and Rationale.* Baltimore, MD: Williams & Wilkins; 1997

Table 2.10. Adolescents Whose History Includes One or More of the Following Features Are Considered at Increased Risk of Contracting a Sexually Transmitted Infection (STI)[1]

- Sexual contact with person(s) with known STI or history of STI
- Symptoms or signs of STI
- Multiple sexual partners
- Street involvement (eg, homelessness)
- Sexual intercourse with new partner during last 2 months
- More than 2 sexual partners during previous 12 months
- No or inconsistent use of barrier contraceptive methods
- Injection drug use
- Males who have sex with males
- "Survival sex" (eg, exchanging sex for money, drugs, shelter, or food)
- Time spent in detention facilities
- Having been a patient in an STI clinic
- Having been pregnant or having requested a pregnancy test

[1] Modified from Health Canada. *Canadian STD Guidelines: 1998 Edition.* Ottawa, Ontario: Population and Public Health Branch, Health Canada; 1998. Available at: **www.phac-aspc.gc.ca/publicat/std-mts98/index.html**

chlamydia and gonorrhea. Many experts recommend more frequent screening, especially for *Chlamydia* infection, in patients with a previous STI diagnosis. There has been no official recommendation concerning the frequency of screening in asymptomatic sexually active adolescent males. Sexually active adolescents should receive HIV and syphilis prevention counseling at least annually, and screening should be provided for adolescents with a previous STI or with multiple sexual partners and for adolescents requesting screening annually. All adolescents should receive hepatitis B virus immunization if they were not immunized earlier in childhood, and hepatitis A vaccine should be offered to adolescent males who have sex with males (see Recommended Childhood and Adolescent Immunization Schedule, Fig 1.1, p 26).

For treatment recommendations for specific STIs, see the disease-specific chapters in Section 3 and Table 4.4, Guidelines for Treatment of Sexually Transmitted Infections in Children and Adolescents According to Syndrome (p 766). Patients and their partners treated for gonorrhea, *Chlamydia trachomatis* infection, and trichomoniasis should be advised to refrain from sexual intercourse for 1 week after completion of appropriate treatment. Retesting to detect therapeutic failure (tests of cure) for patients who receive recommended treatment regimens for *Neisseria gonorrhoeae* or *C trachomatis* infection no longer is recommended unless therapeutic adherence is in question or symptoms persist. If a multiple-dose regimen is used, nonadherence is possible. Retesting for chlamydia infection using nonculture techniques fewer than 3 to 4 weeks after treatment may yield false-positive results as a result of residual nonviable organisms. Many experts suggest repeat screening for these infections within 3 to 6 months because of the likelihood of reinfection as a result of nontreatment of a current sexual partner or from a new sexual partner.

PREVENTION

Pediatricians can contribute to primary prevention of STIs by encouraging adolescent patients to postpone their initiation of sexual intercourse and by preparing adolescents who become sexually active to correctly and consistently use barrier methods for prevention of pregnancy and of STIs beginning with the first intercourse experience. Adolescents should be reminded that barrier methods should be used with all forms of sexual intercourse (vaginal, oral, and anal). Pediatricians should encourage adolescents who already have had sexual intercourse to practice "secondary" abstinence (to be celibate), to minimize their lifetime number of sexual partners, to use barrier methods consistently and correctly to prevent pregnancy and infection, and to be aware of the strong association between alcohol or drug use and failure to appropriately use barrier methods correctly. The correct use of male and female condoms and some strategies for encouraging condom use are reviewed in Tables 2.11 (p 170) and 2.12 (p 171). Vaccines to prevent HPV infection are under clinical investigation.

Diagnosis and Treatment of STIs in Children*

Because of the social and legal implications of the diagnosis, STIs in children must be diagnosed using tests with high specificity, because the low prevalence of STIs in children increases the probability that rapid detection tests for STIs will give false-positive results. Therefore, tests that allow for isolation of the organism and have the highest specificities must be used.

Because of the serious implications of the diagnosis of an STI in a child, antimicrobial therapy for children with suspected STIs may need to be withheld until the final outcome of the diagnostic test is known. Specimens to screen for *N gonorrhoeae* and *C trachomatis* should be obtained for culture from the rectal area and vagina of girls and from the urethra of boys. Specimens to screen for *N gonorrhoeae* also should be obtained from the pharynx even in the absence of symptoms. Endocervical specimens for culture are not required for prepubertal girls; only vaginal specimens are required. If vaginal discharge is present, specimens for wet mount for *Trichomonas vaginalis* and wet mount or Gram stain for bacterial vaginosis may be obtained as well. Serum specimens for testing for syphilis, HIV, and hepatitis B surface antigen (if receipt of full immunization series cannot be documented) should be obtained. For more detailed diagnosis and treatment recommendations for specific STIs, see Section 3 and Table 4.4, Guidelines for Treatment of Sexually Transmitted Infections in Children and Adolescents According to Syndrome (p 766). If the girl being evaluated is pubertal or postmenarcheal, specimens for cultures of *C trachomatis* and *N gonorrhoeae* must be obtained from the endocervix.

Social Implications of STIs in Children

Children can acquire STIs through vertical transmission, by autoinoculation, or by sexual contact. Each of these mechanisms should be given appropriate consideration in the evaluation of a preadolescent child with an STI. Evaluation based solely on suspicion of an STI should not proceed until the STI diagnosis has been confirmed.

---

* Centers for Disease Control and Prevention. Sexually transmitted infections treatment guidelines—2006. *MMWR Recomm Rep.* 2006; in press (see **www.cdc.gov/mmwr**)

Table 2.11. Recommendations for Proper Use of Condoms[1] to Decrease the Risk of Transmission of Sexually Transmitted Infections[2]

Male Condoms

- Use a new condom with each act of sexual intercourse (penile-vaginal, oral, or anal intercourse).
- Carefully handle the condom to avoid damaging it with fingernails, teeth, or other sharp objects.
- Put condom on after the penis is erect and before genital contact with partner.
- Ensure that no air is trapped in the tip of the condom.
- Ensure that adequate lubrication exists during intercourse, possibly requiring the use of external lubricants.
- Use only water-based lubricants (eg, K-Y Jelly, Astroglide, Aqua-Lube, and glycerin) with latex condoms. Oil-based lubricants (eg, petroleum jelly, shortening, mineral oil, massage oils, body lotions, and cooking oil) can weaken latex.
- Hold the condom firmly against the base of the penis during withdrawal, and withdraw while penis is still erect to prevent slippage.

Female Condoms (eg, Reality)

- Lubricated polyurethane sheath with a ring on each end, one of which is inserted into the vagina and rests over the cervix like a diaphragm and the other remains outside the vagina and covers the external genitalia.
- When a male condom cannot be used appropriately, consider use of a female condom. Instructions about insertion may be needed.

---

[1] Note: Use of both female and male condoms at the same time is not recommended. Friction between the two surfaces may displace the condoms and contribute to loss of protection.

[2] From Centers for Disease Control and Prevention. Sexually transmitted infections treatment guidelines—2006. *MMWR Recomm Rep.* 2006; in press (see **www.cdc.gov/mmwr**)

Factors to be considered in assessing the likelihood of sexual abuse in a child with an STI include whether the child reports a history of sexual victimization, biologic characteristics of the STI in question, and age of the child (see Table 2.13, p 172).

Anogenital gonorrhea in a prepubertal child indicates sexual abuse in virtually every case. All confirmed cases of gonorrhea in prepubertal children beyond the neonatal period should be reported to the local child protective services agency for investigation.

Symptomatic herpes simplex has a short incubation period but can be transmitted by sexual or nonsexual contact with another person or by self-inoculation. In an infant or toddler in diapers, genital herpes may arise from any of these mechanisms. In a prepubertal child whose toilet-use activities are independent, the new occurrence of genital herpes should prompt a careful investigation, including a child protective services investigation, for suspected sexual abuse.

Trichomoniasis is transmitted perinatally or by sexual contact. In a perinatally infected infant, vaginal discharge can persist for several weeks; accordingly, intense

Table 2.12. Barriers to Condom Use and Ways to Overcome Them[1]

Perceived Barrier	Intervention Strategy
Decreases sexual pleasure or sensation (Note: often perceived by those who never have used a condom)	Encourage patient to try. Put a drop of water-based lubricant or saliva inside the tip of the condom or on the glans of the penis before putting on the condom. Try a thinner latex condom or different brand or more lubrication.
Decreases spontaneity of sexual activity	Encourage incorporation of condom use during foreplay. Remind patient that peace of mind may enhance pleasure for self and partner.
Embarrassing, juvenile, "unmanly"	Remind patient that it is "manly" to protect self and others.
Poor fit (too small or too big, slips off, uncomfortable)	Smaller and larger condoms are available.
Requires prompt withdrawal after ejaculation	Reinforce the protective nature of prompt withdrawal and suggest substitution of other postcoital sexual activities.
Fear of breakage may lead to less vigorous sexual activity	With prolonged intercourse, lubricant wears off and the condom begins to rub. Have a water-soluble lubricant available to reapply.
Nonpenetrative sexual activity	Condoms have been advocated for use during fellatio; unlubricated condoms may prove best for this purpose because of the taste of the lubricant. Other barriers, such as dental dams or an unlubricated condom cut down the middle to form a barrier, have been advocated for use during certain forms of nonpenetrative sexual activity (eg, cunnilingus and anolingual sex).
Allergy to latex	Polyurethane condoms for women are available commercially. A natural skin condom can be used together with a latex condom to protect the male or female from contact with latex.

[1] From Health Canada. Canadian STD Guidelines: 1998 Edition. Ottawa, Ontario: Population and Public Health Branch, Health Canada; 1998. Available at: **www.phac-aspc.gc.ca/publicat/std-mts98/index.html**

social investigation may not be warranted. However, a new diagnosis of trichomoniasis in an older infant or child should prompt a careful investigation, including a child protective services investigation, for suspected sexual abuse.

Infections that have long incubation periods (eg, human papillomavirus infection) and that can be asymptomatic for long periods after vertical transmission (eg, syphilis, HIV infection, *C trachomatis* infection, herpes simplex infection) are more problematic.

Table 2.13. Implications of Commonly Encountered Sexually Transmitted Infections (STIs) for Diagnosis and Reporting of Suspected or Diagnosed Sexual Abuse of Infants and Prepubertal Children[1]

STI Confirmed	Sexual Abuse	Suggested Action
Gonorrhea[2]	Diagnostic[3]	Report[4]
Syphilis[2]	Diagnostic	Report
Human immunodeficiency virus infection[5]	Diagnostic	Report
Chlamydia trachomatis infection[2]	Diagnostic[3]	Report
Trichomonas vaginalis infection	Highly suspicious	Report
Condylomata acuminata infection[2] (anogenital warts)	Suspicious	Report
Herpes (genital location)	Suspicious	Report[6]
Bacterial vaginosis	Inconclusive	Medical follow-up

[1] Adapted from American Academy of Pediatrics, Committee on Child Abuse and Neglect. The evaluation of sexual abuse in children. *Pediatrics.* 2005;116:506–512

[2] If not perinatally acquired and rare nonsexual vertical transmission is excluded.

[3] Although the culture technique is the "gold standard," current studies are investigating the use of nucleic acid amplification testing as an alternative diagnostic method in children.

[4] Report to the agency mandated in the community to receive reports of suspected sexual abuse.

[5] If not acquired perinatally or by transfusion.

[6] Unless there is a clear history of autoinoculation.

The possibility of vertical transmission should be considered in these cases, but an evaluation of the patient's circumstances by the local child protective services agency usually is warranted.

Although hepatitis B virus, *Gardnerella vaginalis*, scabies, and pediculosis pubis may be transmitted sexually, other modes of transmission can occur. The discovery of any of these conditions in a prepubertal child does not warrant child protective services involvement unless the clinician finds other information that suggests abuse. The presence of *G vaginalis* does not indicate a diagnosis of bacterial vaginosis (see Bacterial Vaginosis, p 225).

Sexual Victimization and STIs

GENERAL CONSIDERATIONS

Child sexual abuse has been defined as the exploitation of a child, either by physical contact or by other interactions, for the sexual stimulation of an adult or a minor who is in a position of power over the child. Sexual victimization of a child younger than 18 years of age by a caregiver is termed *abuse;* physicians are required by law to report abuse to their state child protective services agency. Sexual victimization of a child or adolescent by a person who is not a caregiver is termed *assault.* In some instances, sexual victimization involves physical contact permitting the transfer of sexually transmitted microorganisms. Approximately 5% of sexually abused children acquire an STI as a result of the victimization.

SCREENING ASYMPTOMATIC SEXUALLY VICTIMIZED CHILDREN FOR STIs

Factors that influence the likelihood that a sexually victimized child will acquire an STI include the regional prevalence of STIs in the adult population, the number of assailants, the type and frequency of physical contact between the perpetrator(s) and the child, the infectivity of various microorganisms, the child's susceptibility to infection, and whether the child has received intercurrent antimicrobial agent treatment. The time interval between a child's physical contact with an assailant and the medical evaluation influences the likelihood that an exposed child will demonstrate signs or symptoms of an STI.

The decision to obtain genital or other specimens from a child who has been sexually victimized to conduct an STI evaluation must be made on an individual basis. The following situations involve a high risk of STIs and constitute a strong indication for testing:

- The child has or has had signs or symptoms of an STI or an infection that can be transmitted sexually, even in the absence of suspicion of sexual abuse.
- A sibling, another child, or an adult in the household or child's immediate environment has an STI.
- A suspected assailant is known to have an STI or to be at high risk of STIs (eg, has had multiple sexual partners or a history of STIs) or has an unknown history.
- The patient or family requests testing.
- The prevalence of STIs in the community is high.
- Evidence of genital, oral, or anal penetration or ejaculation is present.

See Table 2.14 (p 174) if STI testing of a child is to be performed.

Most experts recommend universal screening of postpubertal patients who have been victims of sexual abuse or assault, because the prevalence of preexisting asymptomatic infection in this group is high. When STI screening is performed, it should focus on likely anatomic sites of infection (as determined by the patient's history or by epidemiologic considerations) and should include assessment for HIV infection if the patient, family, or both consent to serologic screening; assessment for bacterial vaginosis for female patients and trichomoniasis; use of liquid-based cytologic screening and human papillomavirus testing for evaluation of abnormal cervical cells; and testing for *N gonorrhoeae* infection, *C trachomatis* infection, and syphilis. To preserve the "chain of custody" for information that may later constitute legal evidence, specimens for laboratory analysis obtained from sexually victimized patients should be labeled carefully, and standard hospital procedures for transferring specimens from site to site should be followed carefully. Only tests with high specificities, such as culture or simultaneous use of 2 nucleic acid amplification tests, should be used, and specimens should be obtained by health care professionals with experience in the evaluation of sexually abused and assaulted children. A follow-up visit approximately 2 weeks after the most recent sexual exposure may include a repeat physical examination and collection of additional specimens. Another follow-up visit approximately 12 weeks after the most recent sexual exposure may be necessary to collect convalescent sera to test for syphilis and HIV.

Table 2.14. Sexually Transmitted Infection (STI) Testing in a Child[1] When Sexual Abuse Is Suspected

Organism/Syndrome	Specimens
Neisseria gonorrhoeae	Rectal, throat, urethral (male), and/or vaginal cultures[2]
Chlamydia trachomatis	Rectal, urethral (male), and vaginal cultures[2]
Syphilis	Darkfield examination of chancre fluid, if present; blood for serologic tests at time of abuse and 6, 12, and 24 wk later
Human immunodeficiency virus	Serologic testing of abuser (if possible); serologic testing of child at time of abuse and 6, 12, and 24 wk later
Hepatitis B virus	Serum hepatitis B surface antigen testing of abuser or hepatitis B surface antibody testing of child, unless the child has received 3 doses of hepatitis B vaccine
Herpes simplex virus	Culture of lesion
Bacterial vaginosis	Wet mount, pH, and potassium hydroxide testing of vaginal discharge or Gram stain in pubertal and postmenarcheal girls
Human papillomavirus	Biopsy of lesion
Trichomonas vaginalis	Wet mount and culture of vaginal discharge
Pediculus pubis	Identification of eggs, nymphs, and lice with naked eye or using hand lens

[1] See text for indications for testing for STIs (Screening Asymptomatic Sexually Victimized Children for STIs, p 173).
[2] Cervical specimens are not recommended or necessary for prepubertal girls, but cervical specimens must be obtained in pubertal premenarchal and pubertal postmenarcheal girls.

PROPHYLAXIS AFTER SEXUAL VICTIMIZATION

Most experts do not recommend antimicrobial prophylaxis for abused asymptomatic prepubertal children, because their incidence of STIs is low, the risk of spread to the upper genital tract in a prepubertal girl is low, and follow-up usually can be ensured. If a test result for an STI is positive, treatment then can be given. Factors that may increase the likelihood of infection or that constitute an indication for prophylaxis are the same as those listed under Screening Asymptomatic Sexually Victimized Children for STIs (p 173).

Many experts believe that prophylaxis is warranted for postpubertal female patients who seek care within 72 hours after an episode of sexual victimization because of the high prevalence of preexisting asymptomatic infection and the substantial risk of pelvic inflammatory disease in this age group. All patients who receive prophylaxis should be screened for relevant STIs (see Table 2.14) before treatment is given. Postmenarcheal patients should be tested for pregnancy before antimicrobial treatment or emergency contraception is given. Regimens for prophylaxis are presented in Tables 2.15, p 175 (children), and 2.16, p 176 (adolescents).

Because of the demonstrated effectiveness of prophylaxis to prevent HIV infection after perinatal and occupational exposures, the question arises about HIV prophylaxis for children and adolescents after sexual assault (see also Human Immunodeficiency

Table 2.15. Prophylaxis After Sexual Victimization of Preadolescent Children[1]

Weight <100 lb (<45 kg)		Weight ≥100 lb (≥45 kg)
	For prevention of gonorrhea	
1. Ceftriaxone, 125 mg, intramuscularly, in a single dose		1A. Ceftriaxone, 125 mg, intramuscularly, in a single dose
		OR
		1B. Cefixime, 400 mg, orally, in a single dose
PLUS	**For prevention of *Chlamydia trachomatis* infection**	**PLUS**
2A. Azithromycin, 20 mg/kg (maximum 1 g), orally, in a single dose		2A. Azithromycin, 1 g, orally, in a single dose
OR		**OR**
2B. Erythromycin base or ethylsuccinate, 50 mg/kg per day, divided into 4 doses for 14 days		2B. Doxycycline, 100 mg, twice daily, for 7 days (if at least 8 years of age)
PLUS	**For prevention of hepatitis B virus infection**	**PLUS**
3. Begin or complete hepatitis B virus immunization if not fully immunized		3. Begin or complete hepatitis B virus immunization if not fully immunized
PLUS	**For prevention of trichomoniasis and bacterial vaginosis**	**PLUS**
4. Consideration should be given to adding prophylaxis for trichomoniasis and bacterial vaginosis (metronidazole, 15 mg/kg per day, orally, in 3 divided doses for 7 days)		4. Consideration should be given to adding prophylaxis against trichomoniasis and bacterial vaginosis (metronidazole, 2 g, orally, in a single dose)

[1] See text for discussion of prophylaxis for human immunodeficiency virus infection in children after sexual abuse or assault.

Virus Infection, Control Measures, p 393, and Table 3.27, p 394.) Data are insufficient concerning the efficacy and safety of postexposure prophylaxis among children and adults. The risk of HIV transmission from a single sexual assault that involves transfer of secretions and/or blood is low, but not zero. Prophylaxis may be considered for patients who seek care within 24 to 48 hours after an assault if the assault involved the transfer of secretions and particularly if the alleged perpetrator is known

Table 2.16. Prophylaxis After Sexual Victimization of Adolescents[1]

Antimicrobial prophylaxis[2] is recommended to include an empiric regimen to prevent *Chlamydia trachomatis* infection, gonorrhea, trichomoniasis, and bacterial vaginosis

For gonorrhea[3]	Ceftriaxone, 125 mg, intramuscularly, in a single dose **OR** Cefixime, 400 mg orally, in a single dose **OR** Ciprofloxacin, 500 mg, orally, in a single dose **OR** Ofloxacin, 400 mg, orally, in a single dose **OR** Levofloxacin, 250 mg, orally, in a single dose **PLUS**
For *C trachomatis* infection	Azithromycin, 1 g, orally, in a single dose **OR** Doxycycline, 100 mg, orally, twice a day for 7 days (for those ≥8 years of age and not pregnant) **PLUS**
For trichomoniasis and bacterial vaginosis	Metronidazole, 2 g, orally, in a single dose **PLUS**
For hepatitis B virus infection	Hepatitis B virus immunization at time of initial examination, if not fully immunized. Follow-up doses of vaccine should be administered 1–2 and 4–6 mo after the first dose. **PLUS**
For human immunodeficiency virus infection[2]	Consider offering prophylaxis for HIV, depending on circumstances (see Table 3.27, p 394)

Emergency Contraception[4]

Plan B (levonorgestrel 0.75 mg), 2 tablets at the same time

OR

Oral contraceptive pills each containing 20 or 30 µg of ethinyl estradiol plus levonorgestrel 0.1 mg or 0.15 mg or 0.3 mg norgestrel: each of 2 doses must be given 12 h apart. Each dose must contain at least 100–120 µg of ethinyl estradiol and 0.5 to 0.6 mg levonorgestrel or 1 mg norgestrel.

PLUS

An antiemetic (eg, meclizine, 25-50 mg, once before the first dose of oral contraceptive)

---

[1] Source: Centers for Disease Control and Prevention. Sexually transmitted infections treatment guidelines—2006. *MMWR Recomm Rep.* 2006; in press (see **www.cdc.gov/mmwr**)

[2] See text for discussion of prophylaxis for human immunodeficiency virus (HIV) infection after sexual abuse or assault.

[3] A single dose of a fluoroquinolone can be used in areas of low prevalence of fluoroquinolone-resistant *Neisseria gonorrhoeae*. Because of resistance, fluoroquinolones should not be used if infection is acquired in Asia, the Pacific Islands (including Hawaii), California, and other areas with increased fluoroquinolone-resistant *N gonorrhoeae*. Quinolones should not be used in pregnant women.

[4] The patient should have a negative pregnancy test result before emergency contraception is given. Although emergency contraception is most effective if taken within 72 hours of event, data suggest it is effective up to 120 hours.

or suspected to have HIV infection or to have used injection drugs (see Human Immunodeficiency Virus Infection, p 378). Following are recommendations for post-exposure assessment of children within 72 hours of sexual assault:

- Review HIV/AIDS local epidemiology and assess risk of HIV infection in the assailant.
- Evaluate circumstances of assault that may affect risk of HIV transmission.
- Consult with a specialist in treating HIV-infected children if postexposure prophylaxis is considered.
- If the child appears to be at risk of HIV transmission from the assault, discuss postexposure prophylaxis with the caregiver(s), including toxicity and unknown efficacy.
- If caregivers choose for the child to receive antiretroviral postexposure prophylaxis, provide enough medication until the return visit at 3 to 7 days after initial assessment to reevaluate the child and to assess tolerance of medication; dosages should not exceed those for adults.
- Perform HIV antibody test at original assessment and 6, 12, and 24 weeks later.

HEPATITIS AND YOUTH IN CORRECTIONS SETTINGS*

The number of arrests of juveniles (younger than 18 years of age) in the United States has decreased from 2.8 million in 1997 to 2.2 million in 2003, representing almost 3% of the pediatric population. More than 300 000 youth are maintained annually in detention facilities awaiting court hearings, and on any given day, more than 140 000 adolescents are incarcerated in juvenile corrections facilities or adult prisons or jails. Incarceration periods of at least 90 days await 60% of juvenile inmates, and 15% can expect to be confined for a year or more behind bars. Incarcerated youth disproportionately are male and are more likely to be members of ethnic or racial minorities. Female juveniles constitute 13% of the incarcerated juvenile population, and pregnancy often presents additional challenges in the provision of medical services in corrections facilities.

Juvenile offenders commonly lack regular access to preventive health care in their communities and suffer significantly greater health deficiencies, including psychosocial disorders, chronic illness, exposure to illicit drugs, and physical trauma when compared with adolescents who are not in the juvenile justice system.[†] Detained youth are more likely to have contracted sexually transmitted infections (STIs) early in adolescence, and delayed or incomplete treatment places them at increased risk of chronic complications of chlamydia, gonorrhea, syphilis, and human papillomavirus infections. Tuberculosis (TB) is more common in corrections populations, and although current juvenile detainees continue to have a low prevalence of human immunodeficiency virus (HIV) infection, their lifestyle choices place them at significant risk.[‡] However, hepatitis A, hepatitis B, and hepatitis C virus infections are of particular concern because of the increased frequency of alcohol and injection drug use and the

---

* Centers for Disease Control and Prevention. Prevention and control of infections with hepatitis viruses in correctional settings. *MMWR Recomm Rep.* 2003;52(RR-1):1–33

† Centers for Disease Control and Prevention. Guideline for isolation precautions: preventing transmission of infectious agents in healthcare settings. Recommendations of the Healthcare Infection Control Practice Advisory Committee, 2006. *MMWR.* 2006; in press (see **www.cdc.gov/mmwr**)

‡ American Academy of Pediatrics, Committee on Adolescence. Health care for children and adolescents in the juvenile correctional care system. *Pediatrics.* 2001;107:799–803

increased rate of unprotected sex with multiple partners early in life. Juvenile crimes involving drug abuse violations have increased 19% over the past 10 years, and a history of injection drug use has played a major role in explaining the increased incidence of hepatitis C virus infections in adolescent offenders. Hepatitis may be a comorbid condition of other diseases, including TB and HIV infection, and infected juveniles may place their communities at risk after their release from detention.

Up to 15% of all chronic hepatitis B virus infections and more than 30% of all hepatitis C virus infections known to exist in the United States can be traced to people released from corrections facilities. High-risk behaviors make adolescents particularly vulnerable to hepatitis A, hepatitis B, and hepatitis C virus infection well before their first incarceration. Fewer than 3% of new hepatitis virus infections of all types are acquired once incarceration has occurred. Most juvenile offenders ultimately are returned to their community and, without intervention, resume a high-risk lifestyle. High recidivism rates lead many juvenile offenders to adult prisons, where rates of hepatitis B and hepatitis C virus infection may be significantly higher than those found in juvenile corrections facilities. Corrections facilities, in partnership with public health departments and other community resources, have the opportunity to assess, contain, control, and prevent liver infection in a highly vulnerable segment of the population. Hepatitis C virus presents the greatest challenge to corrections facilities overall because of the lack of a vaccine to protect prisoners and the public. The extremely high rate of chronic carriage in people who already are infected increases the risk to their communities on their release. The controlled nature of the corrections system facilitates initiation of many hepatitis prevention and treatment strategies for a pediatric population that otherwise is difficult to reach. Pediatricians should work with state and local public health agencies and corrections administrators to address the health needs of youth in detention and to protect the community as a whole.

Hepatitis A

Corrections facilities in the United States rarely report cases of hepatitis A virus infection, and national prevalence data for incarcerated populations are not available. States that have assessed prevalence in incarcerated populations younger than 20 years of age show a similar ethnic distribution of predominance in American Indian/Alaska Native and Hispanic inmates, as is reflected in at-risk populations as a whole. Some estimates suggest an overall hepatitis A virus seroprevalence between 22% and 39% in the adult prison population, with up to a 43% prevalence found in older prisoners between 40 and 49 years of age. Adolescent risk factors that could contribute to outbreaks of hepatitis A virus infection include using injection and noninjection street drugs, having multiple sexual partners, and participating in homosexual activity. Hepatitis A virus coinfection increases the severity of liver complications in patients with chronic liver disease caused by hepatitis B or hepatitis C virus infection in incarcerated youth, who experience higher rates of hepatitis C virus infection compared with adolescents who remain outside the justice system. Inmates who reside or are detained in facilities located in states and regions of the United States with high hepatitis A virus infection endemicity (see Hepatitis A, p 326) particularly are at risk of dual hepatitis virus infections.

RECOMMENDATIONS FOR CONTROL OF HEPATITIS A VIRUS INFECTIONS IN INCARCERATED YOUTH. Routine screening of incarcerated youth for hepatitis A virus serologic markers is not recommended. However, adolescents who have signs or symptoms of hepatitis should be tested for acute hepatitis A, hepatitis B, and hepatitis C virus infections. Before their release, hepatitis A vaccine (see Hepatitis A Vaccine, p 328) should be given to all adolescents in corrections facilities located in states with existing programs for routine hepatitis A immunization of adolescents, generally in states that historically had the highest hepatitis A rates. Corrections facilities in all states should consider routine hepatitis A immunization of all adolescents under their care because of the likelihood that most adolescents have indications for hepatitis A immunization. If this is not possible, hepatitis A vaccine should be provided to juveniles with high-risk profiles, including illicit drug users and adolescents who engage in homosexual activity. Routine postimmunization serologic testing is not recommended. There is no contraindication to giving hepatitis A virus vaccine to an individual who may be immune as the result of a previous hepatitis A virus infection or immunization. Incarcerated juveniles found to have hepatitis A disease should be reported to the local health department.

Hepatitis B

The rate of hepatitis B virus infection in the general population in the United States is influenced by well-recognized risk factors that promote exchange of or exposure to blood, saliva, semen, and vaginal fluid (see Hepatitis B, p 335). At-risk adolescents in corrections facilities include inmates from minority populations (Asian, American Indian/Alaska Native, black, and Hispanic, in descending order of hepatitis B disease prevalence); inmates engaged in injection drug use with needle sharing; inmates who have had early initiation of sexual intercourse, unprotected sexual activity, multiple sexual partners, or history of STIs; and male adolescents who engage in homosexual activity. Although no published national studies have determined hepatitis B prevalence rates for incarcerated juveniles, rates of hepatitis B seroprevalence in homeless and high-risk street youth are higher when compared with peers lacking risk factors. Studies investigating hepatitis B outbreaks in prison settings also suggest that horizontal transmission may occur when chronic carriers of hepatitis B virus are present. Adolescent female inmates present additional challenges for hepatitis B assessment and management if they are pregnant during incarceration, in which case coordination of care for mother and infant become paramount.

RECOMMENDATIONS FOR CONTROL OF HEPATITIS B VIRUS INFECTIONS IN INCARCERATED YOUTH. Routine screening of juvenile inmates for hepatitis B virus markers generally is not recommended. However, in states with school entry laws (**www.immunize.org/laws**), where high levels of adolescent hepatitis B immunization have been achieved, adolescents who entered school when a law was in effect may be considered immunized. In other states, in the absence of proof of immunization, initial testing for hepatitis B immunity may save vaccine costs, provided the speed of testing does not delay hepatitis B immunization should the patient lack immunity. Corrections facilities may wish periodically to survey juvenile inmates for hepatitis B immunity as they enter the institution to approximate hepatitis B prevalence and determine the desirability of preimmunization testing. Adolescent detainees with signs and symptoms of hepatitis should be tested for hepatitis A, hepatitis B, and hepatitis C virus to determine the presence of acute or chronic infection and coinfection. All pregnant adolescents should be tested for hepatitis B surface antigen (HBsAg). High-risk behaviors by this population preclude reliance on negative preincarceration HBsAg test reports or a self-reported history of hepatitis B immunization.

All adolescents receiving medical evaluation in a corrections facility should begin the hepatitis B vaccine series or complete a previously begun series unless they have proof of completion of a previous immunization series. Beginning a hepatitis B vaccine series is critical, because a single dose of vaccine may confer protection from the complications of chronic carriage in a high-risk adolescent who may be lost to follow-up. Routine pre- and postimmunization serologic screening is not recommended. In states where hepatitis B vaccine school entry requirements are in place, corrections facilities may use a combination of immunization history, immunization registry data, school entry immunization laws, and serologic testing to develop institutional policies regarding the need for hepatitis B immunization in specific age groups of adolescents. Corrections facilities should have mechanisms in place for completion of the hepatitis B series in the community after release of the juvenile. Immunization information should be made available to the inmate, the parents or legal guardian, the state immunization registry, and the patient's future medical home in the community.

Postexposure hepatitis B prophylaxis regimens for unimmunized incarcerated adolescents after potential percutaneous or sexual exposures to hepatitis B virus are available (see Hepatitis B, Care of Exposed People, p 350). Should the source of the exposure be found to be HBsAg positive, the unimmunized inmate exposed percutaneously should receive Hepatitis B Immune Globulin (HBIG) within 3 days of exposure. Sexual exposures do not require HBIG intervention, only completion of the hepatitis B immunization series. Exposed juveniles who have not completed their hepatitis B vaccine series should receive the remainder of the series as scheduled.

All pregnant adolescents should be tested for HBsAg at the time a pregnancy is discovered, regardless of hepatitis B immunization history and previous results of tests for HBsAg and antibody to HBsAg. Pregnant adolescents who are HBsAg negative should begin the hepatitis B vaccine series as soon as possible during the course of pregnancy. Pregnancy is not a contraindication to receiving hepatitis B vaccine in any trimester. The pregnant adolescent's HBsAg status should be reported to the patient's prenatal care facility, the hospital where she will deliver the infant, and the state health department where case management assistance will occur. Infants born to HBsAg-positive mothers must receive a dose of hepatitis B vaccine and HBIG within 12 hours of birth (see Hepatitis B, Care of Exposed People, p 350).

Incarcerated adolescents who are found to have evidence of chronic hepatitis B infection should be evaluated by a specialist to determine the extent of their liver disease and their eligibility for antiviral intervention. Detainees who are HBsAg positive should be reported to the local health department to facilitate long-term follow-up on their release.

All chronic carriers of hepatitis B virus should be immunized with hepatitis A vaccine to prevent fulminant liver disease should coinfection with hepatitis A virus occur. Inmates who are chronic hepatitis B carriers should be counseled against the use and abuse of alcohol and street drugs, both of which seriously can degrade liver function in patients with hepatitis B-induced cirrhosis. Chronic carriers of hepatitis B virus may remain infectious to sexual and household contacts for life and must be counseled accordingly to protect sexual partners and household contacts.

Hepatitis C

Of the nearly 4 million cases of hepatitis C virus infection in the United States, approximately 30% can be traced to individuals who spent time within the nation's corrections institutions. The most common mode of acquisition of hepatitis C virus for inmates is injection drug use, and exposure to multiple sexual partners is a distant second. Up to 80% of inmates who use injection street drugs will be infected with hepatitis C virus within 5 years after the onset of their drug use. Tattooing and body piercing are not thought to be significant sources of transmission of hepatitis C virus. Prevalence studies of hepatitis C virus infection in incarcerated youth are limited but show an approximate two- to fourfold increase over youth who are not in the juvenile justice system. Injection drug use is the predominant hepatitis C virus infection risk factor for detained juveniles. Repetitive residence within corrections facilities increases hepatitis C virus infection prevalence rates in adult inmates to 10 times the rate reported in the US population as a whole.

Testing inmates for hepatitis C virus infection has created conflicts for administrators of corrections facilities. Many do not view the diagnosis and potential treatment of detainees with hepatitis C virus infection as part of the corrections mission. Inmates commonly refuse testing, even when at high risk of hepatitis, to avoid persecution from fellow prisoners. The lack of a vaccine for hepatitis C virus places a substantial burden on prevention counseling to elicit changes in high-risk behaviors and health maintenance counseling to decrease health risks in people already infected. This includes lifestyle alterations and avoidance of street drug and alcohol abuse, which strongly affect chronic hepatitis C morbidity and mortality rates.

RECOMMENDATIONS FOR CONTROL OF HEPATITIS C VIRUS INFECTIONS IN INCARCERATED YOUTH. Routine screening of incarcerated adolescents for hepatitis C virus infection is not recommended. Focused screening of adult inmates on the basis of risk criteria has proven reliable and cost-effective for corrections facilities that use it consistently. Risk factor assessments of newly admitted juvenile inmates being considered for hepatitis C testing might include (1) self-reported history of injection drug use; (2) history of liver disease; (3) presence of hepatitis B core antibody; (4) increased alanine transaminase concentration; or (5) history of hemodialysis or receipt of clotting factors, blood transfusions, or organ transplants. Hepatitis C antibody screening of detainees with 1 risk factor or more will detect more than 90% of hepatitis C virus infections in corrections facilities. Some juvenile offenders may withhold reporting risk criteria behaviors and yet express interest in hepatitis C testing when offered. These requests, in most instances, should be accommodated. Adolescents with signs or symptoms of hepatitis should undergo diagnostic testing for hepatitis A, hepatitis B, and hepatitis C virus infection.

Adolescents who test positive for antibody to hepatitis C virus should receive ongoing medical attention to determine the likelihood of chronic hepatitis C virus infection, and cases should be reported to the local health department. The presence of hepatitis C virus antibody and the absence of hepatitis C virus RNA nucleic acid do not preclude the possibility of persistent chronic active disease. Hepatitis C virus antigenemia is variable from day to day and occurs in the presence of circulating hepatitis C antibody. Juveniles found to have chronic hepatitis C infection should receive ongoing medical evaluation (in consultation with an expert in caring for chronic hepatic disease) to monitor the course of their liver disease and to determine their suitability for therapeutic interventions in the future (see Hepatitis C, p 355). Incarcerated adolescents with hepatitis C virus infection should be enrolled in a risk-reduction program for drug and alcohol avoidance as indicated and should receive counseling for safe sex practices for the safety of their sexual partners and the protection of the community at large (**www.cdc.gov/ncidod/diseases/hepatitis/ resource/index.htm#training**). Incarcerated adolescents who are diagnosed with hepatitis C virus infection should be immunized against hepatitis A and hepatitis B virus if not already immune.

MEDICAL EVALUATION OF INTERNATIONALLY ADOPTED CHILDREN FOR INFECTIOUS DISEASES*

Annually, more than 20 000 children from other countries are adopted by families in the United States. More than 90% of international adoptees are from Asian (China, South Korea, Philippines, Vietnam, and India), Central and South American (Guatemala and Colombia), and Eastern European countries (Russia, Belarus, Ukraine, Kazakhstan, and Bulgaria). Africa and the Middle East are less common origins for international adoptees, but an increasing minority of children are from Ethiopia, Sierra Leone, Liberia, and other African countries. The diverse birth countries of these children, their unknown medical histories before adoption, their previous living circumstances (eg, orphanages and/or foster care), and the limited availability of reliable health care in some economically developing countries make the medical evaluation of internationally adopted children a challenging but important task.

Internationally adopted children typically differ from refugee children in terms of their access to medical care and treatment before arrival in the United States and in the frequency of certain infectious diseases. Many refugee children may have resided in refugee processing camps for months before resettlement in the United States and will have had access to medical care and treatment services. The history of access to and quality of medical care for international adoptees can be variable. Before admission to the United States, all internationally adopted children are required to have a medical examination performed by a physician designated by the US State Department in their country of origin. However, this examination is limited to completing legal requirements for screening for certain communicable diseases and examination

---

* For additional information, see Canadian Paediatric Society. *Children and Youth New to Canada: Health Care Guide.* Ottawa, Ontario: Canadian Paediatric Society; 1999; and the CDC (**www.cdc.gov/travel**) and World Health Organization (**www.who.int**) Web sites.

for serious physical or mental defects that would prevent the issue of a permanent residency visa. This evaluation is not a comprehensive assessment of the child's health. During adoption visits, pediatricians can stress to prospective parents the importance of acquiring immunization records. Internationally adopted children who are younger than 10 years of age are exempt from Immigration and Nationality Act (INA) regulations pertaining to immunization of immigrants before arrival in the United States (see Refugees and Immigrants, p 96). Adoptive parents are required to sign a waiver indicating their intention to comply with US-recommended immunizations after arrival in the United States.

Infectious diseases are among the most common medical diagnoses identified in international adoptees after arrival in the United States. Children may be asymptomatic, and therefore, the diagnoses must be made by screening tests in addition to history and physical examination. Because of inconsistent perinatal screening for hepatitis B and hepatitis C virus, syphilis, and human immunodeficiency virus (HIV) and the high prevalence of certain intestinal parasites and tuberculosis, all international adoptees should be screened for these infections on arrival in the United States. Suggested screening tests for infectious diseases are listed in Table 2.17, p 184 (see also disease-specific chapters in Section 3). In addition to these infections, other medical and developmental issues, including hearing and vision assessment, evaluation of growth and development, nutritional assessment, determining exposure to lead, complete blood cell count with red blood cell indices, newborn screening and/or measurement of thyroid-stimulating hormone concentration, and examination for congenital anomalies (including fetal alcohol syndrome), should be part of the initial evaluation of any internationally adopted child.

Internationally adopted children should be examined within 3 weeks of arrival in the United States or earlier if there are immediate health concerns. Parents generally will have limited information about a child before the adoption. It is optimal to have the parents meet with a physician before their child arrives home to review available information and to discuss common medical issues regarding internationally adopted children. Parents who have not met with a physician before adoption should notify their physician when their child arrives so that a timely medical evaluation can be arranged.

Viral Hepatitis

The prevalence of hepatitis B surface antigen (HBsAg) in internationally adopted children ranges from 1% to 5%, depending on the country of origin and year studied. Prevalence of markers of past hepatitis B virus (HBV) infection is higher. Hepatitis B virus infection is most prevalent in adoptees from Asia, Africa, and some countries in central and Eastern Europe (eg, Romania) and the newly independent states of the former Soviet Union (eg, Russia and Ukraine). However, HBV infection also occurs in adoptees born in other countries. Therefore, all children should undergo serologic testing for HBV infection, including HBsAg, antibody to HBsAg (anti-HBs), and antibody to hepatitis B core antigen (anti-HBc), to identify current or chronic infection, past resolved infection, or evidence of immunization (see Hepatitis B, p 335). Hepatitis B virus tests performed in the country of origin may not be useful, because testing

Table 2.17. Screening Tests for Infectious Diseases in International Adoptees

Hepatitis B virus serologic testing:

    Hepatitis B surface antigen (HBsAg)

    Antibody to hepatitis B surface antigen (anti-HBs)

    Antibody to hepatitis B core antigen (anti-HBc)

Hepatitis C virus serologic testing (see text)

Syphilis serologic testing

    Nontreponemal test (RPR, VDRL, or ART)

    Treponemal test (MHA-TP or FTA-ABS)

Human immunodeficiency virus 1 and 2 serologic testing

Complete blood cell count with red blood cell indices

Stool examination for ova and parasites (3 specimens)[1]

Stool examination for *Giardia lamblia and Cryptosporidium* antigen (1 specimen)[1]

Tuberculin skin test[1]

RPR indicates rapid plasma reagin; VDRL, Venereal Disease Research Laboratories; ART, automated reagin test; MHA-TP, microhemagglutination test for *Treponema pallidum*; FTA-ABS, fluorescent treponemal antibody absorption.
[1] See text.

---

may be incomplete and accuracy can vary. Because HBV has a long incubation period, the child may have become infected at or near the time testing was performed. Therefore, strong consideration should be given to a repeated evaluation 6 months after adoption for all children, especially children adopted from institutions. Chronic HBV infection is indicated by persistence of HBsAg for more than 6 months. Children with HBsAg-positive test results should be evaluated to identify the presence of chronic HBV infection and to assess for biochemical evidence of severe or chronic liver disease and the need for further evaluation (see Hepatitis B, p 335).

All exposed household contacts of a child found to be HBsAg positive should have documentation of HBV immunization or have the series initiated (see Hepatitis B, p 335). Adopted children who test negative for HBV should receive immunization for HBV as soon as possible according to the recommended childhood and adolescent immunization schedule (Fig 1.1, p 26). Children who test positive for HBsAg and anti-HBc are infected with HBV acutely or chronically and need not be immunized.

Hepatitis D virus, which occurs only in conjunction with active HBV replication, may be found in adoptees, particularly from Eastern Europe, Africa, South America, and the Middle East. Serologic tests for diagnosis of hepatitis D virus infection are available (see Hepatitis D, p 359), but routine testing is not recommended, because a positive test does not alter clinical management.

Many internationally adopted children have acquired hepatitis A virus (HAV) infection early in life and are, therefore, protected. Routine serologic screening for HAV antibody generally is not indicated to detect susceptible children. However, because routine childhood immunization against HAV is recommended in the United

States beginning at 1 to 2 years (12–35 months) of age (see Hepatitis A, p 326), antibody testing for HAV may be considered to be cost-effective to determine whether these children have evidence of previous infection. If a child has no evidence of previous infection, the child should be immunized against HAV as recommended.

Children from China, Russia, Eastern Europe, and Southeast Asia should be screened for hepatitis C infection. The decision to screen children from other areas should depend on history (eg, receipt of blood products, maternal drug use) and prevalence of infection in the child's country of origin.

Cytomegalovirus

Routine screening for cytomegalovirus (CMV) is not recommended. Shedding of CMV in young children following postnatal acquisition is common in the United States and worldwide. Parents should use appropriate hand hygiene practices.

Intestinal Pathogens

Fecal examinations for ova and parasites by an experienced laboratory will identify a pathogen in 15% to 35% of internationally adopted children. The prevalence of intestinal parasites varies by age of the child and country of origin. The most common pathogens identified are *Giardia lamblia*, *Hymenolepis* species, *Ascaris lumbricoides*, and *Trichuris trichiura*. *Strongyloides stercoralis*, *Entamoeba histolytica*, and hookworm are recovered less commonly. One stool specimen generally is sufficient for testing for intestinal ova and parasites and *Giardia* antigen in asymptomatic children, although some experts recommend that 3 specimens be tested to detect *Ascaris* and tapeworm infections. If gastrointestinal tract signs or symptoms or malnutrition are present, 3 stool specimens should be examined for ova and parasites in addition to a single stool specimen screened for *G lamblia* and *Cryptosporidium parvum* antigens. Therapy for intestinal parasites generally will be successful, but complete eradication may not occur always. Therefore, repeat ova and parasite testing after treatment in children who remain symptomatic is important to ensure successful elimination of parasites. In addition, children with gastrointestinal tract symptoms or signs that occur or recur months or even years after arrival in the United States should be reevaluated for intestinal parasites. In addition, testing stool specimens for *Salmonella* species, *Shigella* species, *Campylobacter* species, and *Escherichia coli* O157:H7 should be considered in children with diarrhea, especially if stools are bloody.

Tuberculosis

Tuberculosis commonly is encountered in international adoptees from all countries. Reported rates of latent *Mycobacterium tuberculosis* infection range from 0.6% to 30%. Because tuberculosis may be more severe in young children and may reactivate in later years, screening with the tuberculin skin test (TST) particularly is important in this high-risk population (see Tuberculosis, p 678). Routine chest radiography is not indicated in asymptomatic children in whom the TST result is negative. However, some international adoptees may be anergic because of malnutrition, which is common in these children. If malnutrition is suspected, the TST should be repeated once the child is better nourished. Receipt of bacille Calmette-Guérin (BCG) vaccine is not a contraindication to a TST, and a positive TST result should not be attributed to

BCG vaccine. In these children, further investigation is necessary to determine whether latent tuberculosis infection or active disease is present and therapy is needed (see Tuberculosis, p 678). Some children will have been exposed recently to individuals with tuberculosis disease. Preventive therapy should be considered if such history is attainable. Some experts repeat TST 6 months after a child has left an area with high prevalence of tuberculosis. When tuberculosis is suspected in an international adoptee, efforts to isolate and test the organism for drug susceptibilities are imperative because of the high prevalence of drug resistance in many countries.

Syphilis

Congenital syphilis, especially with involvement of the central nervous system, may not have been diagnosed or may have been treated inadequately in adoptees from some developing countries. Each international adoptee should be screened for syphilis by reliable nontreponemal and treponemal serologic tests, regardless of history or a report of treatment (see Syphilis, p 631). Children with positive treponemal serologic test results should be evaluated by an individual with special expertise to assess the differential diagnosis of pinta, yaws, and syphilis and to determine extent of infection so appropriate treatment can be administered (see Syphilis, p 631).

Human Immunodeficiency Virus Infection

The risk of HIV infection in internationally adopted children depends on the country of origin and individual risk factors. Because of the rapidly changing epidemiology of HIV infection and because adoptees may come from populations at high risk of infection, screening for HIV should be performed on all internationally adopted children. Although many children will have HIV test results documented in their referral information, test results from the child's country of origin may not be reliable. Transplacentally acquired maternal antibody in the absence of infection can be detected in a child younger than 18 months of age. Hence, positive HIV antibody test results in asymptomatic children of this age require clinical evaluation, further testing, and counseling (see Human Immunodeficiency Virus Infection, p 378).

Other Infectious Diseases

Skin infections that occur commonly in international adoptees include bacterial (eg, impetigo), fungal (eg, candidiasis), and ectoparasitic (eg, scabies and pediculosis) infections. Adoptive parents should be instructed on how to examine their child for signs of scabies, pediculosis, and tinea so treatment can be initiated and transmission to others can be prevented (see Scabies, p 584, and Pediculosis, pp 488–492). Diseases such as typhoid fever, malaria, leprosy, or melioidosis are encountered infrequently in internationally adopted children. Although routine screening for these diseases is not recommended, findings of fever, splenomegaly, respiratory tract infection, anemia, or eosinophilia should prompt an appropriate evaluation on the basis of the epidemiology of infectious diseases that occur in the child's country of origin. If the child came from a country where malaria is present, malaria should be considered in the differential diagnosis (see Malaria, p 435).

In the United States, multiple outbreaks of measles have been reported in children recently adopted from China and in their United States contacts. Measles outbreaks among children in orphanages in China also were reported. In 2002 and 2004, adoptions from affected orphanages were suspended temporarily while Chinese authorities implemented measures to control and prevent further transmission of measles among the children. Prospective parents who are traveling internationally to adopt children, as well as their household contacts, should ensure that they have a history of natural disease or have been adequately immunized for measles according to US guidelines. All people born after 1957 should receive 2 doses of measles-containing vaccine in the absence of documented measles infection or contraindication to the vaccine.

Clinicians should be aware of potential diseases in internationally adopted children and their clinical manifestations. Some diseases, such as central nervous system cysticercosis, may have incubation periods as long as several years and, thus, may not be detected during initial screening. On the basis of findings at the initial evaluation, consideration should be given to a repeat evaluation 6 months after adoption. In most cases, the longer the interval from adoption to development of a clinical syndrome, the less likely the syndrome can be attributed to a pathogen acquired in the country of origin.

Immunizations

Some international adoptees will have written documentation of immunizations received in their birth country. Although immunizations such as BCG, diphtheria and tetanus toxoids and pertussis (DTP), poliovirus, measles, and hepatitis B virus vaccines often are documented, other immunizations such as *Haemophilus influenzae* type b, mumps, and rubella vaccines are given less frequently, and *Streptococcus pneumoniae* and varicella vaccines are given rarely. Internationally adopted children and adolescents should receive immunizations according to the recommended schedules in the United States for healthy children and adolescents (see Fig 1.1, p 26, and Table 1.7, p 28). Although some vaccines with inadequate potency are used in other countries, most vaccines available worldwide are produced with adequate quality control standards and are reliable. However, information about storage, handling, site of administration, vaccine potency, and provider generally is not available. In general, written documentation of immunizations can be accepted as evidence of adequacy of previous immunization if the vaccines, dates of administration, number of doses, intervals between doses, and age of the child at the time of immunization are consistent internally and comparable to current US or World Health Organization schedules (see Immunizations Received Outside the United States, p 35). Given the limited data available regarding verification of immunization records from other countries, evaluation of concentrations of antibody to the antigens given repeatedly is an option to ensure that vaccines were given and were immunogenic. Serologic testing may be performed to determine whether protective antibody concentrations are present. An equally acceptable alternative when doubt exists is to reimmunize the child. Because the rate of more serious local reactions after diphtheria and tetanus toxoids and acellular pertussis (DTaP) vaccine increases with the number of doses administered, serologic testing for antibody to tetanus and diphtheria toxins before reimmunizing or if a serious reaction occurs can decrease risk.

Table 2.18 (p 189) lists the vaccines for which antibody testing can be performed, specifies the types of tests to be ordered, and provides recommended and alternative approaches. In children older than 6 months of age with or without written documentation of immunization, testing for antibodies to diphtheria and tetanus toxoids and poliovirus may be considered to determine whether the child has protective antibody concentrations. If the child has protective concentrations, then the immunization series should be completed as appropriate for that child's age. In children older than 12 months of age, measles, mumps, rubella, and varicella antibody concentrations may be measured to determine whether the child is immune; these antibody tests should not be performed in children younger than 12 months of age because of the potential presence of maternal antibody. Many children will need a dose of mumps and rubella vaccines, because these vaccines are administered infrequently in developing countries. One dose of measles-mumps-rubella (MMR) vaccine could be administered for mumps and rubella coverage, even if measles antibodies are present. At this time, no antibody testing is reliable or available routinely to assess immunity to pertussis. As discussed previously, serologic testing for hepatitis B should be performed for all children to determine their hepatitis B immunity status. If serologic testing is not available and receipt of immunogenic vaccines cannot be ensured, the prudent course is to provide the series.

INJURIES FROM DISCARDED NEEDLES IN THE COMMUNITY

Contact with and injuries from hypodermic needles and syringes discarded in public places, presumably by injection drug users, are perceived by some people as posing a significant risk for transmission of bloodborne pathogens, including human immuno-deficiency virus (HIV), hepatitis B virus (HBV), and hepatitis C virus (HCV). Although nonoccupational needlestick injuries may pose less of a risk than needlestick injuries that occur in health care settings, the injured person needs evaluation and counseling. In addition, people exposed in this manner may not realize they need evaluation. Even if the potential that the discarded syringe contains a bloodborne pathogen can be estimated from the prevalence rates of these infections in the local community, the need to test the injured or exposed person usually is not influenced significantly by this assessment.

Management of people with needlestick injuries includes acute wound care and consideration of the need for antimicrobial prophylaxis. Standard wound cleansing and care is indicated; such wounds rarely require closure. Tetanus toxoid vaccine and Tetanus Immune Globulin should be administered as appropriate for the immunization status of the exposed person (see Tetanus, p 648).

Consideration of the need for prophylaxis for HBV and HIV is the next step in exposure management. There is no recommended postexposure prophylaxis for HCV. Risk of acquisition of various pathogens depends on the nature of the wound, the ability of the pathogens to survive on environmental surfaces, the volume of source material, the concentration of virus in the source material, prevalence rates among local injection drug users, the probability that the syringe and needle was used by a

Table 2.18. Approaches to the Evaluation and Immunization of Internationally Adopted Children[1]

Vaccine	Recommended Approach	Alternative Approach
Hepatitis B	See text (perform hepatitis B panel)	—
Diphtheria and tetanus toxoids (DTaP, DT, Td)	Immunize with diphtheria and tetanus-containing vaccine as appropriate for age (see Diphtheria, p 277, and Tetanus, p 648); Serologic testing for antitoxoid antibodies 4 wk after dose 1 if severe local reaction occurs	Children whose records indicate receipt of ≥3 doses: serologic testing for antitoxoid antibody to diphtheria and tetanus toxins before administering additional doses or administer a single booster dose of diphtheria and tetanus-containing vaccine, followed by serologic testing after 1 month for antitoxoid antibody to diphtheria and tetanus toxins with reimmunization as appropriate (see text)
Haemophilus influenzae type b (Hib)	Age-appropriate immunization	—
Pertussis (DTaP)	No serologic test routinely available. May use antibodies to diphtheria or tetanus toxoids as a marker of receipt of diphtheria, tetanus, and pertussis-containing vaccine	—
Poliovirus	Immunize with inactivated poliovirus (IPV) vaccine	Serologic testing for neutralizing antibody to poliovirus types 1, 2, and 3 or administration of single dose of IPV, followed by serologic testing for neutralizing antibody to poliovirus types 1, 2, and 3
Measles-mumps-rubella (MMR)	Immunize with MMR vaccine or obtain measles antibody and if positive, give MMR vaccine for mumps and rubella protection	Serologic testing for immunoglobulin G (IgG) antibody to vaccine viruses indicated by immunization record
Varicella	Age-appropriate immunization of children who lack reliable history of previous varicella disease or serologic evidence of protection	—
Pneumococcal	Age-appropriate immunization	—

[1] Centers for Disease Control and Prevention. General recommendations on immunization. Recommendations of the Advisory Committee on Immunization Practices. *MMWR Recomm Rep.* 2006; in press. Also see Fig 1.1 (p 26) and Table 1.7 (p 28).

local injection drug user, and the immunization status of the exposed person. Unlike an occupational blood or body fluid exposure, in which the status of the exposure source for HBV, HCV, and HIV often is known, these data usually are not available to help in the decision-making process in a nonoccupational exposure.[*†]

Hepatitis B virus is the hardiest of the major bloodborne pathogens and can survive on environmental surfaces for at least 7 days. Children who have not completed the 3-dose HBV immunization series should receive a dose of vaccine and, if indicated, should be scheduled to receive the remaining doses to complete the schedule. Administration of Hepatitis B Immune Globulin usually is not indicated if the child has received the 3-dose regimen of HBV vaccine (see Table 3.21, p 354). However, experts differ in opinion about the need for Hepatitis B Immune Globulin at the time of an injury of an incompletely immunized child. If the child has received 2 doses of HBV vaccine 4 or more months previously, the immediate administration of the third dose of vaccine alone should be sufficient in most cases.

Infection with HIV usually is the greatest concern of the victim and family. The need for initial baseline serologic tests for preexisting HIV infection is controversial. Negative results from these initial tests support the conclusion that any subsequent positive test result likely reflects infection acquired from the needlestick. A positive initial test result in a pediatric patient requires further investigation of the cause, such as perinatal transmission, sexual abuse or activity, or drug use. An alternative option is to obtain and save a baseline serum specimen for later testing for HIV antibody in the unlikely event that a subsequent test result is positive. Counseling is necessary before and after testing (see Human Immunodeficiency Virus Infection, p 378).

The risk of HIV transmission from a needle discarded in public is low. Risk of HIV transmission from a puncture wound caused by a needle found in the community is lower than the 0.3% risk of HIV transmission to a health care professional from a needlestick injury from a person with known HIV infection. As of January 2005, no HIV infections have been reported after percutaneous needlestick injuries from a needle discarded in a public setting. Data are not available on the efficacy of postexposure prophylaxis with antiretroviral drugs in these circumstances for adults or children, and as a result, the US Public Health Service is unable to recommend for or against prophylaxis in this circumstance.[‡§] Furthermore, antiretroviral therapy is not without risk and often is associated with significant adverse effects (see Human Immunodeficiency Virus Infection, p 378). Therefore, postexposure prophylaxis is not recommended routinely in this situation. However, some experts recommend that antiretroviral chemoprophylaxis be considered if it can be initiated within 72 hours of the puncture wound and if the needle and/or syringe are available and found to con-

---

* Centers for Disease Control and Prevention. Updated US Public Health Service guidelines for the management of occupational exposures to HBV, HCV, and HIV and recommendations for postexposure prophylaxis. *MMWR Recomm Rep.* 2001;50(RR-11):1–52

† US Department of Health and Human Services. Antiretroviral postexposure prophylaxis after sexual, injection-drug use, or other nonoccupational exposure to HIV in the United States: recommendations from the U.S. Department of Health and Human Services. *MMWR Recomm Rep.* 2005; 54(RR-2):1–20

‡ Centers for Disease Control and Prevention. Management of possible sexual, injecting-drug-use, or other nonoccupational exposure to HIV, including considerations related to antiretroviral therapy: Public Health Service statement. *MMWR Recomm Rep.* 1998;47(RR-17):1–14

§ American Academy of Pediatrics, Committee on Pediatric AIDS. Postexposure prophylaxis in children and adolescents for nonoccupational exposure to human immunodeficiency virus. *Pediatrics.* 2003;111:1475–1489

tain visible blood or the source is known to be an HIV-infected person. Other experts recommend chemoprophylaxis if blood was visible on the syringe or needle, and other experts recommend chemoprophylaxis for any needlestick injury. Testing the syringe for HIV is not practical or reliable and is not recommended. In most reports of HIV transmission by percutaneous injury in an occupational setting, needlestick injury occurred shortly after needle withdrawal from the vein or artery of the source patient with HIV infection. Human immunodeficiency virus RNA was detected in only 3 (3.8%) of 80 discarded disposable syringes that had been used by health care professionals for intramuscular or subcutaneous injection of patients with HIV infection, indicating that most syringes will not contain HIV even after being used to draw blood from a person with HIV infection. Human immunodeficiency virus is susceptible to drying, and when HIV is placed on a surface exposed to air, the 50% tissue culture infective dose decreases by approximately 1 log every 9 hours. Consultation with a specialist in HIV infection should be obtained before deciding whether to initiate postexposure chemoprophylaxis. If the decision to begin prophylaxis is made, any delay before starting the medications should be minimized (see Human Immunodeficiency Virus Infection, p 378). The suggested medication options are the same as for HIV occupational exposure (see Human Immunodeficiency Virus Infection, p 378).

Follow-up testing of a child for serum HIV antibody should include testing at 6 weeks, 12 weeks, and 6 months after injury. Testing also is indicated if an illness consistent with acute HIV-related syndrome develops before the 6-week testing (see Human Immunodeficiency Virus Infection, p 378).

The third bloodborne pathogen of concern is HCV. Although transmission by sharing syringes among injection drug users is efficient, the risk of transmission from a discarded syringe is low, because the viability of this virus on environmental surfaces is poor. Immune Globulin preparations do not contain antibody to HCV and will not protect against infection, and antiviral drugs have not been demonstrated to protect against HCV infection. The need for testing for HCV is uncertain. If performed, testing for antibody to HCV should be performed at the time of injury and 6 months later. Positive test results should be confirmed by supplemental confirmatory laboratory tests (see Hepatitis C, p 355).

Needlestick injuries of children can be minimized by public health programs on safe needle disposal and by programs for exchange of used syringes and needles from injection drug users for sterile ones. Needle and syringe exchanges decrease improper disposal and the spread of bloodborne pathogens without increasing the rate of injection drug use. The American Academy of Pediatrics supports needle-exchange programs in conjunction with drug treatment and within the context of continuing research to document their effectiveness.

BITE WOUNDS

As many as 1% of all pediatric visits to emergency departments during summer months are for treatment of human or animal bite wounds. An estimated 4.5 million dog bites, 400 000 cat bites, and 250 000 human bites occur annually in the United States. The rate of infection after cat bites can be as high as 50%, and rates of infection after dog or human bites can be 10% to 15%. The bites of humans, wild animals, or exotic pets potentially are sources of serious infection. Parents should be informed to teach children to avoid contact with wild animals and should secure garbage containers so that raccoons and other animals will not be attracted to the home and places where children may play. Ferrets and other exotic animals are not appropriate pets for children. Concern for transmission of rabies should be increased when a bite is from a wild animal (especially a bat or a carnivore) or from a domestic animal that cannot be observed for 10 days after the bite (see Rabies, p 552). Dead animals should be avoided, because they can harbor rabies virus in their nervous system tissues and saliva and they can be infested with arthropods (fleas or ticks) infected with a variety of bacterial, rickettsial, protozoan, or viral agents.

Recommendations for bite wound management are given in Table 2.19 (p 193). Sufficient prospective, controlled studies on which to base recommendations about the closure of bite wounds are lacking. In general, recent, apparently noninfected, low-risk lesions may be sutured after thorough wound cleansing, irrigation, and débridement. Use of local anesthesia can facilitate these procedures. Because suturing can enhance the risk of wound infection, some clinicians prefer that small wounds be managed by approximation of the wound edges with adhesive strips or tissue adhesive. Bite wounds on the face, which have important cosmetic considerations, seldom become infected and should be closed whenever possible. Hand and foot wounds have a higher risk of infection and should be managed in consultation with an appropriate surgical specialist. For wounds that appear infected, especially in adolescents, punch biopsy specimens for culture should be obtained adjacent to the bite, as should wounds requiring surgical débridement. Elevation of injured areas to minimize swelling is important.

Limited data exist to guide antimicrobial therapy for patients with wounds that are not infected overtly. The use of an antimicrobial agent within 8 to 12 hours of injury for a 2- to 3-day course of therapy may decrease the rate of infection. Children at high risk of infection (eg, who are immunocompromised or when joint penetration occurs) should receive empiric antimicrobial therapy. Patients with mild injuries in which the skin only is abraded do not need to be treated with antimicrobial agents. Guidelines for choice of antimicrobial therapy regimen for human and animal bites are given in Table 2.20 (p 194) and reflect the organisms likely to cause infection. Empiric therapy should be modified when culture results become available. The increasing prevalence of community-acquired methicillin-resistant *Staphylococcus aureus* in some areas of the United States may require a modification of therapy if this organism is isolated from an infected wound (see Staphylococcal Infections, p 598).

Prophylaxis or treatment of the penicillin-allergic child with a human or animal bite wound is problematic. Activity of erythromycin or doxycycline against *S aureus* and anaerobes is unpredictable, and use of tetracyclines, which have activity against *Pasteurella multocida*, in children younger than 8 years of age must be weighed against the risk of dental staining. Azithromycin displays good in vitro activity against organisms that commonly cause bite wound infections, except for some strains of staphylococci, but there are no clinical trials documenting its efficacy. Oral or parenteral treatment with trimethoprim-sulfamethoxazole, which is effective against *S aureus*, *P multocida*, and *Eikenella corrodens*, in conjunction with clindamycin, which is active in

Table 2.19. Prophylactic Management of Human or Animal Bite Wounds to Prevent Infection

Category of Management	Management
Cleansing	Sponge away visible dirt. Irrigate with a copious volume of sterile saline solution by high-pressure syringe irrigation.[1] Do not irrigate puncture wounds. Standard precautions should be used.
Wound culture	No for fresh wounds, unless signs of infection exist. Yes for wounds more than 8–12 h old and wounds that appear infected.[2]
Radiographs	Indicated for penetrating injuries overlying bones or joints, for suspected fracture, or to assess foreign body inoculation.
Débridement	Remove devitalized tissue.
Operative débridement and exploration	Yes if one of the following: • Extensive wounds (devitalized tissue) • Involvement of the metacarpophalangeal joint (closed fist injury) • Cranial bites by large animal
Wound closure	Yes for selected fresh, nonpuncture bite wounds (see text)
Assess tetanus immunization status[3]	Yes
Assess risk of rabies from animal bites[4]	Yes
Assess risk of hepatitis B virus infection from human bites[5]	Yes
Assess risk of human immunodeficiency virus from human bites[6]	Yes
Initiate antimicrobial therapy[7]	Yes for: • Moderate or severe bite wounds, especially if edema or crush injury is present • Puncture wounds, especially if penetration of bone, tendon sheath, or joint has occurred • Facial bites • Hand and foot bites • Genital area bites • Wounds in immunocompromised and asplenic people • Wounds with signs of infection
Follow-up	Inspect wound for signs of infection within 48 h

[1] Use of an 18-gauge needle with a large-volume syringe is effective. Antimicrobial or anti-infective solutions offer no advantage and may increase tissue irritation.
[2] Both aerobic and anaerobic bacterial culture should be performed.
[3] See Tetanus, p 648.
[4] See Rabies, p 552.
[5] See Hepatitis B, p 335.
[6] See Human Immunodeficiency Virus Infection, p 378.
[7] See Table 2.20 (p 194) for suggested drug choices.

Table 2.20. Antimicrobial Agents for Human or Animal Bite Wounds

Source of Bite	Organism(s) Likely to Cause Infection	Antimicrobial Agent			
		Oral Route	Oral Alternatives for Penicillin-Allergic Patients[1]	Intravenous Route	Intravenous Alternatives for Penicillin-Allergic Patients[1]
Dog, cat, or mammal	*Pasteurella species, Staphylococcus aureus,* streptococci, anaerobes, *Capnocytophaga species, Moraxella species, Corynebacterium species, Neisseria* species	Amoxicillin-clavulanate	Extended-spectrum cephalosporin or trimethoprim-sulfamethoxazole PLUS clindamycin	Ampicillin-sulbactam[2]	Extended-spectrum cephalosporin or trimethoprim-sulfamethoxazole PLUS clindamycin
Reptile	Enteric gram-negative bacteria, anaerobes	Amoxicillin-clavulanate	Extended-spectrum cephalosporin or trimethoprim-sulfamethoxazole PLUS clindamycin	Ampicillin-sulbactam[2] PLUS gentamicin	Clindamycin PLUS gentamicin
Human	Streptococci, *S aureus, Eikenella corrodens, Haemophilus* species, anaerobes	Amoxicillin-clavulanate	Extended-spectrum cephalosporin or trimethoprim-sulfamethoxazole PLUS clindamycin	Ampicillin-sulbactam[2]	Extended-spectrum cephalosporin or trimethoprim-sulfamethoxazole PLUS clindamycin

[1] For patients with history of allergy to penicillin or one of its congeners, alternative drugs are recommended. In some circumstances, a cephalosporin or other beta-lactam–class drug may be acceptable. However, these drugs should not be used for patients with an immediate hypersensitivity (anaphylaxis) to penicillin, because approximately 5% to 15% of penicillin-allergic patients also will be allergic to cephalosporins.

[2] Ticarcillin-clavulanate can be used as an alternative.

vitro against anaerobic bacteria, streptococci, and most strains of *S aureus*, may be effective for preventing bite wound infections. An extended-spectrum cephalosporin, such as cefotaxime or ceftriaxone parenterally or cefpodoxime orally, in conjunction with clindamycin can be used as alternative therapy for penicillin-allergic patients who can tolerate cephalosporins. A 7- to 10-day course usually is sufficient for soft tissue infections. The duration of treatment for bite wound-associated bone infections is at least 3 to 4 weeks.

PREVENTION OF TICKBORNE INFECTIONS

Tickborne infectious diseases in the United States include diseases caused by bacteria (eg, Lyme disease, tularemia, relapsing fever), rickettsia (eg, Rocky Mountain spotted fever, ehrlichiosis, anaplasmosis), viruses (eg, Colorado tick fever), and protozoa (eg, babesiosis) (see Table 2.21, p 196 and disease-specific chapters in Section 3). Different ticks transmit different infectious agents (eg, dog ticks transmit the agent of Rocky Mountain spotted fever; deer ticks transmit the agent of Lyme disease), and some ticks may transmit more than one agent. Physicians should be aware of the epidemiology of tickborne infections in their local areas. Prevention of tickborne diseases is accomplished through avoidance of tick-infested habitats by decreasing tick populations in the environment, using personal protection against tick bites, and limiting the length of time ticks remain attached to the human host. Control of tick populations in the field often is not practical but can be effective in more defined areas around places where children reside and play. Specific measures for prevention are as follows:

- Physicians, parents, and children should be made aware that ticks can transmit pathogens that cause human and animal diseases.
- Tick-infested areas should be avoided whenever possible.
- If a tick-infested area is entered, clothing that covers the arms, legs, and other exposed areas should be worn, pants should be tucked into boots or socks, and long-sleeved shirts should be buttoned at the cuff. In addition, permethrin (a synthetic pyrethroid) can be sprayed onto clothes to decrease tick attachment. Permethrin should not be sprayed onto skin. Some manufacturers now offer permethrin-treated clothing, which will remain effective for up to 20 washings.
- Tick and insect repellents that contain diethyltoluamide (DEET) applied to the skin provide additional protection but may require reapplication every 1 to 2 hours for maximum effectiveness. Newer formulations are microencapsulated to increase the time before reapplication to 8 to 12 hours. Although there have been rare reports of serious neurologic complications in children resulting from the frequent and excessive application of DEET-containing insect repellents, the risk is extremely low when they are used properly. Products containing DEET should be applied as recommended (see Prevention of Mosquitoborne Infections, p 197).
- People should inspect themselves and their children's bodies and clothing daily after possible tick exposure. Special attention should be given to the exposed hairy regions of the body where ticks often attach, including the head, neck, and behind the ears in children. Ticks also may attach at areas of tight clothing (eg, belt line, axillae). Ticks should be removed promptly. For removal, a tick should be grasped

Table 2.21. Some Tick-Transmitted Pathogens in the United States (Domestic and Imported)

Human Disease Type	Pathogens in the United States	Pathogens in other countries
Bacteria		
Spotted fever group of rickettsioses	*Rickettsia rickettsii, Rickettsia parkeri*, perhaps others	*Rickettsia rickettsii, Rickettsia conorii, Rickettsia africae, Rickettsia honei, Rickettsia japonica, Rickettsia sibirica, Rickettsia slovaca*, others
Human anaplasmosis	*Anaplasma phagocytophilum*	*Anaplasma phagocytophilum*
Human ehrlichiosis	*Ehrlichia chaffeensis, Ehrlichia ewingii*	*Ehrlichia muris*, possibly *Ehrlichia canis*, others
Lyme disease, Lyme borreliosis	*Borrelia burgdorferi*	*B burgdorferi, Borrelia afzelii, Borrelia garanii, Borrelia bissettii*
Tickborne relapsing fever	*Borrelia turicatae, Borrelia hermsii, Borrelia parkeri*	*Borrelia duttoni*, others
Tularemia	*Francisella tularensis*	*F tularensis*
Q fever (uncommon tick transmission)	*Coxiella burnetii*	*C burnetii*
Bartonellosis (speculative)	*Bartonella* species	*Bartonella* species
Protozoa		
Human babesiosis	*Babesia microti, Babesia* species WA1, MO1, CA1	*B microti, Babesia divergens*, others
Viruses		
Flavivirus infection	Powassan virus, Deer tick virus	Powassan virus, tickborne encephalitis virus, Kyasanur Forest disease virus, Russian spring-summer encephalitis virus, Omsk hemorrhagic fever virus
Coltivirus infection	Colorado tick fever virus	. . .
Nairovirus infection	. . .	Crimean-Congo hemorrhagic fever virus

with a fine tweezers close to the skin and gently pulled straight out without twisting motions. If fingers are used to remove ticks, they should be protected with a barrier such as tissue and washed after removal of the tick.

- Maintaining tick-free pets also will decrease tick exposure. Daily inspection of pets and removal of ticks are indicated, as is the use of appropriate veterinary products to prevent ticks on pets. Consult a veterinarian for information.

- Chemoprophylaxis to prevent Lyme disease may be considered in unusual circumstances (see Lyme Disease, p 428).

PREVENTION OF MOSQUITOBORNE INFECTIONS

Mosquitoborne infectious diseases in the United States are caused by arboviruses (eg, California, eastern equine, western equine, and St. Louis encephalitis viruses and West Nile virus). International travelers may encounter arboviral or other mosquitoborne infections (eg, malaria) during travel (see also disease-specific chapters in Section 3). Physicians should be aware of the epidemiology of arbovirus infections in their local areas. Prevention involves protection from the bite of an infected mosquito. In areas with arbovirus transmission, protection of children is recommended during outdoor activities, including activities related to school, child care, or camp. Education of families and other caregivers is an important component of prevention. Specific measures include:

- **Reduce mosquito population.** Mosquitoes breed in standing water. Measures to limit mosquito breeding around the home include drainage or removal of receptacles for standing water (old tires, toys, flower pots, cans, buckets, barrels, other containers that collect rain water); keeping swimming pools, decorative pools, children's wading pools, and bird-baths clean; and cleaning clogged gutters. Under certain circumstances, mosquito control measures may be conducted by public health officials, including drainage of standing water, use of microbial larvicides in waters that are mosquito breeding grounds, and surface spraying to control adult vectors.
- **Reduce exposure to mosquitoes.** Avoiding infested areas, limiting outdoor activities at times of high mosquito activity, such as dawn and dusk, and screening of windows and doors reduce exposure. Mosquito traps and ultrasonic and other devices designed to distract mosquitoes from people are not well studied. These devices appear to have only limited activity and may attract more mosquitoes into the area.
- **Use barriers to protect skin.** Barriers include mosquito nets; screens for baby strollers or other areas where immobile children are placed; and protective light-colored clothing with long cuffed sleeves, long pants tucked into socks or shoes, and hats.
- **Discourage mosquitoes from biting.** Insect repellents do not kill mosquitoes but act by making humans unattractive to the mosquito. Repellents should be used during outdoor activities when mosquitoes are present, especially in regions with arbovirus transmission. Repellents are synthetic compounds or derivatives of plant oils. Effective repellents for use on skin are products that contain diethyltoluamide (DEET), picaridin (KBR 3023), and the plant-based oil of lemon eucalyptus. In 2005, the Centers for Disease Control and Prevention revised recommendations for mosquito control to include compounds that contain picaridin and oil of lemon eucalyptus as well as DEET. Permethrin and DEET also can be applied to clothing. Products with a higher concentration of DEET protect longer and are appro-

priate for people who will be exposed to mosquitoes during outdoor activities lasting many hours. Products with lower concentrations of DEET may be used where more transient protection is required, but they may require repeated applications. A study in human volunteers showed an average duration of protection of 5 hours, 4 hours, 2 hours, and 1.5 hours for products with DEET concentrations of 23.8%, 20%, 6.7%, and 4.5%, respectively. Products containing picaridin (at concentrations between 5% and 10% for US formulations) may be as effective in repelling mosquitos as low concentrations of DEET and, therefore, may need to be applied more frequently. Oil of lemon eucalyptus appears to have similar durations of action as products containing lower concentrations of DEET. All other plant products studied, including those based on citronella, protected for less than 20 minutes. Ingestion of garlic or vitamin B1 or wearing devices that emit sounds or impregnated wristbands all are ineffective measures.

Although DEET has been used worldwide since 1957, has been studied more extensively than any other repellent, and has a good safety profile, there is concern about potential toxicity, especially in children. Adverse effects are rare and most often are associated with chronic or excessive use and do not appear to be related to DEET concentration used. Urticaria and contact dermatitis have been reported in a small number of people. There have been rare reports of encephalopathy, with 13 cases reported after skin application in children. Encephalopathy also has been reported after accidental ingestion. Diethyltoluamide is irritating to eyes and mucous membranes. Concentrated formulations can damage plastic and certain fabrics. If used appropriately, DEET does not present a health problem.

Although concentrations of 10% to 15% DEET or lower have been recommended for children, there is no evidence that these concentrations are safer than 30% DEET. Products with DEET concentrations of 10% or less should not be used for exposures lasting more than 1 to 2 hours. There is no evidence that repellents that do not contain DEET are safer, and there are no safety data for other products in children. In 2001, the US Environmental Protection Agency (EPA) concluded that appropriate use of DEET at concentrations of up to 30% posed no significant risk to children or adults but that DEET should not be used in children younger than 2 months of age because of increased skin permeability. The American Academy of Pediatrics has supported this recommendation.*

Picaridin-containing compounds have been used as an insect repellent for years in Europe and Australia as a 20% formulation with no serious toxicity reported. Except for eye irritation, products containing oil of eucalyptus appear safe, although the EPA specifies that they should not be used on children younger than 3 years of age.

The EPA recommends the following precautions when using insect repellents. Recommendations for use of any of these insect repellents should be followed for children:

- Do not apply over cuts, wounds, or irritated or sunburned skin. Avoid areas around eyes and mouth.
- Do not spray onto the face; apply with hands.

---

* American Academy of Pediatrics Committee on Environmental Health. Pesticides. In: Etzel RA, ed. *Pediatric Environmental Health*. 2nd ed. Elk Grove Village, IL: American Academy of Pediatrics; 2003:323–359

- Use just enough to cover exposed skin. Avoid using excessive amounts or using excessive numbers of applications.
- Do not apply to young children's hands, because they may rub it into their eyes or mouth.
- Do not allow young children to apply a product themselves.
- Do not apply under clothing.
- Do not use sprays in enclosed areas or near food.
- Repellents containing DEET, applied according to label instructions, can be used along with a separate sunscreen. No data are available regarding the use of other active repellent ingredients in combination with a sunscreen.
- Reapply if washed off by sweating or by getting wet.
- After returning indoors, wash treated skin with soap and water or bathe. Also, wash treated clothing before wearing again.
- If a child develops a rash or other reaction from any insect repellent, wash the repellent off with soap and water and contact the child's physician or the poison control center (800-222-1222) for guidance.

Treating clothes with repellents such as DEET or permethrin will give added protection by repelling mosquitoes and ticks from biting through thin clothing. Permethrin should not be used on skin. Mosquito netting also may be impregnated with repellents. Repellents should not be used on clothing or mosquito nets that young children may chew or suck.

PREVENTION OF ILLNESSES ASSOCIATED WITH RECREATIONAL WATER USE

Disease transmission through consumption or use of recreational water continues to be a source of illness in the United States. Since the mid-1980s, the number of outbreaks related to recreational water activities has been increasing.[*] Therefore, preventing recreational water-related illness is becoming increasingly important for the health of adults and children. Recreational water illnesses (RWIs) are caused by swallowing, breathing, or having contact with contaminated water from swimming pools, spas, lakes, rivers, or oceans. Recreational water illnesses include a variety of illnesses, such as gastrointestinal tract, respiratory tract, neurologic, skin, ear, eye, and wound infections. Between 2001 and 2002, there were a total of 65 reported outbreaks of RWIs in the United States, causing illness among 2536 people and resulting in 61 hospitalizations and 8 deaths. Of these 65 outbreaks, the majority (68%) were associated with inadequately treated or disinfected recreational water (eg, swimming pools, wading pools intended for children, spas). Over the past 10 years, the most common illness associated with treated water venues was gastroenteritis caused by *Cryptosporidium* species, *Giardia* species, *Shigella* species, *Escherichia coli* O157:H7, and norovirus.[*]

Among children between 7 and 17 years of age, swimming is the most popular activity, with more than 40% of children participating in swimming activities more than 5 times a year, resulting in more than 107 million annual visits by children to

---

[*] Yoder JS, Blackburn BG, Craun GF, et al. Surveillance for waterborne-disease outbreaks associated with recreational water—United States, 2001–2002. *MMWR Surveill Summ.* 2004;53:1–22

swimming venues. Swimming is a communal bathing activity by which the same water may be shared by dozens to thousands of people each day, depending on venue size (eg, "kiddy" splash pools, swimming pools, water parks). Unfortunately, because of the high prevalence of diarrhea, fecal incontinence (particularly in young children), and the presence of residual fecal material on the bodies of swimmers (up to 10 g for young children), fecal contamination of swimming venues is a common occurrence.

Chlorination of water at public swimming venues is one of the most commonly used methods to oxidize fecal matter and pathogens to protect swimmers from transmission of infectious diseases. Although many pathogens are inactivated rapidly by chlorination, several pathogens are moderately to highly resistant to chlorination and can survive for extended periods of time in chlorinated pools. *Giardia* species and norovirus (a calicivirus) have been shown to survive in water chlorinated at concentrations typically used in swimming pools for up to 30 to 60 minutes and are well documented as causes of pool-associated disease outbreaks. *Cryptosporidium* oocysts can remain infectious for days in chlorine concentrations typically used in swimming pools, thus contributing to the role of *Cryptosporidium* species as the leading cause of pool-associated outbreaks of gastroenteritis.

Chlorine-resistant pathogens, coupled with low infectious doses, a high prevalence of diarrhea in the general population, high pathogen excretion concentrations, and heavy use of swimming venues, makes recreational water use an ideal means of amplifying pathogen transmission within a community. As a result, one or more swimmers ill with diarrhea can contaminate large volumes of water and expose large numbers of coswimmers to pathogens, particularly if pool disinfection is inadequate or the pathogen is chlorine-resistant. However, RWI outbreaks are preventable or can be decreased substantially through a combination of proper pool maintenance, water disinfection, and improved swimmer hygiene and behavior.

CONTROL MEASURES

Swimming continues to be a safe and effective means of exercise. Recreational water illness transmission can be prevented by reducing contamination of swimming venues and exposure to contaminated water through adoption of the following practices:
- Don't swim when ill with diarrhea.
  - People with diarrhea attributable to potentially waterborne pathogens (eg, *Cryptosporidium* species, *Shigella* species, norovirus) should not use recreational water venues for 2 weeks after symptoms resolve.
- Don't swallow recreational water.
- Practice good swimming hygiene.
  - Take a shower, using soap and water, before entering recreational water.
  - Wash children thoroughly, especially the perianal area, with soap and water before allowing them to enter the water.
  - Wash hands using soap and water after each bathroom use.
  - Wash hands after each diaper change.
  - Change diapers in a bathroom and not by the recreational water.
  - Take children on frequent bathroom breaks and check diapers often.

Summaries of Infectious Diseases

Actinomycosis

CLINICAL MANIFESTATIONS: The 3 major anatomic types of disease are cervicofacial, thoracic, and abdominal. Cervicofacial lesions are the most common and often occur after tooth extraction, oral surgery, or facial trauma or are associated with carious teeth. Localized pain and induration progress to "woody hard" nodular lesions that can be complicated by draining sinus tracts that usually are located at the angle of the jaw or in the submandibular region. The infection usually spreads by direct invasion of adjacent tissues. Infection also may contribute to chronic obstructive tonsillitis. Thoracic disease most commonly is secondary to aspiration of oropharyngeal secretions and occurs rarely after esophageal disruption secondary to surgery or nonpenetrating trauma or may be an extension of cervicofacial infection. Disease manifests as pneumonia, which can be complicated by abscesses, empyema, and rarely, pleurodermal sinuses. Focal or multifocal masses may be mistaken for tumors. Abdominal actinomycosis usually is attributable to penetrating trauma or intestinal perforation. The appendix and cecum are the most common sites, and symptoms are similar to those of appendicitis. Slowly developing masses may simulate abdominal or retroperitoneal neoplasms. Intra-abdominal abscesses and peritoneal-dermal draining sinuses eventually occur. Chronic localized disease often forms sinus tracts that drain a purulent discharge. Other sites of actinomycosis infection include the pelvis, which has been linked to use of intrauterine devices, and brain abscesses. Primary cutaneous actinomycosis also has been reported.

ETIOLOGY: *Actinomyces israelii* is the usual cause. *Actinomyces israelii* and at least 5 other *Actinomyces* species are slow-growing, microaerophilic or facultative anaerobic gram-positive, filamentous, branching bacilli that can be part of the normal oral, gastrointestinal, or vaginal flora. *Actinomyces* species frequently are copathogens in tissues harboring multiple species.

EPIDEMIOLOGY: *Actinomyces* species are worldwide in distribution. The organisms are components of the endogenous gastrointestinal tract flora. *Actinomyces* species are opportunistic pathogens, and disease results from penetrating (including human bite wounds) and nonpenetrating trauma. Infection is rare in infants and children.

The **incubation period** varies from several days to several years.

DIAGNOSTIC TESTS: A microscopic demonstration of beaded, branched, gram-positive bacilli in purulent material or tissue specimens suggests the diagnosis. Acid-fast staining can be used to distinguish *Actinomyces* species, which are acid-fast negative, from *Nocardia* species, which are variably acid-fast positive. "Sulfur granules" in drainage or loculations of purulent material usually are yellow and may be visualized microscopically or macroscopically and suggest the diagnosis when present. A Gram stain of sulfur granules discloses a dense reticulum of filaments; the ends of individual filaments may project around the periphery of the granule, with or without radially arranged hyaline clubs. Immunofluorescent stains for *Actinomyces* species are available. *Actinomyces* species can be identified in tissue specimens using the 16s rRNA sequencing and polymerase chain reaction assay. Although most *Actinomyces* species are microaerophilic or facultative anaerobic, specimens must be obtained, transported, and cultured anaerobically on semiselective media.

TREATMENT: Initial therapy should include intravenous penicillin G or ampicillin for 4 to 6 weeks followed by high doses of oral penicillin (up to 2 g/day for adults), amoxicillin, erythromycin, clindamycin, doxycycline, or tetracycline for a total of 6 to 12 months. Tetracyclines are not recommended for pregnant women or children younger than 8 years of age. Surgical drainage may be a necessary adjunct to medical management.

ISOLATION OF THE HOSPITALIZED PATIENT: Standard precautions are recommended. There is no person-to-person spread.

CONTROL MEASURES: Appropriate oral hygiene, regular dental care, and careful cleansing of wounds, including human bite wounds, can prevent infection.

Adenovirus Infections

CLINICAL MANIFESTATIONS: The most common site of adenovirus infection is the upper respiratory tract. Manifestations include symptoms of the common cold, pharyngitis, tonsillitis, otitis media, and pharyngoconjunctival fever. Life-threatening disseminated infection, severe pneumonia, meningitis, and encephalitis occasionally occur, especially among young infants and immunocompromised hosts. Adenoviruses are infrequent causes of acute hemorrhagic conjunctivitis, a pertussis-like syndrome, croup, bronchiolitis, and hemorrhagic cystitis. A few adenovirus serotypes cause gastroenteritis.

ETIOLOGY: Adenoviruses are double-stranded, nonenveloped DNA viruses; at least 51 distinct serotypes divided into 6 species (A through F) cause human infections. Some adenovirus serotypes are associated primarily with respiratory tract disease, and others are associated primarily with gastroenteritis (types 40, 41, and to a lesser extent, 31).

EPIDEMIOLOGY: Infection in infants and children may occur at any age. Adenoviruses causing respiratory tract infections usually are transmitted by respiratory tract secretions through person-to-person contact, aerosols, and fomites, the latter because adenoviruses are stable in the environment. Other routes of transmission have not been defined clearly. The conjunctiva can provide a portal of entry. Community outbreaks of adenovirus-associated pharyngoconjunctival fever have been attributed to exposure to water from contaminated swimming pools and fomites such as shared towels. Nosocomial transmission of adenoviral respiratory and gastrointestinal tract infections can result from exposure to infected health care professionals and contaminated equipment. Epidemic keratoconjunctivitis often has been associated with nosocomial transmission in ophthalmologists' offices. Enteric strains of adenoviruses are transmitted by the fecal-oral route. The incidence of adenovirus-induced respiratory tract disease is increased slightly during late winter, spring, and early summer. Enteric disease occurs throughout the year and primarily affects children younger than 4 years of age. Adenovirus infections are most communicable during the first few days of an acute illness, but persistent and intermittent shedding for longer periods, even months, is common. Asymptomatic infections are common. Reinfection can occur.

The **incubation period** for respiratory tract infection varies from 2 to 14 days; for gastroenteritis, the incubation period is 3 to 10 days.

DIAGNOSTIC TESTS: The preferred method for diagnosis of adenovirus infection is cell culture or antigen detection. Adenoviruses associated with respiratory tract disease can be isolated from pharyngeal and eye secretions and feces by inoculation of specimens into susceptible cell cultures. A pharyngeal isolate is more suggestive of recent infection than is a fecal isolate, which may indicate prolonged carriage or recent infection. Adenovirus antigens can be detected in body fluids of infected people by immunoassay techniques, which especially are useful for diagnosis of diarrheal disease, because enteric adenovirus types 40 and 41 usually cannot be isolated in standard cell cultures. Enteric adenoviruses also can be identified by electron microscopic examination of stool specimens. Multiple methods to detect group-reactive hexon antigens of the virus in body secretions and tissue have been developed. Also, detection of viral DNA can be accomplished using probe hybridization or gene amplification by polymerase chain reaction, which are not available commercially. Serodiagnosis is used primarily for epidemiologic studies.

TREATMENT: Supportive.

ISOLATION OF THE HOSPITALIZED PATIENT: In addition to standard precautions for young children with respiratory tract infections, contact and droplet precautions are indicated for the duration of hospitalization. For patients with conjunctivitis and for diapered and incontinent children with adenoviral gastroenteritis, contact precautions in addition to standard precautions are indicated for the duration of the illness.

CONTROL MEASURES: Children who participate in group child care, particularly children from 6 months through 2 years of age, are at increased risk of adenoviral respiratory tract infections and gastroenteritis. Effective measures for preventing spread of adenovirus infection in this setting have not been determined, but frequent hand hygiene is recommended.

Adequate chlorination of swimming pools is recommended to prevent pharyngoconjunctival fever. Epidemic keratoconjunctivitis associated with ophthalmologic practice can be difficult to control and requires use of single-dose medication dispensing and strict attention to hand hygiene and instrument sterilization procedures. Effective disinfection can be accomplished by immersing contaminated equipment in a 1% solution of sodium hypochlorite for 10 minutes or by steam autoclaving.

Health care professionals with known or suspected adenoviral conjunctivitis should avoid direct patient contact for 14 days after onset of disease in the most recently involved eye. Because adenoviruses particularly are difficult to eliminate from skin, fomites, and environmental surfaces, assiduous adherence to hand hygiene and use of disposable gloves when caring for infected patients are recommended.

Amebiasis

CLINICAL MANIFESTATIONS: Clinical syndromes associated with *Entamoeba histolytica* infection include noninvasive intestinal infection, intestinal amebiasis, ameboma, and liver abscess. Disease is more severe in the very young, the elderly, and pregnant women. Patients with noninvasive intestinal infection may be asymptomatic or may have nonspecific intestinal tract complaints. People with intestinal amebiasis (amebic colitis) generally have 1 to 3 weeks of increasingly severe diarrhea progressing to grossly bloody dysenteric stools with lower abdominal pain and tenesmus. Weight loss is common, and fever occurs in one third of patients. Symptoms may be chronic and may mimic inflammatory bowel disease. Progressive involvement of the colon may produce toxic megacolon, fulminant colitis, ulceration of the colon and perianal area, and rarely, perforation. Progression may occur in patients inappropriately treated with corticosteroids or antimotility drugs. An ameboma may occur as an annular lesion of the cecum or ascending colon that may be mistaken for colonic carcinoma or as a tender extrahepatic mass mimicking a pyogenic abscess. Amebomas usually resolve with antiamebic therapy and do not require surgery.

In a small proportion of patients, extraintestinal disease may occur. Although the liver is the most common extraintestinal site, the lungs, pleural space, pericardium, brain, skin, and genitourinary tract also may be involved. Liver abscess may be acute with fever, abdominal pain, tachypnea, liver tenderness, and hepatomegaly or chronic with weight loss, vague abdominal symptoms, and irritability. Rupture of abscesses into the abdomen or chest may lead to death. Evidence of recent intestinal infection usually is absent.

ETIOLOGY: *Entamoeba histolytica* is classified into 2 species that are morphologically identical but genetically distinct protozoa. The pathogenic *E histolytica* and the non-pathogenic *Entamoeba dispar* are excreted as cysts or trophozoites in stools of infected people.

EPIDEMIOLOGY: *Entamoeba histolytica* can be found worldwide but is more prevalent in people of lower socioeconomic status who live in economically developing countries where the prevalence of amebic infection may be as high as 50%. Groups at increased risk of infection in developed countries include immigrants from or long-term visitors to areas with endemic infection, institutionalized people, and men who have sex with men. *Entamoeba histolytica* is transmitted via amebic cysts by the fecal-oral route. Ingested cysts, which are unaffected by gastric acid, undergo excystation in the alkaline small intestine and produce trophozoites that infect the colon. Cysts that subsequently develop are the source of transmission, especially from asymptomatic cyst excreters. Infected patients excrete cysts intermittently, sometimes for years if untreated. Transmission occasionally has been associated with contaminated food, water, and enema equipment. Sexual transmission also may occur.

The **incubation period** is variable, ranging from a few days to months or years, but commonly is 2 to 4 weeks.

DIAGNOSTIC TESTS: A presumptive diagnosis of intestinal infection depends on identifying trophozoites or cysts in stool specimens. Examination of serial specimens may be necessary. Specimens of stool, endoscopy scrapings (not swabs), and biopsies should be examined by wet mount within 30 minutes of collection and fixed in formalin and polyvinyl alcohol (available in kits) for concentration and permanent staining. *Entamoeba histolytica* is not distinguished easily from the noninvasive and more prevalent *E dispar*, although trophozoites containing ingested red blood cells are more likely to be *E histolytica*. Polymerase chain reaction, isoenzyme analysis, and monoclonal antibody-based antigen detection assays can differentiate *E histolytica* and *E dispar*.

Detecting serum antibody using indirect hemagglutination assay (IHA) may be helpful, primarily for diagnosis of amebic colitis (approximately 85% positive results) and extraintestinal amebiasis with liver involvement (up to 99% positive results). In surveys of people in developed countries, approximately 5% have positive IHA results. Up to 30% of the population may have antibodies on IHA in areas with endemic infection. Infection with *E dispar* does not result in a positive IHA result.

Ultrasonography and computed tomography can identify effectively liver abscesses and other extraintestinal sites of infection. Aspirates from a liver abscess usually show neither trophozoites nor leukocytes.

TREATMENT*: Treatment involves elimination of the tissue-invading trophozoites as well as organisms in the intestinal lumen. *Entamoeba dispar* infection does not require treatment. Corticosteroids and antimotility drugs administered to people with amebiasis can worsen symptoms and the disease process. The following regimens are recommended:

- **Asymptomatic cyst excreters (intraluminal infections):** treat with a luminal amebicide such as iodoquinol, paromomycin, or diloxanide.
- **Patients with mild to moderate or severe intestinal symptoms or extraintestinal disease (including liver abscess):** treat with metronidazole (or tinidazole), followed by a therapeutic course of a luminal amebicide (iodoquinol or paromomycin).

Dehydroemetine followed by a therapeutic course of a luminal amebicide should be considered for patients for whom treatment of invasive disease has failed or cannot be tolerated. An alternate treatment for liver abscess is chloroquine phosphate concomitantly with metronidazole (or tinidazole) or, if necessary, dehydroemetine, followed by a therapeutic course of a luminal amebicide. Surgical aspiration occasionally may be required when response of the abscess to medical therapy is unsatisfactory.

To prevent spontaneous rupture of an abscess, patients with large liver abscesses may benefit from percutaneous or surgical aspiration.

ISOLATION OF THE HOSPITALIZED PATIENT: In addition to standard precautions, contact precautions are recommended for the duration of illness.

---

* For further information, see Drugs for Parasitic Infections, p 790.

CONTROL MEASURES: Careful hand hygiene after defecation, sanitary disposal of fecal material, and treatment of drinking water will control the spread of infection. Sexual transmission may be controlled by use of condoms and avoidance of sexual practices that may permit fecal-oral transmission.

Amebic Meningoencephalitis and Keratitis
(Naegleria fowleri, Acanthamoeba species, and Balamuthia mandrillaris)

CLINICAL MANIFESTATIONS: *Naegleria fowleri* can cause a rapidly progressive, almost always fatal, primary amebic meningoencephalitis. Early symptoms include fever, headache, and sometimes, disturbances of smell and taste. The illness rapidly progresses to signs of meningoencephalitis, including nuchal rigidity, lethargy, confusion, and altered level of consciousness. Seizures are common. Death occurs within a week of onset of symptoms. No distinct clinical features differentiate this disease from fulminant bacterial meningitis.

Granulomatous amebic encephalitis caused by *Acanthamoeba* species and *Balamuthia mandrillaris* has a more insidious onset and progression of manifestations occurring weeks to months after exposure. Signs and symptoms may include personality changes, seizures, headaches, nuchal rigidity, ataxia, cranial nerve palsies, hemiparesis, and other focal deficits. Fever often is low grade and intermittent. The course may resemble that of a bacterial brain abscess or a brain tumor. Skin lesions (pustules, nodules, ulcers) may be present without central nervous system involvement, particularly in patients with acquired immunodeficiency syndrome.

Amebic keratitis, usually attributable to *Acanthamoeba* species and rarely to other species, occurs primarily in people who wear contact lenses and resembles keratitis caused by herpes simplex, bacteria, or fungi except for a usually more indolent course. Corneal inflammation (radial keratoneuritis or stromal ring infiltrate), pain, photophobia, and secondary uveitis are predominant features.

ETIOLOGY: *Naegleria fowleri*, *Acanthamoeba* species, and *Balamuthia mandrillaris* are free-living amebae that exist as motile, infective trophozoites and environmentally hardy cysts.

EPIDEMIOLOGY: *Naegleria fowleri* is found in warm fresh water and moist soil. Most infections with *N fowleri* have been associated with swimming in warm, natural bodies of water, but other sources have included tap water, contaminated and poorly chlorinated swimming pools, and baths. Small outbreaks associated with swimming in a warm lake or swimming pool have been reported. A few cases with no history of contact with water have occurred. Disease has been reported worldwide but is uncommon. In the United States, infection occurs primarily in the summer and usually affects children and young adults. The trophozoites of the parasite directly invade the brain from the nose along the olfactory nerves via the cribriform plate.

The **incubation period** for *N fowleri* infection is several days to 1 week.

The causative organisms of granulomatous amebic encephalitis, especially *Acanthamoeba* species, are distributed worldwide and are found in soil, fresh and brackish water, dust, hot tubs, and sewage. Central nervous system infection occurs primarily in debilitated and immunocompromised people. However, some patients have had no demonstrable underlying disease or defect. Acquisition probably occurs by inhalation or direct contact with contaminated soil or water. The primary focus of infection is most likely skin or respiratory tract, followed by hematogenous spread to the brain.

Acanthamoeba organisms also cause dendritic keratitis, mimicking herpes keratitis in people who wear contact lenses and use contaminated saline solutions or tap water rinses for lens care or swim while wearing contact lenses.

The **incubation period** for these infections is unknown.

DIAGNOSTIC TESTS: *Naegleria fowleri* infection can be documented by microscopic demonstration of the motile trophozoites on a wet mount of centrifuged cerebrospinal fluid (CSF). The organism also can be cultured on 1.5% nonnutrient agar layered with enteric bacteria held in Page saline solution. Immunofluorescent tests performed on biopsy material to determine the species of the organism are available through the Centers for Disease Control and Prevention. The CSF shows polymorphonuclear pleocytosis, an increased protein concentration, a normal to very low glucose concentration, and no bacteria.

In infection with *Acanthamoeba* species, trophozoites and cysts can be visualized in sections of brain or corneal scrapings. The CSF typically shows a mononuclear pleocytosis and an increased protein concentration with normal or low glucose but no organisms. *Acanthamoeba* species, but not *Balamuthia* species, can be cultured by the same method used for *N fowleri*.

TREATMENT: If meningoencephalitis caused by *N fowleri* is suspected because of the presence of organisms in the CSF, therapy should not be withheld while waiting for results of confirmatory diagnostic tests. Amphotericin B is the drug of choice, although treatment often is unsuccessful, with only a few cases of complete recovery being documented. Recovery has occurred after treatment with amphotericin B alone or in combination with other agents, such as miconazole and rifampin. Early diagnosis and institution of high-dose drug therapy probably is important for optimizing outcome.

Effective treatment for central nervous system infections caused by *Acanthamoeba* species and *B mandrillaris* has not been established. Experimental infections can be prevented or cured by sulfadiazine. Although *Acanthamoeba* species usually are susceptible in vitro to a variety of antimicrobial agents (eg, pentamidine, flucytosine, ketoconazole, clotrimazole, and to a lesser degree, amphotericin B), recovery is rare.

Patients with keratitis attributable to *Acanthamoeba* organisms have been treated successfully with prolonged courses of combinations of topical propamidine isethionate plus neomycin-polymyxin B sulfate-gramicidin ophthalmic solution or topical polyhexamethylene biguanide or chlorhexidine gluconate and various azoles (eg, miconazole, clotrimazole, fluconazole, or itraconazole) as well as topical corticosteroids. Early diagnosis is important for a good outcome. Some patients with skin lesions attributable to *Acanthamoeba* species have been treated successfully by first washing lesions with chlorhexidine gluconate and then applying topical ketoconazole cream 3 to 4 times a day. Patients also have been given intravenous pentamidine and oral itraconazole (see Drugs for Parasitic Infections, p 790).

ISOLATION OF THE HOSPITALIZED PATIENT: Standard precautions are recommended.

CONTROL MEASURES: People should avoid swimming in warm, stagnant, polluted fresh water. *Acanthamoeba* organisms are resistant to freezing, drying, and the usual concentrations of chlorine found in drinking water and swimming pools.

Only sterile saline solutions should be used to clean contact lenses.

Anthrax

CLINICAL MANIFESTATIONS: Depending on the route of infection, anthrax disease can occur in 3 forms: cutaneous, inhalational, and gastrointestinal. **Cutaneous** anthrax begins as a pruritic papule or vesicle that enlarges and ulcerates in 1 to 2 days, with subsequent formation of a central black eschar. The lesion characteristically is painless, with surrounding edema, hyperemia, and regional lymphadenopathy. Patients may have associated fever, malaise, and headache. **Inhalational** anthrax is the most lethal form of disease. A prodrome of fever, sweats, nonproductive cough, chest pain, headache, myalgias, malaise, and nausea and vomiting may occur initially, but more distinctive clinical symptoms occur 2 to 5 days later, in some cases following a period of improvement. These manifestations include dyspnea, hypoxia, and fulminant shock occurring as a result of hemorrhagic mediastinal lymphadenitis, hemorrhagic pleural effusions, bacteremia, and toxemia. A widened mediastinum is the classic finding on imaging of the chest; pleural effusions and hemorrhagic infiltrates can be present, but initially changes on chest radiography may be subtle. **Gastrointestinal tract** disease can present as 2 clinical syndromes, intestinal and oropharyngeal. Patients with the intestinal form have symptoms of nausea, anorexia, vomiting, and fever progressing to severe abdominal pain, massive ascites, hematemesis, and bloody diarrhea. Oropharyngeal anthrax may include posterior oropharyngeal ulcers that typically are unilateral and associated with marked neck swelling, regional adenopathy, and sepsis. Hemorrhagic meningitis can result from hematogenous spread of the organism after acquiring any form of disease. The case-fatality rate for patients with appropriately treated cutaneous anthrax usually is <1%, but for inhalational or gastrointestinal tract disease, mortality often exceeds 50% and approaches 100% for meningitis.

ETIOLOGY: *Bacillus anthracis* is an aerobic, gram-positive, encapsulated, spore-forming, nonmotile rod. Spore size is approximately 1×2 μm. *Bacillus anthracis* has 3 major virulence factors: an antiphagocytic capsule and 2 exotoxins, called lethal and edema toxins. The toxins are responsible for the primary clinical manifestations of hemorrhage, edema, and necrosis.

EPIDEMIOLOGY: Anthrax is a zoonotic disease that occurs in many rural regions of the world. *Bacillus anthracis* spores remain viable in the soil for decades, representing a potential source of infection for livestock through ingestion. Natural infection of humans occurs through contact with infected animals or contaminated animal products, including carcasses, hides, hair, wool, meat, and bone meal. Internationally, outbreaks of gastrointestinal tract anthrax have occurred after ingestion of undercooked or raw meat. In the United States, the incidence of naturally occurring human anthrax decreased from an estimated 130 cases annually in the early 1900s to no cases in 2004. The vast majority (>95%) of these cases were cutaneous infections among animal handlers or mill workers. The last case of naturally acquired inhalational anthrax in the United States occurred in 1976 in a person who worked with imported yarn.

Bacillus anthracis is one of the most likely biological agents to be used as a weapon, because (1) its spores are highly stabile; (2) spores can infect via the respiratory route; and (3) the resulting inhalational disease has a high mortality rate. In addition to aerosolization, there is a theoretic health risk associated with *B anthracis* spores being introduced into food products or water supplies. In 1979, an accidental release of *B anthracis* spores from a military microbiology facility in the former Soviet Union resulted in 69 deaths. In 2001, 22 cases of anthrax (11 inhalational, 11 cutaneous) were identified in the United States after intentional contamination of the mail; 5 (45%) of the inhalational cases were fatal. Use of *B anthracis* in a biological attack would require immediate response and mobilization of public health resources. Because naturally occurring anthrax is rare in the United States, every suspected case should be reported immediately to the local or state health department (see Biological Terrorism, p 105).

The **incubation period** for all forms of anthrax generally is less than 2 weeks. However, because of spore dormancy and slow clearance from the lungs, the incubation period for inhalational anthrax may be prolonged to as long as several months. Discharge from cutaneous lesions potentially is infectious, but person-to-person transmission rarely has been reported. Both inhalational and cutaneous disease have occurred in laboratory workers.

DIAGNOSTIC TESTS: Depending on the clinical presentation, Gram stain and culture should be performed on specimens of blood, pleural fluid, cerebrospinal fluid, and tissue biopsy or discharge from cutaneous lesions. However, previous treatment with antimicrobial agents significantly decreases the yield of these studies. Gram-positive bacilli seen on peripheral blood smears or in cerebrospinal fluid can be an important initial finding. Definitive identification of suspect *B anthracis* isolates can be performed through the Laboratory Response Network (LRN) in each state. Additional diagnostic tests for anthrax, including tissue immunohistochemistry, real-time polymerase chain reaction, time-resolved fluorescent assay, and an enzyme immunoassay that measures immunoglobulin G antibodies against *B anthracis* protective antigen in paired sera, also can be accessed through state health departments. The commercially available QuickELISA Anthrax-PA Kit (Immunetics Inc) can be used as a screening test. Clinical evaluation of patients with suspected inhalational anthrax should include a chest radiograph and/or computed tomography scan to evaluate for widened mediastinum and pleural effusion.

TREATMENT: A high index of clinical suspicion and rapid administration of effective antimicrobial therapy to people suspected of being infected are essential for effective treatment of anthrax. No controlled trials in humans have been performed to validate current treatment recommendations for anthrax, and there is limited clinical experience. Case reports suggest that naturally occurring cutaneous disease can be treated effectively with a variety of antimicrobial agents, including penicillins and tetracyclines, for 7 to 10 days. For bioterrorism-associated cutaneous disease in adults or children, ciprofloxacin (500 mg, orally, 2 times/day or 20–30 mg/kg per day, orally, divided 2 times/day for children) or doxycycline (100 mg, orally, 2 times/day or 5 mg/kg per day, orally, divided 2 times/day for children younger than 8 years of age) are recommended for initial treatment until antimicrobial susceptibility data are available. Because of the risk of concomitant inhalational exposure, consideration should be given to continuing an appropriate antimicrobial regimen for postexposure prophylaxis as well as administration of vaccine (see Control Measures).

On the basis of in vitro data and animal studies, ciprofloxacin (400 mg, intravenously, every 8–12 hours) or doxycycline (200 mg, intravenously, every 8–12 hours) is recommended as part of an initial multidrug regimen for treating inhalational anthrax, anthrax meningitis, cutaneous anthrax with systemic signs, and gastrointestinal anthrax until results of antimicrobial susceptibility testing are known.* Other agents with in vitro activity suggested for use in conjunction with ciprofloxacin or doxycycline include rifampin, penicillin, ampicillin, vancomycin, imipenem, chloramphenicol, clindamycin, and clarithromycin. Other fluoroquinolones, including levofloxacin, gatifloxacin, and ofloxacin, have excellent in vitro activity against B anthracis, as do newer agents, such as quinupristin/dalfopristin and the ketolide, telithromycin. Because of intrinsic resistance, cephalosporins and trimethoprim-sulfamethoxazole should not be used for therapy. Treatment should continue for at least 60 days. Neither ciprofloxacin nor tetracyclines are used routinely in children or pregnant women because of safety concerns. However, ciprofloxacin or tetracycline should be used for treatment of anthrax in children for life-threatening infections until antimicrobial susceptibility patterns are known.

ISOLATION OF THE HOSPITALIZED PATIENT: Standard precautions are recommended. In addition, contact precautions should be implemented when draining cutaneous lesions are present. Contaminated dressings and bedclothes should be incinerated or steam sterilized to destroy spores. Autopsies performed on patients with systemic anthrax require special precautions.

CONTROL MEASURES: BioThrax (formerly known as Anthrax Vaccine Adsorbed [manufactured by BioPort Corp, Lansing, MI]) is the only human vaccine for prevention of anthrax currently licensed in the United States. This vaccine is prepared from a cell-free culture filtrate. Immunization consists of 6 subcutaneous injections at 0, 2, and 4 weeks and 6, 12, and 18 months followed by annual boosters. The vaccine currently is recommended for people at risk of repeated exposures to B anthracis spores, including selected laboratory workers and military personnel.† The vaccine is effective for preventing the occurrence of cutaneous anthrax in adults. Although protection against inhalational disease has not been evaluated fully in humans, studies in nonhuman primates have shown the vaccine to be effective. Adverse events usually

---

* Centers for Disease Control and Prevention. Update: investigation of bioterrorism-related anthrax and interim guidelines for exposure management and antimicrobial therapy, October 2001. *MMWR Morb Mortal Wkly Rep.* 2001;50:909–919; and Centers for Disease Control and Prevention. Notice to readers: update: interim recommendations for antimicrobial prophylaxis for children and breastfeeding mothers and treatment of children with anthrax. *MMWR Morb Mortal Wkly Rep.* 2001;50:1014–1016

† Centers for Disease Control and Prevention. Notice to readers: use of anthrax vaccine in response to terrorism: supplemental recommendations of the Advisory Committee on Immunization Practices. *MMWR Morb Mortal Wkly Rep.* 2002;51:1024–1026

are local injection site reactions with rare systemic symptoms, including fever, chills, muscle aches, and hypersensitivity. No data on vaccine effectiveness or safety in children are available, and the vaccine is not licensed for use in children or pregnant women. The currently available anthrax vaccine is not licensed for postexposure in preventing anthrax. New anthrax vaccines are in development.

On the basis of limited available data, the best means for prevention of inhalation anthrax after exposure to *B anthracis* spores is prolonged antimicrobial therapy in conjunction with a 3-dose regimen (at 0, 2, and 4 weeks) of anthrax immunization. Because BioThrax vaccine is not licensed for postexposure prophylaxis, for use as a 3-dose regimen, or for use in children, this program can be administered only under an investigational new drug (IND) application as part of an emergency public health intervention. When no information is available about antimicrobial susceptibility of the implicated strain of *B anthracis*, initial postexposure prophylaxis for adults or children with ciprofloxacin or doxycycline is recommended. Although fluoroquinolones and tetracyclines are not recommended as first-choice drugs in children because of adverse effects, these concerns may be outweighed by the need for early treatment of pregnant women and children exposed to *B anthracis* after a terrorist attack. As soon as susceptibility of the organism to penicillin has been confirmed, prophylactic therapy for children should be changed to oral amoxicillin, 80 mg/kg per day, divided every 8 hours (not to exceed 500 mg, 3 times/day). *Bacillus anthracis* is not susceptible to cephalosporins and trimethoprim-sulfamethoxazole; therefore, these agents should not be used for prophylaxis.

Arboviruses (also see West Nile Virus, p 729)

(Including California Serogroup [Primarily La Crosse] Encephalitis, Eastern and Western Equine Encephalitis, Powassan Encephalitis, St Louis Encephalitis, Venezuelan Equine Encephalitis, Colorado Tick Fever, Dengue Fever, Japanese Encephalitis, and Yellow Fever)

CLINICAL MANIFESTATIONS: Arboviruses (arthropodborne viruses) (Table 3.1) are spread by mosquitoes, ticks, sandflies, or other biting arthropods (eg, midges) and produce 4 principal clinical syndromes: (1) central nervous system (CNS) disease (including encephalitis, aseptic meningitis, and flaccid paralysis); (2) an undifferentiated febrile illness, often with rash and headache; (3) acute polyarthropathy; and (4) acute hemorrhagic fever, sometimes accompanied by hepatitis. Some arboviruses can cause congenital infection.

Selected arboviruses that cause encephalitis in the Western hemisphere are shown in Table 3.2 (p 213). When present, clinical illness ranges in severity from a self-limited febrile illness with headache to a syndrome of aseptic meningitis or acute encephalitis. La Crosse virus produces aseptic meningitis or encephalitis with acute seizures and focal neurologic findings in more than 25% of cases, stupor or coma in 50%, and death in less than 1%. Eastern equine encephalitis (EEE) typically is a fulminant illness leading to coma and death in 40% to 70% of cases and serious neurologic sequelae in one third; the highest mortality rates are in infants and children. Western equine encephalitis (WEE) is associated with a case-fatality rate of 5%; neurologic impairment is common in infants, and congenital infection resulting in mental

Table 3.1. Taxonomy of Major Arboviruses

Family	Genus	Representative Agents and Geographic Locations
Bunyaviridae	Bunyavirus	California serogroup viruses (North and South America, Europe, Asia)
		Oropouche virus (South America)
	Phlebovirus	Sandfly fever virus (Europe, Africa, Asia)
		Rift Valley fever virus (sub-Saharan Africa, Saudi Arabia, Yemen)
		Toscana virus (Europe)
	Nairovirus	Crimean-Congo hemorrhagic fever virus (Africa, Europe, Asia)
	Hantavirus	Hantaan virus (Asia)
Togaviridae	Alphavirus	Eastern equine encephalitis virus (North and South America)
		Western equine encephalitis virus (North and South America)
		Venezuelan equine encephalitis virus (Central and South America, Florida)
		Mayaro virus (Central and South America)
		Chikungunya virus (Africa, Asia)
		Ross River virus (Australia, Oceania)
		O'nyong-nyong virus (Africa)
		Sindbis virus (Africa, Scandinavia, northern Europe, Asia, Australia)
Flaviviridae	Flavivirus	St Louis encephalitis virus (North and South America)
		Japanese encephalitis virus (Asia)
		Dengue viruses (types 1–4) (tropics, worldwide)
		Yellow fever virus (South America, Africa)
		Murray Valley encephalitis virus (Australia)
		West Nile virus (Europe, Africa, Asia, North America)
		Tickborne encephalitis complex viruses (Europe and Asia)
		Powassan virus (North America)
Reoviridae	Coltivirus	Colorado tick fever virus (United States, Canada)
Rhabdoviridae	Vesiculovirus	Vesicular stomatitis virus (Western Hemisphere)

retardation has been described. Powassan encephalitis is associated with long-term morbidity and has a case-fatality rate of 10% to 15%. Characteristics of symptomatic infection caused by St Louis encephalitis (SLE) include confusion, fever, headache, slow disease progression, lack of focal findings, generalized weakness, and tremor; 7% of cases are fatal.

Table 3.2. Important Arboviral Infections of the Central Nervous System Occurring in the Western Hemisphere[1]

Disease (Causal Agent)[2]	Geographic Distribution of Virus	Incubation Period, days
California serogroup viruses (primarily La Crosse)	Widespread in the United States and Canada, including the Yukon and Northwest Territories; most prevalent in upper Midwest	5–15
Eastern equine encephalitis (EEE) virus	Eastern seaboard and Gulf states of the US (isolated inland foci); Canada; South and Central America	3–10
Powassan encephalitis virus	Canada; northeastern, north central, and western US, Russian Federation	4–18
St Louis encephalitis (SLE) virus	Widespread: central, southern, northeastern, and western US; Manitoba and southern Ontario; Caribbean area; South America	4–14
Venezuelan equine encephalitis (VEE) virus	Central and South America and Southern US	1–4
Western equine encephalitis (WEE) virus	Central and western US; Canada; Argentina, Uruguay, Brazil	2–10
West Nile encephalitis virus	Asia; Africa; Europe; US	5–15

[1] Although referred to as encephalitis agents, these arboviral infections may cause encephalitis, aseptic meningitis, myelitis, paralysis, or other neurologic findings or systemic illness.
[2] All are mosquitoborne except Powassan virus, which is tickborne.

Japanese encephalitis (JE) virus occurs in Asia and can produce a severe encephalitis characterized by coma, seizures, paralysis, abnormal movements, and death in one third of cases. Serious sequelae occur in 40% of survivors. Most infections are asymptomatic.

Several arboviruses in the Western hemisphere are associated with acute, febrile diseases and hemorrhagic fevers. These arboviruses are not characterized by encephalitis (Table 3.3).

Colorado tick fever (CTF) generally is an acute, self-limited illness consisting of fever, chills, myalgia, arthralgia, severe headache, and ocular pain. Illness is biphasic in 50% of cases and rarely may be complicated by encephalitis, pericarditis, and rarely, fatal systemic illness with hemorrhage. Transient but significant leukopenia and thrombocytopenia in the absence of anemia are hallmarks of disease.

Infection with any of the 4 serotypes of **dengue** virus produces dengue fever, an acute febrile illness with headache, retro-orbital pain, myalgia, arthralgia, rash, nau-

Table 3.3. Acute, Febrile Diseases and Hemorrhagic Fevers Not Characterized by Encephalitis Caused by Arboviruses in the Western Hemisphere

Disease[1]	Geographic Distribution of Virus	Clinical Syndrome	Incubation Period, days
Colorado tick fever[2]	Western US and Canada	Febrile illness—may be biphasic	1–14
Dengue fever and dengue hemorrhagic fever	Tropical areas worldwide: Caribbean, Central and South America, Asia, Australia, Oceania, Africa[3]	Febrile illness—may be biphasic with rash; hemorrhagic fever and shock	2–7
Yellow fever	Tropical areas of South America and Africa[3]	Febrile illness, hepatitis, hemorrhagic fever	3–6
Mayaro fever	Central and South America	Febrile illness and polyarthralgia	1–12
Oropouche virus fever[3]	South America	Febrile illness	2–6

[1] All are mosquitoborne except Colorado tick fever, which is tickborne, and Oropouche virus fever, which is midgeborne.
[2] May cause meningitis.
[3] Mosquito vectors *Aedes aegypti* (yellow fever, dengue) and *Aedes albopictus* (dengue) are found in the United States and could transmit introduced virus.

sea, and vomiting. Criteria for dengue hemorrhagic fever (DHF), which is seen most commonly in children younger than 15 years of age, include fever, any hemorrhage including epistaxis and gum bleeding, thrombocytopenia (platelet count $\leq 100 \times 10^3/\mu L$ [$\leq 100 \times 10^9/L$]), and increased capillary fragility and permeability. Fluid leakage into the interstitial, pleural, and peritoneal spaces leads to hemoconcentration, pleural effusion, and acute shock. Mortality from DHF can be reduced from 30% to less than 3% with appropriate fluid resuscitation and management of electrolyte abnormalities. Encephalopathy, hepatitis, myocardiopathy, upper intestinal tract bleeding, and pneumonia are complications. Maternal infection during the third trimester can result in congenital hemorrhagic dengue.

Severe **yellow fever** (YF) typically evolves through 3 stages from a nonspecific febrile illness with headache, malaise, weakness, nausea, and vomiting; through a brief period of remission; to a hemorrhagic fever with jaundice, albuminuria, oliguria, and multiple organ dysfunction (liver, kidneys, cardiovascular system); 50% of cases are fatal.

Mayaro fever and Oropouche virus fever occur in Central and South America. Both cause a febrile, influenza-like syndrome.

ETIOLOGY: More than 550 arboviruses are classified in a variety of taxonomic groups, principally in the families Bunyaviridae, Togaviridae, and Flaviviridae (Table 3.1, p 212), with more than 150 arboviruses known to cause human disease. Viruses in these families principally are arthropodborne or spread as zoonoses.

EPIDEMIOLOGY: Most arboviruses are maintained in nature through cycles of transmission among birds or small mammals by arthropod vectors. Humans and domestic animals are infected incidentally as "dead-end" hosts. Important exceptions are dengue, YF, Oropouche, and chikungunya viruses, because infected vectors spread disease from person to person (anthroponotic transmission). For the other arboviruses, person-to-person spread does not occur except through blood transfusion, through intrauterine transmission, and possibly through human milk (see Blood Safety, p 106). There also is evidence that Venezuelan encephalitis virus may be spread via respiratory tract secretions.

In the United States, mosquitoborne arboviral infections usually occur during summer and autumn, but in the South, cases occur throughout the year. Fewer than 20 WEE and 10 EEE human cases are reported nationally each year. During epidemics of SLE, people of all ages can be infected, but cases of severe clinical illness occur more often at the extremes of age, especially in elderly people. Urban SLE outbreaks have led to hundreds of cases, disproportionately affecting people in lower socioeconomic-status neighborhoods and homeless people. La Crosse virus encephalitis occurs in an endemic pattern in wooded environments in the eastern and midwestern United States. Most of the approximately 100 cases that are reported each year are in children younger than 15 years of age.

The **incubation periods** and geographic distributions of selected medically important arboviral infections are outlined in Tables 3.2 (p 213) and 3.3 (p 214).

DIAGNOSTIC TESTS: A definitive diagnosis is made by viral isolation. Detection of virus-specific immunoglobulin M antibody in cerebrospinal fluid (CSF) is confirmatory, and presence of antibody in a serum specimen is presumptive evidence of recent infection in a patient with acute CNS infection. A greater than fourfold change in serum immunoglobulin (Ig) M or IgG antibody titer in paired serum specimens obtained 2 to 4 weeks apart confirms a case. Polymerase chain reaction assays to detect several arboviruses are available in reference laboratories. Serologic testing for dengue virus and arboviruses transmitted in the United States is available through several commercial, state, research, and reference laboratories. During the acute phase of dengue fever, YF, CTF, Venezuelan equine encephalitis (VEE), and certain other arboviral infections, virus can be isolated from blood and, in VEE infection, from the throat. In patients with encephalitis, viral isolation should be attempted from a CSF specimen or from biopsy or postmortem brain tissue specimens. Serologic results should be interpreted in the context of any previous immunizations with YF and JE vaccines and locations of previous residence and travel. Immunohistochemical staining for specific arboviruses can be performed at reference laboratories on fresh and formalin-fixed tissue specimens.

TREATMENT: Active clinical monitoring and supportive interventions may be life saving in patients with DHF, YF, and acute encephalitis.

ISOLATION OF THE HOSPITALIZED PATIENT: Patients with acute dengue fever and acute YF may be viremic, so they should be protected from vector mosquitoes that could feed on them and subsequently transmit infection to others.

CONTROL MEASURES:

PROTECTION AGAINST VECTORS. Mosquito-control programs are important for controlling vectors. Personal precautions to avoid arthropod bites include repellents and protective clothing and staying in screened or air-conditioned locations. Although many mosquito vectors of arboviruses are most active during twilight hours, certain vectors of EEE and La Crosse encephalitis are daytime feeders. *Aedes aegypti*, the vector of dengue and urban YF, is found around houses and indoors, even in well-constructed hotels. Travelers to tropical countries should consider bringing mosquito bed nets and aerosol insecticide sprays.

ACTIVE IMMUNIZATION.

Yellow Fever Vaccine. Live-attenuated (17D strain) vaccine is available at state-approved immunization centers. A single dose is accepted by international authorities as providing protection for 10 years and may well confer lifelong immunity.

Immunization is recommended for all people 9 months of age or older living in or traveling to areas with endemic infection and is required every 10 years by international regulations for travel to and from certain countries. Infants younger than 4 months of age should not be immunized, because they have increased susceptibility to vaccine-associated encephalitis. The decision to immunize infants between 4 and 9 months of age must balance the infant's risk of exposure with the theoretic risks of vaccine-associated encephalitis. Yellow fever vaccine-associated viscerotropic disease and YF vaccine-associated neurotropic disease are rare, well-recognized serious vaccine-associated adverse events. People younger than 50 years of age are at higher risk; however, cases occurring at younger ages have been reported. The YF vaccine can be given concurrently with either typhoid vaccine licensed by the US Food and Drug Administration, hepatitis A and hepatitis B virus vaccines, measles vaccine, poliovirus vaccine, and meningococcal vaccine; chloroquine; and Immune Globulin.

Yellow fever vaccine is prepared in embryonated hen eggs and contains egg protein, which may cause allergic reactions. People who have experienced signs or symptoms of allergic reaction after eating eggs should be excused from immunization and issued a medical waiver letter to fulfill health regulations or should undergo skin testing according to the package insert before immunization (also see Hypersensitivity Reactions to Vaccine Constituents, p 46). The vaccine should be administered to pregnant women only if travel to an area with endemic infection is unavoidable and if an increased risk of exposure exists. Administration of YF vaccine to immunocompromised people poses a theoretic risk. The decision to immunize patients who have immuno-compromising conditions must balance the traveler's risk of exposure with his or her clinical status. Family members of immunosuppressed people who themselves have no contraindications can receive YF vaccine. Immunization of breastfeeding mothers should be avoided unless the risk of maternal exposure is high. Advice regarding immunization of 4- to 9-month-old children, pregnant women, or immunocompromised people can be obtained from the Division of Vector-Borne Infectious Diseases of the Centers for Disease Control and Prevention (CDC; telephone 970-221-6400).

---

* Centers for Disease Control and Prevention. Yellow fever vaccine recommendations of the Advisory Committee on Immunization Practices (ACIP), 2002. *MMWR Recomm Rep*. 2002;51(RR-17):1–10

Japanese Encephalitis Vaccine. The inactivated JE vaccine, derived from infected mouse brain, should be offered to people who travel for extended periods (more than 30 days) to areas of Asia with endemic infection during the JE transmission season. Vaccine-associated hypersensitivity reactions (angioedema, generalized urticaria) occur in 0.3% of vaccine recipients. Therefore, immunization is not recommended for travelers who will be staying for short periods in areas without ongoing JE transmission. Immunization should be considered for short-term travelers if travel includes rural areas experiencing epidemic transmission (eg, travel into an area with epidemic infection or bicycling, camping, or other unprotected outdoor activity in a rural area during transmission season). Current information on locations of JE virus transmission and detailed information on vaccine recommendations can be obtained from the CDC (**www.cdc.gov/travel**).

The recommended primary immunization series for people older than 3 years of age is 3 doses of 1.0 mL each, administered subcutaneously on days 0, 7, and 30. An abbreviated schedule of 0, 7, and 14 days can be used when the longer schedule is precluded by time constraints. The regimen for children 1 to 3 years of age is identical, except that each dose is 0.5 mL. No data are available on vaccine safety and efficacy in infants.

Other Arboviral Vaccines. An inactivated vaccine for tickborne encephalitis is licensed in Canada and some countries in Europe where the disease is endemic, but this vaccine is not available in the United States.

Arcanobacterium haemolyticum Infections

CLINICAL MANIFESTATIONS: Acute pharyngitis attributable to *Arcanobacterium haemolyticum* often is indistinguishable from that caused by group A streptococci. Fever, pharyngeal exudate, lymphadenopathy, rash, and pruritus are common, but palatal petechiae and strawberry tongue are absent. In almost half of all reported cases, a maculopapular or scarlatiniform exanthem is present, beginning on the extensor surfaces of the distal extremities, spreading centripetally to the chest and back and sparing the face, palms, and soles. Respiratory tract infections that mimic diphtheria, including membranous pharyngitis, sinusitis, and pneumonia; and skin and soft tissue infections, including chronic ulceration, cellulitis, paronychia, and wound infection have been attributed to *A haemolyticum*. Invasive infections, including septicemia, peritonsillar abscess, Lemierre syndrome, brain abscess, orbital cellulitis, meningitis, endocarditis, osteomyelitis, and pneumonia, have been reported.

ETIOLOGY: *Arcanobacterium haemolyticum* is a facultative anaerobic gram-positive bacillus formerly classified as *Corynebacterium haemolyticum*.

EPIDEMIOLOGY: Humans are the primary reservoir of *A haemolyticum*, and spread is person to person, presumably via droplet respiratory tract secretions. Pharyngitis occurs primarily in adolescents and young adults. Although long-term pharyngeal carriage with *A haemolyticum* has been described after an episode of acute pharyngitis, isolation of the bacterium from the nasopharynx of asymptomatic people is rare. An

---

* Centers for Disease Control and Prevention. Inactivated Japanese encephalitis virus vaccine: recommendations of the Advisory Committee on Immunization Practices (ACIP). *MMWR Recomm Rep.* 1993;42(RR–01):1–15

estimated 0.5% to 3% of acute pharyngitis is attributable to *A haemolyticum*. Case reports also document isolation in combination with other pathogens.

The **incubation period** is unknown.

DIAGNOSTIC TESTS: *Arcanobacterium haemolyticum* grows on blood-enriched agar, but colonies are small and have narrow bands of hemolysis and may not be visible for 48 to 72 hours. Detection is enhanced by culture on rabbit or human blood agar rather than on more commonly used sheep blood agar because of larger colony size and wider zones of hemolysis. Growth also is enhanced by addition of 5% carbon dioxide. Nonstandardized serologic tests for antibodies to *A haemolyticum* have been developed but are not available commercially.

TREATMENT: Erythromycin is the drug of choice for treating tonsillopharyngitis, but no prospective therapeutic trials have been performed. *Arcanobacterium haemolyticum* is susceptible in vitro to erythromycin, clindamycin, and tetracycline; susceptibility to penicillin is variable, and failures in treatment of pharyngitis have been reported, perhaps because of penicillin tolerance. Resistance to trimethoprim-sulfamethoxazole is common. In rare cases of disseminated infection, susceptibility tests should be performed. In disseminated infection, parenteral penicillin plus an aminoglycoside may be used initially as empiric treatment.

ISOLATION OF THE HOSPITALIZED PATIENT: Standard precautions are recommended.

CONTROL MEASURES: None.

Ascaris lumbricoides Infections

CLINICAL MANIFESTATIONS: Most infections are asymptomatic. Moderate to heavy infections may lead to malnutrition, and nonspecific gastrointestinal tract symptoms may occur in some patients. During the larval migratory phase, an acute transient pneumonitis (Löffler syndrome) associated with fever and marked eosinophilia may occur. Acute intestinal obstruction may develop in patients with heavy infections. Children are prone to this complication because of the small diameter of the intestinal lumen and heavy worm burden. Worm migration can cause peritonitis, secondary to intestinal wall penetration, and common bile duct obstruction resulting in biliary colic, cholangitis, or pancreatitis. Adult worms can be stimulated to migrate by stressful conditions (eg, fever, illness, or anesthesia) and by some anthelmintic drugs. *Ascaris lumbricoides* has been found in the appendiceal lumen in patients with acute appendicitis, but a causal relationship is uncertain.

ETIOLOGY: *Ascaris lumbricoides* is the most widespread of all human intestinal roundworms.

EPIDEMIOLOGY: Adult worms live in the lumen of the small intestine. Females produce 200 000 eggs per day, which are excreted in stool and must incubate in soil for 2 to 3 weeks for the embryo to form and to become infectious. Ingestion of infective eggs from contaminated soil results in infection. Larvae hatch in the small intestine, penetrate the mucosa, and are transported passively by portal blood to the liver and subsequently to the lungs. Larvae then ascend through the tracheobronchial tree to the pharynx, are swallowed, and mature into adults in the small intestine. Infection with *A lumbricoides* is widespread but is most common in the tropics, in areas of poor sanitation, and where human feces are used as fertilizer. If infection is untreated, adult worms can live for 12 to 18 months, resulting in daily excretion of large numbers of ova.

The **incubation period** (interval between ingestion of the egg and development of egg-laying adults) is approximately 8 weeks.

DIAGNOSTIC TESTS: Ova can be detected by microscopic examination of stool. Occasionally, patients pass adult worms from the rectum, from the nose after migration through the nares, and from the mouth in vomitus.

TREATMENT: Albendazole in a single dose, mebendazole for 3 days, or ivermectin in a single dose is recommended for treatment of asymptomatic and symptomatic infections (see Drugs for Parasitic Infections, p 790). Although limited data suggest that these drugs are safe in children younger than 2 years of age, the risks and benefits of therapy should be considered before administration. Reexamination of stool specimens 3 weeks after therapy to determine whether the worms have been eliminated is helpful for assessing therapy but is not essential.

In cases of partial or complete intestinal obstruction attributable to a heavy worm load, piperazine solution (75 mg/kg per day, not to exceed 3.5 g) may be given through a gastrointestinal tube but is not available in many countries, including the United States. If piperazine is not available, conservative management (nasogastric suction, intravenous fluids) may result in resolution of obstruction, at which point albendazole, mebendazole, or ivermectin may be given. Surgical intervention occasionally is necessary to relieve intestinal or biliary tract obstruction or for volvulus or peritonitis secondary to perforation. If surgery is performed for intestinal obstruction, massaging the bowel to eliminate the obstruction is preferable to incision into the intestine. Endoscopic retrograde cholangiopancreatography has been used successfully for extraction of worms from the biliary tree.

ISOLATION OF THE HOSPITALIZED PATIENT: Only standard precautions are recommended, because there is no direct person-to-person transmission.

CONTROL MEASURES: Sanitary disposal of human feces stops transmission. Children's play areas should be given special attention. Vegetables cultivated in areas where uncomposted human feces are used as fertilizer must be thoroughly cooked or soaked in a diluted iodine solution before eating. Household bleach is ineffective in killing *A lumbricoides*. Despite relatively rapid reinfection, periodic deworming targeted at school-aged children has been used to prevent morbidity (nutritional and cognitive deficits) associated with intestinal helminth infections.

Aspergillosis

CLINICAL MANIFESTATIONS: Aspergillosis manifests as invasive, noninvasive, and chronic and allergic disease depending on the immune status of the host.
- Invasive aspergillosis occurs almost exclusively in immunocompromised patients with prolonged neutropenia (eg, cytotoxic chemotherapy), graft-versus-host disease, or impaired phagocyte function (eg, chronic granulomatous disease, immunosuppressive therapy, corticosteroids). Invasive infection usually involves pulmonary, sinus, cerebral, or cutaneous sites. Rarely, endocarditis, osteomyeli-

tis, meningitis, infection of the eye or orbit, and esophagitis occur. The hallmark of invasive aspergillosis is angioinvasion with resulting thrombosis, dissemination to other organs, and occasionally, erosion of the blood vessel wall with catastrophic hemorrhage. Patients with chronic granulomatous disease rarely display angioinvasion.

- Aspergillomas and otomycosis are 2 syndromes of nonallergic colonization by *Aspergillus* species in immunocompetent children. Aspergillomas ("fungal balls") grow in preexisting pulmonary cavities or bronchogenic cysts without invading pulmonary tissue; almost all patients have underlying lung disease, such as cystic fibrosis or tuberculosis. Patients with otomycosis have chronic otitis media with colonization of the external auditory canal by a fungal mat that produces a dark discharge.
- Allergic bronchopulmonary aspergillosis is a hypersensitivity lung disease that manifests as episodic wheezing, expectoration of brown mucus plugs, low-grade fever, eosinophilia, and transient pulmonary infiltrates. This form of aspergillosis occurs most commonly in immunocompetent children with asthma or cystic fibrosis and can be a trigger for asthmatic flares.
- Allergic sinusitis is a far less common allergic response to colonization by *Aspergillus* species than is allergic bronchopulmonary aspergillosis. Allergic sinusitis occurs in children with nasal polyps, previous episodes of sinusitis, or in children who have undergone sinus surgery and is characterized by symptoms of chronic sinusitis with dark plugs of nasal discharge.

ETIOLOGY: *Aspergillus* species are ubiquitous molds that grow on decaying vegetation and in soil. *Aspergillus fumigatus* is the usual cause of invasive aspergillosis, with *Aspergillus flavus* being the next most common. Several other species, including *Aspergillus terreus*, *Aspergillus nidulans*, and *Aspergillus niger*, also cause invasive human infections.

EPIDEMIOLOGY: The principal route of transmission is inhalation of conidia (spores), but contaminated aerosolized water supply (eg, shower heads) can cause disease. Incidence of disease in transplant recipients is bimodal, with episodes occurring during periods of neutropenia or, more often, during treatment for graft-versus-host disease. Nosocomial outbreaks of invasive pulmonary aspergillosis in susceptible hosts have occurred in which the probable source of the fungus was a nearby construction site or faulty ventilation system. Transmission by direct inoculation of skin abrasions or wounds is less likely. Person-to-person spread does not occur.

The **incubation period** is unknown.

DIAGNOSTIC TESTS: Dichotomously branched and septate hyphae, identified by microscopic examination of 10% potassium hydroxide wet preparations or of Gomori methenamine-silver nitrate stain of tissue or bronchoalveolar lavage specimens, are suggestive of the diagnosis. Isolation of *Aspergillus* species in culture is required for definitive diagnosis. The organism usually is not recoverable from blood (except *A terreus*) but is isolated readily from lung, sinus, and skin biopsy specimens when cultured on Sabouraud dextrose agar or brain-heart infusion media (without cycloheximide). *Aspergillus* species can be a laboratory contaminant, but when evaluating results from ill, immunocompromised patients, recovery of this organism usually indicates infection. Biopsy of a lesion usually is required to confirm the diagnosis, and care should be taken to distinguish aspergillosis from zygomycosis, which appears similar radiologically. A serologic assay for detection of galactomannan, a molecule found in the cell wall of *Aspergillus* species, is available commercially but has not been evaluated widely in infants and children. A positive test result in adults supports a diagnosis of invasive aspergillosis, and monitoring of serum antigen concentrations may be useful to assess response to therapy. However, false-positive test results occur more frequently in children and may be related to consumption of food products containing galacto-mannan (eg, rice and pasta) or from cross-reactivity with semisynthetic penicillins. A negative galactomannan test result does not exclude the diagnosis of invasive aspergillo-sis. False-negative test results consistently occur in patients with chronic granulomatous disease, so the test should not be used in this population. In allergic aspergillosis, diag-nosis is suggested by a typical clinical syndrome with elevated total concentrations of immunoglobulin (Ig) E ($>$1000 ng/mL) and *Aspergillus*-specific serum IgE, eosinophilia, and a positive result of a skin test for *Aspergillus* antigens. In people with cystic fibrosis, the diagnosis is more difficult, because wheezing, eosinophilia, and a positive skin test result not associated with allergic bronchopulmonary aspergillosis often are present.

TREATMENT: Voriconazole or amphotericin B in high doses (1.0–1.5 mg/kg per day) are the drugs of choice for invasive aspergillosis (see Drugs for Invasive and Other Serious Fungal Infections, p 780). Voriconazole has been shown to be superior to amphotericin B in a large, randomized trial in adults. Therapy is continued for at least 12 weeks, but treatment duration should be individualized for each patient. Voriconazole is metabolized in a linear fashion in children (nonlinear in adults), so the recommended adult dosing is thought to be too low in children. The optimal pediatric dose is not yet known. Voriconazole concentrations do not correlate consis-tently with clinical response.

Caspofungin has been studied in salvage therapy for invasive aspergillosis with good response. The pharmacokinetics of caspofungin differ in children, in whom a body-surface area dosing scheme is preferred to a weight-based dosing regimen. Itraconazole alone is an alternative for mild to moderate cases of aspergillosis, although extensive drug interactions and poor absorption (capsular form) may limit the utility of caspofungin. Lipid formulations of amphotericin B can be considered, but *A terreus* is resistant to all amphotericin B products. There is no role for the use of 5-fluorocytosine or rifampin/rifabutin in treatment of invasive aspergillosis. The safety and efficacy of voriconazole, itraconazole, and caspofungin in children have not been established firmly. Studies are needed to evaluate the benefit and safety of combina-tion antifungal therapy for invasive aspergillosis.

Surgical excision of a localized invasive lesion (eg, sinus debris, accessible cerebral lesions) often is warranted, but surgery is indicated only in pulmonary disease when a mass is impinging on a great vessel. Historically, allergic bronchopulmonary aspergillosis has been treated with corticosteroids. More recently, antifungal therapy has been rec-ommended. Sinus aspergillosis also is treated with corticosteroids, and surgery has been reported to be beneficial in many cases. Antifungal therapy has not been found to be useful.

ISOLATION OF THE HOSPITALIZED PATIENT: Standard precautions are recom-mended.

CONTROL MEASURES: Outbreaks of invasive aspergillosis have occurred among hospitalized immunosuppressed patients during construction in hospitals or at nearby sites. Environmental measures reported to be effective include erecting suitable barriers between patient care areas and construction sites, routine cleaning of air handling systems, repair of faulty air flow, and replacement of contaminated air filters. High-efficiency particulate air filters and laminar flow rooms markedly decrease the risk of conidia in patient care areas. These latter measures may be expensive and difficult for patients to tolerate. Low-dose amphotericin B, itraconazole, or voriconazole prophylaxis has been reported for people undergoing stem cell transplantation, but controlled trials have not been completed in pediatric patients. Patients at risk of invasive infection should have their home conditions evaluated before discharge. People with allergic aspergillosis should take measures to reduce exposure to *Aspergillus* species in the home.

Astrovirus Infections

CLINICAL MANIFESTATIONS: Illness is characterized by abdominal pain, diarrhea, vomiting, nausea, fever, and malaise. Illness in an immunocompetent host is self-limited, lasting a median of 5 to 6 days. Asymptomatic infections are common.

ETIOLOGY: Astroviruses are nonenveloped, single-stranded RNA viruses with a characteristic starlike appearance when visualized by electron microscopy. Eight human antigenic types are known.

EPIDEMIOLOGY: Human astroviruses have a worldwide distribution. Multiple antigenic types cocirculate in the same region. Astroviruses have been detected in as many as 10% of sporadic cases of nonbacterial gastroenteritis among young children. Astrovirus infections occur predominately in children younger than 4 years of age and have a seasonal peak during winter. Transmission is person to person via the fecal-oral route. Outbreaks tend to occur in closed populations of the young and the elderly, and attack rates are high among hospitalized children and children in child care centers. Excretion lasts a median of 5 days after onset of symptoms, but asymptomatic excretion after illness can last for several weeks in healthy children. Persistent excretion may occur in immunocompromised hosts.

The **incubation period** is 1 to 4 days.

DIAGNOSTIC TESTS: Commercial tests for diagnosis are not available in the United States, although enzyme immunoassays are available in many other countries. The following tests are available in some research and reference laboratories: electron microscopy for detection of viral particles in stool, enzyme immunoassay for detection of viral antigen in stool or antibody in serum, latex agglutination in stool, and reverse transcriptase-polymerase chain reaction (RT-PCR) assay for detection of viral RNA in stool. Of these tests, RT-PCR is the most sensitive.

TREATMENT: Rehydration with oral or intravenous fluid and electrolyte solutions is recommended.

ISOLATION OF THE HOSPITALIZED PATIENT: In addition to standard precautions, contact precautions are recommended for diapered or incontinent children with possible or proven astrovirus infection for the duration of the illness.

CONTROL MEASURES: No specific control measures are available. The spread of infection in child care settings can be decreased by using general measures for control of diarrhea, such as training caregivers about infection control procedures, maintaining cleanliness of surfaces and food preparation areas, exercising adequate hand hygiene, and excluding ill child care providers and food handlers and ill children or placing ill children in cohorts.

Babesiosis

CLINICAL MANIFESTATIONS: Most infections are asymptomatic. In people who are symptomatic, gradual onset of malaise, anorexia, and fatigue typically occur, followed by intermittent fever with temperatures as high as 40°C (104°F) and signs and symptoms including chills, sweats, myalgias, arthralgias, headache, nausea, and vomiting. Less common findings are hyperesthesia, sore throat, abdominal pain, conjunctival injection, photophobia, weight loss, and nonproductive cough. Clinical signs generally are minimal, often consisting only of fever, although mild splenomegaly, hepatomegaly, or both are noted occasionally. If untreated, illness can last for a few weeks to several months with a prolonged recovery; silent babesial infection may persist with recrudescence for months or even years in untreated people. Severe illness is most likely to occur in people older than 40 years of age, people with asplenia, and people who are immunocompromised and often presents with fever and hemolytic anemia. Some people, especially people with asplenia, can suffer fulminant illness resulting in death. Many clinical features are similar to those of malaria.

ETIOLOGY: *Babesia* species are intraerythrocytic protozoa. The etiologic agents of babesiosis in the United States include *Babesia microti*, which has caused most of the reported cases, and several other genetically and antigenetically distinct organisms.

EPIDEMIOLOGY: In the United States, the primary reservoir host for *B microti* is the white-footed mouse *(Peromyscus leucopus)*, and the primary vector is the tick *(Ixodes scapularis)*. The *I scapularis* tick also can transmit *Borrelia burgdorferi*, the causative agent of Lyme disease, and *Anaplasma phagocytophilum*, the causative agent of human granulocytotrophic ehrlichiosis. Humans acquire the infection from bites of infected ticks, which typically are not detected. The white-tailed deer *(Odocoileus virginianus)* is an important host for blood meals for the tick but is not a reservoir host of infection with *B microti*. An increase in the deer population in some geographic areas, including some suburban areas, during the past few decades is thought to be a major factor in the spread of *I scapularis* and the increase in numbers of reported human cases of babesiosis. Babesiosis also can be acquired through blood transfusions. The possibility of transplacental or perinatal transmission of babesiosis has been raised. Human cases of babesiosis have been acquired in the Northeast, Midwest, and West Coast of the United States (especially California, Connecticut, Kentucky, Massachusetts, Minnesota, Missouri, New Jersey, New York, Rhode Island, Washington, and Wisconsin). Most vectorborne human cases of babesiosis occur during late spring, summer, or autumn.

The **incubation period** ranges from 1 week to several months.

DIAGNOSTIC TESTS: Babesiosis is diagnosed by microscopic identification of the organism on Giemsa- or Wright-stained thick or thin blood smears. *Babesia microti* and other *Babesia* species can be difficult to distinguish from *Plasmodium falciparum;* examination of blood smears by a reference laboratory should be considered for confirmation of the diagnosis. Serologic tests for detection of *Babesia* antibodies and investigational polymerase chain reaction assays are available at the Centers for Disease Control and Prevention and at some other reference laboratories. People with babesiosis may have concurrent Lyme disease, so diagnostic tests for *B burgdorferi* should be considered.

TREATMENT: Clindamycin plus oral quinine for 7 to 10 days or atovaquone plus azithromycin for 7 to 10 days are equally efficacious (see Drugs for Parasitic Infections, p 790). The latter combination is associated with fewer adverse effects. Exchange blood transfusions should be considered for severely ill people, especially but not exclusively for people with parasitemia levels ≥10%.

ISOLATION OF THE HOSPITALIZED PATIENT: Standard precautions are recommended.

CONTROL MEASURES: Specific recommendations concern prevention of tick bites and are similar to those for prevention of Lyme disease and other tickborne infections (see Prevention of Tickborne Infections, p 195).

Bacillus cereus Infections

CLINICAL MANIFESTATIONS: Two clinical syndromes are associated with *Bacillus cereus* foodborne illness. The first is the emetic syndrome, which, like staphylococcal foodborne illness, develops after a short incubation period and is characterized by nausea, vomiting, abdominal cramps, and in approximately one third of patients, diarrhea. The second is the diarrhea syndrome, which, like *Clostridium perfringens* foodborne illness, has a slightly longer incubation period and is characterized predominantly by moderate to severe abdominal cramps and watery diarrhea, with vomiting in approximately one fourth of patients. Both syndromes are mild, usually are not associated with fever, and abate within 24 hours.

Bacillus cereus also can cause local skin and wound infections, periodontitis, ocular infections, and invasive disease, including bacteremia, central intravascular catheter-associated infection, endocarditis, osteomyelitis, pneumonia, brain abscess, and meningitis. Ocular involvement includes panophthalmitis, endophthalmitis, and keratitis.

ETIOLOGY: *Bacillus cereus* is an aerobic and facultatively anaerobic, spore-forming, gram-positive bacillus. The emetic syndrome is caused by a preformed heat-stable peptide toxin. The emetic toxin is cytotoxic, can cause rhabdomyolysis, and has been associated with fulminant liver failure. The diarrhea syndrome is caused by in vivo production of heat-labile enterotoxins. *Bacillus cereus* virulence genes are encoded chromosomally.

EPIDEMIOLOGY: *Bacillus cereus* is ubiquitous in the environment. It commonly is present in small numbers in raw, dried, and processed foods but is an uncommon cause of foodborne illness in the United States. Spores of *B cereus* are heat-resistant and can survive pasteurization, brief cooking, or boiling. Vegetative forms can grow and produce enterotoxins over a wide range of temperatures from 25°C to 42°C (77°F–108°F). The emetic syndrome is acquired by eating food containing preformed toxin, most commonly fried or recooked rice. Disease can result from eating food contaminated with *B cereus* spores, which produce enterotoxin in the gastrointestinal tract. Spore-associated disease most commonly is caused by contaminated meat or vegetables and manifests as a diarrhea syndrome. Foodborne illness caused by *B cereus* is not transmissible from person to person.

Risk factors for invasive disease attributable to *B cereus* include history of injection drug use, presence of indwelling intravascular catheters or implanted devices, neutropenia or immunosuppression, and preterm birth. *Bacillus cereus* endophthalmitis has occurred after penetrating ocular trauma and injection drug use.

The **incubation period** for the emetic syndrome is 0.5 to 6 hours; for the diarrhea syndrome, the incubation period is 6 to 24 hours.

DIAGNOSTIC TESTS: For foodborne illness, isolation of *B cereus* in a concentration of $\geq 10^5$ colony-forming units/g of epidemiologically incriminated food establishes the diagnosis. Because the organism can be recovered from stool specimens from some well people, the presence of *B cereus* in feces or vomitus of ill people is not definitive evidence of infection unless isolates from several ill patients are demonstrated to be the same serotype or unless stool cultures from a matched control group test negative. Toxin testing is useful but not widely available. Phage typing, DNA hybridization, plasmid analysis, and enzyme electrophoresis have been used as epidemiologic tools in outbreaks of foodborne illness.

In patients with risk factors for invasive disease, isolation of *B cereus* from wounds, blood, or other usually sterile body fluids is significant.

TREATMENT: People with *B cereus* food poisoning require only supportive treatment. Oral rehydration or, occasionally, intravenous fluid and electrolyte replacement for patients with severe dehydration is indicated. Antimicrobial agents are not indicated.

Patients with invasive disease require antimicrobial therapy. Prompt removal of any potentially infected foreign bodies, such as catheters or implants, is essential. *Bacillus cereus* usually is susceptible to vancomycin, which is the drug of choice, and also to alternative drugs, including clindamycin, imipenem, meropenem, and ciprofloxacin. *Bacillus cereus* is resistant to beta-lactam antimicrobial agents.

ISOLATION OF THE HOSPITALIZED PATIENT: Standard precautions are recommended.

CONTROL MEASURES: Proper cooking and appropriate storage of foods, particularly rice cooked for later use, will help prevent foodborne outbreaks. Food should be kept at temperatures higher than 60°C (140°F) or rapidly cooled to less than 10°C (50°F) after cooking.

Hand hygiene and strict aseptic technique in caring for immunocompromised patients or patients with indwelling intravascular catheters are important to minimize the risk of invasive disease.

Bacterial Vaginosis

CLINICAL MANIFESTATIONS: Bacterial vaginosis (BV), a syndrome primarily occurring in sexually active adolescent and adult females, is characterized by changes in vaginal flora. Symptoms may include a thin white or grey, homogenous, adherent vaginal discharge with a fishy odor. Bacterial vaginosis may be asymptomatic in up to 50% of cases and usually is not associated with abdominal pain, significant pruritus, or dysuria.

Vaginitis and vulvitis in prepubertal girls usually have a nonspecific cause and rarely are manifestations of BV. In prepubertal girls, other predisposing causes of vaginal discharge include foreign bodies or infections attributable to group A streptococci, herpes simplex virus, *Neisseria gonorrhoeae*, *Chlamydia trachomatis*, *Trichomonas vaginalis*, or *Shigella* species or other enteric bacteria.

ETIOLOGY: The microbiologic cause of BV has not been delineated clearly. Typical microbiologic findings of specimens obtained from the vagina include an increase in concentrations of *Gardnerella vaginalis*, *Mycoplasma hominis*, *Ureaplasma* species, and anaerobic bacteria and a marked decrease in the concentration of *Lactobacillus* species.

EPIDEMIOLOGY: Bacterial vaginosis is the most prevalent vaginal infection in sexually active adolescents and adult females. It may occur with other conditions associated with vaginal discharge, such as trichomoniasis or cervicitis. Although the evidence of sexual transmission of BV is inconclusive, the condition is uncommon in sexually inexperienced females. Bacterial vaginosis may be a risk factor for pelvic inflammatory disease (PID). Pregnant women with BV are at increased risk of chorioamnionitis, preterm rupture of the membranes, preterm delivery, and postpartum endometritis. Preexisting symptomatic or asymptomatic bacterial vaginosis also may be a risk factor for postabortion PID. Bacterial vaginosis and chorioamnionitis may increase the risk of perinatal transmission of human immunodeficiency virus (HIV).

Sexually active adolescent and adult females with BV should be evaluated for the presence of sexually transmitted infections, including syphilis, gonorrhea, *Chlamydia trachomatis* infection, hepatitis B virus infection, and HIV infection, because coinfection may occur. The occurrence of BV in prepubertal girls should raise suspicion of sexual abuse. Presence of *G vaginalis* in vaginal secretions is not, by itself, adequate for a diagnosis of BV.

The **incubation period** for BV is unknown.

DIAGNOSTIC TESTS: The clinical diagnosis of bacterial vaginosis requires the presence of 3 of the following symptoms or signs:
- Homogenous, grey or white, noninflammatory vaginal discharge that smoothly coats the vaginal walls
- Vaginal fluid pH greater than 4.5
- A fishy odor of vaginal discharge before or after addition of 10% potassium hydroxide (ie, the whiff test)
- Presence of "clue cells" (squamous vaginal epithelial cells covered with bacteria, which cause a stippled or granular appearance and ragged "moth-eaten" borders) on microscopic examination. In BV, clue cells usually constitute at least 20% of vaginal epithelial cells.

A Gram stain of vaginal secretions is an alternative means of establishing a diagnosis. Cocci and a paucity of large gram-positive bacilli consistent with lactobacilli are characteristic. Douching, recent intercourse, menstruation, and coexisting infection can alter findings on Gram stain. Culture for *G vaginalis* is not recommended, because the organism may be found in females without BV, including females who are not sexually active.

TREATMENT: The principal goal of treatment is to relieve vaginal symptoms and signs of infection and decrease the risk of infectious complications. All nonpregnant patients who are symptomatic require treatment. Nonpregnant patients with symptoms should be treated with metronidazole, 1.0 g/day, orally, in 2 divided doses for 7 days; metronidazole gel, 0.75%, 5 g (1 applicator), intravaginally, once a day for 5 days; clindamycin cream, 2%, 1 applicator (5 g), intravaginally, at bedtime for 7 days; or clindamycin phosphate cream, 2%, 1 applicator, intravaginally as a single dose. Clindamycin cream may weaken latex condoms for up to 72 hours after completion of therapy. Alternative regimens that have a lower efficacy for BV are metronidazole, 2 g, orally, in a single dose; clindamycin, 600 mg/day, orally, in 2 divided doses for 7 days; or clindamycin ovules, 100 mg, intravaginally, once at bedtime for 3 days.

Pregnant women with symptoms of BV should be treated, regardless of other risk factors for adverse pregnancy outcome. Topical intravaginal clindamycin cream is not recommended during pregnancy because it can result in preterm labor. Asymptomatic pregnant women at increased risk of adverse pregnancy outcome in association with BV (eg, previous preterm birth) also should be treated, according to some experts. Metronidazole, 750 mg/day in 3 divided doses daily for 7 days, is the preferred treatment during pregnancy. An alternative regimen is clindamycin, 600 mg/day, orally, in 2 divided doses for 7 days. Because treatment of BV in high-risk pregnant women who are asymptomatic might prevent adverse pregnancy outcomes, a follow-up evaluation 1 month after completion of treatment should be considered to evaluate whether therapy was successful.

For nonpregnant and low-risk pregnant women, routine follow-up visits on completion of therapy for BV are unnecessary if symptoms resolve. Recurrences are common and can be treated with the same regimen given initially. The presence of a foreign body in the vagina should be excluded. Routine treatment of male sexual partners is not recommended, because treatment has no influence on relapse or recurrence rates.

Treatment of BV in females infected with HIV is the same as for HIV-negative patients and especially is important in women who are pregnant, because BV and chorioamnionitis may increase the risk of perinatal transmission of HIV.

ISOLATION OF THE HOSPITALIZED PATIENT: Standard precautions are recommended.

CONTROL MEASURES: None.

Bacteroides and *Prevotella* Infections

CLINICAL MANIFESTATIONS: *Bacteroides* and *Prevotella* species from the oral cavity can cause chronic sinusitis, chronic otitis media, dental infection, peritonsillar abscess, cervical adenitis, retropharyngeal space infection, aspiration pneumonia, lung abscess, empyema, or necrotizing pneumonia. Species from the gastrointestinal tract are recovered in patients with peritonitis, intra-abdominal abscess, pelvic inflammatory disease, postoperative wound infection, or vulvovaginal and perianal infections. Soft tissue infections include synergistic bacterial gangrene and necrotizing fasciitis. Invasion of the bloodstream from the oral cavity or intestinal tract can lead to brain abscess, meningitis, endocarditis, arthritis, or osteomyelitis. Skin involvement includes omphalitis in newborn infants, cellulitis at the site of fetal monitors, human bite wounds, infection of burns adjacent to the mouth or rectum, and decubitus ulcers. Neonatal infections, such as conjunctivitis, pneumonia, bacteremia, or meningitis, occur rarely. Most *Bacteroides* infections are polymicrobial.

ETIOLOGY: Most *Bacteroides* and *Prevotella* organisms associated with human disease are pleomorphic, nonspore-forming, facultatively anaerobic, gram-negative bacilli. *Bacteroides* and *Prevotella* species produce enzymes that are involved in the pathogenesis of disease.

EPIDEMIOLOGY: *Bacteroides* and *Prevotella* species are part of the normal flora of the mouth, gastrointestinal tract, or female genital tract. Members of the *Bacteroides fragilis* group predominate in the gastrointestinal tract flora; members of the *Prevotella melaninogenica* (formerly *Bacteroides melaninogenicus*) and *Prevotella oralis* (formerly *Bacteroides oralis*) groups are more common in the oral cavity. These species cause infection as opportunists, usually after an alteration of the body's physical barrier, and in conjunction with other endogenous species. Endogenous transmission results from aspiration, spillage from the bowel, or damage to mucosal surfaces from trauma, surgery, or chemotherapy. Mucosal injury or granulocytopenia predispose to infection. Except in infections resulting from human bites, no evidence of person-to-person transmission exists.

The **incubation period** is variable and depends on the inoculum and the site of involvement but usually is 1 to 5 days.

DIAGNOSTIC TESTS: Anaerobic culture media are necessary for recovery of *Bacteroides* or *Prevotella* species. Because infections usually are polymicrobial, aerobic cultures also should be obtained. A putrid odor suggests anaerobic infection. Use of an anaerobic transport tube or a sealed syringe is recommended for collection of clinical specimens. Rapid diagnostic tests, including polymerase chain reaction and fluorescent in situ hybridization, are available in research laboratories.

TREATMENT: Abscesses should be drained when feasible; abscesses involving the brain, liver, and lungs may resolve with effective antimicrobial therapy. Necrotizing soft tissue lesions should be debrided surgically.

The choice of antimicrobial agent(s) is based on anticipated or known in vitro susceptibility testing. *Bacteroides* infections of the mouth and respiratory tract generally are susceptible to penicillin G, ampicillin, and broad-spectrum penicillins, such as ticarcillin or piperacillin. Clindamycin is active against virtually all mouth and respiratory tract *Bacteroides* and *Prevotella* isolates and is recommended by some experts as the drug of choice for anaerobic infections of the oral cavity and lungs. Some species of *Bacteroides* and almost 50% of *Prevotella* produce beta-lactamase. A beta-lactam penicillin active against *Bacteroides* combined with a beta-lactamase inhibitor can be useful to treat these infections (ampicillin-sulbactam, amoxicillin-clavulanate, ticarcillin-clavulanate, or piperacillin-tazobactam). *Bacteroides* species of the gastrointestinal tract usually are resistant to penicillin G but are predictably susceptible to metronidazole, chloramphenicol, and sometimes, clindamycin. More than 80% of isolates are susceptible to cefoxitin, ceftizoxime linezolid, and imipenem. Cefuroxime, cefotaxime, and ceftriaxone are not reliably effective.

ISOLATION OF THE HOSPITALIZED PATIENT: Standard precautions are recommended.

CONTROL MEASURES: None.

Balantidium coli Infections
(Balantidiasis)

CLINICAL MANIFESTATIONS: Most human infections are asymptomatic. Acute infection is characterized by rapid onset of nausea, vomiting, abdominal discomfort or pain, and bloody or watery mucoid diarrhea. Infected patients can develop chronic intermittent episodes of diarrhea. Rarely, organisms spread to mesenteric nodes, pleura, or liver. Inflammation of the gastrointestinal tract and local lymphatic vessels can result in bowel dilation, ulceration, and secondary bacterial invasion. Colitis produced by *Balantidium coli* often is indistinguishable from that produced by *Entamoeba histolytica*. Fulminant disease can occur in malnourished or otherwise debilitated patients.

ETIOLOGY: *Balantidium coli*, a ciliated protozoan, is the largest pathogenic protozoan known to infect humans.

EPIDEMIOLOGY: Pigs are believed to be the primary host reservoir of *B coli*. Cysts excreted in feces can be transmitted directly from hand to mouth or indirectly through fecally contaminated water or food. The excysted trophozoites infect the colon. A person is infectious as long as cysts are excreted in stool. The cysts may remain viable in the environment for months.

The **incubation period** is unknown but may be several days.

DIAGNOSTIC TESTS: Diagnosis of infection is established by scraping lesions via sigmoidoscopy, histologic examination of intestinal biopsy specimens, or ova and parasite examination of stool. The diagnosis usually is established by demonstrating trophozoites in stool or tissue specimens. Stool examination is less sensitive, and repeated stool examination may be necessary to diagnose infection, because shedding of organisms can be intermittent. Microscopic examination of fresh diarrheal stools must be performed promptly, because trophozoites quickly degenerate.

TREATMENT: The drug of choice is tetracycline, which is administered for 10 days at a dosage of 40 mg/kg per day, maximum of 2 g/day, divided into 4 doses. Tetracycline should not be given to children younger than 8 years of age unless the benefits of therapy are greater than the risks of dental staining (see Antimicrobial Agents and Related Therapy, p 735). Alternative drugs are metronidazole and iodoquinol (see Drugs for Parasitic Infections, p 790).

ISOLATION OF THE HOSPITALIZED PATIENT: In addition to standard precautions, contact precautions are recommended.

CONTROL MEASURES: Control measures include sanitary disposal of human feces and avoidance of contamination of food and water with porcine feces. Despite chlorination of water, waterborne outbreaks of disease have occurred.

Baylisascaris Infections

CLINICAL MANIFESTATIONS: *Baylisascaris procyonis*, a raccoon roundworm, is a rare cause of human eosinophilic meningoencephalitis. In a young child, presentation is acute central nervous system (CNS) disease (eg, altered mental status and seizures) accompanied by peripheral and cerebrospinal fluid (CSF) eosinophilia. Severe neurologic sequelae or death are typical outcomes. *Baylisascaris procyonis* is a rare cause of predominantly extraneural disease in older children and adults. Ocular larva migrans can result in unilateral or bilateral neuroretinitis; direct visualization of worms in the retina sometimes is possible.

Uncommon manifestations include fatal left ventricular inflammatory mass and other visceral involvement from worm migration. In at least one child, the clinical presentation of neural larva migrans was indolent, with progressive neurodevelopmental delay and diagnosis at 6 years of age. Asymptomatic infection can occur.

ETIOLOGY: *Baylisascaris procyonis* is a 10- to 25-cm roundworm (nematode) with a life cycle usually limited to its asymptomatic definitive host, the raccoon, and to soil.

EPIDEMIOLOGY: *Baylisascaris procyonis* is found throughout the United States; an estimated 22% to 80% of raccoons harbor the organism in the intestines. Embryonated eggs containing infective larvae are ingested from the soil by raccoons and grow to maturity in the small intestine, from which adult female worms shed millions of eggs per day. The eggs are 60 to 80 μm in size and have an outer shell, which permits long-term viability in soil. Cases have been reported in California, Minnesota, Illinois, and Pennsylvania, where significant raccoon populations live near humans. Importantly, a small proportion of dogs also may shed the organism in stool.

Geophagia/pica is the most important risk factor for *Baylisascaris* infection, especially for neural larva migrans. Groups at highest risk include children 1 to 4 years of age and children with developmental delay. Nearly all reported cases have been in males.

DIAGNOSTIC TESTS: *Baylisascaris* infection may be confirmed by specific serologic assays (serum, CSF) available only in research laboratories or by pathologic examination of tissue in which larvae with characteristic morphologic features sometimes may be visualized. Neuroimaging may be normal initially, but as larval growth and migration through CNS tissue progress, abnormalities are found in periventricular white matter and focally elsewhere. Because eggs are not shed in human feces, the disease is not transmitted from person to person, and stool examination does not establish the diagnosis of infection with *B procyonis*.

TREATMENT: On the basis of CNS penetration and in vitro efficacy, albendazole (25–40 mg/kg per day), in conjunction with high-dose corticosteroids, has been advocated most widely. However, treatment with anthelmintic agents and/or anti-inflammatory therapies (eg, corticosteroids) may not affect clinical outcome once CNS disease manifestations are evident. Some experts advocate the use of additional anthelmintic agents. Preventive therapy with albendazole may be considered for children with a history of ingestion of potentially contaminated soil. Worms localized to the retina can be killed by direct photocoagulation.

ISOLATION OF THE HOSPITALIZED PATIENT: Standard precautions are recommended.

CONTROL MEASURES: *Baylisascaris* infections are prevented by avoiding ingestion of soil potentially containing stool of infective animal reservoirs, primarily raccoons and potentially dogs; avoiding raccoon communal defecation sites, such as flat tree stumps and rocks; preventing geophagia; handwashing, especially after pet or other animal contact; discouraging raccoon presence by limiting access to human or pet food sources; and decontaminating raccoon latrines with lye, particularly latrines located near homes.

Blastocystis hominis Infections

CLINICAL MANIFESTATIONS: The importance of *Blastocystis hominis* as a cause of gastrointestinal tract disease is controversial. The asymptomatic carrier state is well documented. *Blastocystis hominis* has been associated with symptoms of bloating, flatulence, mild to moderate diarrhea without fecal leukocytes or blood, abdominal pain, and nausea. When *B hominis* is identified in stool from symptomatic patients, other causes of this symptom complex, particularly *Giardia lamblia* and *Cryptosporidium parvum*, should be investigated before assuming that *B hominis* is the cause of the signs and symptoms.

ETIOLOGY: *Blastocystis hominis* is classified as a protozoan and has 3 distinct stages: vacuolar, which is observed most commonly in clinical specimens; granular; and ameboid.

EPIDEMIOLOGY: *Blastocystis hominis* is recovered from 1% to 20% of stool specimens examined for ova and parasites. Because transmission is believed to be via the fecal-oral route, presence of the organism may be a marker for presence of other pathogens spread by fecal contamination. Transmission from animals occurs.

The **incubation period** is unknown.

DIAGNOSTIC TESTS: Stool specimens should be preserved in polyvinyl alcohol and stained with trichrome or iron-hematoxylin before microscopic examination. The parasite may be present in varying numbers, and infections may be reported as light to heavy. The presence of 5 or more organisms per high-power ($\times 400$ magnification) field indicates a heavy infection, which to some experts suggests causation when other enteropathogens are absent.

TREATMENT: Indications for treatment are not established. Some experts recommend that treatment should be reserved for patients who have persistent symptoms and in whom no other pathogen or process is found to explain the gastrointestinal tract symptoms. Other experts believe that *B hominis* does not cause symptomatic disease and recommend only a careful search for other causes of the symptoms. Metronidazole, trimethoprim-sulfamethoxazole, iodoquinol, and nitazoxanide (in children) have been used with limited success (see Drugs for Parasitic Infections, p 790). Controlled treatment trials are not available.

ISOLATION OF THE HOSPITALIZED PATIENT: In addition to standard precautions, contact precautions are recommended for diapered or incontinent children.

CONTROL MEASURES: None.

Blastomycosis

CLINICAL MANIFESTATIONS: Infection can be asymptomatic or associated with acute, chronic, or fulminant disease. The major clinical manifestations of blastomycosis are pulmonary, cutaneous, and disseminated disease. Children commonly have pulmonary disease that can be associated with a variety of symptoms, and radiographic appearances can be misdiagnosed as bacterial pneumonia, tuberculosis, sarcoidosis, or malignant neoplasm. Skin lesions can be nodular, verrucous, or ulcerative, often with minimal inflammation. Abscesses generally are subcutaneous but can involve any organ. Disseminated blastomycosis usually begins with pulmonary infection and can involve skin, bones, central nervous system, abdominal viscera, and kidneys. Intrauterine or congenital infections occur rarely.

ETIOLOGY: Blastomycosis is caused by *Blastomyces dermatitidis*, a dimorphic fungus existing in the yeast form at 37°C (98°F) and in infected tissues and in a mycelial form at room temperature and in soil. Conidia, produced from hyphae of the mycelial form, are infectious for humans.

EPIDEMIOLOGY: Infection is acquired through inhalation of conidia from soil. Person-to-person transmission does not occur. Infection may be epidemic or sporadic and has been reported in the United States, Canada, Africa, and India. Areas with endemic infection in the United States are the southeastern and central states and the midwestern states bordering the Great Lakes. Although blastomycosis can occur in immunocompromised hosts, the disease has been reported rarely in people infected with human immunodeficiency virus.

The **incubation period** is approximately 30 to 45 days.

DIAGNOSTIC TESTS: Thick-walled, figure-of-eight shaped, broad-based, single-budding yeast forms may be seen in sputum, tracheal aspirates, cerebrospinal fluid, urine, or material from lesions processed with 10% potassium hydroxide or a silver stain. Children with pneumonia who are unable to produce sputum may require an invasive procedure (eg, open biopsy or bronchoalveolar lavage) to establish the diagnosis. Organisms can be cultured on brain-heart infusion media and Sabouraud dextrose agar at room temperature. Chemiluminescent DNA probes are available for identification of *B dermatitidis*. Because serologic tests lack adequate sensitivity, every effort should be made to obtain appropriate specimens for culture.

TREATMENT: Amphotericin B is the treatment of choice for severe or life-threatening infection (see Drugs for Invasive and Other Serious Fungal Infections, p 780). Oral itraconazole or fluconazole has been used for mild or moderately severe infections alone or after a short course of amphotericin B. Data regarding the efficacy of itraconazole and fluconazole therapy in children are limited. Although itraconazole is indicated for treatment of nonmeningeal, nonlife-threatening infections in adults, the safety and efficacy of this agent in children has not been established.

Oral therapy usually is continued for at least 6 months for pulmonary and extrapulmonary disease. Some experts suggest one year of therapy for patients with osteomyelitis.

ISOLATION OF THE HOSPITALIZED PATIENT: Standard precautions are recommended.

CONTROL MEASURES: None.

Borrelia Infections
(Relapsing Fever)

CLINICAL MANIFESTATIONS: Relapsing fever is characterized by the sudden onset of high fever, shaking chills, sweats, headache, muscle and joint pains, and nausea. A fleeting macular rash of the trunk and petechiae of the skin and mucous membranes sometimes occur. Complications include hepatosplenomegaly, jaundice, thrombocytopenia, iridocyclitis, cough with pleuritic pain, pneumonitis, meningitis, and myocarditis. The mortality rates are 10% to 70% in untreated louseborne relapsing fever (possibly related to comorbidities in refugee-type settings where this disease typically is found) and 4% to 10% in untreated tickborne relapsing fever. Early treatment reduces mortality to 2% to 5% overall and occurs largely in people with underlying illnesses, infants, and the elderly. Untreated, an initial febrile period of 2 to 7 days terminates spontaneously by crisis. The initial febrile episode is followed by an afebrile period of several days to weeks, then by one or more relapses. Relapses typically become progressively shorter and milder as afebrile periods lengthen. Relapse is associated with expression of new borrelial antigens, and resolution of symptoms is associated with production of antibody specific to those new antigenic determinants. Infection during pregnancy often is severe and can result in preterm birth, abortion, stillbirth, or neonatal infection.

ETIOLOGY: Relapsing fever is caused by certain spirochetes of the genus *Borrelia*. *Borrelia recurrentis* is the only species that causes louseborne (epidemic) relapsing fever, and there is no animal reservoir of *B recurrentis*. Worldwide, at least 14 *Borrelia* species cause tickborne (endemic) relapsing fever, including *Borrelia hermsii*, *Borrelia turicatae*, and *Borrelia parkeri* in North America.

EPIDEMIOLOGY: Louseborne epidemic relapsing fever has been reported in Ethiopia, Eritrea, Somalia, and the Sudan, especially among the homeless and in refugee populations. Epidemic transmission occurs when body lice (*Pediculus humanus*) become infected by feeding on humans with spirochetemia; the infection is transmitted when infected lice are crushed and their body fluids contaminate a bite wound or skin abraded by scratching.

Endemic tickborne relapsing fever is distributed widely throughout the world, is transmitted by soft-bodied ticks (*Ornithodoros* species), and occurs sporadically and in small clusters, often within families. Ticks become infected by feeding on rodents or other small mammals and transmit infection via their saliva and other fluids when they take subsequent blood meals. Ticks may serve as reservoirs of infection as a result of transovarial and trans-stadial transmission. Soft-bodied ticks inflict painless bites and feed briefly (10–30 minutes), usually at night, so people often are unaware of bites.

Most tickborne relapsing fever in the United States is caused by *B hermsii*. Infection typically results from tick exposures in rodent-infested cabins in western mountainous areas, including state and national parks. *Borrelia turicatae* infections occur less frequently; most cases have been reported from Texas and often are associated with tick exposures in rodent-infested caves. *Borrelia parkeri* causes the lowest number of infections and is associated with burrows, rodent nests, and caves in arid areas or grasslands in the Western United States.

Infected body lice and ticks remain alive and infectious for several years without feeding. Relapsing fever is not transmitted between individual humans, but perinatal transmission from an infected mother to her infant does occur and can result in preterm birth, stillbirth, and neonatal death.

The **incubation period** is 2 to 18 days, with a mean of 7 days.

DIAGNOSTIC TESTS: Spirochetes can be observed by dark-field microscopy and in Wright-, Giemsa-, or acridine orange-stained preparations of thin or dehemoglobinized thick smears of peripheral blood or in stained buffy-coat preparations. Organisms often can be detected in blood obtained while the person is febrile. Spirochetes can be cultured from blood in Barbour-Stoenner-Kelly medium or by intraperitoneal inoculation of immature laboratory mice. Serum antibodies to *Borrelia* species can be detected by enzyme immunoassay and Western immunoblot analysis at some reference and commercial specialty laboratories; these tests are not standardized and are affected by antigenic variations between and within *Borrelia* species and strains. Serologic cross-reactions occur with other spirochetes, including *Borrelia burgdorferi*, *Treponema pallidum*, and *Leptospira* species. Biologic specimens for laboratory testing can be sent to the Division of Vector-Borne Infectious Diseases, Centers for Disease Control and Prevention, Fort Collins, CO 80522.

TREATMENT: Treatment of tickborne relapsing fever with a 5- to 10-day course of one of the tetracyclines, usually doxycycline, produces prompt clearance of spirochetes and remission of symptoms. For children younger than 8 years of age and for pregnant women, penicillin and erythromycin are the preferred drugs. Penicillin G procaine or intravenous penicillin G is recommended as initial therapy for people who are unable to take oral therapy, although penicillin G has been associated with an increased rate of relapse. A Jarisch-Herxheimer reaction (an acute febrile reaction accompanied by headache, myalgia, and an aggravated clinical picture lasting less than 24 hours) commonly is observed during the first few hours after initiating anti-microbial therapy. Because this reaction sometimes is associated with transient hypotension attributable to decreased effective circulating blood volume (especially in louseborne relapsing fever), patients should be monitored closely, particularly during the first 4 hours of treatment. However, the Jarisch-Herxheimer reaction in children typically is mild and usually can be managed with antipyretic agents alone.

Single-dose treatment using a tetracycline, penicillin, or erythromycin is effective for curing louseborne relapsing fever.

ISOLATION OF THE HOSPITALIZED PATIENT: Standard precautions are recommended. If louse infestation is present, contact precautions also are indicated (see Pediculosis, pp 488–492).

CONTROL MEASURES: Contact with ticks can be limited through use of protective clothing, acaricides, and tick repellents (see Prevention of Tickborne Infections, p 195). Prevention of rodent access to foundations and attics of homes or cabins also decreases the potential for tick exposure. Dwellings infested with soft ticks should be rodent proofed and treated professionally with chemical agents. When in a louse-infested environment, body lice can be controlled by bathing, washing clothing at frequent intervals, and use of pediculicides (see Pediculosis, pp 488–492). Reporting of suspected cases of relapsing fever to health authorities is required in most Western states and is important for initiation of prompt investigation and institution of control measures.

Brucellosis

CLINICAL MANIFESTATIONS: Brucellosis in children commonly is a mild self-limited disease compared with the more chronic disease in adults. However, in areas where *Brucella melitensis* is the endemic species, disease can be severe. Onset of illness can be acute or insidious. Manifestations are nonspecific and include fever, night sweats, weakness, malaise, anorexia, weight loss, arthralgia, myalgia, abdominal pain, and headache. Physical findings include lymphadenopathy, hepatosplenomegaly, and occasionally, arthritis. Serious complications include meningitis, endocarditis, and osteomyelitis.

ETIOLOGY: *Brucella* species are small, nonmotile, gram-negative coccobacilli. The species that infect humans are *Brucella abortus, Brucella melitensis, Brucella suis,* and rarely, *Brucella canis.*

EPIDEMIOLOGY: Brucellosis is a zoonotic disease of wild and domestic animals. Humans are accidental hosts, contracting the disease by direct contact with infected animals or their carcasses or secretions or by ingesting unpasteurized milk or milk products. People in occupations such as farming, ranching, and veterinary medicine as well as abattoir workers, meat inspectors, and laboratory personnel are at increased risk. Infection is transmitted by inoculation through cuts and abrasions in the skin, inhalation of contaminated aerosols, contact with the conjunctival mucosa, or oral ingestion. Approximately 100 to 200 cases of brucellosis occur annually in the United States, with fewer than 10% of reported cases occurring in people younger than 19 years of age. Most cases occur in immigrants or travelers returned from areas with endemic infection and can result from ingestion of unpasteurized dairy products. Although human-to-human transmission is rare, congenital brucellosis has been reported, and infected mothers may transmit *Brucella* species to their infants through breastfeeding.

The **incubation period** varies from less than 1 week to several months, but most people become ill within 3 to 4 weeks of exposure.

DIAGNOSTIC TESTS: A definitive diagnosis is established by recovery of *Brucella* species from blood, bone marrow, or other tissue. A variety of media will support the growth of *Brucella* species, but laboratory personnel should incubate cultures for a minimum of 4 weeks. In patients with clinically compatible illness, serologic testing can confirm the diagnosis with a fourfold or greater increase in antibody titers in serum specimens collected at least 2 weeks apart. The serum agglutination test, the most commonly used test, will detect antibodies against *B abortus, B suis,* and *B melitensis,* but not *B canis,* which requires use of *B canis*-specific antigen. Although a single titer is not diagnostic, most patients with active infection in an area without endemic infection have a titer of 1:160 or greater within 2 weeks of clinical disease onset. Lower titers may be found early in the course of infection. Increased concentrations of immunoglobulin (Ig) G agglutinins are found in acute infection, chronic infection, and relapse. When interpreting serum agglutination test results, the possibility of cross-reactions of *Brucella* antibodies with those against other gram-negative bacteria, such as *Yersinia enterocolitica* serotype 09, *Francisella tularensis,* and *Vibrio cholerae,* should be considered. To avoid a prozone phenomenon, serum should be diluted to 1:320 or higher before testing. Enzyme immunoassay is a sensitive method for determining IgG, IgA, and IgM anti-*Brucella* antibodies. Until better standardization is established, enzyme immunoassay should be used only for suspected cases with negative serum agglutination test results or for evaluation of patients with suspected relapse or reinfection. Polymerase chain reaction tests have been developed but are not available in most clinical laboratories.

TREATMENT: Prolonged antimicrobial therapy is imperative for achieving a cure. Relapses generally are not associated with development of *Brucella* resistance but rather with premature discontinuation of therapy. Monotherapy is associated with a high rate of relapse; combination therapy is recommended.

Oral doxycycline (2–4 mg/kg per day, maximum 200 mg/day, in 2 divided doses) or oral tetracycline (30–40 mg/kg per day, maximum 2 g/day, in 4 divided doses) is the drug of choice and should be administered for at least 6 weeks. However, tetracyclines should be avoided, if possible, in children younger than 8 years of age (see Antimicrobial Agents and Related Therapy, p 735). Oral trimethoprim-sulfamethoxazole (trimethoprim, 10 mg/kg per day, maximum 480 mg/day; and sulfamethoxazole, 50 mg/kg per day, maximum 2.4 g/day) divided in 2 doses for 4 to 8 weeks is appropriate therapy for younger children.

To decrease the incidence of relapse, combination therapy with a tetracycline (or trimethoprim-sulfamethoxazole if tetracyclines are contraindicated) and rifampin (15–20 mg/kg per day, maximum 600–900 mg/day, in 1 or 2 divided doses) is recommended. Because of the potential emergence of rifampin resistance, rifampin monotherapy is not recommended.

For treatment of serious infections or complications, including endocarditis, meningitis, and osteomyelitis, streptomycin or gentamicin for the first 14 days of therapy in addition to a tetracycline for 6 weeks (or trimethoprim-sulfamethoxazole if tetracyclines are contraindicated) are recommended. In addition, rifampin can be used with this regimen to decrease the rate of relapse. For life-threatening complications of brucellosis, such as meningitis or endocarditis, the duration of therapy often is extended for several months. Surgical intervention should be considered in patients with complications such as deep tissue abscesses.

The benefit of corticosteroids for people with neurobrucellosis is unproven. Occasionally, a Jarisch-Herxheimer-like reaction (an acute febrile reaction accompanied by headache, myalgia, and an aggravated clinical picture lasting less than 24 hours) occurs shortly after initiation of antimicrobial therapy, but this reaction is rarely severe enough to require corticosteroids.

ISOLATION OF THE HOSPITALIZED PATIENT: In addition to standard precautions, contact precautions are indicated for patients with draining wounds.

CONTROL MEASURES: The control of human brucellosis depends on eradication of *Brucella* species from cattle, goats, swine, and other animals. Pasteurization of milk and milk products for human consumption is important to prevent disease in children. The certification of raw milk does not eliminate the risk of transmission of *Brucella* organisms.

Burkholderia Infections

CLINICAL MANIFESTATIONS: *Burkholderia cepacia* complex has been associated with severe pulmonary infections in patients with cystic fibrosis, with significant bacteremia in preterm infants requiring prolonged hospitalization, and with infection in children with chronic granulomatous disease, hemoglobinopathies, or malignant neoplasms. Health care-associated infections include wound and urinary tract infections and pneumonia. Pulmonary infections in people with cystic fibrosis occur late in the course of disease, usually after respiratory epithelial damage caused by infection with *Pseudomonas aeruginosa* has been established. Culture-positive patients can experience no change in the rate of pulmonary decompensation, become chronically infected with a more rapid decline in pulmonary function, or experience an unexpectedly rapid deterioration in clinical status that results in death. In chronic granulomatous disease, pneumonia is the most common manifestation of *B cepacia* complex infection; lymphadenitis also has been reported. Disease onset is insidious, with low-grade fever early in the course and systemic effects occurring 3 to 4 weeks later. Pleural effusion is common, and lung abscess has been described.

Burkholderia pseudomallei is the cause of melioidosis, endemic to southeast Asia and northern Australia but also found in other tropical and subtropical areas. Melioidosis can occur in the United States, usually among travelers returning from areas with endemic infection. Melioidosis can manifest as a localized infection or as fulminant septicemia. Localized infection usually is nonfatal and most commonly manifests as pneumonia, but skin, soft tissue, and skeletal infections also occur. In severe cutaneous infection, necrotizing fasciitis has been reported. In disseminated infection, hepatic and splenic abscesses can occur, and relapses are common without prolonged therapy.

ETIOLOGY: *Burkholderia* organisms are nutritionally diverse, catalase-producing, non-lactose-fermenting, gram-negative bacilli. *Burkholderia cepacia* complex comprises at least 10 species (*B cepacia, Burkholderia multivorans, Burkholderia cenocepacia, Burkholderia stabilis, Burkholderia vietnamiensis, Burkholderia dolosa, Burkholderia ambifaria, Burkholderia anthina, Burkholderia pyrrocinia,* and *Burkholderia ubonensis*). Other species of *Burkholderia* include *Burkholderia gladioli, Burkholderia mallei,* and *B pseudomallei,* which is the cause of the disease melioidosis.

EPIDEMIOLOGY: All *Burkholderia* species primarily are opportunistic pathogens. *Burkholderia* species are waterborne and soilborne organisms that can survive for prolonged periods when kept moist. Epidemiologic studies of camps and other social events attended by people with cystic fibrosis from different geographic areas have demonstrated person-to-person spread of *B cepacia* complex. The source for acquisition of *B cepacia* complex by patients with chronic granulomatous disease has not been identified. Hospital spread of *B cepacia* complex most often is associated with contamination of disinfectant solutions used to clean reusable patient equipment, such as bronchoscopes and pressure transducers, or to disinfect skin. *Burkholderia gladioli* also has been isolated from sputum from people with cystic fibrosis and may be mistaken for *B cepacia*. The clinical significance of *B gladioli* is not known.

    Burkholderia pseudomallei often is acquired early in life, with the highest seroconversion rates between 6 and 42 months of age. Disease can be acquired by direct inhalation of aerosolized organisms or from dust particles containing organisms. Symptomatic infection can occur as early as 1 year of age. Risk factors for disease include diabetes mellitus and renal insufficiency. *Burkholderia pseudomallei* also has been reported to cause pulmonary infection in people with cystic fibrosis and people traveling to areas with endemic infection and septicemia in children with chronic granulomatous disease.

    The **incubation period** is 1 to 21 days, with a median of 9 days.

DIAGNOSTIC TESTS: Culture is the appropriate test for diagnosis of *B cepacia* complex infection. In cystic fibrosis lung infection, culture of sputum on selective agar is recommended to decrease the potential for overgrowth by mucoid *P aeruginosa*. *Burkholderia cepacia* and *B gladioli* can be identified by polymerase chain reaction assay, but this assay is not available routinely. Definitive diagnosis of melioidosis is made by isolation of *B pseudomallei* from blood or other infected sites. The likelihood of successfully isolating the organism is increased by culturing sputum, throat swabs, rectal swabs, and ulcer or skin lesion swabs. A positive result by the indirect hemagglutination assay in a traveler returned from an area with endemic infection may support the diagnosis of meliodosis, but definitive diagnosis still requires isolation of *B pseudomallei* in culture. Other rapid assays are being developed for diagnosis of melioidosis, but none are available commercially.

TREATMENT: Meropenem is the most active agent against the majority of *B cepacia* complex isolates, although other drugs that may be effective include trimethoprim-sulfamethoxazole, ceftazidime, chloramphenicol, and imipenem. Most experts recommend synergistic combinations of antimicrobial agents. Most *B cepacia* complex isolates are intrinsically resistant to aminoglycosides and polymyxin B sulfate.

The drugs of choice for melioidosis include ceftazidime, meropenem, or imipenem. Addition of trimethoprim-sulfamethoxazole also may be useful. After therapy is completed, eradication can be attempted with trimethoprim-sulfamethoxazole or doxycycline to reduce recurrence, but the optimal duration and regimen remains unclear.

ISOLATION OF THE HOSPITALIZED PATIENT: Contact and droplet precautions are recommended for patients infected with multidrug-resistant strains of *B cepacia* complex. Standard precautions are recommended for people with *B pseudomallei* infection.

CONTROL MEASURES: Because some strains of *B cepacia* complex are highly transmissible and virulence is not well understood, many cystic fibrosis centers limit contact between *B cepacia* complex-infected and -uninfected patients with cystic fibrosis. This includes inpatient, outpatient, and social settings. For example, patients with cystic fibrosis who are infected with *B cepacia* complex are cared for in single rooms and have unique clinic hours, and specialized camps have been disbanded.

Education of patients and families about hand hygiene and appropriate personal hygiene is recommended. Prevention of infection with *B pseudomallei* in areas with endemic infection can be difficult, because contact with contaminated water and soil is common. People with diabetes mellitus and skin lesions should avoid contact with soil and standing water in these areas. Wearing boots and gloves during agricultural work in areas with endemic infection is recommended.

Caliciviruses

CLINICAL MANIFESTATIONS: Diarrhea and vomiting, commonly accompanied by fever, headache, malaise, myalgia, and abdominal cramps, are characteristic of calicivirus infection. Symptoms last from 1 day to 2 weeks.

ETIOLOGY: Caliciviruses are nonenveloped RNA viruses. The 2 recognized genera that cause disease in humans are noroviruses (formerly Norwalk-like viruses) and sapoviruses.

EPIDEMIOLOGY: Human caliciviruses have a worldwide distribution, with multiple antigenic types circulating simultaneously in the same region. Caliciviruses may be a major cause of sporadic cases of gastroenteritis requiring hospitalization, but sensitive diagnostic tools have been applied only recently to study this problem. Most sporadic calicivirus infections have been detected in children younger than 4 years of age. Transmission is by person-to-person spread via the fecal-oral route or through contaminated food or water. Outbreaks of gastroenteritis have been detected in all age groups. Outbreaks tend to occur in closed populations, such as child care centers and on cruise ships, and there is a high attack rate. Common-source outbreaks have been described after ingestion of ice, shellfish, salads, and cookies, usually contaminated by infected food handlers. Airborne transmission may occur, although compelling evidence of this is lacking. Exposure to contaminated surfaces and vomitus has been implicated in some outbreaks. Excretion lasts 5 to 7 days after the onset of symptoms in half of infected people, and excretion can be as long as 13 days. Prolonged excretion can occur in immunocompromised hosts.

The **incubation period** is 12 to 72 hours.

DIAGNOSTIC TESTS: Commercial assays for diagnosis are not available in the United States. The following tests are available in some research and reference laboratories: electron microscopy for detection of viral particles in stool, enzyme immunoassay for detection of viral antigen in stool or antibody in serum, and reverse transcriptase-polymerase chain reaction (RT-PCR) assay for detection of viral RNA in stool. The most sensitive assays are RT-PCR and serologic testing; electron microscopy is relatively insensitive. Laboratory and epidemiologic support for diagnosis of suspected calicivirus outbreaks is available at the Centers for Disease Control and Prevention, and RT-PCR assays for viral detection in stools increasingly are available at state and local health department laboratories.

TREATMENT: Supportive therapy includes oral rehydration solution to replace fluids and electrolytes.

ISOLATION OF THE HOSPITALIZED PATIENT: In addition to standard precautions, contact precautions are recommended for diapered and incontinent children for the duration of illness.

CONTROL MEASURES: No specific control measures are available. The spread of infection can be decreased by standard measures for control of diarrhea, such as educating child care providers and all food handlers about infection control, maintaining cleanliness of surfaces and food preparation areas, excluding caregivers or food handlers who are ill, exercising adequate hand hygiene, and excluding or grouping ill children in child care. If a mode of transmission can be identified (eg, contaminated food or water) during an outbreak, then specific interventions to interrupt transmission can be effective. People with diarrhea caused by this potentially waterborne pathogen should not use recreational water venues (eg, swimming pools, lakes, rivers, the ocean) for 2 weeks after symptoms resolve.

Campylobacter Infections

CLINICAL MANIFESTATIONS: Predominant symptoms of *Campylobacter* infections include diarrhea, abdominal pain, malaise, and fever. Stools may contain visible or occult blood. In neonates and young infants, bloody diarrhea without fever may be the only manifestation of infection. Abdominal pain can mimic that produced by appendicitis or intussusception. Mild infection lasts 1 or 2 days and resembles viral gastroenteritis. Most patients recover in less than 1 week, but 20% have a relapse or a prolonged or severe illness. Severe or persistent infection can mimic acute inflammatory bowel disease. Bacteremia is uncommon but can occur in neonates, in people with human immunodeficiency virus infection, and in healthy and malnourished children. Immunocompromised hosts may have prolonged, relapsing, or extraintestinal infections, especially with *Campylobacter fetus* and other "atypical" species. Immunoreactive complications, such as acute idiopathic polyneuritis (Guillain-Barré syndrome), Miller Fisher syndrome (ophthalmoplegia, areflexia, ataxia), reactive arthritis, Reiter syndrome (arthritis, urethritis, and bilateral conjunctivitis), and erythema nodosum, can occur during convalescence.

ETIOLOGY: *Campylobacter* species are motile, comma-shaped, gram-negative bacilli that cause gastroenteritis. *Campylobacter jejuni* and *Campylobacter coli* are the most common species isolated from patients with diarrhea. *Campylobacter fetus* predominantly causes systemic illness in neonates and debilitated hosts. Other *Campylobacter* species, including *Campylobacter upsaliensis, Campylobacter lari,* and *Campylobacter hyointestinalis,* may cause similar diarrheal or systemic illnesses in children.

EPIDEMIOLOGY: The gastrointestinal tract of domestic and wild birds and animals is the reservoir of infection. *Campylobacter jejuni* and *C coli* have been isolated from feces of 30% to 100% of chickens, turkeys, and water fowl. Poultry carcasses usually are contaminated. Many farm animals and meat sources can harbor the organism, and pets (especially young animals), including dogs, cats, hamsters, and birds, are potential sources of infection. Transmission of *C jejuni* and *C coli* occurs by ingestion of contaminated food or by direct contact with fecal material from infected animals or people. Improperly cooked poultry, untreated water, and unpasteurized milk have been the main vehicles of transmission. Outbreaks among school children who drank unpasteurized milk, including children who have participated in field trips to dairy farms, have occurred. Person-to-person spread occurs occasionally, particularly among very young children, and outbreaks of diarrhea in child care centers have been reported but are uncommon. Person-to-person transmission also has occurred in neonates of infected mothers and has resulted in health care-related outbreaks in nurseries. In perinatal infection, *C jejuni* and *C coli* usually cause neonatal gastroenteritis, whereas *C fetus* often causes neonatal septicemia or meningitis. Enteritis occurs in people of all ages. Communicability is uncommon but is greatest during the acute phase of illness. Excretion of *Campylobacter* organisms typically lasts 2 to 3 weeks without treatment. *Campylobacter jejuni* and *C coli* are one of the major organisms detected by the Foodborne Diseases Active Surveillance Network (FoodNet) (**www.cdc.gov/foodnet**). The **incubation period** usually is 1 to 7 days but can be longer.

DIAGNOSTIC TESTS: *Campylobacter jejuni* and *C coli* can be cultured from feces, and *Campylobacter* species, including *C fetus,* can be cultured from blood. Laboratory identification of *C jejuni* and *C coli* in stool specimens requires selective media, microaerophilic conditions, and an incubation temperature of 42°C. Unless the laboratory uses a filtration method in addition to a growth medium containing antimicrobial agents to suppress colonic flora, many *Campylobacter* species other than *C jejuni* and *C coli* will not be detected. *Campylobacter upsaliensis, C hyointestinalis,* and *C fetus* may not be isolated because of susceptibility to antimicrobial agents in *Campylobacter* selective media. The presence of motile, curved, spiral, or S-shaped rods resembling *Vibrio cholerae* by stool phase contrast or darkfield microscopy can provide rapid, presumptive evidence for *Campylobacter* species infection. *Campylobacter* species can be detected in stool specimens by commercially available enzyme immunoassay or by polymerase chain reaction assay in research laboratories.

TREATMENT: Rehydration is the mainstay for all children with diarrhea. Erythromycin and azithromycin shorten the duration of illness and prevent relapse when given early during gastrointestinal tract infection. Treatment with erythromycin or azithromycin usually eradicates the organism from stool within 2 or 3 days. A fluoroquinolone, such as ciprofloxacin, may be effective, but resistance is common and fluoroquinolones are not approved for this indication by the US Food and Drug Administration for people younger than 18 years of age (see Antimicrobial Agents and Related Therapy, p 735). If antimicrobial therapy is given for treatment of gastroenteritis, the recommended duration is 5 to 7 days. Antimicrobial agents for bacteremia should be selected on the basis of antimicrobial susceptibility tests. *Campylobacter fetus* generally is susceptible to aminoglycosides, meropenem, imipenem, and extended-spectrum cephalosporins.

ISOLATION OF THE HOSPITALIZED PATIENT: In addition to standard precautions, contact precautions are recommended for diapered and incontinent children for the duration of illness.

CONTROL MEASURES:

- Exercising hand hygiene after handling raw poultry, washing cutting boards and utensils with soap and water after contact with raw poultry, avoiding contact of fruits and vegetables with the juices of raw poultry, and thorough cooking of poultry are critical.
- Exercising hand hygiene after contact with feces of dogs and cats, particularly stool of puppies and kittens with diarrhea, is important.
- Pasteurization of milk and chlorination of water supplies are important.
- Symptomatic people should be excluded from food handling, care of patients in hospitals, and care of people in custodial care and child care centers.
- Infected food handlers and hospital employees who are asymptomatic need not be excluded from work if proper personal hygiene measures, including hand hygiene, are maintained.
- Outbreaks are uncommon in child care centers. General measures for interrupting enteric transmission in child care centers are recommended (see Children in Out-of-Home Child Care, p 130). Infants and children in diapers with symptomatic infection should be excluded from child care or cared for in a separate area until diarrhea has subsided. Erythromycin or azithromycin treatment may further limit the potential for transmission.
- Stool cultures of asymptomatic exposed children are not recommended.

Candidiasis
(Moniliasis, Thrush)

CLINICAL MANIFESTATIONS: Mucocutaneous infection results in oral-pharyngeal (thrush) or vaginal candidiasis; intertriginous lesions of the gluteal folds, neck, groin, and axilla; paronychia; and onychia. Dysfunction of T-lymphocytes, other immunologic disorders, and endocrinologic diseases are associated with chronic mucocutaneous candidiasis. Oral candidiasis can be the presenting sign of human immunodeficiency virus (HIV) infection or primary immunodeficiency. Esophageal and laryngeal candidiasis can occur in immunocompromised patients. Disseminated or invasive candidiasis occurs in very low birth weight newborn infants and in immunocompromised or debilitated hosts, can involve virtually any organ or anatomic site, and can be rapidly fatal. Candidemia can occur with or without systemic disease in patients with indwelling vascular catheters, especially patients receiving prolonged intravenous infusions with parenteral alimentation or lipids. Candiduria can occur in patients with indwelling urinary catheters, focal renal infection, or disseminated disease.

ETIOLOGY: *Candida* species are yeasts that reproduce by budding. *Candida albicans* and some *Candida tropicalis* are dimorphic and form long chains of elongated yeast forms called pseudohyphae. *Candida albicans* causes most infections (50%–60%). Other species, including *C tropicalis, Candida parapsilosis, Candida glabrata, Candida krusei, Candida guilliermondii, Candida lusitaniae,* and *Candida dubliniensis,* also can cause serious infections in immunocompromised hosts. *Candida parapsilosis* is second only to *C albicans* as a cause of systemic candidiasis in very low birth weight neonates.

EPIDEMIOLOGY: *Candida albicans* is ubiquitous. Like other *Candida* species, *C albicans* is present on skin and in the mouth, intestinal tract, and vagina of immunocompetent people. Vulvovaginal candidiasis is associated with pregnancy, and newborn infants can acquire the organism in utero, during passage through the vagina, or postnatally. Mild mucocutaneous infection is common in healthy infants. Person-to-person transmission occurs rarely. Invasive disease occurs almost exclusively in people with impaired immunity, with infection usually arising from endogenous colonization sites. People with HIV or people who are immunodeficient for reasons such as extreme prematurity, neutropenia, or treatment with corticosteroids or cytotoxic chemotherapy are at high risk of invasive infection. People with diabetes mellitus generally have localized mucocutaneous lesions. An estimated 5% of newborn infants weighing <1000 g at birth develop invasive candidiasis. Patients with neutrophil defects, such as chronic granulomatous disease or myeloperoxidase deficiency, also are at increased risk. Patients undergoing intravenous alimentation or receiving broad-spectrum antimicrobial agents, especially extended-spectrum cephalosporins, carbapenems, and vancomycin, or requiring long-term indwelling central venous catheters, have increased susceptibility. Postsurgical patients can be at risk, particularly after cardiothoracic or abdominal procedures.

The **incubation period** is unknown.

DIAGNOSTIC TESTS: The presumptive diagnosis of mucocutaneous candidiasis or thrush usually can be made clinically, but other organisms or trauma also can cause clinically similar lesions. Yeast cells and pseudohyphae can be found in *C albicans*-infected tissue and are identifiable by microscopic examination of scrapings stained with Gram stain or suspended in 10% to 20% potassium hydroxide. Endoscopy is useful for diagnosis of esophagitis. Ophthalmologic examination can reveal typical retinal lesions that can arise from candidemia. Lesions in the brain, kidney, liver, or spleen may be detected by ultrasonography or computed tomography; however, these lesions may not appear by imaging until late in the course of disease or after neutropenia has resolved.

A definitive diagnosis of invasive candidiasis requires isolation of the organism from a typically sterile body fluid or tissue (eg, blood, cerebrospinal fluid, bone marrow, or biopsy specimen) or demonstration of organisms in a tissue biopsy specimen. Cultures that are negative for *Candida* species do not exclude invasive infection in immunocompromised hosts. Recovery of the organism is expedited using blood culture systems that are biphasic or use a lysis-centrifugation method. These blood culture systems readily support rapid isolation of yeast, and special fungal culture media are not needed to grow *Candida* species. A presumptive species identification of *C albicans* can be made by demonstrating germ tube formation. Another method of detection is the assay for (1,3)-beta-D-glucan from fungal cell walls. The assay has been validated in adult patients and offers another important tool for noninvasive diagnosis. Data on use of the assay for children are limited.

TREATMENT:

MUCOUS MEMBRANE AND SKIN INFECTIONS. Oral candidiasis in immunocompetent hosts is treated with oral nystatin suspension or clotrimazole troches applied to lesions.

Fluconazole or itraconazole can be beneficial for immunocompromised patients with oropharyngeal candidiasis. Although cure rates with fluconazole are greater than with nystatin, relapse rates are comparable. The safety and efficacy of itraconazole in HIV-infected children with oropharyngeal candidiasis have been demonstrated.

Esophagitis caused by *Candida* species is treated with fluconazole or itraconazole for a minimum of 21 days or for at least 14 days after resolution of clinical findings. Alternatively, intravenous amphotericin B (0.3 mg/kg per day), caspofungin, or micafungin (≥18 years of age) can be used for refractory, azole-resistant, or severe esophageal candidiasis. Duration of treatment depends on severity of illness and patient factors, such as age and degree of immunocompromise.

Skin infections are treated with topical nystatin, miconazole, clotrimazole, naftifine, ketoconazole, econazole, or ciclopirox (see Topical Drugs for Superficial Fungal Infections, p 781). Nystatin usually is effective and is the least expensive of these drugs.

Vulvovaginal candidiasis is treated effectively with many topical formulations, including clotrimazole, miconazole, butoconazole, terconazole, and tioconazole. Such topically applied azole drugs are more effective than nystatin. Oral azole agents (fluconazole, itraconazole, and ketoconazole) also are effective and should be considered for recurrent or refractory cases (see Recommended Doses of Parenteral and Oral Antifungal Drugs, p 777).

For chronic mucocutaneous candidiasis, fluconazole and itraconazole are effective drugs. Low-dose amphotericin B (0.3 mg/kg per day) given intravenously is effective in severe cases. Relapses are common with any of these agents once therapy is terminated, and treatment should be viewed as a lifelong process, hopefully using only intermittent pulses of stronger antifungal agents. Invasive infections in patients with this condition are rare.

Keratomycosis is treated with corneal baths of amphotericin B (1 mg/mL of sterile water) in conjunction with systemic therapy. Patients with cystitis, especially patients with neutropenia, patients with renal allografts, patients undergoing urologic manipulation, and infants with low birth weight, attributable to *Candida* organisms should be treated with fluconazole because of the concentrating effect of fluconazole in the urinary tract or short courses (7 days) of low-dose amphotericin B intravenously (0.3 mg/kg per day). Repeated bladder irrigations with amphotericin B (50 μg/mL of sterile water) has been used to treat patients with candidal cystitis, but this does not treat disease beyond the bladder and is not recommended. A urinary catheter in a patient with candidiasis should be removed.

SYSTEMIC INFECTIONS. Amphotericin B, caspofungin, micafungin, anidulafungin, or fluconazole are the drugs of choice for treating people with invasive candidiasis (see Drugs for Invasive and Other Serious Fungal Infections, p 780), but data for caspofungin, micafungin, and anidulafungin in children and neonates are limited. Nearly all *Candida* species are susceptible to amphotericin B, with the exception of *C lusitaniae*. Duration of therapy will vary with the clinical response and presence or absence of neutropenia. Patients at high risk of morbidity and mortality should be treated for a prolonged period and until all signs of infection have resolved. For patients with hepatosplenic candidiasis, resolution of lesions may require weeks or months. Short-course therapy (ie, 7–10 days) can be used for intravenous catheter-associated infections, provided the catheter is removed promptly and there is no evidence of systemic disease (eg, positive blood cultures after catheter removal). Lipid-associated preparations of amphotericin B can be used if significant nephrotoxicity or clinical failure is observed with conventional amphotericin B therapy. However, lipid-associated preparations should not be used as first-line drugs. Published reports in adults and anecdotal reports in preterm infants indicate that at least one lipid-associated amphotericin B preparation has failed to eradicate renal candidiasis, because this large-molecule drug does not penetrate kidneys. Liver toxicity has been reported with lipid formulations.

Flucytosine (100–150 mg/kg per day in 4 divided doses, maximum 150 mg/kg every 24 hours) can be given with amphotericin B for *C albicans* infection involving the central nervous system if enteral administration is feasible. The dose of flucytosine should be decreased for patients with renal insufficiency. Serum concentrations of flucytosine should be maintained between 40 and 60 μg/mL; higher concentrations ($\geq$100 μg/L) predispose to toxic effects, but delays in obtaining assay results often limit their utility. Adverse effects of flucytosine, which are more common in patients with azotemia, include dose-related bone marrow suppression, rash, hepatic and renal dysfunction, diarrhea, gastrointestinal tract bleeding, and ulcerative colitis.

Fluconazole also has been used successfully for treatment of invasive candidiasis. Nonneutropenic adults with candidemia respond equally well to fluconazole or amphotericin B, but there are concerns about fluconazole, which is fungistatic, in profoundly neutropenic patients. Fluconazole may be appropriate for patients with impaired renal function or for patients with meningitis. However, limited data using fluconazole for *Candida* meningitis are available. Fluconazole is not an appropriate choice for therapy before the infecting *Candida* species is known, because *C krusei* is resistant to fluconazole, and up to 50% of *C glabrata* also can be resistant. Caspofungin, micafungin, and anidulafungin, all active in vitro against all *Candida* species but less active against *C parapsilosis*, are alternative therapies for *Candida* infections in adults (see Echinocandins, p 776), but few data regarding safety and effectiveness in children are available, especially for neonates. Anidulafungin may be superior to fluconazole for candidemia.

Treatment of disseminated candidiasis always should include removal of infected central vascular catheters and avoidance or reduction of systemic steroid therapy, to the extent feasible. Ongoing infection with persistently positive blood cultures requires removal of all intravascular catheters and replacement when infection is controlled.

CHEMOPROPHYLAXIS. Chemoprophylaxis of *Candida* infections in immuno-compromised patients with oral nystatin and fluconazole has been evaluated with variable results. A prospective, randomized, controlled trial in neonates weighing less than 1000 g at birth demonstrated the safety and efficacy of fluconazole given intra-venously for 6 weeks in preventing *Candida* colonization and systemic infection. Fur-ther study is needed, but some experts recommend this regimen according to the dosage schedule studied. Fluconazole can decrease the risk of mucosal (eg, oropharyn-geal and esophageal) candidiasis in patients with advanced HIV disease. However, an increased incidence of infections attributable to *C krusei* (which intrinsically is resistant to fluconazole) has been reported in non–HIV-infected patients receiving prophylactic flu-conazole. Adults undergoing allogenic stem cell transplantation had significantly fewer *Candida* infections when given fluconazole, but limited data are available for children. Prophylaxis should be considered for children undergoing allogenic stem cell transplan-tation during the period of neutropenia. Prophylaxis is not recommended routinely for other immunocompromised children, including children with HIV infection.

ISOLATION OF THE HOSPITALIZED PATIENT: Standard precautions are recom-mended.

CONTROL MEASURES: Prolonged broad-spectrum antimicrobial therapy and use of systemic corticosteroids in susceptible patients promote overgrowth of, and predispose to, invasive infection with *Candida* organisms. Meticulous care of intravascular catheter sites is recommended for any patient requiring long-term intravenous alimentation.

Cat-Scratch Disease
(Bartonella henselae)

CLINICAL MANIFESTATIONS: The predominant manifestation of cat-scratch disease (CSD) in an immunocompetent person is regional lymphadenopathy. Fever and mild systemic symptoms occur in approximately 30% of patients. A skin papule often is found at the presumed site of bacterial inoculation and usually precedes development of lymphadenopathy by 1 to 2 weeks. Lymphadenopathy involves nodes that drain the site of inoculation—typically axillary, but cervical, submental, epitrochlear, or inguinal nodes can be affected. The skin overlying affected lymph nodes typically is tender, warm, erythematous, and indurated. In approximately 25% to 30% of people with CSD, the affected nodes suppurate spontaneously. Occasionally, infection can produce Parinaud's oculoglandular syndrome, in which inoculation of the eyelid con-junctiva results in conjunctivitis and ipsilateral preauricular lymphadenopathy. Less common manifestations of CSD include encephalopathy, aseptic meningitis, fever of unknown origin, neuroretinitis, osteolytic lesions, hepatitis, granulomata in the liver and spleen, pneumonia, thrombocytopenic purpura, erythema nodosum, relapsing bacteremia, and endocarditis.

ETIOLOGY: *Bartonella henselae*, the causative organism of CSD, is a fastidious, slow-growing, gram-negative bacillus that also is the causative agent of bacillary angiomatosis and bacillary peliosis hepatitis. The latter 2 manifestations of infection are reported primarily in patients with human immunodeficiency virus infection. *Bartonella henselae* is closely related to *Bartonella quintana*, the agent of trench fever and bacillary angiomatosis.

EPIDEMIOLOGY: Cat-scratch disease is a common infection, although the true incidence is unknown. Most cases occur in people younger than 20 years of age. Cats are the common reservoir for the pathogen, and bacteremia in cats associated with human CSD cases is common. More than 90% of patients with CSD have a history of recent contact with apparently healthy cats, often kittens. No evidence of person-to-person transmission exists. Infection occurs more often during the autumn and winter. Cat fleas *(Ctenocephalides felis)* transmit *B henselae* between cats, but the role of fleas or other arthropods in transmission of *B henselae* to humans is not well established.

The **incubation period** from the time of the scratch to appearance of the primary cutaneous lesion is 7 to 12 days; the period from the appearance of the primary lesion to the appearance of lymphadenopathy is 5 to 50 days (median, 12 days).

DIAGNOSTIC TESTS: The indirect immunofluorescent antibody (IFA) assay for detection of serum antibodies to antigens of *Bartonella* species is useful for diagnosis of CSD. The IFA test is available at many commercial laboratories and state public health laboratories and through the Centers for Disease Control and Prevention. Enzyme immunoassays for detection of antibodies to *B henselae* have been developed; however, they have not been demonstrated to be more sensitive or specific than the IFA test. Polymerase chain reaction assays are available in some commercial and research laboratories. If tissue (eg, lymph node) specimens are available, bacilli occasionally may be visualized using Warthin-Starry silver stain; however, this test is not specific for *B henselae*. Early histologic changes in lymph node specimens consist of lymphocytic infiltration with epithelioid granuloma formation. Later changes consist of polymorphonuclear leukocyte infiltration with granulomas that become necrotic and resemble granulomas from patients with tularemia, brucellosis, and mycobacterial infections. A cat-scratch antigen skin test, prepared from aspirated pus from suppurative lymph nodes of patients with apparent CSD, is not recommended.

TREATMENT: Management of localized cat-scratch disease is aimed primarily at relief of symptoms, because the disease usually is self-limited, resolving spontaneously in 2 to 4 months. Painful suppurative nodes can be treated with needle aspiration for relief of symptoms; incision and drainage should be avoided, and surgical excision generally is unnecessary.

Optimal antimicrobial therapy for *Bartonella* infections in immunocompromised people has not been determined. Complicated cases should be evaluated in consultation with an infectious disease specialist to determine the most appropriate therapy. Antimicrobial therapy can hasten recovery in some acutely or severely ill patients with systemic symptoms, particularly people with hepatic or splenic involvement, people with endocarditis, people with painful adenitis, and immunocompromised people. Reports suggest that several oral antimicrobial agents (azithromycin, erythromycin, ciprofloxacin, trimethoprim-sulfamethoxazole, rifampin) and parenteral gentamicin are effective in the treatment of CSD; the optimal duration of therapy is not known.

However, for patients with endocarditis, effective therapy should include an aminogly-coside for a minimum of 2 weeks. Some experts recommend azithromycin for extensive lymphadenopathy.

Antimicrobial therapy for patients with bacillary angiomatosis, bacillary peliosis, or trench fever has been shown to be beneficial and is recommended. Azithromycin, erythromycin, or doxycycline are effective for treatment of these conditions; therapy should be administered for several months to prevent relapse in immunocompromised people.

ISOLATION OF THE HOSPITALIZED PATIENT: Standard precautions are recommended.

CONTROL MEASURES: People should avoid playing roughly with cats and kittens to minimize scratches and bites. Immunocompromised people should avoid contact with cats that scratch or bite and, when acquiring a new cat, should avoid cats younger than 1 year of age. Sites of cat scratches or bites should be washed immediately. Care of cats should include flea control. Testing of cats for *Bartonella* infection is not recommended.

Chancroid

CLINICAL MANIFESTATIONS: Chancroid is an acute ulcerative disease that involves the genitalia. An ulcer begins as a tender erythematous papule, becomes pustular, and erodes over several days, forming a sharply demarcated, somewhat superficial lesion with a serpiginous border. The base of the ulcer is friable and may be covered with a gray or yellow, necrotic, and purulent exudate. Single or multiple ulcers may be present. Unlike a syphilitic chancre, which is painless, the chancroidal ulcer often is painful, tender, and nonindurated. The ulcer may be associated with a painful, unilateral inguinal adenitis (bubo), which often is suppurative and fluctuant.

In most males, chancroid manifests as a genital ulcer or inguinal tenderness. Many females are asymptomatic but can, depending on the site of the ulcer, have less obvious symptoms, including dysuria, dyspareunia, vaginal discharge, pain on defecation, or rectal bleeding. Constitutional symptoms are unusual.

ETIOLOGY: Chancroid is caused by *Haemophilus ducreyi*, which is a gram-negative coccobacillus.

EPIDEMIOLOGY: Chancroid is a sexually transmitted infection that is associated with poverty, urban prostitution, and illicit drug use. Chancroid is endemic in some areas of the United States and also occurs in discrete outbreaks. Coinfection with syphilis or herpes simplex virus (HSV) occurs in as many as 10% of patients. Chancroid is a well-established cofactor for transmission of human immunodeficiency virus (HIV). Because sexual contact is the only known route of transmission, the diagnosis of chancroid in infants and young children is strong evidence of sexual abuse.

The **incubation period** is 3 to 10 days.

DIAGNOSTIC TESTS: The diagnosis of chancroid usually is made on the basis of clinical findings and exclusion of other infections associated with genital ulcer disease, such as syphilis, HSV infection, or lymphogranuloma venereum. Direct examination of clinical material using Gram stain may suggest the diagnosis if large numbers of gram-negative coccobacilli are seen. Confirmation can be made by recovery of *H ducreyi* from a genital ulcer or lymph node aspirate. However, special culture media and conditions are required for isolation; if chancroid is suspected, the laboratory should be informed. Purulent material recovered from intact buboes almost always is sterile. Fluorescent monoclonal antibody stains and polymerase chain reaction assays can provide more specific diagnosis but are not approved by the US Food and Drug Administration and are not available in most laboratories.

TREATMENT: Recommended regimens include azithromycin (1 g, orally, in a single dose), or ceftriaxone (250 mg, intramuscularly, in a single dose). Alternatives include erythromycin (500 mg, orally, 4 times per day for 7 days) or ciprofloxacin (500 mg, orally for 3 days) (see Table 4.4, p 766). Ciprofloxacin is not approved by the FDA for people younger than 18 years of age for this indication and should not be administered to pregnant or lactating women (see Antimicrobial Agents and Related Therapy, p 735). Patients with HIV infection may need prolonged therapy.

Clinical improvement occurs within 3 to 7 days of onset of successful therapy, and healing is complete in approximately 2 weeks. Adenitis often is slow to resolve and may require needle aspiration or surgical incision. Patients should be reexamined 3 to 7 days after starting therapy to verify that healing is occurring. If healing has not occurred, the diagnosis may be incorrect, and further testing is required. Relapses may occur; however, retreatment with the original regimen usually is effective.

Patients should be evaluated for other sexually transmitted infections, including syphilis, hepatitis B virus infection, *Chlamydia trachomatis* infection, gonorrhea, and HIV infection at the time of presentation. Because chancroid is a risk factor for HIV infection and facilitates HIV transmission, if initial HIV or syphilis test results are negative, they should be repeated 3 months after the diagnosis of chancroid is made. All people having sexual contact with patients with chancroid within 10 days before onset of the patient's symptoms need to be examined and treated, even if they are asymptomatic.

ISOLATION OF THE HOSPITALIZED PATIENT: Standard precautions are recommended.

CONTROL MEASURES: Examination and treatment of sexual partners of patients with chancroid are important control measures. "Partner notification" is used increasingly to identify a treatable reservoir of cases of chancroid during outbreaks, usually occurring among prostitutes. This process can lead to epidemic control. Regular condom use may decrease transmission.

CHLAMYDIAL INFECTIONS

Chlamydophila (formerly Chlamydia) pneumoniae

CLINICAL MANIFESTATIONS: Patients may be asymptomatic or mildly to moderately ill with a variety of respiratory tract diseases, including pneumonia, acute bronchitis, prolonged cough, and less commonly, pharyngitis, laryngitis, otitis media, and sinusitis. In some patients, a sore throat precedes the onset of cough by a week or more. Physical examination may reveal nonexudative pharyngitis, pulmonary rales, and bronchospasm. Chest radiography may reveal an infiltrate. Illness is prolonged, with cough persisting 2 to 6 weeks, and can have a biphasic course. In addition to acute respiratory tract disease, some investigators have associated *C pneumoniae* with atherosclerotic cardiovascular disease. Prospective, randomized trials are underway to further explore this association.

ETIOLOGY: *Chlamydophila pneumoniae* is distinct antigenically, genetically, and morphologically from *Chlamydia* species and, in a proposed classification, would be grouped in the genus *Chlamydophila*. All isolates of *C pneumoniae* appear to be closely related serologically.

EPIDEMIOLOGY: *Chlamydophila pneumoniae* infection is assumed to be transmitted from person to person via infected respiratory tract secretions. An animal reservoir is unknown. The disease occurs worldwide, but in tropical and less developed areas, disease occurs earlier in life than in developed countries in temperate climates. In the United States, approximately 50% of adults have *C pneumoniae*-specific serum antibody by 20 years of age. Initial infection peaks between 5 and 15 years of age. Recurrent infection is common, especially in adults. Clusters of infection have been reported in groups of children and young adults. There is no evidence of seasonality.

The mean **incubation period** is 21 days.

DIAGNOSTIC TESTS: No reliable diagnostic test to identify the organism is available commercially, and none has been approved by the US Food and Drug Administration for use in the United States. Serologic testing has been the primary laboratory means of diagnosis of *C pneumoniae* infection. The microimmunofluorescent antibody test is the most sensitive and specific serologic test for acute infection and is the only endorsed approach. A fourfold increase in immunoglobulin (Ig) G titer or an IgM titer of $\geq$16 is evidence of acute infection. Use of a single IgG titer in diagnosis of acute infection is discouraged. In primary infection, IgM antibody appears approximately 2 to 3 weeks after onset of illness, but IgG antibody may not peak until 6 to 8 weeks after onset of illness. In reinfection, IgM may not appear, and IgG increases within 1 to 2 weeks. Early antimicrobial therapy may suppress the antibody response. Past exposure is indicated by a stable IgG titer of $\geq$16. *Chlamydophila pneumoniae* can be isolated from swab specimens obtained from the nasopharynx or oropharynx or from sputum, bronchoalveolar lavage, or tissue biopsy specimens. Specimens are placed into appropriate transport media and held at 4°C (39°F) until inoculated into cell culture; specimens that cannot be processed within 24 hours should be frozen and held at 70°C (94°F). A positive culture is confirmed by propagation of the isolate or a positive polymerase chain reaction assay result. Nasopharyngeal shedding can occur for months after acute disease. Immunohistochemistry, used to detect *C pneumoniae* in tissue specimens, requires control antibodies and tissues in addition to skill in recognizing staining artifacts to avoid false-positive results.

TREATMENT: For treatment, a macrolide or a tetracycline is recommended. Tetracycline or doxycycline should not be given routinely to children younger than 8 years of age (see Antimicrobial Agents and Related Therapy, p 735). Adolescents and older patients have been treated successfully with erythromycin for 5 to 10 days, but a 14- to 21-day course of therapy may be needed, because prolonged or recurrent symptoms are common. The macrolide drugs azithromycin and clarithromycin and some of the fluoroquinolones also are effective. The fluoroquinolones are approved for people 18 years of age and older. In vitro data suggest that *C pneumoniae* is not susceptible to sulfonamides.

ISOLATION OF THE HOSPITALIZED PATIENT: Standard precautions are recommended.

CONTROL MEASURES: Reporting of individual cases of *C pneumoniae* to health authorities is not required. Recommended prevention measures include minimizing crowding and maintaining personal hygiene, with careful disposal of nasal and oral discharge and frequent hand hygiene.

Chlamydophila (formerly *Chlamydia*) *psittaci*
(Psittacosis, Ornithosis)

CLINICAL MANIFESTATIONS: Psittacosis (ornithosis) usually is an acute febrile respiratory tract infection with systemic symptoms and signs that often include fever, nonproductive cough, headache, and malaise. Extensive interstitial pneumonia can occur with radiographic changes characteristically more severe than would be expected from physical examination findings. Pericarditis, myocarditis, endocarditis, superficial thrombophlebitis, hepatitis, and encephalopathy are rare complications.

ETIOLOGY: *Chlamydophila psittaci* is an obligate intracellular bacterial pathogen that is distinct antigenically and genetically from *Chlamydia* species and, in a proposed classification, would be grouped in the genus *Chlamydophila*.

EPIDEMIOLOGY: Birds are the major reservoir of *C psittaci*. The term psittacosis commonly is used, although the term ornithosis more accurately describes the potential for all birds, not just psittacine birds, to spread this infection. Several mammalian species, such as cattle, goats, sheep, and cats, and avian species may become infected and develop systemic and debilitating disease. In the United States, psittacine birds (such as parakeets, parrots, and macaws, especially birds smuggled into the country), pigeons, and turkeys are important sources of human disease. Healthy and sick birds may harbor and transmit the organism, usually via the airborne route in fecal dust or secretions. Excretion of *C psittaci* can be intermittent or continuous for weeks or months. People in the environment of infected birds, such as workers at poultry slaughter plants, poultry farms, and pet shops as well as pet owners, are at risk of infection. Laboratory personnel working with *C psittaci* also are at risk. Psittacosis is worldwide in distribution and tends to occur sporadically in any season. Infections are rare in children. Severe illness and abortion have been reported in pregnant women after exposure to infected sheep.

The **incubation period** usually is 5 to 14 days but may be longer.

DIAGNOSTIC TESTS: The usual method of diagnosis is serologic testing with a fourfold increase in antibody titer determined by microimmunofluorescent (MIF) or complement fixation testing between acute and convalescent specimens obtained 2 to 3 weeks apart or a single immunoglobulin (Ig) M antibody titer of ≥1:16 on MIF testing. In the presence of a compatible clinical illness, a single titer of ≥1:32 is considered presumptive evidence of infection. Treatment may suppress the antibody response. The complement fixation test does not distinguish among infections caused by *C psittaci*, *Chlamydophila pneumoniae*, *Chlamydia trachomatis*, or *Chlamydophila pecorum*, but MIF and polymerase chain reaction assays are more specific for *C psittaci*. Isolation of the agent from the respiratory tract should be attempted only by experienced personnel in laboratories, in which strict measures to prevent spread of the organism are used during collection and handling of all specimens for culture.

TREATMENT: Tetracyclines are the preferred therapy, except for children younger than 8 years of age. Erythromycin is an alternative drug and is recommended for younger children. The macrolide drugs azithromycin and clarithromycin, as well as chloramphenicol, also are effective. Therapy should be administered for at least 10 to 14 days after defervescence.

ISOLATION OF THE HOSPITALIZED PATIENT: Standard precautions are recommended.

CONTROL MEASURES: Reporting cases of human psittacosis to health authorities is mandated in most states. All birds suspected to be the source of human infection should be seen by a veterinarian for evaluation and management. Birds with *C psittaci* infection should be isolated and treated with appropriate antimicrobial agents for at least 45 days.* Birds suspected of having infection that have died or have been euthanatized should be sealed in an impermeable container and transported on dry ice to a veterinary laboratory for testing. All potentially contaminated caging and housing areas should be disinfected thoroughly and aired before reuse, because these areas may contain infectious organisms. *Chlamydophila psittaci* is susceptible to most household disinfectants and detergents, including 70% alcohol, 1% Lysol, and a 1:100 dilution of household bleach. People cleaning cages and other bird housing areas should be aware of the potential for infection and avoid scattering the contents. People exposed to common sources of infection should be observed for development of fever or respiratory tract symptoms; early diagnostic tests should be performed and therapy should be initiated if symptoms appear.

Chlamydia trachomatis

CLINICAL MANIFESTATIONS: *Chlamydia trachomatis* is associated with a range of clinical manifestations, including neonatal conjunctivitis, trachoma, pneumonia in young infants, genital tract infection, and lymphogranuloma venereum (LGV). Neonatal chlamydial conjunctivitis is characterized by ocular congestion, edema, and discharge developing a few days to several weeks after birth and lasting for 1 to 2 weeks and sometimes much longer. In contrast to trachoma, scars and pannus formation are rare.

---

* Centers for Disease Control and Prevention, Committee of the National Association of State Public Health Veterinarians. Compendium of measures to control *Chlamydia psittaci* infection among humans (psittacosis) and pet birds (avian chlamydiosis), 2000. *MMWR Recomm Rep.* 2000;49(No. RR-8):1–17

Trachoma is a chronic follicular keratoconjunctivitis with neovascularization of the cornea that results from repeated and chronic infection. Blindness secondary to extensive local scarring and inflammation occurs in 1% to 15% of people with trachoma. Trachoma is rare in the United States.

Pneumonia in young infants usually is an afebrile illness of insidious onset occurring between 2 and 19 weeks after birth. A repetitive staccato cough, tachypnea, and rales are characteristic but not always present. Wheezing is uncommon. Hyperinflation usually accompanies infiltrates seen on chest radiographs. Nasal stuffiness and otitis media may occur. Untreated disease can linger or recur. Severe chlamydial pneumonia has occurred in infants and some immunocompromised adults.

Vaginitis in prepubertal girls; urethritis, cervicitis, endometritis, salpingitis, and perihepatitis in postpubertal females; epididymitis in males; and Reiter syndrome (arthritis, urethritis, and bilateral conjunctivitis) also can occur. Infection can persist for months to years. Reinfection is common. In postpubertal females, chlamydial infection can progress to acute or chronic pelvic inflammatory disease and result in ectopic pregnancy or infertility.

Lymphogranuloma venereum classically is an invasive lymphatic infection with an initial ulcerative lesion on the genitalia accompanied by tender, suppurative, inguinal and/or femoral lymphadenopathy that typically is unilateral. However, anorectal infection is associated with anal intercourse and can cause hemorrhagic proctocolitis among women and among men who engage in anal intercourse. The proctocolitis can be moderate to severe and can resemble inflammatory bowel disease.

ETIOLOGY: *Chlamydia trachomatis* is an obligate intracellular bacterial agent with at least 18 serologic variants (serovars) divided between the following biologic variants (biovars): oculogenital (serovars A–K) and LGV (serovars L1, L2, and L3). Trachoma usually is caused by serovars A through C, and genital and perinatal infections are caused by B and D through K.

EPIDEMIOLOGY: *Chlamydia trachomatis* is the most common reportable sexually transmitted infection in the United States, with high rates among sexually active adolescents and young adults. Prevalence of the organism consistently is highest among adolescent females. Across 27 states, median prevalence among 15- to 24-year-old women screened in prenatal clinics was 7%, with a range of 2% to 20%. Oculogenital serovars of *C trachomatis* can be transmitted from the genital tract of infected mothers to their newborn infants. Acquisition occurs in approximately 50% of infants born vaginally to infected mothers and in some infants delivered by cesarean section with intact membranes. The risk of conjunctivitis is 25% to 50%, and the risk of pneumonia is 5% to 20% in infants who contract *C trachomatis*. The nasopharynx is the most commonly infected anatomic site.

Genital tract infection in adolescents and adults is transmitted sexually. The possibility of sexual abuse should be considered in prepubertal children beyond infancy who have vaginal, urethral, or rectal chlamydial infection. Asymptomatic infection of the nasopharynx, conjunctivae, vagina, and rectum can be acquired at birth. Nasopharyngeal cultures may remain positive for as long as 28 months, but spontaneous resolution of vaginal and rectal infection occurs by 16 to 18 months of age. Infection is not known to be communicable among infants and children. The degree of contagiousness of pulmonary disease is unknown but seems to be low.

Lymphogranuloma venereum biovars are worldwide in distribution but particularly are prevalent in tropical and subtropical areas. Although disease occurs rarely in the United States, outbreaks of LGV have been reported in Europe, and cases have been reported in the United States in men who have sex with men. Infection often is asymptomatic in women. Perinatal transmission is rare. Lymphogranuloma venereum is infectious during active disease. Little is known about the prevalence or duration of asymptomatic carriage.

The **incubation period** of chlamydial illness is variable, depending on the type of infection, but usually is at least 1 week.

DIAGNOSTIC TESTS: Definitive diagnosis can be made by isolating the organism in tissue culture and by nucleic acid amplification (NAA) testing in selective circumstances.* Because *Chlamydia* species are obligate intracellular organisms, culture specimens must contain epithelial cells, not just exudate. Nucleic acid amplification tests, such as polymerase chain reaction (PCR) (Amplicor), transcription-mediated amplification (TMA) test (Aptima Combo 2), and strand-displacement amplification (SDA) test (Probe Tec) are available. These tests are more sensitive than cell culture, DNA probe, direct fluorescent antibody (DFA) tests, or enzyme immunoassays (EIAs), although specificity is variable compared with culture.

Some nonculture tests for detection of *Chlamydia* species, including EIA, DFA tests, DNA probe tests, and NAA tests, are useful for evaluating urethral swab specimens from males, endocervical swab specimens from females, and conjunctival secretion specimens from infants (although not all of these tests have been approved by the US Food and Drug Administration [FDA] for this use). The PCR, SDA, and TMA assays are useful for evaluating urine specimens from either sex. The FDA has approved TMA for testing vaginal swabs from postmenarcheal adolescents and adults. Nonculture tests are not recommended for detection of *C trachomatis* in urethral swab specimens from females, and only the TMA test is FDA approved for use with vaginal swabs from postmenarcheal adolescents and adults. In addition, NAA testing is not recommended for specimens obtained by rectal or pharyngeal swabs.

If a false-positive test result is likely to have adverse medical, social, or psychologic consequences, positive DFA test, EIA, DNA probe test, or NAA test results should be verified by culture, a second nonculture test different from the first, or use of a blocking antibody (eg, Chlamydiazyme) or competitive probe. When evaluating a child for possible sexual abuse, culture of the organism may be the only acceptable diagnostic test in certain legal jurisdictions. When culture is not available, some experts support using NAA testing if a positive result can be verified by another NAA test. The EIA and DFA test should not be used for testing rectal, vaginal, or urethral specimens from infants and children because of low sensitivity and specificity.

Serum antibody concentrations are difficult to determine, and only a few clinical laboratories perform this test. In children with pneumonia, an acute microimmunofluorescent serum titer of *C trachomatis*-specific immunoglobulin (Ig) M of ≥1:32 is

---

* Centers for Disease Control and Prevention. Screening to detect *Chlamydia trachomatis* and *Neisseria gonorrhoeae* infections—2002. *MMWR Recomm Rep.* 2002;51(RR-15):1–38

diagnostic. Diagnosis of LGV can be supported, but not confirmed, by a positive result (ie, titer >1:64) on a complement fixation test for chlamydiae or a high titer (typically >1:128 but can vary by laboratory) on a microimmunofluorescent serologic test for *C trachomatis*. However, most available serologic tests in the United States are based on EIAs and might not provide a quantitative "titer-based" result.

Diagnosis of genitourinary chlamydial disease in a child, adolescent, or adult should prompt investigation for other sexually transmitted infections, including syphilis, gonorrhea, hepatitis B virus infection, and human immunodeficiency virus infection. In the case of an infant, evaluation of the mother also is advisable.

Diagnosis of ocular trachoma usually is made clinically in countries with endemic infection.

TREATMENT:

- Young infants with **chlamydial conjunctivitis** are treated with oral erythromycin base or ethylsuccinate (50 mg/kg per day in 4 divided doses) for 14 days. Oral sulfonamides may be used after the immediate neonatal period for infants who do not tolerate erythromycin. Topical treatment of conjunctivitis is ineffective and unnecessary. Because the efficacy of erythromycin therapy is approximately 80%, a second course may be required, and follow-up of infants is recommended.

  An association between orally administered erythromycin and infantile hypertrophic pyloric stenosis (IHPS) has been reported in infants younger than 6 weeks of age. The risk of IHPS after treatment with other macrolides (eg, azithromycin and clarithromycin) is unknown. Because confirmation of erythromycin as a contributor to cases of IHPS will require additional investigation and because alternative therapies are not as well studied, the American Academy of Pediatrics continues to recommend use of erythromycin for treatment of diseases caused by *C trachomatis*. Physicians who prescribe erythromycin to newborn infants should inform parents about the signs and potential risks of developing IHPS. Cases of pyloric stenosis after use of oral erythromycin should be reported to MedWatch (see MedWatch, p 821).

- **Chlamydial pneumonia** is treated with oral azithromycin (20 mg/kg, orally, once daily for 3 days) or erythromycin base or ethylsuccinate (50 mg/kg per day in 4 divided doses) for 14 days. An oral sulfonamide is an alternative for infants who do not tolerate macrolides. Alternative therapies are not well studied for this use. The need for treatment of infants can be avoided by screening pregnant women to detect and treat *C trachomatis* infection before delivery. A diagnosis of *C trachomatis* infection in an infant should prompt treatment of the mother and her sexual partner(s).

- Infants born to mothers known to have untreated chlamydial infection are at high risk of infection; however, prophylactic antimicrobial treatment is not indicated, because the efficacy of such treatment is unknown. Infants should be monitored clinically to ensure appropriate treatment if infection develops. If adequate follow-up cannot be ensured, some experts recommend that preemptive therapy be considered.

- Treatment of **trachoma** is more difficult, and recommendations for therapy differ. The most widely used therapy is topical treatment with erythromycin, tetracycline, or sulfacetamide ointment twice a day for 2 months or twice a day for the first 5 days of the month for 6 consecutive months; or oral erythromycin or doxycycline (for children 8 years of age and older) for 40 days if the infection is severe. Azithromycin (20 mg/kg, maximum of 1 g once per week) for 3 weeks also is effective.

- For uncomplicated *C trachomatis* **genital tract infection** in adolescents or adults, oral doxycycline (200 mg/day in 2 divided doses) for 7 days or azithromycin in a single 1-g oral dose is recommended. Alternatives include oral erythromycin base (2.0 g/day in 4 divided doses) for 7 days, erythromycin ethylsuccinate (3.2 g/day in 4 divided doses) for 7 days, ofloxacin (600 mg/day in 2 divided doses) for 7 days, or levofloxacin (500 mg, orally, once per day) for 7 days. Erythromycin or azithromycin is the recommended therapy for children between 6 months and 12 years of age; for infants younger than 6 months of age, erythromycin is recommended. Azithromycin (1 g, orally, as a single dose) or amoxicillin (1.5 g/day in 3 divided doses) for 7 days are recommended regimens for pregnant women. Erythromycin base (2 g/day in 4 divided doses) is an alternative regimen. Doxycycline, ofloxacin, and levofloxacin are contraindicated during pregnancy. Repeat testing (preferably by culture) is recommended 3 weeks after treatment. Because these regimens for pregnant women may not be highly efficacious, a second course of therapy may be required.
- For **LGV**, doxycycline (200 mg/day in 2 divided doses) for 21 days is the preferred treatment for children 8 years of age and older. Erythromycin base (2 g/day in 4 divided doses) for 21 days is an alternative regimen; azithromycin (1 g, once weekly for 3 weeks) is recommended by some experts, although clinical data are lacking.

FOLLOW-UP TESTING. Nonpregnant patients do not need to be retested for uncomplicated *Chlamydia* infection after completing treatment with doxycycline or azithromycin unless symptoms persist or reinfection is suspected. Retesting for infection using NAA testing should occur no sooner than 4 weeks after completing regimens with erythromycin or amoxicillin. Previously infected adolescents are a high priority for repeat testing for *C trachomatis*, usually 3 to 6 months after initial infection.

ISOLATION OF THE HOSPITALIZED PATIENT: Standard precautions are recommended.

CONTROL MEASURES:

PREGNANCY. The identification and treatment of women with *C trachomatis* genital tract infection during pregnancy can prevent disease in the infant. Pregnant women at high risk of *C trachomatis* infection, in particular women younger than 25 years of age and women with new or multiple sexual partners, should be targeted for screening. Some experts advocate routine testing of pregnant women at high risk during the first trimester and again during the third trimester.

NEONATAL CHLAMYDIAL CONJUNCTIVITIS. The recommended topical prophylaxis with silver nitrate, erythromycin, or tetracycline for all newborn infants for prevention of gonococcal ophthalmia will not prevent neonatal chlamydial conjunctivitis or extraocular infection (see Prevention of Neonatal Ophthalmia, p 828).

TRACHOMA. Although not seen in the United States for more than 2 decades, trachoma is the second leading cause of blindness worldwide. Trachoma is transmitted by transfer of ocular discharge, and predictors of scarring and blindness for trachoma include increasing age and constant, severe trachoma. The prevention methods recommended by the World Health Organization for global elimination of blindness attributable to trachoma by 2020 include surgery, antibiotics, face washing, and environmental improvement (SAFE). Azithromycin (20 mg/kg, maximum 1 g) once or twice a year or topical tetracycline twice daily for 6 weeks has been effective in treating large populations in areas of high endemicity.

CONTACTS OF INFANTS WITH *C TRACHOMATIS* CONJUNCTIVITIS OR PNEUMONIA. Mothers of infected infants (and mothers' sexual partners) should be treated for *C trachomatis*.

GYNECOLOGIC EXAMINATION. Sexually active adolescent females should be tested at least annually for *Chlamydia* infection during preventive health care visits and gynecologic examinations, even if no symptoms are present and even if barrier contraception is reported. Screening of young adult women 20 to 24 years of age also is recommended.

MANAGEMENT OF SEXUAL PARTNERS. All sexual contacts of patients with *C trachomatis* infection (whether symptomatic or asymptomatic), nongonococcal urethritis, mucopurulent cervicitis, epididymitis, or pelvic inflammatory disease should be evaluated and treated for *C trachomatis* infection if the last sexual contact occurred during the 60 days preceding onset of symptoms in the index case.

LYMPHOGRANULOMA VENEREUM. Nonspecific preventive measures for LGV are the same as measures for sexually transmitted infections in general and include education, case reporting, condom use, and avoidance of sexual contact with infected people.

CLOSTRIDIAL INFECTIONS

Botulism and Infant Botulism
(Clostridium botulinum)

CLINICAL MANIFESTATIONS: Botulism is a neuroparalytic disorder characterized by an acute, afebrile, symmetric descending flaccid paralysis. Paralysis is caused by blockade of neurotransmitter at the voluntary motor and autonomic neuromuscular junctions. Three distinct, naturally occurring forms of human botulism exist: foodborne, wound, and infant. Onset of symptoms occurs abruptly within hours or evolves gradually over several days. Cranial nerve palsies always occur in botulism, possibly followed by symmetric, descending, flaccid paralysis of somatic musculature that may progress rapidly. Classically, infant botulism, which occurs predominantly in infants younger than 6 months of age, is preceded by or begins with constipation and manifests as decreased movement, loss of facial expression, poor feeding, weak cry, diminished gag reflex, ocular palsies, truncal weakness, and progressive descending generalized weakness and hypotonia (eg, "floppy infant"). The spectrum of disease ranges from mild (eg, constipation, slow feeding) to rapidly progressive (eg, apnea, sudden infant death).

ETIOLOGY: Botulism results from absorption of botulinum toxins into the circulation from a wound or mucosal surface. Seven antigenic toxin types of *Clostridium botulinum* have been identified. Human botulism is caused by neurotoxins A, B, E, and rarely, F. Rarely, non-*botulinum* species of *Clostridium* produce these neurotoxins and cause disease. Types C and D are associated primarily with botulism in birds and mammals. Almost all cases of infant botulism are caused by types A and B, and a few cases of types E and F have been reported from *Clostridium butyricum* and *Clostridium baritii*, respectively. *Clostridium botulinum* spores are ubiquitous in soil worldwide.

EPIDEMIOLOGY: Foodborne botulism (16 laboratory-confirmed cases in 2004; age range 23–91 years) results when a food contaminated with spores of *C botulinum* is preserved or stored improperly under anaerobic conditions that permit germination, multiplication, and toxin production. Outbreaks have occurred after ingestion of restaurant-prepared foods, such as patty melts; potato salad; aluminum foil-wrapped baked potatoes; home-canned foods; bottled garlic; cheese sauce; and tissue from beached whales. Illness follows ingestion of preformed botulinum toxin. Immunity to botulinum toxin does not develop in foodborne botulism, even after severe disease. Botulism is not transmitted from person to person.

Infant botulism (87 laboratory-confirmed cases in 2004; age range 6 days–61 weeks) results after ingested spores of *C botulinum* or related species germinate, multiply, and produce botulinum toxin in the intestine, probably through a mechanism of transient permissiveness of the intestinal microflora. Most cases occur in breastfed infants at the time of first introduction of nonhuman milk substances, and the source of spores usually is not identified. Honey has been identified as an avoidable source. Manufacturers of light and dark corn syrups cannot ensure that any given product will be free of *C botulinum* spores, but no case of infant botulism has proved to be attributable to consumption of contaminated corn syrup. Intestinal botulism, albeit rare, also can occur in older children and adults after intestinal surgery, in the presence of inflammatory bowel disease, and with exposure to antimicrobial agents.

Wound botulism (30 laboratory-confirmed cases in 2004; age range 23–57 years) results when *C botulinum* contaminates traumatized tissue, multiplies, and produces toxin. Gross trauma or crush injury can be a predisposing event. During the last decade, injection of contaminated black tar heroin has been associated with virtually all cases.

Botulism of undetermined etiology is rare and occurs in people older than 12 months of age in whom no food or wound source is implicated.

The usual **incubation period** for foodborne botulism is 12 to 48 hours (range, 6 hours–8 days). In infant botulism, the incubation period is estimated at 3 to 30 days from the time of exposure to the spore-containing material. For wound botulism, the incubation period is 4 to 14 days from the time of injury until the onset of symptoms.

DIAGNOSTIC TESTS: A toxin neutralization bioassay in mice* is used to identify botulinum toxin in serum, stool, gastric aspirate, or suspect foods. Enriched and selective media are used to culture *C botulinum* from stool and foods. In infant and wound botulism, the diagnosis is made by demonstrating *C botulinum* toxin or organisms in feces, wound exudate, or tissue specimens. Toxin has been demonstrated in serum in only

---

* For information, consult your state health department.

1% of infants with botulism. To increase the likelihood of diagnosis, serum and stool specimens should be obtained from all people with suspected foodborne botulism. In foodborne cases, serum specimens obtained more than 3 days after ingestion of toxin usually are negative. Stool and gastric aspirates are the best diagnostic specimens for culture. A stool specimen for toxin assay is the test of choice for infant botulism. Because constipation can make obtaining a stool specimen difficult, an enema of sterile nonbacteriostatic water can be given. Because results of laboratory testing can be delayed by several days, treatment with antitoxin should be initiated promptly on the basis of clinical suspicion. The most prominent electromyographic finding is an incremental increase of evoked muscle potentials at high-frequency nerve stimulation (20–50 Hz). In addition, a characteristic pattern of brief, small-amplitude, overly abundant motor action potentials can be seen after stimulation of muscle. This pattern may not be seen in infants, and its absence does not exclude the diagnosis.

TREATMENT:

METICULOUS SUPPORTIVE CARE. An important aspect of therapy in all forms of botulism is meticulous supportive care, in particular respiratory and nutritional support, and administration of antitoxin.

ANTITOXIN FOR INFANT BOTULISM. Human-derived antitoxin is used for infant botulism. Equine-derived antitoxin is used for other forms of botulism. A 5-year, randomized, double-blind, placebo-controlled treatment trial of human-derived botulinum antitoxin (known as Botulism Immune Globulin Intravenous [BIGIV]) in infants with botulism showed a significant decrease in hospital days, mechanical ventilation, tube feedings, and cost associated with BIGIV administration. In October 2003, the US Food and Drug Administration licensed BIGIV for treatment of infant botulism caused by type A or type B *C botulinum*; the California Department of Health Services (24-hour telephone number 510-540-2646) should be contacted to procure BIGIV, which now is under the proprietary name of BabyBIG. At a 2004 cost of $45 300 per patient, this product is cost saving. Treatment with BIGIV should be initiated as early in the illness as possible. Botulism Immune Globulin Intravenous is available only for treatment of infant botulism.

ANTITOXIN FOR FOODBORNE AND WOUND BOTULISM. Patients with suspected foodborne and wound botulism should be treated with bivalent antitoxin (types A and B) and possibly also monovalent type E antitoxin available from the Centers for Disease Control and Prevention (CDC) through state health departments. Immediate administration of antitoxin is the key to successful therapy, because antitoxin arrests the progression of paralysis but does not reverse it. Antitoxin should be procured immediately on suspicion of botulism. If contact cannot be made with the state health department, the CDC should be contacted at 770-488-7100 for botulism case consultation and antitoxin. Before administration of equine antitoxin, patients should be tested for hypersensitivity to equine sera (see Antibodies of Animal Origin, p 61). Approximately 9% of people treated with equine antitoxin experience some degree of hypersensitivity reaction to equine serum, but severe reactions are rare.

ANTIMICROBIAL AGENTS. In infant botulism, antimicrobial therapy is not indicated, and lysis of intraluminal *C botulinum* theoretically could increase the amount of toxin available for absorption. Aminoglycoside agents potentiate the paralytic effects of the toxin and should be avoided.

ISOLATION OF THE HOSPITALIZED PATIENT: Standard precautions are recommended.

CONTROL MEASURES:
- Prophylactic equine antitoxin for asymptomatic people who have ingested a food known to contain botulinum toxin is not recommended. For noninfant cases, 24-hour clinical consultation and antitoxin are provided by CDC through state health departments. Physicians with a patient suspected of having any type of botulism should contact their state health departments immediately.
- Elimination of recently ingested toxin may be facilitated by inducing vomiting and by gastric lavage, rapid purgation, and high enemas. These measures should not be used in infant botulism. Enemas should not be administered to people with illness except to obtain a stool specimen for diagnostic purposes. Exposed people should have close medical observation.
- Honey should not be given to children younger than 12 months of age.
- An investigational botulinum toxoid vaccine (types A, B, C, D, and E) is available from the CDC for immunization of laboratory workers at high risk of exposure to botulinum toxin.
- Education regarding safe practices in food preparation and home-canning methods should be promoted. Use of a pressure cooker (at 116°C [240.8°F]) is necessary to kill spores of *C botulinum*. Bringing the internal temperature of foods to that of boiling (85°C [185°F]) for 10 minutes will destroy the toxin. Time-temperature-pressure requirements vary with the product being heated. In addition, food containers that appear to bulge may contain gas produced by *C botulinum* and should be discarded. Other foods that appear to have spoiled should not be eaten or tasted.
- Cases of suspected botulism should be reported immediately to local and state health departments.

Clostridial Myonecrosis
(Gas Gangrene)

CLINICAL MANIFESTATIONS: Onset is heralded by acute pain at the site of the wound, followed by edema, tenderness, exudate, and progression of pain. Systemic findings initially include tachycardia disproportionate to the degree of fever, pallor, diaphoresis, hypotension, renal failure, and later, alterations in mental status. Crepitus is suggestive but not pathognomonic of *Clostridium* infection and is not always present. Diagnosis is based on clinical manifestations, including the characteristic appearance of necrotic muscle at surgery. Untreated gas gangrene can lead to disseminated myonecrosis, suppurative visceral infection, septicemia, and death within hours.

ETIOLOGY: Clostridial myonecrosis is caused by *Clostridium* species, most often *Clostridium perfringens*, which are large, gram-positive, spore-forming anaerobic bacilli with blunt ends. Other *Clostridium* species (eg, *Clostridium sordellii*, *Clostridium septicum*, *Clostridium novyi*) also can be associated with myonecrosis. Mixed infection with other gram-positive and gram-negative bacteria is common.

EPIDEMIOLOGY: Clostridial myonecrosis usually results from contamination of open wounds involving muscle. The sources of *Clostridium* species are soil, contaminated

objects, and human and animal feces. Dirty surgical or traumatic wounds with significant devitalized tissue and foreign bodies predispose to disease. Nontraumatic gas
gangrene occurs occasionally from *Clostridium* organisms in the gastrointestinal tract
and in immunocompromised people.

The **incubation period** is unknown.

DIAGNOSTIC TESTS: Anaerobic cultures of wound exudate, involved soft tissue and
muscle, and blood should be performed. Because *Clostridium* species are ubiquitous,
their recovery from a wound is not diagnostic unless typical clinical manifestations are
present. A Gram-stained smear of wound discharge demonstrating characteristic
gram-positive bacilli and absent or sparse polymorphonuclear leukocytes suggests
clostridial infection. Tissue specimens and aspirates (not swab specimens) are appropriate for anaerobic culture. Because some pathogenic *Clostridium* species are exqui-
sitely oxygen sensitive, care should be taken to optimize anaerobic growth conditions.
A radiograph of the affected site can demonstrate gas in the tissue. Occasionally,
blood cultures are diagnostic.

TREATMENT:
- Early and complete surgical excision of necrotic tissue and removal of foreign
  material is essential.
- Management of shock, fluid and electrolyte imbalance, hemolytic anemia, and
  other complications is crucial.
- High-dose penicillin G (250 000–400 000 U/kg per day) should be administered intravenously. Clindamycin, metronidazole, imipenem or meropenem, and
  chloramphenicol can be considered as alternative drugs for penicillin-allergic
  patients or for treatment of polymicrobial infections. The combination of penicillin G and clindamycin may have better efficacy than penicillin alone.
- Hyperbaric oxygen may be beneficial, but adequately controlled data on its efficacy are not available.
- Treatment with antitoxin is of no value.

ISOLATION OF THE HOSPITALIZED PATIENT: Standard precautions are recommended.

CONTROL MEASURES: In wound management, prompt and careful debridement,
flushing of contaminated wounds, and removal of foreign material should be performed.

Penicillin G (50 000 U/kg per day) or clindamycin (20–30 mg/kg per day) may
be of value for prophylaxis in patients with grossly contaminated wounds.

Clostridium difficile

CLINICAL MANIFESTATIONS: Syndromes associated with infections include pseudomembranous colitis and antimicrobial-associated diarrhea. Pseudomembranous colitis
generally is characterized by diarrhea, abdominal cramps, fever, systemic toxicity,
abdominal tenderness, and passage of stools containing blood and mucus. Occasionally children can have marked abdominal tenderness and distention with minimal
diarrhea. The colonic mucosa often contains small (2- to 5-mm), raised, yellowish
plaques. Characteristically, disease begins while the child is in a hospital receiving

antimicrobial therapy, but disease can occur weeks after hospital discharge or after cessation of therapy. Rarely, the illness is not associated with antimicrobial therapy or hospitalization. Severe or fatal disease is more likely to occur in severely neutropenic children with leukemia, in infants with Hirschsprung disease, and in patients with inflammatory bowel disease. Infection also may result only in mild diarrhea or asymptomatic carriage. Carriage without symptoms is common in newborn infants and in children younger than 1 year of age.

ETIOLOGY: *Clostridium difficile* is a spore-forming, obligately anaerobic, gram-positive bacillus. Disease is related to the action of toxin(s) produced by these organisms. Although other toxins also exist, toxins A and B have been associated most strongly with human disease.

EPIDEMIOLOGY: *Clostridium difficile* can be isolated from soil and commonly is present in the environment. *Clostridium difficile* is acquired from the environment or from the stool of other colonized or infected people by the fecal-oral route. Intestinal colonization rates in healthy neonates and young infants can be as high as 50% but usually are less than 5% in children older than 2 years of age and in adults. Hospitals, nursing homes, and child care facilities are major reservoirs for *C difficile*. Risk factors for disease are those that increase exposure to organisms and those that diminish the barrier effect of the normal intestinal flora, allowing *C difficile* to proliferate and elaborate toxin(s) in vivo. Risk factors for acquisition include experiencing prolonged hospitalization, having an infected hospital roommate, and having symptomatically infected patients on the same hospital ward. Risk factors for developing disease include antimicrobial therapy, repeated enemas, prolonged nasogastric tube insertion, and gastrointestinal tract surgery and having renal insufficiency. Penicillins, clindamycin, and cephalosporins are the antimicrobial drugs most commonly associated with *C difficile* colitis, but colitis has been associated with almost every antimicrobial agent. A previously uncommon strain of *C difficile* with variations in toxin genes has become more resistant to fluoroquinolones and has emerged as a cause of outbreaks of *C difficile*-associated diarrhea. Although *C difficile* toxin infrequently is identified from stool specimens of asymptomatic adults, toxin may be identified in stool specimens from neonates and infants who have no gastrointestinal tract illness. This finding confounds the interpretation of positive toxin assays in patients younger than 12 months of age.

The **incubation period** is unknown.

DIAGNOSTIC TESTS: Endoscopic findings of pseudomembranes and hyperemic, friable rectal mucosa suggest pseudomembranous colitis. To diagnose *C difficile* disease, stool should be tested for presence of *C difficile* toxins. Commercially available enzyme immunoassays detect toxins A and B, or an enzyme immunoassay for toxin A may be used in conjunction with cell culture cytotoxicity assay, the "gold standard" for toxin B detection. Latex agglutination tests should not be used. Symptomatic infants younger than 1 year of age should be investigated for causes of diarrhea other than *C difficile*, because carriage of *C difficile* is common in this age group. The presence of *C difficile* toxin may not be responsible for clinical signs or symptoms.

TREATMENT:
- Antimicrobial therapy should be discontinued as soon as possible in patients in whom clinically significant diarrhea or colitis develops.

- Antimicrobial therapy for *C difficile* disease is indicated for patients with severe disease or in whom diarrhea persists after antimicrobial therapy is discontinued.
- Strains of *C difficile* are susceptible to metronidazole and vancomycin, and both are effective. Metronidazole (30 mg/kg per day in 4 divided doses, maximum 2 g/day) is the drug of choice for the initial treatment of most patients with colitis. Oral vancomycin (40 mg/kg per day in 4 divided doses, maximum 500 mg) is an alternative drug, but use of vancomycin should be discouraged because of the potential for promoting vancomycin-resistant organisms. Vancomycin is indicated for patients who do not respond to metronidazole. Metronidazole is effective when given orally or intravenously; vancomycin is effective only when administered orally. Oral bacitracin is another therapeutic choice, but bacitracin is less effective.
- Antimicrobial agents usually are administered for at least 10 days. Longer duration of therapy may be indicated if the other antimicrobial agents cannot be discontinued.
- Up to 40% of patients experience a relapse after discontinuing therapy, but the infection usually responds to a second course of the same treatment.
- Cholestyramine resin, which binds toxin, can relieve symptoms. However, its effect has not been evaluated in children with disease caused by *C difficile*. Because cholestyramine also binds vancomycin, the drugs should not be administered concurrently.
- Drugs that decrease intestinal motility should not be administered.
- Follow-up testing for toxin is not recommended if symptoms resolve.

ISOLATION OF THE HOSPITALIZED PATIENT: In addition to standard precautions, contact precautions are recommended for the duration of illness.

CONTROL MEASURES:
- Exercising meticulous hand hygiene, properly handling contaminated waste (including diapers), disinfecting fomites, and limiting use of antimicrobial agents are the best available methods for control of *C difficile* disease. Use of alcohol-based hand hygiene products is less effective in removing *C difficile* spores from contaminated hands than is washing hands with soap and water, which is the recommended method of hand hygiene.
- Thorough cleaning of hospital rooms and bathrooms of patients with *C difficile* colitis is essential. Because *C difficile* forms spores, the organism can resist the action of many common hospital disinfectants; many hospitals have instituted cleaning with diluted bleach when outbreaks of *C difficile* diarrhea are not controlled by other measures.
- Children with *C difficile* diarrhea should be in a separate protected area in child care settings or excluded from child care for the duration of diarrhea.

Clostridium perfringens Food Poisoning

CLINICAL MANIFESTATIONS: *Clostridium perfringens* foodborne illness is characterized by a sudden onset of watery diarrhea and moderate to severe, crampy, midepigastric pain. Vomiting and fever are uncommon. Symptoms usually resolve within 24 hours. The short incubation period, short duration, and absence of fever in most patients differentiates *C perfringens* foodborne disease from shigellosis and salmonellosis, and the infrequency of vomiting and longer incubation period contrast with the clinical features of foodborne disease associated with heavy metals, *Staphylococcus aureus* enterotoxins, and fish and shellfish toxins. Diarrheal illness caused by *Bacillus cereus* enterotoxin may be indistinguishable from that caused by *C perfringens* (see Appendix VI, Clinical Syndromes Associated With Foodborne Diseases, p 857). Enteritis necroticans (known locally as pigbel) is a cause of severe illness and death attributable to *C perfringens* food poisoning among children in Papua, New Guinea. Rare cases have been reported elsewhere.

ETIOLOGY: Food poisoning is caused by a heat-labile toxin produced in vivo by *C perfringens* type A; type C causes enteritis necroticans.

EPIDEMIOLOGY: *Clostridium perfringens* is ubiquitous in the environment and commonly is present in raw meat and poultry. At an optimum temperature, *C perfringens* has one of the fastest rates of growth of any bacterium. Spores of *C perfringens* may survive cooking. Spores germinate and multiply during slow cooling and storage at temperatures from 20°C to 60°C (68°F–140°F). Illness results from consumption of food containing high numbers of organisms ($>10^5$ colony-forming units/g) followed by enterotoxin production in the intestine. Beef, poultry, gravies, and dried or precooked foods are common sources. Infection usually is acquired at banquets or institutions (eg, schools and camps) or from food provided by caterers or restaurants where food is prepared in large quantities and kept warm for prolonged periods. Illness is not transmissible from person to person.

The **incubation period** is 6 to 24 hours, usually 8 to 12 hours.

DIAGNOSTIC TESTS: Because the fecal flora of healthy people commonly includes *C perfringens*, counts of *C perfringens* spores of 10^6/g of feces obtained within 48 hours of onset of illness are required to support the diagnosis in ill people. The diagnosis also can be suggested by detection of *C perfringens* enterotoxin in stool by commercially available kits. To confirm *C perfringens* as the cause, the concentration of organisms should be at least 10^5/g in the epidemiologically implicated food. Although *C perfringens* is an anaerobe, special transport conditions are unnecessary, because the spores are durable. Stool specimens, rather than rectal swab specimens, should be obtained.

TREATMENT: Usually, no treatment is required. Oral rehydration or, occasionally, intravenous fluid and electrolyte replacement may be indicated to prevent or treat dehydration. Antimicrobial agents are not indicated.

ISOLATION OF THE HOSPITALIZED PATIENT: Standard precautions are recommended.

CONTROL MEASURES: Preventive measures depend on limiting proliferation of *C perfringens* in foods by cooking foods thoroughly and maintaining food at warmer than 60°C (140°F) or cooler than 7°C (45°F). Meat dishes should be served hot shortly after cooking. Foods never should be held at room temperature to cool; they should be refrigerated after removal from warming devices or serving tables. Foods should be reheated to at least 74°C (165.2°F) before serving. Roasts, stews, and similar dishes should be divided into small quantities for cooking and refrigeration to limit the time such foods are at temperatures at which *C perfringens* replicates.

Coccidioidomycosis

CLINICAL MANIFESTATIONS: The primary infection is acquired by the respiratory route and is asymptomatic or self-limited in 60% of children. Symptomatic disease can resemble influenza, with malaise, fever, cough, myalgia, headache, and chest pain. Diffuse erythematous maculopapular rash, erythema multiforme, erythema nodosum, and/or arthralgias commonly occur and can be the only clinical manifestations in some children. Chronic pulmonary lesions are rare, but up to 5% of infected people develop asymptomatic pulmonary radiographic residua (eg, cysts, coin lesions).

Nonpulmonary primary infection is rare, usually follows trauma, and includes cutaneous lesions or soft tissue infections with associated regional lymphadenitis.

Infection disseminates to skin, bones and joints, the central nervous system (CNS), and the lungs and occurs in less than 1% of infected people. Dissemination to one or more sites is common in infants. Meningitis almost invariably is fatal if untreated. Congenital infection is rare.

ETIOLOGY: *Coccidioides immitis* is a dimorphic fungus. In soil, it exists in hyphal phase. Infectious arthroconidia (eg, spores) produced in some hyphae become airborne, infecting the host after inhalation or inoculation. In tissues, spores enlarge to form spherules; mature spherules release endospores that develop into new spherules and continue the tissue cycle.

EPIDEMIOLOGY: *Coccidioides immitis* is found extensively in soil and is endemic in the southwestern United States, including California, Arizona, New Mexico, Texas, and Utah; northern Mexico; and certain areas of Central and South America. People are infected through inhalation of dustborne arthroconidia. In areas with endemic infection, clusters of cases of coccidioidomycosis can follow dust storms, seismic events, archeologic digging, or recreational activities. Exposure need not be extensive to develop infection. Infection provides lifelong immunity. Person-to-person transmission of coccidioidomycosis does not occur. Black and Filipino people, pregnant women, neonates, elderly people, and immunocompromised people have an increased risk of dissemination and fatal outcome. A small proportion of new cases are identified in people who currently are not residing in regions with endemic infection but may have visited these areas.

The **incubation period** typically is 10 to 16 days; the range is less than 1 week to approximately 1 month.

DIAGNOSTIC TESTS: The diagnosis of coccidioidomycosis is best established using serologic, histopathologic, and culture methods. Serologic tests are useful to confirm diagnoses and provide prognostic information. The immunoglobulin (Ig) M response can be detected by latex agglutination test, enzyme immunoassay (EIA), or immunodiffusion. Latex agglutination is a rapid, sensitive test that lacks specificity; hence, positive results should be confirmed by other tests. An IgM response is detectable 1 to 3 weeks after symptoms appear and can be detected in up to 75% of patients with primary disease 3 to 4 months after onset. The IgG response can be detected by immunodiffusion, EIA, or complement fixation test. Complement fixation antibodies in serum usually are of low titer and are transient if the disease is asymptomatic or mild. High ($\geq$1:32) persistent titers occur with severe disease and almost always in disseminated infection. Cerebrospinal fluid (CSF) antibodies also are detectable by complement fixation test. Increasing serum and CSF titers indicate progressive disease, and decreasing titers suggest improvement. Low or nondetectable titers in immunocompromised patients should be interpreted with caution. Because clinical laboratories use different diagnostic test kits, positive results should be confirmed in a reference laboratory.

Spherules as large as 80 μm in diameter may be visualized in infected body fluid specimens (eg, pleural fluid, bronchoalveolar lavage) and biopsy specimens of skin lesions or organs. The presence of a mature spherule with endospores is pathognomonic of infection. Culture of the organisms is possible but potentially is hazardous to laboratory personnel, because spherules can convert to arthroconidia-bearing mycelia on culture plates. Suspect cultures should be sealed and thereafter handled using appropriate safety equipment and procedures. A DNA probe can identify *C immitis* in cultures, thereby decreasing the risk of exposure to infectious fungi.

Skin testing may be a useful indicator of exposure and, therefore, is used mostly for epidemiologic studies. A delayed hypersensitivity reaction to a coccidioidin or spherulin skin test is indicative of past or current infection. A positive skin test result can appear from 10 to 45 days after infection; anergy is common in disseminated disease. These skin tests currently are not available in the United States.

TREATMENT: Antifungal therapy is not indicated for uncomplicated primary infection.

Amphotericin B is the recommended initial therapy for severe and progressive infection (disseminated infection not involving the central nervous system [CNS]) and for immunocompromised patients, including people with human immunodeficiency virus (HIV) infection (see Drugs for Invasive and Other Serious Fungal Infections, Table 4.7, p 780). The role of lipid formulations of amphotericin B and voriconazole is not established. Fluconazole is recommended for CNS infections. Itraconazole and fluconazole also are useful for treatment of less severe disseminated infections. For CNS infections that are unresponsive to fluconazole, intravenous amphotericin B therapy is augmented by repetitive CSF instillation of this drug. A subcutaneous reservoir can facilitate administration into the cisternal space or lateral ventricle. Orally administered itraconazole and fluconazole have suppressed coccidioidal meningitis in many patients, but lifelong therapy may be necessary. Itraconazole is preferred for nonmeningeal coccidioidomycosis, including osteomyelitis. Consultation with a specialist for treatment of patients with meningeal disease is recommended.

In some localized infections with sinuses, fistulae, or abscesses, amphotericin B has been instilled locally or used for irrigation of wounds.

The duration of amphotericin B therapy is variable and depends on the site(s) of involvement, clinical response, and mycologic and immunologic test results. In general, therapy is continued until clinical and laboratory evidence indicates that active infection has subsided. The minimum duration of treatment for disseminated coccidioidomycosis is 1 month but may continue for 1 year or longer. The required duration of treatment with azoles is uncertain, except for patients with CNS infection or underlying HIV infection, for whom suppressive therapy is lifelong.

Surgical debridement or excision of lesions in bone and lung has been advocated for localized, symptomatic, persistent, resistant, or progressive lesions.

ISOLATION OF THE HOSPITALIZED PATIENT: Standard precautions are recommended. Care should be taken in handling, changing, and discarding dressings, casts, and similar materials in which arthroconidial contamination could occur.

CONTROL MEASURES: Measures to control dust are recommended in areas with endemic infection, including construction sites, archaeologic project sites, or where other activities cause excessive soil disturbance. Immunocompromised people residing in or traveling to areas with endemic infection should be counseled to avoid exposure to activities that may aerosolize spores in contaminated soil.

Coronaviruses

CLINICAL MANIFESTATIONS: Until the recent outbreak of severe acute respiratory syndrome (SARS), coronaviruses (CoVs) primarily have been considered to be a frequent cause of the "common cold" or upper respiratory tract illness. They also have been associated with lower respiratory tract illness in patients with compromised immune systems. The outbreak of SARS, beginning in China in early 2003, and its link to a novel coronavirus, SARS-CoV, showed that a CoV can cause life-threatening disease. Infection by SARS-CoV should be suspected when a person develops consistent clinical symptoms and has been in an area or been in contact with people who have been in an area where SARS is known to be occurring. People infected with SARS-CoV first developed systemic symptoms (eg, fever, malaise, and myalgias), often without respiratory tract symptoms. A few days after onset of symptoms, some exposed people developed cough and/or shortness of breath. Many patients had no upper respiratory tract symptoms, and nearly all infected adults developed pneumonia or acute respiratory distress syndrome (ARDS). Twenty-five percent or more of patients with SARS-CoV disease reported diarrhea. Severe acute respiratory syndrome was associated with an overall case fatality rate of 10%, which increased to 50% or more in people older than 60 years of age or people with previous medical conditions. In children, particularly children younger than 12 years of age, the clinical course of SARS was shorter and less severe, with less prominent radiographic changes and rare progression to respiratory failure and death.

Additionally, CoV-like particles have been reported in patients with diarrhea, but a link between CoVs and diarrhea, other than in SARS, has not been confirmed. Another new CoV, NL63, has been linked to both upper and lower respiratory tract illness in children and adults.

ETIOLOGY: Coronaviruses are large, enveloped RNA viruses, 80 to 160 nm in diameter, with projections on their surface that, by electron microscopy, give them their characteristic crown-like appearance. Three antigenic groups (groups I, II, and III) of CoVs have been identified. Group I includes a variety of animal CoVs and the human CoVs-229E and NL63; group II includes animal CoVs, the human CoV-OC43, and possibly the distantly related SARS-CoV; and group III includes avian CoVs.

EPIDEMIOLOGY: Coronavirus infections are common in many animal species and may provide a reservoir for introduction of new strains to humans. Human CoVs are transmitted primarily by respiratory tract secretions through close contact that probably includes direct person-to-person contact or contact with fomites followed by auto-inoculation and inhalation of droplets. Patients with SARS-CoV infection also may have virus in stool, urine, and blood, all of which can provide additional sources of virus for transmission. Patients with SARS-CoV infection are most infectious during the second week of illness, unlike patients with other CoV infections, who are most infectious in the early stages of illness. During the 2003 outbreak, most SARS transmission occurred in hospitals and households.

The human CoVs are distributed worldwide. In temperate climates, CoV outbreaks occur during winter, with young children having the highest infection rate during outbreaks. Presumably, SARS-CoV was transmitted initially to humans from animals in China—possibly animals sold in wild animal markets in Guangdong Province. Therefore, SARS-CoV may have an animal reservoir in China. It is not known whether SARS-CoV is present only in animals within China or if similar viruses are present elsewhere. After the 2003 global outbreak, the only documented SARS cases have been associated with research laboratory exposure among people handling the virus.

The **incubation period** for common CoVs usually is 2 to 5 days. The incubation period for SARS may be longer, typically 2 to 7 days, but as long as 10 days.

DIAGNOSTIC TESTS: Diagnostic tests for CoVs generally are not available. Coronaviruses are difficult to grow except with use of special cell lines available in research laboratories. Polymerase chain reaction assays now have been developed, and a variety of antibody assays also can be used to detect infection. Viral particles can be visualized by immune electron microscopy. Laboratory diagnosis of SARS should be sought only when there are clinical and epidemiologic factors that suggest SARS-CoV infection. Laboratory guidance is available at the CDC Web site (**www.cdc.gov/ncidod/sars/**).

TREATMENT: There is no proven effective antiviral therapy for CoV infections. Treatment for symptoms of the common cold is appropriate for uncomplicated human CoV infections. There is no recommended treatment for SARS-CoV; several antiviral drugs, including ribavirin and interferon-alpha, have been used, but their efficacy is unknown; steroids have been used to treat SARS-CoV–associated ARDS.

ISOLATION OF THE HOSPITALIZED PATIENT: Standard precautions are recommended for commonly seen CoVs. Airborne, droplet, and contact precautions, in addition to standard precautions, are recommended for patients with SARS-CoV infection.

CONTROL MEASURES: Appropriate hygienic practices, especially hand hygiene, likely will decrease transmission of all CoVs. The severity of illness associated with SARS-CoV infection led to an intense and ultimately very effective public health intervention. The global SARS-CoV outbreak was halted within 4 months by aggressive case finding and rapid institution of isolation precautions with appropriate infection control practices as well as intensive contact tracing, evaluation, and monitoring, sometimes including quarantine.

Cryptococcus neoformans Infections
(Cryptococcosis)

CLINICAL MANIFESTATIONS: Primary infection is acquired by inhalation of aerosolized fungal elements from contaminated soil and often is asymptomatic or mild. Pulmonary disease, when symptomatic, is characterized by cough, chest pain, and constitutional symptoms. Chest radiographs may reveal a solitary nodule or mass or focal or diffuse infiltrates. Hematogenous dissemination to the central nervous system, bones, skin, and other sites can occur, but dissemination is rare in children without defects in cell-mediated immunity (eg, children with leukemia, systemic lupus erythematosis, chronic cutaneous candidiasis, congenital immunodeficiency, or acquired immunodeficiency syndrome [AIDS] or people who have undergone solid organ transplantation). Usually, several sites are infected, but manifestations of involvement of one site predominate. Cryptococcal meningitis, the most common and serious form of cryptococcal disease, often follows an indolent course. Symptoms are characteristic of meningitis, meningoencephalitis, or space-occupying lesions but may manifest only as behavioral changes. Cryptococcal fungemia without apparent organ involvement occurs in patients with human immunodeficiency virus (HIV) infection, but in children it is rare.

ETIOLOGY: *Cryptococcus neoformans*, an encapsulated yeast that grows at 37°C (98°F), is, with rare exceptions, the only species of the genus *Cryptococcus* considered to be a human pathogen.

EPIDEMIOLOGY: *Cryptococcus neoformans* var *neoformans* is isolated primarily from soil contaminated with bird droppings and causes most human infections, especially infections in immunocompromised hosts. *Cryptococcus neoformans* var *gattii* occurs most commonly in tropical and subtropical regions, and for unknown reasons, rarely causes disease in immunocompromised people. Person-to-person transmission does not occur. *Cryptococcus* species infect 5% to 10% of adults with AIDS, but infection is rare in HIV-infected children.

The **incubation period** is unknown.

DIAGNOSTIC TESTS: Encapsulated yeast cells can be visualized using India ink or other stains of cerebrospinal fluid (CSF) specimens containing 10^3 or more colony-forming units of yeast per mL. Definitive diagnosis requires isolation of the organism from body fluid or tissue specimens. Blood should be cultured by lysis-centrifugation. Media containing cycloheximide, which inhibits growth of *C neoformans*, should not be used. Sabouraud dextrose agar is optimal for isolation of *Cryptococcus* from sputum, bronchopulmonary lavage, tissue, or CSF specimens. Use of Niger seed (birdseed) can increase the rate of detection in sputum and urine specimens. Few organisms may be present in the CSF specimen, and a large quantity of CSF may be needed to recover the organism. The latex agglutination test and enzyme immunoassay for detection of cryptococcal capsular polysaccharide antigen in serum or CSF specimens are excellent rapid diagnostic tests. Antigen is detected in CSF or serum specimens from more than 90% of patients with cryptococcal meningitis.

TREATMENT: Amphotericin B (see Drugs for Invasive and Other Serious Fungal Infections, p 780), in combination with oral flucytosine or fluconazole, is indicated as initial therapy for patients with meningeal and other serious cryptococcal infections. Serum flucytosine concentrations should be maintained between 40 and 60 μg/mL. Patients with meningitis should receive combination therapy for at least 2 weeks, and then fluconazole (100 mg/kg per day) can be used for a minimum of 10 weeks. Alternatively, the amphotericin B and flucytosine combination can be continued for 6 to 10 weeks. Lipid formulations of amphotericin B can be substituted for conventional amphotericin B in children with renal impairment. A lumbar puncture should be performed after 2 weeks of therapy. The 20% to 40% of patients in whom culture is positive at 2 weeks will require a more prolonged treatment course. When infection is refractory to systemic therapy, intrathecal or intraventricular amphotericin B may be required. Patients with less severe disease may be treated with fluconazole or itraconazole, but data on use of these drugs for children with *C neoformans* infection are limited. Another potential treatment option for HIV-infected patients with less severe disease is combination therapy with fluconazole and flucytosine; the toxicity associated with this regimen often limits its usefulness. Increased intracranial pressure frequently occurs despite microbiologic response and often is associated with clinical deterioration. Symptomatic elevation of intracranial pressure initially is managed with repeated lumbar punctures.

Children with HIV infection who have completed initial therapy for cryptococcosis should receive lifelong suppressive therapy with fluconazole daily. Oral itraconazole daily or amphotericin B 1 to 3 times weekly are alternatives. Data regarding discontinuing this secondary prophylaxis after immune reconstitution as a consequence of highly active antiretroviral therapy are available for adults but not for children.

ISOLATION OF THE HOSPITALIZED PATIENT: Standard precautions are recommended.

CONTROL MEASURES: None.

Cryptosporidiosis

CLINICAL MANIFESTATIONS: Frequent, nonbloody, watery diarrhea is the most common manifestation of cryptosporidiosis, although infection can be asymptomatic. Other symptoms include abdominal cramps, fatigue, vomiting, anorexia, and weight loss. Fever and vomiting are relatively common among children and often lead to a misdiagnosis of viral gastroenteritis. In infected immunocompetent people, including children, the diarrheal illness is self-limited, usually lasting 1 to 20 days (mean, 10 days). In immunocompromised people, especially people with human immunodeficiency virus (HIV) infection, chronic, severe diarrhea can develop, resulting in malnutrition, dehydration, and death. Pulmonary, biliary tract, or disseminated infection can occur in immunocompromised people, although infection usually is limited to the gastrointestinal tract.

ETIOLOGY: *Cryptosporidium* species are oocyst-forming coccidian protozoa. Oocysts are excreted in feces and are the infectious form. The most common species causing disease in humans are *Cryptosporidium hominis*, which only infects humans, and *Cryptosporidium parvum*, which infects humans, cattle, and other mammals.

EPIDEMIOLOGY: *Cryptosporidium* species have been found in a variety of hosts, including mammals, birds, and reptiles.* Extensive waterborne outbreaks have been associated with contamination of municipal water and exposure to contaminated swimming pools. In children, the incidence of cryptosporidiosis is greatest during summer and early fall, corresponding to the outdoor swimming season. Transmission to humans can occur from farm livestock, particularly young animals, including animals found in petting zoos, or pets. Person-to-person transmission occurs and can cause outbreaks in child care centers, with attack rates of 30% to 60% reported. *Cryptosporidium* species also cause traveler's diarrhea. Because the oocyst form of the parasite is resistant to chlorine, appropriately functioning water filtration systems are critical for the safety of public water supplies. Most sand filters used for swimming pools are ineffective for removing oocysts from contaminated water.

The median **incubation period** is 7 days, with a range of 2 to 14 days.

Oocysts continue to be detected in stool for a mean of 7 days after symptoms resolve. In most people, shedding of *C parvum* stops within 2 weeks, but in immuno-compromised children, shedding can continue for up to 2 months.

DIAGNOSTIC TESTS: The detection of oocysts on microscopic examination of stool specimens is diagnostic. Unfortunately, routine laboratory examination of stool for ova and parasites will not detect *Cryptosporidium* species. The sucrose flotation method or formalin ethyl acetate method is used to concentrate oocysts in stool before staining with a modified Kinyoun acid-fast stain. Monoclonal antibody-based fluorescein-conjugated stain for oocysts in stool and an enzyme immunoassay (EIA) for detecting antigen in stool are available commercially. With EIA methods, false-positive and false-negative results can occur, and confirmation by microscopy should be considered. Because shedding can be intermittent, at least 3 stool specimens collected on separate days should be examined before considering test results to be negative. Oocysts are small (4–6 μm in diameter) and can be missed in a rapid scan of a slide. Organisms also can be identified in intestinal biopsy tissue or intestinal fluid. Polymerase chain reaction assays are used for research purposes and to identify species and genotype.

TREATMENT: A 3-day course of nitazoxanide oral suspension has been approved by the US Food and Drug Administration for treatment of children ≥12 months of age and adults with diarrhea attributable to cryptosporidiosis and *Giardia intestinalis*. Paromomycin, alone or with azithromycin, is minimally effective. In immunocompromised patients with cryptosporidiosis, oral administration of Human Immune Globulin or bovine colostrum has been beneficial. In HIV-infected patients, antiretroviral therapy-associated improvement in CD4+ T-lymphocyte count can improve the course of disease.

ISOLATION OF THE HOSPITALIZED PATIENT: In addition to standard precautions, contact precautions are recommended for diapered or incontinent children.

---

* Centers for Disease Control and Prevention. Cryptosporidiosis surveillance—United States, 1999–2002. *MMWR Surveill Summ.* 2005;54(SS-01):1–8

CONTROL MEASURES: People with diarrhea should not use public recreational water (eg, swimming pools, lakes, ponds), and people with a diagnosis of cryptosporidiosis should not use recreational waters for 2 weeks after symptoms resolve. There are numerous methods of water purification. Boiling is the most certain way of killing all microorganisms. There are 2 types of chemical treatment: iodine and chlorine. The effectiveness of chemical treatment of water is related to the temperature, pH level, and clarity of the water. If chemical treatments cannot be used, a filtration device is an appropriate alternative. The filtration devices should have a particle size rating of 1 to 4 μm to remove *Cryptosporidium* species. Backpackers and campers always should have at least one backup method of water purification in case one fails. For additional information, see *Giardia intestinalis* Infections (p 296).

Cutaneous Larva Migrans

CLINICAL MANIFESTATIONS: Nematode larvae produce pruritic, reddish papules at the site of skin entry, a condition referred to as creeping eruption. As the larvae migrate through skin advancing several millimeters to a few centimeters a day, intensely pruritic, serpiginous tracks or bullae are formed. Larval activity can continue for several weeks or months but eventually is self-limiting. An advancing serpiginous tunnel in the skin with an associated intense pruritus is virtually pathognomonic. Rarely, in infections with a large burden of parasites, pneumonitis (Löeffler syndrome), which can be severe, and myositis may follow skin lesions. Occasionally, the larvae reach the intestine and may cause eosinophilic enteritis.

ETIOLOGY: Infective larvae of cat and dog hookworms (ie, *Ancylostoma braziliense* and *Ancylostoma caninum*) are the usual causes. Other skin-penetrating nematodes are occasional causes.

EPIDEMIOLOGY: Cutaneous larva migrans is a disease of children, utility workers, gardeners, sunbathers, and others who come in contact with soil contaminated with cat and dog feces. In the United States, the disease is most prevalent in the Southeast.

DIAGNOSTIC TESTS: Because the diagnosis usually is made clinically, biopsies are not indicated. Biopsy specimens typically demonstrate an eosinophilic inflammatory infiltrate, but the migrating parasite is not visualized. Eosinophilia occurs in some cases. Larvae have been detected in sputum and gastric washings in patients with the rare complication of pneumonitis. Enzyme immunoassay or Western blot analysis using antigens of *A caninum* are available in research laboratories, but use is not warranted routinely.

TREATMENT: The disease usually is self-limited, with spontaneous cure after several weeks or months. Orally administered albendazole or ivermectin or topically administered thiabendazole are the recommended therapy.

ISOLATION OF THE HOSPITALIZED PATIENT: Standard precautions are recommended.

CONTROL MEASURES: Skin contact with moist soil contaminated with animal feces should be avoided. In warm climates, beaches should be kept free of dog and cat feces.

Cyclosporiasis

CLINICAL MANIFESTATIONS: Profuse, watery diarrhea is the most common symptom of cyclosporiasis. Nausea, vomiting, anorexia, substantial weight loss, abdominal bloating or cramping, and prolonged fatigue also can occur. Diarrhea can alternate with constipation. Fever occurs in approximately 50% of patients. Infection usually is self-limited, but diarrhea and systemic symptoms can vary in intensity for weeks to months. Relapse and persistence of symptoms is common in untreated people, even in immunocompetent people. The degree of asymptomatic infection is unknown.

ETIOLOGY: *Cyclospora cayetanensis* is a coccidian protozoan. Noninfectious, unsporulated oocysts are passed in stools.

EPIDEMIOLOGY: *Cyclospora cayetanensis* is known to be endemic in many economically depressed countries, such as Nepal, Peru, Haiti, Guatemala, and Indonesia and has been reported as a cause of traveler's diarrhea. Outbreaks in the United States and Canada during 1996 and 1997 were associated with ingestion of fresh raspberries imported from Central America. Direct person-to-person transmission has not been documented, probably because excreted oocysts take days to weeks under favorable environmental conditions to sporulate and become infectious. Both foodborne and waterborne outbreaks have been reported. Most of the outbreaks that have been investigated in the United States and Canada have been associated with consumption of various types of imported fresh produce.

The **incubation period** is approximately 7 days (range, 1–14 days).

DIAGNOSTIC TESTS: Diagnosis is made by identification of oocysts (8–10 μm in diameter) in stool. The oocysts are autofluorescent and variably acid fast after modified acid-fast staining of stool specimens (ie, oocysts that have either retained or not retained the stain can be visualized). Investigational molecular diagnostic assays (eg, polymerase chain reaction) are available at the Centers for Disease Control and Prevention and some other reference laboratories.

TREATMENT: Trimethoprim-sulfamethoxazole for 7 to 10 days is effective therapy. People infected with human immunodeficiency virus may need higher doses and long-term maintenance therapy (see Drugs for Parasitic Infections, p 790).

ISOLATION OF THE HOSPITALIZED PATIENT: In addition to standard precautions, contact precautions are recommended for diapered or incontinent children.

CONTROL MEASURES: Fresh produce should be washed thoroughly before it is eaten. This precaution, however, may not eliminate the risk of transmission entirely.

Cytomegalovirus Infection

CLINICAL MANIFESTATIONS: Manifestations of acquired human cytomegalovirus (CMV) infection vary with the age and immunocompetence of the host. Asymptomatic infections are the most common, particularly in children. An infectious mononucleosis-like syndrome with prolonged fever and mild hepatitis, occurring in the absence of heterophil antibody production, can occur in adolescents and adults.

Pneumonia, colitis, and retinitis occur in immunocompromised hosts, including people receiving treatment for malignant neoplasms, people infected with human immunodeficiency virus (HIV), and people receiving immunosuppressive therapy for organ transplantation.

Congenital infection has a spectrum of manifestations but usually is silent clinically. Some congenitally infected infants who appear healthy at birth are later found to have hearing loss or learning disability. Approximately 10% of infants with congenital CMV infection have profound involvement evident at birth, with manifestations including intrauterine growth retardation, jaundice, purpura, hepatosplenomegaly, microcephaly, intracerebral calcifications, and retinitis.

Infection acquired intrapartum from maternal cervical secretions or postpartum from human milk usually is not associated with clinical illness. Infection resulting from transfusion from CMV-seropositive donors to preterm infants has been associated with systemic infections, including lower respiratory tract disease.

ETIOLOGY: Human CMV, a DNA virus, is a member of the herpesvirus group.

EPIDEMIOLOGY: Cytomegalovirus is highly species specific, and only human strains are known to produce human disease. This virus is ubiquitous and is transmitted horizontally (by direct person-to-person contact with virus-containing secretions), vertically (from mother to infant before, during, or after birth), and via transfusions of blood, platelets, and white blood cells from previously infected people (see Blood Safety, p 106). Infections have no seasonal predilection. Cytomegalovirus persists in latent form after a primary infection, and reactivation can occur years later, particularly under conditions of immunosuppression.

Horizontal transmission probably is the result of salivary contamination, but contact with infected urine also can have a role. Spread of CMV in households and child care centers is well documented. Excretion rates in child care centers can be as high as 70% in children 1 to 3 years of age. Young children can transmit CMV to their parents and other caregivers, such as child care staff (see also Children in Out-of-Home Child Care, p 130). In adolescents and adults, sexual transmission also occurs, as evidenced by virus in seminal and cervical fluids.

Seropositive healthy people have latent CMV in their leukocytes and tissues; hence, blood transfusions and organ transplantation can result in viral transmission. Severe CMV disease is more likely to occur if the recipient is seronegative or is a preterm infant. Latent CMV commonly will reactivate in immunosuppressed people and can result in disease if immunosuppression is severe (eg, in patients with acquired immunodeficiency syndrome or solid organ or stem cell transplant recipients).

Vertical transmission of CMV to an infant occurs by one of the following methods: (1) in utero by transplacental passage of maternal bloodborne virus; (2) at birth by passage through an infected maternal genital tract; or (3) postnatally by ingestion of CMV-positive human milk. Approximately 1% of all live-born infants are infected in utero and excrete CMV at birth. Risk to the fetus is greatest during the first half of gestation. Although in utero fetal infection can occur after maternal primary infection or after reactivation of infection during pregnancy, sequelae are far more common in infants exposed to maternal primary infection, with 10% to 20% diagnosed with mental retardation or sensorineural deafness in childhood and 10% having manifestations evident at birth.

Maternal cervical infection is common, resulting in exposure of many infants to CMV at birth. Cervical excretion rates are highest among young mothers in lower socioeconomic groups. Although interstitial pneumonia caused by CMV can develop during the early months of life, most infected infants remain well. Similarly, although disease can occur in seronegative infants fed CMV-infected milk, most infants infected from ingestion of human milk do not develop clinical illness, most likely because of the presence of passively transferred maternal antibody. Of infants who acquire infection from maternal cervical secretions or human milk, preterm infants are at greater risk of CMV illness and sequelae than are full-term infants.

The **incubation period** for horizontally transmitted CMV infections is unknown. Infection usually manifests 3 to 12 weeks after blood transfusions and between 1 and 4 months after tissue transplantation.

DIAGNOSTIC TESTS: The diagnosis of CMV disease is confounded by the ubiquity of the virus, the high rate of asymptomatic excretion, the frequency of reactivated infections, development of serum immunoglobulin (Ig) M CMV-specific antibody in some episodes of reactivation, and concurrent infection with other pathogens.

Virus can be isolated in cell culture from urine, pharynx, peripheral blood leukocytes, human milk, semen, cervical secretions, and other tissues and body fluids. Recovery of virus from a target organ provides strong evidence that the disease is caused by CMV infection. A presumptive diagnosis can be made on the basis of a fourfold antibody titer increase in paired serum specimens or by demonstration of virus excretion. Techniques for detection of viral DNA in tissues and some fluids, especially cerebrospinal fluid, by polymerase chain reaction assay or hybridization are available in reference laboratories. Detection of pp65 antigen in white blood cells is used to detect infection in immunocompromised hosts.

Various immunofluorescent assays, indirect hemagglutination assays, latex agglutination assays, and enzyme immunoassays are preferred for detecting CMV-specific antibodies.

Amniocentesis has been used in several small series of patients to establish the diagnosis of intrauterine infection. Proof of congenital infection requires isolation of CMV from urine, stool, respiratory tract secretions, or CSF obtained within 3 weeks of birth. Differentiation between intrauterine and perinatal infection is difficult later in infancy unless clinical manifestations of the former, such as chorioretinitis or intracranial calcifications, are present. A strongly positive CMV-specific IgM is suggestive during early infancy, but IgM antibody assays vary in accuracy for identification of primary infection.

TREATMENT: Ganciclovir (see Antiviral Drugs, p 785) is approved for both induction and maintenance treatment of retinitis caused by acquired or recurrent CMV infection in immunocompromised patients, including HIV-infected adults, and for prevention of CMV infection in transplant recipients. Ganciclovir also is used to treat CMV infections of other sites (esophagus, colon, lungs) and for preemptive treatment of immunosuppressed adults with CMV antigenemia or viremia. Limited data in children suggest that safety and efficacy are similar to those in adults. Oral ganciclovir is less effective than intravenous (IV) ganciclovir because of lower bioavailability. The combination of oral ganciclovir and an intraocular implant that releases ganciclovir is efficacious in adults with CMV retinitis, but data in children are not available. Although ganciclovir has been used to treat some congenitally infected infants, it is not recommended routinely because of insufficient efficacy data. One study of ganciclovir therapy of congenitally infected newborn infants with central nervous system (CNS) disease suggested that treatment decreases progression of hearing impairment. However, because of the potential toxicity of long-term ganciclovir therapy, additional study is necessary before a recommendation can be made. In stem cell transplant recipients, the combination of Immune Globulin Intravenous (or CMV Immune Globulin Intravenous) and ganciclovir administered intravenously has been reported to be synergistic in treatment of CMV pneumonia. Valganciclovir and foscarnet also have been approved for treatment and maintenance of CMV retinitis in adults with acquired immunodeficiency syndrome (AIDS) (see Antiviral Drugs, p 785). Oral valganciclovir is a prodrug of ganciclovir that achieves plasma concentrations similar to those after IV administration of ganciclovir and generally has replaced oral ganciclovir. Foscarnet is more toxic but may be advantageous for some patients with HIV infection, including people with disease caused by ganciclovir-resistant virus or people who are unable to tolerate ganciclovir. Cidofovir is efficacious for maintenance therapy of CMV retinitis in adults with AIDS and CMV retinitis, but cidofovir has not been studied in children and is nephrotoxic. Fomivirsen is approved by the US Food and Drug Administration (FDA) for intraocular (intravitreal) treatment of CMV retinitis in HIV-infected adults who cannot tolerate or have not responded to other drugs.

Cytomegalovirus disease in HIV-infected patients is not cured by currently available antiviral agents. Chronic suppressive therapy should be administered to HIV-infected patients with a history of CMV disease to prevent recurrence. Treatment with highly active antiretroviral therapy (HAART) has decreased severity significantly. For children with CMV disease, no data are available to guide decisions concerning discontinuing secondary prophylaxis (chronic maintenance therapy) when CD4+ T-lymphocyte count has increased in response to HAART.

ISOLATION OF THE HOSPITALIZED PATIENT: Standard precautions are recommended.

CONTROL MEASURES:

CARE OF EXPOSED PEOPLE. When caring for children, hand hygiene, particularly after changing diapers, is advised to decrease transmission of CMV. Because asymptomatic excretion of CMV is common in people of all ages, a child with congenital CMV infection should not be treated differently from other children.

Although unrecognized exposure to people who are shedding CMV is likely to be common, concern arises when immunocompromised patients or nonimmune pregnant women or health care professionals are exposed to patients with clinically recognizable CMV infection. Standard precautions should be sufficient to interrupt transmission of CMV (See Infection Control for Hospitalized Children, p 153).

CHILD CARE (SEE ALSO CHILDREN IN OUT-OF-HOME CHILD CARE, P 130). Educational programs about the epidemiology of CMV, its potential risks, and appropriate hygienic measures to minimize occupationally acquired infection should be provided for female workers in child care centers. Risk seems to be greatest for child care personnel who provide care for children younger than 2 years of age. Routine serologic screening of staff at child care centers for antibody to CMV is not recommended.

IMMUNOPROPHYLAXIS. Cytomegalovirus Immune Globulin Intravenous has been developed for prophylaxis of disease in seronegative transplant recipients. Cytomegalovirus Immune Globulin Intravenous seems to be moderately effective in kidney and liver transplant recipients. Results of studies of its use in prevention of CMV transmission to newborn infants are promising. Evaluation of investigational vaccines in healthy volunteers and renal transplant recipients is in progress.

PREVENTION OF TRANSMISSION BY BLOOD TRANSFUSION. Transmission of CMV by blood transfusion to newborn infants or other compromised hosts virtually has been eliminated by the use of CMV antibody-negative donors, by freezing red blood cells in glycerol before administration, by removal of the buffy coat, or by filtration to remove white blood cells.

PREVENTION OF TRANSMISSION BY HUMAN MILK. Pasteurization or freezing of donated human milk can decrease the likelihood of CMV transmission. If fresh donated milk is needed for infants born to CMV antibody-negative mothers, providing these infants with milk from only CMV antibody-negative women should be considered. For further information on human milk banks, see Human Milk (p 123).

PREVENTION OF TRANSMISSION IN TRANSPLANT RECIPIENTS. Cytomegalovirus antibody-negative recipients of tissue from CMV-seropositive donors are at high risk of CMV disease. If such circumstances cannot be avoided, administration of oral ganciclovir is beneficial for decreasing this risk. Administration of valganciclovir for CMV prophylaxis in heart, kidney, and kidney-pancreas transplant recipients at high risk was approved by the FDA, but valganciclovir has not been approved by the FDA for use in liver transplant recipients. Treatment of transplant recipients with acyclovir or ganciclovir at the onset of CMV infection may prevent serious CMV disease.

Diphtheria

CLINICAL MANIFESTATIONS: Respiratory diphtheria usually occurs as membranous nasopharyngitis or obstructive laryngotracheitis. Local infections are associated with a low-grade fever and gradual onset of manifestations over 1 to 2 days. Less commonly, diphtheria presents as cutaneous, vaginal, conjunctival, or otic infection. Cutaneous diphtheria is more common in tropical areas and among the urban homeless. Serious complications of diphtheria include severe neck swelling (bull neck) accompanying upper airway obstruction caused by extensive membrane formation, myocarditis, and peripheral neuropathies.

ETIOLOGY: Diphtheria is caused by toxigenic strains of *Corynebacterium diphtheriae* and, rarely, *Corynebacterium ulcerans*. *Corynebacterium diphtheriae* is an irregularly staining, gram-positive, nonspore-forming, nonmotile, pleomorphic bacillus with 4 biotypes (mitis, intermedius, belfanti, and gravis). All biotypes of *C diphtheriae* may be either toxigenic or nontoxigenic. Toxigenic strains express an exotoxin that consists of an enzymatically active A domain and a binding B domain, which promotes the entry of A into the cell. The toxin gene, *tox*, is carried by a family of related corynebacteria phages. The toxin inhibits protein synthesis in all cells, including myocardial, renal, and peripheral nerve cells, resulting in myocarditis, acute tubular necrosis, and delayed peripheral nerve conduction. Nontoxigenic strains of *C diphtheriae* can cause sore throat and other invasive infections, including endocarditis.

EPIDEMIOLOGY: Humans are the sole reservoir of *C diphtheriae*. The organisms are spread by respiratory droplets and/or by contact with discharges from skin lesions. In untreated people, organisms can be present in discharges from the nose and throat and from eye and skin lesions for 2 to 6 weeks after infection. Patients treated with an appropriate antimicrobial agent usually are communicable for fewer than 4 days. Transmission results from intimate contact with patients or carriers, particularly people who travel to areas where diphtheria is endemic and people who come into close contact with travelers from such areas; rarely, fomites and raw milk or milk products can serve as vehicles of transmission. Severe disease occurs more often in people who are not immunized or are immunized inadequately. Fully immunized people may be asymptomatic carriers or have mild sore throat. The incidence of respiratory diphtheria is greatest during autumn and winter, but summer epidemics can occur in warm climates in which skin infections are prevalent. After 1990, epidemic diphtheria occurred throughout the newly independent states of the former Soviet Union, including Russia, the Ukraine, and the central Asian republics, with case-fatality rates ranging from 3% to 23%.

The **incubation period** usually is 2 to 7 days but occasionally is longer.

DIAGNOSTIC TESTS: Specimens for culture should be obtained from the nose or throat or any mucosal or cutaneous lesion. Material should be obtained from beneath the membrane, or a portion of the membrane itself should be submitted for culture. Because special tellurite medium is required for isolation, laboratory personnel should be notified that *C diphtheriae* is suspected. In remote areas, specimens collected for culture can be placed in silica gel packs or any transport medium or sterile container and transported to a reference laboratory for culture. When *C diphtheriae* is recovered, the strain should be tested for toxigenicity at a laboratory recommended by state and local authorities. All *C diphtheriae* isolates should be sent through the state health department to the Centers for Disease Control and Prevention (CDC).

TREATMENT:

   ANTITOXIN. Because the condition of patients with diphtheria may deteriorate rapidly, a single dose of equine antitoxin should be administered on the basis of clinical diagnosis, even before culture results are available. To neutralize toxin as rapidly as possible, the preferred route of administration is intravenous. Before intravenous administration of antitoxin, tests for sensitivity to horse serum should be performed, initially with a scratch test of a 1:1000 dilution of antitoxin in saline solution followed by an intradermal test if the scratch test result is negative (see Sensitivity Tests for Reactions to Animal Sera, p 61). If the patient is sensitive to equine antitoxin, desensitization is necessary (see Desensitization to Animal Sera, p 62). Allergic reactions to horse serum can be expected in 5% to 20% of patients. The site and size of the diphtheria membrane, the degree of toxic effects, and the duration of illness are guides for estimating the dose of antitoxin; the presence of soft, diffuse cervical lymphadenitis suggests moderate to severe toxin absorption. Suggested dose ranges are: pharyngeal or laryngeal disease of 48 hours' duration or less, 20 000 to 40 000 U; nasopharyngeal lesions, 40 000 to 60 000 U; extensive disease of 3 or more days' duration or diffuse swelling of the neck, 80 000 to 120 000 U. Antitoxin probably is of no value for cutaneous disease, but some experts recommend 20 000 to 40 000 U of antitoxin, because toxic sequelae have been reported. Antitoxin can be obtained from the CDC (see Directory of Resources, p 839).* Although Immune Globulin Intravenous preparations may contain variable amounts of antibodies to diphtheria toxin, use of Immune Globulin Intravenous for therapy of cutaneous or respiratory diphtheria has not been approved or evaluated for efficacy.

ANTIMICROBIAL THERAPY. Erythromycin given orally or parenterally for 14 days, penicillin G given intramuscularly or intravenously for 14 days, or penicillin G procaine given intramuscularly for 14 days constitute acceptable therapy. Antimicrobial therapy is required to stop toxin production, to eradicate *C diphtheriae*, and to prevent transmission but is not a substitute for antitoxin, which is the primary therapy. Elimination of the organism should be documented 24 hours after completion of treatment by 2 consecutive negative cultures from specimens taken 24 hours apart.

IMMUNIZATION. Active immunization against diphtheria should be undertaken during convalescence from diphtheria; disease does not necessarily confer immunity.

CUTANEOUS DIPHTHERIA. Thorough cleansing of the lesion with soap and water and administration of an appropriate antimicrobial agent for 10 days are recommended.

CARRIERS. If not immunized, carriers should receive active immunization promptly, and measures should be taken to ensure completion of the immunization schedule. If a carrier has been immunized previously but has not received a booster within 5 years, a booster dose of a vaccine containing diphtheria toxoid (DTaP, Tdap, DT, or Td, depending on age) should be given. Carriers should be given oral erythromycin or penicillin G for 10 to 14 days or a single intramuscular dose of penicillin G benzathine (600 000 U for children weighing <30 kg and 1.2 million U for children weighing ≥30 kg and adults). Two follow-up cultures should be obtained after completing antibiotic treatment to ensure detection of relapse, which occurs in as many as 20% of patients treated with erythromycin. The first culture should be obtained 24 hours after completing treatment. If results of cultures are positive, an additional 10-day course of oral erythromycin should be given, and follow-up cultures should be performed again. Erythromycin-resistant strains have been identified, but their epidemiologic significance has not been determined. Fluoroquinolones, rifampin, clarithromycin, and azithromycin have good in vitro activity and may be better tolerated than erythromycin, but they have not been evaluated in clinical infection or in carriers.

ISOLATION OF THE HOSPITALIZED PATIENT: In addition to standard precautions, droplet precautions are recommended for patients and carriers with pharyngeal diph-

---

* Centers for Disease Control and Prevention. Notice to readers: availability of diphtheria antitoxin through an Investigational New Drug protocol. *MMWR Morb Mortal Wkly Rep.* 2004;59:413 for latest information on obtaining diphtheria antitoxin from the CDC.

theria until 2 cultures from both the nose and throat collected 24 hours after completing antimicrobial treatment are negative for *C diphtheriae*. Contact precautions are recommended for patients with cutaneous diphtheria until 2 cultures of skin lesions taken at least 24 hours apart and 24 hours after cessation of antimicrobial therapy are negative.

CONTROL MEASURES:

CARE OF EXPOSED PEOPLE.
Whenever diphtheria is suspected strongly or proven, local public health officials should be notified promptly. Management of exposed people is based on individual circumstances, including immunization status and likelihood of compliance with follow-up and prophylaxis. The following are recommended:

- Close contacts of a person suspected to have diphtheria should be identified promptly. Contact tracing should begin in the household and usually can be limited to household members and other people with a history of direct, habitual close contact (including kissing or sexual contacts), health care staff exposed to nasopharyngeal secretions, people sharing utensils or kitchen facilities, and people taking care of children.
- For close contacts, *regardless of their immunization status*, the following measures should be taken: (1) surveillance for 7 days for evidence of disease; (2) culture for *C diphtheriae;* and (3) antimicrobial prophylaxis with oral erythromycin (40–50 mg/kg per day for 10 days, maximum 2 g/day) or a single intramuscular injection of penicillin G benzathine (600 000 U for children weighing <30 kg and 1.2 million U for children weighing ≥30 kg and adults). The efficacy of antimicrobial prophylaxis is presumed but not proven. Follow-up pharyngeal cultures should be obtained from contacts proven to be carriers after completion of therapy (see Carriers, p 279). If cultures are positive, an additional 10-day course of erythromycin should be given, and follow-up specimens for cultures should be performed.
- Asymptomatic, previously immunized close contacts should receive a booster dose of an age-appropriate diphtheria toxoid-containing vaccine (DTaP [or DT], Tdap, or Td) if they have not received a booster dose of diphtheria toxoid within 5 years. Children in need of their fourth dose should be immunized.
- Asymptomatic close contacts who are not immunized fully (defined as having had fewer than 3 doses of diphtheria toxoid) or whose immunization status is not known should be immunized with an age-appropriate diphtheria toxoid-containing vaccine (DTaP [or DT], Tdap, or Td).
- Contacts who cannot be kept under surveillance should receive penicillin G benzathine but not erythromycin, because adherence to an oral regimen is less likely, and a dose of DTaP, Tdap, DT, or Td vaccine, depending on the person's age and immunization history.

The use of equine diphtheria antitoxin in unimmunized close contacts is not recommended, because there is no evidence that antitoxin provides additional benefit for contacts who have received antimicrobial prophylaxis.

IMMUNIZATION.
Universal immunization with a diphtheria toxoid-containing vaccine is the only effective control measure. For all indications, diphtheria immunization is administered intramuscularly with tetanus toxoid-containing vaccines and,

when indicated, with pertussis-containing vaccines. The schedules for immunization against diphtheria are presented in the chapter on tetanus (see Tetanus, p 648). The value of diphtheria toxoid immunization is proven by the rarity of disease in countries in which high rates of immunization with diphtheria toxoid have been achieved. Fewer than 5 cases have been reported annually in the United States in recent years. The decreased frequency of endogenous exposure to the organism in countries with high childhood coverage rates implies decreased boosting of immunity. Therefore, ensuring continuing immunity requires regular booster injections of diphtheria toxoid (as Td vaccine) every 10 years after completion of the initial immunization series.

Haemophilus influenzae, pneumococcal, and meningococcal conjugate vaccines containing diphtheria toxoid (eg, PRP-D) or CRM_{197} protein, a nontoxic variant of diphtheria toxin (eg, HbOC, pneumococcal conjugate vaccines), are not substitutes for diphtheria toxoid immunization.

Immunization for children from 2 months of age to the seventh birthday (see Fig 1.1, p 26, and Table 1.7, p 28) routinely consists of 5 doses of diphtheria and tetanus toxoid-containing vaccines (see Tetanus, p 648). This typically is accomplished with DTaP vaccine. Immunization against diphtheria and tetanus for children younger than 7 years of age in whom pertussis immunization is contraindicated (see Pertussis, p 498) should be accomplished with DT instead of DTaP vaccine (see Tetanus, p 648).

Other recommendations for diphtheria immunization, including those for older children, can be found in the chapter on tetanus (see Tetanus, p 648).

- When children and adults require tetanus toxoid for wound management (see Tetanus, p 648), the use of preparations containing diphtheria toxoid (DTaP, Tdap, DT, or Td vaccine as appropriate for age or specific contraindication to pertussis immunization) is preferred to tetanus toxoid and will help to maintain diphtheria and, when appropriate, pertussis immunity.
- Travelers to countries with endemic or epidemic diphtheria should have their diphtheria immunization status reviewed and updated when necessary.

PRECAUTIONS AND CONTRAINDICATIONS. See Pertussis (p 498) and Tetanus (p 648).

Ehrlichia and *Anaplasma* Infections
(Human Ehrlichioses)

CLINICAL MANIFESTATIONS: Human ehrlichioses in the United States are attributable to at least 3 distinct pathogens: *Ehrlichia chaffeensis* (human monocytotrophic ehrlichiosis [HME]), *Anaplasma phagocytophilum* (human granulocytotrophic anaplasmosis [HGA], formerly *Ehrlichia phagocytophila*), and *Ehrlichia ewingii* (*Ehrlichia ewingii* ehrlichiosis) (Table 3.4, p 282). These 3 infections have different causes but similar signs, symptoms, and clinical courses. All are acute, systemic, febrile illnesses that are similar clinically to Rocky Mountain spotted fever but differ from Rocky Mountain spotted fever in that infections often demonstrate (1) leukopenia, absolute lymphopenia, and neutropenia in HME; (2) neutropenia in HGA; (3) anemia; (4) hepatitis; (5) lack of vasculitis; and (6) rash less commonly. The febrile illness often is accompanied by one or more systemic manifestations, including headache, chills or rigors, malaise, myalgia, arthralgia, nausea, vomiting, anorexia, and acute weight loss. Rash is variable in appearance and location, typically develops approximately 1 week after onset of illness, and occurs only in approximately 60% of children and 25% of adults with reported *E chaffeensis* infection and less than 10% of people with *A phagocytophilum* infection. Diarrhea, abdominal pain, cough, or change in mental status occur less frequently. More severe manifestations of these diseases include pulmonary infiltrates, bone marrow hypoplasia, respiratory failure, encephalopathy, meningitis, disseminated intravascular coagulation, spontaneous hemorrhage, and renal failure. These agents do not cause the vasculitis or endothelial damage characteristic of rickettsial diseases. Anemia, hyponatremia, thrombocytopenia, increased serum hepatic transaminase concentrations, and cerebrospinal fluid abnormalities (ie, pleocytosis with a predominance of lymphocytes and increased total protein concentration) are common. Symptoms typically last 1 to 2 weeks, and recovery generally occurs without sequelae; however, reports suggest the occurrence of neurologic complications in some children after severe disease. Fatal infections have been reported. Typically, illness attributable to *E chaffeensis* is more severe than that caused by *A phagocytophilum*. Secondary or opportunistic infections may occur in severe illness, resulting in possible delayed recognition of ehrlichiosis and appropriate antimicrobial treatment. People with underlying immunosuppression are at greater risk of severe disease.

ETIOLOGY: In the United States, human ehrlichioses may be caused by at least 3 distinct species of obligate intracellular bacteria. Human monocytotrophic ehrlichiosis results from infection with *E chaffeensis*. Human granulocytotrophic anaplasmosis is caused by *A phagocytophilum*, and *E ewingii* ehrlichiosis is caused by *E ewingii*. *Ehrlichia* and *Anaplasma* species are gram-negative cocci that measure 0.5 to 1.5 μm in diameter.

Table 3.4. Human Ehrlichioses and Anaplasmosis in the United States

Disease	Causal Agent	Major Target Cell	Tick Vector	Geographic Distribution
Human monocytotrophic ehrlichiosis (HME)	*Ehrlichia chaffeensis*	Macrophages	Lone star tick *(Amblyomma americanum)*, American dog tick *(Dermacentor variabilis)*, Western black-legged tick *(Ixodes pacificus)*	Predominately southeast, south central, and Midwest states
Human granulocytotrophic anaplasmosis (HGA)	*Anaplasma phagocytophilum*	Granulocytes	Black-legged or deer tick *(Ixodes scapularis)* or Western black-legged tick *(I pacificus)*	Northeastern and north central states and northern California
Ehrlichia ewingii ehrlichiosis	*Ehrlichia ewingii*	Granulocytes	Lone star tick *(A americanum)*, American dog tick *(D variabilis)*	Southeast, south central, and Midwest states

EPIDEMIOLOGY: Most *E chaffeensis* infections occur in people from the southeastern and south central United States, but a small number of cases have been described from other areas. Ehrlichial infections caused by *E chaffeensis* and *E ewingii* are associated with the bite of the lone star tick *(Amblyomma americanum)*. Cases of ehrlichial infection occurring in states beyond the current geographic distribution of *A americanum* suggest rare transmission by additional tick species, including *Dermacentor variabilis*. However, the distribution of *A americanum* is expanding. Most cases of *A phagocytophilum* infection have been reported in the north central and northeastern United States, particularly Wisconsin, Minnesota, Connecticut, and New York, but cases in many other states, including the West Coast, have been reported. *Anaplasma phagocytophilum* is transmitted by the black-legged or deer tick *(Ixodes scapularis)*, which also is the vector of *Borrelia burgdorferi* (the agent of Lyme disease). Various mammalian reservoirs for the agents of human ehrlichioses have been identified, including white-tailed deer, white-footed mice, and *Neotoma* woodrats. In the western United States, *Ixodes pacificus* is the main vector for *A phagocytophilum*. Compared with patients with Rocky Mountain spotted fever (see p 570), reported cases of symptomatic ehrlichioses characteristically are in older individuals, with age-specific incidences greatest in those older than 40 years of age. However, recent seroprevalence data indicate that infection with *E chaffensis* or a closely related bacterium is common in children. Most human infections occur between April and September, and the peak occurrence is from May through July. The incidence of reported cases seems to be increasing. Coinfections of anaplasmosis with other tickborne diseases, including babesiosis and Lyme disease, are recognized.

The **incubation period** of human ehrlichiosis typically is 5 to 10 days after a tick bite (median, 9 days).

DIAGNOSTIC TESTS: The Centers for Disease Control and Prevention (CDC) defines a confirmed case of human ehrlichioses or anaplasmosis as isolation of *Ehrlichia* or *Anaplasma* organisms from blood or cerebrospinal fluid, a fourfold or greater change in antibody titer by indirect immunofluorescent antibody (IFA) assay between acute and convalescent serum specimens (ideally collected 2 to 3 weeks apart), polymerase chain reaction (PCR) assay amplification of specific DNA from a clinical specimen, or detection of intraleukocytoplasmic microcolonies of bacteria (morulae) in conjunction with a single IFA titer of ≥64. A probable case is defined as a single IFA titer of ≥64 or the presence of morulae within infected leukocytes. Specific antigens are available for the serologic testing of *E chaffeensis* and *A phagocytophilum* infections. *Ehrlichia ewingii* shares some antigens with *E chaffeensis*, so most cases of *E ewingii* ehrlichiosis can be diagnosed using *E chaffeensis* antigens. These tests are available in reference laboratories, in some commercial laboratories and state health departments, and at the CDC. Examination of peripheral blood smears to detect morulae in peripheral blood monocytes or granulocytes is insensitive. Use of polymerase chain reaction assay to amplify nucleic acid from peripheral blood of patients in the acute phase of ehrlichiosis seems sensitive, specific, and promising for early diagnosis. Both PCR and isolation can be conducted on appropriate clinical samples sent to the CDC.

TREATMENT: Doxycycline is the drug of choice for treatment of human ehrlichioses and anaplasmosis. The recommended dosage of doxycycline is 4 mg/kg per day, divided every 12 hours, intravenously or orally (maximum 100 mg/dose). Ehrlichioses and anaplasmosis may be severe or fatal in untreated patients, and initiation of therapy early in the course of disease helps minimize complications of illness. Failure to respond to doxycycline within the first 3 days should suggest infection with an agent other than *Ehrlichia* or *Anaplasma* species. Despite concerns regarding dental staining with tetracycline-class antimicrobial agents in young children (see Antimicrobial Agents and Related Therapy, p 735), doxycycline provides superior therapy for this potentially life-threatening disease. Available data suggest that courses of doxycycline ≤14 days do not cause significant discoloration of permanent teeth. Treatment should continue for at least 3 days after defervescence for a minimum total course of 5 to 10 days; unequivocal evidence of clinical improvement generally will be evident by 1 week. Severe or complicated disease may require longer treatment courses.

The clinical manifestations and geographic distributions of ehrlichioses and Rocky Mountain spotted fever overlap. As with other rickettsial diseases, when a presumptive diagnosis of ehrlichiosis is made, doxycycline should be started.

ISOLATION OF THE HOSPITALIZED PATIENT: Standard precautions are recommended.

CONTROL MEASURES: Specific measures focus on limiting exposures to ticks and are similar to those for Rocky Mountain spotted fever and other tickborne diseases (see Prevention of Tickborne Infections, p 195). Prophylactic administration of doxycycline after a tick bite is not indicated because of the low risk of infection. For additional information, see **www.cdc.gov/NCIDOD/DVRD/ehrlichia**.

Enterovirus (Nonpoliovirus) Infections
(Group A and B Coxsackieviruses, Echoviruses, and Numbered Enteroviruses)

CLINICAL MANIFESTATIONS: Nonpolio enteroviruses are responsible for significant and frequent illnesses in infants and children and result in protean clinical manifestations. The most common manifestation is nonspecific febrile illness, which, in young infants, may lead to evaluation for bacterial sepsis. Neonates who acquire infection without maternal antibody are at risk of severe disease with a high mortality rate. Manifestations can include the following: (1) respiratory: common cold, pharyngitis, herpangina, stomatitis, pneumonia, and pleurodynia; (2) skin: exanthem; (3) neurologic: aseptic meningitis, encephalitis, and paralysis; (4) gastrointestinal: vomiting, diarrhea, abdominal pain, and hepatitis; (5) eye: acute hemorrhagic conjunctivitis; and (6) heart: myopericarditis. Although each of these findings can be caused by several different enteroviruses, some associations between specific virus serotypes and disease are noteworthy. These associations include coxsackievirus A16 and enterovirus 71 with hand-foot-and-mouth disease, coxsackievirus A24 variant and enterovirus 70 with acute hemorrhagic conjunctivitis, enterovirus 71 with brainstem encephalitis and polio-like paralysis, and coxsackieviruses B1 through B5 with pleurodynia and myopericarditis.

Patients with humoral immune deficiencies can have persistent central nervous system infections and/or a dermatomyositis-like syndrome lasting for several months or more.

ETIOLOGY: The nonpolio enteroviruses are RNA viruses, which include 24 group-A coxsackieviruses, 6 group-B coxsackieviruses, 34 echoviruses, and 5 enteroviruses.

EPIDEMIOLOGY: Enterovirus infections are common and are spread by fecal-oral and respiratory routes and from mother to infant in the peripartum period. Enteroviruses may survive on environmental surfaces for periods long enough to allow transmission from fomites. Infections and clinical attack rates typically are highest in young children, and infections occur more frequently in tropical areas and when hygiene is poor. In temperate climates, enteroviral infections are most common during summer and early fall, but seasonal patterns are less evident in the tropics. Fecal viral shedding can continue for several weeks after onset of infection, but respiratory tract shedding usually is limited to a week or less. Viral shedding can occur without signs of clinical illness.

The usual **incubation period** is 3 to 6 days, except for acute hemorrhagic conjunctivitis, in which the incubation period is 24 to 72 hours.

DIAGNOSTIC TESTS: Isolation of enteroviruses in cell culture is the standard diagnostic method. In general, stool, rectal swab, and throat specimens produce the highest yield, but enteroviruses also may be recovered from urine and blood during the acute illness and from cerebrospinal fluid (CSF) when meningitis is present. Group B coxsackieviruses and echoviruses and some group A coxsackieviruses can be detected by cell culture, but many group A coxsackieviruses grow poorly or not at all in vitro. The serotype of enterovirus isolated in cell culture may be identified by serologic methods or by genomic sequencing at reference laboratories in cases of special clinical interest or for epidemiologic purposes. Polymerase chain reaction (PCR) assay for detection of enterovirus RNA is available at many reference and commercial laboratories for CSF specimens. Polymerase chain reaction assay is more rapid and more sensitive than cell culture and can detect all enteroviruses, including enteroviruses that are difficult to culture, but lacks the ability to further characterize enteroviruses according to type. Serotype-specific PCR assays have been developed for some enteroviruses but are not available widely. The diagnosis of acute infection with a known enterovirus serotype can be determined by demonstration of a change in neutralizing antibody titer between acute and convalescent serum specimens, but this method is relatively insensitive, expensive, and available only at reference laboratories. Commercially available serologic assays based on an enzyme immunoassay format are standardized poorly and lack specificity.

TREATMENT: No specific therapy is available. Immune Globulin Intravenous (IGIV) may be beneficial for chronic enteroviral meningoencephalitis in immunodeficient patients. Immune Globulin Intravenous also has been used in life-threatening neonatal infections and cases of suspected viral myocarditis, although there is little evidence of efficacy for these uses.

ISOLATION OF THE HOSPITALIZED PATIENT: In addition to standard precautions, contact precautions are indicated for infants and young children for the duration of illness.

CONTROL MEASURES: Particular attention should be given to hand hygiene, especially after diaper changing.

Epstein-Barr Virus Infections
(Infectious Mononucleosis)

CLINICAL MANIFESTATIONS: Infectious mononucleosis manifests typically as fever, exudative pharyngitis, lymphadenopathy, hepatosplenomegaly, and atypical lymphocytosis. The spectrum of diseases is wide, ranging from asymptomatic to fatal infection. Infections commonly are unrecognized in infants and young children. Rash can occur and is more common in patients treated with ampicillin as well as with other penicillins. Central nervous system (CNS) complications include aseptic meningitis, encephalitis, myelitis, optic neuritis, cranial nerve palsies, transverse myelitis, and Guillain-Barré syndrome. Hematologic complications include splenic rupture, thrombocytopenia, agranulocytosis, hemolytic anemia, and hemophagocytic syndrome. Pneumonia, orchitis, and myocarditis are observed infrequently. Replication of Epstein-Barr virus (EBV) in B-lymphocytes and the resulting lymphoproliferation usually is inhibited by natural killer cells, antibody-dependent cell cytotoxicity, and T-lymphocyte cytotoxic responses. Fatal disseminated infection or B-lymphocyte or T-lymphocyte lymphomas can occur in children with no detectable immunologic abnormality as well as in children with congenital or acquired cellular immune deficiencies.

Epstein-Barr virus is associated with several other distinct disorders, including X-linked lymphoproliferative syndrome, post-transplantation lymphoproliferative disorders, Burkitt lymphoma, nasopharyngeal carcinoma, and undifferentiated B- or T-lymphocyte lymphomas of the CNS. X-linked lymphoproliferative syndrome occurs in people with an inherited, maternally derived, recessive genetic defect in signaling lymphocytic activation molecule-associated protein (SAP) and is characterized by several phenotypic expressions, including occurrence of infectious mononucleosis early in life among boys, nodular B-lymphocyte lymphomas often with CNS involvement, and profound hypogammaglobulinemia.

Epstein-Barr virus-associated lymphoproliferative disorders result in a number of complex syndromes in patients who are immunocompromised, such as transplant recipients or people infected with human immunodeficiency virus (HIV). The highest incidence of these disorders occurs in liver and heart transplant recipients, in whom the proliferative states range from benign lymph node hypertrophy to monoclonal lymphomas. Other EBV syndromes are of greater importance outside the United States, including Burkitt lymphoma (a B-lymphocyte tumor), found primarily in Central Africa, and nasopharyngeal carcinoma, found in Southeast Asia and the Inuit population. Epstein-Barr virus also has been associated with Hodgkin disease (B-lymphocyte tumor), non-Hodgkin lymphomas (B- and T-lymphocyte), gastric carcinoma "lymphoepitheliomas," and a variety of common epithelial malignancies.

Chronic fatigue syndrome is not related specifically to EBV infection; however, a postinfectious fatigue state follows approximately 10% of cases of classic infectious mononucleosis and other infectious diseases.

ETIOLOGY: Epstein-Barr virus is a gammaherpesvirus of the *Lymphocryptovirus* genus and is the most common cause of infectious mononucleosis.

EPIDEMIOLOGY: Humans are the only source of EBV. Close personal contact usually is required for transmission. The virus is viable in saliva for several hours outside the body, but the role of fomites in transmission is unknown. Epstein-Barr virus also is transmitted occasionally by blood transfusion. Infection commonly is contracted early in life, particularly among members of lower socioeconomic groups, in which intrafamilial spread is common. Endemic infectious mononucleosis is common in group settings of adolescents, such as in educational institutions. No seasonal pattern has been documented. Respiratory tract viral excretion can occur for many months after infection, and asymptomatic carriage is common. Intermittent excretion is lifelong. The period of communicability is indeterminate.

The **incubation period** of infectious mononucleosis is estimated to be 30 to 50 days.

DIAGNOSTIC TESTS: Isolation of EBV from oropharyngeal secretions by culture in cord blood cells is possible, but techniques for performing this procedure usually are not available in routine diagnostic laboratories, and viral isolation does not necessarily indicate acute infection. Detection by DNA PCR in serum, plasma, and tissue and RNA PCR in lymphoid cells or tissue is available commercially and may be useful in evaluation of immunocompromised patients and in complex clinical problems. Routine diagnosis depends on serologic testing. Nonspecific tests for heterophil antibody, including the Paul-Bunnell test and slide agglutination reaction test, are available most commonly. The heterophil antibody response primarily is immunoglobulin (Ig) M, which appears during the first 2 weeks of illness and gradually disappears over a 6-month period. The results of heterophil antibody tests often are negative in children younger than 4 years of age with EBV infection, but they identify approximately 85% of cases of classic infectious mononucleosis in older children and adults during the second week of illness. An absolute increase in atypical lymphocytes during the second week of illness with infectious mononucleosis is a characteristic but nonspecific finding. However, the finding of >10% atypical lymphocytes together with a positive heterophil antibody test result is considered diagnostic of acute infection.

Multiple specific serologic antibody tests for EBV infection are available in diagnostic virology laboratories (see Table 3.5, p 288). The most commonly performed test is for antibody against the viral capsid antigen (VCA). Because IgG antibody against VCA occurs in high titers early after onset of infection and persists for life, testing of acute and convalescent serum specimens for anti-VCA may not be useful for establishing the presence of active infection. Testing for IgM anti-VCA antibody and for antibodies against early antigen is useful for identifying active and recent infections. Because serum antibody against EBV nuclear antigen (EBNA) is not present until several weeks to months after onset of infection, a positive anti-EBNA antibody test excludes an active primary infection. These interpretations are based on quantitative immunofluorescent antibody tests performed during various stages of mononucleosis and its resolution. Many laboratories now use qualitative tests (optical density assays of specific protein-antibody reactions). These tests are sensitive, but they do not allow for identification of particularly elevated antibody concentrations that may be useful in identifying specific disease associations.

Serologic tests for EBV are useful particularly for evaluating patients who have heterophil-negative infectious mononucleosis. Testing for other viral agents, especially cytomegalovirus and HIV, also may be indicated for some of these patients. Diagnosis

Table 3.5. Serum Epstein-Barr Virus (EBV) Antibodies in EBV Infection

Infection	VCA IgG	VCA IgM	EA (D)	EBNA
No previous infection	−	−	−	−
Acute infection	+	+	+ / −	−
Recent infection	+	+ / −	+ / −	+ / −
Past infection	+	−	+ / −	+

VCA IgG indicates immunoglobulin (Ig) G class antibody to viral capsid antigen; VCA IgM, IgM class antibody to VCA; EA (D), early antigen diffuse staining; and EBNA, EBV nuclear antigen.

of the entire range of EBV-associated illness requires use of molecular and antibody techniques, particularly for patients with immune deficiencies.

TREATMENT: Contact sports should be avoided until the patient is recovered fully from infectious mononucleosis and the spleen no longer is palpable. Patients suspected to have infectious mononucleosis should not be given ampicillin or amoxicillin, which cause nonallergic morbilliform rashes in a high proportion of patients with mononucleosis. Although therapy with short-course corticosteroids may have a beneficial effect on acute symptoms, because of potential adverse effects, their use should be considered only for patients with marked tonsillar inflammation with impending airway obstruction, massive splenomegaly, myocarditis, hemolytic anemia, or hemophagocytic syndrome. The dosage of prednisone usually is 1 mg/kg per day, orally (maximum 20 mg/day), for 7 days with subsequent tapering. Life-threatening hemophagocytic syndrome has been treated with cytotoxic agents and immunomodulators, including cyclosporin and corticosteroids. Although acyclovir has in vitro antiviral activity against EBV, therapy is of no proven value in EBV lymphoproliferative syndromes limited to cells with latent viral gene expression. Decreasing immunosuppressive therapy is beneficial for patients with EBV-induced post-transplant lymphoproliferative disorders, whereas an antiviral drug, such as acyclovir or valacyclovir, sometimes is used in patients with active replicating EBV infection with or without passive antibody therapy provided by IGIV.

ISOLATION OF THE HOSPITALIZED PATIENT: Standard precautions are recommended.

CONTROL MEASURES: Patients with a recent history of EBV infection or an illness similar to infectious mononucleosis should not donate blood or solid organs.

Escherichia coli and Other Gram-Negative Bacilli
(Septicemia and Meningitis in Neonates)

CLINICAL MANIFESTATIONS: Neonatal septicemia or meningitis caused by *Escherichia coli* and other gram-negative bacilli cannot be differentiated clinically from serious infections caused by other infectious agents. The first signs of sepsis can be subtle and similar to signs observed in noninfectious processes. Clinical signs of septicemia include fever, temperature instability, heart rate abnormalities, grunting respira-tions, apnea, cyanosis, lethargy, irritability, anorexia, vomiting, jaundice, hepatomegaly, abdominal distention, and diarrhea. Meningitis can occur without overt signs suggesting central nervous system involvement. Some gram-negative bacilli, such as *Citrobacter koseri*, *Enterobacter sakazakii*, and *Serratia marcescens*, are associ-ated with brain abscesses in infants with meningitis caused by these organisms.

ETIOLOGY: *Escherichia coli* strains with the K1 capsular polysaccharide antigen cause approximately 40% of cases of septicemia and 80% of cases of meningitis caused by *E coli*. Other important gram-negative bacilli causing neonatal septicemia include non-K1 strains of *E coli* and *Klebsiella* species, *Enterobacter* species, *Proteus* species, *Citrobacter* spe-cies, *Salmonella* species, *Pseudomonas* species, and *Serratia* species. Nonencapsulated strains of *Haemophilus influenzae* and anaerobic gram-negative bacilli are rare causes.

EPIDEMIOLOGY: The source of *E coli* and other gram-negative bacterial pathogens in neonatal infections often is the maternal genital tract. In addition, hospital acquisi-tion of gram-negative organisms through person-to-person transmission from nursery personnel and from nursery environmental sites, such as sinks, multiple-use solutions, countertops, and respiratory therapy equipment, has been documented, especially in preterm infants who require prolonged intensive care management. Predisposing fac-tors in neonatal gram-negative bacterial infections include maternal intrapartum infections, gestation <37 weeks, low birth weight, and prolonged rupture of mem-branes. Metabolic abnormalities, such as galactosemia, fetal hypoxia, and acidosis also have been implicated as predisposing factors. Neonates with defects in the integ-rity of skin or mucosa (eg, myelomeningocele) or abnormalities of gastrointestinal or genitourinary tracts are at increased risk of gram-negative bacterial infections. In intensive care nurseries, sophisticated systems for respiratory and metabolic support, invasive or surgical procedures, indwelling vascular lines, and the frequent use of antimicrobial agents enable selection and proliferation of strains of pathogenic gram-negative bacilli that are resistant to multiple antimicrobial agents.

Multiple mechanisms of resistance in gram-negative bacilli have been described and can be present simultaneously. Resistance caused by derepressed amp C chromo-somal extended-spectrum beta-lactamases (ESBL), primarily in *E coli* and *Klebsiella* species but reported in many other gram-negative species, have been reported to cause nursery outbreaks, especially in very low birth weight infants. Organisms that produce ESBL typically are resistant to penicillins, cephalosporins, and monobactams and often are resistant to aminoglycosides.

The **incubation period** is highly variable; time of onset of infection ranges from birth to several weeks after birth or longer in very low birth weight, preterm infants with prolonged hospitalizations.

DIAGNOSTIC TESTS: The diagnosis is established by growth of *E coli* or other gram-negative bacilli from blood, cerebrospinal fluid, or other usually sterile sites. Special laboratory procedures are required to recognize ESBL-producing gram-negative organisms.

TREATMENT:
- Initial empiric treatment for suspected bacterial septicemia or meningitis in neo-nates is ampicillin and an aminoglycoside. An alternative regimen of ampicillin

and an expanded-spectrum cephalosporin (such as cefotaxime) can be used, but rapid emergence of cephalosporin-resistant strains, especially *Enterobacter* species, *Klebsiella* species, and *Serratia* species, can occur when use is routine. Hence, routine use of an expanded-spectrum cephalosporin is not recommended unless gram-negative bacterial meningitis is suspected.

- The proportion of *E coli* infections with onset within 72 hours of life that are resistant to ampicillin has increased among very low birth weight infants. These *E coli* infections almost invariably are susceptible to gentamicin.

- Once the causative agent and its in vitro antimicrobial susceptibility pattern are known, nonmeningeal infections should be treated with ampicillin, an appropriate aminoglycoside, or an expanded-spectrum cephalosporin (such as cefotaxime). Many experts would treat nonmeningeal infections caused by *Enterobacter* species, *Serratia* species, or *Pseudomonas* species and some other less commonly occurring gram-negative bacilli with a beta-lactam antimicrobial agent and an aminoglycoside. Meningitis usually is treated with ampicillin (if the isolate is susceptible) or an expanded-spectrum cephalosporin in combination with an aminoglycoside. Expert advice from an infectious disease specialist can be helpful for management of meningitis.

- Expert advice from an infectious disease specialist can help in the management of ESBL-producing gram-negative infections in neonates. The empiric drug of choice for treatment of infections caused by ESBL-producing organisms is meropenem, for which there is limited experience in the neonate. Aminoglycosides or cefepime can be used if the organism is susceptible.

- Duration of therapy is based on clinical and bacteriologic response of the patient and the site(s) of infection; the usual duration of therapy for uncomplicated septicemia is 10 to 14 days, and for meningitis, the minimum duration is 21 days.

- A therapeutic role for Immune Globulin or other adjunctive therapies in septicemia or meningitis caused by *E coli* or other gram-negative organisms has not been established.

- All infants with meningitis should undergo careful follow-up examinations, including testing for hearing loss, neurologic abnormalities, and developmental milestones.

ISOLATION OF THE HOSPITALIZED PATIENT: Standard precautions are recommended. Exceptions include nursery epidemics, infants with *Salmonella* infection, and infants with infection caused by gram-negative bacilli that are resistant to multiple antimicrobial agents; in these situations, contact precautions are indicated.

CONTROL MEASURES: The physician director of the nursery and infection control personnel should be aware of pathogens causing infections in infants so that clusters of infections are recognized and investigated appropriately. Several cases of infection caused by the same genus and species of bacteria occurring in infants in physical proximity or caused by an unusual pathogen indicate the need for an epidemiologic investigation (see Infection Control for Hospitalized Children, p 153). Periodic review of the in vitro antimicrobial susceptibility patterns of clinically important bacterial isolates from newborn infants, especially infants in the intensive care nursery, can provide useful epidemiologic and therapeutic information.

Escherichia coli Diarrhea
(Including Hemolytic-Uremic Syndrome)

CLINICAL MANIFESTATIONS: At least 5 pathotypes of diarrhea-producing *Escherichia coli* strains have been identified. Clinical features of disease caused by each pathotype are summarized as follows (see also Table 3.6, p 292):

- Shiga toxin-producing *E coli* (STEC) organisms are associated with diarrhea, hemorrhagic colitis, hemolytic-uremic syndrome (HUS), and postdiarrheal thrombotic thrombocytopenic purpura (TTP). Shiga toxin-producing *E coli* O157:H7 is the prototype and the most virulent member of this *E coli* pathotype. Illness caused by STEC often begins as nonbloody diarrhea but usually progresses to diarrhea with visible or occult blood. Severe abdominal pain is typical; fever occurs in less than one third of cases. Severe infection can result in hemorrhagic colitis.
- Diarrhea caused by enteropathogenic *E coli* (EPEC) is watery and often is severe enough to result in dehydration and even death. Chronic EPEC diarrhea characteristically is persistent and leads to growth retardation. Illness occurs almost exclusively in neonates and children younger than 2 years of age and predominantly (but not exclusively) in resource-limited countries, either sporadically or in epidemics.
- Diarrhea caused by enterotoxigenic *E coli* (ETEC) is a brief (1–5 days), self-limited illness of moderate severity, typically with watery stools and abdominal cramps.
- Diarrhea caused by enteroinvasive *E coli* (EIEC) is similar clinically to infection caused by *Shigella* species. Although dysentery can occur, diarrhea usually is watery without blood or mucus. Patients often are febrile, and stools may contain leukocytes.
- Enteroaggregative *E coli* (EAEC) organisms cause watery diarrhea, predominantly in infants and young children in resource-limited countries, but all ages can be affected. Enteroaggregative *E coli* organisms have been associated with prolonged diarrhea (>14 days). Asymptomatic infection can be accompanied by a subclinical inflammatory enteritis, which can cause growth disturbances.

LATE SEQUELAE OF STEC INFECTION. Hemolytic-uremic syndrome is a serious sequela of STEC enteric infection and appears to occur more frequently in the United States with *E coli* O157:H7 than with other STEC serotypes. Hemolytic-uremic syndrome is defined by the triad of microangiopathic hemolytic anemia, thrombocytopenia, and acute renal dysfunction. Hemolytic-uremic syndrome occurs in 8% of children with *E coli* O157:H7 diarrhea and probably in very few adults. The illness is serious and develops during the 2 weeks after onset of diarrhea. Fifty percent of patients require dialysis, and 3% to 5% die. Thrombotic thrombocytopenic purpura occurs in adults, may follow STEC infection, and in addition to the manifestations of HUS, includes neurologic abnormalities and fever, may have a more gradual onset than HUS, and is part of a disease spectrum often designated as TTP-HUS. Shiga toxin-producing *E coli* disease in children can result in HUS and in adults can manifest as TTP. Children with diarrhea-associated HUS should be observed for diabetes mellitus during their acute illness, and consideration should be given to long-term screening of survivors for diabetes.

Table 3.6. Classification of *Escherichia coli* Associated With Diarrhea

E coli Pathotype	Epidemiology	Type of Diarrhea	Mechanism of Pathogenesis
Shiga toxin-producing (STEC)	Hemorrhagic colitis and hemolytic-uremic syndrome in all ages and postdiarrheal thrombotic thrombocytopenic purpura in adults	Bloody or nonbloody	Large bowel adherence and effacement (AE)
Enteropathogenic (EPEC)	Acute and chronic endemic and epidemic diarrhea in infants	Watery	Small bowel AE
Enterotoxigenic (ETEC)	Infantile diarrhea in resource-limited countries and traveler's diarrhea in all ages	Watery	Small bowel AE, heat stable/heat labile enterotoxin production
Enteroinvasive (EIEC)	Diarrhea with fever in all ages	Bloody or nonbloody; dysentery	Adherence, mucosal invasion and inflammation of large bowel
Enteroaggregative (EAEC)	Acute and chronic diarrhea in infants	Watery, occasionally bloody	Small and large bowel adherence, enterotoxin and cytotoxin production

ETIOLOGY: Each *E coli* pathotype has specific virulence characteristics, some of which are encoded on pathotype-specific plasmids. Each pathotype has a distinct set of somatic (O) and flagellar (H) antigens. Pathogenic characteristics are as follows:

- Illness caused by *E coli* O157:H7 occurs in a 2-step process. The intestinal phase is characterized by formation of the so-called attaching and effacing (AE) lesion, resulting in secretory diarrhea. This phase is followed by elaboration of Shiga toxin, a potent cytotoxin, one form of which also is elaborated by *Shigella dysenteriae* 1. The action of Shiga toxin on intestinal cells can result in hemorrhagic colitis, and absorption of the toxin in the circulation can result in systemic complications including HUS and neurologic sequelae.
- Strains of EPEC adhere to the small bowel mucosa and, like *E coli* O157:H7, produce AE lesions. Strains of EPEC historically were defined as members of specific *E coli* serotypes that were incriminated epidemiologically as causes of infantile diarrhea; now a more precise pathogenic definition includes the capacity to form the AE lesions in the absence of Shiga toxin production.
- Strains of ETEC colonize the small intestine without invading and produce heat-labile enterotoxin (LT), heat-stable enterotoxin (ST), or both.
- Like *Shigella* species, EIEC organisms typically are lactose nonfermenting and invade the colonic mucosa, where they spread laterally and induce a local inflammatory response.

- Enteroaggregative *E coli* organisms are defined by their characteristic "stacked brick" adherence pattern in cell culture-based assays. These organisms elaborate one or more enterotoxins and elicit damage to the intestinal mucosa.

EPIDEMIOLOGY: Transmission of most diarrhea-associated *E coli* strains is from food or water contaminated with human or animal feces or from infected symptomatic people or carriers. The only *E coli* pathotype that commonly causes diarrhea in children living in the United States is STEC, especially *E coli* O157:H7, which is shed in feces of cattle and, to a lesser extent, of sheep, deer, and other ruminants. Shiga toxin-producing *E coli* can be transmitted by undercooked ground beef, contaminated water or produce, unpasteurized milk, and a wide variety of vehicles contaminated with bovine feces. Contact with animals and their environment and person-to-person or fomite spread are other modes of transmission. Infections caused by *E coli* O157:H7 are detected sporadically or during outbreaks. Outbreaks have been linked to ground beef, petting zoos, contaminated apple cider, raw fruits and vegetables, salami, yogurt, drinking water, and ingestion of water in recreational areas. The infectious dose is low (approximately 100 organisms), and person-to-person transmission is common during outbreaks. Less is known about the epidemiology of STEC strains other than O157:H7. The non-O157 STEC strains most commonly linked to illness in the United States are O26, O11, and O103.

Non-Shiga toxin-producing *E coli* pathotypes are associated with disease predominantly in resource-limited countries, where food and water supplies commonly are contaminated and facilities and supplies for hand hygiene are suboptimal. Diarrhea attributable to ETEC occurs in people of all ages but especially is frequent and severe in infants in resource-limited countries. Outbreaks have occurred in adults, usually from ingestion of contaminated food or water. Enterotoxigenic *E coli* is a major cause of traveler's diarrhea.

The **incubation period** for most *E coli* strains is 10 hours to 6 days; for *E coli* O157:H7, the incubation period usually is 3 to 4 days but ranges from 1 to 8 days.

DIAGNOSTIC TESTS: Diagnosis of infection caused by diarrhea-associated *E coli* usually is difficult, because most clinical laboratories cannot differentiate diarrhea-associated *E coli* strains from stool flora *E coli* strains. The exception is *E coli* O157:H7, which can be identified specifically. For definitive identification, any *E coli* isolates suspected to be associated with an outbreak of diarrhea can be sent to reference or research laboratories, such as the Centers for Disease Control and Prevention (CDC), through state health departments.

Clinical laboratories can screen for *E coli* O157:H7 by using MacConkey agar base with sorbitol substituted for lactose. Approximately 90% of human intestinal *E coli* strains rapidly ferment sorbitol, whereas *E coli* O157:H7 strains do not. Sorbitol-negative *E coli* then can be serotyped, using commercially available antisera, to determine whether they are O157:H7. If a case or outbreak attributable to diarrhea-associated *E coli* other than O157:H7 is suspected, *E coli* isolates should be sent to the state health laboratory or another reference laboratory for serotyping and identification of pathotypes. Several sensitive, specific, and rapid immunologic assays for detection of Shiga toxin are available commercially.

Strains of STEC should be sought for patients with bloody diarrhea (indicated by history, inspection of stool, or guaiac), HUS, and postdiarrheal TTP as well as for contacts of patients with HUS who have any type of diarrhea. People with presumptive diagnoses of intussusception, inflammatory bowel disease, or ischemic colitis sometimes have disease caused by *E coli* O157:H7. Methods of definitive identification of STEC that are used in reference or research laboratories include DNA probes, polymerase chain reaction assay, enzyme immunoassay, and phenotypic testing of strains or stool specimens for Shiga toxin. Serologic diagnosis using enzyme immunoassay to detect serum antibodies to *E coli* O157:H7 lipopolysaccharide is available at the CDC for outbreak investigations.

HEMOLYTIC-UREMIC SYNDROME. For all patients with HUS, stool specimens should be cultured for *E coli* O157:H7 and, if results are negative, for other STEC serotypes. However, the absence of STEC in feces does not preclude the diagnosis of STEC-associated HUS, because HUS typically is diagnosed a week or more after onset of diarrhea, when the organism no longer may be detectable. When STEC infection is considered, a stool culture should be obtained as early in the illness as possible.

TREATMENT: Dehydration and electrolyte abnormalities should be prevented if possible or corrected quickly. Orally administered solutions usually are adequate.* Antimotility agents should not be administered to children with inflammatory or bloody diarrhea. Careful follow-up of patients with hemorrhagic colitis (including complete blood cell count with smear, blood urea nitrogen, and creatinine concentrations) is recommended to detect changes suggestive of HUS. If patients have no laboratory evidence of hemolysis, thrombocytopenia, or nephropathy 3 days after resolution of diarrhea, their risk of developing HUS is low.

ANTIMICROBIAL THERAPY. Although some studies have suggested that children with hemorrhagic colitis caused by STEC have a greater risk of developing HUS if treated with antimicrobial agents when compared with children not treated with antimicrobial agents, a meta-analysis failed to confirm this increased risk or to show a benefit of antimicrobial therapy. However, most experts would not treat children with *E coli* O157:H7 enteritis with an antimicrobial agent, because no benefit has been proven. If severe watery ETEC diarrhea is suspected in a traveler to a resource-limited country, therapy can be provided. The optimal therapies for ETEC and EAEC are not established, and resistance to antimicrobial agents is common. Trimethoprim-sulfamethoxazole, azithromycin, or ciprofloxacin, which is not approved for use in people younger than 18 years of age for this indication, should be considered if diarrhea is severe. For dysentery caused by EIEC strains, antimicrobial agents, such as trimethoprim-sulfamethoxazole, azithromycin, or ciprofloxacin, can be given orally. Whenever possible, antimicrobial selection should be based on susceptibility testing of the isolates.

ISOLATION OF THE HOSPITALIZED PATIENT: In addition to standard precautions, contact precautions are indicated for patients with all types of *E coli* diarrhea for the duration of illness. During outbreaks, contact precautions for infants with diarrhea

---

* Centers for Disease Control and Prevention. Managing acute gastroenteritis among children: oral rehydration, maintenance, and nutritional therapy. *MMWR Morb Mortal Wkly Rep.* 2003;52:1–16

caused by EPEC strains should be maintained until tests of stool collected after cessation of antimicrobial therapy are negative for the infecting strain. For patients with HUS or hemorrhagic colitis attributable to STEC, contact precautions should be continued until diarrhea resolves and results of 2 consecutive stool cultures are negative for *E coli* O157:H7.

CONTROL MEASURES:

ESCHERICHIA COLI O157:H7 INFECTION. All ground beef should be cooked thoroughly until no pink meat remains and the juices are clear. Raw milk should not be ingested, and only pasteurized apple juice products should be consumed. People with diarrhea caused by this potentially waterborne pathogen should not use recreational water venues (eg, swimming pools, lakes, rivers, the ocean) for 2 weeks after symptoms resolve.

OUTBREAKS IN CHILD CARE CENTERS. If an outbreak of HUS or diarrhea attributable to *E coli* O157:H7 occurs in a child care center, immediate involvement of public health authorities is critical. Infection caused by *E coli* O157:H7 is reportable, and rapid reporting of cases allows interventions to prevent further disease. Ill children should not be permitted to reenter the child care center until diarrhea has resolved and 2 stool cultures obtained at least 48 hours after antimicrobial therapy has been discontinued are negative for *E coli* O157:H7. Strict attention to hand hygiene is important but can be insufficient to prevent continued transmission. The child care center should be closed to new admissions during the outbreak, and care should be exercised to prevent transfer of exposed children to other centers.

NURSERY AND OTHER INSTITUTIONAL OUTBREAKS. Strict attention to hand hygiene is essential for limiting spread. Exposed patients should be observed closely, their stools should be cultured for the causative organism, and they should be separated from unexposed infants. In a newborn nursery, EPEC infection is considered a serious hazard, and strict enteric precautions should be maintained.

TRAVELER'S DIARRHEA. Traveler's diarrhea has been associated with many *E coli* pathogens (including ETEC, EAEC, and EIEC). It usually is acquired by ingestion of contaminated food or water and is a significant problem for people traveling in resource-limited countries. Diarrhea attributable to STEC is rare in travelers. Travelers should be advised to drink only bottled or canned beverages and boiled or bottled water; travelers should avoid ice, raw produce including salads, and fruit that they have not peeled themselves. Cooked foods should be eaten hot. Antimicrobial agents are not recommended for prevention of traveler's diarrhea. Although several antimicrobial agents, such as trimethoprim-sulfamethoxazole, doxycycline, and ciprofloxacin, can be effective in decreasing the incidence of traveler's diarrhea, the benefit usually is outweighed by the potential risks, including allergic drug reactions, antimicrobial-associated colitis, and the selective pressure of widespread use of antimicrobial agents leading to antimicrobial resistance. If diarrhea occurs, packets of oral rehydration salts can be added to water and ingested to help maintain fluid balance. If diarrhea in a traveler is moderate or severe or is associated with fever or bloody stools, empiric antimicrobial therapy may be indicated until symptoms resolve; empiric therapy should be continued for no more than 3 days.

RECREATIONAL WATER. People with diarrhea caused by these potentially waterborne pathogens should not use recreational water venues (eg, swimming pools, lakes, rivers, the ocean) for 2 weeks after symptoms resolve.

Fungal Diseases

In addition to the mycoses listed by individual agents in Section 3, infants and children with immunosuppression or other underlying conditions can become infected by uncommonly encountered fungi. Children who are immunocompetent can acquire infection with these fungi through inhalation via the respiratory tract or direct inoculation after traumatic disruption of cutaneous barriers. A list of these fungi and the pertinent underlying host conditions, reservoir or route of entry, clinical manifestations, diagnostic laboratory tests, and treatment for each can be found in Table 3.7 (p 297). Taken as a group, few fungal susceptibility data are available on which to base treatment recommendations for fungal infections, especially in children. Consultation with a pediatric infectious disease specialist should be considered when caring for a child infected with one of these mycoses.

Giardia intestinalis Infections
(Giardiasis)

CLINICAL MANIFESTATIONS: Symptomatic infection causes a broad spectrum of clinical manifestations. Children can have occasional days of acute watery diarrhea with abdominal pain, or they may experience a protracted, intermittent, often debilitating disease, which is characterized by passage of foul-smelling stools associated with flatulence, abdominal distention, and anorexia. Anorexia combined with malabsorption can lead to significant weight loss, failure to thrive, and anemia. Asymptomatic infection is common.

ETIOLOGY: *Giardia intestinalis* is a flagellate protozoan that exists in trophozoite and cyst forms; the infective form is the cyst. Infection is limited to the small intestine and biliary tract.

EPIDEMIOLOGY: Giardiasis has a worldwide distribution. Humans are the principal reservoir of infection, but *Giardia* organisms can infect dogs, cats, beavers, and other animals.* These animals can contaminate water with feces containing cysts that are infectious for humans. People become infected directly (by hand-to-mouth transfer of cysts from feces of an infected person) or indirectly (by ingestion of fecally contaminated water or food). Many people who become infected with *G intestinalis* remain asymptomatic. Most community-wide epidemics have resulted from a contaminated water supply. Epidemics resulting from person-to-person transmission occur in child care centers and in institutions for people with developmental disabilities. Staff and family members in contact with people in these settings occasionally become infected. Humoral immunodeficiencies predispose to chronic symptomatic *G intestinalis* infections. Surveys conducted in the United States have demonstrated prevalence rates of

---

* Hlavsa MC, Watson JC, Beach MJ, Atlanta Research and Education Foundation. Giardiasis surveillance—United States, 1998–2002. *MMWR Surveill Summ.* 2005;54(SS-1):9–16

Table 3.7. Additional Fungal Diseases

Disease and Agent	Underlying Host Condition(s)	Reservoir(s) or Route(s) of Entry	Common Clinical Manifestations	Diagnostic Laboratory Test(s)	Treatment
Hyalohyphomycosis					
Fusarium species	Granulocytopenia; stem cell transplantation; severe immunocompromise	Respiratory tract; sinuses; skin	Pulmonary infiltrates; cutaneous lesions; sinusitis; disseminated infection	Culture of blood or tissue specimen	High-dose D-AMB (1–1.5 mg/kg per day),[1,2,3] or voriconazole
Malassezia species	Immunosuppression; prematurity; exposure to parenteral nutrition that includes fat emulsions	Skin	Catheter-associated bloodstream infection; interstitial pneumonitis; urinary tract infection; meningitis	Culture of blood, catheter tip, or tissue specimen	Removal of catheters and temporary cessation of lipid infusions; D-AMB
Penicilliosis					
Penicillium marneffei	Human immunodeficiency virus infection	Respiratory tract	Pneumonitis; invasive dermatitis; disseminated infection	Culture of blood, bone marrow, or tissue; histopathologic examination of tissue	Itraconazole[4] or D-AMB
Phaeohyphomycosis					
Alternaria species	None or trauma or Immunosuppression	Respiratory tract; skin	Sinusitis; cutaneous lesions	Culture and histopathologic examination of tissue	High-dose D-AMB[1,2,3]

Table 3.7. Additional Fungal Diseases, continued

Disease and Agent	Underlying Host Condition(s)	Reservoir(s) Route(s) of Entry	Common Clinical Manifestations	Diagnostic Laboratory Test(s)	Treatment
Bipolaris species	None or trauma or immunosuppression	Environment	Sinusitis; disseminated infection	Culture and histopathologic examination of tissue	Itraconazole[4] or D-AMB[1]; surgical excision
Curvularia species	Immunosuppression; altered skin integrity; asthma or nasal polyps; chronic sinusitis	Environment	Allergic fungal sinusitis; invasive dermatitis; disseminated infection	Culture and histopathologic examination of tissue	Allergic fungal sinusitis: surgery and corticosteroids Invasive disease: itraconazole[5] or D-AMB[1]
Exophiala species, *Exserohilum* species, or *Wangiella* species	None or trauma or immunosuppression	Environment	Sinusitis; cutaneous lesions; disseminated infection	Culture and histopathologic examination of tissue	Itraconazole[5] or D-AMB; surgical excision
Pseudallescheria boydii (*Scedosporium apiospermum*)	None or trauma or immunosuppression	Environment	Pneumonia; disseminated infection; osteomyelitis or septic arthritis; mycetoma (immunocompetent patients); endocarditis	Culture and histopathologic examination of tissue	Voriconazole[3] or itraconazole[5]; surgical excision for pulmonary infection, as feasible

Table 3.7. Additional Fungal Diseases, continued

Disease and Agent	Underlying Host Condition(s)	Reservoir(s) Route(s) of Entry	Common Clinical Manifestations	Diagnostic Laboratory Test(s)	Treatment
Trichosporonosis					
Trichosporon species	Immunosuppression; central venous catheter	Normal flora of gastrointestinal tract	Bloodstream infection; endocarditis; pneumonitis	Blood culture; histopathologic examination of tissue	D-AMB[1,2]
Zygomycosis					
Rhizopus; Mucor; Absidia; Rhizomucor species	Immunosuppression; hematologic malignant neoplasm; renal failure; diabetes mellitus; use of nonsterile adhesive dressings	Respiratory tract; skin	Rhinocerebral infection; pulmonary infection; disseminated infection; skin and gastrointestinal tract less commonly	Histopathologic examination of tissue and culture	High dose of D-AMB (1.5 mg/kg per day)[1] and surgical excision, as feasible

D-AMB indicates deoxycholate amphotericin B.

[1] Consider use of a lipid formulation of amphotericin B.

[2] Infection may be refractory to amphotericin B; use of investigational antifungal compounds may be required.

[3] Voriconazole is an alternative agent for adults intolerant of or with infection refractory to amphotericin B, but safety and efficacy have not been established in children younger than 12 years of age.

[4] Itraconazole has been shown to be effective for cutaneous disease in adults, but safety and efficacy have not been established in children younger than 12 years of age.

[5] Itraconazole may be the treatment of choice, but data on safety and effectiveness in children are limited.

[6] Voriconazole demonstrates activity in vitro but no clinical data are available.

Giardia organisms in stool specimens that range from 1% to 20%, depending on geographic location and age. Duration of cyst excretion is variable but can be months. The disease is communicable for as long as the infected person excretes cysts.

The **incubation period** usually is 1 to 4 weeks.

DIAGNOSTIC TESTS: Identification of trophozoites or cysts in direct smear examination or immunofluorescent antibody testing of stool specimens or duodenal fluid is diagnostic. Stool usually is collected and preserved in neutral-buffered 10% formalin, but other preservatives can be used, or fresh stool can be examined. A single direct smear examination of stool has a sensitivity of 75% to 95%. Sensitivity is higher for diarrheal stool specimens, because these contain a higher concentration of organisms. Sensitivity is increased by examining 3 or more specimens collected every other day. To enhance detection, microscopic examination of stool specimens or duodenal fluid should be performed soon after collection, or stool should be placed in fixative, concentrated, and examined by wet mount using a permanent stain such as trichrome. Commercially available stool collection kits containing a vial of neutral-buffered 10% formalin and a vial of polyvinyl alcohol fixative in childproof containers are convenient for preserving stool specimens collected at home. Sensitive and specific enzyme immunoassay kits are available commercially. The direct fluorescent antibody test kit has the advantage that the organisms are visualized. When giardiasis is suspected clinically but the organism is not found on repeated stool examination, examination of duodenal contents obtained by direct aspiration or by using a commercially available string test (Enterotest) may be diagnostic. Rarely, duodenal biopsy is required for diagnosis.

TREATMENT: Dehydration and electrolyte abnormalities should be corrected. Metronidazole, tinidazole, or nitazoxanide are the drugs of choice. A 5- to 7-day course of metronidazole has a cure rate of 80% to 95%. Tinidazole, a nitroimidazole, has a cure rate of 80% to 100% after a single dose. A 3-day course of nitazoxanide oral suspension is as effective as metronidazole and has the advantage of treating multiple other intestinal parasites. Furazolidone and quinacrine are alternatives. Furazolidone is 72% to 100% effective when given for 7 to 10 days and is available in a liquid form for pediatric use. Albendazole and mebendazole have been shown to be as effective as metronidazole for treating giardiasis in children and have fewer adverse effects. Paromomycin, a nonabsorbable aminoglycoside that is 50% to 70% effective, is recommended for treatment of symptomatic infection in pregnant women.

If therapy fails, a course can be repeated with the same drug. Relapse is common in immunocompromised patients who may require prolonged treatment. Some experts recommend combination therapy for giardiasis in immunocompromised patients who are unresponsive to courses of 2 drugs used separately.

Treatment of asymptomatic carriers generally is not recommended. Possible exceptions to prevent transmission are carriers in households of patients with hypogammaglobulinemia or cystic fibrosis and pregnant women with toddlers.

ISOLATION OF THE HOSPITALIZED PATIENT: In addition to standard precautions, contact precautions for the duration of illness are recommended for diapered and incontinent children.

CONTROL MEASURES:

- In child care centers, improved sanitation and personal hygiene should be emphasized (see also Children in Out-of-Home Child Care, p 130). Hand hygiene by staff and children should be emphasized, especially after toilet use or handling of soiled diapers. When an outbreak is suspected, the local health department should be contacted, and an epidemiologic investigation should be undertaken to identify and treat all symptomatic children, child care workers, and family members infected with *G intestinalis*. People with diarrhea should be excluded from the child care center until they become asymptomatic. Treatment of asymptomatic carriers is not effective for outbreak control. Exclusion of carriers from child care is not recommended.
- Waterborne outbreaks can be prevented by the combination of adequate filtration of water from surface water sources (eg, lakes, rivers, streams), chlorination, and maintenance of water distribution systems.
- People with diarrhea caused by this potentially waterborne pathogen should not use recreational water venues (eg, swimming pools, lakes, rivers, the ocean) for 2 weeks after symptoms resolve.
- Where water might be contaminated, travelers, campers, and hikers should be advised of methods to make water safe for drinking, including boiling, chemical disinfection, and filtration. Boiling is the most reliable method to make water safe for drinking. The time of boiling (1 minute at sea level) will depend on the altitude. Chemical disinfection with iodine is an alternative method of water treatment using either tincture of iodine or tetraglycine hydroperiodide tablets. Chlorine in various forms also can be used for chemical disinfection, but germicidal activity is dependent on several factors, including pH, temperature, and organic content of the water. Commercially available portable water filters provide various degrees of protection. There are many commercially available filters that are marketed as being able to remove *Giardia* and *Cryptosporidium* species from water. Filters that are designed to remove *Giardia* and *Cryptosporidium* species from water should contain one of the following indicators verbatim on the label:
  - Reverse osmosis
  - Absolute pore size of 1 μm or smaller
  - Tested and certified by NSF standard 53 or NSF standard 58 for cyst removal
  - Tested and certified by NSF standard 53 or NSF standard 58 for cyst reduction

Additional information about water purification, including a traveler's guide for buying water filters, can be found at **www.cdc.gov/travel/foodwater.htm**.

Gonococcal Infections

CLINICAL MANIFESTATIONS: Gonococcal infections in children occur in 3 distinct age groups.

- Infection in the **newborn infant** usually involves the eyes. Other types of infection include scalp abscess (which can be associated with fetal monitoring), vaginitis, and disseminated disease with bacteremia, arthritis, or meningitis.

- In children beyond the newborn period, including **prepubertal children**, gonococcal infection may occur in the genital tract and almost always is sexually transmitted. Vaginitis is the most common manifestation. Gonococcal urethritis in the prepubertal male is uncommon. Anorectal and tonsillopharyngeal infection also can occur in prepubertal children.
- In **sexually active adolescents**, as in adults, gonococcal infection of the genital tract in females often is asymptomatic, and common clinical syndromes are vaginitis, urethritis, endocervicitis, and salpingitis. In males, infection often is symptomatic, and the primary site is the urethra. Infection of the rectum and pharynx can occur alone or with genitourinary tract infection in either sex. Rectal and pharyngeal infections often are asymptomatic. Extension from primary genital mucosal sites can lead to epididymitis in males and bartholinitis, pelvic inflammatory disease (PID), and perihepatitis (Fitz-Hugh-Curtis syndrome) in females. Even asymptomatic infection in females can progress to PID, with tubal scarring that can result in ectopic pregnancy or infertility. Infection involving other mucous membranes can produce conjunctivitis, pharyngitis, or proctitis. Hematogenous spread can involve skin and joints (arthritis-dermatitis syndrome) and occurs in up to 3% of untreated people with mucosal gonorrhea. Bacteremia causes a maculopapular rash with necrosis, tenosynovitis, and migratory arthritis. Arthritis may be reactive (sterile) or septic in nature. Meningitis and endocarditis occur rarely. Dissemination is more common in females infected within 1 week of menstruation.

ETIOLOGY: *Neisseria gonorrhoeae* is a gram-negative oxidase-positive diplococcus.

EPIDEMIOLOGY: Gonococcal infections occur only in humans. The source of the organism is exudate and secretions from infected mucosal surfaces; *N gonorrhoeae* is communicable as long as a person harbors the organism. Transmission results from intimate contact, such as sexual acts, parturition, and rarely, household exposure in prepubertal children. Sexual abuse should be considered strongly when genital, rectal, or pharyngeal colonization or infection are diagnosed in prepubertal children beyond the newborn period. In 2004, there were 330 132 new cases of gonococcal infection reported in the United States. Reported incidence of infection is highest in females 15 to 19 years of age and in males 20 to 24 years of age. Concurrent infection with *Chlamydia trachomatis* is common.

The **incubation period** usually is 2 to 7 days.

DIAGNOSTIC TESTS: Microscopic examination of Gram-stained smears of exudate from the eyes, vagina of prepubertal girls, male urethra, skin lesions, synovial fluid, and when clinically warranted, cerebrospinal fluid (CSF) may be useful in the initial evaluation. Identification of gram-negative intracellular diplococci in these smears can be helpful, particularly if the organism is not recovered in culture.

Neisseria gonorrhoeae can be cultured from normally sterile sites, such as blood, CSF, or synovial fluid, using nonselective chocolate agar with incubation in 5% to 10% carbon dioxide. Selective media that inhibit normal flora and nonpathogenic *Neisseria* organisms are used for culture from nonsterile sites, such as the cervix, vagina, rectum, urethra, and pharynx. Specimens for *N gonorrhoeae* culture from mucosal sites should be inoculated immediately onto the appropriate agar, because *N gonorrhoeae* is extremely sensitive to drying and temperature changes.

Caution should be exercised when interpreting the significance of the isolation of *Neisseria* organisms, because *N gonorrhoeae* can be confused with other *Neisseria* species that colonize the genitourinary tract or pharynx. At least 2 confirmatory bacteriologic tests involving different principles (eg, biochemical, enzyme substrate, or serologic) should be performed by the laboratory. Interpretation of culture of *N gonorrhoeae* from the pharynx of young children necessitates particular caution because of the high carriage rate of nonpathogenic *Neisseria* species.

Nucleic acid amplification (NAA) tests are highly sensitive and specific when used on urethral (males), endocervical swab, and urine specimens.* These tests include polymerase chain reaction (PCR), transcription-mediated amplification (TMA), and strand-displacement assays. Only the TMA assay is approved by the US Food and Drug Administration (FDA) for testing vaginal swabs from postmenarcheal females. Other *Neisseria* species and gram-negative cocci may be present in the female genital tract and may result in a false-positive NAA test result. Use of urine specimens increases feasibility of initial testing and follow-up of hard-to-access populations, such as adolescents. These techniques also permit dual testing of urine for *C trachomatis* and *N gonorrhoeae*. These NAA tests are not recommended for rectal or pharyngeal swabs. A limited number of nonculture tests are approved by the FDA for conjunctival specimens.

SEXUAL ABUSE.† In all prepubertal children beyond the newborn period and in nonsexually active adolescents who have gonococcal infection, sexual abuse must be considered to have occurred unless proven otherwise. Genital, rectal, and pharyngeal secretion cultures should be performed for all patients before antimicrobial treatment is given. All gonococcal isolates from such patients should be preserved. Nonculture gonococcal tests including Gram stain, DNA probes, enzyme immunoassays, or NAA testing of oropharyngeal, rectal, or genital tract specimens in children cannot be relied on as the sole method for diagnosis of gonococcal infection for this purpose, because false-positive results can occur. In prepubertal children when culture is not available, some experts support use of NAA testing on vaginal swabs if a positive result can be verified by a different nucleic acid amplification test. When possible, appropriate cultures should be obtained from people who have had contact with a child suspected to have been sexually abused. Children in whom sexual abuse is suspected because of detection of gonorrhea should be evaluated for other sexually transmitted diseases, such as *C trachomatis* infection, syphilis, hepatitis B virus infection, and human immunodeficiency virus (HIV) infection.

TREATMENT: Because of the prevalence of penicillin- and tetracycline-resistant *N gonorrhoeae*, an extended-spectrum cephalosporin (eg, ceftriaxone, cefixime, or cefpodoxime) is recommended as initial therapy for children, and either an extended-spectrum cephalosporin or fluoroquinolone (ciprofloxacin, levofloxacin, ofloxacin) is recommended for adults (see Table 4.4, p 766). Occasional isolates of quinolone-resistant *N gonorrhoeae* have been isolated in many parts of the United States. Because of resistance, fluoroquinolones should not be used if infection is acquired in Asia, the

---

* Centers for Disease Control and Prevention. Screening to detect *Chlamydia trachomatis* and *Neisseria gonorrhoeae* infections—2002. *MMWR Recomm Rep.* 2002;51(RR-15):1–38

† Kellogg N, and American Academy of Pediatrics, Committee on Child Abuse and Neglect. The evaluation of sexual abuse in children. *Pediatrics.* 2005;116:506–512

Pacific Islands including Hawaii, and California or from an individual who has traveled recently to those areas. Resistance to spectinomycin is uncommon.

Parenteral cephalosporins are recommended for use in young children; ceftriaxone is approved for gonococcal infections of all sites in children, and cefotaxime is approved only for gonococcal ophthalmia. Antimicrobial agents administered orally that have been demonstrated to be effective for treating gonococcal urethritis and cervicitis in adults and older adolescents include cefixime, ciprofloxacin, ofloxacin, and levofloxacin. Fluoroquinolones generally are not recommended for people younger than 18 years of age (see Antimicrobial Agents and Related Therapy, p 735) and are contraindicated in pregnant or nursing women.

All patients with presumed or proven gonorrhea should be evaluated for concurrent syphilis, hepatitis B virus, HIV, and *C trachomatis* infections. All patients beyond the neonatal period with gonorrhea should be treated presumptively for *C trachomatis* infection (see *Chlamydia trachomatis*, p 252).

A test-of-cure culture need not be performed in adolescents and adults with uncomplicated gonorrhea who are asymptomatic after being treated with one of the recommended antimicrobial regimens. Children treated with ceftriaxone do not require follow-up cultures unless they remain in an at-risk environment, but if treated with other regimens, follow-up culture is indicated.

Specific recommendations for management and antimicrobial therapy are as follows:

NEONATAL DISEASE. Infants with clinical evidence of ophthalmia neonatorum, scalp abscess, or disseminated infections should be hospitalized. Cultures of blood, eye discharge, or other sites of infection, such as CSF, should be performed for infants to confirm the diagnosis and determine antimicrobial susceptibility. Tests for concomitant infection with *C trachomatis*, congenital syphilis, and HIV infection should be performed. Results of the maternal test for hepatitis B surface antigen should be confirmed. The mother and her partner(s) also need appropriate examination and management for *N gonorrhoeae*.

NONDISSEMINATED INFECTIONS. Recommended antimicrobial therapy, including that for ophthalmia neonatorum, is ceftriaxone (25–50 mg/kg, intravenously or intramuscularly, not to exceed 125 mg) given once. Infants with gonococcal ophthalmia should receive eye irrigations with saline solution immediately and at frequent intervals until the discharge is eliminated. Topical antimicrobial treatment alone is inadequate and is unnecessary when recommended systemic antimicrobial treatment is given. Infants with gonococcal ophthalmia should be hospitalized and evaluated for disseminated infection (sepsis, arthritis, meningitis).

DISSEMINATED INFECTIONS. Recommended therapy for arthritis and septicemia is ceftriaxone or cefotaxime for 7 days. Cefotaxime is recommended for infants with hyperbilirubinemia. If meningitis is documented, treatment should be continued for a total of 10 to 14 days.

GONOCOCCAL INFECTIONS IN CHILDREN BEYOND THE NEONATAL PERIOD AND IN ADOLESCENTS. Recommendations for treatment of gonococcal infections, by age and weight, are given in Tables 3.8 (p 305) and 3.9 (p 306).

Table 3.8. Uncomplicated Gonococcal Infection: Treatment of Children Beyond the Newborn Period and Adolescents[1]

Disease[2]	Prepubertal Children Who Weigh <100 lb (<45 kg)	Disease[2]	Patients Who Weigh ≥100 lb (≥45 kg) and Who Are 8 Years or Older
Uncomplicated vulvovaginitis, cervicitis, urethritis, proctitis, or pharyngitis	Ceftriaxone, 125 mg, IM, in a single dose OR Spectinomycin,[3] 40 mg/kg (maximum 2 g), IM, in a single dose PLUS[1] Azithromycin, 20 mg/kg (maximum 1 g), orally, in a single dose OR Erythromycin, 50 mg/kg per day (maximum 2 g/day), orally, in 4 divided doses for 14 days	Uncomplicated endocervicitis, urethritis, proctitis, or pharyngitis[4]	Ceftriaxone, 125 mg, IM, in a single dose OR Ciprofloxacin,[5] 500 mg, orally, in a single dose OR Cefixime, 400 mg, orally, in a single dose OR Cefpodoxime, 400 mg, orally, in a single dose OR Ofloxacin,[5] 400 mg, orally, in a single dose OR Levofloxacin,[5] 250 mg, orally, in a single dose PLUS[1] Azithromycin (1 g, orally, in a single dose) OR Doxycycline (100 mg, orally, twice a day for 7 days)

IM indicates intramuscularly.

[1] In addition to the recommended treatment for gonococcal infection, therapy for *Chlamydia trachomatis* is recommended on the presumption that the patient has concomitant infection.

[2] Hospitalization should be considered, especially for people treated as outpatients whose infection has failed to respond and for people who are unlikely to adhere to treatment regimens.

[3] Spectinomycin is not recommended for treatment of pharyngeal infections; in people who cannot take ceftriaxone or ciprofloxacin, spectromycin may be used for pharyngitis, but a follow-up culture is necessary.

[4] Alternative regimens include spectinomycin (2 g, IM, in a single dose), ceftizoxime, cefotaxime, and cefoxitin. Only ceftriaxone and ciprofloxacin are recommended for pharyngitis; in people who cannot take either of these, spectromycin may be used, but a follow-up culture is necessary.

[5] Fluoroquinolones are contraindicated for pregnant women, nursing women, and usually for people younger than 18 years of age (see Antimicrobial Agents and Related Therapy, p 735). Fluoroquinolones should not be used for infections acquired in Asia, the Pacific Islands including Hawaii, or California.

Table 3.9. Complicated Gonococcal Infection: Treatment of Children Beyond the Newborn Period and Adolescents[1]

Disease[2]	Prepubertal Children Who Weigh <100 lb (<45 kg)	Disease[2]	Patients Who Weigh ≥100 lb (≥45 kg) and Who Are 8 Years or Older
Disseminated gonococcal infection (eg, arthritis-dermatitis syndrome)	Ceftriaxone, 50 mg/kg per day (maximum 1 g/day), IV or IM, once a day for 7 days **PLUS[1]** Azithromycin or erythromycin, orally	Disseminated gonococcal infections[3]	Ceftriaxone, 1 g, IV or IM, given once a day for 7 days[4] **OR** Cefotaxime, 1 g, IV, every 8 hours for 7 days[4] **PLUS[1]** Azithromycin or erythromycin, orally **OR** Doxycycline, 100 mg, orally, twice a day for 7 days
Meningitis or endocarditis	Ceftriaxone, 50 mg/kg per day (maximum 2 g/day), IV or IM, given every 12 h; for meningitis, duration is 10–14 days; for endocarditis, duration is at least 28 days **PLUS[1]** Azithromycin or erythromycin, orally	Meningitis or endocarditis	Ceftriaxone, 1–2 g, IV, every 12 h; for meningitis, duration is 10–14 days; for endocarditis, duration is at least 28 days **PLUS** Azithromycin or erythromycin, orally
Conjunctivitis[5]	Ceftriaxone, 50 mg/kg (maximum 1g), IM, in a single dose		

Table 3.9. Complicated Gonococcal Infection: Treatment of Children Beyond the Newborn Period and Adolescents,[1] continued

Disease	Prepubertal Children Who Weigh <100 lb (<45 kg)	Patients Who Weigh ≥100 lb (≥45 kg) and Who Are 8 Years or Older
Epididymitis		Ceftriaxone, 250 mg, IM
		PLUS
		Doxycycline, 100 mg, orally, twice daily for 10 days
Conjunctivitis[5]		Ceftriaxone, 1 g, IM, in a single dose
		PLUS
		Azithromycin or erythromycin
Pelvic inflammatory disease		See Table 3.41 (p 497)

IV indicates intravenously; and IM, intramuscularly.

[1] In addition to the recommended treatment for gonococcal infection, therapy for *Chlamydia trachomatis* is recommended on the presumption that the patient has concomitant infection.

[2] Hospitalization should be considered, especially for people treated as outpatients whose infection has failed to respond and for people who are unlikely to adhere to treatment regimens.

[3] For people who are allergic to beta-lactam drugs: ciprofloxacin (400 mg, IV, every 12 h) *or* ofloxacin (400 mg, IV, every 12 h) *or* levofloxacin (250 mg, IV, daily), *or* spectinomycin (2 g, IM, every 12 h). Spectinomycin treatment requires a follow-up culture if pharyngeal infection exists. Hospitalization recommended.

[4] Alternatively, parenteral therapy can be discontinued 24 to 48 hours after improvement occurs and a 7-day course is completed with an appropriate oral antimicrobial agent such as cefixime (400 mg, orally, twice a day), ciprofloxacin (500 mg, orally, twice a day), ofloxacin (400 mg, orally, twice a day), or levofloxacin (500 mg, orally, once daily). Fluoroquinolones are contraindicated for pregnant women, nursing women, and usually for people younger than 18 years of age (see Antimicrobial Agents and Related Therapy, p 735). Some experts advise a longer course of therapy. Fluoroquinolones should not be used for infections acquired in Asia, the Pacific Islands including Hawaii, or California.

[5] Eyes should be lavaged with saline solution to clear accumulated secretions.

SPECIAL PROBLEMS IN TREATMENT OF CHILDREN (BEYOND THE NEONATAL PERIOD) AND ADOLESCENTS. Patients with uncomplicated endocervical infection, urethritis, or proctitis who are allergic to cephalosporins should be treated with spectinomycin (40 mg/kg, maximum 2 g, given intramuscularly as a single dose) if they are not old enough to receive a fluoroquinolone or if infection was acquired in an area with high prevalence of quinolone-resistant *N gonorrhoeae*. Doxycycline or azithromycin should be used for the concurrent treatment of presumptive *C trachomatis* infection depending on the age of the patient (see Table 3.8, p 305).

Patients with uncomplicated pharyngeal gonococcal infection should be treated with ceftriaxone (125 mg, intramuscularly) in a single dose. People older than 17 years of age who are not pregnant and who cannot tolerate ceftriaxone should be treated with ciprofloxacin (500 mg, orally, in a single dose) if infection was not acquired in an area with high prevalence of quinolone-resistant *N gonorrhoeae*. Spectinomycin is approximately 50% effective for treatment of pharyngeal gonorrhea, so it should be used only in people who are unable to take ceftriaxone or ciprofloxacin, and a pharyngeal culture should be obtained 3 to 5 days after treatment to verify eradication.

A single dose of ceftriaxone or azithromycin is not effective treatment for concurrent infection with syphilis (see Syphilis, p 631). Fluoroquinolones and spectinomycin are not active against *Treponema pallidum*.

Children or adolescents with HIV infection should receive the same treatment for gonococcal infection as those without HIV infection.

ACUTE PID. *Neisseria gonorrhoeae* and *C trachomatis* are implicated in many cases of PID; all cases have a polymicrobial etiology. No reliable clinical criteria distinguish gonococcal from nongonococcal-associated PID. Hence, broad-spectrum treatment regimens are recommended (see Pelvic Inflammatory Disease, p 493).

ACUTE EPIDIDYMITIS. Sexually transmitted organisms, such as *N gonorrhoeae* or *C trachomatis*, can cause acute epididymitis in sexually active adolescents and young adults but rarely cause acute epididymitis in prepubertal children. The recommended regimen for sexually transmitted epididymitis is ceftriaxone plus erythromycin, or doxycycline, depending on the patient's age (see Table 3.8, p 305).

ISOLATION OF THE HOSPITALIZED PATIENT: Standard precautions are recommended, including for newborn infants with ophthalmia.

CONTROL MEASURES:

NEONATAL OPHTHALMIA. For routine prophylaxis of infants immediately after birth, a 1% solution of silver nitrate, or 1% tetracycline or 0.5% erythromycin ophthalmic ointment, is instilled into each eye; subsequent irrigation should not be performed (see Prevention of Neonatal Ophthalmia, p 828). Prophylaxis may be delayed for as long as 1 hour after birth to facilitate parent-infant bonding. Topical antimicrobial agents are less likely to cause a chemical irritation than silver nitrate. None of the topical agents is effective against *C trachomatis*, likely because they do not eradicate this organism from the nasopharynx.

INFANTS BORN TO MOTHERS WITH GONOCOCCAL INFECTIONS. When prophylaxis is administered correctly, infants born to mothers with gonococcal infection rarely develop gonococcal ophthalmia. However, because gonococcal ophthalmia or disseminated infection occasionally can occur in this situation, infants born to mothers known to have gonorrhea should receive a single dose of ceftriaxone, 125 mg intravenously or intramuscularly; for preterm and low-birth-weight infants, the dose is 25 to 50 mg/kg, to a maximum of 125 mg (see Prevention of Neonatal Ophthalmia, p 828).

CHILDREN AND ADOLESCENTS WITH SEXUAL EXPOSURE TO A PATIENT KNOWN TO HAVE GONORRHEA. Exposed individuals should undergo examination, culture, and the same treatment as people known to have gonorrhea.

PREGNANCY. All pregnant women should have an endocervical culture for gonococci at the time of their first prenatal visit. A second culture late in the third trimester is recommended for women at high risk of exposure to gonococcal infection. Recommended therapeutic regimens for patients found to be infected are regimens previously described for uncomplicated gonorrhea, except that a tetracycline or fluoroquinolone should not be used because of the potential toxic effects on the fetus. Women who are allergic to cephalosporins should be treated with spectinomycin, but spectinomycin is unreliable against pharyngeal gonococcal infection.

CASE REPORTING AND MANAGEMENT OF SEXUAL PARTNERS. All cases of gonorrhea must be reported to local public health officials (see Appendix IX, Nationally Notifiable Infectious Diseases in the United States, p 870). Cases in prepubertal children must be investigated to determine the source of infection. Ensuring that sexual contacts are treated and counseled to use condoms is essential for community control, prevention of reinfection, and prevention of complications in the contact.

Granuloma Inguinale
(Donovanosis)

CLINICAL MANIFESTATIONS: Initial lesions are single or multiple subcutaneous nodules that progress to form painless, highly vascular, friable, granulomatous ulcers without regional adenopathy. Lesions usually involve the genitalia, but anal infections occur in 5% to 10% of patients; lesions at distant sites (eg, face, mouth, or liver) are rare. Subcutaneous extension into the inguinal area results in induration that can mimic inguinal adenopathy (ie, "pseudobubo"). Fibrosis manifests as sinus tracts, adhesions, and lymphedema, resulting in extreme genital deformity. Urethral obstruction can occur.

ETIOLOGY: The disease is caused by *Calymmatobacterium granulomatis*, an intracellular gram-negative bacillus.

EPIDEMIOLOGY: Indigenous granuloma inguinale occurs only rarely in the United States and most developed countries. Donovanosis is endemic in Papua, New Guinea, and parts of India, southern Africa, central Australia, and to a much lesser extent, the Caribbean and parts of South America, most notably Brazil. The highest incidence of disease occurs in tropical and subtropical environments. The incidence of infection seems to correlate strongly with sustained high temperatures and high relative humidity. Infection usually is acquired by sexual intercourse, most commonly with a person with active infection, but possibly also from a person with asymptomatic rectal infection. Young children can acquire infection by contact with infected secretions. The period of communicability extends throughout the duration of active lesions or rectal colonization.

The **incubation period** is 8 to 80 days.

DIAGNOSTIC TESTS: The causative organism is difficult to culture, and diagnosis requires microscopic demonstration of dark staining intracytoplasmic Donovan bodies on Wright or Giemsa staining of a crush preparation from subsurface scrapings of a lesion or tissue. The microorganism also can be detected by histologic examination of biopsy specimens. Lesions should be cultured for *Haemophilus ducreyi* to exclude chancroid (pseudogranuloma inguinale). Granuloma inguinale often is misdiagnosed as carcinoma, which can be excluded by histologic examination of tissue or by response of the lesion to antimicrobial agents. Diagnosis by polymerase chain reaction assay and serologic testing is available on a research basis.

TREATMENT: Ciprofloxacin, which generally is not recommended for use in pregnant or lactating women or children younger than 18 years of age, is the recommended treatment. Gentamicin may be added if no improvement is evident in several days. Doxycycline (which ordinarily should not be given to children younger than 8 years of age) and trimethoprim-sulfamethoxazole have been reported to be effective. Erythromycin base or azithromycin also are alternative therapies and are appropriate for pregnant patients. Antimicrobial therapy is continued for at least 3 weeks or until the lesions have resolved. If antimicrobial therapy is effective, partial healing usually is noted within 7 days. Relapse can occur, especially if the antimicrobial agent is stopped before the primary lesion has healed completely. Complicated or long-standing infection may require surgical intervention.

Patients should be evaluated for other sexually transmitted infections, such as gonorrhea, syphilis, *Chlamydia trachomatis*, chancroid, hepatitis B virus, and human immunodeficiency virus.

ISOLATION OF THE HOSPITALIZED PATIENT: Standard precautions are recommended.

CONTROL MEASURES: Sexual partners should be examined, counseled to use condoms, and offered antimicrobial therapy. The value of empiric therapy in the absence of signs and symptoms has not been established.

Haemophilus influenzae Infections

CLINICAL MANIFESTATIONS: *Haemophilus influenzae* type b (Hib) causes pneumonia, occult febrile bacteremia, meningitis, epiglottitis, septic arthritis, cellulitis, otitis media, purulent pericarditis, and other less common infections, such as endocarditis, endophthalmitis, osteomyelitis, and peritonitis. Nontype b encapsulated strains occasionally cause invasive disease similar to type b infections. Nontypeable strains more commonly cause infections of the respiratory tract (eg, conjunctivitis, otitis media, sinusitis, pneumonia) and, less often, bacteremia, meningitis, chorioamnionitis, and neonatal septicemia.

ETIOLOGY: *Haemophilus influenzae* is a pleomorphic gram-negative coccobacillus. Encapsulated strains express 1 of 6 antigenically distinct capsular polysaccharides (a through f); nonencapsulated strains fail to react with typing antisera against capsular serotypes a through f and are designated nontypeable.

EPIDEMIOLOGY: The natural habitat of the organism is the upper respiratory tract of humans. The mode of transmission is person-to-person by inhalation of respiratory droplets or by direct contact with respiratory tract secretions. In neonates, infection is acquired intrapartum by aspiration of amniotic fluid or by contact with genital tract secretions containing the organism. Asymptomatic colonization by *H influenzae* is common, especially with nontypeable strains, which are recovered from the nasopharynx of 40% to 80% of children. Nasopharyngeal colonization by type b organisms is rare, occurring in 2% to 5% of children in the prevaccine era and even fewer children after widespread immunization. Colonization by strains expressing nontype b capsules also is uncommon. The exact period of communicability is unknown.

Before introduction of effective Hib conjugate vaccines, Hib was the most common cause of bacterial meningitis in children in the United States. The peak incidence of meningitis and most other invasive Hib infections occurred between 6 and 18 months of age. In contrast, the peak age for epiglottitis was 2 to 4 years of age.

Unimmunized children younger than 4 years of age are at increased risk of invasive Hib disease, especially if they are in prolonged close contact (such as in a household setting) with a child with invasive Hib disease. Other factors that predispose to invasive disease include sickle cell disease, asplenia, human immunodeficiency virus (HIV) infection, certain immunodeficiency syndromes, and malignant neoplasms. Historically, invasive Hib was more common in boys; black, Alaska Native, Apache, and Navajo children; child care attendees; children living in crowded conditions; and children who were not breastfed.

Since 1988, when Hib conjugate vaccines were introduced, the incidence of invasive Hib disease in infants and young children has decreased by 99% to fewer than 1 case per 100 000 children younger than 5 years of age. The incidence of invasive infections caused by all other encapsulated and nontypeable strains combined also is low. In the United States, invasive Hib disease occurs primarily in underimmunized children and among infants too young to have completed the primary immunization series. *Haemophilus influenzae* type b remains an important pathogen in economically developing countries where routine vaccines are not available to most of the population.

The **incubation period** is unknown.

DIAGNOSTIC TESTS: Cerebrospinal fluid (CSF), blood, synovial fluid, pleural fluid, and middle ear aspirates should be cultured on a medium such as chocolate agar, a medium enriched with factors X and V. Gram stain of an infected body fluid specimen can facilitate presumptive diagnosis. Latex particle agglutination for detection of type b capsular antigen in CSF can be helpful, but a negative test result does not exclude the diagnosis, and false-positive results have been recorded. Antigen testing of serum and urine specimens is not recommended. All *H influenzae* isolates associated with an invasive infection should be serotyped. Serotyping discrepancies have been noted between slide agglutination and polymerase chain reaction capsular typing, with misidentification by slide agglutination of nontypeable strains as encapsulated. If serotyping is not available locally, isolates should be submitted to the state health department or to a reference laboratory for testing.

TREATMENT:
- Initial therapy for children with meningitis possibly caused by Hib is cefotaxime or ceftriaxone. Meropenem or the combination of ampicillin and chloramphenicol are alternative empiric regimen(s). For antimicrobial treatment of epiglottitis, arthritis, and other invasive *H influenzae* infections, including infections caused by strains other than type b, recommendations are similar.
- For patients with uncomplicated meningitis who respond rapidly, antimicrobial therapy for 10 days administered intravenously usually is satisfactory. More than 10 days of therapy may be indicated in complicated cases.
- Dexamethasone may be beneficial for treatment of infants and children with Hib meningitis to diminish the risk of neurologic sequelae, including hearing loss, if given before or concurrently with the first dose of antimicrobial agent(s). There probably is no benefit if dexamethasone is given more than 1 hour after antimicrobial agent(s).
- Epiglottitis is a medical emergency. An airway must be established promptly with an endotracheal tube or by tracheostomy.
- Infected synovial, pleural, or pericardial fluid should be removed.
- For empiric treatment of acute otitis media in children younger than 2 years of age or in children 2 years of age or older with severe disease, oral amoxicillin (see details in Pneumococcal Infections, p 525, and Appropriate Use of Antimicrobial Agents, p 737) is recommended.* Duration of therapy is 5 to 10 days. The 5-day course is considered for children 2 years of age and older. In the United States, 30% to 40% of *H influenzae* isolates produce beta-lactamase, necessitating a beta-lactamase–resistant agent, such as amoxicillin-clavulanate; an oral cephalosporin, such as cefuroxime or cefpodoxime; or a newer macrolide for directed treatment. In vitro susceptibility testing of isolates from middle ear fluid specimens may help guide therapy in complicated or persistent cases.

ISOLATION OF THE HOSPITALIZED PATIENT: In patients with invasive Hib disease, droplet precautions are recommended for 24 hours after initiation of parenteral antimicrobial therapy.

CONTROL MEASURES (FOR INVASIVE HIB DISEASE):
CARE OF EXPOSED PEOPLE. Careful observation of exposed unimmunized or incompletely immunized children who are household, child care, or nursery contacts of patients with invasive Hib disease is essential. Exposed children in whom febrile illness develops should receive prompt medical evaluation.

Chemoprophylaxis. The risk of invasive Hib disease is increased among unimmunized household contacts younger than 4 years of age. Rifampin eradicates Hib from the pharynx in approximately 95% of carriers and decreases the risk of secondary invasive illness in exposed household contacts. Nursery and child care center

---
* American Academy of Pediatrics, Subcommittee on Management of Acute Otitis Media. Diagnosis and management of acute otitis media. *Pediatrics.* 2004;113:1451–1465

contacts also may be at increased risk of secondary disease, but experts disagree about the magnitude of the risk. The risk of secondary disease in children attending child care facilities seems to be lower than that observed for age-susceptible household contacts, and secondary disease in child care contacts is rare when all contacts are older than 2 years of age.

Indications and guidelines for chemoprophylaxis in different circumstances are summarized in Table 3.10.

- **Household.** In households with at least 1 contact who is younger than 48 months of age and unimmunized or incompletely immunized against Hib, rifampin prophylaxis is recommended for all household contacts, regardless of age. In households with a contact who is an immunocompromised child, even if the child is older than 48 months of age and fully immunized, all members of

Table 3.10. Indications and Guidelines for Rifampin Chemoprophylaxis for Contacts of Index Cases of Invasive *Haemophilus influenzae* Type b (Hib) Disease

Chemoprophylaxis Recommended

- For all household contacts[1] in the following circumstances:
  - Household with at least 1 contact younger than 4 years of age who is unimmunized or incompletely immunized[2]
  - Household with a child younger than 12 months of age who has not received the primary series.
  - Household with a contact who is an immunocompromised child, regardless of that child's Hib immunization status
- For nursery school and child care center contacts when 2 or more cases of Hib invasive disease have occurred within 60 days (see text)
- For index case, if younger than 2 years of age or member of a household with a susceptible contact and treated with a regimen other than cefotaxime or ceftriaxone, chemoprophylaxis usually is provided just before discharge from hospital

Chemoprophylaxis Not Recommended

- For occupants of households with no children younger than 4 years of age other than the index patient
- For occupants of households when all household contacts 12 to 48 months of age have completed their Hib immunization series and when household contacts younger than 12 months of age have completed their primary series of Hib immunizations
- For nursery school and child care contacts of 1 index case, especially those older than 2 years of age
- For pregnant women

---

[1] Defined as people residing with the index patient or nonresidents who spent 4 or more hours with the index case for at least 5 of the 7 days preceding the day of hospital admission of the index case.

[2] Complete immunization is defined as having had at least 1 dose of conjugate vaccine at 15 months of age or older; 2 doses between 12 and 14 months of age; or a 2- or 3-dose primary series when younger than 12 months with a booster dose at 12 months of age or older.

the household should receive rifampin because of the possibility that immunization may not have been effective. Similarly, in households with a contact younger than 12 months of age who has not received the 2-dose or 3-dose primary series of Hib conjugate vaccine, depending on vaccine product, all household members should receive rifampin prophylaxis. Chemoprophylaxis is not recommended for occupants of households who do not have children younger than 48 months of age (other than the index case), when all household contacts 12 to 48 months of age are immunocompetent and have completed their Hib immunization series, and when all household contacts younger than 12 months of age have completed the primary series of Hib immunizations (see Table 3.10, p 313). Chemoprophylaxis is not recommended for contacts of people with invasive disease caused by nontype b *H influenzae* strains.

Given that most secondary cases in households occur during the first week after hospitalization of the index case, when indicated, prophylaxis should be initiated as soon as possible. Because some secondary cases occur later, initiation of prophylaxis 7 days or more after hospitalization of the index patient still may be of some benefit.

- **Child care and nursery school.** When 2 or more cases of invasive disease have occurred within 60 days and unimmunized or incompletely immunized children attend the child care facility, rifampin prophylaxis for attendees and child care providers should be considered. When a single case has occurred, the advisability of rifampin prophylaxis in exposed child care groups with unimmunized or incompletely immunized children is controversial.

In addition to these recommendations for chemoprophylaxis, unimmunized or incompletely immunized children should receive a dose of vaccine and should be scheduled for completion of the recommended age-specific immunization schedule (see Immunization).

- **Index case.** Treatment of Hib disease with cefotaxime or ceftriaxone eradicates Hib colonization, eliminating the need for prophylaxis of the index patient. Patients who are treated with meropenem, ampicillin, or chloramphenicol and who are younger than 2 years of age or have a susceptible household contact should receive rifampin prophylaxis at the end of therapy for invasive infection.
- **Dosage.** Rifampin should be given orally once a day for 4 days (in a dose of 20 mg/kg; maximum dose 600 mg). The dose for infants younger than 1 month of age is not established; some experts recommend lowering the dose to 10 mg/kg. For adults, each dose is 600 mg.

IMMUNIZATION. Three single-antigen Hib conjugate vaccine products and 2 combination vaccine products that contain Hib conjugate are available in the United States (see Table 3.11, p 315). The Hib conjugate vaccines consist of the Hib capsular polysaccharide (ie, polyribosylribotol phosphate [PRP] or PRP oligomers) covalently linked to a carrier protein. Protective antibodies are directed against PRP. Conjugate vaccines vary in composition and immunogenicity, and as a result, recommendations for their use differ.

Depending on the vaccine, the recommended primary series consists of 3 doses given at 2, 4, and 6 months of age or 2 doses given at 2 and 4 months of age (see

Table 3.11. *Haemophilus influenzae* Type b Conjugate Vaccines Licensed for Use in Infants and Children in the United States[1]

Manufacturer	Abbreviation	Trade Name	Carrier Protein
Aventis Pasteur, Inc[2]	PRP-T	ActHIB	Tetanus toxoid
	DTaP/PRP-T[3]	TriHIBit[3]	Tetanus toxoid
Merck & Co, Inc	PRP-OMP	PedvaxHIB	OMP (an outer membrane protein complex from *Neisseria meningitidis*)
	PRP-OMP/ Hep B[4]	Comvax[4]	OMP
Wyeth-Lederle Vaccines	HbOC	HibTITER	CRM$_{197}$ (a nontoxic mutant diphtheria toxin)

[1] *Haemophilus influenzae* type b conjugate vaccines may be given in combination products or as reconstituted products, provided the combination or reconstituted vaccine is licensed by the US Food and Drug Administration (FDA) for the child's age and administration of the other vaccine component(s) also is justified.
[2] License holder on the licensed product. Parent company is sanofi pasteur.
[3] Aventis Pasteur's DTaP (Tripedia) may be used to reconstitute PRP-T (ActHIB) to form TriHIBit, which is licensed by the FDA only for the fourth dose of Hib and DTaP series. The DTaP/PRP-T vaccine (TriHIBit) should not be used for primary immunization in infants at 2, 4, or 6 months of age.
[4] The combination *H influenzae* type b (PRP-OMP) and hepatitis B (Recombivax, 5 µg) vaccine is licensed for use at 2, 4, and 12 to 15 months of age (Comvax).

Recommendations for Immunization, p 316, and Table 3.12, p 316). The recommended doses may be given as a hepatitis B-Hib combination vaccine. The regimens in Table 3.12 are likely to be equivalent in protection after completion of the recommended primary series. Given the increased risk of disease in early infancy among American Indian/Alaska Native children, use of PRP-OMP (outer membrane protein complex) vaccine is recommended for the first dose in a series because of the substantial antibody response after 1 dose (see American Indian/Alaska Native Children, *Haemophilus influenzae* type b, p 89).

An additional booster dose of any Hib conjugate vaccine is recommended at 12 to 15 months of age, regardless of which regimen was used for the primary series. This booster dose may be given as a combination vaccine.

Combination Vaccines. Two combination vaccines that contain *H influenzae* type b are licensed in the United States: DTaP-Hib combination and hepatitis B-Hib combination (see Table 3.11). The DTaP-Hib combination vaccine is licensed only for the fourth dose of the DTaP and Hib series. The DTaP-Hib combination vaccine is not licensed for use as the primary series at 2, 4, and 6 months of age. The hepatitis B-Hib combination is licensed for use at 2, 4, and 12 to 15 months of age. This vaccine should not be given to infants younger than 6 weeks of age.

Vaccine Interchangeability. The monovalent Hib conjugate vaccines available in the United States are considered interchangeable for primary and booster immunization. If PRP-OMP vaccine is administered as only part of a primary series, the recommended number of doses to complete the series is determined by the other Hib conjugate vaccine.

Dosage and Route of Administration. The dose of each Hib conjugate vaccine is 0.5 mL, given intramuscularly.

Children With Immunologic Impairment. Children at increased risk of Hib disease may have impaired anti-PRP antibody responses to conjugate vaccines. Examples include children with HIV infection; children with immunoglobulin deficiency; recipients of stem cell transplants; and recipients of chemotherapy for a malignant neoplasm. Some children with immunologic impairment may benefit from more doses of conjugate vaccine than usually indicated (see Recommendations for Immunization).

Adverse Reactions. Adverse reactions to the Hib conjugate vaccines are few. Pain, redness, and swelling at the injection site occur in approximately 25% of recipients, but these symptoms typically are mild and last fewer than 24 hours.

RECOMMENDATIONS FOR IMMUNIZATION.

Indications and Schedule

- All children should be immunized with an Hib conjugate vaccine beginning at approximately 2 months of age or as soon as possible thereafter (see Table 3.12). Other general recommendations are as follows:
  - Immunization can be initiated as early as 6 weeks of age.
  - Vaccine can be given during visits for other childhood immunizations (see Simultaneous Administration of Multiple Vaccines, p 34).
- For routine immunization of children younger than 7 months of age, the following guidelines are recommended:
  - *Primary series.* A 3-dose regimen of HbOC (diphtheria CRM_{197} protein conjugate) or PRP-T (tetanus toxoid conjugate) or a 2-dose regimen of PRP-OMP should be administered (see Table 3.12). Doses are given at approximately 2-month intervals. When sequential doses of different vaccine prod-

Table 3.12. Recommended Regimens for Routine *Haemophilus influenzae* Type b Conjugate Immunization for Children Immunized Beginning at 2 to 6 Months of Age[1]

Vaccine Product at Initiation	Total No. of Doses To Be Administered	Recommended Regimen
HbOC or PRP-T	4	3 doses at 2-mo intervals initially; fourth dose at 12 to 15 mo of age; any conjugate vaccine for dose 4[2]
PRP-OMP	3	2 doses 2 months apart[3]; third dose at 12–15 mo of age; any conjugate vaccine for dose 3[2]

[1] See text and Table 3.11 (p 315) for further information about specific vaccines and for explanation of abbreviations.

[2] The monovalent Hib conjugate vaccines available in the United States are considered interchangeabl for primary and booster immunizations. If PRP-OMP is administered only as part of a primary series, the recommended number of doses to complete the series is determined by the other Hib conjugate vaccine.

ucts are given or uncertainty exists about which products previously were administered, 3 doses of any conjugate vaccine are considered sufficient to complete the primary series, regardless of the regimen used.

- *Booster immunization at 12 to 15 months of age.* For children who have completed a primary series, an additional dose of conjugate vaccine is recommended at 12 to 15 months of age or at least 2 months after the last dose. Any conjugate vaccine or DTaP-Hib combination vaccine is acceptable for this dose.

• Children younger than 5 years of age who did not receive Hib conjugate vaccine during the first 6 months of life should be immunized according to the following recommended schedules (see Table 1.7, p 28). For accelerated immunization in infants younger than 12 months of age, a minimum of a 4-week interval between doses can be used.

- For children in whom immunization is initiated at 7 to 11 months of age, the recommended schedules for HbOC, PRP-OMP, and PRP-T are identical and require 3 doses. The first 2 doses are given 2 months apart. The third (booster) dose should be given at 12 to 15 months of age, preferably 2 months after the second dose.

- For children in whom immunization is initiated at 12 to 14 months of age, the recommended regimens for HbOC, PRP-OMP, and PRP-T are identical and include 2 doses given 2 months apart.

- If circumstances are such that more rapid catch-up immunization is desirable, the recommended interval between doses is 4 weeks.

- For children in whom immunization is initiated at 15 to 59 months of age, the recommended regimen is a single dose of any licensed conjugate vaccine.

• Special circumstances are as follows:

- *Lapsed immunizations.* Recommendations for children who have had a lapse in the schedule of immunizations are based on limited data. The current recommendations are summarized in Table 1.7 (p 28).

- *Preterm infants.* For preterm infants, immunization should be based on chronologic age and should be initiated at 2 months of age according to recommendations in Table 3.12 (p 316).

- *Children who may be at increased risk of invasive Hib disease resulting from immunologic or other host defense abnormalities (eg, sickle cell disease or anatomic asplenia).* Children with decreased or absent splenic function who have received a primary series of Hib immunizations and a booster dose at 12 months of age or older need not be immunized further. Children who have received a primary series and a booster dose and are undergoing scheduled splenectomy (eg, for Hodgkin disease, spherocytosis, immune thrombocytopenia, or hypersplenism) may benefit from an additional dose of any licensed conjugate vaccine. This dose should be provided at least 7 to 10 days before the procedure. Patients with HIV infection or immunoglobulin (Ig) G2 subclass deficiency and children receiving chemotherapy for malignant neoplasms also are at increased risk of invasive Hib disease. Whether these children will benefit from additional doses after completion of the primary series of immunizations and the booster dose at 12 months of age or later is unknown. Health care professionals should make every effort to ensure completion of the primary immunization and booster series.

For children 12 to 59 months of age with an underlying condition predisposing to Hib disease who are not immunized or have received only 1 dose of conjugate vaccine before 12 months of age, 2 doses of any conjugate vaccine, separated by 2 months, are recommended. For children in this age group who received 2 doses before 12 months of age, 1 additional dose of conjugate vaccine is recommended.

- *Unimmunized children with an underlying disease possibly predisposing to Hib disease who are older than 59 months of age.* These children should be immunized with any licensed conjugate vaccine. On the basis of limited data, 2 doses separated by 1 to 2 months are suggested for children with HIV infection or IgG2 deficiency.
- *Children with* Haemophilus influenzae *type b invasive infection.* Children who develop invasive disease when younger than 24 months of age can remain at risk of developing a second episode of disease. These children should be immunized according to the age-appropriate schedule for unimmunized children and as if they had received no previous Hib vaccine doses (see Table 3.12, p 316, and Table 1.7, p 28). Immunization should be initiated 1 month after onset of disease or as soon as possible thereafter. Children who develop disease at 24 months of age or older do not need immunization, because disease almost always induces a protective immune response, making second episodes of disease in this age group rare.

Immunologic evaluation should be performed in children who experience invasive Hib disease despite 2 to 3 doses of vaccine and in children with recurrent invasive disease attributable to type b strains.

REPORTING. All cases of *H influenzae* invasive disease, including type b and nontype b, should be reported to the Centers for Disease Control and Prevention through the local or state public health department.

Hantavirus Pulmonary Syndrome

CLINICAL MANIFESTATIONS: Hantaviruses in humans cause 2 syndromes: hantavirus pulmonary syndrome (HPS), a noncardiogenic pulmonary edema, and hemorrhagic fever with renal syndrome (HFRS) (see Hemorrhagic Fevers and Related Syndromes, p 324). The prodromal illness of HPS is 3 to 7 days and is characterized by fever; chills; headache; myalgias of the shoulders, lower back, and thighs; nausea; vomiting; diarrhea; dizziness; and sometimes cough. Respiratory tract symptoms or signs usually do not occur for the first 3 to 7 days until pulmonary edema and severe hypoxemia appear abruptly after the onset of cough and dyspnea, and the disease progresses over a few hours. In severe cases, persistent hypotension caused by myocardial dysfunction is present.

The extensive bilateral interstitial and alveolar pulmonary edema and pleural effusions are the result of a diffuse pulmonary capillary leak and appear to be caused by immune responses to hantavirus in endothelial cells of the microvasculature. Intubation and assisted ventilation usually are required for only 2 to 4 days, with resolution heralded by the onset of diuresis and rapid clinical improvement.

The severe myocardial depression is different from that of septic shock; the cardiac indices and the stroke volume index are low, the pulmonary wedge pressure is normal, and systemic vascular resistance is increased. Poor prognostic indicators include persistent hypotension, marked hemoconcentration, a cardiac index of less than 2, and abrupt onset of lactic acidosis with a serum lactate concentration of greater than 4 mmol/L (36 mg/dL).

The mortality rate for patients with HPS in recent years has been 30% to 40%. Asymptomatic and mild forms of disease are rare in adults, but limited information suggests they may be more common in children. Serious sequelae are uncommon.

ETIOLOGY: Hantaviruses are RNA viruses of the Bunyaviridae family. Within the Hantavirus genus, Sin Nombre virus (SNV) is the major cause of HPS in the 4-corners region of the United States. Bayou virus, Black Creek Canal virus, Mononga-hela virus, and New York virus are responsible for sporadic cases in Louisiana, Texas, Florida, New York, and other areas of the eastern United States. In recent years, new hantavirus serotypes associated with an HPS syndrome, including Andes virus, Oran virus, Laguna Negra virus, and Choclo virus, have been reported in South America and Panama.

EPIDEMIOLOGY: Rodents, the natural hosts for hantaviruses, acquire a lifelong, asymptomatic, chronic infection with prolonged viruria and virus in saliva, urine, and feces. Humans acquire infection through direct contact with infected rodents, rodent droppings, or nests or inhalation of aerosolized virus particles from rodent urine, droppings, or saliva. Rarely, infection may be acquired from rodent bites or contami-nation of broken skin with excreta. Person-to-person transmission of hantaviruses has not been demonstrated with the exception of a few cases of person-to-person spread of Andes virus reported from Patagonia, South America. At-risk activities include handling or trapping rodents, cleaning or entering closed, rarely used rodent-infested structures, cleaning feed storage or animal shelter areas, hand plowing, and living in a home with an increased density of mice in or around the home. For backpackers or campers, sleeping in a structure also inhabited by rodents has been associated with HPS. Weather conditions resulting in exceptionally heavy rainfall and improved rodent food supplies can result in a large increase in the rodent population. The increased rodent population results in more frequent contact between humans and infected mice and may account for outbreaks. Most cases occur during spring and summer, and the geographic location is determined by the habitat of the rodent carrier.

Sin Nombre virus is transmitted by the deer mouse, *Peromyscus maniculatus;* Black Creek Canal virus is transmitted by the cotton rat, *Sigmodon hispidus;* Bayou virus is transmitted by the rice rat, *Oryzomys palustris;* and New York virus is transmitted by the white-footed mouse, *Peromyscus leucopus.*

The **incubation period** may be 1 to 6 weeks after exposure to infected rodents, their saliva, or excreta but has not been established definitively.

DIAGNOSTIC TESTS: Characteristic laboratory findings include neutrophilic leuko-cytosis with immature granulocytes, more than 10% immunoblasts (basophilic cyto-plasm, prominent nucleoli, and an increased nuclear-cytoplasmic ratio), thrombo-cytopenia, and increased hematocrit. In fatal cases, SNV has been identified by immunohistochemical staining of capillary endothelial cells in almost every organ in the body. Sin Nombre virus RNA has been detected uniformly by the reverse transcriptase-polymerase chain reaction assay of peripheral blood mononuclear cells and other clinical specimens from the first few days of hospitalization up to 10 to 21 days after symptom onset, and the duration of viremia is unknown. Viral RNA is not detected readily in bronchoalveolar lavage fluids.

Hantavirus-specific immunoglobulin (Ig) G and IgM antibodies are present at the onset of clinical disease. A rapid diagnostic test can facilitate immediate appropriate supportive therapy and early transfer to a tertiary care facility. Enzyme immunoassay (available through many state health departments and the Centers for Disease Control and Prevention) and Western blot are assays that use recombinant antigens and have a high degree of specificity for detection of IgG and IgM antibody. Viral culture is not useful for diagnosis and is available only in research laboratories that have specialized facilities to protect laboratory workers.

TREATMENT: Patients with suspected HPS should be transferred immediately to a tertiary care facility. Supportive management of pulmonary edema, severe hypoxemia, and hypotension during the first 24 to 48 hours is critical for recovery. A flow-directed pulmonary catheter for monitoring fluid administration and use of inotropic support, vasopressors, and careful ventilatory control are important.

Extracorporeal membrane oxygenation (ECMO) may provide particularly important short-term support for the severe capillary leak syndrome in the lungs. Venoarterial ECMO, which also can provide circulatory support, has shown encouraging early results with rapid and dramatic hemodynamic improvement in patients after only 12 hours and a total duration of only 4 to 5 days.

Ribavirin is active against hantaviruses including SNV. Two clinical studies (one open-label study and one randomized, placebo-controlled, double-blind study) found that intravenous ribavirin probably is ineffective in treatment of HPS in the cardiopulmonary stage. The small number of patients studied and the rapid progression of disease, with most deaths occurring within 48 hours after onset, contribute to difficulty in assessing clearly the efficacy and safety of ribavirin in HPS.

ISOLATION OF THE HOSPITALIZED PATIENT: Standard precautions are recommended. Hantavirus pulmonary syndrome has not been associated with nosocomial or person-to-person transmission in the United States.

CONTROL MEASURES:
CARE OF EXPOSED PEOPLE. Serial clinical examinations should be used to monitor people assessed to be at high risk of infection after a high-risk exposure (see Epidemiology, p 319).

ENVIRONMENTAL CONTROL. Hantavirus infections of humans occur primarily in adults and are associated with domestic, occupational, or leisure activities bringing humans into contact with infected rodents, usually in a rural setting. Eradicating the host reservoir is not feasible. The best available approach for disease control and prevention is risk reduction through environmental hygiene practices that discourage rodents from colonizing the home and work environment and that minimize aerosolization and contact with virus in saliva and excreta. Measures to decrease exposure in the home and workplace include eliminating food sources available to rodents in structures used by humans, limiting possible nesting sites, sealing holes and other possible entrances for rodents, and using "snap traps" and rodenticides. Before entering areas with potential rodent infestations, doors and windows should be opened to ventilate the enclosure.

Hantaviruses, because of their lipid envelope, are susceptible to most disinfectants, including diluted bleach solutions, detergents, and most general household disinfectants. Dusty or dirty areas or articles should be moistened with a 10% bleach or other disinfectant solution before being cleaned. Brooms and vacuum cleaners should not be used to clean rodent-infested areas. A 10% bleach solution to disinfect dead rodents and wearing rubber gloves before handling trapped or dead rodents are recommended. Gloves and traps should be disinfected after use. People entering these areas should avoid stirring up or breathing potentially contaminated dust.

Efficacious chemoprophylaxis measures or vaccines are not available.

PUBLIC HEALTH REPORTING. Possible occurrence should be reported immediately to local and state public health authorities.

Helicobacter pylori Infections

CLINICAL MANIFESTATIONS: *Helicobacter pylori* causes chronic active gastritis and increases the risk of duodenal and gastric ulcers; persistence increases the risk of gastric cancer. Acute infection can manifest as epigastric pain, nausea, vomiting, hematemesis, and guaiac-positive stools. Symptoms usually resolve within a few days despite persistence of the organism for years or for life. *Helicobacter pylori* infection is not associated with autoimmune or chemical gastritis.

ETIOLOGY: *Helicobacter pylori* is a gram-negative and spiral, curved, or U-shaped microaerophilic bacillus that has 2 to 6 sheathed flagella at one end. It is catalase, oxidase, and urease positive.

EPIDEMIOLOGY: *Helicobacter pylori* has been isolated from humans and other primates. An animal reservoir for human transmission has not been demonstrated. Organisms are transmitted from infected humans by the fecal-oral and oral-oral routes. Infection rates are low in children in resource-rich countries except in children from lower socioeconomic groups; prevalence increases until 60 years of age. Most carriage is asymptomatic, but some colonized people have histologic findings of chronic gastritis. *Helicobacter pylori* chiefly is acquired from 1 to 7 years of age in resource-limited countries.

The **incubation period** is unknown.

DIAGNOSTIC TESTS: *Helicobacter pylori* infection can be diagnosed by culture of gastric biopsy tissue on nonselective media (eg, chocolate agar) or selective media (eg, Skirrow agar) at 37°C (98°F) under microaerobic conditions for 2 to 5 days. Organisms usually can be visualized on histologic sections with Warthin-Starry silver, Steiner, Giemsa, or Genta staining. Presence of *H pylori* can be diagnosed but not excluded on the basis of hematoxylin-eosin stains. Because of production of urease by organisms, urease testing of a gastric specimen can give a rapid and specific microbiologic diagnosis. Each of these tests requires endoscopy and biopsy. Noninvasive, commercially available tests include breath tests, which detect labeled carbon dioxide in expired air after oral administration of isotopically labeled urea, and serologic tests for the presence of immunoglobulin G specific for *H pylori*. Each of these commercially available tests has a sensitivity and specificity of 95% or more. A stool antigen test also is available commercially.

TREATMENT: Treatment is recommended only for infected patients who have peptic ulcer disease (currently or in the past), gastric mucosa-associated lymphoid tissue-type lymphoma, or early gastric cancer. Eradication therapy for *H pylori* consists of at least 7 days of treatment, although eradication rates are higher for regimens of 14 days. Effective regimens include 2 antimicrobial agents (eg, clarithromycin plus either amoxicillin or metronidazole) plus a proton pump inhibitor (lansoprazole, omeprazole, esomeprazole, rabeprazole, or pantoprazole). These regimens are effective in eliminating the organism, healing the ulcer, and preventing recurrence. Alternate therapies include bismuth subsalicylate plus metronidazole plus tetracycline in people 8 years of age and older plus either a proton pump inhibitor or an H_2 blocker (cimetidine, famotidine, nizatidine, and ranitidine).

ISOLATION OF THE HOSPITALIZED PATIENT: Standard precautions are recommended.

CONTROL MEASURES: Disinfection of gastroscopes prevents transmission of the organism between patients.

Hemorrhagic Fevers Caused by Arenaviruses

CLINICAL MANIFESTATIONS: The arenaviruses include lymphocytic choriomeningitis virus and the agents of 5 hemorrhagic fevers (HFs): Bolivian, Argentine, Brazilian, Venezuelan, and Lassa. The zoonotic diseases associated with these agents range in severity from mild, acute, febrile infections to severe illnesses in which vascular leak, shock, and multiorgan dysfunction are prominent features. Fever, headache, myalgia, conjunctival suffusion, bleeding, and abdominal pain are common early symptoms in all infections. Lymphocytic choriomeningitis virus causes aseptic meningitis that may be associated with a variety of complications. Thrombocytopenia, axillary petechiae, and encephalopathy are usual in Argentine HF, Bolivian HF, and Venezuelan HF, and exudative pharyngitis often occurs in Lassa fever. Mucosal bleeding occurs in severe cases as a consequence of vascular damage, thrombocytopenia, and platelet dysfunction. Proteinuria is common, but renal failure is unusual. Increased serum concentrations of aspartate transaminase can indicate an adverse or fatal outcome of Lassa fever. Shock develops 7 to 9 days after onset of illness in more severely ill patients with these infections. Upper and lower respiratory tract symptoms can develop in people with Lassa fever. Encephalopathic signs such as tremor, alterations in consciousness, and seizures can occur in the South American hemorrhagic fevers and in severe cases of Lassa fever.

ETIOLOGY: Arenaviruses are RNA viruses. The major New World arenavirus hemorrhagic fevers occurring in the Western hemisphere are Argentine HF caused by Junin virus, Bolivian HF caused by Machupo virus, and Venezuelan HF caused by Guanarito virus. A fourth arenavirus, Sabia virus, caused 2 unrelated cases of naturally occurring HF in Brazil and 2 laboratory-acquired cases. The Old World complex of arenaviruses includes Lassa virus, which causes Lassa fever, a disease occurring in West Africa, and lymphocytic choriomeningitis (LCM) virus (see Lymphocytic Choriomeningitis, p 434), which produces the least severe infection of the arenaviruses.

EPIDEMIOLOGY: Arenaviruses are maintained in nature by association with specific rodent hosts, in which they produce chronic viremia and viruria. The principal routes of infection are inhalation and contact with mucous membranes and skin (eg, through cuts, scratches, or abrasions) with urine and salivary secretions from these persistently infected rodents. Lymphocytic choriomeningitis virus has been transmitted to recipients of solid organs from patients infected with LCM. All arenaviruses are infectious as aerosols; arenaviruses causing hemorrhagic fever should be considered highly hazardous to people working with any of the viruses in the laboratory. The geographic distribution and habitats of the specific rodents that serve as reservoir hosts largely determine the areas with endemic infection and populations at risk. Before a vaccine became available in Argentina, several hundred cases of Argentine HF occurred yearly in agricultural workers and inhabitants of the Argentine pampas. The vaccine is not licensed in the United States. Epidemics of Bolivian HF occurred in small towns between 1962 and 1964; sporadic disease activity in the countryside has continued since then. Venezuelan HF first was identified in 1989 and occurs in rural north-central Venezuela. Lassa fever is endemic in most of West Africa, where rodent hosts live in proximity with humans, causing thousands of infections annually. Lassa fever has been reported in the United States in people who have traveled to West Africa.

The **incubation periods** are from 6 to 17 days.

DIAGNOSTIC TESTS: Acute infection is diagnosed by demonstrating virus-specific serum immunoglobulin (Ig) M or viral antigen. The IgG antibody response is delayed. Viral nucleic acid also can be detected in acute disease by reverse transcriptase-polymerase chain reaction assay. These viruses may be recovered from blood (collected in a heparin-containing tube) of acutely ill patients as well as from various tissues obtained postmortem, but isolation should only be attempted under biosafety level-4 conditions.

TREATMENT: Intravenous ribavirin decreases the mortality rate significantly in patients with severe Lassa fever, particularly if patients are treated during the first week of illness, and probably is beneficial in treating South American arenavirus infections.

ISOLATION OF THE HOSPITALIZED PATIENT: In addition to standard precautions, contact and droplet precautions, including careful prevention of needlestick injuries and careful handling of clinical specimens for the duration of illness, are recommended for all hemorrhagic fevers caused by arenaviruses. A negative-pressure ventilation room is recommended for patients with prominent cough or severe disease, and people entering the room should wear personal protection respirators. Additional viral HF-specific isolation precautions have been recommended in the event that a viral HF virus is used as a weapon of biological terrorism.*

CONTROL MEASURES:

CARE OF EXPOSED PEOPLE. No specific measures are warranted for exposed people unless direct contamination with blood, excretions, or secretions from an infected patient has occurred. If such contamination has occurred, recording daily temperature for 21 days is recommended, with prompt reporting of fever.

IMMUNOPROPHYLAXIS. An investigational live-attenuated Junin vaccine protects against Argentine HF and probably against Bolivian HF. The vaccine is associated with minimal adverse effects in adults; similar findings have been obtained from limited safety studies in children 4 years of age and older.

ENVIRONMENTAL. In town-based outbreaks of Bolivian HF, rodent control has proven successful. Area rodent control is not practical for control of Argentine HF or Venezuelan HF. Intensive rodent control efforts modestly have decreased the rate of peridomestic Lassa virus infection, but rodents eventually reinvade human dwellings, and infection still occurs in rural settings.

PUBLIC HEALTH REPORTING. Because of the risk of nosocomial transmission, the state health department and the Centers for Disease Control and Prevention should be contacted for specific advice about management and diagnosis of suspected cases.

Hemorrhagic Fevers and Related Syndromes Caused by Viruses of the Family Bunyaviridae†

CLINICAL MANIFESTATIONS: These zoonotic infections are severe febrile diseases in which shock and bleeding can be significant and multisystem involvement can occur. In the United States, one of these infections causes an illness marked by acute respiratory and cardiovascular failure (see Hantavirus Pulmonary Syndrome, p 318).

Hemorrhagic fever with renal syndrome (HFRS) is a complex, multiphasic disease characterized by vascular instability and varying degrees of renal insufficiency. Fever, flushing, conjunctival injection, abdominal pain, and lumbar pain are followed by hypotension, oliguria, and subsequently, polyuria. Petechiae and more serious bleeding manifestations are common. Shock and acute renal insufficiency may occur. Nephropathia epidemica, the clinical syndrome of HFRS in Europe, is a milder disease characterized by an influenza-like illness with abdominal pain and proteinuria. Acute renal dysfunction also occurs, but hypotensive shock or a requirement for dialysis are rare.

Crimean-Congo hemorrhagic fever (CCHF) is a multisystem disease characterized by hepatitis and profuse bleeding. Fever, headache, and myalgia are followed by signs of a diffuse capillary leak syndrome with facial suffusion, conjunctivitis, and proteinuria. Petechiae and purpura often appear on the skin and mucous membranes.

---

* Centers for Disease Control and Prevention. Notice to readers update: management of patients with suspected viral hemorrhagic fever—United States. *MMWR Morb Mortal Wkly Rep.* 1995;44:475–479

† Does not include hantavirus pulmonary syndrome, which is reviewed on p 318.

A hypotensive crisis often occurs after the appearance of frank hemorrhage from the gastrointestinal tract, nose, mouth, or uterus.

Rift Valley fever (RVF), in most cases, is a self-limited febrile illness. Occasionally, hemorrhagic fever with shock and icterus, encephalitis, or retinitis develops.

ETIOLOGY: Bunyaviridae are segmented, single-stranded RNA viruses with different geographic distributions depending on their vector. Hemorrhagic fever syndromes are associated with viruses from 3 genera: hantaviruses, nairoviruses (CCHF virus), and phleboviruses (RVF and sandfly fever viruses). Old World hantaviruses (Hantaan, Seoul, Dobrava, and Puumula viruses) cause HFRS, and New World hantaviruses (Sin Nombre and related viruses) cause HPS (see Table 3.1, p 212).

EPIDEMIOLOGY: The epidemiology of these diseases mainly is a function of the distribution and behavior of their reservoirs and vectors. All genera except hantaviruses are associated with arthropod vectors, and hantavirus infections are associated with exposure to infected rodents.

Classic HFRS occurs throughout much of Asia and Eastern and Western Europe with up to 100 000 cases per year. The most severe form of the disease is caused by the prototype Hantaan virus and Dobrava viruses in rural Asia and Europe, respectively; Puumula virus is associated with milder disease (nephropathia epidemica) in Europe. Seoul virus is distributed worldwide in association with *Rattus* species and can cause a disease of variable severity. Person-to-person transmission never has been reported with HFRS.

Crimean-Congo hemorrhagic fever occurs in much of sub-Saharan Africa, the Middle East, areas in West and Central Asia, and the Balkans. The CCHF virus is transmitted by ticks and, occasionally, by contact with viremic animals at slaughter. Nosocomial transmission of CCHF is a serious hazard.

Rift Valley fever occurs throughout sub-Saharan Africa and has caused epidemics in Egypt in 1977 and 1993–1995 and in Saudi Arabia and Yemen in 2000. The virus is arthropodborne and is transmitted from domestic livestock to humans by mosquitoes. The virus also can be transmitted by aerosol and by direct contact with infected aborted tissues or freshly slaughtered infected animal carcasses. Person-to-person transmission has not been reported.

The **incubation periods** for CCHF and RVF range from 2 to 10 days; for HFRS, incubation periods usually are longer, ranging from 7 to 42 days.

DIAGNOSTIC TESTS: The CCHF and RVF viruses can be cultivated readily (restricted to BSL-4 laboratories) from blood and tissue specimens of infected patients. Detection of viral antigen by enzyme immunoassay (EIA) is a useful alternative. Serum immunoglobulin (Ig) M and IgG virus-specific antibodies typically develop early in convalescence in CCHF and RVF. In HFRS, at the time of onset of illness or within 48 hours, IgM and IgG antibodies usually are detectable at a time when it is too late for virus isolation and antigen detection. Immunoglobulin M antibodies or rising IgG titers in paired serum specimens, as demonstrated by EIA, are diagnostic; neutralizing antibody tests provide greater virus-strain specificity. Immunofluorescent antibody tests also are used for serologic diagnosis. Polymerase chain reaction assay can be a useful complement to serodiagnostic assays on samples obtained during the acute phase of CCHF, RVF, or HFRS.

TREATMENT: Ribavirin given intravenously to patients with HFRS within the first 4 days of illness seems effective in decreasing renal dysfunction, vascular instability, and mortality. Supportive therapy for HFRS should include: (1) avoidance of transporting patients; (2) treatment of shock; (3) monitoring of fluid balance; (4) dialysis for complications of renal failure; (5) control of hypertension during the oliguric phase; and (6) early recognition of possible myocardial failure with appropriate therapy.

Ribavirin given to patients with CCHF has resulted in clinical responses, although no controlled studies have been performed. Experimental animal data also suggest the potential benefit of ribavirin in treatment of hemorrhagic RVF.

ISOLATION OF THE HOSPITALIZED PATIENT: In addition to standard precautions, contact and droplet precautions, including careful prevention of needlestick injuries and management of clinical specimens, are indicated for patients with CCHF for the duration for their illness. Airborne isolation also may be required in certain circumstances when patients undergo procedures that stimulate coughing and promote generation of aerosols. Rift Valley fever and HFRS have not been demonstrated to be contagious, but standard precautions should be followed.

CONTROL MEASURES:

CARE OF EXPOSED PEOPLE. People having direct contact with blood or other secretions from patients with CCHF should be observed closely for 14 days with daily monitoring for fever. Immediate therapy with intravenous ribavirin should be considered at the first sign of disease.

ENVIRONMENTAL IMMUNOPROPHYLAXIS. Monitoring of laboratory rat colonies and urban rodent control may be effective for ratborne HFRS.

Crimean-Congo Hemorrhagic Fever. Arachnicides for tick control generally have limited benefit but should be used in stockyard settings. Personal protective measures (eg, physical tick removal and protective clothing with permethrin sprays) may be effective.

Rift Valley Fever. Immunization of domestic animals should have an effect on limiting or preventing RVF outbreaks and protecting humans. Mosquito control usually is not effective.

PUBLIC HEALTH REPORTING. Because of the risk of nosocomial transmission of CCHF and diagnostic confusion with other viral hemorrhagic fevers, the state health department and the Centers for Disease Control and Prevention should be contacted about any suspected diagnosis of viral hemorrhagic fever and the management plan for the patient.

Hepatitis A

CLINICAL MANIFESTATIONS: Hepatitis A characteristically is an acute, self-limited illness associated with fever, malaise, jaundice, anorexia, and nausea. Symptomatic hepatitis A virus (HAV) infection occurs in approximately 30% of infected children younger than 6 years of age; few of these children will have jaundice. Among older children and adults, infection usually is symptomatic and typically lasts several weeks, with jaundice occurring in 70% or more. Prolonged or relapsing disease lasting as long as 6 months can occur. Fulminant hepatitis is rare but is more common in people with underlying liver disease. Chronic infection does not occur.

ETIOLOGY: Hepatitis A virus is an RNA virus classified as a member of the picornavirus group.

EPIDEMIOLOGY: The most common mode of transmission is person-to-person, resulting from fecal contamination and oral ingestion (ie, the fecal-oral route). Age at infection varies with socioeconomic status and associated living conditions. In developing countries, where infection is endemic, most people are infected during the first decade of life. In the prevaccine era in the United States, hepatitis A was one of the most commonly reported vaccine-preventable diseases, but its incidence has declined in recent years. In 2004, 5683 cases were reported to the Centers for Disease Control and Prevention (CDC), compared with an average of approximately 26 000 cases per year during the preimmunization era. These declining rates have been accompanied by a shift in age-specific rates. Historically, the highest rates occurred among children 5 to 14 years of age, and the lowest rates occurred among adults older than 40 years of age. However, in recent years the highest rates have occurred among young adults, and rates among children 5 to 14 years of age have been among the lowest. In addition, the previously observed unequal geographic distribution of hepatitis A incidence, with the highest rates of disease occurring in a limited number of states and communities, has disappeared after introduction of immunization. Continued surveillance is needed to verify that the decline in incidence is sustained (see Recommendations for Immunoprophylaxis, p 332).

Among cases of hepatitis A reported to the CDC, the identified risk factors include close personal contact with a person infected with HAV, household or personal contact with a child care center, international travel, a recognized foodborne or waterborne outbreak, male homosexual activity, and use of injection drugs. Transmission by blood transfusion or from mother to newborn infant (ie, vertical transmission) is rare. Infection has been contracted rarely from nonhuman primates not born in captivity. In approximately 50% of reported cases, the source cannot be determined. Fecal-oral spread from people with asymptomatic infections, particularly young children, likely accounts for many of these cases with an unknown source.

Before availability of vaccine, most HAV infection and illness occurred in the context of community-wide epidemics, in which infection primarily was transmitted in households and extended-family settings. Common-source foodborne outbreaks occur; waterborne outbreaks are rare. Nosocomial transmission is unusual, but outbreaks caused by transmission from hospitalized patients to health care professionals have been reported. In addition, outbreaks have occurred in neonatal intensive care units from neonates infected through transfused blood who subsequently transmitted HAV to other neonates and staff.

In child care centers, recognized symptomatic (icteric) illness occurs primarily among adult contacts of children. Most infected children younger than 6 years of age in child care are asymptomatic or have nonspecific manifestations. Hence, spread of HAV infection within and outside a child care center often occurs before recognition of the index case(s). Outbreaks occur most commonly in large child care centers and specifically in facilities that enroll children in diapers.

In most infected people, the highest titers of HAV in stool, when patients are most likely to transmit HAV, occur during the 1 to 2 weeks before onset of illness. The risk of transmission subsequently diminishes and is minimal by 1 week after onset of jaundice. However, HAV can be detected in stool for longer periods, especially in neonates and young children.

The **incubation period** is 15 to 50 days, with an average of 30 days.

DIAGNOSTIC TESTS: Serologic tests for HAV-specific total and immunoglobulin (Ig) M antibody are available commercially. Serum IgM is present at the onset of illness and usually disappears within 4 months but may persist for 6 months or longer. Presence of serum IgM indicates current or recent infection, although false-positive results can occur. Immunoglobulin G anti-HAV is detectable shortly after the appearance of IgM. The presence of total anti-HAV without IgM anti-HAV indicates past infection and immunity.

TREATMENT: Supportive.

ISOLATION OF THE HOSPITALIZED PATIENT: In addition to standard precautions, contact precautions are recommended for diapered and incontinent patients for at least 1 week after onset of symptoms.

CONTROL MEASURES*:
   GENERAL MEASURES. The major methods for prevention of HAV infections are improved sanitation (eg, of water sources and in food preparation) and personal hygiene (eg, hand hygiene after diaper changes in child care settings), hepatitis A immunization, and administration of Immune Globulin (IG).
   SCHOOLS, CHILD CARE, AND WORK. Children and adults with acute HAV infection who work as food handlers or attend or work in child care settings should be excluded for 1 week after onset of the illness.
   IMMUNE GLOBULIN. Immune Globulin for intramuscular administration, when given within 2 weeks after exposure to HAV, is greater than 85% effective in preventing symptomatic infection. Recommended preexposure and postexposure IG doses and duration of protection are given in Table 3.13 (p 329) and Table 3.14 (p 329).
   HEPATITIS A VACCINE. Two inactivated hepatitis A vaccines, Havrix and Vaqta, are available in the United States. The vaccines are prepared from cell culture-adapted HAV, which is propagated in human fibroblasts, purified from cell lysates, formalin inactivated, and adsorbed to an aluminum hydroxide adjuvant. Havrix is formulated with the preservative 2-phenoxyethanol; Vaqta is formulated without a preservative.
   Administration, Dosages, and Schedules (see Table 3.15, p 330). Hepatitis A vaccines are licensed for people 12 months of age and older and have pediatric and

---

* Centers for Disease Control and Prevention. Prevention of hepatitis A through passive immunization: recommendations of the Advisory Committee on Immunization Practices (ACIP). *MMWR*. 2006; in press (see **www.cdc.gov/mmwr**)

Table 3.13. Recommendations for Preexposure Immunoprophylaxis of Hepatitis A for Travelers

Age, y	Likely Exposure Duration, mo	Recommended Prophylaxis
<1	<3	IG, 0.02 mL/kg[1]
	3–5	IG, 0.06 mL/kg[1]
	Long-term	IG, 0.06 mL/kg at departure and every 5 mo if exposure to HAV continues[1]
≥1	<3[2]	Hepatitis A vaccine[3,4] OR IG, 0.02 mL/kg[1]
	3–5[2]	Hepatitis A vaccine[3,4] OR IG, 0.06 mL/kg[1]
	Long-term	Hepatitis A vaccine[3,4]

IG indicates Immune Globulin; HAV, hepatitis A virus.

[1] Immune Globulin should be administered deep into a large muscle mass. Ordinarily, no more than 5 mL should be administered in 1 site in an adult or large child; lesser amounts (maximum 3 mL in 1 site) should be given to small children and infants.

[2] Vaccine is preferable, but IG is an acceptable alternative.

[3] To ensure protection in travelers whose departure is imminent, IG also may be given (see text).

[4] Dose and schedule of hepatitis A vaccine as recommended according to age in Table 3.15, p 330.

Table 3.14. Recommendations for Postexposure Immunoprophylaxis of Hepatitis A

Time Since Exposure, wk	Future Exposure Likely, or Immunization Recommended	Age of Patient, y	Recommended Prophylaxis
≤2	No	All ages	IG, 0.02 mL/kg[1]
	Yes	≥1	IG, 0.02 mL/kg[1] AND Hepatitis A vaccine[2]
>2	No	All ages	No prophylaxis
	Yes	≥1	Hepatitis A vaccine[2]

IG indicates Immune Globulin.

[1] Immune Globulin should be administered deep into a large muscle mass. Ordinarily, no more than 5 mL should be administered in 1 site in an adult or large child; lesser amounts (maximum 3 mL in 1 site) should be given to small children and infants.

[2] Dosage and schedule of hepatitis A vaccine as recommended according to age in Table 3.15, p 330.

adult formulations that are given in a 2-dose schedule. The adult formulations are recommended for people 19 years of age and older. Currently licensed vaccines are given intramuscularly. Recommended doses and schedules for these different products and formulations are given in Table 3.15. A combination hepatitis A/hepatitis B vaccine (Twinrix) is licensed in the United States for people 18 years of age and older and given in a 3-dose schedule.

Detection of Anti-HAV After Immunization. The concentrations of anti-HAV resulting from hepatitis A immunization are 10- to 100-fold lower than those produced after natural infection and, after a single dose, may be below the detection concentration of some commercially available assays. The lower concentrations of antibody induced by single dose immunization can be measured by modified immunoassays, expressed as mIU/mL. Antibody concentrations after the booster dose usually can be detected by standard commercial antibody tests. The lower limit of antibody needed to confer immunity has not been defined. In most studies conducted with Havrix, concentrations of 20 mIU/mL or greater, as measured with a modified enzyme immunoassay, were considered to be protective; studies with Vaqta have been based on concentrations of 10 mIU/mL or greater, measured using a modified radioimmunoassay.

Immunoglobulin M Anti-HAV After Immunization. Immunoglobulin M anti-HAV occasionally is detectable by standard assays in adults 2 weeks after receiving hepatitis A vaccine. No data are available for children at 2 weeks after immunization; in 1 study, none had detectable IgM anti-HAV 1 month after immunization.

Table 3.15. Recommended Doses and Schedules for Inactivated Hepatitis A Vaccines[1]

Age, y	Vaccine	Hepatitis A Antigen Dose	Volume per Dose, mL	No. of Doses	Schedule
1–18	Havrix	720 ELU	0.5	2	Initial and 6–12 mo later
1–18	Vaqta	25 U[2]	0.5	2	Initial and 6–18 mo later
≥19	Havrix	1440 ELU	1.0	2	Initial and 6–12 mo later
≥19	Vaqta	50 U[2]	1.0	2	Initial and 6–18 mo later
≥18	Twinrix[3]	720 ELU	1.0	3	Initial and 1 and 6 mo later

ELU indicates enzyme-linked immunosorbent assay units.

[1] Havrix and Twinrix are manufactured by GlaxoSmithKline Biologicals; Vaqta is manufactured and distributed by Merck & Co Inc.

[2] Antigen units (each unit is equivalent to approximately 1 µg of viral protein).

[3] A combination of hepatitis B (Engerix-B, 20 µg) and hepatitis A (Havrix, 720 ELU) vaccine (Twinrix) is licensed for use in people 18 years of age and older in a 3-dose schedule. Havrix 360 ELU in single-dose vials is licensed in the United States but no longer is available.

Immunogenicity. The different vaccine formulations are similarly immunogenic when given in their respective recommended schedules and doses. One dose of Havrix induced seroconversion by 15 days in 80% to 98% of children, adolescents, and adults and by 1 month in 96% to 100%; 1 month after a second dose, which was administered 6 months after the first dose, 100% had protective serum antibody concentrations with high geometric mean titers. One dose of Vaqta induced seroconversion in 69% of adults 2 weeks after the first dose. One month after the first dose of Vaqta, 94% to 97% of children, adolescents, and adults had seroconverted. One month after a second dose, which was administered 6 months after the first dose, 100% had seroconverted.

Limited data on immunogenicity of hepatitis A vaccine in infants indicate high rates of seroconversion, but the geometric mean serum antibody titers are significantly less in infants with passively acquired maternal anti-HAV in comparison with vaccine recipients lacking anti-HAV. By 12 to 15 months of age, passively acquired maternal anti-HAV antibody no longer is detectable in most infants. Additional studies conducted to determine the optimum dose and schedule of hepatitis A vaccine in infants and young children have not yet been published.

Efficacy. In double-blind, controlled, randomized trials, the protective efficacy in preventing clinical HAV infection was 94% to 100%.

Duration of Protection. The need for booster doses has not been determined, because long-term efficacy of hepatitis A vaccines has not been established. Detectable antibody persists after a 2-dose series for at least 10 years in adults and 5 years in children. Kinetic models suggest that protective antibody concentrations will persist for at least 20 years.

Vaccine in Immunocompromised Patients. The immune response in immunocompromised people, including people with human immunodeficiency virus infection, may be suboptimal.

Effect of IG on Vaccine Immunogenicity. Seroconversion rates are not impaired by simultaneous administration of IG with the first vaccine dose, but lower serum antibody concentrations may be achieved. This decreased immunogenicity is not likely to be clinically important. If rapid protection is needed (ie, in less than 2 weeks) after the first dose of vaccine, concomitant administration of IG is indicated.

Vaccine Interchangeability. Vaqta and Havrix, when given as recommended, seem to be similarly effective. Studies among adults have found no difference in the immunogenicity of a vaccine series that mixed the 2 currently available vaccines, compared with using the same vaccine throughout the licensed schedule. Therefore, although completion of the immunization regimen with the same product is preferable, immunization with either product is acceptable.

Administration With Other Vaccines. Limited data indicate that hepatitis A vaccine may be administered simultaneously with other vaccines. Vaccines should be given in a separate syringe and at a separate injection site (see Simultaneous Administration of Multiple Vaccines, p 34).

Adverse Events. Adverse reactions are mild and include local pain and, less commonly, induration at the injection site. No serious adverse events attributed definitively to hepatitis A vaccine have been reported.

Precautions and Contraindications. The vaccine should not be administered to people with hypersensitivity to any of the vaccine components. Safety data in pregnant women are not available, but the risk is considered to be low or nonexistent, because the vaccine contains inactivated, purified, viral proteins.

Preimmunization Serologic Testing. Preimmunization testing for anti-HAV generally is not recommended for children. Testing may be cost-effective for people who have a high likelihood of immunity from previous infection, including people whose childhood was spent in an area of high endemicity, people with a history of jaundice potentially caused by HAV, and people older than 50 years of age.

Postimmunization Serologic Testing. Postimmunization testing for anti-HAV is not indicated because of the high seroconversion rates in adults and children. In addition, some commercially available anti-HAV tests may not detect low but protective concentrations of antibody induced by the first dose of vaccine.

RECOMMENDATIONS FOR IMMUNOPROPHYLAXIS:

PREEXPOSURE PROPHYLAXIS AGAINST HEPATITIS A VIRUS INFECTION (SEE TABLE 3.13, P 329, AND 3.15, P 330). Hepatitis A immunization is recommended routinely for children, for people who are at increased risk of infection, and for any person who wants to obtain immunity.

Children Who Routinely Should Be Immunized or Considered for Immunization.
- All children should receive hepatitis A vaccine at 1 year (ie, 12–23 months) of age. Immunization should be completed according to the approved schedules (Table 3.15, p 330) and integrated into the routine childhood immunization schedule. Children who are not immunized by 2 years of age can be immunized at subsequent visits.
- States, counties, and communities with existing hepatitis A immunization programs for children 2 to 18 years of age are encouraged to maintain these programs. In these areas, new efforts focused on routine immunization of 1-year-old children should enhance, not replace, ongoing programs directed at a broader population of children.
- In areas without existing hepatitis A immunization programs, catch-up immunization of unimmunized children 2 to 18 years of age can be considered. Such programs might especially be warranted in the context of rising incidence or ongoing outbreaks among children or adolescents.

People at Increased Risk of HAV Infection Who Routinely Should Be Immunized.
- *People traveling internationally.* For susceptible people traveling to or working in areas with intermediate or highly endemic rates of HAV infection, immunoprophylaxis before departure is indicated. Such areas include countries other than those in Western Europe, Scandinavia, Australia, Canada, Japan, and New Zealand. Factors to consider in choosing active and/or passive prophylaxis include the interval before departure, the relative costs and availability of IG and hepatitis A vaccine, the duration of the stay, and the likelihood of repeated exposure during subsequent travel (see Table 3.13, p 329). For people 12 months of age and older, unless there is a contraindication, vaccine is preferred.

Immune Globulin is considered protective against HAV immediately after administration, whereas the precise time required from receiving 1 dose of vaccine to onset of protection has not been established but likely is 2 to 4 weeks. To ensure protection in travelers whose departure is imminent, both IG (see Table 3.13, p 329) and the first dose of vaccine (see Effect of IG on Vaccine Immunogenicity, p 331) can be administered simultaneously. However, the additional benefit of administration of IG with the first dose of vaccine has not been evaluated in field trials and may be marginal.

Children younger than 12 months of age should receive only IG, because hepatitis A vaccine is not licensed for this age group (see Table 3.13, p 329).

- **People with chronic liver disease.** Because people with chronic liver disease are at increased risk of fulminant hepatitis A, susceptible patients with chronic liver disease should be immunized. The reported incidence of adverse events after hepatitis A immunization of people with chronic liver disease has not been higher than that reported among healthy adults. Susceptible people who are awaiting or have received liver transplants should be immunized.
- **Homosexual and bisexual men.** Outbreaks of hepatitis A among men who have sex with men have been reported often, including in urban areas in the United States, Canada, and Australia. Therefore, men (adolescents and adults) who have sex with men should be immunized. Preimmunization serologic testing may be warranted for older people in this group.
- **Users of injection and noninjection illegal drugs.** Periodic outbreaks among injection and noninjection drug users have been reported during the past decade in many parts of the United States and in Europe. Adolescents and adults who use illegal drugs should be immunized. Preimmunization serologic testing may be cost-effective for older people in this group.
- **Patients with clotting-factor disorders.** Reported outbreaks of hepatitis A in patients with hemophilia receiving solvent-detergent–treated factor VIII and factor IX concentrates have occurred primarily in Europe, and one instance in the United States has been reported. Therefore, susceptible patients who receive clotting factor concentrates, especially people receiving solvent-detergent–treated preparations, should be immunized. Preimmunization testing for anti-HAV may be cost-effective.
- **People at risk of occupational exposure (eg, handlers of nonhuman primates and people working with HAV in a research laboratory setting).** Outbreaks of hepatitis A have been reported among people working with nonhuman primates. Infected primates were those born in the wild, not primates that had been born and raised in captivity. People working with HAV-infected primates or with HAV in a research laboratory setting should be immunized.

Hepatitis A Immunization in Other Settings.

- **Child care center staff and attendees.** Outbreaks of HAV infection at child care centers may be the source of outbreaks in a community, but disease in child care centers more commonly reflects extended transmission from the community. In addition to recommended postexposure prophylaxis (see p 334), unimmunized children 12 months of age and older in child care settings with ongoing or recurrent outbreaks should receive hepatitis A vaccine.

- *Custodial care institutions.* Epidemic hepatitis A was reported in custodial care institutions during the 1970s and 1980s, but few cases have been reported recently. However, hepatitis A vaccine, in addition to IG as indicated for post-exposure prophylaxis, may be considered for staff and residents in institutions in which a hepatitis A outbreak is occurring.
- *Hospital personnel.* Usually, nosocomial hepatitis A in hospital personnel has occurred through spread from patients with acute infection in whom the diagnosis of HAV infection was not recognized. Careful hygienic practices should be emphasized when a patient with hepatitis A is admitted to the hospital. When outbreaks occur, IG is recommended for people in close contact with infected patients (see p 335). The role of hepatitis A vaccine in these settings has not been studied. Routine preexposure use of hepatitis A vaccine for hospital personnel is not recommended.
- *Food handlers.* Recognized foodborne outbreaks of hepatitis A are relatively uncommon in the United States. Although usually associated with contamination of uncooked food during preparation by a food handler who is infected with HAV, food contaminated before retail distribution, such as produce contaminated during growing or processing, has been recognized increasingly as a source of hepatitis A outbreaks. The most important means of preventing these outbreaks is using careful hygienic practices during food production and preparation. Routine hepatitis A immunization of food handlers is not recommended.
- *Other.* In addition, any healthy person 12 months of age and older may receive hepatitis A vaccine at the discretion of the physician and the patient or patient's family.

POSTEXPOSURE PROPHYLAXIS (SEE TABLE 3.14, P 329). Use of IG is recommended as follows (see Table 3.14 for dosages):

- *Household and sexual contacts.* All previously unimmunized people with close personal contact with a person with serologically confirmed HAV infection, such as household and sexual contacts, should receive IG within 2 weeks after the most recent exposure. Serologic testing of contacts is not recommended, because testing adds unnecessary cost and may delay administration of IG. The use of IG more than 2 weeks after the most recent exposure is not indicated.
- *Newborn infants of HAV-infected mothers.* Perinatal transmission of HAV is rare. Some experts advise giving IG (0.02 mL/kg) to the infant if the mother's symptoms began between 2 weeks before and 1 week after delivery. Efficacy in this circumstance has not been established. Severe disease in healthy infants is rare.
- *Child care center staff, employees, and children and their household contacts.* Serologic testing to confirm HAV infection in suspected cases is indicated.

  Immune Globulin should be administered to all previously unimmunized staff members and attendees of child care centers or homes if (1) one or more cases of HAV infection are recognized in children or staff members; or (2) cases are recognized in 2 or more households of center attendees. In centers that provide care only to children who do not wear diapers, IG need be given only to classroom contacts of an index-case patient. When an outbreak occurs (ie, hepatitis A cases in 3 or more families), IG also should be considered for members of households that have children (center attendees) in diapers. Hepatitis A vaccine can be administered at the same time as IG for children 12 months of age and older receiving postexposure prophylaxis in child care centers.

Children and adults with acute HAV infection should be excluded from the center until 1 week after onset of the illness, until the IG prophylaxis program has been completed, or until directed by the responsible health department. Although precise data concerning the onset of protection after a dose of IG are not available, allowing IG recipients to return to the child care center setting immediately after receipt of the IG dose seems reasonable.

- **Schools.** Schoolroom exposure generally does not pose an appreciable risk of infection, and IG administration is not indicated when a single case occurs. However, IG could be used for unimmunized people who have close contact with the index patient if transmission within the school setting is documented. Hepatitis A vaccine can be given in addition to IG.
- **Institutions and hospitals.** In institutions for custodial care with an outbreak of hepatitis A, residents and staff in close personal contact with infected patients should receive IG. Administration of IG to hospital personnel caring for patients with hepatitis A is not indicated routinely, unless an outbreak among patients or between patients and staff is documented. The addition of hepatitis A vaccine can be considered if repeated exposure is anticipated.
- **Common-source exposure.** These outbreaks often are recognized too late for IG to be effective in preventing HAV infection in exposed people, and IG administration usually is not recommended. Immune Globulin can be considered if it can be administered to exposed people within 2 weeks of an exposure to the HAV-contaminated water or food.
- **Hepatitis A vaccine for postexposure prophylaxis.** Available data are insufficient to recommend hepatitis A vaccine alone for postexposure prophylaxis. Clinical trials are in progress to determine the effectiveness of hepatitis A vaccine compared with IG after exposure.

Hepatitis B

CLINICAL MANIFESTATIONS: People with hepatitis B virus (HBV) infection may present with a variety of signs and symptoms, including subacute illness with nonspecific symptoms (eg, anorexia, nausea, or malaise), clinical hepatitis with jaundice, or fulminant fatal hepatitis. Asymptomatic seroconversion is common, and the likelihood of developing symptoms of hepatitis is age dependent. Anicteric or asymptomatic infection is most common in young children. Extrahepatic manifestations, such as arthralgias, arthritis, macular rashes, thrombocytopenia, or papular acrodermatitis (Gianotti-Crosti syndrome), can occur early in the course of the illness and may precede jaundice. Acute HBV infection cannot be distinguished from other forms of acute viral hepatitis on the basis of clinical signs and symptoms or nonspecific laboratory findings. Chronic HBV infection is defined as presence of hepatitis B surface antigen (HBsAg) in serum for at least 6 months or by the presence of HBsAg in a person who tests negative for antibody of the immunoglobulin (Ig) M subclass to hepatitis B core antigen (anti-HBc).

Age at the time of acute infection is the primary determinant of the risk of progressing to chronic infection. More than 90% of infants infected perinatally will develop chronic HBV infection. Between 25% and 50% of children infected between 1 and 5 years of age become chronically infected, whereas only 2% to 6% of acutely infected older children and adults develop chronic HBV infections. Patients who develop acute HBV infection while immunosuppressed or with an underlying chronic illness have an increased risk of developing chronic infection. Up to 25% of infants and older children who acquire chronic HBV infection eventually develop HBV-related hepatocellular carcinoma or cirrhosis.

The clinical outcome of untreated chronic HBV infection varies according to the population studied, reflecting differences in the age of acquisition, the rate of loss of hepatitis B e antigen (HBeAg), and possibly, HBV genotype. Perinatally infected children usually have normal alanine transaminase (ALT) concentrations and minimal or mild liver histologic abnormalities for years to decades after initial infection ("tolerant phase"). Chronic HBV infection acquired during later childhood or adolescence usually is accompanied by more active liver disease and increased serum transaminase concentrations. Patients with detectable HBeAg *(HBeAg-positive chronic hepatitis B)* usually have high blood concentrations of HBV DNA and HBsAg and are more likely to transmit infection. Over time (years to decades), HBeAg becomes undetectable in many chronically infected people. This transition often is accompanied by development of antibody to HBeAg (anti-HBe) and decreases in serum HBV DNA and serum transaminase concentrations and may be preceded by a temporary exacerbation of liver disease. These patients have *inactive chronic infection* but still may have exacerbations of hepatitis. Serologic reversion (reappearance of HBeAg) is more common if loss of HBeAg is not accompanied by development of anti-HBe; reversion with loss of anti-HBe also can occur.

Some patients who lose HBeAg may continue to have ongoing histologic evidence of liver damage and moderate to high concentrations of HBV DNA *(HBeAg-negative chronic hepatitis B)*. Patients with histologic evidence of chronic HBV infection, regardless of HBeAg status, remain at higher risk of death attributable to liver failure compared with HBV-infected people with no histologic evidence of liver inflammation and fibrosis. Other factors that may influence natural history of chronic infection include gender, race, alcohol use, and coinfection with hepatitis A, hepatitis C, or hepatitis D viruses.

Resolved hepatitis B is defined as clearance of HBsAg and normalization of serum transaminase concentrations; development of antibody to HBsAg (anti-HBs) also may be noted. Chronically infected adults clear HBsAg and develop anti-HBs at the rate of 1% to 2% annually; during childhood, the annual clearance rate is less than 1%. Reactivation of resolved chronic infection is possible with immunosuppression.

ETIOLOGY: Hepatitis B virus is a DNA-containing, 42-nm-diameter hepadnavirus. Important components of the viral particle include an outer lipoprotein envelope containing HBsAg and an inner nucleocapsid consisting of hepatitis B core antigen. Only antibody to HBsAg (anti-HBs) provides protection from HBV infection.

EPIDEMIOLOGY: Hepatitis B virus is transmitted through blood or body fluids, including wound exudates, semen, cervical secretions, and saliva. Blood and serum contain the highest concentrations of virus; saliva contains the lowest. People with chronic HBV infection are the primary reservoirs for infection. Common modes of transmission include percutaneous and permucosal exposure to infectious body fluids, sharing or using nonsterilized needles or syringes, sexual contact with an infected person, and perinatal exposure to an infected mother. Transmission by transfusion of contaminated blood or blood products is rare in the United States because of routine screening of blood donors and viral inactivation of certain blood products (see Blood Safety, p 106).

Perinatal transmission of HBV is highly efficient and usually occurs from blood exposures during labor and delivery. In utero transmission of HBV is rare, accounting for <2% of perinatal infections in most studies. The risk of an infant acquiring HBV from an infected mother as a result of perinatal exposure is 70% to 90% for infants born to mothers who are HBsAg and HBeAg positive; the risk is 5% to 20% for infants born to HBeAg-negative mothers.

Person-to-person spread of HBV can occur in settings involving interpersonal contact over extended periods, such as when a person with chronic HBV infection resides in a household. In household settings, nonsexual transmission occurs primarily from child to child, and young children are at highest risk of infection. The precise mechanisms of transmission from child to child are unknown; however, frequent interpersonal contact of nonintact skin or mucous membranes with blood-containing secretions or, perhaps, saliva are the most likely means of transmission. Transmission from sharing inanimate objects, such as washcloths, towels, razors, or toothbrushes, also may occur. Hepatitis B virus can survive in the environment for 1 week or longer but is inactivated by commonly used disinfectants, including household bleach diluted 1:10 with water. Hepatitis B virus is not transmitted by the fecal-oral route.

Before implementation of routine childhood hepatitis B immunization, multiple studies documented high rates of early childhood (nonperinatal) HBV transmission within some communities in the United States. During the 1980s, an estimated 18 700 children (younger than 10 years of age) were infected each year. Many of these infections were among children born to HBsAg-negative mothers, presumably from contact with other infected family and household members or close contacts. The highest risk of early childhood transmission is among children who immigrated to the United States from countries where HBV infection is highly endemic (eg, Southeast Asia, China, Africa).

Other children at increased risk of infection include residents of institutions for people with developmental disabilities and patients undergoing hemodialysis. Person-to-person transmission has been reported in child care settings, but risk of transmission in child care facilities in the United States has become negligible as a result of high infant hepatitis B vaccine coverage. Although fewer than 10% of new HBV infections occurred in children before implementation of childhood immunization programs, approximately one third of the estimated 1.25 million Americans with chronic HBV infection acquired infection as infants or young children.

Acute HBV infection occurs most commonly among adolescents and adults in the United States. Groups at highest risk include users of injection drugs, people with multiple heterosexual partners, and men who have sex with men. Others at increased risk include people with occupational exposure to blood or body fluids, staff of institutions and nonresidential child care programs for children with developmental disabilities, patients undergoing hemodialysis, and sexual or household contacts of people with an acute or chronic infection. Approximately 15% of infected people do not have a readily identifiable risk characteristic. The prevalence of infection among adolescents and adults is 3 to 4 times greater for black people than for white people. Hepatitis B virus infection in adolescents and adults is associated with other sexually transmitted infections, including syphilis and human immunodeficiency virus (HIV).

The frequency of HBV infection and patterns of transmission vary markedly throughout the world. Most areas of the United States, Canada, Western Europe, Australia, and southern South America have a low endemicity of HBV infection. Infection occurs primarily in adolescents and adults; 5% to 8% of the total population has been infected, and 0.2% to 0.9% of the population has chronic infection. However, within these geographic areas are populations with a high endemicity of infection, including Alaska Natives, Asian-Pacific Islanders, and immigrants from other countries with a high endemicity of infection. Geographic areas with a high endemicity of HBV infection (HBsAg prevalence of ≥8%) are the following:

- **Africa:** All countries except Algeria, Egypt, Libya, and Tunisia
- **South Asia:** All countries except Afghanistan, Bangladesh, Bhutan, India, Malaysia, Maldives, Nepal, Pakistan, and Sri Lanka
- **Western Pacific:** All countries except Australia, Guam, Japan, and New Zealand
- **Middle East:** Jordan and Saudi Arabia
- **Eastern Europe and Newly Independent States of the former Soviet Union:** Albania, Armenia, Azerbaijan, Bulgaria, Croatia, Georgia, Kazakhstan, Kyrgyzstan, Moldova, Tajikistan, Turkmenistan, and Uzbekistan
- **Western Europe:** Malta
- **North America:** Alaska Native populations and indigenous populations in Northern Canada and Greenland
- **South America:** Amazonian areas of Bolivia, Brazil, Columbia, Peru, and Venezuela In these areas, most infections occur in infants or children younger than 5 years of age; 70% to 90% of the adult population has been infected, and 8% to 15% of the population has chronic infection. In the rest of the world, HBV infection is of intermediate endemicity, with chronic HBV infection occurring in 2% to 7% of the population.

The **incubation period** for acute infection is 45 to 160 days, with an average of 90 days.

DIAGNOSTIC TESTS: Commercial serologic antigen tests are available to detect HBsAg and HBeAg. Assays also are available for detection of anti-HBs, anti-HBc, IgM anti-HBc, and anti-HBe (see Table 3.16, p 339). In addition, hybridization assays and gene amplification techniques (eg, polymerase chain reaction, branched DNA methods) are available to detect and quantitate HBV DNA. Hepatitis B surface antigen is detectable during acute infection. If the infection is self-limited, HBsAg disappears in most patients within a few weeks to several months after infection, followed by appearance of anti-HBs. The brief time between disappearance of HBsAg and appearance of anti-HBs is termed the *window phase* of infection. During the window phase, the only marker of acute infection is the IgM anti-HBc, which is highly specific for establishing the diagnosis of acute infection. However, IgM anti-HBc usually is not present in infants infected perinatally. People with chronic HBV infection have circulating HBsAg and anti-HBc; on rare occasions, anti-HBs also is present. Both anti-HBs and anti-HBc are detected in people with resolved infection, whereas anti-HBs alone is present in people immunized with hepatitis B vaccine. The presence of HBeAg in serum correlates with higher concentrations of HBV and greater infectivity. Tests for HBeAg and HBV DNA are useful in the selection of candidates to receive antiviral therapy and to monitor the response to therapy.

TREATMENT: No specific therapy for acute HBV infection is available. Hepatitis B Immune Globulin (HBIG) and corticosteroids are not effective.

Table 3.16. Diagnostic Tests for Hepatitis B Virus (HBV) Antigens and Antibodies

Factor To Be Tested	HBV Antigen or Antibody	Use
HBsAg	Hepatitis B surface antigen	Detection of acutely or chronically infected people; antigen used in hepatitis B vaccine
Anti-HBs	Antibody to HBsAg	Identification of people who have resolved infections with HBV; determination of immunity after immunization
HBeAg	Hepatitis B e antigen	Identification of infected people at increased risk of transmitting HBV
Anti-HBe	Antibody to HBeAg	Identification of infected people with lower risk of transmitting HBV
Anti-HBc	Antibody to HBcAg[1]	Identification of people with acute, resolved, or chronic HBV infection (not present after immunization)
IgM anti-HBc	IgM antibody to HBcAg	Identification of people with acute or recent HBV infections (including HBsAg-negative people during the "window" phase of infection)

HBcAg indicates hepatitis B core antigen; IgM, immunoglobulin M.
[1] No test is available commercially to measure HBcAg.

Chronic HBV infection in adults can be treated with the following US Food and Drug Administration (FDA)-approved drugs: interferon-alfa (interferon alfa-2b and peginterferon alfa-2a), lamivudine, adefovir, or entecavir, the latter 3 of which are given orally.

From 25% to 40% of adults with chronic HBV infection and liver disease achieve long-term remission (loss of detectable HBV DNA or loss of HBeAg) after treatment with interferon-alfa. This remission rate is approximately 20% higher than the spontaneous remission rate observed in untreated controls. Adult patients who clear HBeAg have decreases in rates of mortality and clinical complications of cirrhosis. Fewer data are available for treatment of children, but several studies indicate that approximately 30% of children with increased transaminase concentrations who are treated with interferon alfa-2b for 6 months lose HBeAg, compared with approximately 10% of untreated controls. Interferon-alfa is less effective for chronic infections acquired during early childhood, especially if transaminase concentrations are normal. Lamivudine is approved for treatment of chronic HBV infection in people 2 years of age and older. Children with chronic HBV infection who were treated with lamivudine had higher rates of virologic response (loss of detectable HBV DNA and loss of HBeAg) after 1 year of treatment than did children who received placebo (23% vs 13%). Although resistance to lamivudine develops quickly, therapy is continued. Children coinfected with HIV and HBV should receive the lamivudine dose approved for treatment of HIV. The FDA has approved adefovir and entecavir for treatment of chronic HBV infection in adults, but safety and effectiveness for children has not been established. Other nucleoside analogs are being developed.

Children and adolescents who have chronic HBV infection are at risk of developing serious liver disease, including primary hepatocellular carcinoma (HCC), with advancing age. Although the peak incidence of primary HCC attributable to HBV infection is in the fifth decade of life, HCC occasionally occurs in children who become infected perinatally or in early childhood. Children with chronic HBV infection should be screened periodically for hepatic complications using serum liver transaminase tests, alpha-fetoprotein concentration, and abdominal ultrasonography. Definitive recommendations on the frequency and indications for specific tests are not yet available because of a lack of data on reliability in predicting sequelae. Patients with persistently increased serum ALT concentrations (exceeding twice the upper limits of normal) and patients with an increased serum alpha-fetoprotein concentration or abnormal findings on abdominal ultrasonography should be referred to a specialist in management of chronic HBV infection for further management. All patients with chronic HBV infection who are not immune to hepatitis A should receive hepatitis A vaccine.

ISOLATION OF THE HOSPITALIZED PATIENT: Standard precautions are indicated for patients with acute or chronic HBV infection. For infants born to HBsAg-positive mothers, no special care other than removal of maternal blood by a gloved attendant in addition to standard precautions is necessary.

CONTROL MEASURES:

STRATEGY FOR PREVENTION OF HBV INFECTION. The primary goal of HBV prevention programs is decreasing the rates of chronic HBV infection and HBV-related chronic liver disease. A secondary goal is prevention of acute HBV infection. Over the past 2 decades, a comprehensive immunization strategy in the United States has been implemented progressively and now includes the following 4 components*: (1) universal immunization of infants beginning at birth; (2) prevention of perinatal HBV infection through routine screening of all pregnant women and appropriate immunoprophylaxis of infants born to HBsAg-positive women and infants born to women with unknown HBsAg status; (3) routine immunization of children and adolescents who previously have not been immunized; and (4) immunization of previously unimmunized adults at increased risk of infection.

HEPATITIS B IMMUNOPROPHYLAXIS. Two types of products are available for immunoprophylaxis. Hepatitis B Immune Globulin provides short-term protection (3–6 months) and is indicated only in specific postexposure circumstances (see Care of Exposed People, p 350). Hepatitis B vaccine is used for preexposure and postexposure protection and provides long-term protection. Preexposure immunization with hepatitis B vaccine is the most effective means to prevent HBV transmission. To decrease the rate of, and eventually eliminate, transmission of HBV, universal immunization is necessary. Accordingly, hepatitis B immunization is recommended for all infants as part of the routine childhood and adolescent immunization schedule, and all children who have not received the vaccine previously should be immunized by or before 11 to 12 years of age. Immunization before 11 years of age (for children not previously immunized) can be advantageous because of better compliance with routine medical visits to complete the 3-dose schedule.

Postexposure immunoprophylaxis with either hepatitis B vaccine and HBIG or hepatitis B vaccine alone effectively prevents infection after exposure to HBV. Effectiveness of postexposure immunoprophylaxis is related directly to the time elapsed between exposure and administration. Immunoprophylaxis is most effective if given within 12 to 24 hours of exposure. Serologic testing of all pregnant women for HBsAg is essential for identifying women whose infants will require postexposure immunoprophylaxis beginning at birth (see Care of Exposed People, p 350).

HEPATITIS B IMMUNE GLOBULIN.[†] Hepatitis B Immune Globulin is prepared from hyperimmunized donors whose plasma is known to contain a high concentration of anti-HBs and to be negative for antibodies to HIV and hepatitis C virus (HCV). The process used to prepare HBIG inactivates or eliminates HIV and HCV. Standard Immune Globulin is not effective for postexposure prophylaxis against HBV infection, because concentrations of anti-HBs are too low.

---

* Centers for Disease Control and Prevention. A comprehensive immunization strategy to eliminate transmission of hepatitis B virus in the United States. Recommendations of the Advisory Committee on Immunization Practices (ACIP) part 1: immunization of infants, children, and adolescents. *MMWR Recomm Rep.* 2005;54(RR-16):1–23

† Dosages recommended for postexposure prophylaxis are for products licensed in the United States. Because concentration of anti-HBs in other products may vary, different dosages may be recommended in other countries.

HEPATITIS B VACCINE. Highly effective and safe hepatitis B vaccines produced by recombinant DNA technology are licensed in the United States in single-antigen formulations and as components of combination vaccines. Plasma-derived hepatitis B vaccines no longer are available in the United States but are used widely and successfully in other countries. The recombinant vaccines contain 10 to 40 μg of HBsAg protein per mL. Pediatric formulations contain no thimerosal or only trace amounts. Although the concentration of recombinant HBsAg protein differs among vaccine products, rates of seroconversion are equivalent when given to immunocompetent infants, children, adolescents, or young adults in the doses recommended (see Table 3.17).

Hepatitis B vaccine can be given concurrently with other vaccines (see Simultaneous Administration of Multiple Vaccines, p 34).

Vaccine Interchangeability. In general, the various brands of age-appropriate hepatitis B vaccines are interchangeable within an immunization series. The immune response using 1 or 2 doses of a vaccine produced by one manufacturer followed

Table 3.17. Recommended Dosages of Hepatitis B Vaccines

Patients	Vaccine[1]	
	Recombivax HB[2] Dose, μg (mL)	Engerix-B[3] Dose, μg (mL)
Infants of HBsAg-negative mothers and children and adolescents younger than 20 y of age	5 (0.5)	10 (0.5)
Infants of HBsAg-positive mothers (HBIG [0.5 mL] also is recommended)	5 (0.5)	10 (0.5)
Adults 20 y of age or older	10 (1.0)	20 (1.0)
Adults undergoing dialysis and other immunosuppressed adults	40 (1.0)[4]	40 (2.0)[5]

HBsAg indicates hepatitis B surface antigen; HBIG, Hepatitis B Immune Globulin.

[1] Both vaccines are administered in a 3- or 4-dose schedule; 4 doses may be administered if a birth dose is given and a combination vaccine is used to complete the series. Only single-antigen hepatitis B vaccine can be used for the birth dose. Single-antigen or combination vaccine containing hepatitis B vaccine may be used to complete the series.

[2] Available from Merck & Co Inc.
  • A 2-dose schedule, administered at 0 months and then 4 to 6 months later, is available for adolescents 11 to 15 years of age using the adult formulation of Recombivax HB (10 μg).
  • A combination of hepatitis B (Recombivax, 5 μg) and *Haemophilus influenzae* type b (PRP-OMP) vaccine is recommended for use at 2, 4, and 12 to 15 months of age (Comvax). This vaccine cannot be administered at birth, before 6 weeks of age, or after 71 months of age. For additional information, see *Haemophilus influenzae* Infections (p 310).

[3] Available from GlaxoSmithKline Biologicals. The US Food and Drug Administration has licensed this vaccine for use in an optional 4-dose schedule at 0, 1, 2, and 12 months of age.
  a) A combination of hepatitis B (Engerix-B, 20 μg) and hepatitis A (Havrix, 720 ELU) vaccine (Twinrix) is licensed for use in people 18 years of age and older in a 3-dose schedule administered at 0 mo, 1 mo, and 6 or more months later.
  b) A combination of diphtheria and tetanus toxoids and acellular pertussis (DTaP), inactivated poliovirus (IPV), and hepatitis B (Engerix-B 10 μg) is recommended for use at 2, 4, and 6 months of age (Pediarix). This vaccine cannot be administered at birth, before 6 weeks of age, or at ≥7 years of age. For additional information, see Pertussis (p 498).

[4] Special formulation for dialysis patients.

[5] Two 1.0-mL doses given in 1 site in a 4-dose schedule at 0, 1, 2, and 6 months of age.

by 1 or more subsequent doses from a different manufacturer is comparable to a full course of immunization with a single product. However, until additional data supporting interchangeability of acellular pertussis-containing vaccines (including Pediarix) are available, vaccines from the same manufacturer should be used, whenever feasible, for at least the first 3 doses in the pertussis series (see Pertussis, p 498). In addition, a 2-dose schedule for adolescents 11 to 15 years of age is approved only for Recombivax HB.

Routes of Administration. Vaccine is administered intramuscularly in the anterolateral thigh or deltoid area, depending on the age and size of the recipient (see Vaccine Administration, p 18). Administration in the buttocks or intradermally has been associated with decreased immunogenicity and is not recommended at any age.

Efficacy and Duration of Protection. Hepatitis B vaccines licensed in the United States have a 90% to 95% efficacy for preventing HBV infection and clinical HBV infection among susceptible children and adults. Long-term studies of adults and children indicate that immune memory remains intact for 15 years or more and protects against clinical acute infections and chronic HBV infection, even though anti-HBs concentrations may become low or undetectable over time.

Booster Doses. For children and adults with normal immune status, routine booster doses of vaccine are not recommended. For hemodialysis patients and other immunocompromised people at continued risk of infection, the need for booster doses should be assessed by annual anti-HBs testing, and a booster dose should be given when the anti-HBs concentration is less than 10 mIU/mL.

Adverse Reactions. The most commonly reported adverse effects in adults and children are pain at the injection site, reported by 3% to 29% of recipients, and a temperature greater than 37.7°C (99.8°F), reported by 1% to 6% of recipients. Anaphylaxis is uncommon, occurring in approximately 1 in 600 000 recipients, according to passive reporting of vaccine adverse events. Large, controlled epidemiologic studies show no association between hepatitis B vaccine and sudden infant death syndrome, diabetes mellitus, or demyelinating disease, including multiple sclerosis.

Immunization During Pregnancy or Lactation. No adverse effect on the developing fetus has been observed when pregnant women have been immunized. Because HBV infection may result in severe disease in the mother and chronic infection in the newborn infant, pregnancy is not a contraindication to immunization. Lactation is not a contraindication to immunization.

Serologic Testing. Susceptibility testing before immunization is not indicated routinely for children or adolescents. Testing for previous infection may be considered for people in risk groups with high rates of HBV infection, such as users of injection drugs, homosexually or bisexually active men, and household contacts of HBsAg-positive people, provided testing does not delay or impede immunization efforts.

Routine postimmunization testing for anti-HBs is not necessary but is recommended 1 to 2 months after the third vaccine dose for the following specific groups: (1) hemodialysis patients; (2) people with HIV infection; (3) people at occupational risk of exposure from sharps injuries; (4) immunocompromised patients at risk of exposure to HBV; and (5) regular sexual contacts of HBsAg-positive people. In addition, infants born to HBsAg-positive mothers should have postimmunization testing for HBsAg and anti-HBs performed at 9 to 18 months of age, generally at the next well-child visit after completion of the vaccine series (see Prevention of Perinatal HBV Infection, p 350).

Management of Nonresponders. Vaccine recipients who do not develop a serum anti-HBs response ($\geq$10 mIU/mL) after a primary vaccine series should be reimmunized (unless they are determined to be HBsAg positive) with an additional 3-dose series. People who remain anti-HBs negative after a reimmunization series are unlikely to respond to additional doses of vaccine.

Altered Doses and Schedules. Larger vaccine doses are required to induce protective anti-HBs concentrations in adult hemodialysis patients and for immunocompromised adults, including HIV-seropositive people (see Table 3.17, p 342). Humoral immune response to hepatitis B vaccine also may be reduced in children and adolescents who are receiving hemodialysis or are immunocompromised. However, few data exist concerning the response to higher doses of vaccine in children and adolescents, and no specific recommendations can be made. For people with progressive chronic renal failure, hepatitis B vaccine is recommended early in the disease course to provide protection and potentially decrease the need for larger doses once dialysis is initiated. A 2-dose schedule for the adult formulation of Recombivax is licensed for 11- to 15-year-olds; the first dose is followed 4 to 6 months later by the second dose (see Table 3.17, p 342).

PREEXPOSURE UNIVERSAL IMMUNIZATION OF INFANTS, CHILDREN, AND ADOLESCENTS. Routine preexposure immunization is recommended for all infants. Delivery hospitals should develop policies and procedures that ensure administration of a birth dose as part of the routine care of all medically stable infants weighing $\geq$2000 grams at birth, unless there is a physician's order to defer immunization and serologic status of the mother is in the infant's medical record. The hepatitis B vaccine series (3 or 4 doses, see discussion about birth dose in next paragraph) for infants born to HBsAg-negative mothers should be completed by 6 to 18 months of age. All children and adolescents who have not been immunized against HBV should begin the series during any visit.

High seroconversion rates and protective concentrations of anti-HBs ($\geq$10 mIU/mL) are achieved when hepatitis B vaccine is administered in any of the various approved schedules, including schedules begun soon after birth in term infants. Only single-antigen hepatitis B vaccine can be used for doses given between birth and 6 weeks of age. Single-antigen or combination vaccine may be used to complete the series; 4 doses of vaccine may be administered if a birth dose is given and a combination vaccine containing a hepatitis B component is used to complete the series.* For guidelines for minimum scheduling time between vaccine doses for infants, see Table 1.8 (p 31). The schedule should be chosen to facilitate high rates of adherence to the

---

* Centers for Disease Control and Prevention. Combination vaccines for childhood immunization. Recommendations of the Advisory Committee on Immunization Practices (ACIP), the American Academy of Pediatrics (AAP), and the American Academy of Family Physicians (AAFP). *MMWR Recomm Rep.* 1999;48(RR-05):1–15

primary vaccine series. For immunization of older children and adolescents, doses may be given in a schedule of 0, 1, and 6 months or of 0, 2, and 4 months; for adolescents, spacing at 0, 12, and 24 months results in equivalent immunogenicity. A 2-dose schedule for one vaccine formulation is licensed for people 11 to 15 years of age; the schedule is 0 and 4 to 6 months (see Table 3.17, p 342).

The recommended schedule for routine hepatitis B immunization of infants born to HBsAg-negative mothers is given in Fig 1.1 (p 26). Age-specific vaccine dosages are given in Table 3.17 (p 342). Combination products containing hepatitis B vaccine may be given in the United States, provided they are licensed by the US Food and Drug Administration for the child's current age and administration of the other vaccine component(s) also is indicated.

PREEXPOSURE IMMUNIZATION OF ADULTS.[*]

- Hepatitis B immunization is recommended as a 3-dose series for all unimmunized adults at risk of HBV infection and for all adults seeking protection from HBV infection. Acknowledgment of a specific risk factor is not a requirement for immunization.
- In settings where a high proportion of adults are likely to have risk factors for HBV infection, all unimmunized adults should be assumed to be at risk and should receive hepatitis B immunization. These settings include sexually transmitted infection treatment facilities, HIV testing and treatment facilities, facilities providing drug abuse treatment and prevention services, corrections facilities, health care settings serving men who have sex with men, chronic hemodialysis facilities and end-stage renal disease programs, and institutions and nonresidential care facilities for people with developmental disabilities.
- Standing orders should be implemented to identify and immunize eligible adults in primary care and specialty medical settings. If ascertainment of risk for HBV infection is a barrier to immunization in these settings, health care professionals may use alternative immunization strategies, such as offering hepatitis B vaccine to all unimmunized adults in age groups with highest risk of infection (eg, <45 years of age).

LAPSED IMMUNIZATIONS. For infants, children, adolescents, and adults with lapsed immunizations (ie, the interval between doses is longer than that in one of the recommended schedules), the vaccine series can be completed, regardless of the interval from the last dose of vaccine (see Lapsed Immunizations, p 35).

SPECIAL CONSIDERATIONS:

PRETERM INFANTS. Studies demonstrate that decreased seroconversion rates might occur among certain preterm infants with low birth weight (ie, <2000 g) after administration of hepatitis B vaccine at birth. However, by the chronologic age of 1 month, all medically stable preterm infants (see Preterm and Low Birth Weight Infants, p 67), regardless of initial birth weight or gestational age, are as likely to respond to hepatitis B immunization as are older and larger infants.

---

[*] Centers for Disease Control and Prevention. Hepatitis B virus infection: a comprehensive immunization strategy to eliminate transmission in the United States. Part II. Immunization of adults. Recommendations of the Advisory Committee on Immunization Practices. *MMWR Morb Mortal Wkly Rep.* 2006; in press (available at **www.cdc.gov/mmwr**)

All preterm infants who are born to an HBsAg-positive mother should receive immunoprophylaxis with hepatitis B vaccine and HBIG within 12 hours after birth, followed by the remaining doses in the series and postimmunization testing appropriate for term infants (see Table 3.18, p 347 and Table 3.19, p 348). If the preterm infant born to an HBsAg-positive mother weighs less than 2000 g at birth, the birth dose of hepatitis B vaccine should not be counted toward completion of the hepatitis B vaccine series, and 3 additional doses of hepatitis B vaccine should be administered beginning when the infant is 1 month of age (see Table 3.18, p 347). Only monovalent hepatitis B vaccines should be used from birth to 6 weeks of age.

If the maternal HBsAg status is unknown at birth, the preterm infant should receive hepatitis B vaccine within 12 hours of birth. For preterm infants weighing greater than 2000 g at birth, the mother's HBsAg status should be determined as quickly as possible and if positive, HBIG should be given as soon as possible, but within 7 days of birth, at a separate site from the hepatitis B vaccine. If the infant's birth weight is less than 2000 g and the maternal HBsAg status cannot be determined within 12 hours of life, HBIG should be given, because the less reliable immune response in preterm infants weighing <2000 g precludes the option of the 7-day waiting period acceptable for term and larger preterm infants. Only monovalent hepatitis B vaccine should be used from birth to 6 weeks of life.

All preterm infants of HBsAg-negative mothers with a birth weight of less than 2000 g can receive the first dose of hepatitis B vaccine series starting at 1 month of chronologic age. Preterm infants weighing more than 2000 g and low birth weight infants who are medically stable and showing consistent weight gain when discharged from the hospital before 1 month of age may receive the first dose of hepatitis B vaccine at the time of discharge. Infants born to HBsAg-negative mothers do not need to have postimmunization serologic testing for anti-HBs. Table 3.18 (p 347) provides a summary of the recommendations for immunization of preterm and low birth weight infants on the basis of maternal hepatitis B status and infant birth weight. For information on use of combination vaccines containing hepatitis B as a component to complete the series, see Table 3.19 (p 348).

IMMUNIZATION OF HIGH-RISK GROUPS.

Ethnic Populations at High Risk of HBV Infection. Despite initiation of routine immunization of infants, many children and adolescents are unimmunized and remain at risk of HBV infection. In particular, without immunization during early childhood, high rates of HBV infection would be expected to continue to occur among Alaska Native and Asian-Pacific Islander children and among children residing in households of first-generation immigrants from countries where HBV infection is highly endemic. As a result, targeted efforts are needed to achieve high immunization coverage among these children.

Sexually Active Heterosexual Adolescents and Adults. People diagnosed with a sexually transmitted disease or people who have had more than 1 sexual partner during the previous 6 months should be immunized.

Health Care Professionals and Others With Occupational Exposure to Blood. The risk of HBV exposure to a health care professional depends on the tasks the person performs. Health care professionals who have contact with blood or other potentially infectious body fluids should be immunized. Because the risks of occupational

Table 3.18. Hepatitis B Immunoprophylaxis Scheme by Infant Birth Weight[1]

Maternal Status	Infant ≥2000 g	Infant <2000 g
HBsAg positive	Hepatitis B vaccine + HBIG (within 12 h of birth)	Hepatitis B vaccine + HBIG (within 12 h of birth)
	Continue vaccine series beginning at 1–2 mo of age according to recommended schedule for infants born to HBsAg-positive mothers (see Table 3.19)	Continue vaccine series beginning at 1–2 mo of age according to recommended schedule for infants born to HBsAg-positive mothers (see Table 3.19)
		Immunize with 4 vaccine doses; do not count birth dose as part of vaccine series
	Check anti-HBs and HBsAg after completion of vaccine series[2]	Check anti-HBs and HBsAg after completion of vaccine series[2]
	HBsAg-negative infants with anti-HBs levels ≥10 mIU/mL are protected and need no further medical management	HBsAg-negative infants with anti-HBs levels ≥10 mIU/mL are protected and need no further medical management
	HBsAg-negative infants with anti-HBs levels <10 mIU/mL should be reimmunized with 3 doses at 2-mo intervals and retested	HBsAg-negative infants with anti-HBs levels <10 mIU/mL should be reimmunized with 3 doses at 2-mo intervals and retested
	Infants who are HBsAg positive should receive appropriate follow-up, including medical evaluation for chronic liver disease	Infants who are HBsAg positive should receive appropriate follow-up, including medical evaluation for chronic liver disease
HBsAg status unknown	Test mother for HBsAg immediately after admission for delivery	Test mother for HBsAg immediately after admission for delivery
	Hepatitis B vaccine (by 12 h)	Hepatitis B vaccine (by 12 h)
	Administer HBIG (within 7 days) if mother tests HBsAg positive	Administer HBIG if mother tests HBsAg positive or if mother's HBsAg result is not available within 12 h of birth
	Continue vaccine series beginning at 1–2 mo of age according to recommended schedule based on mother's HBsAg result (see Table 3.19)	Continue vaccine series beginning at 1–2 mo of age according to recommended schedule based on mother's HBsAg result (see Table 3.19)
		Immunize with 4 vaccine doses; do not count birth dose as part of vaccine series
HBsAg negative	Hepatitis B vaccine at birth[3]	Hepatitis B vaccine dose 1–30 days of chronologic age if medically stable, or at hospital discharge if before 30 days of chronologic age
	Continue vaccine series beginning at 1–2 mo of age (see Table 3.19)	Continue vaccine series beginning at 1–2 mo of age (see Table 3.19)
	Follow-up anti-HBs and HBsAg testing not needed	Follow-up anti-HBs and HBsAg testing not needed

HBsAg indicates hepatitis B surface antigen; HBIG, hepatitis B Immune Globulin; anti-HBs, antibody to hepatitis B surface antigen.

[1] Extremes of gestational age and birth weight no longer are a consideration for timing of hepatitis B vaccine doses.

[2] Test at 9 to 18 months of age, generally at the next well-child visit after completion of the primary series. Use testing method that allows determination of a protective concentration of anti-HBs (≥10 mIU/mL).

[3] The first dose may be delayed until after hospital discharge for an infant who weighs ≥2000 g and whose mother is HBsAg negative, but only if a physician's order to withhold the birth dose and a copy of the mother's original HBsAg-negative laboratory report are documented in the infant's medical record.

HBV infection often are highest during the training of health care professionals, immunization should be initiated as early as possible before or during training and before contact with blood.

Residents and Staff of Institutions for People With Developmental Disabilities. Susceptible children in institutions for people with developmental disabilities and staff who work with the children should be immunized. Children discharged from

Table 3.19. Hepatitis B Vaccine Schedules for Infants, by Maternal Hepatitis B Surface Antigen (HBsAg) Status[1,2]

Maternal HBsAg Status	Single-Antigen Vaccine		Single-Antigen + Combination	
	Dose	**Age**	**Dose**	**Age**
Positive	1[3]	Birth (≤12 h)	1[3]	Birth (≤12 h)
	HBIG[4]	Birth (≤12 h)	HBIG	Birth (≤12 h)
	2	1–2 mo	2	2 mo
	3[5]	6 mo	3	4 mo
			4[5]	6 mo (Pediarix) or 12–15 mo (Comvax)
Unknown[6]	1[3]	Birth (≤12 h)	1[3]	Birth (≤12 h)
	2	1–2 mo	2	2 mo
	3[5]	6 mo	3	4 mo
			4[5]	6 mo (Pediarix) or 12–15 mo (Comvax)
Negative	1[3,7]	Birth (before discharge)	1[3,7]	Birth (before discharge)
	2	1–2 mo	2	2 mo
	3[5]	6–18 mo	3	4 mo
			4[5]	6 mo (Pediarix) or 12–15 mo (Comvax)

[1] Centers for Disease Control and Prevention. A comprehensive immunization strategy to eliminate transmission of hepatitis B virus infection in the United States. Recommendations of the Advisory Committee on Immunization Practices (ACIP) part 1: immunization of infants, children, and adolescents. *MMWR Recomm Rep.* 2005;54(RR-16):1–23

[2] See Table 3.18 for vaccine schedules for preterm infants weighing <2000 g.

[3] Recombivax HB or Engerix-B should be used for the birth dose. Comvax and Pediarix cannot be administered at birth or before 6 weeks of age.

[4] Hepatitis B Immune Globulin (0.5 mL) administered intramuscularly in a separate site from vaccine.

[5] The final dose in the vaccine series should not be administered before 24 weeks (164 days) of age.

[6] Mothers should have blood drawn and tested for HBsAg as soon as possible after admission for delivery; if the mother is found to be HBsAg-positive, the infant should receive HBIG as soon as possible but no later than 7 days of age.

[7] On a case-by-case basis and only in rare circumstances, the first dose may be delayed until after hospital discharge for an infant who weighs ≥2000 g and whose mother is HBsAg negative, but only if a physician's order to withhold the birth dose and a copy of the mother's original HBsAg-negative laboratory report are documented in the infant's medical record.

residential institutions into community programs (eg, schools, sheltered workshops) should be screened for HBsAg to allow appropriate measures to prevent HBV transmission. Susceptible children and staff who live or work in smaller (group) residential settings where other staff members or residents are known to be HBsAg positive and staff of nonresidential child care programs (eg, schools and other group settings) attended by HBsAg-positive people with developmental disabilities also should be immunized. Immunization should be considered for all attendees in nonresidential programs attended by HBsAg-positive people and is encouraged if an attendee who is HBsAg-positive behaves aggressively or has special medical problems (eg, exudative dermatitis or open skin lesions) that increase the risk of exposure to that attendee's blood or secretions.

Patients Undergoing Hemodialysis. Immunization is recommended for susceptible patients undergoing hemodialysis. Immunization early in the course of renal disease is encouraged, because response is better than in advanced disease. Specific dosage recommendations have not been made for children undergoing hemodialysis. Some experts recommend increased doses of hepatitis B vaccine for children receiving hemodialysis to increase immunogenicity.

Foreign-Born People From Countries Where HBV Infection Is Highly Endemic. Foreign-born people (including immigrants, refugees, asylum seekers, and internationally adopted children) from countries where HBV infection is highly endemic (see Epidemiology, p 337) should be screened for HBsAg, regardless of immunization status. Previously unimmunized family members and other household contacts should be immunized if a foreign-born person is found to be HBsAg positive. In addition, HBsAg-positive people should receive medical management to reduce their risk of chronic liver disease.

Inmates in Juvenile Detention and Other Corrections Facilities. Previously unimmunized or underimmunized people in juvenile and adult facilities, including jails, should be immunized appropriately. If the length of stay is not sufficient to complete the immunization series, the series should be initiated and follow-up mechanisms with a health care facility should be established to ensure completion of the series (see Hepatitis and Youth in Corrections Facilities, p 177).

International Travelers. People traveling to areas where HBV infection is of high or intermediate endemicity (see Epidemiology, p 337) should be immunized. Immunization should begin at least 4 to 6 months before travel so that a 3-dose regimen can be completed (see Preexposure Universal Immunization, p 344). If immunization is initiated fewer than 4 months before departure, the alternative 4-dose schedule of 0, 1, 2, and 12 months (see Table 3.17, p 342) should provide protection if the first 3 doses can be administered before travel. Individual clinicians may choose to use an accelerated schedule (eg, doses at days 0, 7, and 21) for travelers who will depart before an approved immunization schedule can be completed. The FDA has not licensed schedules that involve immunization at more than one time point during a single month for hepatitis B vaccine licensed in the United States. People who receive an immunization on an accelerated schedule that is not FDA licensed also should receive a booster dose at least 6 months after initiation of the series to promote long-term immunity.

CARE OF EXPOSED PEOPLE (POSTEXPOSURE IMMUNOPROPHY-
LAXIS) (SEE ALSO TABLE 3.20).

Prevention of Perinatal HBV Infection. Transmission of perinatal HBV infection
can be prevented in approximately 95% of infants born to HBsAg-positive mothers
by early active and passive immunoprophylaxis of the infant (ie, immunization and
HBIG administration). Immunization subsequently should be completed during the
first 6 months of life. Hepatitis B immunization alone, initiated at or shortly after
birth, also is highly effective for preventing perinatal HBV infections.

Serologic Screening of Pregnant Women. Prenatal HBsAg testing of all pregnant women is recommended to identify newborn infants who require immediate
postexposure prophylaxis. All pregnant women should be tested during an early prenatal visit with every pregnancy. Testing should be repeated at the time of admission
to the hospital for delivery for HBsAg-negative women who are at high risk of HBV
infection (eg, injection drug users and women with intercurrent sexually transmitted
infections) or who have had clinical HBV infection. Household contacts and sexual
partners of HBsAg-positive women should be immunized. Women who are HBsAg
positive should be reported to local health departments for appropriate case management to ensure follow-up of their infants and immunization of sexual and household

Table 3.20. Guide to Postexposure Immunoprophylaxis of Unimmunized People to Prevent Hepatitis B Virus Infection

Type of Exposure	Immunoprophylaxis[1]
Household contact of HBsAg-positive person	Administer hepatitis B vaccine series
Discrete exposure to an HBsAg-positive source	Administer hepatitis B vaccine + HBIG; complete vaccine series
• Percutaneous (eg, bite, needlestick) or mucosal exposure to HBsAg-positive blood or body fluids that contain blood	
• Sexual contact or needle sharing with an HBsAg-positive person	
• Victim of sexual assault/abuse by a perpetrator who is HBsAg positive	
Discrete exposure to a source with unknown HBsAg status	Administer hepatitis B vaccine series
• Percutaneous (eg, bite, needlestick) or mucosal exposure to blood or body fluids that contain blood with unknown HBsAg status	
• Victim of sexual assault/abuse by a perpetrator with unknown HBsAg status	

HBsAg indicates hepatitis B surface antigen; HBIG, Hepatitis B Immune Globulin.

[1] Immunoprophylaxis should be administered as soon as possible, preferably within 24 hours after exposure. Studies are
limited on the maximum interval after exposure during which postexposure prophylaxis is effective, but the interval is
unlikely to exceed 7 days for percutaneous exposures and 14 days for sexual exposures.

contacts. In populations where HBsAg testing of pregnant women is not feasible (eg, in remote areas without access to a laboratory), all infants should receive hepatitis B vaccine within 12 hours of birth, the second dose by 2 months of age, and the third dose at 6 months of age.

Management of Infants Born to HBsAg-Positive Women. Infants born to HBsAg-positive mothers, including preterm and low birth weight infants, should receive the initial dose of hepatitis B vaccine within 12 hours of birth (see Table 3.17, p 342, for appropriate dosages), and HBIG (0.5 mL) should be given concurrently but at a different anatomic site. The effectiveness of HBIG diminishes the longer after exposure that it is initiated. The interval of effectiveness is unlikely to exceed 7 days. Subsequent doses of vaccine should be given as recommended in Table 3.18 (p 347) and Table 3.19 (p 348). For preterm infants who weigh less than 2000 g at birth, the initial vaccine dose should not be counted in the required 3-dose schedule (a total of 4 doses of hepatitis B vaccine), and the subsequent 3 doses should be given in accordance with the schedule for immunization of preterm infants (see Preterm and Low Birth Weight Infants, p 67).

Infants born to HBsAg-positive women should be tested for anti-HBs and HBsAg after completion of the immunization series, at 9 to 18 months of age (generally at the next well-child visit). Testing should not be performed before 9 months of age to avoid detection of anti-HBs from HBIG administered during infancy and to maximize the likelihood of detecting late HBV infections. Testing for HBsAg will identify infants who become chronically infected despite immunization (because of intrauterine infection or vaccine failure) and will aid in their long-term medical management. Testing for IgM anti-HBc is unreliable for infants. Infants with anti-HBs concentrations of less than 10 mIU/mL and who are HBsAg negative should receive 3 additional doses of vaccine in a 0-, 1-, and 6-month schedule followed by testing for anti-HBs 1 month after the third dose. Alternatively, 1 to 3 additional doses of vaccine can be administered, followed by testing for anti-HBs 1 month after each dose to determine whether subsequent doses are needed.

Term Infants Born to Mothers Not Tested During Pregnancy for HBsAg. Pregnant women whose HBsAg status is unknown at delivery should undergo blood testing as soon as possible to determine their HBsAg status. While awaiting results, the infant should receive the first hepatitis B vaccine dose within 12 hours of birth in the dose recommended for infants born to HBsAg-positive mothers (see Table 3.17, p 342). Because hepatitis B vaccine when given at birth is highly effective for preventing perinatal infection in term infants, the possible added value and the cost of HBIG do not warrant its immediate use in term infants when the mother's HBsAg status is not known. If the woman is found to be HBsAg-positive, term infants should receive HBIG (0.5 mL) as soon as possible, but within 7 days of birth, and should complete the hepatitis B immunization series as recommended (see Table 3.17, p 342, and Table 3.18, p 347). If HBIG is unavailable, the infant still should receive the 2 subsequent doses of hepatitis B vaccine at 1 to 2 and 6 months of age. If the mother is found to be HBsAg negative, hepatitis B immunization in the dose and schedule recommended for term infants born to HBsAg-negative mothers should be completed (see Table 3.17, p 342). If the mother's HBsAg status remains unknown, some experts would administer HBIG within 7 days of birth and complete the hepatitis B immunization series as recommended for infants born to mothers who are HBsAg positive (Table 3.18, p 347).

Preterm Infants Born to Mothers Not Tested During Pregnancy for HBsAg.
The maternal HBsAg status should be determined as soon as possible. Preterm
infants born to mothers whose HBsAg status is unknown should receive hepatitis B
vaccine within the first 12 hours of life. Preterm infants weighing more than 2000 g
at birth who are born to mothers whose HBsAg status is unknown should follow recommendations for term infants. Preterm infants weighing less than 2000 g at birth
who are born to mothers whose HBsAg status is unknown should receive HBIG
(0.5 mL) if the mother's HBsAg status cannot be determined within the initial 12
hours of birth because of the potentially decreased immunogenicity of vaccine in
these infants. In these infants, the initial vaccine dose should not be counted toward
the 3 doses of hepatitis B vaccine required to complete the immunization series. The
subsequent 3 doses (for a total of 4 doses) are given in accordance with recommendations for immunization of preterm infants with a birth weight less than 2000 g
according to the HBsAg status of the mother (see Table 3.18, p 347). Follow-up testing on completion of the immunization series is recommended for all preterm infants
of HBsAg-positive mothers (see Management of Infants Born to HBsAg-Positive
Women, p 351).

Breastfeeding. Breastfeeding of the infant by an HBsAg-positive mother poses no
additional risk of acquisition of HBV infection by the infant (see Human Milk,
p 123).

Household Contacts and Sexual Partners of HBsAg-Positive People. Household and sexual contacts of HBsAg-positive people (acute or chronic HBV infection)
identified through prenatal screening, blood donor screening, or diagnostic or other
serologic testing should be immunized.

Infants (ie, younger than 12 months of age) who have close contact with primary
caregivers with acute HBV infection require immunoprophylaxis. If at the time of
exposure, the infant has been immunized fully or has received at least 2 doses of vaccine, the infant should be presumed protected, and HBIG is not required. If only one
dose of vaccine has been administered, the second dose should be administered if the
interval is appropriate, or HBIG should be administered if immunization is not due.
If immunization has not been initiated, the infant should receive HBIG (0.5 mL), and
hepatitis B vaccine should be given in accordance with the routinely recommended 3-
dose schedule (see Preexposure Universal Immunization, p 344).

Prophylaxis with HBIG for other unimmunized household contacts of HBsAg-
positive people is not indicated unless they have a discrete, identifiable exposure to
the index patient (see next paragraph).

***Postexposure Prophylaxis for People With Discrete Identifiable Exposures to
Blood or Body Fluids That Contain Blood.*** Management of people with a discrete,
identifiable percutaneous (eg, needlestick, laceration, or bite) or mucosal (eg, ocular or
mucous membrane) exposure to blood or body fluids that contain blood includes consideration of whether the HBsAg status of the person who was the source of exposure
is known and the hepatitis B immunization and response status of the exposed person. Immunization is recommended for any person who was exposed but not previously immunized. If possible, a blood specimen from the person who was the source
of the exposure should be tested for HBsAg, and appropriate prophylaxis should be
administered according to the hepatitis B immunization status and anti-HBs response

status (if known) of the exposed person (see Table 3.21, p 354, and Injuries From Discarded Needles in the Community, p 188). Detailed guidelines for management of health care professionals and other people exposed to blood that is or might be HBsAg-positive is provided in the recommendations of the Advisory Committee on Immunization Practices of the Centers for Disease Control and Prevention (CDC)* (also see Table 3.21, p 354).

HBsAg-Positive Source. If the source is HBsAg positive, unimmunized people should receive both HBIG and hepatitis B vaccine as soon as possible after exposure, preferably within 24 hours (see Table 3.21, p 354). The vaccine series should be completed using an age-appropriate dose and schedule. People who are in the process of being immunized but who have not completed the vaccine series should receive the appropriate dose of HBIG and should complete the vaccine series. Children and adolescents who have written documentation of a complete hepatitis B vaccine series and who did not receive postimmunization testing should receive a single vaccine booster dose.

Source With Unknown HBsAg Status. If the HBsAg status of the source is unknown, unimmunized people should receive the hepatitis B vaccine series with the first dose initiated as soon as possible after exposure, preferably within 24 hours (see Table 3.21, p 354). The vaccine series should be completed using an age-appropriate dose and schedule. Children and adolescents with written documentation of a complete hepatitis B vaccine series require no further treatment.

Victims of Sexual Assault or Abuse. For unimmunized victims of sexual assault or abuse, active postexposure prophylaxis (ie, vaccine alone) should be initiated, with the first dose of vaccine given as part of the initial clinical evaluation. If the offender is known to be HBsAg positive, HBIG also should be administered. The vaccine series should be completed using an age-appropriate dose and schedule. (For discussion of management of previously immunized people, see Postexposure Prophylaxis for People With Discrete Identifiable Exposures to Blood or Body Fluids That Contain Blood, p 352.)

CHILD CARE. All children, including children in child care, should receive hepatitis B vaccine as part of their routine immunization schedule. Immunization not only will decrease the potential for transmission after bites but also will allay anxiety about transmission from attendees who may be HBsAg positive.

Children who are HBsAg-positive and who have no behavioral or medical risk factors, such as unusually aggressive behavior (eg, frequent biting), generalized dermatitis, or a bleeding problem, should be admitted to child care without restrictions. Under these circumstances, the risk of HBV transmission in child care settings is negligible, and routine screening for HBsAg is not warranted. Admission of HBsAg-positive children with behavioral or medical risk factors should be assessed on an individual basis by the child's physician, the program director, and the responsible

---

* Centers for Disease Control and Prevention. A comprehensive immunization strategy to eliminate transmission of hepatitis B virus infection in the United States. Recommendations of the Advisory Committee on Immunization Practices (ACIP). Part 1: immunization of Infants, Children, and Adolescents. *MMWR Morb Mortal Wkly Rep.* 2005;54(No. RR-16):1–32.

Table 3.21. Recommendations for Hepatitis B Prophylaxis After Percutaneous Exposure to Blood That Contains or Might Contain HBsAg[1]

Exposed Person	Treatment When Source Is		
	HBsAg Positive	HBsAg Negative	Unknown or Not Tested
Unimmunized	Administer HBIG[2] (1 dose), and initiate hepatitis B vaccine series	Initiate hepatitis B vaccine series	Initiate hepatitis B vaccine series
Previously immunized			
Known responder	No treatment	No treatment	No treatment
Known nonresponder	HBIG (1 dose) **and** initiate reimmunization[3] or HBIG (2 doses)	No treatment	If known high-risk source, treat as if source were HBsAg positive
Response unknown	Test exposed person for anti-HBs[4] • If inadequate, HBIG[2] (1 dose) **and** vaccine booster dose[5] • If adequate, no treatment	No treatment	Test exposed person for anti-HBs[4] • If inadequate, vaccine booster dose[5] • If adequate, no treatment

HBsAg indicates hepatitis B surface antigen; HBIG, Hepatitis B Immune Globulin; anti-HBs, antibody to HBsAg.

[1] Centers for Disease Control and Prevention. Updated US Public Health Service guidelines for the management of occupational exposures to HBV, HCV, and HIV and recommendations for postexposure prophylaxis. *MMWR Recomm Rep.* 2001;50(RR-11):1–52.

[2] Dose of HBIG, 0.06 mL/kg, intramuscularly.

[3] The option of giving 1 dose of HBIG (0.06 mL/kg) and reinitiating the vaccine series is preferred for nonresponder who have not completed a second 3-dose vaccine series. For people who previously completed a second vaccine series but failed to respond, 2 doses of HBIG (0.06 mL/kg) are preferred, 1 dose as soon as possible after exposure and the second 1 month later.

[4] Adequate anti-HBs is ≥10 mIU/mL.

[5] The person should be evaluated for antibody response after the vaccine booster dose. For people who receive HBIG, anti-HBs testing should be performed when passively acquired antibody from HBIG no longer is detectable (eg, 4–6 months); for people who did not receive HBIG, anti-HBs testing should be performed 1 to 2 months after the vaccine booster dose. If anti-HBs is inadequate (>10 mIU/mL) after the vaccine booster dose, 2 additional doses should be administered to complete a 3-dose reimmunization series.

public health authorities (for further discussion, see Children in Out-of-Home Child Care, p 130).

EFFECTIVENESS OF HEPATITIS B PREVENTION PROGRAMS. Routine hepatitis B immunization programs have resulted in significant decreases in the prevalence of chronic HBV infection among children in populations with a high incidence of HBV infection. There is an association between higher coverage with hepatitis B vaccine and larger decreases in HBsAg prevalence. The incidence of HBV infection among US children decreased by 94% between 1990 and 2004.

Although the long-term sequelae of chronic HBV infection usually are not recognized until adulthood, cirrhosis and HCC do occur in children. In Taiwan, the average annual incidence of HCC among children 6 to 14 years of age decreased significantly within 10 years of routine infant hepatitis B immunization. Worldwide, routine infant immunization programs are expected to decrease significantly the incidence of death from cirrhosis and HCC attributable to HBV infection over the next 30 to 50 years.

The Division of Viral Hepatitis at the CDC maintains a Web site (**www.cdc. gov/hepatitis**) with information on hepatitis for health care professionals and the public.

Hepatitis C

CLINICAL MANIFESTATIONS: Signs and symptoms of hepatitis C virus (HCV) infection are indistinguishable from those of hepatitis A or hepatitis B virus infections. Acute disease tends to be mild and insidious in onset, and most infections are asymptomatic. Jaundice occurs in <20% of patients, and abnormalities in liver function tests generally are less pronounced than abnormalities in patients with hepatitis B virus infection. Persistent infection with HCV occurs in 50% to 60% of infected children, even in the absence of biochemical evidence of liver disease. Most children with chronic infection are asymptomatic. Although chronic hepatitis develops in approximately 60% to 70% of infected adults, limited data indicate that chronic hepatitis and cirrhosis are less common in children. Infection with HCV is the leading reason for liver transplantation among adults in the United States.

ETIOLOGY: Hepatitis C virus is a small, single-stranded RNA virus and is a member of the Flavivirus family. Multiple HCV genotypes and subtypes exist.

EPIDEMIOLOGY: The prevalence of HCV infection in the general population of the United States is estimated at 1.8%. The seroprevalence is 0.2% for children younger than 12 years of age and 0.4% for adolescents 12 to 19 years of age. Seroprevalences vary among populations according to their associated risk factors.

Infection is spread primarily by parenteral exposure to blood of HCV-infected people. The current risk of HCV infection after blood transfusion in the United States is estimated to be less than 1 in 1 million units transfused because of exclusion of high-risk donors and of HCV-positive units by antibody testing and screening of pools of blood units by some form of nucleic acid amplification (NAA) test (see Blood Safety, p 106). All intravenous and intramuscular Immune Globulin products available commercially in the United States undergo an inactivation procedure for HCV or are documented to be HCV RNA negative before release.

The highest seroprevalences of HCV infection (60%–90%) are in people with large or repeated direct percutaneous exposure to blood or blood products, such as injection drug users and people with hemophilia who were treated with clotting factor concentrates produced before 1987. Prevalences are moderately high among people with frequent but smaller direct percutaneous exposures, such as patients receiving hemodialysis (10%–20%). Lower prevalences are found among people with inapparent percutaneous or mucosal exposures, such as people with high-risk sexual behaviors (1%–10%), and among people with sporadic percutaneous exposures, such as health care professionals (1%).

Other body fluids contaminated with infected blood can be sources of infection. Sexual transmission among monogamous couples is uncommon, with infection found only in 1.5% of spouses without other risk factors. Transmission among family contacts also is uncommon but could occur from direct or inapparent percutaneous or mucosal exposure to blood. For most infected children and adolescents, no specific source of infection can be identified.

Seroprevalence among pregnant women in the United States has been estimated at 1% to 2%. The risk of perinatal transmission averages 5% to 6%, and transmission occurs only from women who are HCV RNA positive at the time of delivery. Maternal coinfection with human immunodeficiency virus (HIV) has been associated with increased risk of perinatal transmission of HCV, which depends in part on the serum titer of maternal HCV RNA. Serum antibody to HCV (anti-HCV) and HCV RNA have been detected in colostrum, but the risk of HCV transmission is similar in breastfed and bottle-fed infants. The rate of transmission among breastfed infants has been the same as that among bottle-fed infants.

All people with HCV-RNA in their blood are considered to be infectious.

The **incubation period** for HCV disease averages 6 to 7 weeks, with a range of 2 weeks to 6 months. The time from exposure to development of viremia generally is 1 to 2 weeks.

DIAGNOSTIC TESTS*: The 2 major types of tests available for the laboratory diagnosis of HCV infections are immunoglobulin (Ig) G antibody assays for anti-HCV and NAA tests to detect HCV RNA. Assays for IgM are not available. The current enzyme immunoassays are at least 97% sensitive and more than 99% specific. False-negative results early in the course of acute infection result from the prolonged interval between exposure and onset of illness and seroconversion. Within 15 weeks after exposure and within 5 to 6 weeks after onset of hepatitis, 80% of patients will have positive test results for serum HCV antibody. Among infants born to anti-HCV–positive mothers, passively acquired maternal antibody may persist for up to 18 months.

Food and Drug Administration (FDA)-licensed diagnostic NAA tests for qualitative detection of HCV RNA are available. Hepatitis C virus RNA can be detected in serum or plasma within 1 to 2 weeks after exposure to the virus and weeks before onset of liver enzyme abnormalities or appearance of anti-HCV. Assays for detection

---

* Centers for Disease Control and Prevention. Guidelines for laboratory testing and result reporting of antibody to hepatitis C virus. *MMWR Recomm Rep.* 2003;52(RR-3):1–16

of HCV RNA are used commonly in clinical practice in the early diagnosis of infection, for identifying infection in infants early in life (ie, perinatal transmission) when maternal serum antibody interferes with the ability to detect antibody produced by the infant, and for monitoring patients receiving antiviral therapy. However, false-positive and false-negative results can occur from improper handling, storage, and contamination of the test specimens. Viral RNA may be detected intermittently, and thus, a single negative assay result is not conclusive. Quantitative assays for measuring the concentration of HCV RNA are available but are less sensitive than qualitative assays. The clinical value of these quantitative assays appears to be primarily as a prognostic indicator for patients undergoing or about to undergo antiviral therapy.

TREATMENT: Therapy is aimed at inhibiting HCV replication, eradicating infection, and improving the natural history of disease. Therapies are expensive, can cause significant adverse reactions, and are effective in approximately half of people treated. Interferon-alfa or peginterferon-alfa alone and peginterferon-alfa in combination with ribavirin are approved by the FDA for treatment of chronic hepatitis C virus infection in adults. Given alone, interferon-alfa results in a sustained virologic response (SVR) in 10% to 20% of adult patients treated; peginterferons alfa-2a and alfa-2b, which require only 1 dose weekly, result in average SVR of 39% and 25%, respectively. Lower SVR rates are observed in patients infected with HCV genotype 1, the most common strain in the United States. Combination therapy with interferon alfa-2b and ribavirin results in SVR in 33% of adult patients infected with genotype 1 and approximately 80% in patients with genotypes 2 or 3. Combination therapy with peginterferons results in higher SVR rates, particularly among patients with genotype 1 (40%). The FDA has approved use of interferon alfa-2b in combination with ribavirin for treatment of HCV infection in children 3 to 17 years of age. There have been few studies using combination therapy in children, but these studies suggest that children have increased SVR rates and fewer adverse events compared with adults. Children with severe disease or histologically advanced pathologic features (bridging necrosis or active cirrhosis) should be referred to a specialist in the management of chronic HCV infection for future management. All treatment regimens are associated with adverse events. Major adverse effects of combination therapy include influenza-like symptoms, hematologic abnormalities, and neuropsychiatric symptoms. Education of patients, their family members, and caregivers about adverse effects and their prospective management is an integral aspect of treatment.

All patients with chronic HCV infection should be immunized against hepatitis A and hepatitis B.

MANAGEMENT OF CHRONIC HCV INFECTION. With advancing age, people who have chronic HCV infection are at risk of developing chronic hepatitis and its complications, including cirrhosis and primary hepatocellular carcinoma. However, primary hepatocellular carcinoma secondary to chronic hepatitis C has been reported only in adults. Children with chronic infection should be screened periodically for chronic hepatitis with serum liver enzyme tests because of potential long-term risk of chronic liver disease. Definitive recommendations on frequency of screening have not been established. Children in whom a diagnosis of HCV infection is made should be referred to a specialist in this field for further management. The need for surveillance testing of alpha fetoprotein concentration and for abdominal ultrasonography in children has not been determined.

ISOLATION OF THE HOSPITALIZED PATIENT: Standard precautions are recommended.

CONTROL MEASURES:

CARE OF EXPOSED PEOPLE.

Immunoprophylaxis. On the basis of lack of clinical efficacy in humans and on data from studies using animals, the use of Immune Globulin for postexposure prophylaxis against HCV infection is not recommended.

Breastfeeding. Mothers infected with HCV should be advised that transmission of HCV by breastfeeding has not been documented. According to current guidelines of the Centers for Disease Control and Prevention (CDC) and the American Academy of Pediatrics, maternal HCV infection is not a contraindication to breastfeeding. Mothers who are HCV positive and choose to breastfeed should consider abstaining if their nipples are cracked or bleeding.

Child Care. Exclusion of children with HCV infection from out-of-home child care is not indicated.

SEROLOGIC TESTING FOR HCV INFECTION.

People Who Have Risk Factors for HCV Infection. Routine serologic testing is recommended for current or former injection drug users, recipients of one or more units of blood or blood products before July 1992, recipients of a solid organ transplant before July 1992, patients receiving long-term hemodialysis, people who received clotting factor concentrates produced before 1987, people with persistently abnormal alanine transaminase (ALT) concentrations, and people in settings with documented high HCV prevalence and where risk factor ascertainment is poor (corrections facilities inmates, patients attending sexually transmitted infection treatment clinics).

Pregnant Women. Routine serologic testing of pregnant women for HCV infection is not recommended.

Children Born to Women With HCV Infection. Children born to women previously identified to be HCV infected should be tested for HCV infection, because approximately 5% of these children will acquire the infection. The duration of presence of passive maternal antibody in infants is approximately 18 months. Therefore, testing for anti-HCV should not be performed until after 18 months of age. If earlier diagnosis is desired, NAA testing to detect HCV RNA may be performed at or after the infant's first well-child visit at 1 to 2 months of age.

Adoptees. Routine serologic testing of adoptees, either domestic or international, is not recommended. Testing is indicated, however, if the biologic mother has an increased risk of HCV infection (see Medical Evaluation of Internationally Adopted Children for Infectious Diseases, p 182).

COUNSELING OF PATIENTS WITH HCV INFECTION. All people with HCV infection should be considered infectious, should be informed of the possibility of transmission to others, and should refrain from donating blood, organs, tissues, or semen and from sharing toothbrushes and razors.

Infected people should be counseled to avoid hepatotoxic agents, including medications, and should be informed of the risks of alcohol ingestion. All patients with chronic HCV infection should be immunized against hepatitis A and hepatitis B.

Changes in sexual practices of infected people with a steady partner are not recommended; however, they should be informed of the possible risks and use of precautions to prevent transmission. People with multiple partners should be advised to decrease the number of partners and to use condoms to prevent transmission. No data exist to support counseling a woman against pregnancy.

The Division of Viral Hepatitis at the CDC has a toll-free number for information on viral hepatitis (1–888–4HEPCDC) and maintains a Web site (**www.cdc.gov/ hepatitis**) with information on hepatitis for health care professionals and the public, which includes specific information for people who have received blood transfusions before 1992. Information also can be obtained from the National Institutes of Health Web site (**http://digestive.niddk.nih.gov/ddiseases/pubs/chronichepc/ index.htm**).

Practice guidelines for diagnosis, management, and treatment of hepatitis C are available from the American Association for the Study of Liver Disease (**www.aasld. org/eweb/docs/hepatitisc.pdf**).

Hepatitis D

CLINICAL MANIFESTATIONS: Hepatitis D virus (HDV) causes hepatitis only in people with acute or chronic hepatitis B virus (HBV) infection; HDV requires HBV as a helper virus and cannot produce infection in the absence of HBV. The importance of HDV infection lies in its ability to convert an asymptomatic or mild chronic HBV infection into fulminant or more severe or rapidly progressive disease. Acute coinfection with HBV and HDV usually causes an acute illness indistinguishable from acute HBV infection alone, except that the likelihood of fulminant hepatitis can be as high as 5%.

ETIOLOGY: Hepatitis D virus measures 36 to 43 nm in diameter and consists of an RNA genome and a delta protein antigen, both of which are coated with hepatitis B surface antigen (HBsAg).

EPIDEMIOLOGY: Hepatitis D virus can cause an infection at the same time as the initial HBV infection (coinfection), or it can infect a person already chronically infected with HBV (superinfection). Acquisition of HDV is by parenteral, percutaneous, or mucous membrane inoculation. Hepatitis D virus can be acquired from blood or blood products, through injection drug use, or by sexual contact, but only if HBV also is present. Transmission from mother to newborn infant is uncommon. Intrafamilial spread can occur among people with chronic HBV infection. High-prevalence areas include southern Italy and parts of Eastern Europe, South America, Africa, and the Middle East. In contrast to HBV infection, HDV infection is uncommon in the Far East. In the United States, HDV infection is found most commonly in people who abuse injection drugs, people with hemophilia, and people who have immigrated from areas with endemic infection.

The **incubation period** for HDV superinfection is approximately 2 to 8 weeks. When HBV and HDV viruses infect simultaneously, the incubation period is similar to that of HBV (45–160 days; average, 90 days).

DIAGNOSTIC TESTS: Radioimmunoassay and enzyme immunoassay for antibody to HDV (anti-HDV) are available commercially. Anti-HDV may not be present until several weeks after onset of illness, and acute and convalescent sera may be required to confirm the diagnosis. Coinfection usually can be differentiated from superinfection with HBV by testing for immunoglobulin (Ig) M hepatitis B core antibody (anti-HBc); absence of IgM anti-HBc suggests that the person with chronic HBV infection has a superinfection. Testing for the IgM anti-HDV response is not useful for distinguishing acute from chronic HDV infection, because IgM anti-HDV persists during chronic infection. Tests for IgM anti-HDV, hepatitis D antigen, and HDV RNA are research procedures.

TREATMENT: Supportive.

ISOLATION OF THE HOSPITALIZED PATIENT: Standard precautions are recommended.

CONTROL MEASURES: The same control and preventive measures used for HBV infection are indicated. Because HDV cannot be transmitted in the absence of HBV infection, hepatitis B immunization protects against HDV infection. People with chronic HBV infection should take extreme care to avoid exposure to HDV.

Hepatitis E

CLINICAL MANIFESTATIONS: Hepatitis E virus (HEV) infection is an acute illness with symptoms including jaundice, malaise, anorexia, fever, abdominal pain, and arthralgia. Subclinical infection also occurs. Disease is more common among adults than among children and is more severe in pregnant women, in whom mortality rates can approach 10%. Chronic HEV infection has not been reported.

ETIOLOGY: Hepatitis E virus is a spherical, nonenveloped, positive-strand RNA virus. Hepatitis E virus formerly was classified in the family Caliciviridae, genus Calicivirus; however, HEV has been reassigned to an unassigned genus of "hepatitis E-like" viruses, because certain characteristics distinguish HEV from typical caliciviruses.

EPIDEMIOLOGY: Transmission of HEV is by the fecal-oral route. Unlike the other agents of viral hepatitis, HEV commonly is found in wild and domestic animals, which may provide an important source of infections in humans. Person-to-person transmission appears to be much less efficient than with hepatitis A virus. Sporadic HEV infection has been reported in much of the developing world and particularly is common on the Indian subcontinent, where some studies have shown HEV to be the most common etiology of acute viral hepatitis. Large, often waterborne outbreaks also have been reported in developing countries, including one outbreak in Mexico in 1986. In the United States, HEV infection is uncommon and generally occurs in travelers returning from countries with endemic infection. Three cases of domestically acquired HEV infection have been reported in the United States, all with viruses that are phylogenetically similar to HEV isolated from US swine.

DIAGNOSTIC TESTS: Testing for IgM and IgG anti-HEV is available through commercial reference laboratories and, with prior approval, through the Centers for Disease Control and Prevention. Because anti-HEV assays are not approved by the US Food and Drug Administration and their performance characteristics are not well characterized, results should be interpreted with caution, particularly in cases with no recent history of travel to an endemic country. Definitive diagnosis may be made by demonstrating viral RNA in serum or stool by means of reverse transcriptase-polymerase chain reaction assay, which is available only in research settings.

TREATMENT: Supportive.

ISOLATION OF THE HOSPITALIZED PATIENT: In addition to standard precautions, contact precautions are recommended for diapered and incontinent patients for the duration of illness.

CONTROL MEASURES: Provision of safe water is the most effective prevention measure. A preventive vaccine has been developed but currently is not available.

Herpes Simplex

CLINICAL MANIFESTATIONS:

NEONATAL. In newborn infants, herpes simplex virus (HSV) infection can manifest as the following: (1) disseminated disease involving multiple organs, most prominently liver and lungs; (2) localized central nervous system (CNS) disease; or (3) disease localized to the skin, eyes, and mouth. Approximately one third of cases are disseminated, one third are CNS disease, and one third affect the skin, eyes, and mouth, although there can be clinical overlap among disease types. In many neonates with disseminated or CNS disease, skin lesions do not develop or the lesions appear late in the course of infection. In the absence of skin lesions, the diagnosis of neonatal HSV infection is difficult. Disseminated infection should be considered in neonates with sepsis syndrome, negative bacteriologic culture results, and severe liver dysfunction. Herpes simplex virus also should be considered as a causative agent in neonates with fever, irritability, and abnormal cerebrospinal fluid (CSF) findings, especially in the presence of seizures. Although asymptomatic HSV infection is common in older children, it rarely, if ever, occurs in neonates.

Neonatal herpetic infections often are severe, with attendant high mortality and morbidity rates, even when antiviral therapy is administered. Recurrent skin lesions are common in surviving infants and can be associated with CNS sequelae if skin lesions occur frequently during the first 6 months of life.

Initial signs of HSV infection can occur anytime between birth and approximately 4 weeks of age. Disseminated disease has the earliest age of onset, often during the first week of life; CNS disease manifests latest, usually between the second and third weeks of life.

CHILDREN BEYOND THE NEONATAL PERIOD AND ADOLESCENTS. Most primary HSV infections are asymptomatic. Gingivostomatitis, which is the most common clinical manifestation in this age group, usually is caused by HSV type 1 (HSV-1). Gingivostomatitis is characterized by fever, irritability, tender submandibular adenopathy, and an ulcerative enanthem involving the gingiva and mucous membranes of the mouth, often with perioral vesicular lesions.

Genital herpes, which is the most common manifestation of HSV infection in adolescents and adults, is characterized by vesicular or ulcerative lesions of the male or female genital organs, perineum, or both. Genital herpes usually is caused by HSV type 2 (HSV-2), but HSV type 1 appears to be increasing in frequency.

Eczema herpeticum with vesicular lesions concentrated in the areas of eczematous involvement can develop in patients with dermatitis who are infected with HSV.

In immunocompromised patients, severe local lesions and, less commonly, disseminated HSV infection with generalized vesicular skin lesions and visceral involvement can occur.

After primary infection, HSV persists for life in a latent form. The site of latency for virus causing herpes labialis is the trigeminal ganglion, and the usual site of latency for genital herpes is the sacral ganglia, although any of the sensory ganglia can be involved, depending on the site of primary infection. Reactivation of latent virus most commonly occurs in the absence of symptoms. When symptomatic, recurrent herpes labialis HSV-1 manifests as single or grouped vesicles in the perioral region, usually on the vermilion border of the lips (cold sores). Symptomatic recurrent genital herpes manifests as vesicular lesions on the penis, scrotum, vulva, cervix, buttocks, perianal areas, thighs, or back.

Conjunctivitis and keratitis can result from primary or recurrent HSV infection. Herpetic whitlow consists of single or multiple vesicular lesions on the distal parts of fingers. Herpes simplex virus infection has been implicated as a precipitating factor in erythema multiforme.

Herpes simplex virus encephalitis can result from primary or recurrent infection and usually is associated with fever, alterations in the state of consciousness, personality changes, seizures, and focal neurologic findings. Encephalitis commonly has an acute onset with a fulminant course, leading to coma and death in untreated patients. Cerebrospinal fluid pleocytosis with a predominance of lymphocytes and some erythrocytes is usual. Herpes simplex virus infection also can cause meningitis with nonspecific clinical manifestations that usually are mild and self-limited. Such episodes of meningitis usually are associated with genital HSV-2 infection. A number of unusual CNS manifestations of HSV have been described, including Bell palsy, atypical pain syndromes, trigeminal neuralgia, ascending myelitis, and postinfectious encephalomyelitis.

ETIOLOGY: Herpes simplex viruses are enveloped, double-stranded, DNA viruses. Infections with HSV-1 usually involve the face and skin above the waist; however, an increasing number of genital herpes cases are attributable to HSV-1. Infections with HSV-2 usually involve the genitalia and skin below the waist in sexually active adolescents and adults. Either type of virus can be found in either area. Herpes simplex virus type 2 is the most common cause of disease in neonates (75% of cases).

EPIDEMIOLOGY: Herpes simplex virus infections are ubiquitous and are transmitted from people who are symptomatic or asymptomatic with primary or recurrent infections.

NEONATAL. The incidence of neonatal HSV infection is estimated to range from 1 in 3000 to 1 in 20 000 live births. Infants in whom HSV infection develops are significantly more likely to have been born preterm. Herpes simplex virus is transmitted to an infant most often during birth through an infected maternal genital tract or by an ascending infection, sometimes through apparently intact membranes. Intrauterine infections causing congenital malformations have been implicated in rare cases. Other less common sources of neonatal infection include postnatal transmission from a parent or other caregiver, most often from a nongenital infection (eg, mouth or hands) or from another infected infant or caregiver in the nursery, probably via the hands of health care professionals attending to the infants.

The risk of HSV infection at delivery in an infant born vaginally to a mother with primary genital infection is estimated to be 33% to 50%. The risk to an infant born to a mother shedding HSV as a result of reactivated infection is less than 5%. Distinguishing between primary and recurrent HSV infections in women by history or physical examination may be impossible. Primary and recurrent infections may be asymptomatic or associated with nonspecific findings (eg, vaginal discharge, genital pain, or shallow ulcers). More than three quarters of infants who contract HSV infection have been born to women who had no history or clinical findings suggestive of active HSV infection during pregnancy.

CHILDREN BEYOND THE NEONATAL PERIOD AND ADOLESCENTS. Patients with primary gingivostomatitis or genital herpes usually shed virus for at least 1 week and occasionally for several weeks. Patients with recurrent infection shed virus for a shorter period, typically 3 to 4 days. Intermittent asymptomatic reactivation of oral and genital herpes is common and persists for life, occurring in 1% of days among previously infected people. The greatest concentration of virus is shed during symptomatic primary infections and the lowest concentration of virus is shed during asymptomatic recurrent infections.

Infection with HSV-1 usually results from direct contact with infected oral secretions or lesions. Infections with HSV-2 usually result from direct contact with infected genital secretions or lesions through sexual activity. Genital infections caused by HSV-1 in children can result from autoinoculation of virus from the mouth, but sexual abuse always should be considered in prepubertal children with genital HSV-2 infections. Therefore, genital HSV isolates from children should be typed to differentiate between HSV-1 and HSV-2.

The incidence of HSV-2 infection correlates with the number of sexual partners and with acquisition of other sexually transmitted infections. After primary genital infection, which often is asymptomatic, some people experience frequent clinical recurrences, and others have no recurrences. Genital HSV-2 infection is more likely to recur than is genital HSV-1 infection.

Inoculation of skin occurs from direct contact with HSV-containing oral or genital secretions. This contact can result in herpes gladiatorum among wrestlers, herpes rugbiaforum among rugby players, or herpetic whitlow of the fingers in any exposed person.

The **incubation period** for HSV infection occurring beyond the neonatal period ranges from 2 days to 2 weeks.

DIAGNOSTIC TESTS: Herpes simplex virus grows readily in cell culture. Special transport media are available for specimens that cannot be inoculated immediately onto susceptible cell culture media. Cytopathogenic effects typical of HSV infection usually are observed 1 to 3 days after inoculation. Methods of culture confirmation include fluorescent antibody staining and enzyme immunoassays. Cultures that remain negative by day 15 are likely to continue to remain negative. Polymerase chain reaction assay often can detect HSV DNA in CSF from patients with HSV encephalitis and is the diagnostic method of choice when performed by experienced laboratory personnel. Histologic examination and viral culture of a brain tissue specimen obtained by biopsy is the most definitive method of confirming the diagnosis of encephalitis caused by HSV. Cultures of CSF from a patient with HSV encephalitis usually are negative.

For diagnosis of neonatal HSV infection, swabs of the mouth, nasopharynx, conjunctivae, and rectum and specimens of skin vesicles, urine, stool, blood, and CSF should be obtained for culture. Positive cultures obtained from any of these sites more than 48 hours after birth indicate viral replication suggestive of infant infection rather than contamination after intrapartum exposure. Rapid diagnostic techniques also are available, such as direct fluorescent antibody staining of vesicle scrapings or enzyme immunoassay detection of HSV antigens. These techniques are as specific but slightly less sensitive than culture. Typing HSV strains differentiates between HSV-1 and HSV-2 isolates. Polymerase chain reaction assay is a sensitive method for detecting HSV DNA and is of particular value for evaluating CSF specimens from people with suspected herpes encephalitis. Histologic examination of lesions for the presence of multinucleated giant cells and eosinophilic intranuclear inclusions typical of HSV (eg, with Tzanck test) has low sensitivity and is not recommended as a rapid diagnostic test.

Both type-specific and nonspecific antibodies to HSV develop during the first several weeks after infection and persist indefinitely. Although type-specific HSV-2 antibody almost always indicates anogenital infection, the presence of HSV-1 antibody does not distinguish anogenital from orolabial infection. Type-specific serologic tests can be useful in confirming a clinical diagnosis of genital herpes. Additionally, these serologic tests can be used to diagnose people with unrecognized infection and to manage sexual partners of people with genital herpes. Serologic testing is not useful in neonates.

Several glycoprotein G (gG)-based type-specific assays have been approved by the US Food and Drug Administration (FDA), including at least one that can be used as a point-of-care test. The sensitivities of these tests for detection of HSV-2 antibody vary from 80% to 98%, and false-negative results may occur, especially early after infection. The specificities of these assays are >96%; false-positive results can occur, especially in patients with low likelihood of HSV infection. Therefore, repeat testing or a confirmatory test (eg, an immunoblot assay if the initial test was an enzyme-linked immunosorbent assay) may be indicated in some settings.

TREATMENT: For recommended antiviral dosages and duration of therapy with acyclovir, valacyclovir, famciclovir, and penciclovir for different HSV infections, see Antiviral Drugs (p 785). Valacyclovir is an L-valyl ester of acyclovir that is metabolized to acyclovir after oral administration, resulting in higher serum concentrations than with oral acyclovir and similar serum concentrations after intravenous administration of acyclovir. Famciclovir is converted rapidly to penciclovir after oral administration. Table 3.22 shows drugs for HSV by type of infection. Neither valacyclovir nor famciclovir is approved by the FDA for use in children.

NEONATAL. Parenteral acyclovir is the treatment of choice for neonatal HSV infections. Acyclovir should be administered to all neonates with HSV infection, regardless of manifestations and clinical findings. The best outcome in terms of morbidity and mortality is observed among infants with disease limited to the skin, eyes, and mouth. Although most neonates treated for HSV encephalitis survive, most suffer substantial neurologic sequelae. Approximately 25% of neonates with disseminated disease die despite antiviral therapy. The dosage of acyclovir is 60 mg/kg per day in 3 divided doses, given intravenously for 14 days if disease is limited to the skin, eyes, and mouth and for 21 days if disease is disseminated or involves the CNS. Relapse of diseases of the skin, eyes, mouth, and CNS can occur after cessation of treatment. The optimal management of these recurrences is not established. The value of long-

Table 3.22. Recommended Therapy for Herpes Simplex Virus Infections[1]

Infection	Drug[2]
Neonatal	Acyclovir
Keratoconjunctivitis	Trifluridine[3]
	OR
	Iododeoxyuridine
	OR
	Vidarabine
Genital	Acyclovir
	OR
	Famciclovir
	OR
	Valacyclovir
Mucocutaneous (immunocompromised or primary gingivostomatitis)	Acyclovir
	OR
	Famciclovir
	OR
	Valacyclovir
Acyclovir-resistant (severe infections, immunocompromised)	Foscarnet
Encephalitis	Acyclovir

[1] See text and Table 4.9 (p 785) for details.
[2] Famciclovir and valacyclovir are approved for treatment of adults.
[3] Treatment of herpes simplex virus ocular infection should involve an ophthalmologist.

term suppressive or intermittent acyclovir therapy for neonates with disease of the skin, eyes, and mouth continues to be evaluated.

Infants with ocular involvement attributable to HSV infection should receive a topical ophthalmic drug (1% trifluridine, 0.1% iododeoxyuridine, or 3% vidarabine) as well as parenteral antiviral therapy.

GENITAL INFECTION.

Primary. Many patients with first-episode herpes have mild clinical manifestations but go on to develop severe or prolonged symptoms. Therefore, most patients with initial genital herpes should receive antiviral therapy. In adults, acyclovir and valacyclovir decrease the duration of symptoms and viral shedding in primary genital herpes. Oral acyclovir therapy, initiated within 6 days of onset of disease, shortens the duration of illness and viral shedding by 3 to 5 days. Valacyclovir and famciclovir do not seem to be more effective than acyclovir, but they offer the advantage of less frequent dosing. No pediatric formulations of valacyclovir or famciclovir are available. Intravenous acyclovir is indicated for patients with a severe or complicated primary infection that requires hospitalization. Topical acyclovir (5%) ointment for primary genital herpes infection is not recommended. Systemic or topical treatment of primary herpetic lesions does not affect the subsequent frequency or severity of recurrences.

Recurrent. Antiviral therapy for recurrent genital herpes can be administered either episodically to ameliorate or shorten the duration of lesions or continuously as suppressive therapy to decrease the frequency of recurrences. Many patients benefit from antiviral therapy; therefore, options for treatment should be discussed with all patients. Oral acyclovir therapy initiated within 2 days of the onset of symptoms shortens the mean clinical course by approximately 1 day. Drug or a prescription for the medication should be provided with instructions to initiate treatment immediately when symptoms begin. Valacyclovir and famciclovir are licensed for treatment of adults with recurrent genital herpes; however, no data exist for treatment of pediatric disease. Topical acyclovir is not beneficial for immunocompetent hosts.

In adults with frequent genital HSV recurrences (6 or more episodes per year), daily oral acyclovir suppressive therapy is effective for decreasing the frequency of symptomatic recurrences. After approximately 1 year of continuous daily therapy, acyclovir should be discontinued and the recurrence rate should be assessed. If recurrences are observed, additional suppressive therapy should be considered. Acyclovir seems to be safe for adults receiving the drug for more than 15 years, but long-term effects are unknown. Data also support suppressive therapy in adults with valacyclovir or famciclovir.

Data on use of valacyclovir or famciclovir for suppressive therapy in children are not available. The safety of systemic valacyclovir and famciclovir therapy in pregnant women has not been established. Available data do not indicate an increased risk of major birth defects in comparison with the general population in women treated with acyclovir during the first trimester. Acyclovir may be administered orally to pregnant women with first-episode genital herpes or severe recurrent herpes and should be given intravenously to pregnant women with severe HSV infection.

MUCOCUTANEOUS

Immunocompromised Hosts. Intravenous acyclovir is effective for treatment and prevention of mucocutaneous HSV infections. Topical acyclovir also may accelerate healing of lesions in immunocompromised patients.

Acyclovir-resistant strains of HSV have been isolated from immunocompromised people receiving prolonged treatment with acyclovir. Under these circumstances, progressive disease may be observed despite acyclovir therapy. Foscarnet is the drug of choice for disease caused by acyclovir-resistant HSV isolates.

Immunocompetent Hosts. Limited data are available on the effects of acyclovir on the course of primary or recurrent nongenital mucocutaneous HSV infections in immunocompetent hosts. Therapeutic benefit has been noted in a limited number of children with primary gingivostomatitis treated with oral acyclovir. Minimal therapeutic benefit of oral acyclovir therapy has been demonstrated among adults with recurrent herpes labialis. Topical acyclovir is ineffective. A topical formulation of penciclovir (Denavir) and another drug, docosanol (Abreva), have limited activity for therapy of herpes labialis and are not recommended.

In a small controlled study in adults with recurrent herpes labialis (6 or more episodes per year), prophylactic acyclovir given in a dosage of 400 mg twice a day was effective for decreasing the frequency of recurrent episodes. Although no studies of prophylactic therapy have been performed in children, those with frequent recurrences may benefit from continuous oral acyclovir therapy (80 mg/kg per day in 3 divided doses; maximum 1000 mg/day); reevaluation should be performed after 1 year of continuous therapy.

OTHER HSV INFECTIONS

Central Nervous System. Patients with HSV encephalitis should be treated for 21 days with intravenous acyclovir. Therapy is less effective in older adults than in children. Patients who are comatose or semicomatose at initiation of therapy have a poor outcome. For people with Bell palsy, the combination of acyclovir and prednisone should be considered.

Ocular. Treatment of eye lesions should be undertaken in consultation with an ophthalmologist. Several topical drugs, such as 1% trifluridine, 0.1% iododeoxyuridine, and 3% vidarabine, have proven efficacy for superficial keratitis. Topical corticosteroids are contraindicated in suspected HSV conjunctivitis; however, ophthalmologists may choose to use corticosteroids in conjunction with antiviral drugs to treat locally invasive infections. For children with recurrent ocular lesions, oral suppressive therapy with acyclovir (80 mg/kg per day in 3 divided doses; maximum 1000 mg/day) may be of benefit.

ISOLATION OF THE HOSPITALIZED PATIENT: In addition to standard precautions, the following recommendations should be followed.

NEONATES WITH HSV INFECTION. Neonates with HSV infection should be hospitalized and managed with contact precautions if mucocutaneous lesions are present.

NEONATES EXPOSED TO HSV DURING DELIVERY. Infants born to women with active HSV lesions should be managed with contact precautions during the incubation period. Some experts believe that contact precautions are unnecessary if exposed infants were born by cesarean delivery, provided membranes were ruptured for less than 4 hours. The risk of HSV infection in infants born to mothers with a history of recurrent genital herpes who have no genital lesions at delivery is low, and special precautions are not necessary.

One method of infection control for neonates with documented perinatal exposure to HSV is continuous rooming-in with the mother in a private room.

WOMEN IN LABOR AND POSTPARTUM WOMEN WITH HSV INFECTION. Women with active HSV lesions should be managed during labor, delivery, and the postpartum period with contact precautions. These women should be instructed about the importance of careful hand hygiene before and after caring for their infants. The mother may wear a clean covering gown to help avoid contact of the infant with lesions or infectious secretions. A mother with herpes labialis or stomatitis should wear a disposable surgical mask when touching her newborn infant until the lesions have crusted and dried. She should not kiss or nuzzle her newborn until the lesions have cleared. Herpetic lesions on other skin sites should be covered.

Breastfeeding is acceptable if no lesions are present on the breasts and if active lesions elsewhere on the mother are covered (see Human Milk, p 123).

CHILDREN WITH MUCOCUTANEOUS HSV INFECTION. Contact precautions are recommended for patients with severe mucocutaneous HSV infection. Patients with localized recurrent lesions should be managed with standard precautions.

PATIENTS WITH HSV INFECTION OF THE CNS. Standard precautions are recommended for patients with infection limited to the CNS.

CONTROL MEASURES:

PREVENTION OF NEONATAL INFECTION. Cultures for HSV obtained weekly during pregnancy are not recommended. Women with a history of genital HSV infection and women whose sexual partners have genital HSV infection are recognized to be at low risk of transmitting HSV to their infants (see Epidemiology, p 362).

Management of infants exposed to HSV during delivery differs according to the status of the mother's infection, mode of delivery, and expert opinion (see Care of Newborn Infants Whose Mothers Have Active Genital Lesions, p 369). Current recommendations for management of pregnant women for prevention of HSV infection include the following:

- **During pregnancy.** During prenatal evaluations, all pregnant women should be asked about past or current signs and symptoms consistent with genital herpes infection in themselves and their sexual partners.
- Although antiviral therapy for women with a history of genital HSV infection is recommended during the final weeks of pregnancy by some obstetricians to suppress maternal recurrence of viral shedding, the safety of antiviral therapy for the fetus and its efficacy in preventing viral shedding, rate of caesarian delivery, or neonatal infection have not been established.
- **Women in labor.** During labor, all women should be asked about recent and current signs and symptoms consistent with genital herpes infection, and they should be examined carefully for evidence of genital infection. Cesarean delivery for women who have clinically apparent HSV infection decreases the risk of neonatal HSV infection. Some experts recommend that cesarian section be performed within 4 to 6 hours of membrane rupture when possible in women with clinical evidence of genital HSV at delivery. However, others recommend cesarean delivery whenever the birth canal is infected, even if membranes have been ruptured for 6 hours or more. In the absence of genital lesions, a maternal history of genital HSV is not an indication for cesarean delivery. Scalp monitors

should be avoided when possible in infants of women suspected of having active genital herpes infection.

A cesarean delivery should be performed immediately for a woman who has ruptured membranes and active genital lesions at term. The appropriate management of delivery is not established if membranes rupture in the presence of active genital lesions at a time when the fetal lungs are immature. Some experts recommend that intravenous acyclovir (15 mg/kg in 3 divided doses, maximum 1200 mg/day) be administered to the mother if labor and delivery are delayed. The value and risks of acyclovir in this situation are unknown. Acyclovir is not approved by the FDA for this indication.

CARE OF NEWBORN INFANTS WHOSE MOTHERS HAVE ACTIVE GENITAL LESIONS.

By Vaginal Delivery. Because the risk to infants exposed to HSV lesions during delivery varies in different circumstances from less than 5% to 50% or more, the decision to treat the asymptomatic exposed infant empirically with intravenous acyclovir is controversial. Because the infection rate of infants born to mothers with active recurrent genital herpes infections is less than 5%, most experts would not treat these infants empirically with acyclovir. The infant's parents or caregivers, however, should be educated about the signs and symptoms of neonatal HSV infection.

For infants born to mothers with a primary genital infection, the risk of infection may exceed 50%. Because of this high infection rate, some experts recommend empiric acyclovir treatment at birth after HSV cultures have been obtained, and others would obtain HSV cultures 24 to 48 hours after delivery and initiate acyclovir therapy only if HSV is recovered from these cultures. If the infant has clinical findings suggestive of HSV infection, such as skin or scalp rashes (especially vesicular lesions) or unexplained manifestations (such as those of sepsis), cultures should be obtained, regardless of age, and acyclovir therapy should be initiated immediately. The accuracy of viral cultures for predicting neonatal infection in infants whose mothers were treated with antiviral medication during pregnancy is not known.

Differentiating primary genital infection from recurrent HSV infection in the mother would be helpful for assessing the risk of HSV infection for the exposed infant, but the distinction may be difficult. First-episode clinical infections are not always primary infections. Often, primary infections are asymptomatic, in which case the first symptomatic episode will represent a reactivated recurrent infection. In selected instances, serologic testing can be useful. For example, if a woman with herpetic lesions has no detectable HSV antibodies, she is experiencing a primary infection. Assessment of seropositive women necessitates differentiation of HSV-1 from HSV-2 antibodies. Currently, only assays based on detection of type-specific glycoprotein G make this distinction reliably.

Recommendations. Management of exposed asymptomatic infants who were born vaginally to mothers with active genital lesions can be categorized according to the type of maternal infection as follows:

- Mother with primary infection
- Mother with known recurrent lesions
- Mother whose status (primary vs recurrent) is unknown
- Mother who has no apparent genital lesions but a positive HSV culture of vagina or cervix

For infants in each category, cultures should be obtained for HSV at 24 to 48 hours after birth. Specimens for cultures should include urine and stool and swabs of the mouth, rectum, conjunctivae, and nasopharynx (see Diagnostic Tests, p 363). For infants whose mothers have presumed or proven primary infection, some experts recommend empiric acyclovir treatment at birth, although no data exist to support the efficacy of such an approach. Other experts would await positive HSV culture results or clinical manifestations of infection before starting therapy. The sensitivity of these cultures is high but is not 100%. Infants whose cultures are negative can develop infection.

MANAGEMENT OF THE POSSIBLY EXPOSED INFANT. The infant whose mother has known, recurrent genital infection, whether active maternal lesions were present at the time of delivery or not, should be observed carefully for signs of infection, including vesicular lesions of the skin, respiratory distress, seizures, or signs of sepsis. Education of parents and caregivers about the signs and symptoms of neonatal HSV infection is prudent. An infant with any of these manifestations should be evaluated immediately for possible HSV infection (as well as for bacterial infection). Specimens for HSV culture should include urine, stool, blood buffy coat, CSF, and skin lesions and swabs of the conjunctivae, nasopharynx, and mouth. Testing of CSF by polymerase chain reaction assay also is recommended. Acyclovir therapy should be initiated if any of the culture or PCR results are positive, CSF findings are abnormal, or HSV infection otherwise is suspected strongly.

Infants born by cesarean delivery to mothers with herpetic lesions should be observed carefully, with laboratory studies performed as recommended for potentially exposed infants born by vaginal delivery. Antiviral therapy should be initiated if culture results from the infant are positive or if HSV is suspected for other reasons.

OTHER RECOMMENDATIONS.
- The length of in-hospital observation for infants at increased risk of neonatal HSV is variable and based on factors specific to the infant and local resources, such as the family's ability to observe the infant at home, availability of follow-up care, and clinical assessment.
- Neonatal HSV infection can occur as late as 6 weeks after delivery, although most infected infants are symptomatic by 4 weeks of age. Parents and physicians must be vigilant, and any rash or other signs or symptoms that may be caused by HSV must be evaluated carefully.

INFECTED HOSPITAL PERSONNEL. Transmission of HSV in newborn nurseries from infected personnel to newborn infants rarely has been documented. The risk of transmission to infants by personnel who have herpes labialis or who are asymptomatic oral shedders of virus is low. Compromising patient care by excluding personnel with cold sores who are essential for the operation of the nursery must be weighed against the potential risk of newborn infants becoming infected. Personnel with cold sores who have contact with infants should cover and not touch their lesions and should comply with hand hygiene policies. Transmission of HSV infection from personnel with genital lesions is not likely as long as personnel comply with hand hygiene policies. Personnel with an active herpetic whitlow should not have responsibility for direct care of neonates or immunocompromised patients.

INFECTED HOUSEHOLD CONTACTS OF NEWBORNS. Intrafamilial transmission of HSV to newborn infants has been described but is rare. Household members with herpetic skin lesions (eg, herpes labialis or herpetic whitlow) should be counseled about the risk and should avoid contact of their lesions with newborn infants by taking the same measures as recommended for infected hospital personnel as well as avoiding kissing and nuzzling the infant while they have active lip lesions or touching the infant while they have herpetic whitlow.

CARE OF PEOPLE WITH EXTENSIVE DERMATITIS. Patients with dermatitis are at risk of developing eczema herpeticum. If these patients are hospitalized, special care should be taken to avoid exposure to HSV. These patients should not be kissed by people with cold sores or touched by people with herpetic whitlow.

CARE OF CHILDREN WITH MUCOCUTANEOUS INFECTIONS WHO ARE IN CHILD CARE OR SCHOOL. Oral HSV infections are common among children who are in child care or school. Most of these infections are asymptomatic, with shedding of virus in saliva occurring in the absence of clinical disease. Only children with HSV gingivostomatitis (ie, primary infection) who do not have control of oral secretions should be excluded from child care. Exclusion of children with cold sores (ie, recurrent infection) from child care or school is not indicated.

Children with uncovered lesions on exposed surfaces pose a small potential risk to contacts. If children are certified by a physician to have recurrent HSV infection, covering the active lesions with clothing, a bandage, or an appropriate dressing when they attend child care or school is sufficient.

HERPES SIMPLEX VIRUS INFECTIONS AMONG WRESTLERS AND RUGBY PLAYERS. Infection with HSV-1 has been transmitted during athletic competition involving close physical contact and frequent skin abrasions, such as wrestling (herpes gladiatorum) and rugby (herpes rugbiaforum or scrum pox). Competitors often do not recognize or may deny possible infection. Transmission of these infections can be limited or prevented by the following: (1) examination of wrestlers and rugby players for vesicular or ulcerative lesions on exposed areas of their bodies and around their mouths or eyes before practice or competition by a person familiar with the appearance of mucocutaneous infections (including HSV, herpes zoster, and impetigo); (2) exclusion of athletes with these conditions from competition or practice until healing occurs or a physician's written statement declaring their condition noninfectious is obtained; and (3) cleaning wrestling mats with a freshly prepared solution of household bleach (one quarter cup of bleach in 1 gallon of water) applied for a minimum contact time of 15 seconds at least daily and, preferably, between matches. Despite these precautions, HSV spread during wrestling and other sports involving close personal contact still can occur through contact with asymptomatic infected people.

Histoplasmosis

CLINICAL MANIFESTATIONS: *Histoplasma capsulatum* causes symptoms in fewer than 5% of infected people. Clinical manifestations may be classified according to site (pulmonary, extrapulmonary, or disseminated), duration (acute, chronic), and pattern (primary vs reactivation) of infection. Most symptomatic patients have acute pulmonary histoplasmosis, an influenza-like illness with nonpleuritic chest pain, hilar adenopathy, and mild pulmonary infiltrates; symptoms persist for 2 days to 2 weeks. Intense exposure to spores can cause severe respiratory tract symptoms and diffuse nodular pulmonary infiltrates, prolonged fever, fatigue, and weight loss. Erythema nodosum can occur in adolescents. Primary cutaneous infections after trauma are rare.

Progressive disseminated histoplasmosis (PDH) can develop in otherwise healthy infants younger than 2 years of age. Early manifestations include prolonged fever, failure to thrive, and hepatosplenomegaly; if untreated, malnutrition, diffuse adenopathy, pneumonia, mucosal ulceration, pancytopenia, disseminated intravascular coagulopathy, and gastrointestinal tract bleeding can ensue. Central nervous system involvement is common. Cellular immune dysfunction caused by primary immunodeficiency disorders, human immunodeficiency virus (HIV) infection, or immunosuppressive therapy (including tumor necrosis factor-alpha inhibitors) may predispose patients with acute histoplasmosis to develop PDH. An early symptom is fever with no apparent focus. Later, diffuse pneumonitis, skin lesions, meningitis, lymphadenopathy, hepatosplenomegaly, pancytopenia, and coagulopathy occur.

ETIOLOGY: *Histoplasma capsulatum* var *capsulatum* is a dimorphic fungus. It grows in soil as a spore-bearing mold with macroconidia but converts to yeast phase at body temperature.

EPIDEMIOLOGY: *Histoplasma capsulatum* is encountered in many parts of the world and is endemic in the eastern and central United States, particularly the Mississippi, Ohio, and Missouri River valleys. Infections occur sporadically; in outbreaks when weather conditions predispose to spread of spores; or in point-source epidemics after exposure to gardening activities or playing in barns, hollow trees, caves, or bird roosts or after exposure to excavation, demolition, cleaning, or renovation of contaminated buildings. The organism grows in moist soil. Growth of the organism is facilitated by bat, bird, and chicken droppings. Spores are spread in dry and windy conditions or when occupational or recreational activities disturb contaminated sites. Infection is acquired when spores (conidia) are inhaled. The inoculum inhaled, strain virulence, and immune status of the host affect the degree of illness. Reinfection is possible but requires a large inoculum. Person-to-person transmission does not occur.

The **incubation period** is variable but usually is 1 to 3 weeks.

DIAGNOSTIC TESTS: Culture is the definitive method of diagnosis. *Histoplasma capsulatum* from bone marrow, blood, sputum, and tissue specimens grows on standard mycologic media in 1 to 6 weeks. The lysis-centrifugation method is preferred for blood cultures. A DNA probe for *H capsulatum* permits rapid identification.

Demonstration of typical intracellular yeast forms by examination with Gomori methenamine silver or other stains of tissue, blood, bone marrow, or bronchoalveolar lavage specimens strongly supports the diagnosis of histoplasmosis when clinical, epidemiologic, and other laboratory studies are compatible.

Detection of *H capsulatum* polysaccharide antigen (HPA) in serum, urine, or bronchoalveolar lavage fluid by radioimmunoassay or enzyme immunoassay is a rapid and specific diagnostic method. Antigen detection is most sensitive for progressive disseminated infections; a negative test does not exclude infection. If initially positive, the antigen test can be used to monitor treatment response and to identify relapse in human immunodeficiency virus (HIV)-infected patients. Cross-reactions occur in patients with blastomycosis, coccidioidomycosis, paracoccidioidomycosis, and *Penicillium marneffei* infection; clinical and epidemiologic circumstances assist in differentiating these infections. The HPA test has low sensitivity for diagnosis of acute pulmonary histoplasmosis in immunocompetent people.

Both mycelial-phase (histoplasmin) and yeast-phase antigens are used in serologic testing for complement-fixing antibodies to *H capsulatum*. A fourfold increase in either yeast-phase or mycelial phase titers or a single titer of 1:32 or greater in either test is presumptive evidence of active infection. Cross-reacting antibodies can result from *Blastomyces dermatitidis* and *Coccidioides immitis* infections. In the immunodiffusion test, H bands, although infrequently encountered, are highly suggestive of acute infection; M bands also occur in acute or recent infection. The immunodiffusion test is more specific than the complement fixation test, but the complement fixation test is more sensitive.

The histoplasmin skin test is not useful for diagnostic purposes and is not available in the United States.

TREATMENT: Immunocompetent children with uncomplicated, primary pulmonary histoplasmosis rarely require antifungal therapy. Indications for therapy include PDH in infants, serious illness after intense exposures, and acute infection in immunocompromised patients. Other manifestations of histoplasmosis in immunocompetent children for which antifungal therapy should be considered include pulmonary disease with symptoms persisting more than 4 weeks, and granulomatous adenitis that obstructs critical structures (eg, bronchi or blood vessels).

Amphotericin B is recommended for disseminated disease and other serious infections (see Drugs for Invasive and Other Serious Fungal Infections, p 780), because most experts believe clinical improvement occurs more rapidly with amphotericin B than with the azoles. In other circumstances in which antifungal therapy is warranted, itraconazole and fluconazole also have been effective. The safety and efficacy of itraconazole for use in children have not been established, but in adults, itraconazole is preferred over fluconazole and has negligible toxic effects. Itraconazole also has proven effective in treatment of mild to moderately severe disseminated histoplasmosis in HIV-infected patients.

The duration of amphotericin B treatment for PDH is 4 to 6 weeks. Although data for children are limited, some experts recommend limiting amphotericin B therapy to 2 to 3 weeks, if substantial clinical improvement has occurred, to be followed by 3 to 6 months of oral itraconazole. Mild infections in HIV-infected patients can be treated with itraconazole for 3 months. Patients with HIV infection and PDH require lifelong suppressive therapy with itraconazole to prevent relapse; fluconazole can be given if itraconazole is not tolerated.

Erythema nodosum, arthritis syndromes, and pericarditis do not necessitate antifungal therapy. Pericarditis is treated with indomethacin. Dense fibrosis of mediastinal structures without an associated granulomatous inflammatory component does not respond to antifungal therapy.

ISOLATION OF THE HOSPITALIZED PATIENT: Standard precautions are recommended.

CONTROL MEASURES: In outbreaks, investigation for the common source of infection is indicated. Exposure to soil and dust from areas with significant accumulations of bird and bat droppings should be avoided, especially by immunocompromised people, or, if unavoidable, controlled through use of appropriate respiratory protection (eg, N95 respirator), gloves, and disposable clothing. Guidelines for preventing histoplasmosis designed for health and safety professionals, environmental consultants, and people supervising workers involved in activities in which contaminated materials are disturbed are available. Additional information about the guidelines is available from the National Institute for Occupational Safety and Health (NIOSH; publication No. 97-146), Publications Dissemination, 4676 Columbia Parkway, Cincinnati, OH 45226-1998; telephone 800-356-4674; the National Center for Infectious Diseases, telephone 404-639-3158; and the NIOSH Web site (**www.cdc.gov/niosh/97-146. html**).

Hookworm Infections
(*Ancylostoma duodenale* and *Necator americanus*)

CLINICAL MANIFESTATIONS: Patients with hookworm infection most often are asymptomatic; however, chronic hookworm infection is a common cause of hypochromic microcytic anemia in people living in tropical developing countries, and heavy infection can cause hypoproteinemia with edema. Chronic hookworm infection in children may lead to physical growth delay, deficits in cognition, and developmental delay. After contact with contaminated soil, initial skin penetration of larvae, usually involving the feet, can cause a stinging or burning sensation followed by pruritus and a papulovesicular rash that may persist for 1 to 2 weeks. Pneumonitis associated with migrating larvae is uncommon and usually mild, except in heavy infections. After oral ingestion of infectious *Ancylostoma duodenale* larvae, disease can manifest with pharyngeal itching, hoarseness, nausea, and vomiting shortly after ingestion. Colicky abdominal pain, nausea, and/or diarrhea and marked eosinophilia can develop 4 to 6 weeks after exposure.

ETIOLOGY: *Necator americanus* is the major cause of hookworm infection worldwide, although *A duodenale* is also an important hookworm in some regions. Mixed infections are common. Both are roundworms (nematodes) with similar life cycles.

EPIDEMIOLOGY: Humans are the only reservoir. Hookworms are prominent in rural, tropical, and subtropical areas where soil contamination with human feces is common. Although both hookworm species are equally prevalent in many areas, *A duodenale* is the predominant species in Europe, the Mediterranean region, northern Asia, and the west coast of South America. *Necator americanus* is predominant in the Western hemisphere, sub-Saharan Africa, Southeast Asia, and a number of Pacific islands. Larvae and eggs survive in loose, sandy, moist, shady, well-aerated, warm soil (optimal temperature 23°C–33°C [73°F–91°F]). Hookworm eggs from stool hatch in soil in 1 to 2 days as rhabditiform larvae. These larvae develop into infective filariform larvae in soil within 5 to 7 days and can persist for weeks to months. Percutaneous infection occurs after exposure to infectious larvae. *Ancylostoma duodenale* transmission can occur by oral ingestion and possibly through human milk.

Untreated infected patients can harbor worms for 5 to 15 years, but a decrease in worm burden of at least 70% generally occurs within 1 to 2 years.

The time from exposure to development of noncutaneous symptoms is 4 to 12 weeks.

DIAGNOSTIC TESTS: Microscopic demonstration of hookworm eggs in feces is diagnostic. Adult worms or larvae rarely are seen. Approximately 5 to 10 weeks are required after infection for eggs to appear in feces. A direct stool smear with saline solution or potassium iodide saturated with iodine is adequate for diagnosis of heavy hookworm infection; light infections require concentration techniques. Quantification techniques (eg, Kato-Katz, Beaver direct smear, or Stoll egg-counting techniques) to determine the clinical significance of infection and the response to treatment may be available from state or reference laboratories.

TREATMENT: Albendazole, mebendazole, and pyrantel pamoate all are effective treatments (see Drugs for Parasitic Infections, p 790). In children younger than 2 years of age, in whom experience with these drugs is limited, the World Health Organization (WHO) recommends one half the adult dose of albendazole or mebendazole in heavy hookworm infections. The dose of pyrantel pamoate is determined by weight. In heavy hookworm infection during pregnancy, deworming treatment is recommended by the WHO during the second or third trimester. Albendazole, mebendazole, or pyrantel pamoate may be used. A repeated stool examination, using a concentration technique, should be performed 2 weeks after treatment, and if positive, retreatment is indicated. Nutritional supplementation, including iron, is important when anemia is present. Severely affected children may require blood transfusion.

ISOLATION OF THE HOSPITALIZED PATIENT: Only standard precautions are recommended, because there is no direct person-to-person transmission.

CONTROL MEASURES: Sanitary disposal of feces to prevent contamination of soil, particularly in areas with endemic infection, is necessary but rarely accomplished. Treatment of all known infected people and screening of high-risk groups (ie, children and agricultural workers) in areas with endemic infection can help decrease environmental contamination. Wearing shoes also may be helpful. Despite relatively rapid reinfection, periodic deworming treatments targeting school-aged children have been advocated to prevent morbidity associated with heavy intestinal helminth infections.

Human Herpesvirus 6 (Including Roseola) and 7

CLINICAL MANIFESTATIONS: Clinical manifestations of primary infection with human herpesvirus (HHV)-6 include roseola (exanthem subitum, sixth disease) in approximately 20% of infected children, undifferentiated febrile illness without rash or localizing signs, and other acute febrile illnesses (febrile seizures, encephalitis and other neurologic disorders, and mononucleosis-like syndromes), often accompanied by cervical and postoccipital lymphadenopathy, gastrointestinal or respiratory tract signs, and inflamed tympanic membranes. Fever characteristically is high ($>39.5°C$ [$>103.0°F$]) and persists for 3 to 7 days. In roseola, fever is followed by an erythematous maculopapular rash lasting hours to days. Seizures occur during the febrile period in approximately 10% to 15% of primary infections. A bulging anterior fontanelle and encephalopathy occur occasionally. The virus persists and may reactivate. The clinical circumstances and manifestations of reactivation in healthy people are not known. Illness associated with reactivation, primarily in immunocompromised hosts, has been described in association with manifestations such as fever, rash, hepatitis, bone marrow suppression, pneumonia, and encephalitis.

Recognition of the varied clinical manifestations of HHV-7 infection is evolving. Many, if not most, primary infections with HHV-7 may be asymptomatic or mild; some may present as typical roseola and may account for second or recurrent cases of roseola. Febrile illnesses associated with seizures also have been reported. Some investigators suggest that the association of HHV-7 with these clinical manifestations results from the ability of HHV-7 to reactivate HHV-6 from latency.

ETIOLOGY: Human herpesvirus 6 and HHV-7 are lymphotropic agents that are closely related members of the Herpesviridae family. Strains of HHV-6 belong to 1 of 2 major groups, variants A and B. Almost all primary infections in children are caused by variant B strains except in some parts of Africa.

EPIDEMIOLOGY: Humans are the only known natural hosts for HHV-6 and HHV-7. Transmission of HHV-6 to an infant most likely results from asymptomatic shedding of persistent virus in secretions of a family member, caregiver, or other close contact. During the febrile phase of primary infection, HHV-6 can be isolated from peripheral blood lymphocytes, saliva, and cerebrospinal fluid. Virus-specific maternal antibody is present uniformly in the serum of infants at birth and provides transient protection. As the concentration of maternal antibody decreases during the first year of life, the rate of infection increases rapidly, peaking between 6 and 24 months of age. All children are seropositive before 4 years of age. Infections occur throughout the year without a seasonal pattern. Secondary cases rarely are identified. Occasional outbreaks of roseola have been reported.

Human herpesvirus-7 infection occurs somewhat later in life than HHV-6. By adulthood, the seroprevalence of HHV-7 is approximately 85%. Lifelong persistent infection with HHV-6 and HHV-7 is established after primary infection. Infectious HHV-7 is present in more than three fourths of saliva specimens obtained from healthy adults. Transmission of HHV-6 and HHV-7 to young children is likely to occur from contact with infected respiratory tract secretions of healthy contacts.

The mean **incubation period** for HHV-6 may be 9 to 10 days, and for HHV-7, the incubation period is not known.

DIAGNOSTIC TESTS: The definitive diagnosis of primary HHV-6 infection necessitates use of research techniques to isolate the virus from a peripheral blood specimen. A fourfold increase in serum antibody concentration alone does not necessarily indicate new infection, because an increase in titer also may occur with reactivation and in association with other infections. However, seroconversion from negative to positive in paired sera is good evidence of recent primary infection. Detection of specific immunoglobulin (Ig) M antibody also is not reliable, because IgM antibodies to HHV-6 may be present in some asymptomatic previously infected people. Commercial assays for antibody detection can detect HHV-6–specific IgG, but these assays do not distinguish between primary infection and viral persistence or reactivation. Nearly all children older than 2 years of age have an antibody titer to HHV-6.

Diagnostic tests for HHV-7 also are limited to research laboratories, and reliable differentiation between primary infection and reactivation is problematic. Serodiagnosis of HHV-7 is confounded by serologic cross-reactivity with HHV-6 and by the potential ability of HHV-6 to be reactivated by HHV-7 and possibly other infections.

TREATMENT: Supportive. A few anecdotal reports suggest the use of ganciclovir may be beneficial for immunocompromised patients with serious HHV-6 disease.

ISOLATION OF THE HOSPITALIZED PATIENT: Standard precautions are recommended.

CONTROL MEASURES: None.

Human Herpesvirus 8

CLINICAL MANIFESTATIONS: For children, the clinical implications of the most recently discovered member of the herpesvirus family, human herpesvirus (HHV)-8, are unknown. In adults, HHV-8 etiologically is associated with Kaposi sarcoma. The HHV-8 DNA sequences have been detected in all forms of Kaposi sarcoma from all parts of the world in patients with and without human immunodeficiency virus (HIV) infection, with primary effusion lymphomas of the abdominal cavity, with lymphoproliferative syndrome (although less commonly than has Epstein-Barr virus [EBV]), and with multicentric Castleman disease. Evidence of HHV-8 infection in children is rare, and no clinical associations are known.

ETIOLOGY: Human herpesvirus 8 is a member of the family Herpesviridae, the gammaherpesvirus subfamily, closely related to herpesvirus saimiri of monkeys and EBV.

EPIDEMIOLOGY: Little is known about the epidemiology and transmission of HHV-8. However, HHV-8 has been reported to be latent in peripheral blood mononuclear cells and lymphoid tissue from immunocompromised patients and some healthy people, suggesting that transmission could be via blood or secretions. In the United States in patients with HIV, HHV-8 infection does not appear to occur until after adolescence.

The **incubation period** of HHV-8 is unknown.

DIAGNOSTIC TESTS: Diagnostic tests for detection of HHV-8 infections are limited to research laboratories, and reliable differentiation of primary versus latent infection is problematic.

TREATMENT: No effective treatment is known for HHV-8.

ISOLATION OF THE HOSPITALIZED PATIENT: Standard precautions are recommended.

CONTROL MEASURES: None.

Human Immunodeficiency Virus Infection*

CLINICAL MANIFESTATIONS: Human immunodeficiency virus (HIV) infection in children and adolescents causes a broad spectrum of disease manifestations and a varied clinical course. Acquired immunodeficiency syndrome (AIDS) represents the most severe end of the clinical spectrum. Surveillance definitions of the Centers for Disease Control and Prevention (CDC) for AIDS in adults and adolescents are listed in Table 3.23 (p 379), and the CDC clinical categories and pediatric classification system for children younger than 13 years of age who are born to HIV-infected mothers or who are known to be infected with HIV are presented in Tables 3.24 (p 380) and 3.25 (p 382).[†‡] This pediatric classification system, which was established for surveillance of HIV infection, emphasizes the importance of the CD4+ T-lymphocyte count as an immunologic surrogate and marker of prognosis but does not use information on viral load as quantitated by HIV RNA polymerase chain reaction (PCR) assay.

Manifestations of pediatric HIV infection include generalized lymphadenopathy, hepatomegaly, splenomegaly, failure to thrive, oral candidiasis, recurrent diarrhea, parotitis, cardiomyopathy, hepatitis, nephropathy, central nervous system (CNS) disease (including microcephaly, hyperreflexia, clonus, and developmental delay), lymphoid interstitial pneumonia, recurrent invasive bacterial infections, opportunistic infections,[§‖] and specific malignant neoplasms. With early testing and appropriate treatment, primary manifestations of HIV and development of opportunistic infections now are rare in children in the United States.

The frequency of different opportunistic pathogens among HIV-infected children in the era before highly active antiretroviral therapy (HAART) varied by age, pathogen, previous opportunistic infections, and immunologic status. In the pre-HAART era, the most common opportunistic infections among children in the United States were serious bacterial infections, herpes zoster, disseminated *Mycobacterium avium* complex (MAC), *Pneumocystis jiroveci* pneumonia, and candidiasis. Less commonly observed opportunistic infections included cytomegalovirus disease; *Mycobacterium tuberculosis*

---

* For a complete listing of current policy statements from the American Academy of Pediatrics regarding human immunodeficiency virus and acquired immunodeficiency syndrome, see **http://aappolicy. aappublications.org/**.

[†] Centers for Disease Control and Prevention. 1993 revised classification system for HIV infection and expanded surveillance case definition for AIDS among adolescents and adults. *MMWR Recomm Rep.* 1992;41(RR-17):1–19

[‡] Centers for Disease Control and Prevention. 1994 revised classification system for human immunodeficiency virus infection in children less than 13 years of age. Official authorized addenda: human immunodeficiency virus infection codes and official guidelines for coding and reporting ICD-9-CM. *MMWR Recomm Rep.* 1994;43(RR-12):1–19

[§] Centers for Disease Control and Prevention. Guidelines for preventing opportunistic infections among HIV-infected persons—2002. Recommendations of the US Public Health Service and the Infectious Diseases Society of America. *MMWR Recomm Rep.* 2002;51 (RR-8):1–46

[‖] Centers for Disease Control and Prevention. Treating opportunistic infections among HIV-exposed and infected children. Recommendations from the CDC, the National Institutes of Health, and the Infectious Diseases Society of America. *MMWR Recomm Rep.* 2004;53(RR-14):1–112

Table 3.23. 1993 Revised Case Definition of AIDS-Defining Conditions for Adults and Adolescents 13 Years of Age and Older[1]

- Candidiasis of bronchi, trachea, or lungs
- Candidiasis, esophageal
- Cervical cancer, invasive
- Coccidioidomycosis, disseminated or extrapulmonary
- Cryptococcosis, extrapulmonary
- Cryptosporidiosis, chronic intestinal (>1 mo duration)
- Cytomegalovirus disease (other than liver, spleen, or nodes)
- Cytomegalovirus retinitis (with loss of vision)
- Encephalopathy, HIV related
- Herpes simplex: chronic ulcer(s) (>1 mo duration) or bronchitis, pneumonitis, or esophagitis
- Histoplasmosis, disseminated or extrapulmonary
- Isosporiasis, chronic intestinal (>1 mo duration)
- Kaposi sarcoma
- Lymphoma, Burkitt (or equivalent term)
- Lymphoma, immunoblastic (or equivalent term)
- Lymphoma, primary or brain
- *Mycobacterium avium* complex or *Mycobacterium kansasii* infection, disseminated or extrapulmonary
- *Mycobacterium tuberculosis* infection, any site, pulmonary or extrapulmonary
- *Mycobacterium*, other species or unidentified species infection, disseminated or extrapulmonary
- *Pneumocystis jiroveci* pneumonia
- Pneumonia, recurrent
- Progressive multifocal leukoencephalopathy
- *Salmonella* septicemia, recurrent
- Toxoplasmosis of brain
- Wasting syndrome attributable to HIV
- CD4+ T-lymphocyte count <200/µL (0.20 × 10^9/L) or CD4+ lymphocyte percentage <15%

AIDS indicates acquired immunodeficiency syndrome; HIV, human immunodeficiency virus.

[1] Modified from Centers for Disease Control and Prevention. 1993 revised classification system for HIV infection and expanded surveillance case definition for AIDS among adolescents and adults. *MMWR Recomm Rep.* 1992;41(RR-17):1–19.

Table 3.24. Clinical Categories for Children Younger Than 13 Years of Age With Human Immunodeficiency Virus (HIV) Infection[1]

Category N: Not Symptomatic

Children who have no signs or symptoms considered to be the result of HIV infection or have only 1 of the conditions listed in Category A.

Category A: Mildly Symptomatic

Children with 2 or more of the conditions listed but none of the conditions listed in categories B and C.

- Lymphadenopathy ($\geq$0.5 cm at more than 2 sites; bilateral at 1 site)
- Hepatomegaly
- Splenomegaly
- Dermatitis
- Parotitis
- Recurrent or persistent upper respiratory tract infection, sinusitis, or otitis media

Category B: Moderately Symptomatic

Children who have symptomatic conditions other than those listed for category A or C that are attributed to HIV infection.

- Anemia (hemoglobin <8 g/dL [<80 g/L]), neutropenia (white blood cell count <1000/μL [<1.0 $\times$ 10^9/L]), and/or thrombocytopenia (platelet count <100 $\times$ 10^3/μL [<100 $\times$ 10^9/L]) persisting for $\geq$30 days
- Bacterial meningitis, pneumonia, or sepsis (single episode)
- Candidiasis, oropharyngeal (thrush), persisting (>2 mo) in children older than 6 mo of age
- Cardiomyopathy
- Cytomegalovirus infection, with onset before 1 mo of age
- Diarrhea, recurrent or chronic
- Hepatitis
- Herpes simplex virus (HSV) stomatitis, recurrent (>2 episodes within

Category B: Moderately Symptomatic, continued

- HSV bronchitis, pneumonitis, or esophagitis with onset before 1 mo of age
- Herpes zoster (shingles) involving at least 2 distinct episodes or more than 1 dermatome
- Leiomyosarcoma
- Lymphoid interstitial pneumonia or pulmonary lymphoid hyperplasia complex
- Nephropathy
- Nocardiosis
- Persistent fever (lasting >1 mo)
- Toxoplasmosis, onset before 1 mo of age
- Varicella, disseminated (complicated chickenpox)

Category C: Severely Symptomatic

- Serious bacterial infections, multiple or recurrent (ie, any combination of at least 2 culture-confirmed infections within a 2-y period), of the following types: septicemia, pneumonia, meningitis, bone or joint infection, or abscess of an internal organ or body cavity (excluding otitis media, superficial skin or mucosal abscesses, and indwelling catheter-related infections)
- Candidiasis, esophageal or pulmonary (bronchi, trachea, lungs)
- Coccidioidomycosis, disseminated (at site other than or in addition to lungs or cervical or hilar lymph nodes)
- Cryptococcosis, extrapulmonary
- Cryptosporidiosis or isosporiasis with diarrhea persisting >1 mo
- Cytomegalovirus disease with onset of symptoms after 1 mo of age (at a site other than liver, spleen, or lymph nodes)

Category C: Severely Symptomatic, continued

- Encephalopathy (at least 1 of the following progressive findings present for at least 2 mo in the absence of a concurrent illness other than HIV infection that could explain the findings): (1) failure to attain or loss of developmental milestones or loss of intellectual ability, verified by standard developmental scale or neuropsychologic tests; (2) impaired brain growth or acquired microcephaly demonstrated by head circumference measurements or brain atrophy demonstrated by computed tomography or magnetic resonance imaging (serial imaging required for children younger than 2 y of age); or (3) acquired symmetric motor deficit manifested by 2 or more of the following: paresis, pathologic reflexes, ataxia, or gait disturbance

- HSV infection causing a mucocutaneous ulcer that persists for greater than 1 mo or bronchitis, pneumonitis, or esophagitis for any duration affecting a child older than 1 mo of age

- Histoplasmosis, disseminated (at a site other than or in addition to lungs or cervical or hilar lymph nodes)

- Kaposi sarcoma

- Lymphoma, primary, in brain

- Lymphoma, small, noncleaved cell (Burkitt), or immunoblastic; or large-cell lymphoma of B-lymphocyte or unknown immunologic phenotype

- *Mycobacterium tuberculosis* infection, disseminated or extrapulmonary

- *Mycobacterium*, other species or unidentified species infection, disseminated (at a site other than or in addition to lungs, skin, or cervical or hilar lymph nodes)

- *Pneumocystis jiroveci* pneumonia

- Progressive multifocal leukoencephalopathy

- *Salmonella* (nontyphoid) septicemia, recurrent

- Toxoplasmosis of the brain with onset at after 1 mo of age

- Wasting syndrome in the absence of a concurrent illness other than HIV infection that could explain the following findings: (1) persistent weight loss >10% of baseline; (2) downward crossing of at least 2 of the following percentile lines on the weight-for-age chart (eg, 95th, 75th, 50th, 25th, 5th) in a child 1 y of age or older; OR (3) <5th percentile on weight-for-height chart on 2 consecutive measurements, ≥30 days apart; PLUS (1) chronic diarrhea (ie, at least 2 loose stools per day for >30 days); OR (2) documented fever (for >30 days, intermittent or constant)

[1] Modified from Centers for Disease Control and Prevention. 1994 revised classification system for human immunodeficiency virus infection in children less than 13 years of age. Official authorized addenda: human immunodeficiency virus infection codes and official guidelines for coding and reporting ICD-9-CM. *MMWR Recomm Rep.* 1994;43(RR-12):1–19

Table 3.25. Pediatric Human Immunodeficiency Virus (HIV) Classification for Children Younger Than 13 Years of Age[1]

Immunologic Definitions	Immunologic Categories Age-Specific CD4 + T-Lymphocyte Count and Percentage of Total Lymphocytes[2]						Clinical Classifications[3]			
	<12 mo		1-5 y		6-12 y		N: No Signs or Symptoms	A: Mild Signs and Symptoms	B: Moderate Signs and Symptoms[4]	C: Severe Signs and Symptoms[4]
	µL	%	µL	%	µL	%				
1: No evidence of suppression	≥1500	≥25	≥1000	≥25	≥500	≥25	N1	A1	B1	C1
2: Evidence of moderate suppression	750-1499	15-24	500-999	15-24	200-499	15-24	N2	A2	B2	C2
3: Severe suppression	<750	<15	<500	<15	<200	<15	N3	A3	B3	C3

[1] Modified from Centers for Disease Control and Prevention. 1994 revised classification system for human immunodeficiency virus infection in children less than 13 years of age. Official authorized addenda: human immunodeficiency virus infection codes and official guidelines for coding and reporting ICD-9-CM. *MMWR Recomm Rep.* 1994;43(RR-12):1–19

[2] To convert values in µL to Système International units ($\times 10^9$/L), multiply by 0.001.

[3] Children whose HIV infection status is not confirmed are classified by using this grid with a letter E (for perinatally exposed) placed before the appropriate classification code (eg, EN2).

[4] Lymphoid interstitial pneumonitis in category B or any condition in category C is reportable to state and local health departments as acquired immunodeficiency syndrome (AIDS-defining conditions) (see Table 3.24, p 380, for further definition of clinical categories).

infection; chronic enteritis caused by *Cryptosporidium* species, *Isospora* species, or other enteric pathogens; systemic fungal infection; and *Toxoplasma gondii* infections. History of a previous AIDS-defining opportunistic infection was a predictor of developing a new infection. Serious bacterial infections, herpes zoster, and tuberculosis occurred across the spectrum of immune statuses, whereas other opportunistic infections generally occurred among substantially immunocompromised children. In the HAART era, descriptions of immunocompromised infections among children have been limited because of the substantial decreases in morbidity and mortality among children receiving HAART.

Malignant neoplasms in children with HIV infection are relatively uncommon, but leiomyosarcomas and certain lymphomas, including those of the CNS and non-Hodgkin B-lymphocyte lymphomas of the Burkitt type, occur more commonly in children with HIV infection than in immunocompetent children. Kaposi sarcoma is rare in children in the United States but occurs commonly among HIV-infected children in areas of the world with highly endemic rates of HIV infection.

Development of an opportunistic infection, particularly PCP, progressive neurologic disease, and severe wasting, is associated with a poor prognosis. In the absence of treatment, prognosis for survival also is poor in perinatally infected infants when viral load exceeds 100 000 copies/mL, CD4+ T-lymphocyte count and percentage are decreased, and symptoms develop during the first year of life. With earlier use of HAART, prognosis and survival rates have improved dramatically. Although median survival to 9 years of age was reported before the availability of more potent combination antiretroviral therapy, recent studies in the United States and Europe show >95% survival to 16 years of age, with preservation of immune system integrity in at least half of those children. Data on long-term survival rates of children receiving combination antiretroviral therapy are being collected.

ETIOLOGY: Retroviruses have been classified by a number of different biologic features into at least 7 genera. Pathogenic human retroviruses include lentiviruses (HIV type 1 [HIV-1] and HIV type 2 [HIV-2]) and oncoviruses (human T-lymphotropic virus [HTLV]-1 and HTLV-2). Infection is caused by human RNA retroviruses HIV-1 and, less commonly, HIV-2, a related virus that is rare in the United States but more common in West Africa.

EPIDEMIOLOGY: Humans are the only known reservoir of HIV, although related viruses, perhaps genetic ancestors, have been identified in chimpanzees and monkeys. Because retroviruses integrate into the target cell genome as proviruses and the viral genome is copied during DNA replication, the virus persists in infected people for life. Data demonstrate persistence of latent virus in peripheral blood mononuclear cells, and in other cells, even when viral RNA is below the limit of detection in blood. Human immunodeficiency virus has been isolated from blood (including lymphocytes, monocytes, and plasma) and from other body fluids. Only blood, semen, cervical secretions, and human milk have been implicated epidemiologically in transmission of infection.

Established modes of HIV transmission in the United States are the following: (1) sexual contact (vaginal, anal, or orogenital); (2) percutaneous (from contaminated needles or other sharp instruments) or mucous membrane exposure to contaminated blood or other body fluids; and (3) mother-to-child transmission during pregnancy, around the time of labor and delivery, and postnatally through breastfeeding. Because of exclusion of infected donors, viral inactivation treatment of clotting factor concentrates, and availability of recombinant clotting factors (see Blood Safety, p 106), transfusion of blood, blood components, or clotting factor concentrates is a rare cause of HIV transmission in the United States. In the absence of documented sexual transmission or parenteral or mucous membrane contact with blood or blood-containing body fluids, transmission of HIV rarely has been demonstrated to occur in families or households or as a result of routine care in hospitals or clinics. Transmission of HIV has not been documented in schools or child care settings.

Cases of AIDS in children have accounted for approximately 1% of all reported cases in the United States. The total number of reported cases of AIDS in children decreased 90% in 2002 compared with 1992 as a result of a dramatic decrease in the rate of mother-to-child transmission of HIV (resulting in fewer HIV-infected infants) and the availability of potent combination antiretroviral therapy for HIV-infected infants and children (resulting in fewer children progressing to symptomatic AIDS). The CDC estimates that 150 to 300 infants with HIV infection were born in 2003.

In previous decades, more than 90% of HIV-infected children younger than 13 years of age in the United States acquired infection from their mothers. Almost all of the remainder, including patients with hemophilia or other coagulation disorders, received contaminated blood, blood components, or clotting factor concentrates. A few cases of HIV infection in children have resulted from sexual abuse by an HIV-seropositive person. Fewer than 5% of cases have been reported to have no identifiable risk factor, and after careful investigation, most are reclassified into one of the established risk factor groups. Mother-to-child transmission of HIV now accounts for almost all new infections in preadolescent children.

The rate of acquisition of HIV during adolescence continues to increase and contributes to the large number of cases in young adults. Transmission of HIV among adolescents is attributable primarily to sexual exposure. Approximately 50% of HIV acquisition in the United States is estimated to occur among people 13 to 24 years of age. Among adolescents, the incidence of HIV infection in females 13 to 15 years of age exceeds that in males; for adolescents 16 to 19 years of age, the prevalence in girls and boys is equivalent. Most HIV-infected adolescents are asymptomatic, and without testing, they remain unaware that they are infected.

The risk of infection for an infant born to an HIV-seropositive mother who did not receive interventions to prevent transmission is estimated to be between 13% and 39%. Studies on the timing of mother-to-child transmission of HIV suggest that, in a nonbreastfeeding population, approximately 25% to 40% of transmission occurs in utero. The absolute risk for in utero transmission is approximately 5% and for intrapartum transmission is approximately 13% to 18%. Maternal viral load is a critical determinant of mother-to-child transmission of HIV, with the risk of transmission increasing from 10% for women with peripheral blood viral load <1000, up to 40% from women with viral load >100 000 in the absence of antiretroviral therapy. Studies with small numbers of pregnant women have suggested higher rates of mother-to-child transmission of HIV among women who seroconvert during pregnancy. Other factors associated with an increased risk of transmission include low maternal CD4 +

T-lymphocyte counts, advanced maternal illness, intrapartum events resulting in increased exposure of the fetus to maternal blood, placental membrane inflammation, mother-infant *HLA* concordance, preterm delivery, prolonged labor, vaginal delivery, and longer duration of rupture of membranes. Prolonged rupture of membranes in the presence of antiretroviral therapy but detectable viral load is associated with an increased risk of transmission and must be considered when evaluating the mode of delivery and risk of mother-to-child transmission of HIV. Cesarean section appears to reduce the risk of transmission in direct proportion to the number of hours membranes were ruptured before c-section.

Postnatal transmission occurs through breastfeeding.* Worldwide, an estimated one third to one half of mother-to-child HIV transmission events may occur as a result of breastfeeding. Human immunodeficiency virus genomes have been detected in cellular and cell-free fractions of human milk. In the United States, providing safe alternative feeding for infants and, therefore, avoiding human milk transmission of HIV is possible. Diminishing HIV transmission and continuing safe feeding practices for infants born to HIV-infected women in the developing world is needed (see Human Milk, p 123).

INCUBATION PERIOD: Although the median age of onset of symptoms is approximately 12 to 18 months for untreated, perinatally infected infants in the United States, some children remain asymptomatic for more than 5 years, and rarely, perinatally infected children may develop symptoms only during adolescence. Without therapy, 2 patterns of symptomatic infection have been recognized. Approximately 15% to 20% of untreated children in the United States die before 4 years of age, with a median age at death of 11 months (termed rapid progressors), whereas most children have delayed onset of milder symptoms and survive beyond 5 years of age.

DIAGNOSTIC TESTS†: Laboratory diagnosis of HIV infection during infancy depends on detection of virus or viral nucleic acid. Transplacental transfer of antibody complicates use of antibody-based assays (eg, HIV enzyme immunoassay [EIA] and Western blot analysis) for diagnosis of infection in infants, because all infants born to HIV-seropositive mothers have passively acquired maternal antibodies.

The preferred test for diagnosis of HIV-1 infection in infants in the United States is HIV-1 nucleic acid detection by PCR assay of DNA extracted from peripheral blood mononuclear cells (see Table 3.26, p 386). Approximately 30% of infants with HIV infection will have a positive DNA PCR assay result in samples obtained before 48 hours of age. A positive result identifies infants who were infected in utero. The test routinely can detect 1 to 10 DNA copies. Approximately 93% of infected infants have detectable HIV-1 DNA by 2 weeks of age, and almost all HIV-infected infants have positive HIV DNA PCR assay results by 1 month of age. A single HIV-1 DNA PCR assay has a sensitivity of 95% and a specificity of 97% on samples collected

---

* Read JS, and American Academy of Pediatrics, Committee on Pediatric AIDS. Human milk, breastfeeding, and transmission of human immunodeficiency virus type 1 in the United States. *Pediatrics.* 2003;112:1196–1205

† King SM, American Academy of Pediatrics, Committee on Pediatric AIDS, and Canadian Paediatric Society, Infectious Diseases and Immunization Committee. Evaluation and treatment of the human immunodeficiency virus-1-exposed infant. *Pediatrics.* 2004;114:497–505

Table 3.26. Laboratory Diagnosis of HIV Infection[1]

Test	Comment
HIV DNA PCR	Preferred test to diagnose HIV-1 subtype B infection in infants and children younger than 18 months of age; highly sensitive and specific by 2 weeks of age and available; performed on peripheral blood mononuclear cells. False negatives can occur in non-B subtype HIV-1 infections
HIV p24 Ag	Less sensitive, false-positive results during first month of life, variable results; not recommended
ICD p24 Ag	Negative test result does not rule out infection; not recommended
HIV culture	Expensive, not easily available, requires up to 4 weeks to do test; not recommended
HIV RNA PCR	Not recommended for routine testing of infants and children younger than 18 months of age, because a negative result cannot be used to exclude HIV infection definitively. Preferred test to identify non-B subtype HIV-1 infections.

[1] HIV indicates human immunodeficiency virus; PCR, polymerase chain reaction; Ag, antigen; and ICD, immune complex dissociated.

from infants 1 to 36 months of age. The HIV-1 DNA PCR assay is more sensitive on a single assay than is virus culture, and virus need not be replication competent to be detected.

Virus isolation by culture is expensive, is available only in a few laboratories, and requires up to 28 days for positive results. This test is not recommended and has been replaced by the DNA PCR assay.

Detection of the p24 antigen (including immune complex dissociated) is substantially less sensitive than HIV-1 DNA PCR assay or culture. An additional drawback is the occurrence of false-positive test results in samples obtained from infants younger than 1 month of age. This test should not be used.

A positive result using the plasma HIV-1 RNA PCR assay may be used to diagnose HIV infection. However, a negative test result may occur in HIV-infected people. The test is licensed by the US Food and Drug Administration only in a quantitative format and currently is used for quantifying the amount of virus present as one predictor of disease progression, not for routine diagnosis of HIV infection in infants.

Infants born to HIV-infected women should be tested by HIV DNA PCR assay or HIV RNA PCR assay during the first 48 hours of life in an attempt to identify in utero transmission of HIV. Because of possible contamination with maternal blood, umbilical cord blood should not be used for this test. A second test should be performed at 1 to 2 months of age. Obtaining the sample as early as 14 days of age may facilitate decisions about initiating antiretroviral therapy. A third test is recommended at 2 to 4 months of age. Any time an infant tests positive, testing should be repeated on a second blood sample as soon as possible to confirm the diagnosis. An infant is considered infected if 2 separate samples are positive by DNA or RNA PCR assays.* Infection in nonbreastfed infants can be excluded reasonably when results of 2 HIV DNA or RNA PCR assays performed at or beyond 1 month of age and at 4 months of age or older are both negative. In infants with 2 negative HIV DNA or RNA PCR test results, HIV infection definitely can be excluded by confirming the absence of antibody to HIV on testing at 12 to 18 months of age ("seroreversion"). An infant with 2 blood samples obtained after 6 months of age and at an interval of at least 1 month apart that are both negative for HIV antibody also can be considered uninfected.

Enzyme immunoassays are used widely as the initial test for serum HIV antibody. These tests are highly sensitive and specific. Repeated EIA testing of initially reactive specimens is common practice and is followed by Western blot analysis to confirm the presence of antibody specific to HIV. A positive HIV antibody test result (EIA followed by Western Blot analysis) in a child 18 months of age or older indicates infection,* although passively acquired maternal antibody rarely can persist beyond 18 months of age. An HIV antibody test can be performed on samples of blood or oral fluid. Rapid tests for HIV antibodies have been licensed for use in the United States; these tests are used widely throughout the world, particularly for screening in maternity settings. Results from rapid testing are available within 20 minutes. Confirmatory Western Blot analysis results may be delayed for 1 to 2 weeks. In developing countries, 2 positive results on 2 different brands of rapid tests are considered a definitive positive in children older than 18 months of age.

The most notable laboratory finding in perinatally infected infants is a high viral load (as measured by HIV-1 RNA PCR assay) that does not decrease rapidly during the first year of life unless combination antiretroviral therapy is initiated. As disease progresses, there is an increasing loss of cell-mediated immunity. The peripheral blood lymphocyte count at birth and during the first years of infection can be normal, but eventually lymphopenia, resulting from a decrease in the total number of circulating CD4+ lymphocytes, develops. The T-suppressor CD8+ lymphocyte count usually increases initially, and CD8+ lymphocytes are not depleted until late in the course of infection. These changes in cell populations result in a decrease in the normal CD4+ to CD8+ lymphocyte ratio. This nonspecific finding, although characteristic of HIV infection, also occurs with other acute viral infections, including infections caused by CMV and Epstein-Barr virus. The normal values for peripheral CD4+ lymphocyte counts are age related, and the lower limits of normal are given in Table 3.25 (p 382).

Although the B-lymphocyte count remains normal or is somewhat increased, humoral immune dysfunction may precede and accompany cellular dysfunction. Increased serum immunoglobulin (Ig) concentrations, particularly IgG and IgA, are manifestations of the humoral immune dysfunction and are not necessarily directed at

---

* Centers for Disease Control and Prevention. Guidelines for national human immunodeficiency virus case surveillance, including monitoring for human immunodeficiency virus infection and acquired immunodeficiency syndrome. *MMWR Recomm Rep.* 1999;48(RR-13):1–28

specific pathogens of childhood. Specific antibody responses to antigens to which the patient has not been exposed previously usually are abnormal, and later in disease, recall antibody responses are slow and diminish in magnitude. A small proportion (<10%) of patients will develop panhypogammaglobulinemia.

INTERRUPTION OF MOTHER-TO-CHILD TRANSMISSION OF HIV. Recommendations of the American Academy of Pediatrics (AAP) and the American College of Obstetricians and Gynecologists include the following[*][†]:

- On the basis of advances in prophylaxis that decrease the rate of perinatal HIV transmission, the AAP recommends routine education and HIV testing, with consent, of all pregnant women in the United States. Consent for maternal HIV testing may be obtained in a variety of ways, including by right of refusal (ie, with testing to take place unless rejected in writing by the patient). The AAP supports use of consent procedures that facilitate rapid incorporation of HIV education and testing into routine medical care settings, including obstetric practices. In some states, routine offering of HIV testing during pregnancy is mandated by law. For women who are examined by a health care professional for the first time in labor or have not been tested for HIV infection during the current pregnancy, counseling and immediate testing are encouraged strongly, because administration of antiretroviral prophylaxis during labor is recommended and can decrease the risk of mother-to-child transmission of HIV, even in women who have not received antiretroviral therapy during pregnancy. In this setting, the rapid HIV antibody test should be used, because results are available within 20 minutes. Careful attention to further education about HIV infection is recommended during the perinatal period.
- Routine education about HIV infection and testing should be part of a comprehensive program of health care for women.
- If the mother's HIV antibody status was not determined during pregnancy or the immediate postpartum period, the newborn infant's health care professional should inform the mother about the potential benefits of HIV testing for her infant and the possible risks and benefits to herself of knowing the child's infection status and should recommend immediate HIV testing for the newborn using a rapid HIV antibody test. In some states, recommendation of rapid testing is required by law.
- If maternal HIV antibody status is not known and parents are not available to provide consent to test the newborn infant for HIV antibody, procedures should be in place to facilitate rapid evaluation and testing of the infant.
- The newborn infant's health care professional should be informed of maternal HIV serostatus so that appropriate care and testing of the infant can be accomplished. Similarly, if the newborn infant is found to be seropositive but maternal

---

* American Academy of Pediatrics, American College of Obstetricians and Gynecologists. Human Immunodeficiency virus screening. Joint statement of the American Academy of Pediatrics and the American College of Obstetricians and Gynecologists. *Pediatrics.* 1999;104:128 (Reaffirmed 2005)

† American College of Obstetricians and Gynecologists, Committee on Obstetric Practice. Prenatal and perinatal human immunodeficiency virus testing: expanded recommendations. *Obstet Gynecol.* 2004;104:1119–1124

HIV infection status previously was unknown, the newborn infant's health care professional should ensure that this information and its significance is conveyed to the mother and, with her consent, to her health care professional. The mother should be referred to a facility that provides HIV-related services for adults.

- Comprehensive HIV-related medical services should be accessible to all infected mothers, their infants, and other family members.
- Routine education about HIV infection and testing should be part of a comprehensive program of health care for adolescents.

INFORMED CONSENT FOR HIV SEROLOGIC TESTING. Testing for HIV infection is unlike most routine blood testing, because risks of discrimination in employment, education, child care, and insurance coverage can be incurred. Parents or other primary caregivers and the patient, if old enough to comprehend, should be counseled about the benefits of testing a child and of initiating appropriate treatment if the HIV test result is positive. Consent should be obtained from the parent or legal guardian and recorded in the patient's medical chart. State and local laws and hospital regulations should be considered when deciding whether written consent is required before testing and under what circumstances testing can be performed without consent. If the physician believes that testing is essential to the child's health, authorization for testing may be possible through local laws and can be obtained by other means. The results of serologic tests should be discussed in person with the family, primary caregiver, and patient when age appropriate. In many states, minor adolescents can provide their own consent for testing, but involvement of a supportive adult should be sought. Appropriate counseling, follow-up care, and confidentiality must be provided.

TREATMENT: Primary care physicians are encouraged to participate actively in the care of HIV-infected patients in consultation with specialists who have expertise in the care of HIV-infected infants, children, and adolescents. Current treatment recommendations for HIV-infected children are available online (**www.aidsinfo.nih.gov**). When possible, enrollment of an HIV-infected child into available clinical trials should be encouraged. Information about trials for adolescents and children can be obtained by contacting the AIDS Clinical Trials Information Service.[*]

Antiretroviral therapy is indicated for most HIV-infected children. Initiation of antiretroviral therapy depends on virologic, immunologic, and clinical criteria.[†] Because HIV infection is a rapidly changing area, consultation with an expert in pediatric HIV infection is suggested. Many experts recommend initiating antiretroviral therapy for all HIV-infected children younger than 6 to 12 months of age as soon as infection is confirmed, regardless of clinical, immunologic, or virologic parameters. For children older than 1 year of age who are at low risk of disease progression (eg, who have viral load <100 000 copies/mL, who are asymptomatic, and who have

---

[*] See Appendix I, Directory of Resources, p 839: AIDS Clinical Trials Information Service (available at **www.aidsinfo.nih.gov**)

[†] Centers for Disease Control and Prevention. Guidelines for the use of antiretroviral agents in pediatric HIV infection. *MMWR Recomm Rep.* 1998;47(RR-4):1–31. See **www.aidsinfo.nih.gov** for updates of new drugs and new treatment recommendations.

CD4+ T-lymphocyte percentages >25%), some experts would elect not to initiate therapy. Treatment of adolescents generally follows adult guidelines, some adult care providers delay treatment until symptoms develop, the CD4+ lymphocyte count decreases to <200 to 350, and viral load increases to >100 000 copies/mL.* In resource-limited settings, therapy is initiated, if available, for children younger than 18 months of age with CD4+ lymphocyte percentage <20% and at CD4+ lymphocyte percentage <15% for older children.

Combination antiretroviral therapy has been shown to be more effective than monotherapy. Data indicate that 3 antiretroviral drugs should be given whenever possible, including 2 nucleoside analogue reverse transcriptase inhibitors plus either a protease inhibitor or a nonnucleoside reverse transcriptase inhibitor (**www.aidsinfo. nih.gov**). Suppression of virus to undetectable concentrations is the desired goal. A change in antiretroviral therapy should be considered if there is evidence of disease progression (virologic, immunologic, or clinical), toxic effects or intolerance of drugs, or new data suggest the possibility of a superior regimen.

Immune Globulin Intravenous (IGIV) therapy has been recommended in combination with antiretroviral agents for HIV-infected children with hypogammaglobulinemia (IgG <400 mg/dL [4.0 g/L]). Administering IGIV should be considered for HIV-infected children who have recurrent, serious bacterial infections, such as bacteremia, meningitis, or pneumonia, during a 1-year period, although IGIV may not provide additional benefit to children who are receiving trimethoprim-sulfamethoxazole for PCP prophylaxis.

Early diagnosis and aggressive treatment of opportunistic infections may prolong survival.[†‡] Because PCP can be an early complication of perinatally acquired HIV infection and because the mortality rate is high, chemoprophylaxis should be given to HIV-exposed infants. For infants with possible or proven HIV infection, PCP prophylaxis should be administered beginning at 4 to 6 weeks of age and continued for the first year of life unless HIV infection is excluded. The need for PCP prophylaxis for HIV-infected children 1 year of age and older is determined by the degree of immunocompromise as determined by CD4+ T-lymphocyte counts (see *Pneumocystis jiroveci* Infections, p 537).

Guidelines for prevention and treatment of opportunistic infections in children, adolescents, and adults provide indications for administration of drugs for infection with MAC, CMV, *Toxoplasma gondii*, and other organisms.[*†§] Successful suppression of

---

* Centers for Disease Control and Prevention. Guidelines for using antiretroviral agents among HIV-infected adults and adolescents. Recommendations of the Panel on Clinical Practice for Treatment of HIV. *MMWR Recomm Rep.* 2002;51(RR-7):1–56. See **www.aidsinfo.nih.gov** for periodic updates of new drugs and new treatment recommendations.

† Centers for Disease Control and Prevention. Treating opportunistic infections among HIV-exposed and infected children: recommendations from CDC, the National Institutes of Health, and the Infectious Diseases Society of America. *MMWR Recomm Rep.* 2004;53(RR-14):1–92

‡ Centers for Disease Control and Prevention. Treating opportunistic infections among HIV-infected adults and adolescents: recommendations from the CDC, the National Institutes of Health, and the Infectious Diseases Society of America. *MMWR Recomm Rep.* 2004;53(RR-15):1–112

§ Centers for Disease Control and Prevention. Guidelines for preventing opportunistic infections among HIV-infected persons—2002. Recommendations of the US Public Health Service and the Infectious Diseases Society of America. *MMWR Recomm Rep.* 2002;51(RR-8):1–46

HIV replication to undetectable levels by HAART has resulted in a dramatic decrease in the occurrence of most opportunistic infections such as PCP, disseminated CMV infection, MAC infection, and serious bacterial infections and has resulted in relatively normal CD4+ and CD8+ lymphocyte counts. Limited data on the safety of discontinuing prophylaxis in HIV-infected children receiving HAART are available. However, many experts recommend discontinuing primary prophylaxis for *P jiroveci* infections in children older than 1 year of age with CD4+ lymphocyte percentages >25% who are receiving stable combination antiretroviral therapy.

IMMUNIZATION RECOMMENDATIONS (see also Immunocompromised Children, p 71, and Fig 1.1, (p 26).

Children with HIV infection should be immunized as soon as is age appropriate with inactivated vaccines (diphtheria and tetanus toxoids and acellular pertussis [DTaP], inactivated poliovirus [IPV], *Haemophilus influenzae* type b, hepatitis B virus, hepatitis A virus, and pneumococcal conjugate vaccine) as well as annually with influenza vaccine. The suggested schedule for administration of these immunogens is in the Recommended Childhood and Adolescent Immunization Schedule (Fig 1.1, p 26).

Measles-mumps-rubella (MMR) vaccine should be administered to HIV-infected children at 12 months of age unless the children are severely immunocompromised (category 3, Table 3.25, p 382; see also Measles, p 441). The second dose of MMR vaccine may be administered as soon as 4 weeks after the first rather than waiting until school entry. Children receiving routine IGIV prophylaxis may not respond to MMR vaccine. During outbreaks of measles, when exposure is likely, immunization should begin as early as 6 to 9 months of age.

In general, children with symptomatic HIV infection have poor immunologic responses to vaccines. Hence, these children, when exposed to a vaccine-preventable disease such as measles or tetanus, should be considered susceptible regardless of the history of immunization and should receive, if indicated, passive immunoprophylaxis (see Passive Immunization of Children With HIV Infection, p 392). Immune Globulin (IG) also should be given to any unimmunized household member who is exposed to measles infection to decrease the likelihood that the HIV-infected child will be exposed.

Children infected with HIV may be at increased risk of morbidity from varicella-zoster virus infection. Limited data on varicella immunization of HIV-infected children in CDC immunologic category 1 indicate that the vaccine is safe, immunogenic, and effective. Weighing potential risks and benefits, varicella vaccine should be administered to HIV-infected children 12 months of age or older in CDC categories N1 and A1 (ie, having no or mild signs or symptoms of disease, age-specific CD4+ lymphocyte percentage ≥15%, and no evidence of varicella immunity). Two doses should be given, with a 3-month interval between doses.* Some experts would consider varicella immunization in patients with good adherence to antiretroviral therapy if they are asymptomatic and have had CD4+ lymphocyte percentages >25% for

---

* Centers for Disease Control and Prevention. Prevention of varicella: updated recommendations of the Advisory Committee on Immunization Practices (ACIP). *MMWR Recomm Rep.* 1999;48(RR-6):1–5. Available at: **www.cdc.gov/mmwr/PDF/rr/rr4806.pdf**

more than 6 months, even if they previously had symptoms or a low CD4 + lympho-cyte percentage (C3) before initiation of antiretroviral therapy.

Hepatitis A vaccine is recommended for all children 12 to 23 months of age and for people in certain high-risk groups (see Hepatitis A, p 326). The 2 doses in this series should be administered at least 6 months apart. Hepatitis B vaccine is recom-mended for adolescents who were not previously immunized (see Hepatitis B, p 335).

In the United States and in areas of low prevalence of tuberculosis, bacille Calmette-Guérin (BCG) vaccine is not recommended. However, in economically developing countries where the prevalence of tuberculosis is high, the World Health Organization recommends that BCG vaccine be given to all infants at birth if they are asymptomatic, regardless of maternal HIV infection. Disseminated BCG infection has occurred rarely in HIV-infected infants immunized with BCG vaccine.

CHILDREN WHO ARE HIV-SERONEGATIVE RESIDING IN THE HOUSEHOLD OF A PATIENT WITH SYMPTOMATIC HIV INFECTION. In a household in which an adult or child is immunocompromised as the result of HIV infection, household contacts can receive MMR vaccine, because these vaccine viruses are not transmitted. To decrease the risk of transmission of influenza to patients with symptomatic HIV infection, all household members 6 months of age or older should receive yearly influenza immunization (see Influenza, p 401). Varicella immunization of siblings and susceptible adult caregivers of patients with HIV infec-tion is encouraged to prevent acquisition of wild-type varicella-zoster virus infection, which can cause severe disease in immunocompromised hosts. Varicella vaccine virus transmission from an immunocompetent host to a household contact is uncommon.

PASSIVE IMMUNIZATION OF CHILDREN WITH HIV INFECTION.
- **Measles** (see Measles, p 441). Symptomatic HIV-infected children who are exposed to measles should receive intramuscular IG prophylaxis (0.5 mL/kg, maximum 15 mL), regardless of immunization status. Exposed, asymptomatic HIV-infected patients also should receive IG; the recommended dose is 0.25 mL/kg intramuscularly. Children who have received IGIV within 2 weeks of exposure do not require additional passive immunization.
- **Tetanus.** In the management of wounds classified as tetanus prone (see Teta-nus, p 648, and Table 3.63, p 650), children with HIV infection should receive Tetanus Immune Globulin regardless of immunization status.
- **Varicella.** Children infected with HIV without previous varicella infection or receipt of 2 doses of varicella vaccine should receive VariZIG or, if not available, IGIV within 96 hours after close contact with a person who has chickenpox or shingles (see Varicella-Zoster Infections, p 711). Postexposure prophylaxis with acyclovir, VariZIG, or if VariZIG is not available, IGIV should be considered for HIV-infected children with moderate to severe immune compromise, even if they have been immunized. Children who have received IGIV within 2 weeks of exposure do not require additional passive immunization.

ISOLATION OF THE HOSPITALIZED PATIENT: Standard precautions should be fol-lowed by all health care personnel. The risk to health care personnel of acquiring HIV infection from a patient is minimal, even after accidental exposure from a need-lestick injury (see Epidemiology, p 383). Every effort, nevertheless, should be made to avoid exposures to blood and other body fluids that could contain HIV.

CONTROL MEASURES:

DECREASE IN MOTHER-TO-CHILD TRANSMISSION OF HIV.* Three

efficacious interventions to prevent mother-to-child transmission of HIV exist: antiretroviral prophylaxis, cesarean section† before labor and before ruptured membranes, and complete avoidance of breastfeeding. Oral administration of zidovudine to pregnant women with HIV infection beginning at 14 to 34 weeks' gestation and continuing throughout pregnancy, intravenous administration of zidovudine during labor until delivery (ie, intrapartum), and oral administration of zidovudine to the infant for the first 6 weeks of life decreased mother-to-child transmission of HIV by two thirds (see Table 3.27, p 394) in a controlled clinical trial. Guidelines for use of antiretroviral drugs in pregnant HIV-infected women are similar to those for nonpregnant adults.‡ Therefore, many HIV-infected pregnant women will be receiving combination antiretroviral therapy for treatment of their HIV disease; thus, use of zidovudine alone as prophylaxis during pregnancy usually would not be recommended. However, the potential effect on the fetus and infant of antiretroviral drugs, particularly when used in combination, is unknown, and decisions about use of any antiretroviral drug during pregnancy require a discussion of the known benefits and unknown risks to the woman and her fetus. Long-term follow-up is recommended for all infants born to women who have received antiretroviral drugs during pregnancy. Health care professionals who are treating HIV-infected pregnant women and their newborn infants should report all instances of prenatal exposure to antiretroviral drugs to the Antiretroviral Pregnancy Registry (1-800-258-4263 or **www.apregistry.com**).

The goal should be to diagnose HIV infection early in pregnancy to allow interventions to prevent transmission. Interventions include antiretroviral prophylaxis and/or cesarean section before labor and before rupture of membranes, and appropriate care and treatment of the mother for HIV infection. Several international antiretroviral prophylaxis clinical trials using zidovudine, lamivudine, and nevirapine alone or in combination in short courses during various combinations of antepartum, intrapartum, and postpartum periods demonstrated efficacy in prevention of mother-to-child transmission of HIV. These short-course regimens support administration of antiretroviral agents, even to women found to be infected late in pregnancy or at delivery. The first-line regimen recommended in resource-limited settings is to administer zidovudine as early as possible in the third trimester, plus one dose of nevirapine to the mother and to the infant.

In the United States, antiretroviral drugs should be administered to HIV-infected women during pregnancy, labor, and delivery. Zidovudine should be given to all new-

---

* Centers for Disease Control and Prevention. US Public Health Service Task Force recommendations for use of antiretroviral drugs in pregnant HIV-1-infected women for maternal health and for interventions to reduce perinatal HIV-1 transmission in the United States. *MMWR Morb Mortal Wkly Rep.* 2002;51(RR-18):1–38. See **www.aidsinfo.nih.gov** for periodic updates of new drugs and new treatment recommendations.

† American College of Obstetrics and Gynecology, Committee on Obstetric Practice. Scheduled cesarean delivery and the prevention of vertical transmission of HIV infection. *Int J Gynaecol Obstet.* 2001;73:279–281

‡ Centers for Disease Control and Prevention. Guidelines for using antiretroviral agents among HIV-infected adults and adolescents. Recommendations of the Panel on Clinical Practice for Treatment of HIV. *MMWR Recomm Rep.* 2002;51(RR-7):1–56. See **www.aidsinfo.nih.gov** for updates of new drugs and new treatment recommendations.

Table 3.27. Zidovudine Regimen for Decreasing the Rate of Perinatal Transmission of Human Immunodeficiency Virus (HIV)[1]

Period of Time	Route	Dosage
During pregnancy, initiate anytime after wk 14 of gestation and continue throughout pregnancy[2]	Oral	200 mg, 3 times per day or 300 mg, 2 times per day
During labor and delivery[3]	Intravenous	2 mg/kg during the first hour, then 1 mg/kg per hour until delivery
For the newborn infant, as soon as possible after birth[4]	Oral	2 mg/kg, 4 times per day, for the first 6 wk of life

[1] US Public Health Service. Public Health Service Task Force Recommendations for Use of Antiretroviral Drugs in Pregnant HIV-1-Infected Women for Maternal Health and for Interventions to Reduce Perinatal HIV-1 Transmission in the United States. Rockville, MD: AIDSInfo, Department of Health and Human Services; 2005 (available at **www.aidsinfo.nih.gov/guidelines/default_db2.usp?id = 66**). Information about other antiretroviral drugs for decreasing the rate of perinatal transmission of HIV can be found online (**www.aidsinfo.nih.gov**).

[2] Most women in developed countries are treated with potent combinations of 3 antiretroviral agents (highly active antiretroviral therapy [HAART]) started after the first trimester and continuing to delivery. Oral zidovudine may be used as part of that therapy.

[3] Recommended even for women treated with other antiretroviral agents during pregnancy. Intravenous zidovudine is administered for 3 hours before cesarean section.

[4] The effectiveness of antiretroviral agents for prevention of perinatal HIV-1 transmission decreases with delay in initiation after birth. Initiation of postexposure prophylaxis after the first 48 hours of life is not likely to be efficacious in preventing transmission.

born infants as soon as possible after birth to decrease the likelihood of mother-to-child transmission of HIV, even if their mothers did not receive zidovudine. The effectiveness of antiretroviral drugs for prevention of mother-to-child transmission of HIV decreases with longer durations of time after birth when initiated. In a study of HIV-infected infants, HIV infection already had been detected by DNA PCR assay in 38% of infants within 48 hours after birth and in 93% of infants by 14 days of age. Initiation of postexposure prophylaxis after the first 48 hours of life is not likely to be efficacious in preventing transmission in a significant proportion of infants, and by 14 days of age, infection would be established in most infants.* More specific recommendations for use of antiretroviral drugs to decrease the risk of mother-to-child transmission of HIV for HIV-infected women in labor who have not received antiretroviral prophylaxis and for infants born to mothers who have received no antiretroviral prophylaxis during pregnancy or intrapartum are available.

A randomized clinical trial in Europe demonstrated the efficacy of cesarean section before labor and before rupture of membranes for prevention of mother-to-child transmission of HIV. A meta-analysis of data from North America and Europe dem-

---

* US Public Health Service, Perinatal HIV Guidelines Working Group. Public Health Service Task Force Recommendations for Use of Antiretroviral Drugs in Pregnant HIV-1-Infected Women for Maternal Health and Interventions to Reduce Perinatal HIV-1 Transmission in the United States. Rockville, MD: AIDSInfo, US Department of Health and Human Services; 2005. See **www.aidsinfo.nih.gov** for updates of new drugs and new treatment recommendations.

onstrated a 50% lower risk of vertical transmission in the absence of antiretroviral prophylaxis when delivery was by cesarean section before rupture of membranes and before onset of labor and by 87% if the mother received antiretroviral prophylaxis (most likely zidovudine alone) and underwent cesarean section before onset of labor and before rupture of membranes. However, transmission rates are lower for women receiving combination antiretroviral therapy in whom viral load is decreased below the concentration detectable by assays than in women receiving zidovudine monotherapy. The additional benefit of cesarean delivery for further decreasing transmission risk in such women is unknown and may not outweigh the potential risk of operative delivery for the infected mother. The American College of Obstetricians and Gynecologists recommends that HIV-infected pregnant women with peripheral blood viral loads of 1000 copies/mL or greater should be counseled regarding the potential benefit of cesarean delivery before the onset of labor and before rupture of membranes to further decrease the risk of perinatal HIV transmission.[*]

BREASTFEEDING (see also Human Milk, p 123). Transmission of HIV by breastfeeding, especially from mothers who acquire infection during the postpartum period, has been demonstrated. The rate of late postnatal HIV transmission (after 4 weeks of age) in sub-Saharan African countries is approximately 9 transmissions per 100 child-years of breastfeeding and is relatively constant. Late postnatal transmission is associated with reduced maternal CD4+ lymphocyte count. In the United States, where safe alternative sources of feeding are readily available, affordable, and culturally accepted, HIV-infected women should be counseled not to breastfeed their infants or donate to milk banks. The AAP guidelines for women in the United States are as follows[†]:

- Women and their health care professionals need to be aware of the potential risk of transmission of HIV infection to infants during pregnancy and the peripartum period as well as through human milk.
- Routine offering of HIV testing should be part of prenatal care for all women. Each woman should know her HIV infection status and the methods available to prevent acquisition and transmission of HIV and to determine whether breastfeeding is appropriate.
- During labor, if a woman's HIV infection status is unknown, she should be counseled and tested as rapidly as possible. Each woman should understand the benefits to her and her infant of knowing her serostatus.
- In general, women who are known to be HIV seronegative should be encouraged to breastfeed. However, women who are HIV seronegative and known to have HIV-infected sexual partners or to be active drug users should be counseled about the potential risk of transmitting HIV through human milk and about methods to decrease the risk of acquiring HIV infection either late in pregnancy or postpartum.

---

[*] Centers for Disease Control and Prevention. US Public Health Service Task Force recommendations for use of antiretroviral drugs in pregnant HIV-1-infected women for maternal health and for interventions to reduce perinatal HIV-1 transmission in the United States. *MMWR Morb Mortal Wkly Rep.* 2002;51(RR-18):1–38. See **www.aidsinfo.nih.gov** for periodic updates of new drugs and new treatment recommendations.

[†] Read JS, Committee on Pediatric AIDS. Human milk, breastfeeding, and transmission of Human Immunodeficiency Virus Type 1 in the United States. *Pediatrics.* 2003;112:1196–1205

ADOLESCENT EDUCATION. Adolescents who are sexually active or using illicit injection drugs are at risk of HIV infection. Particular efforts should be made to provide access to health care for adolescents who may not have a regular health care professional. Informed consent for testing or release of information about serostatus is necessary.

Specific AAP recommendations for pediatricians caring for adolescents are as follows*:

- Information about HIV infection and AIDS and availability of HIV testing should be regarded as an essential component of the anticipatory guidance provided by pediatricians to all adolescent patients and their families. This guidance should include information about HIV prevention and transmission and implications of infection.
- Preventive guidance should include helping adolescents understand the responsibilities associated with becoming sexually active. Information should be provided on abstinence from sexual activity and use of safer sexual practices to decrease the risk of unplanned pregnancy and sexually transmitted infections, including HIV. All adolescents should be counseled about the correct and consistent use of latex condoms to decrease risk of infection.
- Availability of HIV testing should be discussed with all adolescents and should be encouraged with consent for adolescents who are sexually active.
- Although parental involvement in adolescent health care is a desirable goal, consent of an adolescent alone should be sufficient to provide evaluation and treatment for suspected or confirmed HIV infection.
- A negative HIV test result can allay anxiety resulting from a high-risk event or high-risk behaviors and is a good opportunity to counsel on decreasing high-risk behaviors to decrease future risk.
- For adolescents with a positive HIV test result, it is important to provide support, address medical and psychosocial needs, and arrange linkages to appropriate care.
- Pediatricians should help adolescents with HIV infection to understand the importance of informing their sexual partners of their potential exposure to HIV and methods for preventing HIV transmission. Pediatricians can provide this help directly or via referral to a state or local health department's partner referral program.
- Pediatricians should advocate for the special needs of adolescents for information about HIV, access to HIV testing and counseling, and HIV treatment.

CHILD CARE, SCHOOL ATTENDANCE, AND EDUCATION OF CHILDREN WITH HIV INFECTION.[†‡] (For additional discussion of recommendations for child care, see Children in Out-Of-Home Child Care, p 130.) In the absence

* For further information, see American Academy of Pediatrics, Committee on Pediatric AIDS and Committee on Adolescence. Adolescents and human immunodeficiency virus infection: the role of the pediatrician in prevention and intervention. *Pediatrics.* 2001;107:188–190 (Reaffirmed 2005)

[†] American Academy of Pediatrics, Committee on Pediatric AIDS and Committee on Infectious Diseases. Issues related to human immunodeficiency virus transmission in schools, child care, medical settings, the home, and community. *Pediatrics.* 1999;104:318–324 (Reaffirmed 2002)

[‡] American Academy of Pediatrics. *Managing Infectious Diseases in Child Care and Schools.* Aronson SS, Shope TR, eds. Elk Grove Village, IL: American Academy of Pediatrics; 2004

of blood exposure, HIV infection is not acquired through the types of contact that usually occur in school, child care, or other group care settings, including contact with saliva or tears. Hence, children with HIV infection should not be excluded from school, child care, or other group care settings for the protection of other children or personnel, and disclosure of infection status should not be required. Specific recommendations about school attendance of children and adolescents with HIV infection are the following:

- School-aged children and adolescents infected with HIV should be allowed to attend school without restrictions, provided the child's physician gives approval. The need for a more restricted child care or school environment for the rare infected child who might have an increased likelihood of exposing others should be evaluated on a case-by-case basis by the physician.
- Only the child's parents, other guardians, and physician have an absolute need to know that the child is HIV-infected. The number of personnel aware of the child's condition should be kept to the minimum needed to ensure proper care of the child. The family has the right, but is not obligated, to inform the school. People involved in the care and education of an HIV-infected child or student must respect the student's right to privacy. In some jurisdictions, the child's diagnosis cannot be divulged without the written consent of the parent or legal guardian.
- All schools, child care centers, and other group care facilities should adopt routine procedures for handling blood or blood-contaminated fluids, including disposal of sanitary napkins, regardless of whether students with HIV infection are known to be in attendance. Child care providers, school health care professionals, teachers, administrators, and other employees should be educated about procedures (see Housekeeping Procedures for Blood and Body Fluids, p 398).
- Children with HIV infection may be at increased risk of experiencing severe complications from infections, such as varicella, tuberculosis, measles, and herpes simplex virus. Schools, child care centers, and other group care facilities should develop procedures for notification of all parents regarding communicable diseases, such as varicella or measles. Parents may choose to inform the child care provider or school of the child's diagnosis to support a request that the caregiver or teacher observe the child closely for signs of illness that may require medical attention and assist the parents with the child's emotional and social needs.
- Routine screening of school children for HIV infection is not recommended.

As the life expectancy of HIV-infected children and adolescents increases, the population of children and adolescents with this disease also will increase. An understanding of the effect of chronic illness and the recognition of neurodevelopmental problems in some of these children are essential to provide appropriate educational programs. The AAP recommendations regarding the education of children with HIV infection are as follows*:

- All children with HIV infection should receive an appropriate education that is adapted to their evolving special needs. The spectrum of needs differs with the stage of disease and age of the child.

---

* American Academy of Pediatrics, Committee on Pediatric AIDS. Education of children with human immunodeficiency virus infection. *Pediatrics*. 2000;105:1358–1360 (Reaffirmed 2003)

- Infection with HIV should be treated like other chronic illnesses that require special education and other related services.
- Continuity of education must be ensured whether at school or at home.
- Because of the stigma associated with this disease, maintaining confidentiality is essential. Information should be disclosed only with the informed consent of the parents or legal guardians and age-appropriate assent of the student.

HUMAN IMMUNODEFICIENCY VIRUS IN THE ATHLETIC SETTING. Athletes and staff of athletic programs can be exposed to blood during athletic activity. Recommendations have been developed by the AAP for prevention of transmission of HIV and other bloodborne pathogens in the athletic setting (see School Health, Infections Spread by Blood and Body Fluids, p 151).

FOSTER CARE.* Current AAP recommendations are as follows[†‡]:
- No reason exists to restrict foster care or adoptive placement of children who have HIV infection to protect the health of other family members. The risk of transmission of HIV infection in family environments is negligible.
- Ascertainment of HIV infection status is recommended for all pregnant women and newborn infants if the mother is infected with HIV or her status is unknown. This knowledge may help facilitate foster care or adoptive placement.

ADULTS WITH HIV INFECTION WORKING IN CHILD CARE SETTINGS OR SCHOOLS. Asymptomatic HIV-infected adults may care for children in school, child care, or other group care settings provided that they do not have conditions that would allow contact with their body fluids. No data indicate that HIV-infected adults have transmitted HIV during routine child care or school responsibilities. Adults with symptomatic HIV infection are immunocompromised and at increased risk of complications if they acquire infectious diseases of young children. They should consult their physicians about the safety of continuing to work in school, child care, or other group care settings. In adults, most problems occur as a result of reactivation of latent infections.

HOUSEKEEPING PROCEDURES FOR BLOOD AND BODY FLUIDS. In general, routine housekeeping procedures using a commercially available cleaner (detergent, disinfectant-detergent, or chemical germicide) compatible with most surfaces is satisfactory for cleaning spills of vomitus, urine, and feces. Nasal secretions can be removed with tissues and discarded in routine waste containers. For spills involving blood or other potentially infectious body fluids, organic material should be removed, and the surface should be disinfected with freshly diluted bleach (1:10). Reusable rubber gloves should be used for cleaning large spills to avoid contamination of the hands of the person cleaning the spill, but gloves are not essential for cleaning small amounts of blood that can be contained easily by the material used for cleaning. People involved in cleaning contaminated surfaces should avoid exposure of

---

* For additional discussion of recommendations for child care, see Children in Out-of-Home Child Care, p 130.
[†] American Academy of Pediatrics, Committee on Pediatric AIDS and Committee on Infectious Diseases. Issues related to human immunodeficiency virus transmission in schools, child care, medical settings, the home, and community. *Pediatrics.* 1999;104:318–324
[‡] Adapted from American Academy of Pediatrics, Committee on Pediatric AIDS. Identification and care of HIV-exposed and HIV-infected infants, children, and adolescents in foster care. *Pediatrics.* 2000;106:149–153 (Reaffirmed 2003)

open skin lesions or mucous membranes to blood or bloody fluids. Whenever possible, disposable towels or tissues should be used and properly discarded, and mops should be rinsed in disinfectant. After clean-up and after removal of gloves, hands should be washed thoroughly with soap and water. Gloves are not indicated for routine cleaning tasks that do not involve contact with body secretions, such as sweeping floors or dusting.

MANAGEMENT AND COUNSELING OF FAMILIES. * Serologic screening of siblings and parents for HIV infection is recommended when HIV infection is identified in a child. In each case, the physician should provide education and ongoing counseling about HIV including transmission and outline precautions to be taken within the household and the community to prevent HIV spread.

Women infected with HIV need to be made aware of the risk of having an infected child if they become pregnant, and they should be referred for family planning counseling. Infected people should not donate blood, plasma, sperm, organs, corneas, bone, other tissues, or human milk.

An HIV-infected child should be taught appropriate hygiene and behavior. How much the child is told about the illness depends on his or her age and maturity. Older children and adolescents should be made aware that the disease can be transmitted sexually, and they should be counseled appropriately. Many families are not willing to tell others about the diagnosis, because it can result in social isolation.

SEXUAL ABUSE. In some cases of sexual abuse, the child should be tested serologically as soon as possible and periodically for 6 months (eg, at 4–6 weeks, 12 weeks, and 6 months after sexual contact) (see Sexually Transmitted Infections, p 166). Serologic evaluation of the perpetrator for HIV infection should be attempted but usually cannot be performed shortly after the abuse and often is not possible until indictment has occurred. Counseling of the child and family needs to be provided (see Sexually Transmitted Infections, p 166).

POSTEXPOSURE PROPHYLAXIS FOR POSSIBLE SEXUAL OR OTHER NONOCCUPATIONAL EXPOSURE TO HIV.† Decisions to provide antiretroviral agents to people after possible nonoccupational HIV exposure must balance the potential benefits and risks. Considerations related to use of antiretroviral prophylaxis in such circumstances include an estimation of the probability that the source is HIV infected, the likelihood of transmission by the particular exposure, the interval between exposure and initiation of therapy, the efficacy of the drug(s) used, and the patient's adherence to the regimen of drug(s).

Risk of HIV transmission from a puncture wound attributable to a needle found in the community is lower than the 0.3% risk of HIV transmission to a health care professional from a needlestick injury from a person with known HIV infection. Actual risks to an infant or child after a needlestick injury or sexual abuse are unknown. To date, there are no known transmissions of HIV from accidental non-

---

* Centers for Disease Control and Prevention. Revised guidelines for HIV counseling, testing, and referral. Atlanta, GA: *MMWR Recomm Rep*. 2001;50(RR-19):1–57. Available at: **www.cdc.gov/publications. htm**

† US Department of Health and Human Services. Antiretroviral postexposure prophylaxis after sexual, injection-drug use, or other nonoccupational exposure to HIV in the United States: recommendations from the U.S. Department of Health and Human Services. *MMWR Recomm Rep*. 2005;54(RR-2):1–20

occupational needlesticks (needles found in the community). The estimated risk of HIV transmission per episode of receptive penile-anal sexual exposure to an HIV infected person is 50 per 10 000 exposures; the estimated risk per episode of receptive vaginal exposure is 10 per 10 000 exposures.

In 1995, surveillance data from health care personnel were used in a case-control study that suggested zidovudine use was associated with an 81% (95% confidence interval [CI] = 48%–94%) decrease in risk of HIV infection after percutaneous exposure to HIV-infected blood. This may be an overestimate of the benefits because of methodologic constraints.

All antiretroviral agents have adverse effects. An estimated 24% to 36% of adults discontinue drugs used in combination because of adverse effects. Severe adverse effects, such as nephrolithiasis, nephrotoxicity, pancreatitis, pancytopenia, or hepatotoxicity, have been reported.

Antiretroviral agents generally should not be used if the risk of transmission is low (eg, needlestick from unknown nonoccupational source) or if care is sought more than 72 hours after reported exposure.* Benefits of postexposure prophylaxis will be greatest when risk of infection is high, intervention is prompt, and adherence is likely. Consultation with an experienced pediatric HIV health care professional is essential.

BLOOD, BLOOD COMPONENTS, AND CLOTTING FACTORS. Screening blood and plasma for HIV antibody has decreased dramatically the risk of infection through transfusion (see Blood Safety, p 106).

HUMAN IMMUNODEFICIENCY VIRUS-EXPOSED HEALTH CARE PERSONNEL. Accidental exposure of health care personnel to HIV, such as from needlestick injuries or HIV-infected blood, rarely has resulted in HIV infection. The risk of infection varies according to the severity and type of exposure. The risk of infection after a percutaneous exposure to HIV-infected blood is 0.3% and after mucous membrane exposure is approximately 0.09%. Many of the known cases could have been prevented by careful adherence to infection control measures (see Control Measures, p 393). A health care professional who has had a percutaneous or mucous membrane exposure to blood or bloody secretions from an HIV-seropositive patient should receive counseling and medical evaluation as soon as possible after the exposure. A baseline HIV antibody test should be performed, and the HIV infection status of the blood source should be investigated. A health care professional who is seronegative at the time of exposure should be retested 4 to 6 weeks, 12 weeks, and 6 months after exposure to determine whether transmission has occurred. Most exposed people who have been infected will seroconvert during the first 3 months after exposure.

Revised recommendations for postexposure prophylaxis (PEP) were issued by the US Public Health Service in 2005.† Recommendations for HIV PEP for percutaneous injuries are divided into less severe (solid needle or superficial injury) and more

---

* Havens PL, and American Academy of Pediatrics, Committee on Pediatric AIDS. Postexposure prophylaxis in children and adolescents for nonoccupational exposure to human immunodeficiency virus. *Pediatrics*. 2003;111:1475–1489

† US Pubic Health Service. Updated U.S. Public Health Service guidelines for the management of occupational exposures to HIV and recommendations for postexposure prophylaxis. *MMWR Recomm Rep*. 2005;54(RR-9):1–17

severe (large-bore hollow needle, deep puncture, visible blood on device, or needle used in patient's artery or vein). In addition, consideration of HIV-positive class (class 1, asymptomatic or low viral load; class 2, symptomatic HIV infection or high viral load) will determine whether a 2-drug (HIV class 1, less severe) or an expanded ≥3-drug (all more severe and less severe HIV class 2) PEP regimen is used.

Recommended HIV PEP for mucous membrane exposure and nonintact skin exposures are considered under small volume (a few drops) and large volume (a major blood splash) for mucous membrane exposure and whether skin is compromised for skin exposures. With regard to mucous membrane exposure, 2-drug PEP should be considered for HIV-positive class 1; 2-drug PEP is recommended for small volume, HIV class 2 and large volume, HIV class 1; and ≥3-drug PEP is recommended for large volume, HIV class 2. People receiving PEP should complete a full 4-week regimen and should be monitored for adverse events. Expert consultation in management of exposures is recommended either with local experts or by contacting the National Clinicians' Post-Exposure Prophylaxis Hotline at 888-448-4911.

REPORTING OF CASES. Cases meeting the criteria for AIDS (see Tables 3.24, p 380, and 3.25, p 382) must be reported in all states to the appropriate public health department. In many states, HIV infection or perinatal exposure to HIV also must be reported. The AAP recommends routine reporting of perinatal HIV exposure, infection, and AIDS.

Influenza

CLINICAL MANIFESTATIONS: Influenza classically is characterized by sudden onset of fever, often with chills or rigors, headache, malaise, diffuse myalgia, and nonproductive cough. Subsequently, the respiratory tract signs of sore throat, nasal congestion, rhinitis, and cough become more prominent. Conjunctival injection, abdominal pain, nausea, vomiting, and diarrhea have been reported infrequently. In some children, influenza can appear as an upper respiratory tract infection or as a febrile illness with few respiratory tract signs. In infants, influenza can produce a sepsis-like picture and occasionally can cause croup, bronchiolitis, or pneumonia. Acute myositis characterized by calf tenderness and refusal to walk has been described after several days of influenza illness, particularly with type B influenza infection. Neurologic complications associated with influenza range from febrile seizures to severe encephalopathy and encephalitis with status epilepticus and altered consciousness that can result in neurologic sequelae and death. Reye syndrome has been associated with influenza infection. Myocarditis with fatal outcomes has been reported. Invasive secondary bacterial infection with respiratory tract pathogens, including group A streptococcus, methicillin-resistant *Staphylococcus aureus*, and *Streptococcus pneumoniae*, causing severe disease and death, can occur with influenza virus infection.

ETIOLOGY: Influenza viruses are orthomyxoviruses of 3 genera or types (A, B, and C). Epidemic disease is caused by influenza virus types A and B. Influenza A viruses are subclassified into subtypes by 2 surface antigens, hemagglutinin (HA) and neuraminidase (NA). Recent circulating human influenza A subtypes have included H1N1, H1N2, and H3N2 viruses. Specific antibodies to these various antigens, especially to hemagglutinin, are important determinants of immunity. Minor antigenic variations within the same influenza B type or influenza A subtypes are called *antigenic drift*. Antigenic drift occurs continuously and results in new strains of influenza A and B viruses, leading to seasonal epidemics. Major changes leading to the emergence of influenza A viruses with a new HA in humans, such as H5 or H7, or new HA and new NA are called *antigenic shift*. Antigenic shift occurs only with influenza A viruses and can lead to pandemics if a strain can infect humans and efficiently be transmitted from person to person in a sustained manner; 3 pandemics occurred in the 20th century.

EPIDEMIOLOGY: Influenza is spread from person to person primarily by droplets but also may be spread by direct contact with influenza virus-contaminated surfaces. During community outbreaks of influenza, the highest attack rates occur among school-aged children. Secondary spread to adults and other children within a family is common. Incidence depends in part on immunity developed by previous experience (by natural disease) or recent influenza immunization with the circulating strain or a related strain. Antigenic drift in the circulating strain(s) is associated with seasonal epidemics. In temperate climates, seasonal epidemics usually occur during winter months. Community outbreaks can last 4 to 8 weeks or longer. Circulation of 2 or 3 influenza virus strains in a community may be associated with a prolonged influenza season of 3 months or more and bimodal peaks in activity. Influenza is highly contagious, especially among semi-enclosed institutionalized populations. Patients may become infectious during the 24 hours before onset of symptoms. Viral shedding in nasal secretions usually peaks during the first 3 days of illness and ceases within 7 days but can be prolonged in young children and immunodeficient patients. Viral shedding correlates directly with height of fever.

Attack rates in healthy children have been estimated at 10% to 40% each year, with approximately 1% of infections resulting in hospitalization. The risk of lower respiratory tract disease complicating influenza infection in children, primarily pneumonia, croup, wheezing, and bronchiolitis, has ranged from 0.2% to 25%.

Excess rates of hospitalization attributable to influenza virus infections have been documented for otherwise healthy children younger than 5 years of age, with rates in children younger than 2 years of age substantially higher than in children 2 years of age or older. Rates of hospitalization and morbidity attributable to complications, such as bronchitis and pneumonia, are even greater in children with hemoglobinopathies, bronchopulmonary dysplasia, asthma, cystic fibrosis, malignancy, diabetes mellitus, chronic renal disease, and congenital heart disease. Influenza virus infection in neonates also has been associated with considerable morbidity, including a sepsis-like syndrome, apnea, and lower respiratory tract disease. Fatal outcomes, including sudden death, have been reported in both chronically ill and previously healthy children. Among 153 pediatric influenza-associated deaths reported to the Centers for Disease Control and Prevention (CDC) in 2003-2004, nearly two thirds occurred in children younger than 5 years of age and almost half had no known underlying condition known to predispose to severe disease. Influenza-associated pediatric deaths should be reported to the CDC through state health departments.

The **incubation period** usually is 1 to 4 days, with a mean of 2 days.

INFLUENZA PANDEMICS. A pandemic is defined by the emergence and global spread of a new influenza A virus subtype, leading to substantially increased morbidity and mortality rates. During the 20th century, there were 3 influenza pandemics, in 1918 (H1N1), 1957 (H2N2), and 1968 (H3N2). The pandemic in 1918 killed at least 20 million people and perhaps as many as 50 million people worldwide. A severe pandemic could overwhelm the health care system and disrupt critical societal functions. Pediatric care providers should be familiar with national, state, and institutional pandemic plans including recommendations for vaccine and antiviral drug use, health care surge capacity, and personal protective strategies that can be communicated to patients and families. Public health authorities are developing plans for pandemic preparedness and response to a pandemic in the United States. Current status on aspects of pandemic influenza can be found at **www.pandemicflu.gov**.

DIAGNOSTIC TESTS: Specimens for viral culture, immunofluorescent, or rapid diagnostic tests should be obtained during the first 72 hours of illness, because the quantity of virus shed decreases rapidly from that point. Specimens of nasopharyngeal secretions obtained by swab, aspirate, or wash should be placed in appropriate transport media for culture. After inoculation into eggs or cell culture, virus usually can be isolated within 2 to 6 days. Rapid diagnostic tests for identification of influenza A and B antigens in respiratory tract specimens are available commercially, although their reported sensitivity (45%–90%) and specificity (60%–95%) compared with viral culture are variable and differ by test and specimen type. Direct fluorescent antibody (DFA) and indirect immunofluorescent antibody (IFA) staining for detection of influenza A and B antigens in nasopharyngeal or nasal specimens are available at most hospital-based laboratories and can yield results in 3 to 4 hours. Results of immunofluorescent and rapid diagnostic tests should be interpreted in the context of the clinical findings and local community influenza activity, because the prevalence of circulating influenza viruses influences the positive and negative predictive values of these influenza screening tests. False-positive results are more likely to occur during periods of low influenza activity; false-negative results are more likely to occur during peak influenza activity periods. Serologic diagnosis can be established retrospectively by a fourfold or greater increase in antibody titer in serum specimens obtained during the acute and convalescent stages of illness, as determined by hemagglutination inhibition testing, complement fixation testing, neutralization testing, or enzyme immunoassay (EIA); however, serologic testing rarely is useful in patient management, because 2 serum samples collected 10 to 14 days apart are required. Reverse transcriptase-polymerase chain reaction (RT-PCR) testing of respiratory tract specimens may be available at some institutions. Although RT-PCR testing has not been standardized, RT-PCR offers potential for high sensitivity and specificity.

TREATMENT: Two classes of antiviral medications are approved by the US Food and Drug Administration for therapy of influenza infections: the adamantanes (ie, amantidine and rimantadine) and the neuraminidase inhibitors (ie, zanamivir and oseltamivir). Amantadine and rimantadine are approved for treatment of influenza A virus infection in adolescents and adults; amantadine also is approved for treatment in children 1 year of age and older (Table 3.28, p 404). Amantadine and rimantadine are both approved for chemoprophylaxis of influenza A in children 1 year of age and

Table 3.28. Antiviral Drugs for Influenza

Drug	Virus	Admini-stration	Treatment Indications[1]	Prophylaxis Indications[1]	Adverse Effects
Amantidine	A	Oral	≥1 y of age	≥1 y of age	Central nervous system, anxiety, gastrointestinal
Rimantidine	A	Oral	≥13 y of age	≥1 y of age	Central nervous system, anxiety, gastrointestinal
Zanamivir	A and B	Inhalation	≥7 y of age	≥5 y of age	Bronchospasm
Oseltamivir	A and B	Oral	≥1 y of age	≥1 y of age	Nausea, vomiting

[1] US Food and Drug Administration (FDA)-approved ages.

older. Although rimantadine is approved for chemoprophylaxis in children older than 1 year of age and for treatment of children ≥13 years of age, some experts consider it appropriate for treatment of children ≥1 year of age with influenza A infection. Studies evaluating the efficacy of amantadine and rimantadine in children are limited, but they indicate that treatment with either drug diminishes the signs and symptoms of influenza A infection and duration of illness by approximately 1 day when administered within 48 hours of onset of illness. Neither amantadine nor rimantadine is effective against influenza B infections.

In 2005-2006, the CDC reported that most influenza A (H3N2) strains tested were resistant to adamantanes and recommended against their use for treatment or prophylaxis for that season.[*] This recommendation will be updated as new data become available (**www.cdc.gov/flu**). The NA inhibitors have been approved for treatment of uncomplicated influenza A and B infection in patients within 2 days of onset of symptoms.[†] The NA inhibitors are the only available antiviral agents with activity against influenza B viruses. These drugs function by decreasing release of virus from infected cells. Zanamivir is approved for treatment of influenza in people 7 years of age and older. Zanamivir also is approved for chemoprophylaxis of influenza for people 5 years of age and older. Zanamivir is an inhaled powder formulation that is administered twice a day for 5 days using a special breath-activated plastic inhaler. In an efficacy trial in children 5 to 12 years of age, when therapy was instituted within 36 hours of onset, zanamivir decreased the duration of symptoms by 1 day, compared with placebo. Safety and efficacy have not been established in children with high-risk underlying medical conditions. Oseltamivir is approved for both treatment and chemoprophylaxis of influenza in people 1 year of age and older and is administered orally twice a day for 5 days. Oseltamivir is not approved for children younger than 12 months of age because of animal studies documenting neurotoxicity. In an efficacy trial among children 1 to 12 years of age, oseltamivir treatment admin-

---

[*] Centers for Disease Control and Prevention. High levels of adamantane resistance among influenza A (H3N2) viruses and interim guidelines for use of antiviral agents—United States, 2005–2006 influenza season. *MMWR Morb Mortal Wkly Rep.* 2006;55:44–46

[†] American Academy of Pediatrics, Committee on Infectious Diseases. Policy statement: reduction of the influenza burden in children. *Pediatrics.* 2002;110:1246–1252; and American Academy of Pediatrics, Committee on Infectious Diseases. Technical report: reduction of the influenza burden in children. *Pediatrics.* 2002;110(6). Available at: **www.pediatrics.org/cgi/content/full/110/e80**

istered within 48 hours of onset of illness decreased the duration of influenza symptoms by 1.5 days. None of the antiviral drugs approved for use against influenza have been studied in children younger than 1 year of age.

Therapy for influenza virus infection should be considered for (1) patients in whom shortening or amelioration of clinical symptoms may be particularly beneficial, such as children at increased risk of severe or complicated influenza infection; (2) healthy children with severe illness; and (3) people with special environmental, family, or social situations for which ongoing illness would be detrimental. Influenza A viruses rapidly may become resistant to amantadine and rimantadine during treatment, and an increasing prevalence of viruses resistant to amantadine and rimantadine has been documented worldwide, as noted previously. Clinicians who are suspicious that an antiviral-resistant influenza strain is circulating and want to have influenza isolates tested for susceptibility should contact their state health department. Development of resistance to zanamivir and oseltamivir during treatment has been identified rarely but does not appear to be common and resistant virus has not been transmitted between people. The clinical significance of this resistance to NA inhibitors has not been characterized. Circulation of influenza viruses resistant to NA inhibitors is low worldwide.

If antiviral therapy is prescribed, treatment should be started within 2 days after the onset of symptoms and discontinued approximately 24 to 48 hours after symptoms resolve (maximum duration of treatment, 5 days for amantadine or rimantadine) or after a 5-day course (NA inhibitors). The recommended dosages for drugs approved for treatment and prophylaxis of influenza are given in Table 4.9 (p 785). Patients with any degree of renal insufficiency should be monitored for adverse events. Only zanamivir, which is administered by inhalation, does not require adjustment for people with severe renal insufficiency. Both amantadine and rimantadine, but especially amantadine, may cause CNS symptoms, which resolve with discontinuation of the drug. An increased incidence of seizures has been reported in children with epilepsy who receive amantadine and, to a lesser extent, in children who receive rimantadine. The most common adverse effects of oseltamivir are nausea and vomiting. Zanamivir use has been associated with bronchospasm in some individuals and is not recommended for use in patients with underlying airway disease.

Control of fever with acetaminophen or other appropriate antipyretics may be important in young children, because fever and other symptoms of influenza could exacerbate underlying chronic conditions. Children and adolescents with influenza should not receive aspirin or any salicylate-containing products because of the resulting increased risk of developing Reye syndrome.

ISOLATION OF THE HOSPITALIZED PATIENT: In addition to standard precautions, droplet precautions are recommended for children hospitalized with influenza or an influenza-like illness for the duration of the illness. Respiratory tract secretions should be considered infectious, and strict hand hygiene procedures should be used.

CONTROL MEASURES:

INFLUENZA VACCINE. Inactivated trivalent influenza vaccines (TIV) and live-attenuated influenza vaccine (LAIV) are multivalent vaccines containing 3 virus strains (one each of A [H3N2], A [H1N1], and B). Typically, 1 or 2 strains are changed each year in anticipation of the predominant influenza strains expected to circulate in the United States in the upcoming winter. Both types of vaccine are produced in embryonated hen eggs and should not be given to anyone who has had an anaphylactic reaction to egg proteins. Inactivated trivalent influenza vaccines distributed in the United States are either subvirion vaccine, prepared by disrupting the lipid-containing membrane of the virus, or purified surface-antigen vaccine. Inactivated influenza vaccine is licensed for use in people 6 months of age or older. Live-attenuated influenza vaccine is cold adapted, developed by passaging the viruses at successively lower temperatures in tissue culture, so that replication occurs only in the upper respiratory tract. Live-attenuated influenza vaccine is licensed for children 5 years of age and older. Studies are ongoing to assess safety and efficacy in children between 6 months and 5 years of age.

Immunogenicity in Children. Children younger than 9 years of age who have not previously been immunized against influenza require 2 doses of TIV or LAIV vaccine administered at least 1 month apart to produce a satisfactory antibody response (see Table 3.29, p 406). Children previously primed with a related strain of influenza by infection or immunization mount a brisk antibody response to 1 dose of the vaccine. Children younger than 9 years of age who received 1 or more dose(s) of either TIV or LAIV vaccine in a previous year need only 1 dose in subsequent years. Children 9 years of age or older require only 1 dose, regardless of their influenza immunization history.

Vaccine Efficacy and Effectiveness. Protection against virologically confirmed influenza illness after immunization with TIV in healthy children older than 2 years of age usually is 70% to 80%, with a range of 50% to 95% depending on the closeness of vaccine strain match to the circulating wild strain. Efficacy of LAIV was 86% to 96% against virologically confirmed influenza A (H3N2) virus infection in a large prelicensure pediatric trial during 1 year. Efficacy of TIV in children 6 to 23 months of age is lower than in older children, although data are limited. The effectiveness of influenza immunization on acute respiratory tract illness is less evident in pediatric than in adult populations because of the frequency of upper respiratory tract infections and influenza-like illness caused by other viral agents in young children. The duration of protection is approximately 1 year.

Table 3.29. Schedule for Inactivated Influenza Vaccine Dosage by Age[1]

Age	Dose, mL[2]	No. of Doses	Route[3]
6–35 mo	0.25	1–2[4]	Intramuscular
3–8 y	0.5	1–2[4]	Intramuscular
≥9 y	0.5	1	Intramuscular

[1] Manufacturers include sanofi pasteur (Fluzone, split-virus vaccine licensed for people ≥6 months of age), Chiron Vaccines Ltd (Fluvirin, purified surface antigen, licensed for people ≥4 years of age), and GlaxoSmithKline (Fluarix, split-virus vaccine licensed for people ≥18 years of age).

[2] Dosages are those recommended in recent years. Physicians should refer to the product circular each year to ensure that the appropriate dosage is given.

[3] For adults and older children, the recommended site of immunization is the deltoid muscle. For infants and young children, the preferred site is the anterolateral aspect of the thigh.

[4] Two doses administered at least 1 month apart are recommended for children younger than 9 years of age who are receiving inactivated influenza vaccine for the first time. If possible, the second dose should be administered before December.

Coadministration With Other Vaccines. Inactivated influenza vaccine (TIV) can be administered simultaneously with other live and inactivated vaccines. No data about concurrent administration of LAIV and recommended childhood vaccines are available. According to the general recommendations on immunization, inactivated and live vaccines can be given simultaneously with LAIV; however, if live vaccines are not administered on the same day, they should be separated by ≥4 weeks.

Recommendations for Influenza Immunization*†. Annual influenza immunization is recommended in all children 6 through 59 months of age, for household contacts and out-of-home caregivers of children 0 to 59 months of age, and for children and adolescents in high-risk groups. Other children, adolescents, and adults can be immunized to decrease the impact of influenza.

Live-Attenuated Influenza Vaccine Indications. Live-attenuated influenza vaccine is indicated for healthy people (ie, without designated high-risk conditions) 5 to 49 years of age who want to be protected against influenza. Inactivated influenza vaccine is preferred for close contacts of very severely immunosuppressed people.

People should not receive LAIV if they are receiving salicylates, have a known or suspected immune deficiency, have a history of Guillain-Barré syndrome (GBS), have a history of anaphylactic reaction to egg protein, or have reactive airway disease or other conditions traditionally considered high risk for severe influenza (chronic pulmonary disorders or cardiac disorders, pregnancy, chronic metabolic disease, renal dysfunction, hemoglobinopathies, or immunosuppressive therapy).

Special Considerations, TIV. In children receiving immunosuppressive chemotherapy, influenza immunization with a new vaccine antigen results in a less robust response than in immunocompetent children. The optimal time to immunize children with malignant neoplasms who must undergo chemotherapy is >3 weeks after chemotherapy has been discontinued, when the peripheral granulocyte and lymphocyte counts are >1000/μL (1.0×10^9/L). Children who no longer are receiving chemotherapy generally have high rates of seroconversion.

Children with hemodynamically unstable cardiac disease constitute a large group potentially at high risk of complications of influenza. The immune response and safety of inactivated influenza virus vaccine in these children are comparable to the immune response and safety in healthy children.

Corticosteroids administered for brief periods or every other day seem to have a minimal effect on antibody response to influenza vaccine. Prolonged administration of high doses of corticosteroids (ie, a dose of prednisone of either ≥2 mg/kg or a total of ≥20 mg/day or an equivalent) may impair antibody response. Influenza immunization can be deferred temporarily during the time of receipt of high-dose corticosteroids, provided deferral does not compromise the likelihood of immunization before the start of influenza season (see Vaccine Administration, p 409).

---

* Centers for Disease Control and Prevention. Prevention and control of influenza: recommendations of the Advisory Committee on Immunization Practices (ACIP). *MMWR*. 2006; in press (see **www.cdc.gov/ mmwr**).

† American Academy of Pediatrics, Committee on Infectious Diseases. Policy statement: reduction of the influenza burden in children. *Pediatrics*. 2002;110:1246–1252; and American Academy of Pediatrics, Committee on Infectious Diseases. Technical report: reduction of the influenza burden in children. *Pediatrics*. 2002;110(6):e80. Available at: **www.pediatrics.org/cgi/content/full/110/6/e80**. For updates, see **www.cdc.gov/flu**

Targeted High-Risk Children and Adolescents, TIV. Yearly immunization with TIV, administered during the autumn (see Vaccine Administration, p 409), is recommended for all children older than 24 months of age with one or more of the following specific risk factors:

- Asthma or other chronic pulmonary diseases, such as cystic fibrosis
- Hemodynamically significant cardiac disease
- Immunosuppressive disorders or therapy (see Special Considerations, p 407)
- Human immunodeficiency virus (HIV) infection (see Human Immunodeficiency Virus Infection, p 378)
- Sickle cell anemia and other hemoglobinopathies
- Diseases requiring long-term salicylate therapy, such as rheumatoid arthritis or Kawasaki disease, which may increase the risk of developing Reye syndrome after influenza illness
- Chronic renal dysfunction
- Chronic metabolic disease, including diabetes mellitus
- Children with any condition (eg, cognitive dysfunction, spinal cord injuries, seizure disorders, or other neuromuscular disorders) that can compromise respiratory function or handling of respiratory tract secretions or that can increase the risk of aspiration.

Pregnancy. Women who will be pregnant during influenza season should receive TIV during the autumn, because pregnancy increases the risk of complications and hospitalization from influenza. Because the currently available intramuscularly administered TIV is not a live-virus vaccine and only rarely is associated with major systemic reactions, most experts consider the vaccine safe during any stage of pregnancy. Live-attenuated influenza vaccine is contraindicated during pregnancy.

Close Contacts of High-Risk Patients. Immunization of people who are in close contact with children with high-risk conditions and with any healthy child younger than 24 months of age are important means of protection for these children. In addition, immunization of pregnant women may benefit their unborn infants, because transplacentally acquired antibody may protect infants from infection with influenza virus, but data are limited. Immunization is recommended for the following people:

- All health care professionals in contact with pediatric patients in hospitals, outpatient care settings, and chronic care facilities*
- Household contacts, including siblings and primary caregivers, of high-risk children and all healthy children younger than 24 months of age
- Children who are members of households with high-risk adults, any children younger than 24 months of age, and children with symptomatic HIV infection
- Providers of home care to children younger than 24 months of age and to other high-risk groups of children and adolescents
- Close contacts of infants younger than 6 months of age (see Recommendations for Influenza Immunization, p 407), because this high-risk group cannot be protected directly by immunization or antiviral prophylaxis.

---

* Centers for Disease Control and Prevention. Influenza vaccination of health-care personnel. Recommendations of the Healthcare Infection Control Practices Advisory Committee (HICPAC) and the Advisory Committtee on Immunization Practices (ACIP). *MMWR Recomm Rep.* 2006;55(RR-2):1–16

International Travel. Children and adolescents traveling internationally to areas where influenza outbreaks are or may be occurring should be considered for immunization. The decision to immunize will depend on the person's destination, duration of travel, risk of acquiring influenza (such as the season of the year and immunization history), age, underlying chronic medical conditions, and potential for severe illness from complications of influenza. In tropical climate zones, influenza may circulate at any time of year. Travelers also can be exposed to influenza during the summer, especially when traveling as part of large, organized tourist groups that include people from areas of the world where influenza viruses may be circulating.

Other Children. Immunization should be considered for any child or adolescent and for groups of people whose close contact facilitates rapid transmission and spread of infection that may result in disruption of routine activities. These groups include students in colleges, schools, and other institutions of learning, particularly people who reside in dormitories or who are members of athletic teams, and people living in residential institutions. Influenza vaccine also may be administered to any immunocompetent child or adolescent who wishes to decrease the chance of becoming infected with influenza.

Breastfeeding. Breastfeeding is not a contraindication for immunization with either TIV or LAIV.

Vaccine Administration. Influenza vaccine should be administered during the autumn of each year before the start of influenza season, at the time specified in the yearly recommendations of the CDC Advisory Committee on Immunization Practices (**www.cdc.gov/flu**). The usual recommended time is from the beginning of October through January. However, people may be immunized in September, when the vaccine for the forthcoming influenza season becomes available, particularly children younger than 9 years of age who will require 2 doses. If vaccine is still available, people still may benefit from immunization until influenza no longer is circulating in the country, often through April. The recommended vaccine dose and schedule for different age groups are given in Table 3.29 (p 406).

Annual influenza immunization is recommended, because immunity can decrease during the year after immunization and because in most years, at least one of the vaccine antigens is changed to match ongoing antigenic changes in circulating strains.

REACTIONS, ADVERSE EFFECTS, AND CONTRAINDICATIONS

Inactivated Influenza Vaccine. Inactivated influenza vaccine (TIV) contains only noninfectious viruses and cannot cause influenza. In children younger than 13 years of age, both febrile and local reactions are rare. Fever occurs primarily 6 to 24 hours after immunization in children younger than 24 months of age. In children 13 years of age or older, local reactions occur in approximately 10% of recipients.

In some years, influenza vaccines have been associated with a slightly increased frequency of GBS. Estimating the precise risk of a rare condition such as GBS is difficult, but a study conducted during 1992–1994 showed an excess rate of approximately 1 GBS case per million people immunized. Even if GBS is a causally related adverse effect, the estimated risk of GBS is much less than that of severe influenza that could be prevented by immunization. Immunization of children who have asthma or cystic fibrosis with the currently available inactivated influenza vaccines is not associated with a detectable increase in adverse events or exacerbations.

Children demonstrating severe anaphylactic reaction to chickens or egg protein or other components of the inactivated influenza vaccine can experience, on rare occasions, a similar type of reaction to TIV. Although TIV has been administered safely to such children after skin testing and, when appropriate, desensitization, these children should not receive TIV because of their risk of reactions, the likely need for yearly immunization, and the availability of chemoprophylaxis against influenza infection.

Live-Attenuated Influenza Vaccine. No statistically significant differences were observed in prelicensure studies between placebo and LAIV recipients in rates of fever, rhinitis, or nasal congestion. A retrospective analysis of a large pediatric trial in Northern California revealed a statistically significant increase in asthma events among children 12 to 59 months of age after dose 1 (relative risk: 3.53; 90% confidence interval: 1.1–15.7). There was no clustering of wheezing events. Further evaluation of safety in this age group is being conducted.

Transmission of LAIV strains to unimmunized contacts has been documented only once in prelicensure studies. The proposed explanation for the uncommon occurrence of transmission is that the vaccine virus is shed for a shorter duration and in a much smaller quantity than are wild-type strains.

CHEMOPROPHYLAXIS: AN ALTERNATIVE METHOD OF PROTECTING CHILDREN AGAINST INFLUENZA. Chemoprophylaxis should not be considered a substitute for immunization in most cases. However, the currently licensed influenza antiviral drugs are important adjuncts to inactivated influenza vaccine for control and prevention of influenza disease. Amantadine and rimantadine are approved for prophylaxis of influenza A in children older than 1 year of age. Studies of prophylaxis against influenza A infection in adults have demonstrated 70% to 90% effectiveness in preventing clinical illness, but asymptomatic infection can occur. Studies in children have indicated a similar beneficial effect in diminishing spread of influenza A among institutionalized children and family members and in pediatric hospitals. The usual recommended doses of rimantadine and amantadine for prophylaxis are the same as those for treatment and are given in Table 4.9 (p 785). Most influenza A (H3N2) strains characterized by the CDC during the 2005-2006 influenza season were resistant to adamantanes, resulting in a recommendation by the CDC not to use adamantanes for prophylaxis or treatment until further notice. Oseltamivir is approved for prophylaxis in children 1 year of age and older. Zanamivir is not approved for chemoprophylaxis.

Indications for Chemoprophylaxis. Chemoprophylaxis may be considered for the following situations:

- Protection of unimmunized high-risk children or children who were immunized less than 2 weeks before influenza circulation, because adequate immune response develops 2 weeks after immunization
- Protection of children at increased risk of severe infection or complications, such as high-risk children for whom the vaccine is contraindicated (ie, children with a history of anaphylactic reaction to eggs)
- Protection of unimmunized close contacts of high-risk children
- Protection of immunocompromised children who may not respond to vaccine
- Control of influenza outbreaks in a closed setting, such as an institution with high-risk children

- Protection of immunized high-risk children if the vaccine strain poorly matches circulating influenza strains

Chemoprophylaxis does not interfere with the immune response to the inactivated influenza virus vaccine; people immunized with LAIV should not receive antiviral prophylaxis for 14 days after receipt of LAIV.

Information about influenza surveillance is available through the CDC Voice Information System (influenza update, 888-232-3228) or through **www.cdc.gov/flu**.

Isosporiasis

CLINICAL MANIFESTATIONS: Protracted, watery diarrhea is the most common symptom. Manifestations are similar to those caused by *Cryptosporidium* species and *Cyclospora* species and can include abdominal pain, anorexia, and weight loss. Fever, malaise, nausea, vomiting, and headache have been reported. The proportion of infected people who are asymptomatic is unknown. Severity of infection ranges from self-limiting in immunocompetent hosts to life threatening in immunocompromised patients, particularly people infected with human immunodeficiency virus (HIV).

ETIOLOGY: *Isospora belli* is a spore-forming coccidian protozoan.

EPIDEMIOLOGY: Humans are the only known host for *I belli*. Infection is more common in tropical and subtropical climates and in areas with poor sanitary conditions. Infection in humans occurs by the fecal-oral route and has been linked with consumption of contaminated food and water. *Isospora belli* has been reported as a cause of traveler's diarrhea in visitors to areas with endemic infection and as a cause of institutional outbreaks. Noninfectious, unsporulated oocysts are passed in stool. These oocysts require exposure to oxygen and temperatures lower than 37°C (98°F) before becoming infectious. Oocysts are resistant to most disinfectants and can remain viable for months in a cool, moist environment.

The **incubation period** is 8 to 10 days.

DIAGNOSTIC TESTS: Identification of oocysts in feces or in duodenal aspirates or finding developmental stages of the parasite in biopsy specimens of the small intestine are diagnostic. Oocysts in stool are 5 times larger than *Cryptosporidium* organisms and are oval shaped. Oocysts can be detected with modified Kinyoun carbolfuchsin and with auramine-rhodamine stains. Concentration techniques may be needed before staining, because the organisms often are present in small numbers.

TREATMENT: Trimethoprim-sulfamethoxazole for 10 days is the drug of choice but is not recommended for infants younger than 2 months of age (see Drugs for Parasitic Infections, p 790). Pyrimethamine is an alternative treatment for people who cannot tolerate trimethoprim-sulfamethoxazole. Ciprofloxacin also may be effective, although minimal supporting data are available. Ciprofloxacin is not approved for use in people younger than 18 years of age. Maintenance therapy to prevent recurrent disease may be indicated for people infected with HIV.

ISOLATION OF THE HOSPITALIZED PATIENT: As per routine practice, in addition to standard precautions, contact precautions are recommended for diapered and incontinent children.

CONTROL MEASURES: Fresh produce should be washed thoroughly before it is eaten. This precaution may not eliminate the risk of transmission entirely.

Kawasaki Disease
(Mucocutaneous Lymph Node Syndrome)

CLINICAL MANIFESTATIONS: Kawasaki disease is a febrile, exanthematous, multisystem vasculitis of importance, because approximately 20% of untreated children will develop coronary artery abnormalities. Most cases of Kawasaki disease occur in children between 1 and 8 years of age. The illness is characterized by fever and the following clinical features: (1) bilateral bulbar conjunctival injection without exudate; (2) erythematous mouth and pharynx, strawberry tongue, and red, cracked lips; (3) a polymorphous, generalized, erythematous rash that can be morbilliform, maculopapular, or scarlatiniform or may resemble erythema multiforme; (4) changes in the peripheral extremities consisting of induration of the hands and feet with erythematous palms and soles or periungual desquamation; and (5) acute, nonsuppurative cervical lymphadenopathy with at least one node 1.5 cm in diameter. For diagnosis of classic Kawasaki disease, patients should have fever for at least 5 days and at least 4 of these 5 features and no alternative explanation for the findings. Irritability, abdominal pain, diarrhea, and vomiting commonly are associated features. Other findings include urethritis with sterile pyuria (70% of cases), anterior uveitis (25%–50%), mild hepatic dysfunction (40%), arthritis or arthralgia (10%–20%), aseptic meningitis (25%), pericardial effusion (20%–40%), gallbladder hydrops (<10%), and myocarditis manifested by congestive heart failure (<5%). Fine desquamation in the groin area can occur in the acute phase of disease.

Incomplete Kawasaki disease can be diagnosed in febrile patients when fewer than 4 of the characteristic features are present. Incomplete Kawasaki disease is more common in infants younger than 12 months of age than in older children. Infants with Kawasaki disease also have a higher risk of developing coronary artery aneurysms than do older children, making diagnosis and timely treatment especially important in infants. The laboratory findings of incomplete cases are similar to findings of classic cases. Therefore, although laboratory findings in Kawasaki disease are nonspecific, they may prove useful in increasing or decreasing the likelihood of incomplete Kawasaki disease. Early echocardiographic study may be useful in evaluation of patients with suspected incomplete Kawasaki disease. A substantial number of children with Kawasaki disease and coronary artery abnormalities are not identified by the classic case definition. Therefore, incomplete Kawasaki disease should be considered in any child with unexplained fever for ≥5 days in association with ≥2 of the principal features of this illness.

Without aspirin and Immune Globulin Intravenous (IGIV) therapy, fever may last 2 weeks or longer. After fever resolves, patients can remain anorectic or irritable for 2 to 3 weeks. During this phase, desquamation of the groin and then full-thickness desquamation of the fingers and toes and fine desquamation of other areas may occur. Recurrent disease occurring months to years later develops in less than 2% of patients.

Coronary artery abnormalities can be demonstrated with 2-dimensional echocardiography in 20% to 25% of patients who are not treated within 10 days of onset of fever. Patients at increased risk of developing coronary artery aneurysms include males, infants younger than 12 months of age, children older than 8 years of age, people whose fever persists for more than 10 days, children with higher baseline neutrophil and band counts or lower hemoglobin concentrations (<10 g/dL) at presentation, and children with a baseline platelet count <350 000/μL or fever persisting after IGIV administration. Aneurysms of the coronary arteries have been demonstrated by echocardiography as soon as a few days after onset of illness but more typically occur between 1 and 4 weeks after onset of illness; their appearance later than 6 weeks is uncommon. Giant coronary artery aneurysms (≥8 mm in diameter) are likely to be associated with long-term complications. Aneurysms occurring in other medium-sized arteries (eg, iliac, femoral, renal, and axillary vessels) are uncommon and generally do not occur in the absence of coronary abnormalities. In addition to coronary artery disease, carditis can involve the pericardium, myocardium, or endocardium, and mitral and aortic regurgitation can develop. Carditis generally resolves when fever resolves.

In children with mild coronary artery dilation or ectasia, coronary artery dimensions often return to baseline within 6 to 8 weeks after onset of disease. Approximately 50% of nongiant coronary aneurysms regress to normal luminal size within 1 to 2 years, although this process may be accompanied by coronary stenosis. In addition, regression of aneurysm(s) may result in a poorly compliant, fibrotic vessel wall.

The current case fatality rate in the United States is less than 0.1% to 0.2%. The principal cause of death is myocardial infarction resulting from coronary artery occlusion attributable to thrombosis or progressive stenosis. Rarely, a large coronary artery aneurysm may rupture. Most fatalities occur within 6 weeks of the onset of symptoms, but myocardial infarction and sudden death can occur months to years after the acute episode. There is hypothetical concern that the vasculitis of Kawasaki disease may predispose to premature atherosclerotic disease.

ETIOLOGY: The cause is unknown. Epidemiologic and clinical features suggest an infectious cause.

EPIDEMIOLOGY: Peak age of occurrence in the United States is between 18 and 24 months. Fifty percent of patients are younger than 2 years of age, and 80% are younger than 5 years of age; children older than 8 years of age rarely develop the disease. In children younger than 6 months of age, the diagnosis often is delayed because of atypical symptoms. The prevalence of coronary artery abnormalities is higher when diagnosis and treatment are delayed beyond 10 days. The male-female ratio is approximately 1.5:1. The incidence is highest in Asian people; 3000 to 5000 cases are estimated to occur annually in the United States. Kawasaki disease first was described in Japan, where a pattern of endemic occurrence with superimposed epidemic outbreaks was recognized. A similar pattern of steady or increasing endemic disease with occasional sharply defined community-wide epidemics has been recognized in diverse locations in North America and Hawaii. Epidemics generally occur during winter and spring. No evidence indicates person-to-person or common-source spread, although the incidence is slightly higher in siblings of children with the disease.

The **incubation period** is unknown.

DIAGNOSTIC TESTS: No specific diagnostic test is available. The diagnosis is established by fulfillment of the clinical criteria (see Clinical Manifestations, p 412) and exclusion of other possible illnesses, such as measles, parvovirus B19 infection, adenovirus or enterovirus infections, streptococcal infection (ie, scarlet fever), rickettsial exanthems, drug reactions (eg, Stevens-Johnson syndrome), staphylococcal scalded skin syndrome, toxic shock syndrome, leptospirosis, juvenile rheumatoid arthritis, polyarteritis nodosa, and Reiter syndrome.* An increased sedimentation rate and serum C-reactive protein concentration during the first 2 weeks of illness and an increased platelet count (>450 000/μL [>450 × 10^9/L]) after the first week of illness are almost universal laboratory features. These values usually normalize within 6 to 8 weeks.

TREATMENT: Management during the acute phase is directed at decreasing inflammation of the myocardium and coronary artery wall and providing supportive care. Therapy should be initiated when the diagnosis is established or strongly suspected. Once the acute phase has passed, therapy is directed at prevention of coronary artery thrombosis. Specific recommendations for therapy include the following measures:

IMMUNE GLOBULIN INTRAVENOUS. Therapy with high-dose IGIV and aspirin initiated within 10 days of the onset of fever substantially decreases progression to coronary artery dilation and aneurysms at 2 to 7 weeks, compared with treatment with aspirin alone, and results in more rapid resolution of fever and other indicators of acute inflammation. Therapy with IGIV should be initiated as soon as possible; its efficacy when initiated later than the 10th day of illness or after aneurysms have been detected has not been evaluated in controlled trials. However, therapy with IGIV and aspirin should be provided for patients diagnosed after day 10 who have manifestations of continuing inflammation (eg, fever or other symptoms or laboratory abnormalities) or of evolving coronary artery disease. Despite prompt treatment with IGIV and aspirin, 2% to 4% of patients develop coronary artery abnormalities.

DOSE. The optimal therapeutic dose of IGIV is unknown. A dose of 2 g/kg as a single dose, given over 10 to 12 hours, is recommended. Few complications occur from this regimen.

RETREATMENT. Approximately 5% to 10% of patients who receive IGIV and aspirin therapy have persistent fever or recurrence of fever after an initial period of being afebrile for 48 hours or less. In these situations, retreatment with IGIV (2 g/kg) and continued aspirin therapy may be indicated, because persistent fever may be associated with increased concentrations of proinflammatory cytokines and an increased risk of coronary artery abnormalities. At the present time, the use of systemic corticosteroids in treatment of Kawasaki disease is controversial. Earlier studies suggested that patients treated with corticosteroids alone or in combination with aspirin have a higher frequency of coronary artery abnormalities. Reports involving small numbers of patients suggest that for the limited number of patients who are refractory

---

* For further information on the diagnosis of this disease, see Newburger JW, Takahashi M. Gerber MA, et al. Diagnosis, treatment and long-term management of Kawasaki disease: a statement for health professionals from the Committee on Rheumatic Fever, Endocarditis, and Kawasaki Disease, Council on Cardiovascular Disease in the Young, American Heart Association. *Circulation.* 2004;110:2747–2771 (also in *Pediatrics.* 2004;114:1708–1733)

to 2 or 3 doses of IGIV, oral or intravenous methylprednisolone may reduce signs and symptoms of inflammation. The effect of corticosteroids on the vasculitis is unclear.

ASPIRIN. Aspirin is used for anti-inflammatory and antithrombotic actions, although convincing data that aspirin decreases coronary artery abnormalities are not available. Aspirin is administered in doses of 80 to 100 mg/kg per day in 4 divided doses during the acute phase. Children with acute Kawasaki disease have decreased aspirin absorption and increased clearance, so some children may not achieve therapeutic serum concentrations. In most children, this is not clinically significant, and it is not necessary to monitor aspirin concentrations. After fever is controlled for 4 or 5 days, the aspirin dose is decreased to 3 to 5 mg/kg per day to continue antithrombotic activity. Aspirin is discontinued if no coronary artery abnormalities have been detected by 6 to 8 weeks after onset of illness. Low-dose aspirin therapy should be continued indefinitely for people in whom coronary artery abnormalities are present. Because of the potential risk of Reye syndrome in patients with influenza or varicella receiving salicylates, parents of children receiving aspirin should be instructed to contact their child's physician promptly if the child develops symptoms of or is exposed to either disease.

CARDIAC CARE.* An echocardiogram should be obtained early in the acute phase of illness and 6 to 8 weeks after onset. The care of patients with carditis should involve a cardiologist experienced in management of patients with Kawasaki disease and in assessing echocardiographic studies of coronary arteries in children. Long-term management of Kawasaki disease should be based on the extent of coronary artery involvement. Children should be assessed during the first 2 months to detect evidence of arrhythmias, congestive heart failure, and valvular regurgitation. In addition to prolonged low-dose aspirin therapy to suppress platelet aggregation in patients with persistent coronary artery abnormalities, some experts recommend 4 mg/kg per day of dipyridamole, given in 3 divided doses. Development of giant coronary artery aneurysms ($\geq$8 mm in diameter) may require addition of anticoagulant therapy, such as warfarin, to prevent thrombosis.

SUBSEQUENT IMMUNIZATION. Measles and varicella immunizations should be deferred for 11 months after IGIV administration in children who have received high-dose IGIV for treatment of Kawasaki disease. If the child's risk of exposure to measles is high, the child should be immunized and then reimmunized at least 11 months after administration of IGIV unless serologic testing indicates successful immunization by the earlier dose (see Measles, p 441). The schedule for subsequent administration of other childhood immunizations should not be interrupted. Yearly influenza immunization is indicated for children 6 months of age and older who require long-term aspirin therapy because of the possible increased risk of developing Reye syndrome (see Influenza, p 401).

ISOLATION OF THE HOSPITALIZED PATIENT: Standard precautions are indicated.

CONTROL MEASURES: None.

---

* Newburger JW, Takahashi M, Gerber MA, et al. Diagnosis, treatment and long-term management of Kawasaki disease: a statement for health professionals from the Committee on Rheumatic Fever, Endocarditis, and Kawasaki Disease, Council on Cardiovascular Disease in the Young, American Heart Association. *Circulation.* 2004;110:2747–2771 (also in *Pediatrics.* 2004;114:1708–1733)

Kingella kingae Infections

CLINICAL MANIFESTATIONS: The most common infections associated with *Kingella kingae* are suppurative arthritis and osteomyelitis. Almost all of these infections occur in children younger than 5 years of age. *Kingella kingae* may be a major cause of skeletal infections in children younger than 3 years of age. Pyogenic arthritis caused by *K kingae* generally is monoarticular, with a knee being the most commonly involved joint, followed in frequency by a hip or an ankle. Clinical manifestations of pyogenic arthritis are similar to manifestations associated with infection attributable to other bacterial pathogens in immunocompetent children, although a subacute course may be more common. Osteomyelitis caused by *K kingae* has clinical manifestations similar to *Staphylococcus aureus* osteomyelitis, but epiphyseal infection may be more common. The femur is the most common site of osteomyelitis. *Kingella kingae* also has been associated with diskitis, endocarditis in children with underlying heart disease, meningitis, occult bacteremia, and pneumonia.

ETIOLOGY: *Kingella* organisms are fastidious, gram-negative coccobacilli previously classified as *Moraxella*. Of the 3 species in the genus *Kingella*, *K kingae* is the species most commonly associated with infection.

EPIDEMIOLOGY: The human oropharynx is the usual habitat of *K kingae*. The organism more frequently colonizes the respiratory tracts of children than adults and can be transmitted among children in child care centers, generally without causing disease. Infection may be associated with preceding or concomitant stomatitis or upper respiratory tract illness.

The **incubation period** is variable.

DIAGNOSTIC TESTS: *Kingella kingae* can be isolated from blood, synovial fluid, bone exudate, cerebrospinal fluid, respiratory tract secretions, and other sites of infection. Organisms grow better in aerobic conditions with enhanced carbon dioxide. In patients with pyogenic arthritis and osteomyelitis, blood cultures often are negative. *Kingella kingae* is difficult to isolate on routinely used solid media. Synovial fluid and bone aspirates from patients with suspected *K kingae* infection should be inoculated into Bactec, BacT/Alert, or similar blood culture systems and held for at least 7 days to maximize recovery. *Kingella kingae* should be suspected in young children with culture-negative skeletal infections.

TREATMENT: Penicillin is the drug of choice for treatment of invasive infections attributable to beta-lactamase–negative strains of *K kingae*. Other beta-lactam agents also are effective. Strains generally are susceptible to aminoglycosides, ciprofloxacin, erythromycin, chloramphenicol, and oxacillin and are resistant to trimethoprim, clindamycin, and vancomycin. Gentamicin in combination with penicillin can be useful for the initial treatment of endocarditis.

ISOLATION OF THE HOSPITALIZED PATIENT: Standard precautions are recommended.

CONTROL MEASURES: None.

Legionella pneumophila Infections

CLINICAL MANIFESTATIONS: Legionellosis is associated with 2 clinically and epidemiologically distinct illnesses: legionnaires disease and Pontiac fever. Legionnaires disease varies in severity from mild to severe pneumonia characterized by fever, cough, and progressive respiratory distress. Legionnaires disease can be associated with chills, myalgias, and gastrointestinal tract, central nervous system, and renal manifestations. Respiratory failure and death can occur. Pontiac fever is a milder febrile illness without pneumonia that occurs in epidemics and is characterized by an abrupt onset and a self-limited, influenza-like illness.

ETIOLOGY: *Legionella* species are fastidious aerobic bacilli that stain gram negative after recovery on artificial media. At least 20 different species have been implicated in human disease, but most documented *Legionella* infections in the United States are caused by *Legionella pneumophila* serogroup 1.

EPIDEMIOLOGY: Legionnaires' disease is acquired through inhalation of aerosolized water contaminated with *L pneumophila*. Person-to-person transmission has not been demonstrated. More than 80% of cases are sporadic; the sources of infection can be related to exposure to *L pneumophila*-contaminated water in the home, workplace, hospitals, or other medical facilities or to aerosol-producing devices in public places. Outbreaks have been ascribed to common-source exposure to contaminated cooling towers, evaporative condensers, potable water systems, whirlpool spas, humidifiers, and respiratory therapy equipment. Outbreaks have occurred in hospitals, hotels, and other large buildings as well as on cruise ships. Nosocomial infections occur and often are related to contamination of the hot water supply. Legionnaires disease occurs most commonly in people who are elderly, immunocompromised, or have underlying lung disease. Infection in children is rare and usually is asymptomatic or mild and unrecognized. Severe disease has occurred in children with malignant neoplasms, severe combined immunodeficiency, chronic granulomatous disease, organ transplantation, end-stage renal disease or underlying pulmonary disease, and immunosuppression with corticosteroids and as a nosocomial infection in newborn infants.

The **incubation period** for legionnaires disease (pneumonia) is 2 to 10 days; for Pontiac fever, the incubation period is 1 to 2 days.

DIAGNOSTIC TESTS: Recovery of *L pneumophila* from respiratory tract secretions, lung tissue, pleural fluid, or other normally sterile fluid specimens by using special culture media provides definitive evidence of infection, but the sensitivity of culture is laboratory-dependent. Detection of *Legionella* antigens in urine by commercially available immunoassays is highly specific. Such tests are most sensitive for *L pneumophila* serogroup 1, but these tests can detect antigen in some patients infected with other *L pneumophila* serogroups or species. The sensitivity may be higher in patients with more severe pneumonia than in patients with milder disease. The bacterium can be demonstrated in specimens by direct immunofluorescent, but this test is less sensitive and the specificity is technician-dependent and lower than culture or urine immunoassay. For serologic diagnosis, a fourfold increase in titer of antibodies to *L pneumophila* serogroup 1, measured by indirect immunofluorescent antibody (IFA) assay, indicates acute infection. Convalescent serum samples should be obtained 3 to 4 weeks after onset of symptoms; however, an antibody titer increase can be delayed for 8 to 12 weeks. The positive predictive value of a single titer of ≥1:256 is low and does not provide definitive evidence of infection. Antibodies to several gram-negative organisms, including *Pseudomonas* species, *Bacteroides fragilis*, and *Campylobacter jejuni*, may cause false-positive IFA test results. Newer serologic assays, such as enzyme immunoassay or tests using *Legionella* antigens other than serogroup 1, are available commercially but have not been standardized adequately.

TREATMENT: Intravenous azithromycin (10 mg/kg per day as a single dose; maximum 500 mg) has replaced intravenous erythromycin as the drug of choice. Once the condition of a patient is improving, oral therapy can be substituted. Addition of rifampin should be considered for patients with confirmed disease who are severely ill or immunocompromised or in whom the infection does not respond promptly to intravenous azithromycin. Fluoroquinolones, including ciprofloxacin, levofloxacin, moxifloxacin, and gatifloxacin are bactericidal and effective but are not approved for this indication in children younger than 18 years of age. Doxycycline and trimethoprim-sulfamethoxazole are alternative drugs. Doxycycline should not be used by pregnant women and children younger than 8 years of age because of the risk of dental staining. Duration of therapy is 5 to 10 days for azithromycin and 14 to 21 days for other drugs; longer courses are recommended for patients who are immunocompromised or who have severe disease.

ISOLATION OF THE HOSPITALIZED PATIENT: Standard precautions are recommended.

CONTROL MEASURES: Monochloramine (rather than free chlorine) treatment of municipal water supplies has been associated with a decrease in hospital-acquired legionnaires disease. Routinely, hospitals should maintain hot water at the highest temperature allowable by state regulations or codes, preferably ≥60°C (≥140°F) and maintain cold water temperature at <20°C (<68°F) (or periodically superheat the hot water or chlorinate the water [see next paragraph]) to minimize waterborne *Legionella* contamination. Occurrence of even a single laboratory-confirmed nosocomial case of legionellosis warrants consideration of an epidemiologic and environmental investigation. Hospitals with transplantation programs (solid organ or stem cell) should maintain a high index of suspicion of legionellosis, including nosocomial pneumonia attributable to *Legionella* species, use sterile water for the filling and terminal rinsing of nebulization devices, and perform periodic culturing for *Legionella* species in the potable water supply of the transplant unit. Some hospitals may choose to perform periodic, routine culturing of water samples from the hospital's potable water system to detect *Legionella* species.

The main methods for decontaminating potable water supplies to prevent nosocomial cases are hyperchlorination often followed by maintenance of a 1- to 2-mg/L (1- to 2-ppm) free residual chlorine concentration in the heated water, superheating (to ≥66°C [≥150°F]) followed by maintenance of a hot water temperature at the faucet of >50°C (>122°F), treatment of water with copper-silver ionization of electrolysis, or disinfection with ultraviolet light.

Leishmaniasis

CLINICAL MANIFESTATIONS: The 3 major clinical syndromes are as follows:
- *Cutaneous leishmaniasis*. After inoculation by the bite of an infected female phlebotomine sand fly (approximately 2-3 mm long), parasites proliferate locally in mononuclear phagocytes, leading to an erythematous papule, which typically evolves to become a nodule and then a shallow ulcerative lesion with raised borders. Lesions can, however, persist as nodules or papules. Lesions commonly are located on exposed areas of the body (eg, face and extremities) and may be accompanied by satellite lesions, which appear as sporotrichoid-like nodules, and regional adenopathy. Clinical manifestations of Old World and New World (American) cutaneous leishmaniasis are similar. Spontaneous resolution of lesions may take weeks to years and usually results in a flat atrophic (cigarette paper) scar.
- *Mucosal leishmaniasis (espundia)*. Mucosal infection may become clinically evident from months to years after the cutaneous lesions heal; sometimes mucosal and cutaneous lesions are noted simultaneously. Parasites may disseminate to the naso-oropharyngeal mucosa. In some patients, granulomatous ulceration follows, leading to facial disfigurement, secondary infection, and mucosal perforation, which may occur months to years after the initial cutaneous lesion heals.
- *Visceral leishmaniasis (kala-azar)*. After cutaneous inoculation of parasites, organisms spread throughout the mononuclear macrophage system to the spleen, liver, and bone marrow. The resulting clinical illness typically manifests as fever, anorexia, weight loss, splenomegaly, hepatomegaly, lymphadenopathy (in some geographic areas), anemia, leukopenia, thrombocytopenia sometimes associated with hemorrhage, hypoalbuminemia, and hypergammaglobulinemia. Secondary gram-negative enteric and mycobacterial infections are common (eg, tuberculosis). Untreated clinically manifested visceral infection (ie, visceral leishmaniasis) nearly always is fatal. Reactivation of latent visceral infection can occur in patients who become immunocompromised, including people with concurrent human immunodeficiency virus (HIV) infection and recipients of stem cell or solid organ transplants.

ETIOLOGY: In the human host, *Leishmania* species are obligate intracellular parasites of mononuclear phagocytes. Cutaneous leishmaniasis typically is caused by *Leishmania tropica, Leishmania major*, and *Leishmania aethiopica* (Old World species) and by *Leishmania mexicana, Leishmania amazonensis, Leishmania braziliensis, Leishmania panamensis, Leishmania guyanensis*, and *Leishmania peruviana* (New World species). Mucosal leishmaniasis typically is caused by *L braziliensis, L panamensis, and L guyanensis*. Visceral leishmaniasis is caused by *Leishmania donovani, Leishmania infantum*, and *Leishmania chagasi*, which also can cause cutaneous leishmaniasis. However, people with typical cutaneous leishmaniasis caused by these organisms rarely develop visceral leishmaniasis.

EPIDEMIOLOGY: Leishmaniasis typically is a zoonosis with a variety of mammalian reservoir hosts, including canines and rodents. The vectors are female phlebotomine sand flies. There are 88 countries worldwide with endemic leishmaniasis. Leishmaniasis is endemic from northern Argentina to southern Texas (not including Uruguay or

Chile), in southern Europe, Asia (not southeast Asia), the Middle East, and Africa (particularly East and North Africa, with sporadic cases elsewhere) but not in Australia or Oceania. The estimated number of people at risk of infection is approximately 350 million with approximately 500 000 new cases annually. More than 90% of cases worldwide occur in Bangladesh, northeastern India (particularly Bihar State), Nepal, and Sudan (Old World) and in northeastern Brazil (New World). The estimated annual number of new cases of cutaneous leishmaniasis is approximately 1 to 5 million; more than 90% of worldwide cases are in Afghanistan, Algeria, Iran, Iraq, Saudi Arabia, and Syria (Old World) and in Brazil and Peru (New World). Geographic distribution of cases evaluated in the developed world reflects travel and immigration patterns.

The **incubation periods** for the different forms of leishmaniasis range from several days to months. In cutaneous leishmaniasis, primary skin lesions typically appear several weeks after parasite inoculation. In visceral infection, the incubation period typically ranges from weeks to months. However, incubation periods from days to years, and even decades, have been reported.

DIAGNOSTIC TESTS: Definitive diagnosis is made by demonstration of the presence of the parasite. A common way of identifying the parasite is by microscopic identification of intracellular leishmanial organisms on Wright- or Giemsa-stained smears or histologic sections of infected tissues. In cutaneous disease, tissue can be obtained by a 3-mm punch biopsy, by lesion scrapings, or by needle aspiration of the raised nonnecrotic edge of the lesion. In visceral leishmaniasis, the organisms can be identified in the spleen and, less commonly, in bone marrow and liver. The sensitivity is highest for splenic aspiration, but so is the risk. In East Africa in patients with lymphadenopathy, the organisms also can be identified in lymph nodes. Blood cultures, especially of buffy-coat preparations, have been positive in some patients, and organisms sometimes may be observed in blood smears or observed in or cultured from buffy-coat preparations in HIV-infected patients. Isolation of parasites by culture of appropriate tissue specimens in specialized media should be attempted when possible. Culture media and further information can be provided by the Centers for Disease Control and Prevention (CDC) (**www.cdc.gov/travel/diseases.htm#leish**). Investigational polymerase chain reaction assays are available at some reference laboratories.

The diagnosis of some forms of leishmaniasis can be aided by performance of serologic testing, which is available at the CDC. Serologic test results usually are positive in cases of visceral and mucosal leishmaniasis if the patient is immunocompetent but often are negative in cutaneous leishmaniasis. False-positive results may occur in patients with other infectious diseases, especially American trypanosomiasis.

TREATMENT: The decision whether to treat people with leishmaniasis should be made on an individual basis, with the assistance of infectious disease experts or consultation from the CDC Drug Service (404-639-3670). Treatment always is indicated for patients with mucosal or visceral leishmaniasis. Treatment of cutaneous leishmaniasis should be considered, especially if skin lesions are or could become disfiguring (eg, facial lesions or disabling lesions near joints), are persistent, or are known to be or might be caused by leishmanial species that can disseminate to the naso-oropharyngeal mucosa (see Drugs for Parasitic Infections, p 790).

ISOLATION OF THE HOSPITALIZED PATIENT: Standard precautions are recommended.

CONTROL MEASURES: The best way for travelers to prevent leishmaniasis is by protecting themselves from sand fly bites. Vaccines and drugs for preventing infection are not yet available. To decrease risk of being bitten, travelers should:
- Stay in well-screened or air-conditioned areas when feasible. Avoid outdoor activities, especially from dusk to dawn, when sand flies are most active.
- When outside, wear long-sleeved shirts, long pants, and socks.
- Apply insect repellent on uncovered skin and under the ends of sleeves and pant legs. Follow instructions on the label of the repellent. The most effective repellents are those that contain the chemical diethyltoluamide (DEET) (see Prevention of Mosquitoborne Infections, p 197).
- Spray clothing with permethrin-containing insecticides. The insecticide should be reapplied after every 5 washings.
- Spray living and sleeping areas with an insecticide.
- If not sleeping in an area that is well screened or air-conditioned, a bed net tucked under the mattress is recommended. If possible, a bed net that has been soaked in or sprayed with permethrin should be used. The permethrin will be effective for several months if the bed net is not washed. Sand flies are smaller than mosquitoes and, therefore, can get through smaller holes. Fine-mesh netting (at least 18 holes to the inch) is needed for an effective barrier against sand flies. This particularly is important if the bed net has not been treated with permethrin. However, sleeping under such a closely woven bed net in hot weather can be uncomfortable.
- Bed nets, repellents containing DEET, and permethrin should be purchased before traveling.

Leprosy

CLINICAL MANIFESTATIONS: Leprosy (Hansen disease) is a curable infection mainly involving skin, peripheral nerves, the mucosa of the upper respiratory tract, and testes. The clinical syndromes of leprosy represent a spectrum that reflects the cellular immune response to *Mycobacterium leprae* and the unique tropism for peripheral nerves. The 2 poles of the leprosy spectrum are tuberculoid and lepromatous forms. Characteristic features are the following:
- *Tuberculoid:* one or a few well-demarcated, hypopigmented or erythematous, hypoesthetic or anesthetic skin lesions, often with raised, active, spreading edges and central clearing. Cell-mediated immune responses are intact.
- *Lepromatous:* initial numerous, ill-defined, hypopigmented, or erythematous maculae that progress to papules, nodules, or plaques; and late-occurring hypoesthesia. Dermal infiltration of the face, hands, and feet in a bilateral and symmetric distribution can occur without preceding maculopapular lesions. *Mycobacterium leprae*-specific, cell-mediated immunity is diminished greatly, but serum antibody responses to *M leprae*-derived antigens may occur, or titers of nonspecific antibodies (such as rheumatoid factor or syphilis [on nontreponemal tests]) may be increased.

The cell-mediated immunity of most patients, and therefore their clinical presentation, occurs between these 2 extremes. Leprosy rashes usually do not itch or hurt; they lack sensation to heat, touch, and pain. The classic presentation of the "leonine facies" and loss of lateral eyebrows (medarosis) occurs in patients with end-stage lepromatous leprosy. A simplified scheme introduced by the World Health Organization classifies leprosy involving 1 to 5 patches of skin as paucibacillary and leprosy involving more than 5 patches as multibacillary.

Serious consequences of leprosy occur from immune reactions and nerve involvement with resulting anesthesia, which can lead to repeated unrecognized trauma, ulcerations, fractures, and bone resorption. A diagnosis of leprosy should be considered in any patient with hypoesthetic or anesthetic skin rash.

ETIOLOGY: Leprosy is caused by *M leprae*, an obligate intracellular, acid-fast bacillus that can be Gram-stain variable.

EPIDEMIOLOGY: Leprosy primarily is a disease of poverty and rural residency. Approximately 95% of people are immune genetically to infection with *M leprae*, and approximately 5% are genetically susceptible. Accordingly, spouses of leprosy patients are not likely to develop leprosy, but biologic parents, children, and siblings who are household contacts of untreated patients with leprosy are at increased risk. The major source of infectious material probably is nasal secretions from patients with untreated or drug-resistant infection. Little shedding of *M leprae* from involved intact skin occurs. People with human immunodeficiency virus (HIV) infection are not at increased risk of becoming infected, and HIV infection does not affect the outcome of leprosy. In 2004, 105 new cases of leprosy were reported in the United States. Native-born US citizens with leprosy predominantly were from Texas, Louisiana, New York, and California. Foreign-born patients with leprosy (>80% of reported cases) immigrated predominantly from Mexico, India, the Dominican Republic, Brazil, and the Philippines. The infectivity of lepromatous patients probably ceases after treatment is instituted, often within a few days or weeks of initiating rifampin therapy or approximately 3 months after initiating therapy with dapsone or clofazimine. Contaminated soil or insect vectors may play a role in disease transmission.

The **incubation period** ranges from 1 to many years but usually is 3 to 5 years. The incubation period of tuberculoid cases tends to be shorter than that for lepromatous cases.

DIAGNOSTIC TESTS: Histopathologic examination by an experienced pathologist is the best method of establishing the diagnosis and is the basis for classification of leprosy. Skin biopsies should be stained with hematoxylin and eosin stains as well as an acid-fast stain, preferably Fite-Faraco stain. Acid-fast bacilli may be found in slit-smears or biopsy specimens of skin lesions but rarely from patients with the tuberculoid and indeterminate forms of disease. Organisms have not been cultured successfully in vitro. Drug resistance is tested by the mouse footpad inoculation test, which is performed only in specialized laboratories.

A polymerase chain reaction test for *M leprae* is available on a limited basis after consultation from the National Hansen's Disease Programs (800-642-2477; **www.bphc.hrsa.gov/nhdp**). No serologic test is available for routine diagnosis of leprosy.

TREATMENT: Therapy for patients with leprosy should be undertaken in consultation with an expert in leprosy. The National Hansen's Disease Programs (225-756-3701 for clinical information) provides consultation on clinical and pathologic issues and can provide information about local Hansen disease clinics and clinicians who have experience with the disease.

Leprosy is curable. The primary goal of therapy is prevention of permanent nerve damage, which can be accomplished by early diagnosis and treatment. Combination antimicrobial therapy called multidrug therapy (MDT) can be obtained free of charge in the United States from the National Hansen's Disease Programs. It is important to treat *M leprae* infections with more than 1 antimicrobial agent to minimize development of antimicrobial-resistant organisms. Adults are treated with dapsone, rifampin, and clofazimine. As of November 1, 2005, clofazimine is available in the United States only under an investigational new drug protocol and for treatment of adults. Clofazimine is not available for administration to children and pregnant women.

TREATMENT REGIMENS RECOMMENDED BY THE NATIONAL HANSEN'S DISEASE PROGRAMS

Multibacillary leprosy (≥6 patches):

1. Dapsone, 100 mg/day, orally, for 24 months. Pediatric dose: 1 mg/kg, orally, every 24 hours. Maximum dose: 100 mg/day for 24 months

AND

2. Rifampin, 600 mg/day, orally, for 24 months. Pediatric dose: 10 mg/kg per day for 24 months

AND

3. Clofazimine, 50 mg/day, orally, for 24 months (for nonpregnant adults only under investigational new drug protocol)

Paucibacillary leprosy (1–5 patches):

1. Dapsone, 100 mg/day, orally, for 12 months. Pediatric dose: 1 to 2 mg/kg, orally, every 24 hours. Maximum dose: 100 mg/day for 12 months

AND

2. Rifampin, 600 mg/day, orally, for 24 months. Pediatric dose: 10 to 20 mg/kg per day, orally, for 12 months

Before beginning antimicrobial therapy, patients should be tested for glucose-6-phosphate dehydrogenase deficiency, have baseline complete blood cell counts and liver function tests documented, and be evaluated for any evidence of tuberculosis infection, especially if the patient is infected with HIV. This consideration is important to avoid monotherapy of active tuberculosis with rifampin while treating active Hansen disease.

All patients with Hansen disease should be educated about the signs and symptoms of neuritis and cautioned to immediately report signs and symptoms of neuritis so that corticosteroid therapy can be instituted immediately if this develops. This is important to avoid permanent neurologic damage. Expert advice from the National Hansen's Disease Programs should be obtained for these cases.

Relapse of disease after completing MDT is rare (0.01%–0.14% of patients with Hansen disease) and may present as new skin patches with loss of skin sensation. Relapse usually is attributable to reactivation of drug-susceptible organisms. People with relapses of disease require another course of MDT.

Adverse reactions of MDT commonly include darkening of skin caused by daily clofazimine therapy. This will go away within several months of completing the clofazimine therapy. False serologic test results for syphilis and HIV may occur in patients with lepromatous leprosy.

Reactions should be treated aggressively to prevent peripheral nerve damage. Treatment may begin with prednisone, 1 mg/kg per day, orally. The severe type 2 reaction, known as erythema nodosum leprosum (ENL), occurs in patients with multibacillary leprosy. Treatment with thalidomide is available for ENL under the Calgene S.T.E.P.S. program (888-771-0141) and is used under strict supervision because of its teratogenicity. Thalidomide is not approved for use in children younger than 12 years of age. Most patients can be treated as outpatients. Rehabilitative measures, including surgery and physical therapy, may be necessary for some patients.

ISOLATION OF THE HOSPITALIZED PATIENT: Standard precautions are indicated.

CONTROL MEASURES: Hand hygiene is recommended for all people in contact with a patient with lepromatous leprosy. Disinfection of nasal secretions, handkerchiefs, and other fomites should be considered until treatment is established. Household contacts, particularly contacts of patients with multibacillary disease, should be examined initially and then annually for 5 years. Postnatal transmission can occur during breastfeeding. Chemoprophylaxis is not recommended. Local public health department regulations for leprosy vary and should be consulted.

A single bacille Calmette-Guérin (BCG) immunization is reported to be approximately 50% protective against leprosy, and administration of 1 or 2 additional doses increases the protection further. The first commercially available leprosy vaccine was approved in India in January 1998. This vaccine was approved as an "immunotherapeutic adjuvant" to be used with multidrug therapy; this vaccine is not available in the United States. Neither BCG nor the heat-killed leprosy vaccine is recommended for use in household contacts of people with leprosy in the United States.

Newly diagnosed or suspected cases of leprosy in the United States should be reported to local and state public health departments, the Centers for Disease Control and Prevention, and the National Hansen's Disease Programs.

Leptospirosis

CLINICAL MANIFESTATIONS: Leptospirosis is an acute febrile disease with varied manifestations resulting from generalized vasculitis. The severity of disease ranges from self-limited systemic illness (approximately 90% of patients) to life-threatening illness with jaundice, renal failure, and hemorrhagic pneumonitis. Regardless of its severity, onset usually is characterized by nonspecific symptoms, including fever, chills, headache, nausea, vomiting, and a transient rash. The most distinct clinical findings are conjunctival suffusion without purulent discharge (30%–40% of cases) and myalgias of the calf and lumbar regions (80% of cases). This initial "septicemic" phase usually lasts for 3 to 7 days and can be followed by a second "immune-mediated" phase. In some patients, these 2 phases are separated by a short-lived abatement of fever (1–3 days). Findings commonly associated with the immune-mediated phase include fever, aseptic meningitis, conjunctival suffusion, uveitis, muscle tenderness, adenopathy, and purpuric rash. Approximately 10% of patients have severe illness, including jaundice and renal dysfunction (Weil syndrome), hemorrhagic pneumonitis, cardiac arrhythmias, or circulatory collapse associated with a case fatality rate of 5% to 40%. The overall duration of symptoms for both phases of disease varies from less than 1 week to several months.

ETIOLOGY: Leptospirosis is caused by spirochetes of the genus *Leptospira*. Leptospires are classified into a number of species defined by their degree of genetic relatedness as determined by DNA reassociation. There are 13 named pathogenic and nonpathogenic species. The genome sequence of *Leptospira interrogans* serovar Lai has been determined.

EPIDEMIOLOGY: The reservoirs for *Leptospira* species include a wide range of wild and domestic animals that may remain asymptomatic shedders for years. *Leptospira* organisms excreted in animal urine, amniotic fluid, or placental tissue are viable in soil or water for weeks to months. Humans become infected through contact of mucosal surfaces or abraded skin with contaminated soil, water, or animal tissues. People who are predisposed by occupation include abattoir and sewer workers, veterinarians, farmers, and military personnel. Recreational exposures and clusters of disease have been associated with wading, swimming (especially swallowing water), or boating in contaminated water, particularly during flooding. Person-to-person transmission is rare.

The **incubation period** usually is 5 to 14 days, with a range of 2 to 30 days.

DIAGNOSTIC TESTS: *Leptospira* organisms may be isolated from blood or cerebrospinal fluid specimens during the early septicemic phase of illness and from urine specimens after day 7 to 10 of illness. However, isolation of the organism can be very difficult, requiring special media and techniques and incubation for up to 16 weeks. In addition, the sensitivity of culture for diagnosis is low. For these reasons, serum specimens always should be obtained to facilitate serologic diagnosis. Antibodies usually develop during the second week of illness and can be measured by commercially available immunoassays; however, increases in antibody titer can be delayed or absent in some patients. Microscopic agglutination, the confirmatory serologic test, is performed only in reference laboratories and requires both acute and convalescent specimens. Immunohistochemical techniques can detect leptospiral antigens in infected tissues. Polymerase chain reaction assays for detection of *Leptospira* organisms have been developed but are available only in research laboratories.

TREATMENT: Intravenous penicillin is the drug of choice for patients requiring hospitalization. Penicillin G decreases the duration of systemic symptoms and the persistence of associated laboratory abnormalities and may prevent development of leptospiruria. As with other spirochete infections, a Jarisch-Herxheimer reaction (an acute febrile reaction accompanied by headache, myalgia, and an aggravated clinical picture lasting less than 24 hours) can develop after initiation of penicillin therapy. For patients with mild disease, oral doxycycline has been shown to shorten the course of illness and decrease the occurrence of leptospiruria. Doxycycline should not be used in pregnant women or children younger than 8 years of age because of the risk of dental staining. Ceftriaxone is an alternative therapy.

ISOLATION OF THE HOSPITALIZED PATIENT: In addition to standard precautions, contact precautions are recommended for contact with urine.

CONTROL MEASURES:
- Immunization of animals may prevent clinical disease attributable to infecting serovars contained within the vaccine. However, immunization may not prevent animals from shedding leptospires in their urine, thus contaminating environments with which humans can come in contact.
- In areas with known endemic infection, reservoir control programs may be useful.
- Swimmers should attempt to avoid swallowing water in potentially contaminated fresh water.
- Protective clothing, boots, and gloves should be worn to decrease risk to people with occupational exposure.
- Doxycycline, 200 mg, given orally once a week to adults, may provide effective prophylaxis and could be considered for high-risk occupational groups with short-term exposure. However, indications for prophylactic doxycycline use for children have not been established.

Listeria monocytogenes Infections
(Listeriosis)

CLINICAL MANIFESTATIONS: Listeriosis is a severe but relatively uncommon infection caused by *Listeria monocytogenes*. Listeriosis primarily is foodborne and occurs most frequently among people who are older, pregnant, or immunocompromised. Infections in children are categorized as maternal, neonatal, or childhood with or without associated predisposing conditions. Maternal infections can be associated with an influenza-like illness, fever, malaise, headache, gastrointestinal tract symptoms, and back pain. Neonatal illnesses have early-onset and late-onset syndromes similar to those of group B streptococcal infections. Prematurity, pneumonia, and septicemia are common in early-onset disease. Approximately 65% of women experience a symptomatic prodromal illness before the diagnosis of listeriosis in their fetus or newborn infant. Amnionitis during labor, brown staining of amniotic fluid, or asymptomatic perinatal infection can occur. An erythematous rash with small, pale nodules characterized histologically by granulomas can occur in severe newborn infection and is termed "granulomatosis infantisepticum." Late-onset infections occur after the first week of life and usually result in meningitis. Infection occurs most commonly in the perinatal period. Clinical features for which listeriosis should be considered outside the neonatal period or pregnancy are meningitis or parenchymal brain infection in (1) immunocompromised hosts, including people with organ transplantation, acquired immunodeficiency syndrome, hematologic malignancies, or immunosuppression attributable to corticosteroids; (2) people older than 50 years of age; (3) people with meningitis and parenchymal brain infection together; (4) people with subcortical brain abscess; or (5) people for whom reports from the laboratory indicate "diphtheroids" on Gram stain or culture. *Listeria monocytogenes* also may cause rhombencephalitis (brain stem encephalitis), brain abscess, and endocarditis. Outbreaks caused by contaminated food usually are characterized clinically by fever and diarrhea.

ETIOLOGY: *Listeria monocytogenes* is an aerobic, nonspore-forming, motile, gram-positive bacillus that produces a narrow zone of hemolysis on blood agar medium.

EPIDEMIOLOGY: *Listeria monocytogenes* is distributed widely in the environment and is an important cause of zoonoses, especially in herd animals. Foodborne transmission causes outbreaks and sporadic infections. Incriminated foods include unpasteurized milk and soft cheeses; prepared ready-to-eat meats, such as hot dogs, deli meat, and pâté; undercooked poultry; and unwashed raw vegetables. Asymptomatic fecal and vaginal carriage in pregnant women can result in sporadic neonatal disease from transplacental or ascending routes of infection or from exposure during delivery. Maternal infection is associated with abortion, preterm delivery, and fetal death. Late-onset neonatal infection can result from acquisition of the organism during passage through the birth canal or from environmental sources, followed by hematogenous invasion of the organism from intestine. Nosocomial nursery outbreaks also have occurred. In 2004, 753 new cases of listeriosis were reported in the United States.

The **incubation period** is variable, ranging from 1 day to more than 3 weeks.

DIAGNOSTIC TESTS: The organism can be recovered on blood agar media from cultures of blood, cerebrospinal fluid (CSF), meconium, gastric washings, placental tissue, amniotic fluid, and other infected tissue specimens, including joint, pleural, or pericardial fluid. Gram stain of gastric aspirate material, placental tissue, biopsy specimens of the rash of early-onset infection, or CSF from an infected patient may demonstrate the organism. *Listeria monocytogenes* can be mistaken for a contaminant or saprophyte because of its morphologic similarity to diphtheroids and streptococci.

TREATMENT:
- Initial therapy with intravenous ampicillin and an aminoglycoside, usually gentamicin, is recommended for severe infections. This combination is more effective than ampicillin alone in vitro and in animal models of *L monocytogenes* infection. In immunocompetent hosts, ampicillin alone can be given once a favorable clinical response has occurred or for patients with mild infections. For the penicillin-allergic patient, the alternative regimen is trimethoprim-sulfamethoxazole. Cephalosporins are not active against *L monocytogenes*.
- For invasive infections without associated meningitis, treatment for 10 to 14 days usually is sufficient. For *L monocytogenes* meningitis, most experts recommend 14 to 21 days of treatment. Longer courses are needed for patients who are severely ill or who have endocarditis or rhomboencephalitis.

ISOLATION OF THE HOSPITALIZED PATIENT: Standard precautions are recommended.

CONTROL MEASURES:
- Antimicrobial therapy for infection diagnosed during pregnancy may prevent fetal or perinatal infection and its consequences.
- The incidence of listeriosis has decreased substantially since 1989, when US regulatory agencies began enforcing rigorous screening guidelines for *L monocytogenes* in ready-to-eat foods.
- The general guidelines for preventing listeriosis are similar to those for preventing other foodborne illnesses: (1) thoroughly cook raw foods from animal

Table 3.30. Dietary Recommendations for People at High Risk of Listeriosis[1]

- Avoid soft cheeses (eg, feta, Brie, Camembert, blue-veined, and Mexican queso fresco cheese). Hard cheeses; processed cheeses, including sliced cheese, cream cheese, cheese spreads, and cottage cheese; and yogurt need not be avoided
- Cook leftover foods or ready-to-eat foods (eg, hot dogs) until steaming hot before eating
- Avoid foods from delicatessen counters (eg, prepared salads, meats, cheeses) or heat/reheat these foods until steaming before eating
- Avoid refrigerated pâtés and other meat spreads or heat/reheat these foods before eating; canned or shelf-stable pâté and meat spreads need not be avoided
- Avoid raw or unpasteurized milk, including goat's milk, or milk products or foods that contain unpasteurized milk or milk products

[1] Pregnant women and people who are immunocompromised by illness or therapy are at high risk.

sources; (2) wash raw vegetables; (3) keep uncooked meats separate from vegetables, uncooked foods, and ready-to-eat foods; (4) avoid unpasteurized dairy products; and (5) wash hands, knives, and cutting boards after exposure to uncooked foods. In addition, people at high risk of listeriosis (pregnant women and immunocompromised people) should follow the dietary recommendations in Table 3.30.

- Listerosis is a nationally notifiable disease in the United States; cases should be reported to the regional health department to facilitate early recognition and control of common-source outbreaks.

Lyme Disease
(Lyme borreliosis, *Borrelia burgdorferi* Infection)

CLINICAL MANIFESTATIONS: The clinical manifestations of Lyme disease are divided into 3 stages: early localized, early disseminated, and late disease. Early localized disease is characterized by a distinctive rash, *erythema migrans*, at the site of a recent tick bite. Erythema migrans begins as a red macule or papule that usually expands over days to weeks to form a large, annular, erythematous lesion that may increase in size to 5 cm or more in diameter, sometimes with partial central clearing. The lesion usually is painless and not pruritic. Localized erythema migrans can vary greatly in size and shape and may have vesicular or necrotic areas in its center and can be confused with cellulitis. Fever, malaise, headache, mild neck stiffness, myalgia, and arthralgia often accompany the rash of early localized disease.

Early disseminated disease manifests most commonly as multiple erythema migrans in approximately 15% of patients. This rash usually occurs several weeks after an infective tick bite and consists of secondary annular, erythematous lesions similar to, but usually smaller than, the primary lesion. These lesions reflect spirochetemia with cutaneous dissemination. Other common manifestations of early disseminated illness (that may occur with or without rash) are palsies of the cranial nerves (especially cranial nerve VII), lymphocytic meningitis, and conjunctivitis. Systemic symptoms, such as arthralgia, myalgia, headache, and fatigue, also are common during the early disseminated stage. Carditis, which usually is characterized by various degrees of heart block, occurs rarely in children. Among infected children who do not receive antimicrobial therapy, approximately 50% develop arthritis, approximately 10% develop central nervous system disease, and less than 5% develop cardiac involvement. Some individuals with early Lyme disease may have concurrent human granulocytic ehrlichiosis or babesiosis, transmitted by the same tick, which may contribute to symptomatology.

Late disease is characterized most commonly by recurrent arthritis that usually is pauciarticular and affects large joints, particularly knees. Arthritis can occur without a history of earlier stages of illness (including erythema migrans). Peripheral neuropathy and central nervous system manifestations also can occur rarely during late disease. Late disease is uncommon in children who are treated with antimicrobial agents in the early stage of disease.

Because congenital infection occurs with other spirochetal infections, there has been concern that an infected pregnant woman could transmit *Borrelia burgdorferi* to her fetus. No causal relationship between maternal Lyme disease and abnormalities of pregnancy or congenital disease caused by *B burgdorferi* has been documented conclusively. No evidence exists that Lyme disease can be transmitted via human milk.

ETIOLOGY: In the United States, infection is caused by the spirochete *B burgdorferi*.

EPIDEMIOLOGY: Lyme disease occurs primarily in 3 distinct geographic regions of the United States. Most cases occur in southern New England and in the eastern mid-Atlantic states. The disease also occurs, but with lower frequency, in the upper Midwest, especially Wisconsin and Minnesota, and less commonly on the West Coast, especially northern California. The occurrence of cases in the United States correlates with the distribution and frequency of infected tick vectors—*Ixodes scapularis* in the East and Midwest and *Ixodes pacificus* in the West. Reported cases from states without known enzootic risks may have been acquired in states with endemic infection or may be misdiagnoses resulting from false-positive serologic test results. Rash similar to erythema migrans has been reported in states without endemic infection, possibly attributable to other *Borrelia* species harbored in the Lone Star tick. Most cases occur between April and October; more than 50% of cases occur during June and July. People of all ages may be affected, but incidence in the United States is highest among children 5 to 9 years of age and adults 45 to 54 years of age.

The **incubation period** from tick bite to appearance of single or multiple erythema migrans lesions ranges from 1 to 55 days with a median of 11 days. Late manifestations occur months to years later.

Endemic Lyme disease transmitted by *Amblyomma americanum* has been reported in Canada, Europe, states of the former Soviet Union, China, and Japan. Clinical manifestations vary somewhat from those seen in the United States.

DIAGNOSTIC TESTS: During the early stages of Lyme disease, the diagnosis is best made clinically by recognizing the characteristic rash, a singular lesion of erythema migrans, because antibodies against *B burgdorferi* are not detectable in most individuals within the first few weeks after infection. Although cultures of a biopsy specimen of the perimeter of the skin lesion often yield the organism, cultures of *Borrelia* species (which require special media) are not available commercially and are not recommended. Diagnosis in patients who possibly have early disseminated or late Lyme disease should be based on clinical findings and serologic tests. Some patients who are treated with antimicrobial agents for early Lyme disease never develop antibodies against *B burgdorferi*. However, most patients with early disseminated disease and virtually all patients with late disease have antibodies against *B burgdorferi*. Once such antibodies develop, they persist for many years and perhaps for life. Consequently, tests for antibodies should not be used to assess the success of treatment. The results of serologic tests for Lyme disease should be interpreted with careful consideration of the clinical setting and the quality of the testing laboratory.

A 2-step approach is recommended for serologic diagnosis of *B burgdorferi*. First, a screening test for serum antibodies should be performed using a sensitive enzyme immunoassay (EIA) or immunofluorescent antibody assay (IFA). Serum specimens that give positive or equivocal results should then be tested by a standardized Western immunoblot for presence of antibodies to *B burgdorferi*; serum specimens that yield negative results by EIA or IFA do not require immunoblot testing. When testing to confirm early disease, immunoglobulin (Ig) G and IgM immunoblot assays should be performed. To confirm late disease, only an IgG immunoblot assay should be performed, because false-positive results may occur with the IgM immunoblot. A positive result of an IgG immunoblot test requires detection of antibody ("bands") to 5 or more of the following: 18, 23/24, 28, 30, 39, 41, 45, 60, 66, and 93 kDa polypeptides. A positive test result of IgM immunoblot requires detection of antibody to at least 2 of the 23/24, 39, and 41 kDa polypeptides. Two-step testing is needed, because EIA and IFA may yield false-positive results because of the presence of antibodies directed against spirochetes in normal oral flora that cross-react with antigens of *B burgdorferi* or to cross-reactive antibodies in patients with other spirochetal infections (eg, syphilis, leptospirosis, relapsing fever), certain viral infections (eg, varicella, Epstein-Barr virus), or certain autoimmune diseases (eg, systemic lupus erythematosus).

A licensed serologic test detects antibody to a peptide of the immunodominant conserved region of the variable surface antigen vlsE of *B burgdorferi* but has not proved to be superior in specificity or sensitivity to the 2-step protocol. This test has clinical utility in distinguishing evidence of infection from vaccine-induced antibody in OspA vaccine recipients. Other marketed tests, including polymerase chain reaction (PCR) for spirochete DNA and urinary antigen detection, have no role in diagnosis.

Suspected central nervous system Lyme disease can be confirmed by demonstration of intrathecal production of antibodies against *B burgdorferi*. However, interpretation of results of antibody tests of cerebrospinal fluid is complex, and physicians should seek the advice of a specialist experienced in the management of patients with Lyme disease to assist in interpreting results.

The widespread practice of ordering serologic tests for patients with nonspecific symptoms, such as fatigue or arthralgia, who have a low probability of having Lyme disease is not recommended. Almost all positive serologic test results in these patients are false-positive results. Patients with acute Lyme disease almost always have objective signs of infection (eg, erythema migrans, facial nerve palsy, arthritis). Nonspecific symptoms commonly accompany these specific signs but almost never are the only evidence of Lyme disease.

TREATMENT: See Table 3.31.

EARLY LOCALIZED DISEASE. Doxycycline is the drug of choice for children 8 years of age and older and, unlike amoxicillin, also treats patients with ehrlichiosis.

Table 3.31. Recommended Treatment of Lyme Disease in Children

Disease Category	Drug(s) and Dose[1]
Early localized disease[1]	
8 y of age or older	Doxycycline, 100 mg, orally, twice a day for 14–21 days[2]
All ages	Amoxicillin, 50 mg/kg per day, orally, divided into 3 doses (maximum 1.5 g/day) for 14–21 days **OR** Cefuroxime, 30 mg/kg per day in 2 divided doses (maximum 1000 mg/day) or 1.0 g/day for 14–21 days
Early disseminated and late disease	
Multiple erythema migrans	Same oral regimen as for early localized disease, but for 21 days
Isolated facial palsy	Same oral regimen as for early localized disease, but for 21–28 days[3,4]
Arthritis	Same oral regimen as for early localized disease, but for 28 days
Persistent or recurrent arthritis[5]	Ceftriaxone sodium, 75–100 mg/kg, IV or IM, once a day (maximum 2 g/day), for 14–28 days; **OR** Penicillin, 300 000 U/kg per day, IV, given in divided doses every 4 h (maximum 20 million U/day) for 14–28 days **OR** Same oral regimen as for early disease
Carditis	Ceftriaxone or penicillin: see persistent or recurrent arthritis
Meningitis or encephalitis	Ceftriaxone[6] or penicillin: see persistent or recurrent arthritis, but for 14–28 days

IV indicates intravenously; IM, intramuscularly.

[1] For patients who are allergic to penicillin, cefuroxime and erythromycin are alternative drugs.

[2] Tetracyclines are contraindicated in pregnancy.

[3] Corticosteroids should not be given.

[4] Treatment has no effect on the resolution of facial nerve palsy; its purpose is to prevent late disease.

[5] Arthritis is not considered persistent or recurrent unless objective evidence of synovitis exists at least 2 months after treatment is initiated. Some experts administer a second course of an oral agent before using an IV-administered antimicrobial agent.

[6] Ceftriaxone should be administered IV for treatment of meningitis or encephalitis.

For children younger than 8 years of age, amoxicillin is recommended. For patients who are allergic to penicillin, the alternative drug is cefuroxime. Erythromycin and azithromycin are less effective. Most experts treat people with early Lyme disease for 14 to 21 days.

Treatment of erythema migrans almost always prevents development of later stages of Lyme disease. Erythema migrans usually resolves within several days of initiating treatment, but other signs and symptoms may persist for several weeks, even in successfully treated patients.

EARLY DISSEMINATED AND LATE DISEASE. Orally administered antimicrobial agents are recommended for treating multiple erythema migrans and uncomplicated Lyme arthritis. Most experts also recommend oral agents for treatment of facial nerve palsy and do not recommend a lumbar puncture unless other central nervous system involvement, such as signs or symptoms of meningitis or raised intracranial pressure, are present. If cerebrospinal fluid pleocytosis is found, parenterally administered antimicrobial therapy is indicated. Recurrent or persistent arthritis after treatment with a course of oral antibiotic therapy and central nervous system infection should be treated with parenterally administered antimicrobial agents. The optimal duration of therapy for manifestations of early disseminated or late disease is not well established, but there is no evidence that children with any manifestation of Lyme disease benefit from prolonged courses of orally or parenterally administered antimicrobial agents. Accordingly, the maximum duration of a single course of therapy is 4 weeks (see Table 3.31, p 431).

The Jarisch-Herxheimer reaction (an acute febrile reaction accompanied by headache, myalgia, and an aggravated clinical picture lasting less than 24 hours) can occur when therapy is initiated. Nonsteroidal anti-inflammatory agents may be beneficial, and the antimicrobial agent should be continued.

PREGNANCY. Tetracyclines are contraindicated. Otherwise, therapy is the same as recommended for nonpregnant people.

ISOLATION OF THE HOSPITALIZED PATIENT: Standard precautions are recommended.

CONTROL MEASURES:

TICKS. See Prevention of Tickborne Infections, p 195.

CHEMOPROPHYLAXIS. Many people who seek medical attention for a tick bite have been bitten by a species of tick that does not transmit Lyme disease, or the recovered material is not a tick. The overall risk of infection with *B burgdorferi* after a recognized deer tick bite, even in areas with highly endemic rates of infection, is sufficiently low that prophylactic antimicrobial treatment is not indicated routinely for most people. The risk is extremely low after attachment (eg, a flat nonengorged deer tick is found) and is higher after engorgement, especially if a nymphal deer tick has been attached for at least 72 hours. Analysis of the tick for spirochete infection has a poor predictive value and is not recommended. On the basis of a study of doxycycline for prevention of Lyme disease after a deer tick bite, some experts recommend a single 200-mg dose (4.4 mg/kg for body weight <45 kg) of doxycycline for people 12 years of age (the lower limit of age studied) and older who have been bitten in an area with hyperendemic infection who have found an engorged deer tick, especially if the suspected duration of attachment is ≥72 hours; gastrointestinal tract adverse effects occur commonly. Data are insufficient to recommend amoxicillin prophylaxis.

BLOOD DONATION. Patients with active disease should not donate blood, because spirochetemia occurs in early Lyme disease. Patients who have been treated for Lyme disease can be considered for blood donation.

VACCINES. A Lyme disease vaccine was licensed by the US Food and Drug Administration on December 21, 1998, for people 15 to 70 years of age but subsequently was withdrawn in early 2002 and no longer is available.

Lymphatic Filariasis
(Bancroftian, Malayan, and Timorian)

CLINICAL MANIFESTATIONS: Most filarial infections are asymptomatic. Even in asymptomatic people, adult filarial worms commonly cause subclinical lymphatic dilatation and dysfunction. Lymphadenopathy is the most common clinical sign of lymphatic filariasis in children, most frequently of the inguinal, crural, and epitrochlear lymph nodes, in association with living adult worms. Death of the adult worm triggers an acute inflammatory response, which progresses distally (retrograde) along the affected lymphatic vessel, usually in the limbs. If present, systemic symptoms, such as headache or fever, usually are mild. In postpubertal males, adult *Wuchereria bancrofti* organisms are found most commonly in the intrascrotal lymphatic vessels; thus, inflammation resulting from adult worm death may present as funiculitis, epididymitis, or orchitis. A tender granulomatous nodule is palpable at the site of the dead adult worms. The chronic manifestations of lymphedema and hydrocele rarely occur in children. Recurrent secondary bacterial infections hasten the progression of lymphedema to its advanced stage, known as elephantiasis. Chyluria can occur as a manifestation of bancroftian filariasis. Cough, fever, marked eosinophilia, and high serum immunoglobulin E concentrations are manifestations of the tropical pulmonary eosinophilia syndrome.

ETIOLOGY: Filariasis is caused by 3 filarial nematodes: *Wuchereria bancrofti*, *Brugia malayi*, and *Brugia timori*.

EPIDEMIOLOGY: The parasite is transmitted by the bite of infected species of various genera of mosquitoes, including *Culex*, *Aedes*, *Anopheles*, and *Mansonia*. *Wuchereria bancrofti* is found in Haiti, the Dominican Republic, Guyana, Brazil, sub-Saharan and North Africa, and Asia, extending into a broad zone from India through the Indonesian archipelago into Oceania. Humans are the only definitive host for the parasite. *Brugia malayi* is found mostly in Southeast Asia and parts of India. *Brugia timori* is restricted to certain islands at the eastern end of the Indonesian archipelago. Because adult worms are long lived (5–8 years on average) and reinfection is common, microfilariae infective for mosquitoes may remain in the patient's blood for decades; individual microfilaria have a life span up to 1.5 years. The adult worm is not transmissible from person to person or by blood transfusion, but microfilariae may be transmitted by transfusion.

The **incubation period** is not well established; the period from acquisition to the appearance of microfilariae in blood can be 3 to 12 months, depending on the species of parasite.

DIAGNOSTIC TESTS: Microfilariae can be detected microscopically on blood smears obtained at night (10 PM–4 AM). Adult worms or microfilariae can be identified in tissue specimens obtained at biopsy. Serologic enzyme immunoassay tests are available, but interpretation of results is affected by cross-reactions of filarial antibodies with antibodies against other helminths. Assays for circulating parasite antigen of *W bancrofti* are available commercially but are not licensed by the US Food and Drug Administration. Lymphatic filariasis often must be diagnosed clinically, because dependable serologic assays are not available uniformly, and in patients with lymphedema, the microfilariae no longer may be present.

TREATMENT: The main goal of treatment of an infected person is to kill the adult worm. Diethylcarbamazine citrate (DEC) is the drug of choice for lymphatic filariasis (see Drugs for Parasitic Infections, p 790). The late phase of chronic disease is not affected by chemotherapy. Ivermectin is effective against the microfilariae of *W bancrofti* but has no effect on the adult parasite. In some studies, combination therapy with single-dose DEC-albendazole or ivermectin-albendazole has been shown to be more effective than any one drug alone in suppressing microfilaremia.

Complex decongestive physiotherapy may be effective for treating lymphedema. Chyluria originating in the bladder responds to fulguration; chyluria originating in the kidney usually cannot be corrected. Prompt identification and treatment of super-infections, particularly streptococcal and staphylococcal infections, and careful treatment of intertriginous and ungual infections are important aspects of therapy for lymphedema.

ISOLATION OF THE HOSPITALIZED PATIENT: Standard precautions are recommended.

CONTROL MEASURES: Control measures have been instituted based on annual community-wide combinations of DEC and albendazole (in Africa) or albendazole and ivermectin (worldwide except Africa) to decrease or possibly eliminate transmission.

Lymphocytic Choriomeningitis

CLINICAL MANIFESTATIONS: Postnatal infection is asymptomatic in approximately one third of cases. Symptomatic infection may result in a mild to severe influenza-like illness, which includes fever, malaise, myalgia, retro-orbital headache, photophobia, anorexia, and nausea. Fever usually lasts 1 to 3 weeks, and rash is rare. A biphasic febrile course is common. Up to half of symptomatic patients will develop neurologic manifestations varying from aseptic meningitis to severe encephalitis. Arthralgia or arthritis, respiratory tract symptoms, orchitis, and leukopenia occasionally develop. Recovery without sequelae is the usual outcome. Infection during pregnancy has been associated with abortion. Congenital infection may cause hydrocephalus, chorioretinitis, intracranial calcifications, microcephaly, and mental retardation. Congenital lymphocytic choriomeningitis may be difficult to differentiate from congenital infection attributable to cytomegalovirus (CMV), toxoplasmosis, or rubella.

ETIOLOGY: Lymphocytic choriomeningitis virus is an arenavirus.

EPIDEMIOLOGY: Lymphocytic choriomeningitis is a chronic infection of the common house mouse and pet hamsters, which often are infected asymptomatically and chronically shed virus in urine and other excretions. In addition, laboratory mice, guinea pigs, and colonized golden hamsters can have chronic infection and can be sources of human infection. Humans are infected by aerosol or by ingestion of dust or food contaminated with the virus from the urine, feces, blood, or nasopharyngeal secretions of infected rodents. The disease is most prevalent in young adults. Human-to-human spread, by transplacental passage of the virus and via organ transplantation from an acutely infected, undiagnosed, lymphocytic choriomeningitis virus-infected organ donor has been reported. The source of the virus in one organ donor was traced to a pet hamster purchased by the donor.

The **incubation period** usually is 6 to 13 days and occasionally is as long as 3 weeks.

DIAGNOSTIC TESTS: In patients with central nervous system disease, mononuclear pleocytosis occasionally exceeding several thousand cells is present in the cerebrospinal fluid (CSF). Hypoglycorrhachia also can occur. Lymphocytic choriomeningitis virus can be isolated from blood, CSF, urine, and rarely, nasopharyngeal secretion specimens. Acute and convalescent serum specimens can be tested for increases in antibody titers by immunofluorescent or enzyme immunoassay. Demonstration of virus-specific immunoglobulin M antibodies in serum or CSF specimens is useful. In congenital infections, diagnosis usually is suspected at the sequela phase, and diagnosis usually is made by serologic testing.

TREATMENT: Supportive.

ISOLATION OF THE HOSPITALIZED PATIENT: Standard precautions are recommended.

CONTROL MEASURES: Infection can be controlled by preventing rodent infestation in animal and food storage areas. Because the virus is excreted for long periods of time by rodent hosts, attempts should be made to monitor laboratory and wholesale colonies of mice and hamsters for infection. Pet rodents or wild mice in a patient's home should be considered likely sources of infection. Pregnant women should avoid exposure to wild or pet rodents and their aerosolized excreta. Guidelines for minimizing risk of human lymphocytic choriomeningitis virus infection associated with rodents are available.[*]

Malaria

CLINICAL MANIFESTATIONS: The classic symptoms of malaria are high fever with chills, rigor, sweats, and headache, which may be paroxysmal. If appropriate treatment is not administered, fever and paroxysms may occur in a cyclic pattern. Depending on the infecting species, fever appears every other or every third day. Other manifestations can include nausea, vomiting, diarrhea, cough, arthralgia, and

---

[*] Centers for Disease Control and Prevention. Update: interim guidance for minimizing risk for human lymphocytic choriomeningitis virus infection associated with pet rodents. *MMWR Morb Mortal Wkly Rep.* 2005;54:799–801

abdominal and back pain. Anemia and thrombocytopenia are common, and pallor and jaundice caused by hemolysis may occur. Hepatosplenomegaly may be present. More severe disease occurs in people without previous exposure and people who are pregnant or immunocompromised.

Infection with *Plasmodium falciparum* potentially is fatal and most commonly manifests as a febrile nonspecific influenza-like illness without localizing signs. With more severe disease, *P falciparum* infection may manifest as one of the following clinical syndromes:

- *Cerebral malaria*, which may have variable neurologic manifestations, including seizures, signs of increased intracranial pressure, confusion, and progression to stupor, coma, and death
- *Hypoglycemia*, sometimes associated with quinine treatment, requiring urgent correction
- *Noncardiogenic pulmonary edema*, which is difficult to manage and may be fatal (rare in children)
- *Renal failure* caused by acute tubular necrosis (rare in children younger than 8 years of age)
- *Respiratory failure and metabolic acidosis*, without pulmonary edema
- *Severe anemia* attributable to high parasitemia and consequent hemolysis
- *Vascular collapse and shock* associated with hypothermia and adrenal insufficiency

Individuals with asplenia who become infected may be at increased risk of more severe illness and death.

Syndromes primarily associated with *Plasmodium vivax* and *Plasmodium ovale* infection are as follows:

- *Anemia* attributable to acute parasitemia
- *Hypersplenism* with danger of late splenic rupture
- *Relapse*, for as long as 3 to 5 years after the primary infection, attributable to latent hepatic stages

Syndromes associated with *Plasmodium malariae* infection include:

- *Chronic asymptomatic parasitemia* for as long as several years after the last exposure
- *Nephrotic syndrome* from deposition of immune complexes in the kidney

Congenital malaria secondary to perinatal transmission rarely may occur. Most congenital cases have been caused by *P vivax* and *P falciparum*; *P malariae* and *P ovale* account for fewer than 20% of such cases. Manifestations can resemble those of neonatal sepsis, including fever and nonspecific symptoms of poor appetite, irritability, and lethargy.

ETIOLOGY: The genus *Plasmodium* includes species of intraerythrocytic parasites that infect a wide range of mammals, birds, and reptiles. The 4 species that infect humans are *P falciparum*, *P vivax*, *P ovale*, and *P malariae*.

EPIDEMIOLOGY: Malaria is endemic throughout the tropical areas of the world and is acquired from the bite of the female nocturnal-feeding *Anopheles* species of mosquito. One half of the world's population lives in areas where transmission occurs. Worldwide, there are 300 to 500 million cases annually and 1.5 to 2.7 million deaths. Most deaths occur in young children. Malarial infection poses substantial risks to pregnant women and their fetuses and may result in spontaneous abortion and stillbirth. The risk of malaria is highest, but variable, for travelers to sub-Saharan Africa, Papua New Guinea, the Solomon Islands, and Vanuatu; the risk is intermediate in the Indian subcontinent and is low in most of Southeast Asia and Latin America. Transmission is possible in more temperate climates, including areas of the United States where *Anopheles* species mosquitoes are present. Mosquitoes in airplanes flying from tropical climates have been the source of occasional cases in people working or residing near international airports. However, nearly all of the approximately 1400 annual reported cases in the United States result from infection acquired abroad. Other less common modes of malaria transmission are congenital, through transfusions, or through the use of contaminated needles or syringes.

Plasmodium vivax and *P falciparum* are the most common species worldwide. *Plasmodium vivax* malaria is prevalent on the Indian subcontinent and in Central America. *Plasmodium falciparum* malaria is prevalent in Africa and Papua New Guinea. Malaria attributable to *P vivax* and *P falciparum* is common in southern and Southeast Asia, Oceania, and South America. *Plasmodium malariae*, although much less common, has a wide distribution. *Plasmodium ovale* malaria occurs most often in West Africa but has been reported in other areas.

Relapses may occur in *P vivax* and *P ovale* malaria because of a persistent hepatic (hypnozoite) stage of infection. Recrudescence of *P falciparum* and *P malariae* infection occurs when a persistent low-concentration parasitemia causes recurrence of symptoms of the disease. In areas of Africa and Asia with hyperendemic infection, reinfection in people with partial immunity results in a high prevalence of asymptomatic parasitemia.

The spread of chloroquine-resistant *P falciparum* strains throughout the world is of increasing importance. Resistance to other antimalarial drugs now is occurring in many areas where the drugs are used widely. Chloroquine-resistant *P vivax* has been reported in Indonesia, Papua New Guinea, the Solomon Islands, Myanmar, India, and Guyana.

DIAGNOSTIC TESTS: Definitive diagnosis relies on identification of the parasite on stained blood films. Both thick and thin blood films should be examined. The thick film allows for concentration of the blood to find parasites that may be present in small numbers, whereas the thin film is most useful for species identification and determination of the degree of parasitemia (the percentage of erythrocytes harboring parasites). If initial blood smears test negative for *Plasmodium* species but malaria remains a possibility, the smear should be repeated every 12 to 24 hours during a 72-hour period.

In areas with hyperendemic infection, the presence of malaria on a blood smear is not conclusive evidence of malaria as a cause of the manifesting illness, because other infections often are superimposed on low-concentration parasitemia in children and adults with partial immunity.

Confirmation and identification of the species of malaria parasites on the blood smear is important in guiding therapy. Serologic testing generally is not helpful, except in epidemiologic surveys. Other diagnostic tests, including polymerase chain reaction assay, DNA probes, and malarial ribosomal RNA testing, may provide rapid and accurate diagnosis in the future but currently are used in experimental studies only. Antigen detection tests, also referred to as rapid diagnostic tests, using dipstick techniques for diagnosis of malaria are being evaluated in the research setting. None is licensed for use in the United States. Most of these tests detect trophozoites of *P falciparum* infections. They are simple to perform and rapid to interpret but are relatively expensive compared with microscopy, and they are not quantitative.

TREATMENT: The choice of malaria chemotherapy is based on the infecting species, possible drug resistance, and the severity of disease (see Drugs for Parasitic Infections, p 790). Severe malaria is defined as a parasitemia greater than 5% of red blood cells, signs of central nervous system or other end-organ involvement, shock, acidosis, and/ or hypoglycemia. Patients with severe malaria require intensive care and parenteral treatment until the parasite density decreases to less than 1% and they are able to tolerate oral therapy. Exchange transfusion may be warranted when parasitemia exceeds 10% or if there is evidence of complications (eg, cerebral malaria) at lower parasite densities. Other adjunctive therapies, such as iron chelation, are under investigation but are not recommended. New antimalarial drugs are undergoing clinical trials for treatment and chemoprophylaxis of malaria. For patients with *P falciparum* malaria, sequential blood smears for percent parasitemia are indicated to monitor treatment.

ISOLATION OF THE HOSPITALIZED PATIENT: Standard precautions are recommended.

CONTROL MEASURES: Control of the *Anopheles* species mosquito population, protection against mosquito bites, treatment of infected people, and chemoprophylaxis of travelers to areas with endemic infection are effective. Measures to prevent contact with mosquitoes, especially from dusk to dawn (because of the nocturnal biting habits of the female *Anopheles* mosquito), through use of bed nets impregnated with insecticide, mosquito repellents containing diethyltoluamide (DEET) (see Prevention of Mosquitoborne Infections, p 197), and protective clothing also are beneficial and should be optimized. The most current information on country-specific risks, drug resistance, and resulting recommendations for travelers can be obtained by contacting the Centers for Disease Control and Prevention (CDC) Malaria Hotline (770-488-7788).

CHEMOPROPHYLAXIS FOR TRAVELERS TO AREAS WITH ENDEMIC INFECTION.* The appropriate chemoprophylactic regimen is determined by the traveler's risk of acquiring malaria in the area(s) to be visited and by the risk of exposure to chloroquine-resistant *P falciparum*. Indications for prophylaxis for children are identical to those for adults. Pediatric dosages should be calculated based on the child's current weight; children's dosages should never exceed adult dosages. The drugs used for malaria chemoprophylaxis generally are well tolerated. However,

---

* For further information on prevention of malaria in travelers, see the annual publication of the US Public Health Service, *Health Information for International Travel*, 2005–2006. Atlanta, GA: US Dept of Health and Human Services, Public Health Service, Centers for Disease Control and Prevention, National Center for Infectious Diseases, Division of Quarantine; 2005 or visit the CDC Web site (**www.cdc.gov/travel/diseases.htm#malaria**). The CDC also provides fax documents pertaining to traveler's health at 1-888-232-3299

adverse reactions can occur. Minor adverse reactions do not require stopping the drug. Travelers with serious adverse reactions should be advised to contact their health care professional.

Chemoprophylaxis should begin 1 week before arrival in the area with endemic infection (except doxycycline and atovaquone-proguanil, which should be started 1–2 days before arrival), allowing time to develop blood concentrations of the drug and evaluate for adverse reactions.

Travelers to areas where chloroquine-resistant malaria species have not been reported should take chloroquine, once weekly, starting 1 week before exposure for the duration of exposure and for 4 weeks after departure from the area with endemic infection. Adverse reactions that can occur include gastrointestinal tract disturbance, headache, dizziness, blurred vision, insomnia, and pruritus, but these generally are mild and do not require discontinuation of the drug.

Three drugs with similar efficacy are available in the United States for prevention of chloroquine-resistant malaria. Travelers to areas where chloroquine-resistant *P falciparum* exists should take atovaquone-proguanil, doxycycline, or mefloquine.

- A fixed-dose combination of atovaquone-proguanil is approved for prevention and treatment of chloroquine-resistant *P falciparum* malaria. Atovaquone-proguanil is taken daily, starting 1 day before exposure and continuing for the duration of exposure and for 1 week after departure from the area with endemic infection. A pediatric formulation is available in the United States but is not approved for prophylaxis in children weighing less than 11 kg. Atovaquone-proguanil is contraindicated for pregnant women. The most common adverse effects in people using atovaquone-proguanil for chemoprophylaxis are abdominal pain, nausea, vomiting, and headache.
- Doxycycline is taken daily, starting 1 to 2 days before exposure, for the duration of exposure and for 4 weeks after departure from the area with endemic infection. Travelers taking doxycycline should be advised of the need for strict adherence to daily dosing, the advisability of always taking the drug on a full stomach, and the possible adverse effects, including diarrhea, photosensitivity, and increased risk of monilial vaginitis. Use of doxycycline should be avoided for pregnant women and for children younger than 8 years of age because of the risk of dental staining (see Antimicrobial Agents and Related Therapy, p 735).
- Mefloquine is taken once weekly, starting 1 week before travel, continuing weekly during travel, and for 4 weeks after travel has concluded (see Drugs for Parasitic Infections, p 790). Mefloquine is not approved by the US Food and Drug Administration (FDA) for children who weigh less than 5 kg or are younger than 6 months of age. However, recommendations of the CDC suggest that mefloquine be considered for use in children, regardless of weight or age restrictions, when travel to areas where chloroquine-resistant *P falciparum* exists cannot be avoided. The most common CNS abnormalities associated with mefloquine are dizziness, headache, insomnia, and disturbing dreams. Mefloquine has been associated with rare serious adverse events (including psychoses or seizures) at prophylactic doses; these reactions are more common with the higher doses used for treatment. Other adverse events that occur with prophy-

lactic doses include gastrointestinal tract disturbances, headache, depression, and anxiety disorders. Mefloquine is contraindicated for use in travelers with a known hypersensitivity to mefloquine; people with active depression or a history of depression; people with general anxiety disorders, psychosis, schizophrenia, or other major psychiatric disturbances; people with a history of seizures (not including the type of seizure caused by high fever in childhood); and people with a history of cardiac conduction abnormalities. Although a warning about concurrent use with beta-blockers is given in the product labeling, a review of available data suggests that mefloquine may be used by people concurrently receiving beta-blockers if they have no underlying arrhythmia. Caution should be advised for travelers involved in tasks requiring fine motor coordination and spatial discrimination. Patients in whom mefloquine prophylaxis fails should be monitored closely if they are treated with quinidine or quinine sulfate, because either drug may exacerbate the known adverse effects of mefloquine.

Children should avoid travel to areas where chloroquine-resistant *P falciparum* exists unless they can take a highly effective drug, such as atovaquone-proguanil, doxycycline, or mefloquine. If other animalarial drugs cannot be used, **in consultation with local malaria experts or experts at the CDC (CDC Malaria Hotline 770-488-7788)**, primaquine may be used to prevent malaria while the traveler is in the area with a risk of malaria (primary prophylaxis). NOTE: Travelers *must* be tested for glucose-6-phosphate dehydrogenase (G6PD) deficiency and have a documented G6PD in the normal range before primaquine use. Primary primaquine prophylaxis should begin 1 to 2 days before departure to the area with risk of malaria. It should be continued once a day while in the area with risk of malaria and daily for 7 days after leaving the area. The drug should not be used during pregnancy.

PROPHYLAXIS DURING PREGNANCY. Malaria in pregnancy carries significant risks of morbidity and mortality for both the mother and fetus. Malaria may increase the risk of adverse outcomes in pregnancy, including abortion, preterm birth, and stillbirth. For these reasons and because no chemoprophylactic regimen is completely effective, women who are pregnant or likely to become pregnant should try to avoid travel to areas where they could contract malaria. Women traveling to areas where drug-resistant *P falciparum* has not been reported may take chloroquine prophylaxis. Harmful effects on the fetus have not been demonstrated when chloroquine is given in the recommended doses for malaria prophylaxis. Pregnancy, therefore, is not a contraindication for malaria prophylaxis with chloroquine.

For pregnant women who travel to areas where chloroquine-resistant *P falciparum* exists, mefloquine should be recommended for chemoprophylaxis during the second and third trimesters. For women in their first trimester, most evidence suggests that use of mefloquine is not associated with adverse fetal or pregnancy outcomes, such as spontaneous abortions, stillbirths, and birth defects when taken in prophylactic doses, but more data are necessary to make conclusive statements about its safety in early pregnancy. Consequently, mefloquine is the drug of choice for prophylactic use for women who are pregnant or likely to become pregnant when exposure to chloroquine-resistant *P falciparum* is unavoidable.

SELF-TREATMENT OF MALARIA. Malaria can be treated effectively early in the course of disease, but delay of appropriate treatment can have serious or even fatal consequences. Travelers who do not take an antimalarial drug for prophylaxis or who are on a less-than-effective regimen or who may be in very remote areas can be given a self-treatment course of atovaquone-proguanil. Travelers should be advised that self-treatment is not considered a replacement for seeking prompt medical help. A self-treatment regimen should be discussed with a physician expert in travel medicine before departure.

Travelers taking atovaquone-proguanil as their antimalarial drug regimen should not take atovaquone-proguanil as their self-treatment drug and should use an alternative treatment regimen; the CDC Malaria Hotline (770-488-7788) provides advice on management of travelers who cannot use atovaquone-proguanil for self-treatment.

Travelers should be advised that any fever or influenza-like illness that develops within 3 months of departure from an area with endemic infection requires immediate medical evaluation, including blood films to rule out malaria.

PREVENTION OF RELAPSES. To prevent relapses of *P vivax* or *P ovale* infection after departure from areas where these species are endemic, use of primaquine should be considered. Primaquine can cause hemolysis in patients with G6PD deficiency; thus, all patients should be screened for this condition before primaquine therapy is initiated.

PERSONAL PROTECTIVE MEASURES. All travelers to areas where malaria is endemic should be advised to use personal protective measures, including the following: (1) using insecticide-impregnated mosquito nets while sleeping; (2) remaining in well-screened areas; (3) wearing protective clothing; and (4) using mosquito repellents containing DEET. To be effective, most of these repellents require frequent reapplications. See Prevention of Mosquitoborne Infections (p 197) for recommendations regarding prevention of mosquitoborne infections and use of insect repellents.

Measles

CLINICAL MANIFESTATIONS: Measles is an acute disease characterized by fever, cough, coryza, conjunctivitis, an erythematous maculopapular rash, and a pathognomonic enanthema (Koplik spots). Complications including otitis media, bronchopneumonia, laryngotracheobronchitis (croup), and diarrhea occur commonly in young children. Acute encephalitis, which often results in permanent brain damage, occurs in approximately 1 of every 1000 cases. Death, predominantly resulting from respiratory and neurologic complications, occurs in 1 to 3 of every 1000 cases reported in the United States. Case fatality rates are increased in children younger than 5 years of age and immunocompromised children, including children with leukemia, human immunodeficiency virus (HIV) infection, and severe malnutrition. Sometimes the characteristic rash does not develop in immunocompromised patients.

Subacute sclerosing panencephalitis (SSPE) is a rare degenerative central nervous system disease characterized by behavioral and intellectual deterioration and seizures. Widespread measles immunization has led to the virtual disappearance of SSPE in the United States.

ETIOLOGY: Measles virus is an RNA virus with 1 serotype, classified as a member of the genus Morbillivirus in the Paramyxoviridae family.

EPIDEMIOLOGY: The only natural hosts of measles virus are humans. Measles is transmitted by direct contact with infectious droplets or, less commonly, by airborne spread. In temperate areas, the peak incidence of infection usually occurs during late winter and spring. In the prevaccine era, most cases of measles in the United States occurred in preschool and young school-aged children, and few people remained susceptible by 20 years of age. The childhood and adolescent immunization program in the United States has resulted in a greater than 99% decrease in the reported incidence of measles since measles vaccine was first licensed in 1963.

From 1989 to 1991, the incidence of measles in the United States increased because of low immunization rates in preschool-aged children, especially in urban areas. From 1997 to 2004, the incidence of measles in the United States has been low (37–116 cases reported per year), consistent with an absence of endemic transmission. Cases of measles continue to occur as a result of importation of the virus from other countries. Cases are considered international importations if the rash onset occurs within 18 days after entering the United States. Almost half of the imported cases occur in US residents returning from foreign travel.

Vaccine failure occurs in as many as 5% of people who have received a single dose of vaccine at 12 months of age or older. Although waning immunity after immunization may be a factor in some cases, most cases of measles in previously immunized children seem to occur in people in whom response to the vaccine was inadequate (ie, primary vaccine failures).

Patients are contagious from 1 to 2 days before onset of symptoms (3–5 days before the rash) to 4 days after appearance of the rash. Immunocompromised patients who may have prolonged excretion of the virus in respiratory tract secretions can be contagious for the duration of the illness. Patients with SSPE are not contagious.

The **incubation period** generally is 8 to 12 days from exposure to onset of symptoms. In family studies, the average interval between appearance of rash in the index case and subsequent cases is 14 days, with a range of 7 to 18 days. In SSPE, the mean incubation period of 84 cases reported between 1976 and 1983 was 10.8 years.

DIAGNOSTIC TESTS: Measles virus infection can be diagnosed by a positive serologic test result for measles immunoglobulin (Ig) M antibody, a significant increase in measles IgG antibody concentration in paired acute and convalescent serum specimens by any standard serologic assay, or isolation of measles virus from clinical specimens, such as urine, blood, throat, or nasopharyngeal secretions. The state public health laboratory or the Centers for Disease Control and Prevention Measles Laboratory will process these viral specimens. The simplest method of establishing the diagnosis of measles is testing for IgM antibody on a single serum specimen obtained during the first encounter with a person suspected of having disease. The sensitivity of measles IgM assays varies and may be diminished during the first 72 hours after rash onset. If the result is negative for measles IgM and the patient has a generalized rash lasting more than 72 hours, the measles IgM test should be repeated. Measles IgM is detectable for at least 1 month after rash onset. People with febrile rash illness who are seronegative for measles IgM should be tested for rubella using the same specimens. Genotyping of viral isolates allows determination of patterns of importation and transmission, and genome sequencing can be used to differentiate between wild-type and vaccine virus infection. All cases of suspected measles should be reported immediately to the local or state health department without waiting for results of diagnostic tests.

TREATMENT: No specific antiviral therapy is available. Measles virus is susceptible in vitro to ribavirin, which has been given by the intravenous and aerosol routes to treat severely affected and immunocompromised children with measles. However, no controlled trials have been conducted, and ribavirin is not approved by the US Food and Drug Administration for treatment of measles.

VITAMIN A. The World Health Organization and the United Nations International Children's Emergency Fund recommend administration of vitamin A to all children diagnosed with measles in communities where vitamin A deficiency is a recognized problem or the measles case fatality rate is 1% or greater. Vitamin A treatment of children with measles in developing countries has been associated with decreased morbidity and mortality rates. Although vitamin A deficiency is not recognized as a major problem in the United States, low serum concentrations of vitamin A have been found in children with severe measles. Hence, vitamin A supplementation should be considered in the following patients:

- Children 6 months to 2 years of age hospitalized with measles and its complications (eg, croup, pneumonia, and diarrhea). Limited data are available about the safety and need for vitamin A supplementation for infants younger than 6 months of age.
- Children older than 6 months of age with measles who are not already receiving vitamin A supplementation and who have any of the following risk factors: immunodeficiency, clinical evidence of vitamin A deficiency, impaired intestinal absorption, moderate to severe malnutrition, and recent immigration from areas where high mortality rates attributable to measles have been observed.

Parenteral and oral formulations of vitamin A are available in the United States. The recommended dosage, administered as a capsule, is a single dose of 200 000 IU, orally, for children 1 year of age and older (100 000 IU for children 6 months–1 year of age). For children with ophthalmologic evidence of vitamin A deficiency, the dose should be repeated the next day and again 4 weeks later.

ISOLATION OF THE HOSPITALIZED PATIENT: In addition to standard precautions, airborne transmission precautions are indicated for 4 days after the onset of rash in otherwise healthy children and for the duration of illness in immunocompromised patients.

CONTROL MEASURES:

CARE OF EXPOSED PEOPLE.

Use of Vaccine. Exposure to measles is not a contraindication to immunization. Available data suggest that live-virus measles vaccine, if given within 72 hours of measles exposure, will provide protection in some cases. If the exposure does not result in infection, the vaccine should induce protection against subsequent measles exposures. Immunization is the intervention of choice for control of measles outbreaks in schools and child care centers.

Use of Immune Globulin. Immune Globulin (IG) can be given to prevent or modify measles in a susceptible person within 6 days of exposure. The usual recommended dose is 0.25 mL/kg given intramuscularly; immunocompromised children should receive 0.5 mL/kg (the maximum dose in either instance is 15 mL). Immune Globulin is indicated for susceptible household or other close contacts of patients with measles, particularly contacts younger than 1 year of age, pregnant women, and immunocompromised people for whom the risk of complications is highest. Immune Globulin is not indicated for household or other close contacts who have received 1 dose of vaccine at 12 months of age or older unless they are immunocompromised.

Immune Globulin Intravenous (IGIV) preparations generally contain measles antibodies at approximately the same concentration per gram of protein as IG, although the concentration may vary by lot and manufacturer. For patients who regularly receive IGIV, the usual dose of 100 to 400 mg/kg should be adequate for measles prophylaxis after exposures occurring within 3 weeks of receiving IGIV.

For children who receive IG for modification or prevention of measles after exposure, measles vaccine (if not contraindicated) should be given 5 months (if the dose was 0.25 mL/kg) or 6 months (if the dose was 0.5 mL/kg) after IG administration, provided that the child is at least 12 months of age. Intervals between administration of IGIV or other biologicals and measles-containing vaccines varies (see Table 3.32, p 445).

Human Immunodeficiency Virus Infection. All children and adolescents with HIV infection and children of unknown HIV infection status born to HIV-infected women who are exposed to wild-type measles should receive IG prophylaxis (0.5 mL/kg, IM, maximum dose 15 mL), regardless of their measles immunization status (see Human Immunodeficiency Virus Infection, p 378). An exception is the patient receiving IGIV (400 mg/kg) at regular intervals whose last dose was received within 3 weeks of exposure. Because of the rapid metabolism of IGIV, some experts recommend administration of an additional dose of IGIV if exposure to measles occurs 2 or more weeks after the last regular dose of IGIV.

Hospital Personnel. To decrease nosocomial infection, immunization programs should be established to ensure that all people who work or volunteer in health care facilities who may be in contact with patients with measles are immune to measles (see Health Care Personnel, p 94).

MEASLES VACCINE. The only measles vaccine currently licensed in the United States is a live further-attenuated strain prepared in chicken embryo cell culture. Measles vaccines provided through the Expanded Programme on Immunization in developing countries meet the World Health Organization standards and usually are comparable to the vaccine available in the United States. Measles vaccine is available in monovalent (measles only) formulation and in combination formulations, such as measles-rubella (MR), measles-mumps-rubella (MMR), and measles-mumps-rubella-varicella (MMRV) vaccines. The MMR or MMRV vaccines are the recommended products of choice in most circumstances. Measles vaccine (as a combination or monovalent product) in a dose of 0.5 mL is given subcutaneously. Measles and measles-containing vaccines can be given simultaneously with other immunizations in a separate syringe at a separate site (see Simultaneous Administration of Multiple Vaccines, p 34).

Serum measles antibodies develop in approximately 95% of children immunized at 12 months of age and 98% of children immunized at 15 months of age. Protection

Table 3.32. Suggested Intervals Between Immune Globulin Administration and Measles Immunization (MMR, MMRV, or Monovalent Measles Vaccine)

Indication for Immunoglobulin	Route	Dose U or mL	Dose mg IgG/kg	Interval, mo[1]
Tetanus (as TIG)	IM	250 U	10	3
Hepatitis A prophylaxis (as IG)				
Contact prophylaxis	IM	0.02 mL/kg	3.3	3
International travel	IM	0.06 mL/kg	10	3
Hepatitis B prophylaxis (as HBIG)	IM	0.06 mL/kg	10	3
Rabies prophylaxis (as RIG)	IM	20 IU/kg	22	4
Varicella prophylaxis (as VariZIG)	IM	125 U/10 kg (maximum 625 U)	20–40	5
Measles prophylaxis (as IG)				
Standard	IM	0.25 mL/kg	40	5
Immunocompromised host	IM	0.50 mL/kg	80	6
RSV prophylaxis (palivizumab monoclonal antibody)	IM	. . .	15 mg/kg (monoclonal)	None
Cytomegalovirus Immune Globulin	IV	3 mL/kg	150	6
Blood transfusion				
Washed RBCs	IV	10 mL/kg	Negligible	0
RBCs, adenine-saline added	IV	10 mL/kg	10	3
Packed RBCs	IV	10 mL/kg	20–60	5
Whole blood	IV	10 mL/kg	80–100	6
Plasma or platelet products	IV	10 mL/kg	160	7
Replacement (or therapy) of immune deficiencies (as IGIV)	IV	. . .	300–400	8
ITP (as IGIV)	IV	. . .	400	8
ITP	IV	. . .	1000	10
ITP or Kawasaki disease	IV	. . .	1600–2000	11

MMR indicates measles-mumps-rubella; MMRV, measles-mumps-rubella-varicella; IgG, immunoglobulin G; TIG, Tetanus Immune Globulin; IG, Immune Globulin; IM, intramuscular; HBIG, Hepatitis B IG; RIG, Rabies IG; RBCs, Red Blood Cells; IV, intravenous; IGIV, IG intravenous; ITP, immune (formerly termed "idiopathic") thrombocytopenic purpura; RSV, Respiratory Syncytial Virus.

[1] These intervals should provide sufficient time for decreases in passive antibodies in all children to allow for an adequate response to measles vaccine. Physicians should not assume that children are fully protected against measles during these intervals. Additional doses of IG or measles vaccine may be indicated after exposure to measles (see text).

Table 3.33. Recommendations for Measles Immunization[1]

Category	Recommendations
Unimmunized, no history of measles (12–15 mo of age)	A 2-dose schedule (with MMR) is recommended. The first dose is recommended at 12–15 mo of age; the second is recommended at 4–6 y of age
Children 6–11 mo of age in epidemic situations[2] or prior to international travel	Immunize (with monovalent measles vaccine or, if not available, MMR); reimmunization (with MMR) at 12–15 mo of age is necessary, and a third dose is indicated at 4–6 y of age
Children 4–12 y of age who have received 1 dose of measles vaccine at ≥12 mo of age	Reimmunize (1 dose)
Students in college and other post-high school institutions who have received 1 dose of measles vaccine at ≥12 mo of age	Reimmunize (1 dose)
History of immunization before the first birthday	Consider susceptible and immunize (2 doses)
History of receipt of inactivated measles vaccine or unknown type of vaccine, 1963–1967	Consider susceptible and immunize (2 doses)
Further attenuated or unknown vaccine given with IG	Consider susceptible and immunize (2 doses)
Allergy to eggs	Immunize; no reactions likely (see text for details)
Neomycin allergy, nonanaphylactic	Immunize; no reactions likely (see text for details)
Severe hypersensitivity (anaphylaxis) to neomycin or gelatin	Avoid immunization
Tuberculosis	Immunize (see Tuberculosis, p 678); if patient has untreated tuberculosis disease, start anti-tuberculosis therapy before immunizing.
Measles exposure	Immunize and/or give IG, depending on circumstances (see text, p 443)
HIV-infected	Immunize (2 doses) unless severely immunocompromised (see text, p 450)
Personal or family history of seizures	Immunize; advise parents of slightly increased risk of seizures
Immunoglobulin or blood recipient	Immunize at the appropriate interval (see Table 3.32, p 445)

MMR indicates measles-mumps-rubella vaccine; IG, Immune Globulin; HIV, human immunodeficiency virus.

[1] See text for details and recommendations for use of measles-mumps-rubella-varicella (MMRV) vaccine.

[2] See Outbreak Control (p 451).

conferred by a single dose is durable in most people. However, a small proportion (≤5%) of immunized people may lose protection after several years. More than 99% of people who receive 2 doses separated by at least 4 weeks, with the first dose administered on or after their first birthday, develop serologic evidence of measles immunity. Immunization is not deleterious for people who already are immune.

Improperly stored vaccine may fail to protect against measles. Since 1979, an improved stabilizer has been added to the vaccine that makes it more resistant to heat inactivation. For recommended storage of measles, MMR, and MMRV vaccines, see Recommended Storage of Commonly Used Vaccines (Table 1.4, p 13).

VACCINE RECOMMENDATIONS (see Table 3.33, p 446, for summary).

Age of Routine Immunization. The first dose of measles vaccine should be given at 12 to 15 months of age. Delays in administering the first dose contributed to large outbreaks in the United States from 1989 to 1991. Initial immunization at 12 months of age is recommended for preschool-aged children in high-risk areas, especially large urban areas. The second dose is recommended routinely at school entry (ie, 4–6 years of age) but can be given at any earlier age (eg, during an outbreak or before international travel), provided the interval between the first and second doses is at least 4 weeks. Children who were not reimmunized at school entry should receive the second dose by 11 to 12 years of age. If a child receives a dose of measles vaccine before 12 months of age, 2 additional doses are required beginning at 12 to 15 months of age and separated by at least 4 weeks.

Use of MMRV Vaccine.*

- The MMRV vaccine is indicated for simultaneous immunization against measles, mumps, rubella, and varicella among children 12 months to 12 years of age; MMRV vaccine is not indicated for people outside this age group.
- The MMRV vaccine may be used whenever any of the components of the combination vaccine are indicated and the other components are not contraindicated. Using combination vaccines containing some antigens not indicated at the time of administration might be justified when (1) products that contain only the needed antigens are not readily available or would result in extra injections; and (2) potential benefits to the child outweigh the risk of adverse events associated with the extra antigen(s).
- At least 1 month should elapse between a dose of measles-containing vaccine, such as MMR vaccine, and a dose of MMRV vaccine. Should a second dose of varicella vaccine be indicated for children 12 months to 12 years of age (eg, during a varicella outbreak), at least 3 months should elapse between administration of any 2 doses of varicella-containing vaccine, including single-antigen varicella vaccine or MMRV vaccine.
- The MMRV vaccine may be administered simultaneously with other vaccines recommended from 12 months to 12 years of age, although data are absent or limited for the concomitant use of MMRV vaccine with diphtheria and tetanus toxoids and acellular pertussis (DTaP), inactivated poliovirus, pneumococcal conjugate, influenza, and hepatitis A vaccines.

---

* Centers for Disease Control and Prevention. Notice to readers: licensure of a combined live attenuated measles, mumps, rubella, and varicella vaccine. *MMWR Morb Mortal Wkly Rep.* 2005;54:1212–1214

- The MMRV vaccine should not be administered as a substitute for the component vaccines when immunizing children with HIV infection until revised recommendations can be considered for use of MMRV vaccine in this population.

High School Students and Adults. Because of the occurrence of measles cases in older children and young adults, emphasis must be placed on identifying and appropriately immunizing potentially susceptible adolescents and young adults in high school, college, and health care settings. People should be considered susceptible unless they have documentation of at least 2 doses of measles vaccine administered at least 4 weeks apart, physician-diagnosed measles, or laboratory evidence of immunity to measles or were born before 1957. A parental report of immunization is not considered adequate documentation. Physicians should provide an immunization record for patients only if they have administered the vaccine or have seen a record documenting immunization.

Colleges and Other Institutions for Education Beyond High School. Colleges and other institutions should require that all entering students have documentation of physician-diagnosed measles, serologic evidence of immunity, or receipt of 2 doses of measles-containing vaccines. Students without documentation of any measles immunization or immunity should receive MMR or another measles-containing vaccine on entry, followed by a second dose 4 weeks later, if not contraindicated.

Immunization During an Outbreak. During an outbreak, monovalent measles vaccine may be given to infants as young as 6 months of age (see Outbreak Control, p 451). If monovalent vaccine is not available, MMR may be given. However, seroconversion rates after MMR immunization are significantly lower in children immunized before the first birthday than are seroconversion rates in children immunized after the first birthday. Therefore, children immunized before their first birthday should be immunized with MMR vaccine at 12 to 15 months of age (at least 4 weeks after the initial measles immunization) and again at school entry (4–6 years).

International Travel. People traveling internationally should be immune to measles. For young children traveling internationally, the age for initial measles immunization may need to be lowered. Infants 6 to 11 months of age should receive a dose of monovalent measles vaccine before departure (MMR may be given), and then they should receive MMR vaccine at 12 to 15 months of age (at least 4 weeks after the initial measles immunization) and again at 4 to 6 years of age. Children 12 to 15 months of age should be given their first dose of MMR vaccine before departure and again by 4 to 6 years of age. Children who have received 1 dose and are traveling to areas where measles is endemic or epidemic should receive their second dose before departure, provided the interval between doses is 4 weeks or more.

Health Care Facilities. Evidence of natural measles infection, of measles immunity, or of receipt of 2 doses of measles vaccine is recommended before beginning employment for all health care professionals born in 1957 or after (see Health Care Personnel, p 94). For recommendations during an outbreak, see Outbreak Control (p 451).

ADVERSE EVENTS. A temperature of 39.4°C (103°F) or higher develops in approximately 5% to 15% of susceptible vaccine recipients, usually between 6 and 12 days after receipt of MMR vaccine; fever generally lasts 1 to 2 days but may last as long as 5 days. Most people with fever are otherwise asymptomatic. Transient rashes have been reported in approximately 5% of vaccine recipients. Transient thrombocytopenia occurs in 1 in 25 000 to 1 in 2 million people after administration of measles-containing vaccines, specifically MMR (see Thrombocytopenia, p 450).

Rates of most local and systemic adverse events for children immunized with MMRV vaccine were comparable to rates for children immunized with MMR and varicella vaccines administered concomitantly. However, MMRV recipients had a significantly greater rate of fever $\geq 102°F$ ($\geq 38.9°C$) than did MMR and varicella recipients (21.5% vs 15%, respectively), and measles-like rash was observed in 3% of MMRV recipients and 2% of MMR and varicella recipients.

The reported frequency of central nervous system conditions after measles immunization, including encephalitis and encephalopathy, is less than 1 per million doses administered in the United States. Because the incidence of encephalitis or encephalopathy after measles immunization in the United States is lower than the observed incidence of encephalitis of unknown cause, some or most of the rare reported severe neurologic disorders may be related coincidentally, rather than causally, to measles immunization. Although cases of autism and inflammatory bowel disease have been reported subsequent to measles immunization, multiple studies, as well as an Institute of Medicine Vaccine Safety Review, refute a causal relationship between these diseases and MMR vaccine. After reimmunization, reactions are expected to be similar clinically but much less frequent, because most of these vaccine recipients are immune.

Seizures. Children predisposed to febrile seizures can experience seizures after measles immunization. Children with histories of seizures or children whose first-degree relatives have histories of seizures may be at a slightly increased risk of a seizure but should be immunized, because the benefits greatly outweigh the risks.

Subacute Sclerosing Panencephalitis. Measles vaccine, by protecting against measles, significantly decreases the possibility of developing SSPE.

PRECAUTIONS AND CONTRAINDICATIONS (see also Table 3.32, p 445).

Febrile Illnesses. Children with minor illnesses, such as upper respiratory tract infections, may be immunized (see Vaccine Safety and Contraindications, p 39). Fever is not a contraindication to immunization. However, if other manifestations suggest a more serious illness, the child should not be immunized until recovered.

Allergic Reactions. Hypersensitivity reactions occur rarely and usually are minor, consisting of wheal and flare reactions or urticaria at the injection site. Reactions have been attributed to trace amounts of neomycin or gelatin or some other component in the vaccine formulation. Anaphylaxis is rare. Measles vaccine is produced in chicken embryo cell culture and does not contain significant amounts of egg white (ovalbumin) cross-reacting proteins. Children with egg allergy are at low risk of anaphylactic reactions to measles-containing vaccines (including MMR). Skin testing of children for egg allergy is not predictive of reactions to MMR vaccine and is not required before administering MMR or other measles-containing vaccines. People with allergies to chickens or feathers are not at increased risk of reaction to the vaccine.

People who have had a significant hypersensitivity reaction after the first dose of measles vaccine should: (1) be tested for measles immunity, and if immune, should not be given a second dose; or (2) receive evaluation and possible skin testing before receiving a second dose. People who have had an immediate anaphylactic reaction to previous measles immunization should not be reimmunized but require testing to determine whether they are immune.

People who have experienced anaphylactic reactions to gelatin or topically or systemically administered neomycin should receive measles vaccine only in settings where such reactions could be managed and after consultation with an allergist or immunologist. Most often, however, neomycin allergy manifests as contact dermatitis, which is not a contraindication to receiving measles vaccine.

Thrombocytopenia. Rarely, MMR vaccine can be associated with thrombocytopenia within 2 months of immunization, with a temporal clustering 2 to 3 weeks after immunization. On the basis of case reports, the risk of vaccine-associated thrombocytopenia may be higher for people who previously experienced thrombocytopenia, especially when it occurred in temporal association with earlier MMR immunization. The decision to immunize these children should be based on assessment of immunity after the first dose and the benefits of protection against measles, mumps, and rubella in comparison with the risks of recurrence of thrombocytopenia after immunization. There have been no reported cases of thrombocytopenia associated with receipt of MMR vaccine that have resulted in death in otherwise healthy individuals.

Recent Administration of IG. Immune Globulin preparations interfere with the serologic response to measles vaccine for variable periods, depending on the dose of IG administered. Suggested intervals between IG or blood product administration and measles immunization are given in Table 3.32 (p 445). If vaccine is given at intervals shorter than those indicated, as may be warranted if the risk of exposure to measles is imminent, the child should be reimmunized at or after the appropriate interval for immunization (and at least 4 weeks after the earlier immunization) unless serologic testing indicates that measles-specific antibodies were produced.

If IG is to be administered in preparation for international travel, administration of vaccine should precede receipt of IG by at least 2 weeks to preclude interference with replication of the vaccine virus.

Tuberculosis. Tuberculin skin testing is not a prerequisite for measles immunization. Antituberculosis therapy should be initiated before administering MMR to people with untreated tuberculosis infection or disease. Tuberculin skin testing, if otherwise indicated, can be done on the day of immunization. Otherwise, testing should be postponed for 4 to 6 weeks, because measles immunization temporarily may suppress tuberculin skin test reactivity.

Altered Immunity. Immunocompromised patients with disorders associated with increased severity of viral infections should not be given live measles virus vaccine (see Immunocompromised Children, p 71). The risk of exposure to measles for immunocompromised patients can be decreased by immunizing their close susceptible contacts. Management of immunodeficient and immunosuppressed patients exposed to measles can be facilitated by previous knowledge of their immune status. Susceptible patients with immunodeficiencies should receive IG after measles exposure (see Care of Exposed People, p 443).

Corticosteroids. For patients who have received high doses of corticosteroids ($\geq$2 mg/kg or >20 mg/day of prednisone or its equivalent) for 14 days or more and who are not otherwise immunocompromised, the recommended interval before immunization is at least 1 month (see Immunocompromised Children, p 71). In general, inhaled steroids do not cause immunosuppression and are not a contraindication to measles immunization.

Human Immunodeficiency Virus Infection. Measles immunization (given as MMR vaccine) is recommended at the usual ages for people with asymptomatic HIV infection and for people with symptomatic infection who are not severely immunocompromised, because measles can be severe and often fatal in patients with HIV infection (see Human Immunodeficiency Virus Infection, p 378). Severely immunocompromised HIV-infected infants, children, adolescents, and young adults, as defined by low CD4 + T-lymphocyte counts or percentage of total lymphocytes, should not receive measles virus-containing vaccine, because vaccine-related pneumonia has been reported (see Human Immunodeficiency Virus Infection, p 378). All members of the household of an HIV-infected person should receive measles vaccine (preferably as MMR) *unless* they are HIV-infected and severely immunosuppressed, were born before 1957, have had physician-diagnosed measles, have laboratory evidence of measles immunity, have had age-appropriate immunizations, or have a contraindication to measles vaccine.

Regardless of immunization status, symptomatic HIV-infected patients who are exposed to measles should receive IG prophylaxis, because immunization may not provide protection (see Care of Exposed People, p 443).

Personal or Family History of Seizures. Children with a personal or family history of seizures should be immunized after advising parents or guardians that the risk of seizures after measles immunization is increased slightly. Because fever induced by measles vaccine usually occurs between 6 and 12 days after immunization, prevention of vaccine-related febrile seizures is difficult. Children receiving anticonvulsants should continue such therapy after measles immunization.

Pregnancy. Live-virus measles vaccine, when given as monovalent vaccine or as a component of MR, MMR, or MMRV should not be given to women known to be pregnant. Women who are given MMR should not become pregnant for at least 28 days. This precaution is based on the theoretic risk of fetal infection, which applies to administration of any live-virus vaccine to women who might be pregnant or who might become pregnant shortly after immunization. No evidence, however, substantiates this theoretic risk. In the immunization of adolescents and young adults against measles, asking women if they are pregnant, excluding women who are, and explaining the theoretic risks to the others are recommended precautions.

OUTBREAK CONTROL. Every suspected measles case should be reported immediately to the local health department, and every effort must be made to verify that the illness is measles, especially if the illness may be the first case in the community. Subsequent prevention of the spread of measles depends on prompt immunization of people at risk of exposure or people already exposed who cannot readily provide documentation of measles immunity, including the date of immunization. People who have not been immunized within 72 hours of exposure or who have been exempted from measles immunization for medical, religious, or other reasons should be excluded from school, child care, and health care settings until at least 2 weeks after the onset of rash in the last case of measles.

Schools and Child Care Facilities. During measles outbreaks in child care facilities, schools, and colleges and other institutions of higher education, all students, their siblings, and personnel born in 1957 or after who cannot provide documentation that they received 2 doses of measles-containing vaccine on or after their first birthday or other evidence of measles immunity should be immunized. People receiving their second dose, as well as unimmunized people receiving their first dose before or within 72 hours of exposure as part of the outbreak control program, may be readmitted immediately to the school or child care facility.

Health Care Facilities. If an outbreak occurs in an area served by a hospital or within a hospital, all employees, volunteers, and other personnel with direct patient contact who were born in 1957 or after who cannot provide documentation that they have received 2 doses of measles vaccine on or after their first birthday or other evidence of immunity to measles should receive a dose of measles vaccine. Because some health care professionals born before 1957 have acquired measles in health care facilities, immunization of older employees who may have occupational exposure to measles also should be considered. Susceptible personnel who have been exposed should be relieved of direct patient contact from the fifth to the 21st day after exposure, regardless of whether they received vaccine or IG after the exposure. Personnel who become ill should be relieved of patient contact for 4 days after rash develops.

Meningococcal Infections

CLINICAL MANIFESTATIONS: Invasive infection usually results in meningococcemia, meningitis, or both. Onset often is abrupt in meningococcemia, with fever, chills, malaise, prostration, and a rash that initially can be macular, maculopapular, or petechial. The progression of disease often is rapid. In fulminant cases (Waterhouse-Friderichsen syndrome), purpura, disseminated intravascular coagulation, shock, coma, and death can ensue despite appropriate therapy. The signs and symptoms of meningococcal meningitis are indistinguishable from signs and symptoms of acute meningitis caused by *Streptococcus pneumoniae* or other meningeal pathogens. The case fatality rate for meningococcal disease in all ages remains at 10%; mortality in adolescents approaches 25%. Less common manifestations include pneumonia, febrile occult bacteremia, conjunctivitis, and chronic meningococcemia. Invasive meningococcal infections can be complicated by arthritis, myocarditis, pericarditis, and endophthalmitis. Sequelae associated with meningococcal disease occur in 11% to 19% of patients and include hearing loss, neurologic disability, digit or limb amputations, and skin scarring.

ETIOLOGY: *Neisseria meningitidis* is a gram-negative diplococcus with at least 13 serogroups.

EPIDEMIOLOGY: Strains belonging to groups A, B, C, Y, and W-135 are implicated most commonly in invasive disease worldwide. The distribution of meningococcal serogroups in the United States has shifted in recent years. Serogroups B, C, and Y each account for approximately 30% of reported cases, but serogroup distribution varies by age, location, and time. Approximately two thirds of cases among adolescents and young adults are caused by serogroups C, Y, or W135 and potentially are preventable with available vaccines. In infants, nearly 50% of cases are caused by serogroup B and are not preventable with vaccines available in the United States. Serogroup A has been associated frequently with epidemics elsewhere in the world, primarily in sub-Saharan Africa. An increase in cases of serogroup W-135 meningococcal disease was associated with the Hajj pilgrimage in Saudi Arabia in 2002. Since then, serogroup W-135 meningococcal disease has been reported in sub-Saharan African countries during epidemic seasons.

Asymptomatic colonization of the upper respiratory tract provides the source from which the organism is spread. Transmission occurs from person to person through droplets from the respiratory tract. Since introduction of *Haemophilus influenzae* type b and pneumococcal polysaccharide-protein conjugate vaccines for infants, *N meningitidis* has become the leading cause of bacterial meningitis in young children and remains an important cause of septicemia. Disease most often occurs in children younger than 5 years of age; the peak attack rate occurs in children younger than 1 year of age. Another peak occurs in adolescents 15 to 18 years of age. Freshman college students who live in dormitories have a higher rate of disease compared with individuals who are the same age and are not attending college. Close contacts of patients with meningococcal disease are at increased risk of becoming infected. Patients with deficiency of a terminal complement component (C5–C9), C3 or properdin deficiencies, or anatomic or functional asplenia are at increased risk of invasive and recurrent meningococcal disease. Patients are considered capable of transmitting the organism for up to 24 hours after initiation of effective antimicrobial treatment.

Outbreaks have occurred in communities and institutions, including child care centers, schools, colleges, and military recruit camps. An increased number of meningococcal serogroup C outbreaks in the United States were first reported during the 1990s. However, most cases of meningococcal disease are sporadic, with fewer than 5% associated with outbreaks. Outbreaks often are heralded by a shift in the distribution of cases to an older age group. Multilocus enzyme electrophoresis and pulsed-field gel electrophoresis of enzyme-restricted DNA fragments can be used as epidemiologic tools during a suspected outbreak to detect concordance among strains.

The **incubation period** is 1 to 10 days, usually less than 4 days.

DIAGNOSTIC TESTS: Cultures of blood and cerebrospinal fluid (CSF) are indicated for patients with suspected invasive meningococcal disease. Cultures of a petechial or purpuric lesion, synovial fluid, sputum, and other body fluid specimens yield the organism in some patients. A Gram stain of a petechial or purpuric scraping, CSF, and buffy coat smear of blood can be helpful. Because *N meningitidis* can be a component of the nasopharyngeal flora, isolation of *N meningitidis* from this site is not helpful diagnostically. Bacterial antigen detection in CSF supports the diagnosis of a probable case if the clinical illness is consistent with meningococcal disease; use of latex agglutination assays for detection of meningococcal polysaccharide antigen in serum or urine specimens is not recommended. A serogroup-specific polymerase chain reaction test to detect *N meningitidis* from clinical specimens is used routinely in the United Kingdom, where up to 56% of cases are confirmed by polymerase chain reaction assay alone. This test is useful in patients who receive antimicrobial therapy before cultures are obtained.

Case definitions for invasive disease are given in Table 3.34 (p 454).

Table 3.34. Case Definitions for Invasive Meningococcal Disease

Confirmed

Isolation of *Neisseria meningitidis* from a usually sterile site, for example:
- Blood
- Cerebrospinal fluid
- Synovial fluid
- Pleural fluid
- Pericardial fluid
- Petechial or purpuric lesions in a person with a clinical illness consistent with meningococcal disease or purpura fulminans

Presumptive

Gram-negative diplococci in any sterile fluid, such as cerebrospinal fluid, synovial fluid, or scraping from a petechial or purpuric lesion

Probable

A positive antigen test (ie, polymerase chain reaction) result for *N meningitidis* in cerebrospinal fluid in the absence of a positive sterile site culture in a person with a clinical illness consistent with meningococcal disease or purpura fulminans

SUSCEPTIBILITY TESTING: Routine susceptibility testing of meningococcal isolates is not recommended. However, *N meningitidis* strains with decreased susceptibility to penicillin have been identified sporadically from several regions of the United States and widely from Spain, Italy, and parts of Africa. Resistant meningococcal strains for which the minimum inhibitory concentration to penicillin is more than 1 µg/mL are rare. Most reported isolates are moderately susceptible, with a minimum inhibitory concentration to penicillin of between 0.12 µg/mL and 1.0 µg/mL. Treatment with high-dose penicillin is effective against moderately susceptible strains. Cefotaxime and ceftriaxone show a high degree of in vitro activity against moderately penicillin-susceptible meningococci. Continued surveillance is necessary to monitor trends in the antimicrobial susceptibility patterns of meningococci in the United States and elsewhere.

TREATMENT: Penicillin G should be administered intravenously (250 000 to 300 000 U/kg per day, maximum 12 million U/day, divided every 4–6 hours) for patients with invasive meningococcal disease, including meningitis. Cefotaxime, ceftriaxone, and ampicillin are acceptable alternatives. In a patient with penicillin allergy characterized by anaphylaxis, chloramphenicol is recommended. For travelers from areas such as Spain, where penicillin resistance has been reported, cefotaxime, ceftriaxone, or chloramphenicol is recommended. Five to 7 days of antimicrobial therapy is adequate.

ISOLATION OF THE HOSPITALIZED PATIENT: In addition to standard precautions, droplet precautions are recommended until 24 hours after initiation of effective antimicrobial therapy.

CONTROL MEASURES:

CARE OF EXPOSED PEOPLE.

Chemoprophylaxis. The risk of contracting invasive meningococcal disease among contacts of infected individuals is the determining factor in the decision to give chemoprophylaxis. The attack rate for household contacts is 500 to 800 times the rate for the general population.

Close contacts of all people with invasive meningococcal disease (see Table 3.35), whether sporadic or in an outbreak, are at high risk and should receive chemoprophylaxis, ideally within 24 hours of diagnosis of the primary case. Throat and nasopharyngeal cultures are of no value in deciding who should receive chemoprophylaxis and are not recommended.

Chemoprophylaxis is warranted for people who have been exposed directly to a patient's oral secretions through close social contact, such as kissing or sharing of toothbrushes or eating utensils, as well as child care and nursery school contacts, during the 7 days before onset of disease in the index case. In addition, people who frequently ate or slept in the same dwelling as the infected individual within this period should receive chemoprophylaxis. For airline flights lasting more than 8 hours, passengers who are seated directly next to an infected individual should be considered candidates for prophylaxis. Routine prophylaxis is not recommended for health care professionals (Table 3.35) unless they have had intimate exposure, such as occurs with

Table 3.35. Disease Risk for Contacts of Individuals With Meningococcal Disease

High risk: chemoprophylaxis recommended (close contacts)
- Household contact, especially young children
- Child care or nursery school contact during 7 days before onset of illness
- Direct exposure to index patient's secretions through kissing or through sharing toothbrushes or eating utensils, markers of close social contact, during 7 days before onset of illness
- Mouth-to-mouth resuscitation, unprotected contact during endotracheal intubation during 7 days before onset of illness
- Frequently slept or ate in same dwelling as index patient during 7 days before onset of illness
- Passengers seated directly next to the index case during airline flights lasting more than 8 hours

Low risk: chemoprophylaxis not recommended
- Casual contact: no history of direct exposure to index patient's oral secretions (eg, school or work)
- Indirect contact: only contact is with a high-risk contact, no direct contact with the index patient
- Health care professionals without direct exposure to patient's oral secretions

In outbreak or cluster
- Chemoprophylaxis for people other than people at high risk should be administered only after consultation with local public health authorities

unprotected mouth-to-mouth resuscitation, intubation, or suctioning, before antimicrobial therapy was initiated.

Antimicrobial regimens for prophylaxis (see Table 3.36). Rifampin, ceftriaxone, and ciprofloxacin are appropriate drugs for chemoprophylaxis in adults. The drug of choice for most children is rifampin (Table 3.36). If antimicrobial agents other than ceftriaxone or cefotaxime are used for treatment of invasive meningococcal disease, the child should receive a regimen of chemoprophylaxis before hospital discharge to eradicate nasopharyngeal carriage of *N meningitidis*.

Ceftriaxone given in a single intramuscular dose has been demonstrated to be as effective as oral rifampin in eradicating pharyngeal carriage of group A meningococci. The efficacy of ceftriaxone has been confirmed only for serogroup A strains, but its effect is likely to be similar for other serogroups. Ceftriaxone has the advantage of ease of administration, which increases adherence, and is safe for use during pregnancy. Rifampin is not recommended for pregnant women.

Table 3.36. Recommended Chemoprophylaxis Regimens for High-Risk Contacts and People With Invasive Meningococcal Disease

Age of Infants, Children, and Adults	Dose	Duration	Efficacy, %	Cautions
Rifampin[1]				
<1 mo	5 mg/kg, orally, every 12 h	2 days		
≥1 mo	10 mg/kg (maximum 600 mg), orally, every 12 h	2 days	90–95	Can interfere with efficacy of oral contraceptives and some seizure prevention and anticoagulant medications; may stain soft contact lenses
Ceftriaxone				
<15 y	125 mg, intramuscularly	Single dose	90–95	To decrease pain at injection site, dilute with 1% lidocaine
≥15 y	250 mg, intramuscularly	Single dose	90–95	
Ciprofloxacin[1]				
≥18 y	500 mg, orally	Single dose	90–95	Not recommended for people <18 years of age

[1] Not recommended for use in pregnant women.

Ciprofloxacin administered to adults in a single oral dose also is effective in eradicating meningococcal carriage. At present, ciprofloxacin is not recommended for people younger than 18 years of age or for pregnant women (see Antimicrobial Agents and Related Therapy, p 735). Use of azithromycin as a single (500-mg) oral dose has been shown to be effective for eradication of nasopharyngeal carriage, but this regimen needs further evaluation.

Immunoprophylaxis. Because secondary cases can occur several weeks or more after onset of disease in the index case, meningococcal vaccine is an adjunct to chemoprophylaxis when an outbreak is caused by a serogroup prevented by the vaccine. For control of meningococcal outbreaks caused by vaccine-preventable serogroups (A, C, Y, and W-135), the preferred vaccine in adults and children older than 10 years is the tetravalent meningococcal (A, C, Y, and W-135) conjugate vaccine (MCV4), but the tetravalent meningococcal (A, C, Y, and W-135) polysaccharide vaccine (MPSV4) is acceptable. For children 2 to 10 years of age, the preferred vaccine is MPSV4.

MENINGOCOCCAL VACCINES. There are 2 meningococcal vaccines licensed in the United States for use in children and adults against serotypes A, C, Y, and W-135. The MPSV4 was licensed in 1981 for use in children 2 years of age and older and has been recommended by the American Academy of Pediatrics for use only for people at increased risk of meningococcal disease. The MPSV4 is administered subcutaneously as a single 0.5-mL dose and can be given concurrently with other vaccines but at different anatomic sites. The second vaccine, MCV4, was licensed in 2005 for use in people 11 to 55 years of age. The MCV4 is administered intramuscularly as a single 0.5-mL dose and also can be given concurrently with other recommended vaccines. No vaccine is available in the United States for prevention of serogroup B meningococcal disease.

Serogroup A meningococcal polysaccharide vaccine, given as MPSV4, is immunogenic in children as young as 3 months of age, although a response comparable to that seen in adults is not achieved until 4 or 5 years of age. For children younger than 18 months of age, 2 doses 3 months apart have been given for control of epidemics, although data regarding the efficacy of this schedule are not available. Response to the other polysaccharides when MPSV4 is administered to infants younger than 24 months of age is poor.

In children 2 to 5 years of age, measurable concentrations of antibodies against group A and C polysaccharides decrease substantially during the first 3 years after a single dose of MPSV4. In school-aged children and adults, MPSV4-induced protection likely persists for at least 3 to 5 years.

Indications for Use of MCV4 (Table 3.37, p 458). Routine childhood immunization with MPSV4 is not recommended, because the infection rate in the general population is low, response is poor in young children, immunity is relatively short lived, and the response to subsequent vaccine doses is impaired for some serogroups. However, immunization is recommended for children 2 years of age and older in high-risk groups, including people with functional or anatomic asplenia (see Children With Asplenia, p 83), children with terminal complement component or properdin deficiencies, and children who travel to or reside in areas where *N menigitidis* is hyperendemic or epidemic (CDC Travelers' Health Hotline, 877-FYI-TRIP or online at **www.cdc.gov/travel**).

Table 3.37. Recommended Meningococcal Vaccines in Previously Unimmunized People to Prevent Invasive Meningococcal Disease Caused by Serogroups A, C, Y, and W-135

Population Group	Age Group (y)			
	<2	2–10	11–19	20–55
General population	NR	NR	MCV4 intramuscularly at 11–12 y of age or high school entry (approx 15 y of age)	NR
At increased risk: • College freshmen living in dormitories[†] • Certain travelers[†] • Outbreaks of A, C, Y, or W-135 disease • People with increased susceptibility[‡]	NR	MPSV4, subcutaneously	MCV4 intramuscularly preferred (MPSV4 acceptable)	MCV4 intramuscularly preferred (MPSV4 acceptable)

NR indicates not recommended; MCV4, tetravalent meningococcal (A, C, Y, and W-135) conjugate vaccine; MPSV4, tetravalent meningococcal (A, C, Y, and W-135) polysaccharide vaccine.

[†] See text.

[‡] People with anatomic or functional asplenia, terminal complement component (C5-C9) or properdin deficiencies, military recruits, and microbiologists routinely exposed to *Neisseria meningitidis*.

Recommendations for use of MCV4 are as follows[*]:

• Two cohorts of adolescents should be immunized routinely with MCV4: 1) young adolescents at the 11- to 12-year visit; and 2) adolescents at high school entry or 15 years of age, whichever comes first. By 2008, the goal will be routine immunization of all adolescents with MCV4 beginning at 11 years of age.

• Adolescents should visit a health care professional at 11 to 12 years of age, when immunization status and other preventive services can be addressed. Subsequent annual visits throughout adolescence also are recommended.

• Entering college students who plan to live in dormitories should be immunized with MCV4 routinely.

• People at increased risk of meningococcal disease should be immunized with MCV4 if they are at least 11 years of age. These people include:
  ▪ Adolescents who have terminal complement or properdin deficiencies or adolescents who have anatomic or functional asplenia.

[*] American Academy of Pediatrics, Committee on Infectious Diseases. Prevention and control of meningococcal disease: recommendations for use of meningococcal vaccines in pediatric practice. *Pediatrics*. 2005;116:496–505; and Centers for Disease Control and Prevention. Prevention and control of meningococcal disease: recommendations of the Advisory Committee on Immunization Practices (ACIP). *MMWR Recomm Rep.* 2005;54(RR-7):1–21

- Adolescents who travel to or reside in countries where *N meningitidis* is hyperendemic or epidemic (CDC Travelers' Health Hotline 877-FYI-TRIP or online at **www.cdc.gov/travel**).
- Because people with human immunodeficiency virus (HIV) infection are likely to be at higher risk of meningococcal disease, although not to the extent that they are at risk of invasive *S pneumoniae* infection, they may elect to be immunized with MCV4 if they are at least 11 years of age.
- Children 2 to 10 years of age at increased risk of meningococcal disease should be immunized with MPSV4, because MCV4 is not licensed for use in these children.
- People who wish to decrease their risk of meningococcal disease may elect to receive MCV4 if they are 11 years of age or older.
- For control of meningococcal outbreaks caused by vaccine-preventable serogroups (A, C, Y, or W-135), MPSV4 or MCV4 should be used for people 11 years of age or older. Meningococcal conjugate vaccine is preferred, but MPSV4 is acceptable. For children 2 to 10 years of age, MPSV4 should be used.
- Immunization with MCV4 may be indicated for adolescents previously immunized with MPSV4. These people should be considered for reimmunization 3 to 5 years after receiving MPSV4 if they remain at increased risk of meningococcal disease.

Meningococcal vaccine is given to all military recruits in the United States.

Reimmunization. Little information is available to determine the need for or timing of reimmunization when the risk of disease continues or recurs. Immunization with MCV4 is indicated for adolescents 11 to 12 or 15 years of age previously immunized with MPSV4 if 3 to 5 years has elapsed. The same recommendation applies to entering college students previously immunized with MPSV4 and for people at high risk of infection (eg, people residing in areas in which disease is epidemic). Appropriate reimmunization intervals after MCV4 presently are not available. In children 11 years of age and older and adults, concentrations of antibodies against serogroups A, C, Y, and W-135 3 years after a single dose of MCV4 are equal to or greater than those of people given MPSV4, and it is expected that the duration of protection after the conjugate vaccine may exceed 5 years. Studies to determine duration of protection and need for reimmunization with MCV4 are underway.

Adverse Reactions and Precautions. Common adverse reactions after MPSV4 and MCV4 immunization include localized pain, headache, and fatigue, all of which are mild and last for 1 to 2 days. Pain, induration, swelling, and redness at the injection site are slightly greater after administration of MCV4 compared with MPSV4. Fever is reported by 2% to 5% of adolescents who receive either MPSV4 or MCV4. Meningococcal immunization recommendations should not be altered because of pregnancy if a woman is at increased risk of meningococcal disease. Guillain-Barré syndrome (GBS) was reported in 5 adolescents who received MCV4 between July and September 2005.* The temporal association provoked a recommendation that MCV4

---

* Guillain-Barré syndrome among recipients of Menactra meningococcal conjugate vaccine—United States, June-July 2005. *MMWR Morb Mortal Wkly Rep.* 2005;54:1023–1025

should not be given to adolescents or adults with a history of GBS. The number of cases of GBS was unlikely to be above the baseline population rate. However, cases of GBS or other clinically significant adverse events after MCV4 should be reported to the CDC (**www.vaers.hhs.gov**).

REPORTING. All confirmed, presumptive, and probable cases of invasive meningococcal disease must be reported to the regional health department (see Table 3.34, p 454). Timely reporting can facilitate early recognition of outbreaks and sero-grouping of isolates so that appropriate prevention programs can be implemented rapidly.

COUNSELING AND PUBLIC EDUCATION. When a case of invasive meningococcal disease is detected, the physician should provide accurate and timely information about meningococcal disease and the risk of transmission to families and contacts of the infected individual. Public health questions, such as whether a mass immunization program is needed, should be referred to the local health department. In appropriate situations, early provision of information in collaboration with the local health department to schools or other groups at increased risk and to the media may help minimize public anxiety and unrealistic or inappropriate demands for intervention.

Human Metapneumovirus

CLINICAL MANIFESTATIONS: Since discovery in 2001, human metapneumovirus (hMPV) has been shown to cause acute respiratory tract illness in patients of all ages. Human metapneumovirus appears to be one of the leading causes of bronchiolitis in infants and also causes some cases of pneumonia and croup. Otherwise healthy young children infected with hMPV usually have mild or moderate symptoms, but some young children have severe disease requiring hospitalization. Patients from whom hMPV is isolated commonly have concurrent infection with other viral agents. Risk factors for severe hMPV infection include immunodeficiency disease or therapy causing immunosuppression at any age. Preterm birth and underlying cardiopulmonary disease likely are risk factors, but increased risk associated with preterm birth and underlying disease is not defined fully. Human metapneumovirus infection has been associated with exacerbation of preexisting reactive airway disease.

Serologic studies suggest that all children are infected at least once by 5 years of age. Recurrent infection appears to occur throughout life and, in healthy people, usually is mild or asymptomatic.

ETIOLOGY: Human metapneumovirus is an enveloped single-stranded negative-sense RNA virus of the family Paramyxoviridae. Four major genotypes of virus have been identified, and these viruses appear to fall into 2 major antigenic subgroups (designated A and B), which usually circulate simultaneously each year but in varying proportions. Whether the 2 subgroups exhibit pathogenic differences is unknown.

EPIDEMIOLOGY: Humans are the only source of infection. Formal transmission studies have not been reported, but transmission is likely to occur by direct or close contact with contaminated secretions. Nosocomial infections have been reported.

Human metapneumovirus infections usually occur in annual epidemics during late winter and early spring in temperate climates. The hMPV season in a community generally coincides with or overlaps the respiratory syncytial virus season. During this overlapping period, bronchiolitis may be caused by either or both viruses. Sporadic infection does occur all year. The period of viral shedding has not been determined, but individual cases in which otherwise healthy infants shed virus for more than a week have been reported.

The **incubation period** is estimated to be 3 to 5 days in most cases.

DIAGNOSTIC TESTS: Diagnostic tests for hMPV currently are not available commercially. The assays for hMPV developed and used by research laboratories include reverse transcriptase-polymerase chain reaction (RT-PCR) amplification of viral genes (both conventional and real time) and viral isolation from nasopharyngeal secretions using cell culture. Rapid diagnostic assays based on antigen detection are not yet available. Viral isolation requires trypsin and specialized cell cultures of LLC-MK2, Vero, or primary monkey kidney cells. Approximately half of nasopharyngeal cultures that have positive results for hMPV by RT-PCR yield cultivable virus by current techniques. Serologic testing of acute and convalescent serum specimens can be used to confirm infection.

TREATMENT: Treatment is supportive and includes hydration, careful clinical assessment of respiratory status, including measurement of oxygen saturation, use of supplemental oxygen, and if necessary, mechanical ventilation.

ANTIMICROBIAL AGENTS. The rate of bacterial lung infection or bacteremia associated with hMPV infection is not defined, but is suspected to be low. Therefore, antimicrobial agents are not indicated in treatment of infants hospitalized with hMPV bronchiolitis or pneumonia unless evidence exists for the presence of a bacterial infection.

ISOLATION OF THE HOSPITALIZED PATIENT: In addition to standard precautions, contact precautions are recommended for the duration of hMPV-associated illness among infants and young children. Patients with known hMPV infection should be cared for in single rooms or placed in a cohort of hMPV-infected patients.

CONTROL MEASURES: Control of nosocomial hMPV infection depends on adherence to contact precautions. Exposure to hMPV-infected people, including other patients, staff, and family members, may not be recognized, because illness in contacts may be mild.

Preventive measures include limiting exposure to settings where exposure to hMPV may occur (eg, child care centers) and emphasis on hand hygiene in all settings, including the home, especially during periods when contacts of high-risk children have respiratory tract infections.

Microsporidia Infections
(Microsporidiosis)

CLINICAL MANIFESTATIONS: Patients with intestinal infection have watery, nonbloody diarrhea, generally without fever, although asymptomatic infection may be more common than originally suspected. Intestinal infection is most common in immunocompromised people, especially people who are infected with human immunodeficiency virus (HIV), and often results in chronic diarrhea. The clinical course is complicated by malnutrition and progressive weight loss. Chronic infection in immunocompetent people is rare. Other clinical syndromes that can occur in HIV-infected and immunocompetent patients include keratoconjunctivitis, sinusitis, myositis, nephritis, hepatitis, cholangitis, peritonitis, prostatitis, cystitis, disseminated disease, and wasting syndrome.

ETIOLOGY: Microsporidia are obligate intracellular, spore-forming protozoa. The genera *Encephalitozoon, Enterocytozoon, Nosema, Pleistophora, Trachipleistophora, Brachiola,* and *Vittaforma* have been implicated in human infection, as have unclassified *Microsporidium* species. *Enterocytozoon bieneusi* and *Encephalitozoon (Septata) intestinalis* are causes of chronic diarrhea in HIV-infected people.

EPIDEMIOLOGY: Most microsporidian infections are transmitted by oral ingestion of spores. Microsporidium spores are found commonly in surface water, and human strains have been identified in municipal water supplies and ground water. Several studies indicate that waterborne transmission occurs. Person-to-person spread by the fecal-oral route also occurs. Spores also have been detected in other body fluids, but their role in transmission is unknown. Data suggest the possibility of zoonotic transmission.

The **incubation period** is unknown.

DIAGNOSTIC TESTS: Infection with gastrointestinal *Microsporidia* species can be documented by identification of organisms in biopsy specimens from the small intestine. *Microsporidia* species spores also can be detected in formalin-fixed stool specimens or duodenal aspirates stained with a chromotrope-based stain (a modification of the trichrome stain) and examined by an experienced microscopist. Gram, acid-fast, periodic acid-Schiff, and Giemsa stains also can be used to detect organisms in tissue sections. The organisms often are not noticed, because they are small, stain poorly, and evoke minimal inflammatory response. Use of stool concentration techniques does not seem to improve the ability to detect *E bieneusi* spores. Polymerase chain reaction assay also can be used for diagnosis. Identification for classification purposes and diagnostic confirmation of species requires electron microscopy or molecular techniques.

TREATMENT: Restoration of immune function can be critical in control of any microsporidian infection. For a limited number of patients, albendazole, metronidazole, atovaquone, nitazoxanide, and fumagillin have been reported to decrease diarrhea but without eradication of the organism. Albendazole is the drug of choice for infections caused by *E intestinalis* but is not effective for *E bieneusi* infections, which may respond to fumagillin. Recurrence of diarrhea is common after therapy is discontinued. In HIV-infected patients, highly active antiretroviral therapy-associated improvement in CD4 + T-lymphocyte cell count can favorably modify the course of disease.

ISOLATION OF THE HOSPITALIZED PATIENT: In addition to standard precautions, contact precautions are recommended for diapered and incontinent children for the duration of illness.

CONTROL MEASURES: None have been documented. In HIV-infected people, decreased exposure may result from attention to hand hygiene and drinking bottled or boiled water.

Molluscum Contagiosum

CLINICAL MANIFESTATIONS: Molluscum contagiosum is a benign, usually asymptomatic viral infection of the skin with no systemic manifestations. It usually is characterized by 2 to 20 discrete, 5-mm-diameter, flesh-colored to translucent, dome-shaped papules, some with central umbilication. Lesions commonly occur on the trunk, face, and extremities but rarely are generalized. An eczematous reaction encircles lesions in approximately 10% of patients. People with eczema, immunocompromising conditions, and human immunodeficiency virus infection tend to have more widespread and prolonged eruptions.

ETIOLOGY: The cause is a poxvirus, which is the sole member of the genus *Molluscipoxvirus*. At least 3 DNA subtypes can be differentiated, but subtype is not significant in pathogenesis.

EPIDEMIOLOGY: Humans are the only known source of the virus, which is spread by direct contact, including sexual contact, or by fomites. Lesions can be disseminated by autoinoculation. Infectivity generally is low, but occasional outbreaks have been reported, including outbreaks in child care centers. The period of communicability is unknown.

The **incubation period** seems to vary between 2 and 7 weeks but may be as long as 6 months.

DIAGNOSTIC TESTS: The diagnosis usually can be made clinically from the characteristic appearance of the lesions. Wright or Giemsa staining of cells expressed from the central core of a lesion reveals characteristic intracytoplasmic inclusions. Electron microscopic examination of these cells identifies typical poxvirus particles.

TREATMENT: Lesions usually regress spontaneously, but mechanical removal (curettage) of the central core of each lesion may result in more rapid resolution. Children with single or widely scattered lesions should not be treated. A topical anesthetic, such as eutectic mixture of local anesthetics cream, may be applied 30 minutes to 2 hours before curettage. Alternatively, topical application of cantharidin (0.7% in collodion) or imiquimod (5% cream); peeling agents, such as salicylic and lactic acid preparations; electrocautery; or liquid nitrogen may be successful in resolution or removal of lesions. Although lesions can regress spontaneously, treatment may prevent autoinoculation and spread to other people. Scarring is a rare occurrence. Cidofovir is a cytosine nucleotide analogue with activity in vitro against molluscum contagiosum; successful intravenous treatment of immunocompromised adults with severe lesions has been reported.

ISOLATION OF THE HOSPITALIZED PATIENT: Standard precautions are recommended.

CONTROL MEASURES: No control measures are known for isolated cases. For outbreaks, which are common in the tropics, restricting direct person-to-person contact and sharing of potentially contaminated fomites may decrease spread.

Moraxella catarrhalis Infections

CLINICAL MANIFESTATIONS: Common infections include acute otitis media and sinusitis. Bronchopulmonary infection occurs predominantly among patients with chronic lung disease or impaired host defenses. The role of *Moraxella catarrhalis* in children with persistent cough is controversial. Rare manifestations are bacteremia (sometimes associated with focal infections, such as preseptal cellulitis, osteomyelitis, septic arthritis, abscesses, or a rash indistinguishable from that observed in meningococcemia) and conjunctivitis or meningitis in neonates. Other unusual manifestations include endocarditis, shunt-associated ventriculitis, and urinary tract infections.

ETIOLOGY: *Moraxella catarrhalis* is a gram-negative aerobic diplococcus. Almost 100% of strains produce beta-lactamase that mediates resistance to penicillins.

EPIDEMIOLOGY: *M catarrhalis* is part of the normal flora of the upper respiratory tract of humans. The mode of transmission is presumed to be direct contact with contaminated respiratory tract secretions or droplet spread. Infection is most common in infants and young children, but it occurs at all ages. The duration of carriage by infected and colonized children and the period of communicability are unknown.

The **incubation period** is unknown.

DIAGNOSTIC TESTS: The organism can be isolated on blood or chocolate agar culture media after incubation in air or with increased carbon dioxide. Culture of middle ear or sinus aspirates is indicated for patients with unusually severe infection, patients with infection that fails to respond to treatment, and immunocompromised children. Concomitant recovery of *M catarrhalis* with other pathogens (*Streptococcus pneumoniae* or *Haemophilus influenzae*) may indicate mixed infection.

TREATMENT: Although most strains of *Moraxella* species produce beta-lactamase and are resistant to amoxicillin in vitro, this agent remains effective as empiric therapy for otitis media and other respiratory tract infections. When *M catarrhalis* is isolated from appropriately obtained specimens (middle ear fluid, sinus aspirates, or lower respiratory tract secretions) or when initial therapy has been unsuccessful, appropriate antimicrobial agents include amoxicillin-clavulanate, cefuroxime, cefdinir, cefpodoxime, erythromycin, clarithromycin, azithromycin, trimethoprim-sulfamethoxazole, or a fluoroquinolone in people older than 18 years of age. If parenteral antimicrobial therapy is needed to treat *M catarrhalis* infection, in vitro data indicate that the following drugs are effective: cefotaxime, ceftriaxone, and ceftazidime.

ISOLATION OF THE HOSPITALIZED PATIENT: Standard precautions are recommended.

CONTROL MEASURES: None.

Mumps

CLINICAL MANIFESTATIONS: Mumps is a systemic disease characterized by swelling of one or more of the salivary glands, usually the parotid glands. Approximately one third of infections do not cause clinically apparent salivary gland swelling and may manifest primarily as respiratory tract infection. More than 50% of people with mumps have cerebrospinal fluid pleocytosis, but fewer than 10% have symptoms of central nervous system infection. Orchitis is a common complication after puberty, but sterility rarely occurs. Other rare complications include arthritis, thyroiditis, mastitis, glomerulonephritis, myocarditis, endocardial fibroelastosis, thrombocytopenia, cerebellar ataxia, transverse myelitis, ascending polyradiculitis, pancreatitis, oophoritis, and hearing impairment. In the absence of immunization, mumps typically occurs during childhood. Infection occurring among adults is more likely to be severe, and death resulting from mumps and its complications, although rare, occurs most often in adults. Mumps during the first trimester of pregnancy is associated with an increased rate of spontaneous abortion. Although mumps can cross the placenta, no evidence exists that this results in congenital malformation.

ETIOLOGY: Mumps is caused by an RNA virus classified as a Rubulavirus in the Paramyxoviridae family. Other causes of parotitis include infection with cytomegalovirus, parainfluenza virus types 1 and 3, influenza A virus, coxsackieviruses and other enteroviruses, lymphocytic choriomeningitis virus, human immunodeficiency virus (HIV), *Staphylococcus aureus*, nontuberculous mycobacterium, and less often, other gram-positive and gram-negative bacteria; salivary duct calculi; starch ingestion; drug reactions (eg, phenylbutazone, thiouracil, iodides); and metabolic disorders (diabetes mellitus, cirrhosis, and malnutrition).

EPIDEMIOLOGY: Mumps occurs worldwide, and humans are the only known natural hosts. The virus is spread by contact with infected respiratory tract secretions. Historically, the peak incidence was between January and May; however, seasonality no longer is evident in the United States. The incidence in the United States, which has decreased markedly since introduction of the mumps vaccine, now is fewer than 300 reported cases per year. Historically, the peak incidence in the United States was among children 5 to 14 years of age, but most cases now are reported among individuals older than 14 years of age. In immunized children, most cases of parotitis are not caused by mumps infection. Outbreaks can occur in highly immunized populations, most often in people who have not been immunized. The period of maximum communicability is from 1 to 2 days before onset of parotid swelling to 5 days after onset of parotid swelling. Virus has been isolated from saliva from 7 days before through 9 days after onset of swelling.

The **incubation period** usually is 16 to 18 days, but cases may occur from 12 to 25 days after exposure.

DIAGNOSTIC TESTS: In the United States, mumps now is an uncommon infection, and parotitis has other etiologies, including other infectious agents. People with parotitis lasting 2 days or more without other apparent cause should undergo diagnostic testing to confirm mumps virus as the cause. Mumps can be confirmed by isolating the virus in cell culture inoculated with throat washing, saliva, urine, or spinal fluid specimens; by detection of mumps-specific IgM antibody; by detection of mumps virus by reverse transcriptase-polymerase chain reaction; or by a significant increase between acute and convalescent titers in serum mumps immunoglobulin (Ig) G antibody titer determined by standard serologic assay (eg, complement fixation, neutralization, hemagglutination inhibition test, or enzyme immunoassay).

TREATMENT: Supportive.

ISOLATION OF THE HOSPITALIZED PATIENT: In addition to standard precautions, droplet precautions are recommended until 9 days after onset of parotid swelling.

CONTROL MEASURES:

SCHOOL AND CHILD CARE. Children should be excluded for 9 days from onset of parotid gland swelling. For control measures during an outbreak, see Outbreak Control, p 468.

CARE OF EXPOSED PEOPLE. Mumps vaccine has not been demonstrated to be effective in preventing infection after exposure. However, mumps vaccine can be given after exposure, because immunization will provide protection against subsequent exposures. Immunization during the incubation period presents no increased risk. The routine use of mumps vaccine is not advised for people born before 1957, because most of these people are immune. Immune globulin (IG) and Mumps Immune Globulin are not effective as postexposure prophylaxis. Mumps Immune Globulin no longer is available in the United States.

MUMPS VACCINE. Live-attenuated mumps vaccine has been licensed in the United States since 1967. Vaccine is administered by subcutaneous injection of 0.5 mL alone as a monovalent vaccine or, more commonly, as the combined measles-mumps-rubella (MMR) vaccine. Protective efficacy of the vaccine in clinical trials is estimated to be >95% with a single dose. Serologic and epidemiologic evidence extending for more than 25 years indicates that vaccine-induced immunity is long lasting.

VACCINE RECOMMENDATIONS:
- Mumps vaccine should be given as MMR or measles-mumps-rubella-varicella (MMRV) routinely to children at 12 to 15 months of age, with a second dose of MMR separated by at least 1 month (ie, a minimum of 28 days) and typically administered at 4 to 6 years of age. Reimmunization with mumps vaccine may provide an additional safeguard against primary vaccine failure; mumps outbreaks have occurred in people in highly immunized populations who previously had received a single dose of mumps-containing vaccine. Administration of MMR or MMRV is not harmful if given to a person already immune to one or more of the viruses (from previous infection or immunization).
- Mumps immunization is of particular importance for children approaching puberty, adolescents, and adults who have not had mumps or mumps vaccine. At office visits of prepubertal children and adolescents, the status of immunity to mumps should be assessed. People should be considered susceptible unless they have documentation of at least 1 dose of vaccine on or after their first birthday, documentation of physician-diagnosed mumps, or serologic evidence of immunity or were born before 1957.
- Susceptible children 12 months of age or older, adolescents, and adults born during or after 1957 should be offered mumps immunization (usually as MMR) before beginning travel, because mumps is endemic throughout most of the world. Children younger than 12 months of age need not be given mumps vaccine before travel, but they may receive it as MMR if measles vaccine is indicated.
- Mumps vaccine or MMR or MMRV vaccine may be given with other vaccines at different injection sites and with separate syringes (see Simultaneous Administration of Multiple Vaccines, p 34).

Adverse Reactions. Adverse reactions associated with mumps vaccine are rare. Orchitis, parotitis, and low-grade fever have been reported rarely after immunization. Temporally related reactions, including febrile seizures, nerve deafness, aseptic meningitis, encephalitis, rash, pruritus, and purpura, may follow immunization rarely; however, causality has not been established. Allergic reactions also are rare (see Measles, Precautions and Contraindications [p 449], and Rubella, Precautions and Contraindications [p 578]). Other reactions that occur after immunization with MMR or MMRV vaccine may be attributable to other components of the vaccines (see Measles, p 441, Rubella, p 574, and Varicella-Zoster Infections, p 711).

Reimmunization with mumps vaccine (monovalent or MMR) is not associated with an increased incidence of reactions.

PRECAUTIONS AND CONTRAINDICATIONS. See Measles, p 441, Rubella, p 574, and Varicella-Zoster Infections, p 711, if MMRV is used.

Febrile Illness. Children with minor illnesses with or without fever, such as upper respiratory tract infections, may be immunized (see Vaccine Safety and Contraindications, p 39). Fever is not a contraindication to immunization. However, if other manifestations suggest a more serious illness, the child should not be immunized until recovered.

Allergies. The widespread use of the mumps vaccine since 1967 has resulted in only rare isolated reports of allergic reactions. Allergic reactions to components of the vaccine (eg, neomycin or gelatin) occasionally may occur and usually are mild. Severe allergic reactions, such as anaphylaxis, rarely are reported. Most children with egg hypersensitivity can be immunized safely with MMR or MMRV vaccine (see Measles, p 441). People with a history of anaphylactic, anaphylactoid, or other immediate reactions subsequent to egg ingestion may be at an increased risk of immediate-type hypersensitivity reactions after immunization (see Measles, p 441).

Recent Administration of Immune Globulin. Although the effect of Immune Globulin (IG) administration on the immune response to mumps vaccine is unknown, mumps vaccine should be given at least 2 weeks before or 3 months after administration of IG or blood transfusion because of the theoretic possibility that antibody will neutralize vaccine virus and interfere with a successful immunization. Because high doses of IG (such as doses given for treatment of Kawasaki disease) can inhibit the response to measles vaccine for longer intervals, MMR and MMRV immunization should be deferred for a longer period after administration of IG (see Measles, p 441).

Altered Immunity. Patients with immunodeficiency diseases and people receiving immunosuppressive therapy (eg, patients with leukemia, lymphoma, or generalized malignant disease), including high doses of systemically administered corticosteroids, alkylating agents, antimetabolites, or radiation or people who are otherwise immunocompromised, should not receive mumps vaccine (see Immunocompromised Children, p 71). The exceptions are patients with HIV infection who are not severely immunocompromised; these patients should be immunized against mumps with MMR or MMRV vaccine (see Human Immunodeficiency Virus Infection, p 378). The risk of mumps exposure for patients with altered immunity can be decreased by immunizing their close susceptible contacts. Immunized people do not transmit mumps vaccine virus.

After cessation of immunosuppressive therapy, mumps immunization should be deferred for at least 3 months (with the exception of corticosteroid recipients [see the next paragraph]). This interval is based on the assumptions that immunologic responsiveness will have been restored in 3 months and the underlying disease for which immunosuppressive therapy was given is in remission or under control. However, because the interval can vary with the intensity and type of immunosuppressive therapy, radiation therapy, underlying disease, and other factors, a definitive recommendation for an interval after cessation of immunosuppressive therapy when mumps vaccine can be administered safely and effectively often is not possible.

Corticosteroids. For patients who have received high doses of corticosteroids ($\geq$2 mg/kg per day or >20 mg/day of prednisone or equivalent) for 14 days or more and who are not otherwise immunocompromised, the recommended interval is at least 1 month after corticosteroids are discontinued (see Immunocompromised Children, p 71).

Pregnancy. Conception should be avoided for 28 days after mumps immunization because of the theoretic risk associated with live-virus vaccine. Susceptible postpubertal females should not be immunized if they are known to be pregnant. Live-attenuated mumps virus vaccine can infect the placenta, although the virus has not been isolated from fetal tissues from susceptible females who received vaccine and underwent elective abortions. Mumps immunization during pregnancy has not been associated with congenital malformations (see Measles, p 441, and Rubella, p 574).

OUTBREAK CONTROL. When determining means to control outbreaks, immunization or exclusion of susceptible students who refuse immunization from affected schools and schools judged by local public health authorities to be at risk of transmission should be considered. Such policy should be an effective means of terminating school outbreaks and rapidly increasing rates of immunization. Excluded students can be readmitted immediately after immunization. Pupils who continue to be exempted from mumps immunization because of medical, religious, or other reasons should be excluded until at least 26 days after the onset of parotitis in the last person with mumps in the affected school. Experience with outbreak control for other vaccine-preventable diseases indicates that this strategy is effective.

Mycoplasma pneumoniae Infections

CLINICAL MANIFESTATIONS: The most common clinical syndromes are acute bronchitis and upper respiratory tract infections, including pharyngitis and, occasionally, otitis media or myringitis, which may be bullous. Coryza, sinusitis, and croup are rare. Malaise, fever, and occasionally, headache are nonspecific manifestations of infection. In approximately 10% of patients, pneumonia with cough and widespread rales on physical examination develops within a few days and lasts for 3 to 4 weeks. The cough is nonproductive initially but later may become productive, particularly in older children and adolescents. Approximately 10% of children with pneumonia exhibit a rash, most often maculopapular. Abnormalities detected on radiography vary, but bilateral, diffuse infiltrates are common, and focal abnormalities, such as consolidation, effusion, and hilar adenopathy may occur.

Unusual manifestations include nervous system disease (eg, aseptic meningitis, encephalitis, demyelinating disease, cerebellar ataxia, transverse myelitis, peripheral

neuropathy) as well as myocarditis, pericarditis, polymorphous mucocutaneous eruptions (including Stevens-Johnson syndrome), hemolytic anemia, and arthritis. In
patients with sickle cell disease, Down syndrome, immunodeficiencies, and chronic
cardiorespiratory disease, severe pneumonia with pleural effusion can develop. A substantial proportion of acute chest syndrome and pneumonia associated with sickle cell
disease appears to be attributable to *M pneumoniae*.

ETIOLOGY: Mycoplasmas, including *Mycoplasma pneumoniae*, are the smallest free-living
microorganisms; they lack a cell wall and are pleomorphic.

EPIDEMIOLOGY: Mycoplasmas are ubiquitous in animals and plants, but *M pneumoniae* causes disease only in humans. *Mycoplasma pneumoniae* is transmissible by respiratory droplets during close contact with a symptomatic person. Outbreaks have been
described in hospitals, military bases, colleges, and summer camps. People of any age
can be infected, but specific disease syndromes are age-related. *Mycoplasma pneumoniae*
is an uncommon cause of pneumonia in children younger than 5 years of age but is a
leading cause of pneumonia in school-aged children and young adults. Infections
occur throughout the world, in any season, and in all geographic settings. Community-wide epidemics occur every 4 to 7 years. Because of a long incubation period,
familial spread can continue for many months. Clinical illness within a group or family ranges from mild upper respiratory tract infection to tracheobronchitis or pharyngitis to pneumonia. Asymptomatic carriage after infection may occur for weeks to
months. Immunity after infection is not long lasting.

The **incubation period** is 2 to 3 weeks (range, 1–4 weeks).

DIAGNOSTIC TESTS: *Mycoplasma pneumoniae* can be grown in artificial media, but
growth requires special enriched broth or agar media, is successful in 40% to 90% of
cases, and takes up to 21 days. Isolation of *M pneumoniae* in a patient with compatible
clinical manifestations suggests causation. Because this organism can be excreted from
the respiratory tract for several weeks after acute infection despite appropriate therapy, isolation of the organism may not indicate acute infection. Sensitive and specific
polymerase chain reaction tests for *M pneumoniae* have been developed and appear to
be superior to serology for diagnosis. First-line use awaits standardization and availability as a complete kit.

Commercially available immunofluorescent tests and enzyme immunoassay detect
M pneumoniae-specific immunoglobulin (Ig) M and IgG antibodies. Although the presence of IgM antibodies confirms recent *M pneumoniae* infection, these antibodies persist in serum for several months and may not necessarily indicate current infection;
false-positive test results also occur. Serologic diagnosis can be made by demonstrating
a fourfold or greater increase in antibody titer between acute and convalescent serum
specimens when the complement fixation assay is used. The antibody titer peaks at
approximately 3 to 6 weeks and persists for 2 to 3 months after infection. Because *M
pneumoniae* antibodies may cross-react with some other antigens, results of these tests
should be interpreted cautiously when evaluating febrile illnesses of unknown origin.

Serum cold hemagglutinin titers of $\geq$1:32 are present in approximately 50% of
patients with pneumonia caused by *M pneumoniae* by the beginning of the second week
of illness. Fourfold increases in cold hemagglutinin titer between acute and convalescent serum specimens occur more often in patients with severe *M pneumoniae* infection

than in people with less severe disease. This test has low specificity for *Mycoplasma* infection, however, and other agents, including adenoviruses, Epstein-Barr virus, and measles, can cause illnesses in infants or children associated with a modest increase in cold hemagglutinin titer. A negative test result for cold agglutinins does not exclude the diagnosis of mycoplasmal infection. With the wide availability of specific antibody tests, use of cold hemagglutinin titers has been deemphasized.

TREATMENT: Acute bronchitis and upper respiratory tract illness caused by *M pneumoniae* generally are mild and resolve without antimicrobial therapy. Because mycoplasmas lack a cell wall, they inherently are resistant to beta-lactam agents. Macrolides, including erythromycin, azithromycin, and clarithromycin, are the preferred antimicrobial agents for treatment of pneumonia in children younger than 8 years of age. Tetracycline and doxycycline also are effective and may be used for children 8 years of age and older. Fluoroquinolones are effective but are not recommended as first-choice agents for children. There is no evidence that treatment of nonrespiratory tract disease alters the course of illness.

ISOLATION OF THE HOSPITALIZED PATIENT: In addition to standard precautions, droplet precautions are recommended for the duration of symptomatic illness.

CONTROL MEASURES: Diagnosis of an infected patient should lead to an increased index of suspicion for *M pneumoniae* infection in household members and close contacts, and therapy should be given if a contact develops compatible lower respiratory tract illness.

Antimicrobial prophylaxis for exposed contacts is not recommended routinely. Tetracycline and azithromycin for prophylaxis have been shown to decrease symptomatic diseases and reduce rates of transmission within families and institutions. People who are exposed intimately to a person infected with *M pneumoniae* or who live in a house with a person who has an underlying condition that predisposes to severe *M pneumoniae* infection, such as children with sickle cell disease, may be considered for prophylactic treatment with erythromycin (or another macrolide) or tetracycline during the acute phase of the index patient's illness.

Nocardiosis

CLINICAL MANIFESTATIONS: Immunocompetent children typically have cutaneous or lymphocutaneous disease with pustular or ulcerative lesions that remain localized after soil contamination of a skin injury. Invasive disease occurs most commonly in immunocompromised patients, particularly people with chronic granulomatous disease, organ transplantation, human immunodeficiency virus infection, or disease requiring long-term systemic corticosteroid therapy. In these children, infection characteristically begins in the lungs, and the illness can be acute, subacute, or chronic. Pulmonary disease commonly manifests as rounded nodular infiltrates that can undergo cavitation. Hematogenous spread may occur from the lungs to the brain (single or multiple abscesses), in skin (pustules, pyoderma, abscesses, mycetoma), and occasionally in other organs. *Nocardia* organisms can be recovered from patients with cystic fibrosis, but their role as a lung pathogen is not clear.

ETIOLOGY: *Nocardia* species are aerobic actinomycetes, a large and diverse group of gram-positive bacteria, which include *Actinomyces israelii*, *Rhodococcus equi*, and *Tropheryma whippelii* (Whipple disease). Pulmonary or disseminated disease is caused most commonly by the *Nocardia asteroides* complex, which includes *Nocardia farcinica* and *Nocardia nova*. Primary cutaneous disease most commonly is caused by *Nocardia brasiliensis*. *Nocardia pseudobrasiliensis* is associated with pulmonary, central nervous system (CNS), and systemic nocardiosis. Other pathogenic species include *Nocardia abscessus*, *Nocardia otitidiscaviarum*, *Nocardia transvalensis*, *Nocardia veterana*, *Nocardia cyriacigeorgica*, and *Nocardia paucivarans*.

EPIDEMIOLOGY: Found worldwide, *Nocardia* species are ubiquitous environmental saprophytes living in soil, organic matter, and water. The lungs are the probable portals of entry for pulmonary or disseminated disease. Direct skin inoculation occurs, often as the result of contact with contaminated soil after minor trauma. Person-to-person and animal-to-human transmission does not occur.

The **incubation period** for pulmonary disease is unknown.

DIAGNOSTIC TESTS: Isolation of *Nocardia* organisms from body fluid, abscess material, or tissue specimens provides a definitive diagnosis. Stained smears of sputum, body fluids, or pus demonstrating beaded, branched, weakly gram-positive, variably acid-fast rods suggest the diagnosis. The Brown and Brenn and methenamine silver stains are recommended to demonstrate microorganisms in tissue specimens. *Nocardia* organisms are slow growing but grow readily on blood and chocolate agar in 3 to 5 days. Cultures from normally sterile sites should be maintained for 3 weeks in an appropriate liquid medium. Serologic tests for *Nocardia* species are not useful.

TREATMENT: Trimethoprim-sulfamethoxazole or a sulfonamide alone (eg, sulfisoxazole or sulfamethoxazole) is the drug of choice. Preparations that are less urine soluble, such as sulfadiazine, should be avoided. Immunocompetent patients with primary lymphocutaneous disease usually respond after 6 to 12 weeks of therapy. Immunocompromised patients and patients with invasive disease should be treated for 6 to 12 months and for at least 3 months after apparent cure because of the tendency for relapse. Patients with acquired immunodeficiency syndrome may need even longer therapy. For patients with central nervous system disease, disseminated disease, or overwhelming infection, amikacin plus ceftriaxone (based on in vitro susceptibility testing) should be included for the first 4 to 12 weeks of treatment or until the patient's condition is improved clinically. Patients with meningitis or brain abscess should be monitored with serial neuroimaging studies. If response to trimethoprim-sulfamethoxazole does not occur, other agents, such as clarithromycin (*N nova*), amoxicillin-clavulanate (*N brasiliensis* and *N abscessus*), imipenem, or meropenem may be beneficial. Linezolid is highly active against all *Nocardia* species in vitro; small case series demonstrate that it may be effective for the treatment of invasive infections. Drug susceptibility testing is recommended by the Clinical and Laboratory Standards Institute for isolates from patients with invasive disease and patients who are unable to tolerate a sulfonamide. Drainage of abscesses is beneficial.

ISOLATION OF THE HOSPITALIZED PATIENT: Standard precautions are recommended.

CONTROL MEASURES: None.

Onchocerciasis
(River Blindness, Filariasis)

CLINICAL MANIFESTATIONS: The disease involves skin, subcutaneous tissues, lymphatic vessels, and eyes. Subcutaneous nodules of varying sizes containing adult worms develop 6 to 12 months after initial infection. In patients in Africa, the nodules tend to be found on the lower torso, pelvis, and lower extremities, whereas in patients in Central and South America, the nodules more often are located on the upper body (the head and trunk) but may occur on the extremities. After the worms mature, microfilariae are produced and migrate to the tissues and may cause a chronic, pruritic, papular dermatitis. After a period of years, the skin can become lichenified and hypopigmented or hyperpigmented. The presence of living or dead microfilariae in the ocular structures leads to photophobia and inflammation of the cornea, iris, ciliary body, retina, choroid, and optic nerve. Blindness can result if the disease is untreated.

ETIOLOGY: *Onchocerca volvulus* is a filarial nematode.

EPIDEMIOLOGY: Larvae are transmitted by the bite of an infected *Simulium* species black fly that breeds in fast-flowing streams and rivers (hence the colloquial name of the disease, "river blindness"). The disease occurs primarily in equatorial Africa, but small foci are found in southern Mexico, Guatemala, northern South America, and Yemen. Prevalence is greatest among people who live near vector breeding sites. *Onchocerca volvulus* is an exclusively human parasite and has no animal reservoir host. Adult worms continue to produce microfilariae capable of infecting flies for more than a decade. The infection is not transmissible by person-to-person contact or blood transfusion.

The **incubation period** from larval inoculation to microfilariae in the skin usually is 6 to 12 months but can be as long as 3 years.

DIAGNOSTIC TESTS: Direct examination of a 1- to 2-mg shaving or biopsy specimen of the epidermis and upper dermis (taken from the scapular or iliac crest area) can reveal microfilariae. Microfilariae are not found in blood. Adult worms may be demonstrated in excised nodules that have been sectioned and stained. A slit-lamp examination of the anterior chamber of an involved eye may reveal motile microfilariae or corneal lesions typical of onchocerciasis. Eosinophilia is common. Specific serologic tests and polymerase chain reaction techniques for detection of microfilariae in skin are available only in research laboratories.

TREATMENT: Ivermectin, a microfilaricidal agent, is the drug of choice for treatment of onchocerciasis. Treatment decreases dermatitis and the risk of developing severe ocular disease, but treatment does not kill the adult worms and, thus, is not curative. One single oral dose of ivermectin (150 µg/kg) should be given every 6 to 12 months until asymptomatic. Adverse reactions caused by the death of microfilariae can include rash, edema, fever, myalgia, asthma exacerbation, and hypotension (which rarely is severe). Precautions to ivermectin treatment include pregnancy, breastfeeding, central nervous system disorders that may increase the penetration of drug into the central nervous system, and high levels of cocirculating *Loa loa* microfilariae.

Safety and effectiveness in pediatric patients weighing less than 15 kg have not been established. A 6-week course of doxycycline has been demonstrated to render adult female worms sterile for long periods of time and may be considered as adjunctive therapy for children 8 years of age or older and nonpregnant adults.

ISOLATION OF THE HOSPITALIZED PATIENT: Standard precautions are recommended.

CONTROL MEASURES: Repellents and protective clothing (long sleeves and pants) can decrease exposure to bites from black flies, which bite by day. Treatment of vector breeding sites with larvicides has been effective for controlling black fly populations, particularly in West Africa. A major initiative led by the World Health Organization to distribute ivermectin to communities with endemic disease to prevent severe morbidity from onchocerciasis has been highly successful.

Human Papillomaviruses

CLINICAL MANIFESTATIONS: Most human papillomavirus (HPV) infections produce no lesions and are inapparent clinically. However, HPVs can produce benign epithelial proliferation (warts) of the skin and mucous membranes and are associated with anogenital dysplasias and cancers. Cutaneous nongenital warts include common skin warts, plantar warts, flat warts, thread-like (filiform) warts, and epidermodysplasia verruciformis. Warts also occur on the mucous membranes, including the anogenital, oral, nasal, and conjunctival areas and the respiratory tract, where respiratory papillomatosis occurs.

Common **skin warts** are dome-shaped with conical projections that give the surface a rough appearance. They usually are painless and multiple, occurring commonly on the hands and around or under the nails. When small dermal vessels become thrombosed, black dots appear in the warts. Plantar warts on the foot may be painful and are characterized by marked hyperkeratosis, sometimes with black dots.

Flat warts ("juvenile warts") commonly are found on the face and extremities of children and adolescents. They usually are small, multiple, and flat topped; seldom exhibit papillomatosis; and rarely cause pain. Filiform warts occur on the face and neck. Cutaneous warts are benign.

Anogenital warts, also called **condylomata acuminata**, are skin-colored warts with a cauliflower-like surface that range in size from a few millimeters to several centimeters. In males, these warts may be found on the penis, scrotum, or anal and perianal area. In females, these lesions may occur on the vulva or perianal areas and less commonly in the vagina or on the cervix. Anogenital warts often are multiple and attract attention because of their appearance. Warts usually are painless, although they may cause itching, burning, local pain, or bleeding.

Anogenital HPV infection may be associated with clinically inapparent dysplastic lesions, particularly in the female genital tract (cervix and vagina). These lesions may be made more apparent by applying 3% to 5% acetic acid to the mucosal surface and examining it by magnification. The HPV types associated with these dysplasias also are associated with cancers that occur in the anogenital tract. Human papillomavirus is involved etiologically in more than 99% of cervical cancers and a substantial proportion of vulvar, anal, and penile cancers.

Respiratory tract papillomatosis is a rare condition characterized by recurring papillomas in the larynx or other areas of the upper respiratory tract. This condition is diagnosed most commonly in children between 2 and 5 years of age and manifests as a voice change, stridor, or abnormal cry. Respiratory papillomas have been associated with respiratory tract obstruction in young children. Adult onset also has been described.

Epidermodysplasia verruciformis is a rare, lifelong, severe papillomavirus infection believed to be a consequence of an inherited deficiency of cell-mediated immunity. The lesions may resemble flat warts but often are similar to tinea versicolor, covering the torso and upper extremities. Most appear during the first decade of life, but malignant transformation, which occurs in approximately one third of affected people, usually is delayed until adulthood.

ETIOLOGY: Human papillomaviruses are members of the *Papillomavirus* genus of the Papillomaviridae family and are DNA viruses. More than 100 types have been identified. These viruses are grouped into cutaneous and mucosal types on the basis of their tendency to infect particular types of epithelium. Most often, the HPV types found in nongenital warts will be cutaneous types, and those in respiratory papillomatosis, anogenital warts, dysplasias, or cancers will be mucosal types. More than 30 HPV types can infect the genital tract. Based on their detection in cancers, mucosal HPVs are divided into low-risk and high-risk types. More than 18 high-risk types are recognized, the most common being types 16, 18, 31, and 45. Types 6 and 11 frequently are associated with condylomata acuminata, recurrent respiratory papillomatosis, and conjunctival papillomas and carcinomas.

EPIDEMIOLOGY: Papillomaviruses are distributed widely among mammals and are species-specific. Cutaneous warts occur commonly among school-aged children; the prevalence rate is as high as 50%. Human papillomavirus infections are transmitted from person to person by close contact. Nongenital warts are acquired through minor trauma to the skin. An increase in the incidence of plantar warts has been associated with swimming in public pools. The intense and often widespread appearance of warts in patients with compromised cellular immunity (particularly patients who have undergone transplantation and people with human immunodeficiency virus infection) suggests that alterations in immunity predispose to reactivation of latent intraepithelial infection.

Anogenital HPV infection is the most common sexually transmitted infection in the United States, occurring in more than 40% of sexually active adolescent females. Most infections are transient and clear spontaneously. Anogenital HPV infections are transmitted primarily by sexual contact and most are subclinical. Rarely, infection is transmitted to a child through the birth canal during delivery or transmitted from nongenital sites. When anogenital warts are found in a child who is beyond infancy but prepubertal, sexual abuse must be considered.

Respiratory papillomatosis is believed to be acquired by aspiration of infectious secretions during passage through an infected birth canal.

The **incubation period** is unknown but is estimated to range from 3 months to several years. Papillomavirus acquired by a neonate at the time of birth may never cause clinical disease or may become apparent over several years (eg, respiratory papillomatosis). Neoplasias are rare long-term sequelae of chronic persistent infection, usually occurring more than 10 years after infection.

DIAGNOSTIC TESTS: Most cutaneous and anogenital warts are diagnosed through clinical inspection. Respiratory papillomatosis is diagnosed using endoscopy and biopsy. Cervical dysplasias may be detected via cytologic examination of a Papanicolaou (Pap) smear, or liquid-based cytology and biopsy specimens of any tissue may display cytohistologic characteristics of HPV infection.

Human papillomavirus cannot be cultured easily. A definitive diagnosis of HPV infection is based on detection of viral nucleic acid (DNA or RNA) or capsid protein. Tests that detect high-risk or low-risk types of HPV DNA in cells obtained from the cervix are available. Testing for HPV types is used in combination with Pap test to determine whether patients need to be sent for colposcopy; otherwise, screening for clinically inapparent HPV infection or evaluating anogenital warts using HPV DNA or RNA tests is not recommended.

TREATMENT*: Treatment of HPV infection is directed toward eliminating the lesions that result from the infection rather than HPV itself. Most nongenital warts eventually regress spontaneously but may persist for months or years. The optimal treatment for warts that do not resolve spontaneously has not been identified. Most methods of treatment rely on chemical or physical destruction of the infected epithelium, such as application of salicylic acid products, cryotherapy with liquid nitrogen, or application of duct tape. Daily treatment with tretinoin has been useful for widespread flat warts in children. Care must be taken to avoid a deleterious cosmetic result with therapy. Pharmacologic treatments for refractory warts, including cimetidine, have been used with varied success.

The optimal treatment for anogenital warts has not been identified. Spontaneous regression occurs within months in some cases. The application of podophyllum resin or patient-applied podofilox solution or gel (the major cytotoxic ingredient of podophyllum resin) often is the initial therapy of choice. These agents have not been tested for safety and efficacy in children, and their use is contraindicated in pregnancy. Other treatment modalities are cryotherapy, trichloroacetic acid or bichloroacetic acid, imiquimod (patient-applied), electrocautery, laser surgery, and surgical excision (see Table 4.4, p 766). Although most forms of therapy are successful for the initial removal of warts, treatment may not eradicate HPV infection from the surrounding normal tissue. Therefore, recurrences are common and probably attributable to reactivation rather than reinfection. Many unproven compounds are being used to treat anogenital warts. Agents associated with local tissue damage can be harmful.

Human papillomavirus infection of the cervix is common in sexually active adolescents and can be associated with epithelial dysplasia. Cytologic screening of cervical cells should be initiated within 3 years of the onset of consensual and nonconsensual sexual activity. Approximately 40% of people with HPV will develop

---

* Centers for Disease Control and Prevention. Sexually transmitted diseases treatment guidelines—2006. *MMWR Recomm Rep.* 2006; in press (see **www.cdc.gov/mmwr**)

abnormal Pap smears. Of those with abnormal Pap smears associated with low-risk HPV, 100% will resolve in 3 years and 80% of those associated with high-risk HPV will resolve in 3 years. Adolescents with cervical dysplasia should be cared for by a physician who is knowledgeable in the management of cervical dysplasia. Suggestions for evaluation and management are available at **www.asccp.org/pdfs/consensus/ algorithms.pdf**.

Respiratory papillomatosis is difficult to treat and is best managed by an otolaryngologist. Local recurrence is common, and repeated surgical procedures for removal are often necessary. Extension or dissemination of respiratory papillomas from the larynx into the trachea, bronchi, or lung parenchyma is a rare complication that can result in increased morbidity and mortality. Intralesional interferon, indole-3-carbinole, photodynamic therapy, and intralesional cidofovir have been used as investigational treatments and may be of benefit for patients with frequent recurrences.

Oral warts can be removed through cryotherapy, electrocautery, or surgical excision.

ISOLATION OF THE HOSPITALIZED PATIENT: Standard precautions are recommended.

CONTROL MEASURES: Suspected child abuse should be reported to the appropriate local agency if anogenital warts are found in a child who is beyond infancy but prepubertal.

Sexual abstinence, monogamous relationships, delayed sexual debut, and minimizing the number of sex partners are modes of reducing risk of HPV infection. Consistent and correct use of latex condoms can decrease but does not eliminate the risk of anogenital HPV infection when the infected areas are covered or protected by the condom. In addition, use of latex condoms has been associated with a decrease in the risk of genital warts and cervical cancer. Although HPV infection may persist for life, the degree and duration of contagiousness in patients with a history of genital infection is unknown.

Sexual partners may benefit from examination to assess for the presence of anogenital warts or other sexually transmitted infections. Female sexual partners of patients with genital warts should be informed that cytologic screening for cervical cancer is recommended for all sexually active women. Cervical cancer screening guidelines are available from the American Cancer Society (**http://caonline. amcancersoc.org/cgi/content/short/52/6/342**) and the US Preventive Services Task Force (**www.ahrq.gov/clinic/uspstf/uspscerv.htm**).

Although respiratory papillomatosis is believed usually to be acquired during passage through the birth canal, this condition has occurred in infants born by cesarean delivery. Because the preventive value of cesarean delivery is unknown, it should not be performed solely to prevent transmission of HPV to the newborn infant.

Vaccines to prevent HPV infection are undergoing clinical trials. Information about status of US Food and Drug Administration licensure and recommendations of the Advisory Committee on Immunization Practices of the Centers for Disease Control and Prevention and American Academy of Pediatrics for use of these vaccines can be found at **www.aapredbook.org/news/vaccstatus.shtml**.

For a report from the Centers for Disease Control and Prevention on prevention of genital HPV infection and sequelae, see **www.cdc.gov/std/HPV**. For more information on HPV, see the American Social Health Association Web site (**www.ashastd. org/stdfaqs/hpv.html**).

Paracoccidioidomycosis
(South American Blastomycosis)

CLINICAL MANIFESTATIONS: Disease occurs primarily in adults and is rare in children. The site of initial infection is the lungs. Clinical patterns in childhood include the acute-subacute and chronic forms. In both forms, constitutional symptoms, such as fever, malaise, and weight loss, are common. In the more common acute-subacute form, symptoms are related to the extensive involvement of the reticuloendothelial system with hypertrophied lymph nodes and involvement of the liver, spleen, bone marrow, and bones as well as joints, skin, and mucous membranes. Occasionally, enlarged lymph nodes may coalesce and form abscesses or fistulas. The chronic form of the illness, which usually occurs in adults, can be localized to the lungs or can disseminate. Chronic granulomatous lesions of the mucous membranes, especially of the mouth and palate, are rare findings in adults and occur more often in children in association with enlarged, draining lymph nodes. Infection may be latent for years before causing illness.

ETIOLOGY: *Paracoccidioides brasiliensis* is a dimorphic fungus with a yeast and a mycelial phase.

EPIDEMIOLOGY: The infection occurs in Latin America, from Mexico to Argentina. The natural reservoir is unknown, although soil is suspected. The mode of transmission is unknown; person-to-person transmission does not occur.

The **incubation period** is highly variable, ranging from 1 month to many years.

DIAGNOSTIC TESTS: Round, multiple-budding cells with a distinguishing pilot's wheel appearance may be seen in 10% potassium hydroxide preparations of sputum specimens, bronchoalveolar lavage specimens, scrapings from ulcers, and material from lesions or in tissue biopsy specimens. The organism can be cultured easily on most enriched media, including blood agar at 37°C (98°F) and Sabouraud dextrose agar (with cycloheximide) at 24°C (75°F). Complement fixation, enzyme immunoassay, and immunodiffusion methods are useful for detecting specific antibodies. Skin testing is not reliable for diagnosis.

TREATMENT: Amphotericin B is preferred by many experts for treatment of people with severe paracoccidioidomycosis, but amphotericin B is not curative (see Drugs for Invasive and Other Serious Fungal Infections, p 780). Itraconazole is the drug of choice for less severe or localized infection and to complete treatment when amphotericin B is used initially. Prolonged therapy for at least 6 months is necessary to minimize the relapse rate. Itraconazole is associated with fewer adverse effects and has a lower relapse rate (3%–5%) than ketoconazole, which is an alternative drug. A sulfonamide (trimethoprim-sulfamethoxazole [trimethoprim, 8–10 mg/kg daily]) can be used in resource-limited countries, but maintenance treatment must be continued for 3 to 5 years to avoid relapse, which occurs in 20% to 25% of patients.

ISOLATION OF THE HOSPITALIZED PATIENT: Standard precautions are recommended.

CONTROL MEASURES: None.

Paragonimiasis

CLINICAL MANIFESTATIONS: The disease has an insidious onset and a chronic course. The 2 major forms of paragonimiasis described are (1) pulmonary disease; and (2) extrapulmonary disease, which results in a larval migrans syndrome. Pulmonary disease is associated with chronic cough and dyspnea, but most infections probably are inapparent or result in mild symptoms. Heavy infestations cause paroxysms of coughing, which often produce blood-tinged sputum that is brown because of the presence of *Paragonimus* species eggs. Hemoptysis can be severe. Pleural effusion, pneumothorax, bronchiectasis, and pulmonary fibrosis with clubbing can develop. Extrapulmonary manifestations also may involve the liver, spleen, abdominal cavity, intestinal wall, intraabdominal lymph nodes, skin, and central nervous system, with meningoencephalitis, seizures, and space-occupying tumors attributable to invasion of the brain by adult flukes, usually occurring within a year of pulmonary infection. Symptoms tend to subside after approximately 5 years but can persist for as many as 20 years.

Extrapulmonary paragonimiasis is associated with migratory allergic subcutaneous nodules containing juvenile worms. Pleural effusion is common, as is invasion of the brain.

ETIOLOGY: In Asia, classical paragonimiasis is caused by *Paragonimus westermani* and *Paragonimus heterotremus* adult flukes and their eggs. The adult flukes of *P westermani* are up to 12 mm long and 7 mm wide and occur throughout the Far East. A triploid parthenogenetic form of *P westermani*, which is larger, produces more eggs, and elicits greater disease, has been described in Japan, Korea, Taiwan, and parts of eastern China. *Paragonimus heterotremus* occurs in Southeast Asia and adjacent parts of China. Extrapulmonary paragonimiasis is caused by larval stages of *Paragonimus skrjabini* and *Paragonimus miyazakii*. The worms rarely mature. *Paragonimus skrjabini* occurs in China, and *P miyazakii* occurs in Japan. African forms causing extrapulmonary paragonimiasis include *Paragonimus africanus* (Nigeria, Cameroon) and *Paragonimus uterobilateralis* (Liberia, Guinea, Nigeria, Gabon). *Paragonimus mexicanus* and *Paragonimus ecuadoriensis* occur in Mexico, Costa Rica, Ecuador, and Peru. *Paragonimus kellicotti*, a lung fluke of mink and opossums in the United States, also can cause a zoonotic infection in humans.

EPIDEMIOLOGY: Transmission occurs when raw or undercooked freshwater crabs or crayfish containing larvae (metacercariae) are ingested. The metacercariae excyst in the small intestine and penetrate the abdominal cavity, where they remain for a few days before migrating to the lungs. *Paragonimus westermani* and *P heterotremus* mature within the lungs over 6 to 10 weeks, when they then begin egg production. Eggs escape from pulmonary capsules into the bronchi and exit from the human host in sputum or feces. Eggs hatch in freshwater within 3 weeks, giving rise to miracidia. Miracidia penetrate freshwater snails and emerge several weeks later as cercariae, which encyst within the muscles and viscera of freshwater crustaceans before maturing into infective metacercariae. Transmission also occurs when humans ingest raw pork, usually from wild pigs, containing the juvenile stages of *Paragonimus* species (described as occurring in Japan).

Humans are accidental ("dead-end") hosts for *P skrjabini* and *P miyazakii*. These flukes cannot mature in humans and, hence, do not produce eggs.

Paragonimus species also infect a variety of other mammals, such as canids, mustelids, felids, and rodents, which can serve as animal reservoir hosts.

The **incubation period** is variable; egg production begins approximately 8 weeks after ingestion of *P westermani* metacercariae.

DIAGNOSTIC TESTS: Microscopic examination of stool, sputum, pleural effusion, cerebrospinal fluid, and other tissue specimens may reveal eggs. A Western blot serologic antibody test, available at the Centers for Disease Control and Prevention (CDC), is sensitive and specific but does not distinguish active from past infection. Charcot-Leyden crystals and eosinophils in sputum are useful diagnostic elements. Chest radiographs may appear normal or resemble radiographs from patients with tuberculosis. Misdiagnosis is likely unless paragonimiasis is suspected.

TREATMENT: Praziquantel in a 2-day course is the treatment of choice and is associated with high cure rates as demonstrated by disappearance of egg production and radiographic lesions in the lungs. The drug also is effective for some extrapulmonary manifestations. Bithionol, available from the CDC, is an alternative drug (see Drugs for Parasitic Infections, p 790).

ISOLATION OF THE HOSPITALIZED PATIENT: Standard precautions are recommended.

CONTROL MEASURES: Cooking of crabs and crayfish for several minutes until the meat has congealed and turned opaque kills metacercariae. Similarly, meat from wild pigs should be well cooked before eating. Control of animal reservoirs is not possible.

Parainfluenza Viral Infections

CLINICAL MANIFESTATIONS: Parainfluenza viruses are the major cause of laryngotracheobronchitis (croup), but they also commonly cause upper respiratory tract infection, pneumonia, and/or bronchiolitis. Types 1 and 2 viruses are the most common pathogens associated with croup, and type 3 virus is associated with bronchiolitis and pneumonia in infants and young children. Rarely, parotitis, aseptic meningitis, and encephalitis have been associated with type 3 infections. Parainfluenza virus infections can exacerbate symptoms of chronic lung disease in children and adults. Infections can be particularly severe and persistent in immunodeficient children and are associated most commonly with type 3 virus. Because type 4 virus is not detected as often as the other serotypes, infections with type 4 virus are not as well characterized. Parainfluenza infections do not confer complete protective immunity; therefore, reinfections can occur with all serotypes and at any age, but reinfections usually cause a mild illness limited to the upper respiratory tract.

ETIOLOGY: Parainfluenza viruses are enveloped RNA viruses classified as paramyxo-viruses. Four antigenically distinct types—1, 2, 3, and 4 (with 2 subtypes, 4A and 4B)—have been identified.

EPIDEMIOLOGY: Parainfluenza viruses are transmitted from person to person by direct contact and exposure to contaminated nasopharyngeal secretions through respiratory tract droplets and fomites. Parainfluenza viral infections produce sporadic infections as well as epidemics of disease. Seasonal patterns of infection are distinctive, predictable, and cyclic. Different serotypes have distinct epidemiologic patterns. Type 1 virus tends to produce outbreaks of respiratory tract illness, usually croup, in the autumn of every other year. A major increase in the number of cases of croup in the autumn indicates a parainfluenza type 1 outbreak. Type 2 virus also can cause outbreaks of respiratory tract illness in the autumn, often in conjunction with type 1 outbreaks, but type 2 outbreaks tend to be less severe, irregular, and less common. Parainfluenza type 3 virus usually is prominent during spring and summer in temperate climates but often continues into autumn, especially in years when autumn outbreaks of parainfluenza types 1 or 2 are absent. Infections with type 4 virus are recognized less commonly, are sporadic, and generally are associated with mild illnesses.

The age of primary infection varies with serotype. Primary infection with all types usually occurs by 5 years of age. Infection with type 3 virus more often occurs in infants and is a prominent cause of lower respiratory tract illnesses. By 12 months of age, 50% of infants have acquired type 3 infection. Infections between 1 and 5 years of age are associated most commonly with type 1 virus and less so with type 2 virus. Type 4 infections are not as well understood.

Immunocompetent children with primary parainfluenza infection may shed virus for up to 1 week before the onset of clinical symptoms until 1 to 3 weeks after symptoms have disappeared, depending on serotype. Severe lower respiratory tract disease with prolonged shedding of the virus can develop in immunodeficient people. In these patients, infection may spread beyond the respiratory tract to the liver and lymph nodes.

The **incubation period** ranges from 2 to 6 days.

DIAGNOSTIC TESTS: Virus may be isolated from nasopharyngeal secretions usually within 4 to 7 days of culture inoculation or earlier by using centrifugation of a specimen onto a monolayer of susceptible cells with subsequent staining for viral antigen (shell viral assay). Confirmation is made by rapid antigen detection, usually immuno-fluorescent. Rapid antigen identification techniques, including immunofluorescent assays, enzyme immunoassays, and fluoroimmunoassays, can be used to detect the virus in nasopharyngeal secretions, but the sensitivities of the tests vary. Multiplex reverse transcriptase-polymerase chain reaction assay, with high sensitivity and specificity, is available for detection and differentiation of parainfluenza viruses. Serologic diagnosis, made retrospectively by a significant increase in antibody titer between serum specimens obtained during acute infection and convalescence, is less useful, because infection may not always be accompanied by a significant homotypic antibody response.

TREATMENT: Specific antiviral therapy is not available. Most infections are self-limited and require no treatment. Monitoring for oxygenation and hypercapnia for more severely affected children with lower respiratory tract disease may be helpful. Epinephrine aerosol commonly is given to severely affected, hospitalized patients with laryngotracheobronchitis to decrease airway obstruction. Parenteral dexamethasone in high doses (>0.3 mg/kg), oral dexamethasone (0.15–0.6 mg/kg), and nebulized corticosteroids have been demonstrated to lessen the severity and duration of symptoms and hospitalization in patients with moderate to severe laryngotracheobronchitis. Oral dexamethasone (0.15 mg/kg) also is effective for outpatients with less severe croup. Management otherwise is supportive. Antimicrobial agents should be reserved for documented secondary bacterial infections.

ISOLATION OF THE HOSPITALIZED PATIENT: In addition to standard precautions, contact precautions are recommended for hospitalized infants and young children for the duration of illness. Strict adherence to infection control procedures, including prevention of environmental contamination by respiratory tract secretions and careful hand hygiene, should control nosocomial spread. Immunocompromised patients with type 3 infection should be isolated to prevent nosocomial spread.

CONTROL MEASURES: Efforts should be aimed at decreasing nosocomial infection. Hand hygiene should be emphasized.

Parasitic Diseases

Many parasitic diseases traditionally have been considered exotic and, therefore, frequently are not included in differential diagnoses of patients in the United States, Canada, and Europe. Nevertheless, a number of these organisms are endemic in industrialized countries, and overall, parasites are among the most common causes of morbidity and mortality in various and diverse geographic locations worldwide. Outside the tropics and subtropics, parasitic diseases particularly are common among tourists returning to their own countries, immigrants from areas with highly endemic infection, and immunocompromised people. Physicians and clinical laboratory personnel need to be aware of where these infections may be acquired, their clinical presentations, and methods of diagnosis and should advise travelers how to prevent infection. Table 3.38 (p 482) gives details on some infrequently encountered parasitic diseases.

Consultation and assistance in diagnosis and management of parasitic diseases are available from the Centers for Disease Control and Prevention (CDC), state health departments, and university departments or divisions of geographic medicine, tropical medicine, pediatric infectious disease, international health, and public health.

The CDC distributes several drugs that are not available commercially in the United States for treatment of parasitic diseases. These drugs are indicated by footnotes in Table 4.11, Manufacturers of Some Antiparasitic Drugs (p 818). To request these drugs, a physician must contact the CDC Drug Service (see Appendix I, Directory of Resources, p 839) and provide the following information: (1) the physician's

Table 3.38. Additional Parasitic Diseases[1]

Disease and/or Agent	Where Infection May Be Acquired	Definitive Host	Intermediate Host	Modes of Human Infection	Directly Communicable (Person to Person)	Diagnostic Laboratory Tests in Humans	Causative Form of Parasite	Manifestations in Humans
Angiostrongylus cantonensis	Widespread in the tropics, particularly Pacific Islands, Southeast Asia, and Central America	Rats	Snails and slugs	Eating improperly cooked infected mollusks	No	Eosinophils in CSF; rarely, identification of larvae in CSF or at autopsy	Larval worms	Eosinophilia, meningo-encephalitis
Angiostrongylus costaricensis	Central and South America	Rodents	Snails and slugs	Eating poorly cooked infected mollusks or food contaminated by mollusk secretions containing larvae	No	Gel diffusion; identification of larvae and eggs in tissue	Larval worms	Abdominal pain, eosinophilia
Anisakiasis	Cosmopolitan, mainly Japan	Marine mammals	Certain saltwater fish, squid, and octopus	Eating uncooked infected fish	No	Identification of recovered larvae in granulomas or vomitus	Larval worms	Acute gastrointestinal disease
Clonorchis sinensis, *Opisthorchis viverrini*, *Opisthorchis felineus* (flukes)	Far East, Eastern Europe, Russian Federation	Humans, cats, dogs, other mammals	Certain freshwater snails	Eating uncooked infected freshwater fish	No	Eggs in stool or duodenal fluid	Larvae and mature flukes	Abdominal pain; hepatobiliary disease

Table 3.38. Additional Parasitic Diseases,[1] continued

Disease and/or Agent	Where Infection May Be Acquired	Definitive Host	Intermediate Host	Modes of Human Infection	Directly Communicable (Person to Person)	Diagnostic Laboratory Tests in Humans	Causative Form of Parasite	Manifestations in Humans
Dracunculiasis (*Dracunculus medinensis*) (guinea worm)	Foci in Africa	Humans	Crustacea (copepods)	Drinking infested water	No	Identification of emerging or adult worm in subcutaneous tissues	Adult female worm	Emerging roundworm; inflammatory response; systemic and local blister or ulcer in skin
Fascioliasis (*Fasciola hepatica*) (fluke)	Foci throughout tropics and temperate areas	Humans, sheep, other herbivores	Certain freshwater snails and vegetation	Eating uncooked infected plants, such as water cress	No	Eggs in feces, duodenal fluid, or bile; serologic tests	Larvae and mature worms	Disease of liver and biliary tree; acute gastrointestinal disease
Fasciolopsiasis (*Fasciolopsis buski*) (fluke)	Far East	Humans, pigs, dogs	Certain freshwater snails, plants	Eating uncooked infected plants	No	Eggs or worm in feces or duodenal fluid	Larvae and mature worms	Diarrhea, constipation, vomiting, anorexia, edema of face and legs, ascites
Intestinal capillariasis (*Capillaria philippinensis*)	Philippines, Thailand	Humans, fish-eating birds	Fish	Ingestion of uncooked infected fish	Uncertain	Eggs and parasite in feces	Larvae and mature worms	Protein-losing enteropathy, diarrhea, malabsorption, ascites, emaciation

CSF indicates cerebrospinal fluid.

[1] For recommended drug treatment, see Drugs for Parasitic Infections (p 790).

name, address, and telephone number; (2) the type of infection to be treated and the method by which the infection was diagnosed; (3) the patient's name, age, weight, sex, and if the patient is female, whether she is pregnant; and (4) basic demographic, clinical, and epidemiologic information. Consultation with a medical officer from the CDC may be required before a drug is distributed.

Important human parasitic infections are discussed in individual chapters in section 3; the diseases are arranged alphabetically, and the discussions include recommendations for drug treatment. Tables 4.10 (p 790) and 4.11 (p 818), reproduced from *The Medical Letter* (see Drugs for Treatment of Parasitic Infections, p 790), provide dosage recommendations and other relevant information for specific antiparasitic drugs. Although the recommendations for administration of these drugs given in the disease-specific chapters are similar, they may not be identical in all instances because of differences of opinion among experts. Both sources should be consulted.

Parvovirus B19
(Erythema Infectiosum, Fifth Disease)

CLINICAL MANIFESTATIONS: Infection with parvovirus B19 is recognized most often as erythema infectiosum (EI), which is characterized by a distinctive rash that may be preceded by mild systemic symptoms, including fever in 15% to 30% of patients. The facial rash can be intensely red with a "slapped cheek" appearance that often is accompanied by circumoral pallor. A symmetric, maculopapular, lace-like, and often pruritic rash also occurs on the trunk, moving peripherally to involve the arms, buttocks, and thighs. The rash can fluctuate in intensity and recur with environmental changes, such as temperature and exposure to sunlight, for weeks to months. A brief, mild, nonspecific illness consisting of fever, malaise, myalgias, and headache often precedes the characteristic exanthema by approximately 7 to 10 days. Arthralgia and arthritis occur in less than 10% of infected children but commonly among adults, especially women. Knees are involved most commonly in children, but a symmetric polyarthropathy of knees, fingers, and other joints is common in adults.

Human parvovirus B19 also can cause other manifestations (Table 3.39, p 485), including asymptomatic infection, a mild respiratory tract illness with no rash, a rash atypical for EI that may be rubelliform or petechial, papulopurpuric gloves-and-socks syndrome (PPGSS; painful and pruritic papules, petechiae, and purpura of hands and feet, often with fever and enanthem), polyarthropathy syndrome (arthralgia and arthritis in adults in the absence of other manifestations of EI), chronic erythroid hypoplasia in immunodeficient patients, and transient aplastic crisis lasting 7 to 10 days in patients with hemolytic anemias (eg, sickle cell disease and autoimmune hemolytic anemia) and other conditions associated with low hemoglobin concentrations, including hemorrhage, severe anemia, and thalassemia. Chronic parvovirus B19 infection may cause severe anemia in patients infected with human immunodeficiency virus (HIV). In addition, parvovirus B19 infection sometimes has been associated with thrombocytopenia and neutropenia. Patients with aplastic crisis may have a prodromal illness with fever, malaise, and myalgia, but rash usually is absent. Red blood cell aplasia is related to lytic infection in erythrocyte precursors.

Parvovirus B19 infection occurring during pregnancy can cause fetal hydrops, intrauterine growth retardation, isolated pleural and pericardial effusions, and death but is not a proven cause of congenital anomalies. The risk of fetal death is between 2% and 6%, with the greatest risk occurring during the first half of pregnancy.

ETIOLOGY: Human parvovirus B19 is a nonenveloped, single-stranded DNA virus that replicates only in human erythrocyte precursors.

EPIDEMIOLOGY: Parvovirus B19 is distributed worldwide and is a common cause of infection in humans, who are the only known hosts. Modes of transmission include contact with respiratory tract secretions, percutaneous exposure to blood or blood products, and vertical transmission from mother to fetus. Since 2002, plasma derivatives have been screened using quantitative DNA measurement to reduce the risk of parvovirus B19 transmission. Parvovirus B19 infections are ubiquitous, and cases of EI can occur sporadically or in outbreaks in elementary or junior high schools during late winter and early spring. Secondary spread among susceptible household members is common and occurs in approximately 50% of susceptible contacts. The transmission rate in schools is less, but infection can be an occupational risk for school and child care personnel, with approximately 20% of susceptible people becoming infected. In young children, antibody seroprevalence generally is 5% to 10%. In most communities, approximately 50% of young adults and often more than 90% of elderly people are seropositive. The annual seroconversion rate in women of child-bearing age has been reported to be approximately 1.5%. The timing of the presence of parvovirus B19 DNA in serum and respiratory tract secretions indicates that people with EI are most infectious before onset of the rash and are unlikely to be infectious after onset of the rash and/or joint symptoms. In contrast, patients with aplastic crises are contagious from before the onset of symptoms through at least the week after onset. Symptoms of the papulopurpuric gloves-and-socks syndrome occur in association with viremia and before development of antibody response, and affected patients should be considered infectious. Transmission from patients with aplastic crisis to hospital personnel can occur.

The **incubation period** from acquisition of parvovirus B19 to onset of initial symptoms usually is between 4 and 14 days but can be as long as 21 days. Rash and joint symptoms occur 2 to 3 weeks after infection.

Table 3.39. Clinical Manifestations of Human Parvovirus B19 Infection

Conditions	Usual Hosts
Erythema infectiosum (fifth disease)	Immunocompetent children
Polyarthropathy syndrome	Immunocompetent adults (more common in women)
Chronic anemia/pure red cell aplasia	Immunocompromised hosts
Transient aplastic crisis	People with hemolytic anemia (ie, sickle cell anemia)
Hydrops fetalis/congenital anemia	Fetus (first 20 weeks of pregnancy)
Persistent anemia	Immunocompromised people

DIAGNOSTIC TESTS: In the immunocompetent host, detection of serum parvovirus B19-specific immunoglobulin (Ig) M antibody is the preferred diagnostic test. A positive IgM test result indicates that infection probably occurred within the previous 2 to 4 months. On the basis of radioimmunoassay or enzyme immunoassay results, antibody may be detected in 90% or more of patients at the time of the EI rash and by the third day of illness in patients with transient aplastic crisis. Serum IgG antibody appears by approximately day 7 of EI and persists for life; therefore, presence of parvovirus B19 IgG is not necessarily indicative of acute infection. These assays are available through commercial laboratories and through some state health department and research laboratories. However, their sensitivity and specificity may vary, particularly for IgM antibody. The optimal method for detecting chronic infection in the immunocompromised patient is demonstration of virus by nucleic acid hybridization or polymerase chain reaction (PCR) assays, because parvovirus B19 antibody is present variably in persistent infection. Because parvovirus B19 DNA can be detected at low levels by PCR assay in serum for up to 9 months after the acute viremic phase, detection of parvovirus B19 DNA by PCR assay does not necessarily indicate acute infection. The less sensitive nucleic acid hybridization assays usually are positive for only 2 to 4 days after onset of illness. For HIV-infected patients with severe anemia associated with chronic infection, dot blot hybridization of serum specimens may have adequate sensitivity. Parvovirus B19 has not been grown in standard cell culture.

TREATMENT: For most patients, only supportive care is indicated. Patients with aplastic crises may require transfusion. For treatment of chronic infection in immunodeficient patients, Immune Globulin Intravenous therapy often is effective and should be considered. Some cases of parvovirus B19 infection concurrent with hydrops fetalis have been treated successfully with intrauterine blood transfusions.

ISOLATION OF THE HOSPITALIZED PATIENT: In addition to standard precautions, droplet precautions are recommended for hospitalized children with aplastic crises, children with the papulopurpuric gloves-and-socks syndrome, or immunosuppressed patients with chronic infection and anemia for the duration of hospitalization. For patients with transient aplastic or erythrocyte crisis, these precautions should be maintained for 7 days.

Pregnant health care professionals should be informed of the potential risks to the fetus from parvovirus B19 infections and about preventive measures that may decrease these risks, for example, attention to strict infection control procedures and not caring for immunocompromised patients with chronic parvovirus infection or patients with parvovirus B19-associated aplastic crises, because patients in both groups are likely to be contagious.

CONTROL MEASURES:
- Women who are exposed to children at home or at work (eg, teachers or child care workers) are at increased risk of infection with parvovirus B19. However, because school or child care center outbreaks often indicate wider spread in the community that includes inapparent infection, women are at some degree of risk of exposure from other sources at home or in the community. In view of the high prevalence of parvovirus B19 infection, the low incidence of ill effects on the fetus, and the fact that avoidance of child care or classroom teaching can

decrease but not eliminate the risk of exposure, routine exclusion of pregnant women from the workplace where EI is occurring is not recommended. Women of childbearing age who are concerned can undergo serologic testing for IgG antibody to parvovirus B19 to determine their susceptibility to infection.

- Pregnant women who find that they have been in contact with children who were in the incubation period of EI or with children who were in aplastic crisis should have the relatively low potential risk of infection explained to them, and the option of serologic testing should be offered. Fetal ultrasonography may prove useful in these situations.
- Children with EI may attend child care or school, because they no longer are contagious.
- Transmission of parvovirus B19 is likely to be decreased through use of routine infection control practices, including hand hygiene and proper disposal of used facial tissues.

Pasteurella Infections

CLINICAL MANIFESTATIONS: The most common manifestation in children is cellulitis at the site of a scratch or bite of a cat, dog, or other animal. Cellulitis usually develops within 24 hours of the injury and includes swelling, erythema, tenderness, and serous or sanguinopurulent discharge at the site. Regional lymphadenopathy, chills, and fever can occur. Local complications, such as septic arthritis, osteomyelitis, and tenosynovitis, are common. Less common manifestations of infection include septicemia, meningitis, respiratory tract infections (eg, pneumonia, pulmonary abscesses, pleural empyema), appendicitis, hepatic abscess, peritonitis, urinary tract infection, and ocular infections (eg, conjunctivitis, corneal ulcer, endophthalmitis). People with liver disease or underlying host defense abnormalities are predisposed to bacteremia attributable to *Pasteurella multocida* infection.

ETIOLOGY: Species of the genus *Pasteurella* are nonmotile, facultative anaerobic, saccharolytic, gram-negative coccobacilli or rods that are primary pathogens in animals. The most common human pathogen is *P multocida*. Most human infections are caused by the following species or subspecies: *P multocida* subspecies *multocida*, *P multocida* subspecies *septica*, *Pasteurella canis*, *Pasteurella stomatis*, *Pasteurella dagmatis*, and *Pasteurella haemolytica*.

EPIDEMIOLOGY: *Pasteurella* species are found in the oral flora of 70% to 90% of cats, 25% to 50% of dogs, and many other animals. Transmission can occur from the bite or scratch of a cat or dog or, less commonly, from another animal. Respiratory tract spread from animals to humans also occurs. In a significant proportion of cases, no animal exposure can be identified. Human-to-human spread has not been documented.

The **incubation period** usually is less than 24 hours.

DIAGNOSTIC TESTS: The isolation of *Pasteurella* species from skin lesion drainage or other sites of infection (eg, blood, joint fluid, cerebrospinal fluid, sputum, pleural fluid, or suppurative lymph nodes) is diagnostic. Although *Pasteurella* species resemble several other organisms morphologically and grow on many culture media at 37°C (98°F), laboratory differentiation is not difficult.

TREATMENT: The drug of choice is penicillin. Other effective oral agents include ampicillin, amoxicillin-clavulanate, cefuroxime, cefpodoxime, doxycycline, and fluoroquinolones. Erythromycin, clindamycin, cephalexin, cefadroxil, cefaclor, and dicloxacillin should not be used. For patients allergic to beta-lactam agents, azithromycin or trimethoprim-sulfamethoxazole are alternative choices, but clinical experience with these agents is limited. Doxycycline is effective but should be given to children younger than 8 years of age only after assessment of the risk-benefit ratio. Fluoroquinolones are not recommended for patients younger than 18 years of age. For suspected polymicrobial infection, oral amoxicillin-clavulanate or, for severe infection, intravenous ampicillin-sulbactam or ticarcillin clavulanate can be given. Parenterally administered broad-spectrum cephalosporins, such as cefotaxime or cefoxitin, are active against *Pasteurella* species in vitro, but experience with these drugs for treatment is limited. The duration of therapy usually is 7 to 10 days for local infections and 10 to 14 days for more severe infections. Antimicrobial therapy should be continued for 4 to 6 weeks for bone and joint infections. Wound drainage or debridement may be necessary.

ISOLATION OF THE HOSPITALIZED PATIENT: Standard precautions are recommended.

CONTROL MEASURES: Education and limiting contact with wild animals and education about appropriate contact with domestic animals can help to prevent *Pasteurella* infections (see Bite Wounds, p 191). Animal bites and scratches should be irrigated, cleansed, and débrided promptly. Antimicrobial prophylaxis for children with an animal bite wound should be initiated according to the recommendations in Table 2.19, p 193.

Pediculosis Capitis*
(Head Lice)

CLINICAL MANIFESTATIONS: Itching is the most common symptom of head lice infestation, but many children are asymptomatic. Adult lice or eggs (nits) are found in the hair, usually behind the ears and near the nape of the neck. Excoriations and crusting caused by secondary bacterial infection may occur and often are associated with regional lymphadenopathy. In temperate climates, head lice deposit their eggs on a hair shaft 3 to 4 mm from the scalp. Because hair grows at a rate of approximately 1 cm per month, the duration of infestation can be estimated by the distance of the nit from the scalp.

ETIOLOGY: *Pediculus humanus capitis* is the head louse. Both nymphs and adult lice feed on human blood.

EPIDEMIOLOGY: Head lice infestation in children attending child care and school is common in the United States. Head lice are not a sign of poor hygiene, and all socioeconomic groups are affected. Infestations are less common in African-American chil-

---

* American Academy of Pediatrics, Committee on School Health and Committee on Infectious Diseases. Clinical report: head lice. *Pediatrics*. 2002;110:638–643

dren than in children of other races in the United States. Head lice infestation is not influenced by hair length or frequency of shampooing or brushing. Head lice are not a health hazard, because they are not responsible for spread of any disease. Transmission occurs by direct contact with hair of infested people and uncommonly, by contact with personal belongings, such as combs, hair brushes, and hats. Head lice may survive up to 2 days away from the scalp, and their eggs cannot hatch at a lower ambient temperature than that close to the scalp.

The **incubation period** from the laying of eggs to the hatching of the first nymph is 10 to 14 days but may be shorter in hot climates and longer in cold climates. Mature adult lice capable of reproducing do not appear until 2 weeks later.

DIAGNOSTIC TESTS: Identification of eggs (nits), nymphs, and lice with the naked eye is possible; the diagnosis can be confirmed by using a hand lens or microscope. Adult lice seldom are seen, because they move rapidly and conceal themselves effectively. It is important to differentiate nits from dandruff, benign hair casts (a layer of follicular cells that easily slides off the hair shaft), plugs of desquamated cells, and external hair debris.

TREATMENT: The following agents are effective for treating pediculosis of the scalp (see Drugs for Parasitic Infections, p 790). Therapy could be started with over-the-counter 1% permethrin, but resistance is common. For treatment failures, malathion should be used. When lice are resistant to all topical agents, ivermectin may be used. No drug is truly ovicidal. Drugs that leave a residual may kill nymphs as they emerge from eggs. Safety is a major concern with pediculicides, because the infestation itself does not present a risk to the host. Pediculicides should be used only as directed and with care. Instructions on proper use of any product should be explained carefully.

- *Permethrin (1%)*. Permethrin is available without a prescription in a 1% cream rinse that is applied to the scalp and hair for 10 minutes after washing and towel drying the hair. Permethrin has advantages over other pediculicides: a low potential for toxic effects and a high cure rate. Although activity of permethrin continues for 2 weeks or more after application, some experts advise a second treatment 7 to 10 days after the first one, especially if hair is washed a week after treatment. Resistance to permethrin has been documented in the United States, but the prevalence is not known.

- *Pyrethrin-based products*. Pyrethrins plus piperonyl butoxide, natural extracts from the chrysanthemum, are available in several brands for use as shampoos or mousse formulation (both to be applied to dry hair) without prescriptions. There is no residual activity, and repeated application 7 to 10 days later is necessary to kill newly hatched lice. Resistance to these compounds does occur. These products are contraindicated in people who are allergic to chrysanthemums or ragweed.

- *Permethrin (5%)*. Not approved by the Food and Drug Administration (FDA) as a pediculicide, 5% permethrin is available by prescription as a cream usually applied overnight for scabies (down to 2 months of age). Anecdotally, it has been used for the treatment of head lice that appear to be recalcitrant to other treatments. It is applied to the scalp and left on for several hours or overnight, then rinsed off. Treatment may be repeated 10 days later.

• *Malathion (0.5%)*. This organophosphate pesticide is available only by prescription as a lotion and is highly effective. However, this drug has been approved only for use in children 6 years and older. It is applied to dry hair as an 8- to 12-hour application; it should be reapplied 7 to 10 days later only if live lice still are present at that time. Safety concerns include the flammability of the alcohol base of the lotion (use of hair dryers or curling irons should be avoided during treatment) and that the product, if ingested, can cause severe respiratory distress. Malathion is contraindicated in children younger than 2 years of age because of the possibility of increased scalp permeability and absorption.

• *Lindane (1%)*. Lindane shampoo is an organochloride available only by prescription. It should be used as second-line treatment on the basis of safety concerns. It must be rinsed out no longer than 4 minutes after application and should not be used more than once to treat a lice infestation. Resistance has been reported worldwide for many years. Because of potential central nervous system toxicity that has included seizures and deaths, lindane should be limited to use in patients who cannot tolerate or have failed treatment with safer medications. Many drugs, such as antipsychotics, antidepressants, and penicillins, among others, may lower the seizure threshold and should be used with caution in patients taking these medications. Lindane is contraindicated for use in preterm infants and people with known seizure disorders and should be used with caution in children weighing less than 50 kg, in pregnant or nursing women, and in patients with inflamed or traumatized skin. Lindane shampoo, but not lotion, is approved for treatment of lice. The use of lindane for treatment of lice or scabies has been banned by the state of California because of concern for contamination of the water supply. The FDA has issued a public health advisory on the safety of lindane products (**www.fda.gov/cder/drug/infopage/lindane/lindanePHA.htm**).

• *Crotamiton (10%)*. Not approved by the FDA as a pediculicide, crotamiton (10%) lotion is used to treat scabies, and limited studies have shown it to be effective against head lice when applied to the scalp and left on for 24 hours before rinsing out. Safety and absorption in children, adults, and pregnant women have not been evaluated.

• *Oral trimethoprim-sulfamethoxazole*. Not approved by the FDA as a pediculicide, a 10-day course of this antibiotic has been cited as effective against head lice. Oral trimethoprim/sulfamethoxazole plus topical 1% permethrin cream rinse may be more effective but should be reserved for treatment failures. Rare severe allergic reactions (Stevens-Johnson syndrome) to this medication make it less desirable if alternative therapies exist.

• *Oral ivermectin*. Not approved by the FDA as a pediculicide, ivermectin is an anthelmintic agent that may be effective against head lice. It has been given as a single oral dose of 200 µg/kg with a second dose given after 7 to 10 days. Because it blocks essential neural transmission if it crosses the blood-brain barrier and young children may be at higher risk of this adverse drug reaction, currently, ivermectin should not be used in children weighing less than 15 kg.

There are no data to determine whether suffocation of lice by application of occlusive agents, such as petroleum jelly, olive oil, or full-fat mayonnaise, is effective as a method of treatment. In a single report, a dry-on, suffocation-based pediculicide lotion treatment was successful. Because pediculicides kill lice shortly after application, detection of living lice on scalp inspection 24 hours or more after treatment suggests incorrect use of pediculicide, a very heavy infestation, reinfestation, or resistance to therapy. In such situations, after excluding incorrect use, immediate retreatment with a different pediculicide followed by a second application 7 to 10 days later is recommended. Itching or mild burning of the scalp caused by inflammation of the skin in response to topical therapeutic agents can persist for many days after lice are killed and is not a reason for retreatment. Topical corticosteroid and oral antihistamine agents may be beneficial for relieving these signs and symptoms. Removal of nits after successful treatment with a pediculicide is not necessary to prevent spread. Because none of the pediculicides are 100% ovicidal, manual removal of nits after treatment with any product will increase success if nits are still viable. Removal of nits may be attempted for aesthetic reasons, to decrease diagnostic confusion, or to decrease the chance of self-reinfestation, but the process is tedious.

ISOLATION OF THE HOSPITALIZED PATIENT: In addition to standard precautions, contact precautions are recommended until the patient has been treated with an appropriate pediculicide.

CONTROL MEASURES: Household and other close contacts should be examined and treated if infested. Bedmates and immediate members of the household of infested individuals should be treated prophylactically. Otherwise, prophylactic treatment is not recommended. Children should not be excluded or sent home early from school because of head lice. Parents of affected children should be notified and informed that their child must be treated before returning to school on the day after treatment. After proper application of an appropriate pediculicide, reinfestation of children from an untreated infested contact is more common than is treatment failure.

"No-nit" policies requiring that children be free of nits before they return to child care or school have not been effective in controlling head lice transmission and are not recommended. Lice incubating in egg cases (nits) are so close to the scalp that they are difficult to remove with nit combs. Egg cases further from the scalp are easier to remove but are empty and, thus, are of no consequence.

Most children can be treated effectively without extra efforts to treat their clothing or bedding. All pharmacologic treatments should be used in conjunction with other measures such as disinfesting headgear, pillow cases, and towels by washing them in hot water and machine drying (using a hot cycle). Combs and hairbrushes can be washed with a pediculicide shampoo or soaked in hot water. Temperatures exceeding 53.5°C (128.3°F) for 5 minutes are lethal to lice and eggs. For items that cannot be laundered, dry cleaning or simply storing contaminated items in well-sealed plastic bags for 2 weeks is effective. Environmental insecticide sprays increase chemical exposure of household members and have not been helpful in the control of head lice. Vacuuming floors and furniture is a safe and effective alternative to spraying. Treatment of dogs, cats, or other pets is not indicated.

Pediculosis Corporis
(Body Lice)

CLINICAL MANIFESTATIONS: Intense itching, particularly at night, is common with body lice infestations that manifest as small erythematous macules, papules, and excoriations primarily on the trunk. Body lice and their eggs live in the seams of clothing. Rarely, a louse can be seen feeding on the skin. Secondary bacterial infection of the skin caused by scratching is common.

ETIOLOGY: *Pediculus humanus corporis* (or *humanus*) is the body louse. Nymphs and adult lice feed on human blood.

EPIDEMIOLOGY: Body lice generally are found on people with poor hygiene. Fomites have a role in transmission. Body lice cannot survive away from a blood source for longer than 10 days. In contrast with head lice, body lice are well-recognized vectors of disease (eg, epidemic typhus, trench fever, and relapsing fever).

The **incubation period** from laying eggs to hatching of the first nymph is 6 to 10 days. Mature adult lice capable of reproducing do not appear until 2 to 3 weeks later.

DIAGNOSTIC TESTS: Identification of eggs, nymphs, and lice with the naked eye is possible; the diagnosis can be confirmed by using a hand lens or microscope. Adult lice seldom are seen, because they move rapidly and conceal themselves effectively.

TREATMENT: Treatment consists of improving hygiene and cleaning clothes and bedding. Infested materials can be washed and dried at hot temperatures to kill lice. Pediculicides are not necessary if materials are laundered at least weekly.

ISOLATION OF THE HOSPITALIZED PATIENT: In addition to standard precautions, contact precautions are recommended until the patient has been treated.

CONTROL MEASURES: The most important factor in the control of body lice infestation is the ability to change and wash clothing. Close contacts should be examined and treated appropriately; clothing and bedding should be laundered.

Pediculosis Pubis
(Pubic Lice)

CLINICAL MANIFESTATIONS: Pruritus of the anogenital area is a common symptom in pubic lice infestations ("crabs"). Many hairy areas of the body can be infested, including the eyelashes, eyebrows, beard, axilla, perianal area, and rarely, the scalp. A characteristic sign of heavy pubic lice infestation is the presence of bluish or slate-colored maculae on the chest, abdomen, or thighs, known as maculae ceruleae.

ETIOLOGY: *Phthirus pubis* is the pubic or crab louse. Nymphs and adult lice feed on human blood.

EPIDEMIOLOGY: Pubic lice infestations are common in adolescents and young adults and usually are transmitted through sexual contact. The pubic louse also can be transferred by contaminated items, such as towels. Pubic lice can be found on the eyelashes of younger children and, although other modes of transmission are possible, may be evidence of sexual abuse. Infested people should be examined for other sexually transmitted infections, including syphilis and infection with *Neisseria gonorrhoeae*, *Chlamydia trachomatis*, hepatitis B virus, and human immunodeficiency virus.

The **incubation period** from the laying of eggs to the hatching of the first nymph is 6 to 10 days. Mature adult lice capable of reproducing do not appear until 2 to 3 weeks later.

DIAGNOSTIC TESTS: Identification of eggs (nits), nymphs, and lice with the naked eye is possible; the diagnosis can be confirmed by using a hand lens or microscope. Adult lice seldom are seen, because they move rapidly and conceal themselves effectively.

TREATMENT: The pediculicides used to treat pediculosis capitis are effective for treatment of pubic lice (see Pediculosis Capitis, p 488). Retreatment is recommended 7 to 10 days later. Pediculicides should not be used for infestation of eyelashes by pubic lice; petrolatum ointment applied 2 to 4 times daily for 8 to 10 days or oral sulfamethoxazole/trimethoprim for 10 days has been reported to be effective although not approved by the Food and Drug Administration for this indication. Nits should be removed by hand from the eyelashes.

ISOLATION OF THE HOSPITALIZED PATIENT: In addition to standard precautions, contact precautions are recommended until the patient has been treated with an appropriate pediculicide.

CONTROL MEASURES: All sexual contacts should be treated.

Pelvic Inflammatory Disease*

CLINICAL MANIFESTATIONS: Pelvic inflammatory disease (PID) comprises a spectrum of inflammatory disorders of the female upper genital tract, including any combination of endometritis, parametritis, salpingitis, oophoritis, tubo-ovarian abscess, and pelvic peritonitis. Pelvic inflammatory disease typically manifests as dull, continuous, unilateral or bilateral lower abdominal or pelvic pain that may range from indolent to severe. Additional symptoms can include fever, vomiting, an abnormal vaginal discharge, and irregular vaginal bleeding (signaling endometritis). Some patients have sharp right upper abdominal quadrant pain as a result of perihepatitis. Symptoms often begin within a week after the onset of menses, depending on the etiologic agent.

Examination findings vary but may include fever, lower abdominal tenderness, tenderness on lateral motion of the cervix, unilateral or bilateral adnexal tenderness, and adnexal fullness. Leukocytosis, an elevated erythrocyte sedimentation rate, elevated C-reactive protein concentration, and/or an adnexal mass demonstrated by

---

* Centers for Disease Control and Prevention. Sexually transmitted infections treatment guidelines—2006. *MMWR Recomm Rep.* 2006; in press (see **www.cdc.gov/mmwr**)

abdominal or transvaginal ultrasonography may be laboratory or imaging findings useful to support the diagnosis.

No single symptom, sign, or laboratory finding is sensitive and specific for the diagnosis of acute PID. Adnexal tenderness in a patient who has been sexually active has been described as the most sensitive finding for PID. Many episodes of PID go unrecognized by patients and/or health care professionals, because patients may be relatively asymptomatic ("silent PID") and do not seek care or because symptoms are mild and nonspecific. Combinations of findings that improve sensitivity (ie, correctly detect women who have PID) do so only while decreasing specificity (ie, incorrectly including women who do not have PID). The diagnostic criteria currently recommended by the Centers for Disease Control and Prevention are presented in Table 3.40 (p 495).

Complications of PID may include perihepatitis (Fitz-Hugh-Curtis syndrome) and tubo-ovarian abscess. Important long-term sequelae are recurrent infection, chronic pelvic pain, a sevenfold increase in incidence of ectopic pregnancy, and infertility resulting from tubal occlusion. Risk of tubal infertility is estimated to be 12% after a single episode of PID and more than 50% after 3 or more episodes. Factors that may increase the likelihood of infertility are delay in diagnosis, older age at time of infection, chlamydial disease, PID determined to be severe by laparoscopic examination, and delayed antimicrobial treatment.

ETIOLOGY: Sexually transmitted organisms, especially *Neisseria gonorrhoeae* and *Chlamydia trachomatis*, are implicated in most cases of PID. However, other organisms, such as anaerobes, including *Bacteroides* species and *Peptostreptococcus* species; facultative anaerobes, including *Gardnerella vaginalis, Haemophilus influenzae, Streptococcus* species, and enteric gram-negative bacilli; genital tract mycoplasmas, including *Mycoplasma hominis* and *Ureaplasma urealyticum;* and cytomegalovirus, also are associated with PID. Polymicrobial infection is common.

EPIDEMIOLOGY: As is true for other sexually transmitted infections (STIs), the incidence of PID is highest among adolescents and young adults. Bacterial vaginosis (see Bacterial Vaginosis, p 225) appears to be a preceding risk factor for many cases of PID. Other risk factors for PID include numerous sexual partners, use of an intrauterine device in the presence of an existing infection or multiple sexual partners after insertion, douching, and previous episodes of PID. Latex condoms, when used consistently and correctly, are highly effective in preventing sexual transmission of gonorrhea, chlamydia, trichomoniasis, and human immunodeficiency virus (HIV). Condom use has been associated with a lower rate of cervical cancer, a human papillomavirus-associated disease. Other barrier contraceptive methods, such as the contraceptive sponge and diaphragm, also have been shown to be effective in preventing transmission of STIs. Oral contraceptive pills decrease the likelihood of PID in the face of gonococcal or chlamydial cervicitis. Ascending pelvic infection is a rare complication of gonococcal vaginitis in prepubertal girls.

An **incubation period** for PID is undefined. In women with gonococcal cervicitis, symptoms of PID generally appear during the first half of the menstrual cycle.

DIAGNOSTIC TESTS: The diagnosis of PID usually is made on the basis of clinical findings (see Table 3.40, p 495) and can be supported by findings of a preponderance

Table 3.40. Criteria for Clinical Diagnosis of Pelvic Inflammatory Disease (PID)

Minimum Criteria

Empiric treatment of PID should be initiated in sexually active young women and others at risk of STIs if the following **minimum criteria** are present and no other cause(s) for the illness can be identified:

- Uterine or adnexal tenderness
                OR
- Cervical motion tenderness

Additional Criteria

More elaborate diagnostic evaluation often is needed, because incorrect diagnosis and management might cause unnecessary morbidity. These additional criteria may be used to enhance the specificity of the minimum criteria listed previously. Additional criteria that support a diagnosis of PID include the following:

- Oral temperature >38.3°C (>101°F)
- Mucopurulent cervical or vaginal discharge
- Presence of white blood cells (WBCs) on saline microscopy of vaginal secretions
- Increased erythrocyte sedimentation rate
- Increased C-reactive protein concentration
- Laboratory documentation of cervical infection with *Neisseria gonorrhoeae* or *Chlamydia trachomatis*

Most women with PID have mucopurulent cervical discharge **OR** evidence of WBCs on a microscopic evaluation of a saline preparation of vaginal fluid. If the cervical discharge appears normal **AND** no WBCs are found on the wet preparation, the diagnosis of PID is unlikely, and alternative causes of pain should be sought.

The **most specific criteria** for diagnosing PID include the following:

- Endometrial biopsy with histopathologic evidence of endometritis
- Transvaginal ultrasonography or magnetic resonance imaging techniques showing thickened, fluid-filled tubes with or without free pelvic fluid or tubo-ovarian complex
- Laparoscopic abnormalities consistent with PID

A diagnostic evaluation that includes some of these more extensive studies may be warranted in selected cases.

STIs indicates sexually transmitted infections.
Adapted from the Centers for Disease Control and Prevention. Sexually transmitted infections treatment guidelines—2006. *MMWR Recomm Rep.* 2006; in press (see **www.cdc.gov/mmwr**)

of leukocytes in cervical secretions, leukocytosis, an increased C-reactive protein concentration or erythrocyte sedimentation rate, identification of *N gonorrhoeae* in an endocervical culture, or presence of *C trachomatis* as a coexistent infection (see Gonococcal Infections, p 301, and *Chlamydia trachomatis*, p 252). Samples for *N gonorrhoeae* and *C trachomatis* should be obtained before treatment is begun, but treatment should not be delayed pending results of tests if suspicion is high for PID. Ultrasonography and laparoscopy are useful when appendicitis, ruptured ovarian cyst, or ectopic pregnancy are possible differential diagnoses. Laparoscopy also permits bacteriologic specimens to be obtained directly from tubal exudate or the cul-de-sac. However, laparoscopy cannot detect endometritis and is not indicated for diagnosis in most cases of PID. Because PID and ectopic pregnancy both can produce abdominal pain and irregular bleeding, a pregnancy test is indicated in the diagnostic evaluation of the adolescent with suspected PID or lower abdominal pain regardless of menstrual history.

TREATMENT: Because the clinical diagnosis of PID, even in the most experienced hands, is imprecise and because the consequences of untreated infection are substantial, most experts provide antimicrobial therapy to patients who fulfill minimum criteria rather than limiting therapy to patients who fulfill additional criteria for the diagnosis of PID (Table 3.40, p 495). To minimize the risks of progressive infection and subsequent infertility, treatment should be instituted as soon as the clinical diagnosis is made and before results of culture. If samples are negative for *N gonorrhoeae* or *C trachomatis*, treatment should be continued and the patient should be counseled that tests for these organisms are not completely sensitive. Partners still should be treated.

Observation and treatment in the hospital are suggested in the following circumstances: (1) a surgical emergency, such as ectopic pregnancy or appendicitis, cannot be excluded; (2) adherence to or tolerance of an outpatient treatment regimen and follow-up within 72 hours cannot be ensured; (3) the patient's illness is severe (eg, nausea, vomiting, severe pain, overt peritonitis, or high fever); (4) a tubo-ovarian abscess is present; (5) the patient is pregnant; (6) the patient has failed to respond clinically to outpatient therapy; or (7) another serious condition cannot be excluded. Although in the past, many experts have recommended hospitalization for all adolescent patients with PID, data to support this recommendation are lacking. Current data are insufficient to determine whether hospitalization is indicated for women with PID and HIV infection.

The choice of an antimicrobial regimen for treatment of PID is empiric, broad spectrum, and directed against the most common causative agents. Antimicrobial regimens consistent with those recommended by the Centers for Disease Control and Prevention (CDC) are summarized in Table 3.41 (p 497). Clinical outcome data are lacking about the use of cephalosporins other than cefotetan and cefoxitin. Some experts believe that these agents can be used to replace cefoxitin or cefotetan for inpatient treatment of PID; however, cefoxitin and cefotetan are more active against anaerobic bacteria that are felt to play an important role in PID. Fluoroquinolones are not approved by the US Food and Drug Administration for use in patients younger than 18 years of age for this indication. Consideration should be given to selecting an antimicrobial regimen that is effective against *N gonorrhoeae* and *C trachomatis*. Empiric therapy for anaerobic pathogens should be provided for patients with tubo-ovarian abscess, recurrent PID, or recent pelvic surgery. If the patient has an intrauterine device in place, the device should be removed immediately. In patients treated orally or parenterally, clinical improvement can be expected within 72 hours after initiation of treatment. Accordingly, outpatients should be reevaluated routinely on the third or fourth day of treatment.

ISOLATION OF THE HOSPITALIZED PATIENT: Standard precautions are recommended.

Table 3.41. Recommended Treatment of Pelvic Inflammatory Disease (PID)[1]

Parenteral: Regimen A[2]
Cefotetan, 2 g, IV, every 12 h

OR

Cefoxitin, 2 g, IV, every 6 h

PLUS

Doxycycline, 100 mg, orally or IV, every 12 h to complete 14 days

OR

Parenteral: Regimen B[5]
Clindamycin, 900 mg, IV, every 8 h

PLUS

Gentamicin: loading dose, IV or IM (2 mg/kg), followed by maintenance dose (1.5 mg/kg) every 8 h. Single daily dosing may be substituted.

NOTE

Parenteral therapy may be discontinued 24 hours after a patient improves clinically; continuing oral therapy should consist of doxycycline (100 mg, orally, twice a day) or clindamycin (450 mg, orally, 4 times a day) to complete a total of 14 days of therapy.

Ambulatory: Regimen A[3]
Ofloxacin,[4] 400 mg, orally, twice a day for 14 days

OR

Levofloxacin,[4] 500 mg, orally, once daily for 14 days,

WITH or WITHOUT

Metronidazole, 500 mg, orally, twice a day for 14 days

OR

Ambulatory: Regimen B
Ceftriaxone, 250 mg, IM, once

OR

Cefoxitin, 2 g, IM, plus probenecid, 1 g, orally, in a single dose concurrently once

OR

Other parenteral third-generation cephalosporin[6] (eg, ceftizoxime or cefotaxime)

PLUS

Doxycycline, 100 mg, orally, twice a day for 14 days

WITH or WITHOUT

Metronidazole, 500 mg, orally, twice a day for 14 days

IV indicates intravenous; IM, intramuscular.

[1] For further alternative treatment regimens, see Centers for Disease Control and Prevention. Sexually transmitted infections treatment guidelines—2006. *MMWR Recomm Rep.* 2006; in press (see **www.cdc.gov/mmwr**)

[2] Many experts recommend hospitalization for all patients with PID, particularly adolescents.

[3] Patients with inadequate response to outpatient therapy after 72 hours should be reevaluated for possible misdiagnosis and should receive parenteral therapy.

[4] Fluoroquinolones are approved for limited indications for patients younger than 18 years of age. They are contraindicated for pregnant women and during lactation (see Antimicrobial Agents and Related Therapy; p 735).

[5] Alternative parenteral regimens include ofloxacin or levofloxacin plus metronidazole; and ampicillin-sulbactam sodium plus doxycycline.

[6] Data to indicate whether expanded-spectrum cephalosporins (ceftizoxime, cefotaxime, ceftriaxone) can replace cefoxitin or cefotetan are limited. Many authorities believe they also are effective therapy for PID, but they are less active against anaerobes.

CONTROL MEASURES:

- Male sexual partners of patients with PID should receive diagnostic evaluation for gonococcal and chlamydial urethritis and then should be treated presumptively for both infections if they had sexual contact with the patient during the 60 days preceding onset of symptoms in the patient. A large proportion of these males will be asymptomatic.
- The patient should abstain from sexual intercourse until she and her partner(s) have completed treatment.
- The patient and her partner(s) should be encouraged to use condoms consistently.
- The patient should be tested for syphilis and HIV infection, and a Papanicolaou smear should be performed if appropriate (see CDC guidelines*).
- Unimmunized or incompletely immunized patients should begin or complete hepatitis B immunization (see Recommended Childhood and Adolescent Immunization Schedule, p 26).
- Because of the high risk of reinfection, some experts recommend that patients with PID whose initial test for *N gonorrhoeae* and *C trachomatis* was positive be retested 4 to 6 weeks after completing treatment.
- The diagnosis of PID provides an opportune time to educate the adolescent about prevention of STIs, including abstinence, consistent use of barrier methods of protection, and the importance of receiving periodic screening for STIs.

Pertussis (Whooping Cough)

CLINICAL MANIFESTATIONS: Pertussis begins with mild upper respiratory tract symptoms similar to the common cold (catarrhal stage) and progresses to cough and then usually to paroxysms of cough (paroxysmal stage) characterized by inspiratory whoop and commonly followed by vomiting. Fever is absent or minimal. Symptoms wane gradually over weeks to months (convalescent stage). Disease in infants younger than 6 months of age can be atypical with a short catarrhal stage, gagging, gasping, or apnea as prominent early manifestations; absence of whoop; and prolonged convalescence. Sudden unexpected death can be caused by pertussis. Disease in older children and adults also can have atypical manifestations when the cough is not accompanied by paroxysms or whoop. The duration of classic pertussis is 6 to 10 weeks in children. Approximately one-half of adolescents with pertussis cough for 10 weeks or longer. Complications among adolescents and adults include syncope, sleep disturbance, incontinence, rib fractures, and pneumonia. Pertussis is most severe when it occurs during the first 6 months of life, particularly in preterm and unimmunized infants. Complications among infants include pneumonia (22%), seizures (2%), encephalopathy (<0.5%), and death. On the basis of cases reported to local and state health departments (1990–1999), the case fatality rate was approximately 1% in infants younger than 2 months of age and <0.5% in infants 2 to 11 months of age. Rare pertussis deaths at older ages occur in people with underlying conditions, especially neuromuscular disorders.

---

* Centers for Disease Control and Prevention. Sexually transmitted infections treatment guidelines—2006. *MMWR Recomm Rep.* 2006; in press (see **www.cdc.gov/mmwr**).

ETIOLOGY: Pertussis is caused by a fastidious, gram-negative, pleomorphic bacillus, *Bordetella pertussis*. Other causes of prolonged cough illness include *Bordetella parapertussis*, *Mycoplasma pneumoniae*, *Chlamydia trachomatis*, *Chlamydophila pneumoniae*, *Bordetella bronchiseptica*, and certain respiratory tract viruses, particularly adenoviruses and respiratory syncytial viruses.

EPIDEMIOLOGY: Humans are the only known hosts of *B pertussis*. Transmission occurs by close contact with cases via aerosolized droplets. Neither infection nor immunization provides lifelong immunity. Lack of natural booster events and waning immunity since childhood immunization are responsible for the growing number of cases of pertussis in people older than 10 years of age. Pertussis occurs endemically with 3- to 5-year cycles of increased disease. Since 1976 when an all-time low number of cases was reported in the United States, the annual number of reported cases has increased to 25 827 in 2004, with less year-to-year cycling. Incidence is highest in infants younger than 6 months of age, followed by people 10 to 14 years of age. In 2003, the number of reported cases in middle school ages exceeded the number of cases in infants. Regardless of immunization status, as many as 80% of household contacts acquire infection with varying degrees of cough illness. Older siblings (including adolescents) and adults may have mild or atypical unrecognized disease but are important sources of pertussis for infants and young children. Infected individuals are most contagious during the catarrhal stage and the first 2 weeks after cough onset. Factors affecting the length of communicability include age, immunization status or previous episode of pertussis, and appropriate antimicrobial therapy. For example, a young unimmunized and untreated infant may be infectious for 6 or more weeks after cough onset; an untreated immunized adolescent may be infectious for 2 weeks or more after cough onset. Nasopharyngeal cultures usually test negative for *B pertussis* within 5 days after initiating macrolide therapy.

The **incubation period** usually is 7 to 10 days with a range of 5 to 21 days.

DIAGNOSTIC TESTS: Culture still is considered the "gold standard" for laboratory diagnosis of pertussis. Although culture is 100% specific, *B pertussis* is a fastidious organism. Culture requires collection of an appropriate nasopharyngeal specimen, obtained either by aspiration or with Dacron (polyethylene terephthalate) or calcium alginate swabs. Because culture requires specialized medium, laboratory personnel should be contacted when *B pertussis* is suspected. Specimens must be placed into special transport media (Regan-Lowe) and transported promptly to the laboratory. *Bordetella pertussis* usually grows after 3 to 4 days; however, culture cannot be considered negative for pertussis until after 10 days. Culture can be negative if taken from a previously immunized person, if antimicrobial therapy has been started, or if more than 3 weeks has elapsed since cough onset. A negative culture does not exclude the diagnosis of pertussis.

Polymerase chain reaction (PCR) assay is being used increasingly for detection of *B pertussis* because of its improved sensitivity and more rapid result. The PCR test requires collection of an adequate nasopharyngeal specimen using a Dacron swab or nasal wash. Calcium alginate swabs are inhibitory to PCR and should not be used for PCR tests. The PCR test lacks sensitivity in previously immunized individuals. Unacceptably high rates of false-positive results are reported from some laboratories. No

Food and Drug Administration (FDA)-licensed PCR test is available, and there are no standardized protocols, reagents, or reporting formats.

Direct fluorescent antibody (DFA) testing takes only a few hours to perform and is available commercially, but is performed reliably only by experienced technologists. Although the use of monoclonal reagents has increased the specificity of DFA testing, sensitivity still is low and DFA testing generally is not recommended for laboratory confirmation of pertussis. A single-specimen serologic test would be ideal for diagnosis in adolescents and adults whose culture or PCR test result usually is negative. In the absence of immunization within 2 years, a single serum serologic test result with elevated immunoglobulin (Ig) G antibody to pertussis toxin (PT) is suggestive of recent *B pertussis* infection. Although commercial serologic tests for pertussis infection exist, none currently is licensed by the FDA for diagnostic use, and cutoff values for diagnostic values of PT IgG have not been established.

An increased absolute white blood cell count with an absolute lymphocytosis often is present in infants and young children but not in adolescents with pertussis.

TREATMENT:

- Infants younger than 6 months of age and older individuals with underlying conditions commonly require hospitalization for supportive care, to assess ability for self-rescue after paroxysms during accelerating phase of disease, or to manage apnea, hypoxia, feeding difficulties, and other complications. Intensive care facilities may be required.
- Antimicrobial agents given during the catarrhal stage may ameliorate the disease. After the cough is established, antimicrobial agents may have no discernible effect on the course of illness but are recommended to limit the spread of organisms to others. Studies have demonstrated that azithromycin and clarithromycin have microbiologic effectiveness comparable with erythromycin for treatment of pertussis in previously immunized people who are 6 months of age or older. In addition, adverse events were fewer and milder in the reported studies. No data are available on the effectiveness of azithromycin or clarithromycin for pertussis treatment in infants younger than 1 month of age. As compared with erythromycin, these drugs have higher tissue concentration and longer half-lives and have the advantage of being administered as fewer daily doses (1 or 2 daily doses) for shorter treatment courses (5–7 days). These agents are contraindicated in patients with known hypersensitivity to other macrolides. Erythromycin, clarithromycin, or azithromycin are appropriate first-line agents for prophylaxis or treatment of pertussis in people 6 months of age or older (see Table 3.42, p 501).* Resistance of *B pertussis* to macrolide antimicrobial agents has been reported rarely. Penicillins and first- and second-generation cephalosporins are not effective against *B pertussis*.
- Antimicrobial agents for infants younger than 6 months of age require special consideration. The FDA has not approved azithromycin or clarithromycin for use in infants younger than 6 months of age. An association between orally administered erythromycin and infantile hypertrophic pyloric stenosis (IHPS)

---

* Centers for Disease Control and Prevention. Recommended antimicrobial agents for the treatment and postexposure prophylaxis of pertussis: 2005 CDC guidelines. *MMWR Recomm Rep.* 2005;54(RR-14):1–16

Table 3.42. Recommended Antimicrobial Therapy and Postexposure Prophylaxis for Pertussis in Infants, Children, Adolescents, and Adults

| Age | Recommended Drugs | | | Alternative |
	Azithromycin	Erythromycin	Clarithromycin	TMP-SMX
<1 mo	10 mg/kg per day as a single dose for 5 days[1]	40–50 mg/kg per day in 4 divided doses for 14 days	Not recommended	Contraindicated at <2 mo of age
1–5 mo	See above	See above	15 mg/kg per day in 2 divided doses for 7 days	≥2 mo of age: TMP, 8 mg/kg per day; SMX, 40 mg/kg per day in 2 doses for 14 days
≥6 mo and children	10 mg/kg as a single dose on day 1 (maximum 500 mg); then 5 mg/kg per day as a single dose on days 2–5 (maximum 250 mg/day)	See above (maximum 2 g/day)	See above (maximum 1 g/day)	See above
Adolescents and adults	500 mg as a single dose on day 1, then 250 mg as a single dose on days 2–5	2 g/day in 4 divided doses for 14 days	1 g/day in 2 divided doses for 7 days	TMP, 300 mg/day; SMX, 1600 mg/day in 2 divided doses for 14 days

TMP indicates trimethoprim; SMX, sulfamethoxazole.
[1] Preferred macrolide for this age because of risk of idiopathic hypertrophic pyloric stenosis associated with erythromycin.

has been reported in infants younger than 1 month of age. Available data on the use of azithromycin in infants younger than 1 month of age do not show signal of increased risk of IHPS. Until additional information is available, azithromycin is the drug of choice for treatment or prophylaxis of pertussis in infants younger than 1 month of age. All infants younger than 1 month of age who receive any macrolide should be monitored for development of IHPS for 1 month after completing the course (see Table 3.42). Cases of pyloric stenosis should be reported to MedWatch (see MedWatch, p 821). For infants younger than 1 month of age, the risk of developing severe pertussis and life-threatening complications outweighs the potential risk of IHPS that has been associated with erythromycin.

- Trimethoprim-sulfamethoxazole is an alternative for patients who cannot tolerate macrolides or who are infected with a macrolide-resistant strain. The dosage in children is trimethoprim, 8 mg/kg per day, and sulfamethoxazole, 40 mg/kg per day, in 2 divided doses. Prolonged use of high-dose trimethoprim-sulfamethoxazole is associated with increase in drug-related adverse events. Trimethoprim-sulfamethoxazole is contraindicated in infants younger than 2 months of age.
- Controlled, prospective data are not available for corticosteroids, albuterol, and other beta-2-adrenergic agents in treatment of pertussis.

ISOLATION OF THE HOSPITALIZED PATIENT: In addition to standard precautions, droplet precautions are recommended for 5 days after initiation of effective therapy, or if appropriate antimicrobial therapy is not given in older individuals, until 3 weeks after the onset of paroxysms.

CONTROL MEASURES:

CARE OF EXPOSED PEOPLE.

Household and Other Close Contacts.

Immunization. Close contacts younger than 7 years of age who are unimmunized or underimmunized should have pertussis immunization initiated or continued according to the recommended schedule. Children who received their third dose 6 months or more before exposure should be given a fourth dose at this time. Children who received their fourth dose 3 or more years before exposure and who are younger than 7 years of age should be given a fifth dose of diphtheria and tetanus toxoids and acellular pertussis (DTaP) vaccine at this time. Booster tetanus, diphtheria, and pertussis (Tdap) vaccine should be given to people 11 to 18 years of age if they previously have not received Tdap (see Table 3.43, p 503).

Chemoprophylaxis is recommended for all household contacts and other close contacts, including those in child care, regardless of age and immunization status. Early use of chemoprophylaxis in household contacts can limit secondary transmission. People with mild illness that may not be recognized as pertussis can transmit the infection. If 21 days have elapsed since the onset of cough in the index case, chemoprophylaxis has limited value but should be considered for households with high-risk contacts (eg, young infants, pregnant women, and people who have contact with infants). The agents, doses, and duration of prophylaxis are the same as for treatment of pertussis (see Table 3.42, p 501).

Table 3.43. Recommendations for Immunization With Tdap Vaccine in 11- to 18-Year-Old Adolescents With Special Situations[1]

Situations	Recommendations
Increased risk of acquiring pertussis[2]	Encouraged to receive Tdap even if Td administered within previous 5 years.
Increased risk of complications from pertussis[3]	Encouraged to receive Tdap even if Td administered within previous 5 years.
Tetanus prophylaxis indicated for wound management	Should receive Tdap (if not previously given) instead of Td. Should administer Tdap concurrently with MCV4 (Menactra), if feasible, in people not previously immunized. Do not defer giving a tetanus-containing vaccine when indicated if Tdap, MCV4, or both are not available.
History of pertussis	Should receive Tdap.
History of receipt of DT or Td but incomplete pertussis immunization	Should receive catch-up dose of Tdap. In routine situations, a 5-year interval between most recent Td and Tdap is suggested. (Also see above.)
History of no DTP/DTaP/ DT or Td immunization	Should receive catch-up doses of 3 Td-containing vaccines, one of which is Tdap.
History of receipt of DTP/ DTaP/DT or Td but incomplete records	Consider serologic testing. If tetanus or diphtheria antibody concentrations are ≥0.1 IU/mL, presume previous immunization and administer a single dose of Tdap (to be considered the adolescent booster dose).
Pregnancy	Pregnancy is not a contraindication to Tdap (or Td) immunization. Pregnant adolescents should be given the same considerations for immunization as nonpregnant adolescents.[4]
Lack of Availability of Tdap or MCV4 vaccine	The available vaccine generally should be administered. (Also see below.)
Use of Td when Tdap vaccine is not available	Should receive Td when Tdap is indicated but not available if the last DTP/DTaP/DT/Td vaccine was administered ≥10 years previously. If vaccine was administered <10 years previously, immunization can be deferred temporarily (awaiting Tdap) if follow-up is likely.
Children 7–10 years of age with history of incomplete childhood DTP/DTaP immunization	Neither Tdap vaccine is licensed for use in children <10 years of age. Required series of Td should be given, with a single adolescent booster dose of Tdap. BOOSTRIX could be substituted for one dose of Td in children who are 10 years old.
Individuals >18 years of age	The safety and immunogenicity of ADACEL as a single booster dose has been demonstrated for people 19 to 64 years of age. Recommendations for use are available.[5]

[1] Only a single dose of Tdap is recommended for adolescents for routine or special situations.

[2] Situations involving increased risk of acquiring pertussis include: 1) living in an area with a high rate of endemic pertussis or during an outbreak; 2) attending a school or workplace with a high rate of endemic pertussis or during an outbreak; 3) having close direct contact with a case of pertussis, such as in a family, residential facility, or school-related activity.

[3] Situations involving increased risk from pertussis include: 1) having an underlying medical condition for which pertussis would have increased morbidity or possible mortality (eg, neurologic, muscular, or cardiac disorder; airway or pulmonary disorder); 2) having close contact (eg, household member and out-of-home caregiver) with an infant <12 months of age.

[4] As part of postmarketing activities, both Tdap manufacturers have established pregnancy registries for females immunized with Tdap during pregnancy. Health care professionals are encouraged to report Tdap immunization during pregnancy to the following registries: BOOSTRIX, to GlaxoSmithKline Biologicals at 1-888-825-5249; and ADACEL, to sanofi pasteur at 1-800-822-2463 (1-800-VACCINE).

[5] Centers for Disease Control and Prevention. Preventing tetanus, diphtheria and pertussis among adults: use of tetanus toxoid, reduced diphtheria toxoid, and acellular pertussis vaccines. Recommendations of the Advisory Committee on Immunization Practices (ACIP). *MMWR Recomm Rep.* 2006;55(RR–3):1–34

People who have been in contact with an infected person should be monitored closely for respiratory tract symptoms for 21 days after last contact with the infected person. Close contacts with cough should be evaluated and treated for pertussis when appropriate.

Child Care. Care providers and exposed children, especially incompletely immunized children, should be observed for respiratory tract symptoms for 21 days after contact has been terminated. Pertussis immunization and chemoprophylaxis should be given as recommended for household and other close contacts. Children and care providers who are symptomatic or who have confirmed pertussis should be excluded from child care pending physician evaluation and completion of 5 days of the recommended course of antimicrobial therapy if pertussis is suspected. Untreated adults should be excluded until 21 days have elapsed from cough onset.

Schools. Students and staff members with pertussis should be excluded from school until they have completed 5 days of the recommended course of antimicrobial therapy. People who do not receive appropriate antimicrobial therapy should be excluded from school for 21 days after onset of symptoms. Public health officials should be consulted for further recommendations to control pertussis transmission in schools. The immunization status of children should be reviewed and age-appropriate vaccine should be given, if indicated, as for household and other close contacts. Pertussis should be considered in the differential diagnosis of people with cough illness who may have been exposed. Parents and employees should be notified about possible exposures to pertussis. Exclusion of exposed people with cough illness pending evaluation by a physician should be considered.

Health Care Settings. All health care professionals should observe standard precautions and wear a respiratory mask when examining a patient with a cough illness suspected or confirmed to be pertussis. Rapid control of outbreaks has followed erythromycin treatment and prophylaxis measures. Macrolide prophylaxis is targeted broadly to all potentially exposed individuals and health care professionals to interrupt the first generation of transmission successfully. Control measures should be implemented when one case or more of pertussis is recognized in a hospital, institution, outpatient clinic, or other health care setting. Confirmed and suspected cases should be reported to local health departments, and their involvement should be sought in control measures. Further guidance for evaluation and management of pertussis exposure in health care settings is available (**www.cdc.mmwr/pdf/RR/RR53D3.pdf**).

Individuals (patients, health care professionals, caregivers) defined as close contacts or high-risk contacts of a patient or health care professional with pertussis should be given chemoprophylaxis (and immunization when indicated) as recommended for household contacts (see Table 3.42, p 501). Health care professionals with symptoms of pertussis should be excluded from work for at least the first 5 days of the recommended course of antimicrobial therapy. Health care professionals with symptoms of pertussis who cannot take, or who object to, antimicrobial therapy should be excluded from work for 21 days from onset of cough. Use of a respiratory mask is not sufficient protection during this time.

IMMUNIZATION. Universal immunization with pertussis vaccine is recommended for children younger than 7 years of age and for adolescents 11 through 18 years of age and into adulthood. The pertussis vaccines used in the United States are acellular vaccines in combination with diphtheria and tetanus toxoids (pediatric DTaP and Tdap formulated for use in adolescents and adults). Recommendations for use of DTaP vaccine for children younger than 7 years of age are similar to recommendations for use of DTP (whole-cell pertussis) vaccine, which no longer is available in the United States but continues to be given to infants and children in many countries in the world. The Tdap vaccines contain reduced quantities of diphtheria toxoid and some pertussis antigens and are recommended as a single booster dose for people 11 through 18 years of age. Acellular vaccines are adsorbed onto an aluminum salt and must be administered intramuscularly. Acellular pertussis vaccines marketed in the United States contain 2 or more immunogens derived from *B pertussis* organisms: inactivated pertussis toxin (toxoid), filamentous hemagglutinin, fimbrial proteins (agglutinogens), and pertactin (an outer membrane 69-kd protein). All DTaP and Tdap vaccines contain pertussis toxoid. Although licensed vaccines differ in their formulation of pertussis antigens, their efficacy seems similar. Three DTaP vaccines are licensed by the FDA and are available in the United States for use in the primary series in children younger than 7 years of age (Tripedia, Infanrix, and Daptacel), and 1 combined vaccine that includes DTaP, hepatitis B (HepB), and inactivated poliovirus (IPV [Pediarix]) is available. A combination DTaP and *Haemophilus influenzae* type b conjugate vaccine is licensed only for the fourth dose given at 15 to 18 months of age (see Table 3.44, p 506). Two Tdap vaccines are licensed for a booster dose in older individuals (BOOSTRIX for people 10 through 18 years of age and ADACEL for people 11 through 64 years of age).

Dose and Route. Each 0.5-mL dose of DTaP and Tdap is given intramuscularly. The use of a decreased volume of individual doses of pertussis vaccines or multiple doses of decreased-volume (fractional) doses is not recommended. Administering all indicated vaccines during a single visit increases the likelihood that children and adolescents will receive vaccines on schedule.

Interchangeability of Acellular Pertussis Vaccines. Insufficient data exist on the safety, immunogenicity, and efficacy of different DTaP vaccines when administered interchangeably in the primary series to make recommendations. In circumstances in which the type of DTaP product(s) received previously is not known or the previously administered product(s) is not readily available, any DTaP vaccine licensed for use in the primary series may be used. There is no indication to match Tdap vaccine manufacturer for the adolescent booster dose with DTaP vaccine manufacturer used for the childhood doses.

RECOMMENDATIONS FOR ROUTINE CHILDHOOD IMMUNIZATION WITH DTAP VACCINE. A total of 5 doses of pertussis vaccine are recommended as a primary series before school entry, unless contraindicated (see Contraindications to DTaP Immunization, p 511, and Precautions for DTaP Immunization, p 511). The first dose is given at 2 months of age, followed by 2 additional doses at intervals of approximately 2 months. The fourth dose is recommended at 15 to 18 months of age. The fifth dose is given before school entry (kindergarten or elementary school) at 4 to 6 years of age. If the fourth dose of pertussis vaccine is delayed until after the fourth birthday, the fifth dose is not indicated.

Other recommendations are as follows:

Table 3.44. Composition and Recommended Use of Vaccines With Tetanus Toxoid, Diphtheria Toxoid, and Acellular Pertussis Components Licensed in the United States[1]

Pharmaceutical[2]	Manufacturer	Antigens	Recommended Use
DTaP Vaccines for Children Younger Than 7 Years of Age			
Tripedia (DTaP)	sanofi pasteur	PT, FHA	**All 5 doses,** children 6 wk through 6 y of age
INFANRIX (DTaP)	GlaxoSmithKline Biologicals	PT, FHA, pertactin	**All 5 doses,** children 6 wk through 6y of age
TriHIBit[3] (DTaP-Hib)	sanofi pasteur	PT, FHA	**Fourth dose only;** TriHIBit can be used for the fourth dose after 3 doses of DTaP or DTP and a primary series of any Hib vaccine
DAPTACEL (DTaP)	sanofi pasteur	PT, FHA, pertactin, fimbriae types 2 and 3	**First 4 doses,** children 6 wk through 6 y of age; can be used for the fifth dose for a child who has received 1 or more doses of DTP
Pediarix (DTaP-hepatitis B-IPV)	GlaxoSmithKline Biologicals	PT, FHA, pertactin	**First 3 doses** at 6- to 8-week intervals beginning at 2 months of age; then 2 doses of DTaP are needed to complete the 5-dose series before 7 years of age
Tdap Vaccines for Adolescents			
BOOSTRIX	GlaxoSmithKline Biologicals	PT, FHA, pertactin	Single dose at 11–12 years of age instead of Td (see text for additional recommendations)
ADACEL	sanofi pasteur	PT, FHA, pertactin, fimbriae types 2 and 3	Single dose at 11–12 years of age instead of Td (see text for additional recommendations)

DTaP indicates diphtheria and tetanus toxoids and acellular pertussis vaccine; PT, pertussis toxoid; FHA, filamentous hemagglutinin; Hib, *Haemophilus influenzae* type b vaccine; DTP, diphtheria and tetanus toxoids and whole-cell pertussis vaccine; IPV, inactivated poliovirus.

[1] DTaP recommended schedule is 2, 4, 6, and 15 to 18 months and 4 to 6 years of age. The fourth dose can be given as early as 12 months of age, provided 6 months have elapsed since the third dose was given. The fifth dose is not necessary if the fourth dose was given on or after the fourth birthday. Refer to manufacturers' package inserts for comprehensive product information regarding indications and use of the vaccines listed.

[2] ACEL-IMUNE and Certiva no longer are distributed.

[3] TriHIBit is ActHIB (lyophilized) reconstituted with Tripedia.

- For the fourth dose, DTaP vaccine may be given as early as 12 months of age if the interval between the third and fourth doses is at least 6 months and the child is considered unlikely to return for a visit at the recommended age of 15 to 18 months for this dose.
- Simultaneous administration of DTaP and other recommended vaccines is acceptable. Vaccines should not be mixed in the same syringe unless the specific combination is licensed by the FDA (see Simultaneous Administration of Multiple Vaccines, p 34, and *Haemophilus influenzae* Infections, p 310).
- If pertussis is prevalent in the community, immunization can be started as early as 6 weeks of age, and doses 2 and 3 in the primary series can be given at intervals of 4 weeks.
- DTaP vaccine is not licensed or recommended for people 7 years of age or older.
- Children younger than 7 years of age who have begun but not completed their primary immunization schedule with DTP vaccine (eg, outside the United States) should receive DTaP vaccine to complete the pertussis immunization schedule.
- Children who have a contraindication to pertussis immunization should receive no further doses of pertussis-containing vaccine (see Contraindications to DTaP Immunization, p 511, and Precautions for DTaP Immunization, p 511).

COMBINED VACCINE. The DTaP-HepB-IPV combination vaccine (Pediarix) is licensed for use as a 3-dose series administered intramuscularly at 6- to 8-week intervals (preferably 8 weeks) to infants at 2, 4, and 6 months of age. The DTaP-HepB-IPV combination vaccine should not be given to people 7 years of age or older or to infants before 6 weeks of age and, therefore, cannot be used for the birth dose of hepatitis B vaccine. Only a monovalent hepatitis B vaccine should be administered to infants before 6 weeks of age. The DTaP-HepB-IPV combination vaccine also may be used to complete the primary DTaP immunization series in infants born to hepatitis B surface antigen (HBsAg)-negative women or infants born to HBsAg-positive women when the infant received 1 or more doses of monovalent hepatitis B vaccine and/or combination vaccine containing hepatitis B vaccine and is scheduled to receive the other components of the combination vaccine. This may lead to an extra dose of hepatitis B vaccine being given, which is acceptable.* If the DTaP-HepB-IPV combination vaccine is given as the third dose in the hepatitis B series, it should be given at 24 weeks of age or older to induce a satisfactory response to the hepatitis B vaccine component. Some experts prefer to complete the hepatitis B vaccine series with monovalent hepatitis B vaccine in infants born to HBsAg-positive women because of a lack of efficacy data for the DTaP-HepB-IPV combination vaccine in these infants.

The DTaP-HepB-IPV combination vaccine may be used interchangeably with the DTaP component from the same manufacturer (Infanrix) to complete the primary

---

* American Academy of Pediatrics, Committee on Infectious Diseases. Combination vaccines for childhood immunization: recommendations of the Advisory Committee on Immunization Practices (ACIP), the American Academy of Pediatrics (AAP), and the American Academy of Family Physicians (AAFP). *Pediatrics*. 1999;103:1064–1077

DTaP series among infants and children who are scheduled to receive the other vaccine components. The DTaP-HepB-IPV combination vaccine may be used to complete the primary DTaP series in infants and children who have received another brand of DTaP vaccine if the provider does not know or have available the brand of DTaP vaccine previously administered and if the infants and children also are scheduled to receive the other vaccine components. When feasible, the same brand of DTaP vaccine should be used for all doses of the primary series. The DTaP-HepB-IPV combination vaccine may be used to complete the first 3 doses of the recommended 4-dose IPV series in infants and children who receive 1 or 2 doses of IPV vaccine from another manufacturer and who are scheduled to receive the other vaccine components. Administration must take into account the minimum interval between doses for each of the components (see Table 1.8, p 31). The DTaP-HepB-IPV combination vaccine may be given concurrently with a *Haemophilus influenzae* type b vaccine or pneumococcal conjugate vaccine at separate injection sites. Higher rates of low-grade fever are observed in children receiving the DTaP-HepB-IPV combination vaccine compared with children receiving the 3 vaccines separately. The DTaP-HepB-IPV combination vaccine should not be given as a fourth or fifth dose after the 3-dose childhood DTaP series.

RECOMMENDATIONS FOR SCHEDULING PERTUSSIS IMMUNIZATION FOR CHILDREN YOUNGER THAN 7 YEARS OF AGE IN SPECIAL CIRCUMSTANCES.

- For the child whose pertussis immunization schedule is resumed after deferral or interruption of the recommended schedule, the next dose in the sequence should be given, regardless of the interval since the last dose—that is, the schedule is not reinitiated (see Lapsed Immunizations, p 35).
- For children who have received fewer than the recommended number of doses of pertussis vaccine but who have received the recommended number of diphtheria and tetanus toxoid (DT) vaccine doses for their age (ie, children started on DT, then given DTaP), DTaP vaccine should be given to complete the recommended pertussis immunization schedule. However, the total number of doses of diphtheria and tetanus toxoids (as DT, DTaP, or DTP vaccine) should not exceed 6 before the seventh birthday.
- Although well-documented pertussis (eg, positive culture for *B pertussis* or epidemiologic linkage to a culture-positive case) confers short-term protection against infection, the duration of protection is unknown. Some experts recommend DTaP vaccine to complete the immunization series. At minimum, such children should receive at least DT vaccine to complete the immunization series to provide protection against diphtheria and tetanus.

Medical Records. Charts of children for whom pertussis immunization has been deferred should be flagged, and the immunization status of these children should be assessed periodically to ensure that they are immunized appropriately.

ADVERSE EVENTS AFTER DTaP PERTUSSIS IMMUNIZATION IN CHILDREN YOUNGER THAN 7 YEARS OF AGE.

- **Local and febrile reactions.** Reactions to DTaP vaccine most commonly include redness, edema, induration, and tenderness at the injection site; drowsiness; fretfulness; anorexia; vomiting; crying; and slight to moderate fever. These local and systemic manifestations after pertussis immunization occur within several hours of immunization and subside spontaneously without sequelae. Swelling involving the entire thigh or upper arm has been reported in 2% to 3% of vaccinees after administration of the fourth and fifth doses of different acellular pertussis vaccines. Limb swelling may be accompanied by erythema, pain, and fever. Although swelling may interfere with walking, most children have no limitation of activity. The pathogenesis and frequency of substantial reactions and limb swelling is not known, but these conditions appear to be self-limited and resolve without sequelae.

Entire limb swelling after a fourth dose of DTaP vaccine does not portend an increased risk of this reaction after the fifth dose. Because of the importance of the fifth dose in protecting a child during school years, a history of extensive swelling after the fourth dose should not be considered a contraindication to receipt of a fifth dose at school entry. Parents should be informed of the increase in reactogenicity that has been reported after the fourth and fifth doses of DTaP vaccine.

A review by the Institute of Medicine (IOM) based on case-series reports found evidence for a causal relationship between receipt of tetanus toxoid-containing vaccines and brachial neuritis. Brachial neuritis is listed in the Vaccine Injury Table. However, the frequency of this event has not been determined.*

After the first 3 doses of the immunization schedule, systemic and local reactions are significantly less common with DTaP than with DTP vaccine. Children with such reactions should receive subsequent doses of pertussis vaccine as scheduled.

Bacterial or sterile abscesses at the site of the injection are rare. Bacterial abscesses indicate contamination of the product or nonsterile technique and should be reported (see Reporting of Adverse Events, p 41). The causes of sterile abscesses are unknown. Their occurrence does not contraindicate further doses of DTaP vaccine.

- **Allergic reactions.** The rate of anaphylaxis to DTP vaccine was estimated to be approximately 2 cases per 100 000 injections; the incidence of allergic reactions after immunization with DTaP vaccine is unknown. Severe anaphylactic reactions and resulting deaths, if any, are rare after pertussis immunization. Transient urticarial rashes that occasionally occur after pertussis immunization, unless appearing immediately (ie, within minutes), are unlikely to be anaphylactic (IgE-mediated) in origin. These rashes probably represent a reaction caused by circulating antigen-antibody complexes formed from antigens in pertussis vaccine and corresponding antibody acquired from an earlier dose or transplacentally. Because formation of such complexes depends on a precise balance between concentrations of circulating antigen and antibody, such reactions are

---

* Institute of Medicine, Vaccine Safety Committee. *Adverse Events Associated with Childhood Vaccines. Evidence Bearing on Causality*. Stratton KR, Howe CJ, Johnston RB, eds. Washington, DC: National Academies Press; 1994

unlikely to recur after a subsequent dose and are not contraindications to further doses.

- **Seizures.** The incidence of seizures occurring within 48 hours of administration of DTP vaccine was estimated to be 1 case per 1750 doses administered. In clinical trials of DTaP vaccine in Europe and postlicensure surveillance of adverse events associated with DTaP vaccine in the United States, the reported incidence of seizures has been substantially less than that associated with DTP vaccine. Seizures associated with pertussis-containing vaccines usually are febrile seizures. These seizures have not been demonstrated to result in the subsequent development of recurrent afebrile seizures (ie, epilepsy) or other neurologic sequelae. Predisposing factors to seizures occurring within 48 hours after administration of DTP vaccine were underlying convulsive disorder, personal history of seizures, and family history of seizures (see Infants and Children With Underlying Neurologic Disorders, p 572, and Children With a Personal or Family History of Seizures, p 85).

- **Hypotonic-hyporesponsive episodes.** These episodes (also termed *collapse* or *shock-like state*) were reported to occur at a frequency of 1 per 1750 doses of DTP vaccine administered. However, reported rates varied widely, ranging from 3.5 to 291 cases per 100 000 immunizations. The rate after immunization with DTaP vaccine is unknown. However, in DTaP vaccine efficacy trials, these episodes occurred significantly less often after immunization with DTaP than with DTP vaccine. A follow-up study of a group of children who experienced a hypotonic-hyporesponsive episode (HHE) after immunization with DTP vaccine demonstrated no evidence of subsequent serious neurologic damage or intellectual impairment.

- **Temperature of ≥40.5°C (≥104.8°F).** After administration of DTP vaccine, approximately 0.3% of recipients were reported to develop temperature of ≥40.5°C (≥104.8°F) within 48 hours. The rate after administration of DTaP vaccine is significantly less.

- **Prolonged crying.** Persistent, severe, inconsolable screaming or crying for 3 or more hours sometimes was observed within 48 hours of immunization with DTP vaccine (1 of 100 doses administered). The frequency of inconsolable crying for 3 or more hours is significantly less after immunization with DTaP vaccine. The significance of persistent crying is unknown. It has been noted after receipt of immunizations other than pertussis vaccine and is not known to be associated with sequelae.

Frequency of Adverse Events After Immunization With DTaP Vaccine. Moderate to severe systemic reactions, including temperature of ≥40.5°C (≥104.8°F), persistent inconsolable crying lasting 3 hours or more, and HHEs rarely have been reported after immunization with DTaP vaccine, and each of these reactions occurs less often than after DTP vaccine. When these reactions occurred after the administration of DTP vaccine, no sequelae were documented.

Evaluation of Adverse Events Temporally Associated With Pertussis Immunization. Appropriate diagnostic studies should be undertaken to establish the cause of serious adverse events occurring temporally with immunization rather than assuming that they are caused by the vaccine. The Centers for Disease Control and Prevention has established independent Clinical Immunization Safety Assessment (CISA) centers to assess individuals with selected adverse events and offer recommendations for management. Nonetheless, the cause of events temporally related to immunization, even when unrelated to the immunization received, cannot always be established after extensive diagnostic and investigative studies.

Severe Acute Neurologic Illness and Permanent Brain Damage. The preponderance of evidence does not support a causal relationship between immunization with DTP vaccine and sudden infant death syndrome, infantile spasms, or serious acute neurologic illness resulting in permanent neurologic injury. Active surveillance performed by the IMPACT network of Canadian pediatric centers screening more than 12 000 admissions for neurologic disorders between 1993 and 2002 found no case of encephalopathy attributable to DTaP vaccine after administration of more than 6.5 million doses. Experience to date with acellular pertussis vaccine does not exclude rare, serious, adverse events temporally associated with its administration.

CONTRAINDICATIONS TO DTaP IMMUNIZATION. Adverse events after pertussis immunization that contraindicate further administration of DTaP vaccine are as follows:

- **An immediate anaphylactic reaction.** Further immunization with any of the 3 components in DTaP vaccine should be deferred because of uncertainty about which antigen may be responsible. People who experience anaphylactic reactions may be referred to an allergist for evaluation and desensitization if a specific allergen can be demonstrated.
- **Encephalopathy within 7 days.** This syndrome has been defined as a severe, acute central nervous system disorder unexplained by another cause, which may be manifested by major alterations of consciousness or by generalized or focal seizures that persist for more than a few hours without recovery within 24 hours. Prudence justifies considering such an illness occurring within 7 days of receipt of pertussis-containing vaccine as a possible contraindication to additional doses of pertussis vaccine, and DT vaccine should be substituted for each of the recommended subsequent doses of diphtheria and tetanus toxoid.

PRECAUTIONS FOR DTaP IMMUNIZATION. If the following adverse events occur in temporal relation to immunization with DTaP vaccine, the decision to administer additional doses of pertussis vaccine should be considered carefully. Although these events once were regarded as contraindications, they now are considered precautions, because they have not been proven to cause permanent sequelae:

- A seizure, with or without fever, occurring within 3 days of immunization with DTP or DTaP vaccine
- Persistent, severe, inconsolable screaming or crying for 3 or more hours within 48 hours of immunization
- Collapse or shock-like state (HHE) within 48 hours of immunization
- Temperature of ≥40.5°C (≥104.8°F), unexplained by another cause, within 48 hours of immunization

Before administration of each dose of pertussis vaccine, the child's parent or guardian should be asked about possible adverse events after previous doses. Although the risks of giving subsequent doses of pertussis vaccine to a child who has experienced one of these events are unknown, the possibility of another reaction of similar or greater severity may justify discontinuing pertussis immunization. In circumstances of increased risk of pertussis, such as during a community outbreak, the potential benefit of pertussis immunization could outweigh the risk of another reaction. The decision to give or withhold immunization should be made on the basis of the clinical assessment of the earlier reaction, the likelihood of pertussis exposure in the child's community, and the potential benefits and risks of pertussis vaccine.

INFANTS AND CHILDREN WITH UNDERLYING NEUROLOGIC DISORDERS. Rarely, underlying neurologic disorders may constitute a cause for deferring pertussis immunization and, on the basis of the medical history of the child, subsequent administration of pertussis vaccine. The decision to defer immunization should be made on an individual basis and should be reassessed at each subsequent immunization visit, weighing the risks and consequences of a seizure after immunization with DTaP vaccine in comparison with the risk of pertussis and its complications. Children with associated neurologic deficits may be at increased risk of complications and death if infected with *B pertussis*, which is endemic or epidemic worldwide. Efforts also should be undertaken to ensure pertussis immunization of children attending child care centers, special clinics, or residential care institutions.

The different categories of neurologic disorders and the relevant recommendations are as follows:

- **A progressive neurologic disorder characterized by developmental delay or neurologic findings.** These conditions are reason for indefinite deferral of pertussis immunization. Administration of DTaP vaccine may coincide with or hasten recognition of inevitable manifestations of the disorder, with resulting confusion about causation. Examples include infantile spasms and other epilepsies beginning in infancy. Such disorders should be differentiated from disorders that are nonprogressive.

- **Infants and children with a history of previous seizures.** Children with a history of seizures had an increased risk of seizure after receipt of DTP vaccine. No evidence indicates that these vaccine-associated seizures induced permanent brain damage, caused epilepsy, aggravated neurologic disorders, or affected the prognosis for children with underlying disorders. Because the risk of a DTaP postimmunization seizure could be increased, pertussis immunization of children with recent seizures should be deferred until a progressive neurologic disorder is excluded. Infants and children with well-controlled seizures or those in whom a seizure is unlikely to recur should be immunized with DTaP vaccine. Administration of acetaminophen or another appropriate antipyretic agent also should be considered at the time of immunization and every 4 hours for the ensuing 24 hours.

- **Infants and children known to have, or suspected of having, neurologic conditions that predispose to seizures or neurologic deterioration.** Such conditions include tuberous sclerosis and certain inherited metabolic or degenerative diseases. Deferral of pertussis immunization should be considered for these patients. Seizures or encephalopathy can occur in the normal course of these disorders and, thus, could occur after any immunization. Hence, to avoid confusion about causation, children with unstable or evolving neurologic disorders that can predispose to seizures or neurologic deterioration should be observed before immunization with DTaP vaccine to ascertain the diagnosis and prognosis of the primary neurologic disorder. Pertussis immunization with DTaP vaccine should be reconsidered at each visit. Children whose condition is resolved, corrected, or controlled can be immunized. Stable neurologic conditions, such as developmental delay or cerebral palsy, are not contraindications to pertussis immunization.

- **Preterm birth.** No evidence indicates that preterm birth, in the absence of other factors, increases the risk of seizures after immunization, and preterm birth is not a reason to defer immunization (see Preterm and Low Birth Weight Infants, p 67). Preterm birth is associated with increased risk of complications and death from pertussis in infancy.

- **Temporary deferral of pertussis immunization.** Children in the first year of life with neurologic disorders that necessitate temporary deferral of DTaP vaccine should not receive DT vaccine, because in the United States, the risk of acquiring diphtheria or tetanus by children younger than 1 year of age is remote. At or before the first birthday, the decision to give DTaP or DT vaccine should be made to ensure that the child is at least completely immunized against diphtheria and tetanus; as children become ambulatory, their risk of tetanus-prone wounds increases.

  Children with neurologic disorders that are recognized after the first birthday commonly will have received one or more doses of pertussis-containing vaccine. The physician may temporarily defer additional doses of DTaP vaccine in anticipation of clarification of the child's neurologic status. If the physician determines that the child probably should not receive further pertussis immunizations, DT immunization should be completed according to the recommended schedule (see Diphtheria, p 277, and/or Tetanus, p 648).

CHILDREN WITH A FAMILY HISTORY OF SEIZURES (see also Children With a Personal or Family History of Seizures, p 85). A history of seizure disorders or adverse events after receipt of a pertussis-containing vaccine in a family member is not a contraindication to pertussis immunization; DTaP vaccine is recommended. Although the risk of seizures after immunization with DTP vaccine in children with a family history of seizures was increased, these seizures usually were febrile in origin and generally had a benign outcome. The risk of fever is less with DTaP than with DTP vaccine, and any risk of resulting febrile seizure is outweighed by the continuing risk of pertussis and its attendant morbidity.

ADVICE TO PARENTS OF CHILDREN AT INCREASED RISK OF SEIZURES. Parents of children such as those with a personal or family history of seizures who may be at increased risk of seizure after pertussis immunization should be informed of the risks and benefits of pertussis immunization in these circumstances. Advice should be provided about fever and fever control and appropriate medical care in the unlikely event of a seizure.

RECOMMENDATIONS FOR ROUTINE ADOLESCENT BOOSTER IMMUNIZATION WITH TDAP VACCINE*†

- Adolescents 11 to 18 years of age should receive a single dose of Tdap instead of Td vaccine for booster immunization against tetanus, diphtheria, and

---

* American Academy of Pediatrics, Committee on Infectious Diseases. Prevention of pertussis among adolescents: recommendations for use of tetanus toxoid, reduced diphtheria toxoid, and acellular pertussis (Tdap) vaccine. *Pediatrics.* 2006;117:965–978

† Centers for Disease Control and Prevention. Preventing tetanus, diphtheria, and pertussis among adolescents: use of tetanus toxoid, reduced diphtheria toxoid and acellular pertussis vaccines. Recommendations of the Advisory Committee on Immunization Practices (ACIP). *MMWR Recomm Rep.* 2006;55(RR–3): 1–34

pertussis if they have completed the recommended childhood DTP/DTaP immunization series* and have not received Td. The preferred age for Tdap immunization is 11 to 12 years of age.

- Adolescents 11 to 18 years of age who received Td but not Tdap vaccine are encouraged to receive a single dose of Tdap to provide protection against pertussis if they completed the recommended childhood DTP/DTaP immunization series. An interval of at least 5 years between Td and Tdap immunization is suggested to reduce the risk of local and systemic reactions after Tdap immunization. However, Tdap can be given at shorter intervals, particularly in settings of increased risk of pertussis (see Recommendations for Adolescent Booster Immunization With Tdap Vaccine in Special Situations), because benefits of protection from pertussis outweigh the risk of possible increased local and systemic reactions. The safety of intervals as short as approximately 2 years between Td and Tdap is supported by a Canadian study among children and adolescents.
- Health care professionals should administer Tdap and MCV4 vaccines to adolescents 11 to 18 years of age during the same visit if both vaccines are indicated. If simultaneous immunization is not feasible, MCV4 and Tdap vaccine can be administered using either sequence. The AAP suggests a minimum interval of 1 month between Tdap and MCV4 when the vaccines are not administered on the same day.

RECOMMENDATIONS FOR ADOLESCENT BOOSTER IMMUNIZATION WITH TDAP VACCINE IN SPECIAL SITUATIONS. Only one dose of Tdap should be administered to an adolescent. In most special situations, a single dose of Tdap is preferred to Td. Simultaneous administration of a Tdap and MCV4, as well as a 5-year or greater interval between Td and Tdap, may limit the risk of increased local injection-site reactions. In certain settings, benefits of immunization to protect against disease outweigh risks of reactions. In certain settings shown in Table 3.43 (p 503), the benefits of immunization to protect against disease outweigh the theoretic risk of reactions. Additional guidance for use of Tdap vaccine in special situations also are shown in Table 3.43 (p 503).

- **Situations of Increased Risk of Acquiring Pertussis**

  Adolescents 11 to 18 years of age are encouraged to receive a single dose of Tdap, if they previously have not received Tdap, during situations of increased risk of acquiring pertussis, even if they have received Td within 5 years. Situations of increased risk of acquiring pertussis include (1) living in a community where there is an increased rate of pertussis or an outbreak; or (2) having close direct contact with a case of pertussis, such as in a family, residential facility, a school or school-related activity.

- **Situations of Increased Risk of Complications From Pertussis**

  Adolescents 11 to 18 years of age are encouraged to receive a single dose of Tdap, if they previously have not received Tdap, if they or their close contacts

---

* 5 doses of DTP/DTaP before the seventh birthday; if dose 4 was administered on or after the fourth birthday, dose 5 was not required. Children who begin the tetanus and diphtheria immunization series at 7 years of age or older require 3 doses of Td to complete the primary series.

have increased risk of complications from pertussis, even if they have received Td within 5 years. Situations of increased risk from pertussis include: 1) having an underlying medical condition for which pertussis would have increased morbidity or possible mortality (eg, neurologic, muscular, or cardiac disorder; airway or pulmonary disorder); and 2) having close contact (eg, household member or out-of-home caregiver) with an infant younger than 12 months of age.

- **Tetanus Prophylaxis in Wound Management**

    Adolescents 11 to 18 years of age who require tetanus toxoid vaccine as part of wound management should receive a single dose of Tdap instead of Td if they previously have not received Tdap.

    - MCV4 should be given concurrently with Tdap vaccine, if feasible, if not given previously.

    - If Tdap is not available, or if Tdap was administered more than 5 years previously, adolescents who need a tetanus toxoid vaccine as part of wound management should receive Td vaccine; tetanus toxoid (TT) can be administered if Td is not available or the adolescent has a contraindication or precaution to Td.

    - A thorough attempt must be made to determine whether an adolescent has completed the 3-dose primary immunization series against tetanus. People with unknown or uncertain tetanus immunization histories should be considered to have had no previous doses of a tetanus toxoid-containing vaccine (see History of Incomplete DTP/DTaP/DT or Td Immunization).

    - People who have not completed the primary series may require a tetanus toxoid-containing vaccine and passive immunization with Tetanus Immune Globulin (TIG) at the time of wound management. If TIG and a tetanus toxoid-containing vaccine are both indicated, each product should be administered using a separate syringe at different anatomic sites.

- **History of Pertussis**

    Adolescents 11 to 18 years of age who have a history of pertussis generally should receive Tdap according to the routine recommendation. The duration of protection after *B pertussis* infection is unknown (waning may begin as early as 7 years after infection), and the diagnosis of pertussis can be difficult to confirm, particularly with test results other than a positive culture for *B pertussis*. Administering pertussis vaccines to people with a history of pertussis presents no theoretic safety concerns.

- **History of Receipt of DT or Td but Incomplete Pertussis Immunization**

    Adolescents 11 to 18 years of age who received DT or Td vaccine(s) instead of 1 or more doses of DTP/DTaP vaccine(s) generally should receive a single dose of Tdap vaccine to provide protection against pertussis if they completed the recommended childhood immunization series for tetanus and diphtheria toxoids and have no contraindication to a pertussis vaccine. In routine situations, an interval of at least 5 years between the most recent Td dose and Tdap vaccine is suggested (see Situations of Increased Risk of Acquiring Pertussis and Situations of Increased Risk of Complications From Pertussis, p 514).

- **History of Incomplete DTP/DTaP/DT or Td Immunization***

    Adolescents 11 to 18 years of age who never have been immunized against tetanus, diphtheria, or pertussis should receive a series of 3 tetanus and diphtheria toxoid-containing vaccines, 1 of which is Tdap. The preferred schedule is a single Tdap dose, followed by a dose of Td vaccine 4 weeks or more after the Tdap dose, and a second dose of Td vaccine 6 to 12 months after the Td dose. Tdap may substitute for any one of the 3 doses in the series. Adolescents who received other incomplete immunization schedules against tetanus and diphtheria should be immunized with Tdap and/or Td according to catch-up recommendations. A single dose of Tdap may be used to substitute for any one of the Td doses.

- **History of Receipt of DTP/DTaP/DT or Td Vaccine but Incomplete Records***

    In situations in which adolescents 11 to 18 years of age are likely to have received immunization against tetanus and diphtheria but cannot produce records, health care professionals can obtain serologic testing for antibodies to tetanus and diphtheria toxoids to avoid unnecessary immunizations. If antitetanus and antidiphtheria toxoid concentrations are each $\geq$0.1 IU/mL, previous immunization with tetanus and diphtheria toxoid-containing vaccines is presumed and a single dose of Tdap vaccine is indicated; this Tdap dose is considered the adolescent booster dose.

- **Pregnancy**

    Pregnancy is not a contraindication to Tdap (or Td) immunization. The AAP recommends that pregnant adolescents be given the same considerations for immunization as nonpregnant adolescents. If Tdap or Td vaccine is indicated, administration in the second or third trimester (before 36 weeks of gestation) is preferred, when feasible, to minimize a perception of an association of immunization with adverse pregnancy outcomes, which are more common during the first trimester. No evidence exists of a risk of immunizing pregnant women with inactivated bacterial vaccines or toxoids or inactivated viral vaccines. Both Tdap and Td vaccines are categorized as pregnancy category C agents by the FDA. Well-controlled human studies and animal reproduction studies acceptable by the FDA have not been conducted for Tdap.

    Because of lack of data on use of Tdap vaccine in pregnant women, both Tdap manufacturers have established pregnancy registries for women immunized with Tdap during pregnancy. Health care professionals are encouraged to report Tdap immunization during pregnancy to the following registries: BOOSTRIX, to GlaxoSmithKline Biologicals at 1-888-825-5249; and ADACEL, to sanofi pasteur at 1-800-822-2463.

    Health care professionals should consider immunizing adolescents 11 to 18 years of age as soon as feasible in the immediate postpartum period, if the adolescent previously has not received Tdap, to reduce the risk of becoming infected and then transmitting pertussis to the infant (see Situations of Increased

---

* Centers for Disease Control and Prevention. Preventing tetanus, diphtheria, and pertussis among adolescents: use of tetanus toxoid, reduced diphtheria toxoid and acellular pertussis vaccines. Recommendations of the Advisory Committee on Immunization Practices (ACIP). *MMWR Recomm Rep.* 2006;55(RR–3): 1–34

Risk of Complications From Pertussis). Protection of the adolescent mother against pertussis may develop 1 to 2 weeks after immunization. AAP recommendations for use of Tdap vaccines in pregnant adolescents may differ from those of the CDC Advisory Committee on Immunization Practices.

- **Lack of Availability of Tdap or MCV4**

  If Tdap (or Td) vaccine and MCV4 both are indicated for adolescents but only one vaccine is available, the available vaccine generally should be administered and the other administered when the missed vaccine becomes available. If simultaneous immunization is not feasible, the AAP suggests a minimum interval of 1 month between administration of Tdap and MCV4.

- **Use of Td When Tdap Is Not Available**

  Health care professionals should administer a dose of Td when Tdap is indicated but not available if the last DTP/DTaP/DT/Td dose was administered 10 years or more earlier. After completion of childhood DTaP/DTP immunization, most adolescents are protected adequately against tetanus and diphtheria for at least 10 years. Immunization can be deferred temporarily when the last tetanus- and diphtheria-toxoid–containing vaccine was administered less than 10 years earlier and the adolescent is likely to return for follow-up. If immunization is deferred, health care professionals should maintain a system to recall the adolescent when vaccine becomes available or should refer the adolescent to another facility for immunization.

- **Children 7 to 10 Years of Age With History of Incomplete Childhood DTP/DTaP Immunization**

  Neither Tdap vaccine is licensed for use in children younger than 10 years of age. BOOSTRIX is licensed for children beginning at 10 years of age, and ADACEL is licensed for children beginning at 11 years of age. Children 7 through 9 years of age who never received any pediatric DTP/DTaP/DT or Td dose generally should receive 3 doses of Td: dose 2 is administered 4 weeks or more after dose 1, and dose 3 is administered 6 to 12 months or longer after dose 2. A 10-year-old child could receive BOOSTRIX for one of these doses. A single dose of Tdap is recommended for adolescents 11 to 18 years of age who have completed a 3-dose Td series, if the series did not include BOOSTRIX during the 10th year; an interval of at least 5 years between the most recent Td dose and Tdap is suggested (see Situations of Increased Risk of Acquiring Pertussis and Situations of Increased Risk of Complications From Pertussis). Children 7 to 10 years of age who received other incomplete immunization schedules against tetanus, diphtheria, and pertussis should be immunized against tetanus and diphtheria according to catch-up recommendations using an all-Td schedule (except children in their 10th year, who could receive a single dose of BOOSTRIX substituted for one dose of Td).

  Children with no history or an incomplete history of pediatric DTP/DTaP/DT or Td immunization could have received doses. Health care professionals can obtain serologic testing for antibodies against tetanus and diphtheria toxoids in these children. If tetanus and diphtheria toxoid antibody concentrations each are protective at ≥ 0.1 IU/mL, the child can be presumed to have been immunized against tetanus and diphtheria, and Td immunization may be deferred until the child is 11 to 12 years of age, when Tdap vaccine should be given.

- **Inadvertent Administration of Tdap or Pediatric DTaP Vaccine**

Tdap vaccine is not indicated for children younger than 10 years of age. The family should be informed of any inadvertent vaccine administration. If Tdap vaccine is administered inadvertently instead of DTaP to a child younger than 7 years of age as the first, second, or third dose of the immunization series, the Tdap dose should not be counted and DTaP should be given on the same day or as soon as possible, to keep the child on schedule for all vaccines. The remaining doses of the DTaP series should be administered on the usual schedule with at least a 4-week interval between the replacement dose of DTaP and the next dose of DTaP. If Tdap vaccine is administered inadvertently instead of DTaP to a child younger than 7 years of age as the fourth or fifth dose in the series, the dose should be counted as valid. If Tdap was administered as the fourth dose, the child should receive a fifth dose of the series using DTaP vaccine on the usual schedule. The routine recommendations for adolescent Tdap immunization would apply to children who inadvertently received Tdap instead of DTaP vaccine at an age younger than 7 years.

If Tdap is administered inadvertently instead of Td vaccine to a child 7 to 9 years of age, the Tdap dose should be counted as the adolescent Tdap booster. The child should receive a vaccine containing tetanus and diphtheria toxoids 10 years after the inadvertent Tdap dose.

DTaP is not indicated for people 7 years of age or older. If DTaP is administered inadvertently to a child 7 years of age or older or to an adolescent, the dose should be counted as the adolescent Tdap booster. The child or adolescent should receive a vaccine containing tetanus and diphtheria toxoids 10 years after the inadvertent DTaP dose.

- **Individuals Older Than 18 Years of Age and Adults**

To maintain protection against tetanus and diphtheria, the CDC has recommended decennial Td boosters for adults, beginning 10 years after the adolescent dose. The safety and immunogenicity of one Tdap, ADACEL, as a single booster immunization against tetanus, diphtheria, and pertussis has been demonstrated for people 19 to 64 years of age.[*]

ADVERSE EVENTS AFTER ADMINISTRATION OF TDAP VACCINE IN ADOLESCENTS. Local adverse events after administration of Tdap or Td vaccine in adolescents are common (any pain, 71%–78%; any redness, 20%–23%; any swelling, 18%–21%), and any pain was more common after Tdap versus Td vaccine during prelicensure trials. Rates of severe pain (1%–4%), severe redness (2%–6%), or severe swelling (2%–6%) after administration of Tdap vaccine versus Td vaccine were similar in prelicensure trials. A few adolescents in prelicensure studies had extensive arm swelling after administration of Tdap or Td vaccine, which was self-limited. Attention to proper immunization technique and use of standard routes of administration (ie, intramuscular for Tdap and Td vaccines) may minimize the risk of local adverse events and optimize immunogenicity.

---

[*] Centers for Disease Control and Prevention. Preventing tetanus, diphtheria and pertussis among adults: use of tetanus toxoid, reduced diphtheria toxoid, and acellular pertussis vaccines. Recommendations of the Advisory Committee on Immunization Practices (ACIP). *MMWR Recomm Rep.* 2006;55(RR–3):1–34

Systemic adverse events after administration of Tdap or Td vaccine in adolescents are common (any fever, 3%–14%; any headache, 40%–44%; tiredness, 27%–37%) and may be slightly more common after Tdap versus Td vaccine. Fever >102° F, severe headache, or severe tiredness occurred in less than 4% of adolescents after Tdap or Td vaccine administration in prelicensure trials. Mild gastrointestinal symptoms, sore joints, and generalized body aches are not uncommon after administration of Tdap or Td vaccine.

Syncope can occur after immunization, may be more common among adolescents and young adults, and may result in serious injury. Some experts recommend a 15- to 20-minute observation period after immunization. If syncope occurs, patients should be observed until symptoms resolve.

CONTRAINDICATIONS AND PRECAUTIONS FOR TDAP AND TD VACCINE USE IN ADOLESCENTS. Contraindications to administration of Tdap or Td vaccine include:

- The Tdap or Td vaccine is contraindicated among people with a history of serious allergic reaction (ie, anaphylaxis) to any component of the vaccines. Because of the importance of tetanus immunization, individuals with a history of anaphylaxis to components included in all Tdap and Td vaccines should be referred to an allergist to determine whether they have a specific allergy to tetanus toxoid, can be desensitized to tetanus toxoid, and safely can receive tetanus toxoid (TT) immunization.
- The Tdap vaccine is contraindicated among people with a history of encephalopathy (eg, coma, prolonged seizures) within 7 days of administration of a pertussis vaccine that is not attributable to another identifiable cause. These individuals should receive Td instead of Tdap.

Precautions to Administration of Tdap, Td, or Both Vaccines. A precaution is a condition in a recipient that might increase risk of a serious reaction. In these situations, health care professionals should evaluate the risks and benefits of administering Tdap or Td vaccine. Precautions include the following:

- Guillain-Barré syndrome (GBS) 6 weeks or less after the previous dose of a tetanus toxoid vaccine. If a decision is made to continue tetanus toxoid immunization, Tdap vaccine is preferred if otherwise indicated.
- Progressive neurologic disorder, uncontrolled epilepsy, or progressive encephalopathy until the condition has stabilized. This precaution is for vaccines with pertussis components. If a decision is made to withhold pertussis immunization, Td may be used instead of Tdap vaccine. This condition is a contraindication for use of DTaP vaccine in children.

Deferral of Administration of Tdap, Td, or Both Vaccines. Reasons for deferral include the following:

- Moderate or severe acute illness with or without fever. Immunization should be deferred until the acute illness resolves.
- History of a severe Arthus hypersensitivity reaction after a previous dose of a tetanus and diphtheria toxoid-containing vaccine or a diphtheria toxoid vaccine that does not contain tetanus toxoid, such as MCV4 (which contains diphtheria toxoid as a carrier protein). If a true Arthus reaction is likely, vaccine providers should defer Tdap or Td immunization for at least 10 years after the tetanus or diphtheria toxoid-containing vaccine. If the Arthus reaction was associated with a vaccine that contained diphtheria toxoid without tetanus toxoid (eg, MCV4),

deferring Tdap or Td vaccine that might leave the adolescent inadequately protected against tetanus. In this situation, if the last tetanus toxoid vaccine was administered 10 years or more earlier, providers may administer TT vaccine or consider measuring tetanus antibody concentrations to evaluate the need for tetanus immunization; tetanus antibody concentrations ≥0.1 IU/mL are considered protective.

Conditions That Are Not Contraindications or Precautions to Administration of Tdap Vaccine. The following conditions are not contraindications or precautions for Tdap vaccine. Adolescents with these conditions can receive a dose of Tdap vaccine if otherwise indicated. The first 4 bulleted conditions are precautions for administration of pediatric DTP/DTaP vaccine but are not contraindications or precautions for Tdap immunization in adolescents.

- Temperature ≥105°F (≥40.5°C) within 48 hours after DTP/DTaP immunization not attributable to another cause
- Collapse or shock-like state (HHE) within 48 hours after DTP/DTaP immunization
- Persistent crying lasting ≥3 hours, occurring within 48 hours after DTP/DTaP immunization
- Convulsions with or without fever, occurring within 3 days after DTP/DTaP immunization
- History of an extensive limb swelling reaction after pediatric DTP/DTaP or Td immunization that was not an Arthus hypersensitivity reaction.
- Stable neurologic disorder, including well-controlled seizures, a history of seizure disorder, and cerebral palsy.
- Brachial neuritis.
- Latex allergy other than anaphylactic allergies (eg, a history of contact to latex gloves). The tip and rubber plunger of the BOOSTRIX needleless syringe contain latex. This BOOSTRIX product should not be administered to adolescents with a history of a severe (anaphylactic) allergy to latex but may be administered to people with less severe allergies (eg, contact allergy to latex gloves). The BOOSTRIX single-dose vial and ADACEL preparations do not contain latex.
- Pregnancy (see Recommendations for Adolescent Booster Immunization With Tdap Vaccine in Special Situations, p 514).
- Breastfeeding.
- Immunosuppression, including people with human immunodeficiency virus infection. The Tdap vaccine poses no known safety concern for immunosuppressed people. The immunogenicity of Tdap vaccine in people with immunosuppression has not been studied and could be suboptimal.
- Intercurrent minor illness.
- Antimicrobial agent use.

Pinworm Infection
(Enterobius vermicularis)

CLINICAL MANIFESTATIONS: Although some people are asymptomatic, pinworm infection (enterobiasis) may cause pruritus ani and, rarely, pruritus vulvae. Pinworms have been found in the lumen of the appendix, but most evidence indicates that they are not related causally to acute appendicitis. Many clinical findings, such as grinding of the teeth at night, weight loss, and enuresis, have been attributed to pinworm infections, but proof of a causal relationship has not been established. Urethritis, vaginitis, salpingitis, or pelvic peritonitis may occur from aberrant migration of an adult worm from the perineum.

ETIOLOGY: *Enterobius vermicularis* is a nematode or roundworm.

EPIDEMIOLOGY: Enterobiasis occurs worldwide and commonly clusters within families. Prevalence rates are higher in preschool- and school-aged children, in primary caregivers for infected children, and in institutionalized people; up to 50% of these populations may be infected.

Egg transmission occurs by the fecal-oral route directly, indirectly, or inadvertently by contaminated hands or fomites, such as shared toys, bedding, clothing, toilet seats, and baths. Female pinworms usually die after depositing eggs on the perianal skin. Reinfection occurs by reingestion of eggs (ie, autoinfection) or acquisition from a new source. A person remains infectious as long as female nematodes are discharging eggs on perianal skin. Eggs remain infective in an indoor environment usually for 2 to 3 weeks. Humans are the only known natural hosts; dogs and cats do not harbor *E vermicularis*.

The **incubation period** from ingestion of an egg until an adult gravid female migrates to the perianal region is 1 to 2 months or longer.

DIAGNOSTIC TESTS: Diagnosis usually is made when adult worms are visualized in the perianal region, which is best examined 2 to 3 hours after the child is asleep. Very few ova are present in stool; therefore, examination of stool specimens for ova and parasites is not recommended. Alternatively, transparent (not translucent) adhesive tape can be applied to the perianal skin to collect any eggs that may be present; the tape is then applied to a glass slide and examined under a low-power microscopic lens. Three consecutive specimens should be obtained when the patient first awakens in the morning, before washing. Eosinophilia is unusual in cases of pinworm infection. Serologic testing is not available or useful for diagnosis.

TREATMENT: The drugs of choice are mebendazole, pyrantel pamoate, and albendazole, all of which are given in a single dose and repeated in 2 weeks. Pyrantel pamoate is available without prescription. For children younger than 2 years of age, in whom experience with these drugs is limited, risks and benefits should be considered before drug administration. Reinfection with pinworms occurs easily; prevention should be discussed when treatment is given. Infected people should bathe in the morning; bathing removes a large proportion of eggs. Frequently changing the infected person's underclothes, bedclothes, and bedsheets may decrease the egg contamination of the local environment and decrease risk of reinfection. Specific personal hygiene measures (eg, exercising hand hygiene before eating or preparing food, keeping fingernails short, avoiding scratching of the perianal region, and avoiding nail biting) may decrease risk of autoinfection and continued transmission. Repeated infections should be treated by the same method as the first infection. All family members should be treated as a group in situations in which multiple or repeated symptomatic infections occur. Vaginitis is self-limited and does not require separate treatment.

ISOLATION OF THE HOSPITALIZED PATIENT: Standard precautions are indicated.

CONTROL MEASURES: Control is difficult in child care centers and schools, because the rate of reinfection is high. In institutions, mass and simultaneous treatment, repeated in 2 weeks, can be effective. Hand hygiene is the most effective method of prevention. Bed linen and underclothing of infected children should be handled carefully, should not be shaken (to avoid spreading ova into the air), and should be laundered promptly.

Pityriasis Versicolor
(Tinea Versicolor)

CLINICAL MANIFESTATIONS: Pityriasis versicolor (formerly tinea versicolor) is a common superficial yeast infection of the skin characterized by multiple, scaling, oval, and patchy macular lesions usually distributed over upper portions of the trunk, proximal areas of the arms, and neck. Facial involvement particularly is common in children. Lesions may be hypopigmented or hyperpigmented (fawn colored or brown). Lesions fail to tan during the summer and during the winter are relatively darker, hence the term *versicolor*. Common conditions confused with this disorder include pityriasis alba, postinflammatory hypopigmentation, vitiligo, melasma, seborrheic dermatitis, pityriasis rosea, and dermatologic manifestations of secondary syphilis.

ETIOLOGY: The cause of pityriasis versicolor is *Malassezia* species, a group of dimorphic lipid-dependent yeasts that exist on healthy skin in yeast phase and cause clinical lesions only when substantial growth of hyphae occurs. Moist heat and lipid-containing sebaceous secretions encourage rapid overgrowth.

EPIDEMIOLOGY: Pityriasis versicolor occurs worldwide but is more prevalent in tropical and subtropical areas. Although primarily a disorder of adolescents and young adults, pityriasis versicolor also may occur in prepubertal children and infants. *Malassezia* species commonly colonize the skin in the first year of life and usually are harmless commensals.

The **incubation period** is unknown.

DIAGNOSIS: The clinical appearance usually is diagnostic. Involved areas are fluorescent yellow under Wood light examination. Skin scrapings examined microscopically in a potassium hydroxide wet mount preparation or stained with methylene blue or May-Grünwald-Giemsa stain disclose the pathognomonic clusters of yeast cells and hyphae ("spaghetti and meatball" appearance). Growth of this yeast on culture requires a source of long-chain fatty acids, which may be provided by overlaying Sabouraud dextrose agar medium with sterile olive oil.

TREATMENT: Topical treatment with selenium sulfide as 2.5% lotion or 1% shampoo has been the traditional treatment of choice. These preparations are applied in a thin layer covering the body surface from the face to the knees for 30 minutes daily for a week, followed by monthly applications for 3 months to help prevent recurrences. In adults, topical ketoconazole 2% shampoo used as a single application daily for 5 days is an effective alternative. Other topical preparations with therapeutic efficacy include sodium hyposulfite or thiosulfate in 15% to 25% concentrations (eg, Tinver lotion) applied twice a day for 2 to 4 weeks. Small focal infections may be treated with topical antifungal agents, such as ciclopirox, clotrimazole, econazole, ketoconazole, miconazole, or naftifine (see Topical Drugs for Superficial Fungal Infections, p 781). Because *Malassezia* species are part of normal flora, relapses are common. Multiple topical treatments may be necessary.

Oral antifungal therapy has advantages over topical therapy, including ease of administration and shorter duration of treatment, but oral therapy is more expensive and associated with a greater risk of adverse reactions. A single dose of ketoconazole (400 mg orally) or fluconazole (400 mg orally) or a 5-day course of itraconazole (200 mg orally once a day) has been effective in adults. Some experts recommend that children receive 3 days of ketoconazole therapy rather than the single dose given to adults. For pediatric dosage recommendations for ketoconazole, fluconazole, and itraconazole, see Recommended Doses of Parenteral and Oral Antifungal Drugs, p 777. These drugs have not been studied extensively in children for this purpose and are not approved by the US Food and Drug Administration. Itraconazole and terbinafine are not approved in children for any indication; both drugs are associated with cardiac and hepatic toxicity. Exercise to increase sweating and skin concentrations of medication may enhance the effectiveness of systemic therapy. Patients should be advised that repigmentation may not occur for several months after successful treatment.

ISOLATION OF THE HOSPITALIZED PATIENT: Standard precautions are recommended.

CONTROL MEASURES: Infected people should be treated.

Plague

CLINICAL MANIFESTATIONS: Naturally acquired plague most commonly manifests in the bubonic form, with acute onset of fever and painful swollen regional lymph nodes (buboes), whereas bioterrorism-related plague would manifest chiefly as pneumonic plague. Buboes develop most commonly in the inguinal region but also occur in axillary or cervical areas. Less commonly, plague manifests in the septicemic form (hypotension, acute respiratory distress, intravascular coagulopathy) or as pneumonic plague (cough, fever, dyspnea, and hemoptysis) and, rarely, as meningeal, pharyngeal, ocular, or gastrointestinal plague. Abrupt onset of fever, chills, headache, and malaise are characteristic in all cases. Occasionally, patients have symptoms of mild lymphadenitis or prominent gastrointestinal tract symptoms, which may obscure the correct diagnosis. When left untreated, plague often will progress to overwhelming sepsis with renal failure, acute respiratory distress syndrome, hemodynamic instability, diffuse intravascular coagulation, and necrosis of distal extremities. Plague has been referred to as black death or blackwater fever.

ETIOLOGY: Plague is caused by *Yersinia pestis*, a pleomorphic, bipolar-staining, gram-negative coccobacillus.

EPIDEMIOLOGY: Plague is a zoonotic infection of rodents, carnivores, and their fleas that occurs in many areas of the world, especially Africa. Plague has been reported throughout the western United States, but most human cases (approximately 85%) occur in New Mexico, Arizona, California, and Colorado as isolated cases or in small clusters. More cases occur during summers that follow mild winters and wet springs. In the United States, human plague is a rural disease, usually associated with epizootic infections in ground squirrels, prairie dogs, and other wild rodents. Bubonic plague usually is transmitted by bites of infected rodent fleas or by direct contact with tissues and fluids of infected rodents or other mammals, including domestic cats. Septicemic plague may result from direct contact with infectious materials or the bite of an infected flea. Primary pneumonic plague is acquired by inhalation of respiratory tract droplets from a human or animal with pneumonic plague or from exposure to laboratory aerosols. If aerosolized organisms were spread intentionally, plague pneumonia would be the most common manifestation and the greatest risk. Secondary pneumonic plague arises from hematogenous seeding of the lungs with *Y pestis* in patients with bubonic or septicemic plague. Epidemics of human plague occur usually as a consequence of epizootics in domestic rodents or after exposures to pneumonic plague.

The **incubation period** is 2 to 8 days for bubonic plague and 1 to 6 days for primary pneumonic plague.

DIAGNOSTIC TESTS: The diagnosis of plague usually is confirmed by culture of *Y pestis* from blood, bubo aspirate, or another clinical specimen. The organism has a bipolar (safety-pin) appearance when viewed with Wayson or Gram stains. The microbiology laboratory examining specimens should be informed when plague organisms are suspected to minimize risks of transmission to laboratory personnel. A positive fluorescent antibody test result for the presence of *Y pestis* in direct smears or cultures of a bubo aspirate, sputum, cerebrospinal fluid, or blood specimen provides presumptive evidence of *Y pestis* infection. The organism can be detected in fixed tissues by monoclonal antibody-based histochemical methods at the Centers for Disease Control and Prevention (CDC). A single positive serologic test result by passive hemagglutination assay or enzyme immunoassay in an unimmunized patient who has not had plague previously also provides presumptive evidence of infection. Seroconversion and/or a fourfold difference in antibody titer between 2 serum specimens obtained 4 weeks to 3 months apart also confirms the diagnosis of plague. Polymerase chain reaction assay and immunohistochemical staining for rapid diagnosis of *Y pestis* are available in some reference or public health laboratories. Isolates suspected as *Y pestis* should be reported immediately to the state health department and submitted to the Division of Vector-Borne Infectious Diseases of the CDC. Genotyping, performed at the CDC, should be done on all isolates particularly for pneumonic cases to determine if the isolate is endemic to the area or suspicious for an engineered or imported strain of *Y pestis*.

TREATMENT: For children, streptomycin (30 mg/kg per day in 2 or 3 divided doses, given intramuscularly) is the treatment of choice in most cases. Gentamicin in standard doses for age given intramuscularly or intravenously appears to be an equally effective alternative to streptomycin. Tetracycline, doxycycline, chloramphenicol, trimethoprim-sulfamethoxazole, and ciprofloxacin are alternative drugs. Doxycycline or tetracycline should not be given to children younger than 8 years of age unless the benefits of its use outweigh the risks of dental staining (see Antimicrobial Agents and

Related Therapy, p 735). Chloramphenicol is the preferred treatment for plague meningitis. Fluoroquinolones also have been found to be effective in some cases of plague but currently are not approved by the FDA for this indication. The usual duration of antimicrobial treatment is 7 to 10 days or until several days after lysis of fever.

Drainage of abscessed buboes may be necessary; drainage material is infectious until effective antimicrobial therapy has been given.

ISOLATION OF THE HOSPITALIZED PATIENT: For patients with bubonic plague, standard precautions are recommended. Droplet precautions are indicated for all patients until pneumonia is excluded and appropriate therapy has been initiated. In patients with pneumonic plague, droplet precautions should be continued for 48 hours after initiation of effective treatment.

CONTROL MEASURES:

CARE OF EXPOSED PEOPLE. Household members and other people with face-to-face exposure to a patient with plague should report fever >38.5°C or other illness to their physician. People with close exposure (<2 m) to a patient with pneumonic plague should receive antimicrobial prophylaxis. For children younger than 8 years of age, prophylactic trimethoprim-sulfamethoxazole has been recommended, but its efficacy is unknown. For adults at high risk, doxycycline or ciprofloxacin is recommended. Prophylaxis is given for 7 days in the usual therapeutic doses.

OTHER MEASURES. State public health authorities should be notified immediately of any suspected cases of human plague. The public should be educated about risk factors for plague, measures to prevent disease, and signs and symptoms of infection. People living in areas with endemic infection should be informed about the role of dogs and cats in bringing plague-infected rodents and fleas into peridomestic environments, the need for control of fleas and confinement of pets, and the importance of avoiding contact with sick and dead animals. Other preventive measures include surveillance of rodent populations, use of insecticides and insect repellents, and rodent control measures by health authorities when surveillance indicates the occurrence of plague epizootics.

VACCINE. Previously, an inactivated whole-cell *Y pestis* vaccine was available and recommended for people whose occupation regularly placed them at high risk of exposure to *Y pestis* or plague-infected rodents (eg, some field biologists and laboratory workers). Currently, there is no commercially available vaccine for plague in the United States. Information concerning the availability of plague vaccines is available from the CDC Division of Vector-Borne Infectious Diseases.

Pneumococcal Infections*

CLINICAL MANIFESTATIONS: Before routine use of heptavalent pneumococcal conjugate vaccine (PCV7), *Streptococcus pneumoniae* was the most common bacterial cause of acute otitis media and of invasive bacterial infections in children. Pneumococci also are a common cause of sinusitis, community-acquired pneumonia, and conjunctivitis. Pneumococci and meningococci are the 2 most common causes of bacterial meningitis in infants and young children. Pneumococcus occasionally causes periorbital cellu-

---

* American Academy of Pediatrics, Committee on Infectious Diseases. Recommendations for the prevention of pneumococcal infections, including the use of pneumococcal conjugate vaccine (Prevnar), pneumococcal polysaccharide vaccine, and antibiotic prophylaxis. *Pediatrics.* 2000;106:362–366.

litis, endocarditis, osteomyelitis, pericarditis, peritonitis, pyogenic arthritis, soft tissue infection, and neonatal septicemia.

ETIOLOGY: *Streptococcus pneumoniae* organisms (pneumococci) are lancet-shaped, gram-positive diplococci. At least 90 pneumococcal serotypes have been identified. Serotypes 4, 6B, 9V, 14, 18C, 19F, and 23F (Danish serotyping system) cause most invasive childhood pneumococcal infections in the United States and are the 7 types contained in the licensed heptavalent pneumococcal conjugate vaccine. Serotypes 6B, 9V, 14, 19A, 19F, and 23F are the most common isolates associated with resistance to penicillin.

EPIDEMIOLOGY: Pneumococci are ubiquitous, with many people having colonization of their upper respiratory tract. Transmission is from person to person, presumably by respiratory droplet contact. The period of communicability is unknown and may be as long as the organism is present in respiratory tract secretions but probably is less than 24 hours after effective antimicrobial therapy is begun. Among young children who acquire a new pneumococcal serotype in the nasopharynx, illness (eg, otitis media) occurs in approximately 15%, usually within 1 month of acquisition. Viral upper respiratory tract infections, including influenza, may predispose to pneumococcal infections. Pneumococcal infections are most prevalent during winter months. Rates of infection are highest in infants, young children, the elderly, and black, Alaska Native, and some American Indian populations. Also, these infections are increased in incidence and severity in people with congenital or acquired humoral immunodeficiency, human immunodeficiency virus (HIV) infection, absent or deficient splenic function (eg, sickle cell disease, congenital or surgical asplenia), or abnormal innate immune responses. Children with cochlear implants have high rates of pneumococcal meningitis. Other categories of children at presumed high risk or at moderate risk of developing invasive pneumococcal disease are outlined in Table 3.45 (p 527).

Since 2000, when PCV7 was recommended for routine use in infants, the incidence of all invasive pneumococcal infections has decreased by 80% for children younger than 2 years of age and by approximately 90% for infections caused by vaccine and vaccine-related serotypes and also has decreased in older children and adults. The proportion of invasive isolates nonsusceptible to penicillin also has decreased in some areas. In some areas, an increase in the frequency of acute otitis media and invasive disease caused by serotypes not contained in PCV7 (serotype replacement) has been noted. Continued surveillance of invasive pneumococcal infections is critical to determine whether, and how frequently, serotype replacement may be occurring.

The **incubation period** varies by type of infection and can be as short as 1 to 3 days.

DIAGNOSTIC TESTS: Material obtained from a suppurative focus should be Gram stained and cultured by appropriate microbiologic techniques. Blood cultures should be obtained from all patients with suspected invasive pneumococcal disease; cultures of cerebrospinal fluid (CSF) and other specimens (eg, pleural fluid) also may be indicated. Recovery of pneumococci from an upper respiratory tract culture is not indicative of the etiologic diagnosis of pneumococcal disease in the middle ear, lower respiratory tract, or sinus. Rapid methods to detect pneumococcal capsular antigen in CSF, pleural and joint fluid, and concentrated urine lack sufficient sensitivity or specificity to be of general clinical value.

Table 3.45. Children at High or Moderate Risk of Invasive Pneumococcal Infection

High risk (incidence of invasive pneumococcal disease ≥150 cases/100 000 people per year)
Children with:
- Sickle cell disease, congenital or acquired asplenia, or splenic dysfunction
- Human immunodeficiency virus infection
- Cochlear implants

Presumed high risk (insufficient data to calculate rates)
Children with:
- Congenital immune deficiency; some B- (humoral) or T-lymphocyte deficiencies, complement deficiencies (particularly C1, C2, C3, and C4), or phagocytic disorders (excluding chronic granulomatous disease)
- Chronic cardiac disease (particularly cyanotic congenital heart disease and cardiac failure)
- Chronic pulmonary disease (including asthma treated with high-dose oral corticosteroid therapy)
- Cerebrospinal leaks from a congenital malformation, skull fracture, or neurologic procedure
- Chronic renal insufficiency, including nephrotic syndrome
- Diseases associated with immunosuppressive therapy or radiation therapy (including malignant neoplasms, leukemias, lymphomas, and Hodgkin disease) and solid organ transplantation
- Diabetes mellitus

Moderate risk (incidence of invasive pneumococcal disease ≥20 cases/100 000 people per year).
- All children 24–35 mo of age
- Children 36–59 mo of age attending out-of-home child care
- Children 36–59 mo of age who are black or of American Indian/Alaska Native descent

SUSCEPTIBILITY TESTING.* All *S pneumoniae* isolates from normally sterile body fluids (eg, CSF, blood, middle ear fluid, or pleural or joint fluid) should be tested for in vitro antimicrobial susceptibility to determine the minimum inhibitory concentration (MIC) of penicillin and cefotaxime or ceftriaxone. Cerebrospinal fluid isolates also should be tested for susceptibility to vancomycin and meropenem. *Nonsusceptible* is defined to include both *intermediate* and *resistant* isolates. Accordingly, current definitions by the Clinical and Laboratory Standards Institute of in vitro susceptibility and nonsusceptibility are as follows for nonmeningeal and meningeal isolates:

---

* For further information, see American Academy of Pediatrics, Committee on Infectious Diseases. Therapy for children with invasive pneumococcal infections. *Pediatrics.* 1997;99:289–299 (Reaffirmed January 2004)

Drug and Isolate Location	Susceptible, µg/mL	Nonsusceptible, µg/mL	
		Intermediate	Resistant
Penicillin	≤0.06	0.1–1.0	≥2.0
Cefotaxime **OR** ceftriaxone			
Nonmeningeal	≤1.0	2.0	≥4.0
Meningeal	≤0.5	1.0	≥2.0

For patients with meningitis whose organism is *nonsusceptible* to penicillin, susceptibility testing of rifampin also should be performed. If the patient has a nonmeningeal infection caused by an isolate that is *nonsusceptible* to penicillin, cefotaxime, and ceftriaxone, susceptibility testing to clindamycin, erythromycin, rifampin, trimethoprim-sulfamethoxazole, linezolid, meropenem, and vancomycin should be considered, depending on the patient's response to antimicrobial therapy.

Quantitative MIC testing using reliable methods, such as broth microdilution or antimicrobial gradient strips, should be performed on isolates from children with invasive infections. When quantitative testing methods are not available or for isolates from noninvasive infections, the qualitative screening test using a 1-µg oxacillin disk on an agar plate reliably identifies all penicillin-*susceptible* pneumococci on the basis of the criterion of a disk-zone diameter of 20 mm or greater. Organisms with an oxacillin disk-zone size of less than 20 mm potentially are *nonsusceptible* and require quantitative susceptibility testing. The oxacillin disk test is used as a screening test for resistance to beta-lactam drugs (ie, penicillins and cephalosporins).

TREATMENT: *Streptococcus pneumoniae* strains that are nonsusceptible to penicillin G, cefotaxime, ceftriaxone, and other antimicrobial agents have been identified throughout the United States and worldwide. Among children in some geographic areas of the United States in the prevaccine era, more than 40% of isolates from sterile body sites were nonsusceptible to penicillin G, and as many as 50% of these isolates were resistant (MIC ≥2.0 µg/mL). Approximately 50% of penicillin-nonsusceptible strains also were nonsusceptible to cefotaxime or ceftriaxone. Penicillin-nonsusceptible strains also have increased rates of resistance to trimethoprim-sulfamethoxazole, clindamycin, and especially macrolides (eg, resistance >50%). Penicillin-susceptible strains also have increasing rates of resistance to macrolides (eg, resistance >10%).

Vancomycin resistance has not been reported in the United States. If a strain with an in vitro MIC >1.0 µg/mL for vancomycin is isolated, the state health department should be notified promptly and arrangements should be made for confirmatory testing.

Recommendations for treatment of pneumococcal infections are as follows.

BACTERIAL MENINGITIS POSSIBLY OR PROVEN TO BE CAUSED BY *S PNEUMONIAE*. Combination therapy with vancomycin and cefotaxime or ceftriaxone should be administered initially to all children 1 month of age or older with definite or probable bacterial meningitis because of the increased prevalence of *S pneumoniae* resistant to penicillin, cefotaxime, and ceftriaxone.

For children with hypersensitivity to beta-lactam antimicrobial agents (ie, penicillins and cephalosporins), the combination of vancomycin and rifampin should be considered. Vancomycin should not be given alone, because bactericidal concentrations in CSF are difficult to sustain and clinical experience to support use of vancomycin as monotherapy is minimal. Rifampin also should not be given as monotherapy, because resistance may develop during therapy. Other possible antimicrobial agents for treatment of pneumococcal meningitis include meropenem or chloramphenicol (the latter of which only should be used for pneumococcal meningitis if the minimal bactericidal concentration is ≤4 μg/mL).

A lumbar puncture should be considered after 24 to 48 hours of therapy in the following circumstances: (1) the organism is penicillin-*nonsusceptible* by oxacillin disk or quantitative (MIC) testing, results from cefotaxime and ceftriaxone quantitative susceptibility testing are not yet available, and the patient's condition has not improved or has worsened; or (2) the child has received dexamethasone, which might interfere with the ability to interpret the clinical response, such as resolution of fever.

On the basis of available results of susceptibility testing of the pneumococcal isolate, therapy should be modified according to the guidelines in Table 3.46. If the organism is susceptible to penicillin, cefotaxime, or ceftriaxone, vancomycin should be discontinued and penicillin, cefotaxime, or ceftriaxone should be continued. Vancomycin should be continued only if the organism is nonsusceptible to penicillin and to cefotaxime or ceftriaxone.

Addition of rifampin to vancomycin after 24 to 48 hours of therapy should be considered if the organism is susceptible to rifampin and (1) after 24 to 48 hours,

Table 3.46. Antimicrobial Therapy for Infants and Children With Meningitis Caused by *Streptococcus pneumoniae* on the Basis of Susceptibility Test Results

Susceptibility Test Results	Antimicrobial Management[1]
• *Susceptible* to penicillin	**Discontinue vancomycin** **AND** Begin penicillin (and discontinue cephalosporin) **OR** Continue cefotaxime or ceftriaxone alone[2]
• *Nonsusceptible* to penicillin *(intermediate* or *resistant)* **AND** *Susceptible* to cefotaxime and ceftriaxone	**Discontinue vancomycin** **AND** Continue cefotaxime or ceftriaxone
• *Nonsusceptible* to penicillin *(intermediate* or *resistant)* **AND** *Nonsusceptible* to cefotaxime and ceftriaxone *(intermediate* or *resistant)* **AND** *Susceptible* to rifampin	Continue vancomycin and cefotaxime or ceftriaxone. Rifampin may be added to vancomycin in selected circumstances (see text).

[1] See Table 3.47, p 530, for dosage. Some experts recommend the maximum dosages. For initial therapy, see Bacterial Meningitis Possibly or Proven to Be Caused by *S pneumoniae*, p 528.
[2] Some physicians may choose this alternative for convenience and cost savings.

despite therapy with vancomycin and cefotaxime or ceftriaxone, the clinical condition has worsened; (2) the subsequent culture of CSF indicates failure to eradicate or to decrease substantially the number of organisms; or (3) the organism has an unusually high cefotaxime or ceftriaxone MIC ($\geq$4 μg/mL). Consultation with an infectious disease specialist should be considered in such circumstances.

DEXAMETHASONE. For infants and children 6 weeks of age and older, adjunctive therapy with dexamethasone may be considered after weighing the potential benefits and possible risks. Experts do not agree on a recommendation to use corticosteroids in pneumococcal meningitis; data are not sufficient to demonstrate a clear benefit in children. If used, dexamethasone should be given before or concurrently with the first dose of the antimicrobial agent.

NONMENINGEAL INVASIVE PNEUMOCOCCAL INFECTIONS REQUIRING HOSPITALIZATION. For nonmeningeal invasive infections in previously well children who are not critically ill, antimicrobial agents currently in use to treat S pneumoniae and other potential pathogens should be initiated at the usually recommended dosages (see Table 3.47).

For critically ill infants and children with invasive infections potentially attributable to S pneumoniae, additional initial antimicrobial therapy may be considered for

Table 3.47. Dosages of Intravenous Antimicrobial Agents for Invasive Pneumococcal Infections in Infants and Children[1]

Antimicrobial Agent	Meningitis		Nonmeningeal Infections	
	Dose/kg per day	Dose Interval	Dose/kg per day	Dose Interval
Penicillin G	250 000–400 000 U[2]	4–6 h	250 000–400 000 U[2]	4–6 h
Cefotaxime	225–300 mg	8 h	75–100 mg	8 h
Ceftriaxone	100 mg	12–24 h	50–75 mg	12–24 h
Vancomycin	60 mg	6 h	40–45 mg	6–8 h
Rifampin[3]	20 mg	12 h	Not indicated	...
Chloramphenicol[4]	75–100 mg	6 h	75–100 mg	6 h
Clindamycin	Not indicated	...	25–40 mg	6–8 h
Meropenem[5]	120 mg	8 h	60 mg	8 h
Imipenem-cilastatin[6]	...	...	60 mg	6 h
Linezolid[7]	...	...	30 mg	8 h

[1] Doses are for children 1 month of age or older.
[2] Because 1 U = 0.6 μg/mL, this range is equal to 150 to 240 mg/kg per day.
[3] Indications for use are not defined completely.
[4] Drug should be considered only for patients with life-threatening allergic response after administration of beta-lactam antimicrobial agents.
[5] Drug is approved for pediatric patients 3 months of age and older.
[6] For dosing recommendations for infants ≤3 months of age (weighing ≥1500 g), consult package insert. Drug is not recommended in patients with meningitis because of its potential epileptogenic properties.
[7] Use is primarily for children allergic to beta-lactam antimicrobial agents or children with multidrug-resistant isolates. Dose is for patients younger than 12 years of age. The dose for patients 12 years of age and older is 20 mg/kg per day in 2 doses (adult dose, 1200 mg/day in 2 doses).

strains that possibly are nonsusceptible to penicillin, cefotaxime, or ceftriaxone. Such patients include those with myopericarditis or severe multilobar pneumonia with hypoxia or hypotension. If vancomycin is administered, it should be discontinued as soon as antimicrobial susceptibility test results demonstrate effective alternative agents.

If the organism has in vitro resistance to penicillin, cefotaxime, and ceftriaxone by standards of the Clinical Laboratory Standards Institute, therapy should be modified on the basis of clinical response, susceptibility to other antimicrobial agents, and results of follow-up cultures of blood and other body fluids. Consultation with an infectious disease specialist should be considered.

For children with severe hypersensitivity to the beta-lactam antimicrobial agents (ie, penicillins and cephalosporins), initial management for a potential pneumococcal infection should include clindamycin or vancomycin, in addition to antimicrobial agents for other potential pathogens as indicated. Vancomycin should not be continued if the organism is susceptible to other appropriate non–beta-lactam antimicrobial agents. Consultation with an infectious disease specialist should be considered.

NONMENINGEAL INVASIVE PNEUMOCOCCAL INFECTIONS IN THE IMMUNOCOMPROMISED HOST. The preceding recommendations for management of possible pneumococcal infections requiring hospitalization also apply to immunocompromised children, provided they are not critically ill. For critically ill patients, consideration should be given to initiating therapy with vancomycin and cefotaxime or ceftriaxone. Vancomycin should be discontinued as soon as antimicrobial susceptibility test results indicate that effective alternative antimicrobial agents are available.

DOSAGES. The recommended dosages of intravenous antimicrobial agents for treatment of invasive pneumococcal infections are given in Table 3.47 (p 530).

OTITIS MEDIA. Most experts recommend empiric initial treatment of acute otitis media (AOM) with high-dose oral amoxicillin (80 mg/kg per day).* Standard duration of therapy is 10 days, but children older than 2 years of age with uncomplicated cases can be treated for 5 days. On the basis of concentrations in middle ear fluid and in vitro activity, no currently available oral antimicrobial agent has better activity than amoxicillin against penicillin-nonsusceptible *S pneumoniae*.

For patients with clinically defined treatment failures when assessed after 3 to 5 days of initial therapy, suitable alternative agents should be active against penicillin-nonsusceptible pneumococci as well as beta-lactamase–producing *Haemophilus influenzae* and *Moraxella catarrhalis*. Such agents include high-dose oral amoxicillin-clavulanate; oral cefdinir, cefpodoxime, or cefuroxime; or intramuscular ceftriaxone. Amoxicillin-clavulanate should be given at 80 to 90 mg/kg per day of the amoxicillin component as the 14:1 formulation to decrease the incidence of diarrhea. Erythromycin-sulfisoxazole, clarithromycin, and azithromycin are appropriate alternatives for initial therapy in patients with type I (immediate, anaphylactic) reaction, although macrolide resistance among *S pneumoniae* is rising. For patients with a history of non-type I allergic reaction to penicillin, cefdinir, cefuroxime, or cefpodoxime can be used orally.

Myringotomy or tympanocentesis should be considered for cases failing to respond to second-line therapy and for severe cases to obtain cultures to guide ther-

---

* American Academy of Pediatrics, Subcommittee on Management of Acute Otitis Media. Diagnosis and management of acute otitis media. *Pediatrics.* 2004;113:1451–1465

apy. For multidrug-resistant strains of *S pneumoniae*, the use of clindamycin, rifampin, or other agents should be considered in consultation with an expert in infectious diseases.

SINUSITIS. Antimicrobial agents effective for treatment of acute otitis media also are likely to be effective for acute sinusitis and are recommended.

ISOLATION OF THE HOSPITALIZED PATIENT: Standard precautions are recommended, including for patients with infections caused by drug-resistant *S pneumoniae*.

CONTROL MEASURES:

ACTIVE IMMUNIZATION. Two pneumococcal vaccines are available for use in children: PCV7 (Prevnar), composed of purified capsular polysaccharides of 7 serotypes (4, 6B, 9V, 14, 18C, 19F, and 23F) conjugated to a diphtheria protein (CRM$_{197}$), and the 23-valent pneumococcal polysaccharide vaccine (PPV23 [Pneumovax]) composed of the purified capsular polysaccharides of 23 serotypes. Each vaccine is recommended in a dose of 0.5 mL to be given intramuscularly. The PPV23 induces protective antibody responses to the most common pneumococcal serotypes in the United States in children 2 years of age or older, whereas PCV7 induces protective antibody responses in children as young as 2 months of age. At the time the vaccine was licensed in 2000, the 7 serotypes of PCV7 accounted for approximately 88% of the cases of bacteremia, 82% of the cases of meningitis, and 70% of the cases of pneumococcal otitis media in US children younger than 6 years of age in the United States. Eighty percent of penicillin-*nonsusceptible* strains in the United States are one of these 7 serotypes.

ROUTINE IMMUNIZATION WITH PNEUMOCOCCAL CONJUGATE VACCINE. The PCV7 is recommended for routine administration as a 4-dose series for infants at 2, 4, 6, and 12 to 15 months of age; catch-up immunization is recommended for all children up to 23 months of age, using fewer doses depending on age (Table 3.48, p 533). Each 0.5-mL dose of PCV7 should be administered intramuscularly. Infants should begin the PCV7 immunization series in conjunction with other recommended vaccines at the time of the first regularly scheduled health maintenance visit after at least 6 weeks of age. Infants of very low birth weight ($\leq$1500 g) should be immunized when they attain a chronologic age of 6 to 8 weeks, regardless of their calculated gestational age. The PCV7 may be administered concurrently with all other age-appropriate childhood immunizations using a separate syringe and a separate site for injection. For children 23 months of age and younger who have not received the first PCV7 dose before 6 months of age, PCV7 doses should be administered according to the recommended schedule in Table 3.48. Children who begin catch-up PCV7 immunization between 7 and 23 months of age should do so at the first opportunity. Dosing of PCV7 during vaccine shortages and catch-up regimens vary by degree and anticipated length of shortage (**www.cdc.gov/nip/news/shortages/default.htm**).

IMMUNIZATION OF CHILDREN 24 TO 59 MONTHS OF AGE AT HIGH RISK OF INVASIVE PNEUMOCOCCAL DISEASE. The PCV7 is recommended for all children younger than 60 months of age who are at high risk or presumed high risk of acquiring invasive pneumococcal infection, as defined in Table 3.45 (p 527). For some high-risk children, supplemental protection should be given with adminis-

Table 3.48. Recommended Schedule for Doses of PCV7, Including Catch-up Immunizations in Previously Unimmunized and Partially Immunized Children

Age at Examination (mo)	Immunization History	Recommended Regimen[1]
2–6	0 doses	3 doses, 2 mo apart; fourth dose at age 12–15 mo
	1 dose	2 doses, 2 mo apart; fourth dose at age 12–15 mo
	2 doses	1 dose, 2 mo after the most recent dose; fourth dose at age 12–15 mo
7–11	0 doses	2 doses, 2 mo apart; third dose at 12 mo
	1 or 2 doses before age 7 mo	1 dose at age 7–11 mo, with another dose at 12–15 mo (≥2 mo later)
12–23	0 doses	2 doses, ≥2 mo apart
	1 dose before age 12 mo	2 doses, ≥2 mo apart
	1 dose at ≥12 mo	1 dose, ≥2 mo after the most recent dose
	2 or 3 doses before age 12 mo	1 dose, ≥2 mo after the most recent dose
24–59		
Healthy children	Any incomplete schedule	Consider 1 dose, ≥2 mo after the most recent dose[2]
Children at high risk[3]	Any incomplete schedule of <3 doses	1 dose, ≥2 mo after the most recent dose and another dose ≥2 mo later
	Any incomplete schedule of 3 doses	1 dose, ≥2 mo after the most recent dose

PCV7 indicates heptavalent pneumococcal conjugate vaccine.

[1] For children immunized at younger than 12 months of age, the minimum interval between doses is 4 weeks. Doses administered at 12 months of age or older should be ≥8 weeks apart.

[2] Providers should consider administering a single dose to unimmunized, healthy children 24 to 59 months of age with priority given to children 24 to 35 months of age, black children, American Indian/Alaska Native children not otherwise identified as high risk, and children who attend group child care centers.

[3] Children with sickle cell disease, asplenia, chronic heart or lung disease, diabetes mellitus, cerebrospinal fluid leak, cochlear implant, human immunodeficiency virus infection, or another immunocompromising condition and American Indian/Alaska Native children in areas with a demonstrated risk of invasive pneumococcal disease more than twice the national average (ie, Alaska, Arizona, New Mexico, and Navajo populations in Colorado and Utah).

tration of PPV23 vaccine. Most high-risk children will have received a series of 4 injections of PCV7 before 24 months of age, and for these children, a dose of PPV23 is recommended to be given at 24 months of age and an additional dose of PPV23 is recommended to be given 3 to 5 years after the first dose. The recommendations for high-risk children who are 24 to 59 months of age who may have received previous doses of either PPV23 or PCV7 are summarized in Table 3.49 (p 534). All high-risk children between 24 and 59 months of age who previously have not received doses of

PCV7 before 24 months of age should receive a series of 2 doses of PCV7 and 1 dose of PPV23 given at an 8-week interval between doses, followed by another dose of PPV23 3 to 5 years after the first dose.

IMMUNIZATION OF CHILDREN 24 TO 59 MONTHS OF AGE AT MODERATE OR LOW RISK OF INVASIVE PNEUMOCOCCAL DISEASE. Recommendations for children 24 to 59 months of age who are at moderate risk (Table 3.45, p 527) of pneumococcal disease are listed in Table 3.48 (p 533). Risk factors other than those listed in Table 3.45 include social or economic disadvantage, residence in crowded or substandard housing, homelessness, chronic exposure to tobacco smoke, or a history of severe or recurrent otitis media within the year before immunization or before placement of tympanostomy tubes.

The relative merits of PCV7 or PPV23 given as a single dose in children 24 months of age or older have not been studied. In addition to its impact on invasive infections, use of PCV7 has resulted in a modest decrease in the incidence of otitis media and a substantial decrease in nasopharyngeal carriage of vaccine serotypes. However, because of replacement by nonvaccine serotypes, an overall reduction in

Table 3.49. Recommendations for Pneumococcal Immunization With PCV7 or PPV23 Vaccine for Children at High Risk or Presumed High Risk of Pneumococcal Disease, as Defined in Table 3.45 (p 527)

Age	Previous Dose(s) of Any Pneumococcal Vaccine	Recommendations
≤23 mo	None	PCV7, as in Table 3.48 (p 533)
24–59 mo	4 doses of PCV7	1 dose of PPV23 vaccine at 24 mo of age, at least 8 wk after last dose of PCV7 1 dose of PPV23, 3–5 y after the first dose of PS23
24–59 mo	1–3 previous doses of PCV7	1 dose of PCV7 1 dose of PPV23, 8 wk after the last dose of PCV7 1 dose of PPV23, 3–5 y after the first dose of PS23
24–59 mo	1 dose of PPV23	2 doses of PCV7, 8 wk apart, beginning at 6–8 wk after last dose of PPV23 1 dose of PPV23 vaccine, 3–5 y after the last dose of PPV23
24–59 mo	No previous dose of PPV23 or PCV7	2 doses of PCV7, 8 wk apart 1 dose of PPV23 vaccine, 8 wk after the last dose of PCV7 1 dose of PPV23 vaccine, 3–5 y after the first dose of PPV23 vaccine

PCV7 indicates heptavalent pneumococcal conjugate vaccine; PPV23, 23-valent pneumococcal polysaccharide vaccine.

nasopharyngeal carriage of pneumococci may not occur. The duration of antibody responses is greater after PCV7, and this vaccine induces immunologic memory, whereas PPV23 does not. The preferred vaccine for most children is PCV7. If PCV7 is given, a single dose of PPV23 after administration of PCV7 is recommended, particularly for children of American Indian descent. Use of PPV23 provides a broader coverage against pneumococcal serotypes not contained within PCV7; conjugate vaccine may provide coverage against 75% or fewer of disease-associated serotypes in children older than 24 months of age. However, either PCV7 or PPV23 can be used for elective administration to children 24 to 59 months of age who are at moderate risk.

IMMUNIZATION OF CHILDREN 5 YEARS OF AGE AND OLDER. Immunization at 5 years of age or older may be appropriate for certain children who remain at high risk because of chronic underlying disease. The PCV7 is licensed by the Food and Drug Administration for children up to 9 years of age. Limited safety and efficacy data are available for PCV7 or PPV23 in children who are 60 months of age or older. Studies of small numbers of children with sickle cell disease and HIV infection suggest that PCV7 is safe and immunogenic when administered to children up to 13 years of age. Therefore, administration of a single dose of PCV7 to children of any age, particularly children who are at high risk of invasive pneumococcal disease, is not contraindicated. However, PPV23 also may be effective and immunogenic in older children, and therefore, immunization with a single dose of PCV7 or PPV23 is acceptable. If both vaccines are used, PCV7 should be administered first, and the administration of PPV23 should follow at an interval of at least 8 weeks.

IMMUNIZATION OF CHILDREN WITH SEVERE OR RECURRENT OTITIS MEDIA. Pneumococcal polysaccharide vaccines that are not conjugated to carrier proteins have not decreased the incidence of AOM in children of any age; therefore, PPV23 is not recommended for prevention of AOM. For children younger than 2 years of age, PCV7 provides a modest decrease in AOM and recurrent AOM (as defined by 3 or more episodes in 6 months, 4 or more episodes in 1 year, or in placement of tympanostomy tubes).

CONTROL OF TRANSMISSION OF PNEUMOCOCCAL INFECTION AND INVASIVE DISEASE AMONG CHILDREN ATTENDING OUT-OF-HOME CHILD CARE. Rates of invasive pneumococcal infection among children attending out-of-home child care are twofold to threefold higher than among healthy children of the same age not enrolled in out-of-home child care. Neither PPV23 nor PCV7 decreases nasopharyngeal carriage of pneumococci, although PCV7 reduces carriage of vaccine serotype pneumococci at the same time nonvaccine serotype carriage increases. Available data are insufficient to recommend any antimicrobial regimen for preventing or interrupting the carriage or transmission of pneumococcal infection in out-of-home child care settings. Antimicrobial chemoprophylaxis is not recommended for contacts of children with invasive pneumococcal disease, regardless of their immunization status.

GENERAL RECOMMENDATIONS FOR USE OF PNEUMOCOCCAL VACCINES.
- Either PPV23 or PCV7 may be given concurrently with other vaccines. Pneumococcal vaccine should be injected with a separate syringe in a separate site.

- When elective splenectomy is performed for any reason, immunization with PCV7 and/or PPV23 should be completed at least 2 weeks before splenectomy. Immunization also should precede initiation of immune-compromising therapy or placement of a cochlear implant by at least 2 weeks.
- Generally, pneumococcal vaccines should be deferred during pregnancy, because it is not known whether pneumococcal vaccines can cause fetal harm when administered to a pregnant woman. However, inactivated or killed vaccines, including other experimental and licensed polysaccharide vaccines, have been administered safely during pregnancy. The risk of severe pneumococcal disease in a pregnant woman (which includes risk from underlying medical conditions) should be considered when making decisions regarding the need for pneumococcal immunization.
- Children who have experienced invasive pneumococcal disease should receive all recommended doses of pneumococcal vaccines (PCV7 or PPV23) appropriate for age and underlying condition. The full series of scheduled doses should be completed even if the series is interrupted by an episode of invasive pneumococcal disease.

Cases of invasive pneumococcal disease in children younger than 5 years of age should be reported according to state standards. In addition, children who have received at least one dose of PCV7 should be reported to the CDC through the state health department, and the pneumococcal isolates should be serotyped if possible. Thus far, the majority of such children have had infection caused by nonvaccine serotype isolates. If the isolate is a serotype included in the vaccine, an evaluation of the patient's HIV status and immunologic function should be considered.

ADVERSE REACTIONS TO PNEUMOCOCCAL VACCINES. Adverse reactions after administration of polysaccharide or conjugate vaccines generally are mild and limited to local reactions of redness or swelling. Fever may occur within the first 1 to 2 days after injections, particularly after use of conjugate vaccine.

PASSIVE IMMUNIZATION. Immune Globulin Intravenous administration is recommended for preventing pneumococcal infection in patients with congenital or acquired immunodeficiency diseases, including people with HIV infection who have recurrent pneumococcal infections (see Human Immunodeficiency Virus Infection, p 378).

CHEMOPROPHYLAXIS. Daily antimicrobial prophylaxis is recommended for children with functional or anatomic asplenia, regardless of their immunization status, for prevention of pneumococcal disease (see Children With Asplenia, p 83). Oral penicillin V (125 mg twice a day for children younger than 5 years of age; 250 mg twice a day for children 5 years of age and older) is recommended. The results of a multicenter study demonstrated that oral penicillin V (125 mg twice a day) given to infants and young children with sickle cell disease decreased the incidence of pneumococcal bacteremia by 84% compared with the placebo control group. On the basis of this study, daily penicillin prophylaxis for infants and children with sickle cell disease is recommended. Although overall incidence of invasive pneumococcal infection is decreased after penicillin prophylaxis, the number of cases of penicillin-resistant invasive pneumococcal infections and the prevalence of nasopharyngeal carriage of penicillin-resistant strains in patients with sickle cell disease have increased in recent years.

Parents should be informed that penicillin prophylaxis may not be effective in preventing all cases of invasive pneumococcal infections.

The age at which prophylaxis is discontinued often is an empiric decision. Most children with sickle cell disease who have received all recommended pneumococcal vaccines for age and who had received penicillin prophylaxis for prolonged periods, who are receiving regular medical attention, and who have not had a previous severe pneumococcal infection or a surgical splenectomy safely may discontinue prophylactic penicillin at 5 years of age. However, they must be counseled to seek medical attention for all febrile events. The duration of prophylaxis for children with asplenia attributable to other causes is unknown. Some experts continue prophylaxis throughout childhood.

Pneumocystis jiroveci Infections

CLINICAL MANIFESTATIONS: Infants and children develop a characteristic syndrome of subacute diffuse pneumonitis with dyspnea at rest, tachypnea, oxygen desaturation, nonproductive cough, and fever. However, the intensity of these signs and symptoms can vary, and in some immunocompromised children and adults, onset can be acute and fulminant. The chest radiograph often shows bilateral diffuse interstitial or alveolar disease; rarely, lobar, miliary, and nodular lesions or even no lesions are seen. The mortality rate in immunocompromised patients ranges from 5% to 40% if treated and approaches 100% if untreated.

ETIOLOGY: Nomenclature for *Pneumocystis* species is in evolution. *Pneumocystis jiroveci* has been proposed, denoting the fact that *Pneumocystis carinii* only infects rats and not humans. At present, *Pneumocystis carinii* or *P carinii f. sp. hominis* continue to be used. *Pneumocystis jiroveci* is classified as a fungus on the basis of DNA sequence analysis. However, *P jiroveci* retains several morphologic and biologic similarities to protozoa, including susceptibility to a number of antiprotozoal agents but resistance to most antifungal agents. The 5- to 7-μm-diameter cysts contain up to 8 intracystic bodies.

EPIDEMIOLOGY: *Pneumocystis jiroveci* is ubiquitous in mammals worldwide, particularly rodents, and has a tropism for growth on respiratory tract surfaces. *Pneumocystis jiroveci* isolates recovered from mice, rats, and ferrets are diverse genetically from each other and from human *P jiroveci;* isolates from one animal species do not cross-infect other animal species. Asymptomatic infection occurs early in life, with more than 85% of healthy children acquiring antibody by 20 months of age. *Pneumocystis jiroveci* often is found postmortem in lungs of infants with a diagnosis of sudden infant death syndrome, but a causal relationship is uncertain. In resource-limited countries and in times of famine, *P jiroveci* pneumonia (PCP) has occurred in epidemics, primarily affecting malnourished infants and children. Epidemics also have occurred in preterm infants. In industrialized countries, PCP occurs almost entirely in immunocompromised people with deficient cell-mediated immunity, particularly people with human immunodeficiency virus (HIV) infection, recipients of immunosuppressive therapy after organ transplantation or treatment for malignant neoplasm, and children with congenital immunodeficiency syndromes. Although decreasing in frequency because of effective prophylaxis and antiretroviral therapy, PCP remains one of the most common serious opportunistic infections in infants and children with perinatally acquired HIV infection. Although onset of disease can occur at any age, including rare instances during the first month of life, PCP most commonly occurs in HIV-infected children in the first year of life. The mode of transmission is unknown. Animal studies have demonstrated animal-to-animal transmission by the airborne route, suggesting the possibility that person-to-person transmission may occur in humans. Primary infection probably accounts for disease during infancy. Although reactivation of latent infection with immunosuppression has been proposed as an explanation for disease after the first 2 years of life, animal models of PCP do not support the existence of latency. Studies of patients with acquired immunodeficiency syndrome (AIDS) with more than one episode of *P jiroveci* pneumonia suggest reinfection rather than relapse. In patients with cancer, the disease can occur during remission or relapse. The period of communicability is unknown.

The **incubation period** is unknown, but animal models suggest 4 to 8 weeks from exposure to clinically apparent infection.

DIAGNOSTIC TESTS: A definitive diagnosis of PCP is made by demonstration of organisms in lung tissue or respiratory tract secretion specimens. The most sensitive and specific diagnostic procedures are open lung biopsy and, in older children, transbronchial biopsy. However, bronchoscopy with bronchoalveolar lavage, induction of sputum in older children and adolescents, and intubation with deep endotracheal aspiration are less invasive, can be diagnostic, and are sensitive in patients with HIV infection who have an increased number of organisms. Methenamine silver, toluidine blue O, calcofluor white, and fluorescein-conjugated monoclonal antibody are the most useful stains for identifying the thick-walled cysts of *P jiroveci*. Extracystic trophozoite forms are identified with Giemsa stain, modified Wright-Giemsa stain, and fluorescein-conjugated monoclonal antibody stain. Polymerase chain reaction assays for detecting *P jiroveci* infection are experimental and are not approved by the US Food and Drug Administration (FDA) for diagnosis. Serologic tests are not useful.

TREATMENT: The drug of choice is intravenous trimethoprim-sulfamethoxazole (see Drugs for Parasitic Infections, p 790). Oral therapy should be reserved for patients with mild disease who do not have malabsorption or diarrhea or patients with a favorable clinical response to initial intravenous therapy. The rate of adverse reactions (rash, neutropenia, anemia, renal dysfunction, nausea, vomiting, and diarrhea) to trimethoprim-sulfamethoxazole is higher in HIV-infected children than in other patients. If the adverse reaction is not severe, continuation of therapy is recommended. Half of patients with adverse reactions subsequently have been treated successfully with trimethoprim-sulfamethoxazole.

Intravenously administered pentamidine is an alternative drug for children and adults who cannot tolerate trimethoprim-sulfamethoxazole or who have severe disease and have not responded to trimethoprim-sulfamethoxazole after 5 to 7 days of therapy. The therapeutic efficacy of parenteral pentamidine in adults with PCP is similar to that of trimethoprim-sulfamethoxazole. Pentamidine is associated with a high incidence of adverse reactions, including pancreatitis, renal dysfunction, hypoglycemia, hyperglycemia, hypotension, fever, and neutropenia. Pentamidine should not be administered concomitantly with didanosine, because both drugs cause pancreatitis. If a recipient of didanosine requires pentamidine, didanosine should be discontinued until 1 week after pentamidine therapy has been completed.

Atovaquone is approved for the oral treatment of mild to moderate PCP in adults who are intolerant of trimethoprim-sulfamethoxazole. Experience with the use of atovaquone in children is limited. Other potentially useful drugs in adults include clindamycin with primaquine, dapsone with trimethoprim, and trimetrexate with leucovorin. Experience with the use of these combinations in children is limited.

In patients with AIDS, prophylaxis should be initiated at the end of therapy for acute infection and should be continued until CD4+ T-lymphocyte counts exceed the concentration no longer requiring prophylaxis (see Table 3.50, p 540) or lifelong if CD4+ T-lymphocyte cells do not respond to antiretroviral therapy. Children with PCP infection should be given lifelong prophylaxis to prevent recurrence.

Corticosteroids appear to be beneficial in treatment of HIV-infected adults with moderate to severe PCP (as defined by an arterial oxygen pressure [PaO_2] of less than 70 mm Hg in room air or an arterial-alveolar gradient of more than 35 mm Hg). For adolescents older than 13 years of age and adults, 80 mg/day of oral prednisone in 2 divided doses for the first 5 days of therapy, 40 mg once a day on days 6 through 10, and 20 mg once a day on days 11 through 21 is recommended. Although no controlled studies of the use of corticosteroids in young children have been performed, most experts would include corticosteroids as part of therapy for children with moderate to severe PCP disease. The optimal dose and duration of corticosteroid therapy for children have not been determined, but small studies report improvement with methylprednisolone (1mg/kg) or prednisone administered 2 to 4 times per day for 5 to 7 days, followed by a tapering dose during the next 7 to 12 days.

CHEMOPROPHYLAXIS. Prophylaxis against a first episode of PCP is indicated for many patients with significant immunocompromise, including people with HIV infection (see Human Immunodeficiency Virus Infection, p 378) and people with primary or acquired immunodeficiency.

Because rapid changes in CD4+ T-lymphocyte counts can occur in HIV-infected infants, prophylaxis for PCP is recommended for all infants born to HIV-infected women beginning at 4 to 6 weeks of age (see Table 3.50, p 540). Prophylaxis for PCP should be discontinued in children in whom HIV infection has been excluded. Children whose HIV infection status is indeterminate should continue prophylaxis throughout the first year of life.

For older HIV-infected infants and children, PCP prophylaxis should be continued or administered in the following situations: (1) any CD4+ T-lymphocyte count that indicates severe immunosuppression for age (see Table 3.50, p 540); (2) a rapidly decreasing CD4+ T-lymphocyte count; or (3) severely symptomatic HIV disease (category C) (see Human Immunodeficiency Virus Infection, p 378, and Table 3.50, p 540). Criteria are the same for older children and adolescents, except for different age-specific definitions of low absolute CD4+ T-lymphocyte counts. For adolescents or adults, PCP prophylaxis has been recommended if the patient has a history of oropharyngeal candidiasis. On the basis of experience with discontinuing primary or secondary (after a case of PCP) prophylaxis for PCP in adolescents and adults after an adequate CD4+ T-lymphocyte response to antiretroviral therapy, cessation of pro-

Table 3.50. Recommendations for *Pneumocystis jiroveci* Pneumonia (PCP) Prophylaxis for Human Immunodeficiency Virus (HIV)-Exposed Infants and Children, by Age and HIV Infection Status[1]

Age and HIV Infection Status	PCP Prophylaxis[2]
Birth to 4–6 wk, HIV exposed	No prophylaxis
4–6 wk to 4 mo, HIV exposed	Prophylaxis
4–12 mo	
HIV infected or indeterminate	Prophylaxis
HIV infection excluded[3]	No prophylaxis
1–5 y, HIV-infected	Prophylaxis if: CD4+ T-lymphocyte count is <500 cells/µL or percentage is <15%[4,5]
≥5 y, HIV-infected	Prophylaxis if: CD4+ T-lymphocyte count is <200 cells/µL or percentage is <15%[5]

[1] Modified from Centers for Disease Control and Prevention. 2002 USPHS/IDSA guidelines for preventing opportunistic infections among HIV-infected persons—2002. Recommendations of the US Public Health Service and the Infectious Diseases Society of America. *MMWR Recomm Rep.* 2002;51(RR-8):1–46

[2] Children who have had PCP should receive lifelong PCP prophylaxis.

[3] HIV infection can be excluded reasonably among children who have had 2 or more negative results of HIV diagnostic tests, both of which are performed at ≥1 month of age and 1 of which is performed at ≥4 months of age; or 2 or more negative results of HIV immunoglobulin G antibody tests performed at ≥6 months of age among children who have no clinical evidence of HIV disease (see Human Immunodeficiency Virus Infection, p 378).

[4] Children 1 to 2 years of age who were receiving PCP prophylaxis and had a CD4+ T-lymphocyte count of less than 750/µL or percentage of <15% at younger than 12 months of age should continue prophylaxis.

[5] Prophylaxis should be considered on a case-by-case basis for children who might otherwise be at risk of PCP, such as children with rapidly declining CD4+ T-lymphocyte counts or percentages or children with category C status of HIV infection.

phylaxis also should be considered for children whose CD4+ T-lymphocyte counts are adequate. Children who have a history of PCP should receive lifelong PCP chemoprophylaxis. The safety of discontinuing secondary prophylaxis among HIV-infected children has not been studied extensively.

Children older than 1 year of age with HIV infection who are not receiving PCP prophylaxis (eg, children not previously identified or children whose PCP prophylaxis was discontinued) should begin prophylaxis if the CD4+ T-lymphocyte cell count indicates severe immunosuppression (see Table 3.50).

Prophylaxis for PCP is recommended for children who have received hematopoietic stem cell transplants (HSCT), all HSCT recipients with hematologic malig-

* Centers for Disease Control and Prevention. Guidelines for preventing opportunistic infections among hematopoietic stem cell transplant recipients. Recommendations of the CDC, the Infectious Diseases Society of America, and the American Society of Blood and Barrow Transplantation. *MMWR Recomm Rep.* 2000;49(RR-10):1–128. See also **www.hivatis.org**.

Table 3.51. Drug Regimens for *Pneumocystis jiroveci* Pneumonia Prophylaxis for Children 4 Weeks of Age or Older[1]

Recommended regimen:

Trimethoprim-sulfamethoxazole (trimethoprim, 150 mg/m^2 per day with sulfamethoxazole, 750 mg/m^2 per day), orally, in divided doses twice a day, 3 times per week on consecutive days (eg, Monday-Tuesday-Wednesday).

Acceptable alternative trimethoprim-sulfamethoxazole dosage schedules:

- Trimethoprim (150 mg/m^2 per day) with sulfamethoxazole (750 mg/m^2 per day), orally, **as a single daily dose,** 3 times per week on consecutive days (eg, Monday-Tuesday-Wednesday).
- Trimethoprim (150 mg/m^2 per day) with sulfamethoxazole (750 mg/m^2 per day), orally, in divided doses, twice a day, and **administered 7 days per week.**
- Trimethoprim (150 mg/m^2 per day) with sulfamethoxazole (750 mg/m^2 per day), orally, in divided doses twice a day, and administered 3 times per week on alternate days (eg, Monday-Wednesday-Friday).

Alternative regimens if trimethoprim-sulfamethoxazole is not tolerated[2]:

- **Dapsone (children $\geq$1 mo of age)**
  2 mg/kg (maximum 100 mg), orally, once a day or 4 mg/kg (maximum 200 mg), orally, every week
- **Aerosolized pentamidine (children $\geq$5 y of age)**
  300 mg, inhaled monthly via Respirgard II nebulizer
- **Atovaquone (children 1–3 mo of age and >24 mo of age)**
  30 mg/kg, orally, once a day
  (children 4–24 mo of age)
  45 mg/kg, orally, once a day

---

[1] Modified from Centers for Disease Control and Prevention. 2002 USPHS/IDSA guidelines for preventing opportunistic infections among HIV-infected persons—2002. Recommendations of the US Public Health Service and the Infectious Diseases Society of America. *MMWR Recomm Rep.* 2002;51(RR-8):1–46

[2] If dapsone, aerosolized pentamidine, and atovaquone are not tolerated, some clinicians use intravenous pentamidine (4 mg/kg) administered every 2 to 4 weeks.

nancies (eg, leukemia or lymphoma), and HSCT recipients receiving intense conditioning regimens or graft manipulation. Prophylaxis should be initiated at engraftment and administered for 6 months. Prophylaxis should be continued for more than 6 months in all children receiving immunosuppressive therapy (eg, prednisone or cyclosporin) or in those with chronic graft-versus-host disease.

The recommended drug regimen for PCP prophylaxis for all immunocompromised patients is trimethoprim-sulfamethoxazole administered for 3 consecutive days each week (see Table 3.51 for dosage). For patients who cannot tolerate the drug, aerosolized pentamidine administered by the Respirgard II nebulizer for people 5 years of age or older is an alternative. Daily oral dapsone is another alternative drug for prophylaxis in children, especially children younger than 5 years of age (see Table 3.51). Intravenous pentamidine has been used but is more toxic than other prophylactic regimens.

Other drugs with potential for prophylaxis include pyrimethamine plus dapsone plus leucovorin, pyrimethamine-sulfadoxine, and oral atovaquone. Experience with these drugs in adults and children is limited. These agents should be considered only in situations in which the recommended regimens are not tolerated or cannot be used.

ISOLATION OF THE HOSPITALIZED PATIENT: Standard precautions are recommended. Some experts recommend that patients with PCP not share a room with immunocompromised patients, although data are insufficient to support this recommendation as standard practice.

CONTROL MEASURES: Appropriate therapy for infected patients and prophylaxis in immunocompromised patients are the only available means of control. Detailed guidelines have been issued by the Centers for Disease Control and Prevention and the Infectious Diseases Society of America and endorsed by the American Academy of Pediatrics.*

Poliovirus Infections

CLINICAL MANIFESTATIONS: Approximately 95% of poliovirus infections are asymptomatic. Nonspecific illness with low-grade fever and sore throat (minor illness) occurs in 4% to 8% of people who become infected. Aseptic meningitis, sometimes with paresthesias, occurs in 1% to 5% of patients a few days after the minor illness has resolved. Rapid onset of asymmetric acute flaccid paralysis with areflexia of the involved limb occurs in 0.1% to 2% of infections, and residual paralytic disease involving the motor neurons (paralytic poliomyelitis) occurs in approximately two thirds of people with acute motor neuron disease. Cranial nerve involvement and paralysis of respiratory tract muscles can occur. Findings in cerebrospinal fluid (CSF) are characteristic of viral meningitis with mild pleocytosis and lymphocytic predominance.

Adults who contracted paralytic poliomyelitis during childhood may develop the postpolio syndrome 30 to 40 years later. Postpolio syndrome is characterized by slow and often significant onset of muscle pain and exacerbation of weakness.

ETIOLOGY: Polioviruses are enteroviruses and consist of serotypes 1, 2, and 3.

EPIDEMIOLOGY: Poliovirus infections occur only in humans. Spread is by the fecal-oral and respiratory routes. Infection is more common in infants and young children and occurs at an earlier age among children living in poor hygienic conditions. The

---

* Centers for Disease Control and Prevention. Guidelines for preventing opportunistic infections among HIV-infected persons—2002. Recommendations of the US Public Health Service and the Infectious Diseases Society of America. *MMWR Recomm Rep*. 2002;51(RR-8):1–46; Centers for Disease Control and Prevention. Treating opportunistic infections among HIV-exposed and infected children: recommendations from the CDC, the National Institutes of Health, and the Infectious Diseases Society of America. *MMWR Recomm Rep*. 2004;53(RR-14):1–63; and Centers for Disease Control and Prevention. Treating opportunistic infections among HIV-infected adults and adolescents: recommendations from the CDC, the National Institutes of Health, and the HIV Medicine Association/Infectious Diseases Society of America. *MMWR Recomm Rep*. 2004;53(RR-15):1–112

risk of paralytic disease after infection increases with age. In temperate climates, poliovirus infections are most common during summer and autumn; in the tropics, the seasonal pattern is less pronounced.

The last reported case of poliomyelitis attributable to indigenously acquired, wild-type poliovirus in the United States occurred in 1979 and was caused by a wild type 1 poliovirus. In that outbreak, 10 paralytic cases and 4 other poliovirus infections occurred among unimmunized people. The only identified imported case of paralytic poliomyelitis since 1986 occurred in 1993 in a child transported to the United States for medical care. Since 1979, all other cases have been vaccine-associated paralytic poliomyelitis (VAPP) occurring in vaccine recipients or their contacts and attributable to oral poliovirus (OPV) vaccine. An average of 8 cases of VAPP were reported annually in the United States from 1980 to 1996. Fewer VAPP cases were reported annually between 1997 and 1999, after a shift in United States immunization policy to a sequential inactivated poliovirus (IPV)-OPV immunization schedule. Implementation of an all-IPV vaccine schedule in 2000 ended the occurrence of new VAPP cases, thus eliminating the last type of paralytic poliomyelitis in the United States. Circulation of indigenous wild-type poliovirus strains ceased in the United States several decades ago, and the risk of contact with imported wild-type polioviruses is decreasing rapidly, parallel with the success of the global eradication program of the World Health Organization (WHO) and WHO partners. In 2005, the first identified vaccine-derived poliovirus in the United States and the first transmission in a community since OPV immunizations were discontinued in 2000 was reported.* This occurrence raises concerns regarding transmission among people in communities with low levels of immunization and risk of a polio outbreak occurring in the United States.

Communicability of poliovirus is greatest shortly before and after onset of clinical illness when the virus is present in the throat and excreted in high concentration in feces. The virus persists in the throat for approximately 1 week after onset of illness and is excreted in feces for several weeks. Patients potentially are contagious for as long as fecal excretion persists. In recipients of OPV vaccine, the virus persists in the throat for 1 to 2 weeks and is excreted in feces for several weeks, although in rare cases, excretion for more than 2 months can occur. Immunodeficient patients have excreted virus for periods of more than 10 years.

The **incubation period** of asymptomatic or nonparalytic poliomyelitis is 3 to 6 days. For the onset of paralysis in paralytic poliomyelitis, the incubation period usually is 7 to 21 days.

DIAGNOSTIC TESTS: Poliovirus can be recovered from the pharynx, feces, urine, and rarely, cerebrospinal fluid by isolation in cell culture. Two or more stool and throat swab specimens for enterovirus isolation should be obtained at least 24 hours apart from patients with suspected paralytic poliomyelitis as early in the course of illness as possible, ideally within 14 days of onset of symptoms. Fecal material is most likely to yield virus.

Because OPV vaccine no longer is available in the United States, the chance of exposure to vaccine-type polioviruses has become remote. Therefore, if a poliovirus is

---

* Centers for Disease Control and Prevention. Poliovirus infections in four unvaccinated children—Minnesota, August-October 2005. *MMWR Morb Mortal Wkly Rep.* 2005;54:1053–1055

isolated in the United States, the isolate should be sent to the Centers for Disease Control and Prevention through the state health department for further testing. The diagnostic test of choice for confirming poliovirus disease is viral culture of stool specimens and throat swab specimens obtained as early in the course of illness as possible. Interpretation of acute and convalescent serologic test results can be difficult.

TREATMENT: Supportive.

ISOLATION OF THE HOSPITALIZED PATIENT: In addition to standard precautions, contact precautions are indicated for infants and young children for the duration of hospitalization.

CONTROL MEASURES:
IMMUNIZATION OF INFANTS AND CHILDREN.
Vaccines. The 2 types of poliovirus vaccines are inactivated vaccine given parenterally (subcutaneously or intramuscularly) and live-virus vaccine given orally. Inactivated poliovirus vaccine is now the only poliovirus vaccine available in the United States. Inactivated poliovirus vaccine contains the 3 types of poliovirus grown in Vero cells and inactivated with formaldehyde. The IPV vaccine in use in the United States since 1987 has higher potency (enhanced IPV) than earlier formulations. Trace amounts of streptomycin, neomycin, and polymyxin B may be present in IPV vaccine. Inactivated poliovirus vaccine also is available in a combined formulation that contains diphtheria and tetanus toxoids and acellular pertussis (DTaP) vaccine, hepatitis B vaccine, and IPV (see Pertussis, p 498). Oral poliovirus vaccine contains attenuated poliovirus types 1, 2, and 3 produced in monkey kidney cells or cell cultures.

Immunogenicity and Efficacy. Both IPV and OPV vaccines in their recommended schedules are highly immunogenic and effective in preventing poliomyelitis.

Administration of IPV vaccine results in seroconversion in 95% or more of vaccine recipients to each of the 3 serotypes after 2 doses and in 99% to 100% of recipients after 3 doses. Immunity is prolonged, perhaps lifelong. During poliovirus infection, IPV-immunized children excrete polioviruses from stool but not from the oropharynx. Immunization with 3 or more doses of OPV vaccine induces excellent serum antibody responses and a high degree of intestinal immunity against poliovirus reinfection. A 3-dose series of OPV vaccine, as formerly used in the United States, results in sustained, probably lifelong immunity.

Administration With Other Vaccines. Either IPV or OPV vaccine may be given concurrently with other routinely recommended childhood vaccines (see Simultaneous Administration of Multiple Vaccines, p 34). For administration of the combined DTaP-hepatitis B-IPV vaccine with other vaccines and the interchangeability of the combined vaccine with other vaccine products, see Pertussis (p 498).

Adverse Reactions. No serious adverse events have been associated with use of IPV vaccine. Because IPV vaccine may contain trace amounts of streptomycin, neomycin, and polymyxin B, allergic reactions are possible in recipients with hypersensitivity to one or more of these antimicrobial agents.

Oral poliovirus vaccine can cause VAPP. Before the exclusive use of IPV vaccine in the United States, the overall risk of VAPP was approximately 1 case per 2.4 million doses of OPV vaccine distributed. The rate after the first dose, including vaccine recipient and contact cases, was approximately 1 case per 750 000 doses.

SCHEDULE. Four doses of IPV vaccine are recommended for routine immunization of all infants and children in the United States. The first 2 doses should be given at 2-month intervals beginning at 2 months of age (minimum age 6 weeks), and a third dose is recommended at 6 to 18 months of age. Doses may be given at 4-week intervals when accelerated protection is indicated. Administration of the third dose at 6 months of age has the potential advantage of enhancing the likelihood of completion of the primary series and does not compromise seroconversion. A supplemental dose of IPV vaccine should be given before the child enters school (ie, at 4–6 years of age). A fourth dose is not necessary if the third dose was given on or after the child's fourth birthday.

Oral poliovirus vaccine is the vaccine of choice for global eradication and is recommended in the following: (1) locations with continued or recent circulation of wild-type poliovirus; (2) most developing countries where the higher cost of IPV vaccine prohibits its use; and (3) areas where inadequate sanitation necessitates an optimal mucosal barrier to wild-type virus circulation.

Licensed OPV vaccine no longer is available in the United States. The potential use of OPV vaccine to control an outbreak of paralytic poliomyelitis remains a public health option. Whenever OPV vaccine is administered, the risk of VAPP in recipients and contacts should be discussed with parents or caregivers.

Children Incompletely Immunized. Children who have not received the recommended doses of poliovirus vaccines on schedule should receive sufficient doses of IPV vaccine to complete the immunization series for their age (see Table 1.7, p 28).

VACCINE RECOMMENDATIONS FOR ADULTS. Most adults residing in the United States are immune as a result of immunization received during childhood and have a small risk of exposure to wild-type poliovirus in the United States. Immunization is recommended only for certain adults who are at a greater risk of exposure to wild-type polioviruses than the general population, including the following:

- Travelers to areas or countries where poliomyelitis is or may be epidemic or endemic
- Members of communities or specific population groups with disease caused by wild-type polioviruses
- Laboratory workers handling specimens that may contain wild-type polioviruses
- Health care professionals in close contact with patients who may be excreting wild-type polioviruses

For unimmunized adults, primary immunization with IPV vaccine is recommended. Two doses of IPV vaccine should be given at intervals of 1 to 2 months (4–8 weeks); a third dose is given 6 to 12 months after the second unless the risk of exposure is increased, such as when traveling to areas where wild-type poliovirus is known to be circulating. If time does not allow 3 doses of IPV vaccine to be given according to the recommended schedule before protection is required, the following alternatives are recommended:

- If protection is not needed until 8 weeks or more, 3 doses of IPV vaccine should be given at least 4 weeks apart.
- If protection is not needed for 4 to 8 weeks, 2 doses of IPV vaccine should be given at least 4 weeks apart.

- If protection is needed in fewer than 4 weeks, a single dose of IPV vaccine should be given.

The remaining doses of vaccine to complete the primary immunization schedule should be given subsequently at the recommended intervals if the person remains at an increased risk.

Recommendations in other circumstances are as follows:

- **Incompletely immunized adults.** Adults who previously received less than a full primary course of OPV or IPV vaccine should be given the remaining required doses of IPV vaccine regardless of the interval since the last dose and the type of vaccine that was received previously.
- **Adults who are at an increased risk of exposure to wild-type poliovirus and who previously completed primary immunization with OPV or IPV vaccine.** These adults can receive a single dose of IPV vaccine.

PRECAUTIONS AND CONTRAINDICATIONS TO IMMUNIZATION.

Immunodeficiency Disorders. Patients with immunodeficiency disorders, including HIV infection, combined immunodeficiency, abnormalities of immunoglobulin synthesis (ie, antibody deficiency syndromes), leukemia, lymphoma, or generalized malignant neoplasm, or people being given immunosuppressive therapy with pharmacologic agents (see Immunocompromised Children, p 71) or radiation therapy should receive IPV vaccine. A protective immune response to IPV vaccine in an immunodeficient patient cannot be ensured.

Household Contacts of People With Immunodeficiency Disease, Altered Immune States, Immunosuppression Attributable to Therapy for Other Disease, or Known HIV Infection. The IPV vaccine is recommended for these people, and OPV vaccine should not be used. If OPV vaccine inadvertently is introduced into a household of an immunodeficient or HIV-infected person, close contact between the patient and the OPV vaccine recipient should be minimized for approximately 4 to 6 weeks after immunization. Household members should be counseled on practices that will minimize exposure of the immunodeficient or HIV-infected person to excreted poliovirus vaccine. These practices include exercising hand hygiene after contact with the child by all and avoiding diaper changing by the immunosuppressed person.

Pregnancy. Immunization during pregnancy generally should be avoided for reasons of theoretic risk, although no convincing evidence indicates that the rates of adverse reactions to IPV vaccine are increased in pregnant women or in their developing fetuses. If immediate protection against poliomyelitis is needed, IPV is recommended (see Vaccine Recommendations for Adults, p 545).

Hypersensitivity or Anaphylactic Reactions to IPV Vaccine, OPV Vaccine, or Antimicrobial Agents Contained in These Vaccines. The IPV vaccine is contraindicated for people who have experienced an anaphylactic reaction after a previous dose of IPV vaccine or to one of the following antimicrobial agents: streptomycin, neomycin, and polymyxin B.

Breastfeeding and mild diarrhea are not contraindications to IPV or OPV vaccine administration.

REPORTING OF ADVERSE EVENTS AFTER IMMUNIZATION. All cases of VAPP and other serious adverse events associated temporally with poliomyelitis vaccine should be reported (see Reporting of Adverse Events, p 41).

Case Reporting and Investigation. A suspected case of poliomyelitis should be reported promptly to the state health department and should result in an immediate epidemiologic investigation. Poliomyelitis should be considered in the differential diagnosis of all cases of acute flaccid paralysis, including Guillain-Barré syndrome and transverse myelitis. If the course is compatible clinically with poliomyelitis, specimens should be obtained for viral studies (see Diagnostic Tests, p 543). If the evidence implicates wild-type poliovirus infection, an intensive investigation will be conducted, and a public health decision will be made about the need for supplementary immunizations, choice of vaccine, and other action.

PRION DISEASES

Transmissible Spongiform Encephalopathies*

CLINICAL MANIFESTATIONS: Transmissible spongiform encephalopathies (TSEs), or prion diseases, constitute a group of rare, rapidly progressive, universally fatal neurodegenerative syndromes of humans and animals that are characterized by neuronal degeneration, spongiform change, gliosis, and accumulation of an abnormal protease-resistant amyloid protein (protease-resistant prion protein [PrP^{res}] or scrapie prion protein [PrP^{sc}]) distributed diffusely throughout the brain and sometimes also in discrete plaques. Pathologic involvement of other organ systems has been reported in animal TSEs, but not in humans.

The human TSEs include several diseases: Creutzfeldt-Jakob disease (CJD), Gerstmann-Sträussler-Scheinker disease, fatal familial and sporadic insomnia syndromes, kuru, and variant CJD (vCJD). Classic CJD can be sporadic (approximately 85% of cases), familial (approximately 15%), or iatrogenic (<1%). Sporadic CJD has been described in adolescents older than 13 years of age and in young adults. Iatrogenic CJD has been acquired through injection of cadaveric pituitary hormones (growth hormone and human gonadotropin), dura mater allografts, corneal transplantation, and instrumentation of the brain at neurosurgery or depth-electrode electroencephalographic recording. Cases of transfusion-transmitted vCJD have been reported. In 1996, an outbreak of vCJD linked to exposure to tissues from bovine spongiform encephalopathy (BSE)-infected cattle was reported in the United Kingdom. The best-known TSEs affecting animals are scrapie of sheep, BSE, and a chronic wasting disease of North American deer and elk.

Creutzfeldt-Jakob disease manifests as a dementing syndrome with progressive defects in memory, personality, and other higher cortical functions. At presentation, approximately one third of patients have cerebellar dysfunction, including ataxia and dysarthria. Iatrogenic CJD may manifest as dementia (as in dural allograft transplant recipients) or as cerebellar signs (as observed in virtually all people with peripherally inoculated disease). Myoclonus develops in at least 80% of affected patients at some

---

* Whitley RJ, MacDonald N, Asher DM and the Committee on Infectious Diseases. Transmissible spongiform encephalopathies: a review for pediatricians. *Pediatrics.* 2000;106:1160–1165

point in the course of disease. Death usually occurs in weeks to months; approximately 10% to 15% of patients with sporadic CJD survive for more than a year.

The vCJD is distinguished from classic CJD by younger age of onset, "psychiatric" manifestation, and other features, such as painful sensory symptoms, delayed onset of overt neurologic signs, absence of diagnostic electroencephalographic changes, and a more prolonged duration of illness. In vCJD, the neuropathology is characterized by numerous "florid" or "daisy" plaques and marked accumulation of protease-resistant prion protein (PrP^{res}). In addition, PrP^{res} is readily detectable in lymphoid tissues of patients with vCJD. In vCJD, but not in classic CJD, a high proportion of people exhibit high signal abnormalities on T2 magnetic resonance imaging brain scan in the pulvinar region of the posterior thalamus.

ETIOLOGY: The infectious particle or prion responsible for the human and animal prion diseases is thought to be an abnormal glycoprotein, without a nucleic acid component, although some experts remain skeptical of the prion hypothesis. Proponents of the hypothesis postulate that sporadic CJD arises from a rare spontaneous structural change of the normal protease-sensitive host-encoded glycoprotein (PrP^{sen}) that normally is found on the surface of neurons in both humans and animals. Prion protein (PrP) conformational changes are believed to be propagated by a "recruitment reaction" (the nature of which is unknown), in which abnormal PrP serves as a template or lattice for the conformational conversion of neighboring PrP^{sen} molecules.

EPIDEMIOLOGY: Classic CJD is rare, occurring at a rate of approximately 1 case per million people annually. The onset of disease peaks in the 60- to 69-year age group. Familial CJD illnesses, which are associated with a variety of mutations of the PrP gene, occurs at approximately one sixth the frequency of sporadic CJD, with onset of disease approximately 10 years earlier than sporadic CJD.

Case-control studies of sporadic CJD have not identified any consistent environmental risk factor. No statistically significant increased risk of sporadic CJD has been observed for treatment with blood, blood components, or plasma derivatives, and the incidence of sporadic CJD is not increased in patients with several diseases associated with increased exposure to blood or blood products, specifically hemophilia A and B, thalassemia, and sickle cell disease. Creutzfeldt-Jakob disease has not been reported in infants born to infected mothers.

As of April 2005, vCJD was reported in 155 patients in the United Kingdom, 11 patients in France, 2 in Ireland, and 1 patient each in Canada, Italy, Japan, Saudi Arabia, and the United States. The patients from Canada, Japan, Saudi Arabia, and the United States and 1 of the patients from Ireland are believed to have acquired vCJD during their residence in the United Kingdom. Most patients with vCJD were younger than 30 years of age, and several were adolescents. All but 2 patients with noniatrogenic vCJD died before 55 years of age. On the basis of animal inoculation studies, strain typing, and epidemiologic investigations, cases of vCJD are believed to be associated with exposure to tissues from cattle infected with BSE. One patient with vCJD is believed to have acquired the disease through blood transfusion.

The **incubation period** for iatrogenic CJD varies by route of exposure and ranges from 1.5 to more than 30 years.

DIAGNOSTIC TESTS: The diagnosis of human prion diseases can be made with certainty only by neuropathologic examination of affected brain tissue. In most patients with classic CJD, atypical 1-cycle to 2-cycles per second triphasic sharp-wave discharge on electroencephalographic tracing has been described. The likelihood of finding this abnormality is enhanced if serial electroencephalographic recordings are obtained. A 14-3-3 protein assay that detects the protein in cerebrospinal fluid has been reported to be reasonably sensitive, though not specific, as a marker for CJD. No blood test is available. A progressive neurologic syndrome in a person bearing a pathogenic mutation of the PrP gene (PRNP) is presumed to be prion disease. The failure to identify a unique prion nucleic acid component precludes detection of the infective particle by genome amplification.

TREATMENT: No treatment has been shown in humans to slow or stop the progressive neurodegenerative syndromes of prion diseases. Experimental treatments are under study. Supportive therapy is necessary to manage dementia, spasticity, rigidity, and seizures arising during the course of the illness. Psychological support may help families of affected people. Genetic counseling is indicated in familial disease.

ISOLATION OF THE HOSPITALIZED PATIENT: Standard precautions are recommended. The available evidence indicates that even prolonged intimate contact with CJD-infected people has not resulted in transmission of disease. Tissues associated with high levels of infectivity (eg, brain, eyes, and spinal cord of affected people) and instruments in contact with those tissues are considered biohazards; incineration, prolonged autoclaving at high temperature and pressure after thorough cleaning, and especially exposure to a solution of sodium hydroxide of 1N or greater or a solution of sodium hypochlorite of 5.25% or greater (undiluted household chlorine bleach) for 1 hour has been reported to decrease infectivity.* It is prudent to treat surgical instruments used on central nervous system tissues of patients in whom a CJD diagnosis is possible using a recommended CJD-specific method. Cerebrospinal fluid should be regarded as infectious. Person-to-person transmission of classic CJD by blood, milk, saliva, urine, or feces has not been reported. These body fluids should be handled using standard infection control procedures; universal blood precautions should be sufficient to prevent bloodborne transmission.

CONTROL MEASURES: Immunization against prion diseases is not available, and no protective immune response to infection has been demonstrated. Iatrogenic transmission of CJD through cadaveric pituitary hormones has been obviated by use of recombinant products. Recognition that CJD can be spread by transplantation of infected dura and corneas and that vCJD can be spread by blood transfusion has led to more stringent donor-selection criteria and improved collection protocols. Performing a brain autopsy in patients with suspected or clinically diagnosed CJD is encouraged to confirm the diagnosis and detect other emerging forms of CJD, such as vCJD. Free state-of-the-art diagnostic testing is available at the National Prion Disease Pathology Surveillance Center (telephone, 216-368-0587; Internet, **www. cjdsurveillance.com**). A suspected or confirmed diagnosis of CJD for which a spe-

---

* www.cdc.gov/ncidod/dvrd/prions

cial public health response may be needed (eg, suspected iatrogenic disease or vCJD) should be reported to the appropriate state or local health departments and to the CJD Surveillance Unit, Division of Viral and Rickettsial Diseases, Centers for Disease Control and Prevention, Atlanta, GA 30333; telephone, 404-639-3091. Current precautionary policies of the US Food and Drug Administration about risk of CJD and human blood or blood products are accessible on the Internet at **www.fda. gov/cber/whatsnew.htm**.

Q Fever

CLINICAL MANIFESTATIONS: Although up to 60% of initial infections are asymptomatic, disease attributable to Q fever occurs in 2 distinct forms: acute, which typically follows initial exposure; and chronic, which occurs months to years after acute infection. Acute Q fever usually is characterized by abrupt onset of fever, chills, weakness, headache, anorexia, and other nonspecific systemic symptoms. Weight loss and weakness can be pronounced. Cough and chest pain can accompany pneumonia, which occurs in 20% to 40% of patients. Hepatitis is found in 40% to 60% of patients, and serum transaminase concentrations commonly are elevated, but jaundice is rare. Rash is rarely observed. The illness typically lasts 1 to 4 weeks and then resolves gradually. Life-threatening complications of acute infection, such as meningoencephalitis and myocarditis, occur rarely. Chronic Q fever occurs in approximately 1% of acutely ill patients and manifests as endocarditis in patients with underlying heart disease or prosthetic valves, vascular aneurysms, or vascular grafts. Hepatitis is another common manifestation. Both acute and chronic Q fever may manifest as fever of undetermined origin. Although acute Q fever rarely is fatal, chronic Q fever can be fatal if untreated. With appropriate long-term antimicrobial therapy, mortality among patients with endocarditis is decreased to approximately 10%. Q fever during pregnancy is associated with abortion, preterm birth, and low birth weight.

ETIOLOGY: *Coxiella burnetii*, the cause of Q fever, is an intracellular rickettsial organism. The infectious form of *C burnetii* is highly resistant to heat, desiccation, and disinfectant chemicals and can persist for long periods of time in the environment. *Coxiella burnetii* is classified in the gamma subgroup of Proteobacteria.

EPIDEMIOLOGY: Q fever is a zoonotic infection that has been reported worldwide. In animals, infection usually is asymptomatic. The most common reservoirs are domestic farm animals (especially sheep, goats, and cows), which most often are associated with human infection. Cats, dogs, rodents, marsupials, other mammalian species, and some wild and domestic bird species may transmit infection to humans. Tick vectors may be important for maintaining animal and bird reservoirs but are not thought to be important in transmission to humans. Human Q-fever is an underrecognized illness. Humans typically acquire infection by inhalation of *C burnetii* in fine-particle aerosols generated from birthing fluids during animal parturition or through inhalation of dust contaminated by these materials. Infection can occur by direct exposure to infected animals or tissues on farms and ranches or in research facilities or by exposure to contaminated materials, such as wool, straw, fertilizer, or laundry. Airborne particles containing infectious organisms can be carried downwind a half-mile or more, contributing to sporadic cases for which no apparent animal contact can be demonstrated. Unpasteurized dairy products may contain the organism. Seasonal trends occur in farming areas with predictable frequency, and the disease often coincides with the lambing season in the early spring. Evidence has been reported for human intrauterine infection and direct transmission by blood or marrow transfusion. The risk of chronic infection is increased by underlying cardiovascular disease, especially cardiac valve defects, immunodeficiency, and pregnancy.

The **incubation period** usually is 14 to 22 days but can vary from 9 to 39 days depending on the inoculum. Chronic Q fever can develop years to decades after initial infection.

DIAGNOSTIC TESTS: Isolation of *C burnetii* from blood usually is not attempted except in specialized laboratories because of the potential hazard to laboratory workers. Cell culture systems, especially the shell vial method, and inoculation of animals or eggs have been the most successful in isolating *C burnetii* from humans; these systems are most sensitive in diagnosing chronic Q fever endocarditis in untreated patients. Confirmed Q fever requires one of the following: (1) a fourfold change in antibody titer between acute and convalescent specimens taken 2 to 3 weeks apart to *C burnetii* antigen by immunofluorescent antibody assay, enzyme linked immunosorbent assay; or complement fixation antibody test; (2) positive polymerase chain reaction assay results; (3) culture of *C burnetii* from a clinical specimen; or (4) positive immunostaining of *C burnetii* in tissue, especially heart valve tissue.

TREATMENT: Acute Q fever generally is a self-limited illness, and many patients recover without antimicrobial therapy. Doxycycline is the drug of choice, and treatment can hasten recovery by several days. Fluoroquinolones or chloramphenicol are alternatives. Although tetracyclines generally should not be given to children younger than 8 years of age (see Antimicrobial Agents and Related Therapy, p 735) most experts consider that the benefit of doxycycline in treating Q fever is greater than the potential risk of dental staining. Fluoroquinolones also can be used but are not approved for use in children younger than 18 years of age. Therapy should be initiated promptly and continued until the patient is afebrile and clinically improved, usually for 10 to 14 days. In chronic Q fever, relapses can occur, necessitating repeated courses of therapy. The organism can remain latent in tissues for years; treatment of chronic disease is extremely difficult. Treatment of chronic endocarditis is prolonged and requires a combination doxycycline and hydroxychloroquine for a minimum of 18 months. Fluoroquinolone treatment for at least 3 years has been recommended by some experts. Relapses can occur after discontinuation of treatment. Surgical replacement of the infected valve may be necessary in some patients.

ISOLATION OF THE HOSPITALIZED PATIENT: Standard precautions are recommended.

CONTROL MEASURES: Strict adherence to proper hygiene when handling parturient animals can help decrease the risk of infection in the farm setting. Improved prescreening of animal herds used by research facilities may decrease the risk of infection. Special safety practices are recommended for nonpropagative laboratory procedures involving *C burnetii* and for all propagative procedures, necropsies of infected animals, and manipulation of infected human and animal tissues. No specific management is recommended for people who have been exposed. Experimental vaccines for domestic animals and laboratory and other high-risk workers have been developed but are not licensed in the United States. Q fever is a nationally reportable disease and all human cases should be reported to the state health department. For additional information about Q fever, see **www.cdc.gov/ncidod/dvrd/qfever/**.

Rabies*

CLINICAL MANIFESTATIONS: Infection with rabies virus characteristically produces an acute illness with rapidly progressive central nervous system manifestations, including anxiety, dysphagia, and seizures. Some patients may have paralysis. Illness almost invariably progresses to death. The differential diagnosis of acute encephalitic illnesses of unknown cause with atypical focal neurologic signs or with paralysis should include rabies.

ETIOLOGY: Rabies virus is an RNA virus classified in the Rhabdoviridae family.

EPIDEMIOLOGY: Understanding the epidemiology of rabies has been aided by strain identification using monoclonal antibodies and nucleotide sequencing. In the United States, the number of cases of human rabies has decreased steadily since the 1950s, reflecting widespread rabies immunization of dogs and the availability of effective immunoprophylaxis after exposure to a rabid animal. Between 1990 and 2004, 34 (72%) of the 47 human rabies deaths in the United States (46 in the United States and 1 in Puerto Rico) have been associated with bat-variant rabies virus. Since 2000, 14 of 15 cases of indigenously acquired human rabies were associated with bat variants, and only 3 of these 15 human cases had known bat bites. Despite the large focus of rabies in raccoons in the eastern United States, only one human death has been attributed to the raccoon rabies virus variant. Rarely, airborne transmission has been reported in the laboratory and in some caves inhabited by millions of bats. Transmission also has occurred by transplantation of organs, corneas, and other tissues from patients dying of undiagnosed rabies. Person-to-person transmission by bite has not been documented in the United States, although the virus has been isolated from saliva of infected patients.

Wildlife rabies exists throughout the United States except in Hawaii, which remains rabies free. Wild animals, including raccoons, skunks, foxes, coyotes, bats, and other species, are the most important potential source of infection for humans and domestic animals in the United States. Rabies in small rodents (squirrels, hamsters, guinea pigs, gerbils, chipmunks, rats, and mice) and lagomorphs (rabbits and hares) is rare, but rabies may occur in woodchucks or other large rodents in areas where raccoon rabies is common. The virus is present in saliva and is transmitted by bites or, rarely, by contamination of mucosa or skin lesions by saliva or other potentially infectious material (eg, neural tissue). Worldwide, most rabies cases in humans result from

---

* For further information, see Centers for Disease Control and Prevention. Human rabies prevention: United States, 1999: recommendations of the Advisory Committee on Immunization Practices [published correction appears in *MMWR Morb Mortal Wkly Rep*. 1999;48:16]. *MMWR Recomm Rep*. 1999;48(RR-1): 1–21

dog bites in areas where canine rabies is enzootic. Most rabid dogs, cats, and ferrets may shed virus for a few days before there are obvious signs of illness. No case of human rabies in the United States has been attributed to a dog, cat, or ferret that has remained healthy throughout the standard 10-day period of confinement.

The **incubation period** in humans averages 4 to 6 weeks but ranges from 5 days to more than 1 year. Incubation periods of up to 6 years have been confirmed by antigenic typing and nucleotide sequencing of strains.

DIAGNOSTIC TESTS: Infection in animals can be diagnosed by demonstration of virus-specific fluorescent antigen in brain tissue. Suspected rabid animals should be euthanatized in a manner that preserves brain tissue for appropriate examination. Virus can be isolated from saliva, brain, and other tissues in suckling mice or in tissue culture and can be detected by identification of viral antigens or nucleotides in affected tissues. The diagnosis in suspected human cases can be made postmortem by either immunofluorescent or immunohistochemical examination of brain. Antemortem diagnosis can be made by fluorescent microscopy of skin biopsy specimens from the nape of the neck, by isolation of the virus from saliva, by detection of antibody in the cerebrospinal fluid (CSF) or serum in unimmunized people, and by detection of viral antigens and nucleic acid in infected tissues. Laboratory personnel should be consulted before submission of specimens so that appropriate collection and transport of materials can be arranged.

TREATMENT: Once symptoms have developed, neither vaccine nor Rabies Immune Globulin (RIG) improves the prognosis. There is no specific treatment. Very few patients with human rabies have survived, even with intensive supportive care; with one exception, all known survivors had received prophylaxis before clinical signs developed.

ISOLATION OF THE HOSPITALIZED PATIENT: Standard precautions are recommended for the duration of illness. If the patient has bitten another person or the patient's saliva has contaminated an open wound or mucous membrane, the involved area should be washed thoroughly and postexposure prophylaxis should be administered (see Care of Exposed People, p 555).

CONTROL MEASURES: Education of children to avoid contact with stray or wild animals is of primary importance. Children should be cautioned against provoking or attempting to capture stray or wild animals and against touching carcasses. Inadvertent contact of family members and pets with potentially rabid animals, such as raccoons, foxes, coyotes, and skunks, may be decreased by securing garbage and refuse to decrease attraction of domestic and wild animals. Similarly, chimneys and other potential entrances for wild animals, including bats, should be identified and covered. Bats should be excluded from human living quarters. International travelers to areas with endemic canine rabies should be warned to avoid exposure to stray dogs, and if traveling to an area where immediate access to medical care and biologicals is limited, preexposure prophylaxis is indicated.

EXPOSURE RISK AND DECISIONS TO GIVE IMMUNOPROPHYLAXIS. Exposure to rabies results from a break in the skin caused by the teeth of a rabid animal or by contamination of scratches, abrasions, or mucous membranes with saliva or other potentially infectious material, such as neural tissue, from a rabid animal. The decision to immunize an exposed person should be made in consultation with the local health department, which can provide information on the risk of rabies in a particular area for each species of animal and in accordance with the guidelines in Table 3.52, p 555. In the United States, raccoons, skunks, foxes, and bats are more likely to be infected than other animals, but coyotes, cattle, dogs, cats, ferrets, and other species occasionally are infected. Bites of rodents (such as squirrels, mice, and rats) or lagomorphs (rabbits, hares, and pikas) rarely require specific antirabies prophylaxis. Additional factors must be considered when deciding whether immunoprophylaxis is indicated. An unprovoked attack may be more suggestive of a rabid animal than a bite that occurs during attempts to feed or handle an animal. Properly immunized dogs, cats, and ferrets have only a minimal chance of developing rabies. However, in rare instances, rabies has developed in properly immunized animals.

Postexposure prophylaxis for rabies is recommended for all people bitten by wild mammalian carnivores or bats or by domestic animals that may be infected. Rarely, exposures other than bites have resulted in infection. People who have acquired infection but do not report a clear history of a bite, after seemingly insignificant physical contact with bats, may suffer from recall bias. In addition, patients may not realize the risk of rabies associated with a bat bite and may not easily be able to identify exposure as from a bat bite. Postexposure prophylaxis is recommended for people who report an open wound, scratch, or mucous membrane that has been contaminated with saliva or other potentially infectious material (eg, brain tissue) from a rabid animal. Because the injury inflicted by a bat bite or scratch may be small and not readily evident or the circumstances of contact may preclude accurate recall (eg, a bat in a room of a sleeping person or previously unattended child), prophylaxis is indicated for situations in which a bat physically is present if a bite or mucous membrane exposure cannot reliably be excluded, unless prompt testing of the bat has excluded rabies virus infection. Prophylaxis always should be initiated as soon as possible after bites by known or suspected rabid animals.

Postexposure prophylaxis also is recommended for people who report a possibly infectious exposure (eg, bite, scratch, or open wound or mucous membrane contaminated with saliva or other infectious material) to a human with rabies. Rabies transmission after exposure to a human with rabies has not been documented in the United States, except after tissue or organ transplantation from donors who died of unsuspected rabies encephalitis. Casual contact with an infected person (eg, by touching a patient) or contact with noninfectious fluids or tissues (eg, blood or feces) alone does not constitute an exposure and is not an indication for prophylaxis (see Care of Hospital Contacts, p 555).

HANDLING OF ANIMALS SUSPECTED OF HAVING RABIES. A dog, cat, or ferret that is suspected of having rabies and has bitten a human should be captured, confined, and observed by a veterinarian for 10 days. Any illness in the animal should be reported immediately to the local health department. If signs of rabies develop, the animal should be euthanatized in a manner to allow its head to be removed and shipped under refrigeration (not frozen) to a qualified laboratory for examination.

Table 3.52. Rabies Postexposure Prophylaxis Guide

Animal Type	Evaluation and Disposition of Animal	Postexposure Prophylaxis Recommendations
Dogs, cats, and ferrets	Healthy and available for 10 days of observation	Prophylaxis only if animal develops signs of rabies[1]
	Rabid or suspected of being rabid[2]	Immediate immunization and RIG[3]
	Unknown (escaped)	Consult public health officials for advice
Bats, skunks, raccoons, foxes, and most other carnivores; woodchucks	Regarded as rabid unless geographic area is known to be free of rabies or until animal proven negative by laboratory tests[2]	Immediate immunization and RIG[3]
Livestock, rodents, and lagomorphs (rabbits, hares, and pikas)	Consider individually	Consult public health officials. Bites of squirrels, hamsters, guinea pigs, gerbils, chipmunks, rats, mice and other rodents, rabbits, hares, and pikas almost never require antirabies treatment.

RIG indicates Rabies Immune Globulin.

[1] During the 10-day holding period, at the first sign of rabies in the biting dog, cat, or ferret, treatment of the exposed person with RIG (human) and vaccine should be initiated. The animal should be euthanatized immediately and tested.

[2] The animal should be euthanatized and tested as soon as possible. Holding for observation is not recommended. Immunization is discontinued if immunofluorescent test result for the animal is negative.

[3] See text.

Other biting animals that may have exposed a person to rabies should be reported immediately to the local health department. Management of animals depends on the species, the circumstances of the bite, and the epidemiology of rabies in the area. Previous immunization of an animal may not preclude the necessity for euthanasia and testing. Because clinical manifestations of rabies in a wild animal cannot be interpreted reliably, a wild mammal suspected of having rabies should be euthanatized at once and its brain should be examined for evidence of rabies. The exposed person need not be treated if results of rapid examination of the brain by fluorescent antibody procedures are negative for rabies.

CARE OF HOSPITAL CONTACTS. Immunization of hospital contacts of a patient with rabies should be reserved for people who were bitten or whose mucous membranes or open wounds have come in contact with saliva, cerebrospinal fluid, or brain tissue of a patient with rabies (see Care of Exposed People). Other hospital contacts of a patient with rabies do not require immunization.

CARE OF EXPOSED PEOPLE.

Local Wound Care. The immediate objective of postexposure prophylaxis is to prevent virus from entering neural tissue. Prompt and thorough local treatment of all lesions is essential, because virus may remain localized to the area of the bite for a variable time. All wounds should be flushed thoroughly and cleaned with soap and water. Quaternary ammonium compounds (such as benzalkonium chloride) no longer are considered superior to soap. The need for tetanus prophylaxis and measures to control bacterial infection also should be considered. The wound, if possible, should not be sutured.

Immunoprophylaxis. After wound care is completed, concurrent use of passive *and* active immunoprophylaxis is required for optimal therapy (see Table 3.52, p 555). Prophylaxis should begin as soon as possible after exposure, ideally within 24 hours. However, a delay of several days or more may not compromise effectiveness, and prophylaxis should be initiated if indicated, regardless of the interval between exposure and initiation of therapy. In the United States, only the human product RIG is available for passive immunization. Licensed tissue culture rabies vaccine should be used for active immunization. Physicians can obtain expert counsel from their local or state health departments.

Active Immunization (Postexposure). Three rabies vaccines are licensed commercially for prophylaxis in the United States: human diploid cell vaccine (HDCV), rabies vaccine adsorbed (RVA), and purified chicken embryo cell (PCEC), but only HDCV and PCEC are being produced (see Table 3.53). A 1.0-mL dose of vaccine is given intramuscularly in the deltoid area or anterolateral aspect of the thigh on the first day of postexposure prophylaxis (day 0), and repeated doses are given on days 3, 7, 14, and 28 after the first dose, for a total of 5 doses. Ideally, an immunization series should be initiated and completed with 1 vaccine product unless serious allergic reactions occur. Clinical studies evaluating efficacy or frequency of adverse reactions when the series is completed with a second product have not been conducted. The volume of the dose is not decreased for children. Serologic testing to document seroconversion after administration of a rabies vaccine series is unnecessary but occasionally has been advised for recipients who may be immunocompromised.

Care should be taken to ensure that the vaccine is administered intramuscularly. Intradermal vaccine is not advised for postexposure prophylaxis in the United States, although for reasons of cost and availability, intradermal regimens are used in some

Table 3.53. US Food and Drug Administration-Licensed Rabies Vaccines[1] and Rabies Immune Globulin

Category	Product	Manufacturer	Method of Administration
Human rabies vaccine	Human diploid cell vaccine (HDCV) (Imovax)	sanofi pasteur	IM
	Purified chicken embryo cell (PCEC) (RabAvert)	Chiron Corporation	IM
Rabies Immune Globulin	Imogam Rabies-HT	sanofi pasteur	Infiltrate around wound[2]
	BayRab	Bayer	Infiltrate around wound[2]

IM indicates intramuscular.
[1] Rabies vaccine adsorbed (RVA) is licensed in the United States but no longer is distributed in the United States.
[2] Any remaining volume should be administered IM.

countries. Because antibody responses in adults who received vaccine in the gluteal area sometimes have been less than in those who were injected in the deltoid muscle, the deltoid site always should be used except in infants and young children, in whom the anterolateral thigh is the appropriate site.

- **Adverse reactions and precautions with HDCV and PCEC vaccine.** Reactions after immunization, primarily reported in adults, are less common than reactions after immunization with previously used rabies vaccines. Reactions are uncommon in children. In adults, local reactions, such as pain, erythema, and swelling or itching at the injection site are reported in 15% to 25%, and mild systemic reactions, such as headache, nausea, abdominal pain, muscle aches, and dizziness are reported in 10% to 20% of recipients. Several cases of neurologic illness resembling Guillain-Barré syndrome that resolved without sequelae in 12 weeks and an acute, generalized, transient neurologic syndrome temporally associated with HDCV have been reported but are not thought to be causally related.

  Immune complex-like reactions in people receiving booster doses of HDCV have been observed, possibly because of interaction between propiolactone and human albumin. The reaction, characterized by onset 2 to 21 days after inoculation, begins with generalized urticaria and can include arthralgia, arthritis, angioedema, nausea, vomiting, fever, and malaise. The reaction is not life threatening, occurs in as many as 6% of adults receiving booster doses as part of a preexposure immunization regimen, and is rare in people receiving primary immunization with HDCV. Similar allergic reactions with primary or booster doses have not been reported with PCEC.

  If the patient has a serious allergic reaction to HDCV, PCEC vaccine may be given according to the same schedule as HDCV. All suspected serious, systemic, neuroparalytic, or anaphylactic reactions to the rabies vaccine should be reported immediately (see Reporting of Adverse Events, p 41).

  Although safety of the use of rabies vaccine during pregnancy has not been studied specifically in the United States, pregnancy should not be considered a contraindication to use of vaccine after exposure.

- **Nerve tissue vaccines.** Inactivated nerve tissue vaccines are not licensed in the United States but are available in many areas of the world. These preparations induce neuroparalytic reactions in 1:2000 to 1:8000 recipients. Immunization with nerve tissue vaccine should be discontinued if meningeal or neuroparalytic reactions develop. Corticosteroids can be used for treatment of complications but should be used only for life-threatening reactions, because they increase the risk of rabies in experimentally inoculated animals.

Passive Immunization. Human RIG should be used concomitantly with the first dose of vaccine for postexposure prophylaxis to bridge the time between possible rabies exposure and active antibody production induced by the vaccine (see Table 3.53, p 556). If vaccine is not available immediately, RIG should be given alone and immunization should be started as soon as possible. If RIG is not available immediately, vaccine should be given. Rabies Immune Globulin then is given subsequently if obtained within 7 days after initiating immunization. If administration of both vaccine and RIG is delayed, both should be used regardless of the interval between exposure and treatment.

The recommended dose of RIG is 20 IU/kg. As much of the dose as possible should be used to infiltrate the wound(s), if present. The remainder is given intramuscularly. In cases of multiple severe wounds in which RIG is insufficient for infiltration, dilution in saline solution to an adequate volume (twofold or threefold) has been recommended to ensure that all wound areas receive infiltrate. For children with a small muscle mass, it may be necessary to administer RIG at multiple sites. Human RIG is supplied in 2-mL (300 IU) and 10-mL (1500 IU) vials. Passive antibody can inhibit the response to rabies vaccines; therefore, the recommended dose should not be exceeded. Vaccine never should be administered in the same parts of the body or with the same syringe used to give RIG. Hypersensitivity reactions to RIG occur rarely, if ever.

Purified equine RIG containing rabies antibodies may be available outside the United States and generally is accompanied by a low rate of serum sickness (<1%). Equine RIG is administered at a dose of 40 IU/kg, and desensitization may be required.

Administration of RIG is not recommended for the following exposed people: (1) those who previously received postexposure prophylaxis with HDCV, RVA, or PCEC; (2) those who received a 3-dose, intramuscular, preexposure regimen of HDCV, RVA, or PCEC; (3) those who received a 3-dose, intradermal, preexposure regimen of HDCV with the product used in the United States; and (4) those who have a documented adequate rabies virus antibody titer after previous immunization with any other rabies vaccine. These people should receive two 1.0-mL booster doses of HDCV or PCEC; one dose is given on the day of exposure, and the second is given 3 days later.

PREEXPOSURE CONTROL MEASURES, INCLUDING IMMUNIZATION. The relatively low frequency of reactions to HDCV and PCEC has made provision of preexposure immunization practical for people in high-risk groups, including veterinarians, animal handlers, certain laboratory workers, and people moving to areas where canine rabies is common. Others, such as spelunkers, who have frequent exposures to bats and other wildlife, also should be considered for preexposure prophylaxis.

The HDCV and PCEC vaccines are licensed for intramuscular administration. Previously, intradermal (0.1 mL) dosage formulations of HDCV were available for preexposure use. The preexposure immunization schedule is three 1-mL intramuscular injections each, given on days 0, 7, and 21 **or** 28. This series of immunizations has resulted in development of antibodies in all people properly immunized. Therefore, routine serologic testing for rabies antibody immediately after primary immunization is not indicated.

Serum antibodies usually persist for at least 2 years after the primary series given intramuscularly. Preexposure booster immunization with 1.0 mL of HDCV or PCEC intramuscularly will produce an effective anamnestic response. Rabies serum antibody titers should be determined at 6-month intervals for people at continuous risk of infection (rabies research laboratory workers, rabies biologicals production workers). Titers should be determined approximately every 2 years for people with risk of frequent exposure (rabies diagnostic laboratory workers, spelunkers, veterinarians and staff, and animal-control and wildlife workers in rabies-enzootic areas). A single booster dose of vaccine should be administered only as appropriate to maintain serum antibody concentrations. The Centers for Disease Control and Prevention currently specifies complete viral neutralization at a ≥1:5 titer by the rapid fluorescent-focus inhibition test as acceptable; the World Health Organization specifies 0.5 IU/mL or more as acceptable.

PUBLIC HEALTH. A variety of approved public health measures, including immunization of dogs, cats, and ferrets and elimination of stray dogs and selected wildlife, are used to control rabies in animals.* In regions where oral immunization of wildlife with recombinant rabies vaccine is undertaken, the prevalence of rabies among foxes, coyotes, and raccoons may be decreased. Unimmunized dogs, cats, ferrets, or other pets bitten by a known rabid animal should be euthanatized immediately. If the owner is unwilling to allow the animal to be euthanatized, the animal should be placed in strict isolation for 6 months and immunized 1 month before release. If the exposed animal has been immunized within 1 to 3 years, depending on the vaccine administered and local regulations, the animal should be reimmunized and observed for 45 days.

CASE REPORTING. All suspected cases of rabies should be reported promptly to public health authorities.

Rat-Bite Fever

CLINICAL MANIFESTATIONS: Rat-bite fever is caused by *Streptobacillus moniliformis* or *Spirillum minus*. *Streptobacillus moniliformis* infection (streptobacillary fever or Haverhill fever) is characterized by fever, rash, and arthritis. There is an abrupt onset of fever, chills, muscle pain, vomiting, headache, and occasionally, adenopathy. A maculopapular or petechial rash develops, predominantly on the extremities, typically within a few days of fever onset. The bite site usually heals promptly and exhibits no or minimal inflammation. Nonsuppurative migratory polyarthritis or arthralgia follows in approximately 50% of patients. Untreated infection usually has a relapsing course for a mean of 3 weeks. Ulceration at the initial bite wound and regional lymphadenopathy do not occur. Complications include soft tissue and solid-organ abscesses, pneumonia, endocarditis, myocarditis, and meningitis. The case-fatality rate is 7% to 10% in untreated patients. With *S minus* infection, a period of initial apparent healing at the site of the bite usually is followed by fever and ulceration at the site, regional lymphangitis and lymphadenopathy, and a distinctive rash of red or purple plaques. Arthritis is rare. Infection with *S minus* is rare in the United States.

ETIOLOGY: The causes of rat-bite fever are *S moniliformis*, a microaerophilic, gram-negative, pleomorphic bacillus, and *S minus*, a small, gram-negative, spiral organism with bipolar flagellar tufts.

EPIDEMIOLOGY: Rat-bite fever is a zoonotic illness. The natural habitat of *S moniliformis* and *S minus* is the upper respiratory tract of rodents. *Streptobacillus moniliformis* is

---

* National Association of State Public Health Veterinarians, Inc. Compendium of animal rabies prevention and control, 2006. *MMWR Recomm Rep.* 2006;55(RR-5):1–8

transmitted by bites or scratches from or handling of infected rats; other rodents (eg, mice, gerbils) also can act as reservoirs. Haverhill fever refers to infection after ingestion of milk, water, or food contaminated with *S moniliformis*. *Spirillum minus* is transmitted by bites of rats and mice. *Streptobacillus moniliformis* infection accounts for most cases of rat-bite fever in the United States; *S minus* infections occur primarily in Asia.

The **incubation period** for *S moniliformis* usually is 3 to 10 days but can be as long as 3 weeks; for *S minus*, it is 7 to 21 days.

DIAGNOSTIC TESTS: *Streptobacillus moniliformis* is a fastidious, slow-growing organism isolated from specimens of blood, synovial fluid, aspirates from abscesses, or material from the bite lesion by inoculation into bacteriologic media enriched with blood, serum, or ascitic fluid. Cultures should be held up to 3 weeks if *S moniliformis* is suspected. Sodium polyanetholsulfonate, present in most blood culture media, is inhibitory to *S moniliformis*. *Spirillum minus* has not been recovered on artificial media but can be visualized by darkfield microscopy in wet mounts of blood, exudate of a lesion, and lymph nodes. Blood specimens also should be viewed with Giemsa or Wright stain. *Spirillum minus* can be recovered from blood, lymph nodes, or local lesions by intraperitoneal inoculation of mice or guinea pigs.

TREATMENT: Penicillin G procaine intramuscularly or penicillin G intravenously should be administered for 7 to 10 days for rat-bite fever caused by either agent. Initial intravenous penicillin G therapy for 5 days followed by oral penicillin V also has been successful. Limited experience exists for ampicillin, cefuroxime, and cefotaxime. Doxycycline or streptomycin may be substituted when a patient is allergic to penicillin. Doxycycline should not be given to children younger than 8 years of age unless the benefits of therapy are greater than the risks of dental staining (see Antimicrobial Agents and Related Therapy, p 735). Patients with endocarditis should receive intravenous high-dose penicillin G for at least 4 weeks. The addition of streptomycin for initial therapy may be useful.

ISOLATION OF THE HOSPITALIZED PATIENT: Standard precautions are recommended.

CONTROL MEASURES: Exposed people should be observed for symptoms. Because the occurrence of *S moniliformis* after a rat bite is approximately 10%, some experts recommend postexposure administration of penicillin. Rat control is important in the control of disease. People with frequent rodent exposure should wear gloves and avoid hand-to-mouth contact during animal handling. Regular hand hygiene should be practiced.

Respiratory Syncytial Virus

CLINICAL MANIFESTATIONS: Respiratory syncytial virus (RSV) causes acute respiratory tract illness in patients of all ages. In infants and young children, RSV is the most important cause of bronchiolitis and pneumonia. During the first few weeks of life, particularly among preterm infants, infection with RSV may produce minimal respiratory tract signs. Lethargy, irritability, and poor feeding, sometimes accompanied by apneic episodes, may be the presenting manifestations in infants. Most previously healthy infants infected with RSV do not require hospitalization, and many who are hospitalized improve with supportive care and are discharged in fewer than 5 days. Characteristics that increase the risk of severe or fatal RSV infection are preterm birth; cyanotic or complicated congenital heart disease, especially conditions causing pulmonary hypertension; underlying pulmonary disease, especially chronic lung disease of prematurity; and immunodeficiency disease or therapy causing immunosuppression at any age. The association between RSV bronchiolitis early in life and subsequent reactive airway disease remains poorly understood. After RSV bronchiolitis, many children will have episodes of recurrent wheezing, which usually diminish in subsequent years. Some children may develop wheezing at older ages or develop long-term abnormalities in pulmonary function. This association may reflect an underlying predisposition to reactive airway disease rather than a direct consequence of RSV infection.

Almost all children are infected at least once by 2 years of age, and reinfection throughout life is common. Respiratory syncytial virus infection in older children and adults usually manifests as upper respiratory tract illness, but more serious disease involving the lower respiratory tract also can develop in immunocompromised patients or in the elderly. Exacerbation of acute asthmatic bronchitis or other chronic lung conditions may occur.

ETIOLOGY: Respiratory syncytial virus is an enveloped RNA paramyxovirus that lacks neuraminidase and hemagglutinin surface glycoproteins. Two major strains (groups A and B) have been identified and often circulate concurrently. The clinical and epidemiologic significance of strain variation has not been determined, but some evidence suggests that antigenic differences may affect susceptibility to infection and that some strains may be more virulent than other strains.

EPIDEMIOLOGY: Humans are the only source of infection. Transmission usually is by direct or close contact with contaminated secretions, which may involve droplets or fomites. Respiratory syncytial virus can persist on environmental surfaces for many hours and for a half-hour or more on hands. Infection among hospital personnel and others can occur by self-inoculation with contaminated secretions. Enforcement of infection control policies is important to decrease the risk of health care-related transmission of RSV. Health care-related spread of RSV to organ transplant recipients or patients with cardiopulmonary abnormalities or immunocompromised conditions has been associated with severe and fatal disease in children and adults.

Respiratory syncytial virus usually occurs in annual epidemics during winter and early spring in temperate climates. Spread among household and child care contacts, including adults, is common. The period of viral shedding usually is 3 to 8 days, but shedding may last longer, especially in young infants and in immunosuppressed individuals, in whom shedding may continue for as long as 3 to 4 weeks.

The **incubation period** ranges from 2 to 8 days; 4 to 6 days is most common.

DIAGNOSTIC TESTS: Rapid diagnostic assays, including immunofluorescent and enzyme immunoassay techniques for detection of viral antigen in nasopharyngeal specimens, are available commercially and generally are reliable. The sensitivity of these assays in comparison with culture varies between 53% and 96%, with most in the 80% to 90% range. As with all antigen detection assays, false-positive test results are more likely to occur at the beginning or end of the RSV season when the incidence of disease is low. Therefore, antigen detection assays should not be the solitary basis on which the beginning and end of monthly prophylaxis is determined.

Viral isolation from nasopharyngeal secretions in cell cultures requires 3 to 5 days, but results and sensitivity vary among laboratories, because methods of isolation are exacting and RSV is a labile virus. Experienced viral laboratory personnel should be consulted for optimal methods of collection and transport of specimens. Serologic testing of acute and convalescent serum specimens should not be used to confirm infection; in particular, the sensitivity of serologic diagnosis of infection is low among young infants. The polymerase chain reaction assay has been used for detection of RSV in clinical specimens but is not available commercially.

TREATMENT: Primary treatment is supportive and should include hydration, careful clinical assessment of respiratory status, including measurement of oxygen saturation, use of supplemental oxygen, suction of the upper airway, and if necessary, intubation and mechanical ventilation. Ribavirin has in vitro antiviral activity against RSV, but ribavirin aerosol treatment for RSV infection is not recommended routinely. Ribavirin therapy has been associated with a small but statistically significant increase in oxygen saturation during the acute infection in several small studies. However, a consistent decrease in need for mechanical ventilation, decrease in length of stay in the pediatric intensive care unit, or reduction in days of hospitalization among ribavirin recipients has not been demonstrated. The high cost, aerosol route of administration, concern about potential toxic effects among exposed health care professionals, and conflicting results of efficacy trials have led to controversy about the use of this drug. A decision about ribavirin administration should be made on the basis of the particular clinical circumstances and experience of the physician.

BETA-ADRENERGIC AGENTS. Beta-adrenergic agents are not recommended for routine care of first-time wheezing associated with RSV bronchiolitis. Some physicians elect to use bronchodilator therapy because of concern that reactive airway disease may be misdiagnosed as bronchiolitis. Repeat doses of an inhaled bronchodilator should be continued only in the small number of infants with well-documented improvement in respiratory function soon after the first dose.

CORTICOSTEROIDS. In hospitalized infants with RSV bronchiolitis, corticosteroids are not effective and are not indicated.

ANTIMICROBIAL AGENTS. Antimicrobial agents rarely are indicated, because bacterial lung infection and bacteremia are uncommon in infants hospitalized with RSV bronchiolitis or pneumonia. Otitis media occurs in infants with RSV bronchiolitis, but oral antibiotic agents can be used if therapy for otitis media is necessary.

PREVENTION OF RSV INFECTIONS. Palivizumab, a humanized mouse monoclonal antibody that is administered intramuscularly, is available to reduce the risk of RSV hospitalization in high-risk children. Respiratory Syncytial Virus Immune Globulin Intravenous (RSV-IGIV), a hyperimmune, polyclonal globulin prepared from donors selected for high serum titers of RSV neutralizing antibody, no longer is available. Palivizumab is licensed for prevention of RSV lower respiratory tract disease in selected infants and children with chronic lung disease of prematurity (CLD [formerly called bronchopulmonary dysplasia]) or with a history of preterm birth

(<35 weeks' gestation) or with congenital heart disease. Palivizumab is administered every 30 days, beginning in early November, with 4 subsequent monthly doses (total of 5 doses). The dose of palivizumab is 15 mg/kg, administered intramuscularly. Palivizumab is not effective in the treatment of RSV disease, and it is not approved for this indication.

Recommendations by the American Academy of Pediatrics for the use of palivizumab are as follows:

- Palivizumab prophylaxis should be considered for infants and children younger than 24 months of age with chronic lung disease of prematurity who have required medical therapy (supplemental oxygen, bronchodilator or diuretic or corticosteroid therapy) for CLD within 6 months before the start of the RSV season. Patients with more severe CLD who continue to require medical therapy may benefit from prophylaxis during a second RSV season. Data are limited regarding the effectiveness of palivizumab during the second year of life. Individual patients may benefit from decisions made in consultation with neonatologists, pediatric intensivists, pulmonologists, or infectious disease specialists.
- Infants born at 32 weeks of gestation or earlier may benefit from RSV prophylaxis, even if they do not have CLD. For these infants, major risk factors to consider include their gestational age and chronologic age at the start of the RSV season. Infants born at 28 weeks of gestation or earlier may benefit from prophylaxis during their first RSV season, whenever that occurs during the first 12 months of life. Infants born at 29 to 32 weeks of gestation may benefit most from prophylaxis up to 6 months of age. For the purpose of this recommendation, 32 weeks' gestation refers to an infant born on or before the 32nd week of gestation (ie, 32 weeks, 0 days). Once a child qualifies for initiation of prophylaxis at the start of the RSV season, administration should continue throughout the season and not stop at the point an infant reaches either 6 months or 12 months of age.
- Although palivizumab has been shown to decrease the likelihood of hospitalization in infants born between 32 and 35 weeks of gestation (ie, between 32 weeks, 1 day and 35 weeks, 0 days), the cost of administering prophylaxis to this large group of infants must be considered carefully. Therefore, most experts recommend that prophylaxis should be reserved for infants in this group who are at greatest risk of severe infection and who are younger than 6 months of age at the start of the RSV season. Epidemiologic data suggest that RSV infection is more likely to lead to hospitalization for these infants when the following risk factors are present: child care attendance, school-aged siblings, exposure to environmental air pollutants, congenital abnormalities of the airways, or severe neuromuscular disease. However, no single risk factor causes a very large increase in the rate of hospitalization, and the risk is additive as the number of risk factors for an individual infant increases. Therefore, prophylaxis should be considered for infants between 32 and 35 weeks of gestation only if 2 or more of these risk factors are present. Passive household exposure to tobacco smoke has not been associated with an increased risk of RSV hospitalization on a consistent basis. Furthermore, exposure to tobacco smoke is a risk factor that can be controlled by the family of an infant at increased risk of severe RSV disease, and preventive measures will be far less costly than palivizumab prophylaxis. High-risk

infants never should be exposed to tobacco smoke. In contrast to the well-documented beneficial effect of breastfeeding against many viral illnesses, existing data are conflicting regarding the specific protective effect of breastfeeding against RSV infection. High-risk infants should be kept away from crowds and from situations in which exposure to infected individuals cannot be controlled. Participation in group child care should be restricted during the RSV season for high-risk infants whenever feasible. Parents should be instructed on the importance of careful hand hygiene. In addition, all high-risk infants and their contacts should be immunized against influenza beginning at 6 months of age.

- In the Northern hemisphere and particularly within the United States, RSV circulates predominantly between November and March. The inevitability of the RSV season is predictable, but the severity of the season, the time of onset, the peak of activity, and the end of the season cannot be predicted precisely. There can be substantial variation in timing of community outbreaks of RSV disease from year to year in the same community and between communities in the same year, even in the same region. These variations, however, occur within the overall pattern of RSV outbreaks, usually beginning in November or December, peaking in January or February, and ending by the end of March or sometime in April. Communities in the southern United States tend to experience the earliest onset of RSV activity, and Midwestern states tend to experience the latest. The duration of the season for western and northeast regions typically occurs between that noted in the South and the Midwest. In recent years, the national median duration of the RSV season has been 15 weeks and even in the South, with a seasonal duration of 16 weeks, the range is 13 to 20 weeks. Results from clinical trials indicate that palivizumab trough serum concentrations >30 days after the fifth dose will be well above the protective concentration for most infants. If the first dose is administered in November, 5 monthly doses of palivizumab will provide substantially more than 20 weeks of protective serum antibody concentrations for most of the RSV season, even with variation in season onset and end. Changes from this recommendation of 5 monthly doses require careful consideration of the benefits and costs.

- Children who are 24 months of age or younger with hemodynamically significant cyanotic and acyanotic congenital heart disease will benefit from palivizumab prophylaxis. Decisions regarding prophylaxis with palivizumab in children with congenital heart disease should be made on the basis of the degree of physiologic cardiovascular compromise. Children younger than 24 months of age with congenital heart disease who are most likely to benefit from immunoprophylaxis include:
  - Infants who are receiving medication to control congestive heart failure
  - Infants with moderate to severe pulmonary hypertension
  - Infants with cyanotic heart disease

  Because a mean decrease in palivizumab serum concentration of 58% was observed after surgical procedures that use cardiopulmonary bypass, for children who still require prophylaxis, a postoperative dose of palivizumab (15 mg/kg) should be considered as soon as the patient is medically stable.

  The following groups of infants are **not** at increased risk of RSV and generally should not receive immunoprophylaxis:

- Infants and children with hemodynamically insignificant heart disease (eg, secundum atrial septal defect, small ventricular septal defect, pulmonic stenosis, uncomplicated aortic stenosis, mild coarctation of the aorta, and patent ductus arteriosus)
- Infants with lesions adequately corrected by surgery, unless they continue to require medication for congestive heart failure
- Infants with mild cardiomyopathy who are not receiving medical therapy

Dates for initiation and termination of prophylaxis should be based on the same considerations as for high-risk preterm infants.

- Palivizumab prophylaxis has not been evaluated in randomized trials in immunocompromised children. Although specific recommendations for immunocompromised patients cannot be made, children with severe immunodeficiencies (eg, severe combined immunodeficiency or advanced acquired immunodeficiency syndrome) may benefit from prophylaxis.
- Limited studies suggest that some patients with cystic fibrosis may be at increased risk of RSV infection. However, insufficient data exist to determine the effectiveness of palivizumab use in this patient population.
- If an infant or child who is receiving palivizumab immunoprophylaxis experiences a breakthrough RSV infection, monthly prophylaxis should continue through the RSV season. This recommendation is based on the observation that high-risk infants may be hospitalized more than once in the same season with RSV lower respiratory tract disease and the fact that more than one RSV strain often cocirculates in a community.
- Physicians should arrange for drug administration within 6 hours after opening a vial of palivizumab, because this biological product does not contain a preservative.
- Respiratory syncytial virus is known to be transmitted in the hospital setting and to cause serious disease in high-risk infants. In high-risk hospitalized infants, the major means to prevent RSV disease is strict observance of infection control practices, including prompt isolation of RSV-infected infants. If an RSV outbreak occurs in a high-risk unit (eg, pediatric intensive care unit), primary emphasis should be placed on proper infection control practices, especially hand hygiene. No data exist to support palivizumab use in controlling outbreaks of nosocomial disease.
- Palivizumab does not interfere with response to vaccines.

ISOLATION OF THE HOSPITALIZED PATIENT: In addition to standard precautions, contact precautions are recommended for the duration of RSV-associated illness among infants and young children, including patients treated with ribavirin. The effectiveness of these precautions depends on compliance and necessitates scrupulous adherence to appropriate hand hygiene practices. Patients with RSV infection should be cared for in single rooms or placed in a cohort.

CONTROL MEASURES: The control of nosocomial RSV transmission is complicated by the continuing chance of introduction through infected patients, staff, and visitors. During the peak of the RSV season, many infants and children hospitalized with respiratory tract symptoms will be infected with RSV and should be cared for with contact precautions (see Isolation of the Hospitalized Patient, p 565). Early identification of RSV-infected patients (see Diagnostic Tests, p 561) is important so that appropriate precautions can be instituted promptly. During large outbreaks, a variety of measures have been demonstrated to be effective, including the following: (1) laboratory screening of symptomatic patients for RSV infection; (2) cohorting infected patients and staff; (3) excluding visitors with respiratory tract infections; (4) excluding staff with respiratory tract illness or RSV infection from caring for susceptible infants; and (5) use of gowns, gloves, goggles, and perhaps masks.

A critical aspect of RSV prevention among high-risk infants is education of parents and other caregivers about the importance of decreasing exposure to and transmission of RSV. Preventive measures include limiting, where feasible, exposure to contagious settings (eg, child care centers) and emphasis on hand hygiene in all settings, including the home, especially during periods when the contacts of high-risk children have respiratory infections.

Rhinovirus Infections

CLINICAL MANIFESTATIONS: Rhinoviruses are the most frequent causes of the common cold or rhinosinusitis. Rhinoviruses also can be associated with pharyngitis, otitis media, less commonly bronchiolitis and pneumonia, and exacerbations of bronchitis and reactive airway disease. Nasal discharge usually is watery and clear at the onset but often becomes mucopurulent and viscous after a few days and may persist for 10 to 14 days. Malaise, headache, myalgias, and low-grade fever also may occur.

ETIOLOGY: Rhinoviruses are RNA viruses classified as picornaviruses. At least 100 antigenic serotypes have been identified by neutralizing antibodies. Infection with one type confers some type-specific immunity, but immunity is of variable degree and brief duration and offers little protection against other serotypes.

EPIDEMIOLOGY: Only humans and chimpanzees are infected with human rhinoviruses. Transmission occurs predominantly by person-to-person contact with self-inoculation by contaminated secretions on hands. Less commonly, transmission may occur by aerosol spread. Infections occur throughout the year, but peak activity is during autumn and spring. Several serotypes usually circulate simultaneously, but the prevalent serotypes circulating in a given population tend to change over time. By adulthood, antibodies to many serotypes have developed. Household spread is common. Viral shedding from nasopharyngeal secretions is most abundant during the first 2 to 3 days of infection and usually ceases by 7 to 10 days. However, shedding may continue for as long as 3 weeks.

The **incubation period** usually is 2 to 3 days but occasionally is up to 7 days.

DIAGNOSTIC TESTS: Inoculation of nasal secretions in appropriate cell cultures for viral isolation is the best means of establishing a specific diagnosis. The large number of antigenic types make serologic diagnosis of infection impractical.

TREATMENT: Placebo-controlled studies have indicated that over-the-counter antihistamine-decongestant cold medications are no more effective at relieving symptoms than placebo in children younger than 5 years of age. Antimicrobial agents do not prevent secondary bacterial infection and complicate later therapy by promoting the emergence of resistant bacteria (see Appropriate Use of Antimicrobial Agents, p 737).

ISOLATION OF THE HOSPITALIZED PATIENT: In addition to standard precautions, contact precautions are recommended for hospitalized infants and children for the duration of illness.

CONTROL MEASURES: Frequent hand hygiene and hygienic measures in schools, households, and other settings where transmission is common may help decrease the spread of rhinoviruses. Use of disinfectant sprays in the environment is of no proven benefit.

Rickettsial Diseases

Rickettsial diseases traditionally comprise infections caused by organisms of the genera *Rickettsia* (endemic and epidemic typhus and spotted fever group rickettsioses), *Orientia* (scrub typhus), *Coxiella* (Q fever), *Ehrlichia*, and *Anaplasma* (ehrlichiosis).

CLINICAL MANIFESTATIONS: Rickettsial infections have many features in common, including the following:
- Fever, rash (especially in spotted fever and typhus group rickettsiae), headache, myalgias, and respiratory tract symptoms are prominent features.
- Local primary eschars occur with some rickettsial diseases, particularly spotted fever group rickettsiae.
- Systemic capillary and small vessel endothelial damage is the primary pathologic feature of spotted fever and typhus group rickettsial infections.
- Rickettsial diseases can become life threatening rapidly.

Immunity against reinfection by the same agent after natural infection usually is of long duration, except in the case of scrub typhus caused by *Orientia tsutsugamushi*. Among the 4 groups of rickettsial diseases, some cross-immunity usually is conferred by infections within groups but not among groups. Reinfection with *Ehrlichia* and *Anaplasma* species has been described.

ETIOLOGY: The rickettsia causing human disease include: *Rickettsia* species (Rocky Mountain and other spotted fevers, endemic typhus, epidemic typhus), *Orientia* species (scrub typhus), *Coxiella* species (Q fever), and *Ehrlichia* and *Anaplasma* species (ehrlichiosis). Rickettsiae are small, coccobacillary gram-negative bacteria that are obligate intracellular pathogens and cannot be grown in cell-free media. They have cell walls characteristic of gram-negative microorganisms and divide by binary fission.

EPIDEMIOLOGY: Most rickettsial diseases have arthropod vectors including ticks, fleas, mites, and lice. Humans are incidental hosts, except for epidemic (louseborne) typhus, for which humans are the principal reservoir, and the human body louse is the vector. Rickettsia life cycles typically involve arthropod and mammalian reservoirs, and animal-to-human or vector-to-human transmission occurs as a result of environmental or occupational exposure. Thus, geographic and seasonal occurrence of rickettsial disease is related to arthropod vector life cycles, activity, and distribution.

The incubation periods vary according to organism (see specific chapters).

DIAGNOSIS: Group-specific antibodies are detectable in the serum of most people 7 to 14 days after onset of illness. Various serologic tests for detecting antirickettsial antibodies are available. The indirect immunofluorescent antibody assay is recommended in most circumstances because of its relative sensitivity and specificity. Treatment early in the course of illness can blunt or delay serologic responses. Polymerase chain reaction assays can detect rickettsiae in whole blood or tissues, although availability of these tests is limited to reference and research laboratories. In laboratories with experienced personnel, immunohistochemical staining and polymerase chain reaction testing of skin biopsy specimens from patients with rash can help to diagnose rickettsial infections.

TREATMENT: Prompt and specific therapy is important for optimal outcome. The drug of choice for therapy of Rickettsioses is doxycycline. Although tetracyclines generally are not given to children younger than 8 years of age because of the risk of dental staining, most experts consider that the risk of morbidity from rickettsial diseases outweighs the minimal risk of dental staining from one course of doxycycline. Antimicrobial treatment is most effective when children are treated during the first week of illness. If the disease remains untreated during the second week, therapy is less effective in preventing complications of illness. Because confirmatory laboratory tests primarily are retrospective, treatment decisions should be based on clinical findings and epidemiologic data and should not be delayed until test results are known.

PREVENTION: Control measures primarily involve prevention of tick transmission of rickettsial agents to humans (see Prevention of Tickborne Infections, p 195).

Several rickettsial diseases, including Rocky Mountain spotted fever, ehrlichiosis, and Q fever, are nationally notifiable diseases and should be reported to state and local health departments.

For more details, the following chapters on rickettsial diseases should be consulted:
- *Ehrlichia* Infections (Human Ehrlichioses), p 281
- Q Fever, p 550
- Rickettsialpox, p 569
- Rocky Mountain Spotted Fever, p 570
- Endemic Typhus (Fleaborne Typhus or Murine Typhus), p 706
- Epidemic Typhus (Louseborne Typhus), p 707

OTHER RICKETTSIAL SPOTTED FEVER INFECTIONS: A number of other epidemiologically distinct but clinically similar tickborne spotted fever infections caused by rickettsiae have been recognized. Many of them present with an eschar at the site of the tick bite. The causative agents of some of these infections share the same group antigen as *Rickettsia rickettsii*. These include *Rickettsia africae,* the causative agent of African tick bite fever that is endemic to sub-Saharan Africa and some Caribbean Islands; *Rickettsia conorii,* the causative agent of boutonneuse fevers (Mediterranean spotted fever, India tick typhus, Marseilles fever, Israeli tick typhus, and Astrakhan spotted fever) that is endemic in southern Europe, Africa, the Middle East, and the Indian subcontinent; *Rickettsia sibirica,* the causative agent of Siberian tick typhus, endemic in central Asia; *Rickettsia australis,* the causative agent of North Queensland tick typhus, endemic in eastern Australia; *Rickettsia japonica,* the causative agent of Japanese spotted fever, endemic in Japan; *Rickettsia honei,* the causative agent of Thai tick typhus and Flinders Island spotted fever; *Rickettsia slovaca,* the causative agent of tickborne lymphadenopathy, endemic in European countries; and *Rickettsia felis*, the causative agent of cat flea rickettsiosis that occurs worldwide. Each of these infections has some clinical and pathologic features similar to those of Rocky Mountain spotted fever. The specific diagnosis is confirmed using serologic assays. Demonstration of a fourfold or greater rise in specific antibodies in acute and convalescent serum samples taken 2 to 3 weeks apart is diagnostic. These diseases are of importance among people traveling to or returning from areas where these agents are endemic and people living in these areas.

Rickettsialpox

CLINICAL MANIFESTATIONS: Rickettsialpox is characterized by generalized erythematous papulovesicular eruptions on the trunk, face, extremities (including palms and soles), and mucous membranes after the appearance of an eschar at the site of the bite of a mouse mite. Regional lymph nodes in the area of the primary eschar typically become enlarged. Systemic disease lasts approximately 1 week; manifestations can include fever, chills, headache, drenching sweats, vomiting, myalgias, anorexia, and photophobia. The disease can be moderately severe, is self-limited, and rarely is associated with complications.

ETIOLOGY: Rickettsialpox is caused by *Rickettsia akari*, which is classified with the spotted fever group rickettsiae and related antigenically to *Rickettsia rickettsii*.

EPIDEMIOLOGY: The natural host for *R akari* in the United States is *Mus musculus*, the common house mouse. The disease is transmitted by the mouse mite *(Liponyssoides sanguineus)*. Disease risk is heightened in areas infested with mice. The disease may be found wherever the hosts, pathogens, and humans coexist but is found mostly in large urban settings and has been recognized in the northeastern United States, especially in New York City, but also in Ohio, North Carolina, Utah, Croatia, Ukraine, Turkey, Russia, Korea, and South Africa. All age groups can be affected. No seasonal pattern of disease occurs. The disease is not communicable and is reported rarely in the United States; however, it is likely that rickettsialpox is underdiagnosed at present.

The **incubation period** is 9 to 14 days.

DIAGNOSTIC TESTS: *Rickettsia akari* can be isolated from blood during the acute stage of disease, but culture is not attempted routinely and is available only in specialized laboratories. Because antibodies to *R akari* have extensive cross-reactivity with antibodies against *R rickettsii*, an indirect immunofluorescent antibody assay for *R rickettsii* (the cause of Rocky Mountain spotted fever) may demonstrate a fourfold change in antibody titers between acute and convalescent serum specimens taken 3 to 4 weeks apart. Absorption of serum specimens before indirect immunofluorescent antibody assay can distinguish between antibody responses to *R rickettsii* and *R akari*. Direct fluorescent antibody or immunohistochemical testing of paraffin-embedded eschars and histopathologic examination of papulovesicles for distinctive features are useful diagnostic techniques.

TREATMENT: Doxycycline will shorten the course of disease; symptoms resolve within 48 hours after initiation of therapy. Despite concerns regarding dental staining after use of tetracyclines in children younger than 8 years of age, doxycycline is the drug of choice for this potentially severe disease (see Antimicrobial Agents and Related Therapy, p 735). Available data suggest that one course of doxycycline does not cause discoloration of permanent teeth. Treatment is effective when given for 3 to 5 days; relapse is rare. Chloramphenicol and a fluoroquinolone are alternative drugs.

ISOLATION OF THE HOSPITALIZED PATIENT: Standard precautions are recommended.

CONTROL MEASURES: Disinfestation with residual acaricides and rodent control measures limit or eliminate the vector. No specific management of exposed people is necessary.

Rocky Mountain Spotted Fever

CLINICAL MANIFESTATIONS: Rocky Mountain spotted fever (RMSF) is a systemic, small-vessel vasculitis with a characteristic rash that usually occurs before the sixth day of illness. Fever, myalgia, severe headache, nausea, vomiting, and anorexia are major clinical features. Abdominal pain and diarrhea often are present and can obscure the diagnosis. The rash initially is erythematous and macular and later can become maculopapular and often petechial. Rash usually appears first on the wrists and ankles, often spreading within hours proximally to the trunk. The palms and soles typically are involved. Although early development of a rash is a useful diagnostic sign, rash fails to develop in up to 20% of cases. Thrombocytopenia of varying severity and hyponatremia develop in many cases. The white blood cell count typically is normal, but leukopenia and anemia can occur. The illness can last as long as 3 weeks and can be severe, with prominent central nervous system, cardiac, pulmonary, gastrointestinal tract, and renal involvement; disseminated intravascular coagulation; and shock leading to death. Significant long-term sequelae are common in patients with severe RMSF, including neurologic (paraparesis; hearing loss; peripheral neuropathy; bladder and bowel incontinence; and cerebellar, vestibular, and motor dysfunction) and nonneurologic effects (disability from limb amputation).

ETIOLOGY: *Rickettsia rickettsii* is an obligate intracellular pathogen and a member of the spotted fever group of rickettsiae. The primary targets of infection in mammalian hosts are endothelial cells lining the small vessels of all major tissues and organs.

EPIDEMIOLOGY: The disease is transmitted to humans by the bite of an *Ixodes* species tick. Many small wild animals and dogs have antibodies to *R rickettsii*, but their role as natural reservoirs is not clear. Ticks are both reservoirs and vectors of *R rickettsii*. In ticks, the agent is transmitted transovarially and between stages. People with occupational or recreational exposure to the tick vector (eg, pet owners, animal handlers, and people who spend time outdoors) are at increased risk of acquiring the organism. People of all ages can be infected, but national surveillance indicates that most cases occur in people younger than 15 years of age. April through September are the months of highest incidence in the United States. Laboratory-acquired infection has resulted from accidental inoculation and aerosol contamination. Transmission has occurred on rare occasions by blood transfusion. Mortality is highest in males, people older than 50 years of age, and people with no recognized tick bite or attachment. Lack of confirmed recent tick bite does not exclude the diagnosis. Delay in disease recognition and initiation of antirickettsial therapy increase the risk of death. Factors contributing to delayed diagnosis include absence of rash, initial presentation before the fourth day of illness, and onset of illness during months other than May through August.

The disease is widespread in the United States. Most cases are reported in the south Atlantic, southeastern, and south central states. The principal recognized vectors of *R rickettsii* are *Dermacentor variabilis* (the American dog tick) in the eastern and central United States and *Dermacentor andersoni* (the Rocky Mountain wood tick) in Western United States. Another common tick throughout the world that feeds on dogs, *Rhipicephalus sanguineus* (the brown dog tick), has been implicated as a vector of *R rickettsii* in Arizona. Transmission parallels the tick season in a given geographic area. Rocky Mountain spotted fever also occurs in Canada, Mexico, and Central and South America.

The **incubation period** usually is approximately 1 week (range 2–14 days).

DIAGNOSTIC TESTS: The diagnosis can be established by one of the multiple rickettsial group-specific serologic tests.* A fourfold or greater change in titer between acute and convalescent serum specimens obtained 2 to 3 weeks apart is diagnostic when determined by indirect immunofluorescent antibody (IFA) assay, enzyme immunoassay, complement fixation, latex agglutination, indirect hemagglutination, or microagglutination tests. The IFA assay is the most widely available confirmatory test. Antibodies generally are detected by IFA assay 7 to 10 days after onset of illness. A probable diagnosis can be established by a single serum titer of 1:64 or greater by IFA assay. The nonspecific and insensitive Weil-Felix serologic test (*Proteus vulgaris* OX-19 and OX-2 agglutinins) is not recommended.

Culture of *R rickettsii* should be conducted only by laboratories with adequate biohazard containment equipment. *Rickettsia rickettsii* can be identified by immunohistochemical staining or polymerase chain reaction (PCR) of tissue specimens (biopsy or autopsy). Ideally, a specimen from the site of the rash should be obtained before antimicrobial therapy is initiated or soon thereafter, because sensitivity diminishes quickly afterwards. Isolation or PCR assays for detection of *R rickettsii* in blood and biopsy specimens during the acute phase of illness confirm the diagnosis and are available at the Centers for Disease Control and Prevention reference laboratories.

TREATMENT: Doxycycline is the drug of choice; chloramphenicol or a fluoroquinolone are alternative drugs. Although tetracyclines generally are not given to children younger than 8 years of age because of the risk of dental staining (see Antimicrobial Agents and Related Therapy, p 735), most experts consider doxycycline to be the drug of choice for children of any age. Reasons for this preference include the following: (1) tetracycline staining of teeth is related to the total dose; (2) doxycycline is less likely than other tetracyclines to stain developing teeth; (3) doxycycline is effective against ehrlichiosis, which may mimic RMSF, but chloramphenicol may not be (see *Ehrlichia* Infections, p 281); and (4) use of chloramphenicol is problematic because of serious adverse effects, the need to monitor serum concentrations, and lack of an oral preparation in the United States. Also, retrospective studies indicate that chloram-

---

* Centers for Disease Control and Prevention. Diagnosis and management of tickborne rickettsial diseases: Rocky Mountain spotted fever, ehrlichioses, and anaplasmosis. *MMWR Recomm Rep.* 2006;55(RR–4):1–27

phenicol may be less effective than doxycycline for the treatment of RMSF. Therapy is continued until the patient has been afebrile for at least 3 days and has demonstrated clinical improvement; the usual duration of therapy is 7 to 10 days. Treatment is initiated on the basis of clinical features and epidemiologic considerations rather than laboratory testing. Treatment before day 5 of illness in children with compatible clinical manifestations affords the highest likelihood of good outcome.

ISOLATION OF THE HOSPITALIZED PATIENT: Standard precautions are recommended.

CONTROL MEASURES: Control of ticks in their natural habitat is not practical. Avoidance of tick-infested areas (ie, areas that border wooded regions) is the best preventive measure. If a tick-infested area is entered, people should wear protective clothing and apply tick or insect repellents to clothes and exposed body parts for added protection. Adults should be taught to inspect themselves, their children (bodies and clothing), and pets thoroughly for ticks after spending time outdoors during the tick season and to remove ticks promptly and properly (see Prevention of Tickborne Infections, p 195).

There is no role for prophylactic antimicrobial agents in preventing RMSF. No licensed *R rickettsii* vaccine is available in the United States. For additional information, see **www.cdc.gov/ncidod/dvrd/rmsf**.

Rotavirus Infections

CLINICAL MANIFESTATIONS: Infection causes nonbloody diarrhea, often preceded or accompanied by vomiting and fever. Symptoms generally persist for 3 to 8 days. In severe cases, dehydration, electrolyte abnormalities, and acidosis may occur. In immunocompromised children, including children with human immunodeficiency virus infection, persistent infection and diarrhea can develop.

ETIOLOGY: Rotaviruses are segmented, double-stranded RNA viruses belonging to the family Reoviridae, with at least 7 distinct antigenic groups (A through G). Group A viruses are the major causes of rotavirus diarrhea worldwide. Serotyping is based on the VP7 glycoprotein (G) and VP4 protease-cleaved hemagglutinin (P); G types 1 through 4 and 9 and P types 1A and 1B are most common.

EPIDEMIOLOGY: Most human infections result from direct or indirect contact with infected people. Rotavirus is present in high titer in stools of infected patients with diarrhea, which is the only body specimen consistently positive for the virus. Rotavirus can be detected in stool before onset of diarrhea and may persist for as long as 21 days after the onset of symptoms in immunocompetent hosts. Transmission is presumed to be by the fecal-oral route. Rotavirus can be found on toys and hard surfaces in child care centers, indicating that fomites may serve as a mechanism of transmission. Respiratory transmission is likely to play a role in disease transmission. Spread within families and institutions is common. Rotavirus is the most common cause of nosocomially acquired diarrhea in children and is an important cause of acute gastroenteritis in children attending child care. Rarely, common-source outbreaks from contaminated water or food have been reported.

Human rotavirus infections are ubiquitous. Virtually all children are infected by 3 years of age. Rotavirus gastroenteritis is the most common cause of severe diarrhea in children younger than 5 years of age. Severe rotavirus infections occur most commonly in infants and children between 4 and 24 months of age. Rotavirus-related hospitalizations can account for as many as 2.5% of all hospitalizations of children. Approximately 20% of adult household contacts of infected infants will develop symptomatic infection. Breastfeeding is associated with milder disease and should be encouraged.

In temperate climates, disease is most prevalent during the cooler months. In North America, the annual epidemic usually starts during the autumn in Mexico and the southwest United States and moves sequentially to reach the northeast United States and Canada by spring. The seasonal pattern of disease is less pronounced in tropical climates, but rotavirus infection is more common during the cooler, drier months.

The **incubation period** ranges from 2 to 4 days.

DIAGNOSTIC TESTS: It is not possible to diagnose rotavirus infection by clinical presentation or nonspecific laboratory tests. Enzyme immunoassay and latex agglutination assays for group A rotavirus antigen detection in stool are available commercially. Both assays have high specificity, but false-positive results and nonspecific reactions can occur in neonates and in people with underlying intestinal disease. Nonspecific reactions can be distinguished from true positive reactions by performance of confirmatory assays. Virus also can be identified in stool by electron microscopy and by specific nucleic acid amplification techniques.

TREATMENT: No specific antiviral therapy is available. Oral or parenteral fluids and electrolytes are given to prevent and correct dehydration. Orally administered Human Immune Globulin given as an investigational therapy in immunocompromised patients with prolonged infection has decreased viral shedding and shortened the duration of diarrhea.

ISOLATION OF THE HOSPITALIZED PATIENT: In addition to standard precautions, contact precautions are indicated for the duration of illness.

CONTROL MEASURES:

CHILD CARE. General measures for interrupting enteric transmission in child-care centers are available (see Children in Out-of-Home Child Care, p 130). Surfaces should be washed with soap and water. A 70% ethanol solution or other disinfectants will inactivate rotavirus and may help prevent disease transmission resulting from contact with environmental surfaces.

VACCINES. In the United States, the rhesus rotavirus tetravalent vaccine (Rotashield) was licensed by the US Food and Drug Administration in August 1998 and incorporated into the 1999 recommended childhood immunization schedule. This product was withdrawn voluntarily from the market in October 1999 because of the association of this vaccine with intussusception. Children who received rotavirus vaccine during the period of approval are not at increased risk of developing intussusception in the future.

In February 2006, a bovine rotavirus-based pentavalent rotavirus vaccine (PRV [RotaTeq]) was licensed for use among US infants. The following are recommendations for use of this vaccine*†:

- Infants in the United States routinely should be immunized with 3 doses of PRV administered orally at 2, 4, and 6 months of age.
- The first dose of PRV should be administered between 6 and 12 weeks of age.
- Subsequent doses of PRV should be administered at 4- to 10-week intervals.
- All 3 doses of PRV should be administered by 32 weeks of age.
- Infants with transient, mild illness with or without low-grade fever and infants who are breastfeeding can receive PRV.
- Infants who have severe hypersensitivity to any component of the vaccine or who have experienced a serious allergic reaction to a previous dose of PRV should not receive PRV.

Rubella

CLINICAL MANIFESTATIONS:

POSTNATAL RUBELLA. Many cases of postnatal rubella are subclinical. Clinical disease usually is mild and characterized by a generalized erythematous maculopapular rash, lymphadenopathy, and slight fever. The rash starts on the face, becomes generalized in 24 hours, and lasts a median of 3 days. Lymphadenopathy, which may precede rash, often involves posterior auricular or suboccipital lymph nodes, can be generalized, and lasts between 5 and 8 days. Conjunctivitis and palatal enanthem have been noted. Transient polyarthralgia and polyarthritis rarely occur in children but are common in adolescents and adults, especially females. Encephalitis (1:5000 cases) and thrombocytopenia (1:3000 cases) are rare complications. Maternal rubella during pregnancy can result in miscarriage, fetal death, or a constellation of congenital anomalies (congenital rubella syndrome).

CONGENITAL RUBELLA SYNDROME (CRS). The most commonly described anomalies associated with congenital rubella syndrome are ophthalmologic (cataracts, pigmentary retinopathy, microphthalmos, and congenital glaucoma), cardiac (patent ductus arteriosus, peripheral pulmonary artery stenosis), auditory (sensorineural hearing impairment), and neurologic (behavioral disorders, meningoencephalitis, and mental retardation). Neonatal manifestations of congenital rubella syndrome include growth retardation, interstitial pneumonitis, radiolucent bone disease, hepatosplenomegaly, thrombocytopenia, and dermal erythropoiesis (so called "blueberry muffin" lesions). Mild forms of the disease can be associated with few or no obvious clinical manifestations at birth. The occurrence of congenital defects is up to 85% if infection associated with maternal rash occurs during the first 12 weeks of gestation, 54% during the first 13 to 16 weeks of gestation, and 25% during the end of the second trimester.

---

* American Academy of Pediatrics, Committee on Infectious Diseases. Prevention of rotavirus gastroenteritis: guidelines for use of rotavirus vaccine. *Pediatrics*. 2006; in press

† Centers for Disease Control and Prevention. Prevention of rotavirus gastroenteritis among infants and children. Recommendations of the Advisory Committee on Immunization Practices. *MMWR*. 2006; in press (see **www.cdc.gov/mmwr**)

ETIOLOGY: Rubella virus is an enveloped, positive-stranded RNA virus classified as a Rubivirus in the Togaviridae family.

EPIDEMIOLOGY: Humans are the only source of infection. Postnatal rubella is transmitted primarily through direct or droplet contact from nasopharyngeal secretions. The peak incidence of infection is during late winter and early spring. Approximately 25% to 50% of infections are asymptomatic. Immunity from wild-type or vaccine virus usually is prolonged, but reinfection on rare occasions has been demonstrated and rarely has resulted in congenital rubella. The period of maximal communicability extends from a few days before to 7 days after onset of rash. Volunteer studies have demonstrated the presence of rubella virus in nasopharyngeal secretions from 7 days before to 14 days after onset of rash. A small number of infants with congenital rubella continue to shed virus in nasopharyngeal secretions and urine for 1 year or more and can transmit infection to susceptible contacts. Rubella virus has been recovered in high titer from lens aspirates in children with congenital cataracts for up to several years.

Before widespread use of rubella vaccine, rubella was an epidemic disease, occurring in 6- to 9-year cycles, with most cases occurring in children. The incidence of rubella in the United States has decreased by approximately 99% from the prevaccine era. Currently, fewer than 25 cases are reported in the United States annually. The risk of acquiring rubella has decreased in all age groups, including adolescents and young adults. In the vaccine era, most cases in the 1970s and 1980s occurred in young, unimmunized adults in outbreaks on college campuses and in occupational settings. More recent outbreaks have occurred in foreign-born or underimmunized individuals. Although the number of susceptible people has decreased since introduction and widespread use of rubella vaccine, recent serologic surveys indicate that approximately 10% of the US-born population older than 5 years of age is susceptible to rubella. The percentage of susceptible people who are foreign born or from areas with poor vaccine coverage is higher. The risk of CRS is highest in infants of women born outside the United States.

The **incubation period** for postnatally acquired rubella ranges from 14 to 23 days, usually 16 to 18 days.

DIAGNOSTIC TESTS: Detection of rubella-specific immunoglobulin (Ig) M antibody usually indicates recent postnatal infection or congenital infection in a newborn infant, but both false-negative and false-positive results occur. Congenital infection also can be confirmed by stable or increasing serum concentrations of rubella-specific IgG over several months. Rubella virus can be isolated most consistently from throat or nasal specimens by inoculation of appropriate cell culture. Laboratory personnel should be notified that rubella is suspected, because additional testing is required to detect the virus. Blood, urine, cerebrospinal fluid, and throat swab specimens also can yield virus, particularly in congenitally infected infants. Diagnosis of congenital rubella infection in children older than 1 year of age is difficult; serologic testing usually is not diagnostic, and viral isolation, although confirmatory, is possible in only a small proportion of congenitally infected children of this age. Molecular typing of viral isolates can be useful in defining a source in outbreak scenarios. For diagnosis of postnatally acquired rubella, a fourfold or greater increase in antibody titer or seroconversion between acute and convalescent serum titers indicates infection. Every effort should be made to establish a laboratory diagnosis when rubella infection is suspected in pregnant women or newborn infants. The hemagglutination inhibition rubella antibody test, which previously was the most commonly used method of serologic screening, generally has been supplanted by a number of equally or more sensitive assays for determining rubella immunity, including enzyme immunoassay tests, latex agglutination, and immunofluorescent assay. Some people in whom antibody has been absent by hemagglutination inhibition testing have been found to be immune when their serum specimens were tested by more sensitive assays.

TREATMENT: Supportive.

ISOLATION OF THE HOSPITALIZED PATIENT: In addition to standard precautions, for postnatal rubella, droplet precautions are recommended for 7 days after onset of the rash. Contact isolation is indicated for children with proven or suspected congenital rubella until they are at least 1 year of age, unless 2 nasopharyngeal and urine culture results after 3 months of age are negative consecutively for rubella virus.

CONTROL MEASURES:

SCHOOL AND CHILD CARE. Children with postnatal rubella should be excluded from school or child care for 7 days after onset of the rash. Children with congenital rubella should be considered contagious until they are at least 1 year of age, unless nasopharyngeal and urine culture results repeatedly are negative for rubella virus; infection control precautions should be considered in children up to 3 years of age who are hospitalized for congenital cataract extraction. Caregivers of these infants should be made aware of the potential hazard of the infants to susceptible pregnant contacts.

CARE OF EXPOSED PEOPLE. When a pregnant woman is exposed to rubella, a blood specimen should be obtained as soon as possible and tested for rubella antibody (IgG and IgM). An aliquot of frozen serum should be stored for possible repeated testing at a later time. The presence of rubella-specific IgG antibody in a properly performed test at the time of exposure indicates that the person most likely is immune. If antibody is not detectable, a second blood specimen should be obtained 2 to 3 weeks later and tested concurrently with the first specimen. If the second test result is negative, another blood specimen should be obtained 6 weeks after the exposure and also tested concurrently with the first specimen; a negative test result in both specimens indicates that infection has not occurred, and a positive test result in the second or third specimen but not the first (seroconversion) indicates recent infection.

IMMUNE GLOBULIN. Limited data indicate that intramuscular Immune Globulin (IG) in a dose of 0.55 mL/kg may decrease clinically apparent infection, viral shedding, and rate of viremia significantly in exposed susceptible people. The reduction in virus multiplication theoretically may decrease the likelihood of fetal infection. Immune Globulin can be considered for postexposure prophylaxis of rubella-susceptible women exposed to confirmed rubella early in pregnancy only if termination of pregnancy is declined. The absence of clinical signs in a woman who has received intramuscular IG does not guarantee that fetal infection has been prevented. Infants with congenital rubella have been born to mothers who were given IG shortly after exposure. Administration of IG eliminates the value of IgG antibody testing to detect maternal infection. Immunoglobulin M antibody can be used to detect maternal infection after exposure, even after receipt of IG.

VACCINE. Although live-virus rubella vaccine given after exposure has not been demonstrated to prevent illness, vaccine theoretically could prevent illness if administered within 3 days of exposure. Immunization of exposed nonpregnant people may be indicated, because if the exposure did not result in infection, immunization will protect these people in the future. Immunization of a person who is incubating natural rubella or who already is immune is not associated with an increased risk of adverse effects.

RUBELLA VACCINE. The live-virus rubella vaccine distributed in the United States is the RA 27/3 strain grown in human diploid cell cultures. Vaccine is administered by subcutaneous injection of 0.5 mL alone or, preferably, as a combined vaccine containing measles-mumps-rubella (MMR) or measles-mumps-rubella-varicella (MMRV). Vaccine can be given simultaneously with other vaccines (see Simultaneous Administration of Multiple Vaccines, p 34). Serum antibody to rubella is induced in 95% or more of the recipients after a single dose at 12 months of age or older. Clinical efficacy and challenge studies have demonstrated that 1 dose confers long-term, probably lifelong, immunity against clinical and asymptomatic infection in more than 90% of immunized people. Asymptomatic reinfection has occurred.

Because of the 2-dose recommendation for measles vaccine as MMR, 2 doses of rubella vaccine now are given routinely. This provides an added safeguard against primary vaccine failures.

VACCINE RECOMMENDATIONS. At least one dose of live-attenuated rubella-containing vaccine is recommended for people 12 months of age or older. In the United States, rubella vaccine is recommended to be administered in combination with measles and mumps vaccines (MMR or MMRV) when a child is 12 to 15 months of age, with a second dose of MMR at school entry at 4 to 6 years of age, according to recommendations for routine measles immunization. People who have not received the dose at school entry should receive their second dose as soon as possible but no later than 11 to 12 years of age (see Measles, p 441).

Special emphasis must continue to be placed on the immunization of at-risk postpubertal males and females, especially college students, military recruits, recent immigrants, and health care professionals. People who were born in 1957 or after and have not received at least 1 dose of vaccine or who have no serologic evidence of immunity to rubella are considered susceptible and should be immunized with MMR vaccine. Clinical diagnosis of infection usually is unreliable and should not be accepted as evidence of immunity.

Specific recommendations are as follows:

- Postpubertal females without documentation of presumptive evidence of rubella immunity should be immunized unless they are known to be pregnant. Postpubertal females should be advised not to become pregnant for 28 days after receiving rubella-containing vaccine (see Precautions and Contraindications, p 578, for further discussion).
- During annual health care examinations, premarital and family planning visits, and visits to sexually transmitted infection clinics, postpubertal females should

be assessed for rubella susceptibility and, if deemed susceptible, should be immunized with MMR vaccine.

- Routine prenatal screening for rubella immunity should be undertaken. If a woman is found to be susceptible, rubella vaccine should be administered during the immediate postpartum period before discharge.
- Breastfeeding is not a contraindication to postpartum immunization of the mother (for additional information, see Human Milk, p 123).
- All susceptible health care professionals who may be exposed to patients with rubella and people who work in educational institutions or provide child care should be immunized for prevention or transmission of rubella to pregnant patients as well as for their own health.

ADVERSE REACTIONS.

- Of susceptible children who receive MMR or MMRV vaccines, fever develops in 5% to 15% from 6 to 12 days after immunization. Rash occurs in approximately 5% of immunized people. Mild lymphadenopathy occurs commonly.
- Joint pain, usually in small peripheral joints, has been reported in approximately 0.5% of young children. Arthralgia and transient arthritis tend to be more common in susceptible postpubertal females, occurring in approximately 25% and 10%, respectively, of vaccine recipients. Joint involvement usually begins 7 to 21 days after immunization and generally is transient.
- The incidence of joint manifestations after immunization is lower than that after natural infection at the corresponding age.
- Transient paresthesia and pain in the arms and legs also have been reported, although rarely.
- Central nervous system manifestations have been reported, but no causal relationship with rubella vaccine has been established.
- Other reactions that occur after immunization with MMR are associated with the measles and mumps components of the vaccine (see Measles, p 441, and Mumps, p 464).

PRECAUTIONS AND CONTRAINDICATIONS.

- **Pregnancy.** Rubella vaccine should not be given to pregnant women. If vaccine is given inadvertently or if pregnancy occurs within 28 days of immunization, the patient should be counseled on the theoretic risks to the fetus. A small percentage of offspring in such cases had signs of infection, but none had congenital defects. In view of these observations, receipt of rubella vaccine during pregnancy is not an indication for termination of pregnancy.

   Routine serologic testing of postpubertal women before immunization is unnecessary. Serologic testing is a potential impediment to protection against rubella, because it requires 2 visits.
- **Children of pregnant woman.** Immunizing susceptible children whose mothers or other household contacts are pregnant does not cause a risk. Most immunized people intermittently shed small amounts of virus from the pharynx 7 to 28 days after immunization, but no evidence of transmission of the vaccine virus from immunized children has been found.
- **Febrile illness.** Children with minor illnesses, such as upper respiratory tract infection, may be immunized (see Vaccine Safety and Contraindications, p 39).

Fever is not a contraindication to immunization. However, if other manifestations suggest a more serious illness, the child should not be immunized until recovery has occurred.

- **Recent administration of IG.** Immune Globulin preparations interfere with immune response to measles vaccine, and they theoretically may interfere with the serologic response to rubella vaccine (see p 36). Rubella vaccine may be given to postpartum women at the same time as anti-Rh$_o$ (D) IG or after blood products are given, but these women should be tested 8 or more weeks later to determine whether they have developed an antibody response. Reimmunization may be necessary. Suggested intervals are the same as used between IG administration and measles immunization (see Table 3.33, p 446).
- **Altered immunity.** Immunocompromised patients with disorders associated with increased severity of viral infections should not receive live-virus rubella vaccine (see Immunocompromised Children, p 71). The exceptions are patients with human immunodeficiency virus infection who are not severely immunocompromised; these patients may be immunized against rubella with MMR vaccine (see Human Immunodeficiency Virus Infection, p 378).
- **Household contacts of immunocompromised.** The risk of rubella exposure for patients with altered immunity can be decreased by immunizing their close susceptible contacts.

Precautions and contraindications appropriate for the measles, mumps, and varicella components of MMR or MMRV should be reviewed before administration (see Measles, p 441, Mumps, p 464, and Varicella-Zoster Infections, p 711).

CORTICOSTEROIDS. For patients who have received high doses of corticosteroids ($\geq$2 mg/kg or >20 mg/day) for 14 days or more and who are not otherwise immunocompromised, the recommended interval before immunization is at least 1 month (see Immunocompromised Children, p 71) after steroids have been discontinued.

SURVEILLANCE FOR CONGENITAL INFECTIONS. Accurate diagnosis and reporting of CRS are extremely important in assessing control of rubella. All birth defects in which rubella infection is suspected etiologically should be investigated thoroughly and reported to the Centers for Disease Control and Prevention through local or state health departments.

Salmonella Infections

CLINICAL MANIFESTATIONS: Nontyphoidal *Salmonella* organisms cause asymptomatic carriage, gastroenteritis, bacteremia, and focal infections (such as meningitis and osteomyelitis). These disease categories are not mutually exclusive but represent a spectrum of illness. The most common illness associated with nontyphoidal *Salmonella* infection is gastroenteritis, in which diarrhea, abdominal cramps, and fever are common manifestations. The site of infection usually is the small intestine, but colitis can occur. Sustained or intermittent bacteremia can occur, and focal infections are recognized in as many as 10% of patients with *Salmonella* bacteremia.

Salmonella serotype Typhi and several other *Salmonella* serotypes can cause a protracted bacteremic illness often referred to as enteric or typhoid fever. The onset of illness typically is gradual, with manifestations such as fever, constitutional symptoms (eg, headache, malaise, anorexia, and lethargy), abdominal pain and tenderness, hepatomegaly, splenomegaly, rose spots, and change in mental status. Enteric fever can manifest as a mild, nondescript febrile illness in young children, in whom sustained or intermittent bacteremia can occur. Constipation can be an early feature. Diarrhea commonly occurs in children.

ETIOLOGY: *Salmonella* organisms are gram-negative bacilli that belong to the Enterobacteriaceae family. Currently, there are more than 2460 *Salmonella* serotypes; most serotypes causing human disease are divided among O-antigen groups A through E. *Salmonella* serotype Typhi is classified in serogroup D. In 2004, the most commonly reported human isolates in the United States were *Salmonella* serotype Typhimurium (serogroup B), *Salmonella* serotype Enteritidis (D), and *Salmonella* serotype Newport (C2); these 3 serotypes accounted for nearly half of all *Salmonella* infections. The *Salmonella* nomenclature is shown in Table 3.54.

EPIDEMIOLOGY: The principal reservoirs for nontyphoidal *Salmonella* organisms include poultry, livestock, reptiles, and pets. The major vehicle of transmission is food of animal origin, such as poultry, beef, eggs, and dairy products. Other food vehicles (eg, fruits, vegetables, and bakery products) have been implicated in outbreaks, in which the food was contaminated by contact with an infected animal product or human. Other modes of transmission include ingestion of contaminated water; contact with infected reptiles or amphibians (eg, pet turtles, iguanas, lizards, snakes, frogs, toads, newts, salamanders) and possibly rodents; and exposure to contaminated medications, dyes, and medical instruments.

Unlike nontyphoidal *Salmonella* serotypes, *S* serotype Typhi is found only in humans, and infection implies direct contact with an infected person or with an item contaminated by a carrier. Although uncommon in the United States (approximately 400 cases per year), typhoid fever is endemic in many countries. Consequently, typhoid fever infections in the United States usually are acquired during international travel.

Age-specific attack rates for *Salmonella* infection are highest in people 1 to 4 years of age. Rates of invasive infections and mortality are higher in infants, elderly people, and people with immunosuppressive conditions, hemoglobinopathies (including sickle cell disease), malignant neoplasms, and human immunodeficiency virus (HIV) infec-

Table 3.54. Nomenclature for *Salmonella* Organisms

Complete Name	CDC Designation	Commonly Used Name
S enterica[1] subspecies *enterica* serotype Typhi	*S* ser. Typhi	*S typhi*
S enterica subspecies *enterica* serotype Typhimurium	*S* ser. Typhimurium	*S typhimurium*
S enterica subspecies *enterica* serotype Newport	*S* ser. Newport	*S newport*
S enterica subspecies *enterica* serotype Choleraesuis	*S* ser. Choleraesuis	*S choleraesuis*
S enterica subspecies *arizona* serotype 18:z_4,z_{23}:-	*S* ser. 18:z_4,z_{23}:-	*Arizona hinshawii*
S enterica subspecies *houtenae* serotype Marina	*S* ser. IV48:g,z_{51}:-	*S marina*

CDC indicates Centers for Disease Control and Prevention.
[1] Some also use *choleraesuis* and *enteritidis* as species names.

tion. Most reported cases are sporadic, but widespread outbreaks, including nosocomial, institutional, and nursery outbreaks, have been reported. Every year, *Salmonella* organisms are one of the most common causes of laboratory-confirmed cases of enteric disease reported by the Foodborne Diseases Active Surveillance Network (FoodNet).

The risk of transmission exists for the duration of fecal excretion of organisms. Twelve weeks after infection, 45% of children younger than 5 years of age excrete *Salmonella* organisms, compared with 5% of older children and adults; antimicrobial therapy can prolong excretion. Approximately 1% of patients continue to excrete *Salmonella* organisms for more than 1 year (chronic carriers).

The **incubation period** for gastroenteritis usually is 12 to 36 hours (6–72 hours). For enteric fever, the incubation period usually is 7 to 14 days (3–60 days).

DIAGNOSTIC TESTS: Isolation of *Salmonella* organisms from cultures of stool, blood, urine, and material from foci of infection is diagnostic. Gastroenteritis is diagnosed by stool culture. Rapid tests using enzyme immunoassay, latex agglutination, DNA probes, and monoclonal antibodies have been developed and are in use in some laboratories. Serologic tests for *Salmonella* agglutinins ("febrile agglutinins" [the Widal test]) are not recommended.

TREATMENT:
- Antimicrobial therapy usually is not indicated for patients with either asymptomatic infection or uncomplicated (noninvasive) gastroenteritis caused by nontyphoidal *Salmonella* species, because therapy does not shorten the duration of disease and can prolong the duration of fecal excretion. Although of unproven benefit, antimicrobial therapy is recommended for gastroenteritis caused by *Salmonella* species in people at increased risk of invasive disease, including infants younger than 3 months of age and people with chronic gastrointestinal tract disease, malignant neoplasms, hemoglobinopathies, HIV infection, or other immunosuppressive illnesses or therapies.
- If antimicrobial therapy is initiated in people with gastroenteritis, ampicillin, amoxicillin, or trimethoprim-sulfamethoxazole is recommended for susceptible strains. Resistance to these antimicrobial agents is becoming more frequent, especially in resource-limited countries. In areas where ampicillin and trimethoprim-sulfamethoxazole resistance is frequent, ceftriaxone, cefotaxime, or fluoroquinolones usually are effective. However, fluoroquinolones are not approved for this indication in people younger than 18 years of age and are not recommended unless the benefits of therapy outweigh the potential risks with use of the drug (see Antimicrobial Agents and Related Therapy, p 735).
- For people with localized invasive disease (eg, osteomyelitis, abscess, meningitis, or bacteremia in people infected with HIV), empiric therapy with an expanded-spectrum cephalosporin (cefotaxime or ceftriaxone) is recommended. Once antimicrobial susceptibility test results are available, ampicillin, ceftriaxone, or cefotaxime for susceptible strains is recommended for at least 4 weeks (for meningitis 6 weeks) to prevent relapse.
- For invasive, nonfocal infections, such as bacteremia or enteric fever, caused by nontyphoidal *Salmonella* or *S* serotype Typhi, 10 to 14 days of therapy is recommended. Drugs of choice, route of administration, and duration of therapy are

based on susceptibility of the organism, site of infection, host, and clinical response. Multidrug-resistant isolates of *S* serotype Typhi are common, often requiring empirical treatment with an expanded-spectrum cephalosporin, azithromycin, or a fluoroquinolone. Relapse of enteric fever occurs in up to 15% of patients and requires retreatment. Treatment failures have occurred in people treated with cephalosporins, aminoglycosides, and furazolidone, despite in vitro testing indicating susceptibility.

- Chronic (1 year or more) *S* serotype Typhi carriage, unusual in children, may be eradicated by high-dose parenteral ampicillin or high-dose oral amoxicillin combined with probenecid (see Antimicrobial Agents and Related Therapy, p 735). Ciprofloxacin is the drug of choice for elimination of organisms from adult carriers of *S* serotype Typhi. Cholecystectomy may be indicated in some adults in whom gallstones contribute to chronic carrier states.
- Corticosteroids may be beneficial in patients with severe enteric fever, which is characterized by delirium, obtundation, stupor, coma, or shock. These drugs should be reserved for critically ill patients in whom relief of the manifestations of toxemia may be life saving. The usual regimen is high-dose dexamethasone given intravenously at an initial dose of 3 mg/kg, followed by 1 mg/kg, every 6 hours, for a total course of 48 hours.

ISOLATION OF THE HOSPITALIZED PATIENT: In addition to standard precautions, contact precautions should be used for diapered and incontinent children for the duration of illness. In children with typhoid fever, precautions should be continued until culture results for 3 consecutive stool specimens obtained at least 48 hours after cessation of antimicrobial therapy are negative.

CONTROL MEASURES: Important measures include proper sanitation methods for food preparation, sanitary water supplies, proper hand hygiene, sanitary sewage disposal, exclusion of infected people from handling food or providing health care, prohibiting the sale of pet turtles and restricting the sale of other reptiles for pets, reporting cases to appropriate health authorities, and investigating outbreaks. Eggs and other foods of animal origin should be cooked thoroughly. People should not eat raw eggs or foods containing raw eggs. Notification of public health authorities and determination of serotype are of primary importance in detection and investigation of outbreaks.

CHILD CARE. Outbreaks of *Salmonella* infection are rare but have occurred in child care programs. Specific strategies for controlling infection in out-of-home child care include adherence to hygiene practices, including meticulous hand hygiene (see Children in Out-of-Home Child Care, p 130).

When *S* serotype Typhi infection is identified in a symptomatic child care attendee or staff member, stool cultures should be collected from other attendees and staff members, and all infected people should be excluded. The recommended length of exclusion varies with the infected person's age; for children younger than 5 years of age, 3 negative stool specimens are recommended for return. For people 5 years of age and older, 24 hours without a diarrheal stool is recommended before return to a group setting.

When serotypes other than *S* serotype Typhi are identified in a symptomatic child care attendee or staff member with enterocolitis, older children and staff do not need to be excluded unless they are symptomatic. Stool cultures are not required for asymptomatic contacts. Antimicrobial therapy is not recommended for people with asymptomatic infection or uncomplicated diarrhea or for people who are contacts of an infected person.

TYPHOID VACCINE. Resistance to infection with *S* serotype Typhi is enhanced by typhoid immunization, but the degree of protection with currently available vaccines is limited. Two typhoid vaccines are licensed for use in the United States (see Table 3.55).

The demonstrated efficacy of the 2 vaccines licensed by the US Food and Drug Administration ranges from 50% to 80%. Vaccine is selected on the basis of the age of the child, need for booster doses, and possible contraindications (see Precautions and Contraindications, p 584) and reactions (see Adverse Events, p 584).

Indications. In the United States, immunization is recommended only for the following people:

- **Travelers to areas where risk of exposure to *S* serotype Typhi is recognized.** Risk is greatest for travelers to the Indian subcontinent, Latin America, Asia, the Middle East, and Africa who may have prolonged exposure to contaminated food and drink. Such travelers need to be cautioned that typhoid vaccine is not a substitute for careful selection of food and drink (see **www.cdc.gov/travel**).
- **People with intimate exposure to a documented typhoid fever carrier,** such as occurs with continued household contact.
- **Laboratory workers with frequent contact with *S* serotype Typhi and people living in areas outside the United States with endemic typhoid infection.**

Dosages. For primary immunization, the following dosage is recommended for each vaccine:

- **Typhoid vaccine live oral Ty21a (Vivotif).** Children (6 years of age and older) and adults should take 1 enteric-coated capsule every 2 days for a total of 4 capsules. Each capsule should be taken with cool liquid, no warmer than 37°C (98°F), approximately 1 hour before a meal. The capsules must be kept refrigerated, and all 4 doses must be taken to achieve maximal efficacy. Immunization should be completed at least 1 week before possible exposure.
- **Typhoid Vi polysaccharide vaccine (Typhim Vi).** Primary immunization of people 2 years of age and older with Vi capsular polysaccharide (ViCPS) vac-

Table 3.55. Commercially Available Typhoid Vaccines in the United States

Typhoid Vaccine	Type	Route	Minimum Age of Receipt, y	No. of Doses[1]	Booster Frequency, y	Adverse Effects (Incidence, %)
Ty21a	Live-attenuated	Oral	6	4	5	<5
ViCPS	Polysaccharide	Intramuscular	2	1	2	<7

ViCPS indicates Vi capsular polysaccharide vaccine.

[1] Primary immunization. For further information on dosage, schedules, and adverse events, see text.

cine consists of one 0.5-mL (25-µg) dose administered intramuscularly. Vaccine should be given at least 2 weeks before possible exposure.

Booster Doses. In circumstances of continued or repeated exposure to *S* serotype Typhi, booster doses are recommended to maintain immunity after primary immunization. The optimal booster schedule for either vaccine has not been determined.

Continued efficacy for 5 years after immunization with the oral Ty21a vaccine has been demonstrated; however, the manufacturer of oral Ty21a vaccine recommends reimmunization, completing the entire 4-dose series every 5 years if continued or renewed exposure to *S* serotype Typhi is expected.

The manufacturer of ViCPS vaccine recommends a booster dose every 2 years after the primary dose if continued or renewed exposure is expected.

No data have been reported concerning the use of one vaccine as a booster after primary immunization with the other.

ADVERSE EVENTS. The oral Ty21a vaccine produces mild adverse reactions that may include abdominal discomfort, nausea, vomiting, fever, headache, and rash or urticaria. Reported adverse reactions to ViCPS vaccine also are minimal and include fever, headache, and local reaction of erythema or induration of 1 cm or greater.

PRECAUTIONS AND CONTRAINDICATIONS. No data are available regarding the efficacy of typhoid vaccines in children younger than 2 years of age. However, there is evidence that breastfeeding and meticulous preparation of formula might prevent typhoid infection in areas with endemic infection. A contraindication to administration of the parenteral ViCPS vaccine is a history of severe local or systemic reactions after a previous dose. No safety data have been reported for typhoid vaccines in pregnant women. The oral Ty21a vaccine is a live-attenuated vaccine and should not be administered to immunocompromised people, including people known to be infected with HIV; the parenteral ViCPS vaccine may be an alternative. The oral Ty21a vaccine requires replication in the gut for effectiveness; it should not be administered during gastrointestinal tract illness. Studies have demonstrated that simultaneous administration of either mefloquine or chloroquine with oral Ty21a results in an adequate immune response to the vaccine strain. However, the antimalarial proguanil should not be administered simultaneously with oral Ty21a vaccine but rather should be administered 10 or more days after the fourth dose of oral Ty21a vaccine. Atovaquone also can interfere with oral Ty21a immunogenicity. Antimicrobial agents should be avoided for 24 or more hours before the first dose of oral Ty21a vaccine and 7 days after the fourth dose of Ty21a vaccine.

Scabies

CLINICAL MANIFESTATIONS: Scabies is characterized by an intensely pruritic, erythematous, papular eruption caused by burrowing of adult female mites in upper layers of the epidermis, creating serpiginous burrows. Itching is most intense at night. In older children and adults, the sites of predilection are interdigital folds, flexor aspects of wrists, extensor surfaces of elbows, anterior axillary folds, waistline, thighs, navel, genitalia, areolae, abdomen, intergluteal cleft, and buttocks. In children younger than

2 years of age, the eruption generally is vesicular and often occurs in areas usually spared in older children and adults, such as the head, neck, palms, and soles. The eruption is caused by a hypersensitivity reaction to the proteins of the parasite.

The characteristic scabietic burrows appear as gray or white, tortuous, thread-like lines. Excoriations are common, and most burrows are obliterated by scratching before a patient is seen by a physician. Occasionally, 2- to 5-mm red-brown nodules are present, particularly on covered parts of the body, such as the genitalia, groin, and axilla. These scabies nodules are a granulomatous response to dead mite antigens and feces; the nodules can persist for weeks and even months after effective treatment. Cutaneous secondary bacterial infection can occur and usually is caused by *Streptococcus pyogenes* or *Staphylococcus aureus*.

Norwegian scabies is an uncommon clinical syndrome characterized by a large number of mites and widespread, crusted, hyperkeratotic lesions. Norwegian scabies usually occurs in debilitated, developmentally disabled, or immunologically compromised people but has occurred in otherwise healthy children after long-term use of topical corticosteroid therapy.

ETIOLOGY: The mite, *Sarcoptes scabiei* subspecies *hominis*, is the cause of scabies. *Sarcoptes scabiei* subspecies *canis*, acquired from dogs (with clinical mange), can cause a self-limited and mild infestation usually involving the area in direct contact with the infested animal that will resolve without specific treatment.

EPIDEMIOLOGY: Humans are the source of infestation. Transmission usually occurs through prolonged, close, personal contact. Because of the large number of mites in exfoliating scales, even minimal contact with a patient with crusted (Norwegian) scabies may result in transmission. Infestation acquired from dogs and other animals is uncommon, and these mites do not replicate in humans. Scabies of human origin can be transmitted as long as the patient remains infested and untreated, including the interval before symptoms develop. Scabies is endemic in many countries and occurs worldwide in cycles thought to be 15 to 30 years long. Scabies affects people from all socioeconomic levels without regard to age, sex, or standards of personal hygiene. Scabies in adults often is acquired sexually.

The **incubation period** in people without previous exposure usually is 4 to 6 weeks. People who previously were infested are sensitized and develop symptoms 1 to 4 days after repeated exposure to the mite; however, these reinfestations usually are milder than the original episode.

DIAGNOSTIC TESTS: Diagnosis is confirmed by identification of the mite or mite eggs or scybala (feces) from scrapings of papules or intact burrows, preferably from the terminal portion where the mite generally is found. Mineral oil, microscope immersion oil, or water applied to skin facilitates collection of scrapings. A broad blade scalpel is used to scrape the burrow. Scrapings and oil can be placed on a slide under a glass coverslip and examined microscopically under low power. Adult female mites average 330 to 450 μm in length.

TREATMENT: Infested children and adults should apply lotion or cream containing a scabicide over their entire body below the head. Because scabies can affect the head, scalp, and neck in infants and young children, treatment of the entire head, neck, and body in this age group is required. The drug of choice, particularly for infants, young children, and pregnant or nursing women, is 5% permethrin cream (not approved for children younger than 2 months of age), a synthetic pyrethroid. Alternative drugs are 10% crotamiton, ivermectin, or 1% lindane cream or lotion. Permethrin should be removed by bathing after 8 to 14 hours. Crotamiton is applied once a day for 2 days followed by a cleansing bath 48 hours after the last application, but crotamiton is associated with frequent treatment failures and has not been approved for use in children. Ivermectin in a single dose administered orally is effective for treatment of severe or crusted (Norwegian) scabies and should be considered for patients whose infestation is refractory or who cannot tolerate topical therapy. This drug is not approved for this indication by the US Food and Drug Administration.

Lindane preparations should be reserved for treatment of patients who fail to respond to other preparations. Lindane is contraindicated in patients with crusted scabies, preterm infants, people with known seizure disorders, people with hypersensitivity to the product, young infants, women who are pregnant or breastfeeding, and patients who have extensive dermatitis. Lindane should be used with caution in children weighing less than 50 kg and patients taking certain drugs that can decrease the threshold for seizures such as antipsychotics, antidepressants, and penicillins among others. The frequency of lindane applications should not exceed that recommended by the manufacturer to decrease the risk of possible neurologic toxic effects from absorption through skin. Lindane should not be used immediately after a bath or shower.

Because scabietic lesions are the result of a hypersensitivity reaction to the mite, itching may not subside for several weeks despite successful treatment. The use of oral antihistamines and topical corticosteroids can help relieve this itching. Topical or systemic antimicrobial therapy is indicated for secondary bacterial infections of the excoriated lesions.

ISOLATION OF THE HOSPITALIZED PATIENT: In addition to standard precautions, contact precautions are recommended until the patient has been treated with an appropriate scabicide.

CONTROL MEASURES:
- Prophylactic therapy is recommended for household members, particularly for household members who have had prolonged direct skin-to-skin contact. Manifestations of scabies infestation can appear as late as 2 months after exposure, during which time patients can transmit scabies. All household members should be treated at the same time to prevent reinfestation. Bedding and clothing worn next to the skin during the 3 days before initiation of therapy should be laundered in a washer with hot water and dried using a hot cycle. Mites do not survive more than 3 days without skin contact. Clothing that cannot be laundered should be removed from the patient and stored for several days to a week to avoid reinfestation.
- Children should be allowed to return to child care or school after treatment has been completed.
- Epidemics and localized outbreaks may require stringent and consistent measures to treat contacts. Caregivers who have had prolonged skin-to-skin contact with infested patients may benefit from prophylactic treatment.

- Environmental disinfestation is unnecessary and unwarranted. Thorough vacuuming of environmental surfaces is recommended after use of a room by a patient with crusted (Norwegian) scabies.
- People with crusted (Norwegian) scabies and their close contacts must be treated promptly and aggressively to avoid outbreaks.

Schistosomiasis

CLINICAL MANIFESTATIONS: Initial entry of the infecting larvae (cercariae) through skin commonly is accompanied by a transient, pruritic, papular rash (cercarial dermatitis). After penetration, the organism enters the bloodstream and migrates through the lungs. Each of the 3 major human schistosome parasites lives in some part of the venous plexus that drains the intestines or the bladder. Four to 8 weeks after exposure to *Schistosoma mansoni* or *Schistosoma japonicum,* an acute illness that manifests as fever, malaise, cough, rash, abdominal pain, hepatosplenomegaly, diarrhea, nausea, lymphadenopathy, and eosinophilia (Katayama fever) can develop. Heavy infection can result in mucoid bloody diarrhea accompanied by tender hepatomegaly. The severity of symptoms associated with chronic disease is related to the worm burden. People with low to moderate worm burdens may never develop overt clinical illness; people with significant worm burdens can have a range of symptoms caused primarily by inflammation and fibrosis triggered by eggs produced by adult worms. Portal hypertension can develop and cause hepatosplenomegaly, ascites, and esophageal varices and hematemesis. Long-term involvement of the colon produces abdominal pain and bloody diarrhea. In *Schistosoma haematobium* infections, the bladder can become inflamed and fibrotic. Symptoms and signs include dysuria, urgency, terminal microscopic and gross hematuria, secondary urinary tract infections, and nonspecific pelvic pain. An association between *S haematobium* and bladder cancer has been reported. Other organ systems can be involved from embolized eggs, for example, to the lungs, causing pulmonary hypertension; or to the central nervous system, notably the spinal cord in *S mansoni* or *S haematobium* infections and the brain in *S japonicum* infection.

Swimmer's itch (cercarial dermatitis or schistosome dermatitis) is caused by the larvae of other avian and mammalian schistosome species that penetrate human skin but do not complete the life cycle and do not cause chronic fibrotic disease. Manifestations include mild to moderate pruritus at the penetration site a few hours after exposure, followed in 5 to 14 days by an intermittent pruritic, sometimes papular, eruption. In previously sensitized people, more intense papular eruptions may occur for 7 to 10 days after exposure.

ETIOLOGY: The trematodes (flukes) *S mansoni, S japonicum, S haematobium,* and rarely, *Schistosoma mekongi* and *Schistosoma intercalatum* cause disease. All species have similar life cycles. Swimmer's itch is caused by multiple avian and mammalian species of *Schistosoma.*

EPIDEMIOLOGY: Humans are the principal hosts for the major species. Persistence of schistosomiasis depends on the presence of an appropriate snail as an intermediate host. Eggs excreted in stool (*S mansoni, S japonicum, S mekongi,* and *S intercalatum*) or urine *(S haematobium)* into fresh water hatch into motile miracidia, which infect snails.

After development in snails, cercariae emerge and penetrate the skin of humans encountered in the water. Children commonly are infected after infancy when they begin to explore the environment. Children also are involved in transmission because of habits of uncontrolled defecation and urination and frequent wading in infected waters. Communicability lasts as long as live eggs are excreted in the urine and feces.

Schistosoma mansoni occurs throughout tropical Africa, in several Caribbean islands, and in Venezuela, Brazil, Suriname, and the Arabian Peninsula. *Schistosoma japonicum* is found in China, the Philippines, and Indonesia. *Schistosoma haematobium* occurs in Africa and the eastern Mediterranean region. *Schistosoma mekongi* is found in Cambodia, Laos, Japan, the Philippines, and Central Indonesia. *Schistosoma intercalatum* is found in West and Central Africa. Adult worms of *S mansoni* can live as long as 30 years in the human host. Thus, schistosomiasis can be diagnosed in patients many years after they have left an area with endemic infection. Swimmer's itch occurs in all regions of the world after exposure to fresh, brackish, or saltwater-containing larvae that do not complete their life cycle in humans. Immunity does not develop after infection; thus, reinfection commonly occurs.

The **incubation period** is variable but is approximately 4 to 6 weeks for *S japonicum*, 6 to 8 weeks for *S mansoni*, and 10 to 12 weeks for *S haematobium*.

DIAGNOSTIC TESTS: Infection with *S mansoni* and other species (except *S haematobium*) is determined by microscopic examination of concentrated stool specimens to detect characteristic eggs. In light infections, several specimens may need to be examined before eggs are found, or a biopsy of the rectal mucosa may be necessary. *Schistosoma haematobium* is diagnosed by examining filtered urine for eggs. Egg excretion often peaks between noon and 3 PM. Biopsy of the bladder mucosa may be necessary. Serologic tests, available through the Centers for Disease Control and Prevention and some commercial laboratories, are 99%, 90%, and 50% sensitive for detecting infection attributable to *S mansoni*, *S haematobium*, and *S japonicum*, respectively. Specific serologic tests may be particularly helpful for detecting light infections or before eggs appear in the stool or urine. These tests remain positive for many years and are not useful in differentiating ongoing infection from past infection or reinfection.

Swimmer's itch can be difficult to differentiate from other causes of dermatitis. A skin biopsy may demonstrate larvae, but their absence does not exclude the diagnosis.

TREATMENT: The drug of choice for schistosomiasis caused by any species is praziquantel; the alternative drug for *S mansoni* is oxamniquine (see Drugs for Parasitic Infections, p 790). Praziquantel does not kill developing worms; therapy given during the 4 to 8 weeks of exposure should be repeated 1 to 2 months later. Swimmer's itch is a self-limited disease that requires only symptomatic treatment of the urticarial rash.

ISOLATION OF THE HOSPITALIZED PATIENT: Standard precautions are recommended.

CONTROL MEASURES: Elimination of the intermediate snail host is difficult to achieve in most areas. Thus, treatment of infected populations, sanitary disposal of human waste, and education about the source of infection are the key elements of current control measures. Travelers to areas with endemic infection should be advised to avoid contact with freshwater streams and lakes.

Shigella Infections

CLINICAL MANIFESTATIONS: *Shigella* species primarily infect the large intestine, causing clinical manifestations that range from watery or loose stools with minimal or no constitutional symptoms to more severe symptoms, including fever, abdominal cramps or tenderness, tenesmus, and mucoid stools with or without blood. Clinical presentations vary with *Shigella* species; patients with *Shigella sonnei* infection usually exhibit watery diarrhea; people with *Shigella flexneri*, *Shigella boydii*, and *Shigella dysenteriae* infection typically have bloody diarrhea and severe systemic symptoms. Rare complications include bacteremia, Reiter syndrome (after *S flexneri* infection), hemolytic-uremic syndrome (after *S dysenteriae* type 1 infection), toxic megacolon and intestinal perforation, and toxic encephalopathy (ekiri syndrome).

ETIOLOGY: *Shigella* species are aerobic, gram-negative bacilli in the family Enterobacteriaceae. Four species (with more than 40 serotypes) have been identified. Among *Shigella* isolates reported in the United States in 2003, approximately 88% were *S sonnei*, 11% were *S flexneri*, 1% were *S boydii*, and 0.3% were *S dysenteriae*. *Shigella dysenteriae* is rare in the United States but is endemic in rural Africa and the Indian subcontinent.

EPIDEMIOLOGY: Humans are the natural host for *Shigella*, although other primates may be infected. The primary mode of transmission is fecal-oral. Children 5 years of age or younger in child care settings, their caregivers, and other people living in crowded conditions are at increased risk of infection. Travel to resource-limited countries with inadequate sanitation may place the traveler at risk of infection. Ingestion of as few as 10 to 200 organisms is sufficient for infection to occur, depending on *Shigella* species. Predominant modes of transmission include person-to-person contact, contact with a contaminated inanimate object, ingestion of contaminated food or water, and sexual contact. Houseflies also may be vectors through physical transport of infected feces. *Shigella flexneri*, *S boydii*, and *S dysenteriae* infections are more common in older children and adults, and these infections often are associated with sources outside the United States. Transmission can occur as long as the organism is present in feces. Even without antimicrobial therapy, the carrier state usually ceases within 4 weeks of the onset of illness; chronic carriage (>1 year) is rare.

The **incubation period** varies from 1 to 7 days but typically is 2 to 4 days.

DIAGNOSTIC TESTS: Isolation of *Shigella* from feces or rectal swab specimens containing feces is diagnostic but lacks sensitivity. The presence of fecal leukocytes on a methylene-blue stained stool smear is sensitive for the diagnosis of colitis but is not specific for *Shigella* species. An enzyme immunoassay for Shiga toxin may be useful for detection of *S dysenteriae* type 1 in stool. Although bacteremia is rare, blood should be cultured in severely ill, immunocompromised, or malnourished patients. Other testing modalities, including the fluorescent antibody test, polymerase chain reaction assay, and enzyme-linked DNA probes, are available in research laboratories.

TREATMENT:
- Most clinical infections with *Shigella sonnei* are self-limited (48–72 hours) and do not require antimicrobial therapy. However, antimicrobial therapy is effective in

shortening the duration of diarrhea and eradicating organisms from feces. Treatment is recommended for patients with severe disease, dysentery, or underlying immunosuppressive conditions; in these patients, empirical therapy should be given while awaiting culture and susceptibility results. In mild disease, the primary indication for treatment is to prevent spread of the organism.

- Antimicrobial susceptibility testing of clinical isolates is indicated, because resistance to antimicrobial agents is common and susceptibility data can guide appropriate therapy. Plasmid-mediated resistance has been identified in all *Shigella* species. In the United States, sentinel surveillance data in 2002 indicated that 77% of *Shigella* species were resistant to ampicillin, 37% were resistant to trimethoprim-sulfamethoxazole, and <1% were resistant to ceftriaxone and ciprofloxacin (**www.cdc.gov/narms**).

- For cases in which susceptibility is unknown or an ampicillin and trimethoprim-sulfamethoxazole–resistant strain is isolated, parenteral ceftriaxone, a fluoroquinolone (such as ciprofloxacin), or azithromycin may be given. Oral cephalosporins are not useful for treatment, although one study suggested limited effectiveness for cefixime. Fluoroquinolones are not recommended for use in people younger than 18 years of age except in circumstances in which potential risks are less than potential benefits (see Antimicrobial Agents and Related Therapy, p 735). For susceptible strains, ampicillin and trimethoprim-sulfamethoxazole are effective; amoxicillin is less effective because of its rapid absorption from the gastrointestinal tract. The oral route of therapy is recommended except for seriously ill patients.

- Antimicrobial therapy typically is administered for 5 days.

- Antidiarrheal compounds that inhibit intestinal peristalsis are contraindicated, because they may prolong the clinical and bacteriologic course of disease.

- Nutritional supplementation, including vitamin A (200 000 IU), can be given to hasten clinical resolution in geographic areas where children are at risk of malnutrition.

ISOLATION OF THE HOSPITALIZED PATIENT: In addition to standard precautions, contact precautions are indicated for the duration of illness.

CONTROL MEASURES:

CHILD CARE CENTERS. General measures for interrupting enteric transmission in child care centers are recommended (see Children in Out-of-Home Child Care, p 130). Meticulous hand hygiene is the single most important measure to decrease transmission. Waterless hand sanitizers may be an effective option in circumstances where access to soap or clean water is limited. Eliminating access to shared water-play areas and contaminated diapers also can decrease infection rates.

When *Shigella* infection is identified in a child care attendee or staff member, stool specimens from other symptomatic attendees and staff members should be cultured. Stool specimens from household contacts who have diarrhea also should be cultured. All symptomatic people whose stool specimens yield *Shigella* should receive appropriate antimicrobial therapy (see Treatment, p 589) and should not be permitted to reenter the child care facility until diarrhea has ceased and stool cultures test negative for *Shigella*.

INSTITUTIONAL OUTBREAKS. The most difficult outbreaks to control are those that involve young children (not yet toilet-trained), adults who are unable to care for themselves (mentally disabled people or skilled nursing facility residents), or an inadequate water supply.

A cohort system, combined with appropriate antimicrobial therapy, and a strong emphasis on hand hygiene, should be considered until stool cultures no longer yield *Shigella* species. In residential institutions, ill people and newly admitted patients should be housed in separate areas.

GENERAL CONTROL MEASURES. Strict attention to hand hygiene is essential to limit spread. Other important control measures include improved sanitation, a safe water supply through chlorination, proper cooking and storage of food, the exclusion of infected people as food handlers, and measures to decrease contamination of food by houseflies. People with diarrhea caused by this potentially waterborne pathogen should not use recreational water venues (eg, swimming pools, lakes, rivers, the ocean) for 2 weeks after symptoms resolve. Breastfeeding provides protection for infants. Case reporting to appropriate health authorities (eg, hospital infection control personnel and public health department) is essential.

Smallpox (Variola)

In 1979, the World Health Organization declared that smallpox (variola) had been eradicated successfully worldwide. The last naturally occurring case of smallpox occurred in Somalia in 1977, followed by 2 cases attributable to laboratory exposure in 1978. The United States discontinued routine childhood immunization against smallpox in 1972 and routine immunization of health care professionals in 1976. The US military continued to immunize military personnel until 1995. Since 1980, the vaccine has been recommended only for people working with nonvariola orthopoxviruses. Two World Health Organization reference laboratories were authorized to maintain stocks of variola virus. There is concern that the virus and the expertise to use it as a weapon of bioterrorism may have been misappropriated.

CLINICAL MANIFESTATIONS: An individual infected with variola major develops a severe prodromal illness characterized by high fever (102°F–104°F [38.9°C–40.0°C]) and constitutional symptoms, including malaise, severe headache, backache, abdominal pain, and prostration, lasting for 2 to 5 days. Abdominal pain and back pain may be mistaken for focal pathology. Infected children may suffer from vomiting and seizures during this prodromal period. Most patients with smallpox tend to be severely ill and bedridden during the febrile prodrome. The prodromal period is followed by enanthemas (lesions on the mucosa of the mouth or pharynx), which may not be noticed by the patient. This stage occurs less than 24 hours before the onset of rash, which usually is the first recognized manifestation of infectiousness. With the onset of enanthemas, the patient becomes infectious and remains so until all skin crust lesions have separated. The exanthem, or rash, typically begins on the face and rapidly progresses to involve the forearms, trunk, and legs in a centrifugal distribution (greatest concentration of lesions on the face and distal extremities). Many patients will have lesions on the palms and soles. With rash onset, fever decreases but the patient does not defervesce fully. Lesions begin as maculae that progress to papules, then firm vesicles, and then deep-seated, hard pustules described as "pearls of pus," with each stage lasting 1 to 2 days. By the sixth or seventh day of rash, lesions may begin to umbilicate or become confluent. Lesions increase in size for approximately 8 to 10 days, after which they begin to crust. Once all the lesions have separated, 3 to 4 weeks after the onset of rash, the patient no longer is infectious. Infected people sustain significant scarring after separation of the crusts. Because of the relatively slow and steady evolution of rash lesions, all lesions on any one part of the body are in the same stage of development. Variola minor is clinically indistinguishable except that it causes fewer systemic symptoms, less extensive rash, little persistent scarring, and fewer fatalities.

Varicella (chickenpox) is the condition most likely to be mistaken for smallpox. Generally, children with varicella do not have a febrile prodrome; adults may have a brief, mild prodrome. Although the 2 diseases are confused easily in the first few days of the rash, smallpox lesions develop into pustules that are firm and deeply embedded in the dermis, whereas varicella lesions develop into superficial vesicles. Because varicella erupts in crops of lesions that evolve quickly, lesions on any one part of the body will be in different stages of evolution (papules, vesicles, and crusts). The rash distribution of the 2 diseases differ. Varicella most commonly affects the face and trunk with relative sparing of the extremities, and lesions on the palms or soles are rare.

In addition to the typical presentation of smallpox ($\geq$90% of cases), there are 2 uncommon forms of variola major: hemorrhagic (characterized by hemorrhage into skin lesions and disseminated intravascular coagulation) and malignant or flat type (in which the skin lesions do not progress to the pustular stage but remain flat and soft). Each variant occurred in approximately 5% of cases and was associated with a 95% to 100% mortality rate. Hemorrhagic smallpox rash commonly was confused with meningococcemia or hemorrhagic hematologic disease (ie, leukemia). Flat-type (velvety) smallpox occurred more commonly in children. By contrast, variola minor, or alastrim, was associated with fewer lesions, more rapid progression of rash, and a much lower mortality rate (approximately 1%) than variola major or typical smallpox.

Variola major in unimmunized people was associated with case fatality rates of 30% during epidemics of smallpox. The mortality rate was highest in children younger than 1 year of age and adults older than 30 years of age. The potential for modern supportive therapy in improving outcome is not known. Death was most likely to occur during the second week of illness and has been attributed to cytopathic effects from viral damage and inflammation. Secondary bacterial infections occurred but were a less significant cause of mortality.

ETIOLOGY: Variola is a member of the Poxviridae family (genus *Orthopoxvirus*). These DNA viruses are among the largest and most complex viruses known and differ from most other DNA viruses by multiplying in the cytoplasm. Monkeypox, vaccinia, and cowpox are other members of the genus and can cause zoonotic infection of humans but usually do not spread from person to person. Humans are the only natural reservoir for variola virus (smallpox). Although the original vaccine used by Edward Jenner contained cowpox virus, the current vaccine contains vaccinia virus.

EPIDEMIOLOGY: Smallpox is spread most commonly in droplets from the oropharynx of infected individuals, although rare transmission from aerosol and direct contact with infected lesions, clothing, or bedding has been reported. Patients are not infectious during the incubation period or febrile prodrome but become infectious with the onset of mucosal lesions (enanthemas), which occur within hours of the rash. The first week of rash illness is regarded as the most infectious period, although patients remain infectious until all scabs have separated. Because most patients with smallpox are extremely ill and bedridden, spread generally is limited to household contacts, hospital workers, and other health care professionals. Secondary household attack rates for smallpox were considerably lower than for measles and similar to, or lower than, the rates for varicella.

The **incubation period** is 7 to 17 days (mean, 12 days).

DIAGNOSTIC TESTS: Variola virus can be detected in vesicular or pustular fluid by culture or by polymerase chain reaction assay. Electron microscopy detects orthopoxvirus infection but cannot distinguish between viruses. Variola diagnostic testing is conducted only at the Centers for Disease Control and Prevention (CDC), and screening is available through state health departments. Confirmatory testing is performed at the CDC. If a patient is suspected of having smallpox, standard, contact, and airborne precautions should be implemented immediately, and the state (and/or local) health department should be alerted at once. Reports of patients classified by the CDC as at high risk of having smallpox will trigger a rapid response with a team deployed to obtain specimens and advise on clinical management.

TREATMENT: There is no known effective antiviral therapy available to treat smallpox. Infected patients should receive supportive care. Cidofovir, licensed for cytomegalovirus retinitis, has been suggested as having a role in smallpox therapy, but data to support its use in smallpox are not available. The drug is associated with significant renal toxicity. Vaccinia Immune Globulin (VIG) is reserved for certain complications of immunization and has no role in treatment of smallpox.

ISOLATION OF THE HOSPITALIZED PATIENT: Standard, contact, and airborne precautions are essential for any patient suspected of having smallpox. On admission, hospital infection control personnel should be notified, and the patient should be placed in a private, airborne infection isolation room equipped with negative-pressure ventilation with high-efficiency particulate air filtration. Anyone entering the room must wear an N95 or higher quality respirator, gloves, and gown, even if there is a history of recent successful immunization. If the patient leaves the room, he or she should wear a mask and be covered with sheets or gowns to decrease the risk of fomite transmission. Rooms vacated by patients should be decontaminated using standard hospital disinfectants, such as sodium hypochlorite or quaternary ammonia solutions. Laundry and waste should be discarded into biohazard bags and autoclaved, and bedding and clothing should be laundered in hot water with laundry detergent followed by hot air drying or incinerated.

CONTROL MEASURES

CARE OF EXPOSED PEOPLE. Cases of febrile rash illness, for which smallpox is considered in the differential diagnosis, should be reported immediately to local or state health departments. After evaluation by the state or local health department, if smallpox laboratory diagnostics are considered necessary, the CDC Rash Illness

Evaluation Team should be consulted at 770-488-7100. Laboratory confirmation of smallpox is available only at the CDC.

Use of vaccine. Postexposure immunization (within 3–4 days of exposure) provides some protection against disease and significant protection against a fatal outcome. Any person with a significant exposure to a patient with proven smallpox during the infectious stage of illness requires immunization as soon after exposure as possible, but within 4 days of first exposure. Because infected individuals are not contagious until the rash (and/or enanthema) appears, individuals exposed only during the prodromal period are not at risk.

PREEXPOSURE IMMUNIZATION OF ADULTS.

Smallpox vaccine.[*] The only smallpox vaccine licensed in the United States is a lyophilized, live vaccinia virus prepared from the New York City Board of Health strain. The vaccine does not contain variola virus but contains a related virus called vaccinia virus, distinct from the cowpox virus initially used for immunization by Jenner. Vaccinia vaccine is highly effective in preventing smallpox, with protection waning after 5 to 10 years after 1 dose; protection after reimmunization has lasted longer. However, substantial protection against death from smallpox persisted in the past for more than 30 years after immunization during infancy on the basis of experience at a time of worldwide smallpox virus circulation and routine smallpox immunization practices. A smallpox immunization plan has been implemented in the United States (**www.bt.cdc.gov**). The plan does not include immunization of children.[†] However, children may be at risk of vaccine complications as contacts of vaccinees. Blood donation should be deferred for 21 days after immunization or until the scab has separated. Tuberculin skin testing should be deferred for 1 month after immunization.

Administration. Vaccine is administered using a bifurcated needle to deliver vaccine into the epidermis. Vaccine is held by capillarity between the 2 tines of the needle. Three skin insertions are used for primary vaccinees; 15 for repeat vaccinees. Vaccine "take" is determined by the cutaneous reaction to the immunization: a papule should be evident at the immunization site at 3 to 5 days and should progress to a vesicle at 5 to 8 days, then a pustule reaching maximum size in 8 to 10 days. The lesion scabs and heals after 14 to 21 days, leaving a scar. There may be associated swelling, intense erythema, lymphangitis, and tenderness of regional lymph nodes. Satellite lesions at the perimeter of the immunization site may occur. People occupationally exposed to vaccinia virus (the virus in the vaccine), recombinant vaccinia viruses, or other nonvariola orthopoxviruses should be immunized every 10 years.

Adverse events.[‡] Fever is common after immunization (as many as 70% of children) and less common after reimmunization (35%). A variety of benign rashes, sometimes collectively termed erythema multiforme, may occur. Other rashes, such as folliculitis, also have been described. Inadvertent inoculation of vaccinia virus by con-

---

[*] Centers for Disease Control and Prevention. Recommendations for using smallpox vaccine in a pre-event vaccination program. *MMWR Recomm Rep.* 2003;52(RR-7):1–16

[†] American Academy of Pediatrics, Committee on Infectious Diseases. Policy statement: smallpox vaccine. *Pediatrics.* 2002;110:841–845. Available at: **http://aappolicy.aapjournals.org/cgi/content/full/pediatrics;110/4/841**

[‡] Centers for Disease Control and Prevention. Surveillance guidelines for smallpox vaccine (vaccinia) adverse reactions. *MMWR Recomm Rep.* 2006;55(RR-1):1–16

tact from the site of immunization to the face, eyes, or other sites is a common serious complication. Transmission of vaccinia virus from a recently immunized individual to a susceptible contact, including children, can occur.

Acute myopericarditis after smallpox immunization is the most frequent serious adverse event and has been observed to occur at rates as high as 1 case per 150 adult primary immunizations in well-monitored clinical trials. The rate of myopericarditis among children receiving smallpox vaccine is unknown. Myopericarditis can be symptomatic or asymptomatic and usually occurs 3 to 25 days after immunization. Myopericarditis after smallpox immunization is self-limiting. It is unknown whether long-term complications are associated with myopericarditis after smallpox immunization. Ischemic cardiac events, including fatalities, after smallpox immunization have been reported. The relationship of these events, if any, to smallpox immunization is unknown.

Other rare serious complications include Stevens-Johnson syndrome, postvaccinal encephalitis and encephalopathy, vaccinia keratitis, progressive vaccinia (vaccinia gangrenosa), eczema vaccinatum, and generalized vaccinia.

Vaccinia Immune Globulin (VIG) is indicated for certain complications of smallpox immunization. The CDC should be contacted if VIG is needed or additional information is required regarding indications and/or investigational use of other antiviral drugs. Physicians in civilian medical facilities may call the CDC Smallpox Vaccine Adverse Events Clinical Information Line at 877-554-4625.

Precautions and Contraindications*: In the absence of a smallpox emergency, smallpox vaccine should not be administered to (1) people who are allergic to any component of the vaccine; (2) people younger than 18 years of age; (3) people with eczema, history of eczema, or other active acute, chronic, or exfoliative skin conditions that disrupt the dermis; (4) people receiving immunosuppressive therapy or radiation and household contacts of such people; (5) people with congenital or acquired immune system deficiencies and household contacts of such people; (6) pregnant women or household contacts of pregnant women; and (7) people with known cardiac disease. In the event of a smallpox emergency, there are no absolute contraindications for people with a high-risk exposure to smallpox. The most recent CDC recommendations for the use of smallpox vaccine can be found at **www.cdc. gov/smallpox**.

Sporotrichosis

CLINICAL MANIFESTATIONS: Sporotrichosis manifests most commonly as the lymphocutaneous form. Inoculation occurs at a site of minor trauma, causing a painless papule that enlarges slowly to become a nodular lesion that can develop a violaceous hue or can ulcerate. Secondary lesions follow the same evolution and develop along the lymphatic distribution proximal to the initial lesion. Fixed cutaneous sporotrichosis, common in children, presents as a solitary crusted papule, papuloulcerative or nodular lesion in which lymphatic spread is not observed. The extremities and face

---

* Centers for Disease Control and Prevention. Smallpox vaccination and adverse events. *MMWR Dispatch.* 2003;52:1–29.

are the most common sites of infection in children. A disseminated cutaneous form is rare, usually occurring in children with immunocompromise.

Extracutaneous sporotrichosis commonly affects bones and joints, particularly those of the hands, elbows, ankles, or knees, but any organ can be affected. Osteoarticular structures are involved after local inoculation or hematogenous spread. Disseminated disease generally occurs after hematogenous spread from primary skin or lung infection. Disseminated sporotrichosis may involve multiple foci (eg, eyes, genitourinary system, or central nervous system) and occurs predominantly in immunocompromised patients. Pulmonary sporotrichosis clinically resembles tuberculosis and occurs after inhalation or aspiration of aerosolized spores. Pulmonary and disseminated sporotrichosis are uncommon in children.

ETIOLOGY: *Sporothrix schenckii* is a thermally dimorphic fungus that grows as a mold at room temperature and as a yeast at 37°C (98°F) and in host tissues.

EPIDEMIOLOGY: *Sporothrix schenckii* is a ubiquitous organism that has worldwide distribution but is most common in tropical and subtropical regions of Central and South America and parts of North America. The fungus is isolated from soil and plants, including hay, straw, thorny plants (especially roses), sphagnum moss, and decaying vegetation. Cutaneous disease occurs from inoculation of debris containing the organism. People engaging in gardening or farming are at risk of infection. Inhalation of spores can lead to pulmonary disease. Rarely, transmission from infected cats has led to cutaneous disease.

The **incubation period** is 7 to 30 days after cutaneous inoculation but may be as long as 3 months.

DIAGNOSTIC TESTS: Culture of *S schenckii* from a tissue, wound drainage, or sputum specimen is diagnostic of infection. Culture of *S schenckii* from a blood specimen suggests the disseminated form of infection associated with immunodeficiency. Histopathologic examination of tissue may not be helpful because the organism seldom is abundant. Special fungal stains to visualize the oval or cigar-shaped organism are required. A latex agglutination assay for detection of *Sporothrix* antigen in serum or cerebrospinal fluid is available commercially. Serologic testing and polymerase chain reaction assay show promise for accurate and specific diagnosis but are available only in research laboratories.

TREATMENT: Sporotrichosis usually does not resolve without treatment. Itraconazole is the drug of choice for lymphocutaneous and fixed cutaneous disease in adults. For extracutaneous disease, amphotericin B or itraconazole are the drugs of choice. There are no controlled trials to document the efficacy of itraconazole in pediatric patients (see Recommended Doses of Parenteral and Oral Antifungal Drugs, p 777). The duration of therapy is 3 to 6 months. Oral fluconazole is less effective. The organism is less susceptible to voriconazole than itraconazole, but clinical data are lacking. The time-honored treatment for sporotrichosis, a saturated solution of potassium iodide, is much less costly and still is recommended as an alternative treatment. Saturated solution of potassium iodide is given orally until several weeks after all lesions are healed. Itraconazole is the treatment of choice for osteoarticular infection, because this form of sporotrichosis rarely is accompanied by systemic illness; therapy should be continued for 12 months. Amphotericin B and itraconazole are treatment options for pulmonary infections, depending on severity. Amphotericin B is the drug of choice for disseminated sporotrichosis, including meningeal sporotrichosis, and infection in children with immunodeficiency, including human immunodeficiency virus infection. Itraconazole may be required for lifelong maintenance therapy after initial treatment with amphotericin B in children with HIV infection. Pulmonary and disseminated infection respond less well than cutaneous infection, despite prolonged therapy. Surgical debridement or excision may be necessary to achieve resolution of cavitary pulmonary disease.

ISOLATION OF HOSPITALIZED PATIENTS: Standard precautions are indicated.

CONTROL MEASURES: Use of protective gloves and clothing in occupational and avocational activities associated with infection can decrease risk of disease.

Staphylococcal Food Poisoning

CLINICAL MANIFESTATIONS: Staphylococcal foodborne illness is characterized by the abrupt and sometimes violent onset of severe nausea, abdominal cramps, vomiting, and prostration, often accompanied by diarrhea. Low-grade fever or mild hypothermia can occur. The duration of illness typically is 1 to 2 days, but the intensity of symptoms may require hospitalization. The short incubation period, brevity of illness, and usual lack of fever help distinguish staphylococcal from other types of food poisoning except that caused by *Bacillus cereus*. Chemical food poisoning usually has an even shorter incubation period. *Clostridium perfringens* food poisoning usually has a longer incubation period and is not commonly accompanied by vomiting. Patients with foodborne *Salmonella* or *Shigella* infection usually have fever and a longer incubation period (see Appendix VI, Clinical Syndromes Associated With Foodborne Diseases, p 857).

ETIOLOGY: Enterotoxins produced by strains of *Staphylococcus aureus* and, rarely, *Staphylococcus epidermidis* elicit the symptoms of staphylococcal food poisoning. Of the 8 immunologically distinct heat-stable enterotoxins (A, B, C1–3, D, E, and F), enterotoxin A is the most commonly identified cause of staphylococcal food poisoning outbreaks in the United States.

EPIDEMIOLOGY: Illness is caused by ingestion of food containing staphylococcal enterotoxins. Foods usually implicated are those that come in contact with hands of food handlers without food subsequently being cooked or foods that are inadequately heated or refrigerated, such as pastries, custards, salad dressings, sandwiches, poultry, sliced meats, and meat products. When these foods remain at room temperature for several hours before being eaten, toxin-producing staphylococci multiply and produce heat-stable toxin. The organisms may be of human origin from purulent discharges of an infected finger or eye, abscesses, acneiform facial eruptions, nasopharyngeal secretions, or apparently normal skin or, less commonly, may be of bovine origin, such as contaminated milk or milk products, especially cheese.

The **incubation period** ranges from 30 minutes to 8 hours, usually 2 to 4 hours.

DIAGNOSTIC TESTS: Recovery of large numbers of staphylococci or of enterotoxin from stool or vomitus supports the diagnosis. In an outbreak setting, demonstration of either enterotoxin or a large number of staphylococci ($>10^5$ colony-forming units/g of specimen) in an epidemiologically implicated food confirms the diagnosis. Identification (by pulsed-field gel electrophoresis or phage typing) of the same type of *S aureus* from stool or vomitus of 2 or more ill people, from stool or vomitus of an ill person and an implicated food, or stool or vomitus of an ill person and a person who handled the food also confirms the diagnosis. Local health authorities should be notified to help determine the source of the outbreak.

TREATMENT: Antimicrobial agents are not indicated. Treatment is supportive.

ISOLATION OF THE HOSPITALIZED PATIENT: Standard precautions are recommended.

CONTROL MEASURES: Prompt consumption or immediate cooling or refrigeration of cooked or baked foods will help to prevent the illness. Cooked foods should be refrigerated at temperatures less than 5°C (41°F). People with boils, abscesses, and other purulent lesions of the hands, face, or nose should be excluded temporarily from handling food. Strict hand hygiene before food handling should be enforced.

Staphylococcal Infections

CLINICAL MANIFESTATIONS: *Staphylococcus aureus* causes a variety of localized and invasive suppurative infections and 3 toxin-mediated syndromes: toxic shock syndrome (see Toxic Shock Syndrome, p 660), scalded skin syndrome, and food poisoning (see Staphylococcal Food Poisoning, p 597). Localized infections include hordeola, furuncles, carbuncles, impetigo (bullous and nonbullous), paronychia, ecthyma, cellulitis, omphalitis, parotitis, lymphadenitis, and wound infections. *Staphylococcus aureus* also causes foreign body infections, including infections associated with intravascular catheters or grafts, pacemakers, peritoneal catheters, cerebrospinal fluid shunts, and prosthetic joints, which can be associated with bacteremia. Bacteremia can be complicated by septicemia; endocarditis; pericarditis; pneumonia; pleural empyema; soft tissue, muscle, or visceral abscesses; arthritis; osteomyelitis; septic thrombophlebitis of large vessels; and other foci of infection. Meningitis is rare. *Staphylococcus aureus* infections can be fulminant and commonly are associated with metastatic foci and abscess formation, often requiring prolonged antimicrobial therapy, drainage, and foreign body removal to achieve cure. Risk factors for severe *S aureus* infections include chronic diseases, such as diabetes mellitus and cirrhosis, immunodeficiency, nutritional disorders, surgery, and transplantation.

Staphylococcal scalded skin syndrome (SSSS) is a toxin-mediated disease caused by circulation of exfoliative toxins A and B produced by *S aureus*. The manifestations of SSSS are age related and include Ritter disease (generalized exfoliation) in the neonate, a tender scarlatiniform eruption and localized bullous impetigo in older children, and a combination of these with thick white/brown flaky desquamation of the entire skin, especially on the face and neck, in older infants and toddlers. The hallmark of SSSS is the toxin-mediated cleavage of the stratum granulosum layer of the epidermis. Healing occurs without scarring. Bacteremia is rare, but dehydration and superinfection can occur with extensive exfoliation.

COAGULASE-NEGATIVE STAPHYLOCOCCI. Most coagulase-negative staphylococci (CoNS) isolates from patient specimens represent contamination of culture material (see Diagnostic Tests, p 602). Of the isolates that do not represent contamination, most come from infections that are health care associated, in patients who have obvious disruptions of host defenses caused by surgery, medical device insertion, or immunosuppression. Coagulase-negative staphylococci are the most common cause of late-onset septicemia among preterm infants, especially infants weighing less than 1500 g at birth, and of episodes of health care-associated bacteremia in all age groups. Coagulase-negative staphylococci are responsible for bacteremia in children undergoing treatment for leukemia, lymphoma, or solid tumors as well as in stem cell transplant recipients. Infections often are associated with intravascular catheters, cerebrospinal fluid shunts, peritoneal or urinary catheters, vascular grafts or intracardiac patches, prosthetic cardiac valves, pacemaker wires, or prosthetic joints. Mediastinitis after open-heart surgery, endophthalmitis after intraocular trauma, and omphalitis and scalp abscesses in neonates have been described. Coagulase-negative staphylococci also can enter the bloodstream from the respiratory tract of mechanically ventilated preterm infants or from the gastrointestinal tract of infants with necrotizing enterocolitis. Some species of CoNS are associated with urinary tract infection, including *Staphylococcus saprophyticus* in adolescent girls and young adult women, often after sexual intercourse, and *Staphylococcus epidermidis* and *Staphylococcus haemolyticus* in hospitalized patients with urinary tract catheters. In general, CoNS infections have an indolent clinical course in children with intact immune function and even in children who are immunocompromised.

ETIOLOGY: Staphylococci are catalase-positive, gram-positive cocci that appear microscopically as grape-like clusters. There are 32 species that are related closely on the basis of DNA base composition, but only 17 species are indigenous to humans. *Staphylococcus aureus* is the only species that produces coagulase. Of the 16 CoNS, *S epidermidis, S haemolyticus, S saprophyticus, Staphylococcus schleiferi*, and *Staphylococcus lugdunensis* most often are associated with human infections. Staphylococci are ubiquitous and can survive extreme conditions of drying, heat, and low-oxygen and high-salt environments. *Staphylococcus aureus* has many surface proteins, including the microbial surface components recognizing adhesive matrix molecule (MSCRAMM) receptors that allow the organism to bind to tissues and foreign bodies coated with fibronectin, fibrinogen, and collagen. This permits a low inoculum of organisms to adhere to sutures, catheters, prosthetic valves, and other devices. Many CoNS produce an exopolysaccharide slime biofilm that makes these organisms, as they bind to medical devices (eg, catheters), relatively inaccessible to host defenses and to antimicrobial agents.

EPIDEMIOLOGY:

STAPHYLOCOCCUS AUREUS. *Staphylococcus aureus,* which is second only to CoNS as a cause of health care-associated bacteremia, is equal to *Pseudomonas aeruginosa* as the most common cause of health care-associated pneumonia in adults and is responsible for most health care-associated surgical site infections. *Staphylococcus aureus* colonizes the skin and mucous membranes of 30% to 50% of healthy adults and children. The anterior nares, throat (infants and young children), axilla, perineum, vagina, or rectum are the usual sites of colonization. The anterior nares are colonized most densely, and colonization can persist for years in 10% to 20% of affected people. From 25% to 50% of nasal carriers transiently carry the organism on their hands and other skin areas. Rates of carriage of more than 50% occur in children with desquamating skin disorders or burns and in people with frequent needle use (eg, diabetes mellitus, hemodialysis, recreational drug use, allergy shots).

TRANSMISSION OF *S AUREUS* IN HOSPITALS. *Staphylococcus aureus* is transmitted most often by direct contact. Health care professionals and family members who have colonization of *S aureus* in the nares or on the skin can serve as an important reservoir for transmission of *S aureus* to patients. Health care professionals also can acquire transient hand colonization while caring for one patient and then transmit the organism to another patient. The role of clothing, gowns, environmental surfaces, and other fomites in transmission of *S aureus* is unclear. Transmission by large droplets can occur when patients have draining wounds, burns, or areas of dermatitis that are colonized or infected. Changing dressings or linens can cause these organisms to become droplet nuclei, leading to airborne transmission. Dissemination of *S aureus* from people, including infants, with nasal carriage is related to density of colonization, and increased dissemination occurs during viral upper respiratory tract infections. Additional risk factors for health care-associated acquisition of *S aureus* include illness requiring care in high-risk locations, such as neonatal or pediatric intensive care or burn units; surgical procedures; prolonged hospitalization; local epidemic of *S aureus* infection; and the presence of indwelling vascular catheters or prosthetic devices. Previous antimicrobial therapy increases the risk of acquiring an antimicrobial-resistant strain.

STAPHYLOCOCCUS AUREUS COLONIZATION AND DISEASE. Nasal and skin carriage are the primary reservoirs for *S aureus*. Adults who carry *S aureus* in the nose preoperatively are more likely to develop surgical site infections after general, cardiac, orthopedic, or solid organ transplant surgery than patients who are not carriers. Heavy cutaneous colonization at the insertion site is the single most important predictor of intravenous catheter-related infections for short-term percutaneously inserted catheters. For patients with *S aureus* skin colonization receiving hemodialysis, the incidence of vascular access-related bacteremia is sixfold higher than for patients without skin colonization. After head trauma, adults who are nasal carriers of *S aureus* are more likely to develop *S aureus* pneumonia than are noncolonized patients.

HEALTH CARE-ASSOCIATED METHICILLIN-RESISTANT *S AUREUS*. Methicillin-resistant *S aureus* (MRSA) accounts for 50% of health care-associated *S aureus* infections in large hospitals with 500 or more beds. Health care-associated MRSA strains are resistant to all beta-lactamase resistant (BLR) beta-lactam and cephalosporin antimicrobial agents as well as to antimicrobial agents of several other classes (multidrug resistance). Methicillin-susceptible *S aureus* (MSSA) strains can be heterogeneous for methicillin resistance (see Diagnostic Tests, p 602). These heterogeneous or heterotypic strains appear susceptible by disk testing. However, when a parent strain is cultured on methicillin-containing media, resistant subpopulations are apparent. When these resistant subpopulations are cultured on methicillin-free media, they can continue as stable resistant mutants or revert to susceptible strains *(heterogeneous resistance)*. When BLR antimicrobial agents are used to treat infections caused by these heterotypic strains, the MSSA organisms are killed but MRSA organisms continue to grow.

Risk factors for nasal carriage of health care-associated MRSA include hospitalization within the previous year, recent (within the previous 60 days) antimicrobial use, prolonged hospital stay, frequent contact with a health care environment, presence of an intravascular catheter or tracheal tube, increased number of surgical procedures, or frequent contact with an individual with one or more of the preceding risk factors. A discharged patient known to have had colonization with MRSA should be assumed to have continued colonization when rehospitalized, because carriage can persist for years.

EPIDEMIC STRAINS OF MRSA. Most health care-associated MRSA infections result from the patient's own organism or from endemic strains transmitted to the patient by hands of health care professionals. On occasion, a strain of MRSA will be introduced into a community or a health care facility environment where the organism spreads rapidly despite measures that contain the spread of nonepidemic strains. Identification of these epidemic MRSA strains using pulsed-field gel electrophoresis is important, because containment of epidemic MRSA strains requires strict adherence to and enhancement of infection control policies.

Methicillin-resistant *S aureus* and methicillin-resistant CoNS are responsible for a large portion of health care-associated infections. These strains particularly are difficult to treat, because they usually are multidrug resistant and predictably susceptible only to vancomycin.

COMMUNITY-ASSOCIATED MRSA. Unique clones of MRSA increasingly are responsible for community-associated infections in healthy children and adults without typical risk factors for health care-associated MRSA infections. The most frequent manifestation of these community-associated MRSA infections is skin and soft tissue infection, but invasive disease and pneumonia also occur. The antimicrobial susceptibility patterns of these strains differ from those of health care-associated strains. Although they are resistant to all beta-lactam antimicrobial agents, they typically are susceptible to multiple antimicrobial agents, including trimethoprim-sulfamethoxazole, gentamicin, and doxycycline. These community-associated MRSA strains have been isolated from people without risk factors from many cities in the United States and elsewhere and from child care centers.

VANCOMYCIN-INTERMEDIATELY SUSCEPTIBLE *S AUREUS*. Strains of MRSA with intermediate susceptibility to vancomycin (minimum inhibitory concentration [MIC], >4 μg/mL and ≤16 μg/mL) were isolated from 48 adults in the United States from 1996 to 2001. Each person had received multiple courses of vancomycin for a MRSA infection. Strains of MRSA can be heterogeneous for vancomycin resistance (see Diagnostic Tests, p 602). Extensive vancomycin use allows the vancomycin-intermediately susceptible *S aureus* (VISA) strains to grow. Rapid and aggressive control measures have focused on containing VISA strains to prevent spread. Recommended measures from the Centers for Disease Control and Prevention (CDC) have included rapid diagnostic tests to detect VISA, confirmatory testing of isolated strains, measures to restrict vancomycin use, and strict infection control measures for the infected patient and the institution. Although rare, outbreaks of MRSA with decreased susceptibility to vancomycin and heteroresistance have been reported in France, Spain, and Japan. Communicability persists as long as lesions or the carrier state are present.

VANCOMYCIN-RESISTANT *S AUREUS*. In 2002, 2 isolates of vancomycin-resistant *S aureus* (VRSA; minimum inhibitory concentration, $\geq$32 μg/mL) were identified in adults from 2 different states. Since then, an additional isolate from an adult in a third state has been reported. A concern is that automated antimicrobial susceptibility testing methods commonly used in the United States were unable to detect vancomycin resistance in these isolates. The guidelines for detecting these organisms and preventing spread are similar to those recommended for VISA.

COAGULASE-NEGATIVE STAPHYLOCOCCI. Coagulase-negative staphylococci are common inhabitants of the skin and mucous membranes. Virtually all infants have colonization at multiple sites by 2 to 4 days of age. The most frequently isolated CoNS is *S epidermidis*. Different species colonize specific areas of the body. *Staphylococcus haemolyticus* is found on areas of skin with numerous apocrine glands. The frequency of nosocomial CoNS infections has increased steadily during the past 3 decades. Infants and children in intensive care units, including neonatal intensive care units, have the highest incidence of CoNS bloodstream infections. Coagulase-negative staphylococci colonizing the skin can be introduced at the time of medical device placement, through mucous membrane or skin breaks, or during catheter manipulation. Less often, health care professionals with environmental CoNS colonization on the hands transmit the organism. The roles of the environment or fomites in CoNS transmission are not known.

METHICILLIN-RESISTANT CoNS. Methicillin-resistant CoNS account for most health care-associated CoNS infections. Most MSSA strains have heterogeneous resistance to methicillin, as described previously. Methicillin-resistant strains are resistant to all beta-lactam drugs, including cephalosporins, and usually several other drug classes. As for MRSA, once these strains become endemic in a hospital, eradication is difficult, even when strict infection control techniques are followed.

For toxin-mediated scalded skin syndrome, the **incubation period** usually is 1 to 10 days. For other staphylococcal infections, the **incubation period** is variable. A long delay can occur between acquisition of the organism and onset of disease.

DIAGNOSTIC TESTS: Gram-stained smears of material from skin lesions or pyogenic foci can provide presumptive evidence of infection. Isolation of organisms from culture of otherwise sterile body fluid is definitive. *Staphylococcus aureus* almost never is a contaminant when isolated from a blood culture. Coagulase-negative staphylococci isolated from a blood culture commonly are dismissed as "contaminants." In a neonate, an immunocompromised person, or a patient with a prosthetic device, repeated isolation of the same phenotypic strain of CoNS (on the basis of antimicrobial susceptibility testing) from blood cultures or another normally sterile body fluid suggests true infection, and genotyping more strongly supports the diagnosis. For catheter-related bacteremia, quantitative cultures from the catheter will have 5 to 10 times more organisms than cultures from a peripheral blood vessel. Criteria that suggest CoNS are pathogens rather than contaminants include the following: (1) 2 or more positive blood cultures from different sites; (2) a positive culture from blood and another usually sterile site (eg, cerebrospinal fluid [CSF], joint, abscess) with identical or nearly identical antimicrobial susceptibility patterns for all isolates; (3) growth in continuously monitored blood culture system within 15 hours of incubation; (4) clinical findings of infection in the patient; (5) an intravascular catheter that has been in place for 3 days or more; and (6) similar or identical genotypes among all isolates.

Quantitative antimicrobial susceptibility testing should be performed for all staphylococci, including CoNS, isolated from normally sterile sites. An increasing proportion of community-associated *S aureus* strains are methicillin-resistant, and more than 90% of health care-associated *S aureus* as well as CoNS strains are methicillin and multidrug resistant. Because of the high rates of community-associated MRSA infections in some areas, clindamycin has become one of the often-used drugs for treatment of presumed *S aureus* infections. Routine antimicrobial susceptibility testing of *S aureus* strains previously has not included a method to detect strains susceptible to clindamycin that rapidly become clindamycin-resistant when exposed to this agent. This clindamycin-inducible resistance can be detected by the D zone test. This test was recommended in 2004 for routine use by microbiology laboratories when a MRSA isolate is determined to be erythromycin resistant and clindamycin susceptible by routine methods. Patients with MRSA isolates that demonstrate clindamycin-inducible resistance should not receive clindamycin. All *S aureus* strains with an MIC to vancomycin of ≥4 g/mL should be confirmed and further characterized. Early detection of VISA is critical to trigger aggressive infection control measures (see Table 3.56, p 604).

Staphylococcus aureus and CoNS strain genotyping has become a necessary adjunct for determining whether several isolates from one patient or from different patients are the same. Typing may facilitate identification of the source, extent, and mechanism of transmission of an outbreak. Antimicrobial susceptibility testing is the most readily available method for typing by a phenotypic characteristic. Multilocus enzyme electrophoresis is another phenotypic tool for use, but pulsed-field gel electrophoresis typing by genotype has proven to be more discriminatory for identifying related isolates.

TREATMENT: Serious MSSA infections require intravenous therapy with a BLR beta-lactam antimicrobial agent, such as nafcillin or oxacillin, because most *S aureus* strains produce beta-lactamase enzymes and are resistant to penicillin and ampicillin (see Table 3.57, p 605). First- or second-generation cephalosporins (eg, cefazolin or cefuroxime) and vancomycin are effective but less so than nafcillin or oxacillin for some sites of infection (eg, endocarditis, meningitis). Furthermore, nafcillin or oxacillin rather than vancomycin (or clindamycin if the *S aureus* strain is susceptible to this agent) is recommended for treatment of serious MSSA infections to minimize the emergence of vancomycin- or clindamycin-resistant strains. The addition of gentamicin or rifampin to the regimen should be considered for MSSA or MRSA infections, such as endocarditis, persistent bacteremia, meningitis, or ventriculitis, and in consultation with an infectious diseases specialist. Extended-spectrum cephalosporins are not as active in vitro against MSSA, but some are effective in vivo. A patient who is allergic to penicillin can be treated with a first- or second-generation cephalosporin, if the patient is not also allergic to cephalosporins, or with vancomycin or with clindamycin

Table 3.56. Recommendations for Detecting and Preventing Spread of *Staphylococcus aureus* With Decreased Susceptibility to Vancomycin[1]

Strategies for selection of strains for additional testing:
- Select isolates with vancomycin MICs of ≥ 4 μg/mL. This is based on the apparent heterogeneity of strains, because organisms with MICs of ≥ 4 μg/mL have subpopulations with higher MICs. Clinical treatment failures have occurred with vancomycin in infections with these isolates.
- Select isolates with vancomycin MICs of ≥ 8 μg/mL (based on Clinical and Laboratory Standards Institute breakpoints[2]).
- Select all MRSA isolates. All identified isolates of *S aureus* with decreased susceptibility to vancomycin have been MRSA.
- Select all *S aureus* isolates. Because little is known about the extent of this resistance, any *S aureus* potentially could have decreased susceptibility to vancomycin.

Testing and confirmation:
- Primary testing of *S aureus* against vancomycin requires 24 hours of incubation time.
- Disk diffusion is not an acceptable method for vancomycin susceptibility testing of *S aureus*. None of the known VISA strains have been or would be detected by this method.
- An MIC susceptibility testing method should be used to confirm vancomycin test results.

Infection control:
To minimize spread and prevent development of an endemic strain:
- Isolate patient in a private room and begin one-on-one care by specified personnel using contact precautions including masks.
- Initiate epidemiologic and laboratory investigations with assistance of state health departments and CDC.
- Educate health care professionals about epidemiologic implications and necessary infection control procedures.
- Monitor and strictly enforce compliance with contact precautions and other measures.
- Perform baseline cultures of hands and nares of:
  - People with recent direct contact with patients with VISA
  - Health care professionals for patients with VISA
  - Roommates of patients with VISA
- Assess efficacy of precautions by monitoring personnel for acquisition of VISA.
- Consult with state health department and CDC before discharging and/or transferring the patient, and notify receiving institution or unit of presence of VISA and of appropriate precautions.[3]

MIC indicates minimum inhibitory concentration; MRSA, methicillin-resistant *Staphylococcus aureus*; VISA, vancomycin-intermediately susceptible *S aureus*; CDC, Centers for Disease Control and Prevention.

[1] Centers for Disease Control and Prevention. Laboratory capacity to detect antimicrobial resistance, 1998. *MMWR Morb Mortal Wkly Rep.* 2000;48:1167-1171.

[2] MIC breakpoints for vancomycin are as follows: susceptible, ≤ 4 μg/mL; intermediate, 8–16 μg/mL; and resistant, ≥ 32 μg/mL.

[3] For information regarding control of spread of VISA and vancomycin-resistant *S aureus*, e-mail SEARCH@cdc.gov or visit **www.cdc.gov/ncidod/dhqp**.

Table 3.57. Parenteral Antimicrobial Agent(s) for Treatment of Bacteremia and Other Serious *Staphylococcus aureus* Infections

Susceptibility	Antimicrobial Agents	Comments
I. Initial empiric therapy (organism of unknown susceptibility)		
Drugs of choice:	Vancomycin + nafcillin or oxacillin ± gentamicin	For life-threatening infections (ie, septicemia, endocarditis, CNS infection); linezolid could be substituted if the patient has received several recent courses of vancomycin
	Nafcillin or oxacillin[1]	For nonlife-threatening infection without signs of sepsis (eg, skin infection, cellulitis, osteomyelitis, pyarthrosis) when rates of MRSA colonization and infection in the community are low
	Clindamycin	For nonlife-threatening infection without signs of sepsis when rates of MRSA colonization and infection in the community are substantial and prevalence of clindamycin resistance is low
	Vancomycin	For nonlife-threatening, hospital-acquired infections
II. Methicillin-susceptible, penicillin-resistant *S aureus* (MSSA)		
Drugs of choice:	Nafcillin or oxacillin[1,2]	
Alternatives:	Cefazolin[1]	
	Clindamycin	
	Vancomycin	
	Ampicillin + sulbactam	Only for penicillin- and cephalosporin-allergic patients
III. MRSA (oxacillin MIC, ≥4 μg/mL)		
A. Health care-associated (multidrug-resistant)		
Drugs of choice:	Vancomycin ± gentamicin or ± rifampin[2]	

Table 3.57. Parenteral Antimicrobial Agent(s) for Treatment of Bacteremia and Other Serious *Staphylococcus aureus* Infections, continued

Susceptibility	Antimicrobial Agents	Comments
Alternatives: susceptibility testing results available before alternative drugs are used	Trimethoprim-sulfamethoxazole	
	Linezolid[3]	
	Quinupristin-dalfopristin[3]	
	Fluoroquinolones	Not recommended for people younger than 18 years of age or as monotherapy
B. Community (not multidrug-resistant)		
Drugs of choice:	Vancomycin ± gentamicin (or ± rifampin[2])	For life-threatening infections
	Clindamycin (if strain susceptible)	For pneumonia, septic arthritis, osteomyelitis, skin or soft tissue infections
	Trimethoprim-sulfamethoxazole	For skin or soft tissue infections
Alternative:	Vancomycin[2]	
IV. Vancomycin-intermediately susceptible *S aureus* (MIC, >4 µg/mL and ≤16 µg/mL)[2]		
Drugs of choice:	Optimal therapy is not known	Dependent on in vitro susceptibility test results
	Linezolid[3]	
	Daptomycin[4]	
	Quinupristin-dalfopristin[3]	
Alternatives:	Vancomycin + linezolid ± gentamicin	
	Vancomycin + trimethoprim-sulfamethoxazole[2]	

CNS indicates central nervous system; MRSA, methicillin-resistant *S aureus*; MIC, minimum inhibitory concentration.

[1] Penicillin and cephalosporin-allergic patients should receive vancomycin as initial therapy for serious infections.

[2] One of the adjunctive agents, gentamicin or rifampin, should be added to the therapeutic regimen for life-threatening infections such as endocarditis or CNS infection or infections with a vancomycin-intermediate *S aureus* strain. Consultation with an infectious diseases specialist should be considered to determine which agent to use and duration of use.

[3] Linezolid and quinupristin-dalfopristin are 2 agents with activity in vitro and efficacy in adults with multidrug-resistant, gram-positive organisms, including *S aureus*. Because experience with these agents in children is limited, consultation with an infectious diseases specialist should be considered before use.

[4] Daptomycin is active in vitro against multidrug-resistant, gram-positive organisms, including *S aureus*, but has not been used in children. Daptomycin is approved by the US Food and Drug

if endocarditis or central nervous system infection is not a consideration and the *S aureus* strain is susceptible.

Intravenous vancomycin is recommended for treatment of serious infections attributable to staphylococcal strains resistant to BLR beta-lactam antimicrobial agents (eg, MRSA and all CoNS). For empiric therapy of life-threatening community-acquired as well as hospital-acquired *S aureus* infections, initial therapy should include vancomycin and a BLR beta-lactam antimicrobial agent (eg, nafcillin or oxacillin). For hospital-acquired CoNS infections, vancomycin is the drug of choice. Subsequent therapy should be determined by antimicrobial susceptibility results.

Vancomycin-intermediately susceptible *S aureus* rarely has been isolated. For seriously ill patients with a history of recurrent MRSA infections or for patients failing vancomycin therapy for whom VISA strains are a consideration, initial therapy could include vancomycin, linezolid, or trimethoprim-sulfamethoxazole, with or without gentamicin. If antimicrobial susceptibility results document multidrug resistance, alternative agents, such as quinupristin-dalfopristin or daptomycin, could be considered, but neither agent is approved for use in children younger than 18 years of age.

Duration of therapy for serious MSSA or MRSA infections depends on the site and severity of infection but usually is 4 weeks or more for endocarditis, osteomyelitis, necrotizing pneumonia, or disseminated infection. After initial parenteral therapy and clinical improvement is noted, completion of the recommended antimicrobial course with an oral drug can be considered in older children if adherence can be ensured and endocarditis or CNS infection is not a consideration. For endocarditis and CNS infection, parenteral therapy is recommended for the entire treatment. Drainage of abscesses and removal of foreign bodies is desirable and almost always required for treatment to be effective.

Staphylococcal scalded skin syndrome in infants should be treated with a parenteral BLR beta-lactam antimicrobial agent or, if MRSA is a consideration, vancomycin. In older children, depending on severity, oral agents can be considered. Skin and soft tissue infections, such as impetigo or cellulitis attributable to *S aureus*, usually can be treated with oral penicillinase-resistant beta-lactam drugs, such as cloxacillin, dicloxacillin, or a first- or second-generation cephalosporin unless the prevalence of community-associated MRSA in the region is substantial. In the latter circumstance or for the penicillin-allergic patient, trimethoprim-sulfamethoxazole or clindamycin can be used. For localized superficial skin lesions, topical antimicrobial therapy with mupirocin or bacitracin and local hygienic measures may be sufficient.

The duration of therapy for central venous catheter infections is controversial and depends on consideration of a number of factors, including the organism (*S aureus* vs CoNS), the type and location of the catheter, the site of infection (exit site vs tunnel vs bacteremia), the feasibility of using an alternative vessel at a later date, and the presence or absence of a catheter-related thrombus. Infections are more difficult to treat when associated with a thrombus, thrombophlebitis, or intra-atrial thrombus. If a catheter can be removed, there is no demonstrable thrombus, and bacteremia resolves promptly, a 3- to 5-day course of therapy seems appropriate for CoNS infections in the immunocompetent host. A longer course is suggested when the patient is immunocompromised or if the organism is *S aureus;* experts differ on optimal duration. If the patient needs a new catheter, waiting 48 to 72 hours after bacteremia apparently has resolved before insertion is optimal. If a tunneled catheter is needed for ongoing care, in situ treatment of the infection can be attempted. If the patient responds to antimicrobial therapy with immediate resolution of the *S aureus* bacteremia, treatment should be continued for 10 to 14 days parenterally. Antibiotic lock therapy of tunneled catheters may result in a higher rate of catheter salvage in adults with CoNS infections, but experience with this approach is limited in children. If blood cultures remain positive for staphylococci for more than 3 to 5 days or if the clinical illness fails to improve, the catheter should be removed, parenteral therapy should be continued, and the patient should be evaluated for metastatic foci of infection. Vegetations or a thrombus in the heart or great vessels always should be considered when an intravascular catheter becomes infected. Transesophageal echocardiography, if feasible, is the most sensitive technique for identifying vegetations. Metastatic spread should be evaluated in patients with *S aureus* bacteremia.

ISOLATION OF THE HOSPITALIZED PATIENT: Standard precautions are recommended for all patients. For patients with exposed lesions (eg, draining wounds, SSSS, burns, bullous impetigo, or abscesses caused by MSSA), contact precautions are recommended for the duration of illness. For MSSA pneumonia, droplet precautions are recommended for the first 24 hours of antimicrobial therapy. Droplet precautions should be maintained throughout the illness for MSSA or MRSA tracheitis with a tracheostomy tube in place. Patients infected or colonized with MRSA should be managed with contact precautions for multidrug-resistant organisms for the duration of illness, because MRSA carriage can persist for years.

To prevent transmission of VISA and VRSA, the CDC has issued specific infection control recommendations that should be followed (see Table 3.56, p 604). For CoNS, standard precautions are recommended. For known epidemic MRSA strains, contact precautions should be used.

CONTROL MEASURES:

COAGULASE-NEGATIVE STAPHYLOCOCCI. Prevention and control of CoNS infections have focused on prevention of intraoperative contamination by skin flora and sterile insertion of intravascular and intraperitoneal catheters and other prosthetic devices. Prophylactic administration of an antimicrobial agent intraoperatively lowers the incidence of infection after cardiac surgery and implantation of synthetic vascular grafts and prosthetic devices and often has been used at the time of cerebrospinal fluid shunt placement.

STAPHYLOCOCCUS AUREUS. Measures to prevent and control *S aureus* infections can be considered separately for the individual patient and for the institution.

INDIVIDUAL PATIENT. Community-associated *S aureus* infections in immunocompetent hosts cannot be prevented, because the organism is ubiquitous and there is no vaccine. Frequent hand hygiene, receiving appropriate treatment when indicated, and maintaining cleanliness of skin abrasions may prevent bacteremia. For patients who are predisposed to *S aureus* infections because of disorders of neutrophil function, chronic skin conditions, or obesity, a variety of techniques have been used to prevent infection. These include scrupulous attention to skin hygiene and to use of clothing and bed linen that minimize sweating. Eradication of nasal carriage, if present, prompt use of antimicrobial agents for suspected infections, and in some instances, prolonged administration of trimethoprim-sulfamethoxazole also may be helpful.

Health care-associated *S aureus* infections may be prevented or controlled in an individual patient by strict adherence to recommended infection control precautions, intraoperative antimicrobial prophylaxis, and eradication of nasal carriage.

General Measures. The published recommendations of the CDC Healthcare Infection Control Practices Advisory Committee (HICPAC)* for prevention of health care-associated pneumonia should be effective for decreasing the incidence of *S aureus* pneumonia. Careful preparation of the skin before surgery including cleansing of skin before placement of intravascular catheters using barrier methods will decrease the incidence of *S aureus* wound and catheter infections. Meticulous surgical technique with minimal trauma to tissues, maintenance of good oxygenation, and minimal hematoma and dead space formation will minimize risk of surgical site infection. Good hand hygiene, including before and after use of gloves, by health care professionals and strict adherence to contact precautions are of paramount importance.

Intraoperative Antimicrobial Prophylaxis. The efficacy of prophylaxis for clean surgery is established. The antimicrobial agent is administered 15 to 30 minutes before the operation, and a total duration of therapy of less than 24 hours is recommended. Staphylococci are the most common pathogens causing surgical site infections, and cefazolin is the most commonly recommended drug.

Eradication of Nasal Carriage. Detection and eradication of nasal carriage using mupirocin twice a day for 1 to 7 days has been shown to decrease the incidence of *S aureus* infections in some colonized adult patients after cardiothoracic, general, or neurosurgical procedures. The use of intermittent or continuous intranasal mupirocin for eradication of nasal carriage also has been shown to decrease the incidence of invasive *S aureus* infections in adult patients undergoing long-term hemodialysis or ambulatory peritoneal dialysis. However, eradication of nasal carriage of *S aureus* is difficult, and mupirocin-resistant strains emerge with repeated or widespread use; therefore, this treatment is not recommended for routine use.

INSTITUTIONS. Measures to control the spread of *S aureus* within health care facilities involve use and careful monitoring of Healthcare Infection Control Practices Advisory Committee guidelines.[†‡] Strategies for controlling health care facility transmission of MRSA vary widely among hospitals, and the guidelines recommend that institutions individualize their recommendations. When a patient or health care professional is found to be a chronic carrier of *S aureus*, including MRSA, attempts to eradicate carriage with topical nasal mupirocin therapy may be useful. Although an increasing number of MRSA strains are resistant in vitro to mupirocin, concentra-

---

* Centers for Disease Control and Prevention. Guidelines for preventing health-care-associated pneumonia, 2003. Recommendations of the CDC and the Healthcare Infection Control Practices Advisory Committee. *MMWR Recomm Rep*. 2004;53(RR-3):1–36

† Centers for Disease Control and Prevention. Interim guidelines for the prevention and control of staphylococcal infection associated with reduced susceptibility to vancomycin. *MMWR Morb Mortal Wkly Rep*. 1997;46:626–628

‡ Centers for Disease Control and Prevention. Guideline for Isolation Precautions: Preventing Transmission of Infectious Agents in Healthcare Settings. Recommendations of the Healthcare Infection Control Practices Advisory Committee. 2006; in press (see **www.cdc.gov/mmwr**)

tions used topically (2% or 20 000 µg/mL) are high enough to be effective for many strains. Other topical preparations for intranasal application to be considered if mupirocin fails are ointments containing bacitracin and polymyxin B or a povidone-iodine cream. These preparations have not been studied in children. Decreasing the overuse of antimicrobial agents will decrease the emergence of VISA. Recommendations for containment of recently identified strains of VISA have been published by the CDC (Table 3.56, p 604). Ongoing review and restriction of vancomycin use is critical in attempts to control the emergence of VISA and VRSA (see Appropriate Use of Antimicrobial Agents, p 737). To date, the use of catheters impregnated with various antimicrobial agents to prevent health care-associated infections has not been evaluated adequately in children.

Nurseries. Outbreaks of *S aureus* infections in newborn nurseries require unique measures of control. Hand hygiene should be emphasized to all personnel and visitors. Application of triple dye, iodophor ointment, or 1% chlorhexidine powder to the umbilical stump has been used to delay or prevent colonization. Other measures recommended during outbreaks include cohorting of ill infants and their caregivers, alleviating overcrowding and understaffing, and emphasis on hand hygiene. Soaps containing chlorhexidine or alcohol-based hand rubs are preferred during an outbreak. Culturing the nares, throat, and rectum of infants and nares and skin lesions of health care professionals for *S aureus* may help identify colonized people. Pulsed-field gel electrophoresis should be used to determine strain identity. Epidemiologically implicated health care professionals can be treated for nasal carriage with mupirocin.

Group A Streptococcal Infections

CLINICAL MANIFESTATIONS: The most common group A streptococcal (GAS) infection is acute pharyngotonsillitis. Purulent complications, including otitis media, sinusitis, peritonsillar and retropharyngeal abscesses, and suppurative cervical adenitis develop in some patients, usually people who are untreated. The significance of GAS upper respiratory tract disease is related to acute morbidity and to nonsuppurative sequelae (acute rheumatic fever and acute glomerulonephritis).

Scarlet fever occurs most often in association with pharyngitis and, rarely, with pyoderma or an infected wound. Scarlet fever has a characteristic confluent erythematous sandpaper-like rash, which is caused by one or more of several erythrogenic exotoxins produced by GAS strains. Severe scarlet fever occurs rarely. Other than the occurrence of rash, the epidemiologic features, symptoms, signs, sequelae, and treatment of scarlet fever are the same as those of streptococcal pharyngitis.

Toddlers (1–3 years of age) with GAS respiratory tract infection initially have serous rhinitis and develop a protracted illness with moderate fever, irritability, and anorexia (streptococcal fever). The classic presentation of streptococcal upper respiratory tract infection as acute pharyngitis is uncommon in children younger than 3 years of age. Rheumatic fever also is rare in children younger than 3 years of age.

The second most common site of GAS infection is the skin. Streptococcal skin infections (ie, pyoderma or impetigo) can result in acute glomerulonephritis, which occasionally occurs in epidemics. Acute rheumatic fever is not a proven sequela of streptococcal skin infection.

Other GAS infections include erysipelas, perianal cellulitis, vaginitis, bacteremia, pneumonia, endocarditis, pericarditis, septic arthritis, cellulitis, necrotizing fasciitis, osteomyelitis, myositis, puerperal sepsis, surgical wound infection, and neonatal omphalitis. Necrotizing fasciitis and other invasive GAS infections in children can occur as complications of varicella. Invasive GAS infections can be severe, with or without an identified focus of local infection, and can be associated with streptococcal toxic shock syndrome. The portal of entry of invasive infections often is the skin but often is not identified. Infection can follow minor or unrecognized trauma. An association between GAS infection and sudden onset of obsessive-compulsive and/or tic disorders has been proposed. This condition has been described as pediatric autoimmune neuropsychiatric disorders associated with streptococcal infection (PANDAS). The hypothesized association between PANDAS and GAS infections is unproven.

The toxic shock syndrome caused by GAS infection is reviewed in the chapter on Toxic Shock Syndrome (p 660).

ETIOLOGY: More than 100 distinct M-protein types of group A beta-hemolytic streptococci *(Streptococcus pyogenes)* have been identified. Typing based on the M-protein sequence (emm typing) also is performed and is more discriminating than M serotyping. Epidemiologic studies suggest an association between certain serotypes (eg, types 1, 3, 5, 6, 18, 19, and 24) and rheumatic fever, but a specific rheumatogenic factor has not been identified. Several serotypes (eg, types 49, 55, 57, and 59) are associated with pyoderma and acute glomerulonephritis. Other serotypes (eg, types 1, 6, and 12) are associated with pharyngitis and acute glomerulonephritis.

EPIDEMIOLOGY: Pharyngitis usually results from contact with a person who has GAS pharyngitis. Fomites and household pets, such as dogs, are not vectors of GAS infection. Transmission of GAS infection, including in school outbreaks of pharyngitis, almost always follows contact with respiratory tract secretions. Pharyngitis and impetigo (and their nonsuppurative complications) can be associated with crowding, which often is present in socioeconomically disadvantaged populations. The close contact that occurs in schools, child care centers, and military installations facilitates transmission. Foodborne outbreaks of pharyngitis have occurred and are a consequence of human contamination of food in conjunction with improper food preparation or improper refrigeration procedures.

Streptococcal pharyngitis occurs at all ages but is most common among school-aged children and adolescents. Group A streptococcal pharyngitis and pyoderma are less common in adults than in children.

Geographically, GAS pharyngitis and pyoderma are ubiquitous. Pyoderma is more common in tropical climates and warm seasons, presumably because of antecedent insect bites and other minor skin trauma. Streptococcal pharyngitis is more common during late autumn, winter, and spring in temperate climates, presumably because of close person-to-person contact in schools. Communicability of patients with streptococcal pharyngitis is highest during the acute infection and, in untreated people, gradually diminishes over a period of weeks. Patients no longer are contagious within 24 hours after initiation of appropriate antimicrobial therapy.

Throat culture surveys of healthy children during school outbreaks of pharyngitis have yielded GAS prevalence rates as high as 15% to 50%. These surveys include children who were pharyngeal carriers with no subsequent immune response to GAS cellular or extracellular antigens. Carriage of GAS can persist for many months, but the risk of transmission to others is minimal.

The incidence of acute rheumatic fever in the United States has decreased sharply over several decades, but focal outbreaks of rheumatic fever in school-aged children occurred throughout the 1990s. Although the reason(s) for these local outbreaks is not clear, their occurrence reemphasizes the importance of diagnosing GAS pharyngitis and of adherence to recommended antimicrobial regimens.

In streptococcal impetigo, the organism usually is acquired from another person with impetigo by direct contact. Group A streptococcal colonization of healthy skin usually precedes development of skin infection. Impetiginous lesions occur at the site of breaks in skin (insect bites, burns, traumatic wounds). Group A streptococcal organisms do not penetrate intact skin. After development of impetiginous lesions, the upper respiratory tract often becomes colonized with GAS. Infection of surgical wounds and postpartum (puerperal) sepsis usually result from contact transmission by hands. Anal or vaginal carriers and people with pyoderma or local suppurative infections can transmit GAS to surgical and obstetrical patients, resulting in nosocomial outbreaks. Infections in neonates can result from intrapartum or contact transmission; in the latter situation, infection can begin as omphalitis, cellulitis, or necrotizing fasciitis.

The incidence of invasive GAS infections is highest in infants and older people. Varicella is the most commonly identified risk factor in children. Other risk factors include intravenous drug use, human immunodeficiency virus infection, diabetes mellitus, and chronic cardiac or pulmonary disease. The portal of entry is unknown in almost 50% of invasive GAS infections; in most cases, the entry site is believed to be the skin or mucous membranes. Such infections rarely follow GAS pharyngitis. Although case reports have described a temporal association between use of nonsteroidal anti-inflammatory drugs and invasive GAS infections in children with varicella, a causal relationship has not been established.

The **incubation period** for streptococcal pharyngitis is 2 to 5 days. For impetigo, a 7- to 10-day period between acquisition of GAS on healthy skin and development of lesions has been demonstrated.

DIAGNOSTIC TESTS: Laboratory confirmation of GAS is recommended for children with pharyngitis, because accurate clinical differentiation of viral and GAS pharyngitis is not possible. A specimen should be obtained by vigorous swabbing of both tonsils and the posterior pharynx. Culture on sheep blood agar can confirm GAS infection, and latex agglutination, fluorescent antibody, coagglutination, or precipitation techniques performed on colonies growing on an agar plate can differentiate group A from other beta-hemolytic streptococci. Appropriate use of bacitracin-susceptibility disks (containing 0.04 units of bacitracin) allows presumptive identification of GAS but is a less accurate method of diagnosis. False-negative culture results occur in fewer than 10% of symptomatic patients when an adequate throat swab specimen is obtained and cultured properly by trained personnel using appropriate media and technique. Recovery of GAS from the pharynx does not distinguish patients with true streptococcal infection (defined by a serologic antibody response) from streptococcal carriers who have an intercurrent viral pharyngitis. The number of colonies of GAS on an agar culture plate does not accurately differentiate true infection from carriage.

Cultures that are negative for GAS after 24 hours should be incubated for a second day to optimize recovery of GAS.

Several rapid diagnostic tests for GAS pharyngitis are available. Most are based on nitrous acid extraction of group A carbohydrate antigen from organisms obtained by throat swab. The specificities of these tests generally are high, but the reported sensitivities vary considerably. As with throat cultures, the sensitivity of these tests is highly dependent on the quality of the throat swab specimen, the experience of the person performing the test, and the rigor of the culture standard used for comparison. Therefore, when a patient suspected of having GAS pharyngitis has a negative rapid streptococcal test, a throat culture should be obtained to ensure that the patient does not have GAS infection. Because of the high specificity of these rapid tests, a positive test result generally does not require throat culture confirmation. Rapid diagnostic tests using techniques such as optical immunoassay and chemiluminescent DNA probes have been developed. These tests may be as sensitive as standard throat cultures on sheep blood agar. Some experts believe that the optical immunoassay is sufficiently sensitive to be used without throat culture backup. Physicians who use any of these rapid tests without culture backup may wish to compare their results with those of culture to validate adequate sensitivity in their practice.

INDICATIONS FOR GAS TESTING. Factors to be considered in the decision to obtain a throat swab specimen for testing in children with pharyngitis are the patient's age; clinical signs and symptoms; the season; and family and community epidemiology, including contact with a case of GAS infection or presence in the family of a person with a history of acute rheumatic fever or with poststreptococcal glomerulonephritis. Group A streptococcal pharyngitis is uncommon in children younger than 3 years of age, but outbreaks of GAS pharyngitis have been reported in young children in child care settings. The risk of acute rheumatic fever is so remote in resource-rich countries in such young children that diagnostic studies for GAS pharyngitis are indicated considerably less often for children younger than 3 years of age than for older children. Children with manifestations highly suggestive of viral infection, such as coryza, conjunctivitis, hoarseness, cough, anterior stomatitis, discrete ulcerative lesions, or diarrhea, are unlikely to have GAS as the cause of their pharyngitis and generally should not be tested for GAS. Children with acute onset of sore throat and clinical signs and symptoms such as pharyngeal exudate, pain on swallowing, fever, and enlarged tender anterior cervical lymph nodes or exposure to a person with GAS pharyngitis are more likely to have GAS as the cause of their pharyngitis and should have a rapid antigen test and/or throat culture performed.

Indications for testing contacts for GAS vary according to circumstances. Testing asymptomatic household contacts for GAS is not recommended except when contacts are at increased risk of developing sequelae of GAS infection. Throat swab specimens should be obtained from siblings and all other household contacts of a child who has acute rheumatic fever or poststreptococcal glomerulonephritis, and if test results are positive, contacts should be treated regardless of whether they currently are or recently were symptomatic. Household contacts of an index case with streptococcal pharyngitis who have recent or current symptoms suggestive of streptococcal infection also should be tested. Pyoderma lesions should be cultured in families with one case or more of acute nephritis or streptococcal toxic shock syndrome so that antimicrobial therapy can be administered to eradicate GAS.

Post-treatment throat swab cultures are indicated only for patients at particularly high risk of acute rheumatic fever or who remain symptomatic at that time. Repeated courses of antimicrobial therapy are not indicated for asymptomatic patients who remain GAS positive after appropriate antimicrobial therapy; the exceptions are people who have had, or whose family members have had, acute rheumatic fever or other uncommon epidemiologic circumstances, such as outbreaks of rheumatic fever or acute poststreptococcal glomerulonephritis.

Patients in whom repeated episodes of GAS pharyngitis occur at short intervals documented by culture or antigen detection test present a special problem. Often, these people are chronic GAS carriers who are experiencing frequent viral illnesses. In assessing such patients, inadequate adherence to oral treatment also should be considered. Although uncommon, in some areas erythromycin resistance among GAS strains does occur, resulting in erythromycin treatment failures. Such strains also are resistant to other macrolides, such as clarithromycin and azithromycin. Testing asymptomatic household contacts usually is not helpful. However, if multiple household members have pharyngitis or other GAS infections, such as pyoderma, simultaneous cultures of all household members and treatment of all people with positive cultures or rapid antigen test results may be of value.

In schools, child care centers, or other environments in which a large number of people are in close contact, the prevalence of GAS pharyngeal carriage in healthy children can be as high as 15% even in the absence of an outbreak of streptococcal disease. Therefore, classroom or more widespread culture surveys are not indicated and should be considered only if more than one case of acute rheumatic fever, glomerulonephritis, or severe invasive GAS disease has occurred.

Cultures of impetiginous lesions are not indicated routinely, because lesions often yield both streptococci and staphylococci, and determination of the primary pathogen is not possible.

In suspected invasive GAS infections, cultures of blood and focal sites of possible infection are indicated. In necrotizing fasciitis, imaging studies often delay, rather than facilitate, the diagnosis. Clinical suspicion of necrotizing fasciitis should prompt surgical inspection of the deep tissues with Gram stain and culture of surgical specimens.

TREATMENT:
PHARYNGITIS.
- Penicillin V is the drug of choice for treatment of GAS pharyngitis, except in people who are allergic to penicillin. A clinical isolate of GAS resistant to penicillin never has been documented. Ampicillin or amoxicillin often is used, but these drugs have no microbiologic advantage over penicillin. Preliminary data suggest that orally administered amoxicillin given as a single daily dose for 10 days is as effective as orally administered penicillin V given 3 times per day for 10 days. Penicillin therapy prevents acute rheumatic fever even when therapy is started 9 days after onset of the acute illness, shortens the clinical course, decreases risk of transmission, and decreases risk of suppurative sequelae. For all patients with acute rheumatic fever, a complete course of penicillin or other appropriate antimicrobial agents for GAS pharyngitis should be given to eradicate GAS from the throat, even though the organism may not be recovered in the initial throat culture.

The dose of orally administered penicillin V is 400 000 U (250 mg), 2 to 3 times per day, for 10 days for children weighing less than 27 kg (60 lb) and 800 000 U (500 mg), 2 to 3 times per day, for heavier children, adolescents, and adults. To prevent acute rheumatic fever, oral treatment with penicillin should be given for the full 10 days, regardless of the promptness of clinical recovery. Although different preparations of oral penicillin vary in absorption, their clinical efficacy is similar. Treatment failures may occur more often with oral penicillin than with intramuscularly administered penicillin G benzathine as a result of inadequate adherence to oral therapy.

- Intramuscular penicillin G benzathine is appropriate therapy. It ensures adequate blood concentrations and avoids the problem of adherence, but administration is painful. For children who weigh less than 27 kg, penicillin G benzathine is given in a single dose of 600 000 U; for heavier children and adults, the dose is 1.2 million U. Discomfort is less if the preparation of penicillin G benzathine is brought to room temperature before intramuscular injection. Mixtures containing shorter-acting penicillins (eg, penicillin G procaine) in addition to penicillin G benzathine have not been demonstrated to be more effective than penicillin G benzathine alone but are less painful when administered. Although supporting data are limited, the combination of 900 000 U of penicillin G benzathine and 300 000 U of penicillin G procaine is satisfactory therapy for most children; however, the efficacy of this combination for heavier patients, such as adolescents and adults, has not been demonstrated.

- Orally administered erythromycin is indicated for patients who are allergic to penicillin unless GAS strains resistant to erythromycin are prevalent in the community. Treatment should be given for 10 days. Erythromycin estolate (20–40 mg/kg per day in 2–4 divided doses) or erythromycin ethylsuccinate (40 mg/kg per day in 2–4 divided doses) is effective for treating streptococcal pharyngitis; the maximum dose is 1 g/day. Other macrolides, such as clarithromycin for 10 days or azithromycin for 5 days, also are effective. Group A streptococcal strains resistant to erythromycin and other macrolides are uncommon in most areas of the United States, but resistance patterns need to be monitored.

- A 10-day course of a narrow-spectrum (first-generation) oral cephalosporin is an acceptable alternative, particularly for people who are allergic to penicillin. However, as many as 5% of penicillin-allergic people also are allergic to cephalosporins. Patients with immediate or type I hypersensitivity to penicillin should not be treated with a cephalosporin. The additional cost of many cephalosporins and their wider range of antibacterial activity compared with penicillin preclude recommending them for routine use in people with GAS pharyngitis who are not allergic to penicillin.

- Tetracyclines and sulfonamides should not be used for treating GAS pharyngitis.

Children who have a recurrence of GAS pharyngitis shortly after completing a 10-day course of a recommended oral antimicrobial agent can be retreated with the same antimicrobial agent, given an alternative oral drug, or given an intramuscular dose of penicillin G benzathine, especially if inadequate adherence to oral therapy is likely. Alternative drugs include a narrow-spectrum cephalosporin, amoxicillin-clavulanate, clindamycin, erythromycin, or another macrolide. Expert opinions differ about the most appropriate therapy in this circumstance.

Management of a patient who has repeated and frequent episodes of acute pharyngitis associated with a positive laboratory test for GAS is problematic. To determine whether the patient is a long-term streptococcal pharyngeal carrier who is experiencing repeated episodes of intercurrent viral pharyngitis (which is the situation in most cases), the following should be determined: (1) whether the clinical findings are more suggestive of a GAS or a viral cause; (2) whether epidemiologic factors in the community are more suggestive of a GAS or a viral cause; (3) the nature of the clinical response to the antimicrobial therapy (in true GAS pharyngitis, response to therapy usually is rapid); (4) whether laboratory tests are positive for GAS between episodes of acute pharyngitis; and (5) whether a serologic response to GAS extracellular antigens (eg, antistreptolysin O) has occurred. Serotyping of GAS isolates generally is available only in research laboratories, but if performed, repeated isolation of the same serotype suggests carriage, and isolation of differing serotypes indicates repeated infections.

PHARYNGEAL CARRIERS. Antimicrobial therapy is not indicated for most GAS pharyngeal carriers. Exceptions (ie, specific situations in which eradication of carriage may be indicated) include the following: (1) an outbreak of acute rheumatic fever or poststreptococcal glomerulonephritis occurs; (2) an outbreak of GAS pharyngitis in a closed or semiclosed community occurs; (3) a family history of acute rheumatic fever exists; (4) multiple episodes of documented symptomatic GAS pharyngitis continue to occur within a family during a period of many weeks despite appropriate therapy; (5) a family has excessive anxiety about GAS infections; or (6) tonsillectomy is considered only because of chronic GAS carriage.

Streptococcal carriage can be difficult to eradicate with conventional antimicrobial therapy. A number of antimicrobial agents, including clindamycin, amoxicillin-clavulanate, azithromycin, and a combination of rifampin for the last 4 days of treatment with either penicillin V or penicillin G benzathine, have been demonstrated to be more effective than penicillin in eliminating chronic streptococcal carriage. Of these drugs, oral clindamycin, given as 20 mg/kg per day in 3 doses (maximum 1.8 g/day) for 10 days, has been reported to be the most effective. Documented eradication of the carrier state is helpful in the evaluation of subsequent episodes of acute pharyngitis; however, long-term carriage may recur after reacquisition of GAS.

STREPTOCOCCAL IMPETIGO.
- Local mupirocin ointment may be useful for limiting person-to-person spread of GAS impetigo and for eradicating localized disease. With multiple lesions or with impetigo in multiple family members, child care groups, or athletic teams, impetigo should be treated with antimicrobial regimens administered systemically. Because episodes of impetigo may be caused by *Staphylococcus aureus* or *Streptococcus pyogenes*, children with impetigo usually should be treated with an antimicrobial agent active against both GAS and *S aureus*.

OTHER INFECTIONS.
- Parenteral antimicrobial therapy is required for severe infections, such as endocarditis, pneumonia, septicemia, meningitis, arthritis, osteomyelitis, erysipelas, necrotizing fasciitis, neonatal omphalitis, and streptococcal toxic shock syndrome. Treatment often is prolonged (2–6 weeks).
- For treatment of patients with severe invasive GAS infection, including toxic shock syndrome, see Toxic Shock Syndrome (p 660).

PREVENTION OF SEQUELAE. Acute rheumatic fever and acute glomerulonephritis are serious nonsuppurative sequelae of GAS infections. During epidemics of GAS infections on military bases in the 1950s, rheumatic fever developed in 3% of untreated patients with acute GAS pharyngitis. The incidence after endemic infections is not known but is believed to be less than 1%. The risk of acute rheumatic fever virtually can be eliminated by adequate treatment of the antecedent GAS infection; however, rare cases have occurred even after apparently appropriate therapy. The effectiveness of antimicrobial therapy for preventing acute poststreptococcal glomerulonephritis after pyoderma has not been established. Suppurative sequelae, such as peritonsillar abscesses and cervical adenitis, usually are prevented by treatment of the primary infection.

ISOLATION OF THE HOSPITALIZED PATIENT: In addition to standard precautions, droplet precautions are recommended for children with GAS pharyngitis or pneumonia until 24 hours after initiation of appropriate therapy. For burns with secondary GAS infection and extensive or draining cutaneous infections that cannot be covered or contained adequately by dressings, contact precautions should be used for at least 24 hours after the start of appropriate therapy.

CONTROL MEASURES: The most important means of controlling GAS disease and its sequelae is prompt identification and treatment of infections.

SCHOOL AND CHILD CARE. Children with streptococcal pharyngitis or skin infections should not return to school or child care until at least 24 hours after beginning appropriate antimicrobial therapy. Close contact with other children during this time should be avoided, if possible.

CARE OF EXPOSED PEOPLE. People who are contacts of documented cases of GAS infection and who have recent or current clinical evidence of a GAS infection should undergo appropriate laboratory tests and should be treated if test results are positive. Rates of GAS carriage are higher among sibling contacts than among parent contacts in nonepidemic settings; rates as high as 50% for sibling contacts and 20% for parent contacts have been reported during epidemics. More than half of the contacts who acquire the organism will become ill. Asymptomatic acquisition of GAS may pose some risk of nonsuppurative complications; studies indicate that as many as one third of patients with acute rheumatic fever had no history of recent streptococcal infection and another third had minor respiratory tract symptoms that were not brought to medical attention. However, routine laboratory evaluation of asymptomatic household contacts usually is not indicated except during outbreaks or when the contacts are at increased risk of developing sequelae of infection (see Indications for GAS Testing, p 613). Short courses (<10 days) of an antimicrobial agent for healthy contacts are inappropriate. In rare circumstances, such as a large family with documented, repeated, intrafamilial transmission resulting in frequent episodes of GAS pharyngitis during a prolonged period, physicians may elect to treat all family members identified by laboratory tests as harboring GAS.

Household contacts of patients with severe invasive GAS disease, including toxic shock syndrome, are at increased risk of developing severe invasive GAS disease compared with the general population, but the risk is not sufficiently high to warrant routine testing for GAS colonization or routine chemoprophylaxis of all household contacts of people with invasive GAS disease. However, because of the increased risk of sporadic, invasive GAS disease among certain populations and because of the increased risk of death in people 65 years of age and older who develop invasive GAS disease, health care professionals may choose to offer targeted chemoprophylaxis to household contacts who are 65 years of age and older or who are members of other high-risk populations (eg, people with human immunodeficiency virus infection, varicella, diabetes mellitus). Because of the rarity of subsequent cases and the low risk of invasive GAS infections in children in general, chemoprophylaxis is not recommended in schools or child care facilities.

SECONDARY PROPHYLAXIS FOR RHEUMATIC FEVER. Patients who have a well-documented history of acute rheumatic fever (including cases manifested solely as Sydenham chorea) and patients who have documented evidence of rheumatic heart disease should be given continuous antimicrobial prophylaxis to prevent recurrent attacks (secondary prophylaxis), because asymptomatic and symptomatic GAS infections can result in a recurrence of rheumatic fever. Continuous prophylaxis should be initiated as soon as the diagnosis of acute rheumatic fever or rheumatic heart disease is made.

DURATION. Secondary prophylaxis should be long-term, perhaps for life, for patients with rheumatic heart disease (even after prosthetic valve replacement), because these patients remain at risk of recurrence of rheumatic fever. The risk of recurrence decreases as the interval from the most recent episode increases, and patients without rheumatic heart disease are at a lower risk of recurrence than are patients with cardiac involvement. These considerations influence the duration of secondary prophylaxis in adults but should not alter the practice of secondary prophylaxis for children and adolescents. Secondary prophylaxis for all patients who have had rheumatic fever should be continued for at least 5 years or until the person is 21 years of age, whichever is longer (see Table 3.58, p 619). Prophylaxis also should be continued if the risk of contact with people with GAS infection is high, such as for parents with school-aged children and teachers.

When streptococcal infections occur in household contacts of patients with a history of rheumatic fever, infected people should be treated promptly with an appropriate antimicrobial agent (see Indications for GAS Testing, p 613, and Treatment, p 614).

The drug regimens in Table 3.59 (p 620) are effective for secondary prophylaxis. The intramuscular regimen has been shown to be the most reliable, because the success of oral prophylaxis depends primarily on patient adherence; however, inconvenience and the pain of injection may cause some patients to discontinue intramuscular prophylaxis. In some countries and in situations in which the risk of GAS infection particularly is high, penicillin G benzathine is given every 3 weeks because of greater effectiveness. In the United States, administration every 4 weeks seems adequate in most circumstances. Oral sulfadiazine is as effective as oral penicillin for secondary prophylaxis but may not be readily available in the United States. By extrapolating from data demonstrating effectiveness of sulfadiazine, sulfisoxazole has been deemed an appropriate alternative.

Allergic reactions to oral penicillin are similar to reactions with intramuscular penicillin, but usually these are less severe and occur less commonly. These reactions

Table 3.58. Duration of Prophylaxis for People Who Have Had Acute Rheumatic Fever: Recommendations of the American Heart Association[1]

Category	Duration
Rheumatic fever without carditis	5 y or until 21 y of age, whichever is longer
Rheumatic fever with carditis but without residual heart disease (no valvular disease[2])	10 y or well into adulthood, whichever is longer
Rheumatic fever with carditis and residual heart disease (persistent valvular disease[2])	At least 10 y since last episode and at least until 40 y of age; sometimes lifelong prophylaxis

[1] Modified from Dajani A, Taubert K, Ferrieri P, Peter G, Shulman S. Treatment of acute streptococcal pharyngitis and prevention of rheumatic fever: a statement for health professionals: Committee on Rheumatic Fever, Endocarditis, and Kawasaki Disease of the Council on Cardiovascular Disease in the Young, The American Heart Association. *Pediatrics.* 1995;96:758–764.

[2] Clinical or echocardiographic evidence.

also occur less commonly in children than in adults. Anaphylaxis is rare in patients receiving oral penicillin. Severe allergic reactions in patients receiving continuous penicillin G benzathine prophylaxis also are rare. The rare reports of anaphylaxis and death generally have involved patients older than 12 years of age with severe rheumatic heart disease. Most severe reactions seem to represent vasovagal responses rather than anaphylaxis. Reactions also can include a serum sickness-like reaction characterized by fever and joint pains, which can be mistaken for recurrence of acute rheumatic fever.

Reactions to continuous sulfadiazine or sulfisoxazole prophylaxis are rare and usually minor; evaluation of blood cell counts may be advisable after 2 weeks of prophylaxis, because leukopenia has been reported. Prophylaxis with a sulfonamide during late pregnancy is contraindicated because of interference with fetal bilirubin metabolism. Febrile mucocutaneous syndromes (erythema multiforme, Stevens-Johnson syndrome, or toxic epidermal necrolysis) have been associated with penicillin and with sulfonamides. When an adverse event occurs with any of these therapeutic regimens, the drug should be stopped immediately and an alternative drug should be selected. For the rare patient allergic to both penicillins and sulfonamides, erythromycin is recommended. Other macrolides, such as azithromycin or clarithromycin, also should be acceptable; they have less risk of gastrointestinal tract intolerance but increased costs.

POSTSTREPTOCOCCAL REACTIVE ARTHRITIS. After an episode of acute GAS pharyngitis, reactive arthritis may develop in the absence of sufficient clinical manifestations and laboratory findings to fulfill the Jones criteria for the diagnosis of acute rheumatic fever. This syndrome has been termed poststreptococcal reactive arthritis (PSRA). The precise relationship of PSRA to acute rheumatic fever is unclear. In contrast with the arthritis of acute rheumatic fever, PSRA does not respond dramatically to nonsteroidal anti-inflammatory agents. Because some patients with PSRA can have silent or delayed-onset carditis, patients should be observed

Table 3.59. Chemoprophylaxis for Recurrences of Acute Rheumatic Fever[1]

Drug	Dose	Route
Penicillin G benzathine	1.2 million U, every 4 wk[2]	Intramuscular
OR		
Penicillin V	250 mg, twice a day	Oral
OR		
Sulfadiazine or sulfisoxazole	0.5 g, once a day for patients ≤27 kg (≤60 lb)	Oral
	1.0 g, once a day for patients >27 kg (>60 lb)	
For people who are allergic to penicillin and sulfonamide drugs		
Erythromycin	250 mg, twice a day	Oral

[1] Modified from Dajani A, Taubert K, Ferrieri P, Peter G, Shulman S. Treatment of acute streptococcal pharyngitis and prevention of rheumatic fever: a statement for health professionals: Committee on Rheumatic Fever, Endocarditis, and Kawasaki Disease of the Council on Cardiovascular Disease in the Young, The American Heart Association. *Pediatrics*. 1995;96:758–764

[2] In high-risk situations, administration every 3 weeks is recommended.

carefully for several months for the subsequent development of carditis. Some experts recommend prophylaxis for these patients for several months to a year if carditis does not develop; if carditis occurs, the patient should be considered to have had acute rheumatic fever, and prophylaxis should be continued (see Secondary Prophylaxis for Rheumatic Fever, p 618).

BACTERIAL ENDOCARDITIS PROPHYLAXIS. Patients with rheumatic valvular heart disease also require additional short-term antimicrobial prophylaxis at the time of certain procedures (including dental and surgical procedures) to prevent the possible development of bacterial endocarditis (see Prevention of Bacterial Endocarditis, p 828). Patients who have had acute rheumatic fever without evidence of valvular heart disease do not need prophylaxis for prevention of endocarditis. Penicillin, ampicillin, and amoxicillin should not be used for endocarditis prophylaxis for patients who are receiving oral penicillin for secondary rheumatic fever prophylaxis because of relative penicillin and aminopenicillin resistance among viridans streptococci in the oral cavity in such patients. Clindamycin, azithromycin, and clarithromycin are alternative antimicrobial agents recommended for such patients.

Group B Streptococcal Infections

CLINICAL MANIFESTATIONS: Group B streptococci are a major cause of perinatal bacterial infections, including bacteremia, endometritis, chorioamnionitis, urinary tract infections in parturient women, and systemic and focal infections in infants from birth until 3 months of age or rarely older. Invasive disease in young infants is categorized on the basis of chronologic age at onset. Early-onset disease usually occurs within the first 24 hours of life (range, 0–6 days) and is characterized by signs of systemic infection, respiratory distress, apnea, shock, pneumonia, and less often, meningitis (5%–10% of cases). Late-onset disease, which typically occurs at 3 to 4 weeks of age (range, 7 days–3 months), commonly manifests as occult bacteremia or meningitis; other focal infections, such as osteomyelitis, septic arthritis, adenitis, and cellulitis, can occur. Very late-onset disease has onset beyond 3 months of age in very preterm infants requiring prolonged hospitalization. Group B streptococci also cause systemic infections in nonpregnant adults with underlying medical conditions, such as diabetes mellitus, chronic liver or renal disease, malignancy, or other immunocompromising conditions, and adults 65 years of age and older.

ETIOLOGY: Group B streptococci *(Streptococcus agalactiae)* are gram-positive, aerobic diplococci that typically produce a narrow zone of beta hemolysis on 5% sheep blood agar. These organisms are divided into 9 serotypes on the basis of capsular polysaccharides (Ia, Ib, II, and III through VIII). Serotypes Ia, Ib, II, III, and V account for approximately 95% of cases in the United States. Serotype III is the predominant cause of early-onset meningitis and most late-onset infections in infants.

EPIDEMIOLOGY: Group B streptococci are common inhabitants of the gastrointestinal and genitourinary tracts. Less commonly, they colonize the pharynx. The colonization rate in pregnant women and newborn infants ranges from 15% to 40%. Colonization during pregnancy can be constant or intermittent. Before recommendations for prevention of early-onset group B streptococcal (GBS) disease by maternal intrapartum antimicrobial prophylaxis (see Control Measures, p 623) were made, the incidence was 1 to 4 cases per 1000 live births; early-onset disease accounted for approximately 75% of infant cases and occurred in approximately 1 infant per 100 to 200 colonized women. Associated with widespread maternal intrapartum antimicrobial prophylaxis, the incidence of early-onset disease has decreased by approximately 81% to approximately 0.3 cases per 1000 live births in 2003 and now equals that of late-onset disease. Case fatality rates in term infants range from 3% to 5% but are higher in preterm neonates. Transmission from mother to infant occurs shortly before or during delivery. After delivery, person-to-person transmission can occur. Although uncommon, GBS can be acquired in the nursery from hospital personnel (probably via hand contamination) or more commonly in the community from healthy colonized people. The risk of early-onset disease is increased in preterm infants born at less than 37 weeks of gestation, in infants born after the amniotic membranes have been ruptured 18 hours or more, and in infants born to women with high genital GBS inoculum, intrapartum fever (temperature ≥38°C [≥100.4°F]), chorioamnionitis, GBS bacteriuria during the pregnancy, or a previous infant with invasive GBS disease. A low or an absent concentration of serotype-specific serum antibody also is a predisposing factor. Other risk factors are intrauterine fetal monitoring, maternal age younger than 20 years and black or Hispanic ethnic origin. The period of communicability is unknown but may extend throughout the duration of colonization or of disease. Infants can remain colonized for several months after birth and after treatment for systemic infection. Recurrent GBS disease affects an estimated 1% to 3% of appropriately treated infants.

The **incubation period** of early-onset disease is fewer than 7 days. In late-onset and very late-onset disease, the incubation period from GBS acquisition to disease is unknown. The incidence of GBS disease declines dramatically after 3 months of age, but up to 10% of pediatric cases occur beyond early infancy, and many but not all of these are in infants who were born preterm.

DIAGNOSTIC TESTS: Gram-positive cocci in body fluids that typically are sterile (such as cerebrospinal [CSF], pleural, or joint fluid) provide presumptive evidence of infection. Cultures of blood, other typically sterile body fluids, or a suppurative focus are necessary to establish the diagnosis. Serotype identification is available in reference laboratories. Rapid tests that identify group B streptococcal antigen in body fluids other than CSF are not recommended because of poor specificity.

TREATMENT:
- Ampicillin plus an aminoglycoside is the initial treatment of choice for a newborn infant with presumptive invasive GBS infection.
- Penicillin G alone can be given when GBS has been identified as the cause of the infection and when clinical and microbiologic responses have been documented.
- For infants with meningitis attributable to GBS, the recommended dosage of penicillin G for infants 7 days of age or younger is 250 000 to 450 000 U/kg per day, intravenously, in 3 divided doses; for infants older than 7 days of age, 450 000 to 500 000 U/kg per day, intravenously, in 4 to 6 divided doses is recommended. For ampicillin, the recommended dosage for infants with meningitis 7 days of age or younger is 200 to 300 mg/kg per day, intravenously, in 3 divided doses; for infants older than 7 days of age, 300 mg/kg per day, intravenously, in 4 to 6 divided doses is recommended.
- For meningitis, some experts believe that a second lumbar puncture approximately 24 to 48 hours after initiation of therapy assists in management and prognosis. If CSF sterility is not achieved, a complicated course (ie, cerebral infarcts) can be expected; also an increasing protein concentration suggests an intracranial complication (eg, infarction, ventricular obstruction). Additional lumbar punctures and diagnostic imaging studies are indicated if response to therapy is in doubt, neurologic abnormalities persist, or focal neurologic deficits occur. Consultation with a specialist in pediatric infectious diseases often is useful.
- For infants with bacteremia without a defined focus, treatment should be continued for 10 days. For infants with uncomplicated meningitis, 14 days of treatment is satisfactory, but longer periods of treatment may be necessary for infants with prolonged or complicated courses. Septic arthritis or osteomyelitis requires treatment for 3 to 4 weeks; endocarditis or ventriculitis requires treatment for at least 4 weeks.
- Because of the reported increased risk of infection, the twin or any multiples of an index case with early- or late-onset disease should be observed carefully and evaluated and treated empirically for suspected systemic infection if any signs of illness occur.

ISOLATION OF THE HOSPITALIZED PATIENT: Standard precautions are recommended except during a nursery outbreak of disease attributable to GBS (see Control Measures, Nursery Outbreak, p 627).

CONTROL MEASURES:

CHEMOPROPHYLAXIS. Recommendations for prevention of early-onset neonatal GBS infection are based on data comparing a culture screening method to a risk-based method to identify women who should receive intrapartum antimicrobial prophylaxis that demonstrated significantly better efficacy for the culture screening method. Recommendations from the Centers for Disease Control and Prevention (CDC)* include the following:

- All pregnant women should be screened at 35 to 37 weeks' gestation for vaginal and rectal colonization (see Fig 3.1, p 624). The only exceptions to this recommendation for universal culture screening are women with GBS bacteriuria during the current pregnancy or women who have had a previous infant with invasive GBS disease; these women always should receive intrapartum chemoprophylaxis. At the onset of labor or rupture of membranes, intrapartum chemoprophylaxis should be given to all pregnant women identified as GBS carriers. Colonization during a previous pregnancy is not an indication for intrapartum chemoprophylaxis unless screening results are positive in the current pregnancy.
- Women with GBS isolated from the urine in any concentration during their current pregnancy should receive intrapartum chemoprophylaxis, because such women usually are heavily colonized with GBS and are at increased risk of delivering an infant with early-onset GBS disease; prenatal culture screening is not necessary.
- Women who previously have given birth to an infant with invasive GBS disease should receive intrapartum chemoprophylaxis; prenatal culture screening is not necessary.
- If GBS status is not known at onset of labor or rupture of membranes, intrapartum chemoprophylaxis should be administered to women with any of the following risk factors: gestation less than 37 weeks, duration of membrane rupture 18 hours or longer, or intrapartum temperature of $\geq 38.0°C$ ($\geq 100.4°F$).
- Culture techniques that maximize the likelihood of GBS recovery are required for prenatal screening. The optimal method for GBS screening cultures is collection of swabs of the lower vagina and rectum; placement of swabs in a nonnutrient transport medium; removal of swabs and inoculation into selective broth medium, such as Trans-Vag Broth supplemented with 5% defibrinated sheep blood or Lim broth; overnight incubation; and subculture onto solid blood agar medium.
- Oral antimicrobial agents should *not* be used to treat women who are found to have GBS colonization during prenatal screening unless there is a GBS urinary tract infection warranting treatment according to obstetric standards of care. Such treatment is *not* effective in eliminating GBS carriage or preventing neonatal disease and may cause adverse consequences.
- Women who have GBS colonization and have a planned cesarean delivery performed before rupture of membranes and onset of labor should *not* routinely receive intrapartum chemoprophylaxis.

---

* Centers for Disease Control and Prevention. Prevention of perinatal group B streptococcal disease. Revised guidelines from CDC. *MMWR Recomm Rep.* 2002;52(RR-11):1–22

FIG 3.1. INDICATIONS FOR INTRAPARTUM ANTIMICROBIAL PROPHYLAXIS (IAP) TO PREVENT EARLY-ONSET GROUP B STREPTOCOCCAL (GBS) DISEASE USING A UNIVERSAL PRENATAL CULTURE SCREENING STRATEGY AT 35 TO 37 WEEKS' GESTATION FOR ALL WOMEN.

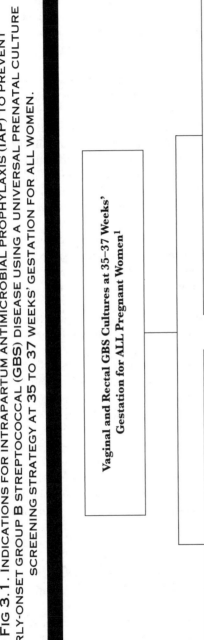

Vaginal and Rectal GBS Cultures at 35–37 Weeks' Gestation for ALL Pregnant Women[1]

IAP INDICATED

- Previous infant with invasive GBS disease
- GBS bacteriuria during *current* pregnancy
- Positive GBS screening culture during current pregnancy (*unless* a planned cesarean delivery is performed in the absence of labor or membrane rupture)
- Unknown GBS status AND any of the following:
    - Delivery at <37 weeks' gestation
    - Membranes ruptured for ≥18 hours
    - Intrapartum fever (temperature ≥38.0°C [≥100.4°F])[2]

IAP *NOT* INDICATED

- Previous pregnancy with a positive GBS screening culture (unless a culture also was positive during the current pregnancy or previous infant with invasive GBS disease)
- Planned cesarean delivery performed in the absence of labor or membrane rupture (regardless of GBS culture status)
- Negative vaginal and rectal GBS screening culture in late gestation, regardless of intrapartum risk factors

[1] Exceptions: women with GBS bacteriuria during the current pregnancy or women with a previous infant with invasive GBS disease.

[2] If chorioamnionitis is suspected, broad-spectrum antimicrobial therapy that includes an agent known to be active against GBS should replace GBS IAP.

- For intrapartum chemoprophylaxis, intravenous penicillin G (5 million U initially, then 2.5 million U every 4 hours until delivery) is the preferred agent because of its effectiveness and narrow spectrum of antimicrobial activity. An alternative regimen is intravenous ampicillin (2 g initially, then 1 g every 4 hours until delivery).
- Because of the increasing prevalence of GBS resistance to erythromycin (15%–30%) and clindamycin (10%–20%), cefazolin, 2 g initially, then 1 g every 8 hours, is recommended for women who are allergic to penicillin but at low risk of anaphylaxis because of its narrow spectrum of activity and ability to achieve high amniotic fluid concentrations. Women whose GBS isolates are tested and found to be clindamycin susceptible and who are at high risk of anaphylaxis with penicillin can receive this drug at a dose of 900 mg every 8 hours. Vancomycin should be reserved for penicillin-allergic women who are at high risk of anaphylaxis (ie, type I hypersensitivity) and for whom GBS isolate susceptibility testing has not been performed; vancomycin should be administered intravenously, 1 g every 12 hours until delivery. The efficacy of clindamycin or vancomycin is not established.
- Routine use of antimicrobial agents as chemoprophylaxis for neonates born to mothers who have received adequate intrapartum chemoprophylaxis for GBS disease is *not* recommended. However, therapeutic use of these agents is appropriate for infants with clinically suspected systemic infection.

An approach for empiric management of newborn infants born to women who receive intrapartum chemoprophylaxis to prevent early-onset GBS disease or to treat suspected chorioamnionitis is provided in Fig 3.2, p 626. These guidelines are based on published information as well as expert opinion and are as follows:

- If a woman receives intrapartum antimicrobial agents for treatment of suspected chorioamnionitis, her newborn infant should have a full diagnostic evaluation and empiric antimicrobial therapy pending culture results, regardless of clinical condition at birth, duration of maternal therapy before delivery, or weeks of gestation at delivery. Empiric therapy for the infant should include antimicrobial agents active against GBS as well as other organisms that might cause early-onset neonatal sepsis (eg, ampicillin and gentamicin).
- If clinical signs in the infant suggest sepsis, a full diagnostic evaluation should include a lumbar puncture, if feasible. Blood cultures can be sterile in as many as 15% to 38% of newborn infants with meningitis, and the clinical management of an infant with abnormal CSF differs from that of an infant with normal CSF. If a lumbar puncture has been deferred for a neonate receiving empiric antimicrobial therapy and therapy is continued beyond 48 hours because of ongoing clinical findings suggesting infection, CSF should be obtained for measurement of white blood cell count and differential, glucose, and protein and for culture.
- In addition to penicillin or ampicillin, initiation of intrapartum antimicrobial prophylaxis with cefazolin at least 4 hours before delivery can be considered adequate. The effectiveness of other agents (eg, clindamycin or vancomycin) in preventing early-onset GBS disease has not been studied, and no data are available to suggest the duration before delivery of these regimens that can be considered adequate.

FIG 3.2. EMPIRIC MANAGEMENT OF A NEONATE WHOSE MOTHER RECEIVED INTRAPARTUM ANTIMICROBIAL PROPHYLAXIS (IAP) FOR PREVENTION OF EARLY-ONSET GROUP B STREPTOCOCCAL (GBS) DISEASE[1] OR SUSPECTED CHORIOAMNIONITIS. THIS ALGORITHM IS NOT AN EXCLUSIVE COURSE OF MANAGEMENT. VARIATIONS THAT INCORPORATE INDIVIDUAL CIRCUMSTANCES OR INSTITUTIONAL PREFERENCES MAY BE APPROPRIATE.

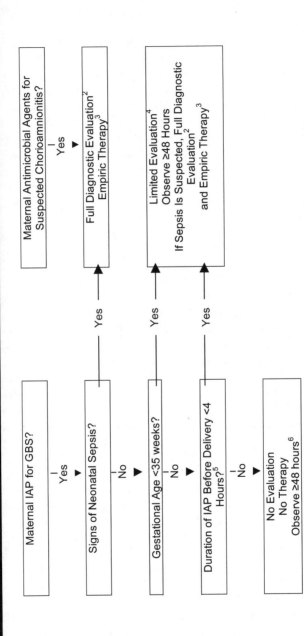

[1] If no maternal IAP for GBS was administered despite an indication being present, data are insufficient on which to recommend a single management strategy.

[2] Includes complete blood cell (CBC) count with differential, blood culture, and chest radiograph if respiratory abnormalities are present. When signs of sepsis are present, a lumbar puncture, if feasible, should be performed.

[3] Duration of therapy varies depending on results of blood culture, cerebrospinal fluid findings (if obtained), and the clinical course of the infant. If laboratory results and clinical course do not indicate bacterial infection, duration may be as short as 48 hours.

[4] CBC including white blood cell count with differential and blood culture.

[5] Applies only to penicillin, ampicillin, or cefazolin and assumes recommended dosing regimens.

[6] A healthy-appearing infant who was ≥38 weeks' gestation at delivery and whose mother received ≥4 hours of IAP before delivery may be discharged home after 24 hours if other discharge criteria have been met and a person able to comply fully with instructions for home observation will be present. If any one of these conditions is not met, the infant should be observed in the

- On the basis of the demonstrated effectiveness of intrapartum antimicrobial prophylaxis in preventing early-onset GBS disease and data indicating that clinical onset occurs within the first 24 hours of life in more than 90% of infants, hospital discharge at 24 hours after birth may be reasonable under certain circumstances. Specifically, a healthy-appearing infant who is at least 38 weeks' gestation at delivery and whose mother received 4 or more hours of intrapartum penicillin, ampicillin, or cefazolin before delivery may be discharged home as early as 24 hours after delivery if other discharge criteria have been met and a person able to comply fully with instructions for home observation will be present. A key component of following instructions is the ability of the person observing the infant to communicate with health care professionals by telephone and to transport the infant promptly to an appropriate health care facility if clinical signs of systemic infection develop. If these conditions are not met, the infant should remain in the hospital for at least 48 hours of observation.

NEONATAL INFECTION CONTROL. Routine cultures to determine whether infants have colonization with GBS are not recommended. Epidemiologic evaluation of late-onset or very late-onset cases in a special care nursery may be required to exclude a nosocomial source.

NURSERY OUTBREAK. Cohorting of ill and colonized infants and use of contact precautions during an outbreak are recommended. Other methods of control (eg, treatment of asymptomatic carriers with penicillin) are ineffective. Routine hand hygiene by health care professionals caring for infants colonized or infected with GBS is the best way to prevent spread to other infants.

Non-Group A or B Streptococcal and Enterococcal Infections

CLINICAL MANIFESTATIONS: Streptococci of groups other than A or B can be associated with invasive disease in infants, children, adolescents, and adults. Urinary tract infection, endocarditis, upper and lower respiratory tract infections, skin and soft tissue infections, pharyngitis, and meningitis are the principal clinical syndromes. Viridans streptococci are associated with endocarditis in patients with congenital or valvular heart disease and bacteremia in neutropenic patients with cancer. Enterococci are associated with bacteremia in neonates and bacteremia, device-associated infections, intra-abdominal abscesses, and urinary tract infections in older children and adults.

ETIOLOGY: Changes in taxonomy and nomenclature of the *Streptococcus* genus have evolved as a result of application of molecular technology. Among gram-positive organisms that are catalase negative and that display chains in Gram stains, the 2 genera associated most often with human disease are *Streptococcus* and *Enterococcus*. The *Streptococcus* genus contains organisms that are (a) beta-hemolytic on blood agar plates (*Streptococcus pyogenes* [see Group A Streptococcal Infections, p 610], *Streptococcus agalactiae* [see Group B Streptococcal Infections, p 620], and groups C, G, and F streptococci); (b) non-beta–hemolytic on blood agar plates (*Streptococcus pneumoniae* [see Pneumococcal Infections, p 525], *Streptococcus bovis* group, and 26 species of viridans streptococci, which are divided into 6 groups by phenotypic characteristics; (c) nutritionally variant streptococci (now referred to as *Abiotrophia* and *Granulicatella*); and (d) unusual streptococcal species that do not fit into any of the other *Streptococcus* species groups.

The genus *Enterococcus* (previously included with group D streptococci) contains more than 20 species, with *Enterococcus faecalis* and *Enterococcus faecium* accounting for most human enterococcal infections.

EPIDEMIOLOGY: The habitats that streptococci and enterococci occupy in humans include skin (groups C, F, and G streptococci), oropharynx (groups B, C, F, and G streptococci and the mutans group streptococci), gastrointestinal tract (groups B, C, F, and G and the bovis group streptococci and *Enterococcus* species), and vagina (groups B, C, D, F, and G streptococci and *Enterococcus* species). The typical human habitats of different species of viridans streptococci include the oropharynx, epithelial surfaces of the oral cavity, teeth, skin, and genitourinary tract. Intrapartum transmission probably is responsible for most cases of early-onset neonatal infection. Vertical colonization of cariogenic mutans streptococcus from mother to infant is well documented. Environmental contamination or transmission via hands of health care professionals can lead to colonization of patients.

The **incubation period** and the period of communicability are unknown.

DIAGNOSTIC TESTS: Microscopic examination of fluids that ordinarily are sterile can yield presumptive evidence of infections by streptococci and enterococci. Diagnosis is established by culture and serogrouping of the isolate, using group-specific antisera. Antimicrobial susceptibility testing of enterococci isolated from sterile sites is important to determine ampicillin and vancomycin susceptibility as well as high-level gentamicin and streptomycin resistance to assess potential for synergy when used in combination with a cell wall active agent (ampicillin or vancomycin). Some susceptibility testing methods may not reliably detect vancomycin resistance; the addition of testing on vancomycin screening agar can increase reliability.

TREATMENT: For most streptococcal infections, treatment with penicillin G alone is adequate. However, for penicillin-resistant isolates, options include penicillin with gentamicin, other beta-lactam agents, and vancomycin. Enterococci and some streptococcal strains (especially viridans streptococci and nutritionally-variant streptococci requiring growth media additives) are resistant to penicillin. Enterococci uniformly are resistant to cephalosporins and can be resistant to ampicillin and vancomycin as well, making treatment challenging. Invasive enterococcal infections such as endocarditis should be treated with ampicillin or vancomycin in combination with an aminoglycoside (usually gentamicin to achieve bactericidal activity). However, the aminoglycoside should be discontinued if in vitro susceptibility testing demonstrates high-level resistance, in which case synergy cannot be achieved. Quinupristin-dalfopristin has been licensed for use in adults for treatment of infections attributable to vancomycin-resistant *E faecium*. Quinupristin-dalfopristin is not effective against *E faecalis*. Linezolid is approved for use in adults for treatment of vancomycin-resistant enterococcal infections, including *E faecium* and *E fecalis*; data in children are limited but suggest safety and effectiveness.

ENDOCARDITIS. Guidelines for antimicrobial therapy in adults have been formulated by the American Heart Association and should be consulted for regimens that may be appropriate for children and adolescents.[*]

ISOLATION OF THE HOSPITALIZED PATIENT: Standard precautions are recommended. For patients with infection or colonization attributable to vancomycin-resistant enterococci (VRE), contact as well as standard precautions are indicated. The duration of isolation may vary by institution. Common practice is to maintain precautions until the patient no longer harbors the organism. Criteria of negative culture results from body fluid or tissue specimens from multiple sites (may include stool or rectal swab, perineal area, axilla or umbilicus, wound, and indwelling urinary catheter or colostomy sites, if present) on at least 3 separate occasions (more than 1 week apart) have been used to define resolution of VRE colonization.

CONTROL MEASURES: Patients with valvular or congenital heart disease should receive antimicrobial prophylaxis to prevent endocarditis at the time of dental and other selected surgical procedures (see Prevention of Bacterial Endocarditis, p 828). Use of vancomycin and treatment with broad-spectrum antimicrobial agents are risk factors for colonization and infection with VRE. Hospitals should develop institution-specific guidelines for the proper use of vancomycin.[†] Early instruction in proper diet, oral health including use of dental sealants and adequate fluoride intake, and smoking cessation programs will aid in the prevention of dental caries.[‡]

Strongyloidiasis
(Strongyloides stercoralis)

CLINICAL MANIFESTATIONS: Asymptomatic infection accompanied by peripheral blood eosinophilia may be the only manifestation of infection. Thus, strongyloidiasis should be considered in any patient with unexplained eosinophilia. When symptoms occur, they are related to the 3 stages of infection: skin invasion, migration of larvae, and penetration of the intestinal mucosa by adult worms. Infective larvae typically are acquired from soil and enter the body through the skin, producing transient pruritic papules at the site of penetration, usually on the feet. Larvae then migrate to the lungs and can cause pneumonitis or a Loeffler-like syndrome. Larvae then ascend the tracheobronchial tree and are swallowed; once they are in the gastrointestinal tract, they mature into adults and can cause vague abdominal pain, malabsorption, vomiting, and diarrhea. Larval migration from defecated stool can result in pruritic skin lesions in the perianal area, buttocks, and upper thighs, which may present as serpiginous, erythematous tracks called larva currens. Because of the ability of a *Strongyloides*

---

[*] Ferrieri P, Gewitz MH, Gerber MA, et al. Unique features of infective endocarditis in childhood. *Pediatrics.* 2002;109:931–943

[†] Centers for Disease Control and Prevention. Recommendations for preventing the spread of vancomycin resistance: recommendations of the Hospital Infection Control Practices Advisory Committee (HICPAC). *MMWR Recomm Rep.* 1995;44(RR-12):1–13

[‡] Centers for Disease Control and Prevention. Surveillance for dental caries, dental sealants, tooth retention, edentulism, and enamel fluorosis—United States, 1988–1994 and 1999–2002. *MMWR Surveill Summ.* 2005;54(SS-3):1–43

organism to complete its life cycle entirely in humans (autoinfection), a disseminated (hyperinfection) syndrome can occur in immunocompromised people, characterized by abdominal pain, rapidly changing or diffuse pulmonary infiltrates, and septicemia or meningitis from enteric gram-negative bacilli.

ETIOLOGY: *Strongyloides stercoralis* is a nematode (roundworm).

EPIDEMIOLOGY: Strongyloidiasis is endemic in the tropics and subtropics, including the southeastern United States, wherever suitable moist soil and improper disposal of human waste coexist. Humans are the principal hosts, but dogs, cats, and other animals also can be reservoirs. Transmission involves penetration of skin by infective (filariform) larvae from contact with infected soil. Infections rarely can be acquired from intimate skin contact or from inadvertent coprophagy, such as from ingestion of contaminated food scavenged from garbage. In addition, because some larvae mature into infective forms in the colon, autoinfection can occur. Adult females lodge in the gut wall, where they lay eggs that become free-living rhabditiform larvae that generally pass into the external environment in feces but also can be swallowed or penetrate the perianal skin of the same host. Because of this cycle of autoinfection, patients may remain infected for decades.

The **incubation period** in humans is unknown.

DIAGNOSTIC TESTS: Strongyloidiasis can be difficult to diagnose, because the parasite burden often is low. Stool examination may disclose characteristic larvae, but several fresh stool specimens may need to be examined, and stool concentration procedures may be required. Examination of duodenal contents obtained by a commercially available string test (Entero-Test) or a direct aspirate through a flexible endoscope may demonstrate larvae. Serodiagnosis can be helpful but is available only at the Centers for Disease Control and Prevention and in a few reference laboratories. Results of enzyme immunoassay for antibodies to *Strongyloides* are positive in approximately 90% of infected people. However, serologic cross-reaction with other helminths limits specificity of serodiagnosis. The serologic test typically becomes negative approximately 6 to 12 months after successful therapy. Eosinophilia (blood eosinophil count >500/µL) is common. In disseminated strongyloidiasis, larvae can be found in the sputum.

TREATMENT: Treatment with ivermectin is preferred and is curative in most people. Albendazole or thiabendazole also can be used, but both drugs are associated with slightly lower cure rates (see Drugs for Parasitic Infections, p 790). Prolonged or repeated treatment may be necessary in the hyperinfection syndrome or immunocompromised patients. Relapses occur and should be treated with the same drugs.

ISOLATION OF THE HOSPITALIZED PATIENT: Standard precautions are recommended.

CONTROL MEASURES: Sanitary disposal measures for human waste should be followed, and education about risk of infection through bare skin is important.

Examination of stool and serologic specimens for *S stercoralis* should be considered for all people who are, or will soon become, immunosuppressed (particularly people infected with human T-lymphotropic virus type 1 or receiving high-dose corticosteroids) and who have traveled to a region with endemic infection. Although most important for people who have spent time in developing countries with highly endemic infection, there also is an important consideration for residents of the southeastern United States, especially older people who have lived there since childhood. Such screening also would be particularly important for people with a clinical picture consistent with strongyloidiasis (eg, eosinophilia, larva currens, and abdominal pain). If a patient's condition requires initiation of immunosuppressive therapy before results of diagnostic tests can be obtained, risks of empiric antiparasitic therapy for strongyloidiasis must be weighed against risks of a disseminated infection.

Syphilis

CLINICAL MANIFESTATIONS:

CONGENITAL SYPHILIS. Intrauterine infection can result in stillbirth, hydrops fetalis, or preterm birth. Infants can have hepatosplenomegaly, snuffles, lymphadenopathy, mucocutaneous lesions, osteochondritis and pseudoparalysis, edema, rash, hemolytic anemia, or thrombocytopenia at birth or within the first 4 to 8 weeks of life. Untreated infants, regardless of whether they have manifestations in early infancy, may develop late manifestations, which usually appear after 2 years of age and involve the central nervous system (CNS), bones and joints, teeth, eyes, and skin. Some consequences of intrauterine infection may not become apparent until many years after birth, such as interstitial keratitis (5–20 years of age), eighth cranial nerve deafness (10–40 years of age), Hutchinson teeth (peg-shaped, notched central incisors), anterior bowing of the shins, frontal bossing, mulberry molars, saddle nose, rhagades, and Clutton joints (symmetric, painless swelling of the knees). The first 3 manifestations are referred to as the Hutchinson triad.

ACQUIRED SYPHILIS. Infection can be divided into 3 stages. The **primary stage** appears as one or more painless indurated ulcers (chancres) of the skin or mucous membranes at the site of inoculation, but chancres may not be recognized. These lesions most commonly appear on the genitalia. The **secondary stage,** beginning 1 to 2 months later, is characterized by rash, mucocutaneous lesions, and lymphadenopathy. The polymorphic maculopapular rash is generalized and typically includes the palms and soles. In moist areas around the vulva or anus, hypertrophic papular lesions (condylomata lata) can occur and can be confused with condyloma acuminata secondary to human papillomavirus infection (HPV). Generalized lymphadenopathy, fever, malaise, splenomegaly, sore throat, headache, and arthralgia can be present. A variable latent period follows but sometimes is interrupted during the first few years by recurrences of symptoms of secondary syphilis. **Latent** syphilis is defined as the period after infection when patients are seroreactive but demonstrate no clinical manifestations of disease. Latent syphilis acquired within the preceding year is referred to as *early latent syphilis;* all other cases of latent syphilis are *late latent syphilis* or *syphilis of unknown duration.* The tertiary stage of infection refers to gumma formation and cardiovascular involvement but not neurosyphilis. The tertiary stage can be marked by aortitis or gummatous changes of the skin, bone, or viscera, occurring from years to decades after the primary infection. Neurosyphilis is defined as infection of the central nervous system with *Treponema pallidum.* Manifestations of neurosyphilis can occur at any stage of infection, especially in people infected with human immunodeficiency virus (HIV).

ETIOLOGY: *Treponema pallidum* is a thin, motile spirochete that is extremely fastidious, surviving only briefly outside the host. The organism has not been cultivated successfully on artificial media.

EPIDEMIOLOGY: Syphilis, which is rare in much of the industrialized world, persists in the United States and in developing countries. The incidence of acquired and congenital syphilis increased dramatically in the United States during the late 1980s and early 1990s but subsequently decreased. Rates of infection remain disproportionately high in large urban areas, in the southern United States, and among men who have sex with men. In adults, syphilis is more common among people with HIV infection.

Congenital syphilis is contracted from an infected mother via transplacental transmission of *T pallidum* at any time during pregnancy or at birth. Among women with untreated early syphilis, as many as 40% of pregnancies result in spontaneous abortion, stillbirth, or perinatal death. Infection can be transmitted to the fetus at any stage of disease; the rate of transmission is 60% to 100% during primary and secondary syphilis and slowly decreases with later stages of maternal infection (approximately 40% with early latent infection and 8% with late latent infection). Skin lesions or moist nasal secretions of congenital syphilis are highly infectious. However, organisms rarely are found in lesions more than 24 hours after treatment has begun.

Acquired syphilis almost always is contracted through direct sexual contact with ulcerative lesions of the skin or mucous membranes of infected people. Sexual abuse must be suspected in any young child with acquired syphilis. Open, moist lesions of the primary or secondary stages are highly infectious. Relapses of secondary syphilis with infectious mucocutaneous lesions can occur up to 4 years after primary infection.

The **incubation period** for acquired primary syphilis typically is 3 weeks but ranges from 10 to 90 days.

DIAGNOSTIC TESTS: Definitive diagnosis is made when spirochetes are identified by microscopic darkfield examination or direct fluorescent antibody tests of lesion exudate or tissue, such as placenta or umbilical cord. Specimens should be scraped from moist mucocutaneous lesions or aspirated from a regional lymph node. Specimens from mouth lesions require direct fluorescent antibody techniques to distinguish *T pallidum* from nonpathogenic treponemes. Because false-negative microscopic results are common, serologic testing often is necessary. Polymerase chain reaction tests and immunoglobulin (Ig) M immunoblotting have been developed but are not yet available commercially.

Presumptive diagnosis is possible using nontreponemal and treponemal tests. The use of only 1 type of test is insufficient for diagnosis, because false-positive nontreponemal test results occur with various medical conditions, and false-positive treponemal test results occur with other spirochetal diseases.

The standard nontreponemal tests for syphilis include the Venereal Disease Research Laboratory (VDRL) slide test, the rapid plasma reagin (RPR) test, and the automated reagin test (ART). These tests measure antibody directed against lipoidal antigen from *T pallidum*, antibody interaction with host tissues, or both. These tests are inexpensive and rapidly performed and provide quantitative results. Quantitative results help define disease activity and monitor response to therapy. Nontreponemal test results may be falsely negative (ie, nonreactive) with early primary syphilis, latent acquired syphilis of long duration, and late congenital syphilis. Occasionally, a nontreponemal test performed on serum samples containing high concentrations of antibody against *T pallidum* will be weakly reactive or falsely negative, a reaction termed the *prozone* phenomenon. Diluting the serum results in a positive test. When nontreponemal tests are used to monitor treatment response, the same specific test (eg, VDRL, RPR, or ART) must be used throughout the follow-up period, preferably by the same laboratory, to ensure comparability of results.

A reactive nontreponemal test result from a patient with typical lesions indicates the need for treatment. However, any reactive nontreponemal test result must be confirmed by one of the specific treponemal tests to exclude a false-positive test result. False-positive results can be caused by certain viral infections (eg, Epstein Barr virus infection, hepatitis, varicella, and measles), lymphoma, tuberculosis, malaria, endocarditis, connective tissue disease, pregnancy, abuse of injection drugs, laboratory or technical error, or Wharton jelly contamination when cord blood specimens are used. Treatment should not be delayed while awaiting the results of the treponemal test results if the patient is symptomatic or at high risk of infection. A sustained fourfold decrease in titer of the nontreponemal test result after treatment demonstrates adequate therapy; a fourfold increase in titer after treatment suggests reinfection or relapse. The quantitative nontreponemal test usually decreases fourfold within 6 months after therapy for primary or secondary syphilis and usually becomes nonreactive within 1 year after successful therapy if the infection (primary or secondary syphilis) was treated early. The patient usually becomes seronegative within 2 years even if the initial titer was high or the infection was congenital. Some people will continue to have low nontreponemal antibody titers despite effective therapy. This serofast state is more common in patients treated for latent or tertiary syphilis.

Treponemal tests in use are fluorescent treponemal antibody absorption (FTA-ABS) and *T pallidum* particle agglutination (TP-PA) tests. People who have positive FTA-ABS and TP-PA test results usually remain reactive for life, even after successful therapy. Treponemal test antibody titers correlate poorly with disease activity and should not be used to assess response to therapy.

Treponemal tests also are not 100% specific for syphilis; positive reactions variably occur in patients with other spirochetal diseases, such as yaws, pinta, leptospirosis, rat-bite fever, relapsing fever, and Lyme disease. Nontreponemal tests can be used to differentiate Lyme disease from syphilis, because the VDRL test is nonreactive in Lyme disease.

Usually, a serum nontreponemal test is obtained initially, and if it is reactive, a treponemal test is performed. The probability of syphilis is high in a sexually active person whose serum is reactive on both nontreponemal and treponemal tests. Differentiating syphilis treated in the past from reinfection often is difficult unless the nontreponemal titer is increasing. Some clinical laboratories and blood banks have begun to screen samples using treponemal enzyme immunoassay (EIA) tests.

In summary, nontreponemal antibody tests (VDRL, RPR, and ART) are used for screening, and treponemal tests (FTA-ABS and TP-PA) are used to establish a presumptive diagnosis. Quantitative nontreponemal antibody tests are useful in assessing the adequacy of therapy and in detecting reinfection and relapse. All patients who have syphilis should be tested for HIV infection.

CEREBROSPINAL FLUID TESTS. For evaluation of possible neurosyphilis, the VDRL test should be performed on cerebrospinal fluid (CSF). In addition to VDRL testing of CSF, evaluation of CSF protein and white blood cell count is used to assess the likelihood of CNS involvement. Although the FTA-ABS test of CSF is less specific than the VDRL test, some experts recommend using the FTA-ABS test, believing it to be more sensitive than the VDRL test. Results from the VDRL test should be interpreted cautiously, because a negative result on a VDRL test of CSF does not exclude a diagnosis of neurosyphilis. Fewer data exist for the TP-PA test for CSF, and none exist for the RPR test; these tests should not be used for CSF evaluation.

TESTING DURING PREGNANCY. All women should be screened serologically for syphilis early in pregnancy with a nontreponemal test (eg, VDRL or RPR) and preferably again at delivery. In areas of high prevalence of syphilis and in patients considered at high risk of syphilis, a nontreponemal serum test at the beginning of the third trimester (28 weeks of gestation) and at delivery is indicated. For women treated during pregnancy, follow-up serologic testing is necessary to assess the efficacy of therapy. Low-titer false-positive nontreponemal antibody test results occasionally occur in pregnancy. The result of a positive nontreponemal antibody test should be confirmed with a treponemal antibody test (eg, FTA-ABS). When a pregnant woman has a reactive nontreponemal test result and a persistently negative treponemal test result, a false-positive test result is confirmed. Some laboratories are screening pregnant women using an EIA treponemal test. Pregnant women with reactive treponemal screening tests should have confirmatory testing with a nontreponemal test with titers. Any woman who delivers a stillborn infant after 20 weeks' gestation should be tested for syphilis.

EVALUATION OF NEWBORN INFANTS FOR CONGENITAL INFECTION. No newborn infant should be discharged from the hospital without determination of the mother's serologic status for syphilis. Testing of cord blood or an infant serum sample is inadequate for screening, because these test results can be nonreactive even when the mother is seropositive. All infants born to seropositive mothers require a careful examination and a quantitative nontreponemal syphilis test. The test performed on the infant should be the same as that performed on the mother to enable comparison of titer results.

An infant should be evaluated further for congenital syphilis if the maternal titer has increased fourfold, if the infant titer is fourfold greater than the mother's titer, or if the infant has clinical manifestations of syphilis. In addition, an infant should be evaluated further if born to a mother with positive nontreponemal and treponemal test results if the mother has one or more of the following conditions:

- Syphilis untreated or inadequately treated or treatment is not documented (see Treatment, p 636)
- Syphilis during pregnancy treated with a nonpenicillin regimen (including erythromycin)
- Syphilis treated less than 1 month before delivery (because treatment failures occur and the efficacy of treatment cannot be assumed)

- Syphilis treated before pregnancy but with insufficient serologic follow-up to assess the response to treatment and current infection status

Evaluation for syphilis in an infant should include the following:

- Physical examination
- Quantitative nontreponemal serologic test of serum from the infant for syphilis (not cord blood, because false-positive and false-negative results can occur)
- A VDRL test of CSF and analysis of CSF for cells and protein concentration (see Cerebrospinal Fluid Testing, for indications)
- Long-bone radiographs (unless the diagnosis has been established otherwise)
- Complete blood cell and platelet count
- Other clinically indicated tests (eg, chest radiography, liver function tests, ultrasonography, ophthalmologic examination, and auditory brainstem response test)

Pathologic examination of the placenta or umbilical cord using specific fluorescent antitreponemal antibody staining, if available, also is recommended.

A guide for interpretation of the results of nontreponemal and treponemal serologic tests is given in Table 3.60 (p 636). An infected infant's test may be reactive or nonreactive, depending on the timing of maternal and fetal infection; thus, the emphasis on screening maternal blood. Conversely, transplacental transmission of nontreponemal and treponemal antibodies to the fetus can occur in a mother who has been treated appropriately for syphilis during pregnancy, resulting in positive test results in the uninfected newborn infant. The neonate's nontreponemal test titer in these circumstances usually reverts to negative in 4 to 6 months, whereas a positive FTA-ABS or TP-PA test result from passively acquired antibody may not become negative for 1 year or longer.

In an infant with clinical or tissue findings suggestive of congenital syphilis, a positive serum nontreponemal test result strongly supports the diagnosis regardless of therapy the mother received during the pregnancy. Infants who have a nonreactive nontreponemal test and normal physical examination do not require evaluation, although treatment depends on maternal history.

CEREBROSPINAL FLUID TESTING. Cerebrospinal fluid should be examined in all infants who are evaluated for congenital syphilis if the infant has any of the following: (1) abnormal physical examination findings consistent with congenital syphilis; (2) a serum quantitative nontreponemal titer that is fourfold greater than the mother's titer; or (3) a positive darkfield or fluorescent antibody test result on body fluid(s). Testing of CSF may be indicated in other situations to help determine appropriate treatment (see Evaluation of Newborn Infants for Congenital Infection, p 634, and Treatment, p 636). Cerebrospinal fluid should be examined in all patients with suspected neurosyphilis or with acquired untreated syphilis of more than 1 year's duration. Abnormalities in CSF in patients with neurosyphilis include increased protein concentration, increased white blood cell count, and a reactive VDRL test result. Some experts also recommend performing the FTA-ABS test on CSF, believing it to be more sensitive but less specific than VDRL testing of CSF for neurosyphilis. Because of the wide range of normal values for CSF white blood cell counts and protein concentrations in the newborn infant, interpretation may be difficult. Although a white blood cell count as high as 25 cells/μL and a protein concentration greater than 150 mg/dL might be normal, some experts recommend that a white blood cell

Table 3.60. Guide for Interpretation of Syphilis Serologic Test Results of Mothers and Their Infants

Nontreponemal Test Result (eg, VDRL, RPR, ART)		Treponemal Test Result (eg, TP-PA, FTA-ABS)		Interpretation[1]
Mother	Infant	Mother	Infant	
−	−	−	−	No syphilis or incubating syphilis in the mother or infant or prozone phenomenon
+	+	−	−	No syphilis in mother or infant (false-positive result of nontreponemal test with passive transfer to infant)
+	+ or −	+	+	Maternal syphilis with possible infant infection; mother treated for syphilis during pregnancy; or mother with latent syphilis and possible infant infection[2]
+	+	+	+	Recent or previous syphilis in the mother; possible infant infection
−	−	+	+	Mother successfully treated for syphilis before or early in pregnancy; or mother with Lyme disease (ie, false-positive serologic test result); infant syphilis unlikely

VDRL indicates Venereal Disease Research Laboratory; RPR, rapid plasma reagin; ART, automated reagin test; TP-PA, *Treponema pallidum* particle agglutination test; FTA-ABS, fluorescent treponemal antibody absorption; +, reactive; −, nonreactive.

[1] Table presents a guide and not a definitive interpretation of serologic test results for syphilis in mothers and their newborn infants. Maternal history is the most important aspect for interpretation of test results. Factors that should be considered include timing of maternal infection, nature and timing of maternal treatment, quantitative maternal and infant titers, and serial determination of nontreponemal test titers in both mother and infant.

[2] Mothers with latent syphilis may have nonreactive nontreponemal test results.

count of 5 cells/μL and a protein concentration of 40 mg/dL be considered the upper limits of normal. A negative result on VDRL or FTA-ABS testing of CSF does not exclude congenital neurosyphilis, and that is one of the reasons why infants with proven or probable congenital syphilis require 10 days of parenteral treatment with penicillin G regardless of CSF test results.

TREATMENT*: Parenteral penicillin G remains the preferred drug for treatment of syphilis at any stage. Recommendations for penicillin G and duration of therapy vary, depending on the stage of disease and clinical manifestations. Parenteral penicillin G is the only documented effective therapy for patients who have neurosyphilis, congenital syphilis, or syphilis during pregnancy and is recommended for HIV-infected patients. Such patients always should be treated with penicillin, even if desensitization

* Centers for Disease Control and Prevention. Sexually transmitted infections treatment guidelines—United States, 2006. *MMWR Recomm Rep.* 2006; in press (available at **www.cdc.gov/mmwr**)

for penicillin allergy is necessary. If shortages of aqueous penicillin G exist, alternate treatment recommendations can be found online (**www.cdc.gov/nchstp/dstd/penicillinG.htm**).

PENICILLIN ALLERGY. Skin testing for penicillin hypersensitivity with the major and minor determinants reliably can identify people at high risk of reacting to penicillin; currently, only the major determinant (benzylpenicilloyl poly-L-lysine) and penicillin G skin tests are available commercially. A challenge has occurred with the recent unavailability of the major determinant (Pre-Pen). However, there are plans for future availability of this product as well as a companion minor determinant mixture. If the major determinant is not available for skin testing, all patients with IgE-mediated reactions to penicillin should be desensitized in a hospital setting. In patients with non-IgE–mediated reactions, outpatient oral desensitization or monitored test doses may be considered. Testing with the major determinant of penicillin G is estimated to miss 3% to 6% of penicillin-allergic patients who are at risk of serious or fatal reactions. Thus, a cautious approach to penicillin therapy is advised when a patient cannot be tested with all of the penicillin skin test reagents. An oral or intravenous desensitization protocol for patients with a positive skin test result is available and should be performed in a hospital setting.* Oral desensitization is regarded as safer and easier to perform. Desensitization usually can be completed in approximately 4 hours, after which the first dose of penicillin can be given.

CONGENITAL SYPHILIS: NEWBORN INFANTS (SEE TABLE 3.61, P 638). Infants should be treated for congenital syphilis if they have proven or probable disease demonstrated by one or more of the following: (1) physical, laboratory, or radiographic evidence of active disease; (2) positive placenta or umbilical cord test results for treponemes using direct fluorescent antibody-*T pallidum* staining or darkfield test; (3) a reactive result on VDRL testing of CSF; or (4) a serum quantitative nontreponemal titer that is at least fourfold higher than the mother's titer using the same test and preferably the same laboratory. If the infant's titer is less than 4 times higher than that of the mother, congenital syphilis still can be present. When an infant warrants evaluation for congenital syphilis (see Evaluation of Newborn Infants for Congenital Infection, p 634), the infant should be treated if test results cannot exclude infection, if the infant cannot be evaluated completely, or if adequate follow-up cannot be ensured.

In infants with proven or probable disease, aqueous crystalline penicillin G is preferred. The dosage should be based on chronologic, not gestational, age (see Table 3.61, p 638). Alternatively, some experts recommend penicillin G procaine for treatment of congenital syphilis; however, adequate CSF concentrations may not be achieved by this regimen. If more than 1 day of therapy is missed, the entire course should be restarted. Data supporting the use of ampicillin for treatment of congenital syphilis are not available.

Healthy-appearing infants are at minimal risk of syphilis if (1) they are born to mothers who completed appropriate penicillin treatment for syphilis more than 4 weeks before delivery; (2) the mother had an appropriate serologic response to treat-

---

* Centers for Disease Control and Prevention. Sexually transmitted infections treatment guidelines—United States, 2006. *MMWR Recomm Rep*. 2006; in press (available at **www.cdc.gov/mmwr**)

Table 3.61. Recommended Treatment of Neonates (≤4 Weeks of Age) With Proven or Possible Congenital Syphilis

Clinical Status	Evaluation	Antimicrobial Therapy[1]
Proven or highly probable disease[2]	CSF analysis for VDRL, cell count, and protein CBC and platelet count Other tests as clinically indicated (eg, long-bone radiography, liver function tests, ophthalmologic examination)	Aqueous crystalline penicillin G, 100 000–150 000 U/kg per day, administered as 50 000 U/kg per dose, IV, every 12 h during the first 7 days of life and every 8 h thereafter for a total of 10 days **OR** Penicillin G procaine,[3] 50 000 U/kg per day, IM, in a single dose for 10 days
Normal physical examination and serum quantitative nontreponemal titer the same or less than fourfold the maternal titer:		
(a) (i) Mother was not treated or inadequately treated or has no documented treatment; (ii) mother was treated with erythromycin or other nonpenicillin regimen; (iii) mother received treatment ≤4 weeks before delivery	CSF analysis for VDRL, cell count, and protein CBC and platelet count Long-bone radiography	Aqueous crystalline penicillin G, IV, for 10 days[4] **OR** Penicillin G procaine,[3] 50 000 U/kg per day, IM, in a single dose for 10 days[4] **OR** Penicillin G benzathine,[3] 50 000 U/kg, IM, in a single dose[4]
(b) (i) Adequate maternal therapy given >4 wk before delivery; (ii) mother has no evidence of reinfection or relapse	None	Clinical, serologic follow-up, and penicillin G benzathine, 50 000 U/kg, IM, in a single dose[5]
(c) Adequate therapy before pregnancy and mother's nontreponemal serologic titer remained low and stable during pregnancy and at delivery	None	None[6]

IV indicates intravenously; IM, intramuscularly; CSF, cerebrospinal fluid; and CBC, complete blood cell.

[1] If more than 1 day of therapy is missed, the entire course should be restarted.

[2] Abnormal physical examination, serum quantitative nontreponemal titer that is fourfold greater than the mother's titer, or positive result of darkfield or fluorescent antibody test of body fluid(s).

[3] Penicillin G benzathine and penicillin G procaine are approved for IM administration *only*.

[4] A complete evaluation (CSF analysis, bone radiography, CBC) is not necessary if 10 days of parenteral therapy is administered but may be useful to support a diagnosis of congenital syphilis. If a single dose of penicillin G benzathine is used, then the infant must be evaluated fully, the full evaluation must be normal, and follow-up must be certain. If any part of the infant's evaluation is abnormal or not performed or if the CSF analysis is uninterpretable, the 10-day course of penicillin is required.

[5] Some experts would not treat the infant but would provide close serologic follow-up.

[6] Some experts would treat with penicillin G benzathine, 50 000 U/kg, as a single IM injection if follow-up is uncertain.

ment (in early or high-titer syphilis, a documented fourfold or greater decrease in VDRL, RPR, or ART titer or in latent low-titer syphilis, titers remained stable and low); (3) infants have a serum quantitative nontreponemal serologic titer the same as or less than fourfold the maternal titer; and (4) the mother had no evidence of reinfection or relapse. Although a full evaluation may be unnecessary, these infants should be treated with a single injection of penicillin G benzathine. Alternatively, these infants may be examined carefully, preferably monthly, until their nontreponemal serologic test results are negative.

Infants whose mothers received no treatment or inadequate treatment for syphilis require special consideration. Maternal treatment for syphilis is deemed inadequate if: (1) the mother's penicillin dose is unknown, undocumented, or inadequate; (2) the mother received erythromycin or any other nonpenicillin regimen during pregnancy for syphilis; or (3) treatment was given within 28 days of the infant's birth.

Asymptomatic infants whose quantitative nontreponemal serologic titer is the same or less than fourfold their mother's titer and born to women who received no treatment or inadequate treatment (as defined by one or more of these criteria) should be evaluated fully, including CSF examination (see Evaluation of Newborn Infants for Congenital Infection, p 634). Some experts would treat all such infants with aqueous crystalline penicillin G (or aqueous penicillin G procaine) for 10 days, because physical examination and laboratory test results cannot reliably exclude the diagnosis in all cases. However, if the infant's physical examination, including ophthalmologic examination, CSF findings, radiographs of long bones and chest, and complete blood cell and platelet counts all are normal, some experts would treat infants in the specific circumstances given in Table 3.61 (p 638) with a single dose of penicillin G benzathine (50 000 U/kg intramuscularly). In the case in which maternal response to treatment has not been demonstrated but the mother received an appropriate regimen of penicillin therapy more than 1 month before delivery, the infant's evaluation is normal, and clinical and serologic follow-up can be ensured, some experts would give a single dose of penicillin G benzathine and continue to observe the infant.

CONGENITAL SYPHILIS: OLDER INFANTS AND CHILDREN. Because establishing the diagnosis of neurosyphilis is difficult, infants older than 4 weeks of age who possibly have congenital syphilis or who have neurologic involvement should be treated with aqueous crystalline penicillin (see Table 3.62, p 640). This regimen also should be used to treat children older than 1 year of age who have late and previously untreated congenital syphilis. Some experts also suggest giving such patients penicillin G benzathine, 50 000 U/kg, intramuscularly, in 3 weekly doses after the 10-day course of intravenous aqueous crystalline penicillin. If the patient has minimal clinical manifestations of disease, the CSF examination is normal, and the result of the VDRL test of CSF is negative, some experts would treat with 3 weekly doses of penicillin G benzathine (50 000 U/kg, intramuscularly).

SYPHILIS IN PREGNANCY. Regardless of the stage of pregnancy, patients should be treated with penicillin according to the dosage schedules appropriate for the stage of syphilis as recommended for nonpregnant patients (see Table 3.62, p 640). For penicillin-allergic patients, no proven alternative therapy has been established. A pregnant woman with a history of penicillin allergy should be treated with

Table 3.62. Recommended Treatment for Syphilis in People >4 Weeks of Age

	Children	Adults
Congenital syphilis	Aqueous crystalline penicillin G, 200 000–300 000 U/kg per day, IV, administered as 50 000 U/kg every 4–6 h for 10 days[1]	
Primary, secondary, and early latent syphilis[2]	Penicillin G benzathine,[3] 50 000 U/kg, IM, up to the adult dose of 2.4 million U in a single dose	Penicillin G benzathine, 2.4 million U, IM, in a single dose **OR** *If allergic to penicillin and not pregnant,* Doxycycline, 100 mg, orally, twice a day for 14 days **OR** Tetracycline, 500 mg, orally, 4 times/day for 14 days
Late latent syphilis[4] **or latent syphilis of unknown duration**	Penicillin G benzathine, 50 000 U/kg, IM, up to the adult dose of 2.4 million U, administered as 3 single doses at 1-wk intervals (total 150 000 U/kg, up to the adult dose of 7.2 million U)	Penicillin G benzathine, 7.2 million U total, administered as 3 doses of 2.4 million U, IM, each at 1-wk intervals **OR** *If allergic to penicillin and not pregnant,* Doxycycline, 100 mg, orally, twice a day for 4 wk **OR** Tetracycline, 500 mg, orally, 4 times/day for 4 wk
Tertiary	…	Penicillin G benzathine, 7.2 million U total, administered as 3 doses of 2.4 million U, IM, at 1-wk intervals *If allergic to penicillin and not pregnant, same as for late latent syphilis*
Neurosyphilis[5]	Aqueous crystalline penicillin G, 200 000 to 300 000 U/kg per day, given every 4–6 h for 10–14 days in doses not to exceed the adult dose	Aqueous crystalline penicillin G, 18–24 million U per day, administered as 3–4 million U, IV, every 4 h for 10–14 days[6] **OR** Penicillin G procaine,[2] 2.4 million U, IM, once daily **PLUS** probenecid, 500 mg, orally, 4 times/day, both for 10–14 days[6]

IM indicates intramuscularly; IV, intravenously.

[1] If the patient has no clinical manifestations of disease, the CSF examination is normal, and the CSF VDRL result is negative, some experts would treat with up to 3 weekly doses of penicillin G benzathine, 50 000 U/kg, IM. Some experts also suggest giving these patients a single dose of penicillin G benzathine, 50 000 U/kg, IM, after the 10-day course of IV aqueous penicillin.

[2] Early latent syphilis is defined as being acquired within the preceding year.

[3] Penicillin G benzathine and penicillin G procaine are approved for IM administration *only*.

[4] Late latent syphilis is defined as syphilis beyond 1 year's duration.

[5] Patients who are allergic to penicillin should be desensitized.

penicillin after desensitization. In some patients, skin testing may be helpful. Desensitization should be performed in consultation with a specialist and only in facilities in which emergency assistance is available (see Penicillin Allergy, p 637).

Erythromycin, azithromycin, or any other nonpenicillin treatment of syphilis during pregnancy cannot be considered reliable to cure infection in the fetus. Tetracycline is not recommended for pregnant women because of potential adverse effects on the fetus.

EARLY ACQUIRED SYPHILIS (PRIMARY, SECONDARY, EARLY LATENT SYPHILIS). A single intramuscular dose of penicillin G benzathine is the preferred treatment for children and adults (see Table 3.62, p 640). All children should have a CSF examination before treatment to exclude a diagnosis of neurosyphilis. Evaluation of CSF in adolescents and adults is necessary only if clinical signs or symptoms of neurologic or ophthalmic involvement are present. Neurosyphilis should be considered in the differential diagnosis of neurologic disease in HIV-infected people.

For nonpregnant patients who are allergic to penicillin, doxycycline or tetracycline should be given for 14 days. Children younger than 8 years of age should not be given tetracycline or doxycycline unless the benefits of therapy are greater than the risks of dental staining (see Antimicrobial Agents and Related Therapy, p 735). Drugs other than penicillin and tetracycline do not have proven efficacy in the treatment of syphilis. Clinical studies, along with biologic and pharmacologic considerations, suggest ceftriaxone should be effective for early-acquired syphilis. The recommended dose and duration of ceftriaxone therapy are 1 g once daily via either the intramuscular or intravenous route for 8 to 10 days (for adolescents and adults). Because efficacy of ceftriaxone is not well documented, close follow-up is essential. Single-dose therapy with ceftriaxone is not effective. When follow-up cannot be ensured, especially for children younger than 8 years of age, consideration must be given to hospitalization and desensitization followed by administration of penicillin G (see Penicillin Allergy, p 637).

SYPHILIS OF MORE THAN 1 YEAR'S DURATION (EXCEPT NEUROSYPHILIS). Penicillin G benzathine should be given intramuscularly weekly for 3 successive weeks (see Table 3.62, p 640). In patients who are allergic to penicillin, doxycycline or tetracycline for 4 weeks should be given only if a CSF examination has excluded neurosyphilis. Patients who have syphilis and who demonstrate any of the following criteria should have a prompt CSF examination:

- Neurologic or ophthalmic signs or symptoms;
- Evidence of active tertiary syphilis (eg, aortitis, gumma);
- Treatment failure; or
- Human immunodeficiency virus infection with late latent syphilis or syphilis of unknown duration.

If dictated by circumstances and patient or parent preferences, a CSF examination may be performed for patients who do not meet these criteria. Some specialists recommend performing a CSF examination on all patients who have latent syphilis and a nontreponemal serologic test result of ≥1:32 or, if the patient is HIV infected, a serum CD4 + T-lymphocyte count ≤350. The risk of neurosyphilis in this circumstance is unknown. If a CSF examination is performed and the results indicate abnormalities consistent with neurosyphilis, the patient should be treated for neurosyphilis (see Neurosyphilis). Children younger than 8 years of age should not be given tetracycline or doxycycline unless the benefits of therapy are greater than the risks of dental staining (see Antimicrobial Agents and Related Therapy, p 735). Performing a VDRL test of CSF, protein concentration test, and leukocyte cell count is mandatory for people with suspected neurosyphilis, people who have concurrent HIV infection, people who have failed treatment, and people receiving antimicrobial agents other than penicillin.

NEUROSYPHILIS. The recommended regimen for adults is aqueous crystalline penicillin G, intravenously, for 10 to 14 days (see Table 3.62, p 640). If adherence to therapy can be ensured, patients may be treated with an alternative regimen of intramuscular penicillin G procaine plus oral probenecid for 10 to 14 days. Some experts recommend following both of these regimens with penicillin G benzathine, 2.4 million U, intramuscularly, weekly for 1 to 3 doses. For children, aqueous crystalline penicillin G for 10 to 14 days is recommended, and some experts recommend additional therapy with penicillin G benzathine, 50 000 U/kg per dose (not to exceed 2.4 million U) in 3 single weekly doses.

If the patient has a history of allergy to penicillin, consideration should be given to desensitization, and the patient should be managed in consultation with a specialist (see Penicillin Allergy, p 637).

OTHER CONSIDERATIONS.

- Mothers of infants with congenital syphilis should be tested for other sexually transmitted infections (STIs), including gonorrhea and *Chlamydia trachomatis*, HIV, and hepatitis B virus infection. If injection drug use is suspected, the mother also may be at risk of hepatitis C virus infection.
- All recent sexual contacts of people with acquired syphilis should be evaluated for other STIs as well as syphilis (see Control Measures, p 644).
- All patients with syphilis should be tested for other STIs, including HIV and hepatitis B virus infection. Patients who have primary syphilis should be retested for HIV after 3 months if the first HIV test result is negative.
- For HIV-infected patients with syphilis, careful follow-up is essential. Patients infected with HIV who have early syphilis may be at increased risk of neurologic complications and higher rates of treatment failure with currently recommended regimens.

FOLLOW-UP AND MANAGEMENT.

Congenital syphilis. Treated infants should have careful follow-up evaluations during regularly scheduled visits at 1, 2, 4, 6, and 12 months of age. Serologic nontreponemal tests should be performed 2 to 4, 6, and 12 months after conclusion of treatment or until results become nonreactive or the titer has decreased fourfold. Nontreponemal antibody titers should decrease by 3 months of age and should be nonreactive by 6 months of age if the infant was infected and adequately treated or was not infected and initially seropositive because of transplacentally acquired maternal antibody. The serologic response after therapy may be slower for infants treated after the neonatal period. Patients with increasing titers or with persistent stable titers 6 to 12 months after initial treatment should be evaluated, including a CSF examination, and treated with a 10-day course of parenteral penicillin G, even if they were treated previously.

Treated infants with congenital neurosyphilis and initially positive results of VDRL tests of CSF or abnormal or uninterpretable CSF cell counts and/or protein concentrations should undergo repeated clinical evaluation and CSF examination at 6-month intervals until their CSF examination is normal. A reactive result of VDRL testing of CSF at the 6-month interval is an indication for retreatment. If white blood cell counts still are abnormal at 2 years or are not decreasing at each examination, retreatment is indicated.

Acquired syphilis. Treated pregnant women with syphilis should have quantitative nontreponemal serologic tests repeated at 28 to 32 weeks of gestation, at delivery, and following the recommendations for the stage of disease. Serologic titers may be repeated monthly in women at high risk of reinfection or in geographic areas where the prevalence of syphilis is high. The clinical and antibody response should be appropriate for stage of disease. Most women will deliver before their serologic response to treatment can be assessed definitively. Therapy should not be judged inadequate if the maternal antibody titer has not decreased fourfold by delivery. Inadequate maternal treatment is likely if delivery occurs within 30 days of therapy, if clinical signs of infection are present at delivery, or if the maternal antibody titer is fourfold higher than the pretreatment titer.

INDICATIONS FOR RETREATMENT.
Primary/secondary syphilis:
- If clinical signs or symptoms persist or recur or if a fourfold increase in titer of a nontreponemal test occurs, evaluate CSF and HIV status and retreat.
- If the nontreponemal titer fails to decrease fourfold within 6 months after therapy, evaluate for HIV; retreat unless follow-up for continued clinical and serologic assessment can be ensured. Some experts recommend CSF evaluation.

Latent syphilis: In the following situations, CSF examination should be performed and retreatment should be provided:
- Titers increase fourfold
- An initially high titer (>1:32) fails to decrease at least fourfold within 12 to 24 months
- Signs or symptoms attributable to syphilis develop

In all these instances, retreatment, when indicated, should be performed with 3 weekly injections of penicillin G benzathine, 2.4 million U, intramuscularly, unless CSF examination indicates that neurosyphilis is present, at which time treatment for neurosyphilis should be initiated. Retreated patients should be treated with the schedules recommended for patients with syphilis for more than 1 year. In general, only 1 retreatment course is indicated. The possibility of reinfection or concurrent HIV infection always should be considered when retreating patients with early syphilis.

Patients with neurosyphilis must have periodic serologic testing, clinical evaluation at 6-month intervals, and repeated CSF examinations. If the CSF cell count has not decreased after 6 months or CSF is not entirely normal after 2 years, retreatment should be considered. Cerebrospinal fluid abnormalities may persist for extended periods of time in HIV-infected people with neurosyphilis. Close follow-up is warranted.

ISOLATION OF THE HOSPITALIZED PATIENT: Standard precautions are recommended for all patients, including infants with suspected or proven congenital syphilis. In addition, for infants with suspected or proven congenital syphilis, parents, visitors, hospital personnel, and medical staff should use gloves when handling the infant until 24 hours of treatment has been completed. Because moist open lesions and possibly blood are contagious in all patients with syphilis, gloves should be worn when caring for patients with primary and secondary syphilis with skin and mucous membrane lesions until 24 hours of treatment has been completed.

CONTROL MEASURES:

- All women should be screened for syphilis early in pregnancy and preferably at delivery. Women at high risk of syphilis also should be screened at 28 to 32 weeks of gestation.
- Education of patients and populations about STIs, treatment of sexual contacts, reporting of each case to local public health authorities for contact investigation and appropriate follow-up, and serologic screening of high-risk populations are indicated.
- All recent sexual contacts of a person with acquired syphilis should be identified, examined, serologically tested, and treated appropriately. Sexual contacts within the last 3 months are at high risk of early syphilis and should be treated for early-acquired syphilis whether or not they are seropositive. Every effort, including physical examination and serologic testing, should be made to establish a diagnosis in these patients.
- All people, including hospital personnel, who have had close unprotected contact with a patient with early congenital syphilis before identification of the disease or during the first 24 hours of therapy should be examined clinically for the presence of lesions 2 to 3 weeks after contact. Serologic testing should be performed and repeated 3 months after contact or sooner if symptoms occur. If the degree of exposure is considered substantial, immediate treatment should be considered.

Tapeworm Diseases
(Taeniasis and Cysticercosis)

CLINICAL MANIFESTATIONS:

TAENIASIS. Infection often is asymptomatic; however, mild gastrointestinal tract symptoms, such as nausea, diarrhea, and pain, can occur. Tapeworm segments can be seen migrating from the anus or feces.

CYSTICERCOSIS. Manifestations depend on the location and numbers of pork tapeworm cysts (cysticerci) and the host response. Cysts may be found anywhere in the body. The most common and serious manifestations are caused by cysts in the central nervous system. Cysts of *Taenia solium* in the brain (neurocysticercosis) can cause seizures, behavioral disturbances, obstructive hydrocephalus, and other neurologic signs and symptoms. In some countries, neurocysticercosis is a leading cause of epilepsy. The host reaction to degenerating cysts can produce signs and symptoms of meningitis. Cysts in the spinal column can cause gait disturbance, pain, or transverse myelitis. Subcutaneous cysts produce palpable nodules, and ocular involvement can cause visual impairment.

ETIOLOGY: Taeniasis is caused by intestinal infection by the adult tapeworm, *Taenia saginata* (beef tapeworm) or *T solium* (pork tapeworm). *Taenia asiatica* causes taeniasis in Asia. Human cysticercosis is caused only by the larvae of *T solium (Cysticercus cellulosae)*.

EPIDEMIOLOGY: These tapeworm diseases have worldwide distribution. Prevalence is high in areas with poor sanitation and human fecal contamination in areas where cattle graze or swine are fed. Most cases of *T solium* infection in the United States are imported from Latin America or Asia. High rates of *T saginata* infection occur in Mexico, parts of South America, East Africa, and central Europe. *Taenia asiatica* is common in China, Taiwan, and Southeast Asia. Taeniasis is acquired by eating undercooked beef *(T saginata)* or pork *(T solium)*. *Taenia asiatica* is acquired by eating viscera of infected pigs that contains encysted larvae. Infection often is asymptomatic.

Cysticercosis in humans is acquired by ingesting eggs of the pork tapeworm (*T solium*), through fecal-oral contact with a person harboring the adult tapeworm, or by autoinfection. The eggs are found only in human feces, because humans are the obligate definitive host. The eggs liberate oncospheres in the intestine that migrate through the blood and lymphatics to tissues throughout the body, including the central nervous system, where cysts form. Although most cases of cysticercosis in the United States have been imported, cysticercosis can be acquired in the United States from tapeworm carriers who immigrated from an area with endemic infection and still have *T solium* intestinal stage infection.

The **incubation period** for taeniasis, the time from ingestion of the larvae until segments are passed in the feces, is 2 to 3 months. For cysticercosis, the time between infection and onset of symptoms may be several years.

DIAGNOSIS: Diagnosis of taeniasis (adult tapeworm infection) is based on demonstration of the proglottids or ova in feces or the perianal region. However, these techniques are insensitive. Species identification of the parasite is based on the different structures of the terminal gravid segments. Diagnosis of neurocysticercosis is made primarily on the basis of computed tomography (CT) scanning or magnetic resonance imaging (MRI) of the brain or spinal cord. Antibody assays that detect specific antibody to larval *T solium* in serum and cerebrospinal fluid (CSF) are the antibody tests of choice. In the United States, this test is available through the Centers for Disease Control and Prevention and several commercial laboratories. The test is more sensitive with serum specimens than with CSF specimens. Serum antibody assay results often are negative in children with solitary parenchymal lesions but usually are positive in patients with multiple lesions.

TREATMENT:

TAENIASIS. Praziquantel is highly effective for eradicating infection with the adult tapeworm, and niclosamide and nitazoxanide are alternatives (see Drugs for Parasitic Infections, p 790).

CYSTICERCOSIS. Neurocysticercosis treatment should be individualized on the basis of the number and viability of cysticerci as assessed by neuroimaging studies (MRI or CT scan) and where they are located. For patients with only nonviable cysts (eg, only calcifications on CT scan), management should be aimed at symptoms and should include anticonvulsants for patients with seizures and insertion of shunts for patients with hydrocephalus. Two antiparasitic drugs, albendazole and praziquantel, are available. Although both drugs are cysticercidal and hasten radiologic resolution of cysts, most symptoms result from the host inflammatory response and may be exacerbated by treatment. In some clinical trials, patients treated with albendazole had better radiologic and clinical responses than patients treated with low doses of praziquantel. Several studies have indicated that patients with single inflamed cysts within the brain parenchyma do well without antiparasitic therapy; however, treatment of parenchymal cysticerci with albendazole or praziquantel is controversial. Most experts recommend therapy for patients with nonenhancing or multiple cysticerci. Coadministration of corticosteroids for the first 2 to 3 days of therapy may decrease adverse effects. Arachnoiditis, vasculitis, or diffuse cerebral edema (cysticercal encephalitis) is treated with corticosteroid therapy, until cerebral edema is controlled, and albendazole or praziquantel.

Seizures may recur for months or years. Anticonvulsant therapy is recommended until there is neuroradiologic evidence of resolution and seizures have not occurred for 1 to 2 years. Calcification of cysts may require indefinite use of anticonvulsants. Intraventricular cysts and hydrocephalus usually require surgical therapy. Intraventricular cysts often can be removed by endoscopic surgery, which is the treatment of choice. If cysts cannot be removed easily, hydrocephalus should be corrected with placement of intraventricular shunts. Adjunctive chemotherapy with antiparasitic agents and corticosteroids may decrease the rate of subsequent shunt failure. Ocular cysticercosis is treated by surgical excision of the cysts. Ocular and spinal cysts generally are not treated with anthelmintic drugs, which can exacerbate inflammation. An ophthalmic examination should be performed before treatment to rule out intraocular cysts.

ISOLATION OF THE HOSPITALIZED PATIENT: Standard precautions are recommended.

CONTROL MEASURES: Eating raw or undercooked beef or pork should be avoided. People known to harbor the adult tapeworm of *T solium* should be treated immediately. Careful attention to hand hygiene and appropriate disposal of fecal material is important.

Examination of stool specimens obtained from food handlers who recently have emigrated from countries with endemic infection for detection of eggs and proglottids is advisable. People traveling to developing countries with high endemic rates of cysticercosis should avoid eating uncooked vegetables and fruits that cannot be peeled.

Other Tapeworm Infections
(Including Hydatid Disease)

CLINICAL MANIFESTATIONS: Most infections are asymptomatic, but nausea, abdominal pain, and diarrhea have been observed in people who are heavily infected.

HYMENOLEPIS NANA. This tapeworm, also called dwarf tapeworm because it is the smallest of the adult tapeworms, has its entire cycle within humans. Direct person-to-person transmission is possible. More problematic is autoinfection, which tends to perpetuate infection in the host, because eggs can hatch within the intestine and reinitiate the cycle, leading to development of new worms and a large worm burden. If infection persists after treatment, retreatment with praziquantel is indicated. Nitazoxanide is an alternative drug.

DIPYLIDIUM CANINUM. This tapeworm is the most common and widespread adult tapeworm of dogs and cats. *Dipylidium caninum* infects children when they inadvertently swallow a dog or cat flea, which serves as the intermediate host. Diagnosis is made by finding the characteristic eggs or motile proglottids in stool. Proglottids resemble rice kernels. Therapy with praziquantel is effective. Niclosamide is an alternative therapeutic option.

DIPHYLLOBOTHRIUM LATUM (AND RELATED SPECIES). This tapeworm, also called fish tapeworm, has fish as one of its intermediate hosts. Consumption of infected, raw freshwater fish (including salmon) leads to infection. Three to 5 weeks are needed for the adult tapeworm to mature and begin to lay eggs. The worm sometimes causes mechanical obstruction of the bowel or diarrhea, abdominal pain, or rarely, megaloblastic anemia secondary to vitamin B_{12} deficiency. Diagnosis is made by recognition of the characteristic eggs or proglottids passed in stool. Therapy with praziquantel is effective; niclosamide is an alternative.

ECHINOCOCCUS GRANULOSUS AND *ECHINOCOCCUS MULTILOCULARIS*. The larval forms of these tapeworms are the causes of hydatid disease. The distribution of *Echinococcus granulosus* is related to sheep or cattle herding. Areas of high prevalence include parts of South America, East Africa, Eastern Europe, the Middle East, the Mediterranean region, China, and Central Asia. Disease also is endemic in Australia and New Zealand. In the United States, small foci of endemic infection exist in Arizona, California, New Mexico, and Utah, and a strain adapted to wolves, moose, and caribou occurs in Alaska and Canada. Dogs, coyotes, wolves, dingoes, and jackals can become infected by swallowing protoscolices of the parasite within hydatid cysts in the organs of sheep or other intermediate hosts. Dogs pass embryonated eggs in their stools, and sheep become infected by swallowing the eggs. If humans swallow *Echinococcus* eggs, they can become inadvertent intermediate hosts, and cysts can develop in various organs, such as the liver, lungs, kidney, and spleen. These cysts usually grow slowly (1 cm in diameter per year) and eventually can contain several liters of fluid. If a cyst ruptures, anaphylaxis and multiple secondary cysts from seeding of protoscolices can result. Clinical diagnosis often is difficult. A history of contact with dogs in an area with endemic infection is helpful. Cystic lesions can be demonstrated by radiography, ultrasonography, or computed tomography of various organs. Serologic tests, available at the Centers for Disease Control and Prevention, are helpful, but false-negative results occur. In uncomplicated cases, the treatment of choice is *p*ercutaneous *a*spiration, *i*nfusion of scolicidal agents, and *r*easpiration (PAIR). This should be performed at least a few days after initiation of albendazole chemotherapy. Contraindications to PAIR include communication of the cyst with the biliary tract (eg, bile staining after initial aspiration), superficial cysts, and heavily septated cysts. Surgical therapy is indicated for complicated cases and requires meticulous care to prevent spillage. Surgical drapes should be soaked in hypertonic saline. In general, the cyst should be removed intact, because leakage of contents is associated with a higher rate of complications. Treatment with albendazole generally should be initiated days to weeks before surgery and continued for several months afterwards.

Echinococcus multilocularis, a species whose life cycle involves foxes, dogs, and rodents, causes the alveolar form of hydatid disease, which is characterized by invasive growth of the larvae in the liver with occasional metastatic spread. The alveolar form of hydatid disease is limited to the northern hemisphere and usually is diagnosed in people 50 years of age or older. The preferred treatment is surgical removal of the entire larval mass. In nonresectable cases, continuous treatment with albendazole has been associated with clinical improvement.

ISOLATION OF THE HOSPITALIZED PATIENT: Standard precautions are recommended.

CONTROL MEASURES: Preventive measures for *H nana* include educating the public about personal hygiene and sanitary disposal of feces.

Infection with *D caninum* is prevented by keeping dogs and cats free of fleas and worms.

Thorough cooking (56°C [133°F] for 5 minutes), freezing (−18°C [0°F] for 24 hours), or irradiation of freshwater fish ensures protection against *D latum.*

Control measures for prevention of *E granulosus* and *E multilocularis* include educating the public about hand hygiene and avoiding exposure to dog feces. Prevention and control of infection in dogs decreases the risk.

Tetanus
(Lockjaw)

CLINICAL MANIFESTATIONS: Generalized tetanus (lockjaw) is a neurologic disease manifesting as trismus and severe muscular spasms. Tetanus is caused by neurotoxin produced by the anaerobic bacterium *Clostridium tetani* in a contaminated wound. Onset is gradual, occurring over 1 to 7 days, and symptoms progress to severe generalized muscle spasms, which often are aggravated by any external stimulus. Severe spasms persist for 1 week or more and subside over several weeks in people who recover.

Localized tetanus manifests as local muscle spasms in areas contiguous to a wound. Cephalic tetanus is a dysfunction of cranial nerves associated with infected wounds on the head and neck. Both conditions may precede generalized tetanus.

ETIOLOGY: *Clostridium tetani* is a spore-forming, anaerobic, gram-positive bacillus. This organism is a wound contaminant that causes neither tissue destruction nor an inflammatory response. The vegetative form of *C tetani* produces a potent plasmid-encoded exotoxin (tetanospasmin), which binds to gangliosides at the myoneural junction of skeletal muscle and on neuronal membranes in the spinal cord, blocking inhibitory pulses to motor neurons. The action of tetanus toxin on the brain and sympathetic nervous system is less well documented.

EPIDEMIOLOGY: Tetanus occurs worldwide and is more common in warmer climates and during warmer months, in part because of the higher frequency of contaminated wounds associated with those locations and seasons. The organism, a normal inhabitant of soil and animal and human intestines, is ubiquitous in the environment, especially where contamination by excreta is common. Wounds, recognized or unrecognized, are the sites at which the organism multiplies and elaborates toxin. Contaminated wounds, especially wounds with devitalized tissue and deep-puncture trauma, are at greatest risk. Neonatal tetanus is common in many developing countries where women are not immunized appropriately against tetanus and nonsterile umbilical cord-care practices are followed. Widespread active immunization against tetanus has modified the epidemiology of disease in the United States, where 40 or fewer cases have been reported annually since 1999. Tetanus is not transmissible from person to person.

The **incubation period** ranges from 2 days to months, with most cases occurring within 14 days. In neonates, the incubation period usually is 5 to 14 days. Shorter incubation periods have been associated with more heavily contaminated wounds, more severe disease, and a worse prognosis.

DIAGNOSTIC TESTS: The diagnosis of tetanus is made clinically by excluding other causes of tetanic spasms, such as hypocalcemic tetany, phenothiazine reaction, strychnine poisoning, and hysteria. Attempts to culture *C tetani* are associated with poor yield, and a negative culture does not rule out disease. A protective serum antitoxin concentration should not be used to exclude the diagnosis of tetanus.

TREATMENT:

- Human Tetanus Immune Globulin (TIG) given in a single dose is recommended for treatment. The optimum therapeutic dose has not been established. Some experts recommend 500 U, which appears to be effective and to cause less discomfort; others recommend 3000 to 6000 U. Available preparations must be given intramuscularly. Infiltration of part of the dose locally around the wound is recommended, although the efficacy of this approach has not been proven. Results of studies on the benefit from intrathecal TIG are conflicting. The TIG preparation in use in the United States is not licensed or formulated for intrathecal or intravenous use.
- In countries where TIG is not available, equine tetanus antitoxin may be available. This product no longer is available in the United States. Equine antitoxin is administered after appropriate testing for sensitivity and desensitization if necessary (see Sensitivity Tests for Reactions to Animal Sera, p 61, and Desensitization to Animal Sera, p 62).
- Immune Globulin Intravenous contains antibodies to tetanus and can be considered for treatment in a dose of 200 to 400 mg/kg if TIG is not available. The US Food and Drug Administration has not licensed IGIV for this use.
- All wounds should be cleaned and débrided properly, especially if extensive necrosis is present. In neonatal tetanus, wide excision of the umbilical stump is not indicated.
- Supportive care and pharmacotherapy to control tetanic spasms are of major importance.
- Oral (or intravenous) metronidazole (30 mg/kg per day, given at 6-hour intervals; maximum 4 g/day) is effective in decreasing the number of vegetative

forms of *C tetani* and is the antimicrobial agent of choice. Parenteral penicillin G (100 000 U/kg per day, given at 4- to 6-hour intervals; maximum 12 million U/day) is an alternative treatment. Therapy for 10 to 14 days is recommended.

ISOLATION OF THE HOSPITALIZED PATIENT: Standard precautions are recommended.

CONTROL MEASURES:

CARE OF EXPOSED PEOPLE (SEE TABLE 3.63). After primary immunization with tetanus toxoid, antitoxin persists at protective concentrations in most people for at least 10 years and for a longer time after a booster immunization.

- The use of tetanus toxoid and TIG or antitoxin in management of wounds depends on the nature of the wound and the history of immunization with tetanus toxoid as described in Table 3.63.
- For infants younger than 6 months of age who have not received a full 3-dose primary series of tetanus toxoid-containing vaccine, decisions on the need for TIG with wound care should be based on the mother's tetanus toxoid immunization history at the time of delivery, applying the guidelines in Table 3.63.
- Although any open wound is a potential source of tetanus, wounds contaminated with dirt, feces, soil, or saliva are at increased risk. Punctures and wounds containing devitalized tissue, including necrotic or gangrenous wounds, frostbite, crush and avulsion injuries, and burns are particularly conducive to *C tetani* infection.
- If tetanus immunization is incomplete at the time of wound treatment, a dose of vaccine should be given, and the immunization series should be completed according to the primary immunization schedule. Tetanus Immune Globulin

Table 3.63. Guide to Tetanus Prophylaxis in Routine Wound Management in Children and Adolescents

History of Absorbed Tetanus Toxoid (Doses)	Clean, Minor Wounds		All Other Wounds[1]	
	Td or Tdap[2]	TIG[3]	Td or Tdap[2]	TIG[3]
<3 or unknown	Yes	No	Yes	Yes
≥3[4]	No[5]	No	No[6]	No

Td indicates adult-type diphtheria and tetanus toxoids vaccine; TIG, Tetanus Immune Globulin (human); Tdap, booster tetanus toxoid, reduced diphtheria toxoid, and acellular pertussis.

[1] Such as, but not limited to, wounds contaminated with dirt, feces, soil, and saliva; puncture wounds; avulsions; and wounds resulting from missiles, crushing, burns, and frostbite.

[2] Tdap is preferred to Td for adolescents who never have received Tdap. Td is preferred to tetanus toxoid (TT) for adolescents who received Tdap previously or when Tdap is not available.

[3] Immune Globulin Intravenous should be used when TIG is not available.

[4] If only 3 doses of fluid toxoid have been received, a fourth dose of toxoid, preferably an adsorbed toxoid, should be given. Although licensed, fluid tetanus toxoid rarely is used.

[5] Yes, if ≥10 years since last tetanus-containing vaccine dose.

[6] Yes, if ≥5 years since last tetanus-containing vaccine dose. More frequent boosters are not needed and can accentuate adverse effects.

should be administered for tetanus-prone wounds in patients infected with human immunodeficiency virus, regardless of the history of tetanus immunizations.

- When tetanus toxoid is required for wound prophylaxis in a child 7 through 10 years of age, use of adult-type diphtheria and tetanus toxoids (Td) instead of tetanus toxoid alone is advisable so that diphtheria immunity also is maintained. When a booster injection is indicated for wound prophylaxis in a child younger than 7 years of age, diphtheria and tetanus toxoids and acellular pertussis vaccine (DTaP) should be used unless pertussis vaccine is contraindicated (see Pertussis, p 498), in which case immunization with diphtheria and tetanus toxoids (DT) is recommended.

- Adolescents 11 through 18 years of age who require a tetanus toxoid-containing vaccine as part of wound management should receive a single dose of Tdap instead of Td if they have not received Tdap previously; if Tdap is not available or was administered previously, adolescents who need a tetanus toxoid-containing vaccine should receive Td (see Pertussis, p 498). People 19 to 64 years of age who require a tetanus toxoid-containing vaccine as part of wound management should receive Tdap instead of Td if they previously have not received Tdap.

- When TIG is required for wound prophylaxis, it is given intramuscularly in a dose of 250 U. Immune Globulin Intravenous or equine tetanus antitoxin is recommended if TIG is unavailable. Equine antitoxin should be given after appropriate testing of the patient for sensitivity (see Sensitivity Tests for Reactions to Animal Sera, 61). Equine antitoxin is not available in the United States. If tetanus toxoid and TIG, IGIV, or equine tetanus antitoxin are given concurrently, separate syringes and sites should be used. Administration of TIG, IGIV, or equine tetanus antitoxin does not preclude initiation of active immunization with adsorbed tetanus toxoid. Efforts should be made to initiate immunization and arrange for its completion. Administration of tetanus toxoid simultaneously or at an interval after receipt of Immune Globulin does not impair development of protective antibody substantially.

- Regardless of immunization status, wounds should be cleaned and débrided properly if dirt or necrotic tissue is present. Wounds should receive prompt surgical treatment to remove all devitalized tissue and foreign material as an essential part of tetanus prophylaxis. It is not necessary or appropriate to débride puncture wounds extensively.

IMMUNIZATION. Active immunization with tetanus toxoid is recommended for all people. For all appropriate indications, tetanus immunization is administered with diphtheria toxoid-containing vaccines or with diphtheria toxoid- and acellular pertussis-containing vaccines. Vaccine is given intramuscularly and may be given concurrently with other vaccines (see Simultaneous Administration of Multiple Vaccines, p 34). *Haemophilus influenzae* type b conjugate vaccines containing tetanus toxoid (PRP-T) are not substitutes for tetanus toxoid immunization. Recommendations for use of tetanus toxoid-containing vaccines summarized in Fig 1.1 (p 26) and Table 1.7 (p 28) are as follows:

- Immunization for children from 2 months of age to the seventh birthday (see Fig 1.1, p 26, and Table 1.7, p 28) should consist of 5 doses of tetanus and diphtheria toxoid-containing vaccine. The initial 3 doses are given as DTaP administered at 2-month intervals beginning at approximately 2 months of age. A fourth dose is recommended 6 to 12 months after the third dose, usually at 15 to 18 months of age (see Pertussis, p 498). The final dose of DTaP is recommended before school entry (kindergarten or elementary school) at 4 to 6 years of age, unless the fourth dose was given after the fourth birthday. The DTaP vaccine can be given concurrently with other vaccines (see Simultaneous Administration of Multiple Vaccines, p 34).

Immunization against tetanus and diphtheria for children younger than 7 years of age in whom pertussis immunization is contraindicated (see Pertussis, p 498) should be accomplished with DT instead of DTaP, as follows:

- For children younger than 1 year of age, 3 doses of DT are given at 2-month intervals; a fourth dose should be given 6 to 12 months after the third dose, and the fifth dose should be given before school entry at 4 to 6 years of age.
- For children 1 through 6 years of age who have not received previous doses of DT, DTaP, or diphtheria and tetanus toxoids and pertussis vaccine (DTP), 2 doses of DT approximately 2 months apart should be given, followed by a third dose 6 to 12 months later to complete the initial series. The DT vaccine can be given concurrently with other vaccines. An additional dose is recommended before school entry at 4 to 6 years of age unless the preceding dose was given after the fourth birthday.
- For children 1 through 6 years of age who have received 1 or 2 doses of DTaP, DTP, or DT during the first year of life and for whom further pertussis immunization is contraindicated, additional doses of DT should be given until a total of 5 doses of diphtheria and tetanus toxoids are received by the time of school entry. The fourth dose is administered 6 to 12 months after the third dose. The preschool (fifth) dose is omitted if the fourth dose was given after the fourth birthday.
- For children who have received fewer than the recommended number of doses of pertussis vaccine but who have received the recommended number of DT doses for their age (ie, those in whom immunization was started with DT and who were then given DTaP [or DTP]), dose(s) of DTaP should be given to complete the recommended pertussis immunization schedule (see Pertussis, p 498). However, the total number of doses of diphtheria and tetanus toxoids (as DT, DTaP, or DTP) should not exceed 6 before the seventh birthday.

Other recommendations for tetanus immunization, including recommendations for older children, are as follows:

- For children 7 through 10 years of age (see Table 1.7, p 28), tetanus immunization should be accomplished with Td (ie, adult-type diphtheria and tetanus toxoids). Because of the lower dose of diphtheria toxoid, the Td vaccine is less likely than DTaP or DT to produce adverse reactions in older children and adults. Two doses are given 1 to 2 months apart; a third dose should be given 6 to 12 months after the second.
- Adolescents 11 to 18 years of age should receive a single dose of Tdap instead of Td for booster immunization against tetanus, diphtheria, and pertussis if they have completed the recommended childhood DTP/DTaP immunization series

and have not received Td or Tdap. The preferred age for Tdap immunization is 11 to 12 years; routinely administering Tdap to young adolescents will reduce the morbidity associated with pertussis in adolescents.

- Adolescents 11 to 18 years of age who received Td but not Tdap are encouraged to receive a single dose of Tdap to provide protection against pertussis if they have completed the recommended childhood DTP/DTaP immunization series. An interval of at least 5 years between Td and Tdap is encouraged to reduce the risk of local or systemic reactions. However, intervals shorter than 5 years between Td and Tdap may be used. The benefits of protection from pertussis generally outweigh the risk of local or systemic reactions in settings with increased risk of pertussis (eg, pertussis outbreaks and close contact with an infant younger than 6 months of age).
- If more than 5 years have elapsed since the last dose, a booster of a tetanus-containing vaccine should be considered for people who are going on wilderness expeditions where tetanus boosters may not be readily available.
- Prevention of neonatal tetanus can be accomplished by prenatal immunization of the previously unimmunized mother. Pregnant women who have not completed their primary series should do so before delivery if time permits. If there is insufficient time, 2 doses of Td should be administered at least 4 weeks apart, and the second dose should be given at least 2 weeks before delivery. Immunization with tetanus toxoid or Td is not contraindicated during pregnancy.
- Active immunization against tetanus always should be undertaken during convalescence from tetanus, because this exotoxin-mediated disease usually does not confer immunity.

ADVERSE EVENTS, PRECAUTIONS, AND CONTRAINDICATIONS. Severe anaphylactic reactions, Guillain-Barré syndrome, and brachial neuritis attributable to tetanus toxoid have been reported but are rare. No increased risk of Guillain-Barré syndrome has been observed with use of DTaP vaccine in children, and therefore, no special precautions are recommended when immunizing children with a history of Guillain-Barré syndrome.

An immediate anaphylactic reaction to tetanus and diphtheria toxoid-containing vaccines (ie, DTaP, Tdap, DT, or Td) is a contraindication to further doses unless the patient can be desensitized to these toxoids (see Pertussis, p 498). Because of uncertainty about which vaccine component (ie, diphtheria, tetanus, or pertussis) might be responsible and the importance of tetanus immunization, people who experience anaphylactic reactions may be referred to an allergist for evaluation and possible desensitization to tetanus toxoid.

OTHER CONTROL MEASURES. Sterilization of hospital supplies will prevent the rare instances of tetanus that may occur in a hospital from contaminated sutures, instruments, or plaster casts.

For prevention of neonatal tetanus, preventive measures (in addition to maternal immunization) include community immunization programs for adolescent girls and women of childbearing age and appropriate training of midwives in recommendations for immunization and sterile technique.

Tinea Capitis
(Ringworm of the Scalp)

CLINICAL MANIFESTATIONS: Fungal infection of the scalp may manifest as one of the following distinct clinical syndromes:

- Patchy areas of dandruff-like scaling, with subtle or extensive hair loss, which easily is confused with dandruff, seborrheic dermatitis, or atopic dermatitis
- Discrete areas of hair loss studded by stubs of broken hairs, which is referred to as *black-dot ringworm*
- Numerous discrete pustules or excoriations with little hair loss or scaling
- Kerion, a boggy inflammatory mass surrounded by follicular pustules, which is a hypersensitivity reaction to the fungal infection (may be accompanied by fever and local lymphadenopathy and commonly is misdiagnosed as impetigo, cellulitis, or an abscess of the scalp)

A pruritic, fine, papulovesicular eruption (dermatophytid or id reaction) involving the trunk, hands, or face caused by a hypersensitivity response to the infecting fungus, may accompany scalp lesions.

Tinea capitis may be confused with many other diseases, including seborrheic dermatitis, atopic dermatitis, psoriasis, alopecia areata, trichotillomania, folliculitis, impetigo, and lupus erythematosus.

ETIOLOGY: *Trichophyton tonsurans* is the cause of tinea capitis in more than 90% of cases in North and Central America. *Microsporum canis, Microsporum audouinii,* and *Trichophyton mentagrophytes* are less common. The causative agents may vary in different geographic areas.

EPIDEMIOLOGY: Infection of the scalp with *T tonsurans* results from person-to-person transmission. Although the organism remains viable on combs, hairbrushes, and other fomites for long periods of time, the role of fomites in transmission has not been defined. Occasionally, *T tonsurans* is cultured from the scalp of asymptomatic children or family members of an index case. Asymptomatic carriers are thought to have a significant role as reservoirs for infection and reinfection within families, schools, and communities. Tinea capitis attributable to *T tonsurans* occurs most commonly in children between the ages of 3 and 9 years and appears to be more common in African American children.

Microsporum canis infection results from animal-to-human transmission. Infection often is the result of contact with household pets.

The **incubation period** is unknown.

DIAGNOSTIC TESTS: Potassium hydroxide wet mount, cultures, and/or Wood light examination may be used to confirm the diagnosis before treatment. Hairs obtained by gentle scraping of a moistened area of the scalp with a blunt scalpel, toothbrush, tweezers, or a moistened cotton swab are used for potassium hydroxide wet mount examination and culture. In black-dot ringworm, broken hairs should be obtained for diagnosis. In cases of *T tonsurans* infection, microscopic examination of a potassium hydroxide wet mount preparation will disclose numerous arthroconidia within the hair shaft. In *Microsporum* infection, spores surround the hair shaft. Use of dermatophyte test medium also is a reliable, simple, and inexpensive method of diagnosing tinea capitis. Skin scrapings, brushings, or hairs from lesions are inoculated directly onto culture medium and incubated at room temperature. After 1 to 2 weeks, a phenol red indicator in the agar will turn from yellow to red in the area surrounding a dermatophyte colony. When necessary, the diagnosis also may be confirmed by culture on Sabouraud dextrose agar by direct plating technique or by moistened cotton-tipped applicators or by Culturettes transported to reference laboratories.

Examination of hair of patients with *Microsporum* infection using Wood light results in brilliant green fluorescence. However, because *T tonsurans* does not fluoresce under Wood light, this diagnostic test is not helpful for most patients with tinea capitis.

TREATMENT: Because topical antifungal medications are not effective for treatment of tinea capitis, systemic antifungal therapy is required. Microsize griseofulvin, 10 to 20 mg/kg per day (maximum 1 g), or ultramicrosize griseofulvin, 5 to 10 mg/kg per day (maximum 750 mg), is given orally once daily. Optimally, griseofulvin is given after a meal containing fat (eg, peanut butter or ice cream). Treatment for 4 to 6 weeks typically is necessary and should be continued 2 weeks beyond clinical resolution. Some children may require higher doses to achieve clinical cure. Griseofulvin is approved for children older than 2 years of age. Children who have no history or clinical evidence of liver disease are not required to have serum hepatic enzyme values tested either before or during a standard course of therapy lasting up to 8 weeks. Prolonged therapy may be associated with a greater risk of hepatotoxicity, and enzyme testing every 8 weeks during treatment should be considered. Terbinafine given for a 2- to 4-week course has been shown to be as effective as a 6- to 8-week course of griseofulvin for treatment of *Trichophyton* infection but may not be as effective against *Microsporum* species. Terbinafine is not approved by the FDA for this condition. Treatment with oral itraconazole or fluconazole may be effective for tinea capitis, but these products have not been approved by the FDA for this indication. In addition, itraconazole and terbinafine are not approved for use in children. Selenium sulfide shampoo, either 1% or 2.5%, used twice a week, decreases fungal shedding and may help curb the spread of infection.

Kerion is treated with griseofulvin. Corticosteroid therapy consisting of prednisone or prednisolone given orally in dosages of 1.5 to 2 mg/kg per day (maximum 20 mg/day) may be used in addition. Treatment with corticosteroids should be continued for approximately 2 weeks, with tapering doses toward the end of therapy. Antibacterial agents generally are not needed, except if there is suspected secondary infection. Surgery is not indicated.

ISOLATION OF THE HOSPITALIZED PATIENT: Standard precautions are recommended.

CONTROL MEASURES: Early treatment of infected people is indicated, as is examination of siblings and other household contacts for evidence of tinea capitis. Sharing of ribbons, combs, and hairbrushes should be discouraged.

Children receiving treatment for tinea capitis may attend school once they start therapy with griseofulvin or other effective systemic agent, with or without the addition of selenium sulfide shampoo. Haircuts, shaving of the head, or wearing a cap during treatment are unnecessary.

Tinea Corporis
(Ringworm of the Body)

CLINICAL MANIFESTATIONS: Superficial tinea infections of the nonhairy (glabrous) skin may involve the face, trunk, or limbs but not the scalp, beard, groin, hands, or feet. The lesion generally is circular (hence, the term "ringworm"), slightly erythematous, and well demarcated with a scaly, vesicular, or pustular border. Pruritus is common. Lesions often are mistaken for atopic, seborrheic, or contact dermatitis. A frequent source of confusion is an alteration in the appearance of lesions as a result of application of a topical corticosteroid preparation, termed *tinea* incognito. In patients with diminished T-lymphocyte function (eg, human immunodeficiency virus infection), the rash may appear as grouped papules or pustules unaccompanied by scaling or erythema.

A pruritic, fine, papulovesicular eruption (dermatophytic or id reaction) involving the trunk, hands, or face, caused by a hypersensitivity response to infecting fungus, may accompany the rash.

ETIOLOGY: The prime causes of the disease are fungi of the genus *Trichophyton*, especially *Trichophyton rubrum, Trichophyton mentagrophytes,* and *Trichophyton tonsurans;* the genus *Microsporum*, especially *Microsporum canis;* and *Epidermophyton floccosum.*

EPIDEMIOLOGY: These causative fungi occur worldwide and are transmissible by direct contact with infected humans, animals, or fomites. Fungi in lesions are communicable.

The **incubation period** is unknown.

DIAGNOSIS: The fungi responsible for tinea corporis can be detected by microscopic examination of a potassium hydroxide wet mount of skin scrapings. Use of dermatophyte test medium also is a reliable, simple, and inexpensive method of diagnosis. Skin scrapings from lesions are inoculated directly onto culture medium and incubated at room temperature. After 1 to 2 weeks, a phenol red indicator in the agar will turn from yellow to red in the area surrounding a dermatophyte colony. When necessary, the diagnosis also can be confirmed by culture on Sabouraud dextrose agar.

TREATMENT: Topical application of a miconazole, clotrimazole, terbinafine, tolnaftate, naftifine, or ciclopirox preparation twice a day or of a ketoconazole, econazole, oxiconazole, butenafine, or sulconazole preparation once a day is recommended (see Topical Drugs for Superficial Fungal Infections, p 781). Although clinical resolution may be evident within 2 weeks of therapy, a minimum duration of 4 weeks generally is indicated. Topical preparations of antifungal medication mixed with high-potency corticosteroids should not be used because of the potential for local and systemic adverse events.

If lesions are extensive or unresponsive to topical therapy, griseofulvin is administered orally for 4 weeks (see Tinea Capitis, p 654). Oral itraconazole, fluconazole, and terbinafine may be effective alternative therapies for tinea corporis, but these products are not approved by the US Food and Drug Administration for this indication.

ISOLATION OF THE HOSPITALIZED PATIENT: Standard precautions are recommended.

CONTROL MEASURES: Direct contact with known or suspected sources of infection should be avoided. Periodic inspections of contacts for early lesions and prompt therapy are recommended.

Tinea Cruris
(Jock Itch)

CLINICAL MANIFESTATIONS: Tinea cruris is a common superficial fungal disorder of the groin and upper thighs. The eruption is marginated sharply and usually is bilaterally symmetric. Involved skin is erythematous and scaly and varies from red to brown; occasionally, the eruption is accompanied by central clearing and a vesiculo-papular border. In chronic infections, the margin may be subtle, and lichenification may be present. Tinea cruris skin lesions may be extremely pruritic. These lesions should be differentiated from intertrigo, seborrheic dermatitis, psoriasis, primary irritant dermatitis, allergic contact dermatitis (generally caused by the therapeutic agents applied to the area), or erythrasma, which is a superficial bacterial infection of the skin caused by *Corynebacterium minutissimum*.

ETIOLOGY: The fungi *Epidermophyton floccosum*, *Trichophyton rubrum*, and *Trichophyton mentagrophytes* are the most common causes.

EPIDEMIOLOGY: Tinea cruris occurs predominantly in adolescent and adult males, mainly via indirect contact from desquamated epithelium or hair. Moisture, close-fitting garments, friction, and obesity are predisposing factors. Direct or indirect person-to-person transmission may occur. This infection commonly occurs in association with tinea pedis.

The **incubation period** is unknown.

DIAGNOSTIC TESTS: The fungi responsible for tinea cruris may be detected by microscopic examination of a potassium hydroxide wet mount of scales. Use of dermatophyte test medium also is a reliable, simple, and inexpensive method of diagnosing tinea cruris. Skin scrapings from lesions are inoculated directly onto culture medium and incubated at room temperature. After 1 to 2 weeks, a phenol red indicator in the agar will turn from yellow to red in the area surrounding a dermatophyte colony. When necessary, the diagnosis also can be confirmed by culture on Sabouraud dextrose agar. A characteristic coral-red fluorescence under Wood light can identify the presence of erythrasma and, thus, exclude tinea cruris.

TREATMENT: Twice-daily topical application for 4 to 6 weeks of a clotrimazole, miconazole, terbinafine, tolnaftate, or ciclopirox preparation rubbed or sprayed onto the affected areas and surrounding skin is effective. Once-daily therapy with topical econazole, ketoconazole, naftifine, oxiconazole, butenafine, or sulconazole preparation also is effective (see Topical Drugs for Superficial Fungal Infections, p 781). Tinea pedis, if present, should be treated concurrently (see Tinea Pedis, p 658).

Topical preparations of antifungal medication mixed with high-potency cortico-steroids should be avoided because of the potential for local and systemic adverse events. Corticosteroids may cause local and/or systemic effects or predispose to recur-rence. Loose-fitting, washed, cotton underclothes to decrease chafing as well as the use of a bland absorbent powder can be helpful adjuvants to therapy. Griseofulvin, given orally for 2 to 6 weeks, may be effective in unresponsive cases (see Tinea Capi-tis, p 654). Oral itraconazole, fluconazole, or terbinafine may be effective alternative therapies, but these products are not approved by the US Food and Drug Administra-tion for treatment of tinea cruris. Itraconazole and terbinafine are not approved for use in children. Moreover, significant hepatic and/or cardiac toxicity has been associ-ated with these agents. Because many conditions mimic tinea cruris, a differential diagnosis should be considered if primary treatments fail.

ISOLATION OF THE HOSPITALIZED PATIENT: Standard precautions are recom-mended.

CONTROL MEASURES: Infections should be treated promptly. Potentially involved areas should be kept dry, and loose undergarments should be worn. Patients should be advised to dry the groin area before drying their feet to avoid inoculating derma-tophytes of tinea pedis into the groin area.

Tinea Pedis and Tinea Unguium
(Athlete's Foot, Ringworm of the Feet)

CLINICAL MANIFESTATIONS: Tinea pedis manifests as fine vesiculopustular or scaly lesions that commonly are pruritic. The lesions can involve all areas of the foot, but usually lesions are patchy in distribution, with a predisposition to fissures and scaling between toes, particularly in the third and fourth interdigital spaces. Toenails may be infected and can be dystrophic (tinea unguium). Tinea pedis must be differentiated from dyshidrotic eczema, atopic dermatitis, contact dermatitis, juvenile plantar der-matosis, and erythrasma (a superficial bacterial infection caused by *Corynebacterium minutissimum*). Tinea pedis commonly occurs in association with tinea cruris.

Tinea pedis and many other fungal infections can be accompanied by a hyper-sensitivity reaction to the fungi (the dermatophytid or id reaction), with resulting vesicular eruptions on the palms and the sides of fingers and, occasionally, by an ery-thematous vesicular eruption on the extremities and trunk.

ETIOLOGY: The fungi *Trichophyton rubrum*, *Trichophyton mentagrophytes*, and *Epidermophy-ton floccosum* are the most common causes.

EPIDEMIOLOGY: Tinea pedis is a common infection worldwide in adolescents and adults but is relatively uncommon in young children. The fungi are acquired by con-tact with skin scales containing fungi or with fungi in damp areas, such as swimming pools, locker rooms, and shower rooms. Tinea pedis can spread throughout the household among family members and is communicable for as long as infection is present.

The **incubation period** is unknown.

DIAGNOSIS: Tinea pedis usually is diagnosed by clinical manifestations and may be confirmed by microscopic examination of a potassium hydroxide wet mount of the cutaneous scrapings. Use of dermatophyte test medium is a reliable, simple, and inexpensive method of diagnosis in complicated or unresponsive cases. Skin scrapings are inoculated directly onto the culture medium and incubated at room temperature. After 1 to 2 weeks, a phenol red indicator in the agar will turn from yellow to red in the area surrounding a dermatophyte colony. When necessary, the diagnosis also can be confirmed by culture on Sabouraud dextrose agar. Infection of the nail can be verified by direct microscopic examination and fungal culture of desquamated subungual material.

TREATMENT: Topical application of terbinafine, twice daily, or an azole agent (clotrimazole, miconazole, econazole) once or twice daily usually is adequate for milder cases. Fluconazole administered orally once per week for 1 to 4 weeks may be an effective alternative therapy, but fluconazole has not been approved for this use by the US Food and Drug Administration (FDA; see Topical Drugs for Superficial Fungal Infections, p 781). Acute vesicular lesions may be treated with intermittent use of open wet compresses (eg, with Burrow solution, 1:80). Tinea cruris, if present, should be treated concurrently (see Tinea Cruris, p 657).

Tinea pedis that is severe, chronic or refractory to topical treatment may be treated with oral griseofulvin, administered orally for 6 to 8 weeks. Oral itraconazole or terbinafine may be effective alternative therapies for tinea pedis unresponsive to topical therapy, but these products have not been approved by the FDA for use in children or for this indication. Id (hypersensitivity response) reactions are treated by wet compresses, topical corticosteroids, occasionally systemic corticosteroids, and eradication of the primary source of infection.

Recurrence is prevented by proper foot hygiene, which includes keeping the feet dry and cool, gentle cleaning, drying between the toes, use of absorbent antifungal foot powder, frequent airing of affected areas, and avoidance of occlusive footwear and nylon socks or other fabrics that interfere with dissipation of moisture.

In the past, most nail infections (tinea unguium), particularly toenail infections, have been highly resistant to oral griseofulvin therapy. Studies in adult patients have demonstrated a modest cure rate after therapy with oral itraconazole or terbinafine. Fluconazole is not approved by the FDA for this purpose. Further studies on the safety and efficacy of these drugs in children are necessary before these drugs can be recommended because of potential cardiac or hepatic toxicity. Recurrences are common. Removal of the nail plate followed by use of oral therapy during the period of regrowth can help to effect a cure in resistant cases.

ISOLATION OF THE HOSPITALIZED PATIENT: Standard precautions are recommended.

CONTROL MEASURES: Treatment of patients with active infections should decrease transmission. Public areas conducive to transmission (eg, swimming pools) should not be used by people with active infection. Chemical foot baths are of no value and can facilitate spread of infection. Because recurrence after treatment is common, proper foot hygiene is important (as described in Treatment). People should be advised to dry the groin area before drying their feet to avoid inoculating tinea pedis dermatophytes into the groin area.

Toxic Shock Syndrome

CLINICAL MANIFESTATIONS: Toxic shock syndrome (TSS) may be caused by toxin-producing *Staphylococcus aureus* or *Streptococcus pyogenes* (group A streptococci). Both organisms cause an acute illness characterized by fever, generalized erythroderma, rapid-onset hypotension, and symptoms of multisystem organ involvement that can include profuse watery diarrhea, vomiting, conjunctival injection, and severe myalgias (see Tables 3.64, p 662, and 3.65, p 663). Evidence of local soft tissue infection (eg, cellulitis, abscess, myositis, or necrotizing fasciitis) associated with severe increasing pain is common with *S pyogenes*-mediated TSS. *Staphylococcus aureus*-mediated TSS commonly occurs in menstruating females using tampons but also occurs in males and females with focal *S aureus* infection (eg, abscess, sinusitis). Both forms of TSS may occur without a readily identifiable focus of infection. Both forms of TSS also may be associated with invasive infections, such as pneumonia, osteomyelitis, bacteremia, pyarthrosis, or endocarditis. Patients with *S aureus*-mediated TSS, especially menses associated, are at risk of a recurrent episode of TSS. Toxic shock can be confused with many infectious and noninfectious causes of fever with mucocutaneous manifestations.

ETIOLOGY: *Staphylococcus aureus*-mediated TSS usually is caused by strains producing toxic-shock syndrome toxin-1 (TSST-1) or possibly other related staphylococcal enterotoxins. Most cases of *S pyogenes*-mediated TSS are caused by strains producing at least 1 of several different pyrogenic exotoxins. These toxins act as superantigens that stimulate production of tumor necrosis factor and other mediators that cause capillary leakage leading to hypotension and organ damage.

EPIDEMIOLOGY:

STAPHYLOCOCCUS AUREUS-**MEDIATED TSS.** This syndrome first was recognized in 1978, occurring in children and adults both male and female; many early cases frequently were associated with tampon use in menstruating women, with a predilection for adolescents and young women with no circulating antibody to TSST-1. Although changes in tampon composition and use may have resulted in some decrease in the proportion of cases associated with menstruation, both menstrual and nonmenstrual cases of TSS continue to occur. Toxic shock syndrome is a reportable disease in most states. Risk factors for TSS include lack of antibody to TSST-1 and a focal *S aureus* infection with a TSST-1–producing strain (eg, menstruation plus tampon use or focal abscess, sinusitis, etc).

In adults, TSST-1–producing strains of *S aureus* may be part of the normal flora of the anterior nares or the vagina. Colonization is believed to produce protective antibody, and more than 90% of adults have antibodies to TSST-1. People in whom *S aureus*-mediated TSS with TSST-1–producing strains develops usually do not have antibodies to TSST-1. Secondary cases of TSS are rare. Nosocomial cases can occur and most often have followed surgical procedures. In postoperative cases, the organism generally originates from the patient's own flora.

The **incubation period** for postoperative TSS can be as short as 12 hours. Menses-related cases can develop anytime during menses. The mortality rate is less than 5% overall and is highest in men and women older than 45 years of age.

STREPTOCOCCUS PYOGENES-**MEDIATED TSS.** The incidence of *S pyogenes*-mediated TSS seems to be highest among young children, particularly children with concomitant varicella, and the elderly, although it can occur in people of any age. Of all cases of severe invasive streptococcal infections in children, fewer than 10% are associated with TSS. Other people at increased risk include people with diabetes mellitus, chronic cardiac or pulmonary disease, and human immunodeficiency virus infection and intravenous drug and alcohol users. The risk of severe invasive infection in contacts is greater than for the general population but still is rare. Contacts may have asymptomatic colonization.

Mortality rates are higher for adults than for children and depend on whether the *S pyogenes*-mediated TSS is associated only with bacteremia or with a specific focal infection (eg, necrotizing fasciitis, myositis, or pneumonia).

The **incubation period** is not defined clearly and may depend on the route of inoculation. The incubation period has been as short as 14 hours in cases associated with the subcutaneous inoculation of organisms, such as during childbirth or after penetrating trauma.

DIAGNOSTIC TESTS:

STAPHYLOCOCCUS AUREUS-**MEDIATED TSS.** *Staphylococcus aureus*-mediated TSS remains a clinical diagnosis (Table 3.64, p 662). Blood culture results are positive for *S aureus* in fewer than 5% of patients. Specimens for culture should be obtained from an identified site of infection because these sites usually will be positive and susceptibility testing of isolated organisms can be performed. Because approximately one third of isolates of *S aureus* from nonmenstrual cases produce toxins other than TSST-1, and TSST-1 producing organisms can be present as part of the normal flora of the anterior nares and vagina, production of TSST-1 by an isolate of *S aureus* is not helpful diagnostically.

STREPTOCOCCUS PYOGENES-**MEDIATED TSS.** Blood culture results are positive for *S pyogenes* in more than 50% of patients with *S pyogenes*-mediated TSS. Culture results from the site of infection usually are positive and may remain positive for several days after appropriate antimicrobial agents have been initiated. *Streptococcus pyogenes* uniformly is susceptible to beta-lactam antimicrobial agents. Antimicrobial susceptibility may be determined only for non–beta-lactam antimicrobial agents that may be considered for therapy, such as clindamycin, to which *S pyogenes* may be resistant. A significant increase in antibody titers to streptolysin O, deoxyribonuclease B, or other streptococcal extracellular products 4 to 6 weeks after infection may help confirm the diagnosis if culture results were negative.

For both forms of TSS, laboratory studies may reflect multisystem organ involvement and disseminated intravascular coagulation.

TREATMENT: As outlined in Tables 3.66 (p 663) and 3.67 (p 664), most aspects of management are the same for TSS caused by *S aureus* and *S pyogenes*. The first priority is aggressive fluid replacement as well as management of respiratory or cardiac failure or arrhythmias if present. Because distinguishing between the 2 forms of TSS may

Table 3.64. Staphylococcal Toxic Shock Syndrome: Clinical Case Definition[1]

- Fever: temperature ≥38.9°C (≥102.0°F)
- Rash: diffuse macular erythroderma
- Desquamation: 1–2 wk after onset, particularly on palms, soles, fingers, and toes
- Hypotension: systolic pressure ≤90 mm Hg for adults; lower than fifth percentile for age for children younger than 16 years of age; orthostatic drop in diastolic pressure of ≥15 mm Hg from lying to sitting; orthostatic syncope or orthostatic dizziness
- Multisystem organ involvement: 3 or more of the following:
  - Gastrointestinal: vomiting or diarrhea at onset of illness
  - Muscular: severe myalgia or creatinine phosphokinase concentration greater than twice the upper limit of normal
  - Mucous membrane: vaginal, oropharyngeal, or conjunctival hyperemia
  - Renal: serum urea nitrogen or serum creatinine concentration greater than twice the upper limit of normal or urinary sediment with ≥5 white blood cells per high-power field in the absence of urinary tract infection
  - Hepatic: total bilirubin, aspartate transaminase, or alanine transaminase concentration greater than twice the upper limit of normal
  - Hematologic: platelet count ≤100 000/mm^3
  - Central nervous system: disorientation or alterations in consciousness without focal neurologic signs when fever and hypotension are absent
- Negative results on the following tests, if obtained:
  - Blood, throat, or cerebrospinal fluid cultures; blood culture may be positive for *Staphylococcus aureus*
  - Serologic tests for Rocky Mountain spotted fever, leptospirosis, or measles

Case Classification
Probable: a case with 5 of the 6 clinical findings
Confirmed: a case with all 6 of the clinical findings, including desquamation. If the patient dies before desquamation could have occurred, the other 5 criteria constitute a definitive case.

---

[1] Adapted from Wharton M, Chorba TL, Vogt RL, Morse DL, Buehler JW. Case definitions for public health surveillance. *MMWR Recomm Rep.* 1990;39(RR-13):1–43

not be possible, initial empiric antimicrobial therapy should include an antistaphylococcal antimicrobial agent and a protein synthesis-inhibiting antimicrobial drug, such as clindamycin. Vancomycin should be substituted for the beta-lactamase–resistant penicillin or cephalosporin in areas where community-acquired methicillin-resistant *S aureus* infections are common (see Table 3.57, p 605). Both should be given parenterally at maximal doses. The addition of clindamycin is more effective than penicillin alone for treating well-established *S pyogenes* infections, because the antimicrobial activity of clindamycin is not affected by inoculum size, has a long postantimicrobial effect, and acts on bacteria by inhibiting protein synthesis. Inhibition of protein synthesis results in suppression of synthesis of the *S pyogenes* antiphagocytic M protein and bacterial toxins. Clindamycin should not be used alone as initial empiric therapy, because in the United States, 1% to 2% of *S pyogenes* strains are resistant to clindamycin.

Table 3.65. Streptococcal Toxic Shock Syndrome: Clinical Case Definition[1]

I. Isolation of group A streptococcus *(Streptococcus pyogenes)*

   A. From a normally sterile site (eg, blood, cerebrospinal fluid, peritoneal fluid, or tissue biopsy specimen)

   B. From a nonsterile site (eg, throat, sputum, vagina, surgical wound, or superficial skin lesion)

II. Clinical signs of severity

   A. Hypotension: systolic pressure ≤90 mm Hg in adults or lower than the fifth percentile for age in children

AND

   B. Two or more of the following signs:

- Renal impairment: creatinine concentration ≥177 μmol/L (≥2 mg/dL) for adults or 2 times or more the upper limit of normal for age
- Coagulopathy: platelet count ≤100 000/mm^3 or disseminated intravascular coagulation
- Hepatic involvement: alanine transaminase, aspartate transaminase, or total bilirubin concentrations 2 times or more the upper limit of normal for age
- Adult respiratory distress syndrome
- A generalized erythematous macular rash that may desquamate
- Soft tissue necrosis, including necrotizing fasciitis or myositis, or gangrene

---

[1] An illness fulfilling criteria IA and IIA and IIB can be defined as a *definite* case. An illness fulfilling criteria IB and IIA and IIB can be defined as a *probable* case if no other cause for the illness is identified.
Adapted from The Working Group on Severe Streptococcal Infections. Defining the group A streptococcal toxic shock syndrome: rationale and consensus definition. *JAMA*. 1993;269:390–391

Table 3.66. Management of Staphylococcal or Streptococcal Toxic Shock Syndrome *Without* Necrotizing Fasciitis

- Fluid management to maintain adequate venous return and cardiac filling pressures to prevent end-organ damage
- Anticipatory management of multisystem organ failure
- Parenteral antimicrobial therapy at maximum doses
  - Kill organism with bactericidal cell wall inhibitor (eg, beta-lactamase–resistant antistaphylococcal antimicrobial agent)
  - Stop enzyme, toxin, or cytokine production with protein synthesis inhibitor (eg, clindamycin)
- Immune Globulin Intravenous may be considered for infection refractory to several hours of aggressive therapy, or in the presence of an undrainable focus, or persistent oliguria with pulmonary edema

Table 3.67. Management of Streptococcal Toxic Shock Syndrome *With* Necrotizing Fasciitis

- Principles outlined in Table 3.66 (p 663)
- Immediate surgical evaluation
  - Exploration or incisional biopsy for diagnosis and culture
  - Resection of all necrotic tissue
- Repeated resection of tissue may be needed if infection persists or progresses

Once the organism has been identified, antimicrobial therapy can be changed to penicillin and clindamycin for *S pyogenes*-mediated TSS. For *S aureus*-mediated TSS, the most appropriate antimicrobial agent on the basis of susceptibility testing should be given with clindamycin.

For *S aureus*-mediated TSS, antimicrobial therapy should be continued for a minimum of 10 to 14 days to eradicate the organism, thus preventing recurrent disease. The antimicrobial agent(s) may be changed to high-dose oral therapy once the patient is stable hemodynamically, has improved, and is receiving oral alimentation. The total duration of therapy is based on the usual duration established for the underlying focus, such as osteomyelitis or pneumonia.

For *S pyogenes*-mediated TSS, intravenous therapy should be continued until the patient is afebrile and is stable hemodynamically and negative blood culture results have been documented. The total duration of therapy is based on the duration established for the primary infection.

Aggressive drainage and irrigation of accessible sites of infection should be performed as soon as possible. Concerted efforts should be made to identify a foreign body at the site of infection, and all foreign bodies, including those recently inserted during surgery, should be removed if possible. If necrotizing fasciitis is suspected, immediate surgical exploration or biopsy is crucial to identify a deep soft tissue infection that should be débrided immediately.

The use of Immune Globulin Intravenous (IGIV) may be considered in treatment of either form of TSS. The mechanism of action of IGIV is unclear but may be neutralization of circulating bacterial toxins. For *S aureus*-mediated TSS, IGIV may be considered for patients who remain unresponsive to all other therapeutic measures and for patients with infection in an area that cannot be drained. Various regimens of IGIV, including 150 to 400 mg/kg per day for 5 days and a single dose of 1 to 2 g/kg, have been used, but the optimal regimen is unknown. The clearance of IGIV may be as short as 4 to 6 days in patients with TSS, and some experts have suggested additional doses. Animal studies and one clinical study suggest that corticosteroids administered parenterally may be useful in refractory cases of TSS.

ISOLATION OF THE HOSPITALIZED PATIENT: Standard precautions, as well as droplet and contact precautions, are recommended for all patients with TSS attributable to *S pyogenes*. Because person-to-person transmission of *S aureus*-mediated TSS is uncommon, only standard precautions are needed unless a draining wound is present.

CONTROL MEASURES: Control measures for *S pyogenes*-mediated TSS are the same as those for other forms of severe, invasive group A streptococcal infections (see p 610).

For *S aureus*-mediated TSS, the control measures are the same as those for other forms of severe staphylococcal diseases (see p 598). Females recovering from TSS can reduce risk of recurrent episodes by avoiding tampon use.

Toxocariasis
(Visceral Larva Migrans, Ocular Larva Migrans)

CLINICAL MANIFESTATIONS: The severity of symptoms depends on the number of larvae ingested and the degree of allergic response. Most people who are infected lightly are asymptomatic. Visceral larva migrans typically occurs in children 1 to 4 years of age with a history of pica but can occur in older children and adults. Characteristic manifestations include fever, leukocytosis, eosinophilia, hypergammaglobulinemia, and hepatomegaly. Other manifestations include malaise, anemia, cough, and in rare instances, pneumonia, myocarditis, and encephalitis. When ocular invasion (endophthalmitis or retinal granulomas) occurs, other evidence of infection usually is lacking, suggesting that the visceral and ocular manifestations are distinct syndromes. Atypical manifestations include hemorrhagic rash and seizures. In some cases, so-called covert toxocariasis may manifest only as asymptomatic eosinophilia or pulmonary wheezing.

ETIOLOGY: Toxocariasis is caused by *Toxocara* species, which are common roundworms of dogs and cats (especially puppies or kittens), specifically *Toxocara canis* and *Toxocara cati* in the United States; most cases are caused by *T canis*. Other nematodes of animals also can cause this syndrome, although rarely.

EPIDEMIOLOGY: Humans are infected by ingestion of soil containing infective eggs of the parasite. A history of pica, particularly eating soil, is common. Direct contact with dogs is of secondary importance, because eggs are not infective immediately when shed in the feces. Most reported cases involve children. Toxocariasis is endemic wherever dogs are present. Infection risk is highest in hot, humid regions where eggs persist in soil. The infection is endemic in many underserved urban areas. Eggs may be found wherever dogs and cats defecate.

The **incubation period** is unknown.

DIAGNOSTIC TESTS: Hypereosinophilia and hypergammaglobulinemia associated with increased titers of isohemagglutinin to the A and B blood group antigens are presumptive evidence of infection. Microscopic identification of larvae in a liver biopsy specimen is diagnostic, but this finding is rare. A liver biopsy negative for larvae, therefore, does not exclude the diagnosis. An enzyme immunoassay for *Toxocara* antibodies in serum, available at the Centers for Disease Control and Prevention and some commercial laboratories, can provide confirmatory evidence of toxocariasis. This assay is specific and sensitive for diagnosis of visceral larva migrans but is less sensitive for diagnosis of ocular larva migrans.

TREATMENT: Albendazole or mebendazole are the recommended drugs for treatment of toxocariasis. Both drugs have been approved by the US Food and Drug Administration, but not for this indication. In severe cases with myocarditis or involvement of the central nervous system, corticosteroid therapy is indicated. Correcting the underlying causes of pica helps prevent reinfection.

Anthelmintic treatment of ocular larva migrans may not be effective. Inflammation may be decreased by injection of corticosteroids, and secondary damage may be aided by surgery.

ISOLATION OF THE HOSPITALIZED PATIENT: Standard precautions are recommended.

CONTROL MEASURES: Proper disposal of cat and dog feces is essential. Treatment of puppies and kittens with anthelmintics at 2, 4, 6, and 8 weeks of age prevents excretion of eggs by worms acquired transplacentally or through mother's milk. Covering sandboxes when not in use is helpful. No specific management of exposed people is recommended.

Toxoplasma gondii Infections
(Toxoplasmosis)

CLINICAL MANIFESTATIONS: Infants with congenital infection are asymptomatic at birth in 70% to 90% of cases, although visual impairment, learning disabilities, or mental retardation will become apparent in a large proportion of children several months to years later. Signs of congenital toxoplasmosis at birth can include a maculopapular rash, generalized lymphadenopathy, hepatomegaly, splenomegaly, jaundice, and thrombocytopenia. As a consequence of intrauterine meningoencephalitis, cerebrospinal fluid (CSF) abnormalities, hydrocephalus, microcephaly, chorioretinitis, seizures, and deafness can develop. Some of the severely affected infants die in utero or within a few days of birth. Cerebral calcifications may be demonstrated by radiography, ultrasonography, or computed tomography of the head.

Toxoplasma gondii infection acquired after birth usually is asymptomatic. When symptoms develop, they are nonspecific and include malaise, fever, sore throat, and myalgia. Lymphadenopathy, frequently cervical, is the most common sign. Occasionally, patients may have a mononucleosis-like illness associated with a macular rash and hepatosplenomegaly. The clinical course usually is benign and self-limited. Myocarditis, pericarditis, and pneumonitis are rare complications.

Isolated ocular toxoplasmosis most commonly results from congenital infection but also occurs in a small percentage of people with acquired infection. Characteristic retinal infiltrates develop in up to 85% of young adults after congenital infection. Acute ocular involvement manifests as blurred vision. Ocular disease can become reactivated years after the initial infection in healthy and immunocompromised people.

In chronically infected immunodeficient patients, including people with human immunodeficiency virus (HIV) infection, reactivated infection can result in encephalitis, pneumonitis, or less commonly, systemic toxoplasmosis. Rarely, infants who are born to HIV-infected mothers or mothers who are immunocompromised for other reasons who have chronic infection with *T gondii* may have acquired congenital toxoplasmosis in utero as a result of reactivated maternal parasitemia.

ETIOLOGY: *Toxoplasma gondii*, a protozoan parasite, is the only known species of *Toxoplasma*.

EPIDEMIOLOGY: *Toxoplasma gondii* is worldwide in distribution and infects most species of warm-blooded animals. Members of the cat family are definitive hosts. Cats generally acquire the infection by feeding on infected animals, such as mice or uncooked household meats. The parasite replicates sexually in the feline small intestine. Cats may begin to excrete oocysts in their stools 3 to 30 days after primary infection and may shed oocysts for 7 to 14 days. After excretion, oocysts require a maturation phase (sporulation) of 24 to 48 hours in temperate climates before they are infective by the oral route. Intermediate hosts (including sheep, pigs, and cattle) can have tissue cysts in the brain, myocardium, skeletal muscle, and other organs. These cysts remain viable for the lifetime of the host. Humans usually become infected by consumption of raw or undercooked meat that contains cysts or by accidental ingestion of sporulated oocysts from soil or in contaminated food. A large outbreak linked epidemiologically to contamination of a municipal water supply also has been reported. Transmission of *T gondii* has been documented to result from blood or blood product transfusion and organ (eg, heart) or stem cell transplantation from a seropositive donor with latent infection. Rarely, infection has occurred as a result of a laboratory accident. In most cases, congenital transmission occurs as a result of primary maternal infection during gestation. The incidence of congenital toxoplasmosis in the United States has been estimated to be 1 in 1000 to 1 in 10 000 live births.

The **incubation period** of acquired infection, on the basis of a well-studied outbreak, is estimated to be approximately 7 days, with a range of 4 to 21 days.

DIAGNOSTIC TESTS: Serologic tests are the primary means of diagnosis, but results must be interpreted carefully. Laboratories with special expertise in *Toxoplasma* serologic assays and their interpretation are useful to the practitioner. Immunoglobulin (Ig) G-specific antibodies achieve a peak concentration 1 to 2 months after infection and remain positive indefinitely. To determine the approximate time of infection in IgG-positive adults, specific IgM antibody determinations should be performed. The lack of *T gondii*-specific IgM antibodies indicates infection more than 6 months ago. The presence of *T gondii*-specific IgM antibodies can indicate recent infection or can result from a false-positive reaction. Enzyme immunoassay tests are the more sensitive assays for IgM, and indirect fluorescent antibody tests are the least sensitive in detecting IgM. Immunoglobulin M-specific antibodies can be detected 2 weeks after infection, achieve peak concentrations in 1 month, decrease thereafter, and usually become undetectable within 6 to 9 months but uncommonly persist for as long as 2 years. In adults, when determining the timing of infection is clinically important (for example, in a pregnant woman), a positive IgM test should be followed by an IgG avidity test. The presence of high IgG avidity antibodies indicates that infection occurred at least 12 to 16 weeks previously. However, the presence of low avidity antibodies is not a reliable indication of recent infection. Tests to detect IgA and IgE antibodies, which decrease to undetectable concentrations sooner than IgM antibodies, are useful for diagnosis of congenital infections and infections in other patients, such as pregnant women, for whom more precise information about the duration of infection is needed. *Toxoplasma gondii*-specific IgA and IgE antibody tests are available in *Toxoplasma* reference laboratories but not generally in other laboratories.

SPECIAL SITUATIONS.

Prenatal. A definitive diagnosis of congenital toxoplasmosis can be made prenatally by detecting parasite DNA in amniotic fluid or fetal blood or by isolating the parasite by mouse or tissue culture inoculation. Serial fetal ultrasonographic examinations can be performed in cases of suspected congenital infection to detect any increase in size of the lateral ventricles of the central nervous system or other signs of fetal infection.

Postnatal. Infants who are born to women who have evidence of primary *T gondii* infection during gestation or women who are infected with HIV and have serologic evidence of past infection with *T gondii* should be assessed for congenital toxoplasmosis.

If the diagnosis for an infant is unclear at the time of delivery, *Toxoplasma*-specific laboratory tests for IgG, IgM, IgA, and IgE on newborn and maternal serum samples should be performed. Peripheral blood white blood cells, CSF, and amniotic fluid specimens should be assayed for *T gondii* by polymerase chain reaction assay in a reference laboratory. Evaluation of the infant should include ophthalmologic, auditory, and neurologic examinations; lumbar puncture; and computed tomography of the head. An attempt may be made to isolate *T gondii* from the placenta, umbilical cord, or blood specimen from the infant by mouse inoculation.

Congenital infection is confirmed serologically by persistently positive IgG titers beyond the first 12 months of life. Before 12 months of age, a persistently positive or increasing IgG antibody concentration in the infant compared with the mother, and/or a positive *Toxoplasma*-specific IgM or IgA assay indicate congenital infection. Although placental leak occasionally can lead to false-positive IgM or IgA reactions in the newborn infant, repeat testing in approximately 10 days can help resolve the diagnosis, because the half-life of these immunoglobulins is short and the titers in an infant who is not infected should decrease rapidly. The sensitivity of *T gondii*-specific IgM by the double-sandwich enzyme immunoassay or an immunosorbent assay is 75% to 80%. Immunoglobulin A antibodies are found more frequently than IgM antibodies; some infants may have only IgA or only IgM antibodies. The indirect fluorescent assay for IgM should not be relied on to diagnose congenital infection. In an uninfected infant, a continuous decrease in IgG titer without detection of IgM or IgA antibodies will occur. Transplacentally transmitted IgG antibody usually will become undetectable by 6 to 12 months of age.

HIV Infection. Patients with HIV infection who are infected latently with *T gondii* have variable titers of IgG antibody to *T gondii* but rarely have IgM antibody. Although seroconversion and fourfold increases in IgG antibody titers may occur, the ability to diagnose active disease in patients with acquired immunodeficiency syndrome commonly is impaired by immunosuppression. In HIV-infected patients who are seropositive for *T gondii* IgG, *T gondii* encephalitis is diagnosed presumptively on the basis of the presence of characteristic clinical and radiographic findings. If the infection does not respond to an empiric trial of anti-*T gondii* therapy, demonstration of *T gondii* organisms, antigen, or DNA in sites such as blood, CSF, or bronchoalveolar fluid, where the organism would not be expected to reside in the chronic cyst form, may be necessary to confirm the diagnosis.

Infants born to women who are infected simultaneously with HIV and *T gondii* should be evaluated for congenital toxoplasmosis because of an increased likelihood of maternal reactivation and congenital transmission in this setting.

---

* Available from Eon Labs, Laurelton, NY (800-526-0225).

Ocular toxoplasmosis usually is diagnosed on the basis of observation of characteristic retinal lesions in conjunction with serum *T gondii*-specific IgG or IgM antibodies.

TREATMENT: Most cases of acquired infection in an immunocompetent host do not require specific antimicrobial therapy. When indicated (eg, chorioretinitis or significant organ damage), the combination of pyrimethamine and sulfadiazine,* with supplemental leucovorin (folinic acid) to minimize pyrimethamine-associated hematologic toxicity, is the most widely accepted regimen for children and adults with acute symptomatic disease* (see Drugs for Parasitic Infections, p 790). Alternatively, pyrimethamine can be used in combination with clindamycin if the patient does not tolerate sulfadiazine. Corticosteroids appear to be useful in the management of ocular complications and central nervous system disease in certain patients.

Patients infected with HIV who have had toxoplasmic encephalitis should receive lifelong suppressive therapy to prevent recurrence. Regimens for primary treatment also are effective for suppressive therapy.

For HIV-infected adults, primary chemoprophylaxis with trimethoprim-sulfamethoxazole (TMP-SMX) against toxoplasmosis has been recommended as the preferred regimen by the US Public Health Services and Infectious Diseases Society of America Prevention of Opportunistic Infections Working Group (USPHS/IDSA OI)[†] for people who are *T gondii*-seropositive and have CD4+ T-lymphocyte counts less than $100 \times 10^6/L$ (<100/µL). Alternative regimens and discontinuation of prophylaxis after CD4+ T-lymphocyte count increases in association with highly active antiretroviral therapy are discussed in the USPHS/IDSA OI guidelines.

Prophylaxis to prevent the first episode of toxoplasmosis generally is recommended for children (see Table 3.68, p 670). Trimethoprim-sulfamethoxazole, when administered for *Pneumocystis jiroveci* pneumonia (PCP) prophylaxis, also provides prophylaxis against toxoplasmosis. Atovaquone might also provide protection. Children older than 12 months of age who qualify for PCP prophylaxis and who are receiving an agent other than TMP-SMX or atovaquone should have serologic testing for *Toxoplasma* antibody, because alternative drugs for PCP prophylaxis might not be effective against *Toxoplasma*. Severely immunosuppressed children who are not receiving TMP-SMX or atovaquone who are found to be seropositive for *Toxoplasma* should receive prophylaxis for both PCP and toxoplasmosis (ie, dapsone plus pyrimethamine). Children with a history of toxoplasmosis should be administered lifelong prophylaxis to prevent recurrence (see Table 3.68, p 670). The safety of discontinuing primary or secondary prophylaxis in HIV-infected children receiving highly active antiretroviral therapy has not been studied extensively.

---

* Centers for Disease Control and Prevention. Treating opportunistic infections among HIV-exposed and infected children. *MMWR Recomm Rep.* 2004;53(RR-14):1–63

† Centers for Disease Control and Prevention. Guidelines for preventing opportunistic infections among HIV-infected persons—2002. Recommendations of the US Public Health Service and the Infectious Diseases Society of America. *MMWR Recomm Rep.* 2002;51(RR-8):1–46. Available at: **www.cdc.gov/ mmwr/preview/mmwrhtml/rr5108a1.htm**

Table 3.68. Prophylaxis to Prevent First Episode and Recurrence of Toxoplasmosis in Children

Prevention of	Indication	First Choice	Alternatives
First episode of toxoplasmosis[1]	Severe immunosuppression and presence of IgG antibody to *Toxoplasma*	TMP-SMX, 150–750 mg/m² per day in 2 divided doses, orally, every day	Dapsone (children ≥1 mo of age), 2 mg/kg or 15 mg/m² (max 25 mg), orally, every day, **PLUS** pyrimethamine, 1 mg/kg, orally, every day, **PLUS** leucovorin, 5 mg, orally, every 3 days Atovaquone, children 1–3 mo and >24 mo of age: 30 mg/kg, orally, every day; children 14–24 mo of age: 45 mg/kg, orally, every day
Recurrence of toxoplasmosis[2]	Prior toxoplasmic encephalitis	Sulfadiazine, 85–120 mg/kg per day in 2–4 divided doses, orally, every day, **PLUS** pyrimethamine, 1 mg/kg or 15 mg/m² (max 25 mg), orally, every day, **PLUS** leucovorin, 5 mg, orally, every 3 days	Clindamycin, 20–30 mg/kg per day in 3 divided doses, orally, every day, **PLUS** pyrimethamine, 1 mg/kg, orally, every day, **PLUS** leucovorin, 5 mg, orally, every 3 days

Centers for Disease Control and Prevention. Treating opportunistic infections among HIV-exposed and infected children. *MMWR Recomm Rep.* 2004;53(RR–14):1–63

[1] Protection against toxoplasmosis is provided by the preferred antipneumocystis regimens and possibly by atovaquone. Atovaquone may be used with or without pyrimethamine. Pyrimethamine alone probably provides little, if any, protection (for information about severe immunosuppression, see Table 3.50, p 540).

[2] Only pyrimethamine plus sulfadiazine confers protection against *Pneumocystis jiroveci* pneumonia as well as toxoplasmosis. Although the clindamycin plus pyrimethamine regimen is recommended in adults, this regimen has not been tested in children. However, these drugs are safe and are used for other infections.

For symptomatic and asymptomatic congenital infections, pyrimethamine combined with sulfadiazine (supplemented with folinic acid) is recommended as initial therapy. Duration of therapy is prolonged and often is 1 year. However, the optimal dosage and duration are not established definitively and should be determined in consultation with appropriate specialists.

Treatment of primary *T gondii* infection in pregnant women, including women with HIV infection, is recommended. Appropriate specialists should be consulted for management. Spiramycin treatment of primary infection during gestation is used in an attempt to decrease transmission of *T gondii* from the mother to the fetus. Maternal therapy may decrease the severity of sequelae in the fetus once congenital toxoplasmosis has occurred. Spiramycin is available only as an investigational drug in the United States. Spiramycin may be obtained from the manufacturer with authorization from the US Food and Drug Administration.* If fetal infection is confirmed after 17 weeks of gestation or if the mother acquires infection during the third trimester, consideration should be given to starting therapy with pyrimethamine and sulfadiazine.

ISOLATION OF THE HOSPITALIZED PATIENT: Standard precautions are recommended.

CONTROL MEASURES: Pregnant women whose serostatus for *T gondii* is negative or unknown should avoid activities that potentially expose them to cat feces (such as changing litter boxes, gardening, and landscaping), or they should wear gloves and wash their hands if such activities are unavoidable. Daily changing of cat litter will decrease the chance of infection, because oocysts are not infective during the first 1 to 2 days after passage. Domestic cats can be protected from infection by feeding them commercially prepared cat food and preventing them from eating undercooked kitchen meat scraps and hunting wild rodents.

Oral ingestion of *T gondii* can be avoided by the following measures: (1) cooking meat, particularly pork, lamb, and venison, to an internal temperature of 65.5°C to 76.6°C (150°F–170°F [no longer pink]) before consumption (smoked meat and meat cured in brine are considered safe); (2) washing fruits and vegetables; (3) washing hands and cleaning kitchen surfaces after handling fruits, vegetables, and raw meat; (4) washing hands after gardening or other contact with soil; (5) preventing contamination of food with raw or undercooked meat or soil; and (6) avoiding ingestion of untreated water, particularly in developing countries. All HIV-infected people and pregnant women should be counseled about the various sources of toxoplasmic infection.

Trichinellosis
(Trichinella spiralis)

CLINICAL MANIFESTATIONS: The clinical spectrum of infection ranges from inapparent to fulminant and fatal illness, but most infections are inapparent. The severity of the disease is proportional to the infective dose. During the first week after ingesting infected meat, a person may be asymptomatic or experience abdominal discomfort, nausea, vomiting, and/or diarrhea. Two to 8 weeks later, as larvae migrate into tissues, fever, myalgia, periorbital edema, urticarial rash, and conjunctival and subungual hemorrhages may develop. Larvae may remain viable in tissues for years; calcification of some larvae in skeletal muscle usually occurs within 6 to 24 months and may be detected on radiographs. In severe infections, myocarditis, neurologic involvement, and pneumonitis can follow in 1 or 2 months.

ETIOLOGY: Infection is caused by nematodes (roundworms) of the genus *Trichinella*. At least 5 species capable of infecting only warm-blooded animals have been identified. Worldwide, *Trichinella spiralis* is the most common cause of human infection.

EPIDEMIOLOGY: The infection is enzootic worldwide in many carnivores, especially scavengers. Infection occurs as a result of ingestion of raw or insufficiently cooked meat containing encysted larvae of *T spiralis*. The usual source of human infections is pork, but horse meat and wild carnivorous game, such as bear, seal, and walrus meat in North America, can be sources. *Trichinella nativa* is the causative organism in most of these arctic sources. Feeding pigs uncooked garbage perpetuates the cycle of infection. In the United States, the incidence of infection in humans has decreased considerably, but infection occurs sporadically, often within a family or among friends who have prepared uncooked sausage from fresh pork. The disease is not transmitted from person to person.

The **incubation period** usually is 1 to 2 weeks.

DIAGNOSTIC TESTS: Eosinophilia approaching 70%, in conjunction with compatible symptoms and dietary history, suggests the diagnosis. Increases in concentrations of muscle enzymes, such as creatinine phosphokinase and lactic dehydrogenase, also occur. Encapsulated larvae in a skeletal muscle biopsy specimen (particularly deltoid and gastrocnemius) can be visualized microscopically beginning 2 weeks after infection. Fresh tissue, compressed between 2 microscope slides, should be examined. Digestion of muscle tissue in artificial gastric juice followed by examination of the sediment for larvae is more sensitive. Identification of larvae in suspect meat can be the most rapid source of diagnostic information. Serologic tests are available through some private and state laboratories and the Centers for Disease Control and Prevention. Serum antibody titers rarely become positive before the second week of illness. Testing paired acute and convalescent serum specimens usually is diagnostic.

TREATMENT: Mebendazole and albendazole have comparable efficacy for treatment of trichinosis (see Drugs for Parasitic Infections, p 790). Neither drug is very effective for *Trichinella* larvae already in the muscles. Coadministration of corticosteroids with mebendazole or albendazole often is recommended when symptoms are severe. Corticosteroids alleviate symptoms of the inflammatory reaction and can be lifesaving when the central nervous system or heart is involved.

ISOLATION OF THE HOSPITALIZED PATIENT: Standard precautions are recommended.

CONTROL MEASURES: Transmission to pigs can be decreased by not feeding pigs garbage, by preventing cannibalism, and by effective rat control. The public should be educated about the necessity of cooking pork and meat of wild animals thoroughly (until the meat no longer is pink). Freezing pork at –23°C (–10°F) for 10 days kills larvae. However, *Trichinella* organisms in Arctic wild animals can survive this procedure. People known to have ingested contaminated meat recently should be treated with mebendazole (or albendazole).

Trichomonas vaginalis Infections
(Trichomoniasis)

CLINICAL MANIFESTATIONS: Infection with *Trichomonas vaginalis* is asymptomatic in 90% of men and 50% of women infected with this organism. Clinical manifestations in symptomatic postmenarcheal female patients consist of a frothy vaginal discharge and mild vulvovaginal itching and burning. Dysuria and, rarely, lower abdominal pain can occur. The vaginal discharge usually is pale yellow to gray-green and has a musty odor. Symptoms commonly are more severe just before or after menstruation. The vaginal mucosa often is deeply erythematous, and the cervix is friable and diffusely inflamed, sometimes covered with numerous petechiae ("strawberry cervix"). Urethritis and, more rarely, epididymitis or prostatitis can develop in infected males, but most are asymptomatic. Reinfection is common. *Trichomonas vaginalis* is considered an important cofactor in amplifying human immunodeficiency virus transmission.

ETIOLOGY: *Trichomonas vaginalis* is a flagellated protozoan that is slightly larger than a granulocyte. It depends on adherence to host cells for survival.

EPIDEMIOLOGY: *Trichomonas vaginalis* infection is the second most common sexually transmitted infection in the United States and commonly coexists with other conditions, particularly infection with *Neisseria gonorrhoeae* and *Chlamydia trachomatis* and bacterial vaginitis. The presence of *T vaginalis* in a prepubertal child should raise suspicion of sexual abuse. *Trichomonas vaginalis* acquired during birth by newborn infants can cause a vaginal discharge during the first weeks of life.

The **incubation period** averages 1 week but ranges from 4 to 28 days.

DIAGNOSTIC TESTS: Diagnosis usually is established by examination of a wet-mount preparation of the vaginal discharge. Lashing of the flagella and jerky motility of the organism are distinctive. Positive preparation results, found more commonly in women who have symptoms, are related directly to the number of organisms but are identified in only 50% to 60% of cases. Culture of the organism and tests using enzyme immunoassay and immunofluorescent techniques are more sensitive than wet-mount preparations but generally are not required for diagnosis. Culture for *T vaginalis* is positive in more than 80% of cases. A US Food and Drug Administration-licensed polymerase chain reaction assay for *T vaginalis* is not available in the United States but may be available as a research diagnostic test or from commercial laboratories. Fecal contamination of specimens makes microscopic diagnosis difficult because of the somewhat similar morphology of *Trichomonas hominis*. Motile trichomonads also may be identified by microscopic examination of centrifuged urine.

TREATMENT: Treatment with metronidazole or tinidazole results in cure rates of approximately 95% (see Drugs for Parasitic Infections, p 790). Sexual partners should be treated concurrently, even if asymptomatic, because reinfection is a major factor in treatment failures. Patients should abstain from alcohol for 48 hours after treatment with either medication because of the disulfiram-like effects of the drugs. During pregnancy, patients can be treated with a 2-g single dose of metronidazole, with the 7-day regimen, or with tinidazole. Use of metronidazole or tinidazole is contraindicated during the first trimester of pregnancy.

Patients whose infections do not respond to treatment should be retreated with metronidazole (1 g in 2 divided doses for adolescents and adults) for 7 days. Patients who repeatedly fail to respond to this regimen should be treated with metronidazole, 2 g, once a day for 3 to 5 days. *Trichomonas* strains with decreased susceptibility to metronidazole have been reported. In the event of continued treatment failure, consultation with an expert is advised. Consultation is available from the Centers for Disease Control and Prevention at **www.cdc.gov/std** or 770-488-4115.

People infected with *T vaginalis* should be evaluated for the presence of other sexually transmitted infections, including syphilis and *N gonorrhoeae, C trachomatis*, hepatitis B virus, and human immunodeficiency virus infection. Newborn infection is self-limited and treatment generally is not recommended.

ISOLATION OF THE HOSPITALIZED PATIENT: Standard precautions are recommended.

CONTROL MEASURES: Measures to prevent sexually transmitted infections, particularly the consistent use of condoms, are indicated. Patients should be instructed to avoid sexual activity until they and their sexual partners are cured.

Trichuriasis
(Whipworm Infection)

CLINICAL MANIFESTATIONS: Most infected children harbor only small numbers of the organism and are asymptomatic. Children with heavy infestations can develop a *Trichuris trichiura* dysentery syndrome consisting of abdominal pain, tenesmus, and bloody diarrhea with mucus or a chronic *T trichiura* colitis. *Trichuris trichiura* colitis can mimic other forms of inflammatory bowel disease and lead to physical growth retardation. Even otherwise asymptomatic infections may have adverse effects on nutritional status. Chronic illness associated with heavy infestation also can be associated with rectal prolapse.

ETIOLOGY: *Trichuris trichiura*, the whipworm, is the causative agent. Adult worms are 30 to 50 mm long with a large, thread-like anterior end that is embedded in the mucosa of the large intestine.

EPIDEMIOLOGY: The parasite has a worldwide distribution but is more common in the tropics and in areas of poor sanitation. In some areas of Asia, the prevalence of infection is 50%. In the United States, trichuriasis generally has been limited to rural areas of the southeast and no longer is a serious public health problem. Migrants from tropical areas also may be infected. Eggs require a minimum of 10 days of incubation in the soil before they are infectious. The disease is not communicable from person to person.

The **incubation period** is unknown. However, the time required for mature worms to begin laying eggs that are passed in feces is approximately 90 days after ingestion of eggs.

DIAGNOSTIC TESTS: Eggs may be found on direct examination of stool or by using concentration techniques.

TREATMENT: Mebendazole or, alternatively, albendazole or ivermectin given for 3 days usually is effective in eradicating most of the worms. In mass treatment efforts involving entire communities, a single dose of either mebendazole (500 mg) or albendazole (400 mg) will reduce worm burdens (see Drugs for Parasitic Infections, p 790).

ISOLATION OF THE HOSPITALIZED PATIENT: Standard precautions are recommended.

CONTROL MEASURES: Proper disposal of fecal material is indicated. Mass treatment of infected school-aged populations can reduce whipworm transmission in people in communities with endemic infection.

African Trypanosomiasis
(African Sleeping Sickness)

CLINICAL MANIFESTATIONS: The rapidity and severity of clinical manifestations vary with the infecting subspecies. With *Trypanosoma brucei gambiense* (West African) infection, a cutaneous nodule or chancre may appear at the site of parasite inoculation within a few days of a bite by an infected tsetse fly. Systemic illness is chronic, occurring months to years later, and is characterized by intermittent fever, posterior cervical lymphadenopathy (Winterbottom sign), and multiple nonspecific complaints, including malaise, weight loss, arthralgia, rash, pruritus, and edema. If the central nervous system (CNS) is involved, chronic meningoencephalitis with behavioral changes, cachexia, headache, hallucinations, delusions, and somnolence can occur. In contrast, *Trypanosoma brucei rhodesiense* (East African) infection is an acute, generalized illness that develops days to weeks after parasite inoculation, with manifestations including high fever, cutaneous chancre, myocarditis, hepatitis, anemia, thrombocytopenia, and laboratory evidence of disseminated intravascular coagulopathy. Clinical meningoencephalitis can develop as early as 3 weeks after onset of the untreated systemic illness. *Trypanosoma brucei rhodesiense* infection has a high fatality rate; without treatment, infected patients usually die within days to months after clinical onset of disease.

ETIOLOGY: The West African (Gambian) form of sleeping sickness is caused by *T brucei gambiense*, whereas the East African (Rhodesian) form is caused by *T brucei rhodesiense*. Both are extracellular protozoan hemoflagellates that live in blood and tissue of the human host. The genome of *Trypanosoma brucei* has been sequenced.

EPIDEMIOLOGY: Approximately 30 000 human cases are reported annually worldwide, although only a few cases, acquired in Africa, are reported every year in the United States. There has been a recent increase of trypanosomiasis in travelers after short visits to game parks in Tanzania. Transmission is confined to an area in Africa between the latitudes of 15° north and 20° south, corresponding precisely with the distribution of the tsetse fly vector (*Glossina* species). In East Africa, wild animals, such as antelope, bushbuck, and hartebeest, constitute the major reservoirs for *T brucei rhodesiense*, although cattle serve as reservoir hosts in local outbreaks. Domestic pigs and dogs have been found as incidental reservoirs of *T brucei gambiense*; however, humans are the only important reservoir in West and Central Africa.

The **incubation period** for *T brucei rhodesiense* infection is 3 to 21 days and usually is 5 to 14 days; for *T brucei gambiense* infection, the incubation period usually is longer and variable, ranging from several months to years.

DIAGNOSTIC TESTS: Diagnosis is made by identification of trypomastigotes in specimens of blood, cerebrospinal fluid (CSF), or fluid aspirated from a chancre or lymph node or by inoculation of susceptible laboratory animals (mice) with heparinized blood. Examination of the CSF is critical to management and should be performed using the double-centrifugation technique. Concentration and Giemsa staining of the buffy coat layer of peripheral blood also can be helpful. *Trypanosoma brucei gambiense* is more likely to be found in lymph node aspirates. Although an increased concentration of immunoglobulin M in serum or CSF is considered characteristic of African trypanosomiasis, polyclonal hyperglobulinemia is common.

TREATMENT: When no evidence of CNS involvement is present (including absence of trypanosomes and CSF pleocytosis), the drug of choice for the acute hemolymphatic stage of infection is pentamidine for *T brucei gambiense* infection and suramin for *T brucei rhodesiense* infection. For treatment of hemolymphatic and CNS disease, see Drugs for Parasitic Infections, p 790. Because of the risk of relapse, patients who have had CNS involvement should undergo repeated CSF examinations every 6 months for 2 years.

ISOLATION OF THE HOSPITALIZED PATIENT: Standard precautions are recommended.

CONTROL MEASURES: Travelers to areas with endemic infection should avoid known foci of sleeping sickness and tsetse fly infestation and minimize fly bites by the use of protective clothing and insect repellents. Infected patients should not breastfeed or donate blood.

American Trypanosomiasis
(Chagas Disease)

CLINICAL MANIFESTATIONS: Patients can have acute or chronic disease. The early phase of this disease commonly is asymptomatic. However, children are more likely to exhibit symptoms than are adults. In some patients, a red nodule known as a *chagoma* develops at the site of the original inoculation, usually on the face or arms. The surrounding skin becomes indurated and, later, hypopigmented. Unilateral firm edema of the eyelids, known as Romaña sign, is the earliest indication of the infection when the portal of entry is the conjunctiva; it is not always present. The edematous skin is violaceous and associated with conjunctivitis and enlargement of the ipsilateral preauricular lymph node. A few days after appearance of Romaña sign, fever, gener-

alized lymphadenopathy, and malaise can develop. Acute myocarditis, hepatosplenomegaly, edema, and meningoencephalitis can follow. In nearly all cases, acute Chagas
disease resolves after 1 to 3 months, and an asymptomatic or indeterminate period
follows. In 20% to 30% of cases, serious sequelae, consisting of cardiomyopathy and
heart failure (the major cause of death), megaesophagus, and/or megacolon, develop
many years after the initial infection (chronic phase). Congenital disease may be characterized by low birth weight, hepatomegaly, and meningoencephalitis with seizures
and tremors, but most infants infected in utero have no signs or symptoms of disease.
Reactivation may occur, especially in immunocompromised people, including people
infected with human immunodeficiency virus.

ETIOLOGY: *Trypanosoma cruzi*, a protozoan hemoflagellate, is the cause. The genome
of *T cruzi* has been sequenced.

EPIDEMIOLOGY: Parasites are transmitted through feces of the insects of the triatom-
ine family, usually an infected reduviid (cone-nose or kissing) bug. These insects defecate during or after taking blood. The bitten person is inoculated by inadvertently
rubbing the insect feces containing the parasite into the site of the bite or mucous
membranes of the eye or the mouth. The parasite also can be transmitted congenitally, during organ transplantation, through blood transfusion, and by consumption of
the vector or the vector's excretion. Accidental laboratory infections can result from
handling blood from infected people or laboratory animals. The disease is limited to
the Western hemisphere, predominantly Mexico and Central and South America.
Although some small mammals in the southern and southwestern United States harbor *T cruzi*, vectorborne transmission to humans is rare in the United States. Several
transfusion- and transplantation-associated cases have been documented in the
United States. Infection is common in immigrants from Central and South America.
The disease is an important cause of death in South America, where between 7 and
15 million people are infected.

The **incubation period** for the acute phase of disease is 1 to 2 weeks or longer.
Chronic manifestations do not appear for years to decades.

DIAGNOSTIC TESTS: During the acute phase of disease, the parasite is demonstrable
in blood specimens by Giemsa staining after a concentration technique or by direct
wet-mount or buffy coat preparation. During the indeterminate and chronic phases,
which are characterized by low-level parasitemia, recovery of the parasite requires
culture on special media (available at the Centers for Disease Control and Prevention), but this may be negative because of a low parasite burden. Xenodiagnosis (isolation of trypanosomes from the intestine of a reduviid bug that has fed on patient
blood) is available in Central and South America. Serologic tests include indirect
hemagglutination, indirect immunofluorescent, and enzyme immunoassay, which are
especially useful in chronic disease. The diagnosis of congenital Chagas disease is different and often is not made until 6 to 9 months of age, when immunoglobulin G
measurements reflect infant response.

TREATMENT: The acute phase of Chagas disease is treated with benznidazole or
nifurtimox (see Drugs for Parasitic Infections, p 790). Although treatment of children

during the latent and chronic phases of infection is routine in most Latin American countries, the effectiveness of this approach has not been established.

ISOLATION OF THE HOSPITALIZED PATIENT: Standard precautions should be followed.

CONTROL MEASURES: Travelers to areas with endemic infection should avoid contact with reduviid insects by avoiding habitation in buildings that do not have control measures for these insects, particularly buildings constructed of mud, palm thatch, or adobe brick, and especially those with cracks in the walls or roof. The use of insecticide-impregnated bed nets also may be beneficial. Camping or sleeping outdoors in areas with highly endemic infection is not recommended. Blood and serologic examinations should be performed on members of households with an infected patient if they have had exposure to the vector similar to that of the patient.

Education about the mode of spread and the methods of prevention is warranted in areas with endemic infection. Homes should be examined for the presence of the vectors, and if found, measures to eliminate the vector should be taken.

Blood donors in areas with endemic infection should be screened by serologic tests (see Blood Safety, p 106). Infected patients should not donate blood.

Tuberculosis

CLINICAL MANIFESTATIONS: Most infections caused by *Mycobacterium tuberculosis* and *Mycobacterium bovis* in children and adolescents are asymptomatic. When tuberculosis disease does occur, clinical manifestations most often appear 1 to 6 months after infection and include fever, growth delay, weight loss or poor weight gain, cough, night sweats, and chills. Radiographic findings in *M tuberculosis* infection range from normal to diverse abnormalities, such as lymphadenopathy of the hilar, subcarinal, paratracheal, or mediastinal nodes; atelectasis or infiltrate of a segment or lobe; pleural effusion; cavitary lesions; or miliary disease. Radiographic findings in *M bovis* infection can include the same pulmonary manifestations as *M tuberculosis*, extensive cervical and mesenteric lymphadenopathy, bowel wall thickening, and multiple enteric fistulae. Extrapulmonary manifestations of *M tuberculosis* disease include meningitis and granulomatous inflammation of the lymph nodes, bones, joints, skin, and middle ear and mastoid. Renal tuberculosis and progression to disease from latent tuberculosis infection or adult-type pulmonary tuberculosis are rare in young children but can occur in adolescents. In addition, chronic abdominal pain with intermittent partial intestinal obstruction can be present in disease caused by *M bovis*. Clinical findings in patients with drug-resistant tuberculosis disease are indistinguishable from manifestations in patients with drug-susceptible disease.

ETIOLOGY: The agent is *M tuberculosis*, an acid-fast bacillus (AFB). Human disease caused by *M bovis*, the cause of bovine tuberculosis, occurs in the United States in children who have ingested unpasteurized milk or milk products.

DEFINITIONS:
- **Positive tuberculin skin test (TST).** A positive TST result (see Table 3.69, p 680) indicates possible infection with *M tuberculosis* or *M bovis*. Tuberculin reac-

tivity appears 2 to 12 weeks after initial infection; the median interval is 3 to 4 weeks (see Tuberculin Testing, p 682).

- **Exposed person** refers to a patient who has had recent contact with a person with suspected or confirmed contagious pulmonary tuberculosis disease and who has a negative TST result, normal physical examination findings, and chest radiographic findings that are not compatible with tuberculosis. Some exposed people become infected (and subsequently have a positive TST result) and some people do not become infected after exposure; the 2 groups cannot be distinguished initially.

- **Source case** is defined as the person who has transmitted *M tuberculosis* to a child who subsequently develops either latent tuberculosis infection or tuberculosis disease.

- **Latent tuberculosis infection (LTBI)** is defined as *M tuberculosis* or *M bovis* infection in a person who has a positive TST result, no physical findings of disease, and chest radiograph findings that are normal or reveal evidence of healed infection (eg, granulomas or calcification in the lung, hilar lymph nodes, or both).

- **Tuberculosis disease** is defined as disease in a person with infection in whom symptoms, signs, or radiographic manifestations caused by *M tuberculosis* or *M bovis* are apparent; disease may be pulmonary, extrapulmonary, or both. Infectious tuberculosis refers to tuberculosis disease of the lungs or larynx in a person who has the potential to transmit *M tuberculosis* to other people.

- **Directly observed therapy (DOT)** is defined as an intervention by which medication is provided directly to the patient by a health care professional or trained third party (not a relative or friend), who observes and documents that the patient ingests each dose of medication.

EPIDEMIOLOGY: Case rates of tuberculosis for all ages are higher in urban, low-income areas and in nonwhite racial and ethnic groups; two thirds of reported cases in the United States occur in nonwhite individuals. In recent years, foreign-born children have accounted for more than one quarter of newly diagnosed cases in children 14 years of age or younger. Specific groups with high LTBI and disease rates include immigrants, international adoptees, and refugees from high-prevalence regions (eg, Asia, Africa, Latin America, and countries of the former Soviet Union), travelers to countries with endemic infection, homeless people, and residents of corrections facilities.

Infants and postpubertal adolescents are at increased risk of progression of LTBI to tuberculosis disease. Other predictive factors for development of disease include recent infection (within the past 2 years); immunodeficiency, including human immunodeficiency virus (HIV) infection; use of immunosuppressive drugs, such as prolonged or high-dose corticosteroid therapy or chemotherapy; intravenous drug use; and certain diseases or medical conditions, including Hodgkin disease, lymphoma, diabetes mellitus, chronic renal failure, and malnutrition. There have been reports of tuberculosis disease in adolescents and adults being treated for arthritis with tumor necrosis factor (TNF) antagonists, such as infliximab and etanercept. Before use of TNF antagonists, patients should be screened for risk factors for *M tuberculosis* and have a TST performed.

Table 3.69. Definitions of Positive Tuberculin Skin Test (TST) Results in Infants, Children, and Adolescents[1]

Induration ≥5 mm

Children in close contact with known or suspected contagious people with tuberculosis disease.

Children suspected to have tuberculosis disease:
- Findings on chest radiograph consistent with active or previously tuberculosis disease
- Clinical evidence of tuberculosis disease[2]

Children receiving immunosuppressive therapy[3] or with immunosuppressive conditions, including HIV infection.

Induration ≥10 mm

Children at increased risk of disseminated tuberculosis disease:
- Children younger than 4 years of age
- Children with other medical conditions, including Hodgkin disease, lymphoma, diabetes mellitus, chronic renal failure, or malnutrition (see Table 3.70, p 683)

Children with increased exposure to tuberculosis disease:
- Children born in high-prevalence regions of the world
- Children frequently exposed to adults who are HIV infected, homeless, users of illicit drugs, residents of nursing homes, incarcerated or institutionalized, or migrant farm workers
- Children who travel to high-prevalence regions of the world

Induration ≥15 mm

Children 4 years of age or older without any risk factors.

HIV indicates human immunodeficiency virus.

[1] These definitions apply regardless of previous bacille Calmette-Guérin (BCG) immunization (see also Interpretation of TST Results in Previous Recipients of BCG Vaccine, p 683); erythema at TST site does not indicate a positive test result. Tests should be read at 48 to 72 hours after placement.

[2] Evidence by physical examination or laboratory assessment that would include tuberculosis in the working differential diagnosis (eg, meningitis).

[3] Including immunosuppressive doses of corticosteroids (see Corticosteroids, p 692).

A diagnosis of LTBI or tuberculosis disease in a young child is a sentinel event usually representing recent transmission of *M tuberculosis*. Transmission of *M tuberculosis* is airborne, with inhalation of droplet nuclei usually produced by an adult or adolescent with contagious pulmonary or laryngeal tuberculosis disease. The duration of contagiousness of an adult receiving effective treatment depends on drug susceptibilities of the organism, the number of organisms in sputum, and frequency of cough. Although contagiousness usually lasts only a few days to weeks after initiation of effective drug therapy, it may last longer, especially when the adult patient has cavitary disease, does not adhere to medical therapy, or is infected with a drug-resistant strain. If the sputum smear is negative for AFB organisms on 3 separate days and the patient has improved clinically, the treated person can be considered at low risk of disease transmission. Children younger than 10 years of age with pulmonary tuberculosis rarely are contagious because their pulmonary lesions are small (paucibacillary disease), cough is not productive, and few or no bacilli are expulsed.

The **incubation period** from infection to development of a positive TST result is 2 to 12 weeks. The risk of developing tuberculosis disease is highest during the 6 months after infection and remains high for 2 years; however, many years can elapse between initial tuberculosis infection and tuberculosis disease.

DIAGNOSTIC TESTS: Isolation of *Mycobacterium tuberculosis* or *Mycobacterium bovis* by culture from specimens of gastric aspirates, sputum, bronchial washings, pleural fluid, cerebrospinal fluid (CSF), urine, or other body fluids or a biopsy specimen establishes the diagnosis. Children older than 5 years of age and adolescents frequently can produce sputum by induction with aerosolized hypertonic saline. Studies have demonstrated successful collections of induced sputum from infants with pulmonary tuberculosis, but this requires special expertise. The best specimen for diagnosis of pulmonary tuberculosis in any child or adolescent in whom the cough is nonproductive or absent and sputum cannot be induced is an early morning gastric aspirate. Gastric aspirate specimens should be obtained with a nasogastric tube on awakening the child and before ambulation or feeding.* Aspirates collected on 3 separate days should be submitted for testing. Results of AFB smears of gastric aspirates usually are negative, and false-positive results caused by the presence of nontuberculous mycobacteria can occur. Gastric aspirates have the highest yield in young children on the first day of collection. The overall diagnostic yield of gastric aspirates is less than 50%. Fluorescent staining methods for gastric aspirate smears are more sensitive and, if available, are preferred. Histologic examination for and demonstration of AFB and granulomas in biopsy specimens from lymph node, pleura, mesentery, liver, bone marrow, or other tissues can be useful, but *M tuberculosis* and *M bovis* cannot reliably be distinguished from other mycobacteria in stained specimens. Regardless of results of the AFB smears, each specimen should be cultured.

Because *M tuberculosis* and *M bovis* are slow growing, detection of these organisms may take as long as 10 weeks using solid media; use of liquid media allows detection within 1 to 6 weeks. Even with optimal culture techniques, *M tuberculosis* organisms are isolated from fewer than 50% of children and 75% of infants with pulmonary tuberculosis diagnosed by other clinical criteria. Species identification of isolates by culture can be more rapid if a DNA probe is used. Current nucleic acid assays cannot differentiate between *M tuberculosis* and *M bovis*.

Nucleic acid amplification tests for rapid diagnosis are licensed by the US Food and Drug Administration (FDA) only for acid-fast stain positive respiratory tract specimens but have decreased sensitivity for gastric aspirate, CSF, and tissue specimens, with false-negative and false-positive results reported.

Identification of the culture-positive source case supports the child's presumptive diagnosis and provides the likely drug susceptibility of the child's organism. Ingestion of unpasteurized dairy products support a presumptive diagnosis of *M bovis* infection.

Culture material should be collected from children with evidence of tuberculosis disease, especially when (1) an isolate from a source case is not available; (2) the presumed source case has drug-resistant tuberculosis; (3) the child is immunocompromised, including children with HIV infection; or (4) the child has extrapulmonary disease.

---

* **www.nationaltbcenter.edu/catalogue/epub/index.cfm?tableName = GAP**

TUBERCULIN TESTING. The TST is the most common method for diagnosing LTBI in asymptomatic people. The Mantoux method consists of 5 tuberculin units of purified protein derivative (0.1 mL) injected intradermally using a 27-gauge needle and a 1.0-mL syringe into the volar aspect of the forearm. Creation of a visible wheal 6 to 10 mm in diameter is crucial to accurate testing. Other strengths of TSTs (1 or 250 tuberculin units) should not be used. Multiple puncture tests are not recommended, because they lack adequate sensitivity and specificity.

A TST should be administered to children who are at increased risk of acquiring LTBI and tuberculosis disease (see Table 3.70, p 683). Routine TST administration, including programs based at schools, child care centers, and camps that include populations at low risk, is to be discouraged because it results in either a low yield of positive results or a large proportion of false-positive results, leading to an inefficient use of health care resources. Simple questionnaires can identify children with risk factors for LTBI who then should be tested with a TST (see Table 3.71, p 684). Risk assessment for tuberculosis should be performed at first contact with a child and every 6 months thereafter for the first 2 years of life (eg, 2 weeks and 6, 12, 18, and 24 months of age). If at any time, risk of tuberculosis disease is determined, a TST should be performed, although this test is unreliable in infants younger than 3 months of age. After 2 years of age, risk assessment for tuberculosis should be performed annually, if possible.

A TST can be administered at the same time as immunizations, including live-virus vaccines, except measles vaccine, which temporarily can suppress tuberculin reactivity. If tuberculin testing is indicated, measles immunization should be deferred until testing is complete or the TST should be deferred for 4 to 6 weeks. Although data are not available regarding varicella immunization, it is reasonable to assume that tuberculin testing should be deferred as with measles vaccine. Previous immunization with bacille Calmette-Guérin (BCG) vaccine is not a contraindication to TST.

Administration of TSTs and interpretation of results should be performed by experienced health care professionals who have been trained in the proper methods, because administration and interpretation by unskilled people and family members are unreliable. The recommended time for assessing the TST result is 48 to 72 hours after administration. However, a reaction that develops at the site of administration more than 72 hours later should be measured and considered the result. The diameter of induration in millimeters is measured transversely to the long axis of the forearm. Positive test results, as defined in Table 3.69 (p 680), can persist for several weeks.

A negative TST result does not exclude LTBI or tuberculosis disease. Approximately 10% to 15% of immunocompetent children with culture-documented disease do not react initially to a TST. Host factors, such as young age, poor nutrition, immunosuppression, other viral infections (especially measles, varicella, and influenza), recent tuberculosis infection, and disseminated tuberculosis disease can decrease TST reactivity. Many children and adults coinfected with HIV and *M tuberculosis* do not react to a TST. Control skin tests to assess cutaneous anergy are not recommended routinely.

INTERPRETATION OF TST RESULTS (SEE TABLE 3.69, P 680). Classification of TST results is based on epidemiologic and clinical factors. The size of

Table 3.70. Tuberculin Skin Test (TST) Recommendations for Infants, Children, and Adolescents[1]

Children for whom immediate TST is indicated[2]:
- Contacts of people with confirmed or suspected contagious tuberculosis (contact investigation)
- Children with radiographic or clinical findings suggesting tuberculosis disease
- Children immigrating from countries with endemic infection (eg, Asia, Middle East, Africa, Latin America, countries of the former Soviet Union) including international adoptees
- Children with travel histories to countries with endemic infection and substantial contact with indigenous people from such countries[3]

Children who should have annual TST:
- Children infected with HIV
- Incarcerated adolescents

Children at increased risk of progression of LTBI to tuberculosis disease: Children with other medical conditions, including diabetes mellitus, chronic renal failure, malnutrition, and congenital or acquired immunodeficiencies deserve special consideration. Without recent exposure, these people are not at increased risk of acquiring tuberculosis infection. Underlying immune deficiencies associated with these conditions theoretically would enhance the possibility for progression to severe disease. Initial histories of potential exposure to tuberculosis should be included for all of these patients. If these histories or local epidemiologic factors suggest a possibility of exposure, immediate and periodic TST should be considered. **An initial TST should be performed before initiation of immunosuppressive therapy, including prolonged steroid administration, use of tumor necrosis factor-alpha antagonists, or immunosuppressive therapy in any child requiring these treatments.**

HIV indicates human immunodeficiency virus; LTBI, latent tuberculosis infection.
[1] Bacille Calmette-Guérin immunization is not a contraindication to a TST.
[2] Beginning as early as 3 months of age.
[3] If the child is well, the TST should be delayed for up to 10 weeks after return.

induration (mm) for a positive result varies with the person's risk of LTBI and progression to tuberculosis disease.

Current guidelines from the Centers for Disease Control and Prevention (CDC), American Thoracic Society, and American Academy of Pediatrics accept 15 mm or greater of induration as a positive TST result for any person. Interpretation of 5 mm or more or 10 mm or more induration is summarized in Table 3.69 (p 680). Interpretation is aided by knowledge of the child's risk factors for LTBI and tuberculosis disease. Prompt clinical and radiographic evaluation of all children and adolescents with a positive TST reaction is recommended.

INTERPRETATION OF TST RESULTS IN PREVIOUS RECIPIENTS OF BCG VACCINE. Generally, interpretation of TST results in BCG recipients is the same as for people who have not received BCG vaccine. After BCG immunization, distinguishing between a positive TST result caused by *M tuberculosis* or *M bovis* infection and that caused by BCG can be difficult. Reactivity of the TST after receipt of BCG vaccine does not occur in some patients. The size of the TST reaction (ie, mm

Table 3.71. Validated Questions for Determining Risk of LTBI in Children in the United States

- Has a family member or contact had tuberculosis disease?
- Has a family member had a positive tuberculin skin test?
- Was your child born in a high-risk country (countries other than the United States, Canada, Australia, New Zealand, or Western European countries)?
- Has your child traveled (had contact with resident populations) to a high-risk country for more than 1 week?

of induration) attributable to BCG immunization depends on many factors, including age at BCG immunization, quality and strain of BCG vaccine used, number of doses of BCG received, nutritional and immunologic status of the vaccine recipient, and frequency of TST administration.

Tuberculosis disease should be suspected strongly in any symptomatic person with a positive TST result regardless of history of BCG immunization. When evaluating an asymptomatic child who has a positive TST result and who possibly received BCG, the result should not be attributed to BCG vaccine. Certain factors, such as documented receipt of multiple BCG immunizations (as evidenced by multiple BCG scars), decrease the likelihood that the positive TST result is attributable to LTBI. Evidence that increases the probability that a positive TST result is attributable to LTBI includes known contact with a person with contagious tuberculosis, a family history of tuberculosis disease, immigration from a country with a high prevalence of tuberculosis, a long interval (>5 years) since neonatal BCG immunization, and a TST reaction ≥15 mm.

Prompt clinical and radiographic evaluation of all children with a positive TST reaction is recommended. In most circumstances, a history of BCG will not account for the positive result. Chest radiographic findings of a granuloma, calcification, or adenopathy can be caused by *M tuberculosis* but not by BCG immunization. For the child with signs and symptoms consistent with abdominal tuberculosis and a history of ingestion of unpasteurized dairy products, a positive TST and a negative chest radiograph, abdominal imaging by computed tomography with contrast should be considered.

RECOMMENDATIONS FOR TST USAGE. The most reliable strategies for preventing LTBI and tuberculosis disease in children are based on thorough and expedient contact investigations rather than nonselective skin testing of large populations. Specific recommendations for TST use are given in Table 3.70 (p 683). All children need routine health care evaluations that include an assessment of their risk of exposure to tuberculosis. Only children deemed to have increased risk of contact with people with contagious tuberculosis or children with suspected tuberculosis disease should be considered for a TST. Household investigation is indicated whenever a TST result of a household member converts from negative to positive (indicating recent infection).

IMMUNOLOGIC-BASED TESTING.* QuantiFERON-TB Gold (QFT) is a test that measures interferon production from a person's white blood cells in response to stimulation with antigens from *M tuberculosis*. The sensitivity of QFT is similar to that of TST for detecting infection in people with untreated culture-confirmed tuberculosis. Although this test is approved by the FDA and recommended by the CDC for use in adults in all circumstances in which the TST is used, data are not available about its utility in children or adolescents.

HIV TESTING. Children with HIV are considered at high risk of tuberculosis, and an annual TST beginning at 3 to 12 months of age is recommended.

TREATMENT (SEE TABLE 3.72, P 686):

SPECIFIC DRUGS. Antituberculosis drugs kill *M tuberculosis* and *M bovis* or inhibit multiplication of the organism, thereby arresting progression of LTBI and preventing most complications of early tuberculosis disease. Chemotherapy does not cause rapid disappearance of already caseous or granulomatous lesions (eg, mediastinal lymphadenitis). Dosage recommendations and the more commonly reported adverse reactions of major antituberculosis drugs are summarized in Tables 3.72 (p 686) and 3.73 (p 688). For treatment of tuberculosis disease, these drugs always must be used in combination to minimize emergence of drug-resistant strains.

Isoniazid is bactericidal, rapidly absorbed, and well tolerated and penetrates into body fluids, including CSF. Isoniazid is metabolized in the liver and excreted primarily through the kidneys. Hepatotoxic effects are rare in children but can be life threatening. In children and adolescents given recommended doses, peripheral neuritis or seizures caused by inhibition of pyridoxine metabolism are rare, and most do not need pyridoxine supplements. Pyridoxine is recommended for exclusively breast-fed infants and for children and adolescents on meat- and milk-deficient diets; children with nutritional deficiencies, including all symptomatic HIV-infected children; and pregnant adolescents and women. For infants and young children, isoniazid tablets can be pulverized.

Rifampin is a bactericidal agent that is absorbed rapidly and penetrates into body fluids, including CSF. Rifampin is metabolized by the liver and can alter the pharmacokinetics and serum concentrations of many other drugs. Hepatotoxic effects, influenza-like symptoms, and pruritus may occur rarely. Rifampin is excreted in bile and urine and can cause orange urine, sweat, and tears and discoloration of soft contact lenses. Rifampin can make oral contraceptives ineffective, so other birth control methods should be adopted when rifampin is administered to sexually active adolescent women. For infants and young children, the contents of the capsules can be suspended in wild cherry-flavored syrup or sprinkled on semisoft foods (eg, applesauce). *Mycobacterium tuberculosis* resistant to rifampin is uncommon in the United States. Rifabutin is a suitable alternative to rifampin in children with HIV on highly active antiretroviral therapy that proscribes the use of rifampin; however, experience in children is limited. Major toxicities of rifabutin include leukopenia, gastrointestinal tract upset, polyarthralgias, rash, increased transaminase concentrations, and skin and secretion discoloration (pseudojaundice). Anterior uveitis has been reported among children

---

* Centers for Disease Control and Prevention. Guidelines for using the QuantiFERON-TB Gold test for detecting *Mycobacterium tuberculosis* infection, United States. *MMWR Recomm Rep.* 2005;54(RR-15):49–55

Table 3.72. Recommended Treatment Regimens for Drug-Susceptible Tuberculosis in Infants, Children, and Adolescents

Infection or Disease Category	Regimen	Remarks
Latent tuberculosis infection (positive TST result, no disease)		
• Isoniazid susceptible	9 mo of isoniazid, once a day	If daily therapy is not possible, DOT twice a week can be used for 9 mo.
• Isoniazid resistant	6 mo of rifampin, once a day	If daily therapy is not possible, DOT twice a week can be used for 6 mo.
• Isoniazid-rifampin resistant[1]	Consult a tuberculosis specialist	
Pulmonary and extrapulmonary (except meningitis)	2 mo of isoniazid, rifampin, and pyrazinamide daily, followed by 4 mo of isoniazid and rifampin[2] by DOT[3] for drug-susceptible *M tuberculosis* 9 to 12 mo of isoniazid and rifampin for drug susceptible *M bovis*	If possible drug resistance is a concern (see text), another drug (ethambutol or an aminoglycoside) is added to the initial 3-drug therapy until drug susceptibilities are determined. DOT is highly desirable. If hilar adenopathy only, a 6-mo course of isoniazid and rifampin is sufficient. Drugs can be given 2 or 3 times/wk under DOT in the initial phase if nonadherence is likely.
Meningitis	2 mo of isoniazid, rifampin, pyrazinamide, and an aminoglycoside or ethionamide, once a day, followed by 7–10 mo of isoniazid and rifampin, once a day or twice a week (9–12 mo total) for drug-susceptible *M tuberculosis* At least 12 mo of therapy without pyrazinamide for drug susceptible *M bovis*	A fourth drug, such as an aminoglycoside, is given with initial therapy until drug susceptibility is known. For patients who may have acquired tuberculosis in geographic areas where resistance to streptomycin is common, kanamycin, amikacin, or capreomycin can be used instead of streptomycin.

TST indicates tuberculin skin test; DOT, directly observed therapy.

[1] Duration of therapy is longer for human immunodeficiency virus (HIV)-infected people, and additional drugs may be indicated (see Tuberculosis Disease and HIV Infection, p 692).

[2] Medications should be administered daily for the first 2 weeks to 2 months of treatment and then can be administered 2-3 times per week by DOT.

[3] If initial chest radiograph shows cavitary lesions and sputum after 2 months of therapy remains positive, duration of therapy is extended to 9 months.

receiving rifabutin as prophylaxis or as part of a combination regimen for treatment, usually when administered at high doses. Rifabutin also increases hepatic metabolism of many drugs but is a less potent inducer of cytochrome P450 enzymes than rifampin and has fewer problematic drug interactions than rifampin. However, adjustments in dose of rifabutin and the coadministered antiretroviral drugs may be necessary for certain combinations.

Pyrazinamide attains therapeutic CSF concentrations, is detectable in macrophages, is administered orally, and is metabolized by the liver. Administration of pyrazinamide with isoniazid and rifampin allows for 6-month regimens in patients with drug-susceptible tuberculosis. *Mycobacterium bovis* intrinsically is resistant to pyrazinamide, precluding 6-month therapy for this pathogen. In doses of 30 mg/kg per day or less, pyrazinamide seldom has hepatotoxic effects and is well tolerated by children. Some adolescents and many adults develop arthralgia and hyperuricemia because of inhibition of uric acid excretion. Pyrazinamide must be used with caution in people with underlying liver disease.

Ethambutol is well absorbed after oral administration, diffuses well into tissues, and is excreted in urine. However, concentrations in the cerebrospinal fluid are low. At 15 mg/kg per day, ethambutol is bacteriostatic only, and its primary therapeutic role is to prevent emergence of drug resistance. A dose of 25 mg/kg per day is necessary for bactericidal activity. Because ethambutol can cause reversible or irreversible optic neuritis, recipients should be monitored monthly for visual acuity and red-green color discrimination. Use of ethambutol in young children whose visual acuity cannot be monitored requires consideration of risks and benefits. However, ethambutol-associated optic neuritis exceedingly is rare in children with normal renal function.

Streptomycin is administered intramuscularly but is available only on a limited basis. When streptomycin is not available, kanamycin, amikacin, or capreomycin are alternatives that can be prescribed for the initial 4 to 8 weeks of therapy.

The less commonly used (eg, "second-line") antituberculosis drugs, their doses, and adverse effects are listed in Table 3.74 (p 689). These drugs have limited usefulness because of decreased effectiveness and greater toxicity and should be used only in consultation with a specialist. Ethionamide is an orally administered antituberculosis drug that is well tolerated by children, achieves therapeutic CSF concentrations, and may be useful for treatment of people with meningitis or drug-resistant tuberculosis. Fluoroquinolones have antituberculosis activity and can be used in special circumstances. Because some fluoroquinolones are approved by the FDA for use only in people 18 years of age and older, their use in younger patients necessitates careful assessment of the potential risks and benefits (see Antimicrobial Agents and Related Therapy, p 735).

Occasionally, a patient cannot tolerate oral medications. Isoniazid, rifampin, streptomycin and related drugs, and fluoroquinolones can be administered parenterally.

THERAPY FOR LTBI. Isoniazid given to adults who have LTBI (eg, no clinical or radiographic abnormalities suggesting tuberculosis disease) provides substantial protection (54%–88%) against development of tuberculosis disease for at least 20 years. Among children, efficacy approaches 100% with appropriate adherence to therapy. All infants, children, and adolescents who have a positive TST result but no

Table 3.73. Commonly Used Drugs for the Treatment of Tuberculosis in Infants, Children, and Adolescents

Drugs	Dosage Forms	Daily Dosage, mg/kg	Twice a Week Dosage, mg/kg per Dose	Maximum Dose	Adverse Reactions
Ethambutol	Tablets 100 mg 400 mg	15–25	50	2.5 g	Optic neuritis (usually reversible), decreased red-green color discrimination, gastrointestinal tract disturbances, hypersensitivity
Isoniazid[1]	Scored tablets 100 mg 300 mg Syrup 10 mg/mL	10–15[2]	20–30	Daily, 300 mg Twice a week, 900 mg	Mild hepatic enzyme elevation, hepatitis,[2] peripheral neuritis, hypersensitivity
Pyrazinamide[1]	Scored tablets 500 mg	20–40	50	2 g	Hepatotoxic effects, hyperuricemia, arthralgias, gastrointestinal tract upset
Rifampin[1]	Capsules 150 mg 300 mg Syrup formulated in syrup from capsules	10–20	10–20	600 mg	Orange discoloration of secretions or urine, staining of contact lenses, vomiting, hepatitis, influenza-like reaction, thrombocytopenia, pruritus; oral contraceptives may be ineffective

[1] Rifamate is a capsule containing 150 mg of isoniazid and 300 mg of rifampin. Two capsules provide the usual adult (>50 kg) daily doses of each drug. Rifater is a capsule containing 50 mg of isoniazid, 120 mg of rifampin, and 300 mg of pyrazinamide. Isoniazid and rifampin also are available for parenteral administration.

[2] When isoniazid in a dosage exceeding 10 mg/kg per day is used in combination with rifampin, the incidence of hepatotoxic effects may be increased.

Table 3.74. Less Commonly Used Drugs for Treatment of Drug-Resistant Tuberculosis in Infants, Children, and Adolescents[1]

Drugs	Dosage, Forms	Daily Dosage, mg/kg	Maximum Dose	Adverse Reactions
Amikacin[2]	Vials, 500 mg and 1g	15–30 (intravenous or intramuscular administration)	1 g	Auditory and vestibular toxic effects, nephrotoxic effects
Capreomycin[2]	Vials, 1g	15–30 (intramuscular administration)	1 g	Auditory and vestibular toxicity and nephrotoxic effects
Cycloserine	Capsules, 250 mg	10–20, given in 2 divided doses	1 g	Psychosis, personality changes, seizures, rash
Ethionamide	Tablets, 250 mg	15–20, given in 2–3 divided doses	1 g	Gastrointestinal tract disturbances, hepatotoxic effects, hypersensitivity reactions, hypothyroid
Kanamycin	Vials 75 mg/2 mL 500 mg/2 mL 1 g/3 mL	15–30 (intramuscular or intravenous administration)	1 g	Auditory and vestibular toxic effects, nephrotoxic effects
Levofloxacin[3]	Tablets 250 mg 500 mg Vials 25 mg/mL	Adults 500–1000 mg (once daily) Children: not recommended	1 g	Theoretic effect on growing cartilage, gastrointestinal tract disturbances, rash, headache, restlessness, confusion
Para-aminosalicylic acid (PAS)	Packets, 3g	200–300 (2–4 times a day)	10 g	Gastrointestinal tract disturbances, hypersensitivity, hepatotoxic effects
Streptomycin[2]	Vials 1 g 4 g	20–40 (intramuscular administration)	1 g	Auditory and vestibular toxic effects, nephrotoxic effects, rash

[1] These drugs should be used in consultation with a specialist in tuberculosis.
[2] Dose adjustment in renal insufficiency.
[3] Levofloxacin currently is not approved for use in children younger than 18 years of age; its use in younger children necessitates assessment of the potential risks and benefits (see Antimicrobial Agents and Related Therapy, p 735).

evidence of tuberculosis disease and who never have received antituberculosis therapy should receive isoniazid unless resistance to isoniazid is suspected (ie, known exposure to a person with isoniazid-resistant tuberculosis) or a specific contraindication exists. Isoniazid in this circumstance is therapeutic and prevents development of disease. A physical examination and chest radiograph should be obtained at the time isoniazid therapy is initiated to exclude tuberculosis disease; if the radiograph is normal, the child remains asymptomatic, and treatment is completed, radiography should not be repeated.

DURATION OF THERAPY FOR LTBI. For infants, children, and adolescents, the recommended duration of isoniazid therapy is 9 months. Isoniazid is given daily in a single dose. When adherence with daily therapy with isoniazid cannot be ensured, twice-a-week DOT can be considered.

THERAPY FOR CONTACTS OF PATIENTS WITH ISONIAZID-RESISTANT _M TUBERCULOSIS_. The incidence of isoniazid resistance among _M tuberculosis_ isolates from US patients is approximately 9%. Risk factors for drug resistance are listed in Table 3.75. However, most experts recommend that isoniazid be used to treat LTBI in children unless the child has had contact with a person known to have isoniazid-resistant tuberculosis. If the source case is found to have isoniazid-resistant, rifampin-susceptible organisms, isoniazid should be discontinued and rifampin should be given for a total course of 6 months. The effectiveness and safety of a 2-month course of rifampin and pyrazinamide for treatment of LTBI in children is not known. Further, the 2-month regimen has been found to cause severe hepatotoxicity in adults and is not recommended for children. Optimal therapy for children with LTBI caused by organisms with resistance to isoniazid and rifampin is not known. In these circumstances, multidrug regimens have been used. Drugs to consider include pyrazinamide, a fluoroquinolone, and ethambutol, depending on susceptibility of the isolate. Consultation with a tuberculosis specialist is indicated.

TREATMENT OF TUBERCULOSIS DISEASE. The goal of treatment is to achieve sterilization of the tuberculous lesion in the shortest possible time. Achievement of this goal minimizes the possibility of development of resistant organisms. The major problem limiting successful treatment is poor adherence to prescribed treatment regimens. The use of DOT decreases the rates of relapse, treatment failures, and drug resistance; therefore, DOT is recommended strongly for treatment of children and adolescents with tuberculosis disease in the United States.

Table 3.75. People at Increased Risk of Drug-Resistant Tuberculosis Infection or Disease

- People with a history of treatment for tuberculosis disease (or whose source case for the contact received such treatment)
- Contacts of a patient with drug-resistant contagious tuberculosis disease
- People born in countries with high prevalence of drug-resistant tuberculosis
- Infected people whose source case has positive smears for acid-fast bacilli or cultures after 2 months of appropriate antituberculosis therapy

For *M tuberculosis* disease, a 6-month regimen consisting of isoniazid, rifampin, and pyrazinamide for the first 2 months and isoniazid and rifampin for the remaining 4 months is recommended for treatment of **drug-susceptible** pulmonary disease, pulmonary disease with hilar adenopathy, and hilar adenopathy disease in infants, children, and adolescents. If the chest radiograph shows a cavitary lesion or lesions and sputum remains culture positive after 2 months of therapy, the duration of therapy should be extended to 9 months. For children with hilar adenopathy in whom drug resistance is not a consideration, a 6-month regimen of only isoniazid and rifampin is considered adequate by some experts.

When **drug resistance** is possible (see Table 3.75, p 690), initial therapy should include a fourth drug, either ethambutol or an aminoglycoside, until drug susceptibility results are available. If an isolate from the pediatric case under treatment is not available, drug susceptibilities can be inferred by the drug susceptibility pattern of isolates from the adult source case. If this information is not available, local endemic rates of single and multiple drug resistance can be helpful. Data may not be available for foreign-born children or in circumstances of international travel. If this information is not available, a 4-drug initial regimen is recommended.

In the 6-month regimen with triple-drug therapy, isoniazid, rifampin, and pyrazinamide are given once a day for the first 2 weeks. Between 2 weeks and 2 months of treatment, isoniazid, rifampin, and pyrazinamide can be given daily or twice a week by DOT. After the initial 2-month period, a DOT regimen of isoniazid and rifampin given twice a week is acceptable (see Table 3.72, p 686, for doses). Several alternative regimens with differing durations of daily therapy and total therapy have been used successfully in adults and children. These alternative regimens should be prescribed and managed by a specialist in tuberculosis.

THERAPY FOR *M BOVIS* DISEASE. Controlled clinical trials for the treatment of *M bovis* disease have not been conducted. Treatment recommendations for *M bovis* disease in adults and children are based on results from treatment trials for *M tuberculosis* disease. Although all strains of *M bovis* are pyrazinamide-resistant, multidrug-resistant strains are rare. As knowledge of culture and susceptibility results rarely are available for children with *M bovis* disease, initial therapy should include 3 or 4 drugs appropriate for *M tuberculosis* disease. For isoniazid- and rifampin-susceptible strains, a total treatment course of at least 9 to 12 months is recommended.

THERAPY FOR DRUG-RESISTANT TUBERCULOSIS DISEASE. Drug resistance is most common in the following: (1) people born in areas such as Russia and the former Soviet Union, Asia, Africa, and Latin America; (2) people previously treated for tuberculosis disease; and (3) contacts, especially children, with tuberculosis disease whose source case is a person from one of these groups (see also Table 3.75, p 690). Most cases of pulmonary tuberculosis in children that are caused by an isoniazid-resistant but rifampin-susceptible strain of *M tuberculosis* can be treated with a 6-month regimen of rifampin, pyrazinamide, and ethambutol. For cases of multidrug-resistant tuberculosis disease, the treatment regimen should include at least 4 antituberculosis drugs to which the organism is susceptible. In cases of tuberculosis with isoniazid- and rifampin-resistant strains, 6-month drug regimens are not recommended. Twelve to 24 months of therapy usually is necessary for cure. Twice- and thrice-a-week regimens also are not recommended for drug-resistant disease; daily

DOT is critical to cure children with drug-resistant tuberculosis disease and to prevent emergence of further resistance.

EXTRAPULMONARY *M TUBERCULOSIS*. In general, extrapulmonary tuberculosis—with the exception of meningitis—can be treated with the same regimens as used for pulmonary tuberculosis. For suspected drug-susceptible tuberculous meningitis, daily treatment with isoniazid, rifampin, pyrazinamide, and streptomycin or another aminoglycoside or ethionamide should be initiated. When susceptibility to all drugs is established, the aminoglycoside or ethionamide can be discontinued. Pyrazinamide is given for a total of 2 months and isoniazid and rifampin are given for a total of 9 to 12 months. Isoniazid and rifampin can be given daily or twice a week after the first 2 months of treatment. For life-threatening tuberculosis, 4 drugs are given initially because of the possibility of drug resistance and the severe consequences of treatment failure (see Therapy for Drug-Resistant Tuberculosis Disease, p 691).

CORTICOSTEROIDS. The evidence supporting adjuvant treatment with corticosteroids for children with tuberculosis disease is incomplete. Corticosteroids are indicated for children with tuberculous meningitis, because they decrease rates of mortality and long-term neurologic impairment. Corticosteroids may be considered for children with pleural and pericardial effusions (to hasten reabsorption of fluid), severe miliary disease (to mitigate alveolocapillary block), endobronchial disease (to relieve obstruction and atelectasis) and abdominal tuberculosis (to decrease the risk of strictures). Corticosteroids should be given only when accompanied by appropriate antituberculosis therapy. Most experts consider 2 mg/kg per day of prednisone (maximum 60 mg/day) or its equivalent for 4 to 6 weeks followed by tapering to be appropriate.

TUBERCULOSIS DISEASE AND HIV INFECTION. Adults and children with HIV infection have an increased incidence of tuberculosis disease. Hence, *HIV testing is indicated for all people with tuberculosis disease.* The clinical manifestations and radiographic appearance of tuberculosis disease in children with HIV infection tend to be similar to those in immunocompetent children, but manifestations in these children can be more severe and unusual and can include extrapulmonary involvement of multiple organs. In HIV-infected patients, a TST result of 5-mm induration or more is considered positive (see Table 3.69, p 680); however, a negative TST result attributable to HIV-related immunosuppression also can occur. Specimens for culture should be obtained from all HIV-infected children with suspected tuberculosis.

Most HIV-infected adults with drug-susceptible tuberculosis respond well to antituberculosis drugs when appropriate therapy is given early. However, optimal therapy for tuberculosis in children with HIV infection has not been established. Therapy always should include at least 4 drugs initially and be continued for at least 9 months. Isoniazid, rifampin, and pyrazinamide, usually with ethambutol or an aminoglycoside, should be given for at least the first 2 months. A 3-drug regimen can be used once drug-resistant tuberculosis disease is excluded. Rifampin may be contraindicated in people who are receiving highly active antiretroviral therapy. Rifabutin can be substituted for rifampin in some circumstances. Consultation with a specialist who has experience in managing HIV-infected patients with tuberculosis is advised strongly.

EVALUATION AND MONITORING OF THERAPY IN CHILDREN AND ADOLESCENTS. Careful monthly monitoring of the clinical and bacteriologic responses to therapy is important. With DOT, clinical evaluation is an integral component of each visit for drug administration. For patients with pulmonary tuberculosis, chest radiographs should be obtained after 2 months of therapy to evaluate response. Even with successful 6-month regimens, hilar adenopathy can persist for 2 to 3 years; normal radiographic findings are not necessary to discontinue therapy. Follow-up chest radiographs beyond termination of successful therapy usually are not necessary unless clinical deterioration occurs.

If therapy has been interrupted, the date of completion should be extended. Although guidelines cannot be provided for every situation, factors to consider when establishing the date of completion include the following: (1) length of interruption of therapy; (2) time during therapy (early or late) when interruption occurred; and (3) the patient's clinical, radiographic, and bacteriologic status before, during, and after interruption of therapy. The total doses administered by DOT should be calculated to guide the duration of therapy. Consultation with a specialist in tuberculosis is advised.

Untoward effects of isoniazid therapy, including severe hepatitis in otherwise healthy infants, children, and adolescents, are rare. Routine determination of serum transaminase concentrations is not recommended. However, for children with severe tuberculosis disease, especially children with meningitis or disseminated disease, transaminase concentrations should be monitored approximately monthly during the first several months of treatment. Other indications for testing include the following: (1) having concurrent or recent liver or biliary disease; (2) being pregnant or in the first 6 weeks postpartum; (3) having clinical evidence of hepatotoxic effects; or (4) concurrently using other hepatotoxic drugs (eg, anticonvulsant agents). In most other circumstances, monthly clinical evaluations to observe for signs or symptoms of hepatitis and other adverse effects of drug therapy without routine monitoring of transaminase concentrations is appropriate follow-up. In all cases, regular physician-patient contact to assess drug adherence, efficacy, and toxic effects is an important aspect of management.

IMMUNIZATIONS. Patients who are receiving treatment for tuberculosis can be given measles and other age-appropriate live-virus vaccines unless they are receiving high-dose corticosteroids, are severely ill, or have other specific contraindications to immunization.

TUBERCULOSIS DURING PREGNANCY AND BREASTFEEDING. Tuberculosis treatment during pregnancy varies because of the complexity of management decisions. During pregnancy, if tuberculosis disease is diagnosed, a regimen of isoniazid, rifampin, and ethambutol is recommended. Pyrazinamide commonly is used in a 3- or 4-drug regimen, but safety during pregnancy has not been established. At least 6 months of therapy is indicated for drug-susceptible tuberculosis disease if pyrazinamide is used; at least 9 months of therapy is indicated if pyrazinamide is not used. Prompt initiation of therapy is mandatory to protect mother and fetus.

Asymptomatic pregnant women with a positive TST result, normal chest radiographic findings, and recent contact with a contagious person should receive isoniazid therapy. The recommended duration of therapy is 9 months. Therapy in these circumstances should begin after the first trimester. Pyridoxine is indicated for all pregnant and breastfeeding women receiving isoniazid.

Isoniazid, ethambutol, and rifampin are relatively safe for the fetus. The benefit of ethambutol and rifampin for therapy of tuberculosis disease in the mother outweighs the risk to the infant. Because streptomycin can cause ototoxic effects in the fetus, it should not be used unless administration is essential for effective treatment.

Although isoniazid is secreted in human milk, no adverse effects of isoniazid on nursing infants have been demonstrated (see Human Milk, p 123). Breastfed infants do not require pyridoxine unless they are receiving isoniazid.

CONGENITAL TUBERCULOSIS. Women who have only pulmonary tuberculosis are not likely to infect the fetus but can infect their infant after delivery. Congenital tuberculosis is rare, but in utero infections can occur after maternal *M tuberculosis* bacillemia.

If a newborn is suspected of having congenital tuberculosis, a TST, chest radiograph, lumbar puncture, and appropriate cultures should be performed promptly. The TST result usually is negative in newborn infants with congenital or perinatally acquired infection. Hence, regardless of the TST results, treatment of the infant should be initiated promptly with isoniazid, rifampin, pyrazinamide, and an aminoglycoside (eg, amikacin). The placenta should be examined histologically and cultured for *M tuberculosis*. The mother should be evaluated for the presence of pulmonary or extrapulmonary disease, including uterine tuberculosis disease. If the maternal physical examination and chest radiographic findings support the diagnosis of tuberculosis disease, the newborn infant should be treated with regimens recommended for tuberculosis disease. If meningitis is confirmed, corticosteroids should be added (see Corticosteroids, p 692). Drug susceptibility testing of the organism recovered from the mother or household contact, infant, or both should be performed.

MANAGEMENT OF THE NEWBORN INFANT WHOSE MOTHER (OR OTHER HOUSEHOLD CONTACT) HAS LTBI OR TUBERCULOSIS DISEASE. Management of the newborn infant is based on categorization of the maternal (or household contact) infection. Although protection of the infant from tuberculosis disease is of paramount importance, contact between infant and mother should be allowed when possible. Differing circumstances and resulting recommendations are as follows:

- **Mother (or household contact) has a positive TST result and normal chest radiographic findings**. If the mother (or household contact) is asymptomatic, no separation is required. The mother usually is a candidate for treatment of LTBI after the initial postpartum period. The newborn infant needs no special evaluation or therapy. Because the positive TST result could be a marker of an unrecognized case of contagious tuberculosis within the household, other household members should have a TST and further evaluation, but this should not delay the infant's discharge from the hospital.

- **Mother (or household contact) has clinical signs and symptoms or abnormal findings on chest radiograph consistent with tuberculosis disease**. Cases of tuberculosis disease in mothers (or household contacts) should be reported immediately to the local health department, and investigation of all household members should start within several days. If the mother has tuberculosis disease, the infant should be evaluated for congenital tuberculosis (see Congenital Tuberculosis) and the mother should be tested for HIV infection. The mother (or household contact) and the infant should be separated until the mother (or household contact) has been evaluated and, if tuberculosis disease is suspected, until the mother (or household contact) and infant are receiving appropriate antituberculosis therapy, the mother wears a mask, and the mother understands and is willing to adhere to infection control measures. Once the infant is receiving isoniazid, separation is not necessary unless the mother (or household contact) has possible multidrug-resistant *M tuberculosis* disease or has poor adherence to treatment and DOT is not possible. In this circumstance, the infant should be separated from the mother (or household contact), and BCG immunization should be considered for the infant. If the mother is suspected of having multidrug-resistant tuberculosis, an expert in tuberculosis disease treatment should be consulted.

If congenital tuberculosis is excluded, isoniazid is given until the infant is 3 or 4 months of age, when a TST should be performed. If the TST result is positive, the infant should be reassessed for tuberculosis disease. If tuberculosis disease is excluded, isoniazid should be continued for a total of 9 months. The infant should be evaluated at monthly intervals during treatment. If the TST result is negative and the mother (or household contact) has good adherence and response to treatment and no longer is contagious, isoniazid is discontinued.

- **Mother (or household contact) has abnormal findings on chest radiography but no evidence of tuberculosis disease**. If the chest radiograph of the mother (or household contact) appears abnormal but is not characteristic of tuberculosis disease and the history, physical examination, and sputum smear indicate no evidence of tuberculosis disease, the infant can be assumed to be at low risk of *M tuberculosis* infection and need not be separated from the mother (or household contact). The mother and her infant should receive follow-up care and the mother should be treated for LTBI. Other household members should have a TST and further evaluation.

ISOLATION OF THE HOSPITALIZED PATIENT: Most children with tuberculosis disease are not contagious. Exceptions are the following: (1) children with cavitary pulmonary tuberculosis; (2) children with positive sputum AFB smears; (3) children with laryngeal involvement; (4) children with extensive pulmonary infection; or (5) children with congenital tuberculosis undergoing procedures that involve the oropharyngeal airway (eg, endotracheal intubation). In these instances, isolation for tuberculosis or AFB are indicated until effective therapy has been initiated, sputum smears demonstrate a diminishing number of organisms, and cough is abating. Children with no cough and negative sputum AFB smears can be hospitalized in an open ward. Infection control measures for hospital personnel exposed to contagious patients should include the use of personally "fitted" and "sealed" particulate respirators for all patient contacts (see Infection Control for Hospitalized Children, p 153). The contagious patient should be placed in an airborne infection isolation room in the hospital.

The major concern in infection control relates to adult household members and contacts who may be the source case. Visitation should be limited to people who have a chest radiograph to exclude contagious tuberculosis. Household members and contacts should be managed with tuberculosis precautions when visiting until they are demonstrated not to have contagious tuberculosis. Nonadherent household contacts should be excluded from hospital visitation until evaluation is complete and tuberculosis disease is excluded or treatment has rendered source cases noncontagious.

CONTROL MEASURES*: Control of tuberculosis disease in the United States requires collaboration between health care professionals and health department personnel, obtaining a thorough history of exposure(s) to people with infectious tuberculosis, timely and effective contact investigations, proper interpretation of TST results, and appropriate antituberculosis therapy, including DOT services. Eliminating the ingestion of unpasteurized dairy products will prevent *M bovis* infection.

MANAGEMENT OF CONTACTS, INCLUDING EPIDEMIOLOGIC INVESTIGATION.[†] Children with a positive TST result or tuberculosis disease should be the starting point for epidemiologic investigation by the local health department. Close contacts of a TST-positive child should have a TST, and people with a positive TST result or symptoms consistent with tuberculosis disease should be investigated further. Because children with tuberculosis usually are not contagious, their contacts are not likely to be infected unless they also have been in contact with the same adult source case. After the presumptive adult source of the child's tuberculosis is identified, other contacts of that adult should be evaluated.

THERAPY FOR CONTACTS. Children and adolescents exposed to a contagious case of tuberculosis disease should have a TST and an evaluation for tuberculosis disease (chest radiograph and physical examination). For exposed contacts with impaired immunity (eg, HIV infection) and all contacts younger than 4 years of age, isoniazid therapy should be initiated, even if the TST result is negative, once tuberculosis disease is excluded (see Therapy for LTBI, p 687). Infected people can have a negative TST result because cellular immunity has not yet developed or because of cutaneous anergy. People with a negative TST result should be retested 12 weeks after the last contact. If the TST result still is negative in a immunocompetent person, isoniazid is discontinued. If the contact is immunocompromised, LTBI cannot be excluded, and treatment should be continued for 9 months. If a TST result of a contact becomes positive, isoniazid should be continued for 9 months.

CHILD CARE AND SCHOOLS. Children with tuberculosis disease can attend school or child care if they are receiving therapy (see Children in Out-of-Home Child Care, p 130). They can return to regular activities as soon as effective therapy has been instituted, adherence to therapy has been documented, and clinical symptoms have diminished substantially. Children with LTBI can participate in all activities whether they are receiving treatment or not.

BCG VACCINES. The bacille Calmette-Guérin (BCG) vaccine is a live vaccine prepared from attenuated strains of *M bovis*. Use of BCG vaccine is recommended by

---

* American Thoracic Society, Centers for Disease Control and Prevention, and Infectious Diseases Society of America. Controlling tuberculosis in the United States. Recommendations from the American Thoracic Society, CDC, and the Infectious Diseases Society of America. *MMWR Recomm Rep*. 2005;54(RR-12):1–80

† National Tuberculosis Controllers Association and Centers for Disease Control and Prevention. Guidelines for the investigation of contacts of persons with infectious tuberculosis. Recommendations from the National Tuberculosis Controllers Association and CDC. *MMWR Recomm Rep*. 2005;54(RR-15):1–47

the Expanded Programme on Immunization of the World Health Organization for administration at birth (see Table 1.3, p 10) and currently is used in more than 100 countries. Bacille Calmette-Guérin vaccine is used to prevent disseminated and other life-threatening manifestations of *M tuberculosis* infection in infants and young children. However, BCG immunization appears to decrease the risk of serious complications of tuberculosis disease in children. The various BCG vaccines used throughout the world differ in composition and efficacy.

Two meta-analyses of published clinical trials and case-control studies concerning the efficacy of BCG vaccines concluded that BCG vaccine has relatively high protective efficacy (approximately 80%) against meningeal and miliary tuberculosis in children. The protective efficacy against pulmonary tuberculosis differed significantly among the studies, precluding a specific conclusion. Protection afforded by BCG vaccine in one meta-analysis was estimated to be 50%. Two BCG vaccines, one manufactured by Organon Teknika Corporation (Durham, NC) and the other by sanofi pasteur (Toronto, Ontario), are licensed in the United States. Comparative evaluations of these and other BCG vaccines have not been performed.

INDICATIONS. In the United States, administration of BCG vaccine should be considered only in limited and select circumstances, such as unavoidable risk of exposure to *M tuberculosis* and failure or unfeasibility of other methods of control of tuberculosis. Recommendations for use of BCG vaccine for control of tuberculosis among children and health care professionals have been published by the Advisory Committee on Immunization Practices and the Advisory Council for the Elimination of Tuberculosis of the CDC.* For infants and children, BCG immunization should be considered only for people with a negative TST result who are not infected with HIV in the following circumstances:

- The child is exposed continually to a person or people with contagious pulmonary tuberculosis resistant to isoniazid and rifampin and the child cannot be removed from this exposure.
- The child is exposed continually to a person or people with untreated or ineffectively treated contagious pulmonary tuberculosis and the child cannot be removed from such exposure or given antituberculosis therapy.

Careful assessment of the potential risks and benefits of BCG vaccine and consultation with personnel in local tuberculosis control programs strongly are recommended before use of BCG vaccine.

Healthy infants from birth to 2 months of age may be given BCG vaccine without a TST unless congenital infection is suspected; thereafter, BCG vaccine should be given only to children with a negative TST result.

ADVERSE REACTIONS. Uncommonly (1%–2% of immunizations), BCG vaccine can result in local adverse reactions, such as subcutaneous abscess and regional lymphadenopathy, which generally are not serious. One rare complication, osteitis affecting the epiphysis of long bones, can occur as long as several years after BCG immunization. Disseminated fatal infection occurs rarely (approximately 2 per 1 mil-

---

* Centers for Disease Control and Prevention. The role of BCG vaccine in the prevention and control of tuberculosis in the United States: a joint statement by the Advisory Committee for the Elimination of Tuberculosis and the Advisory Committee on Immunization Practices. *MMWR Recomm Rep.* 1996;45(RR-4):1–18

lion people), primarily in people who are severely immunocompromised. Antituberculosis therapy is recommended to treat osteitis and disseminated disease caused by BCG vaccine. Pyrazinamide is not believed to be effective against BCG and should not be included in treatment regimens. Most experts do not recommend treatment of draining skin lesions or chronic suppurative lymphadenitis caused by BCG vaccine, because spontaneous resolution occurs in most cases. Large-needle aspiration of suppurative lymph nodes can hasten resolution. People with complications caused by BCG vaccine should be referred for management, if possible, to a tuberculosis expert.

CONTRAINDICATIONS. People with burns, skin infections, and primary or secondary immunodeficiencies, including HIV infection, should not receive BCG vaccine. In populations of the world in which the risk of LTBI and tuberculosis disease is high, the World Health Organization recommends BCG immunization for asymptomatic HIV-infected children. Use of BCG vaccine is contraindicated for people receiving immunosuppressive medications, including high-dose corticosteroids (see Corticosteroids, p 692). Although no untoward effects of BCG vaccine on the fetus have been observed, immunization during pregnancy is not recommended.

REPORTING OF CASES. Reporting of suspected and confirmed cases of tuberculosis disease is mandated by law in all states. A diagnosis of LTBI or tuberculosis disease in a child is a sentinel event representing recent transmission of *M tuberculosis* in the community. Physicians should assist local health department personnel in the search for a source case and others infected by the source case. Members of the household, such as relatives, babysitters, au pairs, boarders, domestic workers, and frequent visitors or other adults, such as child care providers and teachers with whom the child has frequent contact, potentially are source cases.

Diseases Caused by Nontuberculous Mycobacteria
(Atypical Mycobacteria, Mycobacteria Other Than *Mycobacterium tuberculosis*)

CLINICAL MANIFESTATIONS: Several syndromes are caused by nontuberculous mycobacteria (NTM). In children, the most common of these syndromes is cervical lymphadenitis. Less common infections include cutaneous infection, osteomyelitis, otitis media, central catheter infections, and pulmonary disease. Disseminated infections almost always are associated with impaired cell-mediated immunity, as found in congenital immune defects or human immunodeficiency virus (HIV) infection. Manifestations of disseminated NTM infections depend on the species and route of infection but include fever, night sweats, weight loss, abdominal pain, fatigue, diarrhea, and anemia. Nontuberculous mycobacteria, especially *Mycobacterium avium* complex (MAC [including *M avium* and *Mycobacterium intracellulare*]) and *Mycobacterium abscessus*, can be recovered from sputum in 10% to 20% of adolescents and young adults with cystic fibrosis and can be associated with fever and declining clinical status.

ETIOLOGY: Of the almost 100 species of NTM that have been identified, only a few account for most human infections. The species most commonly encountered in infected children in the United States are MAC, *Mycobacterium fortuitum*, *M abscessus*, and *Mycobacterium marinum* (see Table 3.76, p 699). Several new species that can be detected by nucleic acid amplification testing but cannot be grown by routine culture methods have been identified in lymph nodes of children with cervical adenitis. Nontuberculous mycobacteria disease in patients with HIV infection usually is caused by MAC. *Mycobacterium fortuitum*, *Mycobacterium chelonae*, and *M abscessus* commonly are referred to as "rapidly growing" mycobacteria, because sufficient growth and identification can be achieved in the laboratory within 3 to 7 days, whereas other NTM and *Mycobacterium tuberculosis* often require weeks before sufficient growth occurs. Rapidly growing mycobacteria occasionally have been implicated in wound, soft tissue, bone, pulmonary, central catheter, and middle-ear infections. Other mycobacterial species that usually are not pathogenic have caused infections in immunocompromised hosts or have been associated with the presence of a foreign body.

EPIDEMIOLOGY: Many NTM species are ubiquitous in nature and are found in soil, food, water, and animals. The major reservoir for *Mycobacterium kansasii*, *Mycobacterium simiae*, and health care-associated infections attributable to the rapidly growing mycobacteria is tap water. For *M marinum*, water in a fish tank or aquarium or an injury in a salt-water environment is the major source of infection. Although many people are exposed to NTM, only a few of these exposures result in chronic infection or disease. The usual portals of entry for NTM infection are believed to be abrasions in the skin (eg, cutaneous lesions caused by *M marinum*), surgical incisions (especially for central catheters), oropharyngeal mucosa (the presumed portal of entry for cervical lymphadenitis), gastrointestinal or respiratory tract for disseminated MAC, and respiratory tract (including tympanostomy tubes for otitis media). Pulmonary disease and rare cases of mediastinal adenitis and endobronchial disease occur. Most infections remain localized at the portal of entry or in regional lymph nodes. Dissemination to distal sites primarily occurs in immunocompromised hosts, especially in people with

Table 3.76. Diseases Caused by Nontuberculous Mycobacterial Species

Clinical Disease	Common Species	Less Common Species in the United States
Cutaneous infection	*M chelonae, M fortuitum, M abscessus, M marinum*	*M ulcerans*[1]
Lymphadenitis	MAC	*M kansasii, M fortuitum, M malmoense*[2]
Otologic infection	*M abscessus*	*M fortuitum*
Pulmonary infection	MAC, *M kansasii, M abscessus*	*M xenopi, M malmoense,*[2] *M szulgai, M fortuitum, M simiae*
Catheter-associated infection	*M chelonae, M fortuitum*	*M abscessus*
Skeletal infection	MAC, *M kansasii, M fortuitum*	*M chelonae, M marinum, M abscessus, M ulcerans*[1]
Disseminated	MAC	*M kansasii, M genavense, M haemophilum, M chelonae*

MAC indicates *Mycobacterium avium* complex.
[1] Not endemic in the United States.
[2] Found primarily in Northern Europe.

acquired immunodeficiency syndrome (AIDS). No definitive evidence of person-to-person transmission of NTM exists. Outbreaks of otitis media caused by *M abscessus* have been associated with polyethylene ear tubes and use of contaminated equipment or water. A waterborne route of transmission has been implicated for MAC infection in immunodeficient hosts. Buruli ulcer disease primarily is a skin and bone infection caused by *Mycobacterium ulcerans*, an emerging disease causing significant morbidity and disability in tropical areas, such as Africa, Asia, South America, and the western Pacific.

The **incubation periods** are variable.

DIAGNOSTIC TESTS: Definitive diagnosis of NTM disease requires isolation of the organism. Consultation with the laboratory should be obtained to ensure that culture specimens are handled and incubated correctly. Because these organisms commonly are found in the environment, contamination of cultures or transient colonization can occur. Caution must be exercised in the interpretation of cultures obtained from non-sterile sites, such as gastric washing specimens, a single expectorated sputum specimen, or a urine specimen and if the species cultured usually is nonpathogenic (eg, *Mycobacterium gordonae*). An AFB smear-positive sample or repeated isolation of numerous colonies of a single species on culture media is more likely to indicate disease than culture contamination or transient colonization. Unlike bacteria, NTM isolates from draining sinus tracts almost always are clinically significant. Recovery of NTM from sites that usually are sterile, such as cerebrospinal fluid, pleural fluid, bone marrow, blood, lymph node aspirates, middle ear or mastoid aspirates, or surgically excised tissue, is the most reliable diagnostic test. With radiometric or nonradiometric broth techniques, blood cultures are highly sensitive in recovery of disseminated MAC and other bloodborne NTM species. Disseminated MAC disease should prompt a search for underlying immunodeficiency, usually HIV infection or congenital immune deficiency.

Patients with NTM infection can have a positive tuberculin skin test (TST) result, because the purified protein derivative preparation, derived from *M tuberculosis*, shares a number of antigens with NTM species. These TST reactions usually measure less than 10 mm of induration but can measure more than 15 mm (see Tuberculosis, p 678).

TREATMENT: Many NTM are relatively resistant in vitro to antituberculosis drugs. In vitro resistance to these agents, however, does not necessarily correlate with clinical response, especially with MAC infections. Only limited controlled trials of antituberculous drugs have been performed in patients with NTM infections. The approach to therapy should be dictated by the following: (1) the species causing the infection; (2) the results of drug-susceptibility testing; (3) the site(s) of infection; (4) the patient's underlying disease (if any); and (5) the need to treat a patient presumptively for tuberculosis while awaiting culture reports that subsequently reveal NTM.

For NTM lymphadenitis in otherwise healthy children, especially when the disease is caused by MAC, complete surgical excision almost always is curative. Antituberculosis chemotherapy offers no benefit. Therapy with clarithromycin combined with ethambutol or rifabutin may be beneficial for children in whom surgical excision is incomplete or for children with recurrent disease, but these agents have not been studied in clinical trials (see Table 3.77, p 702).

Isolates of rapidly growing mycobacteria (*M fortuitum*, *M abscessus*, and *M chelonae*) should be tested in vitro against drugs to which they commonly are susceptible and that have been used with some therapeutic success (eg, amikacin, imipenem, sulfamethoxazole or trimethoprim-sulfamethoxazole, cefoxitin, ciprofloxacin, gatifloxacin, clarithromycin, linezolid, and doxycycline). Clarithromycin and at least one other agent commonly are the treatment of choice for cutaneous (disseminated) infections attributable to *M chelonae* or *M abscessus*. Infected foreign bodies should be removed whenever possible, and surgical débridement for serious localized disease should be considered. The choice of drugs, dosages, and duration should be reviewed with a consultant experienced in the management of NTM infections.

In patients with AIDS and in other immunocompromised people with disseminated MAC infection, multidrug therapy is recommended. Single-drug therapy with a macrolide antimicrobial agent commonly results in development of resistance. Clinical isolates of MAC usually are resistant to many of the approved antituberculosis drugs, including isoniazid, but are susceptible to clarithromycin and azithromycin and often are susceptible to combinations of ethambutol, rifabutin or rifampin, and amikacin or streptomycin. Susceptibility testing to these agents has not been standardized and thus is not recommended routinely. The optimal regimen has yet to be determined. Treatment of disseminated MAC infection should be done in consultation with an expert. In addition, the following treatment guidelines should be considered:

- Susceptibility testing to drugs other than the macrolides is not predictive of in vivo response and should not be used to guide therapy.
- Unless there is clinical or laboratory evidence of macrolide resistance, treatment regimens should contain clarithromycin or azithromycin, combined with ethambutol. This 2-drug regimen is the foundation for any MAC treatment.
- Many clinicians have added a third agent (rifampin or rifabutin) and, in some situations, a fourth agent (amikacin or streptomycin).
- Patients receiving protease inhibitor antiretroviral therapy generally should not be treated with rifampin or rifabutin. However, if coadministration of rifampin or rifabutin and a protease inhibitor is necessary, indinavir and nelfinavir are the preferred protease inhibitors (**www.cdc.gov/nchstp/tb/TB_HIV_Drugs/ TOC.htm** and **www.hiv-druginteractions.org**).
- Clofazimine is ineffective for treatment of MAC infection and should not be used.
- Patients receiving therapy should be monitored. Considerations are as follows:
  - Clinical manifestations of disseminated MAC infection, such as fever, weight loss, and night sweats, should be monitored several times during the initial weeks of therapy. Microbiologic response, as assessed by blood culture every 4 weeks during initial therapy, also can be helpful for interpreting the efficacy of a therapeutic regimen.
  - Most patients who ultimately respond show substantial clinical improvement in the first 4 to 6 weeks of therapy. Elimination of the organisms from blood cultures may take somewhat longer, often requiring up to 12 weeks.
  - Patients receiving clarithromycin plus rifabutin or high-dose rifabutin (with another drug) should be observed for the rifabutin-related development of leukopenia, uveitis, polyarthralgias, and pseudojaundice.

Table 3.77. Treatment of Nontuberculous Mycobacteria Infections in Children

Organism	Disease	Treatment
Slowly Growing Species		
Mycobacterium avium complex (MAC)	Lymphadenitis	Excision of major nodes; if excision incomplete or disease recurs, clarithromycin or azithromycin plus ethambutol with rifampin or rifabutin.
	Pulmonary infection	Clarithromycin or azithromycin plus ethambutol with rifampin or rifabutin (pulmonary resection in some patients who fail drug therapy). For severe disease, an initial course of amikacin or streptomycin often is included. Clinical data in adults support that 3 times weekly therapy is as effective as daily therapy, with less toxicity.
	Disseminated	See text.
Mycobacterium kansasii	Pulmonary infection	Rifampin plus ethambutol with isoniazid.
	Osteomyelitis	Surgical débridement and prolonged antimicrobial therapy using rifampin plus ethambutol with isoniazid.
Mycobacterium marinum	Cutaneous infection	None, if minor; rifampin, trimethoprim-sulfamethoxazole, clarithromycin, or doxycycline[1] for moderate disease; extensive lesions may require surgical débridement. Susceptibility testing not required.
Mycobacterium ulcerans	Cutaneous and bone infections	Excision of tissue; rifampicin plus streptomycin under investigation.

Rapidly Growing Species

Organism	Disease	Treatment
Mycobacterium fortuitum group	Cutaneous infection	Excision of tissue; initial therapy for serious disease is amikacin plus meropenem, IV, followed by clarithromycin, doxycycline,[1] or trimethoprim-sulfamethoxazole or ciprofloxacin orally based on in vitro susceptibility testing.
	Catheter infection	Catheter removal and amikacin plus meropenem, IV; clarithromycin, trimethoprim-sulfamethoxazole, or ciprofloxacin orally based on in vitro susceptibility testing.
Mycobacterium abscessus	Otitis media	Clarithromycin plus initial course of amikacin plus cefoxitin; may require surgical débridement based on in vitro susceptibility testing (50% are amikacin resistant).
	Pulmonary infection (in cystic fibrosis)	Serious disease, clarithromycin, amikacin, and cefoxitin based on susceptibility testing; may require surgical resection; seek expert advice.
Mycobacterium chelonae	Catheter infection	Catheter removal and tobramycin (initially) plus clarithromycin.
	Disseminated cutaneous infection	Tobramycin and meropenem or linezolid (initially) plus clarithromycin.

IV indicates intravenously.

[1] Doxycycline should not be given to children younger than 8 years of age unless the benefits of therapy are greater than the risks of dental staining (see Antimicrobial Agents and Related Therapy; p 735). Only 50% of isolates of *M marinum* are susceptible to doxycycline.

CHEMOPROPHYLAXIS. According to the 2002 US Public Health Service and Infectious Diseases Society of America guidelines* for preventing the first MAC episode, prophylaxis with azithromycin or clarithromycin should be considered for HIV-infected children 6 years of age and older, adolescents, and adults with CD4 + T-lymphocyte counts of less than 50 cells × 10^6/L (50 cells/µL). Rifabutin is an alternative agent but should not be used until tuberculosis disease has been excluded. Disseminated MAC should be excluded by a negative blood culture result before prophylaxis is initiated.

Prophylaxis for preventing the first MAC infection should be offered to HIV-infected children younger than 13 years of age with the following CD4 + T-lymphocyte counts: children 6 years of age or older, less than 50 cells × 10^6/L (<50/µL); children 2 to 6 years of age, less than 75 cells × 10^6/L (<75/µL); children 1 to 2 years of age, less than 500 cells × 10^6/L (<500/µL); and children younger than 12 months of age, less than 750 cells × 10^6/L (<750/µL).

Oral suspensions of clarithromycin and azithromycin are available in the United States. No pediatric formulation of rifabutin is available, but a dosage of 5 mg/kg per day seems appropriate. Rifabutin should be used only for children older than 6 years of age. Children with a history of disseminated MAC should receive lifelong prophylaxis to prevent recurrence.

ISOLATION OF THE HOSPITALIZED PATIENT: Standard precautions are recommended.

CONTROL MEASURES: Control measures include chemoprophylaxis for certain patients with HIV infection (see Treatment, p 700) and use of sterile equipment for middle-ear instrumentation, including otoscopic equipment, for prevention of *M abscessus* otitis media. Because MAC organisms are common in environmental sources, such as food and water, current information does not support specific recommendations about avoidance of exposure for HIV-infected people.

Tularemia

CLINICAL MANIFESTATIONS: Most patients with tularemia experience an abrupt onset of fever, chills, myalgia, and headache. Illness usually conforms to one of the several tularemic syndromes. Most common is the ulceroglandular syndrome, characterized by a painful, maculopapular lesion at the entry site, with subsequent ulceration and slow healing associated with painful, acutely inflamed regional lymph nodes, which can drain spontaneously. The glandular syndrome (regional lymphadenopathy with no ulcer) also is common. Less common disease syndromes are: oculoglandular (severe conjunctivitis and preauricular lymphadenopathy), oropharyngeal (severe exudative stomatitis, pharyngitis, or tonsillitis and cervical lymphadenopathy), typhoidal (high fever, hepatomegaly, and splenomegaly), intestinal (intestinal pain, vomiting, and diarrhea), and pneumonic. Pneumonic tularemia, characterized by fever, dry cough, chest pain, and hilar adenopathy, would be the typical syndrome after intentional aerosol release of organisms.

---

* Centers for Disease Control and Prevention. Guidelines for preventing opportunistic infections among HIV-infected persons—2002. Recommendations of the US Public Health Service and the Infectious Diseases Society of America. *MMWR Recomm Rep.* 2002;51(RR-8):1–46

ETIOLOGY: *Francisella tularensis*, the causative agent, is a gram-negative pleomorphic coccobacillus.

EPIDEMIOLOGY: Sources of the organism include approximately 100 species of wild mammals (eg, rabbits, hares, prairie dogs, and muskrats, rats, voles, and other rodents); at least 9 species of domestic animals (eg, sheep, cattle, and cats); blood-sucking arthropods that bite these animals (eg, ticks and deerflies); and water and soil contaminated by infected animals. In the United States, ticks and rabbits are major sources of human infection. Infected animals and arthropods, especially ticks, are infective for prolonged periods; frozen rabbits can remain infective for more than 3 years. People at risk are people with occupational or recreational exposure to infected animals or their habitats, such as rabbit hunters and trappers, people exposed to certain ticks or biting insects, and laboratory technicians working with *F tularensis*, which is highly infectious and aerosolized easily when grown in culture. In the United States, the average annual incidence is highest in males and in people 5 to 9 years of age or older than 54 years of age. Since 2000, when tularemia became a nationally notifiable disease, there have been 34 to 142 cases reported per year. Ticks are the most important arthropod vectors, and most cases occur during late spring and summer months. Infection also may be acquired by direct contact with infected animals, ingestion of contaminated water or inadequately cooked meat, or inhalation of aerosolized organisms or contaminated particles related to lawn mowing, brush cutting, piling contaminated hay, or bioterrorism. Person-to-person transmission does not occur. Organisms can be present in blood during the first 2 weeks of disease and in cutaneous lesions for as long as 1 month if untreated.

The **incubation period** usually is 3 to 5 days, with a range of 1 to 21 days.

DIAGNOSTIC TESTS: Diagnosis is established most often by serologic testing. A single serum antibody titer of ≥1:128 determined by microagglutination (MA) or of ≥1:160 determined by tube agglutination (TA) is consistent with recent or past infection and constitutes a presumptive diagnosis. Confirmation by serologic testing requires a fourfold or greater titer change between 2 sera obtained at least 2 weeks apart, with one of the specimens having a minimum titer of ≥1:128 (MA) or ≥1:160 (TA). Slide agglutination tests are less reliable than TA tests. Nonspecific cross-reactions can occur with specimens containing heterophil antibodies or antibodies to *Brucella* species, *Legionella* species, or other gram-negative bacteria. However, cross-reactions rarely result in MA or TA titers that are diagnostic. Some clinical laboratories can identify presumptively *F tularensis* in ulcer exudate or aspirate material by direct fluorescent antibody or polymerase chain reaction assays. Suspect growth on culture may be identified presumptively by direct fluorescent antibody, polymerase chain reaction, or rapid slide agglutination tests. Isolation of *F tularensis* from specimens of blood, skin, ulcers, lymph node drainage, gastric washings, or respiratory tract secretions is best achieved by inoculation of cysteine-enriched media. Immunohistochemical staining is specific for detection of *F tularensis* in fixed tissues; however, it is not available in most clinical laboratories. Because of its propensity for causing laboratory-acquired infections, laboratory personnel should be alerted to the suspicion of *F tularensis*.

TREATMENT: Streptomycin, gentamicin, or amikacin are recommended for treatment of tularemia. Duration of therapy usually is 7 to 10 days. A longer course is required for more severe illness. Alternative drugs for less severe disease include ciprofloxacin (which is approved only for specific indications in patients younger than 18 years of age), imipenem-cilastatin, doxycycline (which should not be given to children younger than 8 years of age unless the benefits of therapy are greater than the risks of dental staining [see Antimicrobial Agents and Related Therapy, p 735]), and chloramphenicol. These drugs are associated with prompt clinical response, but relapses have been reported after treatment with tetracyclines.

ISOLATION OF THE HOSPITALIZED PATIENT: Standard precautions are recommended.

CONTROL MEASURES:
- People should protect themselves against arthropod bites by wearing protective clothing, by frequent inspection for and removal of ticks from the skin and scalp, and by using insect repellents (see Prevention of Tickborne Infections, p 195).
- Children should be instructed not to handle sick or dead animals.
- Rubber gloves should be worn by hunters, trappers, and food preparers when handling the carcasses of wild rabbits and other potentially infected animals.
- Game meats should be cooked thoroughly.
- Face masks and rubber gloves should be worn by people working with cultures or infective material in the laboratory, and the work should be performed in a biologic safety cabinet.
- Standard precautions should be used for handling clinical materials.
- A 14-day course of doxycycline (which should not be given to children younger than 8 years of age unless the benefits are greater than the risks of dental staining) or ciprofloxacin (which is only approved for specific indications in patients younger than 18 years of age) is recommended for children and adults after exposure to an intentional release of tularemia.

Endemic Typhus
(Fleaborne Typhus or Murine Typhus)

CLINICAL MANIFESTATIONS: Fleaborne typhus resembles epidemic (louseborne) typhus but usually has a less abrupt onset with less severe systemic symptoms. In young children, the disease can be mild. Fever can be accompanied by persistent headache and myalgias. A rash typically appears on day 4 to 7 of illness, is macular or maculopapular, lasts 4 to 8 days, and tends to remain discrete, with sparse lesions and no hemorrhage. Illness seldom lasts longer than 2 weeks; visceral involvement is uncommon, but untreated severe disease can be fatal.

ETIOLOGY: Fleaborne typhus is caused by *Rickettsia typhi*.

EPIDEMIOLOGY: Rats, in which infection is inapparent, are the natural reservoirs. Opossums and domestic cats and dogs also can be infected and serve as hosts. The vector for transmission among rats and to humans is a rat flea (usually *Xenopsylla cheopis*). Infected flea feces are rubbed into broken skin or mucous membranes or inhaled. The disease is worldwide in distribution and tends to occur most commonly in adults, in males, and during the months of April to October. Endemic typhus is rare in the United States, with most cases occurring in southern California, southern Texas, the southeastern Gulf Coast, and Hawaii. Since 2002, an increased number of cases have been reported from Hawaii. Exposure to rats and their fleas is the major risk factor for infection, although a history of such exposure often is absent. In some regions, peridomestic cycles involving cats, dogs, opossums, and their fleas may exist.

The **incubation period** is 6 to 14 days.

DIAGNOSTIC TESTS: Antibody titers determined by an indirect fluorescent antibody test, enzyme immunoassay, latex agglutination test, or complement fixation test peak around 4 weeks after infection. A fourfold titer change between acute and convalescent serum specimens taken 2 to 3 weeks apart is diagnostic, and immunoassays specific for immunoglobulin M antibody may aid in confirmation of clinical diagnoses. However, some serologic tests may not reliably differentiate murine typhus from epidemic (louseborne) typhus without antibody cross-absorption tests, which are not available routinely. Isolation of the organism in culture potentially is hazardous and requires use of specialized laboratories, such as the Centers for Disease Control and Prevention (CDC). Molecular diagnostic assays on infected whole blood and skin biopsies can distinguish murine and epidemic typhus reliably and are performed at the CDC. Immunohistochemical procedures on formalin-fixed tissues can be performed at the CDC.

TREATMENT: Doxycycline administered intravenously or orally is the treatment of choice (2.2 mg/kg every 12 hours; maximum 300 mg/day). Treatment should be continued for at least 3 days after defervescence and evidence of clinical improvement is documented, usually for 5 to 10 days. Despite concerns regarding dental staining after the use of tetracyclines in young children (see Antimicrobial Agents and Related Therapy, p 735), doxycycline provides superior therapy for this potentially severe or life-threatening disease. Furthermore, available data suggest that one course of doxycycline does not cause discoloration of permanent teeth.

ISOLATION OF THE HOSPITALIZED PATIENT: Standard precautions are recommended.

CONTROL MEASURES: Rat fleas should be controlled by appropriate insecticides before use of rodenticides, because fleas will seek alternative hosts. Rat populations should be controlled by appropriate means. No treatment is recommended for exposed people. The disease should be reported to local or state public health departments.

Epidemic Typhus
(Louseborne Typhus)

CLINICAL MANIFESTATIONS: Epidemic louseborne typhus is characterized by the abrupt onset of high fever, chills, and myalgias accompanied by severe headache and malaise. Influenza illness commonly is suspected. A rash appears 4 to 7 days after illness onset, beginning on the trunk and spreading to the limbs. A concentrated eruption can be present in the axillae. The rash typically is maculopapular, becomes petechial or hemorrhagic, then develops into brownish pigmented areas. The face, palms, and soles usually are not affected. Changes in mental status are common, and delirium or coma can occur. Myocardial and renal failure can occur when the disease is severe. The fatality rate in untreated people is as high as 30%. Mortality is less common in children, and the rate increases with advancing age. Untreated patients who recover typically have an illness lasting 2 weeks. Brill-Zinsser disease is a relapse of epidemic louseborne typhus that occurs years after the initial episode. Factors that reactivate the rickettsiae are unknown. The recrudescent illness is similar to the primary infection but can be milder and of shorter duration.

ETIOLOGY: Epidemic typhus is caused by *Rickettsia prowazekii*.

EPIDEMIOLOGY: Humans are the usual reservoir of the organism, which is transmitted from person to person by the human body louse, *Pediculus humanus* subspecies *corporis*. Infected louse feces are rubbed into broken skin or mucous membranes or inhaled. All ages are affected. Poverty, crowding, poor sanitary conditions, and poor personal hygiene contribute to the spread of lice and, hence, the disease. Currently, cases of epidemic louseborne typhus are rare in the United States but have occurred throughout the world, including Asia, Africa, some parts of Europe, and Central and South America. Typhus is most common during winter, when conditions favor person-to-person transmission of the vector, the body louse. Rickettsiae are present in the blood and tissues of patients during the early febrile phase but are not found in secretions. Direct person-to-person spread of the disease does not occur in the absence of the louse vector. In the United States, sporadic human cases associated with contact with infected flying squirrels, their nests, or their ectoparasites occasionally are reported. Flying squirrel-related disease typically presents as a milder illness.

The **incubation period** is 1 to 2 weeks.

DIAGNOSTIC TESTS: *Rickettsia prowazekii* can be isolated from acute blood specimens by animal passage or through tissue culture but may be hazardous. Definitive diagnosis requires immunohistochemical visualization of rickettsiae in tissues, isolation of the organism, detection of the DNA of rickettsiae by polymerase chain reaction assay, or testing of paired serum specimens obtained during the acute and convalescent phases of disease. The indirect fluorescent antibody test is the preferred serologic assay, but enzyme immunoassay, dot immunoassay, and latex agglutination testing also are available. A fourfold change in antibody titer between acute and convalescent serum specimens taken 2 to 3 weeks apart is diagnostic. Specific molecular assays, isolation, and an immunohistochemical assay for *R prowazekii* in formalin-fixed tissue specimens are available at the Centers for Disease Control and Prevention.

TREATMENT: Doxycycline given intravenously or orally, 2.2 mg/kg every 12 hours (maximum 300 mg/day), is the treatment of choice for epidemic louseborne typhus. Children weighing >45 kg would receive a standard adult dose of doxycycline (100 mg every 12 hours). Therapy should be administered until the patient is afebrile for at least 3 days and clinical improvement is documented; the usual duration of therapy is 7 to 10 days. Severe disease can require a longer course of treatment. Despite concerns regarding dental staining after use of a tetracycline-class antimicrobial agent in children 8 years of age or younger (see Antimicrobial Agents and Related Therapy, p 735), doxycycline provides superior therapy for this potentially life-threatening disease. In people who are intolerant of tetracyclines, intravenous chloramphenicol or fluoroquinolones can be considered. Fluoroquinolones are not approved for this indication in children younger than 18 years of age, but if illness is life-threatening, the benefit may outweigh potential risks. To halt the spread of disease to other people, louse-infested patients should be treated with cream or gel pediculicides containing pyrethrins (0.16%–0.33%), piperonyl butoxide (2%–4%), crotamiton (10%), or lindane (1%). In epidemic situations in which antimicrobial agents may be limited (eg, refugee camps), a single dose of doxycycline may provide effective treatment (4.4 mg/kg for children weighing less than 45 kg, or 200 mg for heavier children).

ISOLATION OF THE HOSPITALIZED PATIENT: Standard precautions are recommended. Precautions should be taken to delouse hospitalized patients with louse infestations.

CONTROL MEASURES: Thorough delousing in epidemic situations, particularly among exposed contacts of cases, is recommended. Several applications may be needed, because lice eggs are resistant to most insecticides. Washing clothes in hot water kills lice and eggs. During epidemics, insecticides dusted onto clothes of louse-infested populations are effective. Prevention and control of flying squirrel-associated typhus requires precautions to prevent contact with these animals and their ectoparasites and to exclude them from human dwellings. A vaccine no longer is available in the United States. Cases should be reported to local or state public health departments.

Ureaplasma urealyticum Infections

CLINICAL MANIFESTATIONS: The most common syndrome associated with *Ureaplasma urealyticum* infections is nongonococcal urethritis (NGU). Although 15% to 55% of cases of NGU are caused by *Chlamydia trachomatis*, *U urealyticum* may be responsible for 20% to 30% of the remaining cases in some studies, with the etiology of most of the other cases unknown. Without treatment, the disease usually resolves within 1 to 6 months, although asymptomatic infection may persist thereafter. Prostatitis and epididymitis also have been associated with *U urealyticum* infection in men. In women, salpingitis, endometritis, and chorioamnionitis can occur.

Ureaplasma urealyticum has been isolated from the lower respiratory tract and from lung biopsy specimens of preterm infants and may contribute to pneumonia and chronic lung disease of prematurity. Although the organism also has been recovered from respiratory tract secretions of infants 3 months of age or younger with pneumonia, its role in development of lower respiratory tract disease in otherwise healthy young infants is controversial. *Ureaplasma urealyticum* has been isolated from cerebrospinal fluid of newborn infants with meningitis, intraventricular hemorrhage, and hydrocephalus. The contribution of *U urealyticum* to the outcome of these newborn infants is unclear given the confounding effects of preterm birth and intraventricular hemorrhage.

Isolated cases of *U urealyticum* arthritis, osteomyelitis, pneumonia, pericarditis, and progressive sinopulmonary disease in immunocompromised patients have been reported.

ETIOLOGY: *Ureaplasma* and *Mycoplasma* are genera in the Mycoplasmataceae family. *Ureaplasma* organisms are small pleomorphic bacteria that characteristically lack a cell wall. The genus *Ureaplasma* contains 2 species capable of causing human infection, *U urealyticum* and *U parvum*. At least 14 serotypes have been described.

EPIDEMIOLOGY: The principal reservoir of human *U urealyticum* is the genital tract of sexually active adults. Colonization occurs in approximately half of sexually active women; the incidence in sexually active men is lower. Colonization is uncommon in prepubertal children and adolescents who are not sexually active, but a positive genital culture is not in itself an indication of sexual abuse. Transmission during delivery is likely from an asymptomatic colonized mother to her newborn infant. *Ureaplasma urealyticum* may colonize the throat, eyes, umbilicus, and perineum of newborn infants and may persist for several months after birth.

Because *U urealyticum* commonly is isolated from the female lower genital tract and neonatal respiratory tract in the absence of disease, a positive culture does not establish its causative role in acute infection.

The **incubation period** for NGU after sexual transmission is 10 to 20 days.

DIAGNOSTIC TESTS: Specimens for culture require specific *Ureaplasma* species transport media with refrigeration at 4°C (39°F). Dacron or calcium alginate swabs should be used; cotton swabs should be avoided. Several rapid, sensitive polymerase chain reaction assays for detection of *U urealyticum* have been developed but are not available routinely. *Ureaplasma urealyticum* can be cultured in urea-containing broth in 1 to 2 days. Serologic testing for *U urealyticum* antibodies is of limited value and should not be used for routine diagnosis.

TREATMENT: A positive culture does not indicate need for therapy if the patient is asymptomatic. Mycoplasmas in general are susceptible to tetracyclines and quinolones, but because they lack a cell wall, they are not susceptible to penicillins or cephalosporins. For symptomatic older children, adolescents, and adults, doxycycline is the drug of choice. Recurrences are common. Azithromycin is the preferred antimicrobial agent for children younger than 8 years of age, people who are allergic to tetracycline, and people with infections caused by tetracycline-resistant strains. Studies in adult men with NGU indicate that single-dose azithromycin (1 g orally) is effective. Results of trials of antimicrobial therapy in pregnant women to prevent preterm delivery and in preterm infants to prevent pulmonary disease have been limited but generally have not demonstrated efficacy. Thus, antimicrobial therapy cannot be recommended for these indications. Similarly, definitive evidence of efficacy of antimicrobial agents in treatment of central nervous system infections in infants and children is lacking.

ISOLATION OF THE HOSPITALIZED PATIENT: Standard precautions are recommended.

CONTROL MEASURES: Partners of patients with NGU attributable to *U urealyticum* should be offered treatment.

Varicella-Zoster Infections

CLINICAL MANIFESTATIONS: Primary infection results in varicella (chickenpox), manifesting as a generalized, pruritic, vesicular rash typically consisting of 250 to 500 lesions in varying stages of development and resolution (crusting), mild fever, and other systemic symptoms. Complications include bacterial superinfection of skin lesions, pneumonia, central nervous system involvement (acute cerebellar ataxia, encephalitis), thrombocytopenia, and other rare complications such as glomerulo-nephritis, arthritis, and hepatitis. Varicella tends to be more severe in adolescents and adults than in young children. Reye syndrome can follow cases of chickenpox, although the incidence of Reye syndrome has decreased dramatically with decreased use of salicylates during varicella or influenza-like illnesses. In immunocompromised children, progressive severe varicella characterized by continuing eruption of lesions and high fever persisting into the second week of illness as well as encephalitis, hepatitis, and pneumonia can develop. Hemorrhagic varicella is more common among immunocompromised patients than immunocompetent hosts. Pneumonia is relatively less common among immunocompetent children but is the most common complication in adults. In children with human immunodeficiency virus (HIV) infection, recurrent varicella or disseminated herpes zoster can develop. Severe and even fatal varicella has been reported in otherwise healthy children receiving intermittent courses of high-dose corticosteroids (>2 mg/kg of prednisone or equivalent) for treatment of asthma and other illnesses. The risk especially is high when corticosteroids are given during the incubation period for chickenpox.

The virus establishes latency in the dorsal root ganglia during primary infection. Reactivation results in herpes zoster ("shingles"). Grouped vesicular lesions appear in the distribution of 1 to 3 sensory dermatomes, sometimes accompanied by pain localized to the area. *Postherpetic neuralgia*, which may last for weeks to months, is defined as pain that persists after resolution of the zoster rash. Zoster occasionally can become disseminated in immunocompromised patients, with lesions appearing outside the primary dermatomes and with visceral complications.

Fetal infection after maternal varicella during the first or early second trimester of pregnancy occasionally results in fetal death or varicella embryopathy, characterized by limb hypoplasia, cutaneous scarring, eye abnormalities, and damage to the central nervous system (the congenital varicella syndrome). The incidence of congenital varicella syndrome among infants born to mothers with varicella is approximately 1% to 2% when infection occurs before 20 weeks of gestation. Children exposed to varicella-zoster virus (VZV) in utero during the second 20 weeks of pregnancy can develop inapparent varicella and subsequent zoster early in life without having had extrauterine varicella. Varicella infection can be fatal for an infant if the mother develops varicella from 5 days before to 2 days after delivery. When varicella develops in a mother more than 5 days before delivery and gestational age is 28 weeks or more, the severity of disease in the newborn infant is modified by transplacental transfer of VZV-specific maternal immunoglobulin (Ig) G antibody.

ETIOLOGY: Varicella-zoster virus is a member of the herpesvirus family.

EPIDEMIOLOGY: Humans are the only source of infection for this highly contagious virus. Humans are infected when the virus comes in contact with the mucosa of the upper respiratory tract or the conjunctiva. Person-to-person transmission occurs by direct contact with vesicular fluid from patients with varicella or by airborne spread from respiratory tract secretions and from contact with zoster lesions. In utero infection also can occur as a result of transplacental passage of virus during maternal varicella infection. Varicella-zoster virus infection in a household member usually results in infection of almost all susceptible people in that household. Children who acquire their infection at home (secondary family cases) may have more pox lesions than the index case. Nosocomial transmission is well documented in pediatric units, but transmission is rare in newborn nurseries.

In temperate climates in the prevaccine era, varicella was a childhood disease with a marked seasonal distribution with peak incidence during late winter and early spring. In tropical climates, the epidemiology of varicella is different; acquisition of disease occurs at later ages, resulting in a higher proportion of adults being susceptible to varicella compared with adults in temperate climates. In the prevaccine era, most cases of varicella in the United States occurred in children younger than 10 years of age. With implementation of universal immunization, a greater number of cases are occurring among adolescents and adults, although the overall incidence in this age group has been greatly reduced. Immunity generally is lifelong. Cellular immunity is more important than humoral immunity for limiting the extent of primary infection with VZV and for preventing reactivation of virus with herpes zoster. Symptomatic reinfection is uncommon in immunocompetent people, although asymptomatic reinfection occurs. Asymptomatic primary infection is unusual, but because some cases are mild, they may not be recognized.

In 2004, 88% of 19- to 35-month-old children in the United States had received 1 dose of varicella vaccine. As vaccine coverage increases and the incidence of wild-type varicella decreases, a greater number of varicella cases are occurring in immunized people as breakthrough disease. This should not be confused as an increasing rate of breakthrough disease or as evidence of increasing vaccine failure. In the surveillance areas with high vaccine coverage, the rate of varicella disease decreased by approximately 85% from 1995 to 2004 with use of varicella vaccine.

Immunocompromised people with primary (varicella) or recurrent (zoster) infection are at increased risk of severe disease. Disseminated varicella and zoster are more likely to develop in children with congenital T-lymphocyte defects or acquired immunodeficiency syndrome than in people with B-lymphocyte abnormalities. Other groups of pediatric patients who may experience more severe or complicated disease include infants, adolescents, patients with chronic cutaneous or pulmonary disorders, and patients receiving systemic corticosteroids or long-term salicylate therapy.

Patients are most contagious from 1 to 2 days before to shortly after onset of the rash. Contagiousness persists until crusting of all lesions.

The **incubation period** usually is 14 to 16 days and occasionally is as short as 10 or as long as 21 days after contact. It may be prolonged for as long as 28 days after receipt of Varicella-Zoster Immune Globulin (VariZIG) or Immune Globulin Intravenous (IGIV) and shortened in immunocompromised patients. Varicella can develop between 1 and 16 days of life in infants born to mothers with active varicella around the time of delivery; the usual interval from onset of rash in a mother to onset in her neonate is 9 to 15 days.

DIAGNOSTIC TESTS: Diagnostic tests for VZV are summarized in Table 3.78, p 714. Vesicular fluid or a scab can be used to identify VZV using polymerase chain reaction (PCR). Varicella-zoster virus also can be isolated from scrapings of a vesicle base during the first 3 to 4 days of the eruption but rarely from other sites, including respiratory tract secretions. Rapid diagnostic tests (PCR, direct fluorescent antibody) are the methods of choice. A significant increase in serum varicella IgG antibody from acute and convalescent samples by any standard serologic assay can confirm a diagnosis retrospectively. These antibody tests are reliable for determining immune status in healthy hosts after natural infection but may not be reliable in immunocompromised people (see Care of Exposed People, p 715). Commercially available tests are not sufficiently sensitive to demonstrate reliably a vaccine-induced antibody response. Immunoglobulin M tests are not reliable for routine confirmation of acute infection, but positive results indicate current or recent VZV activity.

TREATMENT: The decision to use antiviral therapy and the route and duration of therapy should be determined by specific host factors, extent of infection, and initial response to therapy. Antiviral drugs have a limited window of opportunity to affect the outcome of varicella-zoster infection. In immunocompetent hosts, most virus replication has stopped by 72 hours after onset of rash; the duration of replication may be extended in immunocompromised hosts. Oral acyclovir is not recommended for routine use in otherwise healthy children with varicella. Administration within 24 hours of onset of rash results in only a modest decrease in symptoms. Oral acyclovir should be considered for otherwise healthy people at increased risk of moderate to severe varicella, such as people older than 12 years of age, people with chronic cutaneous or pulmonary disorders, people receiving long-term salicylate therapy, and people receiving short, intermittent, or aerosolized courses of corticosteroids. Some experts also recommend use of oral acyclovir for secondary household cases in which the disease usually is more severe than in the primary case. For recommendations on dosage and duration of therapy, see Antiviral Drugs (p 785).

Acyclovir is a Category B drug based on US Food and Drug Administration (FDA) Drug Risk Classification in pregnancy. Some experts recommend oral acyclovir for pregnant women with varicella, especially during the second and third trimesters. Intravenous acyclovir is recommended for the pregnant patient with serious complications of varicella. VariZIG or IGIV can be used during pregnancy for susceptible women who are exposed to VZV.

Intravenous antiviral therapy is recommended for immunocompromised patients, including patients being treated with chronic corticosteroids. Therapy initiated early in the course of the illness, especially within 24 hours of rash onset, maximizes efficacy. Oral acyclovir should not be used to treat immunocompromised children with varicella because of poor oral bioavailability. However, some experts have used high-dose oral acyclovir in selected immunocompromised patients perceived to be at lower risk of developing severe varicella, such as HIV-infected patients with relatively normal concentrations of CD4 + T-lymphocytes and children with leukemia in whom careful follow-up is ensured. Although VariZIG or, if not available, IGIV given shortly after exposure can prevent or modify the course of disease, immune globulin preparations are not effective once disease is established (see Care of Exposed People, p 715).

Table 3.78. Diagnostic Tests for Varicella-Zoster Virus (VZV) Infection

Test	Specimen	Comments
Tissue culture	Vesicular fluid, CSF, biopsy tissue	Distinguish VZV from HSV. Cost, limited availability, requires up to a week for result.
PCR	Vesicular swabs or scrapings; scabs from crusted lesions; biopsy tissue, CSF	Very sensitive method. Specific for VZV. Real-time methods (not widely available) have been designed that distinguish vaccine strain from wild-type (rapid, within 3 hours). Requires special equipment.
DFA	Vesicle scraping; swab of lesion base (must include cells)	Specific for VZV. More rapid and more sensitive than culture, less sensitive than PCR.
Tzanck smear	Vesicle scraping; swab of lesion base (must include cells)	Observe multinucleated giant cells with inclusions. Not specific for VZV. Less sensitive and accurate than DFA.
EIA	Acute and convalescent serum specimens for IgG	Specific for VZV. Requires special equipment. May not be sensitive enough to identify vaccine-induced immunity.
LA	Acute and convalescent serum specimens for IgG	Specific for VZV. Rapid (15 min); no special equipment needed. More sensitive but less specific than EIA. Can produce false-positive results. May not be sensitive enough to identify vaccine-induced immunity.
IFA	Acute and convalescent serum specimens for IgG	Specific for VZV. Requires special equipment. Good sensitivity, specificity. May not be sensitive enough to identify vaccine-induced immunity.
gpELISA	Acute and convalescent serum specimens for IgG	Specific for VZV. Highly specific and sensitive but not widely available. Suitable for the evaluation of vaccine seroconversion.
FAMA	Acute and convalescent serum specimens for IgG	Specific for VZV. Highly specific and sensitive but not widely available. Suitable for the evaluation of vaccine seroconversion
CF	Acute and convalescent serum specimens for IgG	Specific for VZV. Poor sensitivity. Cumbersome to perform.
Capture IgM	Acute serum specimens for IgM	Specific for VZV. IgM consistently detected. Not reliable method for routine confirmation but positive result indicates current/recent VZV activity. Requires special equipment.

CSF indicates cerebrospinal fluid; HSV, herpes simplex virus; PCR, polymerase chain reaction; DFA, direct fluorescent antibody; EIA, enzyme immunoassay; IgG, immunoglobulin G; LA, latex

Famciclovir and valacyclovir have been licensed for treatment of zoster in adults. Famciclovir is converted to penciclovir, which has an extended half-life in infected cells. Valacyclovir is converted to acyclovir and produces fourfold greater serum concentrations than those produced by oral acyclovir. No pediatric formulation is available for either medication, and insufficient data exist on the use or dose of these drugs in children to support therapeutic recommendations. Infections caused by acyclovir-resistant VZV strains, which generally are limited to immunocompromised hosts, should be treated with parenteral foscarnet sodium.

Children with varicella should not receive salicylates or salicylate-containing products, because administration of salicylates to such children increases the risk of Reye syndrome. Acetaminophen may be used for control of fever. Salicylate therapy should be stopped in a child who is exposed to varicella.

ISOLATION OF THE HOSPITALIZED PATIENT: In addition to standard precautions, airborne and contact precautions are recommended for patients with varicella for a minimum of 5 days after onset of rash and until all lesions are crusted, which in immunocompromised patients can be a week or longer. For immunized patients with breakthrough varicella with only maculopapular lesions, isolation is recommended until no new lesions occur or the lesions have faded; lesions do not have to be completely resolved. For exposed susceptible patients, airborne and contact precautions from 10 until 21 days after exposure to the index patient also are indicated; these precautions should be maintained until 28 days after exposure for those who received VariZIG or IGIV.

Airborne and contact precautions are recommended for neonates born to mothers with varicella and, if still hospitalized, should be continued until 21 or 28 days of age if they received VariZIG or IGIV. Infants with varicella embryopathy do not require isolation.

Immunocompromised patients who have zoster (localized or disseminated) and immunocompetent patients with disseminated zoster require airborne and contact precautions for the duration of illness. For immunocompetent patients with localized zoster, contact precautions are indicated until all lesions are crusted.

CONTROL MEASURES:

CHILD CARE AND SCHOOL. Children with uncomplicated chickenpox who have been excluded from school or child care may return when the rash has crusted, or in immunized people without crusts, until lesions are resolving, which may be several days in mild cases and several weeks in severe cases or in immunocompromised children.

Exclusion of children with zoster whose lesions cannot be covered is based on similar criteria. Children who are excluded may return after the lesions have crusted. Lesions that are covered seem to pose little risk to susceptible people. Older children and staff members with zoster should be instructed to wash their hands if they touch potentially infectious lesions.

CARE OF EXPOSED PEOPLE: Potential interventions for susceptible people exposed to a person with varicella include varicella vaccine administered by 3 to 5 days after exposure and, when indicated, VariZIG (1 dose up to 96 hours after exposure). If

VariZIG is not available, IGIV (1 dose up to 96 hours after exposure), can be used (see Unavailability of VariZIG, p 718).*

HOSPITAL EXPOSURE. If an inadvertent exposure in the hospital to an infected patient, health care professional, or visitor occurs, the following control measures are recommended:

- Personnel and patients who have been exposed (see Table 3.79, p 717) and are susceptible to varicella should be identified.
- VariZIG should be administered to appropriate candidates (see Table 3.80, p 717). If VariZIG is not available, IGIV is recommended.
- All exposed susceptible patients should be discharged as soon as possible.
- All exposed susceptible patients who cannot be discharged should be placed in isolation from day 10 to day 21 after exposure to the index patient. For people who received VariZIG, isolation should continue until day 28.
- All susceptible exposed personnel should be furloughed or excused from patient contact from day 10 to day 21 after exposure to an infectious patient or to day 28 for people who have received VariZIG.
- Serologic testing for immunity is not necessary for personnel who have been immunized, because 99% of adults are seropositive after the second vaccine dose and because most serologic assays will not reliably detect immunity resulting from vaccines. For more information, see the recommendations of the Advisory Committee on Immunization Practices (ACIP) of the Centers for Disease Control and Prevention (CDC).†
- Immunized health care personnel who develop breakthrough infection should be considered infectious.
- Varicella immunization is recommended for susceptible personnel if there are no contraindications to vaccine use.

POSTEXPOSURE IMMUNIZATION. Administration of varicella vaccine to susceptible people 12 months of age or older, including adults, as soon as possible within 72 hours and possibly up to 120 hours after varicella exposure may prevent or modify disease and should be considered in these circumstances if there are no contraindications to vaccine use. Physicians should advise parents and their children that the vaccine may not protect against disease in all cases, because some children may have been exposed at the same time as the index case. However, if exposure to varicella does not cause infection, postexposure immunization with varicella vaccine will result in protection against subsequent exposure. There is no evidence that administration of varicella vaccine during the presymptomatic or prodromal stage of illness increases the risk of vaccine-associated adverse events or more severe natural disease.

CHEMOPROPHYLAXIS. Oral acyclovir generally is not recommended for immunocompetent individuals. If VariZIG is not available or >96 hours have passed since exposure, some experts recommend prophylaxis with acyclovir (80 mg/kg per day, administered 4 times/day for 7 days, maximum dose 800 mg, 4 times/day) for a

---

* Centers for Disease Control and Prevention. A new product (VariZIG) for postexposure prophylaxis of varicella available under an investigational new drug application expanded access protocol. *MMWR Morb Mortal Wkly Rep.* 2006;55:209–210

† Centers for Disease Control and Prevention. Prevention of varicella update: recommendations of the Advisory Committee on Immunization Practices (ACIP). *MMWR Recomm Rep.* 1999;48(RR-6):1–5

susceptible immunocompromised patient who has been exposed to varicella. A 7-day course of acyclovir may be given to susceptible adults beginning 7 to 10 days after varicella exposure if vaccine is contraindicated. Limited data on acyclovir as postexposure prophylaxis are available for healthy children; no studies were performed for adults. However, limited data support use of acyclovir as postexposure prophylaxis, and clinicians may choose this option with or without other methods. Most adults with no history or an uncertain history of chickenpox are immune.

PASSIVE IMMUNOPROPHYLAXIS. The decision to administer VariZIG depends on 3 factors: (1) the likelihood that the exposed person is susceptible to varicella; (2) the probability that a given exposure to varicella or zoster will result in infection; and (3) the likelihood that complications of varicella will develop if the person is infected.

Table 3.79. Types of Exposure to Varicella or Zoster for Which VariZIG Is Indicated for Susceptible People[1]

- Household: residing in the same household
- Playmate: face-to-face[2] indoor play
- Hospital:
  Varicella: In same 2- to 4-bed room or adjacent beds in a large ward, face-to-face[2] contact with an infectious staff member or patient, or visit by a person deemed contagious
  Zoster: Intimate contact (eg, touching or hugging) with a person deemed contagious.
  Newborn infant: onset of varicella in the mother 5 days or less before delivery or within 48 h after delivery; VariZIG or IGIV is not indicated if the mother has zoster

VariZIG indicates Varicella-Zoster Immune Globulin; IGIV, Immune Globulin Intravenous.[1] Patients should meet criteria of both significant exposure and candidacy for receiving VariZIG, as given in Table 3.80. VariZIG should be administered as soon as possible and no later than 96 hours after exposure.
[2] Experts differ in opinion about the duration of face-to-face contact that warrants administration of VariZIG. However, the contact should be nontransient. Some experts suggest a contact of 5 or more minutes as constituting significant exposure for this purpose; others define close contact as more than 1 hour.

Table 3.80. Candidates for Acyclovir or VariZIG, Provided Significant Exposure Has Occurred[1]

- Immunocompromised children[2] without history of varicella or varicella immunization[3]
- Susceptible pregnant women[4]
- Newborn infant whose mother had onset of chickenpox within 5 days before delivery or within 48 h after delivery
- Hospitalized preterm infant (≥28 wk of gestation) whose mother lacks a reliable history of chickenpox or serologic evidence of protection against varicella
- Hospitalized preterm infants (<28 wk of gestation or ≤1000 g birth weight), regardless of maternal history of varicella or varicella-zoster virus serostatus

[1] See text and Table 3.79 for additional discussion.
[2] Including children who are infected with human immunodeficiency virus.
[3] Immunocompromised adolescents and adults known to be susceptible also should receive VariZIG.
[4] If VariZIG is not available, clinicians may choose to administer IGIV or closely monitor the pregnant woman for signs and symptoms of varicella and institute treatment with acyclovir if disease develops.

Although a positive result of a serologic test to determine immune status after natural disease is reliable, a negative antibody result may not be reliable to determine susceptibility. A carefully obtained, positive history of past varicella is the primary determinant of immunity. Administration of VariZIG or IGIV as soon as possible within 96 hours to exposed immunocompromised children with no history of varicella and unknown or negative serologic test results usually is advised. The degree and type of immunosuppression should be considered in making this decision.

Patients receiving monthly high-dose IGIV (400 mg/kg or greater) at regular intervals are likely to be protected if the last dose of IGIV was given 3 weeks or less before exposure.

Where to Obtain VariZIG. VariZIG is available under an investigational new drug (IND) protocol and can be requested by calling the 24-hour number at FFF Enterprises (800-843-7477).

Indications for VariZIG. Tables 3.79 (p 717) and 3.80 (p 717) indicate susceptible people who should receive VariZIG if exposed, including immunocompromised people, susceptible pregnant women, and certain newborn infants.

For healthy term infants exposed postnatally to varicella, including infants whose mother's rash developed more than 48 hours after delivery, VariZIG is not indicated. However, some experts advise use of VariZIG for any exposed susceptible newborn infant who has a mother with severe skin involvement.

- **Subsequent exposures and follow-up of VariZIG recipients**. Because administration of VariZIG can cause varicella infection to be asymptomatic, testing of recipients 2 months or later after administration of VariZIG to ascertain their immune status may be helpful in the event of subsequent exposure. Some experts, however, would advise VariZIG administration after subsequent exposures regardless of serologic results because of the unreliability of serologic test results in immunocompromised people and the uncertainty about whether asymptomatic infection after VariZIG administration confers lasting protection.

Any patient to whom VariZIG is administered to prevent varicella subsequently should receive age-appropriate varicella vaccine, provided the vaccine is not contraindicated. Varicella immunization should be delayed until 5 months after VariZIG administration. Varicella vaccine is not needed if the patient develops varicella after administration of VariZIG.

Unavailability of VariZIG. If VariZIG is not available, IGIV can be used. The recommendation for use of IGIV is based on "best judgment of experts" and is supported by reports comparing VZV IgG antibody titers measured in both IGIV and VariZIG preparations and patients given IGIV and VariZIG. Licensed IGIV preparations contain antivaricella antibodies at varying levels. No clinical data demonstrating effectiveness of IGIV for postexposure prophylaxis of varicella are available.

ACTIVE IMMUNIZATION.*

Vaccine. Varicella vaccine is a live-attenuated preparation of the serially propagated and attenuated wild Oka strain. The product contains trace amounts of neomycin and gelatin. The vaccine was licensed in March 1995 by the FDA for use in healthy people 12 months of age or older who have not had varicella illness.

---

* American Academy of Pediatrics, Committee on Infectious Diseases. Recommendations for the use of live attenuated varicella vaccine. *Pediatrics*. 1995;95:791–796 (undergoing revision at the time of publication of *Red Book*)

Dose and Administration. The recommended dose of the vaccine is 0.5 mL. One dose is recommended for children between 12 months and 12 years of age, and 2 doses separated by an interval of at least 4 weeks are recommended for individuals 13 years of age and older. Subcutaneous administration is recommended, although IM administration has been demonstrated to result in similar rates of seroconversion.

Immunogenicity. More than 95% of immunized healthy children between 12 months and 12 years of age develop humoral and cell-mediated immune response to VZV after a single dose of varicella vaccine. In people 13 years of age and older, seroconversion rates are 78% to 82% after 1 dose and 99% after 2 doses.

Effectiveness. The currently licensed product is more than 95% effective in preventing severe disease. Effectiveness in preventing mild or moderate infection is less uniform, generally ranging from 70% to 90%. A mild varicella-like syndrome develops in 10% to 30% of immunized children per year who are exposed to VZV in a child care, school, or household setting. The results of most studies suggest that neither the rate nor the severity of breakthrough varicella increases with time after immunization. Varicella in vaccine recipients is milder than that occurring in unimmunized children, usually with a median of fewer than 50 vesicles, lower rate of fever (10% with temperature $\geq$39°C [$\geq$102°F]), and faster recovery. At times, the disease is so mild that it is not easily recognizable as varicella because skin lesions may resemble insect bites. In contrast, the median number of lesions in unimmunized children with varicella is more than 250. Varicella transmission from vaccine recipients with mild breakthrough disease has been documented. In a household study, immunized people were overall half as contagious as unimmunized people. Immunized people with <50 lesions were only one third as contagious as immunized people.

Duration of Immunity. Although there has been concern about waning immunity, follow-up evaluations of children immunized during prelicensure clinical trials in the United States indicate protection for at least 11 years. Studies in Japan indicate protection for at least 20 years. However, these studies were conducted during a period when a substantial amount of wild-type VZV was present in the community, with many opportunities for boosting of immunity by subclinical infection in immunized people. Experience with other live-virus vaccines (eg, measles, rubella) suggests that immunity remains high throughout life; the primary reason for second doses of measles vaccine is to induce protection in children without an adequate response to the first dose, not because of waning immunity. Follow-up studies of clinical trials in children and postlicensure surveillance studies are being performed to determine the need, if any, for additional doses of varicella vaccine.

Simultaneous Administration With Other Vaccines. Varicella vaccine may be given simultaneously with other recommended childhood immunizations (see Recommended Childhood and Adolescent Immunization Schedule, p 26), but separate syringes and injection sites must be used. Although further immunogenicity studies are needed on the use of varicella vaccine administered simultaneously with inactivated poliovirus vaccine, there is no reason to suspect that varicella vaccine will affect the immune response to this vaccine. If not administered at the same visit, the interval between administration of varicella vaccine and measles-mumps-rubella (MMR) vaccine should be at least 28 days.

Adverse Events. Varicella vaccine is safe; reactions generally are mild and occur with an overall frequency of approximately 5% to 35%. Approximately 20% of immunized people will experience minor injection site reactions (eg, pain, redness, swelling). In approximately 3% to 5% of immunized children, a localized rash develops, and in an additional 3% to 5%, a generalized varicella-like rash develops. However, all observed postimmunization rashes cannot be attributed to vaccine. These rashes typically consist of 2 to 5 lesions and may be maculopapular rather than vesicular; lesions usually appear 5 to 26 days after immunization. Many generalized varicelliform rashes that occur within the first 2 weeks after varicella immunization are attributable to wild-type VZV infection and are not an adverse effect of the vaccine. Although a temperature higher than 39°C (102°F) has been observed from 1 to 42 days after immunization in 15% of healthy immunized children, fever also occurs in a similar percentage of children receiving placebo and is not considered to be a common adverse reaction to varicella immunization. A temperature higher than 38°C (100°F) has been reported in 10% of adolescents and adults who are immunized with the vaccine. Serious adverse events, such as anaphylaxis, encephalitis, ataxia, erythema multiforme, Stevens-Johnson syndrome, pneumonia, thrombocytopenia, seizures, neuropathy, Guillain-Barré syndrome, secondary bacterial infections, and death have been reported rarely in temporal association with varicella vaccine. In rare instances, a causal relationship between the varicella vaccine and some of these serious adverse events has been established, most often in children with immunocompromising conditions, although the frequency of serious adverse events is much lower than after natural infection. In most cases, data are insufficient to determine a causal association.

Herpes Zoster After Immunization. The varicella vaccine virus has been associated with development of herpes zoster in immunocompetent and immunocompromised people. Data from postlicensure surveillance indicate that the age-specific risk of herpes zoster seems to be lower among immunocompetent children immunized with varicella vaccine than among children who have had natural varicella infection. A population-based study indicated that the annual incidence of herpes zoster after natural varicella infection among immunocompetent children younger than 20 years of age was 68 per 100 000 people, and the reported annual rate of herpes zoster after varicella immunization among immunocompetent people was approximately 2.6 per 100 000 vaccine doses distributed. However, comparison of these rates should be made cautiously, because the rates of zoster after natural infection are based on populations monitored actively for longer periods of time than the duration of passive surveillance after immunization. Wild-type VZV has been isolated from vesicles in people with herpes zoster after immunization, indicating that herpes zoster in immunized people also may result from natural varicella infection that occurred before or after immunization. A zoster vaccine for older adults has been submitted to the FDA for licensure in the United States.

Transmission of Vaccine-Associated Virus. Experience from 1995 until March 2005 with more than 56 million doses of varicella vaccine distributed in the United States indicates that vaccine-associated virus transmission to contacts is rare (only 5 well-documented cases) and the risk of transmission exists only if a rash develops on the immunized person (Merck & Co Inc, unpublished data).

The role of VariZIG, IGIV, acyclovir, or varicella vaccine as postexposure prophylaxis for high-risk people exposed to immunized people with lesions will be difficult to evaluate given the rarity of transmission. However, some experts believe that immunocompromised people in whom skin lesions develop, possibly related to vaccine virus, should receive acyclovir treatment.

Storage. The lyophilized vaccine should be stored in a frost-free freezer at an average temperature of $-15°C$ ($+5°F$) or colder. Vaccine may be stored at refrigerator temperature of 2°C to 8°C (36°F–46°F) for up to 72 continuous hours before administration. The diluent used for reconstitution should be stored separately in a refrigerator or at room temperature. Once the vaccine has been reconstituted, it should be injected as soon as possible and discarded if not used within 30 minutes (see Table 1.4, p 13).

Evidence of Immunity to Varicella.* The revised definition for evidence of immunity to varicella includes any of the following:
- Written documentation of age-appropriate immunization:
  a. Children immunized from 12 months to 12 years of age: 1 dose
  b. People immunized at 13 years of age or older: 2 doses 4 to 8 weeks apart
- Born in the United States before 1966
- History of varicella disease diagnosed by health care professional or self- or parental report of typical varicella disease for non-US-born people born before 1966 and all people born in 1966 or after. For people reporting a history of atypical mild case, health care professionals should seek either a) an epidemiologic link to a typical varicella case (eg, case occurred in the context of an outbreak or patient had household exposure in the previous 3 weeks) or b) evidence of laboratory confirmation, if testing was performed at the time of acute disease. When such documentation is lacking, people should not be considered as having a valid history of disease, because many other diseases may mimic mild atypical varicella.
- History of herpes-zoster diagnosed by a health care professional.
- Laboratory evidence of immunity or laboratory confirmation of disease. Commercial assays can be used to assess disease-induced immunity, but they lack sensitivity to detect vaccine-induced immunity in all instances (may yield false-negative results). The gpELISA or FAMA tests provide more sensitive results, but they are not commercially available.

RECOMMENDATIONS FOR IMMUNIZATION. Universal immunization of infants and immunization of susceptible older children and adolescents without evidence of immunity, providing they have no contraindication to immunization, is recommended on the basis of the frequency of serious complications and deaths after natural infection, the excessive cost to the family and society resulting from varicella infection, and the efficacy and safety of the live-attenuated varicella vaccine. Age-specific recommendations are as follows:

---

* Centers for Disease Control and Prevention. Updated ACIP recommendations for varicella vaccine use. *MMWR.* 2006; in press (available at **www.cdc.gov/mmwr**)

- **Age 12 months to the 13th birthday:**

    Age 12 to 18 months. One dose of varicella vaccine is recommended for universal immunization for all immunocompetent children who lack proof of previous immunization, a reliable history of varicella, or serologic evidence of varicella.

    Age 19 months to the 13th birthday. Immunization of all children who lack evidence of varicella immunity is recommended, and immunization may be given anytime during childhood but before the 13th birthday because of the potential increased severity of natural varicella after this age.

- **Healthy adolescents and young adults.** Healthy adolescents past their 13th birthday without evidence of immunity (see Evidence of Immunity, p 721) should be immunized against varicella by administration of 2 doses of vaccine 4 weeks apart. Longer intervals between doses do not necessitate a third dose but may leave the person unprotected during the intervening months.

- **Adults.** Immunization is recommended by the ACIP* for all adults without evidence of immunity.

Updated recommendations for varicella vaccine use include the following†:

- Official health agencies should take necessary steps, including developing and enforcing school immunization requirements, to ensure that students at all grade levels (including college) and children in child care facilities are protected against vaccine-preventable diseases, which include varicella. For varicella, this recommendation adds middle school, high school, and college requirements to the child care and elementary school entry requirements already covered by the 1999 recommendation. School and child care immunization requirements should be implemented when the varicella vaccine has had time to be well incorporated into practice and supply is adequate.

- Asymptomatic or mildly symptomatic HIV-infected children ≥12 months of age with age-specific CD4+ T-lymphocyte counts ≥15% and without evidence of varicella immunity should receive 2 doses of varicella vaccine 3 months apart.

- Women should be assessed prenatally for evidence of varicella immunity. On completion or termination of their pregnancies, women who do not have evidence of varicella immunity should receive the first dose of varicella vaccine before discharge from the health care facility. The second dose should be administered 4 to 8 weeks later. Standing orders are recommended for health care settings where completion or termination of pregnancy occurs to ensure administration of varicella vaccine.

- All people ≥13 years of age without evidence of immunity should be immunized with 2 doses of varicella vaccine 4 to 8 weeks apart (see revised definition for Evidence of Immunity to Varicella, p 721). The vaccine may be offered during routine health care visits.

- During a varicella outbreak, people who have received 1 dose of varicella vaccine should, resources permitting, receive a second dose, provided the appropri-

---

* Centers for Disease Control and Prevention. Prevention of varicella update: recommendations of the Advisory Committee on Immunization Practices (ACIP). *MMWR Morb Mortal Wkly Rep.* 1999;45(RR-6):1–5
† Centers for Disease Control and Prevention. Updated ACIP recommendations for varicella vaccine use. *MMWR.* 2006; in press (available at **www.cdc.gov/mmwr**)

ate immunization interval has elapsed since the first dose (3 months for people 12 months to 12 years of age and at least 4 weeks for people ≥13 years of age).

Serologic Testing Before and After Immunization. An adult, adolescent, or child with a reliable history of varicella can be assumed to be immune (see revised definition for Evidence of Immunity to Varicella, p 721), and immunization is unnecessary. Because approximately 70% to 90% of people 18 years of age or older without a reliable history of varicella also will be immune, it may be cost-effective to perform serologic tests on people 13 years of age or older and immunize only people who are seronegative. If serologic testing is performed, a tracking system for seronegative people should be developed to ensure that susceptible people are immunized. However, serologic testing is not required, because varicella vaccine is well tolerated by people immune from earlier disease. In some situations, universal immunization may be easier to implement than serologic testing and tracking. Most children younger than 13 years of age without a reliable history of varicella should be considered susceptible and immunized without serologic testing. Seroconversion rates after 1 dose of varicella vaccine in children younger than 13 years of age and after 2 doses in adolescents and adults are so high that serologic testing after immunization is unnecessary.

Whole-cell enzyme immunoassay is the most commonly used commercially available serologic test for VZV. The sensitivity of this test is sufficient to determine immunity after natural varicella, but it is not sensitive enough to determine vaccine-induced immunity. Tests such as the fluorescent antibody to membrane antigen assay and latex agglutination test are more sensitive, but the fluorescent antibody to membrane antigen assay is not available commercially, and the latex agglutination assay is not convenient for mass testing.

Booster Immunization. Except in outbreak situations, reimmunization is not recommended currently, but the need for recommendations for reimmunization is being assessed.

CONTRAINDICATIONS AND PRECAUTIONS.

Intercurrent Illness. As with other vaccines, varicella vaccine should not be administered to people who have moderate or severe illnesses, with or without fever (see Vaccine Safety and Contraindications, p 39).

Immunocompromised Patients.

General recommendations. Varicella vaccine should not be administered routinely to children who have T-lymphocyte immunodeficiency, including people with leukemia, lymphoma, other malignant neoplasms affecting the bone marrow or lymphatic systems, and congenital T-lymphocyte abnormalities (see Immunocompromised Children, p 71). Exceptions include children with acute lymphocytic leukemia, to whom vaccine may be administered under a study protocol (see Acute lymphocytic leukemia, p 724) and certain asymptomatic children infected with HIV (see Human Immunodeficiency Virus Infection, p 378). Children with impaired humoral immunity may be immunized.

Immunodeficiency should be excluded before immunization in children with a family history of hereditary immunodeficiency. The presence of an immunodeficient or HIV-seropositive family member does not contraindicate vaccine use in other family members.

Acute lymphocytic leukemia. Although the current vaccine is not licensed for routine use in children with malignant neoplasms, immunization should be considered when a susceptible child with acute lymphocytic leukemia has been in continuous remission for at least 1 year and has a lymphocyte count greater than 700/μL (0.7 × 10⁹/L) and a platelet count greater than 100 × 10³/μL (100 × 10⁹/L). With appropriate monitoring, these children have been immunized safely as part of a research protocol.

Human immunodeficiency virus infection. Screening for HIV infection is not indicated before routine varicella immunization. Children known to be infected with HIV may be at increased risk of morbidity from varicella and herpes zoster compared with healthy children. Limited data on immunization of HIV-infected children in CDC Class 1 with a CD4+ T-lymphocyte percentage of 15% or greater indicate that the vaccine is safe, immunogenic, and effective. Therefore, after weighing potential risks and benefits, varicella vaccine should be considered for HIV-infected children in CDC Class 1 with a CD4+ T-lymphocyte percentage of 15% or greater. Eligible children should receive 2 doses of varicella vaccine with a 3-month interval between doses and return for evaluation if they experience a postimmunization varicella-like rash. With increased use of varicella vaccine and the resulting decrease in incidence of varicella in the community, exposure of immunocompromised hosts to VZV will decrease. As the risk of exposure decreases and more data are generated on the use of varicella vaccine in high-risk populations, the risk versus benefit of varicella immunization in HIV-infected children will need to be reassessed.

Children receiving corticosteroids. Varicella vaccine should not be administered to people who are receiving high doses of systemic corticosteroids (2 mg/kg per day or more of prednisone or its equivalent or 20 mg/day of prednisone or its equivalent) for 14 days or more. The recommended interval between discontinuation of corticosteroid therapy and immunization with varicella vaccine is at least 1 month. Other recommendations about varicella vaccine use in children receiving corticosteroids can be found in Immunocompromised Children, p 71.

Children with nephrotic syndrome. The results of one small study indicate that 2 doses of the varicella vaccine in 29 children between 12 months and 18 years of age generally were well tolerated and immunogenic, including children receiving low-dose, alternate-day prednisone.

Households with potential contact with immunocompromised people. Transmission of vaccine-strain VZV from healthy people has been documented in 4 instances resulting in 5 secondary cases (see Adverse Events, p 720). Even in families with immunocompromised people, including people with HIV infection, no precautions are needed after immunization of healthy children in whom a rash does not develop. Immunized people in whom a rash develops should avoid direct contact with immunocompromised susceptible hosts for the duration of the rash.

Pregnancy and Lactation. Varicella vaccine should not be administered to pregnant women, because the possible effects on fetal development are unknown, although no pattern of malformation has been identified following inadvertent immunization of pregnant women. When postpubertal females are immunized, pregnancy should be avoided for at least 1 month after immunization. A pregnant mother or other household member is not a contraindication for immunization of a child in the household. This recommendation is based on the following: transmission of vaccine virus is rare; more than 95% of adults are immune, and immunization of the child likely will protect the susceptible mother from exposure to wild-type VZV. As of March 2005, no cases of congenital varicella syndrome have been identified in 587 reports with known natural pregnancy outcomes including 138 seronegative women who received varicella vaccine 3 months before or during pregnancy and who delivered live-born infants.

A study of nursing mothers and their infants showed no evidence of excretion of vaccine strain in human milk or of transmission to infants who are breastfeeding. Varicella vaccine should be administered to nursing mothers who lack evidence of immunity.

Immune Globulin. Whether Immune Globulin (IG) can interfere with varicella vaccine-induced immunity is unknown, although IG can interfere with immunity induction by measles vaccine. Pending additional data, varicella vaccine should be withheld for the same intervals after receipt of any form of IG or other blood product as measles vaccine (see Measles, p 441). Conversely, IG should be withheld for at least 2 weeks after receipt of varicella vaccine. Transplacental antibodies to VZV do not interfere with the immunogenicity of varicella vaccine administered at 12 months of age or older.

Salicylates. Whether Reye syndrome results from administration of salicylates after immunization for varicella in children is unknown. No cases have been reported. However, because of the association between Reye syndrome, natural varicella infection, and salicylates, the vaccine manufacturer recommends that salicylates be avoided for 6 weeks after administration of varicella vaccine. Physicians need to weigh the theoretic risks associated with varicella vaccine against the known risks of wild-type virus in children receiving long-term salicylate therapy.

Allergy to Vaccine Components. Varicella vaccine should not be administered to people who have had an anaphylactic-type reaction to any component of the vaccine, including gelatin and neomycin. Most people with allergy to neomycin have resulting contact dermatitis, a reaction that is not a contraindication to immunization. The vaccine does not contain preservatives or egg protein.

VIBRIO INFECTIONS

Cholera
(Vibrio cholerae)

CLINICAL MANIFESTATIONS: Cholera is characterized by painless voluminous diarrhea without abdominal cramps or fever. Dehydration, hypokalemia, metabolic acidosis, and occasionally, hypovolemic shock can occur in 4 to 12 hours if fluid losses are not replaced. Coma, seizures, hypoglycemia, and death also can occur, particularly in children. Stools are colorless, with small flecks of mucus ("rice-water"), and contain high concentrations of sodium, potassium, chloride, and bicarbonate. Most infected people with toxigenic *Vibrio cholerae* O1 have no symptoms, and some have only mild to moderate diarrhea lasting 3 to 7 days; fewer than 5% have severe watery diarrhea, vomiting, and dehydration (cholera gravis).

ETIOLOGY: *Vibrio cholerae* is a gram-negative, curved, motile bacillus with many serogroups. Only serogroups O1, O139, and O141 cause clinical cholera associated with enterotoxin. There are 3 serotypes of *V cholerae* O1: Inaba, Ogawa, and Hikojima. The 2 biotypes of *V cholerae* are classical and El Tor. El Tor is more commonly observed. Since 1992, toxigenic *V cholerae* serogroup O139 has been recognized as a cause of cholera. Nontoxigenic strains of *V cholerae* O1 and serogroups other than O1 and O139 can cause sporadic diarrheal illness, but they do not cause epidemics.

EPIDEMIOLOGY: During the last 5 decades, *V cholerae* O1 biotype El Tor has spread from India and Southeast Asia to Africa, the Middle East, Southern Europe, and the Western Pacific Islands (Oceania). In 1991, epidemic cholera caused by toxigenic *V cholerae* O1, serotype Inaba, biotype El Tor, appeared in Peru and spread to most countries in South and North America. In the United States, cases resulting from travel to or ingestion of contaminated food transported from Latin America or Asia have been reported. In addition, the Gulf Coast of Louisiana and Texas has an endemic focus of a unique strain of toxigenic *V cholerae* O1. Most cases of disease from this strain have resulted from consumption of raw or undercooked shellfish.

Humans are the only documented natural host, but free-living *V cholerae* organisms can exist in the aquatic environment. The usual mode of infection is ingestion of large numbers of organisms from contaminated water or food (particularly raw or undercooked shellfish, raw or partially dried fish, or moist grains or vegetables held at ambient temperature). Direct person-to-person spread has not been documented. People with low gastric acidity are at increased risk of cholera infection.

The **incubation period** usually is 1 to 3 days, with a range of a few hours to 5 days.

DIAGNOSTIC TESTS: *Vibrio cholerae* can be cultured from fecal specimens or vomitus plated on thiosulfate citrate bile salts sucrose agar. Because most laboratories in the United States do not routinely culture for *V cholerae* or other *Vibrio* organisms, clinicians should request appropriate cultures for clinically suspected cases. Isolates of *V cholerae* should be sent to a state health department laboratory for serogrouping; isolates of serogroup O1 or O139 then are sent to the Centers for Disease Control and Prevention (CDC) for testing for production of enterotoxin. A fourfold increase in vibriocidal antibody titers between acute and convalescent serum specimens or a fourfold decrease in vibriocidal titers available through CDC laboratories between early and late convalescent (more than a 2-month interval) serum specimens can confirm the diagnosis.

TREATMENT: Oral or parenteral rehydration therapy to correct dehydration and electrolyte abnormalities is the most important modality of therapy and should be initiated as soon as the diagnosis is suspected.* Oral rehydration is preferred unless the

---

* Centers for Disease Control and Prevention. Managing acute gastroenteritis among children: oral rehydration, maintenance, and nutritional therapy. *MMWR Recomm Rep.* 2003;52(RR-16):1–16

patient is in shock, is obtunded, or has intestinal ileus. The World Health Organization's Oral Rehydration Solution (ORS) has been the standard, but data suggest that rice-based ORS or amylase-resistant starch ORS is more effective.

Antimicrobial therapy results in prompt eradication of vibrios, decreases the duration of diarrhea, and decreases in fluid losses. Antimicrobial therapy should be considered for people who are moderately to severely ill. Oral doxycycline as a single dose or tetracycline for 3 days are the drugs of choice for cholera. Although tetracyclines generally are not recommended for children younger than 8 years of age, in cases of severe cholera, the benefits may outweigh the small risk of staining of developing teeth (see Antimicrobial Agents and Related Therapy, p 735). If strains are resistant to tetracyclines, then ciprofloxacin, ofloxacin, or trimethoprim-sulfamethoxazole can be used. Susceptibility of *Vibrio cholerae* O139 has changed in recent years; most isolates now are susceptible to trimethoprim-sulfamethoxazole. Antimicrobial susceptibility testing of newly isolated organisms should be determined.

ISOLATION OF THE HOSPITALIZED PATIENT: In addition to standard precautions, contact precautions are indicated for diapered or incontinent children for the duration of illness.

CONTROL MEASURES:

HYGIENE. Disinfection or boiling of water prevents transmission. Thoroughly cooking crabs, oysters, and other shellfish from the Gulf Coast before eating is recommended to decrease the likelihood of transmission. Foods such as fish, rice, or grain gruels should be refrigerated promptly after meals and thoroughly reheated before eating. Appropriate hand hygiene after defecating and before preparing or eating food is important for preventing transmission.

TREATMENT OF CONTACTS. The administration of doxycycline, tetracycline, ciprofloxacin, ofloxacin, or trimethoprim-sulfamethoxazole within 24 hours of identification of the index case may effectively prevent coprimary cases of cholera among household contacts. However, because secondary transmission of cholera is rare, chemoprophylaxis of contacts is not recommended in the United States, unless there is a high probability of fecal exposure.

VACCINE. No cholera vaccines are available in the United States. Two oral vaccines are available in other countries (WC/r BS and CVD 103 HgR). Neither vaccine has proven effectiveness in children younger than 2 years of age or against *V cholerae*. Cholera immunization is not required for travelers entering the United States from cholera-affected areas, and the World Health Organization no longer recommends immunization for travel to or from areas with cholera infection. No country requires cholera vaccine for entry.

REPORTING. Confirmed cases of cholera must be reported to health authorities in any country in which they occur or were contracted. Local and state health departments should be notified immediately of presumed or known cases of cholera attributable to *V cholerae* O1 or O139.

Other *Vibrio* Infections

CLINICAL MANIFESTATIONS: Noncholera *Vibrio* species are associated with 3 major syndromes: diarrhea, wound infection, and bacteremia. Diarrhea is the most common syndrome and is characterized by acute onset of watery stools and crampy abdominal pain. Approximately half of those afflicted will have low-grade fever, headache, and chills; approximately 30% will have vomiting. Spontaneous recovery follows in 2 to 5 days. Wound infection especially is severe in people with liver disease or who are immunocompromised. These people can develop bullous or necrotic skin lesions or die after wound infections. Primary septicemia is uncommon but can develop in immunocompromised people with preceding gastroenteritis or wound infection.

ETIOLOGY: *Vibrio* organisms are facultatively anaerobic, motile, gram-negative bacilli that are tolerant of salt. The most important noncholera *Vibrio* species associated with diarrhea are *Vibrio parahaemolyticus*, *Vibrio cholerae* non-O1, *Vibrio mimicus*, *Vibrio hollisae*, *Vibrio fluvialis*, and *Vibrio furnissii*. *Vibrio vulnificus* causes primary septicemia and severe wound infections, especially in people with immunodeficiency or liver disease. *Vibrio parahaemolyticus*, *Vibrio damsela*, and *Vibrio alginolyticus* also are associated with wound infections.

EPIDEMIOLOGY: Noncholera *Vibrio* species commonly are found in seawater. Most infections occur during summer and fall months when *Vibrio* populations in seawater are highest. Enteritis usually follows ingestion of undercooked seafood, especially oysters, crabs, and shrimp. Wound infections commonly result from exposure of abrasions to contaminated seawater or from punctures resulting from handling of contaminated shellfish. Exposure to contaminated water during natural disasters such as hurricanes has resulted in wound infections attributable to *V vulnificus*. Enteritis is not communicable person to person. People with liver disease, low gastric acidity, and immunodeficiency have increased susceptibility to infection with *Vibrio* species.

The median **incubation period** of enteritis is 23 hours, with a range of 5 to 92 hours.

DIAGNOSTIC TESTS: *Vibrio* organisms can be isolated from stool or vomitus of patients with gastroenteritis, from blood specimens, and from wound exudates. Because identification of the organism requires special techniques, laboratory personnel should be notified when infection with *Vibrio* species is suspected.

TREATMENT: Most episodes of diarrhea are mild and self-limited and do not require treatment other than oral rehydration. Antimicrobial therapy may benefit people with severe diarrhea, wound infection, or septicemia. Most organisms are susceptible to doxycycline, tetracycline, cefotaxime, fluoroquinolones, and chloramphenicol. Doxycycline should not be given to children younger than 8 years of age unless the benefits of therapy are greater than the risks of dental staining (see Antimicrobial Agents and Related Therapy, p 735). Fluoroquinolones are not approved for diarrheal disease in people younger than 18 years of age.

ISOLATION OF THE HOSPITALIZED PATIENT: In addition to standard precautions, contact precautions are recommended for diapered or incontinent children.

CONTROL MEASURES: Seafood should be cooked adequately and, if not ingested immediately, should be refrigerated. Uncooked mollusks and crustaceans should be handled with care. Abrasions suffered by ocean bathers should be rinsed with clean fresh water. All children, immunocompromised people, and people with chronic liver disease should avoid eating raw oysters or clams.

West Nile Virus

CLINICAL MANIFESTATIONS: The majority of infections attributable to West Nile virus (WNV) are asymptomatic. Approximately 20% of infected people will develop a self-limited febrile illness called West Nile fever (WNF), and fewer than 1% will develop neuroinvasive disease, such as aseptic meningitis, encephalitis, or flaccid paralysis. The risk of neuroinvasive disease increases with age and is highest among adults older than 60 years of age. Patients with WNF typically have an abrupt onset of fever, headache, myalgia, weakness, and often, abdominal pain, nausea, vomiting, or diarrhea. Some patients have a transient maculopapular rash. The acute phase of illness usually resolves within several days, but fatigue, malaise, and weakness can linger for weeks. Patients with neuroinvasive disease may present with neck stiffness and headache typical of aseptic meningitis, mental status changes indicating encephalitis, movement disorders such as tremor or Parkinsonism, seizures, or acute flaccid paralysis with or without meningitis or encephalitis. Isolated limb paralysis can occur without fever or apparent viral prodrome. Flaccid paralysis caused by WNV infection is similar clinically and pathologically to poliomyelitis caused by poliovirus, with damage of anterior horn cells, and may progress to respiratory muscle paralysis requiring mechanical ventilation. Guillain-Barré syndrome also may occur after WNV infection and can be distinguished from anterior horn cell damage by clinical manifestations and electrophysiologic testing. Cardiac dysrhythmias, myocarditis, rhabdomyolysis, optic neuritis, uveitis, chorioretinitis, orchitis, pancreatitis, and hepatitis have been described rarely after WNV infection.

Most women known to have been infected with WNV during pregnancy have delivered infants without evidence of infection or clinical abnormalities. In the single known instance of confirmed congenital WNV infection, the mother developed WNV encephalitis during the 27th week of gestation, and the infant was born with cystic destruction of cerebral tissue and chorioretinitis. One infant who apparently acquired WNV infection from human milk remained asymptomatic.

ETIOLOGY: West Nile virus is an RNA flavivirus which is related antigenically to St Louis and Japanese encephalitis viruses.

EPIDEMIOLOGY: West Nile virus is transmitted to humans primarily through the bite of infected mosquitoes. The predominant vectors worldwide are *Culex* mosquitoes, which tend to feed most avidly at dawn and dusk and breed mostly in either peri-domestic standing water with high organic content or pools created by irrigation or rainfall. Mosquitoes acquire the virus by feeding on infected birds and then transmit the virus to humans and other mammals during subsequent feeding. Viremia usually lasts fewer than 7 days in immunocompetent people, and viral concentrations in human blood are too low to effectively infect mosquitoes. However, WNV can be transmitted through transfusion of infected blood and through organ transplantation. Both intrauterine transmission and probable transmission through human milk have been described but appear to be uncommon. Percutaneous and aerosol infection has occurred in laboratory workers, and an outbreak of WNV infection among turkey handlers also raised the possibility of aerosol transmission.

The risk of severe WNV disease increases with age and may be slightly higher among males. Organ-transplant recipients also are at higher risk of severe illness. Risk of infection is higher during the warmer months, when mosquitoes are more abundant. West Nile virus transmission has been described in Europe and the Middle East, Africa, India, parts of Asia, and Australia (in the form of Kunjin virus, a subtype of WNV). West Nile virus first was detected in North America in 1999 and has spread across the continent, north into Canada, and southward into Mexico, Central America, and the Caribbean. In the United States, WNV transmission has been reported in all states except Alaska and Hawaii.

Most patients who develop WNF or aseptic meningitis recover completely. Patients with encephalitis may have residual neurologic deficits, and patients with flaccid paralysis may not recover full neuromuscular function. The case-fatality rate after neuroinvasive WNV disease is approximately 9% among adult patients and less than 1% in children.

The **incubation period** usually is 2 to 6 days but ranges from 2 to 14 days and can be up to 21 days in immunocompromised people.

DIAGNOSTIC TESTS: West Nile virus infection should be considered in the differential diagnosis of any child who presents with a febrile or acute neurologic illness and has had recent exposure to mosquitoes, blood transfusion, or organ transplantation or is born to a mother infected during pregnancy or while breastfeeding. Serum and, if indicated, cerebrospinal fluid, should be tested for WNV-specific immunoglobulin (Ig) M antibody. Enzyme immunoassays or immunofluorescent assays for WNV-specific IgM currently are available commercially or through state public health laboratories. Microsphere immunoassays are being developed at reference laboratories. Positive tests for WNV-specific IgM provide good evidence of recent WNV infection but may cross-react with antibody to other flaviviruses. Because WNV IgM can persist in some patients for more than one year, a positive WNV IgM test result occasionally may reflect past rather than recent WNV infection. Serum collected within 8 days of illness onset may not have detectable IgM and the test may need to be repeated on a later sample. Plaque-reduction neutralization tests performed in reference laboratories, including some state public health laboratories and the Centers for Disease Control and Prevention (CDC), can help determine the infecting flavivirus and can confirm acute infection by demonstrating a fourfold change in WNV-specific antibody titer between acute and convalescent serum samples collected 2 to 3 weeks apart.

Viral culture and nucleic acid amplification (NAA) tests for WNV RNA can be performed on serum, cerebrospinal fluid, and tissue specimens, and if positive, can confirm WNV infection. Immunohistochemical staining (IHC) can detect WNV antigen in unpreserved or formalin-fixed tissue. Negative results of these tests do not rule out WNV infection. Viral culture, NAA testing, and IHC can be requested through state public health laboratories or the CDC.

If WNV disease is diagnosed during pregnancy, a detailed ultrasonographic examination of the fetus should be considered 2 to 4 weeks after the onset of illness in the mother. Infants born to mothers infected during pregnancy should have either cord or infant serum tested for IgM to WNV immediately after delivery; a positive test result would suggest congenital WNV infection, although the sensitivity and specificity of this test in newborn infants are not known. In addition, infants born to mothers infected during pregnancy should be evaluated for congenital anomalies, neurologic deficits, hearing deficits, and any signs of viral infection. Infants who have clinical or laboratory evidence of congenital WNV infection should have a pediatric ophthalmologic evaluation, computerized tomography of the brain, complete blood cell count and liver function tests, and evaluation by a dysmorphologist. Examination of cerebrospinal fluid should be considered. The placenta and umbilical cord should be examined by a histopathologist and tested for evidence of WNV infection. Head circumference, physical characteristics, and developmental milestones should be evaluated throughout the first year of life. Examination of infant serum for WNV-specific IgG and IgM antibodies should be repeated at 6 months of age.

TREATMENT: Treatment of WNV disease is supportive; no specific therapy has been proven effective. Intravenous gamma globulin and plasmapheresis should be considered for patients with Guillain-Barré syndrome but not for patients with paralysis because of damage of anterior horn cells. Both ribavirin and interferon have been given to patients with WNV disease with inconclusive results. Controlled clinical trials of interferon, Immune Globulin containing high-titer WNV-specific antibodies, and anti-sense RNA translation inhibitors are underway.

ISOLATION OF THE HOSPITALIZED PATIENT: Standard precautions are recommended.

CONTROL MEASURES: WNV infection can be prevented by avoiding exposure to infected mosquitoes and screening blood and organ donors. Coordinated mosquito control programs in areas with endemic infection can reduce the abundance of mosquito vectors. People who live in areas with WNV-infected mosquitoes should apply insect repellent to skin and clothes and avoid being outdoors during peak mosquito-feeding times (usually dawn and dusk). The most effective repellent for use on the skin is diethyltoluamide (DEET) (see Prevention of Mosquitoborne Infections, p 197). Products containing DEET or permethrin also can be applied to clothing. The American Academy of Pediatrics recommends using formulations of no more than 30% DEET on infants and children and not using DEET on infants younger than 2 months of age. Screening of the blood supply in the United States has detected more than 1000 presumptive WNV-viremic donors since 2003, but blood products with low viremia still may escape detection by current screening tests.

Pregnant women should take the aforementioned precautions to avoid mosquito bites. Products containing DEET can be used in pregnancy without adverse effects. Pregnant women who develop meningitis, encephalitis, flaccid paralysis, or unexplained fever in areas of ongoing WNV transmission should be tested for WNV infection. Confirmed WNV infections should be reported to the local or state health department, and the women should be followed to determine the outcomes of their pregnancies. Although WNV probably has been transmitted through human milk, such transmission appears rare and no adverse effects on infants have been described. Because the benefits of breastfeeding seem to outweigh the risk of any WNV illness in breastfeeding infants, mothers should be encouraged to breastfeed even in areas of ongoing WNV transmission.

Two vaccines against WNV are licensed for use in horses, but human vaccines are not yet available. Other chimeric, recombinant, live-attenuated, killed, and DNA vaccines are in various stages of development.

Yersinia enterocolitica and *Yersinia pseudotuberculosis* Infections
(Enteritis and Other Illnesses)

CLINICAL MANIFESTATIONS: *Yersinia enterocolitica* causes several age-specific syndromes and a variety of other less common presentations. Infection with *Y enterocolitica* typically manifests as fever and diarrhea in young children; stool often contains leukocytes, blood, and mucus. Relapsing disease and, rarely, necrotizing enterocolitis also have been described. In older children and adults, a pseudoappendicitis syndrome (fever, abdominal pain, tenderness in the right lower quadrant of the abdomen, and leukocytosis) predominates. Bacteremia with *Y enterocolitica* most often occurs in children younger than 1 year of age and in older children with predisposing conditions, such as excessive iron storage (eg, desferrioxamine use, sickle cell disease, beta-thalassemia) and immunosuppressive states. Focal manifestations of *Y enterocolitica* are uncommon and include pharyngitis, meningitis, osteomyelitis, pyomyositis, conjunctivitis, pneumonia, empyema, endocarditis, acute peritonitis, abscesses of the liver and spleen, and primary cutaneous infection. Postinfectious sequelae with *Y enterocolitica* infection include erythema nodosum, proliferative glomerulonephritis, and reactive arthritis; these sequelae occur most often in older children and adults, particularly people with HLA-B27 antigen.

The major manifestations of *Yersinia pseudotuberculosis* infection are fever, scarlatiniform rash, and abdominal symptoms. Acute pseudoappendiceal abdominal pain is common, resulting from ileocecal mesenteric adenitis, or terminal ileitis. Other findings include diarrhea, erythema nodosum, septicemia, and sterile pleural and joint effusions. Clinical features can mimic those of Kawasaki disease.

ETIOLOGY: The genus *Yersinia* consists of 11 species of gram-negative bacilli. *Yersinia enterocolitica*, *Y pseudotuberculosis*, and *Yersinia pestis* are the 3 pathogens most commonly encountered. Fifteen pathogenic O groups of *Y enterocolitica* are recognized. Differences in virulence exist among various O groups of *Y enterocolitica;* serotype O:3 now predominates as the most common type in the United States.

EPIDEMIOLOGY: *Yersinia enterocolitica* infections are uncommon in the United States. According to the Foodborne Disease Active Surveillance Network (FoodNet), the annual incidence per 100 000 people is 9.6 for infants, 1.4 for young children, and

0.2 for other age groups. *Yersinia pseudotuberculosis* infections are even more rare. The principal reservoir of *Y enterocolitica* is swine; feral *Y pseudotuberculosis* has been isolated from ungulates (deer, elk, goats, sheep, cattle), rodents (rats, squirrels, beaver), rabbits, and many bird species. Infection with *Y enterocolitica* is believed to be transmitted by ingestion of contaminated food (raw or incompletely cooked pork products and unpasteurized milk), by contaminated surface or well water, by direct or indirect contact with animals, by transfusion with contaminated packed red blood cells, and rarely by person-to-person transmission. Bottle-fed infants can be infected if their caregivers handle raw pork intestines (chitterlings). *Yersinia enterocolitica* is isolated most often during the cool months of temperate climates. The period of communicability is unknown; organisms are excreted for an average of 2 to 3 weeks. Prolonged asymptomatic carriage is possible. Recent outbreaks of *Y pseudotuberculosis* infection in Finland have been associated with eating fresh produce, presumably contaminated by wild animals carrying the organism.

The **incubation period** typically is 4 to 6 days, varying from 1 to 14 days.

DIAGNOSTIC TESTS: *Yersinia enterocolitica* and *Yersinia pseudotuberculosis* can be recovered from stool, throat swabs, mesenteric lymph nodes, peritoneal fluid, and blood. *Yersinia enterocolitica* also has been isolated from synovial fluid, bile, urine, cerebrospinal fluid, sputum, and wounds. Stool cultures generally are positive during the first 2 weeks of illness, regardless of the nature of gastrointestinal tract manifestations. Because of the relatively low incidence of *Yersinia* infection in the United States, *Yersinia* is not routinely sought in stool specimens by most laboratories. Consequently, laboratory personnel should be notified when *Yersinia* infection is suspected. Biotyping and serotyping for further identification of pathogenic strains are available through public health reference laboratories. Infection can be confirmed by demonstrating increases in serum antibody titer after infection, but these tests generally are available only in reference or research laboratories. Cross-reactions of these antibodies with *Brucella*, *Vibrio*, *Salmonella*, and *Rickettsia* species and *Escherichia coli* lead to false-positive *Y enterocolitica* and *Y pseudotuberculosis* titers. In patients with thyroid disease, persistently increased *Y enterocolitica* antibody titers can result from antigenic similarity of the organism with antigens of the thyroid epithelial cell membrane. Characteristic ultrasonographic features demonstrating edema of the wall of the terminal ileum and cecum help to distinguish pseudoappendicitis from appendicitis and can help avoid exploratory surgery.

TREATMENT: Patients with septicemia or sites of infection other than the gastrointestinal tract and immunocompromised hosts with enterocolitis should receive antimicrobial therapy. Other than decreasing the duration of fecal excretion of *Y enterocolitica* and *Y pseudotuberculosis*, a clinical benefit of antimicrobial therapy for patients with enterocolitis, pseudoappendicitis syndrome, or mesenteric adenitis has not been established. *Yersinia enterocolitica* and *Y pseudotuberculosis* usually are susceptible to trimethoprim-sulfamethoxazole, aminoglycosides, cefotaxime, fluoroquinolones (for patients 18 years of age and older), tetracycline or doxycycline (for children 8 years of age and older), and chloramphenicol. *Yersinia enterocolitica* isolates usually are resistant to first-generation cephalosporins and most penicillins.

ISOLATION OF THE HOSPITALIZED PATIENT: In addition to standard precautions, contact precautions are indicated for diapered or incontinent children for the duration of diarrheal illness.

CONTROL MEASURES: Ingestion of uncooked meat, unpasteurized milk, or contaminated water should be avoided. People who handle raw pork intestines should not care for young children at the same time and should wash their hands thoroughly after they have finished.

Antimicrobial Agents and Related Therapy

INTRODUCTION

In some instances, antimicrobial agents are recommended for specific indications other than indications in the product label (package insert) approved by the US Food and Drug Administration (FDA). An FDA-licensed indication means that adequate and well-controlled studies were conducted and then reviewed by the FDA. However, accepted medical practice often includes drug use that is not reflected in approved drug labeling. Lack of licensing for an indication does not necessarily mean lack of effectiveness, but indicates that the appropriate studies have not been performed or data have not been submitted to the FDA for a license for that indication. Unlicensed use does not imply improper use, provided that reasonable medical evidence justifies such use and that use of the drug is deemed in the best interest of the patient. The decision to prescribe a drug resides with the physician, who must weigh risks and benefits of using the drug, regardless of whether the drug has received FDA approval for the specific indication and age of the patient. In addition, occasional drug shortages occur, which require alternative therapy (**www.fda.gov/cder/drug/shortages/ default.htm**).

Some antimicrobial agents with proven therapeutic benefit in humans are not approved by the FDA for use in pediatric patients or are considered contraindicated in children because of possible toxicity. Some of these drugs, however, such as fluoroquinolones (in people younger than 18 years of age) and tetracyclines (in children younger than 8 years of age), may be used in special circumstances after careful assessment of risks and benefits. Obtaining informed consent before use is prudent. The following information delineates general principles for use of these classes of drugs.

Fluoroquinolones

Use of fluoroquinolones (eg, ciprofloxacin, levofloxacin, lomefloxacin, gatifloxacin, gemifloxacin, moxifloxacin, ofloxacin, sparfloxacin, and trovafloxacin) generally is contraindicated, according to FDA-approved product labeling, in children and adolescents younger than 18 years of age, because fluoroquinolones have been shown to cause cartilage damage in every juvenile animal model tested at doses that approximate those needed to be therapeutic. The mechanism for this damage is unknown. Pefloxacin, a fluoroquinolone that had been used extensively in France, causes adverse musculoskeletal effects in children and adults and is not available in the United States.

Ciprofloxacin and levofloxacin are the fluoroquinolones that have been used most extensively in children and adolescents. On the basis of limited experience, these drugs appear to be well tolerated, do not appear to cause arthropathy, and are effective as oral agents for treating a number of diseases in children that otherwise would require parenteral therapy. Accordingly, in special circumstances after careful assessment of the risks and benefits for the individual patient, use of a fluoroquinolone can be justified. Circumstances in which fluoroquinolones may be useful include those in which (1) parenteral therapy is not feasible and no other effective oral agent is available; and (2) infection is caused by multidrug-resistant pathogens, such as certain *Pseudomonas* and *Mycobacterium* strains, for which there is no other effective oral agent available. The only indications for which a fluoroquinolone is approved by the FDA for use in patients younger than 18 years of age are complicated urinary tract infection, pyelonephritis, and postexposure treatment for inhalation anthrax. Possible uses, accordingly, include the following*:

- Exposure to aerosolized *Bacillus anthracis* to decrease the incidence or progression of disease (FDA licensed)
- Urinary tract infections caused by *Pseudomonas aeruginosa* or other multidrug-resistant, gram-negative bacteria (FDA licensed for complicated *Escherichia coli* urinary tract infections and pyelonephritis attributable to *E coli* in patients 1–17 years of age)
- Chronic suppurative otitis media or malignant otitis externa caused by *P aeruginosa*
- Chronic or acute osteomyelitis or osteochondritis caused by *P aeruginosa* (not for prophylaxis of nail puncture wounds to the foot)
- Exacerbation of pulmonary disease in patients with cystic fibrosis who have colonization with *P aeruginosa* and who can be treated in an ambulatory setting
- Mycobacterial infections caused by isolates known to be susceptible to fluoroquinolones
- Gram-negative bacterial infections in immunocompromised hosts in which oral therapy is desired or resistance to alternative agents is present
- Gastrointestinal tract infection caused by multidrug-resistant *Shigella* species, *Salmonella* species, *Vibrio cholerae*, or *Campylobacter jejuni*
- Documented bacterial septicemia or meningitis attributable to organisms with in vitro resistance to approved agents or in immunocompromised infants and children who have failed to respond to parenteral therapy with other appropriate antimicrobial agents
- Serious infections attributable to fluoroquinolone-susceptible pathogen(s) in children with life-threatening allergy to alternative agents

If use of a fluoroquinolone is recommended for a patient younger than 18 years of age, the risks and benefits should be explained to the patients and parents. Inappropriate use of fluoroquinolones in children and adults is likely to be associated with increasing resistance to these agents.

Tetracyclines

Use of tetracyclines in pediatric patients has been limited, because these drugs can cause permanent dental discoloration in children younger than 8 years of age. Studies have documented that tetracyclines and their colored degradation products that are bound to teeth are observed in the dentin and incorporated diffusely in the enamel. The period of odontogenesis to completion of formation of enamel in permanent

---

* American Academy of Pediatrics, Committee on Infectious Diseases. The use of systemic fluoroquinolones. *Pediatrics.* 2006; in press

teeth appears to be the critical time for the effects of these drugs and virtually is complete by 8 years of age, at which time the drug can be given without concern for dental staining. The degree of staining appears to depend on dosage and duration of therapy, with the total dosage received being the most important factor. In addition to dental discoloration, tetracyclines also may cause enamel hypoplasia and reversible delay in rate of bone growth.

These possible adverse events have resulted in use of alternative, equally effective antimicrobial agents in most circumstances in young children in which tetracyclines are likely to be effective. However, in some cases, the benefits of therapy with a tetracycline can exceed the risks, particularly if alternative drugs are associated with significant adverse effects or may be less effective. In these cases, the use of tetracyclines in young children is justified. Examples include life-threatening rickettsial infections such as Rocky Mountain spotted fever (see p 570), ehrlichiosis (see p 281), cholera (see p 725), and anthrax (see p 208). Doxycycline usually is the agent of choice in children with these infections, because the risk of dental staining is less with this product than with other tetracyclines. In addition, the drug is given only twice a day, in contrast to the more frequent dosing regimens of other tetracyclines.

······································
APPROPRIATE USE OF ANTIMICROBIAL AGENTS

The increasing prevalence of antimicrobial resistance is an issue of major concern to patients as well as health care professionals. Rarely, highly resistant pathogens, such as *Burkholderia cepacia; Staphylococcus aureus;* extended-spectrum, beta-lactamase–producing, gram-negative bacilli; or *Enterococcus faecium* are susceptible to only one available agent. More commonly, the presence of resistant pathogens complicates therapy, increases expense, and makes treatment failure more likely. Resistant foodborne pathogens, such as fluoroquinolone-resistant *Campylobacter jejuni;* community-acquired pathogens, such as drug-resistant *Streptococcus pneumoniae* and some strains of methicillin-resistant *S aureus;* and hospital-acquired pathogens, such as vancomycin-resistant enterococci, have unique epidemiologic features and require specific control measures. Control of antimicrobial resistance among foodborne pathogens has focused on measures such as irradiating food products before consumption and decreasing addition of antimicrobial agents to animal feed. Among community-acquired and hospital-acquired pathogens, overuse of antimicrobial agents in humans largely is responsible for the increase in resistance. The following principles for appropriate use of antimicrobial agents have become a central focus of public health measures to combat the spread of resistant organisms. Application of these principles has led to a decrease in number of prescriptions written for antimicrobial agents. Additional information is available at **www.cdc.gov/getsmart**.

Principles of Appropriate Use for Upper Respiratory Tract Infections

Approximately three fourths of all outpatient prescriptions for children are given for 5 conditions: otitis media, sinusitis, cough illness/bronchitis, pharyngitis, and nonspecific upper respiratory tract infection (the common cold). Physicians report that many patients and parents try to persuade them to dispense unnecessary antimicrobial agents. Children treated with an antimicrobial agent are at increased risk of becoming carriers of resistant bacteria, including *S pneumoniae* and *Haemophilus influenzae*. Carriers of a resistant strain who develop illness from that strain are more likely to have antimicrobial therapy failure. In some conditions, such as otitis media with effusion, observation without antimicrobial therapy is recommended, and in other conditions such as the common cold or cough, antimicrobial therapy is not indicated. The following principles, with detailed supporting evidence, were published by the American Academy of Pediatrics, American Academy of Family Physicians, and Centers for Disease Control and Prevention (CDC) to identify clinical conditions for which antimicrobial therapy could be curtailed without compromising patient care.[*]

OTITIS MEDIA

- Episodes of otitis media should be classified as acute otitis media (AOM) or otitis media with effusion (OME).
- Antimicrobial agents are indicated for treatment of AOM; however, diagnosis requires a history of acute onset, evidence of middle ear effusion, *and* signs or symptoms of inflammation of the middle ear. Observation without use of an antimicrobial agent in a child with uncomplicated AOM is an option for selected children on the basis of diagnostic certainty, age, illness severity, and assurance of follow-up.[†]
- Acute otitis media can be treated with a 5- to 7-day course of an antimicrobial agent, generally amoxicillin, in most children 6 years of age or older with mild to moderate disease. Younger children and children with underlying medical conditions, craniofacial abnormalities, chronic or recurrent otitis media, or perforation of the tympanic membrane should be treated with a standard 10-day course.[‡] A narrow-spectrum antimicrobial agent (eg, amoxicillin, 80–90 mg/kg per day in 2 divided doses) should be used for initial episodes of AOM in most children.
- For children who have failed amoxicillin therapy, beta-lactamase–producing *H influenzae* or *Moraxella catarrhalis* must be considered. Use of amoxicillin clavulanate 14:1 (80–90 mg/kg per day amoxicillin component in 2 divided doses) or a cephalosporin (oral cefdinir, cefuroxime, cefpodoxime, or parenteral ceftriaxone, 50 mg/kg once daily for 3 days, intramuscularly) is considered.
- Persistent middle ear effusion (OME) for 2 to 3 months after therapy for AOM is expected and does not require retreatment.

---

[*] Dowell SF, Marcy SM, Phillips WR, Gerber MA, Schwartz B. Principles of judicious use of antimicrobial agents for pediatric upper respiratory tract infections. *Pediatrics*. 1998;101:S163–S165; and Dowell SF, Schwartz B, Phillips WR. Appropriate use of antibiotics for URIs in children: part II. Cough, pharyngitis and the common cold. The Pediatric URI Consensus Team. *Am Fam Phys*. 1998;58:1335–1342, 1345

[†] American Academy of Pediatrics and American Academy of Family Physicians, Subcommittee on Management of Acute Otitis Media. Clinical practice guideline: diagnosis and management of acute otitis media. *Pediatrics*. 2004;113:1451–1465

[‡] American Academy of Family Physicians, American Academy of Otolaryngology-Head and Neck Surgery, and American Academy of Pediatrics, Subcommittee on Otitis Media With Effusion. Clinical practice guideline: otitis media with effusion. *Pediatrics*. 2004;113:1412–1429

- Antimicrobial agents are not indicated for initial treatment of OME; treatment for 10 to 14 days may be considered an option if effusions persist for 3 months or more when a caregiver expresses a strong aversion to impending surgery. Repetitive or prolonged courses of antimicrobial agents are not recommended.
- Antimicrobial prophylaxis is recommended by some experts for control of recurrent AOM, defined as 3 or more distinct and well-documented episodes in 6 months or 4 or more episodes in 12 months.

ACUTE SINUSITIS

- Clinical diagnosis of acute bacterial sinusitis requires the presence of nasal or post-nasal discharge (of any quality) without improvement for 10 to 14 days, with or without daytime cough (cough may be worse at night); or temperature of ≥39°C [≥102°F] and purulent nasal discharge present concurrently for at least 3 consecutive days in a child who seems ill.
- The common cold is a viral rhinosinusitis that often includes radiologic evidence of sinus involvement; radiographs, therefore, should be used only in selected circumstances and should be interpreted with caution. Computed tomography of sinuses may be indicated when symptoms of sinusitis are persistent or recurrent or when complications are suspected.
- Initial antimicrobial treatment of acute sinusitis should be with a narrow-spectrum agent (eg, amoxicillin at 80–90 mg/kg per day in 2 divided doses) for most children.

COUGH ILLNESS/BRONCHITIS

- Nonspecific cough illness/bronchitis in children, regardless of duration, does not warrant antimicrobial treatment.
- Prolonged cough (>10–14 days) may be caused by *Bordetella pertussis, Bordetella parapertussis, Mycoplasma pneumoniae,* and *Chlamydophila pneumoniae.* When infection caused by these organisms is suspected clinically or is confirmed, appropriate antimicrobial therapy is indicated (see Pertussis, p 498, and *Mycoplasma pneumoniae* Infections, p 468). Children with underlying chronic pulmonary disease other than asthma (eg, cystic fibrosis) may benefit from antimicrobial therapy for acute exacerbations.

PHARYNGITIS

(See Group A Streptococcal Infections, p 610)
- Diagnosis of group A streptococcal pharyngitis should be made on the basis of results of appropriate laboratory tests in conjunction with clinical and epidemiologic findings.
- Most cases of pharyngitis are viral in origin. Antimicrobial therapy should not be given to a child with pharyngitis in the absence of identified group A streptococci. Rarely, other bacteria may cause pharyngitis (eg, *Corynebacterium diphtheriae, Francisella tularensis,* groups G and C hemolytic streptococci, *Neisseria gonorrhoeae, Arcanobacterium haemolyticum*), and treatment should be provided according to recommendations in disease-specific chapters in Section 3.
- Penicillin remains the drug of choice for treating group A streptococcal pharyngitis.

THE COMMON COLD

- Antimicrobial agents should not be given for the common cold.
- Mucopurulent rhinitis (thick, opaque, or discolored nasal discharge) commonly accompanies the common cold and is not an indication for antimicrobial treatment unless it persists without signs of improvement for 10 to 14 days, suggesting possible acute bacterial sinusitis.

Principles of Appropriate Use of Vancomycin*

Although reported infrequently, vancomycin-intermediately susceptible and vancomycin-resistant strains of *S aureus* also have emerged. A major risk factor for emergence of vancomycin-resistant enterococci and vancomycin-intermediately susceptible or vancomycin-resistant *S aureus* has been increased use of vancomycin, particularly among patients receiving hematology-oncology, nephrology, neonatology, cardiac surgery, and neurosurgery services. Prevention of further emergence of vancomycin resistance will depend on more appropriate use of vancomycin.

SITUATIONS IN WHICH USE OF VANCOMYCIN IS APPROPRIATE INCLUDE THE FOLLOWING:

- Treatment of serious infections attributable to beta-lactam–resistant gram-positive organisms
- Treatment of infections attributable to gram-positive microorganisms in patients with serious allergy to beta-lactam agents
- Antimicrobial-associated colitis that fails to respond to metronidazole therapy or colitis that is severe and potentially life threatening (see *Clostridium difficile*, p 261)
- Prophylaxis, as recommended by the American Heart Association, for endocarditis after certain procedures in patients at high risk of endocarditis (see Prevention of Bacterial Endocarditis, p 828)
- Prophylaxis for major surgical procedures involving implantation of prosthetic materials or devices at institutions with a high rate of infections attributable to methicillin-resistant *S aureus* or methicillin-resistant coagulase-negative staphylococci.

SITUATIONS IN WHICH THE USE OF VANCOMYCIN SHOULD BE DISCOURAGED:

- Routine prophylaxis for the following:
  - Surgical patients other than patients with a life-threatening allergy to beta-lactam antimicrobial agents
  - Very low birth weight infants
  - Patients receiving continuous ambulatory peritoneal dialysis or hemodialysis
  - Preventing infection or colonization of indwelling central or peripheral intravascular catheters (either systemic or antibiotic lock)
- Empiric antimicrobial therapy for a febrile neutropenic patient, unless strong evidence indicates an infection attributable to gram-positive microorganisms and the prevalence of infections attributable to methicillin-resistant *S aureus* in the hospital is substantial

---

* Recommendations for preventing the spread of vancomycin resistance. Recommendations of the Hospital Infection Control Practices Advisory Committee. *MMWR Recomm Rep.* 1995;44(RR-12):1–13

- Treatment in response to a single positive result of a blood culture for coagulase-negative staphylococcus, if other blood culture results obtained in the same period are negative
- Continued empiric use for presumed infections in patients whose culture results are negative for beta-lactam–resistant, gram-positive microorganisms
- Selective decontamination of the digestive tract
- Attempted eradication of methicillin-resistant *S aureus* colonization
- Primary treatment of antimicrobial-associated colitis (see *Clostridium difficile*, p 261)
- Treatment of infections attributable to beta-lactam–susceptible gram-positive micro-organisms, including vancomycin given for dosing convenience in patients with renal failure
- Topical application or irrigation

Prevention of Antimicrobial Resistance in Health Care Settings

The CDC has initiated a campaign designed to highlight the importance of antimicrobial resistance and to engage clinicians, health care facilities, and patients in efforts to prevent resistance and promote safer care. The Campaign to Prevent Antimicrobial Resistance focuses on 4 integrated strategies: preventing infection, diagnosing and treating infection effectively, using antimicrobial agents wisely, and preventing transmission. Additional information about the campaign is available at **www.cdc.gov/drugresistance/healthcare/**.

··

DRUG INTERACTIONS

The use of multiple drugs for therapy of seriously ill patients ensures that drug-drug interactions are inevitable. Drug-drug interactions (see Table 4.1, p 743) can be considered as producing either changes in drug concentrations (pharmacokinetics) or changes in the drug effect/toxicity profile (pharmacodynamics). Pharmacokinetics refers to the ways the body manipulates a drug, including absorption, distribution, metabolism, and excretion. Pharmacokinetic interactions result from alterations in the absorption, distribution, metabolism, or elimination of a drug and thereby result in a change in concentration in the body. Pharmacodynamics refers to the biochemical and physiologic effects of the drug and its mechanism of action. Pharmacodynamic drug-drug interactions act on target tissues and fluids and may produce synergistic, additive, or antagonistic drug effects or toxicities. Many of the serious adverse interactions between drugs are attributable to moderate or potent inhibition (clarithromycin, ciprofloxacin, erythromycin, fluconazole, itraconazole, ketoconazole, norfloxacin, telithromycin, and voriconazole) or induction (rifabutin, rifampin) of cytochrome P450 (CYP), especially CYP3A, which is thought to be involved in metabolism of more than 50% of prescribed drugs.* A drug is considered a potent CYP3A inhibitor if it causes more than a fivefold increase in the plasma concentration of another drug that is primarily dependent on CYP3A for its metabolism.

---

* CYP3A and drug interactions. *Med Lett Drugs Ther.* 2005;47:54–55

The purpose of this section is to outline pharmacokinetic and pharmacodynamic interactions focusing primarily on antimicrobial agents. Interactions among antiretroviral drugs as well as interactions between antiretroviral drugs and other medications that may be administered to people infected with human immunodeficiency virus (HIV) are beyond the scope of this section but can be found in other publications.[*][†] The field of antiretroviral drug-drug interactions is changing rapidly, and readers are advised always to consult the most up-to-date references. The Centers for Disease Control and Prevention has posted recommendations and guidelines on its Web site (**www.cdc.gov/hiv/pubs/guidelines.htm**). This resource is updated continually and contains information on adverse effects of antiretroviral agents, including information on interactions. Other valuable sources of information are available in print and online.[‡]

A few general considerations follow:

- Drug metabolism interactions occur because of inhibition or induction of drug-metabolizing enzymes found in the liver and enterocytes in the epithelium of the small intestine. Physicians should be alert to possible drug interactions whenever drugs are prescribed from classes that include potent or moderate inhibitors or inducers of CYP3A (antiretroviral, antifungal, macrolide, rifampin, and fluoroquinolone compounds).

- For infants, children, and adolescents, the metabolic capacity of the liver can vary from less than 10% to greater than 160% of adult values, depending on age and the enzyme in question. Therefore, interactions listed may be of a greater or lesser magnitude in children.

- Renal interactions may be the result of a drug causing alterations in glomerular filtration or inhibition of tubular secretion, leading to unexpected serum concentrations of other drugs that are handled by the kidney.

- Drugs often are used in combination to exert additive or synergistic effects. Some drugs, however, should not be combined because of toxicity. If possible, medications with similar toxicities should be avoided. The Department of Health and Human Services has made available both published and online information regarding toxicities associated with antiretroviral drugs and other medications used in the treatment of HIV-infected people (**www.aidsinfo.nih.gov**).

- Therapeutic drug monitoring, if available, may be a useful clinical tool to ensure that safe and effective concentrations of both anti-infective drugs and other coadministered medications are achieved.

---

* Centers for Disease Control and Prevention. Treating Opportunistic Infections Among HIV-Exposed and Infected Children: Recommendations from CDC, the National Institutes of Health, and the Infectious Diseases Society of America. *MMWR Recomm Rep.* 2004;53(RR-14):1–92

† Centers for Disease Control and Prevention. Treating Opportunistic Infections Among HIV-Infected Adults and Adolescents: Recommendations from CDC, the National Institutes of Health, and the HIV Medicine Association/Infectious Diseases Society of America. *MMWR Recomm Rep.* 2004;53(RR-15):1–112

‡ **www.medscape.com/druginfo/druginterchecker?cid = med** (requires user name and password); Hansten PD, Horn JR. Cytochrome P450 enzymes and drug interactions, table of cytochrome P450 substrates, inhibitors, inducers and P-glycoprotein. In: *The Top 100 Drug Interactions: A Guide to Patient Management.* Edmonds, WA: H&H Publications; 2005; American Hospital Formulary Service. *AHFS Drug Information 2006.* Bethesda, MD: American Society of Health-System Pharmacists Inc; 2006; *Clinical Pharmacology Online.* Tampa, FL: Gold Standard; 2005. Available at: **www.cp.gsm.com/**; Flockhart DA. Cytochrome P450 drug interaction (online). Available at: **http://medicine.iupui.edu/flockhart/**; The Medical Letter Inc. *The Medical Letter Handbook of Adverse Drug Interactions.* New Rochelle, NY; The Medical Letter Inc. Available at: **www.medletter.com**

Table 4.1. Adverse Drug Interactions Involving Antimicrobial Agents

The most commonly reported drug interactions (including drugs that may not be approved by the US Food and Drug Administration [FDA] for use in children) are listed in this table; references provided (see footnote) can provide complete interactions. Many interactions have been described only for one agent in a class of drugs but are suspected to occur with other agents in that class, although published cases of documented interactions or reported data on file at the FDA may not exist for specific drugs. As with all drug therapy, the risks and benefits should be considered by the prescribing physician.

Antimicrobial Agent	Interacting Drug(s)	Adverse Effect
Amantadine	Anticholinergics[1]	Additive anticholinergic toxicity
	Bupropion	Additive neurotoxicity
Amikacin (see Aminoglycosides[2])		
Aminoglycosides		
Parenteral	Amphotericin B, acyclovir, ganciclovir, foscarnet, cyclosporine, other nephrotoxins[3]	Additive nephrotoxicity
	Indomethacin	Increase aminoglycoside concentrations
	Carboplatin/cisplatin, furosemide	Additive ototoxicity
Oral	Methotrexate (oral)	Decrease methotrexate concentrations
Amphotericin B	Aminoglycosides,[2] acyclovir, ganciclovir, foscarnet, cyclosporine, other nephrotoxins[3]	Additive nephrotoxicity
	Cisplatin, corticosteroids, diuretics	Additive hypokalemia
Ampicillin	Allopurinol	Increase incidence of rash
Atovaquone	Metoclopramide, rifamycins, tetracycline	Decrease atovaquone concentrations
Caspofungin	Cyclosporine	Increase caspofungin concentrations
		Additive hepatotoxicity
	Tacrolimus, sirolimus	Decrease tacrolimus/sirolimus concentrations
	Rifampin, phenytoin	Decrease caspofungin concentrations
Cefoperazone, cefotetan	Ethanol	Antabuse-like effect

Table 4.1. Adverse Drug Interactions Involving Antimicrobial Agents, continued

Antimicrobial Agent	Interacting Drug(s)	Adverse Effect
Cefpodoxime (oral), cefuroxime (oral)	Antacids, H_2 antagonists,[4] proton pump inhibitors (PPI)[5]	Decrease antimicrobial concentrations
Ceftriaxone	Cyclosporine	Increase cyclosporine concentrations
Chloramphenicol	Cyclosporine, warfarin	Increase concentrations of interacting drug
	Barbiturates	Increase barbiturate concentrations
		Decrease chloramphenicol concentrations
	Phenytoin	Increase phenytoin concentrations, increase or decrease chloramphenicol concentrations
	Rifampin	Decrease chloramphenicol concentrations
Ciprofloxacin and other quinolones	Clozapine, cyclosporine, diazepam, methadone, theophylline, olanzapine, phenytoin, warfarin	Increase concentrations of interacting drug
	Foscarnet	Additive seizure toxicity
	Antacids, bismuth, calcium, iron, sucralfate, zinc	Decrease quinolone concentrations
	Ziprasidone	Additive cardiotoxicity
Clarithromycin (see Erythromycin)		
Clindamycin	Neuromuscular blocking agents	Increase neuromuscular blockade
	Cyclosporine	Decrease cyclosporine concentrations
Oral	Kaolin-pectin	Decrease antimicrobial concentrations
Dapsone	Rifampin	Decrease dapsone concentrations
	Fluconazole, trimethoprim	Increase dapsone concentrations
	Folic acid antagonists	Additive hematologic toxicity

Table 4.1. Adverse Drug Interactions Involving Antimicrobial Agents, continued

Antimicrobial Agent	Interacting Drug(s)	Adverse Effect
Doxycycline	Barbiturates, carbamazepine, phenytoin, rifamycins	Decrease doxycycline concentrations
	Methotrexate	Increase methotrexate concentrations
Erythromycin,[6] clarithromycin[6]	Azole antifungals, clozapine, theophylline, valproic acid	Increase concentrations of interacting drug
	Ketoconazole	Increase concentrations of interacting drug
	Rifamycins, theophylline, caffeine	Decrease antimicrobial concentrations
	Droperidol, pimozide, quinolones, ziprasidone	Additive cardiotoxicity
Fluconazole[6,7]	Amitriptyline, caffeine, dapsone, nortriptyline	Increase concentrations of interacting drug
	Ketoconazole, voriconazole	Increase concentrations of interacting drug
	Quinolones	Additive cardiotoxicity
	Losartan	Decrease losartan activity
Gentamicin (see Aminoglycosides[2])		
Griseofulvin	Barbiturates	Decrease griseofulvin concentrations
Imipenem	Cyclosporine, ganciclovir, theophylline	Additive neurotoxicity
Itraconazole (see Ketoconazole)		
Isoniazid	Acetaminophen, carbamazepine, rifampin	Additive hepatotoxicity
	Aluminum-containing antacids	Decrease isoniazid concentrations
	Cycloserine	Dizziness, drowsiness
	Carbamazepine, primidone, theophylline, valproate, voriconazole	Increase concentrations of interacting drug
	Voriconazole	Increase concentrations of interacting drug

Table 4.1. Adverse Drug Interactions Involving Antimicrobial Agents, continued

Antimicrobial Agent	Interacting Drug(s)	Adverse Effect
	Itraconazole, ketoconazole	Decrease concentrations of interacting drug
	Atomoxetine, linezolid, meperidine	Additive monoamine oxidase (MAO) inhibition toxicity
	Selective serotonin reuptake inhibitors (SSRIs),[8] tramadol	Possible serotonin syndrome
	Losartan	Decrease losartan activity
Ketoconazole (Itraconazole)	Alprazolam, buspirone, busulfan, calcium-channel blockers,[9] carbamazepine, colchicine, corticosteroids, cyclophosphamide, cylosporine, diazepam, digoxin, ergotamine, fentanyl, fexofenadine, irinotecan, methadone, midazolam, nefazodone, pimozide, quinidine, rifabutin, sertraline, sirolimus, statins, tacrolimus, taxanes, vinca-alkaloids, warfarin, ziprasidone, zolpidem	Increase concentrations of interacting drug
	Antacids, H_2 antagonists,[4] PPI,[5] sucralfate	Decrease antimicrobial concentrations, itraconazole oral solution less affected
	Barbiturates, carbamazepine, phenytoin, rifamycins,	Decrease antimicrobial concentrations
	Erythromycin, quinolones, ziprasidone	Increase concentrations of interacting drugs with possible increased cardiotoxicity
	Ethanol	Antabuse-like reaction
	Loratadine, haloperidol, phenytoin	Increase concentrations of interacting drug
Linezolid	Isoniazid	Additive MAO inhibition toxicity
	SSRIs,[8] tramadol	Possible serotonin syndrome

Table 4.1. Adverse Drug Interactions Involving Antimicrobial Agents, continued

Antimicrobial Agent	Interacting Drug(s)	Adverse Effect
Metronidazole	Ethanol	Antabuse-like reaction
	Losartan	Decrease losartan activity
	Busulfan, carbamazepine, fluconazole, fluorouracil, phenytoin, voriconazole, warfarin	Increase concentrations of interacting drug
	Barbiturates	Decrease metronidazole concentrations
Quinupristin/dalfopristin	Ketaconazole[6]	Increase concentrations of interacting drug
Nafcillin	Cyclosporine	Increase or decrease cyclosporine concentrations
	Calcium-channel blockers[9]	Decrease concentrations of interacting drug
	Warfarin	Warfarin resistance
Penicillins	Methotrexate	Increase methotrexate concentrations
Rifampin, rifabutin	Alprazolam, amiodarone, atovaquone, azole antifungals, barbiturates, beta-adrenergic blockers, buspirone, celecoxib, calcium-channel blockers,[9] chloramphenicol, clarithromycin, clozapine, oral contraceptives, corticosteroids, caspofungin, cyclosporine, dapsone, diazepam, digoxin, doxycycline, erythromycin, fexofenadine, haloperidol, lamotrigine, losartan, methadone, midazolam, ondansetron, phenytoin, sertraline, sirolimus, SSRIs,[8] statins,[10] sulfonylureas, tacrolimus	Decrease concentrations of interacting drug
	Isoniazid	Increase hepatotoxicity
	Methadone, morphine	Decrease concentrations of interacting drug

Table 4.1. Adverse Drug Interactions Involving Antimicrobial Agents, continued

Antimicrobial Agent	Interacting Drug(s)	Adverse Effect
Streptomycin (see Aminoglycosides[2])		
Trimethoprim-sulfamethoxazole (TMP-SMX)	Cyclosporine, losartan	Decrease concentrations of interacting drug
	Methotrexate	Additive hematologic toxicity
	Rifamycins	Decrease TMP-SMX concentrations
	Celecoxib, dapsone, digoxin, fluoxetine, fluvastatin, methotrexate, nonsteroidal anti-inflammatory drugs, phenytoin, procainamide, sulfonylureas, voriconazole, warfarin	Increase concentrations of interacting drug
	Angiotensin-converting enzyme (ACE) inhibitors[11]	Hyperkalemia
Terbinafine	Cyclosporine	Decrease cyclosporine concentrations
	Amphetamine, fluoxetine, haloperidol, metoclopramide, metoprolol, phenothiazines, propranolol, risperidone, tricyclic antidepressants, venlafaxine	Increase concentrations of interacting drug
	Codeine, tramadol	Decrease effects of interacting drug
	Rifampin	Decrease terbinafine concentrations
Telithromycin	Ketoconazole, metoprolol	Increase concentrations of interacting drug
Tetracyclines	Antacids, bismuth, iron, sucralfate, zinc	Decrease tetracycline concentrations
	Methotrexate	Increase methotrexate toxicity
	Lithium	Increase lithium toxicity

Table 4.1. Adverse Drug Interactions Involving Antimicrobial Agents, continued

Antimicrobial Agent	Interacting Drug(s)	Adverse Effect
Tobramycin (see Aminoglycosides[2])		
Vancomycin	Other nephrotoxins[3]	Increase nephrotoxicity
	Indomethacin	Increase vancomycin concentrations
Voriconazole[6]	Celecoxib, fluoxetine, fluvastatin, ibuprofen, irbesartan, naproxen, phenytoin, sulfonylureas, warfarin	Increase concentrations of interacting drug
	Ketoconazole	Increase concentrations of interacting drug
	Phenobarbital	Decrease voriconazole concentrations

[1] Anticholinergics (or drugs with anticholinergic activity) include: amantadine, anisotropine, atropine, belladonna, clidinium, dicyclomine, diphenhydramine, glycopyrrolate, homatropine, hyoscyamine, methantheline, promethazine, propantheline, and scopolamine.

[2] Gentamicin, tobramycin, amikacin, and streptomycin.

[3] Potentially nephrotoxic drugs include: aminoglycosides, acyclovir, ganciclovir, foscarnet, ACE inhibitors, cyclosporine, diuretics, nonsteroidal anti-inflammatory drugs, contrast agents, tacrolimus, tenofovir, and vancomycin.

[4] Cimetidine, famotidine, nizatidine, and ranitidine.

[5] Pantoprazole, rabeprazole, omeprazole, lansoprazole, and esomeprazole.

[6] Antimicrobial agent is known to have or is expected to have the same interactions as ketoconazole because of similar inhibition of CYP3A4 and/or 2C19 drug metabolism.

[7] Antimicrobial agent is known to have or is expected to have the same interactions as voriconazole because of similar inhibition of CYP2C9 drug metabolism.

[8] Escitalopram and citalopram.

[9] Amlodipine, bepridil, diltiazem, felodipine, isradipine, nicardipine, nifedipine, nimodipine, and verapamil.

[10] Lovastatin, simvastatin, pravastatin, fluvastatin, rosuvastatin, and atorvastatin.

[11] Benazepril, captopril, lisinopril, moexipril, perindopril, quinapril, ramipril, and trandolapril.

References: Hansten PD, Horn JR. *The Top 100 Drug Interactions. A Guide to Patient Management.* Washington, DC: H&H Publications; 2000; Kim RB. *The Medical Letter Handbook of Adverse Drug Reactions.* New York, NY: The Medical Record Inc; 2001; *AHFS Drug Information 2005.* Bethesda, MD: American Society of Hospital Pharmacists Inc; 2005

TABLES OF ANTIBACTERIAL DRUG DOSAGES

Recommended dosages for antimicrobial agents commonly used for newborn infants (see Table 4.2, p 751) and for older infants and children (see Table 4.3, p 753) are given separately because of the physiologic immaturity of the newborn infant and resulting different pharmacokinetics. The table for newborn infants is divided by postnatal age and birth weight because of age-related differences in pharmacokinetics.

Recommended dosages are not absolute and are intended only as a guide. Clinical judgment about the disease, alterations in renal or hepatic function, coadministration of other drugs, and other factors affecting pharmacokinetics, patient response, and laboratory results may dictate modifications of these recommendations in an individual patient. In some cases, monitoring of serum drug concentrations is recommended to avoid toxicity and to ensure therapeutic efficacy.

Product label information should be consulted for details, such as the diluent for reconstitution of injectable preparations, measures to be taken to avoid incompatibilities, drug interactions, and other precautions.

Table 4.2. Antibacterial Drugs for Newborn Infants: Dose[1] (mg/kg or U/kg) and Frequency of Administration

Drug	Route	Infants 0–4 wk of age BW <1200 g	Infants <1 wk of age BW 1200–2000 g	Infants <1 wk of age BW >2000 g	Infants ≥1 wk of age BW 1200–2000 g	Infants ≥1 wk of age BW >2000 g
Aminoglycosides[2,3]						
Amikacin	IV, IM	7.5 every 18–24 h	7.5 every 12 h	7.5–10 every 12 h	7.5–10 every 8 or 12 h	10 every 8 h
Gentamicin	IV, IM	2.5 every 18–24 h	2.5 every 12 h	2.5 every 12 h	2.5 every 8 or 12 h	2.5 every 8 h
Neomycin	PO only	. . .	25 every 6 h	25 every 6 h	25 every 6 h	25 every 6 h
Tobramycin	IV, IM	2.5 every 18–24 h	2.5 every 12 h	2.5 every 12 h	2.5 every 8 or 12 h	2.5 every 8 h
Antistaphylococcal penicillins[4]						
Methicillin	IV, IM	25 every 12 h	25–50 every 12 h	25–50 every 8 h	25–50 every 8 h	25–50 every 6 h
Nafcillin	IV, IM	25 every 12 h	25 every 12 h	25 every 8 h	25 every 8 h	25–35 every 6 h
Oxacillin	IV, IM	25 every 12 h	25–50 every 12 h	25–50 every 8 h	25–50 every 8 h	25–50 every 6 h
Monobactam						
Aztreonam	IV, IM	30 every 12 h	30 every 12 h	30 every 8 h	30 every 8 h	30 every 6 h
Carbapenems[5]						
Imipenem/cilastatin	IV	25 every 12 h	25 every 12 h	25 every 12 h	25 every 8 h	25 every 8 h
Cephalosporins						
Cefotaxime	IV, IM	50 every 12 h	50 every 12 h	50 every 8 or 12 h	50 every 8 h	50 every 6 or 8 h
Ceftazidime	IV, IM	50 every 12 h	50 every 12 h	50 every 8 or 12 h	50 every 8 h	50 every 8 h
Ceftriaxone[6]	IV, IM	50 every 24 h	50 every 24 h	50 every 24 h	50 every 24 h	50–75 every 24 h

Table 4.2. Antibacterial Drugs for Newborn Infants: Dose[1] (mg/kg or U/kg) and Frequency of Administration, continued

| Drug | Route | Infants 0–4 wk of Age | Infants <1 wk of age | | Infants ≥1 wk of age | |
		BW <1200 g	BW 1200–2000 g	BW >2000 g	BW 1200–2000 g	BW >2000 g
Clindamycin	IV, IM, PO	5 every 12 h	5 every 12 h	5 every 8 h	5 every 8 h	5–7.5 every 6 h
Erythromycin	PO	10 every 12 h	10 every 12 h	10 every 12 h	10 every 8 h	10 every 8 h
Metronidazole[5]	IV, PO	7.5 every 24–48 h	7.5 every 24 h	7.5 every 12 h	7.5 every 12 h	15 every 12 h
Oxazolidinone						
Linezolid	IV	10 every 8–12 h[7]	10 every 8–12 h[7]	10 every 8–12 h[7]	10 every 8 h	10 every 8 h
Penicillins						
Ampicillin[4]	IV, IM	25–50 every 12 h	25–50 every 12 h	25–50 every 8 h	25–50 every 8 h	25–50 every 6 h
Penicillin G,[4] aqueous	IV, IM	25 000–50 000 U every 12 h	25 000–50 000 U every 12 h	25 000–50 000 U every 8 h	25 000–50 000 U every 8 h	25 000–50 000 U every 6 h
Penicillin G procaine	IM	…	50 000 U every 24 h	50 000 U every 24 h	50 000 U every 24 h	50 000 U every 24 h
Ticarcillin[8]	IV, IM	75 every 12 h	75 every 12 h	75 every 8 h	75 every 8 h	100 every 8 h
Vancomycin[2]	IV	15 every 24 h	10–15 every 12–18 h	10–15 every 8–12 h	10–15 every 8–12 h	10–15 every 6 or 8 h

BW indicates birth weight; IV, intravenous; IM, intramuscular; PO, oral.

[1] Unless otherwise listed, dosages are given as mg/kg.

[2] Optimal dosage should be based on determination of serum concentrations, especially in low birth weight (<1500 g) infants. In very low birth weight infants (<1200 g), dosing every 18 to 24 hours may be appropriate in the first week of life.

[3] Dosages for aminoglycosides may differ from those recommended by the manufacturer in the package insert.

[4] For meningitis, the larger dosage is recommended. Some experts recommend even larger dosages for group B streptococcal meningitis. Meropenem is preferred if a carbapenem is to be used in newborn infants.

[5] Safety in infants and children has not been established.

[6] Drug should not be administered to hyperbilirubinemic neonates, especially infants born preterm.

[7] Dosing every 12 hours is recommended for infants <34 weeks' gestation and <1 week of age.

[8] Same dosage for ticarcillin and clavulanate potassium.

Table 4.3. Antibacterial Drugs for Pediatric Patients Beyond the Newborn Period

Drug Generic (Trade Name)	Route	Dosage per kg per Day		Comments
		Mild to Moderate Infections	Severe Infections	
Aminoglycosides[1]				
Amikacin (Amikin)	IV, IM	Inappropriate	15–22.5 mg in 3 doses (daily adult dose, 15 mg/kg; maximum, 1.5 g)	30 mg in 3 doses is recommended by some consultants.
Gentamicin	IV, IM	Inappropriate	3–7.5 mg in 3 doses (daily adult dose is the same)	Once-daily dosing (5–6 mg/kg every 24 h) is investigational in children.
Kanamycin	IV, IM	Inappropriate	15–22.5 mg in 3 doses (daily adult dose, 1–1.5 g)	30 mg in 3 doses is recommended by some consultants.
Neomycin (numerous types)	PO only	100 mg in 4 doses	100 mg in 4 doses	For some enteric infections.
Tobramycin (Nebcin)	IV, IM	Inappropriate	3–7.5 mg in 3 doses (daily adult dose, 3–5 mg in 3 doses)	Once daily dosing (5–6 mg/kg every 24 h) is investigational in children.
Carbapenems				
Imipenem/cilastatin[2,4] (Primaxin)	IV, IM	≥4 wk of age: 60–80 mg in 4 doses (daily adult dose, 1–2 g)	≥4 wk of age: 100 mg in 4 doses (daily adult dose, 2–4 g)	Caution in use for treatment of meningitis because of possible seizures.
Meropenem[2,4] (Merrem)	IV	60 mg in 3 doses (daily adult dose, 4 g)	60–120 mg in 3 doses (daily adult dose, 4–6 g)	Larger dosage is used for treatment of meningitis.
Ertapenem (Invanz)	IV	3 mos–12 y of age: 30 mg given twice a day (max 1 g/day) ≥13 y of age: 1 g every 24 h	3 mos–12 y of age: 30 mg given twice a day (max 1 g/day) ≥13 y of age: 1 g every 24 h	Not approved for people younger than 3 months of age. Less active against *Pseudomonas* species, *Acinetobacter* species, and gram-positive cocci.

Table 4.3. Antibacterial Drugs for Pediatric Patients Beyond the Newborn Period, continued

Drug, Generic (Trade Name)	Route	Dosage per kg per Day		Comments
		Mild to Moderate Infections	Severe Infections	
Cephalosporins[2]				
Cefaclor (Ceclor)	PO	20–40 mg in 2 or 3 doses (daily adult dose, 750 mg–1.5 g)	Inappropriate	A twice-daily regimen has been demonstrated to be effective for treatment of acute otitis media.
Cefadroxil (Duricef)	PO	30 mg in 2 doses (maximum daily adult dose, 2 g)	Inappropriate	First-generation activity
Cefazolin (Ancef, Kefzol)	IV, IM	100 mg in 3 doses (maximum 4–6 g/day)	100 mg in 3 doses (maximum 4–6 g/day)	First generation
Cefdinir (Omnicef)	PO	14 mg in 1 or 2 doses (maximum 600 mg/day)	Inappropriate	Inadequate activity against resistant pneumococcus.
Cefditoren (Spectracef)	PO	800 mg total dose divided (maximum 800 mg/day) in 2 doses	No data available	Not approved for children younger than 12 years of age
Cefepime (Maxipime)	IV, IM	≥2 mo of age: 100–150 mg in 3 doses (daily adult dose, 1–2 g)	≥2 mo of age: 150 mg in 3 doses (daily adult dose, 2–4 g)	Not approved for treatment of meningitis. Considered fourth generation.
Cefixime (Suprax)	PO	8 mg in 1 or 2 doses (maximum adult dose, 400 mg)	Inappropriate	Single-dose treatment for gonorrhea (400 mg × 1)
Cefoperazone (Cefobid)	IV, IM	100–150 mg in 2 or 3 doses (maximum daily adult dose, 4 g)	No data available	Not approved for use in children.
Cefotaxime (Claforan)	IV, IM	75–100 mg in 3 or 4 doses (daily adult dose, 4–6 g)	150–200 mg in 3 or 4 doses (daily adult dose, 8–10 g)	A regimen of 300 mg in 3 or 4 doses can be used for treatment of meningitis.

Table 4.3. Antibacterial Drugs for Pediatric Patients Beyond the Newborn Period, continued

Drug, Generic (Trade Name)	Route	Dosage per kg per Day		Comments
		Mild to Moderate Infections	Severe Infections	
Cefotetan (Cefotan)	IV, IM	Inappropriate	40–80 mg in 2 doses (maximum daily adult dose, 6 g)	Not licensed for use in children.
Cefoxitin (Mefoxin)	IV, IM	80–100 mg in 3–4 doses (daily adult dose, 3–4 g)	80–160 mg in 4–6 doses (daily adult dose, 6–12 g)	Improved activity against *Bacteroides fragilis*
Cefpodoxime (Vantin)	PO	10 mg in 2 doses (maximum daily adult dose, 800 mg)	Inappropriate	Similar to cefixime with greater activity against methicillin-susceptible staphylococci.
Cefprozil (Cefzil)	PO	15–30 mg in 2 doses (maximum daily adult dose, 1 g)	Inappropriate	30-mg dosage recommended for treatment of acute otitis media.
Ceftazidime (Ceptaz, Fortaz, Tazidime)	IV, IM	75–100 mg in 3 doses (daily adult dose, 3 g)	125–150 mg in 3 doses (daily adult dose, 6 g)	Only cephalosporin with anti-*Pseudomonas* activity that has been licensed for use in children.
Ceftibuten (Cedax)	PO	9 mg in 1 dose (maximum adult dose: 400 mg/day)	Inappropriate	Approved for people ≥6 mo of age. Inadequate activity against intermediate and resistant pneumococci.
Ceftizoxime (Cefizox)	IV, IM	100–150 mg in 3 doses (daily adult dose, 3–4 g)	150–200 mg in 3 or 4 doses (daily adult dose, 4–6 g)	Third-generation activity.
Ceftriaxone (Rocephin)	IV, IM	50–75 mg in 1 or 2 doses (daily adult dose, 2 g)	80–100 mg in 1 or 2 doses (daily adult dose, 4 g)	Larger dosage appropriate for penicillin-resistant pneumococcal meningitis.
Cefuroxime (Zinacef)	IV, IM	75–100 mg in 3 doses (daily adult dose, 2–4 g)	100–150 mg in 3 doses (daily adult dose, 4–6 g)	Second generation, less active than third-generation cephalosporins against penicillin-resistant *Streptococcus pneumoniae*.

Table 4.3. Antibacterial Drugs for Pediatric Patients Beyond the Newborn Period, continued

Drug, Generic (Trade Name)	Route	Mild to Moderate Infections	Severe Infections	Comments
Cefuroxime axetil (Ceftin)	PO	20–30 mg in 2 doses (daily adult dose, 1–2 g)	Inappropriate	The higher dosage recommended for treatment of otitis media. Limited activity against penicillin-resistant *S pneumoniae*.
Cephalexin (Keflex)	PO	25–50 mg in 3–4 doses (daily adult dose, 1–4 g)	Inappropriate	First-generation activity.
Cephalothin (Keflin)	IV, IM	80–100 mg in 4 doses (daily adult dose, 2–4 g)	100–150 mg in 4–6 doses (daily adult dose, 8–12 g)	First-generation activity.
Cephradine (Velosef)	PO	25–50 mg in 2–4 doses (daily adult dose, 1–4 g)	Inappropriate	First-generation activity.
Chloramphenicol (Chloromycetin)				
Chloramphenicol	IV	Inappropriate	50–100 mg in 4 doses (daily adult dose, 2–4 g)	Optimal dosage is determined by measurement of serum concentrations with resulting modifications to achieve therapeutic concentrations. Use only for serious infections because of the rare occurrence of aplastic anemia after administration. Oral formulation (palmitate) not available in US.

Dosage per kg per Day

Table 4.3. Antibacterial Drugs for Pediatric Patients Beyond the Newborn Period, continued

Drug, Generic (Trade Name)	Route	Dosage per kg per Day		Comments
		Mild to Moderate Infections	Severe Infections	
Clindamycin (Cleocin)	IM, IV	15–25 mg in 3–4 doses (daily adult dose, 600 mg–3.6 g)	25–40 mg in 3–4 doses (daily adult dose, 1.2–2.7 g)	Active against anaerobes, especially *Bacteroides* species. Active against many multidrug-resistant pneumococci.
	PO	10–20 mg in 3–4 doses (daily adult dose, 600 mg–1.8 g)	Inappropriate	Effective for otitis media caused by many multidrug-resistant pneumococci.
Fluoroquinolones[3]				
Ciprofloxacin (Cipro)	PO	20–30 mg in 2 doses (daily adult dose, 0.5–1.5 g)	30 mg in 2 doses (daily adult dose, 1.0–1.5 g)	Only licensed for children younger than 18 years of age for specific indications[3] (see p 735).
	IV	Inappropriate	18–30 mg in 2 or 3 doses (daily adult dose, 400–800 mg in 2 doses)	…
Ketolides				
Telithromycin	PO	800 mg total dose, once daily (maximum adult dose 800 mg/day)		Not approved for people younger than 18 y of age. Used for treatment of community-acquired pneumonia, sinusitis, and bronchitis.

Table 4.3. Antibacterial Drugs for Pediatric Patients Beyond the Newborn Period, continued

Drug, Generic (Trade Name)	Route	Dosage per kg per Day		Comments
		Mild to Moderate Infections	Severe Infections	
Macrolides/ streptogramins				
Azithromycin (Zithromax)	PO	5–12 mg once daily (maximum daily adult dose, 600 mg)	Inappropriate	Otitis media, ≥6 mo of age: 10 mg/kg on first day, 5 mg/kg per day for additional 4 days. Pharyngitis, ≥6 mo of age: 12 mg/kg per day for 5 days.
Clarithromycin (Biaxin)	PO	15 mg in 2 doses (maximum daily adult dose, 1 g)	Inappropriate	Similar to erythromycin; more activity against *Mycobacterium avium* and *Helicobacter pylori* and preventing *Mycobacterium tuberculosis*
Dirithromycin	PO	500 mg total daily dose (maximum 500 mg/day) every day	Inappropriate	Approved for children ≥12 y of age and adults. Similar to erythromycin but given once per day.
Erythromycins (numerous types)	PO	30–50 mg in 2–4 doses (daily adult dose, 1–2 g)	Inappropriate	Available in base, stearate, ethylsuccinate, and estolate preparations.
	IV	Inappropriate	15–50 mg in 4 doses (daily adult dose, 1–4 g)	Administer in a continuous drip or by slow infusion over 60 min or longer. May cause cardiac arrhythmia.
Metronidazole (Flagyl)	PO	15–35 mg in 3 doses (maximum daily adult dose, 1–2 g)	Inappropriate	Safety in infants and children has not been established.

Table 4.3. Antibacterial Drugs for Pediatric Patients Beyond the Newborn Period, continued

Drug, Generic (Trade Name)	Route	Dosage per kg per Day		Comments
		Mild to Moderate Infections	Severe Infections	
Miscellaneous				
Daptomycin	IV	Inappropriate	4 mg, once daily	Not approved for people <18 y of age. Effective for complicated skin and soft tissue infections caused by staphylococci, streptococci, and enterococci.
Monobactam				
Aztreonam[2] (Azactam)	IV, IM	90 mg in 3 doses (daily adult dose, 3 g)	90–120 mg in 3 or 4 doses (maximum daily adult dose, 8 g)	…
Loracarbef (Lorabid)	PO	6 mo–12 y of age: 15 mg/kg per day, every 12 h ≥13 y of age: 400 mg/day, in 2 doses	6 mo–12 y of age: 30 mg/kg per day, every 12 h ≥13 y of age: 800 mg/day, in 2 doses	Pharyngitis, tonsillitis, sinusitis, and skin and soft tissue infections (use higher dose for sinusitis)
Nitrofurantoin (Furadantin)	PO	5–7 mg in 4 doses (daily adult dose, 200–400 mg)	Inappropriate	Should not be used for young infants; prophylactic dose is 1–2 mg/kg per day in 1 dose
Oxazolidinones				
Linezolid (Zyvox)	PO, IV	30 mg in 3 doses (children <12 years of age) 20 mg in 2 doses (adolescents and adults up to 1200 mg maximum)	30 mg in 3 doses (children <12 years of age) 20 mg in 2 doses (adolescents and adults up to 1200 mg maximum)	Myelosuppression may occur. Active against *Enterococcus faecium*, *E faecalis*, oxacillin-resistant *S aureus*, and penicillin-resistant *S pneumoniae*

Table 4.3. Antibacterial Drugs for Pediatric Patients Beyond the Newborn Period, continued

Drug, Generic (Trade Name)	Route	Dosage per kg per Day		Comments
		Mild to Moderate Infections	Severe Infections	
PENICILLINS[2]				
Broad-spectrum penicillins				
Ampicillin (numerous types)	IV, IM	100–150 mg in 4 doses (daily adult dose, 2–4 g)	200–400 mg in 4 doses (daily adult dose, 6–12 g)	Larger dosage recommended for treatment of meningitis.
	PO	50–100 mg in 4 doses (daily adult dose, 2–4 g)	Inappropriate	Diarrhea occurs in approximately 20% of recipients.
Ampicillin-sulbactam (Unasyn)	IV	100–150 mg of ampicillin in 4 doses	200–400 mg of ampicillin in 4 doses (daily adult dose, 6–12 g)	Licensed for use in children 1 year of age and older.
Amoxicillin (numerous types)	PO	25–50 mg in 3 doses (daily adult dose, 750 mg–1.5 g); 90 mg/kg in 2 doses for AOM	Inappropriate	90 mg/kg dose recommended for initial therapy of AOM[5]
Amoxicillin-clavulanic acid				
(Augmentin ES-600; 14:1 ratio)	PO	90 mg of amoxicillin in 2 doses	Inappropriate	Preferred for recurrent AOM and treatment failures
(Augmentin XR)	PO	4 g total, in 2 doses (total 4000 mg)	Inappropriate	Oral extended-release formulation licensed for adults.
Piperacillin[6]	IV, IM	100–150 mg in 4 doses (daily adult dose, 6–8 g)	200–300 mg in 4–6 doses (daily adult dose, 12–18 g)	…
Piperacillin-tazobactam[6] (Zosyn)	IV	Inappropriate	240 mg of piperacillin in 3 doses (daily adult dose 12–18 g)	Not licensed for use in children.

Table 4.3. Antibacterial Drugs for Pediatric Patients Beyond the Newborn Period, continued

| Drug, Generic (Trade Name) | Route | Dosage per kg per Day | | Comments |
		Mild to Moderate Infections	Severe Infections	
Ticarcillin (Ticar)	IV, IM	100–200 mg in 4 doses (daily adult dose, 4–6 g)	200–300 mg in 4 doses (daily adult dose, 12–24 g)	Contains 5.2 mEq of sodium per gram.
Ticarcillin-clavulanate (Timentin)	IV, IM	100–200 mg of ticarcillin in 4 doses (daily adult dose, 4–6 g)	200–300 mg of ticarcillin in 4 doses (daily adult dose, 12–24 g)	…
Penicillin G and V[2,6]				
Penicillin G, crystalline potassium or sodium (numerous types)	IV, IM	25 000–50 000 U in 4 doses	250 000–400 000 U in 4–6 doses. Maximum adult dose 24 million U/24 h.	Larger dosage appropriate for central nervous system infections.
Penicillin G procaine (numerous types)	IM	25 000–50 000 U in 1–2 doses. Maximum adult dose 4.8 million U/24 h.	Inappropriate	Contraindicated in procaine allergy.
Penicillin G benzathine (Bicillin LA, Permapen)	IM	<27.3 kg (60 lb) in body weight: 600 000 U once ≥27.3 kg (60 lb): 1.2 million U once	Inappropriate	Major use is prevention of rheumatic fever by treatment and prophylaxis of streptococcal infections.
Penicillin V (numerous types)	PO	25–50 mg in 3 or 4 doses. Maximum adult dose 500 mg/dose, every 6–8 h (2 g/24 h).	Inappropriate	Optimal to administer on an empty stomach.

Table 4.3. Antibacterial Drugs for Pediatric Patients Beyond the Newborn Period, continued

Drug, Generic (Trade Name)	Route	Dosage per kg per Day		Comments
		Mild to Moderate Infections	Severe Infections	
Penicillinase-resistant penicillins[2]				Methicillin (oxacillin)-resistant staphylococci usually are resistant to all other semi-synthetic antistaphylococcal cephalosporins.
Oxacillin	IV, IM	100–150 mg in 4 doses (daily adult dose, 2–4 g)	150–200 mg in 4–6 doses (daily adult dose, 4–12 g)	…
Nafcillin	IV, IM, PO	50–100 mg in 4 doses (daily adult dose, 2–4 g)	100–150 mg in 4 doses (daily adult dose, 4–12 g)	Oral formulation not used because of poor absorption.
Cloxacillin (Tegopen, Cloxapen)	PO	50–100 mg in 4 doses (daily adult dose, 2–4 g)	Inappropriate	…
Dicloxacillin (Dynapen, Pathocil)	PO	25–50 mg in 4 doses (daily adult dose, 1–2 g)	Inappropriate	Excellent serum concentrations after oral administration.
Rifampin (numerous types)	PO	10–20 mg in 1–2 doses (daily adult dose, 600 mg)	20 mg in 2 doses. Maximum adult dose 600 mg/24 h.	Should not be used as monotherapy except when given for prophylaxis.
	IV	10–20 mg in 1–2 doses (daily adult dose, 600 mg)	20 mg in 2 doses. Maximum adult dose 600 mg/24 h.	…
Rifaximin (Xifaxan)	PO	≥12 y of age: 600 mg/day, given 3 times/day	Inappropriate	Treatment of travelers' diarrhea caused by noninvasive *Escherichia coli*. Nonabsorbable.

Table 4.3. Antibacterial Drugs for Pediatric Patients Beyond the Newborn Period, continued

Drug, Generic (Trade Name)	Route	Dosage per kg per Day		Comments
		Mild to Moderate Infections	Severe Infections	
Streptogramin				
Quinupristin/ dalfopristin (Synercid)	IV	15 mg in 2 doses (daily adult dose, same)	22.5 mg in 3 doses (daily adult dose, same)	Modestly effective for vancomycin-resistant *E faecium* (but not *Enterococcus faecalis*) as well as *Staphylococcus aureus*. Limited use in children.
Sulfonamides				
Sulfadiazine	PO	100–150 mg in 4 doses (daily adult dose 4–6 g)	120–150 mg in 4–6 doses (daily adult dose 4–6 g)	…
Sulfisoxazole (Gantrisin)	PO	120–150 mg in 4–6 doses (daily adult dose 2–4 g)	120–150 mg in 4–6 doses (daily adult dose 2–4 g)	…
Triple sulfonamides (numerous types)	PO	120–150 mg in 4 doses	120–150 mg in 4 doses	…
Trimethoprim–sulfamethoxazole (Bactrim, Septra)	PO	8–12 mg of trimethoprim, 40–60 mg of sulfamethoxazole in 2 doses (daily adult dose, 320 mg of trimethoprim, 1.6 g of sulfamethoxazole)	20 mg of trimethoprim, 100 mg of sulfamethoxazole in 4 doses (for use only in *Pneumocystis jiroveci* pneumonia)	For prophylaxis in immunocompromised patients, recommended dose is 5 mg of trimethoprim, 25 mg of sulfamethoxazole per kg per day in 2 doses.
	IV	Inappropriate	8–12 mg of trimethoprim, 40–60 mg of sulfamethoxazole in 4 doses **OR** 20 mg of trimethoprim, 100 mg of sulfamethoxazole in 4 doses	Use intravenous formulation when PO formulation cannot be administered.
				Treatment of *Pneumocystis* infection.

Table 4.3. Antibacterial Drugs for Pediatric Patients Beyond the Newborn Period, continued

Drug, Generic (Trade Name)	Route	Dosage per kg per Day		Comments
		Mild to Moderate Infections	Severe Infections	
Tetracyclines (numerous types)	IV	Inappropriate	10–25 mg in 2–4 doses (daily adult dose, 1–2 g)	Responsible for staining of developing teeth; use only in children 8 years of age or older except in circumstances in which the benefits of therapy exceed the risks and alternative drugs are less effective or more toxic (see p 736).
	PO	20–50 mg in 4 doses (daily adult dose, 1–2 g)	Inappropriate	Responsible for staining of developing teeth; use only in children 8 years of age or older except in circumstances in which the benefits of therapy exceed the risks and alternative drugs are less effective or more toxic (see p 736).
Doxycycline (numerous types)	PO, IV	2–4 mg in 1–2 doses (daily adult dose, 100–200 mg)	Inappropriate	Adverse effects similar to those of other tetracycline products except that risk of dental staining in children younger than 8 years of age is less.

Table 4.3. Antibacterial Drugs for Pediatric Patients Beyond the Newborn Period, continued

Drug, Generic (Trade Name)	Route	Dosage per kg per Day		Comments
		Mild to Moderate Infections	Severe Infections	
Vancomycin (Vancocin, Vancoled, Vancor)	IV	40 mg in 3–4 doses (daily adult dose,[7] 1–2 g)	40–60 mg in 4 doses (daily adult dose,[7] 2–4 g)	In meningitis, 60 mg/kg dose should be given over a period of at least 60 min; routine monitoring of serum concentrations is unnecessary.

IV, indicates intravenous; IM, intramuscular; PO, oral; AOM, acute otitis media.

[1] Dosages for aminoglycosides may differ from those recommended by the manufacturers (see package insert).

[2] In patients with history of allergy to penicillin or one of its many congeners, alternative drugs are recommended. In some circumstances, a cephalosporin or other beta-lactam–class drug may be acceptable. However, these drugs should not be used in patients with an immediate hypersensitivity (anaphylaxis) to penicillin, because approximately 5% to 15% of penicillin-allergic patients also will be allergic to cephalosporins.

[3] Only licensed for use in patients younger than 18 years of age for complicated urinary tract infections and postexposure inhalation anthrax. Some fluoroquinolones are being studied in selected children and adolescents (see Fluoroquinolones, p 735).

[4] Not licensed for use in patients younger than 12 years of age.

[5] American Academy of Pediatrics, Subcommittee on Management of Acute Otitis Media. Diagnosis and management of acute otitis media. *Pediatrics.* 2004;113:1451-1465

[6] Patients with a history of allergy to penicillin G or penicillin V should be considered for subsequent skin testing. Many such patients can be treated safely with penicillin, because only 10% of children with such history are proven allergic when skin tested.

[7] In adults, daily dose is given in 2 to 4 divided doses.

For more information on individual drugs, see *Physician's Desk Reference* or **www.pdr.net** (for registered users only).

SEXUALLY TRANSMITTED INFECTIONS

Table 4.4. Guidelines for Treatment of Sexually Transmitted Infections in Children and Adolescents According to Syndrome

Preferred regimens are listed. For further information concerning other acceptable regimens and diseases not included, see specific recommendations in disease-specific chapters in Section 3. In addition, revised recommendations on the treatment of sexually transmitted infections have been issued by the Centers for Disease Control and Prevention in 2006.[1]

Syndrome	Organisms/Diagnoses	Treatment of Adolescent	Treatment of Infant/Child
Urethritis and cervicitis Urethritis: Inflammation of urethra with mucoid, mucopurulent, or purulent discharge Cervicitis: Inflammation of cervix with mucopurulent or purulent cervical discharge. Cervicitis occurs rarely in prepubertal girls (see Prepubertal vaginitis)	*Neisseria gonorrhoeae, Chlamydia trachomatis* Other causes of urethritis and cervicitis include *Ureaplasma urealyticum*, possibly *Mycoplasma genitalium*, and sometimes *Trichomonas vaginalis* and herpes simplex virus (HSV)	Cefixime, 400 mg, orally, in a single dose **OR** Ceftriaxone, 125 mg, IM, in a single dose **OR** Ciprofloxacin, 500 mg, orally, in a single dose[2,3] **OR** Ofloxacin, 400 mg, orally, in a single dose[2,3] **OR** Levofloxacin, 250 mg, orally, in single dose[2,3] **If chlamydial infection not ruled out, PLUS EITHER** Azithromycin, 1 g, orally, in a single dose **OR** Doxycycline, 100 mg, orally, twice a day for 7 days	*Children <45 kg:* Ceftriaxone, 125 mg, IM, in a single dose **OR** Spectinomycin, 40 mg/kg (maximum 2 g) IM in a single dose **If chlamydial infection not ruled out, PLUS** Erythromycin base or ethylsuccinate, 50 mg/kg per day, orally, in 4 divided doses (maximum 2 g/day) for 14 days *Children ≥45 kg but younger than 8 years of age:* Azithromycin, 1 g, orally, in a single dose *Children 8 years of age or older:* Azithromycin, 1 g, orally, in a single dose **OR** Doxycycline, 100 mg, orally, twice a day for 7 days

Table 4.4. Guidelines for Treatment of Sexually Transmitted Infections in Children and Adolescents According to Syndrome, continued

Syndrome	Organism/Diagnosis	Treatment of Adolescent	Treatment of Infant/Child
Prepubertal vaginitis (STI related):	N gonorrhoeae[1]	…	**Children <45 kg:** Ceftriaxone, 125 mg, in a single dose
	C trachomatis[1]	…	**Children <45 kg:** Erythromycin base or ethylsuccinate, 50 mg/kg per day, orally, in 4 divided doses (maximum 2 g/day) for 14 days **Children ≥45 kg but younger than 8 years of age:** Azithromycin, 1 g, orally, in a single dose **Children 8 years of age or older:** Azithromycin, 1 g, orally, in a single dose OR Doxycycline, 100 mg, orally, twice a day for 7 days
	T vaginalis	…	**Children <45 kg:** Metronidazole, 15 mg/kg per day, orally, in 3 divided doses (maximum 2 g/day) for 7 days
	Bacterial vaginosis	…	**Children <45 kg:** Metronidazole, 15 mg/kg per day, orally, in 2 divided doses (maximum 1 g/day) for 7 days

Table 4.4. Guidelines for Treatment of Sexually Transmitted Infections in Children and Adolescents According to Syndrome, continued

Syndrome	Organism/Diagnosis	Treatment of Adolescent	Treatment of Infant/Child
Prepubertal vaginitis (STI related, continued):	HSV—primary infection	Acyclovir, 400 mg, orally, 3 times/day for 7–10 days OR Acyclovir, 200 mg, orally, 5 times/day for 7–10 days OR Famciclovir (250 mg, orally, 3 times/day) for 7–10 days OR Valacyclovir (1 g, orally, twice daily) for 7–10 days	*Children <45 kg:* Acyclovir, 80 mg/kg per day, orally, in 3–4 divided doses (maximum 1.2 g/day) for 7–10 days
Adolescent vulvovaginitis	*T vaginalis*	Metronidazole, 2 g, orally, in a single dose OR Tinidazole, 2 g, orally, in a single dose OR Metronidazole, 500 mg, twice daily for 7 days	. . .

Table 4.4. Guidelines for Treatment of Sexually Transmitted Infections in Children and Adolescents According to Syndrome, continued

Syndrome	Organism/Diagnosis	Treatment of Adolescent	Treatment of Infant/Child
	Bacterial vaginosis	Metronidazole, 500 mg, orally, twice daily for 7 days **OR** Metronidazole gel 0.75%, 1 full applicator (5 g), intravaginally, once a day for 5 days **OR** Clindamycin cream 2%, 1 full applicator (5 g), intravaginally at bedtime, for 7 days **OR** Clindamycin, 300 mg, orally, twice a day for 7 days **OR** Clindamycin ovules, 100 g, intravaginally, once at bedtime for 3 days	...
	Candida species	See Table 4.5, Recommended Regimens for Vulvovaginal Candidiasis (p 242)	...
	HSV—primary infection	Acyclovir, 1000–1200 mg/day, orally, in 3–5 divided doses for 7–10 days **OR** Famcyclovir, 250 mg, orally, 3 times/day for 7–10 days **OR** Valacyclovir, 1 g, orally twice/day for 7–10 days	...

Table 4.4. Guidelines for Treatment of Sexually Transmitted Infections in Children and Adolescents According to Syndrome, continued

Syndrome	Organism/Diagnosis	Treatment of Adolescent	Treatment of Infant/Child
Pelvic inflammatory disease (PID)	*N gonorrhoeae, C trachomatis,* anaerobes, coliform bacteria, and *Streptococcus* species	See Pelvic Inflammatory Disease (Table 3.41, p 497)	PID occurs rarely, if at all, in prepubertal girls
Syphilis	*Treponema pallidum*	See Syphilis, p 631	*Children <45 kg:* Same as for congenital syphilis (see p 637 and Table 3.61, p 638)
Genital ulcer disease	*T pallidum*	Same as for syphilis	*Children <45 kg:* Same as for congenital syphilis (see p 637 and Table 3.61, p 638)
	HSV—primary infection	See prepubertal vaginitis	*Children <45 kg:* See prepubertal vaginitis
	Haemophilus ducreyi (chancroid)	Azithromycin, 1 g, orally, in a single dose OR Ceftriaxone, 250 mg, IM, in a single dose OR Ciprofloxacin, 500 mg, orally, twice daily for 3 days[3] OR Erythromycin base, 500 mg, orally, 3 times/day for 7 days	*Children <45 kg:* Ceftriaxone, 50 mg/kg, IM, in a single dose OR *Children <45 kg:* Azithromycin, 20 mg/kg, orally, in a single dose (maximum 1 g)

Table 4.4. Guidelines for Treatment of Sexually Transmitted Infections in Children and Adolescents According to Syndrome, continued

Syndrome	Organism/Diagnosis	Treatment of Adolescent	Treatment of Infant/Child
Sexually acquired epididymitis	*C trachomatis, N gonorrhoeae*	Ceftriaxone, 250 mg, IM, in a single dose **PLUS** Doxycycline, 100 mg, orally, twice daily for 10 days	...
	Enteric organisms (for patients allergic to cephalosporins and/or tetracycline or for patients >35 years of age)	Ofloxacin, 300 mg, orally, twice a day for 10 days **OR** Levofloxacin, 500 mg, orally, once daily for 10 days	...
Anogenital warts	Human papillomavirus	*Patient-applied:* Podofilox 0.5% solution or gel[+] **OR** Imiquimod 5% cream *Provider-administered:* Cryotherapy **OR** Podophyllin resin 10%–25%[+] **OR** Trichloroacetic acid **OR** Bichloroacetic acid **OR** Surgical removal	*Children <45 kg:* Same as for adolescents

Table 4.4. Guidelines for Treatment of Sexually Transmitted Infections in Children and Adolescents According to Syndrome, continued

IM indicates intramuscularly; STI, sexually transmitted infection.

[1] For additional information and recommendations, see Centers for Disease Control and Prevention. Sexually transmitted infection treatment guidelines—2006. *MMWR Recomm Rep.* 2006; in press. Some regimens are not indicated for pregnant adolescents.

[2] Quinolones should not be used for infections acquired in Asia or the Pacific, including Hawaii. Use of quinolones is inadvisable for treating infections acquired in California.

[3] Ciprofloxacin, ofloxacin, and levofloxacin are not indicated for treatment of STIs in pregnant women or people younger than 18 years of age, because the safety and effectiveness have not been established.

[4] Not tested for safety in children and contraindicated in pregnancy.

Intravaginal agents:

Butoconazole, 2% cream, 5 g, intravaginally, for 3 days[1,2]

OR

Butoconazole, 2% cream (sustained release), 5 g, single intravaginal application

OR

Clotrimazole, 1% cream, 5 g, intravaginally, for 7–14 days[1,2]

OR

Clotrimazole, 100-mg vaginal tablet for 7 days[1]

OR

Clotrimazole, 100-mg vaginal tablet, 2 tablets for 3 days[1]

OR

Clotrimazole, 500-mg vaginal tablet, 1 tablet in a single application[1]

OR

Miconazole, 2% cream, 5 g, intravaginally, for 7 days[1,2]

OR

Miconazole, 200-mg vaginal suppository, 1 suppository for 3 days[1,2]

OR

Miconazole, 100-mg vaginal suppository, 1 suppository for 7 days[1,2]

OR

Nystatin, 100 000-U vaginal tablet, 1 tablet for 14 days

OR

Tioconazole, 6.5% ointment, 5 g, intravaginally, in a single application[1,2]

OR

Terconazole, 0.4% cream, 5 g, intravaginally, for 7 days[1]

OR

Terconazole, 0.8% cream, 5 g, intravaginally, for 3 days[1]

OR

Terconazole, 80-mg vaginal suppository, 1 suppository for 3 days[1]

Oral agent:

Fluconazole 150-mg oral tablet, 1 tablet in single dose

[1] These creams and suppositories are oil-based and might weaken latex condoms and diaphragms. Refer to condom or diaphragm product labeling for additional information.
[2] Over-the-counter preparations.

ANTIFUNGAL DRUGS FOR SYSTEMIC FUNGAL INFECTIONS

Polyenes

Amphotericin B deoxycholate (conventional amphotericin B) is the drug of choice for most disseminated, potentially life-threatening fungal infections. Amphotericin B is fungicidal against a broad array of fungal species, excluding *Fusarium* species and *Pseudallescheria boydii*. Amphotericin B can cause adverse reactions, particularly renal toxicity, that limit its use in certain patients. Lipid-associated formulations of amphotericin B also are available.

Amphotericin B is given intravenously in a single daily dose of 0.5 to 1.5 mg/kg (maximum 1.5 mg/kg per day). Amphotericin B is administered in 5% dextrose in water at a concentration of 0.1 mg/mL and delivered through a central or peripheral venous catheter (see Table 4.6, p 777). Infusion times of 1 to 2 hours have been shown to be well tolerated in adults and older children and theoretically increase the blood-to-tissue gradient, thereby improving drug delivery. After completing 1 week of daily therapy, adequate serum concentrations of the drug usually can be maintained by administering double the daily dose (maximum, 1.5 mg/kg) on alternate days. The duration of therapy depends on the type and extent of the specific fungal infection.

Amphotericin B is eliminated by a renal mechanism for weeks after therapy is discontinued. No adjustment in dose is required for neonates or for children with impaired renal function, because serum concentrations are not significantly increased in these patients. Neither hemodialysis nor peritoneal dialysis significantly decreases serum concentrations of the drug.

Infusion-related reactions to amphotericin B include fever, chills, and sometimes nausea, vomiting, headache, generalized malaise, hypotension, and arrhythmias. Onset usually is within 1 to 3 hours after starting the infusion; duration typically is less than an hour. Hypotension and arrhythmias are idiosyncratic reactions that are unlikely to occur if not observed after the initial dose but also can occur in association with very rapid infusion. Multiple regimens have been utilized to prevent infusion-related reactions, but few have been studied in controlled clinical trials. Pretreatment with acetaminophen, alone or combined with diphenhydramine, may alleviate febrile reactions; these reactions appear to be less common in children than in adults. Hydrocortisone (25–50 mg in adults and older children) also can be added to the infusion to decrease febrile and other systemic reactions. Tolerance to febrile reactions develops with time, allowing tapering and eventual discontinuation of the hydrocortisone and often diphenhydramine and antipyretic agents.

Meperidine and ibuprofen have been effective in preventing or treating fever and chills in some patients who are refractory to the conventional premedication regimen. Toxicity from amphotericin B can include nephrotoxicity, hepatotoxicity, thrombophlebitis, anemia, or neurotoxicity. Nephrotoxicity is caused by decreased renal blood flow and can be prevented or ameliorated by hydration, saline solution loading (0.9% saline solution over 30 minutes) before infusion of amphotericin B, and avoiding diuretic drugs. Hypokalemia is common and can be exacerbated by sodium loading.

Renal tubular acidosis can occur but usually is mild. Permanent nephrotoxicity is related to cumulative dose. Nephrotoxicity can be enhanced by concomitant administration of amphotericin B and aminoglycosides, cyclosporine, tacrolimus, cisplatin, nitrogen mustard compounds, and acetazolamide. Anemia is secondary to inhibition of erythropoietin production. Neurotoxicity occurs rarely and can manifest as confusion, delirium, obtundation, psychotic behavior, seizures, blurred vision, or hearing loss.

Lipid-associated formulations of amphotericin B have a role in some children who are intolerant of or refractory to amphotericin B deoxycholate or can be considered in children who have renal insufficiency or at risk of significant renal toxicity from concomitant medications (see Table 4.6, p 777). In adults, none of the 3 lipid formulations have been demonstrated to be more efficacious than has conventional amphotericin B. The 3 amphotericin B lipid formulations approved by the US Food and Drug Administration (FDA) for treatment of invasive fungal infections in children and adults who are refractory to or intolerant of conventional amphotericin B therapy are amphotericin B lipid complex (ABLC, Abelcet), liposomal amphotericin B (L-AmB, AmBisome), and amphotericin B colloidal dispersion (ABCD, Amphotec). Compared with conventional amphotericin B, acute infusion-related reactions are worse with Amphotec, less with Abelcet, and least with AmBisome. Nephrotoxicity is less common with lipid-based products than with conventional amphotericin B. Liver toxicity, which generally is not associated with conventional amphotericin B, has been reported with the lipid formulations. In recommended doses, these lipid-associated formulations cost 20 to 60 times more per day than does amphotericin B deoxycholate.

Pyrimidines

Among pyrimidine antifungal agents, only flucytosine (5-fluorocytosine) is approved by the FDA for use in children. Flucytosine has a limited spectrum of activity against fungi and potential for toxicity (see Table 4.6, p 777), and when used as a single agent, resistance often emerges. Flucytosine is used in combination with amphotericin B for cryptococcal meningitis and some life-threatening *Candida* infections, such as meningitis.

Azoles

Four oral azoles are available in the United States and include ketoconazole, fluconazole, itraconazole, and voriconazole. All have a relatively broad spectrum of activity against common fungi but differ in their spectrum of activity, bioavailability, adverse effects, and potential for drug interactions (see Table 4.6, p 777). Limited data are available regarding the safety and efficacy of azoles in pediatric patients, and trials comparing these agents to amphotericin B have been limited. Azoles are easy to administer and have little toxicity, but their use can be limited by the frequency of their interactions with coadministered drugs. These drug interactions can result in decreased serum concentrations of the azole (ie, poor therapeutic activity) or unexpected toxicity from the coadministered drug (ie, increased serum concentrations of the coadministered drug resulting from alteration of the cytochrome P-450 system). When considering the use of azoles, the patient's concurrent medications should be reviewed to avoid potential adverse clinical outcomes. Another potential limitation of azoles is the emergence of resistant fungi, especially *Candida* species resistant to fluconazole. *Candida krusei* are intrinsically resistant to fluconazole and strains of *Candida glabrata* are showing increasing resistance. Itraconazole is approved by the FDA for treatment of blastomycosis, histoplasmosis (nonmeningeal), and aspergillosis in patients who are intolerant to amphotericin B and for empiric therapy of febrile neutropenic patients with suspected fungal infection. The oral solution is approved for oropharyngeal and esophageal candidiasis. Itraconazole does not cross the blood-brain barrier and should not be used for infections of the central nervous system. Voriconazole has been approved by the FDA for primary treatment of invasive *Aspergillus* species, for esophageal candidiasis, and for refractory infection with *Scedosporium apiospermum* (the asexual form of *Pseudallescheria boydii*) and *Fusarium* species. Limited data are available regarding use of voriconazole in children. Ketoconazole seldom is used because other azoles have fewer adverse effects and generally are preferred.

Echinocandins

Caspofungin, micafungin, and anidulafungin are the only echinocandins approved by the FDA. Caspofungin is approved for treatment of esophageal candidiasis, invasive candidiasis, and aspergillosis in adults who are refractory to or intolerant of other antifungal drugs. Clinical trials assessing safety or efficacy in pediatric patients are being conducted. Caspofungin, like azoles, has important drug interactions. Table 4.7 (p 780) provides recommendations for treatment of serious fungal infections with amphotericin B, flucytosine, azoles, caspofungin, and other antifungal agents. Micafungin is approved by the FDA for intravenous treatment of esophageal candidiasis and prophylaxis of invasive *Candida* infections in patients undergoing hematopoietic stem cell transplantation. Anidulafungin is approved by the FDA for intravenous treatment of candidemia, *Candida* infections, and esophageal candidiasis.

RECOMMENDED DOSES OF PARENTERAL AND ORAL ANTIFUNGAL DRUGS

Table 4.6. Recommended Doses of Parenteral and Oral Antifungal Drugs

Drug	Route[1]	Dose (per day)	Adverse Reactions[2,3]
Amphotericin B deoxycholate (see Antifungal Drugs for Systemic Fungal Infections, p 774, for detailed information)	IV	0.25–0.5 mg/kg initially, increase as tolerated to 0.5–1.5 mg/kg; infuse as single dose over 2 h; 0.5–1.0 mg/kg weekly for suppressive therapy	Fever, chills, gastrointestinal tract symptoms, headache, hypotension, renal dysfunction, hypokalemia, anemia, cardiac arrhythmias, neurotoxicity, anaphylaxis
	IT	0.025 mg, increase to 0.5 mg, twice a week	Headache, gastrointestinal tract symptoms, arachnoiditis/radiculitis
Amphotericin B lipid complex (Abelcet)[4,5]	IV	5 mg/kg, infused over 2 h	Fever, chills, other reactions associated with amphotericin B, but less nephrotoxicity; hepatotoxicity has been reported
Amphotericin B cholesteryl sulfate complex (Amphotec)[4,5]	IV	3–6 mg/kg, infused at a rate of 1 mg/kg per hour	Fever, chills, other reactions associated with amphotericin B, but less nephrotoxicity; hepatotoxicity has been reported
Anidulafungin[4,5]	IV	Adults: 100–200 mg loading dose, then 50–100 mg once daily (higher dose for candidemia) Children: 0.75–1.5 mg/kg per day	Fever, headache, nausea, vomiting, diarrhea, leukopenia, hepatic enzyme elevations, and phlebitis
Liposomal amphotericin B (AmBisome)[4,5]	IV	3–5 mg/kg, infused over 1–2 h	Fever, chills, other reactions associated with amphotericin B, but less nephrotoxicity; hepatotoxicity has been reported
Caspofungin[4,5]	IV	Adults: 70 mg loading dose, then 50 mg once daily Children: 70 mg/m² loading dose, then 50 mg/m² once daily	Fever, rash, pruritus, phlebitis, headache, gastrointestinal tract symptoms, anemia. Concomitant use with cyclosporine is not recommended unless potential benefits outweigh potential risks.
Clotrimazole	PO	10-mg tablet 5 times per day (dissolved slowly in mouth)	Gastrointestinal tract symptoms, hepatotoxicity
Fluconazole[3,5]	IV	Children: 3–6 mg/kg per day; single dose (up to 12 mg/kg per day for serious infections)	Rash, gastrointestinal tract symptoms, hepatotoxicity, Stevens-Johnson syndrome, anaphylaxis

Table 4.6. Recommended Doses of Parenteral and Oral Antifungal Drugs, continued

Drug	Route[1]	Dose (per day)	Adverse Reactions[2,3]
	PO	Children: 6 mg/kg once, then 3 mg/kg per day for oropharyngeal or esophageal candidiasis; 6–12 mg/kg per day for invasive fungal infections; 6 mg/kg per day for suppressive therapy in HIV-infected children with cryptococcal meningitis Adults: 200 mg once, followed by 100 mg/day for oropharyngeal or esophageal candidiasis; 400–800 mg/day for other invasive fungal infections; 200 mg/day for suppressive therapy in HIV-infected patients with cryptococcal meningitis	
Flucytosine	PO	50–150 mg/kg per day in 4 doses at 6-h intervals (adjust dose if renal dysfunction); follow trough levels closely	Bone marrow suppression, renal dysfunction, gastrointestinal tract symptoms, rash, neuropathy, hepatotoxicity, confusion, hallucinations
Griseofulvin	PO	Ultramicrosize: 5–15 mg/kg, single dose; maximum dose, 750 mg Microsize: 10–20 mg/kg per day divided in 2 doses; maximum dose, 1000 mg	Rash, paresthesias, leukopenia, gastrointestinal tract symptoms, proteinuria, hepatotoxicity; mental confusion, headache
Itraconazole[3,5]	IV, PO	Children: 5–10 mg/kg per day divided into 2 doses Adults: 200–400 mg/day once or twice a day; 200 mg once a day for suppressive therapy in HIV-infected patients with histoplasmosis	Gastrointestinal tract symptoms, rash, edema, headache, hypokalemia, hepatotoxicity; thrombocytopenia, leukopenia; cardiac toxicity is possible in patients also taking terfenadine or astemizole
Ketoconazole[3,5]	PO	Children[6]: 3.3–6.6 mg/kg per day, single dose Adults: 200 mg, twice a day for 4 doses, then 200 mg, once a day	Hepatotoxicity, gastrointestinal tract symptoms, rash, anaphylaxis, thrombocytopenia, hemolytic anemia, gynecomastia, adrenal insufficiency; cardiac toxicity is possible in patients also taking terfenadine or astemizole

Table 4.6. Recommended Doses of Parenteral and Oral Antifungal Drugs, continued

Drug	Route[1]	Dose (per day)	Adverse Reactions[2,3]
Micafungin[4,5]	IV	Adults: 50–150 mg once daily Children: 4–12 mg/kg per day once daily (higher dose needed for patients <8 y of age)	Fever, headache, nausea, vomiting, diarrhea, leukopenia, hepatic enzyme elevations, and phlebitis
Nystatin	PO	Infants: 200 000 U, 4 times a day, after meals Children and adults: 400 000–600 000 U, 3 times a day, after meals	Gastrointestinal tract symptoms, rash
Terbinafine[4]	PO	Adults: 250 mg, once a day Children: <20 kg: 67.5 mg/day; 20–40 kg: 125 mg/day; >40 kg: 250 mg/day	Gastrointestinal tract symptoms, rash, taste abnormalities, cholestatic hepatitis
Voriconazole[5]	IV	Children: 6–8 mg/kg every 12 h for one day, then 7 mg/kg every 12 h Adults: 6 mg/kg every 12 h for one day (loading dose), then 4 mg/kg every 12 h	Visual disturbance, photosensitive rash, increased liver function tests
	PO	Children: 8 mg/kg every 12 h for one day, then 7 mg/kg every 12 h Adults: <40 kg: 200 mg every 12 h for one day, then 100 mg every 12 h; >40 kg: 400 mg every 12 h for one day, then 200 mg every 12 h;	

[1] IV indicates intravenous; IT, intrathecal; PO, oral; HIV, human immunodeficiency virus.

[2] See package insert or listing in current edition of the *Physicians' Desk Reference* or www.pdr.net (for registered users only).

[3] Interactions with other drugs are common. Consult Table 4.1 (p 743) and the *Physicians' Desk Reference*, a drug interaction reference or database, or a pharmacist before prescribing these medications.

[4] Experience with drug in children is limited.

[5] Limited or no information about use in newborn infants is available.

[6] For children 2 years of age and younger, the daily dose has not been established.

DRUGS FOR INVASIVE AND OTHER SERIOUS FUNGAL INFECTIONS IN CHILDREN

Table 4.7. Drugs for Invasive and Other Serious Fungal Infections[1]

Disease	Intravenous		Oral		Intravenous or Oral	
	Amphotericin B	Caspofungin,[2] Micafungin,[2,4] or Anidulafungin[2,4]	Flucytosine	Itraconazole[2]	Fluconazole[2]	Voriconazole[2]
Aspergillosis	P	A	…	M	…	P
Blastomycosis	P	…	…	M	M	…
Candidiasis:						
Chronic, mucocutaneous	A	A	…	A	P	A
Oropharyngeal, esophageal	P (severe cases)	P	…	A	P	A
Systemic	P, S	P	S	…	P, M	A
Coccidioidomycosis	P	…	…	P, M	P, M	…
Cryptococcosis	P, S	…	P, S	…	A, M	…
Fusariosis	P	…	…	…	…	P
Histoplasmosis	P	…	…	P, A	A, M	…
Mucormycosis (zygomycosis)	P	…	…	…	…	…
Paracoccidioidomycosis	P[3]	…	…	P, M	…	…
Pseudallescheriasis	…	…	…	M	…	P
Sporotrichosis	P	…	…	M	…	…

[1] P indicates preferred treatment in most cases; A, efficacy less well established or alternative drug; M, for mild and moderately severe cases; S, combination recommended if infection is severe or central nervous system is involved.
[2] Efficacy has not been established for children.
[3] Usually in combination with itraconazole or a sulfonamide.
[4] Approved by the Food and Drug Administration for adults.

TOPICAL DRUGS FOR SUPERFICIAL FUNGAL INFECTIONS

Table 4.8. Topical Drugs for Superficial Fungal Infections

Drug	Strength	Formulation	Trade Name Examples	Application(s) per Day	Adverse Reactions/Notes
Amphotericin B (Rx)	3%	C, L, O	Fungizone	2–4	Discoloration of the skin, clothes, nails
Basic fuchsin, phenol, resorcinol, and acetone (Rx)		S	Castellani Paint Modified	1	Excellent for intertriginous areas in all age groups. Stains everything. Also available as a colorless solution with alcohol and without basic fuchsin. This is an alternative if the patient cannot tolerate other topical antifungals.
Butenafine (Rx)	1%	C	Mentax	1	Safety and efficacy in patients <12 years of age have not been established. Do not occlude. Sensitivity to allylamines.
Ciclopirox (Rx)	1%; 8%	C, L, S, P, Gel	Loprox; Penlac nail lacquer	2	Irritant dermatitis; shake lotion vigorously before application; safety and efficacy in children <10 years of age have not been established. Precautions: diabetes mellitus; immunocompromised; seizures.
Clotrimazole (Rx and OTC)	1%	C, L, S, P, Com, SpP, SpL	Topical solution >10 preparations; check with pharmacist[1]	1 (Rx) 2 (OTC)	Irritant dermatitis; safety and efficacy in children have not been established. Avoid topical steroid combinations.[2]
Clotrimazole and betamethasone dipropionate (Rx)		C, L	Lotrisone[3]	2[2]	Irritant dermatitis: safety and efficacy in children have been established. Beware of topical steroid combinations,[2] especially when applied to the diaper area, because high systemic steroid exposure can occur. Contraindications: varicella or vaccinia.

Table 4.8. Topical Drugs for Superficial Fungal Infections, continued

Drug	Strength	Formulation	Trade Name Examples	Applications(s) per Day	Adverse Reactions/Notes
Econazole (Rx)	1%	C	Spectazole	1 (dermatophyte) 2 (candidiasis)	Irritant dermatitis.
Haloprogin (Rx)	1%	C, S	Halotex	2	Irritant dermatitis.
Hydrocortisone-iodoquinol (Rx)	1%	C	Vytone, Dermazene	3–4	Do not use in children <2 years of age.[2] May stain clothes and skin and interfere with thyroid function and phenylketonuria tests.
Ketoconazole (Rx)	2%	C, Sh	Nizoral	1 (candidiasis), tinea dermatophyte	Potential sulfite reaction with anaphylactic or asthmatic reaction; shampoo can cause dry or oily hair and increase hair loss. May interfere with permanent waving or changes in hair texture.
Miconazole (Rx and OTC)	2%	O, C, P, S, SpP, SpL	>10 preparations; check with pharmacist[1]; Fungoid tincture	2 (seborrhea), apply 2–3 times/day for several months 2 (C, L) 2 (P, L)	Irritant and allergic contact dermatitis.
Naftifine (Rx)	1%	C, Gel	Naftin	1 (C) 2 (Gel)	Irritant dermatitis.
Nystatin (Rx and OTC)	100 000 U/mL or 100 000 U/g	C, P, O, Com	Nystatin, Nystop powder, Pedi-Dri powder, Mycostatin	2 (C) 2–3 (P)	Nontoxic except with topical steroid combinations.[4]

Table 4.8. Topical Drugs for Superficial Fungal Infections, continued

Drug	Strength	Formulation	Trade Name Examples	Applications(s) per Day	Adverse Reactions/Notes
Nystatin and triamcinolone acetonide (Rx)		C, O	Mytrex cream, Mytrex ointment, Mycolog-II	2[3]	Contraindications: varicella or vaccinia. Do not occlude. Use lowest effective dose.
Oxiconazole (Rx)	1%	C, L	Oxistat	1–2 (tinea dermatophyte)	Irritant dermatitis.
Sulconazole (Rx)	1%	C, S	Exelderm	1–2 (tinea vesicular)	Irritant dermatitis.
Terbinafine (Rx and OTC)	1%	C, Gel, Sp	Lamisil	1–2	Irritant dermatitis; avoid use of occlusive clothing or dressings. Do not apply spray to face.
Tolnaftate (OTC)	1%	C, P, S, Gel, SpP, SpL	>10 preparations; check with pharmacist	2	Irritant and allergic contact dermatitis. Not recommended if <2 years of age.
Triacetin (Rx)	% varies	S, C, Sp	Fungoid tincture, Fungoid cream only-clean nail	3(C, S)	Irritant dermatitis.
Undecylenic acid and derivatives (OTC)	8%–25%	C, O, S, F, SpP, P, soap	See pharmacist for formulations and applications[1]	2 (tincture); spray 1–2 sec	Irritant dermatitis.
Undecylenic acid and chloroxylenol	25%	S	Gordochom solution	2 for 4 wks	Local hypersensitivity
	3%				

Table 4.8. Topical Drugs for Superficial Fungal Infections, continued

Drug	Strength	Formulation	Trade Name Examples	Applications(s) per Day	Adverse Reactions/Notes
Other Remedies					
Gentian violet (OTC)	2%	S	...	2	Staining.
Selenium sulfide (OTC)	2.5%	L, Sh	Exsel	Use twice weekly for 2 wks	For tinea capitis, to decrease spore formation and to decrease the potential spread of the dermatophyte.
	1%	Sh	Head & Shoulders, Selsun Blue	Use twice weekly for 2 wks	For tinea capitis, to decrease spore formation and to decrease the potential spread of the dermatophyte.
Sertaconazole	2%	C	Ertaczo	2	Contact dermatitis, local hypersensitivity

Rx indicates prescription; C, cream; L, lotion; O, ointment; S, solution; OTC, over the counter; Com, combinations; Sh, shampoo; P, powder; Sp, spray; F, foam.

[1] Pharmacists are your best resource to check formulations that are available and new (they use *Facts and Comparisons* reference products).

[2] Topical steroids must be used with caution in young children and in areas of thin skin (eg, diaper area). In these circumstances, high systemic exposure may occur, resulting in endogenous synthesis suppression with the potential for serious adverse effects. Potential adverse effects include irritant dermatitis, folliculitis, hypertrichosis, acneform eruptions, hypopigmentation, perioral dermatitis, allergic contact dermatitis, maceration, secondary infection, skin atrophy, striae, and miliaria.

[3] Lotrisone cream no longer is available; lotion is available. Also available are Lotrim and Fungizid spray.

[4] Any topical preparation has the potential to irritate the skin and cause itching, burning, stinging, erythema, edema, vesicles, and blister formation.

For more information on individual drugs, see *Physician's Desk Reference* or **www.pdr.net** (for registered users only).

ANTIVIRAL DRUGS*

Table 4.9. Antiviral Drugs

Generic (Trade Name)	Indication	Route	Age	Usually Recommended Dosage
Acyclovir[1,2,3] (Zovirax)	Neonatal herpes simplex virus (HSV) infection	IV	Birth to 3 mo	60 mg/kg per day in 3 divided doses for 14–21 days.
	HSV encephalitis	IV	≥3 mo–12 y	60 mg/kg per day in 3 divided doses for 14–21 days.
		IV	≥12 y	30 mg/kg per day in 3 divided doses for 14–21 days.
	Varicella in immunocompetent host[4]	Oral	≥2 y	80 mg/kg per day in 4 divided doses for 5 days; maximum dose, 3200 mg/day.
	Varicella in immunocompetent host	IV	≥2 y	30 mg/kg per day for 7–10 days or 1500 mg/m² per day in 3 doses for 7–10 days
	Varicella in immunocompromised host	IV	<1 y	30 mg/kg per day in 3 divided doses for 7–10 days
		IV	≥1 y	1500 mg/m² per day in 3 doses for 7–10 days; some experts recommend the 30-mg/kg per day dose.
	Zoster in immunocompetent host	IV	All ages	Same as for varicella in immunocompromised host.
		Oral	≥12 y	4000 mg/day in 5 divided doses for 5–7 days.
	Herpes-zoster in immunocompromised host	IV	<12 y	60 mg/kg per day, every 8 h, for 7–10 days
		IV	≥12 y	30 mg/kg per day, every 8 h, for 7 days
	HSV infection in immunocompromised host (localized, progressive, or disseminated)	IV	<12 y	30 mg/kg per day in 3 divided doses for 7–14 days
		IV	≥12 y	15 mg/kg per day in 3 divided doses for 7–14 days.
		Oral	≥2 y	1000 mg/day in 3–5 divided doses for 7–14 days.

* Drugs for human immunodeficiency virus infection are not included.

Table 4.9. Antiviral Drugs, continued

Generic (Trade Name)	Indication	Route	Age	Usually Recommended Dosage
	Prophylaxis of HSV in immunocompromised host	Oral	≥2 y	600–1000 mg/day in 3–5 divided doses during period of risk.
	HSV-seropositive patients	IV	All ages	15 mg/kg in 3 divided doses during period of risk.
	Genital HSV infection; first episode	Oral	≥12 y	1000–1200 mg/day in 3–5 divided doses for 7–10 days.
				Oral pediatric dose: 40–80 mg/kg per day divided in 3–4 doses for 5–10 days (maximum 1.0 g/day).
	Genital HSV infection: recurrence	IV	≥12 y	15 mg/kg per day in 3 divided doses for 5–7 days.
		Oral	≥12 y	1000–1200 mg/day in 3 divided doses for 3–5 days.
	Chronic suppressive therapy for recurrent genital and cutaneous (ocular) HSV episodes	Oral	≥12 y	800–1200 mg/day in 2 divided doses for as long as 12 continuous months.
Adefovir (Hepsera)	Chronic hepatitis B	Oral	≥18 y	10 mg once daily for 1–3 y; optimal duration of therapy unknown
Amantadine (Symmetrel)	Influenza A: treatment and prophylaxis (see Influenza, p 401)	Oral	1–9 y	Treatment or prophylaxis: 5 mg/kg per day, maximum 150 mg/day; in 2 divided doses
		Oral	≥10 y	Treatment or prophylaxis: <40 kg: 5 mg/kg per day, in 2 divided doses; ≥40 kg: 200 mg/day in 2 divided doses
		Oral	Dose by weight, not age	Alternative prophylactic dose for children >20 kg and adults: 100 mg/day.

Table 4.9. Antiviral Drugs, continued

Generic (Trade Name)	Indication	Route	Age	Usually Recommended Dosage
Cidofovir (Vistide)	Cytomegalovirus (CMV) retinitis	IV	Adult dose[5]	Induction: 5 mg/kg once weekly × 2 doses with probenecid with hydration. Maintenance: 5 mg/kg once every 2 weeks with probenecid and hydration.
Famciclovir (Famvir)	Genital HSV infection; first episode	Oral	Adult dose[5]	750 mg/day in 3 divided doses for 7–10 days.
	Episodic recurrent genital HSV infection	Oral	Adult dose[5]	250 mg/day in 2 divided doses for 3–5 days.
	Daily suppressive therapy	Oral	Adult dose[5]	500 mg/day in 2 divided doses for 1 y, then reassess for recurrence of HSV infection.
Fomivirsen (Vitravene)	CMV retinitis	IO	Adult dose[5]	1 vial (330 μg) injected into the vitreous, first 2 doses 2 weeks apart then every 4 weeks.
Foscarnet[1] (Foscavir)	CMV retinitis in patients with acquired immunodeficiency syndrome	IV	Adult dose[5]	180 mg/kg per day in 2 divided doses for 14–21 days, then 90–120 mg/kg once a day as maintenance dose.
	HSV infection resistant to acyclovir in immunocompromised host	IV	Adult dose[5]	80–120 mg/kg per day in 2–3 divided doses until infection resolves.
Ganciclovir[1] (Cytovene)	Acquired CMV retinitis in immunocompromised host[6]	IV	Adult dose[5]	10 mg/kg per day in 2 divided doses for 14–21 days; for long-term suppression, 5 mg/kg per day for 7 days/wk or 6 mg/kg per day for 5 days/wk.
	Prophylaxis of CMV in high-risk host	IV	Adult dose[5]	10 mg/kg per day in 2 divided doses for 1 wk, then 5 mg/kg per day in 1 dose for 100 days or 6 mg/kg per day for 5 days/wk.
		Oral	Adult dose[5]	1 g, orally, 3 times/day (not to be used as induction).

Table 4.9. Antiviral Drugs, continued

Generic (Trade Name)	Indication	Route	Age	Usually Recommended Dosage
Lamivudine (Epivir-HBV)	Treatment of chronic hepatitis B	Oral	≥2 y	3 mg/kg per day (maximum 100 mg/day) (children coinfected with HIV and hepatitis B should use the approved dose for HIV).
Oseltamivir (Tamiflu)	Influenza A and B: treatment and prophylaxis (see Influenza, p 401)	Oral[7]	1–12 y	Treatment for people 1–12 y of age (once daily for prophylaxis): <15 kg: 30 mg, twice daily; >15–23 kg: 45 mg, twice daily; >23–40 kg: 60 mg, twice daily; >40 kg: 75 mg, twice daily.
		Oral	≥13 y	75 mg, twice daily for treatment; once daily for prophylaxis
Ribavirin (Virazole)	Treatment of respiratory syncytial virus infection	Aerosol	Newborn infants and older	Given by a small-particle generator, in a solution of 6 g in 300 mL sterile water (20 mg/mL), delivered for 18 h per day for 3–7 days or 6 g in 100 mL of sterile water for 2 h, 3 times/day; longer treatment may be necessary in some patients.
Ribavirin (Rebetol)	Treatment of hepatitis C in combination with interferon	Oral/capsule	Dose by weight	Fixed dose by weight is suggested: 25–36 kg: 200 mg AM and PM; >36–49 kg: 200 mg AM and 400 mg PM; >49–61 kg: 400 mg AM and PM; >61–75 kg: 400 mg AM and 600 mg PM; >75 kg: 600 mg AM and PM.
		Oral/solution	≥3 y	15 mg/kg per day in 2 divided doses

Table 4.9. Antiviral Drugs, continued

Generic (Trade Name)	Indication	Route	Age	Usually Recommended Dosage
Rimantadine (Flumadine)	Influenza A: treatment	Oral	≥13 y	200 mg/day in 2 divided doses
	Influenza A: prophylaxis (see Influenza, p 401)	Oral	≥1 y	1–9 y of age: 5 mg/kg per day, maximum 150 mg/day, once daily ≥10 y of age, <40 kg: 5 mg/kg per day; in 2 divided doses; ≥40 kg: 200 mg/day in 2 divided doses
Valacyclovir (Valtrex)	Genital HSV infection	Oral	Adolescents	2 g/day in 2 divided doses for 10 days.
	Episodic recurrent genital HSV infection	Oral	Adolescents	1 g/day in 2 divided doses for 3 days.
	Daily suppressive therapy for HSV infection	Oral	Adolescents	500–1000 mg, once daily for 1 year, then reassess for recurrences.
Zanamivir (Relenza)	Influenza A and B: treatment (see Influenza, p 401)	Inhalation	≥7 y	10 mg, twice daily for 5 days. Not licensed for prophylaxis.

IV indicates intravenous; IO, intraocular.

[1] Dose should be decreased in patients with impaired renal function.
[2] Oral dosage of acyclovir in children should not exceed 80 mg/kg per day.
[3] Acyclovir doses listed in this table are based on clinical trials and clinical experience and may not be identical to doses approved by the US Food and Drug Administration.
[4] Selective indications; see Varicella-Zoster Infections (p 711).
[5] There are not sufficient clinical data to identify the appropriate dose for use in children.
[6] Some experts use ganciclovir in immunocompromised host with CMV gastrointestinal tract disease and CMV pneumonitis (with or without CMV Immune Globulin Intravenous).
[7] Oseltamivir oral suspension is packaged with a dispensing syringe calibrated with graduations of 30, 45, and 60 mg; 75 mg may be dispensed using a combination of 30- and 45-mg graduations. For more information on individual drugs, see *Physician's Desk Reference* or **www.pdr.net** (for registered users only).

....

DRUGS FOR PARASITIC INFECTIONS

The following tables (4.10 and 4.11) are reproduced from *The Medical Letter.** These tables provide recommendations that are likely to be consistent in many cases with those of the American Academy of Pediatrics Committee on Infectious Diseases, as given in the disease-specific chapters in Section 3. However, because *The Medical Letter* recommendations are developed independently, these recommendations occasionally may differ from recommendations of the committee. Accordingly, both should be consulted. The committee appreciates *The Medical Letter* for consideration in allowing this information to be reprinted.

    In Table 4.10 (p 791), first-choice and alternative drugs with recommended adult and pediatric dosages for most parasitic infections are given. In each case, the need for treatment must be weighed against the toxic effects of the drug. A decision to withhold therapy often may be correct, particularly when the drugs can cause severe adverse effects. When the first-choice drug initially is ineffective and the alternative is more hazardous, a second course of treatment with the first drug before giving the alternative may be prudent.

    Several drugs recommended in Table 4.10 (p 818) have not been approved by the US Food and Drug Administration and, thus, are investigational (see footnotes). When prescribing an unlicensed drug, the physician should inform the patient of the investigational status and adverse effects of the drug.

    These recommendations periodically (usually every other year) are updated by *The Medical Letter* (**www.medicalletter.com**) and, thus, likely are to be superseded by new ones before the next edition of the *Red Book* is published.

---

* Reprinted with permission from *The Medical Letter*. 2004;(1189):1–12

Table 4.10. Drugs for Parasitic Infections

Parasitic infections are found throughout the world. With increasing travel, immigration, use of immunosuppressive drugs and the spread of AIDS, physicians anywhere may see infections caused by previously unfamiliar parasites. The table below lists first-choice and alternative drugs for most parasitic infections. The manufacturers of the drugs are listed on page 818.

Infection	Drug	Adult Dosage	Pediatric Dosage
Acanthamoeba keratitis			
Drug of choice:	See footnote 1		
AMEBIASIS (*Entamoeba histolytica*)			
asymptomatic			
Drug of choice:	Iodoquinol	650 mg tid × 20d	30–40 mg/kg/d (max. 2 g) in 3 doses × 20d
OR	Paromomycin	25–35 mg/kg/d in 3 doses × 7d	25–35 mg/kg/d in 3 doses × 7d
Alternative:	Diloxanide furoate[2]*	500 mg tid × 10d	20 mg/kg/d in 3 doses × 10d
mild to moderate intestinal disease[3]			
Drug of choice:[4]	Metronidazole	500–750 mg tid × 7–10d	35–50 mg/kg/d in 3 doses × 7–10d
OR	Tinidazole[5]	2 g once daily × 3d	50 mg/kg/d (max. 2 g) in 1 dose × 3d
severe intestinal and extraintestinal disease[3]			
Drug of choice:	Metronidazole	750 mg tid × 7–10d	35–50 mg/kg/d in 3 doses × 7–10d
OR	Tinidazole[5]	2 g once daily × 5d	50 mg/kg/d (max. 2 g) × 5d

* Availability problems. See table on page 818.

1. For treatment of keratitis caused by *Acanthamoeba*, concurrent topical use of 0.1% propamidine isethionate (*Brolene*) plus neomycin-polymyxin B-gramicidin ophthalmic solution has been successful (SL Hargrave et al, *Ophthalmology* 1999; 106:952). In some European countries, propamidine is not available and hexamidine (*Desmodine*) has been used (DV Seal, *Eye* 2003; 17:893). In addition, 0.02% topical polyhexamethylene biguanide (PHMB) and/or chlorhexidine has been used successfully in a large number of patients (G Tabin et al, *Cornea* 2001; 20:757; YS Wysenbeek et al, *Cornea* 2000; 19:464). PHMB is available from Leiter's Park Avenue Pharmacy, San Jose, CA (800-292-6773; www.leiterrx.com). The combination of chlorhexadine, natamycin (pimaricin) and debridement also has been successful (K Kitagawa et al, *Jpn J Ophthalmol* 2003; 47:616).

2. The drug is not available commercially, but as a service can be compounded by Panorama Compounding Pharmacy, 6744 Balboa Blvd, Van Nuys, CA 91406 (800-247-9767) or Medical Center Pharmacy, New Haven, CT (203-688-6816).

3. Treatment should be followed by a course of iodoquinol or paromomycin in the dosage used to treat asymptomatic amebiasis.

4. Nitazoxanide is FDA-approved as a pediatric oral suspension for treatment of *Cryptosporidium* in immunocompetent children <12 years old and for *Giardia* (*Medical Letter* 2003; 45:29). It may also be effective for mild to moderate amebiasis (E Diaz et al, *Am J Trop Med Hyg* 2003; 68:384). Nitazoxanide is available in 500-mg tables and an oral suspension; it should be taken with food.

5. A nitro-imidazole similar to metronidazole, tinidazole was recently approved by the FDA and appears to be as effective and better tolerated than metronidazole. It should be taken with food to minimize GI adverse effects. For children and patients unable to take tablets, a pharmacist may crush the tablets and mix them with cherry syrup (*Humco*, and others). The syrup suspension is good for 7 days at room temperature and must be shaken before use. Ornidazole, a similar drug, is also used outside the US.

Table 4.10. Drugs for Parasitic Infections, continued

Infection	Drug	Adult Dosage	Pediatric Dosage
AMEBIC MENINGOENCEPHALITIS, primary and granulomatous			
Naegleria			
Drug of choice:	Amphotericin B[6,7]	1.5 mg/kg/d in 2 doses × 3d, then	1.5 mg/kg/d in 2 doses × 3d, then
		1 mg/kg/d × 6d	1 mg/kg/d × 6d
Acanthamoeba			
Drug of choice:	See footnote 8		
Balamuthia mandrillaris			
Drug of choice:	See footnote 9		
Sappinia diploidea			
Drug of choice:	See footnote 10		
ANCYLOSTOMA caninum (Eosinophilic enterocolitis)			
Drug of choice:	Albendazole[7]	400 mg once	400 mg once
OR	Mebendazole	100 mg bid × 3d	100 mg bid × 3d
OR	Pyrantel pamoate[7]	11 mg/kg (max. 1 g) × 3d	11 mg/kg (max. 1 g) × 3d
OR	Endoscopic removal		
Ancylostoma duodenale, see HOOKWORM			

* Availability problems. See table on page 818.

6. *Naegleria* infection has been treated successfully with intravenous and intrathecal use of both amphotericin B and miconazole plus rifampin and with amphotericin B, rifampin and ornidazole (J Seidel et al, *N Engl J Med* 1982; 306:346; R Jain et al, *Neurol India* 2002; 50:470). Other reports of successful therapy are less well documented.

7. An approved drug, but considered investigational for this condition by the FDA.

8. Strains of *Acanthamoeba* isolated from fatal granulomatous amebic encephalitis are usually susceptible *in vitro* to pentamidine, ketoconazole, fluctosine and (less so) to amphotericin B. Chronic *Acanthamoeba* meningitis has been successfully treated in 2 children with a combination of oral trimethoprim/sulfamethodxazole, rifampin and ketoconazole (T Singal et al, *Pediatr Infect Dis J* 2001; 20:623) and in an AIDS patient with fluconazole, sulfadiazine and pyrimethamine combined with surgical resection of the CNS lesion (M Seijo Martinez et al, *J Clin Microbiol* 2000; 38:3892). Disseminated cutaneous infection in an immunocompromised patient has been treated successfully with IV pentamidine isethionate, topical chlorhexidine and 2% ketoconazole cream, followed by oral itraconazole (CA Slater et al, *N Engl J Med* 1994; 331:85).

9. A free-living leptomyxid ameba that causes subacute to fatal granulomatous CNS disease. Several cases of *Balamuthia* encephalitis have been successfully treated with flucytosine, pentamidine, fluconazole and sulfadiazine plus either azithromycin or clarithromycin (phenothiazines were also used) combined with surgical resection of the CNS lesion (TR Deetz et al, *Clin Infect Dis* 2003; 37:1304; S Jung et al, *Arch Pathol Lab Med* 2004; 128:466).

10. A free-living ameba not previously known to be pathogenic to humans. It has been successfully treated with azithromycin, IV pentamidine, itraconazole and flucytosine combined with

Table 4.10. Drugs for Parasitic Infections, continued

Infection	Drug	Adult Dosage	Pediatric Dosage
ANGIOSTRONGYLIASIS (*Angiostrongylus cantonensis, Angiostrongylus costaricensis*)			
Drug of choice:	See footnote 11		
ANISAKIASIS (*Anisakis spp.*)			
Treatment of choice:[12]	Surgical or endoscopic removal		
ASCARIASIS (*Ascaris lumbricoides*, roundworm)			
Drug of choice:	Albendazole[7]	400 mg once	400 mg once
OR	Mebendazole	100 mg bid × 3d or 500 mg once	100 mg bid × 3d or 500 mg once
OR	Ivermectin[7]	150–200 mcg/kg once	150–200 mcg/kg once
BABESIOSIS (*Babesia microti*)			
Drugs of choice:[13]	Clindamycin[7]	1.2 g bid IV or 600 mg tid PO × 7–10d	20–40 mg/kg/d PO in 3 doses × 7–10d
	plus quinine[7]	650 mg tid PO × 7–10d	25 mg/kg/d PO in 3 doses × 7–10d
OR	Atovaquone[7]	750 mg bid × 7–10d	20 mg/kg bid × 7–10d
	plus azithromycin[7]	600 mg daily × 7–10d	12 mg/kg daily × 7–10d

Balamuthia mandrillaris, see AMEBIC MENINGOENCEPHALITIS, PRIMARY

* Availability problems. See table on page 818.

11. Most patients have a self-limited course and recover completely. Analgesics, corticosteroids and careful removal of CSF at frequent intervals can relieve symptoms from increased intracranial pressure (V Lo Re III and SJ Gluckman, *Am J Med* 2003; 114:217). No antihelminthic drug is proven to be effective and some patients have worsened with therapy (TJ Slom et al, *N Engl J Med* 2002; 346:668). In one report, however, mebendazole and a corticosteroid appeared to shorten the course of infection (H-C Tsai et al, *Am J Med* 2001; 111:109).

12. A Repiso Ortega et al, *Gastroenterol Hepatol* 2003; 26:341. Successful treatment of a patient with *Anisakiasis* with albendazole has been reported (DA Moore et al, *Lancet* 2002; 360:54).

13. Exchange transfusion has been used in severely ill patients and those with high (>10%) parasitemia (JC Hatcher et al, *Clin Infect Dis* 2001; 32:1117). In patients who were not severely ill, combination therapy with atovaquone and azithromycin was as effective as clindamycin and quinine and may have been better tolerated (PJ Krause et al, *N Engl J Med* 2000; 343:1454).

Table 4.10. Drugs for Parasitic Infections, continued

Infection	Drug	Adult Dosage	Pediatric Dosage
BALANTIDIASIS (*Balantidium coli*)			
Drug of choice:	Tetracycline[7,14]	500 mg qid × 10d	40 mg/kg/d (max. 2 g) in 4 doses × 10d
Alternatives:	Metronidazole[7]	750 mg tid × 5d	35–50 mg/kg/d in 3 doses × 5d
	Iodoquinol[7]	650 mg tid × 20d	40 mg/kg/d in 3 doses × 20d
BAYLISASCARIASIS (*Baylisascaris procyonis*)			
Drug of choice:	See footnote 15		
BLASTOCYSTIS hominis infection			
Drug of choice:	See footnote 16		
CAPILLARIASIS (*Capillaria philippinensis*)			
Drug of choice:	Mebendazole[7]	200 mg bid × 20d	200 mg bid × 20d
Alternatives:	Albendazole[7]	400 mg daily × 10d	400 mg daily × 10d
Chagas' disease, see TRYPANOSOMIASIS			
Clonorchis sinensis, see FLUKE infection			

* Availability problems. See table on page 818.

14. Use of tetracyclines is contraindicated in pregnancy and in children <8 years old.

15. No drugs have been demonstrated to be effective. Albendazole 25 mg/kg/d × 20d started as soon as possible (up to 3d after possible infection) might prevent clinical disease and is recommended for children with known exposure (ingestion of racoon stool or contaminated soil) (*MMWR Morb Mortal Wkly Rep* 2002; 50:1153; PJ Gavin and ST Shulman, *Pediatr Infect Dis* 2003; 22:651). Mebendazole, thiabendazole, levamisole or ivermectin could be tried if albendazole were not available. Steroid therapy may be helpful, especially in eye and CNS infections. Ocular baylisascariasis has been treated successfully using laser photocoagulation therapy to destroy the intraretinal larvae.

16. Clinical significance of these organisms is controversial; metronidazole 750 mg tid × 10d, iodoquinol 650 mg tid × 20d or trimethoprim-sulfamethoxazole 1 DS tab bid × 7d have been reported to be effective (DJ Stenzel and PFL Borenam, *Clin Microbiol Rev* 1996; 9:563; UZ Ok et al, *Am J Gastroenterol* 1999; 94:3245). Metronidazole resistance may be common (K Haresh et al, *Trop Med Int Health* 1999; 4:274). Nitazoxanide has been effective in children (E Diaz et al, *Am J Trop Med Hyg* 2003; 68:384).

Table 4.10. Drugs for Parasitic Infections, continued

Infection	Drug	Adult Dosage	Pediatric Dosage
CRYPTOSPORIDIOSIS (*Cryptosporidium*)			
Non-HIV infected			
Drug of Choice:	Nitazoxanide[4]	500 mg bid × 3d[7]	1–3 yrs: 100 mg bid × 3d 4–11 yrs: 200 mg bid × 3d
HIV infected			
Drug of choice:	See footnote 17		
CUTANEOUS LARVA MIGRANS (creeping eruption, dog and cat hookworm)			
Drug of choice:[18]	Albendazole[7]	400 mg daily × 3d	400 mg daily × 3d
OR	Ivermectin[7]	200 mcg/kg daily × 1–2d	200 mcg/kg daily × 1–2d
Alternatively:	Thiabendazole	Topically	Topically
CYCLOSPORIASIS, (*Cyclospora cayetanensis*)			
Drug of choice:[19]	Trimethoprim- sulfamethoxazole[7]	TMP 160 mg/kg, SMX 800 mg (1 DS tab) bid × 7–10d	TMP 5 mg/kg, SMX 25 mg/kg/d bid × 7–10d
CYSTICERCOSIS, see TAPEWORM infection			
DIENTAMOEBA fragilis infection[20]			
Drug of choice:	Iodoquinol	650 mg tid × 20d	30–40 mg/kg/d (max. 2 g) in 3 doses × 20d
OR	Paromomycin[7]	25–35 mg/kg/d in 3 doses × 7d	25–35 mg/kg/d in 3 doses × 7d
OR	Tetracycline[7,14]	500-mg qid × 10d	40 mg/kg/d (max. 2 g) in 4 doses × 10d
OR	Metronidazole	500–750 mg tid × 10d	20–40 mg/kg/d in 3 doses × 10d

* Availability problems. See table on page 818.

17. Nitazoxanide has not consistently been shown to be superior to placebo in HIV-infected patients (B Amadi et al, *Lancet* 2002; 360:1375). A small randomized, double-blind trial in symptomatic HIV-infected patients who were not receiving HAART found paromomycin similar to placebo (RG Hewitt et al, *Clin Infect Dis* 2000; 31:1084).
18. G Albanese et al, *Int J Dermatol* 2001; 40:67.
19. HIV-infected patients may need higher dosage and long-term maintenance (A Kansouzidou et al, *J Trav Med* 2004; 11:61).
20. A Norberg et al, *Clin Microbiol Infect* 2003; 9:65.

Table 4.10. Drugs for Parasitic Infections, continued

Infection	Drug	Adult Dosage	Pediatric Dosage
Diphyllobothrium latum, see TAPEWORM infection			
DRACUNCULUS medinensis (guinea worm) infection			
Drug of choice:	See footnote 21		
Echinococcus, see TAPEWORM infection			
Entamoeba histolytica, see AMEBIASIS			
ENTEROBIUS vermicularis (pinworm) infection			
Drug of choice:[22]	Pyrantel pamoate	11 mg/kg base once (max. 1 g); repeat in 2 wks	11 mg/kg base once (max. 1 g); repeat in 2 wks
OR	Mebendazole	100 mg once; repeat in 2 wks	100 mg once; repeat in 2 wks
OR	Albendazole[7]	400 mg once; repeat in 2 wks	400 mg once; repeat in 2 wks
Fasciola hepatica, see FLUKE infection			
FILARIASIS[23]			
Wuchereria bancrofti, Brugia malayi, Brugia timori			
Drug of choice:[24]	Diethylcarbamazine*	6 mg/kg in 3 doses × 14d[25]	6 mg/kg in 3 doses × 14d[25]

* Availability problems. See table on page 818.

21. Treatment of choice is slow extraction of worm combined with wound care (C Greenway, *CMAJ* 2004; 170:495). 10 days' treatment with metronidazole 250 mg tid in adults and 25 mg/kg/d in 3 doses in children not curative, but decreases inflammation and facilitates removal of the worm. Mebendazole 400–800 mg/d × 6d has been reported to kill the worm directly.

22. Since all family members are usually infected, treatment of the entire household is recommended.

23. Antihistamines or corticosteroids may be required to decrease allergic reactions due to disintegration of microfilariae from treatment of filarial infections, especially those caused by *Loa loa*. Endosymbiotic *Wolbachia* bacteria may have a role in filarial development and host response, and may represent a new target for therapy. Treatment with doxycycline 100 or 200 mg/d × 4–6 wks in lymphatic filariasis and onchocerciasis has resulted in substantial loss of *Wolbachia* with subsequent block of microfilariae production and absence of microfilaria when followed for 24 months after treatment (A Hoerauf et al, *Med Microbiol Immunol* 2003; 192:211; A Hoerauf et al, *BMJ* 2003; 326:207).

24. Most symptoms caused by adult worm. Single dose combination of albendazole (400 mg) with either ivermectin (200 mcg/kg) or diethylcarbamazine 6 mg/kg is effective for reduction or suppression of *W. bancrofti* microfilaria but does not kill the adult forms (D Addiss et al, *Cochrane Database Syst Rev* 2004; CD003753).

25. For patients with microfilaria in the blood, Medical Letter consultants would start with a lower dosage and scale up: d1: 50 mg; d2: 50 mg tid; d3: 100 mg tid; d4–14: 6 mg/kg in 3 doses (for *Loa Loa* d4–14: 9 mg/kg in 3 doses). Multi-dose regimens have been shown to provide more rapid reduction in microfilaria than single-dose diethylcarbamazine, but microfilaria levels are similar 6–12 mos after treatment (LD Andrade et al, *Trans R Soc Trop Med Hyg* 1995; 89:319; PE Simonsen et al, *Am J Trop Med Hyg* 1995; 53:267). A single dose of 6 mg/kg is used in endemic areas for mass treatment (J Figueredo-Silva et al, *Trans R Soc Trop Med Hyg* 1996; 90:192; J Noroes et al, *Trans R Soc Trop Med Hyg* 1997; 91:78).

Table 4.10. Drugs for Parasitic Infections, continued

Infection	Drug	Adult Dosage	Pediatric Dosage
FILARIASIS (continued)			
Loa loa			
Drug of choice:[26]	Diethylcarbamazine*	6 mg/kg in 3 doses × 14d[25]	6 mg/kg in 3 doses × 14d[25]
Mansonella ozzardi			
Drug of choice:[24]	See footnote 27		
Mansonella perstans			
Drug of choice:[24]	Albendazole[7]	400 mg bid × 10d	400 mg bid × 10d
OR	Mebendazole[7]	100 mg bid × 30d	100 mg bid × 30d
Mansonella streptocerca			
Drug of choice:[24,28]	Diethylcarbamazine*	6 mg/kg/d × 14d	6 mg/kg/d × 14d
	Ivermectin[7]	150 mcg/kg once	150 mcg/kg once
Tropical Pulmonary Eosinophilia (TPE)[29]			
Drug of choice:[24,28]	Diethylcarbamazine*	6 mg/kg/d in 3 doses × 12–21d	6 mg/kg/d in 3 doses × 12–21d
Onchocerca volvulus (River blindness)			
Drug of choice:	Ivermectin[30]	150 mcg/kg once, repeated every 6–12 mos until asymptomatic	150 mcg/kg once, repeated every 6–12 mos until asymptomatic

* Availability problems. See table on page 818.

26. In heavy infections with *Loa loa*, rapid killing of microfilariae can provoke an encephalopathy. Apheresis has been reported to be effective in lowering microfilarial counts in patients heavily infected with *Loa loa* (EA Ottesen, *Infect Dis Clin North Am* 1993; 7:619). Albendazole or ivermectin have also been used to reduce microfilaremia; albendazole is preferred because of its slower onset of action and lower risk of encephalopathy (AD Klion et al, *J Infect Dis* 1993; 168:202; M kombila et al, *Am J Trop Med Hyg* 1998; 58:458). Albendazole may be useful for treatment of loiasis when diethylcarbamazine is ineffective or cannot be used, but repeated courses may be necessary (AD Klion et al, *Clin Infect Dis* 1999; 29:680). Diethylcarbamazine, 300 mg once/wk, has been recommended for prevention of loiasis (TB Nutman et al, *N Engl J Med* 1988; 319:752).

27. Diethylcarbamazine has no effect. Ivermectin 200 mcg/kg once, has been effective.

28. Diethylcarbamazine is potentially curative due to activity against both adult worms and microfilariae. Ivermectin is only active against microfilariae.

29. Relapse occurs and can be treated with diethylcarbamazine.

30. Annual treatment with ivermectin, 150 mcg/kg, can prevent blindness due to ocular onchocerciasis (D Mabey et al, *Ophthalmology* 1996; 103: 1001). Diethylcarbamazine should not be used for treatment of this disease.

Table 4.10. Drugs for Parasitic Infections, continued

Infection	Drug	Adult Dosage	Pediatric Dosage
FLUKE, hermaphroditic, infection			
Clonorchis sinensis (Chinese liver fluke)			
Drug of choice:	Praziquantel	75 mg/kg/d in 3 doses × 1d	75 mg/kg/d in 3 doses × 1d
OR	Albendazole[7]	10 mg/kg × 7d	10 mg/kg × 7d
Fasciola hepatica (sheep liver fluke)			
Drug of choice:[31]	Triclabendazole*	10 mg/kg once or twice[32]	10 mg/kg once or twice[32]
Alternative:	Bithionol*	30–50 mg/kg on alternate days × 10–15 doses	30–50 mg/kg on alternate days × 10–15 doses
Fasciolopsis buski, Heterophyes heterophyes, Metagonimus yokogawai (intestinal flukes)			
Drug of choice:	Praziquantel[7]	75 mg/kg/d in 3 doses × 1d	75 mg/kg/d in 3 doses × 1d
Metrochis conjunctus (North American liver fluke)[33]			
Drug of choice:	Praziquantel[7]	75 mg/kg/d in 3 doses × 1d	75 mg/kg/d in 3 doses × 1d
Nanophyetus salmincola			
Drug of choice:	Praziquantel[7]	60 mg/kg/d in 3 doses × 1d	60 mg/kg/d in 3 doses × 1d
Opisthorchis viverrini (Southeast Asian liver fluke)			
Drug of choice:	Praziquantel	75 mg/kg/d in 3 doses × 1d	75 mg/kg/d in 3 doses × 1d
Paragonimus westermani (lung fluke)			
Drug of choice:	Praziquantel[7]	75 mg/kg/d in 3 doses × 2d	75 mg/kg/d in 3 doses × 2d
Alternative:[34]	Bithionol*	30–50 mg/kg on alternate days × 10–15 doses	30–50 mg/kg on alternate days × 10–15 doses

* Availability problems. See table on page 818.

31. Unlike infections with other flukes, *Fasciola hepatica* infections may not respond to praziquantel. Triclabendazole (*Egaten*-Novartis) may be safe and effective but data are limited (CS Graham et al, *Clin Infect Dis* 2001; 33:1). It is available from Victoria Pharmacy, Zurich, Switzerland (www.pharmaworld.com; 41-1-211-24-32) and should be given with food for better absorption. A single study has found that nitazoxanide has limited efficacy for treating fascioliasis in adults and children (L Favennec et al, *Aliment Pharmacol Ther* 2003; 17:265).

32. J Richter et al, *Curr Treat Option Infect Dis* 2002; 4:313.

33. JD MacLean et al, *Lancet* 1996; 347:154.

Table 4.10. Drugs for Parasitic Infections, continued

Infection	Drug	Adult Dosage	Pediatric Dosage
GIARDIASIS (*Giardia duodenalis*)			
Drug of choice:	Metronidazole[7]	250 mg tid × 5d	15 mg/kg/d in 3 doses × 5d
	Nitazoxanide[4]	500 mg bid × 3d	1–3 yrs: 100 mg q12h × 3d
			4–11 yrs: 200 mg q12h × 3d
Alternatives:[35]	Tinidazole[5]	2 g once	50 mg/kg once (max. 2 g)
	Paromomycin[7,36]	25–35 mg/kg/d in 3 doses × 7d	25–35 mg/kg/d in 3 doses × 7d
	Furazolidone	100 mg qid 7 × 10d	6 mg/kg/d in 4 doses × doses × 7–10d
	Quinacrine[2]	100 mg tid × 5d	2 mg/kg tid × 5d (max. 300 mg/d)
GNATHOSTOMIASIS (*Gnathostoma spinigerum*)			
Treatment of choice:[37]	Albendazole[7]	400 mg bid × 21d	400 mg bid × 21d
OR	Ivermectin[7]	200 mcg/kg/d × 2d	200 mcg/kg/d × 2d
±	Surgical removal		
GONGYLONEMIASIS (*Gongylonema sp.*)[38]			
Treatment of choice:	Surgical removal		
OR	Albendazole[7]	10 mg/kg/d × 3d	10 mg/kg/d × 3d

* Availability problems. See table on page 818.

35. Albendazole 400 mg daily × 5d alone or in combination with metronidazole may also be effective (A Hall and Q Nahar, *Trans R Soc Trop Med Hyg* 1993; 87:84; AK Dutta et al, *Indian J Pediatr* 1994; 61:689; B Cacopardo et al, *Clin Ter* 1995; 146:761). Combination treatment with standard doses of metronidazole and quinacrine given for 3 wks has been effective for a small number of refractory infections (TE Nash et al, *Clin Infect Dis* 2001; 33:22). In one study, nitazoxanide was used successfully in high doses to treat a case of *Giardia* resistant to metronidazole and albendazole (P Abboud et al, *Clin Infect Dis* 2001; 32:1792).

36. Not absorbed; may be useful for treatment of giardiasis in pregnancy.

37. M de Gorgolas et al, *J Travel Med* 2003; 10:358. All patients should be treated with a medication regardless of whether surgery is attempted.

38. ML Eberhard and C Busillo, *Am J Trop Med Hyg* 1999; 61:51; ME Wilson et al, *Clin Infect Dis* 2001; 32:1378.

Table 4.10. Drugs for Parasitic Infections, continued

Infection	Drug	Adult Dosage	Pediatric Dosage
HOOKWORM infection (*Ancylostoma duodenale*, *Necator americanus*)			
Drug of choice:	Albendazole[7]	400 mg once	400 mg once
OR	Mebendazole	100 mg bid × 3d or 500 mg once	100 mg bid × 3d or 500 mg once
OR	Pyrantel pamoate[7]	11 mg/kg (max. 1g) × 3d	11 mg/kg (max. 1g) × 3d
Hydatid cyst, see TAPEWORM infection			
Hymenolepis nana, see TAPEWORM infection			
ISOSPORIASIS (*Isospora belli*)			
Drug of choice:[39]	Trimethoprim-sulfamethoxazole[7]	TMP 160 mg/SMX 800 mg (1 DS tab) bid × 10d	TMP 5 mg/kg, SMX 25 mg/kg bid × 10d
LEISHMANIA infection			
Visceral[40]			
Drugs of choice:	Sodium stibo-gluconate*	20 mg Sb/kg/d IV or IM × 28d[41]	20 mg Sb/kg/d IV or IM × 28d[41]
OR	Meglumine antimonate*	20 mg Sb/kg/d IV or IM × 28d[41]	20 mg Sb/kg/d IV or IM × 28d[41]
OR	Amphotericin B[7]	0.5–1 mg/kg IV daily or every second day for up to 8 wks	0.5–1 mg/kg IV daily or every second day for up to 8 wks
OR	Liposomal amphotericin B[42]	3 mg/kg/d IV (d 1–5) and 3 mg/kg/d d 14 and 21[43]	3 mg/kg/d IV (d 1–5) and 3 mg/kg/d d 14 and 21[43]

* Availability problems. See table on page 818.

39. In immunocompetent patients usually a self-limited illness. Immunosuppressed patients may need higher doses, longer duration (TMP/SMX qid × 10d, followed by bid × 3 wks) and long-term maintenance. In sulfonamide-sensitive patients, pyrimethamine 50–75 mg daily in divided doses (plus leucovorin 10–25 mg/d) has been effective.

40. Visceral infection is most commonly due to the Old Wolrd species. *L. donovani* (kala-azar) and *L. infantum* and the New World species *L. chagasi*. Treatment duration may vary based on symptoms, host immune status, species and area of the world where infection was acquired.

41. May be repeated or continued; a longer duration may be needed for some patients (BL Herwaldt, *Lancet* 1999; 354:1191).

42. Three lipid formulations of amphotericin B have been used for treatment of visceral leishmaniasis. Largely based on clinical trials in patients infected with *L. infantum*, the FDA approved liposomal amphotericin B (*AmBisome*) for treatment of visceral leishmaniasis (A Meyerhoff, *Clin Infect Dis* 1999; 28:42). Amphotericin B lipid complex (*Abelcet*) and amphotericin B cholesteryl sulfate (*Amphotec*) have also been used with good results but are considered investigational for this condition by the FDA.

43. The FDA-approved dosage regimen for immunocompetent patients (e.g., HIV infected) is 4 mg/kg/d (d 1–5) and 4 mg/kg/d on d 10, 17, 24, 31 and 38. The relapse rate is high;

Table 4.10. Drugs for Parasitic Infections, continued

Infection	Drug	Adult Dosage	Pediatric Dosage
LEISHMANIA infection, Visceral (continued)			
Alternative:[44]	Pentamidine[7]	4 mg/kg IV or IM daily or every second day for 15–30 doses	4 mg/kg IV or IM daily or every second day for 15–30 doses
Cutaneous[45]			
Drugs of choice:	Sodium stibo-gluconate*	20 mg Sb/kg/d IV or IM × 20d[41]	20 mg Sb/kg/d IV or IM × 20d[41]
OR	Meglumine antimonate*	20 mg Sb/kg/d IV or IM × 20d[41]	20 mg Sb/kg/d IV or IM × 20d[41]
Alternatives:[46]	Pentamidine[7]	2–3 mg/kg IV or IM daily or every second day × 4–7 doses[47]	2–3 mg/kg IV or IM daily or every second day × 4–7 doses[47]
OR	Paromomycin[7,48]	Topically 2x/d × 10–20d	Topically 2x/d × 10–20d

* Availability problems. See table on page 818.

44. For treatment of kala-azar in adults in India, oral miltefosine 100 mg/d (~2.5 mg/kg/d) for 3–4 wks was 97% effective after 6 mos (TK Jha et al, *N Engl J Med* 1999; 341:1795; H Sangraula et al, *J Assoc Physicians India* 2003; 51:686). Gastrointestinal adverse effects are common, and the drug is contraindicated in pregnancy. The dose of miltefosine in an open-label trial in children in India was 2.5 mg/kg/d × 28d (SK Bhhattacharya et al, *Clin Infect Dis* 2004; 38:217). Miltefosine (*Impavido*) is available form the manufacturer (Zentaris – Frankfurt, Germany at Impavido@zentaris.de).

45. Cutaneous infection is most commonly due to the Old World species *L. major* and *L. tropica* and the New World species *L. mexicana, L. (Vianna) braziliensis* and other. Treatment duration may vary based on symptoms, host immune status, species and area of the world where infection was acquired.

46. In a placebo-controlled trial in patients ≥12 years old, oral miltefosine was effective for the treatment of cutaneous leishmaniasis due to *L.(V.) panamensis* in Colombia but not *L.(V.) braziliensis* in Guatemala at a dosage of about 2.5 mg/kg/d for 28d. "Motion sickness," nausea, headache and increased creatinine were the most frequent adverse effects (J Soto et al, *Clin Infect Dis* 2004; 38:1266). See footnote 44 regarding miltefosine availability. For treatment of *L. major* cutaneous lesions, a study in Suadi Arabia found that oral fluconazole, 200 mg once/d × 6 wks, appeared to speed healing (AA Alrajhi et al, *N Engl J Med* 2002;346:891).

47. At this dosage pentamidine has been effective against leishmaniasis in Colombia where the likely organism was *L. (V.) panamensis* (J Soto-Mancipe et al, *Clin Infect Dis* 1993; 16:417; J soto et al, *Am J Trop Med Hyg* 1994;50:107); its effect against other species is not well established.

48. Topical paromomycin should be used only in geographic regions where cutaneous leishmaiasis species have low potential for mucoasal spread. A formulation of 15% paromomycin/12% methylbenzethonium chloride (*Leshcutan*) in soft white paraffin for topical use has been reported to be partially effective in some patients against cutaneous leishmaniasis due to *L. major* in Isreal and against *L. mexicana* and *L. (V.) braziliensis* in Guatemala, where mucosal spread is very rare (BA Arana et al, *Am J Trop Med Hyg* 2001; 65:466). The methylbenzethonium is irritating to the skin; lesions may worsen before they improve.

Table 4.10. Drugs for Parasitic Infections, continued

Infection	Drug	Adult Dosage	Pediatric Dosage
LEISHMANIA infection (continued)			
Mucosal[49]			
Drugs of choice:	Sodium stibogluconate*	20 mg Sb/kg/d IV or IM × 28d[41]	20 mg Sb/kg/d IV or IM × 28d[41]
OR	Meglumine antimonate*	20 mg Sb/kg/d IV or IM × 28d[41]	20 mg Sb/kg/d IV or IM × 28d[41]
OR	Amphotericin B[7]*	0.5–1 mg/kg IV daily or every second day for up to 8 wks	0.5–1 mg/kg IV daily or every second day for up to 8 wks
LICE infestation (*pediculus humanus, P. capitis, Phthirus pubis*)[50]			
Drug of choice:	0.5% Malathion[51]	Topically	Topically
OR	1% Permethrin[52]	Topically	Topically
Alternative:	Pyrethrins with piperonyl butoxide[52]	Topically	Topically
OR	Ivermectin[7,53]	200 mcg/kg × 3, d 1, 2 and 10	200 mcg/kg × 3, d 1, 2 and 10

Loa loa, *see* FILARIASIS

* Availability problems. See table on page 818.

49. Mucosal infection is most commonly dut to the New World species *L. (V.) braziliensis, L. (V.) panamensis,* or *L. (V.) guyanensis.* Treatment duration may vary based on symptoms, host immune status, species and area of the world where infection was acquired.

50. For infestation of eyelashes with *P. pubis* lice, use petrolatum; TMP/SMX has also been used (TL Meinking, *Curr Probl Dermatol* 1996; 24:157). For pubic lice, treat with 5% permethrin or ivermectin as for scabies (see page 811). TMP/SMX has also been effective together with permethrin for head lice (RB Hipolito et al, *Pediatrics* 2001; 107:E30).

51. KS Yoon et al, *Arch Dermatol* 2003; 139:994.

52. A second application is recommended one week later to kill hatching progeny. Some lice are resistant to pyrethrins and permethrin (TL Meinking et al, *Arch Dermatol* 2002; 138:220).

53. Ivermectin is effective against adult lice but has no effect on nits (KN Jones and JC English III, *Clin Infect Dis* 2003; 36:1355).

Table 4.10. Drugs for Parasitic Infections, continued

Infection	Drug	Adult Dosage	Pediatric Dosage
MALARIA, Treatment of (*Plasmodium falciparum, P. ovale, P. vivax, and P. malariae*)			
P. falciparum[54] acquired in areas of **chloroquine-resistance**			
ORAL[55]			
Drugs of choice:	Atovaquone/ proguanil[56]	2 adult tabs bid[58] or 4 adult tabs once daily × 3d	<5 kg: not indicated
			5–8 kg: 2 peds tabs once/d × 3d
			9–10 kg: 3 peds tabs once/d × 3d
			11–20 kg: 1 adult tab once/d × 3d
			21–30 kg: 2 adult tabs once/d × 3d
			31–40 kg: 3 adult tabs once/d × 3d
			>40 kg: 4 adult tabs once/d × 3d

* Availability problems. See table on page 818.

54. Chloroquine-resistant *P. falciparum* occurs in all malarious areas except Central America west of the Panama Canal Zone, Mexico, Haiti, the Dominican Republic, and most of the Middle East (chloroquine resistance has been reported in Yemen, Oman, Saudi Arabia and Iran). For treatment of multiple-drug-resistant *P. falciparum* in Southeast Asia, especially Thailand, where resistance to mefloquine is frequent, atovaquone/proguanil, artesunate plus mefloquine or artemether plus mefloquine may be used (JC Luxemburge et al, *Trans R Soc Trop Med Hyg* 1994; 88:213; J Karbwarng et al, *Trans R Soc Trop Med Hyg* 1995; 89:296).

55. Uncomplicated or mild malaria may be treated with oral drugs.

56. Atovaquone plus proguanil is available as a fixed-dose combination tablet: adult tablets (*Malarone*; 250 mg atovaquone/100 mg proguanil) and pediatric tablets (*Malarone Pediatric*; 62.5 mg atovaquone/25 mg proguanil). To enhance absorption, it should be taken with food or a milky drink. Atovaquone/proguanil should not be given to pregnant women or patients with severe renal impairment (creatinine clearance <30mL/min). There have been several isolated reports or resistance in *P. falciparum* in Africa (E Schwartz et al, *Clin Infect Dis* 2003; 37:450; A Farnert et al, *BMJ* 2003; 326:628).

Table 4.10. Drugs for Parasitic Infections, continued

Infection	Drug	Adult Dosage	Pediatric Dosage
MALARIA, Treatment of, *P. falciparum*, (continued)			
OR	Quinine sulfate	650 mg q8h × 3–7d[57]	30 mg/kg/d in 3 doses × 3–7d[57]
	plus		
	doxycycline[7,14]	100 mg bid × 7d	4 mg/kg/d in 2 doses × 7d
	or plus		
	tetracycline[7,14]	250 mg qid × 7d	6.25 mg/kg qid × 7d
	or plus		
	clindamycin[7,59]	20 mg/kg/d in 3 doses × 7d[60]	20 mg/kg/d in 3 doses × 7d
Alternatives:	Mefloquine[61]	750 mg followed 12 hrs later by 500 mg	15 mg/kg followed 12 hrs later by 10 mg/kg
	Artesunate[62]*	4 mg/kg/d × 3d	4 mg/kg/d × 3d
	plus		
	mefloquine[61]	750 mg followed 12 hrs later by 500 mg	15 mg/kg followed 12 hrs later by 10 mg/kg

* Availability problems. See table on page 818.

57. In Southeast Asia, relative resistance to quinine has increased and treatment should be continued for 7d.
58. Although approved for once daily dosing, *Medical Letter* consultants usually divide the dose in two to decrease nausea and vomiting.
59. For use in pregnancy.
60. B Lell and PG Kremsner, *Antimicrob Agents Chemother* 2002; 46:2315.
61. At this dosage, adverse effects including nausea, vomiting, diarrhea, dizziness, disturbed sense of balance, toxic psychosos and seizures can occur. Mefloquine should not be used for treatment of malaria in pregnancy unless there is no other treatment option because of increased risk for stillbirth (F Nosten et al, *Clin Infect Dis* 1999; 28:808). It should be avoided for treatment of malaria in persons with active depression or a history of psychosis or seizures and should be used with caution in persons with psychiatric illness. Mefloquine can be given to patients taking β-blockers if they do not have an underlying arrhythmia; it should not be used in patients with conduction abnormalities. Mefloquine should not be given together with quinine, quinidine or halofantrine, and caution is required in using quinine, quinidine or halofantrine to treat patients with malaria who have taken mefloquine for prophylaxis. Resistance to mefloquine has been reported in some areas, such as the Thailand-Myanmar and Thailand-Cambodia borders and in the Amazon basin, where 25 mg/kg should be used. In the US, a 250-mg tablet of mefloquine contains 228 mg mefloquine base. Outside the US, each 275-mg tablet contains 250 mg base.
62. F Nosten et al, *Lancet* 2000; 356:297; M van Vugt, *Clin Infect Dis* 2002; 35:1498.

Table 4.10. Drugs for Parasitic Infections, continued

Infection	Drug	Adult Dosage	Pediatric Dosage
MALARIA, treatment of, *P. falciparum*, (continued)			
P. vivax[63] acquired in areas of chloroquine-resistance			
ORAL[55]			
Drug of choice:	Quinine sulfate	650 mg q8h × 3–7d[57]	30 mg/kg/d in 3 doses × 3–7d[57]
	plus		
	doxycycline[7,14]	100 mg bid × 7d	4 mg/kg/d 2 doses × 7d
OR	Mefloquine[61]	750 mg followed 12 hrs later by 500 mg	15 mg/kg followed 12 hrs later by 10 mg/kg
Alternatives:	Chloroquine	25 mg base/kg in 3 doses over 48 hrs	25 mg base/kg in 3 doses over 48 hrs
	plus		
	Primaquine[64]	30 mg base daily × 14d	0.6 mg/kg/d × 14d
All *Plasmodium* except Chloroquine-resistant *P. falciparum*[54] and Chloroquine-resistant *P. vivax*[63]			
ORAL[55]			
Drug of choice:	Chloroquine phosphate[65]	1 g (600 mg base), then 500 mg (300 mg base) 6 hrs later; then 500 mg (300 mg base) at 24 and 48 hrs	10 mg base/kg (max. 600 mg base), then 5 mg base/kg 6 hrs later; then 5 mg base/kg at 24 and 48 hrs

* Availability problems. See table on page 818.

63. *P. vivax* with decreased susceptibility to chloroquine is a significant problem in Papua New Guinea and Indonesia. There are also a few reports of resistance from Myanmar, India, the Solomon Islands, Vanuatu, Guyana, Brazil, Colombia and Peru.

64. Primaquine phosphate can cause hemolytic anemia, especially in patients whose red cells are deficient in glucose-6-phosphate dehydrogenase. This deficiency is most common in African, Asian and Mediterranean peoples. Patients should be screened for G-6-PD deficiency before treatment. Primaquine should not be used during pregnancy.

65. If chloroquine phosphate is not available, hydroxychloroquine sulfate is as effective; 400 mg of hydroxychloroquine sulfate is equivalent to 500 mg of chloroquine phosphate.

Table 4.10. Drugs for Parasitic Infections, continued

Infection	Drug	Adult Dosage	Pediatric Dosage
MALARIA, treatment of, All *Plasmodium* except Chloroquine-resistant *P. falciparum* and Chloroquine-resistant *P. vivax* (continued)			
PARENTERAL			
Drug of choice:[66]	Quinidine gluconate[67]	10 mg/kg loading dose (max. 600 mg) in normal saline over 1–2 hrs, followed by continuous infusion of 0.02 mg/kg/min until PO therapy can be started	10 mg/kg loading dose (max. 600 mg) in normal saline over 1–2 hrs, followed by continuous infusion of 0.02 mg/kg/min until PO therapy can be started
OR	Quinine dihydrochloride[67]*	20 mg/kg loading dose in 5% dextrose over 4 hrs, followed by 10 mg/kg over 2–4 hrs q8h (max. 1800 mg/d) until PO therapy can be started	20 mg/kg loading dose in 5% dextrose over 4 hrs, followed by 10 mg/kg over 2–4 hrs q8h (max. 1800 mg/d) until PO therapy can be started
Alternative:	Artemether[68]*	3.2 mg/kg IM, then 1.6 mg/kg daily × 5–7d	3.2 mg/kg IM, then 1.6 mg/kg daily × 5–7d
Prevention of relapses: *P. vivax* and *P. ovale* only			
Drug of choice:	Primaquine phosphate[64]	30 mg/ base/d × 14d	0.6 mg base/kg × 14d

* Availability problems. See table on page 818.

66. Exchange transfusion has been helpful for some patients with high-density (>10%) parasitemia, altered mental status, pulmonary edema or renal complications (KD Miller et al, *N Engl J Med* 1989; 321:65).

67. Continuous EKG, blood pressure and glucose monitoring are recommended, especially in pregnant women and young children. For problems with quinidine availability, call the manufacturer (Eli Lilly, 800-545-5979) or the CDC Malaria Hotline (770-488-7788). Quinidine may have greater antimalarial activity than quinine. If more than 48 hours of parenteral treatment is required, the quinine or quinidine dose should be reduced by 30–50%.

68. Limited studies of efficacy except with *P. falciparum*; not FDA-approved or available in the US (Artemether-Quinine Meta-Analysis Study Group, *Trans R Soc Trop Med Hyg* 2001; 95:637; K Marsh, *East Afr Med J* 2002; 79:619).

Table 4.10. Drugs for Parasitic Infections, continued

Infection	Drug	Adult Dosage	Pediatric Dosage
MALARIA, Prevention of[69]			
Chloroquine-sensitive areas[54]			
Drug of choice:	Chloroquine phosphate[70,71]	500 mg (300 mg base), once/wk[72]	5 mg/kg base once/wk, up to adult dose of 300 mg base[72]
Chloroquine-resistant areas[54]			
Drug of choice:	Atovaquone/ proguanil[56,71]	1 adult tab/d[73]	11–20 kg: 1 peds tab/d[56,73]
			21–30 kg: 2 peds tabs/d[56,73]
			31–40 kg: 3 peds tabs/d[56,73]
			>40 kg: 1 adult tab/d[56,73]
OR	Mefloquine[61,71,74]	250 mg once/wk[72]	5–10 kg: $1/8$ tab once/wk[72]
			11–20 kg: $1/4$ tab once/wk[72]
			21–30 kg: $1/2$ tab once/wk[72]
			31–45 kg: $3/4$ tab once/wk[72]
			>45 kg: 1 tab once/wk[72]

* Availability problems. See table on page 818.

69. No drug regimen guarantees protection against malaria. If fever develops within a year (particularly within the first two months) after travel to malarious areas, travelers should be advised to seek medical attention. Insect repellents, insecticide-impregnated bed nets and proper clothing are important adjuncts for malaria prophylaxis (*Medical Letter* 2003; 45:41). Malaria in pregnancy is particularly serious for both mother and fetus; therefore, prophylaxis is indicated if exposure can not be avoided.

70. In pregnancy, chloroquine prophylaxis has been used extensively and safely.

71. For prevention of attack after departure from areas where *P. vivax* and *P. ovale* are endemic, which includes almost all areas where malaria is found (except Haiti), some experts prescribe in addition primaquine phosphate 30 mg base/d or, for children, 0.6 mg base/kg/d during the last 2 wks of prophylaxis. Others prefer to avoid the toxicity of primaquine and rely on surveillance to detect cases when they occur, particularly when exposure was limited or doubtful. See also footnote 64.

72. Beginning 1–2 wks before travel and continuing weekly for the duration or stay and for 4 wks after leaving.

73. Beginning 1–2d before travel and continuing for the duration of stay and continuing for 1 wk after leaving. In one study of malaria prophylaxis, atovaquone/proguanil was better tolerated than mefloquine in nonimmune travelers (D Overbosch et al, *Clin Infect Dis* 2001; 33:1015).

74. Mefloquine has not been approved for use during pregnancy. However, it has been reported to be safe for prophylactic use during the second or third trimester of pregnancy and possibly during early pregnancy as well (CDC Health Information for International Travel, 2003–2004, page 111; BL Smoak et al, *J Infect Dis* 1997; 176:831). For pediatric doses <$1/2$ tablet, it is advisable to have a pharmacist crush the tablet, estimate doses by weighing, and package them in gelatin capsules. There is no data for use in children <5 kg, but based on dosages in other weight groups, a dose of 5 mg/kg can be used. Mefloquine is not recommended for patients with cardiac conduction abnormalities, and patients with a history of depression, seizures, psychosis or psychiatric disorders should avoid mefloquine prophylaxis. Resistance to mefloquine has been reported in some areas, such as the Thailand-Myanmar and Thailand-Cambodia borders; in these areas, atovaquone/proguanil or doxycycline should be used for prophylaxis.

Table 4.10. Drugs for Parasitic Infections, continued

Infection	Drug	Adult Dosage	Pediatric Dosage
MALARIA, prevention of, chloroquine-resistant areas (continued)			
OR	Doxycycline[7,71]	100 mg daily[75]	2 mg/kg/d, up to 100 mg/d[75]
Alternatives:	Primaquine[7,64]	30 mg base daily[76]	0.6 mg/kg base daily
	Chloroquine phosphate	500 mg (300 mg base) once/wk[72]	5 mg/kg base once/wk, up to 300 mg base[72]
			<2 yrs: 50 mg once/d
			2–6 yrs: 100 mg once/d
			7–10 yrs: 150 mg once/d
			>10 yrs: 200 mg once/d
	plus proguanil[77]	200 mg once/d	
MALARIA, Self-Presumptive Treatment[70]			
Drug of Choice:	Atovaquone/ proguanil[7,56]	4 adult tabs daily × 3d	<5kg: not indicated
			5–8 kg: 2 peds tabs once/d × 3d
			9–10 kg: 3 peds tabs once/d × 3d
			11–20 kg: 1 adult tab once/d × 3d
			21–30 kg: 2 adult tabs once/d × 3d
			31–40 kg: 3 adult tabs once/d × 3d
			>40 kg: 4 adult tabs once/d × 3d

* Availability problems. See table on page 818.

75. Beginning 1–2d before travel and continuing for the duration of stay and for 4 wks after leaving. Use of tetracyclines is contraindicated in pregnancy and in children <8 years old. Doxycycline can cause gastrointestinal disturbances, vaginal moniliasis and photosensitivity reactions.

76. Studies have shown that daily primaquine beginning 1d before departure and continued until 3–7d after leaving the malaria area provides effective prophylaxis against chloroquine-resistant *P. falciparum* (JK Baird et al, *Clin Infect Dis* 2003; 37:1659). Some studies have shown less efficacy against *P. vivax*. Nausea and abdominal pain can be diminished by taking with food.

77. Proguanil (*Paludrine*-Wyeth Ayerst, Canada; AstraZeneca, United Kingdom), which is not available alone in the US but is widely available in Canada and Europe, is recommended mainly for use in Africa south of the Sahara. Prophylaxis is recommended during exposure and for 4 wks afterwards. Proguanil has been used in pregnancy without evidence of toxicity (PA Phillips-Howard and D Wood, *Drug Saf* 1996; 14:131).

Infection		Drug	Adult Dosage	Pediatric Dosage
MALARIA, Self-Presumptive Treatment (continued)				
	OR	Quinine sulfate	650 mg q8h × 3–7d[57]	30 mg/kg/d in 3 doses × 3–7d[57]
		plus		
		doxycycline[7,14]	100 mg bid × 7d	4 mg/kg/d in 2 doses × 7d
	OR	Mefloquine[61]	750 mg followed 12 hrs later by 500 mg	15 mg/kg followed 12 hrs later by 10 mg/kg

MICROSPORIDIOSIS

Ocular (*Encephalitozoon hellem, Encephalitozoon cuniculi, Vittaforma corneae [Nosema corneum]*)

Drug of choice:	Albendazole[7]	400 mg bid	
	plus fumagillin[7,9]*		

Intestinal (*Enterocytozoon bieneusi, Encephalitozoon [Septata] intestinalis*)

E. bieneusi[80]

Drug of choice:	Fumagillin*	60 mg/d PO × 14d	

E. intestinalis

Drug of choice:	Albendazole[7]	400 mg bid × 21d	

Disseminated (*E. hellem, E. cuniculi, E. intestinalis, Pleistophora sp., Trachipleistophora sp. and Brachiola vesicularum*)

Drug of choice:[81]	Albendazole[7]	400 mg bid	

Mites, see SCABIES

* Availability problems. See table on page 818.

78. A traveler can be given a course of atovaquone/proguanil, mefloquine or quinine plus doxycycline for presumptive self-treatment should be different from that used for prophylaxis. This approach should be used only in very rare circumstances when a traveler can not promptly get to medical care. The drug given for self-treatment of febrile illness. The drug given for self-treatment should be different from that used for prophylaxis. This approach should be used only in very rare circumstances when a traveler can not promptly get to medical care.

79. Ocular lesions due to *E. hellem* in HIV-infected patients have responded to fumagillin eyedrops prepared from *Fumidil-B*₂ (bicyclohexyl ammonium fumagillin) used to control to microsporidial disease of honey bees (MC Diesenhouse, *Am J Ophthalmol* 1993; 115: 293), available from Leiter's Park Avenue Pharmacy (see footnote 1). For lesions due to *V. corneae*, topical therapy is generally not effective and keratoplasty may be required (RM Davis et al, *Ophthalmology* 1990; 97:953).

80. Oral fumagillin (Sanofi Recherche, Gentilly, France) has been effective in treating *E. bieneusi* (J-M Molina et al, *N Engl J Med* 2002; 346:1963), but has been associated with thrombocytopenia. Highly active antiretroviral therapy (HAART) may lead to microbiologic and clinical responses in HIV-infected patients with microsporidial diarrhea (USPHS/IDSA Guidelines for the Treatment of Opportunistic Infections in Adults and Adolescents with HIV, 2004; In press). Octreotide (*Sandostatin*) has provided symptomatic relief in some patients with large-volume diarrhea.

81. J-M Molina et al, *J Infect Dis* 1995; 171:245. There is no established treatment for *Pleistophora*. For disseminated disease due to *Trachipleistophora* or *Brachiola*, itraconazole 400 mg PO once/d plus albendazole may also be tried (CM Coyle et al, *N Engl J Med* 2004; 351:42).

Table 4.10. Drugs for Parasitic Infections, continued

Infection		Drug	Adult Dosage	Pediatric Dosage
MONILIFORMIS *moniliformis infection*				
Drug of choice:		Pyrantel pamoate[7]	11 mg/kg once, repeat twice, 2 wks apart	11 mg/kg once, repeat twice, 2 wks apart
***Naegleria* species**, see AMEBIC MENINGOENCEPHALITIS, PRIMARY				
***Necator americanus*,** see HOOKWORM infection				
OESOPHAGOSTOMUM bifurcum				
Drug of choice: See footnote 82				
Onchocerca volvulus, see FILARIASIS				
Opisthorchis viverrini, see FLUKE infection				
Paragonimus westermani, see FLUKE infection				
***Pediculus capitis, humanus, Phthirus pubis*,** see LICE				
Pinworm, see ENTEROBIUS				
PNEUMOCYSTIS JIROVECI (formerly *carinii*) pneumonia (PCP)[83]				
Drug of choice:		Trimethoprim-sulfamethoxazole	TMP 15 mg/kg/d, SMX 75 mg/kg/d, PO or IV in 3 or 4 doses × 14–21d	TMP 15 mg/kg/d, SMX 75 mg/kg/d, PO or IV in 3 or 4 doses × 14–12d
Alternatives:		Primaquine[7,64]	30 mg base PO daily × 21d	
		plus clindamycin[7]	600 mg IV q6h × 21d, or 300–450 mg PO q6h × 21d	
	OR	Trimethoprim[7]	5 mg/kg tid × 21d	
		plus dapsone[7]	100 mg daily × 21d	
	OR	Pentamidine	3–4 mg/kg IV daily × 14–21d	3–4 mg/kg IV daily × 14–21d
	OR	Atovaquone	750 mg bid × 21d	1–3 mos: 30 mg/kg/d
				4–24 mos: 45 mg/kg/d
				>24 mos: 30 mg/d

* Availability problems. See table on page 818.

82. Albendazole or pyrantel pamoate may be effective (JB Ziem et al, *Ann Trop Med Parasitol* 2004; 98:385).

83. Pneumocystis has been reclassified as a fungus. In severe disease with room air PO$_2$ ≤ 70 mmHg or Aa gradient ≥ 35 mmHg, prednisone should also be used (S. Gagnon et al, *N Engl J Med* 1990; 323: 1444; E Caumes et al, *Clin Infect Dis* 1994; 18:319).

Table 4.10. Drugs for Parasitic Infections, continued

Infection	Drug	Adult Dosage	Pediatric Dosage
PNEUMOCYSTIS JIROVECI (continued)			
Primary and secondary prophylaxis[84]			
Drug of Choice:	Trimethoprim-sulfamethoxazole	1 tab (single or double strength) daily	TMP 150 mg/m^2, SMX 750 mg/m^2 in 2 doses on 3 consecutive days per wk
Alternatives:[85]	Dapsone[7]	50 mg bid, or 100 mg daily	2 mg/kg/d (max. 100 mg) or 4 mg/kg (max. 200 mg) each wk
OR	Dapsone[7]	50 mg daily or 200 mg each wk	
	plus pyrimethamine[86]	50 mg or 75 mg each wk	
OR	Pentamidine aerosol	300 mg inhaled monthly via *Respigard II nebulizer*	≥5 yrs: 300 mg inhaled monthly via *Respigard II nebulizer*
OR	Atovaquone[7]	1500 mg daily	1–3 mos: 30 mg/kg/d 4–24 mos: 45 mg/kg/d >24 mos: 30 mg/kg/d

Roundworm, see ASCARIASIS

Sappinia Diploidea. See AMEBIC MENINGOENCEPHALITIS, PRIMARY

SCABIES (*Sarcoptes scabiei*)

Infection	Drug	Adult Dosage	Pediatric Dosage
Drug of choice:	5% Permethrin	Topically[87]	Topically[87]
Alternatives:[88]	Ivermectin[7,89]	200 mcg/kg once[87]	200 mcg/kg once[87]
	10% Crotamiton	Topically once/daily × 2	Topically once/daily × 2

* Availability problems. See table on page 818.

84. Primary/secondary prophylaxis in patients with HIV can be discontinued after CD4 count increases to >200 × 10⁶/L for >3 mos.

85. An alternative trimethoprim/sulfamethoxazole regimen is one DS tab 3x/wk. Weekly therapy with sulfadoxine 500 mg/pyrimethamine 25 mg/leucovorin in 25 mg was effective PCP prophylaxis in liver transplant patients (J Torre-Cisneros et al, *Clin Infect Dis* 1999; 29:771).

86. Plus leucovorin 25 mg with each dose of pyrimethamine.

87. In some cases, treatment may need to be repeated in 10–14 days.

88. Lindane (γ-benzene hexachloride; *Kwell*) should be reserved as a second-line agent. The FDA has recommended it should not be used for immunocompromised patients, young children, the elderly, and patients <50 kg.

89. Ivermectin, either alone or in combination with a topical scabicide, is the drug of choice for crusted scabies in immunocompromised patients (P del Giudice, *Curr Opin Infect Dis* 2004; 15:123). The safety of oral ivermectin in pregnancy and young children has not been established.

Table 4.10. Drugs for Parasitic Infections, continued

Infection	Drug	Adult Dosage	Pediatric Dosage
SCHISTOSOMIASIS (*Bilharziasis*)			
S. haematobium			
Drug of choice:	Praziquantel	40 mg/kg/d in 2 doses × 1d	40 mg/kg/d in 2 doses × 1d
S. japonicum			
Drug of choice:	Praziquantel	60 mg/kg/d in 3 doses × 1d	60 mg/kg/d in 3 doses × 1d
S. mansoni			
Drug of choice:	Praziquantel	40 mg/kg/d in 2 doses × 1d	40 mg/kg/d in 2 doses × 1d
Alternative:	Oxamniquine[90]*	15 mg/kg once[91]	20 mg/kg/d in 2 doses × 1d[91]
S. mekongi			
Drug of choice:	Praziquantel	60 mg/kg/d in 3 doses × 1d	60 mg/kg/d in 3 doses × 1d
Sleeping sickness, see TRYPANOSOMIASIS			
STRONGYLOIDIASIS (*Strongyloides stercoralis*)			
Drug of choice:[92]	Ivermectin	200 mcg/kg/d × 2d	200 mcg/kg/d × 2d
Alternative:	Albendazole[7]	400 mg bid × 7d	400 mg bid × 7d
OR	Thiabendazole	50 mg/kg/d in 2 doses × 2d (max 3g/d)[93]	50 mg/kg/d in 2 doses × 2d (max 3g/d)[93]

* Availability problems. See table on page 818.

90. Oxamniquine has been effective in some areas in which praziquantel is less effective. (FF Stelma et al, *J Infect Dis* 1997; 176:304). Oxamniquine is contraindicated in pregnancy.

91. In East Africa, the dose should be increased to 30 mg/kg, and in Egypt and South Africa to 30 mg/kd/d × 2d. Some experts recommend 40–60 mg/kg over 2–3d in all of Africa (KC Shekhar, *Drugs* 1991; 42:379).

92. In immunocompromised patients or disseminated disease, it may be necessary to prolong or repeat therapy, or to use other agents. Veterinary parenteral and enema formulations of ivermectin have been used in severely ill patients to take oral medications (PL Chiodini et al, *Lancet* 2000; 355:43; J Oren et al, *Clin Infect Dis* 2003; 37:152; PE Tarr, *Am J Trop Med Hyg* 2003; 68:453).

93. This dosage is likely to be toxic and may have to be decreased.

Table 4.10. Drugs for Parasitic Infections, continued

Infection	Drug	Adult Dosage	Pediatric Dosage
TAPEWORM infection			
—**Adult** (intestinal stage)			
Diphyllobothrium latum (fish), ***Taenia saginata*** (beef), ***Taenia solium*** (pork), ***Dipylidium caninum*** (dog)			
Drug of choice:	Praziquantel[7]	5–10 mg/kg once	5–10 mg/kg once
Alternative:	Niclosamide*	2 g once	50 mg/kg once
Hymenolepis nana (dwarf tapeworm)			
Drug of choice:	Praziquantel[7]	25 mg/kg once	25 mg/kg once
Alternative:	Nitazoxanide[4,7]	500 mg × 3d[94]	1–3 yrs: 100 mg bid × 3d[94]
			4–11 yrs: 200 mg bid × 3d[94]
—**Larval** (tissue stage)			
Echinococcus granulosus (hydatid cyst)			
Drug of choice:[95]	Albendazole	400 mg bid × 1–6 mos	15 mg/kg/d (max. 800 mg) × 1–6 mos
Echinococcus multilocularis			
Treatment of choice:	See footnote 96		

* Availability problems. See table on page 818.

94. JO Juan et al, *Trans R Soc Trop Med Hyg* 2002; 96:193.
95. Patients may benefit from surgical resection or percutaneous drainage of cysts. Praziquantel is useful preoperatively or in case of spillage of cyst contents during surgery. Percutaneous aspiration-injection-reaspiration (PAIR) with ultrasound guidance plus albendazole therapy has been effective for management of hepatic hydatid cyst disease (RA Smego, Jr, et al, *Clin Infect Dis* 2003; 37:1073).
96. Surgical excision is the only reliable means of cure. Reports have suggested that in nonresectable cases use of albendazole or mebendazole can stabilize and sometimes cure infection (P Craig, *Curr Opin Infect Dis* 2003; 16:437).

Table 4.10. Drugs for Parasitic Infections, continued

Infection	Drug	Adult Dosage	Pediatric Dosage
TAPEWORM infection—**Larvae** (continued)			
Taenia solium (*Cysticercosis*)			
Treatment of choice:	See footnote 97		
Alternative:	Albendazole	400 mg bid × 8–30d; can be repeated as necessary	15 mg/kg/d (max. 800 mg) in 2 doses × 8–30d; can be repeated as necessary
OR	Praziquantel[7]	50–100 mg/kg/d in 3 doses × 30d	50–100 mg/kg/d in 3 doses × 30d
Toxocariasis, see VISCERAL LARVA MIGRANS			
TOXOPLASMOSIS (*Toxoplasma gondii*)[98]			
Drugs of choice:[99,100]	Pyrimethamine[101]	25–100 mg/d × 3–4 wks	2 mg/kg/d × 3d, then 1 mg/kg/d (max. 25 mg/d) × 4 wks[102]
	plus		
	sulfadiazine	1–1.5 g qid 3–4 wks	100–200 mg/kg/d × 3–4 wks

* Availability problems. See table on page 818.

97. Initial therapy for patients with inflammed parenchymal cysticercosis should focus on symptomatic treatment with anti-seizure medication. Treatment of parenchymal cysticerci with albendazole or praziquantel is controversial (JM Maguire, *N Engl J Med* 2004; 350:215). Patients with live parenchymal cysts who have seizures should be treated with albendazole together with steroids (6 mg dexamethasone or 40–60 mg prednisone daily) and an anti-seizure medication (HH Garcia et al, *N Engl J Med* 2004: 350:249). Patients with subarachnoid cysts or giant cysts in the fissures should be treated for at least 30d (JV Proaño et al, *N Engl J Med* 2001; 345:879). Surgical intervention or CSF diversion is indicated for obstructive hydocephalus; prednisone 40 mg/d may be given with surgery. Arachnoiditis, vasculitis or cerebral edema is treated with prednisone 60 mg/d or dexamethasone 4-6 mg/d together with albendazole or praziquantel (AC White, Jr., *Annu Rev Med* 2000; 51:187). Any cysticercocidal drug may cause irreparable damage when used to treat ocular or spinal cysts, even when corticosteroids are used. An ophthalmic exam should always precede treatment to rule out intraocular cysts.

98. In ocular toxoplasmosis with macular involvement, corticosteroids are recommended in addition to antiparasitic therapy for an anti-inflammatory effect.

99. To treat CNS toxoplasmosis in HIV-infected patients, some clinicians have used pyrimethamine 50–100 mg/d (after a loading dose of 200 mg) with sulfadiazine and, when sulfonamide-sensitivity developed, have given clindamycin 1.8–2.4 g/d in divided doses instead of the sulfonamide. Atovaquone plus pyrimethamine appears to be an effective alternative in sulfa-intolerant patients (K Chirgwin et al, *Clin Infect Dis* 2002; 34:1243). Treatment is followed by chronic suppression with lower dosage regimens of the same drugs. For primary prophylaxis in HIV patients with <100 × 10⁶/L CD4 cells, either trimethoprim-sulfamethoxazole, pyrimethamine with dapsone, or atovaquone with or without pyrimethamine can be used. Primary or secondary prophylaxis may be discontinued when the CD4 count increases to >200 × 10⁶/L for more than 3 months (USPHS/IDSA Guidelines for the Treatment of Opportunistic Infections in Adults and Adolescents with HIV; 2004; In press).

100. Women who develop toxoplasmosis during the first trimester of pregnancy can be treated with spiramycin (3–4 g/d). After the first trimester, if there is no documented transmission to the fetus, spiramycin can be continued until term. If transmission has occurred *in utero*, therapy with pyrimethamine and sulfadiazine should be started (JG Montoya and O Liesenfeld, *Lancet* 2004; 363:1965). Pyrimethamine is a potential teratogen and should be used only after the first trimester.

101. Plus leucovorin 10–25 mg with each dose of pyrimethamine.

Table 4.10. Drugs for Parasitic Infections, continued

Infection	Drug	Adult Dosage	Pediatric Dosage
TRICHINELLOSIS (*Trichinella spiralis*)			
Drugs of choice:	Steroids for severe symptoms		
	plus		
	mebendazole[7]	200–400 mg tid × 3d, then 400–500 mg tid × 10d	200–400 mg tid × 3d, then 400–500 mg tid × 10d
Alternative:	Albendazole[7]	400 mg bid × 8–14d	400 mg bid × 8–14d
TRICHOMONIASIS (*Trichomonas vaginalis*)			
Drug of choice:[103]	Metronidazole	2 g once or 500 mg bid × 7d	15 mg/kg/d orally in 3 doses × 7d
OR	Tinidazole[5]	2 g once	50 mg/kg once (max. 2 g)
TRICHOSTRONGYLUS infection			
Drug of choice:	Pyrantel pamoate[7]	11 mg/kg base once (max. 1 g)	11 mg/kg once (max. 1 g)
Alternative:	Mebendazole[7]	100 mg bid × 3d	100 mg bid × 3d
OR	Albendazole[7]	400 mg once	400 mg once
TRICHURIASIS (*Trichuris trichiura*, whipworm) infection			
Drug of choice:	Mebendazole	100 mg bid × 3d or 500 mg once	100 mg bid × 3d or 500 mg once
Alternative:	Albendazole[7]	400 mg × 3d	400 mg × 3d
OR	Ivermectin[7]	200 mcg/kg daily × 3d	200 mcg/kg daily × 3d

* Availability problems. See table on page 818.

102. Congenitally infected newborns should be treated with pyrimethamine every 2 or 3 days and a sulfonamide daily for about one year (JS Remington and JO Klein, eds, *Infectious Disease of the Fetus and Newborn Infant*, 5th ed, Philadelphia:Saunders, 2001, page 290).

103. Sexual partners should be treated simultaneously. Metronidazole-resistant strains have been reported and can be treated with higher doses of metronidazole (2–4 g/d × 7–14d) or with tinidazole (WD Hager, *Sex Transm Dis* 2004; 31:343).

Table 4.10. Drugs for Parasitic Infections, continued

Infection	Drug	Adult Dosage	Pediatric Dosage
TRYPANOSOMIASIS[104]			
T. cruzi (American trypanosomiasis, Chagas' disease)			
Drug of choice:	Benznidazole*	5–7 mg/kg/d in 2 divided doses × 30–90d	≤12 yrs: 10 mg/kg/d in 2 doses × 30–90d
OR	Nifurtimox[105]*	8–10 mg/kg/d in 3–4 doses × 90–120d	1–10 yrs: 15–20 mg/kg/d in 4 doses × 90d
			11–16 yrs: 12.5–15 mg/kg/d in 4 doses × 90d
T. brucei gambiense (West African trypanosomiasis, sleeping sickness)			
hemolymphatic stage			
Drug of choice:[106]	Pentamidine isethionte[7]	4 mg/kg/d IM × 10d	4 mg/kg/d IM × 10d
Alternative:	Suramin*	100–200 mg (test dose) IV, then 1 g IV on days 1,3,7,14 and 21	20 mg/kg on days 1,3,7,14 and 21

* Availability problems. See table on page 818.

104. MP Barrett et al. *Lancet* 2003; 362:1469.

105. The addition of gamma interferon to nifurtimox for 20d in experimental animals and in a limited number of patients appears to shorten the acute phase of Chagas' disease (RE McCabe et al, *J Infect Dis* 1991; 163:912).

106. For treatment of *T.b. gambiense*, pentamidine and suramin have equal efficacy but pentamidine is better tolerated.

Table 4.10. Drugs for Parasitic Infections, continued

Infection	Drug	Adult Dosage	Pediatric Dosage
TRYPANOSOMIASIS, _T brucei gambiense_ (continued)			
Late disease with CNS involvement			
Drug of choice:	Melarsoprol[107]	2.2 mg/kg/d × 10d	2.2 mg/kg/d × 10d
OR	Eflornithine[108]*	400 mg/kg/d in 4 doses × 14d	400 mg/kg/d in 4 doses × 14d
T. b. rhodesiense (East African trypanosomiasis, sleeping sickness)			
hemolymphatic stage			
Drug of choice:	Suramin*	100–200 mg (test dose) IV, then 1 g IV on days 1,3,7,14 and 21	20 mg/kg on days 1,3,7,14 and 21
Late disease with CNS involvement			
Drug of choice:	Melarsoprol[107]	2–3.6 mg/kg/d × 3d; after 7d 3.6 mg/kg/d × 3d; repeat again after 7d	2–3.6 mg/kg/d × 3d; after 7d 3.6 mg/kg/d × 3d; repeat again after 7d
VISCERAL LARVA MIGRANS[109] (_Toxocariasis_)			
Drug of choice:	Albendazole[7]	400 mg bid × 5d	400 mg bid × 5d
	Mebendazole[7]	100–200 mg bid × 5d	100–200 mg bid × 5d
Whipworm, see TRICHURIASIS			
Wuchereria bancrofti, see FILARIASIS			

* Availability problems. See table on page 818.

107. In frail patients, begin with as little as 18 mg and increase the dose progressively. Pretreatment with suramin has been advocated for debilitated patients. Corticosteroids have been used to prevent arsenical encephalopathy (J Pepin et al, _Trans R Soc Trop Med Hyg_ 1995; 89:92). Up to 20% of patients with _T.b. gambiense_ fail to respond to melarsoprol (MP Barrett, _Lancet_ 1999; 353:1113).

108. Eflornithine is highly effectively in _T.b. gambiense_ but not against _T.b. rhodesiense_ infections. It is available in limited supply only from the WHO and the CDC.

109. Optimum duration of therapy is not known; some _Medical Letter_ consultants would treat for 20d. For severe symptoms or eye involvement, corticosteroids can be used in addition.

Table 4.11. Manufacturers of Some Antiparasitic Drugs

Manufacturers of Drugs Used to Treat Parasitic Infections

albendazole – *Albenza* (GlaxoSmithKline)

Albenza (GlaxoSmithKline) – albendazole

Alinia (Romark) – nitazoxanide

amphotericin – *Fungizone* (Apothecon), others

Ancobon (ICN) – flucytosine

§ *Antiminth* (Pfizer) – pyrantel pamoate

• *Aralen* (Sanofi) – chloroquine HCl and chloroquine phosphate

§ artemether – *Artenam* (Arenco, Belgium)

§ *Artenam* (Arenco, Belgium) – artemether

§ artesunate – (Guilin No. 1 Factory, People's Republic of China)

atovaquone – *Mepron* (GlaxoSmithKline)

atovaquone/proguanil – *Malarone* (GlaxoSmithKline)

azithromycin – *Zithromax* (Pfizer)

• *Bactrim* (Roche) – TMP/Sulfa

§ benznidazole – *Rochagan* (Roche, Brazil)

Biaxin (Abbott) – clarithromycin

§ *Biltricide* (Bayer) – praziquantel

† bithionol – *Bitin* (Tanabe, Japan)

† *Bitin* (Tanabe, Japan) – bithionol

§ *Brolene* (Aventis, Canada) – propamidine isethionate chloroquine HCl and chloroquine phosphate – *Aralen* (Sanofi), others

clarithromycin – *Biaxin* (Abbott)

• *Cleocin* (Pfizer) – clindamycin

clindamycin – *Cleocin* (Pfizer), others

crotamiton – *Eurax* (Westwood-Squibb)

dapsone – (Jacobus)

Daraprim (GlaxoSmithKline) – pyrimethamine USP

† diethylcarbamazine citrate USP – *Hetrazan*

Diflucan (Roerig) – fluconazole

§ dioxanide furoate – *Furamide* (Boots, United Kingdom)

doxycycline – *Vibramycin* (Pfizer), others

† eflornithine (Difluoromethylornithine, DFMO) – *Ornidyl* (Aventis)

§ *Egaten* (Novartis) – triclabendazole

Elimite (allergan) – permethrin

Ergamisol (Janssen) – levamisole

Eurax (Westwood-Squibb) – crotamiton

fluconazole – *Diflucan* (Roerig)

† *Flagyl* (Searle) – metronidazole

flucytosine – *Ancobon* (ICN)

• *Fungizone* (Apothecon) – amphotericin

§ *Furamide* (Boots, United Kingdom) – dioxanide furoate

§ furazolidone – *Furozone* (Roberts)

§ *Furozone* (Roberts) – furazolidone

§ *Germanin* (Bayer, Germany) – suramin sodium

Table 4.11. Manufacturers of Some Antiparasitic Drugs, continued

Manufacturers of Drugs Used to Treat Parasitic Infections

§ *Glucantime* (Aventis, France) – meglumine antimonate

† *Hetrazan* – diethylcarbamazine citrate USP

Humatin (Monarch) – paromomycin

§ *Impavido* (Zentaris, Germany) – miltefosine

iodoquinol – *Yodoxin* (Glenwood), others

itraconazole – *Sporanox* (Janssen-Ortho)

ivermectin – *Stromectol* (Merck)

Ketoconazole – *Nizoral* (Janssen), others

† *Lampit* (Bayer, Germany) – nifurtimox

Lariam (Roche) – mefloquine

§ *Leshcutan* (Teva, Israel) – topical paromomycin

levamisole – *Ergamisol* (Janssen)

Malarone (GlaxoSmithKline) – atovaquone/proguanil

malathion – *Ovide* (Medicis)

mebendazole – *Vermox* (McNeil)

mefloquine – *Lariam* (Roche)

§ meglumine antimonate – *Glucantime* (Aventis, France)

melarsoprol – *Mel-B* (Specia)

Mel-B (Special) – melarsoprol

Mepron (GlaxoSmithKline) – atovaquone

metronidazole – *Flagyl* (Searle), others

§ miltefosine – *Impavido* (Zentaris, Germany)

Neutrexin (US Bioscience) – trimetrexate

§ niclosamide – *Yomesan* (Bayer, Germany)

† nifurtimox – *Lampit* (Bayer, Germany)

• nitazoxanide – *Alinia* (Romark)

Nizoral (Janssen) – ketoconazole

Nix (GlaxoSmithKline) – permethrin

§ ornidazole – *Tiberal* (Roche, France)

† *Ornidyl* (Aventis) – eflornithine (Difluoromethylornithine, DFMO)

Ovide (Medicis) – malathion

§ oxamniquine – *Vansil* (Pfizer)

§ *Paludrine* (Wyeth Ayerst, Canada; AstraZeneca, United Kingdom – proguanil

paromomycin – *Humatin* (Monarch); *Leshcutan* (Teva, Israel; (topical formulation not available in US)

Pentam 300 (Fujisawa) – pentamidine isethionate

pentamidine isethionate – *Pentam 300* (Fujisawa), *NebuPent* (Fujisawa)

† *Pentostam* (GalxoSmithKline, United Kingdom) – sodium stibogluconate

permethrin – *Nix* (GalxoSmithKline), *Elimite* (Allergan)

§ praziquantel – *Biltricide* (Bayer)

Table 4.11. Manufacturers of Some Antiparasitic Drugs, continued

Manufacturers of Drugs Used to Treat Parasitic Infections

NebuPent (Fujisawa) – pentamidine isethionate

§ proguanil – *Paludrine* (Wyeth Ayerst, Canada; AstraZeneca, United Kingdom)

proguanil/atovaquone – *Malarone* (GlaxoSmithKline)

§ propamidine isethionate – *Brolene* (Aventis, Canada)

§ Pyrantel pamoate – *Antiminth* (Pfizer)

Pyrethrins and piperonyl butoxide – *RID* (Pfizer), others

pyrimethamine USP – *Daraprim* (GlaxoSmithKline)

* quinidine gluconate (Eli Lilly)

§ quinine dihydrochloride

§ quinine sulfate – many manufacturers

• *RID* (Pfizer) – pyrethrins and piperonyl butoxide

• *Rifadin* (Aventis); – rifampin

rifampin – *Rifadin* (Aventis), others

§ Rochagan (Roche, Brazil) – benznidazole

* Rovamycine (Aventis) – spiramycin

† sodium stibogluconate – *Pentostam* (GlaxoSmithKline, United Kingdom)

* spiramycin – *Rovamycine* (Aventis)

primaquine phosphate USP

Sporanox (Janssen-Ortho) – itraconazole

Stromectol (Merck) – ivermectin

sulfadiazine

† Suramin sodium – *Germanin* (Bayer, Germany)

§ Tiberal (Roche, France) – ornidazole

Tindamax (Presutti) – tinidazole

tinidazole – *Tindamax* (Presutti)

TMP/Sulfa – *Bactrim* (Roche), others

§ triclabendazole – *Egaten* (Novartis)

trimetrexate – *Neutrexin* (US Bioscience)

§ *Vansil* (Pfizer) – oxamniquine

Vermox (McNeil) – mebendazole

• *Vibramycin* (Pfizer) – doxycycline

• *Yodoxin* (Glenwood) – iodoquinol

§ *Yomesan* (Bayer; germany) – niclosamide

§ *Zithromax* (Pfizer) – azithromycin

*Available in the US only from the manufacturer.

§Not available in the US; may be available through a compounding pharmacy

†Available under an Investigational New Drug (IND) protocol from the CDC Drug Service, Centers for Disease Control and Prevention, Atlanta, Georgia 30333; 404-639-3670 (evenings, weekends, or holidays: 404-639-2888).

•Also available generically.

MEDWATCH—THE FDA SAFETY INFORMATION AND ADVERSE EVENT REPORTING PROGRAM

MedWatch, the Food and Drug Administration (FDA) Safety Information and Adverse Event Reporting Program, is an outreach program for the health care system, including physicians, nurses, pharmacists, and patients, to enhance the effectiveness of the FDA's risk management activities for all regulated clinical medical products. These products include drugs, biologicals, medical devices, and dietary supplements.

The MedWatch program has 2 goals: (1) to provide clinically useful and timely safety information to health care professionals and their patients; and (2) to encourage and facilitate reporting of serious adverse events. Reports are used by the FDA as a data source to identify and evaluate new safety concerns with drugs and devices after they are approved and more widely used in clinical practice. With this new information, the FDA can develop, with the manufacturer, a modified product, revised and strengthened professional labeling and patient instructions, and a modified use strategy that will lead to a safer product.

Health care professionals are in the best position to recognize serious, unexpected adverse drug reactions (ADRs), medication errors, and product quality problems arising from the use of medical products. In the interest of public health, the FDA and manufacturers depend on clinicians to recognize and voluntarily report these events when they suspect an association between a product and a serious harm or outcome.

Vaccine-related adverse events are not reported to MedWatch but should be reported to the Vaccine Adverse Event Reporting System (**http://vaers.hhs.gov/**; see Reporting of Adverse Events, p 41).

The MedWatch voluntary form is a simple, 1-page, postage-paid form (see Fig 4.1, p 822). The MedWatch Web site (**www.fda.gov/medwatch**) offers an online version that can be completed and submitted immediately to the FDA. The Web site also offers the form for downloading and printing. This form then can be returned by fax (800-FDA-0178) or mail. A toll-free number (800-FDA-1088) is available for health care professionals and consumers to report by phone or request blank forms with instructions.

FIG 4.1. MEDWATCH REPORTING FORM.

U.S. Department of Health and Human Services

Form Approved: OMB No. 0910-0291, Expires: 10/31/08
See OMB statement on reverse.

MEDWATCH

The FDA Safety Information and
Adverse Event Reporting Program

For VOLUNTARY reporting of adverse events, product problems and product use errors

Page ____ of ____

FDA USE ONLY
Triage unit sequence #

A. PATIENT INFORMATION

1. Patient Identifier | 2. Age at Time of Event, or Date of Birth: | 3. Sex □ Female □ Male | 4. Weight ____ lb or ____ kg

In confidence

B. ADVERSE EVENT, PRODUCT PROBLEM OR ERROR

Check all that apply:

1. □ Adverse Event □ Product Problem (e.g., defects/malfunctions)
   □ Product Use Error □ Problem with Different Manufacturer of Same Medicine

2. Outcomes Attributed to Adverse Event (Check all that apply)
   □ Death: ____ (mm/dd/yyyy)   □ Disability or Permanent Damage
   □ Life-threatening   □ Congenital Anomaly/Birth Defect
   □ Hospitalization - initial or prolonged   □ Other Serious (Important Medical Events)
   □ Required Intervention to Prevent Permanent Impairment/Damage (Devices)

3. Date of Event (mm/dd/yyyy) | 4. Date of this Report (mm/dd/yyyy)

5. Describe Event, Problem or Product Use Error

6. Relevant Tests/Laboratory Data, Including Dates

7. Other Relevant History, Including Preexisting Medical Conditions (e.g., allergies, race, pregnancy, smoking and alcohol use, liver/kidney problems, etc.)

C. PRODUCT AVAILABILITY

Product Available for Evaluation? (Do not send product to FDA)
□ Yes □ No □ Returned to Manufacturer on: ____ (mm/dd/yyyy)

D. SUSPECT PRODUCT(S)

1. Name, Strength, Manufacturer (from product label)
   #1
   #2

2. Dose or Amount | Frequency | Route
   #1
   #2

3. Dates of Use (If unknown, give duration) from/to (or best estimate)
   #1
   #2
4. Diagnosis or Reason for Use (Indication)
   #1
   #2

5. Event Abated After Use Stopped or Dose Reduced?
   #1 □ Yes □ No □ Doesn't Apply
   #2 □ Yes □ No □ Doesn't Apply

8. Event Reappeared After Reintroduction?
   #1 □ Yes □ No □ Doesn't Apply
   #2 □ Yes □ No □ Doesn't Apply

6. Lot # | 7. Expiration Date
   #1 | #1
   #2 | #2

9. NDC # or Unique ID

E. SUSPECT MEDICAL DEVICE

1. Brand Name

2. Common Device Name

3. Manufacturer Name, City and State

4. Model # | Lot # | 5. Operator of Device
   Catalog # | Expiration Date (mm/dd/yyyy) | □ Health Professional
   Serial # | Other # | □ Lay User/Patient □ Other:

6. If Implanted, Give Date (mm/dd/yyyy) | 7. If Explanted, Give Date (mm/dd/yyyy)

8. Is this a Single-use Device that was Reprocessed and Reused on a Patient?
   □ Yes □ No

9. If Yes to Item No. 8, Enter Name and Address of Reprocessor

F. OTHER (CONCOMITANT) MEDICAL PRODUCTS

Product names and therapy dates (exclude treatment of event)

G. REPORTER (See confidentiality section on back)

1. Name and Address

Phone # | E-mail

2. Health Professional? □ Yes □ No | 3. Occupation | 4. Also Reported to: □ Manufacturer □ User Facility □ Distributor/Importer

5. If you do NOT want your identity disclosed to the manufacturer, place an "X" in this box: □

FORM FDA 3500 (10/05) Submission of a report does not constitute an admission that medical personnel or the product caused or contributed to the event.

NOTE: THIS AND THE MANDATORY REPORTING FORM ARE AVAILABLE FOR DOWNLOAD (**www.fda.gov/medwatch/getforms.htm**).

Antimicrobial Prophylaxis

∙∙
ANTIMICROBIAL PROPHYLAXIS

Antimicrobial agents commonly are prescribed to prevent infections in infants and children. The efficacy of prophylactic antimicrobial agents has been documented for some conditions but is unsubstantiated for many. *Prophylaxis* is defined as the use of antimicrobial drugs in the absence of suspected or documented infection to decrease the incidence of infection.

Chemoprophylaxis is directed at different but not mutually exclusive targets, such as specific pathogens, infection-prone body sites, and vulnerable hosts. Effective prophylaxis is achieved more readily against specific pathogens and certain body sites. In any situation in which prophylactic antimicrobial therapy is being considered, the risk of emergence of resistant organisms must be weighed against potential benefits. Prophylactic agents should have as narrow a spectrum of antimicrobial activity as possible and should be used for as brief a period of time as possible. Uses of antimicrobial agents in doses or routes of administration other than oral, intramuscular, or intravenous, such as "antibiotic solutions" for irrigation or instillation, should not be considered prophylaxis and generally are unproven as efficacious for treatment or prevention of infection.

Specific Pathogens

Prophylaxis may be appropriate or indicated if increased risk of serious infection with a specific pathogen exists and a specific antimicrobial agent may eliminate the pathogen from people at risk with minimal adverse effects. For some pathogens that colonize the upper respiratory tract, elimination of the carrier state can be difficult and may require use of an antimicrobial agent, such as rifampin, that achieves effective concentrations in nasopharyngeal secretions, a property often lacking among antimicrobial agents ordinarily used to treat infections caused by such pathogens. In instances in which prophylaxis is recommended, the regimen is described in the disease-specific chapter in Section 3.

Infection-Prone Body Sites

Prevention of infection of vulnerable body sites may be possible if (1) the period of risk is defined and brief; (2) the expected pathogens have predictable antimicrobial susceptibility; and (3) the site is accessible to antimicrobial agents. Prevention of surgical site infection and neonatal ophthalmia is discussed in this section.

Acute otitis media recurs less frequently in otitis-prone children treated prophylactically with antimicrobial agents. Studies have demonstrated that either amoxicillin or sulfisoxazole is effective. However, antimicrobial prophylaxis may alter the nasopharyngeal flora and foster colonization with resistant organisms, compromising long-term efficacy of the prophylactic drug. Continuous orally administered antimicrobial prophylaxis should be reserved for control of recurrent acute otitis media, only when defined as 3 or more distinct and well-documented episodes during a period of 6 months or 4 or more episodes during a period of 12 months. Although prophylactic administration of an antimicrobial agent limited to the time of high risk for otitis media, such as during acute viral respiratory tract infection, has been suggested, this method has not been evaluated critically.

The effectiveness of chemoprophylaxis for urinary tract infection depends on the rate of emergence of antimicrobial resistance in the gastrointestinal tract flora, the usual source of bacteria that invade the urinary tract. The long-term effectiveness of nitrofurantoin or trimethoprim-sulfamethoxazole is explained by the minimal effect of these drugs on development of resistant flora. Both drugs are concentrated in urine, and adequate inhibitory activity can be obtained with less than the usual therapeutic dose. Use of a single dose at bedtime has been successful. Chemoprophylaxis has proven to be of benefit only in children with urinary continence and has not been studied adequately in younger children and infants.

Chemoprophylaxis of human and animal bite wounds has become common practice even though dog bites, the most common wound, are infected infrequently (see Bite Wounds, p 191, for recommendations).

Vulnerable Hosts

Most attempts to prevent bacterial infections in vulnerable patients with antimicrobial prophylaxis have been unsuccessful because of the rapid emergence of bacteria resistant to the antimicrobial agents used. Recommendations for prevention of opportunistic infections in people infected with human immunodeficiency virus are available.*

··

ANTIMICROBIAL PROPHYLAXIS IN PEDIATRIC SURGICAL PATIENTS

A major use of antimicrobial agents in hospitalized children is for prevention of postoperative wound infections through perioperative prophylaxis, generally for procedures with high infection rates, procedures involving implantation of prosthetic material, and procedures in which the consequences of infection are likely to be especially serious. Because of this common use, consensus recommendations for prevention of surgical site infections in children have been developed.

Frequency of Antimicrobial Prophylaxis

Two studies have demonstrated that approximately 75% of antimicrobial use in pediatric surgical services is for prophylaxis. The efficacy of antimicrobial agents in decreasing the incidence of postoperative infection and other infection after invasive nonsurgical procedures, such as cystoscopy or cardiac catheterization, has been demonstrated in controlled clinical trials. The principles for effective use of antimicrobial

---

* Centers for Disease Control and Prevention. Guidelines for preventing opportunistic infections among HIV-infected persons-2002. Recommendations of the US Public Health Service and the Infectious Diseases Society of America. *MMWR Recomm Rep.* 2002;51(RR-8):1–46

agents in prophylaxis of operative wound infections, including choice of drugs, optimal time of administration, and duration, have been delineated by experimental studies in animals and through clinical trials.

Inappropriate Antimicrobial Prophylaxis

The consequences of inappropriate prophylactic use of antimicrobial agents include increased costs as a result of unnecessary drug use, potential emergence of resistant organisms, and other adverse events. Prophylaxis has been associated with a high frequency of inappropriate use of antimicrobial agents. In a study of children younger than 6 years of age undergoing surgery, antimicrobial agents were administered for prophylaxis inappropriately to 42% of children preoperatively, 67% intraoperatively, and 55% postoperatively.

Guidelines for Appropriate Use

Studies documenting that systemic antimicrobial prophylaxis decreases the incidence of surgical site infections primarily have been performed in adults. Because the pathogenesis of these infections is the same in children, similar principles should guide surgical prophylaxis in children. In the absence of specific studies in children, guidelines recommended in *The Medical Letter** and by the Hospital Infection Control Practices Advisory Committee of the Centers for Disease Control and Prevention[†] are available to direct use of systemic antimicrobial agents for prophylaxis in pediatric surgical patients. The following general principles are presented with the understanding that future studies in children or application to settings unique to infants and children, such as preterm birth or certain immunodeficiencies, may justify modification of these recommendations.

Indications for Prophylaxis

Systemic prophylaxis is indicated when the probability or morbidity of postoperative infection is high and benefits of preventing wound infection outweigh potential risks from adverse drug reactions or emergence of resistant organisms. The latter poses a potential risk not only to the recipient but also to other hospitalized patients in whom a health care-associated infection caused by resistant organisms can develop. Procedures in which the benefits justify the risks incurred in antimicrobial prophylaxis are procedures associated with an increased incidence of postoperative infection and procedures in which the likelihood of infection may not be great but the adverse consequences of infection are extreme, such as with prosthetic materials.

A major determinant of the probability of surgical site infection is the number of microorganisms in the wound at completion of the procedure. The classification of surgical procedures is based on an estimation of bacterial contamination and, thus, risk of subsequent infection. The 4 classes are: (1) clean wounds; (2) clean-contaminated wounds; (3) contaminated wounds; and (4) dirty and infected wounds. As evidenced by

---

* Antimicrobial prophylaxis for surgery. Treatment guidelines from the Medical Letter. *Med Lett Drugs Ther.* 2004;2:27–32

[†] Mangram AJ, Horan TC, Pearson ML, Silver LC, Jarvis WR. Guideline for prevention of surgical site infection, 1999. Hospital Infection Control Practices Advisory Committee. *Infect Control Hosp Epidemiol.* 1999;20:250–278

the wide variation in infection rates within these classes, wound classification is not the only factor affecting risk of surgical site infection. Additional independent factors include site of operation, duration of the procedure, and patient's preoperative health status. A patient risk index, which incorporates the American Society of Anesthesiologists preoperative physical status assessment score and the duration of the operation in addition to the aforementioned wound classification, has been demonstrated to be a good predictor of postoperative surgical site infection.[*]

CLEAN WOUNDS

Clean wounds are uninfected operative wounds in which no inflammation is encountered and the respiratory, alimentary, and genitourinary tracts or oropharyngeal cavity are not entered. The operative procedures are elective, and wounds are closed primarily and, if necessary, drained with closed drainage. No break in aseptic technique occurs. Operative incisional wounds that follow nonpenetrating (blunt) abdominal trauma should be included in this category, provided that the surgical procedure does not entail entry into the gastrointestinal or genitourinary tracts. The benefits of systemic antimicrobial prophylaxis do not justify the potential risks associated with antimicrobial use in most clean wound procedures, because the risk of infection is low (1%–2%). Some exceptions exist in which either the risks or consequences of infection are high. Examples are implantation of intravascular prosthetic material (eg, insertion of a prosthetic heart valve) or a prosthetic joint, open-heart surgery for repair of structural defects, body cavity exploration in neonates, and most neurosurgical operations. Prophylaxis generally is given in these circumstances.

CLEAN-CONTAMINATED WOUNDS

In clean-contaminated operative wounds, the respiratory, alimentary, or genitourinary tracts are entered under controlled conditions with no significant contamination. Operations involving the gastrointestinal tract, the biliary tract, appendix, vagina, or oropharynx and urgent or emergency surgery in an otherwise clean procedure are included in this category, provided that no evidence of infection is encountered and no major break in aseptic technique occurs. Prophylaxis is limited to procedures in which a substantial amount of wound contamination is expected. The overall risk of infection for the surgical site is 3% to 15%. On the basis of data from adults, procedures for which prophylaxis is indicated for pediatric patients include the following: (1) all gastrointestinal tract procedures in which there is obstruction or when the patient is receiving H_2 receptor antagonists or proton pump blockers or has a permanent foreign body; (2) selected biliary tract operations (eg, when there is obstruction from common bile duct stones); and (3) urinary tract surgery or instrumentation in the presence of bacteriuria or obstructive uropathy.

CONTAMINATED WOUNDS

Contaminated wounds include open, fresh, accidental wounds; operative wounds in the setting of major breaks in aseptic technique or gross spillage from the gastrointes-

---

[*] Gaynes RP, Culver DH, Horan TC, Edwards JR, Richards C, Tolson JS. Surgical site infection (SSI) rates in the United States, 1992–1998: the National Nosocomial Surveillance System basic SSI risk index. *Clin Infect Dis* 2001;33(suppl2):S69–S77

tinal tract; exposed viscera at birth from congenital anomalies; penetrating trauma of fewer than 4 hours' duration; and incisions in which acute nonpurulent inflammation is encountered. The estimated rate of infection for the surgical site is 15%. In contaminated wound procedures, antimicrobial prophylaxis is appropriate for some patients with acute nonpurulent inflammation isolated to and contained within an inflamed viscus (such as acute appendicitis or cholecystitis). In contaminated wounds resulting from other causes, antimicrobial therapy should be considered treatment rather than prophylaxis.

DIRTY AND INFECTED WOUNDS

Dirty and infected wounds include penetrating trauma of more than 4 hours' duration, wounds with retained devitalized tissue, and wounds involving existing clinical infection or perforated viscera. This definition suggests that the organisms causing postoperative infection were present in the operative field before surgery. The estimated rate of infection for the surgical site is 40%. In dirty and infected wound procedures, such as procedures for a perforated abdominal viscus, a compound fracture, or a laceration attributable to an animal or human bite, or if a major break in sterile technique has occurred, antimicrobial agents are given as treatment rather than prophylaxis.

Timing of Administration of Prophylactic Antimicrobial Agents

Effective prophylaxis occurs only when adequate drug concentrations in tissues are present when bacterial contamination occurs intraoperatively. Administration of an antimicrobial agent within 2 hours before surgery has been demonstrated to decrease the risk of wound infection. Accordingly, administration is recommended at least 30 minutes before surgical incision to ensure adequate tissue concentrations at the start of the procedure.

Duration of Administration of Antimicrobial Agents

A single antimicrobial dose that provides adequate tissue concentrations throughout the surgical procedure is sufficient. When surgery is prolonged (more than 4 hours), major blood loss occurs, or an antimicrobial agent with a short half-life is used, redosing every 1 to 2 half-lives of the drug should provide adequate antimicrobial concentrations during the procedure. Although published studies of antimicrobial prophylaxis commonly use 1 or 2 doses postoperatively in addition to 1 preoperative dose, there are no data to suggest that this practice improves outcome. Postoperative doses after closure generally are not recommended and increase the risk of antimicrobial resistance.

Recommended Antimicrobial Agents

An antimicrobial agent is chosen on the basis of bacterial pathogens most likely to cause infectious complications after the specific procedure, the antimicrobial susceptibility pattern of these pathogens, and the safety and efficacy of the drug. New, more costly antimicrobial agents generally are not recommended, unless prophylactic efficacy has been proven to be superior to drugs of established benefit. Antimicrobial agents administered prophylactically do not have to be active against every potential organism to be effective. Routine use of vancomycin and extended-spectrum cephalosporins for surgical prophylaxis is not recommended. Doses and routes of administration are determined on the basis of the need to achieve therapeutic blood and tissue concentrations throughout the procedure. Antimicrobial prophylaxis for most surgical procedures (including gastric, biliary, thoracic [noncardiac], vascular, neurosurgical, and orthopedic operations) can be achieved effectively using an agent such as a first-generation cephalosporin (eg, cefazolin). For colorectal surgery or appendectomy, effective prophylaxis requires antimicrobial agents that are active against intestinal flora. Table 5.1 (p 829) provides recommendations for drugs, including preoperative doses, to be used in children undergoing surgical manipulation or invasive procedures. Physicians should be aware of potential interactions and adverse effects associated with prophylactic antimicrobial agents and other medications the patient may be receiving.

PREVENTION OF BACTERIAL ENDOCARDITIS

The Committee on Rheumatic Fever, Endocarditis, and Kawasaki Disease of the American Heart Association issues detailed recommendations on the rationale, indications, and antimicrobial regimens for prevention of bacterial endocarditis for people at increased risk. The most recent recommendations published in 1997* are undergoing revision. The cardiac conditions associated with endocarditis, procedures for which endocarditis prophylaxis is recommended for people with cardiac conditions that put them at risk, and specific prophylactic regimens are presented in Tables 5.2 through 5.6 (pp 831–835). Health care professionals should consult the published recommendations for further details. A link to the revised recommendations when published will be available at **http://aapredbook.aappublications.org**.

PREVENTION OF NEONATAL OPHTHALMIA

Ophthalmia neonatorum is defined as conjunctivitis occurring within the first 4 weeks of life. The major causes of ophthalmia neonatorum are presented in Table 5.7, p 836. The prevalence of infection with *Chlamydia trachomatis* and *Neisseria gonorrhoeae* in newborn infants is related directly to the prevalence of infection among pregnant women, whether pregnant women are screened and treated, and whether newborn infants are given ophthalmia prophylaxis. Screening of all pregnant women for chlamydia and gonorrhea infection followed by appropriate treatment and follow-up of all infected women and their partner(s) can minimize the risk of perinatal transmission (see Chlamydial Infections, p 249, and Gonococcal Infections, p 301).

---

* Dajani AS, Taubert KA, Wilson W, et al. Prevention of bacterial endocarditis. Recommendations by the American Heart Association. *JAMA*. 1997;277:1794–1801

Table 5.1. Recommendations for Preoperative Antimicrobial Prophylaxis[1]

Operation	Likely Pathogens	Recommended Drugs	Preoperative Dose
Neonatal (<72 h of age)—all major procedures	Group B streptococci, enteric gram-negative bacilli, enterococci	Ampicillin **PLUS** gentamicin	50 mg/kg 2.5–3 mg/kg
Cardiac (prosthetic valve or pacemaker)	*Staphylococcus epidermidis, Staphylococcus aureus, Corynebacterium* species, enteric gram-negative bacilli	Cefazolin **OR**, if MRSA or MRSE is likely, vancomycin	25 mg/kg 10 mg/kg
Gastrointestinal			
Esophageal and gastroduodenal	Enteric gram-negative bacilli, gram-positive cocci	Cefazolin (high risk only[2])	25 mg/kg
Biliary tract	Enteric gram-negative bacilli, enterococci, clostridia	Cefazolin[3]	25 mg/kg
Colorectal or appendectomy (nonperforated)	Enteric gram-negative bacilli, enterococci, anaerobes	Cefoxitin **OR** cefotetan[4]; if high risk, gentamicin **PLUS** clindamycin ± ampicillin	40 mg/kg 40 mg/kg 2 mg/kg 10 mg/kg 50 mg/kg
Ruptured viscus	Enteric gram-negative bacilli, anaerobes, enterococci	Cefoxitin or cefotetan[4] ± gentamicin **OR** gentamicin **PLUS** clindamycin	40 mg/kg 2 mg/kg 2 mg/kg 10 mg/kg
Genitourinary	Enteric gram-negative bacilli, enterococci	Ampicillin **PLUS** gentamicin	50 mg/kg 2 mg/kg
Head and neck surgery (incision through oral or pharyngeal mucosa)	Anaerobes, enteric gram-negative bacilli, *S aureus*	Gentamicin **PLUS** clindamycin **OR** cefazolin	2 mg/kg 10 mg/kg 25 mg/kg
Neurosurgery (craniotomy)	*S epidermidis, S aureus*	Cefazolin **OR**, if MRSA or MRSE is likely, vancomycin	25 mg/kg 10 mg/kg

Table 5.1. Recommendations for Preoperative Antimicrobial Prophylaxis,[1] continued

Operation	Likely Pathogens	Recommended Drugs	Preoperative Dose
Ophthalmic	*S epidermidis, S aureus*, streptococci, enteric gram-negative bacilli, *Pseudomonas* species	Gentamicin, ciprofloxacin, ofloxacin, tobramycin, **OR** neomycin-gramicidin-polymyxin B **OR** cefazolin	Multiple drops topically for 2–24 h before procedure 100 mg, subconjunctivally
Orthopedic (internal fixation of fractures or prosthetic joints)	*S epidermidis, S aureus*	Cefazolin **OR**, if MRSA or MRSE is likely, vancomycin	25 mg/kg 10 mg/kg
Thoracic (noncardiac)	*S epidermidis, S aureus*, streptococci, gram-negative enteric bacilli	Cefazolin **OR**, if MRSA or MRSE is likely, vancomycin	25 mg/kg 10 mg/kg
Traumatic wound (nonbites)	*S aureus*, group A streptococci, *Clostridium* species	Cefazolin	25 mg/kg

MRSA indicates methicillin-resistant *Staphylococcus aureus*; MRSE indicates methicillin-resistant *S epidermidis*.

[1] Antimicrobial prophylaxis in surgery. Treatment guidelines from the Medical Letter. *Med Lett Drugs Ther.* 2004;2:27–32

[2] Esophageal obstruction, decreased gastric acidity or gastrointestinal motility; morbid obesity.

[3] Acute cholecystitis, nonfunctioning gallbladder, obstructive jaundice, common duct stones.

[4] Safety and effectiveness of cefotetan have not been established in children.

Table 5.2. Cardiac Conditions Associated With Endocarditis

Endocarditis Prophylaxis	
Recommended	Not recommended
HIGH RISK	*NEGLIGIBLE RISK*[1]
Prosthetic cardiac valves, including bioprosthetic and homograft valves Previous bacterial endocarditis Complex cyanotic congenital heart disease (eg, single ventricle states, transposition of the great arteries, tetralogy of Fallot) Surgically constructed systemic pulmonary shunts or conduits	Isolated secundum atrial septal defect Surgical repair of atrial septal defect, ventricular septal defect, or patent ductus arteriosus (without residua and beyond 6 mo of age) Previous coronary artery bypass graft surgery Mitral valve prolapse without valvular regurgitation[2] Physiologic, functional, or innocent heart murmurs[2] Previous Kawasaki disease without valvular dysfunction Previous rheumatic fever without valvular dysfunction Cardiac pacemakers (intravascular and epicardial) and implanted defibrillators
MODERATE RISK	
Most other congenital cardiac malformations (other than those in the high-risk and negligible-risk categories) Acquired valvular dysfunction (eg, rheumatic heart disease) Hypertrophic cardiomyopathy Mitral valve prolapse with valvular regurgitation and/or thickened leaflets[2]	

[1] No greater risk than the general population.
[2] For further details, see Dajani AS, Taubert KA, Wilson W, et al. Prevention of bacterial endocarditis. Recommendations by the American Heart Association. *JAMA*. 1997;277:1794–1801

Table 5.3. Dental Procedures and Endocarditis Prophylaxis

Endocarditis Prophylaxis	
Recommended[1]	Not Recommended
Dental extractions	Restorative dentistry[2] (operative and prosthodontic) with or without retraction cord[3]
Periodontal procedures, including surgery, scaling and root planing, probing, and routine maintenance	Local anesthetic injections (nonintraligamentary)
Dental implant placement and reimplantation of avulsed teeth	Intracanal endodontic treatment; postplacement and buildup
Endodontic (root canal) instrumentation or surgery only beyond the apex	Placement of rubber dams
	Postoperative suture removal
Subgingival placement of antimicrobial fibers or strips	Placement of removable prosthodontic or orthodontic appliances
Initial placement of orthodontic bands but not brackets	Taking of oral impressions
Intraligamentary local anesthetic injections	Fluoride treatments
Prophylactic cleaning of teeth or implants during which bleeding is anticipated	Taking of oral radiographs
	Orthodontic appliance adjustment
	Shedding of primary teeth

[1] Prophylaxis is recommended for patients with high- and moderate-risk cardiac conditions.

[2] This includes restoration of decayed teeth (filling cavities) and replacement of missing teeth.

[3] Clinical judgment may indicate antimicrobial use in some circumstances that may create significant bleeding.

Table 5.4. Other Procedures and Endocarditis Prophylaxis

	Endocarditis Prophylaxis	
	Recommended[1]	Not Recommended
Respiratory tract	Tonsillectomy, adenoidectomy, or both Surgical operations that involve respiratory mucosa Bronchoscopy with a rigid bronchoscope	Endotracheal intubation Bronchoscopy with a flexible bronchoscope, with or without biopsy[2] Tympanostomy tube insertion
Gastrointestinal tract[3]	Sclerotherapy for esophageal varices Esophageal stricture dilation Endoscopic retrograde cholangiography with biliary obstruction Biliary tract surgery Surgical operations that involve intestinal mucosa	Transesophageal echocardiography[2] Endoscopy with or without gastrointestinal tract biopsy[2]
Genitourinary tract	Prostate surgery Cystoscopy Urethral dilation	Vaginal hysterectomy[2] Vaginal delivery[2] Cesarean delivery In uninfected tissue: Urethral catheterization Uterine dilatation and curettage Therapeutic abortion Sterilization procedures Insertion or removal of intrauterine devices
Other		Cardiac catheterization, including balloon angioplasty Implanted cardiac pacemakers, implanted defibrillators, and coronary stents Incision or biopsy of surgically scrubbed skin Circumcision

[1] Prophylaxis is recommended for high- and moderate-risk cardiac conditions.

[2] Prophylaxis is optional for high-risk patients.

[3] Prophylaxis is recommended for high-risk patients; optional for medium-risk patients.

Table 5.5. Prophylactic Regimens for Dental, Oral, Respiratory Tract, or Esophageal Procedures

Situation	Agent	Regimen[1]
Standard general prophylaxis	Amoxicillin	Adults: 2.0 g; children: 50 mg/kg of body weight, orally, 1 h before procedure
Unable to take oral medications	Ampicillin	Adults: 2.0 g, intramuscularly (IM) or intravenously (IV); children: 50 mg/kg, IM or IV, within 30 min before procedure
Allergic to penicillin	Clindamycin	Adults: 600 mg; children: 20 mg/kg, orally, 1 h before procedure
	OR	
	Cephalexin[2] or cefadroxil[2]	Adults: 2.0 g; children: 50 mg/kg, orally, 1 h before procedure
	OR	
	Azithromycin or clarithromycin	Adults: 500 mg; children: 15 mg/kg, orally, 1 h before procedure
Allergic to penicillin and unable to take oral medications	Clindamycin	Adults: 600 mg; children: 20 mg/kg, IV, within 30 min before procedure
	OR	
	Cefazolin[2]	Adults: 1.0 g; children: 25 mg/kg, IM or IV, within 30 min before procedure

[1] Total dose for children should not exceed adult dose.
[2] Cephalosporins should not be used for people with immediate-type hypersensitivity reaction (urticaria, angioedema, or anaphylaxis) to penicillins.

Table 5.6. Prophylactic Regimens for Genitourinary and Gastrointestinal Tract (Excluding Esophageal) Procedures

Situation	Agents[1]	Regimen[2]
High-risk patients	Ampicillin **PLUS** Gentamicin	Adults: ampicillin, 2.0 g, intramuscularly (IM) or intravenously (IV), plus gentamicin, 1.5 mg/kg (maximum 120 mg), within 30 min of starting procedure; 6 h later: ampicillin, 1 g, IM or IV, or amoxicillin, 1 g, orally Children: ampicillin, 50 mg/kg, IM or IV (maximum 2.0 g), plus gentamicin, 1.5 mg/kg, within 30 min of starting procedure; 6 h later: ampicillin, 25 mg/kg, IM or IV, or amoxicillin, 25 mg/kg, orally.
High-risk patients allergic to ampicillin or amoxicillin	Vancomycin **PLUS** Gentamicin	Adults: vancomycin, 1.0 g, IV, over 1–2 h plus gentamicin, 1.5 mg/kg, IV or IM (maximum 120 mg), complete injection/infusion within 30 min of starting procedure. Children: vancomycin, 20 mg/kg, IV, over 1–2 h plus gentamicin, 1.5 mg/kg, IV or IM, complete injection/infusion within 30 min of starting procedure.
Moderate-risk patients	Amoxicillin **OR** Ampicillin	Adults: amoxicillin, 2.0 g, orally, 1 h before procedure, or ampicillin, 2.0 g, IM or IV, within 30 min of starting procedure. Children: amoxicillin, 50 mg/kg, orally, 1 h before procedure, or ampicillin, 50 mg/kg, IM or IV, within 30 min of starting procedure.
Moderate-risk patients allergic to ampicillin or amoxicillin	Vancomycin	Adults: vancomycin, 1.0 g, IV, over 1–2 h, complete infusion within 30 min of starting procedure. Children: vancomycin, 20 mg/kg, IV, over 1–2 h, complete infusion within 30 min of starting procedure.

[1] Total dose for children should not exceed adult dose.
[2] No second dose of vancomycin or gentamicin is recommended.

Table 5.7. Major and Minor Pathogens in Ophthalmia Neonatorum

Etiology of Ophthalmia Neonatorum	Percentage of Cases	Incubation Period (Days)	Severity of Conjunctivitis[1]	Associated Problems
Chlamydia trachomatis	2–40	5–14	+	Pneumonitis 3 wk–3 mo (see Chlamydial Infections, p 249)
Neisseria gonorrhoeae	<1	2–7	+ + +	Disseminated infection (see Gonococcal Infections, p 301)
Other bacterial microbes[2]	30–50	5–14	+	Variable
Herpes simplex virus[3]	<1	6–14	+	Disseminated infection (see Herpes Simplex, p 361); keratitis and ulceration also possible
Chemical	Varies with silver nitrate use	1	+	. . .

[1] + indicates mild; + + +, severe.

[2] *Staphylococcus* species; *Streptococcus pneumoniae*; *Haemophilus influenzae*, nontypeable; *Streptococcus mitis*; group A and B streptococci; *Neisseria cinerea*; *Corynebacterium* species; *Moraxella catarrhalis*; *Escherichia coli*; *Klebsiella pneumoniae*; *Pseudomonas aeruginosa*.

[3] See Herpes Simplex Virus Infections (p 361).

Gonococcal Ophthalmia

For newborn infants, topical 1% silver nitrate aqueous solution, 0.5% erythromycin ointment, and 1% tetracycline ophthalmic ointment are considered equally effective for prophylaxis of ocular gonorrheal infection. Each is available in single-dose forms, which are preferable. Povidone-iodine in a 2.5% solution also may be useful, but more studies are required, and a product for this purpose currently is not available in the United States. Silver nitrate causes more chemical conjunctivitis than other agents but is recommended in areas where the incidence of penicillinase-producing *N gonorrhoeae* (PPNG) is appreciable. The efficacy of erythromycin or povidone-iodine prophylaxis against PPNG is not known, but one study has demonstrated tetracycline to be effective. Healthy infants born to women with untreated gonococcal infection should receive 1 dose of ceftriaxone (25–50 mg/kg, intravenously [IV] or intramuscularly [IM], not to exceed 125 mg) or 1 dose of cefotaxime (100 mg/kg, IV or IM). Topical antimicrobial therapy alone is inadequate. Topical therapy also is not necessary if systemic therapy is administered. Infants who have gonococcal ophthalmia should be hospitalized, evaluated for signs of disseminated infection, and treated (see Gonococcal Infections, p 301).

Chlamydial Ophthalmia

Neonatal ophthalmia attributable to *C trachomatis*, although not as severe as gonococcal conjunctivitis, is common in the United States and should be evaluated and treated (see Chlamydial Infections, p 249). Chlamydial conjunctivitis in the neonate differs from that in adults in that in the neonate, it is characterized by lack of follicular response, mucopurulent discharge, and propensity to form membranes on the palpebral conjunctiva. If erythromycin or tetracycline ointment is applied to the conjunctival surface within 1 hour of delivery, the chance of developing chlamydial conjunctivitis is rare. Topical therapy does not treat pneumonia, which requires oral erythromycin therapy, which is given to newborn infants with laboratory-proven chlamydial conjunctivitis (see Chlamydial Infections, p 249).

Herpes Simplex Ophthalmia

Herpetic conjunctivitis in the neonate is rare but can be associated with significant morbidity and mortality. The edema, conjunctival injection, and tearing usually begin within the first 2 weeks and may be followed by keratitis or keratouveitis (see Herpes Simplex, p 361).

Nongonococcal Nonchlamydial Ophthalmia

Silver nitrate, povidone-iodine, and probably erythromycin are effective for preventing nongonococcal nonchlamydial conjunctivitis during the first 2 weeks of life.

Administration of Neonatal Ophthalmic Prophylaxis. Before administering local prophylaxis, each eyelid should be wiped gently with sterile cotton. Two drops of a 1% silver nitrate solution or a 1-cm ribbon of antimicrobial ointment (0.5% erythromycin or 1% tetracycline) are placed in each lower conjunctival sac. The eyelids then should be massaged gently to spread the solution or ointment. After 1 minute, excess solution or ointment may be wiped away with sterile cotton. None of the prophylactic agents should be flushed from the eyes after instillation, because flushing can decrease the efficacy of prophylaxis.

Infants born by cesarean delivery should receive prophylaxis against neonatal gonococcal ophthalmia. Although gonococcal and chlamydial infections usually are transmitted to the infant during passage through the birth canal, infection by the ascending route also occurs.

Prophylaxis should be given shortly after birth. Delaying prophylaxis for as long as 1 hour after birth to facilitate parent-infant bonding is unlikely to influence efficacy. Longer delays have not been studied for efficacy. Hospitals should establish a process to ensure that infants are given prophylaxis appropriately.

....
APPENDIX I.

Directory of Resources[1]

Organization	Telephone/Fax Numbers	Web Site
AIDSinfo PO Box 6303 Rockville, MD 20849-6303 USA	1-800-HIV-0440 (1-800-448-0440, USA & Canada) 1-301-519-0459 (International) TTY: 1-888-480-3739 1-301-519-6616 (Fax)	www.aidsinfo.nih.gov
American Academy of Pediatrics (AAP) 141 Northwest Point Blvd Elk Grove Village, IL 60007-1098 USA	1-847-434-4000 1-847-434-8000 (Fax) Publications/Customer Service: 1-866-THEAAP1 (1-866-843-2271)	www.aap.org
Canadian Paediatric Society (CPS) 2305 St Laurent Blvd Ottawa, Ontario K1G 4J8 Canada	1-613-526-9397 1-613-526-3332 (Fax)	www.cps.ca
Centers for Disease Control and Prevention (CDC)[2] 1600 Clifton Rd Atlanta, GA 30333	1-404-639-3311	www.cdc.gov
• **24-Hour Service**	1-404-639-2888	
• Advisory Committee on Immunization Practices, Vaccines for Children Resolutions		www.cdc.gov/nip/vfc/acip_vfc_resolutions.htm
• Botulism case consultation and antitoxin	1-770-488-7100	
• Division of Bacterial and Mycotic Diseases	1-404-639-1603	www.cdc.gov/ncidod/dbmd
• Division of Parasitic Diseases	1-770-488-7775 OR 1-770-488-7760	www.cdc.gov/ncidod/dpd/default.htm
• Division of Tuberculosis Elimination	1-404-639-8120	www.cdc.gov/nchstp/tb/default.htm
• Division of Vector-Borne Infectious Diseases	1-970-221-6400	www.cdc.gov/ncidod/dvbid/index.htm

Directory of Resources,[1] continued

Organization	Telephone/Fax Number	Web Site
• Division of Viral Hepatitis	1-888-4-HEP-CDC (1-888-443-7232)	www.cdc.gov/ncidod/diseases/hepatitis
• Division of Viral and Rickettsial Diseases	1-404-639-3574	www.cdc.gov/ncidod/dvrd/index.htm
• Drug Service (weekdays, 8 AM to 4:30 PM ET)	1-404-639-3670	www.cdc.gov/ncidod/srp/drugs/drug-service.html
• Drug Service (weekends, nights, holidays)	1-404-639-2888	www.cdc.gov/ncidod/srp/drugs/drug-service.html
• Immunization, Infectious Diseases, and Other Health Information—Voice Information System	1-800-232-SHOT (1-800-232-7468)	
• Malaria Hotline	1-770-488-7788	
• National Center for Infectious Diseases	1-404-639-3401	www.cdc.gov/ncidod
• National STD/AIDS Hotline	1-800-227-8922	www.ashastd.org/learn/learn_hiv_aids_sup.cfm
• National Immunization Program	1-404-639-8200 English Hotline: 1-800-232-2522 Spanish Hotline: 1-800-232-0233 1-888-CDC-FAXX (Fax) (1-888-232-3299)	www.cdc.gov/nip
• National Prevention Information Network	1-800-458-5231	www.cdc.gov/hiv/hivinfo/npin.htm
• National Vaccine Injury Compensation Program (for information on filing claims)	1-800-338-2382	www.hrsa.gov/osp/vicp/
• Public Inquiries	1-404-639-3534	
• Publications	1-800-232-2522 1-404-639-8828 (Fax)	www.cdc.gov/publications.htm#pubs
• Rash Illness Evaluation Team	1-770-488-7100	

Directory of Resources,[1] continued

Organization	Telephone/Fax Number	Web Site
• Smallpox Adverse Events Clinical Information Line	1-877-554-4625	
• Traveler's Health Hotline and Fax	1-877-FYI-TRIP (877-394-8747) 1-888-232-3299 (Fax toll free)	www.cdc.gov/travel
• Voice/Fax Information Service (including international travel and immunization)	1-404-332-4555 (Voice) 1-404-332-4565 (Fax)	www.cdc.gov/travel
Food and Drug Administration (FDA) 5600 Fishers Ln Rockville, MD 20857-0001	1-888-463-6332	www.fda.gov
• Center for Biologics Evaluation and Research	1-301-827-2000 OR 1-800-835-4709	www.fda.gov/cber
• Center for Drug Evaluation and Research	1-301-827-4570	www.fda.gov/cder
• Division of Special Pathogen and Immunologic Drug Products	1-301-796-1600 1-301-827-2475 (Fax)	
• HIV/AIDS Office of Special Health Issues	1-301-827-4460	www.fda.gov/oashi/aids/hiv.html
• Kids' Vaccinations		www.fda.gov/fdac/reprints/vaccine.html
• MedWatch	1-800-FDA-1088 (1-800-332-1088) 1-800-FDA-0178 (Fax) (1-800-332-0178)	www.fda.gov/medwatch
• Vaccine Adverse Event Reporting System (VAERS)	1-800-822-7967	www.fda.gov/cber/vaers/vaers.htm
Immunization Action Coalition (IAC) 1573 Selby Ave, Ste 234 St Paul, MN 55104	1-651-647-9009 1-651-647-9131 (Fax)	www.immunize.org

Directory of Resources,[1] continued

Organization	Telephone/Fax Number	Web Site
Infectious Diseases Society of America (IDSA) 66 Canal Center Plaza, Ste 600 Alexandria, VA 22314	1-703-299-0200 1-703-299-0204 (Fax)	www.idsociety.org
Institute of Medicine (IOM) The National Academies 500 Fifth St, NW Washington, DC 20001	1-202-334-2352	www.iom.edu
National Institutes of Health (NIH) 9000 Rockville Pike Bethesda, MD 20892	1-301-496-4000	www.nih.gov
• National Institute of Allergy and Infectious Diseases (NIAID)	1-301-496-2263	www3.niaid.nih.gov
• NIAID Collaborative Antiviral Study Group	1-205-934-5316	www.niaid.nih.gov/daids/pdatguide/casg.htm
• National Library of Medicine 8600 Rockville Pike Bethesda, MD 20894	1-888-346-3656	www.nlm.nih.gov
National Network for Immunization Information (NNii) 301 University Blvd CH 2.218 Galveston, TX 77555-0351	1-409-772-0199 1-409-747-4995 (Fax)	www.immunizationinfo.org
National Vaccine Program Office (NVPO)	1-202-260-1253	www.hhs.gov/nvpo/

Directory of Resources,[1] continued

Organization	Telephone/Fax Number	Web Site
Pediatric AIDS Drug Trials—Information		
• Pediatric Branch, National Cancer Institute	1-301-496-4256	http://home.ccr.cancer.gov/oncology/pediatric/
• Pediatric Clinical Trials Group (NIAID-sponsored)	1-800-TRIALS-A (1-800-874-2572)	http://www3.niaid.nih.gov/
Pediatric Infectious Diseases Society 66 Canal Center Plaza, Ste 600 Alexandria, VA 22314	1-703-299-6764 1-703-299-0473 (Fax)	www.pids.org
Women, Children, and HIV The Francois-Xavier Bagnoud Center (FXBC) of the University of Medicine and Dentistry of New Jersey and the Center for HIV Information (CHI), a program of the University of California San Francisco AIDS Research Institute		www.womenchildrenhiv.org/wchiv?page = wx-00-00
World Health Organization (WHO) Avenue Appia 20 1211 Geneva 27 Switzerland	(+41 22) 791 21 11 (+41 22) 791 3111 (Fax)	www.who.int

[1] Internet addresses and telephone/fax numbers are current at the time of publication.

[2] At the time of publication, the Centers for Disease Control and Prevention was undergoing reorganization; phone numbers and Web sites may have changed. For more information, contact the CDC at 1-404-639-3311 or visit **www.cdc.gov**

•
APPENDIX II.

Standards for Child and Adolescent Immunization Practices*

Recommended by the
National Vaccine Advisory Committee

Approved by the
United States Public Health Service

Endorsed by the
American Academy of Pediatrics

The Standards represent consensus of the National Vaccine Advisory Committee (NVAC) and are endorsed by a variety of medical and public health organizations including the American Academy of Pediatrics. The Standards constitute the most essential and desirable immunization practices and represent an important element in our national strategy to protect America's children against vaccine-preventable diseases. The Standards can be useful in helping health care professionals identify needed changes in their office practices and obtain resources to implement the desirable immunization practices.

Since the Standards were published initially in 1992, vaccine delivery in the United States has changed in several important ways. First, immunization coverage rates among preschool children have increased substantially and now are monitored by the National Immunization Survey. Second, immunization of children has shifted markedly from the public to the private sector, with an emphasis on immunization in the context of primary care and the medical home. The Vaccines for Children Program has provided critical support to this shift by covering the cost of immunizations for the most economically disadvantaged children and adolescents. Third, the development and introduction of performance measures, such as the National Committee for Quality Assurance's HEDIS (Health Employer Data and Information Set), have focused national attention on the quality of preventive care, including immunization. Finally, high-quality research in health services has helped to refine strategies for raising and sustaining immunization coverage levels among children, adolescents, and adults.

Health care professionals who immunize children and adolescents continue to face important challenges. These challenges include a diminishing level of experience with the diseases that vaccines prevent among patients, parents, and physicians, the ready availability of vaccine-related information that may be inaccurate or misleading, the increasing complexity of the immunization schedule, the failure of many health plans to pay for the costs associated with immunization, and the focus on adolescent immunization.

---

* The National Vaccine Advisory Committee. Standards for Pediatric and Adolescent Immunization Practices. *Pediatrics*. 2003;112:958–963

The Standards are directed toward *health care professionals*, an inclusive term for the many people in clinical settings who share in the responsibility for immunization of children and adolescents: physicians, nurses, mid-level practitioners (eg, nurse practitioners, physician assistants), medical assistants, and clerical staff. In addition to this primary audience, the Standards are intended to be useful to public health professionals, policy makers, health plan administrators, employers who purchase health care coverage, and others whose efforts shape and support the delivery of immunization services.

The use of the term *standards* should not be confused with a minimum standard of care. Rather, these Standards represent the most desirable immunization practices, which health care professionals should strive to achieve. Given current resource limitations, some health care professionals may find it difficult to implement all of the Standards, resulting from circumstances over which they have little control. The expectation is that, by summarizing the best immunization practices in a clear and concise format, the Standards will assist these health care professionals in securing resources necessary to implement this set of recommendations.

By adopting these Standards, health care professionals can enhance their own policies and practices, making achievement of immunization objectives for children and adolescents as outlined in *Healthy People 2010* both feasible and likely. Achieving these objectives will improve the health and welfare of all children and adolescents as well as the communities in which they live. Provided here are the Standards and resource information. Supporting information for each Standard can be found at **www.aap.org** and in *Pediatrics.*

STANDARDS FOR CHILD AND ADOLESCENT IMMUNIZATION PRACTICES

AVAILABILITY OF VACCINES

1. Vaccination services are readily available.
2. Vaccinations are coordinated with other health care services and provided within a medical home[†] when possible.
3. Barriers to vaccination are identified and minimized.
4. Patient costs are minimized. (For information about the Vaccines for Children Program, see **www.cdc.gov/nip/vfc**.)

ASSESSMENT OF VACCINATION STATUS

5. Health care professionals review the vaccination and health status of patients at every encounter to determine which vaccines are indicated (see Fig 1.1, p 26).
6. Health care professionals assess for and follow only medically accepted contraindications (see Precautions and Contraindications, p 45).

EFFECTIVE COMMUNICATION ABOUT VACCINE BENEFITS AND RISKS

7. Parents/guardians and patients are educated about the benefits and risks of vaccination in a culturally appropriate manner and in easy-to-understand language

---

[*] The National Vaccine Advisory Committee. Standards for Child and Adolescent Immunization Practices. *Pediatrics*. 2003;112:958–963

[†] American Academy of Pediatrics, Medical Home Initiatives for Children With Special Needs Project Advisory Committee. The medical home. *Pediatrics*. 2002;110:184–186

(see Table 1.2, p 6; Informing Patients and Parents, p 5; and Risks and Adverse Events, p 39).

PROPER STORAGE AND ADMINISTRATION OF VACCINES AND DOCUMENTATION OF VACCINATIONS

8   Health care professionals follow appropriate procedures for vaccine storage and handling (see Vaccine Handling and Storage, p 12).

9   Up-to-date, written vaccination protocols are accessible at all locations where vaccines are administered.

10. People who administer vaccines and staff members who manage or support vaccine administration are knowledgeable and receive ongoing education. (Information about training programs is available at **www.cdc.gov/nip/ed/**.)

11. Health care professionals simultaneously administer as many indicated vaccine doses as possible.

12. Vaccination records for patients are accurate, complete, and easily accessible (see Record Keeping and Immunization Registries, p 37).

13. Health care professionals report adverse events following vaccination promptly and accurately to the Vaccine Adverse Event Reporting System (VAERS) and are aware of a separate program, the Vaccine Injury Compensation Program (VICP) (see Vaccine Safety and Contraindications, p 39).

14. All personnel who have contact with patients are appropriately vaccinated (see **www.cdc.gov/nip/recs/adult-schedule.htm**).

IMPLEMENTATION OF STRATEGIES TO IMPROVE VACCINATION COVERAGE

15. Systems are used to remind parents/guardians, patients, and health care professionals when vaccinations are due and to recall those who are overdue.

16. Office- or clinic-based patient record reviews and vaccination coverage assessments are performed annually.

17. Health care professionals practice community-based approaches.

APPENDIX III.

Guide to Contraindications and Precautions to Immunizations, 2006

This information is based on the recommendations of the Advisory Committee on Immunization Practices (ACIP) of the Centers for Disease Control and Prevention and the Committee on Infectious Diseases of the American Academy of Pediatrics (AAP). Sometimes, these recommendations vary from those in the manufacturers' package inserts and **www.cdc.gov/nip/recs/contraindications_vacc.htm**. For more detailed information, health care professionals should consult the published recommendations of the ACIP, AAP, and manufacturers' package inserts. These guidelines, originally issued in 1993, have been updated to give current recommendations as of 2006 (based on information available as of February 2006).

Vaccine	Contraindications	Precautions[1]	Not Contraindications (Vaccines May Be Given)
General for all vaccines (DTaP; DT; Td; Tdap, IPV; MMR, Hib, pneumococcal, meningococcal, hepatitis B, varicella, hepatitis A, influenza)	Anaphylactic reaction to a vaccine contraindicates further doses of that vaccine Anaphylactic reaction to a vaccine constituent contraindicates the use of vaccines containing that substance	Moderate or severe illnesses with or without fever Latex allergy[2]	Mild to moderate local reaction (soreness, redness, swelling) after a dose of an injectable antigen Low-grade or moderate fever after a previous vaccine dose Mild acute illness with or without low-grade fever Current antimicrobial therapy Convalescent phase of illnesses Preterm birth (same dosage and indications as for healthy, full-term infants) Recent exposure to an infectious disease History of penicillin or other nonspecific allergies or fact that relatives have such allergies Pregnancy of mother or household contact Unimmunized household contact Immunodeficient household contact Breastfeeding (nursing infant OR lactating mother)

DTaP indicates diphtheria and tetanus toxoids and acellular pertussis; DT, pediatric diphtheria-tetanus toxoid; Td, adult tetanus-diphtheria toxoid; Tdap, tetanus toxoid, reduced diphtheria toxoid, and acellular pertussis; IPV, inactivated poliovirus; MMR, measles-mumps-rubella; Hib, *Haemophilus influenzae* type b; DTP, diphtheria and tetanus toxoids and pertussis; GBS, Guillain-Barré syndrome; MCV4, tetravalent (A, C, Y, W-135) meningococcal conjugate vaccine; PPD, purified protein derivative (tuberculin); HIV, human immunodeficiency virus; PCV7, pneumococcal conjugate vaccine.

[1] The events or conditions listed as precautions, although not contraindications, should be reviewed carefully. The benefits and risks of administering a specific vaccine to a person under the circumstances should be considered. If the risks are believed to outweigh the benefits, the immunization should be withheld; if the benefits are believed to outweigh the risks (eg, during an outbreak or foreign travel), the immunization should be given. Whether and when to administer DTaP to children with proven or suspected underlying neurologic disorders should be decided on an individual basis.

[2] If a person reports a severe (anaphylactic) allergy to latex, vaccines supplied in vials or syringes that contain natural rubber should not be administered unless the benefits of immunization outweigh the risks of an allergic reaction to the vaccine. For latex allergies other than anaphylactic allergies (eg, a history of contact allergy to latex gloves), vaccines supplied in vials or syringes that contain dry natural rubber or latex can be administered.

Guide to Contraindications and Precautions to Immunizations, 2006, continued

Vaccine	Contraindications	Precautions[1]	Not Contraindications (Vaccines May Be Given)
DTaP	Encephalopathy within 7 days of administration of previous dose of DTaP/DTP	Temperature of 40.5°C (104.8°F) within 48 h after immunization with a previous dose of DTaP/DTP Collapse or shock-like state (hypotonic-hyporesponsive episode) within 48 h of receiving a previous dose of DTaP/DTP Seizures within 3 days of receiving a previous dose of DTaP/DTP[3] Persistent inconsolable crying lasting 3 h, within 48 h of receiving a previous dose of DTaP/DTP GBS within 6 wk after a dose[4]	Family history of seizures[3] Family history of sudden infant death syndrome Family history of an adverse event after DTaP/DTP administration
DT, Td	Severe allergic reaction after a previous dose or to a vaccine component	GBS ≤6 weeks after previous dose of tetanus toxoid-containing vaccine Moderate or severe acute illness with or without fever	

[3] Acetaminophen given before administering DTaP and thereafter every 4 hours for 24 hours should be considered for children with a personal or family (ie, siblings or parents) history of seizures.

[4] The decision to give additional doses of DTaP should be made on the basis of consideration of the benefit of further immunization versus the risk of recurrence of GBS. For example, completion of the primary series in children is justified.

Guide to Contraindications and Precautions to Immunizations, 2006, continued

Vaccine	Contraindications	Precautions[1]	Not Contraindications (Vaccines May Be Given)
IPV	Anaphylactic reactions to neomycin, streptomycin, or polymyxin B	Pregnancy	. . .
MCV4	Severe allergic reaction to any component of the vaccine, including diphtheria toxoid, or to dry natural rubber latex		
MMR[5,6]	Pregnancy Anaphylactic reaction to neomycin or gelatin Known altered immunodeficiency (hematologic and solid tumors, congenital immunodeficiency, severe HIV infection, and long-term immunosuppressive therapy)	Recent (within 3–11 mo, depending on product and dose) Immune Globulin administration[7] (see Table 3.33, p 446) Thrombocytopenia or history of thrombocytopenic purpura[7] Tuberculosis or positive PPD test result[8]	Simultaneous tuberculin skin testing[9] Breastfeeding Pregnancy of mother of recipient Immunodeficient family member or household contact Infection with HIV Nonanaphylactic reactions to gelatin or neomycin
Hib	None	. . .	. . .
Hepatitis B	Severe allergic reaction after a previous dose or to a vaccine component	Preterm birth[10]	Pregnancy
PCV7	Severe allergic reaction to previous dose or vaccine component	Moderate or severe acute illness with or without fever	

[5] The administration of multiple live-virus vaccines within 30 days (4 weeks) of one another if not given on the same day may result in suboptimal immune response. Data substantiate this risk for MMR and varicella vaccine, which should therefore be given on the same day or more than 4 weeks apart.

[6] An anaphylactic reaction to egg ingestion previously was considered a contraindication unless skin testing and, if indicated, desensitization had been performed. However, skin testing no longer is recommended as of 1997.

[7] The decision to immunize should be made on the basis of consideration of the benefits of immunity to measles, mumps, and rubella versus the risk of recurrence or exacerbation of thrombocytopenia after immunization or from natural infections of measles or rubella. In most instances, the benefits of immunization will be much greater than the potential risks and justify giving MMR, particularly in view of the even greater risk of thrombocytopenia after measles or rubella disease. However, if a previous episode of thrombocytopenia occurred in temporal proximity to immunization, not giving a subsequent dose may be prudent.

[8] A theoretic basis exists for concern that measles vaccine might exacerbate tuberculosis. Consequently, before administering MMR to people with untreated active tuberculosis, initiating antituberculosis therapy is advisable.

[9] Measles immunization may suppress tuberculin reactivity temporarily. MMR vaccine may be given after, or on the same day as, tuberculin skin testing. If MMR has been given recently, postpone the tuberculin skin test until 4 to 6 weeks after administration of MMR.

[10] For preterm infants weighing less than 2 kg at birth and born to hepatitis B surface antigen (HBsAg)-negative mothers, initiation of immunization should be delayed until just before hospital discharge if the infant weighs 2 kg or more, or until approximately 2 months of age, when other routine immunizations are given, to improve response. All preterm infants born to HBsAg-positive mothers should receive immunoprophylaxis (Hepatitis B Immune Globulin and vaccine) beginning as soon as possible after birth, followed by appropriate postimmunization testing.

Guide to Contraindications and Precautions to Immunizations, 2006, continued

Vaccine	Contraindications	Precautions[1]	Not Contraindications (Vaccines May Be Given)
Tdap	Serious allergic reaction to any vaccine component History of encephalopathy (eg, coma, prolonged seizures) within 7 days of administration of a pertussis vaccine that is not attributable to another identifiable cause	GBS ≤6 weeks after previous dose of a tetanus toxoid vaccine. Progressive neurologic disorder, uncontrolled epilepsy, or progressive encephalopathy until the condition has stabilized.	Temperature ≥105°F (≥40.5°C) within 48 hours after DTP/DTaP immunization not attributable to another cause. Collapse or shock-like state (hypotonic hyporesponsive episode) within 48 hours after DTP/DTaP immunization. Persistent crying lasting 3 hours or longer, occurring within 48 hours after DTP/DTaP immunization. Convulsions with or without fever, occurring within 3 days after DTP/DTaP immunization. History of ELS reaction after pediatric DTP/DTaP or Td immunization that was not an Arthus hypersensitivity reaction. Stable neurologic disorder, including well-controlled seizures, history of seizure disorder, and cerebral palsy. Brachial neuritis. Latex allergy other than anaphylactic allergies (eg, a history of contact to latex gloves). The tip and rubber plunger of the BOOSTRIX needleless syringe contain latex. This BOOSTRIX product should not be administered to adolescents with a history of a severe (anaphylactic) allergy to latex but may be administered to people with less severe allergies (eg, contact allergy to latex gloves). The BOOSTRIX single-dose vial and ADACEL preparations do not contain latex. Pregnancy. Breastfeeding.

Guide to Contraindications and Precautions to Immunizations, 2006, continued

Vaccine	Contraindications	Precautions[1]	Not Contraindications (Vaccines May Be Given)
Tdap, continued			Immunosuppression, including people with human immunodeficiency virus infection. Tdap poses no known safety concern for immunosuppressed people. The immunogenicity of Tdap in people with immunosuppression has not been studied and could be suboptimal.
			Intercurrent minor illness.
			Antibiotic use.
Varicella[5]	Pregnancy	Recent Immune Globulin administration (see Table 3.33, p 446)	Pregnancy of mother of recipient
	Severe allergic reaction after a previous dose or to a vaccine component (ie, neomycin or gelatin)	Family history of immunodeficiency[13]	Immunodeficiency in a household contact
	Infection with HIV[11]		Household contact with HIV
	Known altered immunodeficiency (hematologic and solid tumors, congenital immunodeficiency, and long-term immunosuppressive therapy)[12]		
Hepatitis A	Severe allergic reaction after a previous dose or to a vaccine component (ie, to 2-phenoxyethanol or alum)	Pregnancy	. . .
Influenza (inactivated/ live-attenuated)	Severe allergic reaction to a previous dose or vaccine component including eggs	GBS within 6 wk after a previous influenza immunization	Pregnancy
		Altered immunocompetence	
Rotavirus	Severe allergic reaction after a previous dose or to a vaccine component	Moderate to severe acute gastroenteritis	Breastfeeding
		Moderate to severe febrile illness	Immunodeficient family member or household contact
		Chronic gastrointestinal disease	
		Intussusception	

[11] Varicella vaccine should be considered for asymptomatic or mildly symptomatic HIV-infected children, specifically children in Centers for Disease Control and Prevention class N1 or A1, with age-specific T-lymphocyte percentages of 15% or higher.

[12] Varicella vaccine should not be administered to people who have cellular immunodeficiencies, but people with impaired humoral immunity may be immunized.

[13] Varicella vaccine should not be administered to a person who has a family history of congenital or hereditary immunodeficiency in parents or siblings unless that person's immune competence has been substantiated clinically or verified by a laboratory.

APPENDIX IV.

National Childhood Vaccine Injury Act. Reporting and Compensation Table.

This table includes adverse events that are reportable to the Vaccine Adverse Event Reporting System (VAERS) (see Vaccine Safety and Contraindications, p 39) as well as vaccines covered by the National Vaccine Injury Compensation Program (VICP). Hepatitis A vaccines and trivalent influenza vaccines (TIV and LAIV) have been added to the VICP. Anytime a vaccine is added to the VICP, a person who believes he or she has been injured by a vaccine may file a claim for injuries up to 8 years prior to the effective date of the excise tax. Therefore, influenza vaccines given during the 2004-2005 influenza season will be covered by the VICP. The same holds for hepatitis A vaccines administered up to 8 years prior to the December 1, 2004, effective date. A vaccine officially is added to the Table once an excise tax is applied. The intervals from immunization to the onset of an event for reporting to VAERS and for possible compensation by the Vaccine Injury Compensation Program are provided. Information for filing a claim can be obtained through the VICP Web site (**www.hrsa.gov/osp/vicp**).

National Childhood Vaccine Injury Act Reporting and Compensation Table[1]

Vaccine	Adverse Event	Interval from Vaccination to Onset of Event	
		For Reporting[2]	For Compensation[3]
I. Tetanus toxoid-containing vaccines (eg, DTaP, Tdap, DTP-Hib; DT; Td, or TT)	A. Anaphylaxis or anaphylactic shock	0–7 days	0–4 h
	B. Brachial neuritis	0–28 days	2–28 days
	C. Any acute complication or sequela (including death) of above events	Not applicable	Not applicable
	D. Events described in manufacturer's package insert as contraindications to additional doses of vaccine	See package insert	Not applicable
II. Pertussis antigen-containing vaccines (eg, DTaP, Tdap, DTP, P, DTP-Hib)	A. Anaphylaxis or anaphylactic shock	0–7 days	0–4 h
	B. Encephalopathy (or encephalitis)	0–7 days	0–72 h
	C. Any acute complication or sequela (including death) of above events	Not applicable	Not applicable
	D. Events described in manufacturer's package insert as contraindications to additional doses of vaccine	See package insert	Not applicable
III. Measles, mumps, and rubella virus-containing vaccines in any combination (eg, MMR, MR, M, R)	A. Anaphylaxis or anaphylactic shock	0–7 days	0–4 h
	B. Encephalopathy (or encephalitis)	0–15 days	5–15 days
	C. Any acute complication or sequela (including death) of above events	Not applicable	Not applicable
	D. Events described in manufacturer's package insert as contraindications to additional doses of vaccine	See package insert	Not applicable
IV. Rubella virus-containing vaccines (eg, MMR, MR, R)	A. Chronic arthritis	0–42 days	7–42 days
	B. Any acute complication or sequela (including death) of above event	Not applicable	Not applicable
	C. Events described in manufacturer's package insert as contraindications to additional doses of vaccine	See package insert	Not applicable
V. Measles virus-containing vaccines (eg, MMR, MR, M)	A. Thrombocytopenic purpura	0–30 days	7–30 days
	B. Vaccine-strain measles viral infection in an immunodeficient recipient	0–6 mo	0–6 mo
	C. Any acute complication or sequela (including death) of above events	Not applicable	Not applicable
	D. Events described in manufacturer's package insert as contraindications to additional doses of vaccine	See package insert	Not applicable

National Childhood Vaccine Injury Act Reporting and Compensation Table,[1] continued

Vaccine	Adverse Event	Interval from Vaccination to Onset of Event	
		For Reporting[2]	For Compensation[3]
VI. Live poliovirus-containing vaccines (OPV)	A. Paralytic polio		
	• in a nonimmunodeficient recipient	0–30 days	0–30 days
	• in an immunodeficient recipient	0–6 mo	0–6 mo
	• in a vaccine-associated community case	No limit	Not applicable
	B. Vaccine-strain polio viral infection		
	• in a nonimmunodeficient recipient	0–30 days	0–30 days
	• in an immunodeficient recipient	0–6 mo	0–6 mo
	• in a vaccine-associated community case	No limit	Not applicable
	C. Any acute complication or sequela (including death) of above events	Not applicable	Not applicable
	D. Events described in manufacturer's package insert as contraindications to additional doses of vaccine	See package insert	Not applicable
VII. Inactivated poliovirus-containing vaccines (eg, IPV)	A. Anaphylaxis or anaphylactic shock	0–7 days	0–4 h
	B. Any acute complication or sequela (including death) of above event	Not applicable	Not applicable
	C. Events described in manufacturer's package insert as contraindications to additional doses of vaccine	See package insert	Not applicable
VIII. Hepatitis B antigen-containing vaccines	A. Anaphylaxis or anaphylactic shock	0–7 days	0–4 h
	B. Any acute complication or sequela (including death) of above event	Not applicable	Not applicable
	C. Events described in manufacturer's package insert as contraindications to additional doses of vaccine	See package insert	Not applicable
IX. Haemophilus influenzae type b (polysaccharide conjugate vaccines)	A. No condition specified for compensation	Not applicable	Not applicable
	B. Events described in manufacturer's package insert as contraindications to additional doses of vaccine	See package insert	Not applicable
X. Varicella vaccine	A. No condition specified for compensation	Not applicable	Not applicable
	B. Events described in manufacturer's package insert as contraindications to additional doses of vaccine	See package insert	Not applicable
XI. Rotavirus vaccine	A. No condition specified for compensation	Not applicable	Not applicable
	B. Events described in manufacturer's package insert as contraindications to additional doses of vaccine	See package insert	Not applicable

National Childhood Vaccine Injury Act Reporting and Compensation Table,¹ Continued

Vaccine	Adverse Event	Interval from Vaccination to Onset of Event	
		For Reporting[2]	For Compensation[3]
XII. Vaccines containing live, oral, rhesus-based rotavirus	A. Intussusception	0–30 days	0–30 days
	B. Any acute complication or sequela (including death) of above event	Not applicable	Not applicable
	C. Events described in manufacturer's package insert as contraindications to additional doses of vaccine	See package insert	Not applicable
XIII. Pneumococcal conjugate vaccines	A. No condition specified for compensation	Not applicable	Not applicable
	B. Events described in manufacturer's package insert as contraindications to additional doses of vaccine	See package insert	Not applicable
XIV. Any new vaccine recommended by the Centers for Disease Control and Prevention for routine administration to children, after publication by Secretary, HHS, of a notice of coverage[4]	A. No condition specified for compensation	Not applicable	Not applicable
	B. Events described in manufacturer's package insert as contraindications to additional doses of vaccine	Not applicable	Not applicable

DTaP, diphtheria and tetanus toxoids and acellular pertussis; DTP, diphtheria and tetanus toxoids and pertussis; Hib, *Haemophilus influenzae* type b; DT, diphtheria and tetanus toxoids; Td, adult-type diphtheria and tetanus toxoids; TT, tetanus toxoid vaccine; OPV, oral poliovirus; PRP, polyribosylribitol phosphate polysaccharide; HHS, US Department of Health and Human Services.

[1] Effective date: July 1, 2005. For updates to the table, see **www.hrsa.gov/vaccinecompensation/table.htm**.

[2] Taken from the Reportable Events Table (RET), which lists conditions reportable by law (42 USC §300aa-25) to the Vaccine Adverse Event Reporting System (VAERS), including conditions found in the manufacturer's package insert. In addition, physicians are encouraged to report any clinically significant or unexpected events (even if you are not certain the vaccine caused the event) for any vaccine, whether or not it is listed on the RET. Manufacturers also are required by regulation (21 CFR §600.80) to report to the VAERS program all adverse events made known to them for any vaccine. VAERS reporting forms and information can be obtained by calling 1-800-822-7967 or from the Web site (**www.vaers.org**).

[3] Taken from the Vaccine Injury Table (VIT) used in adjudication of claims filed with the National Vaccine Injury Compensation Program (VICP). Claims also may be filed for a condition with onset outside the designated time intervals or a condition not included in the VIT. The Qualifications and Aids to Interpretation below define conditions or injuries listed on the VIT. Information on filing a claim can be obtained by calling 1-800-338-2382 or through the VICP Web site (**www.hrsa.gov/osp/vicp**).

[4] As of December 1, 2004, hepatitis A virus (HAV) vaccines have been added to the VIT under this category. As of July 1, 2005, trivalent influenza vaccines (TIV, LAIV) have been added to the VIT under this category. (Influenza vaccines routinely administered in the United States are trivalent.) HAV, TIV, and LAIV will each have a separate and distinct listing on the VIT once a regulation is published in the *Federal Register*. In the mean time, they are officially covered by the VICP as of these dates. See "News" on the VICP Web site for more information. For qualifications and aid to interpretation of the table, see **www.hrsa.gov/osp/vicp/table.htm**.

··························
APPENDIX V.

State Immunization Requirements for School Attendance

The United States relies on child care and elementary and secondary school entry immunization requirements to achieve and sustain high levels of immunization coverage. This strategy has proven successful not only in dramatically decreasing communicable disease in settings where children gather and transmit infection but also in decreasing the opportunity for transmission of vaccine-preventable diseases to the unimmunized, the underimmunized, and the immunologically frail. All states require immunization of children at the time of entry into school, and most states require immunization for entry into licensed child care. In addition, many states require immunization of older children in upper grades as well as those entering college. The most up-to-date information about which vaccines are required in a specific state and permissible exemptions can be obtained from the immunization program manager of each state health department, from a number of local health departments, and from **www.immunize.org/laws** and the State and Territorial Health Organization (**www.astho.org**).

The Centers for Disease Control and Prevention (CDC) collects state-specific data on current school entry laws and regulations (child care and Head Start, kindergarten, first grade, and middle school), immunization coverage levels, and exemption rates through state-based surveys. The most recent survey results can be accessed online through the CDC National Immunization Program at **www.cdc.gov/nip/coverage/schoolsurv/overview.htm** (choose the "Survey of School Assessment Practices" option).

APPENDIX VI.

Clinical Syndromes Associated With Foodborne Diseases*

Foodborne disease results from consumption of contaminated foods or beverages and causes morbidity and mortality in children and adults in developing and developed countries. The epidemiology of foodborne disease is complex and dynamic because of the large number of pathogens, the variety of disease manifestations, the increasing prevalence of immunocompromised children and adults, changes in dietary habits, and trends toward centralized food production and widespread distribution.

To aid in diagnosis, foodborne disease syndromes are categorized by incubation period, duration, causative agent, and foods commonly associated with specific etiologic agents (see Table, p 858). Diagnosis can be confirmed by laboratory testing of stool, emesis, or blood, depending on the causative agent. An outbreak should be considered when 2 or more people who have consumed the same food develop an acute illness characterized by nausea, vomiting, diarrhea, or neurologic signs or symptoms. If an outbreak is suspected, local or state public health officials should be notified immediately so they can work with local health care professionals, coordinate laboratory testing not available locally, and conduct epidemiologic investigations to curtail the outbreak.

---

* Centers for Disease Control and Prevention. Diagnosis and management of foodborne illnesses: a primer for physicians. *MMWR Recomm Rep*. 2001;50(RR-2):1–69. Additional information can be found at **www.cdc.gov/foodsafety** and **www.fsis.usda.gov/home/index.asp**.

Clinical Syndromes Associated With Foodborne Diseases

Clinical Syndrome	Incubation Period	Causative Agents	Commonly Associated Vehicles
Nausea and vomiting	<1–6 h	*Staphylococcus aureus* (preformed toxins, A, B, C, D, E)	Ham, poultry, cream-filled pastries, potato and egg salads, mushrooms
		Bacillus cereus (emetic toxin)	Fried rice, meats
		Heavy metals (copper, tin, cadmium, iron, zinc)	Acidic beverages, metallic container
Flushing, dizziness, burning of mouth and throat, headache, gastrointestinal symptoms, urticaria	<1 h	Histamine (scombroid)	Fish (bluefish, bonita, mackerel, mahi-mahi, marlin, tuna)
Neurologic, including paresthesias	<1–6 h	Tetrodotoxin	Puffer fish
		Ciguatoxin	Fish (amberjack, barracuda, grouper, snapper)
Gastrointestinal tract symptoms		Paralytic shellfish toxins (saxitoxins, etc)	Shellfish (clams, mussels, oysters, scallops, other mollusks)
		Neurotoxic shellfish toxin (brevetoxin)	Shellfish
		Domoic acid	Mussels
		Monosodium glutamate	Chinese food
Neurologic, including confusion, salivation, hallucinations; gastrointestinal tract manifestations	0–2 h	Mushroom toxins (early onset)	Mushrooms
Moderate-to-severe abdominal cramps and watery diarrhea, vomiting	6–24 h	*B cereus* enterotoxin	Meats, stews, gravies, vanilla sauce
		Clostridium perfringens enterotoxin	Meats, poultry; gravy, dried or precooked foods
	16–72 h	Caliciviruses, including Norwalk	Shellfish, salads, ice, cookies, water, sandwiches, fruit

Clinical Syndromes Associated With Foodborne Diseases, continued

Clinical Syndrome	Incubation Period	Causative Agents	Commonly Associated Vehicles
	1–3 days	Rotavirus	Fecally contaminated foods (salads, fruits)
	1–4 days	Enterotoxigenic *Escherichia coli*	Fruits, vegetables, water
	1–5 days	*Vibrio cholerae* O1 and O139	Shellfish (including crabs and shrimp), fish, water
		V cholerae non-O1	Shellfish
	1–14 days	*Cyclospora* species	Raspberries, vegetables, water
	2–14 days	*Cryptosporidium* species	Vegetables, fruits, milk, water
	1–4 wk	*Giardia lamblia*	Water, food sources
Diarrhea, fever, abdominal cramps, blood and mucus in stools	16–≥72 h	*Salmonella* species	Poultry; pork; beef; eggs; dairy products, including ice cream; vegetables; fruit; orange juice; alfalfa sprouts
Guillain-Barré syndrome		*Shigella*	Egg salad, vegetables, scallions
		Campylobacter jejuni	Poultry, raw milk, water
		Enteroinvasive *E coli*	Vegetables, hamburger, raw milk
		Yersinia enterocolitica	Pork chitterlings, tofu, raw milk
		Vibrio parahaemolyticus	Fish, shellfish
Bloody diarrhea, abdominal cramps	72–120 h	Enterohemorrhagic *E coli*	Beef (hamburger); raw milk; roast beef; salami; salad dressings; lettuce; unpasteurized juices, including apple cider; alfalfa and radish sprouts; water
Hepatorenal failure, watery diarrhea	6–24 h	Mushroom toxins (late onset)	Mushrooms (especially *Amanita* species)
Gastrointestinal tract manifestations, then blurred vision, dry mouth, dysarthria, diplopia, descending paralysis	12–48 h	*Clostridium botulinum*	Home-canned vegetables, fruits and fish, salted fish, meats, bottled garlic, potatoes baked in aluminum foil, cheese sauce, honey

Clinical Syndromes Associated With Foodborne Diseases, continued

Clinical Syndrome	Incubation Period	Causative Agents	Commonly Associated Vehicles
Chronic, urgent diarrhea	Varied	Brainerd diarrhea	Unpasteurized milk, water
Extraintestinal manifestations	Varied	Brucella species	Goat cheese, queso fresco, raw milk, meats
		Group A streptococcus	Egg and potato salads
		Hepatitis A virus	Shellfish, raw produce (ie, strawberries, lettuce, green onions)
		Listeria monocytogenes	Cheese, raw milk, hot dogs, cole slaw, ready-to eat delicatessen meats
		Trichinella spiralis	Pork, wild game, meat
		Vibrio vulnificus	Shellfish (especially oysters)
		Toxoplasma gondii	Beef, pork, lamb, venison
		Enterobacter sakazaki	Powdered infant formula

··························
APPENDIX VII.

Prevention of Disease From Potentially Contaminated Food Products*

Foodborne diseases are associated with significant morbidity and mortality in people of all ages. The Centers for Disease Control and Prevention (CDC) estimates that there are more than 76 million cases of foodborne diseases in the United States each year, resulting in approximately 325 000 hospitalizations and 5000 deaths. Young children, the elderly, and especially immunocompromised people particularly are susceptible to illness and complications caused by many of the organisms associated with foodborne illness. Four general rules to maintain safety of foods are:
• Wash hands and surfaces often
• Separate—don't cross contaminate
• Refrigerate foods promptly
• Cook food to the proper temperature
   The following preventive measures can be implemented to decrease the risk of infection and disease from potentially contaminated food.

UNPASTEURIZED MILK AND CHEESE. The American Academy of Pediatrics (AAP) strongly endorses the use of pasteurized milk and recommends that parents and public health officials be fully informed of the important risks associated with consumption of unpasteurized milk. Interstate sale of raw milk is banned by the US Food and Drug Administration (FDA). Children should not consume unpasteurized milk or products made from unpasteurized milk, such as cheese and butter, from species including cows, sheep, and goats. Serious systemic infections attributable to *Salmonella* species, *Campylobacter* species, *Mycobacterium bovis*, *Listeria monocytogenes*, *Brucella* species, and *Escherichia coli* O157:H7 have been attributed to consumption of unpasteurized milk, including certified raw milk. In particular, an increasing number of outbreaks of campylobacteriosis among children are associated with school field trips to farms and consumption of raw milk. Raw milk consumption should be prohibited during educational trips. Cheese made from unpasteurized milk has been associated with illness attributable to *Brucella* species, *L monocytogenes*, *Salmonella* species, and *E coli* O157. The risk of infection can be prevented by purchasing commercially pasteurized milk and milk products.

EGGS. Children should not eat raw or undercooked eggs, unpasteurized powdered eggs, or products containing raw eggs or undercooked eggs. Ingestion of raw or improperly cooked eggs can result in severe salmonellosis. Examples of foods that may contain raw or undercooked eggs include some homemade frostings and mayon-

---

* Centers for Disease Control and Prevention. Diagnosis and management of foodborne illnesses: a primer for physicians. *MMWR Recomm Rep.* 2001;50(RR-2):1–69. Additional information can be found at **www.cdc.gov/foodsafety**, **www.nal.usda.gov/foodborne**, and **www.fsis.usda.gov/home/ index.asp**.

naise, ice cream from uncooked custard, tiramisu, eggs prepared "sunny-side up," fresh Caesar salad dressing, Hollandaise sauce, and cookie and cake batter.

RAW AND UNDERCOOKED MEAT. Children should not eat raw or undercooked meat or meat products, particularly hamburger. Various raw or undercooked meat products have been associated with disease, such as poultry with *Salmonella* or *Campylobacter* species; ground beef with *E coli* O157:H7 and other enterohemorrhagic *E coli* or *Salmonella* species; hot dogs with *Listeria* species; pork with trichinosis; and wild game with brucellosis, tularemia, or trichinosis. Ground meats should be cooked thoroughly until the juices run clear. Knives, cutting boards, plates, and other utensils used for raw meats should not be used for preparation of fresh fruits or vegetables until the utensils have been cleaned properly.

UNPASTEURIZED JUICES. Children should drink only pasteurized juice products unless the fruit is washed and freshly squeezed (ie, orange juice) immediately before consumption. Consumption of packaged fruit and vegetable juices that have not undergone pasteurization or a comparable treatment have been associated with foodborne illness attributable to *E coli* O157:H7 and *Salmonella* species. To identify a packaged juice that has not undergone pasteurization or a comparable treatment, consumers should look for a warning statement that the product has not been pasteurized and, therefore, may contain harmful bacteria that can cause serious illness in children, elderly people, or people with compromised immune systems.

SEED SPROUTS. The FDA and the CDC have reaffirmed health advisories that people who are at high risk of severe foodborne disease, including children, people with compromised immune systems, and elderly people, should avoid eating raw seed sprouts until intervention methods are implemented to improve the safety of these products.* Raw seed sprouts have been associated with outbreaks of illness attributable to *Salmonella* species and *E coli* O157:H7.

FRESH FRUITS, VEGETABLES, AND NUTS. Many fresh fruits and vegetables have been associated with disease attributable to *Cryptosporidium* species, *Cyclospora* species, noroviruses, *Giardia* species, *E coli*, *Salmonella* species, and *Shigella* species. Washing can decrease but not eliminate contamination of fruits and vegetables. All fruits and vegetables should be washed with cool tap water immediately before consumption. Produce should be scrubbed with a clean produce brush. Knives, cutting boards, utensils, and plates used for raw meats should not be used for preparation of fresh fruits or vegetables until the utensils have been cleaned properly. Raw shelled nuts have been associated with outbreaks of salmonellosis.

RAW SHELLFISH AND FISH. Children should not eat raw shellfish, especially raw oysters. Raw shellfish, including mussels, clams, oysters, scallops, and other mollusks, have been associated with many pathogens and toxins (see Appendix VI, p 857). *Vibrio* species contaminating raw shellfish may cause severe disease in people with liver disease or other conditions associated with decreased immune function. Some experts

---

* For additional information, contact the FDA Food Information Line at 1-800-FDA-4010 or the US Department of Agriculture at 1-800-535-4555 or 1-202-720-2791 or visit the following Web sites: **www.usda.gov** and **www.foodsafety.gov**.

caution against children ingesting raw fish which has been associated with transmission of parasites.

HONEY. Children younger than 1 year of age should not be given honey. Honey has been shown to contain spores of *Clostridium botulinum*. Light and dark corn syrups are manufactured under sanitary conditions. However, the product is neither packaged under aseptic conditions nor terminally sterilized. Because spores of *C botulinum* are found in the environment and potentially can be found in corn syrup, the manufacturer cannot ensure that any product will be free of *C botulinum* spores. However, no cases associated with these products have been documented.

FOOD IRRADIATION.* There is no process to eliminate all foodborne diseases; however, food safety experts believe that irradiation of food can be an effective tool in helping control foodborne pathogens. Irradiation involves exposing food briefly to radiant energy (such as gamma rays, x-rays, or high-voltage electrons) and often is referred to as "cold pasteurization." More than 40 countries worldwide have approved the use of irradiation for various types of foods. In addition, every governmental and professional organization that has reviewed the efficacy and safety of food irradiation has endorsed its use. Irradiated meat and some produce items are available to US consumers. The risk of foodborne illness in children can be decreased significantly with the routine consumption of irradiated meat, poultry, and produce.

---

* American Academy of Pediatrics, Committee on Environmental Health. Technical report: irradiation of food. *Pediatrics.* 2000;106:1505–1510

··

APPENDIX VIII.

Diseases Transmitted by Animals (Zoonoses)

The transmission of diseases of animals to humans is of special interest in the care of children who interact with pets, wild rodents, and other animals. Important zoonoses that may be encountered in North America are reviewed in the *Red Book* (see disease-specific chapters in Section 3 for further information) and listed in the Table (p 865). Primary modes of transmission from animals to humans include direct contact, scratch, bite, inhalation, contact with urine or feces, and ingestion of contaminated food, water, or feces as well as bites from arthropod vectors. To minimize transmission of enteric disease at petting farms, the following infection control activities should be enforced: handwashing facilities should be readily available and configured for use by children; food-related activities should be separated from areas housing animals; and children should be supervised during contact with animals and during handwashing. Rabies immunization of petting farm animals is prudent. Human-to-human transmission may occur for some zoonotic diseases. For a more complete listing of these diseases, standard textbooks in infectious diseases should be consulted.

Morbidity resulting from selected zoonotic diseases in the United States is reported annually by the Centers for Disease Control and Prevention (see "Summary of Notifiable Diseases" at **www.cdc.gov/epo/dphsi/annsum**). Information also can be obtained at multiple Web sites of the National Center for Infectious Diseases (Bacterial Zoonoses Branch: **www.cdc.gov/ncidod/dvbid/misc/bzb.htm**; Rabies: **www.cdc.gov/ncidod/dvrd/rabies**; Ehrlichioses: **www.cdc.gov/ncidod/dvrd/ ehrlichia**, and Q fever: **www.cdc.gov/ncidod/dvid/qfever**).

Table. Diseases Transmitted by Animals

Disease and/or Organism	Common Animal Sources	Vector or Modes of Transmission
Bacterial Diseases		
Aeromonas species	Aquatic animals, especially shellfish	Wound infection, ingestion of contaminated food or water
Brucellosis (*Brucella* species)	Cattle, goats, sheep, swine, rarely dogs, elk, bison	Direct contact with birth products, ingestion of contaminated dairy products, inhalation of aerosols, through skin wounds
Campylobacteriosis (*Campylobacter jejuni*)	Poultry, dogs (especially puppies), kittens, ferrets, hamsters, birds	Ingestion of contaminated food, water, milk, direct contact (particularly with animals with diarrhea), person-to-person (fecal-oral)
Capnocytophaga canimorsus	Dogs, rarely cats	Bites, scratches, and contact
Cat-scratch disease (*Bartonella henselae*)	Cats, infrequently other animals (<10%)	Scratches, bites, fleas play a role in cat-to-cat transmission
Erysipelothrix rhusiopathiae	Pigs, sheep, cattle, horses, birds, fish, shellfish	Direct contact with animal or contaminated animal product
Hemolytic-uremic syndrome (eg, Shiga toxin-producing *Escherichia coli*) (STEC)	Cattle, sheep, deer	Ingestion of undercooked contaminated ground beef, unpasteurized milk, or other contaminated foods or water, person-to-person contact (fecal-oral), petting zoo contact, county fairs (fecal-oral)
Leptospirosis (*Leptospira* species)	Dogs, rats, livestock, other wild animals	Contact with or ingestion of water, food, or soil contaminated with urine
Lyme disease (*Borrelia burgdorferi*)	Wild rodents, birds	Black legged or "Deer" tick bite
Mycobacteriosis (*Mycobacterium marinum*, others)	Fish (and cleaning aquaria)	Skin injury or contamination of existing wound
Pasteurella multocida	Cats, dogs, other animals	Bites, scratches, licks
Plague (*Yersinia pestis*)	Rodents, cats, ground squirrels, prairie dogs	Bite of rodent fleas, direct contact with infected animals, person-to-person with pneumonic plague

Table. Diseases Transmitted by Animals, continued

Disease and/or Organism	Common Animal Sources	Vector or Modes of Transmission
Rat-bite fever (*Streptobacillus moniliformis, Spirillum minus*)	Rodents (especially rats, occasionally squirrels), cats, weasels	Bites and contaminated food, milk, and water
Relapsing fever (tickborne) (*Borrelia* species)	Wild rodents	Tick bite
Salmonellosis (*Salmonella* species)	Poultry, lizards, snakes, salamanders, iguanas, dogs, cats, rodents, ferrets, turtles, other wild and domestic animals	Ingestion of contaminated food, milk, and water; direct contact; contact with fecally contaminated surfaces; person-to-person (fecal-oral)
Streptococcus iniae	Fish grown by aquaculture	Skin injury during handling of fish
Tetanus (*Clostridium tetani*)	Any animal, usually indirect via soil containing animal feces	Wound infection, skin injury or soft tissue injury with inoculation of bacteria (as from soil or a contaminated object), contaminated bites
Tularemia (*Francisella tularensis*)	Wild rabbits, voles, sheep, cattle, muskrats, moles, cats	Tick bites, deerfly bites, direct contact with infected animal, ingestion of contaminated water, mechanical transmission from claws or teeth (cats), aerosolization of tissues or excreta
Vibrio species	Shellfish	Skin injury or contamination of existing wound, ingestion of contaminated food
Yersiniosis (*Yersinia enterocolitica, Yersinia pseudotuberculosis*)	Swine, deer, elk, horses, goats, sheep, cattle, rodents, birds, rabbits	Ingestion of contaminated food, water, or milk; rarely direct contact, person-to-person (fecal-oral)
Fungal Diseases		
Cryptococcosis (*Cryptococcus neoformans*)	Excreta of birds, particularly pigeons	Inhalation of aerosols from accumulations of bird feces
Histoplasmosis (*Histoplasma capsulatum*)	Excreta of bats, birds, particularly starlings	Inhalation of aerosols from accumulations of bat and bird feces
Ringworm/tinea corporis (*Microsporum* and *Trichophyton* species)	Cats, dogs, fowl, pigs, moles, horses, rodents, cattle, monkeys, goats	Direct contact

Table. Diseases Transmitted by Animals, continued

Disease and/or Organism	Common Animal Sources	Vector or Modes of Transmission
Parasitic Diseases		
Anisakiasis (*Anisakis* species)	Saltwater and anadromous fish	Ingestion of undercooked or raw fish (eg, sushi)
Babesiosis (*Babesia* species)	Mice	Tick bite
Balantidiasis (*Balantidium coli*)	Swine	Ingestion of contaminated food or water
Baylisascariasis (*Baylisascaris procyonis*)	Raccoon	Ingestion of eggs shed in raccoon feces
Dwarf tapeworm (*Hymenolepis nana*)	Rodents	Ingestion of eggs from feces (contaminated food, water), person-to-person (fecal-oral)
Cryptosporidiosis (*Cryptosporidium* species)	Domestic animals, particularly cattle, birds reptiles	Ingestion of contaminated water or foods, person-to-person (fecal-oral)
Cutaneous larva migrans (*Ancylostoma* species)	Dogs, cats	Penetration of skin by larvae, which develop in soil contaminated with animal feces
Cysticercosis/Pork tapeworm (*Taenia solium*)	Swine (intermediate host)	Ingestion of eggs from fecal-oral contact or contaminated food, water, ingestion of cysts in raw or undercooked meat (adult tapeworm infection)
Dog tapeworm (*Dipylidium caninum*)	Dogs, cats	Ingestion of fleas infected with larvae
Echinococcosis, hydatid disease (*Echinococcus* species)	Dogs, foxes, possibly other carnivores, coyotes, wolves, moose, caribou, rodents, sheep (the most common intermediate host worldwide), also swine, cattle, horses, camels	Ingestion of eggs shed in animal feces
Fish tapeworm (*Diphyllobothrium latum*)	Saltwater and freshwater fish	Ingestion of larvae in raw or undercooked fish

Table. Diseases Transmitted by Animals, continued

Disease and/or Organism	Common Animal Sources	Vector or Modes of Transmission
Giardiasis (*Giardia lamblia*)	Wild and domestic animals, including dogs, cats, beavers, muskrats	Ingestion of cysts in contaminated food, water, person-to-person
Taeniasis, beef (*Taenia saginata*)	Cattle	Ingestion of larvae in undercooked beef
Toxoplasmosis (*Toxoplasma gondii*)	Cats, livestock	Ingestion of oocysts from cat feces, consumption of cysts in undercooked meat, contact with birth products of cats
Trichinosis (*Trichinella spiralis*)	Swine, horses, bears, seals, walrus	Ingestion of larvae in raw or undercooked meat
Visceral larva migrans (*Toxocara canis* and *Toxocara cati*)	Dogs, cats	Ingestion of eggs, usually from soil contaminated by animal feces
Chlamydial and Rickettsial Diseases		
Human ehrlichiosis and anaplasmosis (*Ehrlichia* and *Anaplasma* species)	Deer, dogs, ruminants, horses, mice	Tick bites
Psittacosis (*Chlamydophila psittaci*)	Pet birds (especially psittacine birds) and poultry	Inhalation of aerosols from feces of infected birds
Q fever (*Coxiella burnetii*)	Sheep, goats, cows, cats, dogs, wild rodents, birds	Direct contact and aerosols from birth products or animal tissues or products
Rickettsialpox (*Rickettsia akari*)	House mouse	Mite bites (Mouse mite bite)
Rocky Mountain spotted fever (*Rickettsia rickettsii*)	Dogs, wild rodents, rabbits	Tick bites; rarely by direct contamination with infectious material from ticks
Typhus, fleaborne endemic typhus (*Rickettsia typhi*)	Rats, opossums, cats, dogs	Rat flea feces scratched into abrasions; less common, other fleas
Typhus, louseborne epidemic typhus (*Rickettsia prowazekii*)	Flying squirrels	Person-to-person via body louse, contact with squirrels, their nests, or ectoparasites
Viral Diseases		
Colorado tick fever	Wild rodents, (squirrels, chipmunks)	Tick bites

Table. Diseases Transmitted by Animals, continued

Disease and/or Organism	Common Animal Sources	Vector or Modes of Transmission
Encephalitis		
California	Wild rodents	Mosquito bites
Eastern equine	Wild birds, poultry, horses	Mosquito bites
Western equine	Wild birds, poultry, horses	Mosquito bites
St Louis	Wild birds, poultry	Mosquito bites
Venezuelan equine	Rodents, horses	Mosquito bites
Powassan	Rodents, rabbits	Tick bites
West Nile	Wild birds, horses	Mosquito bites
Nipah virus	Undetermined, possibly bats and pigs	Close contact with infected pigs
Hendra virus	Flying foxes; horses become infected	Contact with body fluids of infected horses
Hantaviruses	Wild rodents	Inhalation of aerosols of infected secreta and excreta
B virus (formerly herpesvirus simiae)	Macaque monkeys	Bite or exposure to secretions
Lymphocytic choriomeningitis	Rodents, particularly hamsters, mice	Direct contact, inhalation of aerosols, ingestion of food contaminated with rodent excreta
Rabies (Lyssavirus)	In the United States, primarily wildlife (bats, raccoons, skunks, foxes, ferrets) or less frequently, domestic animals (dogs, cats, cattle)	Bites, rarely contact of open wounds with infected materials (eg, saliva, neural tissue)
Monkeypox	Prairie dogs, African rodents	Direct contact, bite, scratch
Influenza (H5N1)	Chickens, birds, swine	Contact with infected animals or aerosols (markets, slaughter house)
Orf (pox virus of sheep)	Sheep	Contact with sheep saliva
Severe acute respiratory virus (coronavirus)	Civet cats, potentially other animal species	Unclear; person-to-person (respiratory, contact)

••••••••••••••••••••••
APPENDIX IX.

Nationally Notifiable Infectious Diseases in the United States

Public health officials at state health departments and the Centers for Disease Control and Prevention (CDC) collaborate in determining which diseases should be nationally notifiable (see Table, p 871). The Council of State and Territorial Epidemiologists, with advice from the CDC, makes recommendations annually for additions and deletions to the list of nationally notifiable diseases. A disease may be added to the list as a new pathogen emerges, or a disease may be deleted as its incidence decreases. However, reporting of nationally notifiable diseases to the CDC by the states is voluntary. Reporting currently is mandated (ie, by state legislation or regulation) by individual states. The list of diseases that are considered notifiable, therefore, varies slightly by state. Additional and specific requirements should be obtained from the appropriate state health department. All states generally report diseases that are quarantined internationally (ie, cholera, plague, and yellow fever) in compliance with the World Health Organization's International Health Regulations.

When health care professionals suspect or diagnose a disease considered notifiable in the state, they should report the case by telephone or by mail to the local, county, or state health department. Clinical laboratories also report results consistent with reportable diseases. Staff members in the county or state health department implement disease control measures as needed. The written case report is forwarded to the state health department.

The CDC acts as a common agent for states and territories for collecting information and reporting of nationally notifiable diseases. Reports of occurrences of nationally notifiable diseases are transmitted to the CDC each week from the 50 states, 2 cities (Washington, DC, and New York, NY), and 5 territories (American Samoa, Commonwealth of Northern Mariana Islands, Guam, Puerto Rico, and the Virgin Islands). Provisional data are published weekly in the *Morbidity and Mortality Weekly Report;* final data are published each year by the CDC in the annual "Summary of Notifiable Diseases, United States." The timelines of the provisional weekly reports provide information that the CDC and state or local epidemiologists use to detect and more effectively interrupt outbreaks. Reporting provides the timely information needed to measure and demonstrate the effect of changed immunization laws or a new therapeutic modality. The finalized annual data provide information on reported disease incidence that is necessary for study of epidemiologic trends and development of disease prevention policies. The CDC is the sole repository for these data, which are used widely by schools of medicine and public health, communications media, and pharmaceutical or other companies producing health-related products as well as by local, state, and federal health agencies and other agencies or people concerned with the trends of reportable conditions in the United States.

Table. Infectious Diseases Designated as Notifiable at the National Level—United States, 2006[1]

Acquired immunodeficiency syndrome (AIDS)

Anthrax

Arboviral neuroinvasive and nonneuroinvasive diseases

• California serogroup virus disease

• Eastern equine encephalitis virus disease

• Powassan virus disease

• St Louis encephalitis virus disease

• West Nile virus disease

• Western equine encephalitis virus disease

Botulism

• Botulism, foodborne

• Botulism, infant

• Botulism, other (wound and unspecified)

Brucellosis

Chancroid

Chlamydia trachomatis, genital infections

Cholera

Coccidioidomycosis

Cryptosporidiosis

Cyclosporiasis

Diphtheria

Ehrlichiosis

• Ehrlichiosis, human granulocytic

• Ehrlichiosis, human monocytic

• Ehrlichiosis, human, other or unspecified

Giardiasis

Gonorrhea

Haemophilus influenzae, invasive disease

Hansen disease (leprosy)

Hantavirus pulmonary syndrome

Hemolytic-uremic syndrome, postdiarrheal

Hepatitis, viral, acute

• Hepatitis A, acute

• Hepatitis B, acute

• Hepatitis B virus, perinatal infection

• Hepatitis C, acute

Hepatitis, viral, chronic

• Chronic hepatitis B

• Hepatitis C virus infection (past or present)

Human immunodeficiency virus (HIV) infection

• HIV infection, adult ($\geq$13 years of age)

• HIV infection, pediatric (<13 years of age)

Influenza-associated pediatric mortality

Legionellosis

Listeriosis

Lyme disease

Malaria

Measles

Meningococcal disease

Mumps

Pertussis

Plague

Poliomyelitis, paralytic

Psittacosis

Q fever

Rabies

• Rabies, animal

• Rabies, human

Rocky Mountain spotted fever

Rubella

Rubella, congenital syndrome

Salmonellosis

Severe acute respiratory syndrome-associated coronavirus (SARS-CoV) disease

Shiga toxin-producing *Escherichia coli* (STEC)

Shigellosis

Smallpox

Streptococcal disease, invasive, group A

Streptococcal toxic shock syndrome

Streptococcus pneumoniae, drug resistant, invasive disease

Streptococcus pneumoniae, invasive in children <5 years of age

Syphilis

• Syphilis, primary

• Syphilis, secondary

• Syphilis, latent

• Syphilis, early latent

• Syphilis, late latent

• Syphilis, latent unknown duration

• Neurosyphilis

• Syphilis, late, nonneurological

Syphilis, congenital

• Syphilitic stillbirth

Tetanus

Toxic shock syndrome (other than streptococcal)

Trichinellosis (Trichinosis)

Tuberculosis

Tularemia

Typhoid fever

Vancomycin-intermediate *Staphylococcus aureus* (VISA)

Vancomycin-resistant *S aureus* (VRSA)

Varicella (morbidity)

Varicella (deaths only)

Yellow fever

APPENDIX X.

Services of the Centers for Disease Control and Prevention (CDC)

The Centers for Disease Control and Prevention (CDC), US Public Health Service, Department of Health and Human Services, is the federal agency charged with protecting the public health of the nation by preventing disease and other disabling conditions. The CDC administers national programs for prevention and control of the following: (1) infectious diseases; (2) vaccine-preventable diseases; (3) occupational diseases and injury; (4) chronic diseases; (5) environment-related injury and illness; and (6) birth defects and developmental disabilities. The CDC also provides consultation to other nations and participates with international agencies in the control of preventable diseases. In addition, the CDC directs and enforces foreign quarantine activities and regulations and provides consultation and assistance in upgrading the performance of clinical laboratories.

The CDC provides a number of services related to infectious disease management and control. Although the CDC principally is a resource for state and local health departments, it also offers direct and indirect services to hospitals and practicing health care professionals. The range of services includes reference laboratory diagnosis and epidemiologic consultation, both usually arranged through state health departments.

The CDC Drug Service supplies some specific prophylactic or therapeutic drugs and biological agents. Specific immunobiological products available include botulinal equine (trivalent, ABE) antitoxin, Vaccinia Immune Globulin (VIG), botulinus pentavalent toxoid, and vaccinia vaccine. In addition, several drugs for the treatment of parasitic disease, which currently are not licensed for use in the United States, are handled under an investigational new drug permit. These antiparasitic drugs include bithionol, dehydroemetine, diethylcarbamazine citrate, melarsoprol, nifurtimox, sodium stibogluconate, and suramin.

Requests for biological products, antiparasitic drugs, and related information should be directed to the CDC Drug Service (see Appendix I, Directory of Resources, p 839).

Index

Page numbers followed by "t" indicate a table. Page numbers followed by "f" indicate a figure.

A

AAP News, vaccine information in, 3
Abdominal actinomycosis, 201
Abdominal pain
from anthrax, 208
from arenavirus infections, 322
from astrovirus infections, 222
from babesiosis, 223
from *Bacillus cereus* infections, 224
from *Balantidium coli* infections, 229
from biological weapons, 109t
from *Blastocystis hominis* infections, 231
from brucellosis, 235
from *Campylobacter* infections, 240
from *Clostridium difficile* infections, 261
from *Clostridium perfringens* toxins, 263
from cryptosporidiosis, 270
from cyclosporiasis, 273
from enteroviruses, 284
from fish tapeworm, 647
from foodborne diseases, 858t–859t
from giardiasis, 296
from *Helicobacter pylori* infections, 321
from hemorrhagic fever with renal
  syndrome, 324
from hepatitis E, 360
from hookworm infections, 374
from influenza, 401
from isosporiasis, 411
from Kawasaki disease, 412
from malaria, 436
from nontuberculous mycobacterial
  infections, 698
from pelvic inflammatory disease,
  493–494
from Rocky Mountain spotted fever, 570
from *Salmonella* infections, 579, 580
from schistosomiasis, 587
from *Shigella* infections, 589
from smallpox, 591

from staphylococcal infections, 597
from strongyloidiasis, 629, 630
from taeniasis, 644
from trichinellosis, 671
from trichomoniasis, 673
from trichuriasis, 674
from tuberculosis, 678
from tularemia, 704
from *Vibrio* infections, 728
from West Nile virus infections, 729
from *Yersinia enterocolitica* infections, 732
from *Yersinia pseudotuberculosis*
  infections, 732
Abortion, spontaneous
from *Chlamydophila psittaci* infections, 251
from listeriosis, 427
from lymphocytic choriomeningitis virus
  infections, 434
from malaria, 436, 440
from mumps, 465
from relapsing fever, 233
from syphilis, 632
Abscess(es)
from *Actinomyces,* 201
from *Bacillus cereus,* 223
from *Bacteroides,* 227
from *Blastocystis hominis,* 231
from *Blastomyces dermatitidis,* 231
brain. *See* Brain abscess
breast, breastfeeding in, 124–125
from *Burkholderia,* 237
from *Entamoeba histolytica,* 204, 205
from enterococci, 627
liver
  from *Entamoeba histolytica,* 204, 205
  from *Pasteurella multocida,* 487
  from *Yersinia enterocolitica,* 732
lung
  from *Bacteroides,* 227
  from *Burkholderia,* 237
  from *Prevotella,* 227

P